D1039649

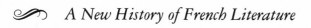 *A New History of French Literature*

A NEW HISTORY *of* FRENCH LITERATURE

EDITED BY
DENIS HOLLIER

WITH

R. Howard Bloch
Peter Brooks
Joan DeJean
Barbara Johnson
Philip E. Lewis
Nancy K. Miller
François Rigolot
Nancy J. Vickers

Harvard University Press
Cambridge, Massachusetts
London, England

Copyright © 1989, 1994 by the President and Fellows of Harvard College
All rights reserved
Printed in the United States of America
Second printing, 1994

First Harvard University Press paperback edition, 1994

Library of Congress Cataloging-in-Publication Data

A New history of French literature / edited by Denis Hollier.
    p.   cm.
  Bibliography: p.
  Includes index.
  ISBN 0-674-61565-4 (cloth)
  ISBN 0-674-61566-2 (pbk.)
   1. French literature—History and criticism. I. Hollier, Denis.
PQ119.N48   1989   88-27027
840'.9—dc19   CIP

ℰ℘ Contents

viii

xvi

ℰ𝒫꙰ Introduction

Conceived for the general reader, this volume presents French literature not as a simple inventory of authors or titles, but rather as a historical and cultural field viewed from a wide array of contemporary critical perspectives. Neither of the traditional modes of encyclopedic presentation—continuous historical narrative or alphabetical "dictionary"—seemed adequate for such an undertaking. The latter, while attempting complete coverage, introduces masses of often irrelevant information, and the former artificially homogenizes literature into linear genealogies.

Insofar as the essays that follow are each introduced by a date and are arranged in chronological order, they observe the general presentation of a history of literature. But both individually and cumulatively they question our conventional perception of the historical continuum. Each date is followed by a "headline," evoking an event, which specifies not so much the essay's content as its chronological point of departure. Usually the event is literary—typically the publication of an original work, of a journal, or of a translation; the first performance of a play; the death of an author. But some events are literary only in terms of their repercussions, and some of those repercussions are far removed from their origins in time or place. The juxtaposition of these events is designed to produce an effect of heterogeneity and to disrupt the traditional orderliness of most histories of literature: essays devoted to a genre coexist with essays devoted to one book, institutions are presented alongside literary movements, large surveys next to detailed analysis of specific landmarks.

No article is conceived as a comprehensive presentation of a single author. There are, for example, several Rousseaus: the Rousseau of the *Essai sur l'origine des langues* (1754? *Essay on the Origin of Languages*), the Rousseau of the *Lettre à M. d'Alembert sur les spectacles* (1758; *Letter to M. d'Alembert on the Theater*), the Rousseau of *Du contrat social* (1762; *On the Social Contract*), and the Rousseau of *Les confessions* (1782–1789). Proust also appears through various lenses: fleetingly, in connection with Antoine Galland's translation of *The Thousand and One Nights* (1704; *Les mille et une nuits*); in 1898, in connection with the Dreyfus

Affair; in 1905, on the occasion of the law on the separation of church and state; in 1911, in relation to Gide and their different treatments of homosexuality; and in 1922 on the occasion of his death. The concept of *period* has undergone a fragmentation analogous to that of author. Rather than following the usual periodization schemes by centuries, as often as possible we have favored much briefer time spans and focused on nodal points, coincidences, returns, resurgences.

Without pretending to cover every author, work, and cultural development since the Serments de Strasbourg in 842, this history attempts to be both informative and critical. It presents the classical canon next to both its rivals and its opponents. In setting forth not only their knowledge but also their points of view and their choices, the contributors offer encounters with the major methodological and ideological positions in today's literary studies.

Although each essay is conceived as an independent entity, connections to discussions of related interest in the volume are flagged by a *See also* at the conclusion of many essays. Titles of French works are followed at their first occurrence by their date of publication and a translation of the title in parentheses. Old spellings of proper names and titles have been modernized. All quotations are given in English and are followed by a brief reference to a source listed in the bibliography following each article.

The Editors

On Writing Literary History

One of the most selfless of today's international humanitarian institutions is called Médecins sans Frontières, Doctors without Borders. Literature, however, selfless or not, never comes without borders. Not only, as Rousseau said, does language distinguish humans from animals, but also, as he added, languages distinguish nations from one another.

National borders are not the only ones dividing literature. Borders also exist between genders, classes, and generations, between the oral and the written, between writing and reading; and all these are significant. It is also true that the linguistic map of the world is not identical with the political one, and that the nationalistic celebration of borders is not the only way of accounting for their existence. Works of literature are not as tightly bound to place as are architectural ones, or to time as are political acts. The most significant aspects of the Western idea of literature are embodied in the book, a physical object that circulates more easily through the world than any oral utterance; able to overstep the borders enclosing vernacular languages, it is less tightly anchored to local history and geography. But despite this kind of freedom, literature's production and consumption remain for the most part shaped by the nonuniversality of languages, framed by the experience of frontiers. The necessity of translation (as well as its many impossibilities) is part of its definition: literature is both lost and found in translation. Esperanto might be a linguistic utopia; but it will remain a language with no literature.

This linguistic anchorage is responsible for the commonly held idea that literary historians ought to belong to the same linguistic background as their object: literary history has to be written by natives, from within; one is entitled to write only the history of one's own literature. This almost autobiographical dimension was underlined by Chateaubriand when he remarked in his *Essai sur la littérature anglaise* (1836; *Essay on English Literature*): "It's hilarious to find out who our great writers are in London, Vienna, Berlin, Petersburg, Munich, Leipzig, Göttingen, Cologne" (*Essai,* 2:235). And, having written his survey of English literature in Paris, he must admit the inevitable corollary for his own effort: "I have just expressed my opinion on a whole crowd of English authors:

it is very possible . . . that my judgments will seem impertinent and grotesque on the other side of the Channel" (p. 236).

Chateaubriand's worries, of course, are more those of a writer than of a scholar, as much about being known as about knowing. And after expressing his concerns for "our great writers" he joins their ranks and speaks in his own name—"we great men"—bitterly depicting the aspect of the Romantic departmentalization of literature to which his desire for fame made him most sensitive, the end of universal literary glory: "In Vienna, Petersburg, Berlin, London, Lisbon, Madrid, Rome, Paris, no one will ever have the same and identical view of a German, English, Portuguese, Spanish, Italian, French poet, as we do with Virgil and Homer . . . We great men count on filling the world with our fame, but, whatever we do, it will scarcely cross the borders at which our language expires" (*Essai,* 2:237–238). Modernity has brought the loss of universal standards. With the European republic of letters now divided into national literatures, no nation willingly ratifies the local fame of its competitors. Fame, now tied to languages, ends just where languages do.

The nationalization of literary fame is coeval with the Romantic vision of literature inaugurated in France by Germaine de Staël's *De la littérature considérée dans ses rapports avec les institutions sociales* (1801; *The Influence of Literature upon Society*). Staël's work is rightly considered to be the charter of the twin decanonizing disciplines, literary history and comparative literature. From this date on, literary studies sought to contextualize the productions of the mind, to present them as conforming to a cultural ecology, to reconstruct, as biology does for living organisms, the milieu that allowed them to appear and to grow. Tastes, which are a function of context, took the place of rules, which are not: each era, each nation, came to be viewed in terms of its own values, its own style. Despite the singular *littérature* in its title, Staël's book has a pluralizing message: *Des littératures.*

Such contextualization also rooted literary works in their geographic soil: the *genius loci,* like Sartre's legendary bananas, could be tasted only on the spot. Whether oral or written, they traveled no longer. *Scripta restant.* Instead, readers started traveling specifically as readers. Reflecting the Romantics' taste for *couleur locale,* most early French literary historians drew their inspiration from what we would call today anthropology (or cultural tourism), concerning themselves with non-French as well as with proto and early French literatures. Staël's career as a historian of literature, for example, was a consequence of exile: she wrote *De l'Allemagne* (1813; *On Germany*) because Napoleon, instead of asking the most brilliant *femme de lettres* of his time to influence society, banished her from Paris. Similarly, Chateaubriand's *Essai* owes everything to his sojourns in England, first as an exile, later as an ambassador. Jean-Jacques Ampère, who introduced the term *littérature comparée* in French, described his speciality as "traveling criticism" (*critique en voyage*); an active globetrotter, he visited Germany and Sweden before writing about "Northern Literatures," and Greece before writing about Homer. The challenge was to bridge the historical or geographic gap separating the contexts of the work and of its Romantic revival.

For the French, who, throughout the Enlightenment, considered their language to be the voice of the universal, this nationalization almost came to mean their own cultural death. As late as 1784, for example, Antoine de Rivarol had read in Berlin a somewhat immodest discourse, *De l'universalité de la langue française* (*On the Universality of the French Language*), in which he declared bluntly: "The time has come to call the world French" (p. 2); and the arrogance of such a statement did not prevent Prussia's Frederick the Great from acclaiming it. Yet even then the time had in fact passed for calling a sizable part of the world French: in the 1763 Treaty of Paris, France had given up Canada to England and Louisiana to Spain, a geopolitical reapportionment that resulted in France's "exclusion from the world where the human race begins anew" (Chateaubriand, *Mémoires d'outre-tombe* [1849; *Memoirs from beyond the Grave*], 1:317). The Romantic view of literature also was at odds with the neoclassical agenda that ruled most French cultural institutions after the Revolution, typified by the very name—*lycée* (lyceum)—given by Bonaparte in 1802 to secondary schools. Accordingly, the first histories of French literature, which sought above all else to defend classical stability against Romantic relativism, were resolutely antihistorical. Désiré Nisard's *Histoire de la littérature française* (1841–1861) praised "what is constant, essential, immutable in *l'esprit français*" (1:9); it presented this French mind as untouched by evolution, as "always identical with itself" (4:540). In his 1810 letter censoring *De l'Allemagne*, Napoleon's police minister had told Staël: "We are not yet reduced to looking for models among the nations you admire" (*De l'Allemagne*, 1:39). Nisard, thirty years later, still wanted to spare French literature the vicissitudes of change, the trials of otherness: looking beyond the borders of France for inspiration could only be fatal for it. French literature was different from all others precisely because in it there was nothing "merely local" (1:18). The same "chauvinisme transcendantal," as Charles Augustin Sainte-Beuve (*Causeries du lundi* [1859; *Monday Chats*], 11:465) characterized Nisard's position, was expressed even more graphically, around the same time, in the concept of *nationalité,* still a neologism when Emile Littré included an article on it in his 1866 *Dictionnaire de la langue française.* His dissymmetrical definition contrasted a statement about the phenomenon elsewhere ("the principle of nationalities is in the process of transforming Germany") with a disclaimer about its operativeness in France, allegedly derived from Napoleon Bonaparte: "Les Français n'ont point de nationalité" ("French people have no nationality at all"). This blindness to one's own nationalism survived the 19th century. Ingrained against the most obvious goodwill, it would lead Sartre himself, in the same year that he wrote his diatribe against "La nationalisation de la littérature" (1947; "The Nationalization of Literature"), to publish *Qu'est-ce que la littérature?* (*What Is Literature?*), a dazzling short history of French literature whose title seems to imply that for him there simply was no literature outside France.

Nisard, as director of the Ecole Normale Supérieure from 1857 until the fall of the Second Empire in 1870, practically controlled the teaching of literature in French secondary schools. In institutionalizing the rhetorical resistance against the progress of history, he delayed in France the defeat of rhetoric by science. Elsewhere in Europe, the mid-19th century witnessed the development of a growing gap between history and literature. History, seeking legitimation as a scientific discipline, entered the university by withdrawing from the epublic of letters. Modern historians wanted to be admired not for the way they wrote, but for what they wrote. This change in focus from eloquence to research transformed the teaching of literature in high schools: students were required no longer to admire and imitate, to compete with the eloquence of classical models, but to analyze, describe, and judge. Gérard Genette summarizes this pedagogical shift in his essay "Rhétorique et enseignement" (1969; "Rhetoric and Teaching"): "From a model, literature turned into an object; scholarly discourse was no longer a literary discourse but a discourse about literature" (*Figures II*, p. 30). Gustave Lanson's 1895 *Histoire de la littérature française* is, in that sense, the first work to deserve (and to claim fully) the status of history. As director of the same Ecole Normale Supérieure in the 1920s, Lanson thus exerted the same influence that Nisard had on the teaching of literature, but to an opposite end. For him, literary history had a political function as a tool of national reconciliation; in its space, former enemies— Catholics and Protestants, the Ancients and the Moderns, the classics and the Romantics—were able to coexist. The emergence of the discipline of comparative literature fulfilled an identical function, but at the international level. Comparative literature is the 20th-century version of the 18th-century republic of letters.

For the Romantics, the chief border affecting literary history was the linguistic one separating nations; for the positivist historians it was the epistemological border separating a scientific discourse from its object. For the comparativists there is yet a third, implicit border: the one separating the literary and the nonliterary. "Like humanity, Literature is one," René Wellek and Austin Warren proclaim in their *Theory of Literature* (p. 50). But in overcoming the conflicts of nationalities, comparative literature also obliterates the singularity of idioms. Thus, although Wellek and Warren analyze what the status of a poem owes to its being oral or written, to being read aloud or read silently, to what extent it is dependent on its typographical presentation, and even whether it can be affected by the occurrence of typographical errors, they never address the fact that the signs of a literary work of art also belong— for reasons that are essential to its definition—to a given idiom. The question of translation is totally ignored. Literature's independence of languages is a prerequisite for enclosing the literary work of art within its own border.

Such an essentialism does not preclude per se a historical approach to literature. Wellek claims on the contrary that it provides the ground for a true literary history. Replacing both a theory of literature unable to account for its evolution and a view of history unable to account for the literary, a formalist literary history will finally grasp literature's own historicity, literature changing as literature and for literary reasons. Methodological debates concerning literary history traditionally focus on the relations between what is inside and what is outside a literary work, between its content and its context. Whether they intend to demonstrate literature's independence of any contextual influence, its enforced responsiveness to what occurs in its surroundings, or its evolution according to its own laws, all these versions of literary history require that it always be clear what is inside and what outside, where literature starts and where it ends, where one enters and where one leaves literature.

Today it is increasingly difficult to draw one solid line of demarcation between the inside and the outside of a work of art; sometimes it is even impossible to distinguish between form and background. Context itself has been "textualized": Georges Bataille and Maurice Blanchot define modern art as being "out of work"; Hans Robert Jauss moves it outward toward its reception; Gérard Genette is concerned with the editorial procedures by which a text is severed from its author—the "paratextual," external presentation that makes a book out of it; Jacques Derrida insists on margins, on frames, on the parergon, the "hors-livre" that his translator renders as the "outwork." One enters literature by leaving it. There is no reliable checkpoint; it is impossible to say where it starts and where it ends. Literature is engrossed by what takes its place. The possibility of a history of literature is thus dependent on both literature's resistance to history and literature's resistance to literature. Literature wants to be everything—but beside itself. As a result, the question today is no longer, as it still was for Sartre, "What is literature?" but rather, "What is not?"

For us, the space of literature is mapped according to more complex and more delicate strategies, which, though not denying the inescapable partisanships that go with the politics of language, are no longer contained by national politics. Its focus has shifted from the assertion of borders through literature and the presentation of a literature within borders, to a questioning that results in the proliferation of those borders. Such a questioning, occurring both within and outside literature, both constitutes and undoes literature.

What French person, asked Chateaubriand, would not smile at the idea of a history of French literature composed outside France's own frontiers? This *New History of French Literature* has been written from both sides of as many borders as possible.

Bibliography: François-René de Chateaubriand, *Essai sur la littérature anglaise et considérations sur le génie des hommes, des temps et des révolutions,* 2 vols. (Paris: Gosselin et Furne, 1836). Chateaubriand, *Mémoires d'outre-tombe,* ed. Maurice Levaillant, 4 vols. (Paris: Garnier, 1964). Gérard Genette, *Figures II* (Paris: Seuil, 1969). Désiré Nisard, *Histoire de la littérature française,* 4 vols. (Paris: Firmin-Didot, 1883). Antoine de Rivarol, *De l'universalité de la langue française,* in *Oeuvres complètes,* vol. 2 (Paris: Léopold Collin, 1808). Charles Augustin Sainte-Beuve, *Causeries du lundi,* vol. 11 (Paris: Garnier, n.d.). Jean-Paul Sartre, *What Is Literature? and Other Essays* (Cambridge, Mass.: Harvard University Press, 1988). Germaine de Staël, *De l'Allemagne,* ed. Simone Balayé, 2 vols. (Paris: Garnier-Flammarion, 1968). Austin Warren and René Wellek, *Theory of Literature* (New York: Harcourt Brace Jovanovich, 1977).

Denis Hollier

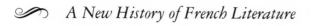 *A New History of French Literature*

Roland Dies at Roncevaux

Entering the Date

In matters of literary history, assigning dates is far more problematic for medieval works than for modern ones: most printed books bear dates provided by the printers themselves, first as a matter of bibliographic convention and soon afterward as a matter of law, whereas most literary texts produced in the Middle Ages are undated (administrative documents were, of course, a different matter). In the later Middle Ages scribes copying manuscripts started to indicate in a colophon at the end of the text their names, the place (usually a monastery) at which they were working, the date they had finished copying the work, or all three. The first book printed with a dated colophon appeared in Mainz in 1457, and the practice was introduced in France, in Lyons, in 1473. But no law required the provision of such information, and in the last decade of the 15th century almost half the books printed in Europe, like most manuscripts, contained no statement identifying either their producer or the time of their production. In the 16th century more and more printers noted their names and the date and place of publication. Legal requirements soon reinforced this practice. In 1521 Francis I forbade the sale in France of books that had not been examined by the University of Paris, and in 1563 Charles IX prohibited printing in France without permission. To show their compliance with the law and the exclusive publishing rights (or privilege) given them by the crown, printers began to display the words *cum privilegio* and the year on the title page (an innovation originating in Venice in 1476 and introduced in France in 1486). Slowly, publishers had taken the first steps toward today's bibliographic processing by the Bibliothèque Nationale or the Library of Congress and the registration of an International Standard Book Number.

Literary historians have developed a useful distinction among "oral," "manuscript," and "print" cultures, despite the fact that in a given society two or all three of these modes of transmission may coexist, as print and television media do today. In terms of literary transmission the classical world of the late Roman Republic and Empire was a manuscript culture, indeed a very highly developed one. Cicero wrote for an active book trade, and Atticus may be said to have served as his "publisher." There were public libraries (Augustus founded two), and Virgil, Horace, and Ovid saw their works become part of the usual school curriculum during their lifetimes. Classical authors commonly followed the example of the Greek lyric poet Theognis and made sure that their names appeared like a seal somewhere in their works. Occasionally they wrote something about the circumstances of composition, even a reference to when a text was completed, as Virgil did at the end of the *Georgics*. But the concept of dating a work precisely by year or consulship, or even of providing information that would allow posterity to assign an exact date, was almost unknown.

In contrast, the Germanic peoples who overthrew the Roman Empire had an oral culture. In such a culture the only dates that are relevant for poems, songs, or tales are the dates of the events portrayed in them. An oral work may be said to have first appeared at a certain date, but because each successive performance is both a repetition and a new presentation, as long as the work continues to be told or sung directly to an actual audience it cannot be assigned a definitive date of composition. Even when an oral narrative has been committed to writing, as in the case of the *Chanson de Roland* (*Song of Roland*), attempting to determine *a* date is a futile exercise. Although some of the phrases in the Oxford manuscript of the *Chanson de Roland*, which was probably copied in the second quarter of the 12th century, are remarkably similar to those used by Pope Urban II at the Council of Clermont in 1095, and although the language of this manuscript is that used at the turn of the 12th century, it is clear that much of the material dates from a much earlier period and reflects a long oral poetic evolution. The geographic bounds of the earthquake that occurs at the time of Roland's death—"from Saint-Michel-du-Péril to Saintes and from Besançon to Wissant"—correspond roughly to the limits of the 10th-century kingdom of Francia. Is the *Chanson de Roland*, then, a 10th-century work, as the traces of its earliest versions suggest? Is it a late 11th-century work, as the state of its language and certain historically rooted phrases suggest? Or is it a mid-12th-century work, as suggested by the probable date of the earliest manuscript copy on which our modern edition is based? The idea of precise dating has little or no meaning in a society in which events are normally remembered rather than recorded. In northern France, until the middle of the 12th century even administrative documents such as charters were often undated.

Before 1155 the written versions of what we call vernacular literature contained no references to a date of composition, just as they hardly ever contained an indication of authorship. Besides the occasional scribes who signed their work, dated it, or both, the only exceptions to this rule were those quasi-authors: translators. Like the editors of late antiquity, translators of Greek or Arabic texts into Latin often appended a date to their efforts. For example, when Adelard of Bath translated a volume of Arabic astronomical tables into Latin, he noted the Christian date, 26 January 1126, along with the Muslim equivalent; and the *explicit* that concludes Hermann of Carinthia's translation of another astronomical work gives the date as 3 kalends October 1138. Like-

2

wise, the first Old French texts to supply dates were translations. The Norman poet Robert Wace concluded his free translation of Geoffrey of Monmouth's Latin *Historia Regum Britanniae* (ca. 1136; *History of the Kings of Britain*), the *Roman de Brut* (*Brutus*), with the statement that he had "made" it in 1155. To the best of my knowledge, this is the earliest work in French given a date by its author.

Another work from the 12th century dated by its author is Aimon de Varennes's romantic and fabulous tale *Florimont,* about the grandfather of Alexander the Great. Aimon, a most self-conscious author, mentions his own name eighteen times in the poem. At the end, he declares that he "made" his romance in 1188, but by his own account his French composition was a translation: elsewhere in the poem he says that he had come upon or heard a Greek "story" (*istoire*) in Greece at Philippopolis (now Plovdiv in Bulgaria), that he had brought back a written Latin version, and from that he had later "made" his French romance, which he wrote at his home near Lyons. Aimon probably visited Philippopolis as a member of a crusading army or armed band of pilgrims taking the land route through Hungary and Bulgaria to Adrianople; Lyons was part of the German empire, and on the Third Crusade the army of Frederick Barbarossa stopped at Philippopolis for five weeks in 1189. Aimon's date of 1188 for the completion of the French text seems to rule out the possibility that he visited Greece as part of that army, but even a precise and apparently sure date must be viewed critically in the light of other knowledge about a text. Although 1188 (".M. [et] .C. .IIIIXX. et .VIII. ans") is the editor's preferred reading, numbers may easily be transmitted incorrectly: other manuscripts have "Mil et .C. et .IIII. v. ans" (which makes no sense) and "M .C. et .XXIIII. ans" (which, depending on spacing and punctuation, can be read as either 1124 or 1180).

Early in the 13th century several translations from Latin were given dates by their French authors. The prologue to the second or "Johannes" version of the *Pseudo-Turpin Chronicle,* a prose translation, announces a date of 1206. The translator may have been Pierre de Beauvais, who made a prose translation into French of a related text, *Translation et miracles de saint Jacques* (*Translation and Miracles of Saint James*), and stated at the end that he had done his work in 1212 at Beauvais. An Anglo-Norman verse translation, *La vie de saint Grégoire* (*The Life of Saint Gregory*), was made by a canon of St. Frideswide in Oxford named Angier, who stated in a Latin *explicit* that he had completed his work on Friday ("feria .vi.") of the fourth week of November in 1212 (".mᵒ . ccᵒ . x iiᵒ "), the eve ("vigilia") of St. Andrew the apostle. Scholars have debated whether Angier made a mistake about the day of the week or dropped a stroke from the year, for in 1212 the eve or vigil of St. Andrew fell on Thursday rather than Friday. Since we have the translator's holograph manuscript, that is, the manuscript entirely written by the translator himself, it seems that Angier himself is responsible for our confusion. In any case, he attempted to date with precision the completion of his work.

Soon a few French authors began to ascribe dates to vernacular works that were not translations. For example, Gossouin (Goswin) of Metz noted in both the preface and the conclusion of the first version of his scientific encyclopedia, *L'image du monde* (*The Image of the World*), that it had been made at Les Roises (in Lorraine) on Epiphany in the year 1245 (by the old calendar). Geufroi of Paris, of whom we know little but the name, stated in the epilogue to his *Bible des sept états du monde* (*Bible of the Seven Estates of the World*), a scissors-and-paste presentation of vernacular works by other authors, that he compiled his work in 1243. Robert de l'Oulme noted in the epilogue to his original poem, *Dit des sept serpents* (*Poem of the Seven Snakes*), that he finished his work in 1266 on the third day after Trinity Sunday (26 May). Master Ermengaud recorded that he *began* his Provençal *Bréviaire d'amour* (*Love's Breviary*) in 1288.

In the second half of the 13th century a large proportion of precisely dated works in French continued to be translations: Alexandre du Pont's *Roman de Mohammed* (1258; *Romance of Mahomet*), Guillaume d'Oyes's *La vie de saint Thibaut* (July 1267; *The Life of Saint Thibaut*), Hagin's translation from Hebrew of Abraham ibn Ezra's *The Beginning of Wisdom,* the translation of the first two books of Andreas Capellanus' *De Amore* (ca. 1185; *The Art of Courtly Love*) by Drouart la Vache (1290). In 1280 Pieros du Riés completed Gautier de Belleperche's rather free translation of the biblical book of Maccabees, *La chevalerie de Judas Macchabée* (*The Knighthood of Judas Maccabaeus*), and in 1285 the same Pieros or an anonymous author produced another *Chevalerie de Judas Macchabée et de ses nobles frères* (*The Knighthood of Judas Maccabaeus and of His Noble Brothers*), which borrowed heavily from the work of Gautier de Belleperche.

Toward the middle of the 13th century changes in the techniques of book production, notably the development of commercially organized workshops and the beginning of mass production, gave book producers increased control over the diffusion of a given work. Manuscript copies were often dated, and those dates were often repeated verbatim in later copies, creating a class of falsely dated manuscripts to confuse paleographers. The active book trade and mass production were not controlled by the author. Indeed, dating and the attendant sense that an author had finished a work and had let it go extended even to such apparently ephemeral (or timeless?) compositions as songs; the troubadour Guiraud Riquier kept a record of the dates of many of his songs, and rubricators noted dates for songs by his contemporaries Raimon Gaulcelm and Joan Estève of Béziers.

Although even in the 14th and 15th centuries a significant majority of authors took no interest in informing their readers of the dates of composition of their works, there are a few detailed authorial accounts. One chronologically self-conscious 14th-century author is instructive for a study of dating. Guillaume de Deguilleville told his readers that he began the *Le pèlerinage de la vie humaine* (*The Pilgrimage of Human Life*) in 1330 at the age of thirty-five. He completed this work two years later, copies went into circulation, and this first "edition" was highly successful, as the existence of over seventy-five manuscripts attests. But Guillaume was not satisfied with his work and came back to the poem twenty-five years later. As he announced in the prologue of his revised "second edition," his first text had been "taken" from him "without his

4

knowledge and against his will," before he had had a chance to make the corrections he thought necessary. Although it is doubtful that Guillaume was as innocent of responsibility for the first circulation of his work as he claimed, his prologue shows that he regretted the loss of control over his work entailed by its "premature" circulation.

Under ideal circumstances authors could keep their personal copies of a manuscript for many years, allowing other copies to be made at different stages of development but maintaining their capability to shape the work, correct it, and allow it to develop. Copies of such texts made at different dates are like sketches of a growing child, each an authentic representation of a given stage, no one more authoritative than another. But a medieval work varied also with the copyists. Some scribes were careless; some ignorantly misunderstood their exemplars; others, too bright for their readers' good, introduced "corrections" where none were needed. In addition, the scribes who copied medieval French texts felt remarkably free to introduce deliberate changes. For example, a Picard scribe who copied a poem written in the dialect of neighboring Champagne might alter words at the ends of the line, and others if necessary, or might change the order of lines, so that his product would rhyme in his own dialect. Under such circumstances, a "copy" was not so much a copy as a new version. Two "copies" of what we take to be the same work may vary significantly in length, in the episodes they contain, and even in the order of lyric strophes. Authorial revision? Scribal intervention? We often have no way of knowing.

Not all texts were altered with the same freedom, of course. The Bible, liturgical books, and "authoritative works" (*auctoritates*) were treated with great respect, and the licensed system of piecework copying developed at the University of Paris in the 13th century was created in part in order to protect textbooks from contamination. In general, vernacular texts were more freely edited by copyists than Latin ones, and poetry was more subject to change than prose. To the degree that a work could easily be revised either by its original author or in the process of transmission, any given text would be seen more as part of a process than as a datable object. The medieval text was constantly subject to a multiplicity of hands and minds that contributed to its evolution, up to and including modern editors, who must choose among the different manuscript versions and printed variants what could be considered—anachronistically—to be a definitive work.

There is no notion more alien to the conditions of medieval literary creation than that of precise dating, which is the obsession of 19th- and 20th-century literary historians who conjecture about chronology on the basis of comparisons between information contained in a particular work and what we know from other sources about the events of the period, or on the basis of internal linguistic information. This is another way of saying that the date assigned medieval works is always the result of a conscious, and therefore somewhat arbitrary, decision as to what constitutes its "date"—the hypothetical date of composition; the date of a first performance; the date on which an oral song or legend was supposedly first transcribed; the dates of subsequent transcriptions or

5

copies; the date ascribable to language, which may be archaic with respect to any given copy; the date of revision, either by the original author or by someone else; or the date of translation. The complex assumptions that go into the attribution of a date emphasize the extreme fluidity of the medieval text, whose origin, and thus whose originality, depends upon thoroughly modern notions of what defines not only a date, but also at what moment the text as a literary object is constituted.

Medieval poets' and scribes' lack of attention to dating reflects a fundamental difference between the idea of literary property and the means of literary production in the Middle Ages and in the modern era. Literature produced before the period of increasing literary privilege—that is, before the period beginning with Francis I's requirement that books be scrutinized and culminating in the copyright laws of the 18th century—were not conceived to be the possession of an individual author who in essence "owned," or owned the rights to, his or her work. The work, in turn, has no precise moment of origin. This is why so many of the poems known before the 13th century are anonymous, and why, when we do know the name of the poet (which sometimes is no more than a common first name), we often know little else. In an age in which literary invention seems to have been based upon memory as well as upon the skillful use of received rhetorical devices, poetry, like performance, the manufacture of paper, or the copying of manuscripts, was conceived as a craft, as a product neither of divine inspiration, as in classical times, nor of individual genius, as in the Romantic period. The medieval poet was, after all, less a creator than a *trouvère*—one who finds.

See also 1123, 1202, 1214, 1342, 1555 (13 September).

Bibliography: Jean Delorme, *Chronologie des civilisations* (Paris: Presses Universitaires de France, 1969). Reginald Land Poole, *Medieval Reckonings of Time* (London: Society for Promoting Christian Knowledge, 1918). R. Dean Ware, "Medieval Chronology," in *Medieval Studies: An Introduction,* ed. James M. Powell (Syracuse: Syracuse University Press, 1976), pp. 213–237.

John Benton

 842

Louis the German and Charles the Bald, Grandsons of Charlemagne, Ratify the Serments de Strasbourg

The First Document and the Birth of Medieval Studies

The Serments de Strasbourg (the Oaths of Strasbourg), a treaty between two sons of Louis the Pious, Charlemagne's grandsons, are generally recognized as the earliest document in any Romance language. According to the Frankish chronicler Nithard, himself a grandson of Charlemagne, whose history of the sons of Louis the Pious (*Nithardi Historiarum Libri III* [*Nithard's Three Books of History*], Bibliothèque Nationale Ms. lat. 9768) contains the record of the event, Louis the German met Charles the Bald on 14 February 842 in the city of Argentoratum (Strasbourg) for the purpose of resolving the quarrel with their eldest brother Lothair over the "middle kingdom" between Germany and France (modern-day Alsace and Lorraine) (see map). After haranguing his army in his native tongue, each swore in the language of the other a solemn promise of mutual assistance. Thus Louis:

For the love of God and the salvation of the Christian people and our common salvation, from this day forward, in so far as God grants me knowledge and power, I will succor this my brother Charles in aid and in everything, as one ought by right to succor one's brother, provided that he do likewise by me, and I will never undertake an engagement with Lothair which, by my consent, may be of harm to this my brother Charles.   (Quoted in Ewert, *The French Language,* p. 352)

Both military chiefs then elicited, again in their own language, confirmation from their vassals.

The Strasbourg Oaths, written at a time when the idiom spoken in Carolingian Gaul seems to have become sufficiently distinct from classical Latin to constitute a separate tongue, tell us much about the status of language at the time of Charlemagne. Nithard's juxtaposition of tongues—the Latin narrative framing the promises in Romance and in Rhenish Franconian German—attests to the fact that Latin represented the only medium suitable for writing, and especially for drafting documents, even though people may have communicated orally in the vernacular. More important, the hybrid structure of the "lingua romana" referred to by Nithard, with its Latin archaisms alongside forms anticipatory of Old French, offers unique evidence of what such a spoken language might have been in the period between late antiquity and the so-called Renaissance of the 12th century.

Yet certain unresolved issues still perplex those who study this oldest Romance document. Indeed, the history of scholarship dealing with this document offers ample evidence that many of the urgent issues of medieval studies remain without definite solution and that much of what we do know remains conjecture. We do not, for example, understand adequately the process by which a

7

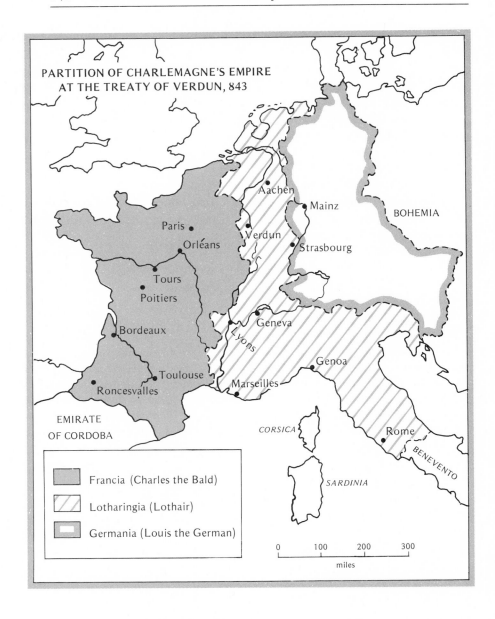

PARTITION OF CHARLEMAGNE'S EMPIRE
AT THE TREATY OF VERDUN, 843

BOHEMIA

Aachen

Mainz

Paris

Orléans

Verdun

Strasbourg

Tours

Poitiers

Geneva

Lyons

Bordeaux

Genoa

Toulouse

Marseilles

Roncesvalles

EMIRATE
OF CORDOBA

CORSICA

Rome

BENEVENTO

SARDINIA

■ Francia (Charles the Bald)

▨ Lotharingia (Lothair)

□ Germania (Louis the German)

0   100   200   300
miles

scribe might have transliterated a language for the first time and precisely what that language, still in the process of formation, might have been. Because the only surviving manuscript of Nithard's *Historiarum Libri III* dates from the end of the 10th century, we cannot know with certainty whether the Romance version of the oaths was in fact pronounced at Strasbourg in 842. We do not know whether our record is a glossed commentary on some preexisting text, or a later addition. We have no way of telling how many copyists might have worked on intermediary versions between Nithard's original and our rendition, or to what extent supposed errors or inconsistencies in the text—unclear divi-

8

sion of words, variant spellings, syntactic differences between the Romance and German versions—are the results of scribal ignorance, carelessness, mistranslation, or deliberate emendation. Nithard does not reveal whether he actually participated in the swearing, and, if so, whether his role was that of author, redactor, court recorder, or eyewitness. He gives no clue as to whether the oaths were read aloud from a written copy or whether the written version is a record of what was said. We will most likely never know if the Oaths of Strasbourg were originally composed in the vernacular or translated from Latin, if the Romance served as a model for the German or the German took precedence, or, finally, if they were composed by the same person.

The difficulties attached to the transcription of a language with no fixed system for the graphic rendering of sounds makes one wonder about both the language in which the oaths might actually have been pronounced and the relation of such a linguistic event to its transcription by Nithard. It has been suggested, for example, that the Romance Strasbourg Oaths and the Latin that frames them are in reality a single tongue transcribed in different ways, their difference one between the uniform archaic way in which Latin was habitually written and some cruder attempt at phonetic transcription. The question remains, in other words, whether what Nithard's text calls "lingua romana" is indeed Old French or Latin. If Latin, is it spoken or Gallo-Latin or a form of notarial Latin (that used at the Carolingian court for official documents) deliberately vulgarized? If, on the other hand, the "lingua romana" can indeed be considered an example of Romance vernacular, to which region of linguistically fragmented Gaul does it belong? Scholars have maintained variously and with equal conviction that the dialect of the Strasbourg Oaths is that of Burgundy, Lyons, Lorraine, Picardy, Ponthieu, Poitou, the Rhône; that it is an example of Old Northern French, Old Southern French, "West Romance," "pre-French."

Speculation about how to classify the inaugural transcription of a language cannot be divorced from the difficulties of reading a tongue devoid of context, and simply of identifying meaningful graphic signs upon the parchment page. Scholars have quarreled bitterly, for example, about how to transliterate into Roman characters the oath of Charles's vassals as it appears in the manuscript:

Indeed, the question of how to write, in the most literal sense, the Strasbourg Oaths determines how to read them, or how to make sense out of an apparently incomprehensible phrase such as **n loftanæ**. The parallelism of the oath sworn in German ("If Charles keeps the oath . . . and Louis breaks it") is upset in Romance by the illogicality of the *lo,* which seems to refer syntactically to Louis's oath and not, as the situation suggests, to that of Charles; by the masculine possessive pronoun *suo* modifying the feminine noun *partem;* and by the abbreviation *n* for *non,* which seems to negate the purpose of the hypothetical clause. Thus various specialists have proposed that when the scribe wrote **n loftanne,** he really intended *non los tanit, non lo se tanit, non lo stanit* or *l'ostanit, non lo frangit, non lo suon tint, lo suon fraint, non lo fraint, non l'enfraint, de suo partem lo fraint, de suo part in lo s[agramen]t anit, non loftanit, non lo s[en] tanit, de sua part lo suon infraint.* Such disagreement about how even to decipher certain words means that we remain unable to read with certainty the Oaths of Strasbourg. "We are ready to confess that all our reasonings about this text are mere gropings in the dark," observed the noted editor Ernest Muret (*Romania,* 1921, p. 426). Yet the very mystery surrounding the Oaths of Strasbourg demonstrates the inseparability of the linguistic and material conditions of early medieval literature and at the same time makes it ideal for our understanding of medieval studies in France.

Speculation about a founding cultural document such as the Strasbourg Oaths is necessarily as ideologically determined by the present as by the past. Thus it can be no accident either that the discipline of medieval studies came into being in France in the period between the Franco-Prussian War and World War I (1870–1914) or that scholars from the beginning used what they could not know with certainty about such early texts for their own nationalistic purposes. At a time when nation-states were deciding militarily whether Alsace and Lorraine—that is, Strasbourg—were to be French or German, specialists debated passionately whether Europe's earliest literary monuments were of French or German origin.

Medieval specialists around 1870, whose views still inform our own, perceived erudition as a form of war, and France as a laggard in classical and medieval studies and in paleographic and philological methods. This was in part a demographic perception. Germans were not only outbreeding the French but outpublishing them as well. "The German people have in erudition the same qualities as in war," wrote the eminent historian Numa Fustel de Coulanges, "that is, numbers and discipline. Their historians form an organized army" (*Revue des deux mondes,* 1872, p. 245). Léon Gautier, whose *Epopées françaises* (1868; *The French Epic*) had appeared just before the Franco-Prussian War, later blamed the French defeat of 1870 upon scholarly defects: "We find before us a nation that makes war scientifically . . . The Prussian fights in the same way he criticizes a text, with the same precision and method" (*Revue des questions historiques,* 1870, p. 496). Gautier lamented that more Germans in a single town (Marburg) were working on the *chanson de geste* than in all of France, that the two medieval journals of France were outmatched by ten beyond the Rhine, that German universities gave more courses on Old French literature, and that their students had more stamina and force. In fact, in Germany by 1875 the publication of primary medieval sources had become a matter of state, aided by the resources of empire and uniting the Academies of Berlin, Munich, and Vienna. The establishment of a chair of Romance philology at Strasbourg in 1872 was merely a symptom of the proliferation after 1860 of such posts in a country where study of the Middle Ages represented, to a greater degree than in France, a catalyst of national identity. The study of ancient texts was considered a German science, and those who were instrumental in the founding of historical and literary studies in France were obliged to go abroad for training—Michel Bréal to Berlin for Sanskrit with Franz Bopp, Gaston Paris to Bonn for philology with Friedrich Diez, Gabriel Monod to Berlin for paleography with Philipp Jaffé. In an essay published on the eve of World War I, Henri Massis complained that "there is a clear, logical link between our system of classical studies and the capitulation of Metz, as, of course, between the methodology of German universities and the invasion of Paris" (*Les jeunes gens d'aujourd'hui* [*Today's Young Men*], p. 107).

French reaction to the losses of 1870 largely emulated the German model. In the four years from 1876 to 1879, 250 new chairs of literature and history, supported by university libraries, were endowed. Journals dedicated to medieval culture came slowly into being. Supplementing the *Revue des questions historiques,* with its Catholic, legitimist, anti-Revolutionary, and nationalist predilections, which had done much to encourage interest in the Middle Ages before the war, were the philological journals *Revue des langues romanes* (1870), *Romania* (1872), *Revue de philologie française et provençale* (1887), *Le moyen âge* (1888), and *Annales du Midi* (1889), many of which are still in existence.

Most of all, however, the publication of Old French *chansons de geste,* intended to rival German scholarly production, was accompanied by new ways of reading France's oldest poetic work, the *Chanson de Roland* (ca. 1100; *Song of Roland*), which, like the Strasbourg Oaths in the realm of linguistics, came to constitute for literature the determining limit case. Hardly considered in a patriotic context before the Franco-Prussian War, *Roland* came suddenly to occupy pride of place in the French national heritage. Even as the Germans encircled the capital, Gaston Paris affirmed from his chair at the Collège de France that "in its simple verses . . . vibrated already the voice of France . . . this male heroic voice which has so often resounded in battle . . . this voice of the nation. Let us recognize in ourselves," he urged, "the sons of those who died at Roncevaux [Roncesvalles] and those who avenged them" (*La poésie au moyen âge* [*Poetry in the Middle Ages*], p. 118). The *Chanson de Roland* penetrated the university curriculum as part of the program of the *agrégation* (national teachers examination) in 1877, then secondary education (1880), where it was to serve as the vehicle through which students would learn to love France: "What we want is for you to read, with a vibrating voice and a heart full of emotion," Gautier addressed high school teachers, "a translation of our oldest poem . . . and especially that you take the occasion of this reading to say to these young Frenchmen, 'You see, my children, how great France already was and how she was loved more than eight centuries ago'" (*Epopées,* p. 749).

At the center of medieval studies from the beginning lay the troubling suspicion that French literature may in fact be German. Gaston Paris, who did more than anyone else to institutionalize the discipline at the end of the 19th century, also did more to adapt to the Old French *chanson de geste* German Romantic explanations (those of Friedrich Wolf, Karl Lachmann, Johann Herder, August and Friedrich von Schlegel, and Jacob and Wilhelm Grimm) for the origin of epic. According to Paris' *Histoire poétique de Charlemagne* (1865; *The Poetic History of Charlemagne*), the earliest elements of the *Chanson de Roland*, in the form of songs (*cantilènes*), emanated from witnesses, perhaps even participants, in the events of Roncevaux (778); underwent gradual crystallization into legends; and, some two centuries later, emerged as epics and, eventually, heroic cycles. The implication is, of course, that some embryonic species of the Old French *chanson de geste*, sung by Charlemagne's Frankish warriors, was a function of the Germanization of Gallo-Roman culture, that is, the product of an earlier invasion of France by its neighbor from the East. "The father [of *Roland*] may come from beyond the Rhine," Paris asserted defensively in 1884, "but the mother is still Gallic . . . The germ is German, but the development Roman" (*Romania*, 1884, pp. 613–614).

The issue of the origins of the *Chanson de Roland* is further charged ideologically by certain questions of language of the kind that haunt the Strasbourg Oaths—that is, whether the idiom in which France's oldest literary monument was composed was Germanic, Latin, or Gallo-Romance. Which is another way of asking what the words *Franc, Franceis*, or the phrase repeated in *Roland* "Francs de France," might have meant in the 9th century. For if, as suggested by Paris' thesis of early composition, *Franc* meant "Frank," then French literature was from the start Frankish, or at best a translation. Such a prior linguistic claim might easily be translated into a territorial one, and Strasbourg would in that case be Strassburg. Thus the application to *Roland* of Romantic notions of the epic could only excite the worst fears of the French that France was really Germany in disguise. "'German spirit in a French form,' this," wrote Paris, "is exactly what the word *français* expresses so precisely, with its German root and Latin suffix" (*Romania*, p. 626).

The appearance of Joseph Bédier's four-volume *Les légendes épiques* (1908–1913; *Epic Legends*), just before World War I, repudiated Paris' *Histoire poétique* and, in offering an alternative explanation for the early epic, came to constitute the second major pole of medieval studies. In the place of Paris' early, collective, popular (oral)—that is, Germanic—origins, Bédier asserted individual authorship and late composition of *Roland* (11th century) on the basis of learned (written) sources found along Spanish pilgrimage routes. The strategic effect of such a thesis was threefold. First, it displaced the origin of French literature as far from the "breezes of German forests" (Grimm cited apocryphally by Paris) as possible. Second, it transformed *Roland* into the work of genius of a single poet rather than the quasi-mystical, amorphous by-product of something like "soul of the people." Bédier's equation of the origin of the epic with a singular act of writing both made the *chanson de geste* conform to classical aesthetic criteria and established continuity between the classicism of the 17th century and the Middle Ages. Third, and finally, by rejecting the Germanic notion of

12

natural epic poetry, Bédier's *Légendes épiques* naturalized *Roland* as French, since, by the 11th century, "Franc" could mean nothing else. "Even if we hardly know the name of the author of the *Chanson de Roland*," Bédier alleged, "at least we know he was a 'Frenchman of France' [*Franc de France*], and we find in his work that which is most specifically national in our poetry: a classical sense of proportion, clarity, sobriety, harmonious force" (*Légendes,* 3:451). The French should not give up *Roland* to the Germans, the great medievalist concluded, until the Germans had returned to the Scyths their *Nibelungenlied.*

What this debate suggests is that the founding discourse of medieval studies allows no distinction between explanations of the genesis of France's earliest linguistic and literary monuments and the identity of the nation. Bédier's thesis, which makes "French" synonymous with "free," legitimated the French claim to the lands between Germany and France—the Lotharingia—disputed since at least 842. Referring to the supposed poet of *Roland,* Bédier insisted: "This Turold who, eight hundred years ago caressed our country with names— 'Sweet France,' 'France the Free,'—showed us how simply French unity could be made. His 'Sweet France' is exactly ours with the Lorraines as today, with the Gascons, the Normans, and those of Provence" (*Légendes,* 3:452). The terms of debate over the status of the Strasbourg Oaths and the *Chanson de Roland* were, in other words, identical with conflicting claims over the status of Strasbourg; and the quarrel over the "middle kingdom," which the treaty supposedly concluded, was merely prolonged by the Franco-Prussian and First World wars, out of which medieval studies, displaced and occulted, were born.

See also 1895.

Bibliography: Joseph Bédier, *Les légendes épiques,* 4 vols. (Paris: Champion, 1908–1913). W. D. Elcock, *The Romance Languages* (London: Faber and Faber, 1960), pp. 334–344. Alfred Ewert, *The French Language* (London: Faber and Faber, 1964). Léon Gautier, *Les épopées francaises: Etude sur les origines et l'histoire de la littérature nationale,* 2d ed. (Paris: Librairie Universitaire, 1892). H. U. Gumbrecht, "Un souffle d'Allemagne ayant passé: Friedrich Diez, Gaston Paris, and the Genesis of National Philologies," *Romance Philology,* 40 (1986), 1–37. Henri Massis, *Les jeunes gens d'aujourd'hui* (Paris: Plon, 1913). Gaston Paris, *La poésie au moyen âge,* vol. 1 (Paris: Hachette, 1887). Roger Wright, *Late Latin and Early Romance in Spain and Carolingian France* (Liverpool: Francis Cairns, 1982), pp. 122–126.

R. Howard Bloch

 1050?

An Unidentified Copyist from Normandy, Probably from Rouen, Writes the Hagiographic *Vie de saint Alexis*

Saints' Lives

La vie de saint Alexis (*The Life of Saint Alexius*), probably composed around the middle of the 11th century, is the first sustained narrative in Old French and as such marks the starting point of the history of French literature. The poem recounts the ascetic deeds of a 5th-century scion of a noble Roman family who abandons his wife on the wedding night, leaves for Syria to live a life of poverty, and returns home unrecognized, to spend his last seventeen years as a beggar. After his death, a letter written by Alexis himself reveals his identity to an admiring citizenry, and thus begins the fame and celebration of his life.

In the predominantly Latin culture of the 11th century, *La vie de saint Alexis* constitutes a linguistic and literary document of great significance. Its hero is not only a saint but also a clerk writing down his own story; Alexis' posthumous letter attests and confirms his holiness while glorifying the power of the word. The saint's achievement thus assumes a dual significance, both spiritual and poetic. The originality of *La vie de saint Alexis* lies in its emphasis—new in vernacular writing—on the written text.

One particular episode, that of the discovery of Alexis the saint in the guise of a destitute and anonymous beggar, illustrates the preeminent role of literacy. Following a divine revelation that a "man of God" is to be found in the house of Eufemiien—Alexis' father—the pope and the emperor of Rome go to see him. At this very moment Eufemiien is told that the beggar living in his house has just died. He sees his son's body without recognizing him, notices that Alexis holds a letter in his hand, but is unable to remove it. In contrast,

> The pope stretches out his hand for the letter,
> Saint Alexius opens his to him;
> He surrenders it to him who was pope of Rome.
> He did not read it, nor does he look inside;
> He holds it out to a worthy and learned clerk.
>
> The chancellor, whose duty this was,
> He read the letter; the others listened. (*The Life of Saint Alexius*, pp. 122–123)

The saint's hitherto unrecognized presence is revealed through the written text. Knowledge coincides not with the visible—his appearance as a beggar has in fact prevented his father and wife from recognizing him—but with the less tangible mode of truth produced by textuality. For Alexis the autobiographer as well as for the Norman author of his story—perhaps, according to Gaston Paris, Tedbalt of Vernon, canon at Rouen—immortality results from a transformation of the flesh into words.

The revelation in this episode produces two opposite reactions: Alexis' family mourns his loss; the pope rejoices at the discovery of the holy man. Each of these reactions reflects a specific attitude toward language. On the one hand, the pope, representing doctrinal and scriptural authority, serves as mediator between the written world of the saint and the oral world of his family; he treats Alexis' letter as a sacred text that belongs to those who have mastered learning. By contrast, the inability of Alexis' father to take the letter symbolizes his ignorance and illiteracy, which are compensated by the chancellor's reading the document aloud. The layman's access to knowledge, then, is indirect, through an oral narration orchestrated by church dignitaries. Alexis' death itself effects a decisive separation between the temporal and the spiritual worlds.

Alexis' funeral occasions another contrast. While his family mourns his loss, the people of Rome join the pope and the emperor in a joyful celebration of the saint. And the celebration in turn presents contrasting attitudes toward the sacred: whereas the nobles of the city are eager to honor the saint by giving him a proper and quick funeral, the people flock to see and touch Alexis' body. For them, the revelation of holiness is a visible and tangible benefit, one to be enjoyed as long as possible. Thus they reject the Roman lords' attempt to seduce them away with gold and silver and "by force keep him seven days above the ground" (*Life,* p. 137). Alexis' family likewise emphasize the visible as they evoke his "tender flesh" and "handsome form" (pp. 129–131). The miracles unleashed through the hero's body are more valuable than the gold and silver of the Roman nobles or the hero's life and personal accomplishments (p. 137):

> No one sick, whatever his infirmity,
> Who, when he calls upon him, fails at once to be restored to health.
> Some walk, some are carried.
> God has shown them such true miracles
> That whoever arrives in tears, he has him go home with song.

Whereas flesh becomes word in the scriptural sanctification of the hero, word returns to flesh when popular devotion is concerned. Through the common medium of the vernacular, *La vie de saint Alexis* thus distinguishes between two modes of behavior and expression: that of the church, which seeks to regulate and to control the transmission of truth; and that of the laypeople of the community, whose contact with the sacred involves gestures and concrete expectations.

Originally sung or recited to an illiterate audience in northern France but transmitted to us in written form, *La vie de saint Alexis* effects several interactions between orality and textuality. These interactions play a fundamental role in the vernacular portrayal of sanctity and in the distance it establishes between sacred and profane, as revealed in the poet's final apostrophe to his public (*Life,* p. 141):

> My lords, let us keep alive the memory of that holy man,
> And let us pray that he deliver us from all evil;
> That in this life he may obtain for us peace and joy,
> And in that other one, everlasting glory
> In the Word Itself. And so let us say: Pater Noster.
> Amen.

For an audience unable to understand Latin and on the whole untouched by abstract doctrinal considerations, remembrance of Alexis involves invoking his protection against "all evil," whereas Alexis' mastery over language allows him to address God (the "Word Itself") in the name of the faithful. This epilogue emphasizes the value of prayers yet openly distinguishes between the inventive dimension of Alexis' discourse and the faithful's reliance on invocation of his name and on liturgical recitation ("Pater Noster"). By writing an autobiographical letter, Alexis the clerk has disclosed the existence of Alexis the saint;

in both capacities, he represents a level of competence and excellence that the illiterate faithful can neither imitate nor emulate.

Like all of early vernacular Lives, this devotional work addressed to the feudal community of 11th-century northern France is much indebted to orality, for it grew out of the church's effort—starting with the Council of Tours in 813—to preach to and edify the uneducated faithful. The recitation of holy legends entailed the development of a new poetic genre, versified hagiography, of which *La vie de saint Alexis* is still regarded as the finest example. Following the Latin hagiographic tradition of the preceding five centuries, the poem extols the virtues of asceticism and worldly renunciation. Like the 10th-century Latin version generally regarded as its source, it demonstrates the church's superiority to and dominance over feudal genealogy, which she supplants and governs. But the French narrative goes even further than the Latin *Vita* in articulating the difference between clergy and laity, and thus between the holy and the ordinary. Whereas in the *Vita* Alexis' parents display saintly attitudes, in the French version they are almost exclusively concerned with family ambitions regarding their only heir; worldly genealogical tensions and conflicts are much more prominent, and saintly renunciation more nearly coincides with active rejection of the world. Alexis' refusal to see himself as Eufemiien's son or as his betrothed's husband enables him to become the "man of God." The breaking of the human genealogical chain is a precondition to integration into God's family and to sainthood. In terms of the continuation of the species, it is also the mark of exceptional behavior.

The French version of the Life emphasizes more than its predecessors the curative and protective function of the saint's exceptional behavior. In the 5th-century Syriac text believed to be the earliest source of the legend, Alexis dies at Edessa; but his body is nowhere to be found and only his rags remain in the tomb. The slightly later Greek version, which also ends with the saint's death in Syria, omits mention of the empty tomb. In the 10th-century Latin composite, Alexis returns to Rome, and his body is recognized as directly benefiting Rome's spiritual leadership. But in *La vie de saint Alexis* the cult of Alexis centers on his dead body as a material talisman against disorder and disease. Alexis, having rejected the roles of son and spouse, by his death becomes a powerful mediator between man and God. His behavior in relation to contemporary 11th-century societal norms is of greater consequence than his eastern ties to Christ or his role as founder of Christian Rome.

The enormous popularity of the cult of the saints—attested by about 200 versified French Lives surviving from the Middle Ages—reveals the faithful's fear of earthly and infernal dangers and their consequent need for protectors. The saints' Lives responded more directly than sermons, edifying tales (the exemplum and the miracle), and liturgical lyrics to the common people's desire for refuge from a troubled world. As intercessors with God these holy heroes were a safeguard against "all evil" and a guarantee of salvation at the hour of death. Most of the saints celebrated in the vernacular throughout the Middle Ages were early martyrs (Agnes, Alban, Barbara, Catherine, Edmund,

Lawrence, Margaret, Sylvester) and hermits (Alexis, Brendan, Euphrosina, Gregory, Marina, Mary the Egyptian, Thais) who were regarded as powerful mediators: their bodies, through their self-sacrifice, became relics producing cures and salvation.

This focus prevails throughout vernacular hagiography. Rutebeuf's 13th-century *La vie de sainte Elysabel* (*The Life of Saint Elizabeth of Hungary*), one of the rare vernacular Lives devoted to a contemporary saint, forcefully illustrates the saint's sacrificial function. Though neither a martyr nor a hermit, Elizabeth of Hungary is nevertheless the object of "persecutive veneration": "In great haste, a crowd came to cut out a piece of her. Parts of her hair and breast were cut; her toes, her fingernails were likewise cut, and perhaps more parts also; and they would have dismembered her totally, if they had not been prevented from doing so" (*Elysabel,* p. 162). Popular recognition of Elizabeth's sanctity leads to a violent appropriation of her body. Dismemberment, which transforms the heroine into talismanic fragments, also indicates that all the saints celebrated in vernacular hagiography are essentially martyrs. The faithful's manifest attraction for, and participation in, spectacular suffering suggests that the saints' essential function is to serve as substitutes and founding victims. Venerated for their role in promoting the physical and spiritual welfare of the devout, these protagonists are scapegoats through whom social order is achieved. As legends engendering Christian communal harmony—the "peace and joy" evoked in the *Alexis* epilogue—vernacular saints' Lives constitute a religious mythology about origins. The death of one individual becomes both fundamental and necessary for the survival of the many. This is why, in the French version of the Alexis legend, the saint's tomb is not empty; as if only a tangible victim could ensure collective redemption.

As a clerk and as a saint, Alexis achieves admirable perfection; his posthumous letter helps ennoble and authenticate the written vernacular. In the epilogue, however, it is as a provider that he is commemorated, in connection with the immediate and concrete benefits unleashed by his death. Focusing on devotional practices that invoke events (miraculous curing), on gestures (the carrying of relics), and on speech acts (the naming of the saint) belonging above all to the realm of orality, the epilogues of vernacular saints' Lives return to the contemporary present and subordinate the saint's historical or authorial reality to his or her protective efficiency. In the process, the individual and original identity of the protagonists disappears, proving that their lives are indeed less important than their posthumous transmutation into miracle-workers. The saints celebrated in vernacular hagiography are thus not imitable models but shields ensuring the worshiper's welfare. Their function being to suffer and die on behalf of the faithful, these heroes are the product of a sacrificial mentality whereby only a victim can engender spiritual and terrestrial salvation.

See also 1123, 1215.

Bibliography: R. H. Bloch, *Etymologies and Genealogies: A Literary Anthropology of the French Middle Ages* (Chicago: University of Chicago Press, 1983). Brigitte Cazelles, *Le corps de sainteté: D'après "Jehan Bouche d'Or," "Jehan Paulus" et quelques vies des XIIe et XIIIe siècles* (Geneva: Droz, 1982). P. A. Johnson and Brigitte Cazelles, *"Le Vain Siècle Guerpir": A Literary Approach to Sainthood through Old French Hagiography of the Twelfth Century* (Chapel Hill: University of North Carolina Press, 1979). *The Life of Saint Alexius in the Old French Version of the Hildesheim Manuscript,* trans. Carl J. Odenkirchen (Brookline, Mass., and Leiden: Classical Folio Editions, 1978). D. L. Maddox, "Pilgrimage Narrative and Meaning in Manuscripts L and A of the *Vie de saint Alexis,"* *Romance Philology,* 27 (1973), 143–157. Rutebeuf, *La vie de sainte Elysabel,* in *Oeuvres complètes de Rutebeuf,* ed. Edmond Faral and Julia Bastin, vol. 2 (Paris: Picard, 1969). *La vie de saint Alexis, poème du XIe siècle et renouvellements des XIIe, XIIIe et XIVe siècles,* ed. Gaston Paris and Léopold Pannier (1872; reprint, Paris: Champion, 1967).

Brigitte Cazelles

✐ 1095

Pope Urban II at the Council of Clermont Proclaims the First Crusade

The Epic

When Pope Urban II preached the First Crusade to the Orient in 1095 at Clermont, the vernacular literature of France consisted of epic poems (*chansons de geste*), saints' Lives, and lyric poetry. Most of these works were still being passed on orally rather than being written down. The immensely popular *chansons de geste* include several of the finest works in medieval French literature: the *Chanson de Roland* (ca. 1100; *Song of Roland*), *Raoul de Cambrai, Garin le Lorrain,* the *Chanson de Guillaume, Girart de Roussillon,* and *Huon de Bordeaux.* They were sung at fairs, weddings, and coronations, in public squares and in castles. Over 120 of them have survived, and the corpus totals more than a million lines. Many of the poems were translated into other medieval languages. In the 14th and 15th centuries, the most popular were reworked in prose, and several of these were among the first texts to be printed in the late 15th century. They continued to be read well into the 1800s in the Bibliothèque Bleue and other popular collections.

The French epic was largely the creation of jongleurs, itinerant performers who not only composed *chansons de geste* and performed the lyric poetry of the trouvères (inventors) of northern France and the troubadours of the south, but also juggled, did acrobatic tricks, exhibited trained animals, played instruments, and staged mimes and other entertainments. Jongleurs depended for their livelihood on the generosity of audiences; thus their songs can be taken to reflect the types of narrative diversion that the public desired. From the pronouncements of ecclesiastical officials, it is obvious that jongleurs belonged to the lowest level of medieval society. Female jongleurs, for example, were routinely assumed to engage in prostitution. Since literacy was confined almost entirely to the clergy and the higher nobility in the period in which the *chansons de geste* flourished, it appears that most jongleurs were illiterate. In any case, in medieval iconography jongleurs are never seen using books in their performances. Apparently they were able to perform *chansons de geste* of considerable length—examples of the genre range from 800 to 35,000 lines—through the use of an improvisational technique that has been solidly documented in other preliterate cultures: jongleurs developed a repertoire of stock scenes and phrases to aid them in reproducing, often in more or less the same form but sometimes with considerable modification, the songs that they heard others perform. In keeping with this oral and traditional transmission, the vast majority of the poems are anonymous.

Medieval illuminations show jongleurs playing a stringed instrument called the *vielle,* and treatises report that they sang the entire story to a chantlike melody. *Chansons de geste* are divided into *laisses,* stanzas of varying length, each characterized by a single assonance or rhyme; the lines are ten or twelve syllables long (though in one text, *Gormont et Isembart,* eight), and each is marked by a pause, or caesura. Variations in melody probably marked the first and last lines of the *laisse,* and the hiatus between *laisses* may have been filled with instrumental music.

Evidence for the existence of a thriving literature of epic song before the First Crusade is found in several precious texts: in his chronicle of the abbey of Saint-Riquier (completed in 1088), the monk Hariulf incorporates into his narrative an event from *Gormont et Isembart;* the Nota Emilianense, from the third quarter of the 11th century, summarizes a version of the *Chanson de Roland;* and the Fragment of the Hague, an attempt around the year 1000 to render into a nostalgically classicized Latin the story of a fictional siege of Gerona, places there a number of heroes from what was later to be the cycle of epic poems recounting the deeds of Guillaume d'Orange, his forebears, and his nephews. The two other major epic cycles of *chansons de geste* (so divided by the 12th-century poet Bertrand de Bar-sur-Aube) are that of the kings of France, sometimes referred to as the cycle of Charlemagne, and that of the rebellious vassals, treacherous or recalcitrant barons who are conceived as having all belonged to the same lineage. Several indications, including references to episodes from other songs in the early 12th-century *Chanson de Guillaume* and the presence of Guillaume-cycle heroes in the Fragment of the Hague, lead to the conclusion that the cycles had begun to develop well before the earliest *chanson de geste* to be preserved, the Oxford *Chanson de Roland* (Bodleian Library Ms. Digby 23), was copied in the second quarter of the 12th century. Not mentioned by Bertrand is the cycle that purports to give an account of the First Crusade: its content is, with the notable exception of the *Chanson d'Antioche,* almost entirely fictitious.

As a body of literature, then, the *chansons de geste* were conceived of genealogically. Typically each of the great heroes was the subject of a major song: examples are the *Chanson de Roland,* the *Chanson de Guillaume, Renaut de Montauban, Girart de Roussillon,* and *Raoul de Cambrai.* The process of cyclical development led to the composing of songs that told of the heroes' childhood exploits, or *enfances* (the *Enfances Guillaume,* the *Enfances Vivien*); their young manhood or *chevalerie* (the *Chevalerie Ogier de Danemark,* the *Chevalerie Vivien*); their conversions to the monastic life, or *moniage* (the *Moniage Guillaume,* the

Moniage Renouart); and their deaths (the *Mort Charlemagne;* the *Mort Aimeri de Narbonne,* which recounts the demise of Guillaume's father). The deeds of great heroes are set in the context of their kinship alliances, reflecting the medieval legal principle that one was responsible for the acts of one's relatives: thus in the Oxford *Chanson de Roland,* Roland is the son of Charlemagne as well as his nephew; Guillaume is the brother of six other heroes, each of whom sets out to conquer a different land (*Les Narbonnais*), and the uncle of the tragic Vivien; the traitor Ganelon of the *Roland* is viewed as having been related to other untrustworthy knights, like him descended from the eponymous hero of *Doon de Mayence.* This emphasis on genealogy in the *chansons de geste* is hardly surprising: *geste* signifies not only "deeds" and "tale about a hero's exploits" but also "lineage" and "cycle of songs about a lineage."

The seemingly sudden profusion of French texts after the First Crusade has frequently been viewed as the product of a great burst of authorial energy. Much of that textual production, however, resulted simply from the writing down of an oral literature that was in full blossom long before the crusade got under way. Although debates about the origins of French literature are often confined to the few hagiographic texts that were actually copied before the crusade, such as the late 9th-century *Cantilène* or *Séquence de sainte Eulalie* (*Sequence of Saint Eulalie*) and *La vie de saint Alexis* (ca. 1050), in a very real sense there were no discrete origins, since it appears that the oral literature of France came into being along with the French language as it developed out of popular Latin.

Viewed in that light, the relationship between the *chanson de geste* and history takes on added significance. Many of the earliest and most famous of the songs have at their center a historical kernel, frequently a great battle. Thus the *Chanson de Guillaume* recalls William of Toulouse's capture of Barcelona from the Moors in 803; the battle of Saucourt in 881, in which Louis III defeated a Viking force that had attacked and burned the monastery of Saint-Riquier, inspired the tradition that produced *Gormont et Isembart;* the attack of Raoul, son of a certain Raoul de Gouy, on the county of Vermandois in 943 is at the core of *Raoul de Cambrai.* Sometimes surprisingly accurate details are preserved in the epics, such as the name of William of Toulouse's wife, Witburgh, which comes down in works of the Guillaume cycle in the corresponding French form Guibourc. Generally the historical events found in the *chanson de geste* date from the Carolingian period, although names and occurrences from as early as the Merovingian monarchy and as late as the taking of Antioch in 1098 figure in the French epic, and the Occitan *chanson de geste,* composed south of the Loire, contains material from as late as the civil war in Navarre of 1276–77. The preservation of events for as long as 300 years says much about the conservatism of the oral tradition.

Nonetheless, only a modicum of the tens of thousands of events recounted in the epics have a basis in history, and even in those cases the facts have been adapted to the dramatic and mythical requirements of the genre. The poets appropriated the details of history to their own needs—compositional, socio-economic, and occasionally even propagandistic—shaping a vision of the

French past that centered on the achievements of legendary figures from the formative period in which the consciousness of national identity had begun to appear. In the process, they sometimes merged the deeds of historical figures who shared the same name, assigned one person's actions to another, created independent heroes from the same historical prototype, ascribed straightforward military defeats to the machinations of traitors, and took other liberties with the facts that had entered their ken. Still, they claimed that their songs were true, as a result of which the *chansons de geste* were viewed as history by many a medieval cleric; and modern readers have not been exempt from the tendency to accept their testimony. In fact the *chanson de geste* embodied a popular form of historiography that competed with both the official annalists and chroniclers and the ecclesiastical historians.

Chansons de geste were sometimes used to spread the news of great historical events. The late 12th-century chronicler of the house of Guines, Lambert d'Ardre, tells a revealing anecdote concerning Arnold de Guines, who took part in the siege of Antioch during the First Crusade. A jongleur singing a *Chanson d'Antioche* one day offered to include Arnold's deeds in his tale in exchange for a pair of scarlet shoes. When Arnold rejected the bargain, the jongleur excluded him from his version of the song. This example of the use of a *chanson de geste* to propagate the news of a recent event is also valuable for the insight it provides into the economic mentality of jongleurs, who did not hesitate to exact a price for the fame they were capable of spreading. That noble families did indeed pay attention to the songs that told of their putative ancestors' achievements is indicated by the fact that, from the last quarter of the 12th century on, the viscounts of Narbonne began to call their heirs "Aimeri" in obvious emulation of the epic—and probably fictitious—Aimeri de Narbonne of the Guillaume cycle.

Legends from the *chansons de geste* were also invoked for purposes of persuasion. The First Crusade offers a salient instance: the chronicler Robert of Reims, an eyewitness to Urban II's speech launching the idea of the crusade, reports that the pope called upon the assembled nobles to follow the example of their predecessors Charlemagne and his son Louis, who destroyed pagan kingdoms and extended the boundaries of the holy church. In the context of the struggle against Islam, this image of Charlemagne and Louis corresponds more closely to their deeds as transformed in the *chansons de geste* than to their historical undertakings, and suggests that the fictional story of Charlemagne's journey to the Holy Land, told in the *Pèlerinage de Charlemagne,* provided an ideal precedent for French knights to take the cross.

Thus it is very likely that the *Chanson de Roland* and similar militant poems helped to shape the mentalities that made the crusades possible. Struggles between paganism and Christendom are predominant themes in the *chansons de geste,* and the ways in which the French Crusaders imagined Islam and the Arabs could not help but be shaped by their depiction in the epics. Not that the forces who opposed the Crusaders can simply be equated with the Saracens of the *chansons de geste.* The inclusion among the latter of such diverse tribes as the

Ireis (Irish), the Argoilles (Scottish Argyles), the Esclavon (Slavs), the Ermines (Armenians), the Avers (Avars), the "people of Samuel" (Bulgars of Macedonia), the Hums (Huns), and the Hungres (Hungarians) renders it plausible that the Saracens represent all the external forces of paganism that were perceived as threats in early medieval France. Understanding of the tenets of Islam did not figure in the stock of knowledge available to the Crusaders, most of whom probably held a notion of that religion informed by the *chansons de geste:* the Saracens are said in the epics to worship many gods in the form of idols and to keep pigs—characteristics that are not only alien to Islam but abhorrent to its followers. That Mohammed is included among the gods of the Saracens is perhaps the crowning distortion. But rather than an anti-Islam conceived in calculated fashion, this depiction of the pagans who held Spain, North Africa (whose chief city in the epics is "Babylone," that is, Cairo), and the Holy Land represents a failure to differentiate between, on the one hand, the Germanic, Scandinavian, and Slavic pagans, many of whom did indeed worship idols, and, on the other, the monotheists emanating from Arabia, Persia, and Turkey. These reminiscences of the earlier threat of northern and eastern paganism are an archaism in the epic conception of the world: just as many of the subjects of the *chansons de geste* hark back to the Carolingian era, when the poems presumably first began to take shape, so the view of the non-Christian world represented in them reflects a popular historiography of the 8th through 11th centuries rather than the view of Islam that men of learning began to develop in the 12th century.

The acknowledged masterpiece of the genre, the *Chanson de Roland,* has traditionally been viewed as the story of Charlemagne's nephew, but an obscure reference to the emperor's confessor, St. Giles, in lines 2096–98 reveals that the poet composed his work in full awareness of the legend that Charlemagne had committed incest with his sister, who as a consequence gave birth to Roland. These events are detailed in the First Branch of the *Karlamagnus Saga,* a Norse text of the mid-13th century that is based on lost French epics of the 11th and 12th centuries. The most renowned of the *chansons de geste* is thus the tale of the tragic death of Charlemagne's son, the genealogically pure offspring of the Frankish royal family, whose death, caused not by the Saracens but rather by his own extraordinary effort in sounding the horn to call for help after he and his men have fallen into a trap arranged by his stepfather Ganelon, is no doubt a punishment for his father's sin. Hence the *Chanson de Roland* belongs among a range of myths concerning heroes and gods born of incest—Heracles, Romulus, Mordred, Zeus, Apollo, Freyr, and in particular Sinfjotli in the *Völsunga Saga,* son of a brother (Sigmund) and a sister (Signy), who refuses to call for his father's help in a fight against overwhelming odds and who dies young and without offspring through his stepmother's treachery. The *Chanson de Roland* is a foundation myth, the story of the suffering and eventual triumph of Charlemagne, the figure who in the national consciousness is the founder of the French collectivity, on the occasion of his own son's death. In keeping with the character of the *chansons de geste,* however, the myth is anchored in a historical event, the defeat of Charlemagne's rearguard in the Pyrenees in the year 778. The evidence for Roland's historical existence is fragile and ambiguous.

The *Chanson de Roland* exemplifies the mutually beneficial relationship between the jongleurs and history: the poets preserved in their songs fragmentary memories of historical events, which they embellished for artistic purposes, while historical figures such as Urban II appropriated and exploited the epic legends to further their political and social agendas.

See also 1202, 1214.

Bibliography: Robert F. Cook, *The Sense of the "Song of Roland"* (Ithaca: Cornell University Press, 1987). Joseph J. Duggan, *The "Song of Roland": Formulaic Style and Poetic Craft* (Berkeley: University of California Press, 1973). *Karlamagnus Saga: The Saga of Charlemagne and His Heroes,* trans. Constance Hieatt, 3 vols. (Toronto: Pontifical Institute of Medieval Studies, 1975–1980). *The Song of Roland,* trans. Frederick Goldin (New York: Norton, 1978). Eugene Vance, *Reading the "Song of Roland"* (Englewood Cliffs, N.J.: Prentice-Hall, 1970). Frederick Whitehead, ed., *The Song of Roland* (Oxford: Blackwell, 1946).

Joseph J. Duggan

✌🏵 1123?

A Richly Illustrated Latin Psalter Prefaced by a Vernacular *Chanson de saint Alexis* Is Produced at the English Monastery of St. Albans for Christina of Markyate

Manuscripts

The earliest surviving vernacular version of the *Chanson de saint Alexis* (*Song of Saint Alexius*) is one of several texts prefacing a magnificently illustrated Latin psalter produced at the English monastery of St. Albans, probably around 1123, for use by Christina of Markyate, an English noblewoman who became a recluse. This manuscript has been in Germany for centuries; it is currently owned by St. Godehard's Church in Hildesheim, which acquired it from the abbey of Lamspringe, the home, in the mid-17th century, of English Benedictine monks who apparently brought the St. Albans Psalter with them from England. Modern editorial convention designates this manuscript not as the St. Albans *Alexis,* as I shall do here, but as the Hildesheim or L (for Lamspringe) version, thereby dissociating the text from the place and social conditions of its inscription.

Because of its relatively early date, the St. Albans *Alexis* has received more scholarly attention than any of the later vernacular versions of the poem. Yet it was not until 1956 (in a note in *Modern Language Review*) that Mary Dominica Legge pointed out to literary scholars intent on dating and defining origins the importance of *Alexis'* manuscript context: the St. Albans Psalter. Legge brought

23

to our attention the book on the St. Albans Psalter published in 1895 by the art historian Adolph Goldschmidt, who judged that the St. Albans *Alexis* is a copy of a vernacular poem composed in England for performance at the dedication of a chapel to St. Alexius at St. Albans between 1115 and 1119. Goldschmidt, however, treated the vernacular text like a foreign object lodged by chance, or merely because it was on hand, within the body of the Latin liturgical manuscript.

In viewing the vernacular literary text as a *corpus alienum,* or foreign body, in a manuscript collection of texts, the art historian lent support to literary scholars' practice of editing "individual" texts rather than whole manuscript collections. Many modern editions do not even mention the texts surrounding the one edited. The conventional set of questions that the modern editor must answer about the physical conditions of a medieval text—page size, number of lines and columns per page, distinction of scribal hands, and so forth—does not extend to more difficult problems involving contextual relationships. In his critical edition of the St. Albans *Alexis,* for example, Christopher Storey limits his description of the manuscript to the pages on which the prologue and text of *Alexis* are inscribed. In his 1872 edition, which was considered to mark a new era in meticulously scholarly editing, Gaston Paris relegated to an endnote the vernacular prose prologue introducing the St. Albans *Alexis,* even though it is the work of the same scribe. Alienation of the medieval vernacular text from its manuscript context in these ways makes the task of editing more manageable—but at the expense of censoring information present in the manuscript context about how the scribe, patron, or medieval interpretative community understood and used the text.

Our tendency to ignore medieval manuscript contexts is encouraged not only by editorial pragmatism but also by literary scholars' need to search for the "original" text, a goal that devalues existing "later, corrupt" texts and contexts in favor of hypothetical reconstructions of "pure and authoritative" ancestral ones. Another strong encouragement to disregard medieval manuscript contexts while studying "individual" texts is the very nature of medieval manuscript collections, which are often extremely diverse and exist today in states that we know to be fragmentary or much revised and reformed. The "original" manuscript collection—its form at the time of a poem's inscription in it—has rarely survived. For example, the earliest written text of the Old Provençal *Chanson de sainte Foi* (*Song of Saint Faith*), nearly contemporary with the St. Albans *Alexis,* is currently bound in a library in Leiden with a later text on portents, while the Latin liturgical offices of St. Foy, with which the original manuscript began, are bound with other texts in Paris, and the ending of the original manuscript survives in a manuscript in Orléans. According to Ernest Hoepffner, part of this dispersion is recent, the work of Libri, the famous 19th-century book thief. Nevertheless, similar kinds of breaking up and recombining of manuscripts also happened in the Middle Ages in order to meet the various needs and uses of different owners.

The compilation of a manuscript often spanned a long period, because writing and illuminating texts on parchment was very laborious and expensive, and also because the medieval codex was something of a library in the form of a book. The manuscript written by hand on leather pages bound together between wooden covers was a relatively compact, effective way of preserving texts that circulated or were inscribed in more precarious forms: in human memory, on wax tablets, on single leather sheets called charters or briefs, carved in wood, woven into the images of tapestries, painted on walls or other objects. In the 10th through 12th centuries, the compilers of manuscripts were mostly religious institutions with scriptoria, either cathedral chapters (such as Clermont, today's Clermont-Ferrand, which, in the early 11th century, inscribed on blank pages of a mid-10th-century Latin dictionary the vernacular *Passion de Jésus Christ* and the *Vie de saint Léger* [*Life of Saint Léger*]) or monasteries such as Saint-Martial of Limoges (the Provençal *Sponsus* [*Bridegroom*] and a number of other short vernacular religious playlets) and Saint-Benoît-sur-Loire, also known as Fleury (the Provençal *Boeci* [*Boethius*], a bilingual dawn song, and the *Chanson de sainte Foi*).

Manuscripts surviving from this early period contain, almost exclusively, Latin liturgical texts. These form the manuscript contexts of virtually all early vernacular verse, much of which is accompanied by musical notation, as is liturgical song, and most of which, like the St. Albans *Alexis* or the late 9th-century text of the *Cantilène* or *Séquence de sainte Eulalie* (*Sequence of Saint Eulalie*), present saints' Lives or "Passions" and seem to have been used to gloss or "illuminate" certain liturgical offices, to bring the liturgy to life. Thus three early vernacular texts—a fragment in a Saint-Martial liturgical collection, the Clermont-Ferrand *Passion de Jésus Christ,* and the St. Albans *Alexis*—call themselves "explanations" (*razo* or *raizun* or, in the prose prologue to *Alexis,* "spiritel raisun").

Even if a medieval manuscript did not change hands, its owner might decide to add to it or change its contents in some way. For example, the presence of *Alexis* and of the entire second section of the St. Albans Psalter manuscript seems to be the result of a decision to try to tailor the psalter (already prefaced by its liturgical calendar) more specifically to the uses and experiences of Christina of Markyate and the women who congregated around her. The St. Albans Psalter as it now exists is probably not the "original" manuscript but the "revised" version. This revision has made the manuscript *more,* not less, valuable to us, for it has given us additional texts, including *Alexis,* and enabled art historians to date the manuscript far more precisely than is usual with such early manuscripts. Otto Pächt, C. R. Dodwell, and Francis Wormald have carried Goldschmidt's earlier discovery of a change of plans in the compilation of the manuscript to interesting conclusions about the ideas motivating this change and about how *Alexis* and the second section (which Goldschmidt had treated as a foreign body) create a new whole.

In the "revised" St. Albans Psalter, two sections precede the psalter proper. The first section is a gathering (a sheaf of pages folded together) of eight folios (manuscript leaves with both front and back, recto and verso, counted as one page) devoted to a Latin liturgical calendar listing festive dates. The second section has four gatherings, of eight, ten, two, and eight folios, respectively; the first three of these gatherings present a highly original series of full-page biblical illuminations (color illustrations) focusing on the life of Christ and concluding with a full-page image of King David playing a contemporary jongleur's rebec (fig. 1). This secularized figure of David introduces *Alexis* on the facing recto, which begins the fourth gathering of the second section. The half-page tinted drawing at the top of folio 29 recto shows three moments from Alexis' story glossed by Latin captions (fig. 1). The bottom half of the page is devoted to a vernacular prose prologue introducing the poem. The verse text of *Alexis* begins on folio 29 verso (fig. 2) with an initial *B* (of the song's first phrase, "Bons fut li secles" [The world was good]) that prefigures, in form and ornament, the initial *B* (fig. 2) beginning the first phrase of the later psalter ("Beatus vir" [Blessed the man]). Inscribed immediately after *Alexis* are a Latin version and a French prose translation of Gregory the Great's apology for the use of images in teaching the illiterate. Next come three full-page tinted drawings of Christ's encounter with two disciples on the road to Emmaus. This gathering ends with another image of King David framed not by the usual ornamental border but by an exegetical gloss relating the activity of psalmody to the two mounted knights fighting each other with drawn swords at the top of the page; according to the gloss, both psalmist and knights represent spiri-

1. *Left:* King David playing the rebec, St. Albans Psalter, fol. 28 verso; *right:* Illustration of and prologue to the *Chanson de saint Alexis,* St. Albans Psalter, fol. 29 recto. St. Godehard's Church, Hildesheim. (Courtesy of the Warburg Institute, London.)

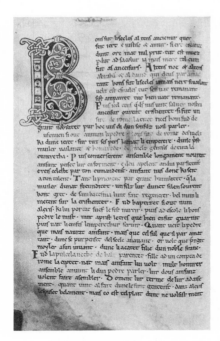

2. *Left:* Beginning of the *Chanson de saint Alexis,* St. Albans Psalter, fol. 29 verso; *right:* King David playing the harp or Psalmody as combat, St. Albans Psalter, fol. 36 verso. St. Godehard's Church, Hildesheim. (Courtesy of the Warburg Institute, London.)

tual athletes fighting against sin. In this second presentation of David, he sits in a large initial *B* harping with one hand and displaying the psalter with the other, while a huge dove sticks its beak into his ear in representation, according to the inscription on the displayed psalter, of the "Annunciation of the Holy Spirit," that is, the divine inspiration of the psalms to follow (fig. 2).

Of the five hands that Wormald has identified in the St. Albans Psalter, one anonymous scribe, whom I shall call the *Alexis* scribe, wrote the entire second section as well as, in the psalter itself, the verse captions that designate which psalm is illustrated by the human figures depicted inside the large initials beginning each chapter. The *Alexis* scribe's handwriting appears only once elsewhere in the manuscript: in the liturgical calendar, in an additional entry noting the date of death and dedicating "this psalter" to the memory of Roger the Hermit (Christine of Markyate's teacher and protector, whose cell she shared for four years and continued to occupy after his death). From historical sources, C. R. Dodwell has discovered that Roger the Hermit died in 1120 or 1121 and has reasoned that if Roger's obituary was entered soon after his death (although this is not always the case with such entries), the liturgical calendar and also the psalter, which is mentioned in the obituary, must have been completed by 1123. Otto Pächt has suggested, further, that the *Alexis* scribe added Roger's obituary to the calendar at the same time he inserted between the calendar and the psalter a section of his own execution that shaped the manuscript to the experiences of Christina of Markyate. Wormald has reinterpreted Dodwell's and Pächt's arguments somewhat more broadly, suggesting a date of 1123–1130 for the entire manuscript.

The logic of these arguments is convincing, and the assumptions that underpin them seem relatively sound; nevertheless, we would do well to take 1123 only as a fairly close approximation of the date of inscription of the St. Albans *Alexis*. The Emmaus cycle of illustrations in the fifth gathering of the second section indicates that this section may have been executed as long as fifteen to twenty years after 1123. The 14th-century Latin *Vita* (*Life*) of Christina of Markyate, based on Markyate priory's lost 12th-century Latin *Vita* of its foundress, recounts two occasions when Christina encountered Christ disguised as a pilgrim. The dates of these meetings are not given, but they are narrated quite near the end of the chronologically ordered *Vita,* which breaks off with events of 1142. On the first occasion, a very handsome, grave-mannered pilgrim came to Christina's hermitage and sat down to a meal with her and her sister, but he barely tasted the fish they offered, and he left, after blessing them, without revealing his identity. This brief visit, however, made such an impression on Christina that she was forever wishing for the pilgrim to return—which he duly did on the day after Christmas, participated in the procession, and then mysteriously disappeared from the locked church before anyone had had a chance to talk with him.

In the St. Albans Psalter, the three full-page illustrations of the Emmaus story (Christ's appearance as a pilgrim to two disciples, their meal of fish and bread together, and Christ's sudden—and iconographically unusual—disappearance by ascension) are set apart from the rest of the full-page illustrations of Christ's life in a sequence following *Alexis*. Pächt has rightly suggested that this deliberate juxtaposition of Alexis with Emmaus makes the story of the anonymous pilgrim Alexis prefigure that of the anonymous pilgrim Christ. The Emmaus picture cycle thus glosses or brings out the true significance of the Alexis story (as the compilers of the St. Albans Psalter saw it). There is probably at least one other reason for the positioning of the Emmaus illustrations after the *Alexis* poem: figuratively, both recapitulate and commemorate important events in Christina of Markyate's life. Like Alexis, Christina made a vow of chastity in her youth and kept it by refusing the noble marriage her parents made for her; she escaped from the persecution of her parents and husband to live the life of a recluse in Roger the Hermit's cell, barricaded by day, to escape detection, for four years in a tiny enclosure (even more constraining than Alexis' closet under the staircase). As a reward for her great virtue, Christina received visions of Mary and Christ and also, according to her *Vita,* actual meetings with Christ (encounters that obviously replay biblical story).

The second section of the St. Albans Psalter, especially its illustrations and the prose prologue introducing *Alexis,* glorifies Christina and the holy, virginal woman as a type in other ingenious ways as well. In the series of twenty biblical illustrations with which the gathering begins, Pächt has remarked the innovative presentation of the Virgin Mary *reading* (instead of spinning or weaving the veil of the Temple) at the moment of the Annunciation. Equally extraordinary is the representation of the descent of the Holy Spirit at Pentecost, with the Virgin Mary pictured larger than the disciples and stationed at the center of the group (instead of Peter). It may be no coincidence that the priory Christina founded at Markyate in 1145 was dedicated to the Holy Spirit. Whereas illustrations of saints' Lives before this period almost always represent the saints' virtuous deaths, the half-page illustrations of Alexis' Life in the St. Albans Psalter focus on three earlier moments.

The purpose of this break with iconographic tradition is to devote more attention to Alexis' bride. Indeed, the illustrations of the St. Albans Psalter give the bride a more central position in the structure of the visual image than she has even in the verbal text of the St. Albans *Alexis* (which, however, devotes more attention to the bride than do earlier Latin hymns or prose Lives of Alexis) (see fig. 1). On the left, in the bedroom scene, the dove of the Holy Spirit at his ear inspires Alexis to give his ring and swordbelt (with his sword) to his bride. This gesture appears to be as much an investment of confidence in her as a renunciation of worldly things. In the second moment chosen for emphasis, the bride is framed, columnar as a statue, within the central arch of the picture; with one hand held at the side of her face in a gesture of patient grief, she bids Alexis farewell. Meanwhile Alexis steps toward the open door to the right, with his eyes and hands raised to God. In the outdoor scene to the right of this, with the hand of God directing him, Alexis takes ship and gives coins to the oarsman in a sequentially represented gesture. The Latin gloss over the head of Alexis' bride in the bedroom scene, "O sponsa beata semper gemebunda" (O blessed bride ever lamenting), attributes to her a *saintly* status like that of Alexis.

Composed earlier, probably for the dedication of a chapel to St. Alexis, the St. Albans *Alexis* is made, through the pointing of these visual and verbal glosses, to apply more clearly to the life of Christina of Markyate: on one level, Alexis' renunciation of a marriage of the flesh recollects Christina's own analogous action; on another level, Alexis' bride's experience represents Christina's—and the Christian's—experience of separation from Christ and continual expectation of Christ-the-bridegroom's eventual return. The French prose prologue further points the meaning of the poem to make it apply to "those who live purely in chastity," whose delight is in "heavenly joys and virginal marriage" (to Christ).

The mind that directed the compilation of the St. Albans Psalter was the mind of an exegete, a teacher who wanted to make the liturgy and the Christian story relevant to contemporary lives. To this purpose he was willing to use images (whose efficacy in teaching the illiterate he justified by citing Gregory the Great) and also vernacular poems such as *Alexis*. This mind directed the hand that inscribed the French text and prologue of *Alexis;* the Latin glosses around David as psalmist, at the side of the Emmaus ascension, and above the *Alexis* illustrations; and the captions (phrases from the psalms) indicating which psalms would be illustrated within the large initials of the psalter. The person who chose these phrases was responsible for the mise-en-scène of the psalter, that is, the visualization of significant postures and gestures—the invention of simple mime plays—within the frames of the capital letters beginning each chapter of the psalms.

This mind (and hand) may well have belonged to a great admirer and supporter of Christina, Geoffrey of Gorron (in the present-day département of Mayenne), abbot of St. Albans from 1119 to 1147, who came to England as a schoolteacher and staged religious plays as part of his didactic efforts before becoming a monk at St. Albans. Otto Pächt has quite plausibly suggested that Geoffrey may have been responsible for the inclusion of *Alexis* in the St. Albans Psalter. It seems likely that he was also responsible for the visual and verbal glosses that would make the *Alexis* poem more meaningful to Christina of Markyate, for whom he intended the manuscript, to be used in the performance of daily worship by her and the female recluses who gathered about her, not all of whom were able to read Latin—or even French. The pictures of the St. Albans Psalter might teach these women biblical story and serve as mnemonic devices for recollecting song texts they had previously heard performed; in this way, the psalter might also serve to teach reading, the association of aural images with visual ones. The manuscript context of the St. Albans *Alexis,* by the various ways it glosses the text both visually and verbally, suggests how a particular teaching community at a particular period *used* the poem.

See also 778, 1050.

Bibliography: Adolph Goldschmidt, *Der Albani-Psalter in Hildesheim und seine Beziehung zur symbolischen Kirchensculptur des XII. Jahrhunderts* (Berlin: Siemens, 1895). Ernest Hoepffner and Prosper Alfaric, eds., *La chanson de sainte Foi* (Paris: Belles Lettres, 1926). Mary Dominica Legge, "Archaism and the Conquest," *Modern Language Review,* 51 (1956), 227–229. *The Life of Christina of Markyate: A Twelfth-Century Recluse,* ed. and trans. C. H. Talbot (Oxford: Oxford University Press, 1959). Otto Pächt, C. R. Dodwell, and Francis Wormald, *The St. Albans Psalter* (London: Warburg Institute, 1960). *La vie de saint Alexis: Texte du manuscrit de Hildesheim (L),* ed. Christopher Storey (Geneva: Droz, 1968); translated by Carl J. Odenkirchen as *The Life of St. Alexius in the Old French Version of the Hildesheim Manuscript* (Brookline, Mass., and Leiden: Classical Folio Editions, 1978).

Laura Kendrick

 1127

Death of William IX of Aquitaine, the First Troubadour

The Old Provençal Lyric

In 1127 the richest, most powerful aristocrat in Western Europe died. In his own day, William, ninth duke of Aquitaine and seventh count of Poitou, was known for his considerable wealth, his military campaigns against neighboring lords, a crusade to Palestine in which his army was destroyed before reaching the Holy Land, and disputes with the church that led to his excommunication on two occasions. Chroniclers tell us that he was a notorious womanizer; licentiousness was certainly a contributing factor in one of his excommunications.

But today William of Aquitaine is remembered for the same reasons for which medieval contemporaries and historians honored him above other great lords: as the first lyric poet to write in the vernacular, the first troubadour. The vernacular in William's case was the language of southern France, *langue d'oc* or Provençal. In 1127, from northern France to Italy, it was the language of high culture, known by poets and aristocrats, so prestigious in fact that two centuries later Dante called it "the mother tongue" of all vernacular poetry.

Almost single-handedly, William changed the literary landscape of Western Europe by creating a new genre, the complex love lyric, which fused music with poetry. In this new form the human voice played a crucial role. For the first time the singer was not simply lending his voice to perform a narrative but took on a poetic identity: the speaking subject was also the subject of the poem.

William IX seems an unlikely innovator of the European love lyric. Given his military exploits and political machinations, one would expect him to have been more at home with the epic literature of the period, which focused on the holy war between Saracens and Christians or on the revolts of barons against their king. Indeed, Frank Chambers suggests that one metrical form used by William "exhibits a number of features . . . in common with epic verse" (*Old Provençal Versification*, p. 17). And echoes of epic events are also mentioned in William's songs, as when he laments the danger in which his departure for foreign lands will leave his son and heir, in the second stanza of what is often held to be his last song, "Pos de chantar m'es pres talentz" ("Since I've Got the Urge to Sing"):

> For now I'm going far away,
> sorely troubled, sorely tried,
> since I shall be leaving my son at war,
> and his neighbors will do him harm.

We find other traces of feudal mentality in his poems, such as the presumptions that a mistress and a good horse are both signs of knightly status, and that vassals' wives, like neighbors' lands, are legitimate objects of depredation.

Unlike epic, however, William's songs are not concerned primarily with social or political issues. They are rather a vehicle, the first in a modern European language, for showing how poetic voice, the articulated language of a speaking subject, situates itself between an inherited culture in flux and a particular unconscious, expressed in lyrics as individual consciousness finding or questioning its identity. The role of that speaking voice was also to discover or to expose the relationship between the speaking subject (the "I"), nature, and the social world embodied by the *domna,* or beloved woman, a role apparent not only in the songs themselves but also in the names given to the poet and to the process of composition. *Trobar,* an Old Provençal word, means "to invent by finding or discovering," thence "to compose musical verse." *Troubadour,* literally "the inventor," designates the poet-composer.

But *trobar* denotes only the discovery phase, the silent part of the poet's work. Performance, the ensuing "envoicement" of the song, completes the process, and so William coined a second term, *chantar,* "to sing," to describe the poetic activity he invented. The attraction of troubadour verse lay in the sophisticated tension maintained between the inner, silent process of invention (*trobar*) and the voicing of that discovery in the socialized world of performance (*chantar*), which led to the names, *vers* or *canso* (song), by which the most refined lyric genre was known.

The troubadour lyric thus has a double orientation: self-reflexive and retro-spective (past tense) when speaking of the act of creation, gregarious and imme-diate (present tense) when addressing its audience directly. In the generation after William IX, Bernard de Ventadour made the circular movement from inward discovery to outward performance a condition for the best *cansos* in his "Chantars no pot gaire valer" ("There Is No Use in Singing," lines 1–4):

> There is no use in singing
> If the song does not spring from the heart;
> And the song cannot spring from the heart
> If there is no true love there.

The *canso,* then, is alternately a process of resistance to and celebration of physical sexuality. The transference of the sexual to the verbal incorporates this ambivalence in the speaking subject's attempts to discover (*trobar*) why and how love and poetry are so closely linked.

The direct antecedent to Bernard de Ventadour's lines is the beginning of "Ben vuelh que sapchon li plusor" ("I Want Everyone to Tell"), a song in which William IX works out the elements of lyric resistance and transference and shows the double bind of the process of invention, simultaneously repressing and expressing the subject's desire. In the first stanza, the sexual desire that motivates the poem is concealed rather than uncovered by the "colors" or images the poet forges in his "workshop":

> I want everyone to tell
> Whether there's good color to this *vers*
> That I have brought out of my workshop [*obrador*]
> For I'm the one who wins the laurel in this craft
> And that's the truth,
> And I'll call this *vers* to witness
> When it is all laced up.

In this, one of William's more sexually evocative songs, the image of the poet-artisan seems to efface the poet-lover's body, whose desires inspire the song. The body and its desires have not been effaced, but transferred to the performative level, where they are formulated by the poetic voice. Like the common medieval image of nature at her forge fashioning human bodies, the poet fashions the poetic voice as the vehicle for conveying suppressed desire. The movement from making to singing is thus a form of refashioning body into voice, a substitution of the part for the whole. Performance—singing—thereby represents both a repression and a release of the desire that motivated the song.

In William's poetry, the voice is the voice of the body in all its erotic physicality. The body, the song, and the subject generate an equivocal identity from the *joc d'amor* (game of love), which from William IX on became a synonym for the love lyric. The final stanzas of "Ben vuelh que sapchon li plusor" show how sexual desire is normalized through wordplay and rhetorical game, how the libidinal dimension of sexual narrative is transposed into public entertainment:

> For they call me "mister sureshot":
> That's right, my little friend will never have me for a night
> Without wanting to have me again next day;
> For in this craft—that's right, I boast of it—I'm so expert
> I could earn my bread by it . . .

> She didn't help with her chiding:
> "My Lord, kind of small, your dice
> So I'll raise you double!"
> But I shot back: "I wouldn't fold
> If they gave me Montpellier!"
> And I raised her game board some
> With both my arms.

> And when I'd lifted that board
> The dice thickened:
> And two were nice and square
> And the third was loaded.

Fin'amors (the medieval term for courtly love) was based on the underlying tension between the real and the ideal, the erotic and the spiritual, the spoken and the unsaid. William invokes this tension by forcing the reader/listener to translate the equivocal phrases . . . or to choose not to.

The lyric form he developed encouraged such dynamics. Indeed, the complex poetic form and language themselves played important roles in concealing and releasing erotic tensions. This lyric form (later known as the *canso*) used a loose poetic form: the number of stanzas and meter, rhyme scheme, and stanza length vary in each *canso*. The first stanza establishes the music, rhythm, and rhyme scheme for the song, and the subsequent stanzas repeat these patterns to different words, allowing the listener to become aware of their sophisticated dimensions. As Christopher Page notes, the complex melodic and rhythmic interrelationships "do not necessarily materialize when we hear the first stanza . . . As the performance proceeds, our sense of coherence and focus on the rhapsodic flow of the music becomes more pronounced" (*Voices and Instruments*, p. 14). The stanza is thus the principal unit of expression. Significantly, the technical terms used to describe the stanza during the period, *frons* (head) for the first part and *cauda* (tail) for the second, suggest the extent to which the

33

body was a metaphor for the lyric form itself. The bipartite stanzaic structure is repeated at the level of individual lines and in the musical setting. All these disparate elements came together in the voice, the speaking subject of the "body" (stanza) of the song.

Even though the early troubadours used complex rhetorical, poetic, and linguistic techniques of the sort we associate with written poetry, their songs were composed for the ear rather than for the eye. And music, a link between human voice and nature, provided another image for the repression of the body and the sublimation of its desires. The troubadours themselves continually refer to the dual dimensions of word and sound. The terms *motz* (words) and *sonetz* (musical sounds) occur as linked pairs in William IX, Marcabru (1129–1150), and Jaufré Rudel (1126–1148), to name only three of the earliest. Jaufré Rudel, lord of Blaye, Pons, and Bergerac in the southwest, and thus one of William IX's vassals, evokes the voice in its double role as musical and verbal instrument in the first stanza of "No sap chantar qui so no di" ("He Who Can't Carry a Tune Doesn't Know How to Sing"):

> He who can't carry a tune [*qui so no di*] doesn't know how to sing
> Nor how to create poems if he does not make the words [*qui motz no fa*]
> Nor does he understand how rhyme works
> If he does not understand reasoning [discourses, *razos*] within himself;
> That's why my song begins this way
> And why the more you hear it the better it will sound.

Song was not a matter of mere entertainment. In the early Middle Ages the "envoicing" of the lyric word conveyed ethical implications. "Harmony" did not refer only to musical sound, but also to the relation between the body and the world. The word *music* itself, through complex etymological mediations, blended aesthetics and theology in ways that seem strange today. The philosopher Philo of Alexandria, who influenced early Christian interpretation of the Bible, argued that the original language spoken by Adam when he named all things in the Garden of Eden was the language closest to God's ideas at the time of the Creation. Etymology was therefore a way to recover divine meanings lost after the Fall, when the single tongue of Eden was fractured into the many languages of the historical world.

Etymological interpretation, the linguistic science of the Middle Ages, offered theologians a device for connecting the historical world to the divine Word in a universal history. From a single syllable they would construct an etymology—and, from the etymology, spin out a narrative linking history and theology. The more culturally significant a word, the richer its etymologies. So it proved with *music*. Well before the troubadours, ingenious etymologies had built complex links between music and nature, especially music and water. The root, *mus–*, was thought to join the Greek concept of the muses—viewed as nymphs or aquatic deities—with the Hebrew prophet Moses, so called because he was found by the water. Moses, in turn, according to Philo of Alexandria, assigned names to things that were manifest images of the things, so that the name and the thing are inevitably the same. Music also represented the sound of nature, since medieval theory held that humans first learned to make music by imitating the sound of water they had heard in streams and fountains.

Enacting the merging of culture and nature, the singing voice, beyond its pleasing mixing of words and tune, replicated on a smaller scale the infinitely greater and more harmonious music of the spheres. Music brought the body into harmony with nature in accordance with the divine plan.

The troubadours established a close link between love, singing, and nature. Often *cansos* begin with an evocation of a natural setting, generally in spring, as in William IX's "Ab la dolchor del temps novel" ("In the Sweetness of This New Season"):

> In the sweetness of this new season
> The woods leaf out, the birds
> Sing each one in its Latin
> To the melody of this new song.

Not infrequently a fountain, the sign of the muses as well as of music and lyric, figures in such natural settings, signifying the concord between the natural music of birds and water and the artificial music of the poetic text and music. But the singing voice, as well as the feminine object of the poem, may nevertheless be portrayed as in disharmony with the natural setting as a result of the pains of love.

Jaufré Rudel's "Quan lo rius de la fontana" ("When the Stream from the Spring") is an extended development of this theme. In a setting (a garden with a fountain) from which the speaking voice takes inspiration for its own harmonies, an idyllic evocation of the sources of music gives way brusquely in the second stanza to a discordant note arising from the poet's own body. He literally cannot "find [*trobar*] medicine," that is, make music (like the fountain), because of his physical pain (discord). The key verb *trobar,* here applied to the medicine, that is, the music that could put him once again in harmony with the world, links the fountain, the source of natural music, and the body, the source of artificial (human) music in Jaufré Rudel's song.

The natural world provided other topoi through which poets both repressed and recovered images of the body. One of the most moving is Bernard de Ventadour's metaphor of the bird that flies so high toward the sun that it falls into an ecstasy, loses consciousness, and plunges back to earth. Bernard's song, "Can vei la lauzeta mover . . . ," begins: "When I see the lark beat / its wings in sheer delight at the sun's rays." It is accompanied by one of the most beautiful troubadour melodies, whose sound imitates the rise and fall of the lark/poet's body while symbolizing the meeting of nature and culture in the human voice.

These and other major achievements by poets of the later Provençal school recall William IX's ambition to make the poet's movement from *trobar* to *chantar,* a celebration of the body's quest for pleasure, concur with the audience's quest for the pleasure of the song. Subsequent generations of troubadours refined this goal but did not alter it.

35

en deu quascus lo joy jauzir
don es jauzens

It is right that each man enjoy the joy
That makes him rejoice
("Pus vezem de novel florir" ["Now When We See the Meadows Once Again
in Flower"], stanza 1)

See also 1225, 1401.

Bibliography: Bernard de Ventadour, *The Songs of Bernart de Ventadorn,* ed. Stephen G. Nichols et al. (Chapel Hill: University of North Carolina Press, 1962). Frank M. Chambers, *An Introduction to Old Provençal Versification* (Philadelphia: American Philosophical Society, 1985). Frederick Goldin, *Lyrics of the Troubadours and Trouvères* (New York: Anchor, 1973). Jaufré Rudel, *The Songs of Jaufré Rudel,* ed. Rupert T. Pickens (Toronto: Pontifical Institute of Medieval Studies, 1978). Stephen G. Nichols, "The Promise of Performance: Discourse and Desire in Early Troubadour Lyric," in *The Dialectic of Discovery,* ed. J. D. Lyons and N. J. Vickers (Lexington, Ky.: French Forum, 1984), pp. 93–108. Nichols, "Towards an Aesthetic of the Provençal Canso," in *Disciplines of Criticism,* ed. Peter Demetz, Thomas Greene, and Lowry Nelson (New Haven: Yale University Press, 1968), pp. 349–374. Christopher Page, *Voices and Instruments of the Middle Ages: Instrumental Practice and Songs in France, 1100–1300* (Berkeley: University of California Press, 1986). James J. Wilhelm, *Medieval Song: An Anthology of Hymns and Lyrics* (New York: Dutton, 1971). William IX, *Guglielmo IX d'Aquitania: Poesie,* ed. Nicolo Pasero (Modena: STEM Mucchi, 1973).

Stephen G. Nichols

 1152

The Second Council of Beaugency Annuls the Marriage of Louis VII
and Eleanor of Aquitaine

The Romances of Antiquity

The rise of *romance* coincided with a divorce and subsequent remarriage that made history seem like a romantic novel. On 18 March 1152 the Second Council of Beaugency declared the marriage contracted in 1137 between the Capetian king Louis VII and Eleanor of Aquitaine as void, for reasons of consanguinity. Aquitaine, Limousin, Poitou, and Berry were thus separated from the French kingdom (see map). Scarcely two months later, Eleanor brought these same territories as a dowry to Henry Plantagenet (1133–1189), who ascended the English throne as Henry II in 1154 to reign over an area reaching from Scotland to Spain. Love thus refashioned Western European political space through the quarrel between Capetian and Plantagenet imprinted so boldly upon the history of the High Middle Ages. These events were preserved in Latin chronicles, but they found their true significance in vernacular romances that situated them within the tradition of the romances of antiquity and thus enabled them to participate in the genesis of the genre of the novel.

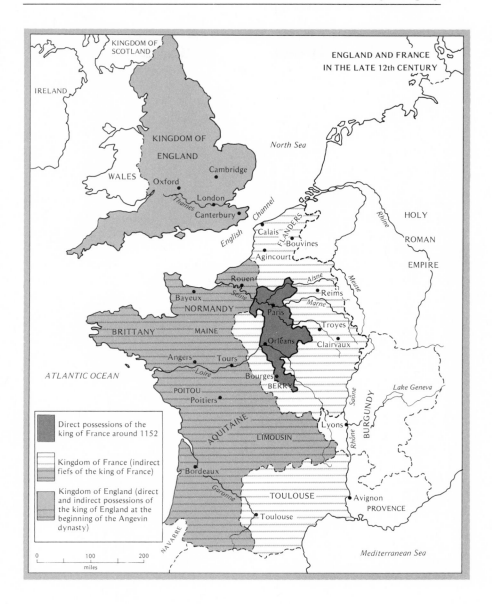

In the middle of the 12th century the romances of antiquity marked the rise of the novel by breaking with one tradition and asserting the continuity of another. The break was a formal one: the abandonment of the *laisse assonancée* (set of assonant lines) characteristic of the *chansons de geste,* which had aided memorization of textual units in a period of oral diffusion, in favor of the couplets of rhymed octosyllabic verses, which reinforced the musicality of the Romance language and gave it a flexibility more adequate to the depiction of psychological life. The desire for continuity was apparent in the subject matter of the texts, which reflected a concern to reestablish a connection with classical

37

culture, a humanist gesture that inscribed the sudden appearance of the romances of antiquity in what has been called the Renaissance of the 12th century. The term *roman* (novel or romance) referred to Romance, the language of the "illitterati" ignorant of Latin. The romances of antiquity were presented as Romance "translations" of prestigious Latin texts that had been read, spoken, and endlessly glossed in the schools for clerics. Thus the *Roman de Thèbes* (ca. 1152–1154) appeared as a "translation" of the *Thebaid* by the Latin poet Statius, the *Roman d'Enéas* (ca. 1154–1156) as a Romance version of Virgil's *Aeneid,* and Benoît de Sainte-Maure's *Roman de Troie* (ca. 1165) as a transposition of two late Latin compilations, Dares Phrygius' *De Excidio Trojae Historia* (*History of the Fall of Troy*) and Dictys Cretensis' *Ephemeris Belli Trojani* (*A Journal of the Trojan War*). Other examples include Albéric de Pisançon's *Roman d'Alexandre* (ca. 1130) and Robert Wace's *Roman de Brut* (ca. 1155; *Brutus*). Benoît de Sainte-Maure, a cleric from Normandy who served in the entourage of Henry II, wrote for him the vast *Chronique des ducs de Normandie* (ca. 1170; *Chronicle of the Dukes of Normandy*). The idiom of the *romans,* as it survives in 13th-century copies, suggests that they were composed in one of Henry II's continental domains, in Normandy or elsewhere in the west of France.

In the prologue to the *Roman de Troie,* Benoît de Sainte-Maure presents himself as a translator, making traditional texts accessible to the "illitterati": "And thus I want to work to begin a History, which, from the Latin in which I found it, I will translate into Romance, if I have the intelligence and ability, so that those who do not understand the letter can take pleasure in the romance" (*Troie,* lines 33–39). Yet none of the medieval "translators" of the romances of antiquity felt bound to a scrupulous fidelity to the original text, which was itself enriched by additions, commentary, and late compilations. Thus the unknown author of the *Roman d'Enéas* augmented the Virgilian epic with glosses inherited from the late Latin commentators Servius and Fulgentius and the poets Claudian and Apollinaris Sidonius. He borrowed from Donatus, the 4th-century grammarian, the account of the apple thrown into the pantheon of goddesses, to explain the misfortunes of the Trojans. He gave to Virgil's lovers words right out of Ovid's *Ars amatoria.*

Such additions bear witness to something specifically novelistic, that something conceived as a surplus meaning added to the Latin model. This freedom of translation extended to a partial rewriting of the original text or even to a complete transformation of its narrative structure. For example, the model for *ordo artificialis* (artificial order, in which one does not start with the beginning), Virgil's *Aeneid,* begins with Aeneas' arrival at Carthage, where he recounts the fall of Troy to Dido. The author of the *Enéas,* in contrast, reestablishes the *ordo naturalis* by beginning with the sack of Troy, the cause of the wandering that brings the hero to Carthage. These additions, abridgments, and displacements show that the romances of antiquity were rewritings more than translations, more rewritings "against" than rewritings "with." Benoît de Sainte-Maure illustrates this phenomenon when he discovers in the clerk Ditis, who "rewrote the history against Dares [Phrygius]" (line 24400), a double who reflects his own practice. The relation between the original text and the romance of antiquity involved a rivalry aimed at the substitution of the authority of the vernacular for the *auctoritas* of the model.

The romances of antiquity appeared at the turning point of what the historian Marc Bloch called the "second feudal age." Feudalism was characterized by a restructuring of political and social space after the collapse of the Carolingian empire, in the 9th century. As centralized institutions failed and government became increasingly fragmented, individual social ties grew stronger and assumed greater economic and territorial importance. With vassalage, based upon the need for self-protection, there arose a class of warriors, the knights, who soon became indistinguishable from the aristocracy. Feudalism also coincided with a change in kinship structures around the year 1000: the gradual substitution of patrilineal for matrilineal filiation. Georges Duby's study of aristocratic lineages in the north of France shows that toward 1100 the ancestors of the father supplanted those of the mother in familial memory. The father thus acquired a decisive significance: he was the guardian both of the memory of the lineage and of the name that gave him its symbolic inscription. Although commemoration seemed rarely to go further back than three or four generations, it always came to rest on a first name, belonging to a mythical ancestor who had married a woman of higher rank than his own before dying a violent death. The genealogical accounts (in Latin) thus suggest an equation between the father, an encounter with a woman, and death.

The romances of antiquity transport this equation into Romance literature. Parricide is a recurrent theme that borders upon obsession. Significantly, the anonymous author of the *Roman de Thèbes* added to his transcription of Statius' *Thebaid* a "pre-text" of more than 500 lines (32–558) relating the legend of Oedipus, who "killed his father the king." The history of Oedipus' sons, Eteocles and Polynices, opens with a similar *péché* (sin). Horrified at the very idea of the desire through which they were conceived, they crush beneath their feet, in a frenzy of hatred, the eyes that Oedipus, in order not to see the outcome of his irredeemable fault, had just torn from himself. In the *Roman de Troie,* the oneiromancers, interpreting one of Ulysses' dreams, encourage him to mistrust his son. He imprisons Telemachus in vain, for another son, Telegonus, ignorant of his father's identity until the fatal moment, deals him the mortal blow. "Telegonus sees and understands that he . . . has sinned and killed his father. Father, he says to Ulysses . . . I am your son Telegonus" (*Troie,* lines 30189–211).

The heroes of antiquity depicted in these first *romans* seem compelled to take the same parricidal route; even when an author resisted that path, his successors exerted themselves to recall him there. In his *Alexandre,* Albéric de Pisançon denies that the hero is the son of the enchanter Neptanabus (or Natanabus, or Nectanabus) in order to refute the possibility of misconduct by Queen Olympia, wife of Philip of Macedonia. But one of his successors, the anonymous author of the *Alexandre de Paris* (ca. 1170–1180), confirms the suspicion of bastardy by recounting the denial and then adding the announcement that Alexander has murdered the enchanter. Thomas of Kent, in the Anglo-Norman *Alexandre*

39

(ca. 1180), takes an additional step by showing how Neptanabus indeed engendered Alexander. At the end of his version, Alexander, a father figure, ends up victim of a certain Antipater (Antifather). The successive rewritings of the *geste* of Alexander thus seem to release progressively what remained repressed in Albéric's text, bringing to the forefront the relentless theme of the parricide.

Paradoxically, the romances of antiquity also opened Romance literature to the subject of femininity, starting with the topic of love. Full of combats between men, the *chansons de geste,* though not completely ignoring women (Guibourc, in Guillaume d'Orange's cycle, is more than a shadow), did not make them central figures. The romances, however, inherited from their antique models a number of feminine characters. They changed the roles of these characters by setting them in a feudal universe, describing beauty at length and devoting attention to amorous complaints. This trend gradually intensified. Thus, in the *Roman de Thèbes,* Argeia, Deiphyle, Antigone, and Ismene play only a secondary role, emphasizing by their lamentation the unsurpassable prowess of the beloved hero, too soon struck down by death. Dido and Lavinia, in the *Roman d'Enéas,* support the narrative by their opposition. Whereas in Virgil's *Aeneid* Dido emerges as a much stronger, more vivid character than Lavinia, in the medieval version Lavinia wakens to a desire whose suspense and agony are described at some length. The vast *Roman de Troie* (more than 30,000 lines) multiplies the feminine characters: the individual and painful destiny of each inscribes itself perfectly in that grandiose apocalypse, the Trojan War, which allows the chivalric class to exorcise its tensions and which already anticipates that twilight of heroes, the 13th-century *La mort du roi Arthur* (*The Death of King Arthur*). In these *romans* woman gains a value that was not possible in antiquity: she inherits a coveted piece of territory that enables the young male hero to establish himself and puts an end to his quest, both economically and sexually. From this perspective, the conflict between Turnus and Aeneas over Lavinia and "la terre du roi Latin" (the land of King Latinus) acquires an emblematic value emphasizing the critical nature of the competition for women in the chivalric world.

With the romances of antiquity, vernacular literature discovered love at the same time that it discovered woman. The art of love, elaborated in the *Roman d'Enéas* and the *Roman de Troie,* owes more to Ovid's *Ars amatoria* than to the *fin'amors* (courtly love) sung by the troubadours since the dawn of the 12th century. The Latin poets provided an amorous symptomatology: love, above all, is suffering; long interior monologues complaining of agony and sleeplessness permit a movement from ignorance to an enunciation of the word *amor* (love), confirming a diagnosis of the malady.

Love is also contagious. The one who loves at once wounds the beloved. In the *Enéas,* Dido fails while Lavinia succeeds in touching the Trojan hero's heart with the arrow of her gaze. As a victim of love, the man lets speak within himself a femininity that, by foretelling defeat to an individual accustomed to vanquishing, becomes security for the marriage union.

The nuptial focus of the romances of antiquity had strong implications. In telling the history of a successful or failed, impossible or annulled, marriage, and in assessing its consequences, the genre shared the preoccupations of the chivalric class in its frantic quest for heiresses who would provide land and assure the continuance of a lineage. Certainly it understood marriage as nothing other than a father's gift of a woman to a man, who thus will himself achieve paternity. The romances of antiquity thus overcome the incompatibility between marriage and love. Love that does not culminate in the marriage bed dooms one to madness and death. Chrétien de Troyes and those who anticipated the Tristan legend abandoned this truth in order to reinterrogate the *fin'amors,* the adulterous love, through which Western romantic love is born.

See also 842, 1095, 1165.

Bibliography: Marc Bloch, *Feudal Society,* trans. L. A. Manyon (Chicago: University of Chicago Press, 1964). *The Death of King Arthur,* trans. James Cable (Harmondsworth: Penguin, 1971). Benoît de Sainte-Maure, *Le roman de Troie de Benoît de Sainte-Maure,* ed. Louis Constans, 6 vols. (Paris: Firmin-Didot, 1904–1912). *Chronique des ducs de Normandie,* ed. Carin Fahlin, 4 vols. (Uppsala: Almquist & Wiksells, 1951–1979). Dictys of Crete: *The Trojan War: The Chronicles of Dictys of Crete and Dares the Phrygian,* trans. Richard McIlwaine Frazer, Jr. (Bloomington: Indiana University Press, 1966). Georges Duby, *Medieval Marriage: Two Models from Twelfth-Century France,* trans. Elborg Forster (Baltimore: Johns Hopkins University Press, 1978). *Enéas: A Twelfth-Century French Romance,* ed. John A. Yunck (New York: Columbia University Press, 1974). Jean-Charles Huchet, *Le roman médiéval* (Paris: Presses Universitaires de France, 1984). *The Medieval French Roman d'Alexandre,* ed. Alfred Foulet, 7 vols. (Princeton: Princeton University Press, 1949–1955). *Le roman de Thèbes,* 2 vols., trans. John S. Coley (New York: Garland, 1986). Thomas of Kent, *The Anglo-Norman Alexander: Le roman de toute chevalerie,* ed. Brian Foster and Ian Short (London: Anglo-Norman Text Society, 1976). Robert Wace, *Roman de Brut de Wace,* ed. Ivor Arnold, 2 vols. (Paris: Société des Anciens Textes Français, 1938–1940).

Jean-Charles Huchet

 1165

Chrétien de Troyes, from the County of Champagne, Writes in Verse the First Arthurian Romance

Erec et Enide

In 1165 a stunningly brilliant vernacular narrative poem about the knights of Arthur's Round Table appeared in Troyes, the seat (since 1152) of what had recently emerged as the county of Champagne. It was written by Chrétien de Troyes, author of five other distinguished romances and two known lyric poems.

Called a "romance" because it was written in the Old French vernacular (*li romans*) instead of in Latin, *Erec et Enide* (*Erec and Enide*) brought sudden prestige to the Champenois dialect, which was the first of northern French culture to distinguish itself (as had the Provençal language of the south) through the achievement of poetic perfection. But *Erec et Enide* played an inaugural role for European vernacular fiction as well, in its mastery of so many narrative techniques that have prevailed in the West ever since.

Erec et Enide was part of a new literary vogue that drew upon legends that were both old and diverse, isolated in their Celtic habitat until the Norman Conquest (1066) began to open new axes of communication between the cultures of England and those of other European vernaculars. Because Chrétien's Arthurian material was not drawn from scripture, from Carolingian epic, or from the classical authors, but from legends whose historical validity had been only tenuously asserted in England and France, Chrétien was relatively free to explore the potential of fiction (*fabula*) not to lie, but to constitute its own mode of poetic truth. This truth devolved not from claims that a story might make about the real world, but from the internal coherence of his story—its *conjointure*, to use Chrétien's own term.

Erec et Enide is a story about the initiation of a young man and woman into adulthood. Its tightly interwoven episodes of knightly combat and courteous erotic love fall into three major parts: first, a young knight's experience of love that culminates in marriage; second, the testing of the conjugal bond; third, the accession of the pair as mature adults to a hereditary throne.

The story begins as Arthur's court takes up the customary hunt for the white stag, whose troubling terms dictate that the slayer of the stag must publicly kiss the fairest lady of the court. In the tradition of the great Latin poet Ovid (Chrétien's most important classical source), the hunt for a marvelous beast and the warrior's quest for unknown dangers are both subtly eroticized: that is, they are exploited as metaphors for exploring the psychic violence of love in the human soul.

Dressed in a shiny tunic from Constantinople, ermine furs, and silken slippers, Erec wanders aimlessly and with no weapon but a sword. He is hardly ready to do combat, but is conspicuously ready to love and be loved. He encounters Arthur's wife, Guenevere, and offers her his company. When they wander into the forest, an unknown knight insults the queen, and suddenly Erec has his first quest: to avenge Guenevere. Wandering still unarmed, Erec comes upon the domain of a *vavasseur* (a minor noble) who is impoverished by endless war and who has a daughter to marry off, preferably to someone of higher status. It is the time of the feast of the falcon, whose custom dictates that the boldest knight summon his lady to claim the hunting falcon as her prize. If necessary, the hunter-knight will defend his lady's claim.

The vavasor's unmarried daughter, Enide, arms Erec with weapons provided by her own father and then claims the falcon. Erec overthrows the previously uncontested prizewinner, Yder, who is none other than the knight who insulted Guenevere. Erec returns to Arthur's court, accompanied by Enide, whom the queen welcomes by bestowing on her a new dress. Judged by all to be the most beautiful lady of the court, Enide receives the kiss of the white stag from Arthur. The parallel strands of the erotic hunt and the erotic quest have now converged and are fulfilled in the marriage of Erec and Enide. Up to now this has been a story of male victories. In the sweeter skirmishes of the wedding bed, however, Enide will prove herself the hardier of the pair. In all his romances, Chrétien is intrigued by strong women.

Now comfortably married, Erec spends so much time abed with his wife that he neglects his chivalry. Through his *recréance* (weakness), Erec becomes an object of *médisance* (badmouthing) among the knights of his own court. When Enide tearfully discloses their slander to him, Erec is outraged and commands that they set out on a quest to restore their honor.

The conditions that Erec foolishly imposes on the quest are as follows: Enide must keep her silence as they wander, no matter what danger to Erec arises. But each time Enide perceives that Erec's life is threatened by unseen aggressors, she speaks out, thereby breaking his orders but saving his life. When Erec has been apparently wounded to the death, Enide resists, to the verge of martyrdom, a violent marriage suit by the Count of Limors, although he beats her in public for her recalcitrance. After his wife has been tested to the limit, Erec revives and slays the violent suitor.

Certain now that his wife's loyalty to him is stronger than her fear of transgressing his foolish commands (to obey them would be false loyalty), Erec is ready to undertake the most difficult quest of all, called the "Joy of the Court." In a marvelous orchard with invisible walls, Erec defeats the knight Mabonagrain. To his astonishment, the loser rejoices at this outcome. The enigma of Mabonagrain's "joy" in defeat is explained: as a young man he had sworn never to leave the company of his lady in this enchanted orchard until such time as he might be conquered by someone stronger. Mabonagrain has thus remained for years a hostage of his own honor to respect that vow—and of the lady who would not release him from it. Thus Erec and Enide are witnessing a welcome breach of female domination. The pertinence of this episode to their own conjugal life is reinforced by the discovery that Mabonagrain's lady is Enide's cousin. The Joy of the Court, therefore, is the legitimation of love by free consent, of love which transcends the tyrannical passions and fear that characterize "Ovidian" love at first sight. But this curious episode explores an abiding paradox: in love (but not war), loss can produce gain; defeat, victory.

The brief final section of the romance describes the coronation of Erec and Enide in Arthur's court. The ceremony is an occasion for displaying unprecedented material opulence. Moreover, the exotic finery abounding at the event comes conspicuously from afar: ivory thrones decorated with leopards and crocodiles, and a royal robe woven with gold and embroidered with exotic animals from India that eat only spices—ginger and cloves. Just as important, the treasures of this new culture are intellectual as well: Erec's robe is ornamented not only with exotic animals but also with emblems of the quadrivium, the four "sciences of things" (as they were then called): geometry, mathematics, music, and astronomy. But even better, Erec's scepter is adorned with the forms of every living thing in nature, as if to tell us that encyclopedic knowledge is a virtue of kings as well as of philosophers.

There are many reasons why the court of Champagne where Chrétien wrote

43

should have nurtured the flowering of Arthurian romance in France. We know nothing about the identity of Chrétien himself, but we know a great deal about his patrons and their literary tastes. In a later romance, *Perceval, ou le conte du Graal* (ca. 1181; *Perceval, or the Story of the Grail*), Chrétien identifies Marie, countess of Champagne, as a patroness with a strong will and, indeed, with a few too many ideas of her own. Marie was the daughter of Eleanor of Aquitaine and Louis VII. But her pedigree was poetical as well as political: her mother was the daughter of William IX of Aquitaine, a great poet as well as a duke, whose language was not French (*la langue d'oïl*), spoken in the north of France, but Provençal (*la langue d'oc*), spoken south of the Loire.

Marie's husband, Henri the Liberal, was the great-grandson of William the Conqueror and nephew of King Stephen of England. Like Chrétien's fictive heroines, both Henri's wife and mother-in-law were strong feminine models, as were several of his direct female ancestors. But the cultivation of Arthurian romance, whose material was imported from the British Isles—as opposed, for instance, to the more indigenous material of Carolingian epic—had ideological motives that reached beyond Henri's genealogical connection with Normandy and England. Recent political and economic relationships between Champagne and Louis VII had been at worst hostile (Louis had invaded Champagne in 1142), at best fragile: desperate for a son and heir, Louis had married Henri's sister in 1160. At a time when the Capetian kings were inventing as many ancestral links as possible to Charlemagne and to the dream empire that he symbolized, Henri was cultivating feudal networks with the Normans and the Flemish to the west of Paris and with the Germans to the east, all to the dismay of Louis. Thus Henri remained indifferent both to any blood links with Charlemagne and to Carolingian epic, despite its important genealogical subtexts.

Henri's feudal network served as the political foundation of a massive economic revival in Western Europe. Its very center was the commercial fairs of Champagne. Actively promoted by Henri, these fairs brought together merchants from Flanders bearing high-quality wool imported from England and woven in Flanders and merchants from Italy bearing spices, silk, precious metals, and many other objects of luxury. Whereas the great French epic the *Chanson de Roland* (put into writing sometime in the first third of the 12th century) had looked on the finery of the East with contempt, in the marriage of Erec and Enide Chrétien hyperbolically lauded the fruits of international trade: even Alexander and Caesar, he announces, have been outdone. The *Roland* poet loved well-made armor and swords. Chrétien loved them too, but he loved exotic textiles and fine clothes even more. Chrétien was the first vernacular poet to give heroic status to the consumer mentality.

Chrétien's fantasy of economic (as opposed to military) preeminence embedded in the portrait of Arthur's court was no doubt alluring to Count Henri himself. Nearly twenty years before, Bernard of Clairvaux had sent Henri to Constantinople to be dubbed knight by the Byzantine emperor Manuel I Comnenus, presumably to arouse sympathy for the upcoming Second Crusade, which would be led by Louis VII himself. However, the crusade had not only ended in a resounding military disaster in the Holy Land, but had left the French just as deeply intimidated by the cultural splendors of Constantinople. As the abbé Suger (an architect both in his own right and of Capetian political ambition) had tried to rival the Byzantine Greeks by building at Saint-Denis a sumptuous sanctuary rivaling St. Sophia in Constantinople, Chrétien (who was himself influenced by Byzantine romances) put the now-hated Greeks in their (fictional) place with a stroke of the pen.

Addressing a rapidly changing world, Chrétien faced a delicate task. On the one hand, he had to respect the values of a warfaring, landed aristocracy whose privilege of ruling was now becoming hereditary; on the other, he had to inflect these codes so as to address the economic realities of an urban barter economy swiftly transforming itself into an international market based on liquid assets and the miracle of credit.

The new economics of Champagne favored the bourgeoisie, the clergy, and the high nobility, who were its patrons. It disfavored the lesser, chivalric nobility, who had the land but not the precious metal, and who had to be tamed if merchants were to cross their territory unscathed. Chivalric combat was becoming outmoded, and so too were its ideals. Henri himself had created an armed, mounted sergeantry of non-nobles to keep the merchant's and the churchman's peace. Paradoxically, the fiction of the wandering knight emerged when the chivalric joust was tending to move from the battlefield into the list: chivalry lent itself equally well to sport and to fiction. Like Enide's father, many of the minor knightly nobles of Champagne were impoverished not by war alone but also by their economic marginality. The errant knights of Chrétien's romances who bring back to the court fine tales of heroic adventures (and finer women to wed) may be a poetic fiction, but underneath this fiction was an encoded message to Chrétien's aristocratic audience: the altar, the wedding bed, the cradle, and the inheritance—not the battlefield—were now the surer paths to power.

Thus the new heroism favored warriors-turned-breeders, and Henri himself was something of a paradigm. He had returned a personal hero from the otherwise disastrous Second Crusade and soon afterward inherited the newly constituted county of Champagne. One of Henri's first political deeds was to become engaged, in 1153, to Marie, then only eight years old. They did not marry until 1164, precisely when Chrétien must have been hard at work marrying Erec to Enide in his romance.

As a vernacular writer whose training had very likely been ecclesiastical (though some have thought that he was a converted Jew), Chrétien navigated among a variety of well-established "textual communities" in northern France, subgroups within feudal society whose social identities were based on specific models of reading and writing. There were several important textual communities in Champagne: a distinguished Jewish community (dominated by the 11th-century commentator Rashi); the Christian mystics of the Cistercian order, led by Bernard of Clairvaux; and (more recently) Peter Abelard's philosophical school, the Paraclete. (The forward-looking Marie and Henri named

45

one of their daughters Scholastica.) Chrétien's own humanistic cast of mind seems to reflect deep affinities with the cathedral school of Chartres. All of these highly learned textual communities interacted in various ways with Chrétien's own texts. There were also less orthodox textual communities in Troyes, notably the curious, semiplayful, semiserious (but in any case antimarital) "Love Court" presided over by Marie herself, with Andreas Capellanus as its Latin chronicler.

But 12th-century Champagne also inaugurated new vernacular textual communities. One of the most remarkable, which Chrétien helped to promulgate, was that of the so-called Champagne circle of lyric poets, who exchanged elegant and highly artificial courtly songs about love. If such love was not sincere, why were the nobles of Champagne so eager to write about it? Perhaps, confronted by the rise of commerce and the new techniques for keeping written accounts, and perhaps also threatened by Henri's increasing political exploitation of the archive of written records and contracts, the nobles of Champagne were now eager to acquire and master the art of writing—though in an emblematic discourse of their own.

Several generations of fine critics have taught us much about Chrétien's craft as a poet and storyteller, about his rhetoric and irony, and about the poetic influences at work in his texts. Chrétien's art is obviously the work of an individual genius, but it was still a patronized art. Although we are unlikely ever to know anything about Chrétien as a historical person, we can at least understand much more about the social and economic conditions that summoned (or allowed) Chrétien and his fellow poets of Champagne to lay down such firm discursive foundations for the literary traditions of medieval and Renaissance France and beyond.

See also 1127, 1181, 1209.

Bibliography: Chrétien de Troyes, *Erec et Enide,* ed. Mario Roques (Paris: Champion, 1958). Jean Frappier, *Chrétien de Troyes: The Man and His Work,* trans. Robert J. Cormier (Athens: Ohio University Press, 1982). Norris J. Lacy, *The Craft of Chrétien de Troyes: An Essay on Narrative Art* (Leiden: Brill, 1980). Donald Maddox, *Structure and Sacring: The Systematic Kingship in Chrétien's "Erec et Enide"* (Lexington, Ky.: French Forum, 1978).

Eugene Vance

 1175

Comic Animal Stories Are Collected in *Le roman de Renart*

Fables and Parodies

The name Renart needs little introduction. The praenomen quickly came to function, in Old French, as the common name for "fox," carrying with it connotations of slyness, deceit, and cruelty. Renart is an incorrigible creature endowed with speech, intelligence, a will to deceive, and impossible desires. This fox has enjoyed a time-honored popularity as the wily trickster hero, comic in his shifts from ravenous beast to rational man. *Le roman de Renart* (referred to in English as *Renard the Fox*) is a specifically medieval reworking of the universal fables best known to modern readers from the collection of Aesop. The character of Renart himself first appears in medieval Latin literature in approximately 1150, in the cleric Nivard's satire *Ysengrimus*. Although *Ysengrimus* draws on the same body of material, it is not a direct source of the Old French *Roman de Renart*. In later medieval versions, such as Rutebeuf's *Renart le bestourné* (second half of the 13th century; *Renard Corrupted*) and *Le couronnement de Renart* (ca. 1251; *The Coronation of Renard*), the fox symbolizes political machinations and monastic corruption. In modern literature Renart appears in a variety of texts, from those of Goethe to James Fenimore Cooper. In each period the Renart character expresses the mentality of the historical period that gives him literary life. Accordingly, we can learn a great deal about the literature and culture of 12th-century France from consideration of this comic text.

The second half of the 12th century witnessed a great outpouring of Old French literature in Champagne, Normandy, Picardy, and the Ile-de-France. The earliest twelve "branches," or collections of comic episodes, that make up *Le roman de Renart* were created, performed, and became popular between 1175 and 1205, in the same period that the works of Marie de France, Chrétien de Troyes, Béroul, Thomas, and the northern troubadours achieved fame.

Roman, a medieval word, denotes first and foremost the language of the text: vernacular French, as opposed to learned Latin. But it also links the comic fables of *Le roman de Renart* to the great new genre, romance. The generic title raises a question: What is the relation between these tales of wolves, lions, and bears and the chivalric romances recounting the quest for the Grail or the love of Tristan and Iseut? In *Le roman de Renart* the word *roman* is in fact used ironically: the work is a literary parody of canonical romance, a rewriting and a distortion of canonical literature. In this role *Le roman de Renart* typifies a fundamental tendency of all medieval French literature.

Since the 19th century medievalists have classified *Le roman de Renart* as a satire of medieval society, of the indifference of Louis VII, of the chaos of French feudalism, of the violence of men and the lascivious cunning of women. Both satire and parody are forms of distorted reproduction or imitations of a model, usually comic. But the two can be distinguished in terms of their target. The target of satire is extraliterary, the world outside: mores, institutions, attitudes, and practices, whether social, political, or religious. Satire has often been described as a mirror in which the vices of the real world are reflected. Parody, on the other hand, targets literary models and aesthetic conventions. In recent decades literary critics have begun to point out the sophisticated literary parody in the comic fables of *Le roman de Renart*.

To call *Le roman de Renart* "sophisticated" may at first seem inappropriate. After all, these apparently simple animal tales look somewhat like children's literature: the animals steal chickens, lose their tails, and try to trick one

47

another by playing dead. On the other hand, the adventures of Renart the fox and Ysengrin the wolf contain scatological pranks, obscenities, and sexual violence that would hardly qualify them for inclusion in the canon of great books.

But it is precisely in this use of naturalism as a vehicle for literary parody that the sophistication and canonicity of *Le roman de Renart* episodes are revealed. This 12th-century collection of beast fables demonstrates the medieval understanding that literature is a construct and consequently can be taken apart and played with. The lion-king's court with its bears, camels, beavers, and snails is an image not of the court of Louis VII but rather of contemporary literary paradigms: the knights of King Arthur, in Arthurian romance, or the barons of King Marc, in the Tristan stories. The erotic entanglements of the she-wolf Hersent with her husband, Ysengrin, and his nephew, Renart, are not so much references to the perfidy of real French women as a comic rewriting of the story of Iseut with Marc and his nephew Tristan. When Renart manages to pay a sly visit to Hersent, for example, she coyly beckons him into their den and chastises the fox for coming so infrequently (VIIa, lines 5752–65):

> Lady, as God is my witness, if I did not come earlier it was not out of malevolence or ill will on my part. On the contrary, I would have taken great pleasure in seeing you, but Master Ysengrin watches my comings and goings. I do not know what else to do to avoid the hatred of your husband, who, moreover, is wrong to behave in this way. May I be hanged if ever I committed an action that justifies his rancor. He claims that I am in love with you.

The naturalism of the scene's setting (a fox and a she-wolf in her lair, with the fox cubs about) establishes a highly ironic contrast with Renart's courtly discourse, echoing as it does Béroul's *Roman de Tristan*.

The depiction of rustic farmers in "La ruée épique" ("The Epic Charge"; VIIb), as they take up their pitchforks in a bathetic charge against thieving animals, again reveals the text's pleasure in parodically juxtaposing the naturalism of animal fables with the solemn scenes of chivalric literature. The author displays his skill and literary knowledge in playing with the overblown style of the epic battle scene: the thronging rush of horsemen; the enumeration of their elaborate patronyms, such as Tiegier Flatcakebreaker, Roger Icebreaker, Femeris Emptyplate; the pretentious description of their arms (here rustic clubs, whips, and arrows). *Le roman de Renart* comically rewrites the epic *chanson de geste* in the naturalistic space of the beast fable tradition: "Onward, great lords, onward, follow that bear!" (XIIb, line 7061). A scene in the king's court, where an Italian camel presides over a divorce case, speaking incomprehensible legal jargon, is a spoof of medieval romance's predilection for trials and legal technicalities in the matter of marriage vows and infidelity: "*Prego*, Signore, hear me, hear me. We findeth in written decree laws that *expressissimo* forbid of matrimonial violatings" (VIIb, lines 6269–72). The portrait of the Italian camel also offers an example of the self-conscious literary wordplay so prevalent in *Le roman de Renart*. Similarly, the high-minded intellectual constructs of the 12th century are mocked in the following exchange between the fox and Tibert the cat: "'Renart, you devil, are you drunk? What are you doing with my books? . . . Do you know anything about dialectics?' 'Yes, all kinds of quick-quackalectics'" (XI, lines 12173–74, 12179–80).

An episode of Branch I, called "Renart teinturier" ("Renard the Dyer"), shows most clearly how *Le roman de Renart* plays with the contemporary paradigms of lofty canonical literature. Renart attempts to escape from his nemesis, the wolf, by pretending to be a jongleur from a foreign land (I, lines 2428–30, 2435–41):

> "Ja, ja, I am screwing good chongleur,
> but yesterday screwing robbers beat me
> and my screwing lute stolen.
>
> . . .
>
> I know good screwing Breton lays
> about Melon the magician
> and King Arfer and Sir Dristan,
> about the Horny Suckle, and about Saint Brendan."
> "And do you know the lay of Lady Isolde?"
> "Ja, ja," said he, "by Godsdiddle,
> I will be knowing them all whole thing."

Thus the "wild animal," deep in the forest, cleverly catalogues the literary best-sellers of the day, implicitly challenging the very notion of the canon.

Parody is more prevalent throughout medieval French literature than was formerly thought. It is not limited to the later Middle Ages or to periods of decline in which models have degenerated and become unpopular. Parody plays with well-established literary conventions, but it also flourishes whenever a new mode or genre reaches popularity. It is a sign not of decadence but of new life. An obvious parody of the epic tradition, the anonymous *Audigier,* dates from about 1150. Just as the genealogical epic reaches the height of its popularity, *Audigier* rewrites it, imitating its literary form to perfection but transposing it to a scatological context. *Audigier* plays with the rules of medieval literature by juxtaposing aristocratic characters and rural peasants and by combining the epic matrix and scatological humor of various comic genres.

Medieval parody is not always comic; it includes a serious tendency in which literary rulebreaking is not a moral lowering but a thoughtful rewriting. In some texts the earthly signs of secular literature are reworked in religious codes. The anonymous *La quête du saint Graal* (ca. 1220; *The Quest for the Holy Grail*) exemplifies this noncomic parody; it draws on the quest pattern of secular chivalric romance, translating it as a spiritual quest for salvation.

The date 1175 and *Le roman de Renart* are a fitting introduction to the rich parodic traditions of the Middle Ages. Medieval parody deconstructs canonical literary genres and traditional poetics. Its intention, in *Le roman de Renart* as in other parodic texts, is not to judge or criticize but to play. It is not the crude art of childlike buffoons, but the witty play of talented and knowledgeable poets. Parody revels in literary trends and history, reworking old models and studying new fashions.

49

Parody in medieval France is not a decadent or cynical art form, but a central tradition, a finely wrought dialogue of literary forms and conventions. Parody pays homage to the stability of existing traditions and delights in counterfeiting the latest literary modes. It is the practice of a culture that takes pleasure and pride in its own literary talents and predilections. It teaches us that medieval literature was, from the outset, highly conscious of itself.

See also 1210, 1460, 1668.

Bibliography: John Flinn, *Le roman de Renart dans la littérature française et dans les littératures étrangères au moyen âge* (Paris: Presses Universitaires de France, 1963). Kathryn Gravdal, *Vilain et Courtois: Transgressive Parody in French Literature of the 12th and 13th Centuries* (Lincoln: University of Nebraska Press, 1989). Hans Robert Jauss, *Untersuchungen zur mittelalterlischen Tierdichtung* (Tübingen: Max Niemeyer, 1959). Omer Jodogne, "*Audigier* et la chanson de geste, avec une édition nouvelle du poème," *Le moyen âge,* 66 (1960), 495–526. *Renard the Fox,* trans. Patricia Terry (Boston: Northeastern University Press, 1983) (portions of Branches I, II, Va, and VIII). *Le roman de Renart,* ed. Mario Roques, 5 vols. (Paris: Champion, 1958–1982). Rutebeuf, *Le couronnement de Renart,* ed. Alfred Foulet (Princeton: Princeton University Press, 1929). Rutebeuf, *Renart le bestourné,* in *Oeuvres complètes de Rutebeuf,* ed. Edmond Faral and Julia Bastin, vol. 2 (Paris: Picard, 1969), pp. 145–146.

Kathryn Gravdal

✍ *1180?*

A Frenchwoman in England Writes for a Norman Court

Marie de France

Since we have no definite dates for Marie de France and can say only that she wrote in the latter part of the 12th century, 1180 is at best an arbitrary or symbolic date for her. But it is a moment central to related historical figures and to her literary culture. Marie wrote during the first flowering of French chivalric romance, when the adaptations of classical stories, the Arthurian poems of Chrétien de Troyes, and the first written versions of the Tristan story were composed. Her *lais,* though considerably shorter than the romances, are written in the same verse form, octosyllabic couplets, for the same kind of audience, a French-speaking court, with similar interests: love, the inner life of the individual, and the claims of society.

About Marie herself we know almost nothing, except her name, which she gives in each of the works attributed to her, the *Lais,* the *Fables,* and the disputed *Purgatoire de saint Patrice* (*Purgatory of Saint Patrick*). There is little in the works to connect them with each other or with the same Marie, beyond a clear authorial interest in edifying her audience, which is scarcely distinctive in medieval literature, and a concern with social responsibility in the public and private realms that runs through the fables and the *lais.* Marie declares at the end of the *Fables* that she is from France ("Marie is my name, I am from

France"), and she writes in French, but the scattered occurrences of English words and English places in the *Lais* suggest that she was writing for a French-speaking Norman audience in England. The *Lais* are dedicated to a noble king, presumed to be Henry II, who reigned from 1154 to 1189, the most likely period for their composition.

The events and interconnections between the English and French royal families are thus part of her milieu. In 1180 two rulers died: Louis VII of France, whose first wife was Eleanor of Aquitaine, now married to Henry II of England; and Manuel I Comnenus of Byzantium. Manuel was succeeded by his son Alexius II Comnenus, who was married to one of Louis's daughters. In the same year Henry the Lion, duke of Saxony, was deprived of his fiefs and would go into exile within two years at the court of Henry II. Henry the Lion was married to one of the daughters of Henry II and Eleanor; one of their sons was married to a daughter of Louis. Louis's two daughters by Eleanor were married to the French counts of Champagne and Blois, and both were patrons of poets, as their mother was. Henry II's wife and several of his sons were technically vassals of Louis. The very complicated family and feudal relations and marital arrangements were part of the daily reality of Marie's life and may well have encouraged her interests in the problems of women married to men they did not love, a situation that obtains in more than half of the *lais*.

The fact that Eleanor was imprisoned by her husband from 1174 to 1189 because of her part in political conspiracies may also be reflected in the *lais* about imprisoned wives ("Guigemar" and "Yonec") and in Marie's concern with women's need to free themselves, by the mind and the will, from oppressive situations. Eleanor was not the only example of a forceful woman available to Marie. In 1179 Hildegard of Bingen had died after a long and impressive career as abbess, philosophical visionary, and medical writer, but particularly as author of letters to figures throughout Europe, in which she did not hesitate to reprove and correct popes, emperors, and lesser public figures—which Marie also does frequently, if not so directly as Hildegard, particularly in her fables. About fifteen years earlier, another distinguished abbess had died, Héloïse, known for her great learning and for her affair with Peter Abelard, before she won the respect of the world as the abbess of the Paraclete. Both abbesses seem to have gained control over their lives, indeed to have made themselves powerful figures in their world by their intellect and strength of will. Although Marie seeks secular solutions in the *lais,* she does turn in the last and longest, "Eliduc," to a religious one, at least in the pattern of life; both women in the story retire from marriage to a monastery, where the friendship they share seems to be more satisfying than their earlier lives.

Marie is concerned in both the *Lais* and the *Fables* with problems of daily reality, but she also shows the influence of her literary milieu. By the time she began to write, there was an established tradition of courtly love lyric in Provençal and the beginning of one in French. That tradition is reflected in the composition of the *lai* in "Chaitivel" and probably in the love debates in "Equitan," which may also have some connection with the debates recorded by

Marie's contemporary, Andreas Capellanus. The classical romances, translations into French of Latin poems with highly expanded love stories, were popular; indeed it is likely that Marie is referring to them when she says she considered translating a story from Latin into Romance, but instead decided to record the *lais* she had heard, perhaps preferring a form that gave greater scope to her imagination and more freedom to introduce the problems that interested her. She may have known the Tristan romances of Béroul and Thomas; her Tristan, "Chèvrefeuille," is the only *lai* for which she claims a written source, and motifs from the Tristan stories are scattered through the *lais*. Chrétien de Troyes had probably already composed some of his romances. Although no direct influence has been shown, both poets are concerned with the conflicting needs of society and of the individual, and with the potential for corruption even in the "ideal" Arthurian court, which Marie depicts in "Lanval" as cynically as Chrétien does in *Yvain* and *Lancelot*. Chrétien drew most of his material from Celtic oral sources, the same sources Marie claims for virtually every one of her *lais*.

Marie's intent is at least partly serious in all her works, with explicit morals in the *Fables* and the *Purgatoire,* and in a few of the *lais,* "Equitan," "Frêne," and "Bisclavret." In the prologue to the *Lais* she talks about the difficulties and obscurities built into ancient texts, the need to interpret them to get at the meaning, with the strong implication that one has to do the same with her poems. Even in the prologue to the *Fables,* despite their built-in lessons for the improvement of the audience, she says that people wondered at Aesop's putting his mind to such a task, but that there is some wisdom to be gained from any fable, however foolish.

The need to justify her work and call attention to its serious message may have been occasioned by accusations of frivolity, such as the comments of Denis Piramus at the beginning of *La vie de saint Edmond le roi* (1190–1200? *The Life of Saint Edmund the King*). Dismissing as unrealistic the work of some fashionable writers of the day, perhaps with some envy for their success, he gives thirteen lines to Marie, as the author of *lais* in verse that "are not at all true, and yet she is praised for them and her poetry loved by all" (lines 35–47). In an invaluable testimony to her popularity, Denis tells us that counts, barons, and knights cherish her, love her writings, and take delight in having them read often, and that ladies derive joy from hearing them, because "they suit their desires." Gautier d'Arras in *Ille et Galeron* (ca. 1170) had also alluded to *lais* that "seem to have been dreamt" (lines 935–937).

Marie appears to be aware of such views and perhaps to be answering them in one of her fables, "De Leone et Homine" ("About the Lion and the Man"), where she distinguishes between a fable that is a lie or a painting that is a dream, and the truth that is revealed by experience. In the *lais,* too, she continually asserts the truth of the experiences she relates, and shows how art is fashioned from life (as in "Chaitivel," "Chèvrefeuille," and "Laüstic" ["Nightingale"]) and how life can imitate art ("Yonec"). Part of the problem, of course, lies with the genre. The *lai,* as far as we know from the extant examples, seems to have dealt primarily with love stories, usually with a good dose of the supernatural. The same is true of Marie's *lais,* although in comparing them with other versions of the story when available, several scholars have noted that Marie's invariably play down the supernatural elements. Indeed, she employs supernatural motifs sparingly and usually combines them with realistic symbols. The werewolf phase of the hero in "Bisclavret" represents the potential for violence in any of us, which is kept in check by the usages of civilized life, the clothes he must put on to return to his human form. The unmanned boat in "Guigemar," which appears when needed to carry both the hero and the heroine to new lives, may represent fate, which must be driven by their wills. It is contrasted with both the tower in which the heroine's husband imprisons her and the knots that the lovers make for each other, representing the self-imposed bonds of love, far more effective than the claims of an oppressive marriage. The bird-knight of "Yonec" represents a love that is not earthbound, that can appear when needed, that can penetrate the imprisoning towers of oppressed marriages and bring joy and relief and yet is vulnerable to the violence of a jealous husband; but he leaves the heroine with the very realistic symbols of the ring of fidelity and the sword of revenge. And the *lai* that follows, "Laüstic," features a real bird, the nightingale, which becomes the symbol of a love stifled by the husband's threat of violence, its carcass preserved in a rich casket, a love with superficial trappings and no substance.

Marie, however, focuses far more on natural and realistic symbols, because the kind of love she is concerned with is not romantic fluff, but mutual commitment and support. It can offer to women relief from the suffering of bad marriages, to men a satisfaction that worldly pursuits do not. But it cannot be self-indulgent or irresponsible. The fact that the love presented in many *lais* is adulterous does not mean that it is amoral. If the order of the *lais* as they appear in the one complete manuscript is the order established by Marie when she put them together, then she intentionally balanced positive and negative characteristics. The odd *lais* (first, third, and so on) proclaim the need for love ("Guigemar"), the qualities essential to love—loyalty, generosity, self-sacrifice ("Frêne," "Lanval," "Chèvrefeuille")—and the gifts of love—relief from suffering ("Guigemar," "Yonec"), progeny ("Yonec," "Milun"), joy ("Chèvrefeuille"). The even *lais* condemn and punish the abuse of love for self-interest or self-indulgence: the ambitious wife and irresponsible king of "Equitan" are boiled alive in the tubs prepared for her husband; the wife who betrayed her werewolf husband loses her nose and her lover is mauled in "Bisclavret"; the possessive father loses his daughter and the overconfident lover his life in "Les deux amants" ("The Two Lovers"); the frivolous lovers of "Laüstic" lose the pretense for their encounters, although they preserve and glorify it as the lifeless symbol of their love; and the vain lady of "Chaitivel" who refuses to give up any of her admirers loses three of them and the services of the fourth. The last *lai,* "Eliduc," if not so overtly negative, gently shows up the limitations of earthly love and reveals the satisfactions of a disinterested human love and devotion to God. The message that emerges from the twelve *lais* is that love can offer the greatest rewards and solace in human life, but only to those who deserve them by their selflessness, suffering, courage, and devotion.

Good love for Marie is fruitful, either in progeny or in art; bad love is sterile. This point is made in a variety of ways, most directly in "Yonec" and "Milun," where the marriages are childless but the love produces a son. From the beginning of the first *lai*, "Guigemar," where the hero's need for love is expressed by a hind accompanied by its fawn, Marie implies that love should be fruitful. In "Frêne" the hero's men reject the heroine because she is fruitless (like her namesake, the ash, since she has been deprived of her identity and cannot marry) and propose that he marry her sister Coudre (Hazel), who offers the promise of an heir like the nut-bearing tree. Although the love of Tristan and Iseut produces no child, it does inspire Tristan's *lai,* from which Marie says she derives hers, and it is rich in literary progeny. On the negative side, the unjustified affair in "Equitan" leads only to the death of the lovers; the fruit of the treacherous wife's union in "Bisclavret" is tainted (born noseless); the only thing to emerge from the abortive affair in "Laüstic" is the elaborate casket to house the dead nightingale; the possessive father in "Les deux amants" cuts his only child off from a fruitful life and ultimately from life itself, leaving him too with nothing but an elaborate tomb; and the woman in "Chaitivel," whose selfishness has destroyed three suitors and left the fourth sterile, can only compose a *lai* to glorify her loss.

Marie's sense of commitment and responsibility does not apply only to love relations. Although she focuses on those in the *lais,* she does not lose sight of the claims of society. We know from her fables how interested she was in social questions. Barely a third of the fables are concerned with personal morality. Many more deal with the effects of one's actions on others, particularly the effects of deception and treachery; several show the inequities between rich and poor or the effects of bad leadership, of selfish, weak, or sick kings whose courts are dominated by the self-serving and unscrupulous; and a considerable number stretch far to derive social morals from their stories, to condemn corruption and exploitation in courts of law, to criticize evil lords, or to preach the mutual responsibilities of lords and subjects. But such concerns are also evident in the *lais.* Marie does not attack the issue directly, but she does present a number of kings, in varying attitudes of inadequacy, and for the most part allows us to draw our own conclusions.

The king in "Equitan" neglects his public responsibilities to make love to his seneschal's wife while the seneschal runs the country for him; he dies appropriately in his own trap, whereas in "Lanval" King Arthur, who fails to reward a loyal and worthy knight and allows his queen to bring the man to trial on a false accusation, loses no more than the man's service. In "Eliduc," the hero's king exiles him without trial despite his good service on the word of envious courtiers and restores him only when he needs him, by which time the man has incurred obligations to a new lord. The father who sacrifices his only child and a good knight to his possessive love in "Les deux amants" is a king about whose judgment in public affairs we must have serious reservations. Only in "Bis-clavret" do we see a king whose wisdom recognizes worth in the most unlikely guise and who is able to restore a loyal subject and punish his betrayers.

Secular society is portrayed with many defects in the *lais,* both in the political sphere and in the familial: families marry their daughters to inappro-priate husbands, husbands abuse their wives, wives betray good husbands, a mother rejects her daughter, a father destroys his. But this is not to say either that Marie rejects secular society—quite the contrary—or that she presents the religious life as a better way. The church plays a very small role in the *lais:* the presence of a eunuch priest in the service of a possessive husband emphasizes the latter's sterility; the care an abbess gives a rejected child contrasts with the mother's selfishness, but the child leaves the convent for worldly love. Even in "Eliduc," where all three main characters finally retire to a monastery, the emphasis is more on the shift away from married love to friendship than on religious devotion.

For Marie, the ideal life involves mutual love in a social context. Lovers cannot live for long in isolation no matter how powerful their love. Society will always intrude and must be served as in "Guigemar," where they cannot remain together in the tower, but must be separated, suffer, and return to the world before they can be reunited. Tristan and Iseut cannot remain alone in the woods, but must return to their social roles and hope for an end to their separation. Not even Eliduc, who is rejected by his society, can remain with his new love but must return to his obligations to king and to wife; when he and the two women retire from the world, they do not leave society, but move into a dif-ferent form of society within the monastery. The love idyll in "Frêne" is dis-rupted by the social responsibilities imposed on the man and cannot be continued until the woman is restored to her family and thereby to her proper social position. Only Lanval, who is rejected by his society until he finds some-thing better and then is threatened and abused by that society, is allowed to leave it and go off with his love. Men who try to cut their wives or daughters off from society lose them; the king who ignores his social responsibilities is killed. The man who is forced to live outside society, Bisclavret, is a werewolf, an animal, despite his worth, until he is able to resume the trappings of civi-lized life. But at the same time, the lover in "Milun" who pursues chivalric glory at the cost of his obligations to love has to sacrifice that glory before he can be reunited with his love. Society must be served, but it is best served by those who love and who suffer and sacrifice for that love.

Bibliography: Glyn S. Burgess, *Marie de France: An Analytical Bibliography* (London: Grant and Cutler, 1977). Burgess, *Marie de France: Text and Context* (Athens: University of Georgia Press, 1987). Denis Piramus, *La vie de seint Edmund le rei,* ed. Hilding Kjellman (Göteborg: Elanders Boktryckeri Aktiebolag, 1935). Gautier d'Arras, *Ille und Galeron von Walter von Arras,* ed. Werdelin Foerster (Halle: Niemeyer, 1891). Robert Hanning and Joan Ferrante, *The Lais of Marie de France,* 2d ed. (Durham, N.C.: Laby-rinth, 1982). Marie de France, *The Fables of Marie de France,* trans. Mary L. Martin (Birmingham, Ala.: Summa, 1984). Marie de France, *Les lais de Marie de France,* ed.

Jean Rychner (Paris: Champion, 1966). Emanuel J. Mickel, *Marie de France* (New York: Twayne, 1974). Robert Sturges, "Texts and Readers in Marie de France's *Lais*," *Romanic Review,* 71 (1980), 244–264.

Joan M. Ferrante

✐ *1181?*

Chrétien de Troyes Composes *Perceval, ou le conte du Graal*

The Grail

The drafting of Chrétien de Troyes's *Perceval, ou le conte du Graal* (*Perceval, or the Story of the Grail*), dedicated to Philippe, count of Flanders (1143–1191), can be dated to between 1180 and 1190. The unfinished text of 9,234 octosyllabic lines gave rise to four sequels totaling more than 70,000 lines (attributed to the pseudonymous continuators Wauchier de Denain, Gerbert de Montreuil, and Manessier); to an adaptation in verse, *Le roman de l'histoire du Graal,* attributed to a pseudonymous Robert de Boron (ca. 1200); and to an anonymous prose *Perlesvaus* (ca. 1215). Moreover, it was integrated in the cyclical prose rendering attributed to various pseudonymous authors and known as the Arthurian Cycle (ca. 1215–1235; published as *The Vulgate Version of the Arthurian Romances*).

The fiction is divided into two parts: the first one is devoted to Perceval's initiation into knighthood and the court of Artu, King of the Bretons (Arthur, King of the Britons); the second part follows Gauvain, Artu's nephew, in his quests. It is the first text in Old French to use the word *graal* (grail, from Low Latin *cratale* or *gradale*), which has had a vast influence upon art ever since. At once a novel of initiation, a reflection on the meaning of chivalry, a Christianizing adaptation of Celtic mythology, and a meditation on the art of writing, *Le conte du Graal* is the most complex and enigmatic of Chrétien de Troyes's works.

At the beginning Perceval, a young *valet* (the son of a noble family not yet dubbed a knight), grows up ignorant of the courtly world of chivalry. His mother, the Veuve Dame (Widow Lady), who has confined him in a forest rendered sterile by a mysterious curse, reveals to him that chivalry is responsible for the death of his father and two brothers; thus the world of heraldry is associated with death from the outset of the narration. For the mortal refinements of chivalry, the Widow Lady has substituted an education rooted in the Bible. The sylvan setting of the romance metaphorically refers to a style identified by classical rhetoric as *sylva,* the natural style of a "draft," written, according to Quintilian's *De institutione oratoria,* under the "heat and élan of inspiration" (10.3. 17). In Chrétien's theocentric worldview, this setting immerses Perceval in a divinely inspired *natura* (nature), whose signs he must learn to decipher in order to understand God's will. Through the emblematic presence of the widow mother, the forest finally symbolizes also a femininity deserted by a male principle, this principle having itself rejected God. These converging indices identify Perceval's environment with Dante's *parlar materno* (maternal tongue), a language rooted in the divine and emblematizing the dignity of the vernacular.

But Perceval totally rejects the maternal *ensaing* (teaching, wisdom; line 119). Early in the tale, when five knights irrupt into the forest, this intrusion being in itself an act of violence perpetrated against *natura,* the Widow Lady's instruction does not prevent him from being at once and irreversibly seduced by chivalry: a second "nature" suddenly takes over, the one he inherited from his knight father. His rejection of maternal wisdom almost provokes a blasphemous confusion. Perceval at first takes the knights for devils, then, dazzled by the sparkling of their armor, for God and his angels. He then learns that these marvels come from the court of Artu, "the king who manufactures knights" (line 333), a revelation that links chivalry to *ars* (art), to the artificiality of *technē* (technical mastery), to *fabrication.*

In Chrétien's cultural context, Great and Little Brittany—the Celtic lands of wonders and sorcery—function as the enigmatic source of stories composing the *matière de Bretagne* (Breton themes); this region becomes, then, the privileged territory of fiction. It is the kingdom of Artu, its passive sovereign, whose principal occupation is to delight in the adventure stories told him by his knights. For example, in *Le conte du Graal,* the vanquished opponent in each of Perceval's combats must go to the court to relate his defeat. Thus Arthurian chivalry is above all, as Jean de Meun portrayed it in *Le roman de la rose* (ca. 1275; *The Romance of the Rose*), a literary chivalry ("chevalerie de letreüre"): weapons and combats are metaphors for a rhetorical and aesthetic battle (and vice versa), the main goal of which is always the production of an elegant narrative. From this perspective, the errant knights' quests are a passage into the lands of fiction, a rhetorical *via* that recurs obsessively in the figures of the road, its twists, turns, and detours. Following the traditional opposition of *ars* and *natura,* the passage toward courtly rhetoric (another passage toward *ars* and *technē*) opposes in a radical way the theocentric teachings of *natura* that Perceval's mother tried to instill in him in vain. This opposition can be seen at three different levels. (1) Generally speaking, Arthurian *ars* has its source in myths of the Other World, of the good or evil fairy, whose deliberately pagan character and Celtic origins were taken for granted in the 12th century. (2) By leaving his mother, Perceval will provoke her death; his fascination for Arthurian chivalry is thus the antithesis of what the Widow Lady symbolizes. (3) In the episode in which Perceval, on his way to Artu's court, is initiated into the subtleties of the courtly and chivalric code by the vassal (no doubt Artu's) Gornemant de Gohort, the latter agrees to dub him only on condition that Perceval will leave off his constant references to his mother and shed the simple garments she gave him at his departure. Perceval's consent to Gornemant's demand entails a double rejection of his mother's wisdom, since clothing in *Le conte du Graal* has the sense both of a symbolic investiture and of a rhetorical ornament (the *vestitio*) that haunts the story to its end.

It is in this sense that Perceval must renounce the original language of maternal wisdom in favor of an acculturation into the chivalry of letters. Such is the price to be paid for admission into the virile world of chivalry, the place of his dead father. Everything in Le conte du Graal underscores the profound antithesis between the maternal and paternal worlds, for which the opposition between nature and culture does not entirely account. Given his second, paternal "nature," Perceval learns the handling of arms and courtly rhetoric with astonishing ease.

This irremediable contradiction is strikingly emphasized in the episode of the grail. Trying to return to his mother, Perceval arrives at the manor of the Riche Roi Pêcheur (Rich Fisher King), who is, as he learns only later, his maternal uncle. Because it is a common practice in medieval narratives to use family relations to indicate a symbolic affinity, the Rich Fisher King's manor thus participates in the world of the mother. Though sitting in a small boat, on the river that separates his manor from the surrounding land, the Rich Fisher King does not offer his services as pilot. He leaves Perceval to reach his domain by his own means. In the manor, Perceval first receives a sword covered with writing and destined to break in two at the first battle. Next appears the grail procession: a lance carried by a *valet* and bleeding from its tip (reminiscent of the lance that pierced the side of Christ); then two golden candelabra, also carried by *valets;* then the grail, carried by a maiden. The brightness of the grail eclipses that of the twenty candles (it contains, we later learn, a consecrated wafer): "A girl who came in with the boys, fair and comely and beautifully adorned, was holding a grail between her hands. When she entered holding the grail, so brilliant a light appeared that the candles lost their brightness like the stars or the moon when the sun rises . . . The grail, which went ahead, was made of fine, pure gold; and in it were set precious stones of many kinds, the richest and most precious in the earth or the sea: those in the grail surpassed all other jewels, without a doubt" (*Perceval, the Story of the Grail*, p. 35).

This celebrated scene, which struck Chrétien's successors as well as his commentators, is marked with mystery. Although its intrinsic religious significance is undeniable, its meaning should not be separated from its narrative context. Obeying Gornemant de Gohort's advice never to talk too much, Perceval refrains from asking why the lance is bleeding and who is being served from the grail. Had he asked, not only would he have restored the original splendor of the deserted forest, but he would also have had access to a narration unveiling the secret of the grail. His silence, like a curse, seals the mystery forever, implicitly condemning all the knightly art of Gornemant's teaching.

The next day, after he has left the now deserted manor, his first cousin, a young girl, informs him that he failed to speak because he has strayed from maternal wisdom. At the same time, he receives the revelation of his name, Perceval le Gallois (Perceval the Welshman; line 3575). Thus his failure before the grail coincides with his baptism. But, still blind to the warning concealed in this failure, Perceval returns to Artu's court, where Gauvain, Artu's nephew, gives him a robe symbolizing his complete integration into the world of

Arthurian fiction. A blind and evil fairy appears, allowing the narrative to start anew. She proposes different quests to Artu's knights and reminds Perceval of his failure. Whereas Gauvain, in typical courtly fashion, proposes to save a virgin and to cleanse his honor, sullied by the accusation that he murdered the king of Escavalon, Perceval "says something very different" (line 4727): he will seek the truth of the lance and the grail, with their clear religious significance.

At this point, the story splits; for 1,400 lines it follows the adventures of Gauvain, inserts a brief Perceval episode, and returns to Gauvain's quest. When the narrative takes up with him, Perceval has been wandering for five years, during which time he has tested his knightly valor but also completely forgotten God. So, when he meets some penitents in a desert preparing to celebrate Easter, they catechize him, reminding him of his Christian duty. The penitents then send him to a hermit living in a forest who turns out to be yet another maternal uncle, reinforcing the link between Christian religion and Perceval's maternal lineage. The hermit explains to Perceval again why he has failed before the grail: "Your sin cut off your tongue," he says (line 6409), reminding him of his abandonment of maternal wisdom. He also reveals that Perceval's other uncle, the Rich Fisher King, is the one who is served by the grail, and teaches him a prayer containing the secret names of God, to be used only in grave danger. Having confessed, Perceval takes communion and so returns to the Christian fold. At this point the narration abandons Perceval and returns to Gauvain, implying that this is the end of Perceval's quest.

Gauvain's adventures appear at first to be opposed to those of Perceval: motivated by the desire to restore his sullied honor, they belong to the profane values of chivalry. Gauvain's rhetorical skills also oppose him to Perceval: he is accused of "selling his words," of bringing Perceval back to the court not by means of a hard fight, but by verbal persuasion: "Obviously you know the way to make your polished language pay" (lines 4384–85). The theme of the marketable word recurs at Tintagel, where Gauvain is mistaken for a salesman. And finally the knight Greoras accuses him of being a *fableor,* a jongleur, a minstrel (lines 8679–80). Thus, whereas Perceval remains silent because he has forgotten the original foundation of language, Gauvain embodies the ultimate stage of this oblivion. Language, as he practices it, no longer has ties to truth. Gauvain, accused throughout his quest of being a liar, symbolizes the part lying takes in the making of fiction and the mastery of rhetoric, especially in Breton themes: for French writers of the Middle Ages, the adjective "Breton" is often the equivalent of "liar." The different challenges Gauvain meets in his progress are thus opportunities to test the lies of Breton fiction. Furthermore, through Gauvain, Chrétien de Troyes frames the transcendent quest for the grail within the immanent terms of chivalry: when, at Escavalon, Gauvain is challenged to find the bleeding lance, this quest takes the place of the trial by combat that would have absolved him of the murder charge. Chrétien's narrative thus subtly frames the holy quest *inside* a chivalric challenge.

After prevailing in an array of worldly tests, Gauvain arrives at the border of Galvoie, a land whose name oddly resembles his own. Its border is none other than the entrance to the Underworld, arrived at through the services of a ferryman who evokes Charon. Residing there are two queens, Ygerne, Artu's mother, dead for eighty years, and Gauvain's, dead for twenty. The Queens' Palace has two doors, one of ivory, one of ebony; following a Homeric and Virgilian tradition familiar to medieval writers, they indicate that Galvoie is also the land of dreams. It is finally the land of art, full of enchantments manufactured by "a clerk, wise in astronomy" (line 7458). Contrasting strongly with Perceval's primitive forest, this palace embodies the native artifice of Breton fiction, linked to the unconscious and to death. Gauvain, the knight who symbolizes Arthurian chivalry, relies upon this source for his art and has no trouble mastering its traps: like Gérard de Nerval's Orpheus, he has "twice unvanquished crossed the Acheron"; he is the only knight to return from the land of shadows and, of course, to turn it into narrative.

Gauvain's wanderings in the land of dreams and death are obviously antithetical to Perceval's experience and the world of Christian doctrine. Nevertheless, many troubling similarities can be noted: (1) the Rich Fisher King's manor, like the Queens' Palace, is separated from the Arthurian territory by a river; (2) the presence of the Rich Fisher King as a pilot in the episode of Perceval doubles that of the ferryman on the border of Galvoie; (3) Perceval's fascination with Arthurian chivalry is epitomized by his desire for friendship with Gauvain (line 4490), a friendship emblematic of that chivalry. All these similarities suggest that Perceval might also be looked at as a double of Gauvain. There is, indeed, something profoundly ambiguous in the romance: it is as if Breton writing were erected upon an amnesia of origins and of God. Gauvain, the mirror of Perceval, represents an art of death and nothingness (echoed in the *vain* of his name), which dissimulates its void in the splendor of its rhetorical ornamentation, in its abundant decor, in the luxuriance of its gilt. Moreover, these symbols are already present in the figure of the golden grail, embedded with jewels. The grail then becomes the paradoxical symbol of Arthurian literature, even though at first it seems to stand in contradiction to its emptiness: it encloses, dissimulates, and frames the consecrated wafer (the sign of Christ's transubstantiation), suggesting theology's dependence on a fictional container. The secret of Brittany's silent rhetoric, concentrated in its king's name (*Art-tu*: the silenced art), is the hidden but violent transformation of a writing anchored in God's word into an antitheological fiction. From there to the more general conclusion that literature, even in the Middle Ages, stands in radical conflict with theology is but one short step, a step that many other texts from the period invite us to take. In particular, the immense corpus of continuations in verse and prose stemming from Chrétien's story in the late 12th and early 13th centuries will insistently confront the blasphemy of literature in a theocentric age.

See also 1165, 1209.

Bibliography: Chrétien de Troyes, *Le roman de Perceval, ou le conte du Graal,* ed. William Roach (Geneva: Droz, 1959); translated by Nigel Bryant as *Perceval, the Story of the Grail* (Cambridge: D.S. Brewer, 1982). Roger Dragonetti, *La vie de la lettre au moyen âge (le "Conte du Graal")* (Paris: Seuil, 1980). Alexandre Leupin, *Le Graal et la littérature* (Lausanne: L'Age d'Homme, 1982). Charles Mela, "Perceval," in *Literature and Psychoanalysis,* ed. Shoshana Felman (Baltimore: Johns Hopkins University Press, 1982). Mela, *La reine et le Graal: La conjointure dans les romans du Graal, de Chrétien de Troyes au "livre de Lancelot"* (Paris: Seuil, 1984).

Alexandre Leupin

✑ 1202

Nicolas of Senlis Translates from Latin the Legendary Account of Charlemagne's Expedition to Spain Known as the *Pseudo-Turpin Chronicle*

Old French Prose Historiography

In the opening decades of the 13th century historical writing in Old French moved to prose, marking a radical departure from the chanted verse histories and *chansons de geste* hitherto preferred by the medieval lay aristocracy. The earliest products of the movement toward vernacular prose historiography were translations of the *Historia Karoli Magni et Rotholandi* (*The History of Charlemagne and Roland*), an audacious clerical rewriting of the largely legendary account of Charlemagne's expedition to Spain and the epic matter of Roncevaux (Roncesvalles), best known through the verses of the *Chanson de Roland* (ca. 1100; *Song of Roland*). Scholars refer to this apocryphal eyewitness account, whose author pretends to be the Archbishop of Reims Turpin (himself a central figure in the epic narrative), as the *Pseudo-Turpin Chronicle*. Between 1202 and 1230, no fewer than six independent translations of the *Turpin* were made within the French realm (as well as an Anglo-Norman version by William of Briane, which dates from the same period). All of these translations were commissioned by members of the French-speaking Flemish aristocracy of northern France. This extreme chronological and geographic concentration suggests that Old French prose historiography in general, and *Turpin* in particular, addressed particular needs of the local aristocracy at a moment of crisis and that historiographic innovation was, at least in part, a response to social and political changes then affecting the aristocracy.

The first Old French translation of the *Pseudo-Turpin Chronicle* was made by Nicolas of Senlis at the request of Yolande, countess of Saint-Pol, and her husband, Hugh IV, about the year 1202. Yolande was the sister of Count Baldwin VIII of Flanders, who, sometime between 1180 and 1189, had commissioned his clerks to procure a copy of the *Pseudo-Turpin Chronicle*. He did this because, according to Nicolas of Senlis, "the good count Baldwin of Hainaut loved Charlemagne greatly, but he was unable to believe the things that were sung about him; thus he had a search conducted throughout the libraries of all the fine abbeys of France in order to know if a true history [of the emperor] could be found" (*Poitevinische Pseudo-Turpin,* p. 6). This text—the apocryphal *Turpin,* in all likelihood recovered from the abbey of Saint-Denis—Baldwin bequeathed to Yolande at his death in 1195, requesting that "out of love for him she guard the book for as long as she lived" (ibid.). It was in Yolande's possession when it came to serve as the Latin source for Nicolas's translation.

Additional translations in Old French rapidly followed. One, executed by a "Master Johannes" shortly before 1206, was combined with Pierre de Beauvais's translation of Charlemagne's legendary journey to Jerusalem (the *Descriptio Qualiter Karolus Magni Clavum et Coronam a Constantinopoli Transtulit*), and it was in this combined form, as a *Descriptio-Turpin*, that Johannes' text was to find favor at the courts of the Flemish aristocracy. In 1206 Renaud of Dammartin, count of Boulogne, sponsored a transcription of the Johannes *Turpin*, and in the same or the following year another copy was made for Michel III, lord of Harnes and justiciar of Flanders. Another offshoot of this redaction appears in a version commissioned by William of Cayeux, a lord of Ponthieu, of which only a fragment survives. A fifth translation from Artois dates from about 1218; it was subsequently used by an anonymous Artesian minstrel in the employ of Robert VII of Béthune, who inserted the *Turpin* chronicle into a history of France from the beginning to the wars between King John Lackland of England and King Philip Augustus of France. The sixth and final translation of the *Pseudo-Turpin Chronicle* from this period was made in Hainaut in the decade between 1220 and 1230. It is the work of an anonymous translator who, in all likelihood, lived and worked in that same region bordering the counties of Hainaut, Flanders, and Artois that was the center for the diffusion of the vernacular *Turpin*. The translation of *Turpin,* and with it the creation of vernacular prose historiography, thus seems to respond to the interests and needs of a small group of Franco-Flemish lords circulating in the orbit of the count of Flanders in the opening decades of the 13th century.

Many scholars of the first phase of vernacular historiography have been frankly puzzled at the choice of *Turpin* for translation. Others, including Ronald Walpole, have attributed it to an awakening French patriotism, which settled on *Turpin* because of its exaltation of the French monarchy in the guise of Charlemagne. In Walpole's opinion, the growing prestige of the French monarchy under Philip Augustus (1180–1223) led French national feeling to crystallize around the legendary figure of Charlemagne as a symbol of the emerging power and high ideals of the Capetian kings of France. According to this view, the patronage of *Turpin* translations expressed the desire of French lords to merge their pasts with the future destinies of the Capetian royalty. But a closer examination reveals that every single patron of an early vernacular *Turpin* was either centrally or peripherally involved in the Flemish struggle against the rising power of the French monarchy, which ended with the defeat of Flanders at Bouvines in 1214. Hugh of Saint-Pol, William of Cayeux, Renaud of Boulogne, and Robert of Béthune were mainstays of the English (anti-Capetian) party in Flanders. Even Michel of Harnes, a devoted partisan of Philip Augustus at the battle of Bouvines, cannot be placed in the Capetian camp until 1208 at the earliest, and secure evidence of his alliance with the French monarchy is not found until 1212.

When the dust had settled after Bouvines, two-thirds of the Flemish aristocracy were in French prisons, including Count Ferrand of Flanders, Renaud of Boulogne, and Robert of Béthune (Hugh of Saint-Pol had died). Only Michel of Harnes escaped the ruin visited upon his countrymen, having defected to the French party. After Bouvines, reports the Anonymous of Béthune, "there was no longer anyone who dared to make war against the king; his *baillis* [bailiffs] had placed all the land of Flanders in such servitude that all those who heard tell of it marveled at how it could be endured" (*Chronique des rois de France*, p. 770). Eight centuries later, Henri Pirenne concurred in this judgment: "After Bouvines," he asserted, "the power of the French king became preponderant, so much so that at the end of the 13th century, the Low Countries seemed no more than an annex of the Capetian monarchy" (*Histoire de Belgique*, p. 232).

At first glance, however, the declining political fortunes of the Flemish aristocracy would appear unrelated to any motives that might have inspired such extensive patronage of *Turpin* chronicles in the courts of Flanders. What possible connection could there be between the fields of Flanders and the fantasies of Charlemagne's exploits in the Spanish hills of Roncevaux (Roncesvalles), between the all-too-real sting of political defeat at home and the all-too-illusory glory of chivalric combat, distant in both time and place? If clearly not patriotism, what explains the ubiquity of *Turpin* as the originating text of prose historiography, and what special attraction did it hold for the Flemish lords who commissioned the translations? And, in the broadest sense of the question to which the *Turpin* translations are merely the first (and partial) response, what problematic aspects of aristocratic experience or ideology, or both, were being defined and expressed with the rise of the prose vernacular chronicle? Clues to the answer to these questions are to be found in the prologues to the translations, which at the same time allow us to situate the *Turpin* histories within this sociopolitical context.

The *Turpin* prologues are surprisingly unanimous concerning the motives and goals of the translators. Four programmatic statements are present to varying degrees in all the texts: first, a desire to revive chivalric virtues deemed to be in decline; second, a belief in the exemplary value of Charlemagne and the moral profit to be gained from a knowledge of his crusading deeds; third, a less overtly stated but nonetheless clear pride in Charlemagne as the distant progenitor of the patron's own lineage, for whom the *Pseudo-Turpin Chronicle* functions as ancestral history; and, finally, the explicit adoption of prose as the proper language of history, with a corollary condemnation of epic and romance styles of historical writing. Taken together, these statements frame the terms of the revolution in historical writing represented by the rise of the vernacular prose chronicle.

The first of the chronicle's stated aims—to revive chivalric virtues—indicates a desire to recover the moral and political conditions of an earlier age of aristocratic glory as a form of ethical reassurance to an aristocratic public fully conscious of a crisis in its code of behavior and in those values of honor and courage to which it lent support. The translators' assumption of the power of history to

63

provide such an ethical stimulus is accompanied by a belief that it was the neglect of the past, the inattention paid to the "deeds of *prud'hommes* [great men] and ancient histories," that resulted in the loss of moral virtue and courage to begin with—a criticism leveled not only, one suspects, at contemporary ethical behavior but also at the relative neglect of history itself as a result of the rise of romance genres in the second half of the 12th century. The vogue of romance genres had diverted aristocratic literary preferences away from the public recitation of chivalric *chansons de geste* and had led, the prologues seem to suggest, to a decline in chivalric values. Also embedded in this claim is the typical medieval belief in the exemplary power of history, whose primary function is seen as the encouragement of virtue and the disparagement of evil through an objective narration of examples drawn from the past.

In the *Pseudo-Turpin Chronicle* the principal exemplary subject matter was the crusading exploits of Charlemagne in Spain, the "truth of Spain" as the translators call it. The personal backgrounds of the patrons were doubtless a conditioning factor in the popularity of *Turpin,* for Flemish participation in the Third and Fourth crusades ran high. Of far greater significance, however, was the use of *Turpin* as ancestral history. The sponsors of vernacular history, as the prologues make clear, turned to *Turpin* not because it presented them with a vehicle through which they could give form to inchoate sentiments of patriotism, but because they saw in it the history of their own, most glorious progenitor. As Nicolas of Senlis had asserted, Count Baldwin had searched far and wide for a copy of *Turpin* because "he loved Charlemagne greatly," from whom he claimed descent through Judith, a daughter of Charles the Bald. Interestingly, the one patron not of Flemish descent, Renaud of Boulogne, appended to his text a false genealogy of the counts of Boulogne and of Flanders in which he pretended descent, through Ermengarde, from Charles of Lorraine, Hugh Capet's rival for the throne of France in 987. Virtually every prologue affirms the importance of the knowledge of ancestral deeds to be gained by the recitation and reading of *Turpin,* written down "so that it might remain in the memory of the living and great men . . . and remind them of their ancestors" (Bibliothèque Nationale Ms. fr. 1621, folio 208). Far from being protonationalist, the vernacular chronicle erects an ideology based on family origins and to that extent is ethnocentric in focus and, it could be argued, antiroyalist or, more exactly, anti-Capetian in motive.

The idealized portrayal of Charlemagne as presented through the legitimating lens of the original ecclesiastical author of *Turpin* made him an apt figure for the aesthetic correction of the present on the basis of what the past had been. Like Arthur in courtly romance, Charlemagne could be set forth as an alternative model to the increasingly assertive French monarchy under Philip Augustus. Viewed in this perspective, *Turpin* served as a mediated criticism of Capetian kingship by a group of Flemish lords acutely aware of the challenge to their independence posed by the revival of royal power. Clearly intended as a performed text, *Turpin* functioned, in this sociopolitical setting, as a ritualistic confirmation of the shared values of an aristocracy in the throes of social change and as a historiography of resistance, verbalizing hostility to the monarchy in the guise of a widely shared fantasy masquerading as historical fact concerning a glorious, collective past that, in medieval historical consciousness, was potentially present in each succeeding generation of noble heirs. Such an interpretation of the vernacular *Turpin* connects it to the tradition of the French epic of revolt—the 12th-century *chansons de geste,* whose plots often turned on royal injustices to feudal vassals, driving them to break their bonds of fidelity and to revolt against their sovereign. In a more general sense, it indicates the fundamental affinity between vernacular historiography and Arthurian romance as well, that is, that whole body of courtly literature created for and by the French aristocracy through which it sought to explore and legitimate its own ideological premises in opposition to the hegemonic aspirations of monarchy.

This affinity naturally raises the question as to why the epic and romance stopped being perceived as adequate modes of discourse for the expression of aristocratic ideology, since the translation of *Turpin* is conducted in the context of a militant rejection of verse and an equally militant insistence on prose as the necessary medium for history. According to the first translator, Nicolas of Senlis, "Many people had heard recounted and sung [the deeds of Charlemagne], but never were so many lies told as by those singers and jongleurs who spoke and chanted it" (*Poitevinische Pseudo-Turpin,* p. 6). This was so because "no rhymed tale is true; all that it speaks is lies, for it knows nothing but hearsay" (ibid.). The translations, in contrast, were "written in French without rhyme according to the order of the Latin in the true history by Archbishop Turpin" (Walpole, *Old French Johannes Translation,* p. 130). The vernacular *Turpin,* therefore, makes an exclusive claim to authority based on its use of an authentic Latin text that is accurately reconstituted in French by means of a literal prose translation.

The assertions of truthfulness and accuracy that abound in the prologues bespeak a desire to create or answer a demand for a new form of historical discourse more relevant to the historical needs of its public than the versified histories of epic and romance. The problem of the prose chronicle's rise to generic autonomy is, therefore, necessarily also the problem of the failure of these two earlier forms of courtly literature to continue to satisfy the requirements of courtly audiences for historical edification and orientation.

Scholars concerned with the beginning of prose history have interpreted the *Turpin* prologues as demands for greater factual accuracy and realism on the part of an increasingly sophisticated and literate public. Although the ultimate results of the adoption of prose may have been greater realism and accuracy in historical writing, these consequences are not necessarily identical with the chroniclers' initial motives for using prose. Rather, the substitution of prose for verse can be linked to an ideological initiative on the part of an aristocracy whose political dominance was being threatened by the rise of Capetian royal power during the very period that witnessed the birth of vernacular prose historiography. The adoption of prose enhanced the credibility of aristocratic ideology by grounding it in a language of apparent factuality, in contradistinction

65

to the overt use of fantasy in romance. This evolution suggests that the failure of romance occurred on the level of metaphor, in the sense that the specific literary devices employed by courtly romance, and to a lesser extent by epic, were no longer perceived as an adequate means of articulating the aristocracy's sense of crisis. *Turpin* met this need by appropriating the inherent authority of an earlier Latin text, now employed for the legitimation of aristocratic ideology, and by adapting prose for the historicization of aristocratic literary language. For Franco-Flemish lords of the early 13th century, the Carolingian legend embodied in the *Pseudo-Turpin Chronicle* supplied a medium for the propagation of a historiography of resistance to royal centralization and did so with the borrowed authority of an ecclesiastical Latin text set forth in the newly historicized language of vernacular prose. Out of this process vernacular prose historiography emerges as a literature of fact, integrating on a literary level the historical experience and expressive language proper to the aristocracy. No longer the expression of a shared, collective image of the community's social past, vernacular prose history becomes instead a partisan record intended to serve the interests of a particular social group and inscribes, in the very nature of its linguistic choice, an ideologically motivated assertion of the aristocracy's place and prestige in medieval society.

See also 1095, 1209, 1214, 1566, 1677.

Bibliography: Anonymous of Béthune, *Chronique des rois de France,* ed. L.-V. Delisle, in *Recueil des historiens des Gaules et de la France,* vol. 24 (Paris, 1904), 750–775. André de Mandach, *Naissance et développement de la chanson de geste en Europe,* vol. 1: *La geste de Charlemagne et de Roland* (Geneva: Droz, 1961). Nicolas de Senlis, *Die Sogenannte Poitevinische Übersetzung des Pseudo-Turpin nach den Handschriften Mitgetheilt,* ed. Theodor Auracher (Halle: Niemeyer, 1877). Henri Pirenne, *Histoire de Belgique* (Brussels: Renaissance du Livre, 1948–1952). Diana Tyson, "Patronage of French Vernacular History Writers in the Twelfth and Thirteenth Centuries," *Romania,* 100 (1979), 180–222. Ronald N. Walpole, *The Old French Johannes Translation of the Pseudo-Turpin Chronicle: A Critical Edition,* 2 vols. (Berkeley: University of California Press, 1976).

Gabrielle M. Spiegel

✍ *1209?*

Death of Walter Map, a Scholar at the Court of Henry II

Arthurian Romance in Prose

Walter Map was a royal clerk, a justice, a canon and precentor for Henry II of England. He became chancellor of Lincoln in 1186 and archdeacon of Oxford in 1197. A well-traveled scholar and court satirist, he was noted by medieval English chroniclers for his wit and his ability as a storyteller. According to his contemporary Gerald of Wales, "the famous and eloquent Walter Map" used to boast of his overwhelming literary popularity: "Master Gerald," he told him once, "you have written and are still writing much, and I have spoken many things. You have uttered writings, and I words. Your writings are far more praiseworthy than my words; yet because mine are easy to follow and in the vernacular, while yours are in Latin, which is understood by fewer folk, I have carried off a reasonable reward while you and your distinguished writings have not been adequately rewarded" (quoted in *De Nugis Curialium,* p. xxii).

This claim to popularity, however accurate or fanciful it may be, is significant not only because it presents Walter Map as a master storyteller, but also because it outlines a conflict between two competing narrative traditions that surround the birth of French prose in the first quarter of the 13th century. Contrasting the authoritative Latin document with the more pleasurable fictive accounts recited aloud by vernacular storytellers, Map sketches the backdrop for a complex conflict between the accuracy of the written word and the fictiveness of the oral account that reflects a crucial stage in the development of French letters.

In the first decade of the 13th century Arthurian verse romances—previously delivered orally—were recast into prose. Vernacular prose, like its Latin counterpart, had formerly been reserved largely for recording legal and religious truths in juridical texts, charters, translations of the Bible, and sermons. Prose had also been used to document historical events in the chronicles of Geoffroi de Villehardouin, Robert of Clari, and Henri of Valenciennes. But obviously fictive tales of Arthurian knights and ladies had previously appeared only in verse. As prose became an accepted medium, in the early 13th century, for telling stories of love and adventure, the distinction between the orally delivered tale and more "distinguished writings" began to collapse. The scope of the courtly narrative became simultaneously more historical and more religious, and the resultant prose romances called attention to their new role by incorporating frequent and overt claims to authenticity and veracity. One of the earliest literary monuments to attest this shift from verse to prose is the Arthurian Vulgate Cycle (ca. 1215–1235), published as *The Vulgate Version of the Arthurian Romances.* The reputed author of major portions of the cycle is none other than Walter Map.

The Vulgate Cycle recounts the adventures of knights at King Arthur's court through a kind of literary summa that reflects, in its vast scale, contemporary theological summae. Combining the ideals of the courtly knight with those of the religious quester, these prose narratives create an overtly fictive tale that presents itself as a rival to scripture, often claiming the authority of the sacred word. Episodic verse romances that in the preceding century had focused on the exploits of an individual knight such as Lancelot or Perceval are here expanded into a vast cyclic prose narrative chronicling the deeds of whole generations of knights and spanning the entire history of the grail quest from its origin in the Passion of Christ to its successful accomplishment by the chosen Arthurian hero. In keeping with the tradition of rewriting popular tales, established by continuations of Chrétien de Troyes's *Perceval* (ca. 1181), the Vulgate Cycle elaborates the love story of Lancelot and Guenevere into a lengthy *Lancelot en prose* (ca. 1215; *Prose Lancelot*); combines that with an embellished narrative of the grail quest, *La quête du saint Graal* (ca. 1220; *The Quest for the Holy Grail*); and adds to these an account of Arthur's tragic demise, *La mort du roi Arthur* (ca. 1225; *The Death of King Arthur*). The popularity of these romances— collectively identified as the Lancelot-Grail Cycle—prompted the composition of precursors to the cycle: *L'histoire du saint Graal* (ca. 1230; *The Story of the Holy Grail*) chronicles the evangelization of the East and West by Joseph of Arimathea and his son, Joséphé, the official keepers of the holy vessel; and *L'histoire de Merlin* (ca. 1235; *The Story of Merlin*) depicts the remarkable feats of the prophet-enchanter who engineered the birth of the future King Arthur and ensured his military and political supremacy.

Walter Map's name appears twice in the Vulgate Cycle. In the closing lines of *La quête du saint Graal* he is credited with having translated a preexisting archival document from Latin into French: "When they had dined, King Arthur summoned his clerks who were keeping a record of all the adventures undergone by the knights of his household. When Bors had related to them the adventures of the holy grail as witnessed by himself, they were written down and the record kept in the library at Salisbury, whence Master Walter Map extracted them in order to make his book about the holy grail for love of his lord King Henry, who had the story translated from Latin into French" (*Quest*, p. 284). The epilogue of *La mort du roi Arthur* attributes to Map the composition of the entire Lancelot-Grail trilogy. And three passages in the *Lancelot en prose* detail the same process of oral deposition and scribal copying, though without mentioning Map by name.

This textual genealogy outlines two types of literary provenance for the Vulgate Cycle that echo those mentioned by Walter Map to Gerald of Wales. But the roles are reversed. Map appears here as an author-translator responsible for a written version of the Vulgate Cycle (ultimately in the vernacular), and the role of riveting storyteller is displaced to Arthur's knights. However, even the oral accounts delivered by Bors and his companions at the Round Table are given a distinctly historical cast. As chivalric heroes who first seek "adventures worth telling" and then recount their exploits at court, they do not offer tall tales of their own invention; instead, they claim for their narratives the status of eyewitness accounts, accurate renderings of actual historical events.

Such a claim indicates the allure that historiography held for prose romancers of the early 13th century. By advancing the name of Walter Map, an author who supposedly drew on documents written in Latin, the Vulgate Cycle refers for its literary validation not only to patristic authorities but also to Latin chroniclers. By presenting a host of author-heroes who provide a record of events they have personally undertaken, it further reinforces the link with the chronicler's firsthand account. Through the combination of Bors's oral deposition and Map's recovery of an archival document, the Arthurian adventure story in prose acquires quasi-historical status.

These texts reflect not so much a desire to establish accurate historical detail as an effort to create the illusion of historical veracity. In fact Walter Map's actual contribution to the Vulgate Cycle is, to say the least, no more verifiable than that of his wholly fictitious counterpart, Bors. Map died around 1209, approximately five to ten years before the composition of the first volume of tales that bear his name. But Map was a known historical personage whose association with Henry II's court was well established. And Henry enjoyed a legendary association with King Arthur. What better way to assert the historicity of Arthurian adventure than to make it flow from the pen of a master storyteller who had rubbed shoulders with the very king reputed to have found the tombs of Arthur and Guenevere at Glastonbury?

If Map's link with kings, historical and legendary, made him a viable candidate for authorship of the Vulgate Cycle, his relation to Arthurian historiography may also have increased his appeal. Map was an author in his own right; his *De Nugis Curialium* (1181–1193; *Courtiers' Trifles*) offers the kind of pseudo-history that continues the tradition of Latin prose chronicles established by Geoffrey of Monmouth's *Historia Regum Britanniae* (ca. 1136; *History of the Kings of Britain*). A loose collection of anecdotes in Latin prose about life at Henry's court, Map's text is interspersed with satiric invective, moral tales, reports of miracles, and even ghost stories. Mixing fact with fiction in the manner common to early medieval chroniclers, Map sometimes draws directly on antique tales mentioned in Geoffrey's *Historia,* recasting them to suit his purposes, just as Geoffrey had done with his own sources. Yet both authors insist on the historical value of their works, Geoffrey by saying that his text is a translation of a work given to him by the archdeacon of Oxford, and Map by claiming to record only what he sees. In both instances the authors' declarations of authenticity seem to have amply overshadowed the text's obvious lack of it.

This is precisely the attitude of 13th-century prose romancers wishing to lend an air of truth to their large-scale histories of Arthurian lineage and grail lore. Romance narratives of the 12th century had already often claimed literary or rhetorical superiority to other contemporary works. But they made no clear claim to historical veracity. In contrast, Walter Map's assertion that he simply records the "sayings and doings" of people at court establishes a precedent for Bors's supposedly accurate account of knights at Arthur's court. And the historical Map's assertion, in *De Nugis Curialium,* that he is "no writer of lies" strangely heralds the Vulgate Cycle's portrait of the fictive character Walter Map as an authoritative truthteller: "At this point Master Walter Map will end the story of Lancelot because he has brought everything to a proper conclusion, according to the way it happened, and he finishes his book here so completely that no one can afterwards add anything to the story that is not completely false" (*Death of King Arthur,* p. 235).

In reiterating the opposition between the authoritative book and inconsequential literary fabrication, these last lines of the last volume of the Vulgate Cycle carve out a special place for the Arthurian prose romance. As "distinguished writings" the prose narratives are presented as no mere stories. They faithfully record past events in a way that cannot be altered, improved upon, or repeated. Through the agency of a voice linked to one Walter Map, however

69

fictive or fabricated this link may be, the adventure story is absorbed into history. Map is cast as the teller of a tale, as someone who recounts the "story of Lancelot," but the words he uses to discharge this task are not to be considered either undistinguished or exaggerated. They carry the weight and the force of books that record what really happened.

See also 1165, 1181, 1202, 1214.

Bibliography: E. Jane Burns, *Arthurian Fictions: Rereading the Vulgate Cycle* (Columbus: Ohio State University Press, 1985). *The Death of King Arthur,* trans. James Cable (Harmondsworth: Penguin, 1971). Jean Frappier, "Le roman en prose en France au 13e siècle," in *Grundriss der Romanischen Literaturen des Mittelalters,* ed. Jean Frappier and Reinhold R. Grimm (Heidelberg: Carl Winter, 1978). Walter Map, *De Nugis Curialium: Courtiers' Trifles,* ed. and trans. M. R. James, rev. C. N. L. Brooke and R. A. B. Mynors (Oxford: Clarendon Press, 1983). *The Quest of the Holy Grail,* trans. P. M. Matarasso (Baltimore: Penguin, 1969). *The Vulgate Version of the Arthurian Romances,* ed. H. Oskar Sommer, 5 vols. (Washington, D.C.: Carnegie Institute, 1908–1912).

E. Jane Burns

✑ 1210
Death of Jean Bodel, the Poet of Arras

The Fabliaux

Concerning the origins of the fabliaux, Knut Togeby has observed: "The only firm date is that of the death of Jean Bodel in 1210, . . . before which he had written at least eight fabliaux" ("Les fabliaux," p. 89). Togeby offers good reasons for regarding Bodel—popular poet of Arras and author of the comic and religious drama *Le jeu de saint Nicolas* (*The Play of Saint Nicholas*) and the epic *Chanson des Saisnes* (*Song of the Saxons*)—as the father of this genre of realistic and mostly comic tales in verse. At any rate, it is very much a genre of the 13th century; although few can be securely dated, it is clear that most of the 150-odd fabliaux that have survived were written between 1200 and 1340.

They seem to have been primarily an "after dinner" genre, told for amusement, in a mood of relaxation and confidence, and, despite their frequently bawdy subject matter, in mixed company. They were composed and recited both by jongleurs—professional entertainers—and by amateurs; thus a traveling clerk might pay a family for his meal and night's lodging by reciting a couple of fabliaux. Clerks, indeed, are so often the erotic heroes in fabliau triangle plots that it is likely that many of these poems were composed as well as recited by clerks. Individual fabliaux were freely copied and often re-edited to suit different audiences during this period, but the general absence of immediate literary precursors—although they have many analogues in folklore from antiquity to the present—indicates that most of the stories were taken from oral tradition. Garin, the author of *La grue* (*The Crane*), says that he is using material he "heard tell about at Vézelay in front of the Exchange" (Montaiglon and Raynaud, *Recueil général*, 5:151).

Although there has been some disagreement as to precisely which poems to include in the canon, the general character of the genre is reasonably secure. Over sixty of the fabliaux are so labeled in medieval texts (the word is Picard dialect for "fable," plus a diminutive ending), and another ninety can be admitted to the canon without debate. Still, they are a diverse lot. In length they range from a few dozen verses to more than a thousand. There are small masterpieces of plotting and characterization—such as *Le boucher d'Abbeville* (*The Butcher of Abbeville*), *Boivin de Provins*, *La bourgeoise d'Orléans* (*The Townswoman of Orléans*), and *Auberée de Compiègne*—and such remarkably inept productions as the four by the scribbler Haiseau, who touched nothing that he did not damage. There are texts of almost courtly delicacy, and a few almost combatively disgusting. Some are wildly funny, others marginally solemn, hardly different from moral exempla. But all have a certain realism—of style, tone, or ethos—that sets them off from other genres of the period.

The stylistic realism of the fabliau is the realism of comedy. "A comic subject," wrote the medieval rhetorician Geoffrey of Vinsauf, "rejects artfully labored diction. It requires plain words only" (*Poetria Nova*, p. 255). This style freely admits comic exaggeration, grotesquerie, and caricature, but its basic world is determinedly the familiar and the local. Its imagery, though not always dense, is overwhelmingly mundane and concrete; it is a world of things, as the fabliau titles make clear: *Les braies au Cordelier* (*The Friar's Breeches*); *Brunain, la vache au prêtre* (*Browny, the Priest's Cow*); *Le chevalier à la corbeille* (*The Knight with the Basket*); *La crotte* (*The Turd*); *Le cuvier* (*The Tub*); *Le prévôt à l'aumusse* (*The Provost with the Hood*); *La sourisette des étoupes* (*The Mouse in the Tow*). The plots of about a third of the poems are closely bound up with such images.

Furthermore, a good deal of this imagery seems to exceed the demands of the plot, as if included for its own sake. The fabliaux occasionally parody courtly style, and in doing so present some descriptions of superlative places and things. But most often their descriptions evoke the texture of ordinary life, as in the proud inventory of pots, pans, and bedclothes in *La veuve* (*The Widow*), the hilariously padded bill for dinner and lodging in *Le prêtre et le chevalier* (*The Priest and the Knight*), the delighted descriptions of a peasant disguise in *Boivin de Provins*, and of a poor minstrel's rags in *Le prêtre et les deux ribauds* (*The Priest and the Two Rascals*). An obvious savoring of this texture, a sometimes ironical recognition and enjoyment of how things really are, explains the attraction of the many poems whose weak plots or otherwise meager narrative features would not alone have ensured their survival.

The fabliaux are generally too short to permit realistic characterization (which in this period would have been unusual in any case). Characters tend to be types—the jealous husband, the clever clerk, the gullible maiden, the faithless wife, the stupid peasant, the rich and/or lecherous priest—individualized, if at all, in single traits: a big head, a talent for theft, a taste for berries, a huge penis, an intolerance of dirty words. But although few characters are complex, they are still realistic in the sense that they come mainly from the audience's own world, and they are caught and recorded with just that shrewd, practical, reductive abbreviation typical of the conduct of ordinary life.

The realistic style of the fabliaux not only evokes a particular world but also supports a particular ethos: materialist, hedonistic, and finally ironic. The fabliaux are endlessly concerned with pleasure. They are, for instance, a compendium of medieval food and wine. A whole plot turns on the disposition of some roast partridges, another on a roast goose. Unsympathetic characters are known and judged by their diets: a peasant's son has no feeling for chivalry but loves tarts and custards; a hungry peasant is insulted by a seneschal as a "gulper of peas"; a buffoon and his new wife eat smelly sow-meat with pepper and juniper. Conversely hospitality, and especially that of satisfied love, is underlined by the sharing of splendid meals, whose menus are lovingly detailed, along with good wine—"clear as tears"—and often a warm tub.

The only rival to the pleasure of gastronomy in the fabliaux is that of sex. Sex is, as often as not, presented explicitly, almost never elaborately, but always with approval or enthusiasm. There is hardly a trace of the Christian-puritan taboo on sex for its own sake and, more remarkably, much less than one might expect of a mood of confrontation in the easy violations of that taboo. Of course, the fabliaux's ample treatment of sex among the celibate clergy always carries some satiric or ironic effect, but not at the expense of sex. Except for brushes with sadism in four or five poems, and for some comically epic instances of sexual prowess, sex in these poems is the normal, pleasurable thing; it is an apt subject of comedy for many reasons, but usually not just because the church forbids it.

The fabliaux are uninhibitedly concerned also with money. The subject is hedged about with a certain amount of mechanical moralizing—avarice is the root of evil—but their basic materialism is never threatened; they are endlessly concerned with large and small coins, profits, losses, bargains, prices, bribes, bills, gifts, and debts.

The final preoccupation of the fabliaux is with *engin* (wit, cleverness). Cleverness will get you money, food, and sex, and it is also pleasurable in itself. The fabliaux celebrate champion thieves and confidence men and, par excellence, clever women. Fabliau authors are not as antifeminist as they pretend to be. The woman who deceives her jealous husband to have a much better time with her lover is presented with admiration. Like other comic genres, the fabliaux are thus a mildly subversive literature. They favor the dispossessed, reward ingenuity at the expense of law and privilege, and suggest throughout that the conventional rules of morality and justice simply do not hold.

For all the material solidity of the world of the fabliau, then, its plots and ethos suggest an ambiance of instability, of insecurity, surprise, and irony. This perhaps explains its taste for wordplay and double meaning; some forty-seven fabliaux or major episodes in them turn on words rather than on actions. They range from the verbal wit sustained through the whole of *Le roi d'Angleterre et le jongleur d'Ely* (*The King of England and the Minstrel of Ely*) to the central misunderstanding of *La male honte* (*Honte's Bag* = *Evil Shame*), to plentiful incidental punning, especially on the monosyllable pronounced *vi* (face, alive, penis) and the common prefix *con—* (vagina).

About two-thirds of the fabliaux contain some sort of moral or proverbial saying. This fact has given rise to the unlikely theory that the genre itself somehow evolved from the moral fable. But for the most part these prefatory or terminal or inserted "morals" rarely have a close connection with the actions of the tales they comment upon. They seem to have been included partly in response to the familiar medieval notion—based on St. Paul—that there is profitable doctrine in every text; partly as a reflex of the common rhetorical teaching that beginnings and endings call for a proverb; partly as play with the medieval habit of sententiousness itself; and perhaps partly as a means of protection from puritanical criticism. In one sense, however, they provide valuable insight into the fabliau ethos: if they do not comment directly on the tales, they mirror through their very commonplaceness the everyday wisdom of their audience.

This wisdom is almost never specifically Christian; it is overwhelmingly practical—and ironic: "Don't behave against your nature." "A fool never gives up." "The more forbidden, the more incentive." "With a mild shepherd, the wolf shits wool." "Who goes, feasts; who sits, dries up." "Troubles you can cook and eat are better than ones that give no pleasure." "Often the innocent pays the penalty." "He wiped my nose with my own sleeve." "He's a fool who believes his wife more than himself." This overt general "wisdom" ultimately harmonizes rather well with the ethos generated by the action and texture of the stories themselves. It is a wisdom of practical experience, mingling the securities of profit and pleasure with a shrewd and ironic awareness of the uncertainty of almost everything.

A central question remains: Why were these stories written up in literary form at this time? For half a century the dominant view was that of Joseph Bédier, who in 1893 identified the fabliaux as the poetry of the newly arising bourgeoisie and contrasted it with the refined literature of the courtly class: "The fabliaux are . . . the poetry of the little people. Down to earth realism, a merry and ironic conception of life, all the distinctive traits of the fabliau . . . show likewise the features of the bourgeois. On the other hand, the worship of woman, dreams of fairyland, idealism, all the traits that distinguish the lyric poetry and the romances of the Round Table, also mark out the features of the knightly class" (*Les fabliaux*, p. 371).

Bédier grants that there was some mixing of genres and classes in the 13th century, but his basic location of the origin of the genre in a specific social class commanded general assent until 1957, when Per Nykrog reopened the whole subject and led a worldwide revival of interest in the genre. His central idea is that fabliaux "were not only read and appreciated in courtly milieus, but . . . are so profoundly penetrated by the manner of thinking of these circles that to understand them well it is necessary to consider them a sort of courtly genre" (*Les fabliaux*, p. 18). Nykrog, significantly, did not challenge Bédier's theory

73

of the class origins of the genre; but he emphatically substituted one class for another. His argument that fabliaux must have *coexisted* with courtly literature as favored entertainment for some audiences has lasting merit, and he significantly deepened our sensitivity to the element of parody in some of them—which would presuppose their audience's appreciation of courtly convention.

But thirty years of further research show that the idea of a class origin for the fabliaux will not hold. What external evidence there is indicates that they were circulated among aristocrats, the bourgeoisie, and wealthy peasants alike; and in the 13th century, city dwellers did not have a monopoly on tastes and attitudes that we have since come to think of as materialistic and "bourgeois." The century's economic expansion—the shift to a money economy, the weakening of social ties, the consequent weakening of fortunes based on feudal privilege, and the opening of opportunity for the newly liberated—affected all classes and is amply reflected in the fabliaux themselves. We must imagine the whole culture to have been influenced by the same climate that attended the rise of cities, the emergence of an urban middle class, and the appearance of the fabliau as a literary genre.

The fabliaux, then, are not a class literature, but reveal a stratum of sensibility that resides in the whole culture and coexists along with other strata—the courtly and the Christian, for instance—with remarkably little sense of strain or conflict. Fabliaux do contain some parody or burlesque of the courtly, and some satire of religious hypocrisy, but they do not, contrary to a common supposition, exist merely as a marginal and reactive response to establishment values. They are not a truant or temporary "carnival" literature. They express, rather, a set of cultural norms of some weight and coherence, and of great persistence.

The integrity and importance of this literature as an index of 13th-century sensibility is confirmed by its relatively robust survival. It is almost the only record we have of the moods of relaxed, unbuttoned, confidential conviviality in a period that tended to preserve only its "serious" and official documents. Fabliaux would always, of course, have been censored in the most puritanical of quarters. In later periods, as the newly forming genteel tradition of behavior and diction gathered strength, as fabliau language and attitudes increasingly lost their unselfconsciousness, and as the term *vulgar* took on increasingly pejorative moral and social connotations, further censorship must have ensued. In this light, the survival of 150 texts in forty-six manuscripts or fragments is impressive. In the major manuscripts, which are private literary collections, the texts exist side by side with pieces of every other kind—courtly tales, moral poems, translations from the Latin—as if to illustrate their easy naturalization within the sensibility of the time.

The fabliaux represent a mood and a set of values that in the history of culture by far antedate the courtly tradition, and indeed they reflect here and there a response to the new courtly taboos imposed on certain references and on four- (in French, three-) letter words in the 13th century. Their ethos probably antedates the Christian one as well. But the elaboration of a new literary genre embodying this ethos attests to a new force, or interest, or validity that a hedonistic, materialist, and ironic sensibility enjoys at this time. This stratum of sensibility is as authentic a part of the identity of the French 13th century as are those attested by courtly allegory, the cult of the Virgin, or the great cathedrals.

See also 1460.

Bibliography: Joseph Bédier, *Les fabliaux* (Paris: Champion, 1893). R. H. Bloch, *The Scandal of the Fabliaux* (Chicago: University of Chicago Press, 1986). Thomas D. Cooke and Benjamin L. Honeycutt, eds., *The Humor of the Fabliaux* (Columbia: University of Missouri Press, 1974). Geoffrey of Vinsauf, *Poetria Nova,* in *Les arts poétiques du XIIe et du XIIIe siècles,* ed. Edmond Faral (Paris: Champion, 1924). Robert Harrison, trans., *Gallic Salt: Eighteen Fabliaux Translated from the Old French* (Berkeley: University of California Press, 1974). Anatole de Montaiglon and Gustave Raynaud, *Recueil général et complet des fabliaux,* 6 vols. (Paris: Librairie des Bibliophiles, 1872–1890). Charles Muscatine, *The Old French Fabliaux* (New Haven: Yale University Press, 1986). Willem Noomen and Nico van den Boogard, *Nouveau recueil complet des fabliaux,* 3 vols. to date (Assen: Van Gorcum, 1983–). Per Nykrog, *Les fabliaux* (Copenhagen: Ejnar Munksgaard, 1957). Knut Togeby, "Les fabliaux," *Orbis Litterarum,* 12 (1957), 85–98.

Charles Muscatine

✍ *1214, 27 July*
King Philip Augustus Defeats an Anglo-German Army
at Bouvines, Flanders

Literature and History in the Late Feudal Age

In 1214 the territorial conflicts (mostly over Normandy) that pitted the English king John Lackland against the French king Philip II (Augustus) came to a head: John formed an alliance with the German emperor Otto IV and the Flemish aristocracy; Philip Augustus ravaged Flanders. In the summer of that same year, John attacked the French from the southwest while the German-Flemish army moved in from the north. On 27 July a decisive French victory consolidated the power of Philip Augustus (see map).

The defeat of the Anglo-Flemish-German coalition seemed to give new legitimacy to Philip's expansionist aims. Already he had tripled the territory subject to the French monarchy, an achievement that had inspired the chronicler Rigord to dub him Augustus. This surname, with its echoes of the Roman Empire, expressed both Philip's accomplishments and his aspirations and could be helpful in sustaining his imperial ideology. One of the chroniclers of Philip Augustus' reign, Guillaume le Breton, even went so far as to cast Philip's life in Virgilian terms, when in *La Philippide* (ca. 1214 and 1224) he recreated Philip as a second Aeneas.

King Henry II of England, the father of Philip's enemy John Lackland, had had similar aspirations, and his reign, like Philip's, was marked by the appear-

75

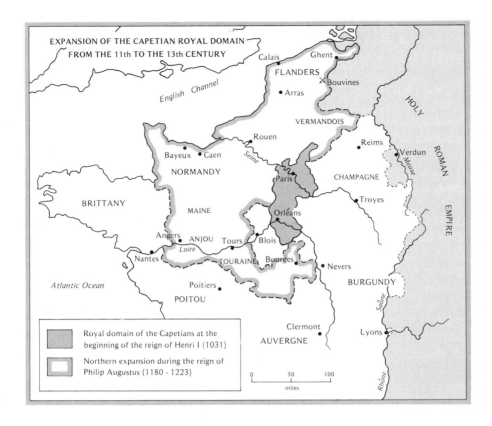

EXPANSION OF THE CAPETIAN ROYAL DOMAIN FROM THE 11th TO THE 13th CENTURY

Royal domain of the Capetians at the beginning of the reign of Henri I (1031)

Northern expansion during the reign of Philip Augustus (1180 - 1223)

ance of texts showing a new interest in ancient history. It seems clear that these literary productions were closely related to the two kings' political aims and preoccupations.

In France, epic literature had served, at least in part, to create a national past and at the same time to lend support to contemporary ideologies and politics. For Henry's new Angevin dynasty no such literary support existed. It was probably for his court that in the mid-12th century the stories of Thebes (used as a cautionary tale against civil war), Troy, and the founding of Rome were told in French for the first time in a group of texts known as the romances of antiquity. At the same time, Robert Wace, a clerk from Caen, established the connection between the Britons and the Trojans in his *Roman de Brut* (ca. 1155; *Brutus*). These texts established (imaginary) genealogical roots for the new ruling class of Britain. Other nations followed the British example, and by the 13th century the obsession with Trojan origins had spread through most of Europe: it was easy to claim Trojan forebears because Troy no longer existed and its exact geographic location was unknown.

To establish links to ancient Rome was more problematic. Not only did Rome still exist, but also, because the conflict over who was the true heir to the Holy Roman Empire of Charlemagne was still very much alive in France and Germany, the history of ancient Rome could not be exploited as easily as the history of Troy and was more subject to the vicissitudes of political and ideological developments. Around 1214, however, no fewer than three texts— *Les faits des Romains* (*The Deeds of the Romans*), *Histoire ancienne jusqu'à César* (*Ancient History up to Julius Caesar*), and the Champenois clerk Calendre's *Les empereurs de Rome* (*The Roman Emperors*)—were written that dealt in various ways with Roman history. The first two, both anonymous, are among the earliest examples of French prose; the third was in verse.

Semantically and functionally, it was not easy to distinguish between the genres of medieval romance and history: in Old French the word *estoire* can refer to either a story or history. Beginning in the early 13th century, vernacular chronicles and accounts of ancient history were written in the same two forms as literary works, verse or prose, thus blurring any possible distinction between literature and history. Nor was there much of a functional distinction, at least in the case of the romances of antiquity. The *matière de Rome* (matter of Rome), as the poet Jean Bodel referred to themes from antiquity, aimed at instruction, whereas the romances and the *matière de Bretagne* (matter of Brittany) were deemed to be "vain and pleasant," that is, purely entertaining. This contemporary judgment (Bodel wrote around 1200) reveals that ancient history, whether in romance or "historical" form, could teach moral—and political—lessons to a medieval audience.

The *Histoire ancienne jusqu'à César* was probably composed for Roger, castellan of Lille. It is a universal history; that is, starting with the creation of the world, it was designed to work its way through biblical and ancient history up to the present. The Roman part was based largely on Orosius' 5th-century *Adversus Paganos Historiarum Libri VI* (*Six Books of History against the Pagans*), whereas the sections on Thebes, Troy, and Aeneas' founding of Rome represent prose versions of the 12th-century verse romances dealing with these topics. The account was meant to include all the Roman emperors, but it breaks off with Caesar's invasion of Flanders, possibly because the author of the *Histoire* learned of the existence of *Les faits* (telling the life of Julius Caesar) and felt that his efforts would be redundant even though he did not use the same sources. There is no explicit political propaganda in the *Histoire,* and three separate passages extolling the benefits of peace, "which we are at present enjoying," seem to place the text before the battle of Bouvines, which devastated the very regions closest to the author's heart. He seems to identify himself with the Belgians, and it is possible that the final passage of his text contains a veiled message: breaking off as it does in midsentence, the story that stretched from Genesis all the way to Julius Caesar comes to a sudden halt—history ends with the destruction of Flanders. Philip Augustus brought the same destruction as Julius Caesar: for the inhabitants of Flanders the exemplarity of Roman history had become only too clear.

What makes the *Histoire* interesting from a literary point of view is its use of verse interpolations in the prose text. Given the controversy in the early 13th century about the relative merits of verse and prose (which usually ended with a condemnation of the "lying" verse), the alternation between these two forms is important. The author uses the verse passages to establish his own moralizing voice, which comments on the events recounted in the prose passages. His technique shows an awareness of literary form and its rhetorical possibilities and helps characterize the nature of historical writing in this period when historical events were often used as a pretext for moralizing.

Calendre's *Les empereurs de Rome* is a free translation of Orosius and Alfred the Great's translation/adaptation of Orosius. *Les empereurs* was written in octo-syllabic rhyming couplets, the standard form of medieval romance. If the success of a given work can be measured by the number of surviving manuscripts, Calendre's was a failure: it survives only in the famous Guiot manuscript of the Bibliothèque Nationale, which also contains the romances of Chrétien de Troyes. Perhaps the verse form was deemed unsuitable for a text dealing with ancient history, or the market may have been saturated with Roman histories (especially since the *Histoire ancienne* used the same source as Calendre).

Of the three texts under consideration, only Calendre's *Les empereurs* goes beyond Julius Caesar to the reigns of Arcadius and Honorius, who in the 5th century A.D. divided the Roman Empire into a western and an eastern empire. Calendre is most interested in the various emperors' attitudes toward the Christians; the emperor Tiberius, for example, is shown as having foreknowledge of the Passion. Calendre dramatically narrates Nero's gruesome legend, which became extremely popular in the Middle Ages. His view of history is intensely personal, and he presents most political conflicts in terms of individual incompatibilities: he ignores larger political patterns and zeroes in on petty personal quarrels. Anachronistically, in the account of Julius Caesar he refers to Gaul as the "kingdom of France." He generally exalts the courage of the French, whom he consistently refers to as "les Français" even though he admits at one point that "then they were not called French." Despite its patriotic cast, Calendre's work left no lasting mark on French culture.

By contrast, the success of *Les faits des Romains* was immense and long-lasting. Over sixty manuscripts are still extant; in one group of manuscripts *Les faits* is preceded by the *Histoire ancienne*.

Two of the three texts are based on Orosius' *History against the Pagans*, a title that makes its Christian bias clear. *Les faits*, on the other hand, draws almost exclusively on pagan authors. Nevertheless, all three prologues sound similar notes: they aim for moral edification; we, the readers, should learn from historical examples; it is the duty of the clerk to transmit historical truth and knowledge to posterity. Most of these familiar topoi are drawn from classical texts, but often with very telling modifications. The prologue of *Les faits*, for example, is a translation of Sallust. To render classical Latin into French was no easy task; to adapt a pagan framework to a Christian context without losing the Roman "authenticity" was even harder.

How had 12th-century poets dealt with such problems? The adaptations of classical texts found in the romances of antiquity were characterized by medievalization and anachronism. In the story of Thebes, for example, the pagan priest Amphiares is represented as a bishop; Theban people go to church to worship; they use feudal terminology and follow medieval customs. Rather than being outgrowths of the poets' naïveté, these adaptations must be seen as conscious efforts to stress to their audience the contemporary relevance of these ancient stories. The process of medievalization becomes especially clear in manuscript illuminations: medieval towns serve as a backdrop for battles between "Roman" soldiers in medieval armor. In one particularly splendid 15th-century manuscript of Jean Mansel's *Histoires romaines* (*Roman Histories*), Julius Caesar is being married by a bishop in front of an elaborate Gothic cathedral (fig. 1); but in another manuscript from the same period, Caesar is shown as adoring pagan idols. To a medieval audience, this intertwining of ancient history and contemporary reality did not seem incongruous.

Translators of ancient history had to find ways to combine a sense of the "otherness" of past centuries with enough parallels to contemporary times and mores to underline the usefulness of historical knowledge. In the prologue of *Les faits,* for example, the medieval author supplements Sallust's *Bellum Catilinae* (*Catilinarian Conspiracy*): whereas Sallust stressed the duty of all men to distinguish themselves from animals through their reason and their intellectual

1. Julius Ceasar being married by a bishop in front of a Gothic cathedral, in Jean Mansel, *Histoires romaines,* fol. 43 recto (Bibliothèque de l'Arsenal, Paris, Ms. 5088, 15th century). (Courtesy of the Bibliothèque Nationale, Paris.)

endeavors, the medieval adapter introduces God as the one who has given reason to man in the first place. In the same vein, the Roman concept of Nature is replaced by the Christian notion of the Creator. The lessons that the reader is supposed to learn from *Les faits* are also couched in Christian vocabulary. And even though ancient Cato is still posited as a moral exemplar in Sallustian terms, the author's diatribe against the Christian sin of *luxure* (lechery) is a far cry from Sallust's more restrained passage.

The addition of a personal and profoundly Christian perspective to a pagan model establishes a link with the medieval present, which the author reinforces with a remarkable and amusing allusion to Philip Augustus. As he is speaking of Julius Caesar, who apparently always wore his belt too loose, he adds: "When I think of Julius Caesar, whom Lucius Silla called the 'badly girded' [*mau ceint*], I recall Monseigneur Philip, the king of France, whom one could well call the 'badly combed' [*mau pingnié*] because in his youth his hair was always ruffled" (*Faits*, p. 18). In addition to this rather lighthearted evocation of the French king, there are other passages tying the Romans of *Les faits* to the contemporary French. One passage in particular reflects the pre-Bouvines political climate: the author/translator judges the English and Normans to be crazy if they plan to ally themselves with "Otto the excommunicated" (of Germany) in order to invade France (p. 365). (The Normans were still suspect because Philip had only a few years previously seized Normandy from his vassal John, who also happened to be the king of England.) A diatribe against the Germans in a text praising Roman greatness had great propaganda value, especially given the continuing conflicts about the legitimate heir to Charlemagne's imperium. Another, rather delicate, problem facing the translator was the fact that Caesar had invaded and subjugated Gaul. He modifies Caesar's text in order to show not only that the Gauls (that is, the French) were extremely courageous but also that they were not exactly defeated; rather, they saw that it was reasonable to ally themselves with Caesar. Caesar himself (who in the Middle Ages was not known to have been the author of *De bello gallico; On the Gallic War*) is presented as a courteous and chivalric hero whose honorable behavior serves as a justification for this alliance. That Caesar was meant to be an exemplary hero is clear from the author/translator's adaptation of Lucan's *Pharsalia* (*The Civil War*), a thoroughly anti-Caesarean text. Despite some unavoidably negative connotations, Caesar emerges as a courageous fighter. Since the parallel between Caesar and Philip is implicit throughout the text and stated explicitly at least once, a consistently positive image of Caesar was obligatory.

The rewriting of Roman history in *Les faits* reflects the chauvinistic anti-German and anti-Norman atmosphere in France just before 1214. Through skillful modifications of his Latin models, the medieval author/translator weaves all these sentiments into his compilation.

Despite its political propaganda, *Les faits* enjoyed considerable popularity in other centuries and countries, where it was received primarily as a book of ancient wisdom. The original text was transmitted in a large number of manuscripts. There were also direct translations (into Italian and Portuguese, for example) and loose adaptations; parts of the text were frequently incorporated into other works, especially in France and Italy. For instance, whenever a passage on the birth of Julius Caesar was needed, the text of *Les faits* would be used. Based on Isidore of Seville's 7th-century *Etymologiae* (*Etymologies*), this passage helped spread the (erroneous) legend that Julius Caesar was born by caesarean section. The story reappears in *Renart le contrefait* (*Renard the Hypocrite*) in the 14th century, in Jean Mansel's *Histoires romaines* in the 15th, and was even included in a preface to 15th-century French translations of Caesar's *De bello gallico*. The "loosely belted" Caesar also reappears in many later texts.

The original text of *Les faits* experienced several distinct waves of popularity. In the 13th and early 14th centuries its greatest success was in northern France and Italy; the late 14th and 15th centuries added Burgundy and the Flemish regions. The latter produced some of the most magnificent illuminated manuscripts still extant.

Readers of *Les faits* ranged from learned clerks to princes and kings. The former found their preferred *auctores,* their models for Latin grammar and rhetoric, translated in an entertaining and instructive text; the latter found models for chivalric and kingly behavior as well as shrewd remarks on strategy and diplomacy. At least one powerful ruler found *Les faits* an absolute necessity: Charles the Bold of Burgundy, obsessed with the figure of Julius Caesar, claimed that he could not go to sleep without having a passage from the text read to him.

The success of *Les faits* came to an end only when Renaissance humanism required new and different translations of the classics. The techniques and preoccupations of 13th-century clerks, often amounting to what today would be considered falsifications of the original texts, were no longer acceptable to a learned public. The case of the exemplary nature of Roman history, however, was probably stated more forcefully and convincingly by these "falsifiers" than by their humanist successors.

See also 1202, 1517.

Bibliography: Jeanette M. A. Beer, *A Medieval Caesar* (Geneva: Droz, 1976). Renate Blumenfeld-Kosinski, "Moralization and History: Verse and Prose in the *Histoire ancienne jusqu'à César* (in B.N. f.fr. 20125)," *Zeitschrift für romanische Philologie,* 97 (1981), 41–46. Calendre, *Les empereors de Rome,* ed. Galia Millard (Ann Arbor: University of Michigan Press, 1957). Georges Duby, *Le dimanche de Bouvines* (Paris: Gallimard, 1973). *Li fet des Romains. Compilé ensemble de Salluste, de Suétone et de Lucan,* ed. L.-F. Flutre and Kornelis Sneyders de Vogel (Paris: Droz, 1936). *Histoire ancienne jusqu'à César* (Bibliothèque Nationale, Ms. fr. 20125). Paul Meyer, "Les premières compilations françaises d'histoire ancienne," *Romania,* 14 (1885), 1–81.

Renate Blumenfeld-Kosinski

✑ 1215, November

The Fourth Lateran Council Prescribes That Adult Christians
Confess at Least Once a Year

The Impact of Christian Doctrine on Medieval Literature

From the beginning, French literature, like all the other vernacular literatures of medieval Europe, was strongly religious. In addition to Lives and miracles of the saints, pious tales, plays enacting scenes from scripture, and hymns and songs about the love of "sweet Jesus" and his beautiful mother, even essentially worldly works assumed a Christian public and contained Christian themes. But the Fourth Lateran Council, held in Rome in November 1215 under the pontificate of Innocent III, contributed significantly to a transformation of the way in which people understood, lived, and wrote about their faith.

Innocent was concerned not only with the dignity of the papacy but also with the need for reform in the church, including improvement in the moral and intellectual life of the clergy, and for a strengthening of the spiritual and moral life of laypeople. The council's work consisted largely in approving decrees set before it by Innocent to achieve these purposes. Thus one decree declared that every diocese must establish theologians to teach the clergy everything necessary for the "care of souls"; another, aimed at strengthening laypeople's faith, mandated more preaching to them; and another prescribed that adult Christians must confess at least once a year. Innocent's prestige, as well as the large and ecumenical attendance, ensured that the council's decrees were promoted in Europe by many bishops.

From the council flowed three great overlapping waves of eloquence in France and Anglo-Norman England—indeed throughout Europe. This literature was generated by the council's charge to preachers and teachers that they instill in ordinary believers a better grasp of what it meant to be a Christian. The faith, as understood by laymen through the 12th century, had tended on the one hand to be external: Roland died for his faith more than he lived it, and the characters in romances were commonly Christians only in that they were shown attending mass and praying for the outcome of combat. Insofar as it was internalized, on the other hand, religious faith tended to be highly emotional: repentant sinners in pious tales wept copious tears for their sins, and poets sang in affective, courtly language of divine love. The new, postconciliar emphasis was both more internal and less emotional. The church was to teach laymen what the sacraments were, meant, and did. Christians now had to confess regularly—and not only on battlefield or deathbed, or when burdened with a particularly heinous sin. People were to be taught how and what to confess; thus, how to examine their consciences. To do so, they had to be able to recognize sin—and virtue. Such considerations account for the vast proliferation of "mirror" literature, all the many *specula* in which medieval men and women were invited to look at themselves and to reflect not only on what they were but also on what they should be. Later developments in autobiographical—"confessional"—literature would probably have been impossible without this training in introspection.

The first wave of Lateran literature consisted of works intended ultimately for the laity but mediated through the clergy and through Latin. Later developments in religious themes and genres in French (and in the other vernacular literatures) are best understood as a continuation of this first great wave.

These Latin works included four general categories: manuals on penance, treatises on the vices and virtues, collections of sermons, and collections of exempla. The *Summa de Poenitentia et Matrimonio* (ca. 1235; *Summa on Penitence and Matrimony*), by the Catalan Dominican Raymond of Peñafort, furnishes an example of the new approach to penance. Instead of providing blanket penances for categories of sin, as earlier penitential books did, Peñafort emphasizes the importance of intentionality and looks at the concrete circumstances of each particular "case" of sin or moral choice (whence the science of "casuistry"), in which the age, sex, profession, and circumstances of the individual are taken into account. Treatises on the vices and virtues, such as those of Peñafort's contemporary and fellow Dominican Guillaume Perrault (Peraldus), updated ancient traditions. Moving beyond the old static paired opposites (such as Pride versus Humility), Perrault analyzes in detail the many different forms that sin could take; thus he took up not only the various manifestations of gluttony, pride, and other deadly sins but also (for example) the sins of the tongue—including "guilty silence." Between 1220 and 1240 the great Jacques de Vitry wrote his French sermons *ad status* (to the different "estates" of men and women), which were later collected and published in Latin so that other preachers could make use of them as they tried to reach people of different conditions. Finally, collections of exempla—memorable stories illustrating the vices and virtues—were often taken out of books of sermons (such as those of Jacques de Vitry). One of the most famous was that of the Cistercian Caesarius of Heisterbach (ca. 1170–ca. 1240), *Dialogus Miraculorum* (*The Dialogue of Miracles*). Many an exemplum book was a Franciscan's "companion," for the Franciscans began early on to be known for their use of stories in preaching; after all, their founder, Francis of Assisi (1182–1226), was God's jongleur, or storyteller. Their exempla illustrated vices and virtues but were also earthy and sensual. Like the related fabliaux, these stories frequently provide valuable glimpses into medieval life.

Many of these collections are dry warehouses of catechetical or devotional "commonplaces," providing only bare bones of homily or story, but they were meant not so much to be read as to be consulted, used—and fleshed out, brought to life, by the eloquence of preachers. One of the few exceptions that actually invite reading is the *Legenda Aurea* (ca. 1260; *The Golden Legend*), a summa of short saints' Lives, by the Dominican Jacobus de Voragine.

This Latin Lateran literature emerged largely outside the vast intellectual development for which the 13th century is famous (such as the rise of the universities, the rediscovery of Aristotle, and the work of such major figures as

Bonaventura and Aquinas). Although the council stressed the importance of an educated clergy, and although the new understanding of penance was fed by scholars, the primary emphasis was not on learning—still less on scholastic disputation—but on powerful preaching to the people. Robert Grosseteste, bishop of Lincoln, refused to allow a priest under his authority to pursue advanced studies, reminding him that Jesus told Peter to feed his sheep with God's Word—not to give lectures to the flock. Although medieval religious literature is commonly classified as "didactic," it is often best understood as catechetical and devotional. After all, what the council called for was essentially oral instruction (Greek *katechein,* to learn by heart and "echo back"), whose purpose was to move the heart and will. Although the Lateran literature has a strong reflective component, required by the necessity to examine one's conscience, the self-knowledge involved is connected to action, to the eradication of vice and the exercise of virtue, rather than to the more abstract idea of knowledge implied in the Greek *didaskein,* "to teach."

The second great wave of Lateran literature consisted of works composed by the clergy in French rather than in Latin. Written directly for laymen and the lower clergy, who could not read Latin, these works tended to be more appealing and more personal in tone than the dry Latin models on which they were generally based. Although some of these works (especially the later ones) were intended for private reading, most were clearly meant to be read aloud. Unlike the Latin texts, which were almost invariably in prose, these French works were commonly in verse, which was associated with the oral, performed tradition and thus invited listeners or readers to learn parts by heart.

One of the first and most important of these works intended for laymen was *Le manuel des péchés* (ca. 1260; *The Manual of Sins*), an Anglo-Norman work (that is, written in England in French, which was the language of the upper classes until well into the 14th century). England was particularly rich in such productions, probably because English bishops gave strong support to the Lateran program, and a council at Oxford in 1222 reinforced Lateran decrees. The *Manuel* was composed in octosyllabic rhymed couplets by an unknown cleric. Clearly inspired by the Fourth Lateran Council, it provided a guide for the examination of conscience, setting out the basics of the faith—the Twelve Articles of Faith, the Ten Commandments, the Seven Deadly Sins, the Roots of Sacrilege, the Seven Sacraments—as well as sections on "why sin should be hated," "what things are damaging and what things profitable to confession," "what the power of holy prayer is," and a section containing prayers to Christ and to "sweet Mother Mary." Mingled in are many exempla, such as that of Pierre the usurer, converted by a dream in which he stood before the throne of God awaiting judgment.

Catechetical summae varied somewhat in content, reflecting preachers' different emphases, but all enumerated and explained basic teachings of the faith, and all were organized numerically—by "sevens" (the Sacraments, Vices, Virtues), by "tens," and so on—making for easy retention. A continental cousin to the *Manuel* was the immensely influential *Somme du roi* (1279; *The King's*

Summa), written in prose for Philip III by his confessor, the Dominican Brother Laurent. Though similar in content to the *Manuel,* it has a more positive emphasis, with sections on the Seven Virtues and the Seven Gifts of the Holy Spirit and less stress on sin and confession.

Some attractive works of imagination also belong to this wave: allegories such as *Le besant de Dieu* (before 1230; *God's Coin*), based on the parable of the talents, by the Norman clerk Guillaume. Guillaume (like various other writers of the period) draws on Innocent III's ascetic work *De Miseria Conditionis Humanae* (1195; *On the Misery of the Human Condition*), adding a clear satirical message. The work has a strong personal quality: Guillaume begins by saying that he wishes to speak—to make good use of the coin God has given him—while he still has time, for, he says (*Besant,* lines 5–6),

> I do not know when He will come,
> Nor at what hour He will summon me.

The work is full of personal exhortation (lines 3706–07, 3717–20):

> Let's go seek the cross of Jesus Christ!
> Let's make good use of the talents God has given us!
> . . .
> Let's wash ourselves through confession
> So that in the high procession
> We may go with the angels
> And praise the King of glory!

Here there is no sense of a clerical "we" as distinct from—superior to— "them," the laity. Guillaume speaks, as do many other eloquent preachers, out of a common Christian identity.

Pious tales and exempla—some of which had already been put into French in the 12th century—continued to be popularized in the 13th. For example, an Anglo-Norman Templar, Henri d'Arci, around midcentury set quite freely into verse old Latin works about the early desert hermits: the *Vitae Patrum* (*Lives of the Fathers*). Such stories emphasize the power of confession, often stressing that no sin, however terrible—even infanticide, incest—is beyond God's forgiveness.

The translation of Latin prayers and hymns, especially those devoted to the Virgin, stimulated new, often moving, compositions—all of which contributed to the growth of lay devotions. One of these, the rosary, emerged as the illiterate layman's equivalent of the 150 psalms recited daily in monasteries. Books of hours arose as the layman's breviary, containing a variable set of prayers, hymns, and readings from scripture in the vernacular, along with devotional pictures.

The third great wave of catechetical and devotional literature of lay writers preaching to the laity—and to the clergy—began by the mid-13th century, as laymen were increasingly drawn into the program launched by the Lateran Council. One of this wave's strongest voices was that of Rutebeuf (ca.

1245–1280), a professional poet working in almost all the devout genres of the period (as well as composing violent polemics and vulgar fabliaux). Among his many works is the *Voie de paradis* (ca. 1265; *Path to Paradise*), commissioned for use in Lent, when believers prepared their annual confession. Rutebeuf tells of a dream in which he is on a pilgrimage to paradise. On the road he is given hospitality by Charity's husband, Pity, who explains to him that to reach paradise he must go through the City of Confession and describes to him the vices and virtues he will meet along the way, explaining how he will recognize them. Here is Envy (lines 337–341, 345–353, 357–358):

> The person whom Envy controls
> Never has joy or pleasure;
> Every day his face is pale,
> Every day his words are evil;
> He laughs when his neighbor weeps
>
> . . .
>
> Now you can know the life
> That he who is envious leads.
> Envy makes men kill
> And makes them move boundary stones
> And steal other men's land,
> Envy brings war into the world,
> Envy makes husband and wife
> Hate each other, Envy destroys the soul,
> Envy puts discord between brothers,
>
> . . .
>
> Envy confounds Charity
> And destroys Humility.

At the end Rutebeuf praises the City of Repentance (lines 874–875):

> For no evil can come to
> The man who sojourns therein.

Rutebeuf also wrote about his personal sense of contrition and need for confession in *La mort de Rutebeuf* (*Rutebeuf's Death*); about the former prostitute and extraordinary penitent Mary of Egypt; and about Theophilus, who had made a pact with the devil but was snatched from the jaws of hell by his repentance and his devotion to the Virgin—in whose honor Rutebeuf also composed poems and prayers.

From the mid-13th century on, in French and Anglo-Norman letters laymen began to speak out on matters that had up to then been largely reserved for the clergy, composing devotional works and prayers and calls to repentance. In *Les trois morts et les trois vifs* (ca. 1295; *The Three Dead and the Three Living*), the minstrel Baudoin de Condé conjures up rotting but alarmingly animated and articulate skeletons who confront high-living young men, calling them to confession. Laymen even wrote manuals on the moral and religious life. Sometimes they stressed the discrepancy between what the faithful professed and the way they really lived, as in the anonymous 13th-century *Patenôtre de l'usurier* (*The Usurer's "Our Father"*), thus assuming a new awareness of what Christians were *supposed* to be and do. Secular works such as Henri d'Andeli's entertaining *Lai d'Aristote* (ca. 1250; *Lay of Aristotle*) often made casual references to mortal sin, lust, and other concepts taken from moral theology. Both parts of *Le roman de la rose* (*The Romance of the Rose*)—that of Guillaume de Lorris (ca. 1225) and that of Jean de Meun (ca. 1275)—show a similar impact, as in the "Vices" portrayed on the outer walls of the Garden (in Guillaume's part), and in Nature's lengthy confession to her priest (Jean's part).

The first laymen involved in the Lateran agenda were professional writers such as Rutebeuf and members of the educated upper classes. Jean de Joinville wrote a *Vie de saint Louis* (1309; *Life of Saint Louis*), a blend of memoir, chronicle, and hagiography, and a paraphrase of the Apostles' Creed, whose purpose was to help dying men struggle with doubt. Eventually middle-class and nonprofessional writers joined in. One of the last and most memorable voices of Anglo-Norman literature was that of John Gower, apparently a wealthy wool merchant. Working in French in the 1370s, he wrote for his fellow laymen a *Miroir de l'homme* (*Mirror of Man*). This massive work—over 30,000 octosyllables—differs from the catechetical summae in that it has a strong unifying principle and was intended as a literary effort: it has symmetry and poetic ornament and contains many interesting lines. It was apparently meant to be read in bits and snatches for both devotion and literary pleasure. Gower also wrote in Latin; and he wrote in English: his masterpiece, the pseudoautobiographical *Confessio Amantis* (ca. 1390; *A Lover's Confession*) is a strange blend of Jean de Meun's *Rose*—starring Venus' chaplain, Genius, as confessor—and a review of the Seven Deadly Sins!

Through the efforts of these three waves of writers, by the latter 14th century the Fourth Lateran Council had to a substantial degree borne the fruit intended by Innocent III: "the faith strengthened" and "virtues implanted."

See also 1609.

Bibliography: E. J. Arnould, ed., *Le manuel des péchés* (Paris: Droz, 1940). John Fleming, *An Introduction to the Franciscan Literature of the Middle Ages* (Chicago: Franciscan Herald Press, 1977). Guillaume le Clerc de Normandie, *Le besant de Dieu*, ed. Ernst Martin (1869; reprint, Geneva: Slatkine, 1975). Guillaume de Lorris and Jean de Meun, *The Romance of the Rose*, trans. Harry W. Robbins (New York: Dutton, 1972). Henri d'Andeli, *The Lay of Aristotle*, in *Gallic Salt: Eighteen Fabliaux Translated from the Old French*, trans. Robert Harrison (Berkeley: University of California Press, 1974). Jean de Joinville, *The Life of Saint Louis*, in Jean de Joinville and Villehardouin, *Chronicles of the Crusades*, trans. M. R. B. Shaw (New York: Penguin, 1963). Ch.-V. Langlois, *La vie en France au moyen âge, du XIIe au milieu du XIVe siècle: La vie spirituelle: Enseignements, méditations & controverses, d'après les écrits en français à l'usage des laïcs* (Paris: Hachette, 1928). Mary Dominica Legge, *Anglo-Norman Literature and Its Background* (Oxford: Clarendon Press, 1963). G. C. Macaulay, *The Complete Work of John Gower, Edited from the Manuscripts with Introductions, Notes, and Glossaries*, 3 vols. (Oxford: Clarendon Press, 1899). André Mary, *Anthologie poétique française du moyen âge*, 2 vols. (Paris: Garnier-

Flammarion, 1967). Jean-Marcel Paquette, ed., *Poèmes de la mort, de Turold à Villon* (Paris: Union Générale d'Editions, 1979). Jean-Charles Payen, *Le motif du repentir dans la littérature française médiévale des origines à 1230* (Geneva: Droz, 1967). Rutebeuf, *Oeuvres complètes de Rutebeuf,* ed. Edmond Faral and Julia Bastin, 2 vols. (Paris: Picard, 1969). Jacques de Vitry, *The Exempla or Illustrative Stories from the Sermones Vulgares of Jacques de Vitry,* ed. Thomas F. Crane (1890; reprint, New York: Burt Franklin, 1971).

Evelyn Birge Vitz

✍ 1225?

Guillaume de Lorris Writes the Prologue to the First Part of
Le roman de la rose

Generic Hybrids

French literature of the 13th century is characterized by extensive experimentation with generic forms. Preexisting literary genres are fused, deconstructed, and recombined in a dazzling variety of hybrids, which in turn give rise to further innovations. This vital process of generic transformation is central to the anonymous *Aucassin et Nicolette* (ca. 1225–1260) at every level. In its use of language and its narrative structure, the work combines essential features from courtly romance and chivalric epic. The resulting contrasts and contradictions establish the upside-down universe of *Aucassin et Nicolette* and shape the reader's response to the text. These effects are compounded by the presence of various constructs from several other literary genres: saint's Life, troubadour and trouvère lyric, Byzantine adventure story, *pastourelle,* and fabliau.

Formally speaking, the hybrid status of *Aucassin et Nicolette* is its defining feature. Its forty-one sections alternate between verse and prose. Rubrics call for the verse sections to be sung and the prose sections to be spoken. In the concluding section a unique generic designation is applied to the work as a whole, derived from its double discourse: *chantefable* (song-story). No other example of this explicitly mixed vernacular generic form survives. There was, however, an important Latin analogue in the *prosimetrum* (prose-verse) tradition, in particular in Boethius' *De Consolatione Philosophiae* (ca. 524; *The Consolation of Philosophy*), which Jean de Meun translated into French in the mid-13th century. In both Boethius' work and *Aucassin et Nicolette* the relation between prose and verse is a dialogic one, and there is much overlap: many sections in lyric verse advance the narrative; many sections in narrative prose contain lyric set pieces. Unlike Boethius' *Consolation,* however, the subject matter of *Aucassin et Nicolette* is literary rather than philosophical.

The story line is relatively simple. The two title characters are young lovers against whom a variety of circumstances conspire. They are twice separated and twice reunited. A kind of telescoping occurs: the second cycle has a faster narrative pace and a correspondingly abbreviated articulation. It is Nicolette who effects both reunions, who successfully overcomes the obstacles presented by the

88

two externally imposed separations. Her success results from a striking combination of intellectual astuteness and linguistic inventiveness. On the first occasion she leads Aucassin to her hiding place in the forest by means of a set of carefully encoded messages that simultaneously disguise and reveal her identity and location. By engaging in this signifying activity at the level of plot, Nicolette functions as an index of the author. On the second occasion she escapes from captivity in Spain and journeys to Aucassin's castle in Beaucaire, disguised as a jongleur (poet-minstrel). In this disguise she performs an abbreviated version of the very adventures that have befallen the lovers in the *chantefable*. Her public performance within the story line thus doubles in miniature the public performance of the author-jongleur for the text as a whole. Here, Nicolette functions as an emblem—even a specular double—of the author, at the same time as she advances the plot.

As the work progresses, the author is represented with increasing explicitness by Nicolette. This process simultaneously involves a redefinition of the key term *prouesse* (prowess, valor, exploits) by yet another sort of generic transformation. The prologue has presented the two protagonists in conventional chivalric/courtly terms from both epic and romance: "Who would like to hear a good poem about how an old man separated two beautiful young children, Nicolette and Aucassin; about the torments that this latter suffered and the exploits [*prouesses*] he accomplished for his beloved with the radiant face?" (sec. 1, lines 1–7). Nicolette is presented as passive love object and Aucassin as active subject. In the course of the story the chivalric *prouesse* initially associated with Aucassin is programatically undercut, displaced by a newly defined *prouesse* associated with the artful and efficacious manipulation of discourse, embodied by Nicolette. By the end of the work she is explicitly revealed as a poet figure whose power and efficaciousness—derived from her discourse—are demonstrated by her successful reunions of the lovers. The corrective reworking of the prologue that opens her song *qua* jongleur is particularly significant: "Hear me, noble lords, whether seated low or high: Would you like to hear a song about Aucassin, a noble lord, and about the valiant Nicolette [*Nicolette la prous*]?" (sec. 39, lines 14–18). Here the initial epic and romance formulas are subverted: Nicolette is substituted for Aucassin as doer of *prouesses*. In this witty, playful, and highly self-conscious remotivation of the preexisting generic systems that serve as the *chantefable*'s point of departure, *Aucassin et Nicolette* highlights the literary process that has to a large degree generated it, and may be read as a generic hybrid "about" the hybridization of genres.

In Guillaume de Lorris' *Le roman de la rose* (ca. 1225; *The Romance of the Rose*), a different kind of generic mixing had important implications for subsequent literary history. Guillaume's prologue conflates the first-person lover of courtly lyric with the first-person narrator of courtly romance. Before Guillaume's *Rose*, these two personae—indeed, the two genres—had been mutually exclusive: the clerkly romance narrator was not a lover; the lyric lover was not a clerkly narrator. Guillaume's brilliant structural innovation involves a new kind of "autobiographical" discourse. An older narrator tells the story of his own experience

89

of love when he was twenty. The clerkly perspective of the romance narrator (including his bookish authority) is combined with the lyric perspective of the first-person love experience. Romance narrative techniques are used to articulate lyric subject matter. It is as if Lancelot were to recount his love affair with Guenevere from the more mature perspective of a Chrétien de Troyes. An important result of this conflation is that the experience of the first-person narrator-protagonist seems to acquire a universal validity: his particular story functions simultaneously as an amatory treatise, an *ars amandi.* Guillaume is explicitly aware of his innovation: "The subject matter is both good and new" (line 39). At the same time, the narrator is himself still a lover, and the entire romance is presented as a lyric offering to a beloved who exists outside the text: "She who is so precious and is so worthy to be loved that she should be called Rose" (*Romance,* lines 42–44).

Guillaume's entire text is presented as a dream that has already come true, and thus acquires a double kind of authenticity: the protagonist has himself lived through the dream-events, and these have been confirmed in waking reality. The story line recounts (largely in terms of personification allegory) the protagonist's love for a beautiful rosebud. Although his suit is intermittently successful, the romance concludes with a poignant lament by the lover (lines 3920–4028), who is definitively separated from his rose by the recently con-structed castle of Jealousy.

This lament also fuses the lover-protagonist with the poet-narrator. Recounted almost exclusively from a present perspective, the lament is pre-sented as equally applicable to the rose of the story line and to the extratextual lady called Rose. In effect, then, Guillaume's romance is both complete and incomplete, and this paradox is a direct result of the work's status as generic hybrid. As narrative, the romance is clearly unfinished. The narrator's own voice signals this by intervening in the story (lines 3482–86) to state that he will recount his successful capture of Jealousy's castle, which will constitute the end of the story. This, obviously, does not take place. At the same time, the status of the romance as lyric offering to the narrator's extratextual lady in the present makes such a narrative closure impossible in terms of courtly convention, since the dream is presented as having already come true in the fiction of the text. An explicit depiction of the successful taking of the rose by the protagonist would be both presumptuous and profoundly uncourtly with regard to the nar-rator's lady, Rose, since it would presuppose her having already accepted him as her lover. The discreetly unfinished narrative, on the other hand, allows the text to function as a (strategically effective) lyric love request. Guillaume de Lorris' *Rose* is thus simultaneously unfinished as narrative and finished as lyric. The work's status as a generic hybrid is therefore essential to its reception by its readers. At the same time, the opposition between lyric and narrative that is so central to Guillaume's *Rose* is not articulated at the formal level: a single verse form (octosyllabic rhyming couplets) is employed throughout.

In Jean Renart's romance of the same name (also composed ca. 1225, most likely after Guillaume de Lorris'), a different kind of opposition between lyric and narrative obtains, for there is a clear formal distinction between the two generic modes: Renart's *Rose* (often referred to as *Le roman de la rose ou de Guillaume de Dole,* to differentiate it from Lorris' work) consists of a narrative in rhyming octosyllabic couplets in which a series of forty-six lyric set pieces is intercalated, each presented as being sung by one or more characters.

The narrative involves a love quest in which the emperor of Germany offers his hand in marriage to Liénor, the sister of his recently appointed courtier Guillaume de Dole, having heard of her unsurpassed beauty and virtue from Jouglet, his court minstrel. The emperor's wicked seneschal attempts to sabotage the marriage by claiming to have slept with the maiden, offering as proof his knowledge of a rose-shaped birthmark on her thigh. By a clever ruse Liénor exposes his story as a lie and ends by marrying the emperor.

The intercalated songs form, in the words of the work's most recent editor, Félix Lecoy, "a veritable anthology of [contemporary] French lyric production." Two broad categories are discernible: a relatively homogeneous group of sixteen "aristocratic," courtly love songs (*chansons courtoises*), often attributed (or attributable) to specific trouvères or troubadours such as Gace Brulé, the châtelain de Coucy, Renaut de Beaujeu, the Vidame de Chartres, Jaufré Rudel, and Bernard de Ventadour; and a much more heterogeneous group of thirty pieces (virtually all anonymous) drawn from the "popular" lyric tradition. These include twenty dance songs (*chansons à danser*), six ballads (including three *chansons de toile,* laments traditionally sung by women weaving), two *pastourelles* (in which a knight sings of his erotic love for a shepherdess), and two songs of praise (to a patron and to a lady). There is in addition an intercalated epic strophe (*laisse*) from the *chanson de geste Gerbert de Metz.*

In the prologue to his romance, Renart is explicitly aware of the kind of generic innovation in which he is engaged: "For just as one dyes cloth to gain praise and esteem, so are the songs and melodies placed into this *Roman de la rose,* which is a new thing" (lines 8–12).

At the same time, two important developments have been effected in relation to the *Rose* of Guillaume de Lorris. One is that in Renart's romance the female object of desire has become an active agent rather than a passive object in the story. The other is a change in the rose's function as signifier: as Michel Zink has observed, in Guillaume de Lorris the rose signifies *metaphorically*—it resembles the lady and the lady resembles it; in Jean Renart, by contrast, the rose signifies *metonymically*—it is itself a literal part of the lady's identity.

Renart's *Rose* initiated a hybrid form that was quickly imitated. Within a very short time Gerbert de Montreuil composed *Le roman de la violette* (ca. 1230; *The Romance of the Violet*), which incorporated some forty songs (including a strophe from the 12th-century epic *Aliscans*) into its narrative structure. The opening episode reworks the basic plot line of Renart's *Rose,* but with several important differences. First, the false accusation against the heroine, Euriaut, results from a bet in which her lover, Gerart, stakes his land on her fidelity. Further, Euriaut, unlike Renart's Liénor, remains more a passive object than an active subject: she is unable to expose the imposture and clear her name.

Finally, Euriaut's distinguishing mark or sign (*saing*) is a violet-shaped birthmark on her right breast, which signifies metonymically the lady's sexual identity and whose concealment guarantees her fidelity to her lover. Like Renart, Gerbert is quite explicitly conscious in his prologue of the hybrid status of his work: "For one can both read and sing it; and the sung part goes so well with the recited part that I call anyone who hears it to be my witness" (lines 38–41).

Around 1250 Tibaut's *Le roman de la poire* (*The Romance of the Pear*) combined the first-person love allegory of Guillaume de Lorris with the female protagonist of Jean Renart and Gerbert de Montreuil. The songs intercalated in Tibaut's narrative are refrains sung by allegorical characters and involve a series of reciprocal messages between the lover and the lady. In addition, there is, immediately after the prologue, an extended sequence of stanzaic verses (mostly twelve-syllable) in which Cupid, Fortune, and four exemplary past lovers (Cligès, Tristan, Pyramus, and Paris) speak in the first person to introduce the *Poire*'s lover and his lady. The central rhetorical figure has also been modified, for the pear of the title both symbolizes and initiates the reciprocal relationship between the romance's lovers: the first-person protagonist falls in love after tasting the pear that the lady offers to him after tasting it herself. At the same time, the pear seems to be a metaphor for the romance itself, which is a medium of communication between the lovers and a record of their dialogue. In addition, the pear involves a positive rewriting of the apple of Adam and Eve, as well as of the pear from book 2 of St. Augustine's *Confessions*.

With *Le roman du châtelain de Coucy et de la dame de Fayel* (ca. 1285; *The Romance of the châtelain of Coucy and the Lady of Fayel*), Jakemes produced a new kind of relationship between lyric interpolations and narrative story line. Here the protagonist is the historically "real" trouvère, the châtelain de Coucy (flourished ca. 1186–1203), whose existing love and crusade songs generate the pseudobiographical story line of the romance in which they are intercalated. Seven of the trouvère's songs (four of certain attribution) are integrated into the narrative, which, among other things, claims to explain how they came to be written. The result is a self-conscious northern French poeticization of the process that produced the Provençal *vidas* (biographies) of the troubadours. Three additional songs sung by other characters function narratively in a similar fashion.

By the end of the 13th century the narrative poem with intercalated lyrics—originally a generic hybrid—had become a canonical form, figuring in a variety of discursive registers: Henri d'Andeli's *Lai d'Aristote* (ca. 1250; *Lay of Aristotle*), an antiuniversity satire utilizing fabliau elements; Adenet le Roi's *Cléomadès* (ca. 1280), a fantastic adventure romance; Adam de la Halle's *Le jeu de Robin et Marion* (ca. 1285; *Play of Robin and Marion*), a theatrical version of the lyric *pastourelle;* Jacques Bretel's *Le tournoi de Chauvency* (ca. 1285; *The Chauvency Tournament*), a courtly pageant involving historically real characters; and Jacquemart Giélée's *Renart le nouvel* (ca. 1288; *The New Renard*), a parodic blend of animal epic and courtly romance. Collectively, these late 13th-century mixed forms point the way to the 14th-century generic entity known as the *dit* (story).

Nicole de Margival's *Dit de la panthère d'amour* (ca. 1310; *Story of the Panther of Love*) is of particular importance as a transitional text. It is a first-person love allegory with two different kinds of intercalated lyrics: eight songs (complete or excerpted) by Adam de la Halle, who functions as an external, didactic authority on love; and eleven by Nicole himself, which function as lyric love requests (both direct and indirect) to his lady, who exists outside the text. The central metaphor—the panther—is taken from the bestiary tradition and represents both the lady (in the dream that constitutes the *dit* proper) and the inadequacies of metaphoric discourse, that is, the distance between lady and metaphor (in the epilogue to the dream). By the late 14th century, the newly canonical narrative *dit* with intercalated lyrics would produce such masterpieces as Guillaume de Machaut's *Remède de Fortune* (ca. 1342; *Fortune's Cure*) and *Le livre du vrai dit* (ca. 1365; *The Book of the True Story*), as well as Jean Froissart's *La prison amoureuse* (ca. 1372; *The Prison of Love*) and *Le joli buisson de jeunesse* (ca. 1373; *The Pretty Bush of Youth*).

See also 1277.

Bibliography: Aucassin et Nicolette, ed. Mario Roques (Paris: Champion, 1969); translated by Glyn S. Burgess and Anne Cobby in *"The Pilgrimage of Charlemagne" and "Aucassin and Nicolette"* (New York: Garland, 1988). Kevin Brownlee, "Discourse as *Proueces* in *Aucassin et Nicolette,"* *Yale French Studies,* 70 (1986), 167–182. Gerbert de Montreuil, *Le roman de la violette,* ed. Douglas L. Buffum (Paris: Champion, 1928). Guillaume de Lorris, *The Romance of the Rose,* trans. Charles Dahlberg (Princeton: Princeton University Press, 1971). David Hult, *Self-Fulfilling Prophecies: Readership and Authority in the First "Roman de la Rose"* (Cambridge: Cambridge University Press, 1986). Sylvia Huot, *From Song to Book: The Poetics of Writing in Old French Lyric and Lyrical Narrative Poetry* (Ithaca: Cornell University Press, 1987). Jean Renart, *Le roman de la rose ou de Guillaume de Dole,* ed. Félix Lecoy (Paris: Champion, 1969). Tibaut, *Le roman de la poire,* ed. Christiane Marchello-Nizia (Paris: Picard, 1984). Michel Zink, *Roman rose et rose rouge: Le "Roman de la rose ou de Guillaume de Dole" de Jean Renart* (Paris: Nizet, 1979).

Kevin Brownlee

 1267

In *Le livre du trésor* Brunetto Latini First Teaches the Art of Writing in the French Language

Medieval Rhetoric

The third section of Brunetto Latini's *Le livre du trésor* (1267; *The Book of Treasure*), an encyclopedia in French, is a treatise on rhetoric. Even though it deals with both oral and written eloquence (oratory, letter writing, and composition in verse and prose) in a rather traditional way, its medium constitutes a significant break: it teaches Latin theory of composition as understood in the High Middle Ages, but does it in and for the French language. Latini's treatise marks the definitive shift from the Latin tradition, transmitted through the schools since antiquity, to the competing French one, which emerged in the 12th century and triumphed by the 14th and 15th. By then several more or less formal treatises and manuals—such as Eustache Deschamps's *Art de dicter* (1392; *The Art of Versifying*) and Jean Molinet's *Art de rhétorique vulgaire* (1493; *Art of Vernacular Rhetoric*)—had followed Latini's example, presenting composition and versification in French and using French literary works as models.

Although Latini's view of the function and aim of rhetoric—it "teaches us to speak fully and completely in public and private matters, and to do so for the purpose of convincing auditors of what is being said" (vol. 3, chap. 2, para. 1)—goes back to Cicero's *De inventione* (*On Invention*), it highlights two essential features of medieval literature: orality and the composition of the audience. The only difference between Cicero's time and Latini's was that the vernacular was French, not Latin.

From Latini's chapter through Jacques Le Grand's early 15th-century *Archiloge sophie* (*The Fair Speech of Wisdom*), medieval manuals and treatises continued to emphasize elocution, or oral delivery of a written text. Many of the tales first committed to writing in the Middle Ages were themselves the product of a centuries-old oral tradition; the *chansons de geste,* for example, successively composed, sung, and retold by jongleurs from at least as early as the 9th century, were not written down until the 11th or 12th. Medieval literature in all its genres was an oral literature. The words surviving in manuscripts were not intended for silent reading, but for declamation before an audience, whether that audience was oneself alone, a small group, or large groups gathered at festivities and entertainments to celebrate, say, a marriage or a royal entrance into a town.

The words used in any text had to be understandable, credible, and appropriate to the audience for which it was composed. Thus the language and commonplaces (topoi) used in romances and lyric poetry, destined for worldly aristocrats, should differ from those used in saints' Lives, aimed at a more pious audience. Language was also the medium for debate and judgment. Issues of importance to the aristocracy were raised in exemplary narratives that presented different points of view, sometimes suggesting a solution, sometimes leaving the solution ambiguous, a matter for further discussion or debate by the audience. Contrasting points of view were also embedded in courtly lyric or debate poems (*tensos, jeux-partis*). Love poetry throughout the medieval period has a singer/narrator figure who adapts his or her words to a projected audience, which might be asssumed to change as often as each stanza, from the loved one to a circle of connoisseurs or rivals, to a patron dispensing largesse. In the prose romances of the 13th century, fictional or semirealistic narrators—the knights of the Round Table, Merlin, Jesus Christ, Walter Map, anonymous scribes— alternately narrate and interpret their tales. These narrators, like orators, define authorial intention and context to suit their audience's expectations.

In the Latin tradition, skill in writing was acquired by the study (including practice and imitation) of grammar (the art of speaking correctly) and rhetoric (the art of speaking well). The major medieval treatises in Latin poetic and prose composition appeared in France between about 1170 and 1250. The most influential and representative were those by Matthew of Vendôme, Geoffrey of Vinsauf, and John of Garland. Offering practical instruction in elementary composition in verse and prose, they drew more or less systematically on a Latin tradition that extended back to antiquity. They also relied on models of "good" literature, represented by prescribed authors (such as Virgil and Statius as well as medieval writers), and the theories of accepted authorities on good writing (such as Horace and Cicero). In the study of these models, commentary (elucidating principles of the art of poetry and prose) and composition (exercises imitating the prescribed authors and applying the recommended features of the art) were the two fundamental activities. Correction could be formal, essentially saying the same thing, but more "artfully," or substantive, drawing a new and different meaning from the original. Commentary, formal glossing to explain a given text, could be external—either separate disquisitions or marginal or interlinear glosses—or internal. In the latter case the commentary became an integral part of the text and hence produced a new work. Thus the 12th-century *Roman d'Enéas* was an adaptation and recreation of Virgil's *Aeneid* for a French-speaking aristocratic audience.

The essential technique for internal commentary and correction was topical invention, which used "commonplaces" (*koinoi topoi* in Greek, *loci communes* in Latin) to create a new context. Commonplaces were physical, sartorial, or internal features distinctive of certain widely accepted human "types." They could show forth and elaborate on the quality of a character and thus distinguish a beautiful person from an ugly one, a knight from a carpenter or banker, and a lady from a shepherdess. As a rhetorical technique, topical invention urged listeners or readers to accept a certain vision of the world or confirmed their beliefs as mirrored in the characters and actions of the written work. French writers in the Latin tradition used topical invention extensively. Marie de France refers to it in the prologue to her *Lais* (ca. 1180) when telling how authors draw hidden meaning from their sources; and Chrétien de Troyes refers to it when he claims to be articulating the *matière* (source material) and *sens* (context or signification) his patron gave him in a romance about Lancelot and Guenevere, *Lancelot ou le chevalier à la charrette* (ca. 1170; *Lancelot, or the Knight of the Cart*).

Medieval writers did not think of artistic invention as creation; only God could create. Rather, they saw themselves as translating the past by adapting it to current ideals. Latini himself integrated translations from Latin works into the *Trésor,* including extensive excerpts from Cicero, Sallust, and Geoffrey of Vinsauf in the section on rhetoric. As the vernacular became more widely accepted as a medium for the arts and sciences, translation from Latin into French became more common. At about the time Latini wrote the *Trésor,* Jean de Meun translated Boethius, Vegetius, and the letters of Héloïse and Abélard. He also amalgamated a variety of sources in *Le roman de la rose* (ca. 1275; *The Romance of the Rose*), drawing new meaning from old matter in adapting it to new contexts and purposes. This kind of translation transmitted the past to the present, the foreign to the native, by commentary, correction, and rearrangement.

Throughout the medieval period what came to be called *poétrie* consisted of fables, exempla, and other kinds of stories drawn from the poet's memory and from literary and biblical sources. By digression, description, allegory, example, personification, and other devices, the poet used pleasing, ornate language to transform or "translate" these stories into different modes or genres, rearranging and recombining them to fit his or her intended meaning. As such, the poet was still a commentator and corrector, presenting his or her truth in an agreed-upon context, for a given audience, and in one or more of the three traditional modes of translation, adaptation, and allegory. *Le roman de la rose* was the first great vernacular poetic work to use allegory to give to a literal text another meaning from historical, scientific, or moral sources and models. It was followed by historical, scientific, exegetical, moral, and love allegories such as the 14th-century *Ovide moralisé* (*Moralization of Ovid*) and the dream visions of late medieval writers such as Guillaume de Machaut, Jean Froissart, Christine de Pisan, and René d'Anjou.

French poets of the late Middle Ages understood these kinds of poetic invention as imagination. In the critical introduction to his collected works, the *Prologue,* written just before his death in 1377, Guillaume de Machaut defines imagination as the faculty the artist uses to invent images. The truth or validity of the images depends on their representation of an accepted model. For example, the poet who wishes to show a religious or moral truth will model the persons and things represented in the work on the life of Christ, or portray personifications of vices or virtues whose attributes define or describe the moral abstractions they represent. In social or amatory contexts, definitions of love and exemplary schemes such as the *gradus amoris,* the stages in love from sight to consummation, form and inform the poet's matter.

Le Grand's *Archiloge sophie* (a translation and adaptation into French of his Latin *Sophilogium*) offers the most extensive instruction in and illustration of the accommodation of topical invention and imagination since the *Trésor.* Like his predecessors in the Latin tradition, Le Grand begins with grammar and rhetoric. But he emphasizes *poétrie* and rhetoric. For Le Grand, *poétrie* is "a science that teaches how to feign, to make fictions that are confirmed by reason and analogous to those things about which one proposes to speak" (bk. 1, chap. 25, lines 2–3). This is imagination. Literature is an essentially metaphorical medium wherein a poet adapts or allegorizes received images in analogy with preconceived models.

The diversity of French literature and its final triumph over Latin resulted from transmission and adaptation, not revolution against earlier traditions. The literary art was essentially a rhetoric in Latini's sense: speech public and private designed to convince an audience of the truth of what was sung or declaimed in narrative, dream vision, or lyric statement.

See also 1342, 1493.

Bibliography: Frederick Goldin, "An Array of Perspectives in the Early Courtly Love Lyric," in *In Pursuit of Perfection: Courtly Love in Medieval Literature,* ed. Joan M. Ferrante and George Economou (Port Washington, N.Y.: Kennikat Press, 1975), pp. 51–100.

Douglas Kelly, *The Arts of Poetry and Prose* (Turnhout: Brepols, 1989). Kelly, "*Translatio studii:* Translation, Adaptation, and Allegory in Medieval French Literature," *Philological Quarterly,* 57 (1978), 287–310. Brunetto Latini, *Li livres dou tresor,* ed. Francis J. Carmody (Berkeley: University of California Press, 1948). Jacques Le Grand, *Archiloge sophie/Livre de bonnes meurs,* ed. Evencio Beltran (Paris: Champion, 1986). Paul Zumthor, *La lettre et la voix de la "littérature" médiévale* (Paris: Seuil, 1987).

Douglas Kelly

✑ 1277, 7 March
The Bishop of Paris Condemns as Errors 219 Propositions
Taught at the University of Paris

Jean de Meun's Continuation of Le roman de la rose

On 7 March 1277 the bishop of Paris, Etienne Tempier, following a papal mandate to investigate the doctrinal orthodoxy of instruction at the Faculty of Arts of the University of Paris, issued an official condemnation listing 219 propositions, termed "errors," that had been culled from written works in the arts curriculum and from actual lectures delivered by certain of the professors. Tempier's decidedly overzealous response, coupled with its threat of excommunication, undoubtedly aimed to suppress the thriving and, for some, subversive influence of Thomism and neo-Aristotelianism in theological circles. Its undiscriminating comprehensiveness, however, shows it to have been more a defense against innovation in any form. To be sure, the list contains a large number of Aristotelian ideas filtered to the Latin West through the influential commentaries of the Arab philosopher Averroës and another fifteen that can be traced to the writings of Thomas Aquinas (d. 1274). But the document also mentions by name, somewhat incongruously, Andreas Capellanus' popular guide to social manners in a courtly setting, *De Amore* (ca. 1185; *The Art of Courtly Love*). By all accounts, the immediate effect of the condemnation was impressive: the teaching career of the university's leading Averroist, Siger de Brabant, was abruptly terminated, and the official proscription of Aquinas' writings persisted in Paris until 1325, two years after his canonization.

Although it is unlikely that a churchman such as Tempier would have taken notice of any literary or philosophical production in the vernacular, the following propositions related to moral errors could have been lifted directly from a contemporary work in French destined for a phenomenal popularity, Jean de Meun's *Le roman de la rose* (ca. 1275; *The Romance of the Rose*):

> That simple fornication, namely, that of an unmarried man with an unmarried woman, is not a sin.
>
> That a sin against nature, such as abuse in intercourse, is not against the nature of the individual, although it is against the nature of the species.
>
> That continence is not essentially a virtue.   (Lerner and Mahdi, *Medieval Political Philosophy,* p. 353)

Numerous other passages in Jean's work demonstrate his close ties with, and intimate knowledge of, the university milieu; but the fact that Jean conceived it as a romance in the vernacular strongly suggests that it was destined to be circulated at the fringes of that community, possibly as a source of entertainment satirizing intellectual issues without incurring the kinds of ideological strictures imposed upon writings in Latin. No precise date for *Le roman de la rose* is available, but we can infer from Jean's retelling of an important historical event, Charles of Anjou's conquest of Sicily (1266–1268), that his poem was conceived and written within the decade preceding Tempier's condemnation. Jean de Meun died in Paris in 1305.

Jean de Meun's *Rose* is one of several texts marking a change in vernacular literary culture in the third quarter of the 13th century. Fresh inspiration in the courtly genres had dwindled by this time, and even those who continued the tradition turned increasingly to the didactic (as in Richard of Fournival's midcentury *Bestiaire d'amour; Bestiary of Love*). The continued vogue for romance took a similar turn: in its lengthy prose version, the hitherto secular Arthurian saga became the vehicle for a Christianized version of world history; chivalric romances in verse written later in the century, though less explicitly didactic, looked backward in a nostalgic and highly derivative fashion. The audience's broadening taste, in the moralistic as well as in the bawdy, reflected the fact that centers of literary activity had shifted from the closely monitored and culturally inbred patronage of the provincial courts to the heterogeneous atmosphere, both clerical and popular, of the cities, chief among them Arras, with an increasingly active bourgeoisie made affluent by the cloth industry, and Paris, in which a vibrant intellectual life had developed around the university. An increase in literacy brought with it not solely a revival in Latin learning and writing but also a growing demand for texts in the vernacular; correspondingly, book production, now a commercial enterprise, began catering to that demand. A variety of topics previously thought appropriate only for Latin were now sought after in the vernacular: rhetoric, history, philosophy, science, and mythography.

That vernacular literature could also be used as a propagandistic tool had already been amply demonstrated by Jean de Meun's elder contemporary Rutebeuf, who, some fifteen years before, had written a series of pamphleteering poems commenting on university polemics in the 1250s. But unlike Rutebeuf and Adam de la Halle (d. ca. 1288), the prominent Artesian trouvère (as poets from the north of France were called), whose celebrity waned in a couple of generations, Jean's poem has survived in some 250 manuscripts (many of them lavishly illustrated)—more than any other medieval vernacular work in Western Europe except Dante's *Divina Commedia* (*Divine Comedy*)—and ran to twenty-one printed editions by 1538. It remains to be seen not only what Jean de Meun's *Rose* meant to his contemporaries but also why it became the most widely read, and most controversial, poem of the late Middle Ages and early Renaissance.

As he reveals in the midst of his own poem, albeit obliquely, through the voice of the God of Love, Jean de Meun came across an unfinished poem, a certain *Roman de la rose* undertaken by Guillaume de Lorris "more than forty years" before, and decided to conclude the work—as it turned out, adding some 17,500 lines of octosyllabic verse to the original 4,000-line fragment. With all the delicacy, finesse, and artifice of a poet steeped in courtly lyric and its rhetorical intricacies, Guillaume recounts in the first person an allegorical dream vision in which he seeks his beloved, figured by the rose, in the garden of Diversion until stymied by forces contrary to the fulfillment of amorous desire: Jealousy and her cohorts Shame, Fear, Refusal, and Evil Tongue. As society's mores, personified, dash the lover's aspirations, he ends with a solitary plaint outside the defensive fortifications built by Jealousy, a subtle request for his lady's good graces that replicates the courtly lover's archetypal stance.

It is unclear how Jean de Meun came across this fragile, and possibly obscure, courtly poem or why it even caught his attention. Perhaps he perceived in it an exemplary text, representative not only of a depleted literary genre but also of an outmoded worldview. The continuation of another author's work was fairly common in romance composition as early as the late 12th century, but no one before Jean de Meun produced such a strikingly self-conscious example of literary continuation as a mode of rewriting or of critical reinterpretation.

Jean's approach to allegory diverges significantly from that of his predecessor. Whereas much of Guillaume's poem (with the exception of a lengthy episode devoted to the God of Love's teachings) translates intangible feelings into physical action (as in the following summary of one episode: "Fair Welcome grants the Lover entry into the enclosure of rose bushes, but then Evil Tongue alerts Jealousy, who chases the Lover away"), Jean eschews allegorical action in favor of a sequence of disquisitions (ranging from 1,000 to 3,000 lines) by various authorities: Reason, Nature, the Old Lady, False Seeming, and so on. The characters are defined less by what they do than by what they say, and their identity in turn confers authority on the content of their speeches as it contextualizes them. In lieu of actions, Jean provides words; in lieu of feelings, he traffics in ideas. The topics dealt with range from friendship to sexual abstinence, from optics to details of feminine hygiene, from jealousy to sodomy. Jean does, however, return intermittently to allegorical action, and most notably in the final, rousing scene: championed by Genius, Nature's confessor, who is portrayed as a high priest of promiscuity, and Venus with her flaming torch, the Lover penetrates Jealousy's protective castle wall and, in no uncertain terms, deflowers the rose.

This massive and centrifugal text, characterized by large-scale digressions and repetitious wordplay, defies attempts to control its meaning, to identify a unified message. Some readers will side with Reason, the first personification in the Lover's long series of encounters, who counsels a chaste love and an avoidance of passion. In such a case the rest of the poem would describe a downhill movement, treating with ironic detachment the Lover's stubborn efforts to make contact with the rose. Other readers will find that Nature and Genius provide the key, expressing, contrariwise, an earthy naturalism that highlights the contradictions between the obvious imperative to perpetuate the species and the church's growing emphasis on chastity. According to the latter reading,

Jean's obscene ending, with its faintly disguised impregnation of the rose, would proclaim the triumph of a secularized worldview over the rarefaction of inapplicable dogmas.

Either of these interpretations presupposes that Jean was trying to formulate a specific idea or doctrine, that his poem achieves a kind of synthesis through an ultimate agreement among the "authorities" or through according preeminence to one of them. But as previous scholarship has amply demonstrated, Jean's ideas, far from being innovative, are largely derivative and, on occasion, downright banal. Jean himself confesses to being a "re-citer" or reteller, a claim borne out by the fact that thousands of lines are direct quotations from such disparate figures as Ovid, Alan of Lille, Boethius, Guillaume de Saint-Amour, and Juvenal. Furthermore, the poem's narrative structure bespeaks a plurality of ideas and points of view. Just as a fundamentally dual focus is suggested by Jean de Meun's fictional elaboration of the poem's two authors, so the poem taken as a whole embodies the spirit of disputation and debate made common currency in intellectual circles by the influential scholastic tradition. Allegory through personification proves to be a perfect vehicle for this kind of enterprise, given its potential for creating phantom authorities and conflicting doctrinal messages. Indeed, the genre of personification allegory was conceived within the metaphor of armed conflict: its founding text was Prudentius' *Psychomachia* (4th century; *The Battle of the Soul*).

Jean's brilliance resides in his submission of ideas to the broader question of epistemological inquiry, which becomes the central aspect of the fictional frame. Ultimately, he calls into question rigid systems of belief by stimulating the reader's awareness of his own interpretative faculties. The narrator's last words addressed directly to his audience underscore this point: "Thus things go by contraries; one is the gloss of the other. If one wants to define one of the pair, he must remember the other, or he will never, by any intention, assign a definition to it; for he who has no understanding of the two will never understand the difference between them, and without this difference no definition that one can make can come to anything" (*The Romance of the Rose*, p. 351).

Jean's words here provide an implicit critique of the type of normative gesture made by Etienne Tempier, thus showing the convergence of these two documents to be not totally fortuitous, regardless of whether the bishop was taking aim at the vernacular poem. For Jean, things can be known only through their opposites—orthodoxy through heresy, morality through pornography. Tempier's condemnation functions according to Jean's rule of opposites, even though its desired effect is to legislate the banishment of all that is contrary to orthodoxy. But what, after all, is the difference between Jean's fictional quotation of thoughts and ideas ascribed to others, and Tempier's condemnation (and delineation) of a sequence of propositions he has gathered from masters of theology at the university? Is the good bishop to be praised or blamed for presenting us with a list of objectionable ideas that we are then supposed to recant? Is he not, by condemning these ideas, also perpetuating them? Jean's fictional formulation of an irreducible intellectual heterodoxy successfully reveals the double edge of any effort aimed at the suppression of ideas based upon moral or other grounds: in order to condemn, one must, in some way, understand and even appreciate.

The combined scandalousness and fascination of Jean's poem results from his articulation of the limits of propriety. His principal tool in this endeavor is irony. Classical rhetoric defines irony as a particular subspecies of allegory, a trope that expresses one idea or opinion and means its opposite. The detection of irony within a speech or a written discourse is dependent upon factors of voice or of context. Jean de Meun has constructed his poem in such a way that every voice, even that of the narrator, lends itself to recontextualization and thus to interpretation in another, sometimes contrary, light. The ironic play of voices becomes, on occasion, quite complex. For example, the most outrageous (and most frequently criticized) instance of antifeminist haranguing occurs in the speech of the "jealous husband" that is used as an illustrative example by the allegorical character Friend (Ami), who is, in turn, interacting with the Lover inside the allegorical dream construct. No fewer than three distinct fictional frames separate him from the voice of the narrator. What justification, then, do we have for deeming Jean de Meun a misogynist? Moreover, the poem's refusal to adhere to any single viewpoint creates the uncanny impression of a transcendent authorial presence, intangible yet omniscient. This paradoxical authorial presence certainly proved instrumental in the development of the cult that later surrounded Jean de Meun.

Above and beyond attitudes toward love and sexuality, one leitmotif runs through the various discourses in *Le roman de la rose:* the troubled relationship between intention and linguistic expression. Not only are few ideas directly ascribable to the narrator, whose comments are mostly limited to the elaboration of the narrative events, but even the narrator's persona evolves in the course of the poem, as he gradually distances himself from the character of the Lover. Some of the work's most suggestive episodes, such as the elaborate retelling of the Pygmalion story near the end, which substitutes a myth of productive sexuality for one of sterile self-involvement as symbolized by Guillaume de Lorris' Narcissus, involve virtually no interpretative commentary.

A noteworthy exception to the narrator's inscrutability occurs somewhat past the middle of the poem, when he interrupts his story momentarily to defend himself against detractors, real or imagined. He asserts initially that he has discussed "bawdy or silly" topics only because his "subject matter demanded these things" (p. 258). Using a quotation from still another ancient author, Sallust, he transforms this statement into praise for the writer, who must struggle to approximate deeds with words, becoming a hero in his own right. This point gains in richness when considered alongside a passage some 8,000 lines before, the debate between Reason and the Lover over the relationship between words and things. Briefly, the Lover objects to Reason's use of an obscene word, "balls," which he considers inappropriate "in the mouth of a courteous girl." The verbal irony of the joke exploits in its own way the conceptual problem of dissociating language from its referent, while the situational irony that arises from the prudish Lover's inadvertent creation of an image of oral copulation (through words) successfully demonstrates the concomitant innocence and provocativeness of the verbal arts. Obscenity can be regarded as a spontaneous and irrepressible offshoot of language.

The narrator provides a further defense, one based upon the nature of poetic traditions. Specifically addressing possible objections to misogyny in the text, he states that writing everything down is essential to our instruction: "It is good to know everything" (p. 259). Moreover, since he is only repeating what the ancient authors said on these subjects, they are the ones to be reproached: "I do nothing but retell." Perhaps the most interesting narratorial defense addresses False Seeming, the religious hypocrite whose portrayal approaches, somewhat provocatively, a contemporary social "type," a member of one of the mendicant religious orders that had become a salient, and controversial, presence in 13th-century Paris. The denunciation of such hypocrisy is compared to the shooting of arrows, and "if it happens that any man is pleased to put himself in the way of the arrow and receive a shot . . . and then complains because I have wounded him, it is not my fault" (pp. 259–260). Culpability shifts from the writer to the reader, whose interpretative activity entails a risk, that of viewing in the mirror of literature what he does not wish to know about himself. In other words, by Jean de Meun's logic, he who criticizes or condemns is truly the most guilty. Throughout this discourse Jean is uncannily setting up a pattern for his poem's reception, including the controversies that will surround it.

Readers were undoubtedly fascinated by *Le roman de la rose,* at least in part because they could find anything they wanted within the poem's labyrinthine folds. Response to it appears to have been immediate, not just as a text to be studied or consulted, as one might an encyclopedia, but also as a model for a genre that was being revitalized, the moralizing or doctrinal allegory. As early as 1290 an otherwise unknown cleric, Gui de Mori, composed an edited, moralized version of the poem. In the 14th century "Master Jean de Meun" became a celebrity, garnering praise as a learned doctor, and his cult probably reached its culmination with Honoré Bouvet's allegory featuring Jean as a character in his own right, *L'apparition de maître Jean de Meun* (1398; *The Apparition of Master Jean de Meun*). The *Rose* itself spawned a rich allegorical progeny, from the erotic *Les échecs d'amour* (1370–1380; *The Chessgame of Love*), to the moralistic *Pèlerinage de la vie humaine* (1330; *Pilgrimage of Human Life*), to Philippe de Mézières's political *Songe du vieux pèlerin* (1389; *Dream of the Elderly Pilgrim*), to the anonymous social commentary *Renart le contrefait* (ca. 1320; *Renard the Hypocrite*).

The prolific 15th-century writer Christine de Pisan, objecting to Jean de Meun's ribaldry and, most adamantly, to his shabby treatment of women, sparked what has been called France's first literary debate (1401–02)—an epistolary exchange that engaged champions and opponents of the notorious *Rose* author. The dispute curiously ends up mirroring the romance's own debate structure. Even more interesting is the stance of Jean's principal defender, Pierre Col, who demonstrates his affinity with the master by turning to concerns of an epistemological nature. He summarily defends the content of the poem but then turns the tables on Jean's detractors by subtly impugning their piety, suggesting that even the intent of their letters might be turned to an opposite effect. After bemusedly considering and then dismissing possible reasons for their excessive dislike of *Le roman de la rose* (personal hatred for Jean de Meun, envy of his success, or simple ignorance), he arrives at a final, more cynical possibility: "Perhaps you merely pretend to blame the said book in order to exalt it, that is, by causing your hearers to read it. And you know well that he who reads it will find there much worthy teaching, the opposite of your criticism. And if this is your intent, you and the critics of the work should be held excused. For such purpose would be good, whatever the means" (*La Querelle*, p. 112). In an increasingly sophisticated literary climate, no verbal artifact can be considered safe.

Le roman de la rose provides, if not the first, certainly the most elaborate expression in medieval French literature of the power of the written word and the dangerous privilege constituted by the act of interpretation. The critical debates it has provoked from the 14th century to the present day attest to the centrality of these issues in our understanding of fiction. At a time when the French language was just beginning to gain acceptance as a functional and versatile written medium, Jean de Meun staked out, by means of a powerful formal strategy, a daring epistemological quest in a space that was relatively free of ideological censorship precisely because of the vernacular's marginal position in intellectual circles. In addition, he managed to transfer a sense of authority to his first readers, for whom predigested answers in a world overflowing with new information were becoming insufficient. He also perhaps taught his most important lesson for literary criticism of any period: Even if words can do harm, we all nonetheless have the power, the responsibility, to enter the fray.

Bibliography: Heather M. Arden, *The Romance of the Rose* (Boston: Twayne, 1987). D. F. Hult, *Self-Fulfilling Prophecies: Readership and Authority in the First Roman de la Rose* (Cambridge: Cambridge University Press, 1986). Ralph Lerner and Muhsin Mahdi with Ernest L. Fortin, eds., *Medieval Political Philosophy: A Sourcebook* (Ithaca: Cornell University Press, 1972). Maxwell Luria, *A Reader's Guide to the Roman de la Rose* (Hamden, Conn.: Archon, 1982). *La Querelle de la Rose: Letters and Documents*, trans. Joseph L. Baird and John R. Kane (Chapel Hill: University of North Carolina Press, 1978). *The Romance of the Rose by Guillaume de Lorris and Jean de Meun*, trans. Charles Dahlberg (Princeton: Princeton University Press, 1971).

David F. Hult

 1300?

The Passion of Christ Is Copied for the First Time
in the Vernacular and in a Dramatic Form

Medieval Vernacular Drama

The Passion of Christ is among the most prevalent biblical accounts in medieval literature. One of the earliest monuments of French literature is a Franco-

Provençal narrative known as the Clermont-Ferrand *Passion,* dating from the late 11th century. Its 129 quatrains narrate events in the life of Jesus from Palm Sunday to the Ascension. The Virgin Mary is already given considerable prominence as the Mater Dolorosa whose profound grief at the foot of the Cross is offset by her comprehension of the divine mystery of the Resurrection. Later French Passion narratives, such as the 12th-century *La Passion des jongleurs* (*The Minstrels' Passion*) or the 14th-century *Livre de la Passion* (*The Passion Book*), will continue to supplement the narrative tradition of the gospels with the lyric and affective experience of Mary.

Given the early appearance and subsequent persistence of this affectively humanized Passion in medieval vernacular narrative, it is surprising that the first known French dramatic work devoted to the Passion—*La Passion du Palatinus*—does not appear until around 1300. So named after the sole extant manuscript (Vatican Library, Palatinus Latinus 1969), this play lies near the chronological midpoint of the most literarily productive centuries of the French Middle Ages. By the time the *Palatinus* was composed, French literature had already passed through an initial, late 12th-century "classical" maturity, followed throughout the 13th by a rich and prolific phase of self-conscious, innovative reworking of earlier subjects. But the year 1300 is a relatively early one as regards vernacular drama. During the century and a half before the *Palatinus,* no single dramatic type had established itself as part of a sustained tradition. There survives only a small but important handful of earlier plays, frequently designated as such by the term *jeu* (play).

The earliest of these (between 1146 and 1174) is the *Ordo Representacionis Ade,* or *Le jeu d'Adam* (*The Play of Adam*), which inventively amplifies scenes from Genesis (the Fall, the murder of Abel), followed by a procession of prophets of Christ. The survival of two fragments of *La sainte Résurrection* (ca. 1175; *The Holy Resurrection*), both depicting episodes following the Crucifixion, suggests that vernacular dramatization of at least some events from the Passion had occurred well before 1300. During the 13th century, four plays—works from the prolific literary center of Arras, in Artois—disclose a trend toward more secular themes and a tendency to blend matters from a wide variety of literary traditions. Jean Bodel's *Le jeu de saint Nicolas* (ca. 1200; *The Play of Saint Nicholas*) combines epic conflict and hagiographic legend, perhaps to stimulate interest in the Fourth Crusade; and in the anonymous *Courtois d'Arras* (before 1228; *The Prodigal of Arras*), a prodigal son from rural Picardy wastes his substance in a seamy tavern. Two plays by Adam de la Halle round out this group: *Le jeu de la feuillée* (ca. 1276; *Adam's Farewell*) features urban— and urbane—satire involving a motley assortment of conventional literary figures as well as representatives of the local citizenry; the somewhat later *Jeu de Robin et Marion* (ca. 1285) dramatizes a lyric *pastourelle:* the conventional encounter between knight and shepherdess occurs in a rural setting of rustic games and dances. Of these four works by playwrights from Picardy only *Robin et Marion* does not feature a tavern as a locus of dramatic action. Treating a legend involving a demonic pact, *Le miracle de Théophile* (ca. 1265; *The Miracle of The-*

ophilus), by the Parisian poet Rutebeuf, is the first known miracle play depicting the Virgin as intercessor; it precedes by nearly a century a collection of some forty plays known as *Les miracles de Notre Dame* (14th century; *The Miracles of the Virgin*). Finally, a brief comic skit, *Le garçon et l'aveugle* (after 1266; *The Boy and the Blind Man*), depicting a sightless, worldly beggar cruelly deceived by a young scoundrel, foreshadows the myriad farces that proliferated near the end of the Middle Ages.

Whence among these earliest French plays a varied assortment of sacred and secular, serious and comic veins. The relative dearth of religious drama in the vernacular before the *Passion du Palatinus* has prompted some scholars to conclude that the French Passion play was a direct outgrowth of liturgical drama—the Latin music-drama of the medieval church. As early as the 9th century, brief verbal and melodic ornaments known as tropes or sequences began to be interpolated at specific points in the liturgy. It has been suggested that two of these, originally augmentations of the Mass at Easter and at Christmas, were elaborated over time into brief liturgical plays celebrating, respectively, the Resurrection and the Nativity. The supposed "evolution" of these plays, as of liturgical drama in general, raises a number of unresolved questions. The hypothesis that vernacular religious drama evolved in successive stages from liturgical drama has recently been cast into doubt by O. B. Hardison. For example, the *Jeu d'Adam*'s use of nine liturgical responses found in the Gregorian *Liber Responsalis,* or the *Jeu de saint Nicolas*'s adaptation of an earlier Latin play with liturgical features, does not suggest continuous, quasi-"organic" development from liturgical to French religious drama. Nor does the latter show any direct indebtedness to the far more modest and sober Latin Passion play that predates it by nearly two centuries. To the degree that early theories of the origins of medieval vernacular drama adhered to evolutionist doctrines, they obscured the extent to which religious plays in the vernacular rely on nondramatic elements, such as legend, folktale, apocryphal and hagiographic themes, and features from epic, romance, and lyric genres.

In this regard, the *Passion du Palatinus* is typical of the spirit of independence, even of antagonism, that marks the breach between liturgical and vernacular traditions. On the one hand, its narrative line follows the account of the Passion in the gospels from the Entry into Jerusalem to the moment of recognition when the three Marys, on their way to anoint the body of Jesus, discover the empty tomb and hear the angelic proclamation that the Savior is risen. In affective terms, the play traces the same progression from grief to recognition, and thence to rejoicing, found in many liturgical plays. On the other hand, the real vitality of the play stems from its heavy reliance on nonliturgical and nondramatic traditions. Its primary source is the narrative *Passion des jongleurs,* from which it derives, often verbatim, much of its popular flavor. In addition, the lengthy lyric lament of Mary and John, the tirades of Pilate and Herod, and the debates of the infernal characters are among the many elements that suggest a blending of the oral traditions of the jongleurs with rhetorical flourishes more typical of the schooled clerical writer. Above all, symbolic replication of the gospels in order to signify their sacred import has been supplanted by a far more worldly orientation, one suggestive of a popular culture combining a long-standing agrarian mentality with an awareness of developing patterns of urban organization.

Accordingly, the play lingers over, indeed savors, a host of largely unsavory details, most of which are nowhere to be found in either the gospels or the liturgy. The betrayal by Judas is of course indispensable to the minimal narrative of the Passion, but in this play Judas laments the "shameful waste" of an expensive balm with which Mary Magdalene anoints the feet of Jesus, then haggles with the Jews over the fact that only twenty-eight of the agreed-upon thirty pieces of silver have been paid. Near the end of the play the three Marys encounter a merchant of unguents—a self-styled "physician" from Salerno— who, in a monologue reminiscent of Rutebeuf's *Dit de l'herberie* (*In Praise of Elixirs*), extols at length the virtues of his various herbal remedies for the senile, the loveless and the lovelorn, the impotent, and even the dead! Throughout the central scenes of trial and crucifixion, torture and cruelty abound, as do the oaths and obscenities of the numerous accessories of evil. The futile beating inflicted upon a stoic Jesus in the presence of Pilate is followed by the equally grotesque labor of Haquin and Mossé as they build a cross and attach its victim. Their grim task is interrupted only by an errand to fetch three nails, obligingly forged by the smith's swarthy wife when her spouse's hands are suddenly paralyzed. At the upper level of the hierarchy, Caiaphas, on behalf of the Jews, denounces Jesus before Pilate, who defers to Herod, who in turn refers back to Pilate, who consults "all the masters of the law" before returning the matter to the instigators of the trial. Among the many other scenes of negotiation, Joseph of Arimathea requests Pilate's permission to inter the body, in a scene that expands upon the apocryphal Gospel of Nicodemus; Pilate also authorizes the Jews' hiring of four soldiers to guard the tomb, although they flee in terror as the stone is rolled aside.

It has been said that medieval comic drama—whose origins are also much debated—owes much to humorous interludes such as that of the spice merchant or the boastful soldiers. Along with humor and the grotesque goes an apparent fascination with the mechanisms of secular culture. In the *Palatinus* the Passion is negotiated, executed, and commemorated beyond the confines of the sanctuary, within the economic sphere of the marketplace, and it is carried out by artisans in the service of a political hierarchy whose elaborate protocol is enacted in minute detail.

In this new abundance of transactional realism, there is scant indebtedness to the signifying practices of liturgical drama, in which the pure redundance of ritual yields only slightly to a rudimentary, altar-centered representational space. Liturgical symbolism is restricted to a monovalent and transcendental plane, to which time is assimilated *in illo tempore*. By contrast, the space-time of the *Palatinus* oscillates between the ritually redundant course of events in salvation history, where absolute predictability obtains, and ceaseless deferral of this christological movement through time. The invariant sequence—Last Supper, Mount of Olives, Trial, Crucifixion, Resurrection—remains intact, but the play defies any ritually conditioned expectation of this progression by depicting nonessential events that connote the eschatological intensification of evil and prolong the uncertainty that good will ultimately triumph. This temporalization of dramatic action, characterized by expansion of the trivial at the expense of the ritually significant, has the effect of reintroducing strangeness into a sacred story whose familiarity had emptied it of all suspense. Thus, whereas liturgical drama iterates the ritually knowable so as to celebrate and to console by evoking the mythic time of origins, the vernacular Passion defamiliarizes the ritually known by introducing mundane and anecdotal elements that renew its contemporaneity and popular appeal. In consequence, the public is confronted by an image of itself that is both specular and spectacular. In the *Mystère de la Passion* (after 1450; *The Mystery of the Passion*), Arnoul Gréban will in fact comment at length on the Passion as a "mirror" for the public.

Along with this tendency to solicit the public's identification with the scene of the Passion, the *Palatinus* ritualizes secular time by having the actors describe, in a plethora of present and future tenses, the gestures being enacted. As holy scripture is transposed to mimetic script, the gestures of the vicious no less than those of the celebrants serve to coordinate the verbal and the representational planes. In addition, thanks to the staging, in which all the loci of action are represented simultaneously as individual "mansions," the cosmos itself is secularized. The tongues of men and of angels are identical. The denizens of hell resemble those of urban lowlife. In a quasi-antiphonal *altercatio* Sathanas (Satan) boasts of having corrupted Judas and foretells the imminent triumph of vice; Enfers, hell's sentry, warns that Jesus is coming and counsels flight, whereupon Sathanas sets out for Lombardy.

Despite the flagrantly transgressive distortions of the canonical Passion, representational innovations never fully subvert a sense of theological integrity. Various characters help to condition the audience's assent to the reality of the transcendental. The lamentations of Mary and John at midpoint elicit spiritual understanding as well as pathos; the miracle of the blind Longinus, healed by the sacred blood on the lance, facilitates belief in the efficacy of divine power. Early on, the ingenuously human qualities of Mary Magdalene are set in opposition to the cunning evil of Judas, and at the very end it is she who assumes the homiletic role of preacher as she admonishes the audience to share in her prayer for righteousness and redemption.

The drama's aesthetic distance is, thus dissolved as the public is enabled to find in the represented events of salvation history the expression of profoundly human concerns similar to its own. This helps to explain why these increasingly worldly spectacles enjoyed widespread popularity in late medieval Europe. As plagues and warfare ravaged the populace in successive waves, the Passion play served as a stabilizing influence. It nurtured a vivid collective memory of universal history, from Creation to Last Judgment, against the background of which the immediate terrors and tribulations of secular society could seem less catastrophic. The secularized Passion play provided a potential space for depicting worldly evil in its countless guises while demonstrating the viability of the Christian paradigm as a means of conquering it. Whence a psychically cathartic mechanism, one that helped to allay social anxieties by dramatically reawakening them and working them through within the context of a positive metaphysical design.

By later standards, the *Palatinus* is a relatively short text; it consists of only 1,996 lines, most of them octosyllabic couplets, with occasional metric variation to achieve lyric effects. Over the two ensuing centuries, the vernacular Passion play will burst at the seams. The mid-14th-century Sainte-Geneviève *Passion* exceeds 4,000 octosyllables; the Passion plays of Semur and Arras, both from the early 15th century, exceed 9,000 and 25,000 verses, respectively. The Semur *Passion* is divided into two *journées*, or playing "days." It includes numerous scenes ranging from the Creation to the public life of Jesus, as does a collection of processional plays from Lille. *La Passion d'Arras*, by Eustache Mercadé, depicts, in four *journées*, only the life of Jesus, from birth to Ascension. So does Arnoul Gréban's better-known *Mystère de la Passion*, extant in many manuscripts. Gréban's massive play is notable for its aesthetic charm and grace as well as for its wide range of both learned and popular sources. It was presented often both in Paris and in the provinces, and was soon appropriated and expanded by Jean Michel. Several other sizable plays devoted to religious themes attest to the late medieval popularity of religious spectacle, as do the records of many artisanal groups and brotherhoods, or *confréries*, which provided the institutional framework for these ambitious productions. In 1548 the Parlement of Paris officially forbade the playing of *mystères sacrés*. Yet the mass appeal of the Passion persisted into the early 17th century.

Bibliography: Maurice Accarie, *Le théâtre sacré de la fin du moyen âge: Etude sur le sens moral de la Passion de Jean Michel* (Geneva: Droz, 1979). Richard Axton and John Stevens, eds., *Medieval French Plays* (Oxford: Clarendon Press, 1971) (contains Adam de la Halle's *Adam's Farewell* and *The Play of Robin and Marion*, Jean Bodel's *The Play of Saint Nicholas*, Rutebeuf's *The Miracle of Theophilus*, and the anonymous *The Prodigal of Arras*, *The Boy and the Blind Man*, *The Play of Adam*, and *The Holy Resurrection*). J.-P. Bordier, "Lectures du Palatinus," *Le moyen âge*, 80 (1974), 429–482. Grace Frank, *The Medieval French Drama* (Oxford: Clarendon Press, 1954). O. B. Hardison, Jr., *Christian Rite and Christian Drama in the Middle Ages: Essays in the Origin and Early History of Modern Drama* (Baltimore: Johns Hopkins Press, 1965). *La Passion du Palatinus*, ed. Grace Frank (Paris: Champion, 1930). Sandro Sticca, *The Latin Passion Play: Its Origins and Development* (Albany: SUNY Press, 1970). Rainer Warning, "On the Alterity of Medieval Religious Drama," *New Literary History*, 10 (1979), 265–292. Karl Young, *The Drama of the Medieval Church* (Oxford: Clarendon Press, 1933).

Donald Maddox

ᥱᢈᢙ 1342?

Guillaume de Machaut Writes His *Remède de fortune*

Lyricism in the Age of Allegory

Guillaume de Machaut (ca. 1300–1377) is a pivotal figure in the development of the late medieval lyric in France: at once "the last of the trouvères" and the first systematic, authoritative practitioner of the *formes fixes* (fixed forms) that were to dominate French lyric poetry until the time of François Villon. His *Remède de fortune* (ca. 1342; *Fortune's Cure*) played a key role in the redefinition of the lyric effected by his overall literary production, which establishes a new conception of authorial identity—nothing less than the first adumbration of such fundamental modern literary notions as "author," "poet," and "book." Self-consciously expanding the parameters of the earlier vernacular literary tradition in France, Machaut conjoined the clerkly narrator figure of Old French hagiography and romance, the first-person voice of medieval courtly love lyric (the *grand chant courtois*), and a new conception of the professional artist—in part a development of 13th-century scribal activity in "editing" and organizing codices. This extraordinary expansion of the range of the lyric-based, first-person poetic voice allowed for great generic and linguistic diversity while providing a unifying element.

Machaut's career, an epitome of 14th-century French cultural history, formed also an essential component of the new poetic identity that Machaut assumed in his almost exclusively first-person literary work. He was educated as a cleric, but his patrons and protectors belonged to the highest ranks of contemporary courtly society. Born in Champagne, Machaut had by 1323 entered the service of Jean de Luxembourg, king of Bohemia, one of the most admired rulers of his age, a model of both *chevalerie* and *courtoisie.* In his capacity as "clerk, secretary, and companion," Machaut accompanied his royal master on campaigns in Silesia, Poland, and Lithuania in the 1320s and 1330s. By 1340 he was installed as canon in Reims, although he continued in Jean's service until the latter's death in 1346 at the battle of Crécy. From 1359 on Machaut worked for the French royal family, especially Charles of Normandy (the future Charles V) and Jean de Berry, both of whom were among his major patrons during the final decades of his life. In 1371 both Amadeus VI of Savoy and Jean de Berry purchased luxury manuscripts of Machaut's works, probably completed under the poet's supervision. He died at the height of his fame.

Machaut's enormous artistic output encompassed narrative verse, lyric verse, and music. The *Remède* combines all three in a single, coherent work (lavishly illuminated in Bibliothèque Nationale Ms. fr. 1584 and 1586) and thus serves as an epitome of his entire artistic achievement. Formally speaking, the *Remède* belongs to the late medieval hybrid genre known as the *dit* (story). Presented simultaneously as an *ars amandi* (guide for lovers) and an *ars poetica* (poetic handbook), this first-person narrative poem contains a series of seven intercalated lyric pieces set to music, one superlative example of each of the major "fixed-forms" of the 14th century, arranged in order of decreasing difficulty. The *Remède's* explicit treatment of the process of lyric composition transforms the way the relationship between love, inspiration, and song was conceived: in the course of the *dit* the first-person voice of the narrator-protagonist is increasingly differentiated from that of Machaut the author figure.

The story line of the *Remède* is relatively simple: the first-person narrator-protagonist recounts the birth and evolution of his love for an unnamed lady. In a basic tripartite structure, two narrative segments set in the courtly world frame a scene of isolation and withdrawal. After a brief prologue, which stresses the didactic nature of the work to follow, the narrator recounts the first stage of his love, a period in which he serves his lady long and well but secretly, since he fears her presence. This courtly love service is synonymous with poetic activity, for a crucial aspect of the narrator's identity as lover is his self-presentation as love poet. His experience of love at once generates and authenticates song, which reciprocally validates the love experience. "Inspiration" transforms the love experience into lyric poetry. Almost immediately after the narrator's self-presentation as lyric poet, the *lai* "Qui n'auroit autre déport" ("He who would have no other pleasure"; lines 431–680) describes the narrator-protagonist's condition at the time of writing: although he considers being in love (and writing love poetry) to be its own reward, he also wants his lady to know of his love, but for fear of a possible refusal he dares not declare his feelings to her. The lyric advances the narrative in which it is embedded: the lady discovers the *lai,* has the lover read it to her, then asks him who wrote it. Unable either to admit that it is his (since this would involve confessing his love) or to lie to his lady, the abashed and fearful lover is reduced to silence. Without taking proper leave he flees and wanders aimlessly until he arrives at the Park of Hedin, the site of the second and longest narrative segment.

Within this delightful enclosed garden, after the narrator-protagonist voices an extended *complainte* against Amour and Fortune, a mysterious but authoritative lady appears, offering consolation. Modeled on Boethius' Lady Philosophy, Machaut's Lady Espérance (Hope) explains the true nature of Love and Fortune, combining a quasi-philosophical narrative exposition with a *chanson royale* (a lyric poem set to music), and convinces the lover that his situation is in fact very positive. Having fully educated the narrator-protagonist on the fundamental importance of hope in love, Espérance ends her lesson with a second song, a *balladelle.* The now-joyful lover sings a ballade in response to celebrate his newfound knowledge as he leaves the confines of the park.

The third and final segment of the *Remède,* a palinode to the first, recounts the lover's ostensible success with his lady once he has rejoined courtly society. His performance of a virelay at her request leads to the declaration of love he was earlier incapable of making. He celebrates her acceptance of his suit by singing a rondeau, the last of the *Remède's* intercalated lyrics, which coincides with the apex of the narrator-protagonist's amatory success within the story line.

The *dit*'s final episode, however, casts this success into doubt. The lover falls into painful uncertainty and "great melancholy" after his lady greets him coldly and ignores him (line 4161). When he demands that she tell him outright if she has ceased to love him, she explains that her previous coldness was a ruse to deceive *médisants* (slanderers). Even though the lover intensely desires to believe his lady, the episode closes ambiguously. He returns to the same verbal attitude toward her as initially, but with one difference: the first-person narrator *qua* lover now possesses hope. The reality of the love experience within the story is thus put into question. If his status as lover remains doubtful, however, his status as poet does not: the *dit* has been written, and this fact is repeatedly emphasized in the epilogue. In sharp contrast to the uncertainties of the narrator-protagonist's final status as a lover stands the "fact" that the poet-author's service to Amour has produced the *Remède de fortune*.

The effect of such an ending is to emphasize implicitly the relationship between the author and his text rather than that between the protagonist and his love experience. In this context the full significance of the didactic prologue becomes evident: the intercalated lyrics of the *Remède* are made to function collectively as a poetic handbook. Presenting each of the contemporary major lyric forms (which after Machaut became fixed for at least three generations) as a poetic model to be imitated, the *Remède de fortune* is an implicit *ars poetica*. Moreover, an important correspondence emerges between the *dit*'s story line and its didactic dimension: just as—at the level of plot—the protagonist fails as lover whereas the author succeeds as poet, so the *Remède de fortune* fails as *ars amandi* but succeeds as *ars poetica*.

As an *ars poetica*, the *Remède*'s originality derives from both the author's elaborate and authoritative self-presentation and his radical differentiation from the first-person narrator-protagonist, whose identity he subsumes. Machaut accomplishes this result by self-consciously transforming the Old French narrative poem with intercalated lyrics, a subgenre extending back to Jean Renart's *Le roman de la rose* (ca. 1225; *The Romance of the Rose,* also called *Le roman de Guillaume de Dole*), and elaborating at the same time Nicole de Margival's embryonic use in *Dit de la panthère d'amour* (ca. 1310; *Story of the Panther of Love*) of intercalated lyrics as poetic exempla. Because the poet-author's service to love is above all poetic service, the *Remède de fortune* presents Machaut as an *exemplum poetae,* a model to be imitated. But the authority that implicitly guarantees this presentation is in the broadest sense lyric-based. It resides nowhere else than in the identity of the poet-author himself.

Later, in both the *Jugement du roi de Navarre* (1349; *The King of Navarre's Judgment*) and *Le livre du vrai dit* (ca. 1365; *The Book of the True Story*), Machaut consistently links the activity of composing poetry and music with the transcription and circulation of manuscripts and the business of patronage. In the *Vrai dit* Machaut is explicitly concerned with supervising the arrangement and copying of editions of his collected works. The poet-author no longer simply composes verses, songs, or *dits* but also concerns himself with the composition of a codex. By depicting himself as supervising the transcription and arrangement of his own complete works, Machaut raises the codex to the level of literary artifact and moves one step beyond the accomplishments of 13th-century scribes (who in the ordering of codices often exercised considerable editorial license).

This level of authorial involvement is confirmed by manuscript evidence. Each of the major manuscripts reveals an explicit concern with the arrangement and ordering of the whole, which was almost certainly the result of Machaut's personal supervision. Thus Bibliothèque Nationale Ms. fr. 1584 opens with the superscription "Here is the order that G. de Machaut wants his book to have." It is also clear that Machaut viewed his various works as forming a coherent oeuvre: near the end of his life, he wrote his *Prologue* (ca. 1370) to stand at the beginning of his collected, complete works. The *Prologue* not only serves as a formal unifying element; it also explicitly establishes the poetic voice that will be speaking in all the works that follow. A carefully constructed poetic persona— a complex first-person poet-narrator—unifies the corpus. The clerk, the lover, and the poetic craftsman are conflated into a single but multifaceted poetic voice. This new poet-author figure is acutely aware of the dignity of his calling, highly conscious of his technical expertise, and proud of the breadth and diversity of his artistic production. Machaut's poet figure is no longer bound by the lyric convention that requires him to sing only of his own love experience.

Machaut's creation of a new kind of authorial identity led to his being the first French vernacular writer to be termed a *poète,* a term previously reserved for the classical Latin *auctores.* The earliest occurrences are in two ballades written by Eustache Deschamps (1346–1406), Machaut's self-described "disciple," to commemorate his master's death. In the first, Deschamps speaks of Machaut as "the flower of all flowers, noble poet [*poète*] and renowned maker [*faiseur*], truer remedy of Love than Ovid" (no. 447). Deschamps seems to feel that the term *poète* requires a gloss, *faiseur,* a term already used to designate vernacular poets. In "Sur la mort de Guillaume de Machaut" (1377; "On the Death of Guillaume de Machaut"), Deschamps uses the term in a context that links the classical poetic inspiration of the *auctores* with the contemporary vernacular master: "It is fitting that Circe's fountain and the spring of Helicon, of which you were the stream and the canal, and at which poets study, be silent—which makes me very sad" (no. 124). The idea of *auctor* is thus built into, fused with, the idea of *poète* in its expanded sense.

The *ars poetica* that was (perhaps necessarily) implicit in Machaut's *Remède* is developed in Deschamps's *Art de dicter* (1392; *The Art of Versifying*), which— after the treatise on rhetoric contained in Brunetto Latini's *Le livre du trésor* (1267; *The Book of Treasure*)—is the first French vernacular poetic treatise written in expository, didactic prose. Brief descriptive definitions of the major fixed forms are followed by illustrative examples. Machaut's discourse (deriving from his identity as *poète*) no longer seems to be sufficient for writing "about" poetry. In addition, Deschamps redefines vernacular lyric by explicitly separating poetry from music: his model lyric pieces are not sung. Machaut's status as *exemplum poetae* in the *Remède,* however, authorizes a similar stance by his disciple: all the exemplary fixed-form lyrics in the *Art de dicter* are Deschamps's own (with the significant exception of certain rondeaux taken from Machaut).

Beginning with Deschamps's *Art de dicter,* Machaut's innovative concept of poetic identity (and in particular the *Remède*) both inspired and authorized subsequent developments in medieval French rhetorical and poetic theory. Similarly, the new poet figure he created significantly influenced French literary practice. Deschamps simultaneously extended and transformed the achievement of his acknowledged master. In addition to Machaut's classic courtly discourse, Deschamps makes extensive use of two other registers, always in a lyric context: the moralizing, didactic register of the sermon and the humorous, "realistic" register of the satire. Although Deschamps's global poetic "I," like Machaut's, unifies his numerous and varied literary works, it does so in a different way. The sense of ordered progression found in Machaut's great manuscripts is absent. The Bibliothèque Nationale Ms. fr. 840, which contains his collected works (82,000 lines), includes 1,500 ballades, rondeaux, virelays, and *chansons royales* grouped with minimal concern for thematic coherence. As a result, the smallest formal units are invested with great importance. But this fragmentation itself serves in part to define the poetic identity of a particular individual whose oeuvre is uniquely his own.

Jean Froissart (1333?–1405?) further expanded the possibilities inherent in Machaut's strengthened lyric "I." First, he carefully supervised the arrangement of his poetic works, both lyric and narrative, in at least two surviving manuscripts (Bibliothèque Nationale Mss. fr. 830 and 831). According to Daniel Poirion, these two collections present Froissart's amorous and didactic poems "according to a logical and formal order, analogous to that of Machaut" (*Le poète et le prince,* p. 206).

The great lyric poets of the 15th century—Christine de Pisan (1363?–1431), Alain Chartier (ca. 1385–ca. 1435), and Charles d'Orléans (1394–1465)—continued to build on and to modify Machaut's achievement in several important ways. First, they cultivated the lyric *formes fixes* that he had definitively and systematically authorized in the *Remède de fortune:* the *lai,* the *chanson royale,* the ballade, the virelay, the rondeau. Like Deschamps and Froissart, however, they did not compose musical settings for their lyric poems. In this respect Machaut may be seen as the culmination of the earlier lyric tradition of the trouvères: he was the last great French lyric poet to set his own words to music. Paradoxically, Machaut's greatly strengthened lyric "I" resulted in the perception that music was no longer an essential component of lyric poetry. The culmination of this new lyricism was *Le testament* (wr. ca. 1461, pub. 1489; also called *Grand testament* [*The Testament*]) of François Villon, the supreme masterpiece of 15th-century French poetry and the last great example of the first-person *dit.*

See also 1127, 1267, 1460, 1493.

Bibliography: Kevin Brownlee, *Poetic Identity in Guillaume de Machaut* (Madison: University of Wisconsin Press, 1984). William Calin, *A Poet at the Fountain: Essays on the*

Narrative Verse of Guillaume de Machaut (Lexington: University of Kentucky Press, 1974). Jacqueline Cerquiglini, *"Un engin si soutil": Guillaume de Machaut et l'écriture au XIVe siècle* (Paris: Champion, 1985). Eustache Deschamps, *Oeuvres complètes de Eustache Deschamps,* ed. Marquis Queux de Saint-Hilaire and Gaston Raynaud, 10 vols. (Paris: Société des Anciens Textes Français, 1878–1901). Guillaume de Machaut, *Oeuvres de Guillaume de Machaut,* ed. Ernest Hoepffner, 3 vols. (Paris: Société des Anciens Textes Français, 1908–1921). Machaut, *"Le jugement dou roy de Behaigne" and "Remède de fortune,"* ed. and trans. James I. Wimsatt and William W. Kibler, music ed. Rebecca A. Baltzer (Athens: University of Georgia Press, 1988). Daniel Poirion, *Le poète et le prince: L'évolution du lyrisme courtois de Guillaume de Machaut à Charles d'Orléans* (Paris: Presses Universitaires de France, 1965).

Kevin Brownlee

✐ 1401, *St. Valentine's Day*
The Charter of La Cour Amoureuse Is Read Aloud in the Hôtel d'Artois

Trials of Eros

On 6 January 1400 (Epiphany) according to the old calendar, a number of great lords and poets assembled in the hôtel of the duke of Burgundy and founded La Cour Amoureuse, a literary and legal association dedicated to honoring women and encouraging poetic creation. This meeting produced a document known as the charter of the Love Court, which was "published"—that is, was "read in public"—on St. Valentine's Day of the same year (for us, 1401). And although there is a good deal of discussion about what may have preceded the drafting of this document (one later copy of which is preserved in Bibliothèque Nationale Ms. fr. 5233) and what the function of the Love Court actually might have been, the charter asserts that the Love Court was created "to pass the time more graciously" in the midst of an epidemic of the plague (*La cour amoureuse,* p. 36). Thus it recalls Boccaccio's *Decameron* (1353), whose storytellers, under similar circumstances (the plague of 1348), sought "pleasing pastimes," as is said at the opening of the collection. Dedicated to two virtues, humility and loyalty, "in honor, praise, recommendation, and service of all ladies and damsels," the Love Court was to hold "a joyous literary festival [*puy d'amour*]" on the first Sunday of each month and on other dates chosen for their symbolic value, such as St. Valentine's Day, a day in May, or one of the five festivals of the Virgin (pp. 36, 39, 40). Its activities included the composition of ballads on a given refrain and poems in honor of the Virgin, dinners, and masses as well as debates and decisions on questions of love, which hark back to those contained in book 2 of Andreas Capellanus' *De Amore* (ca. 1185; *The Art of Courtly Love*) or even to the debate poems—the *jeux-partis* and *tensos*—of the troubadours. The purpose of the Love Court was therefore at once literary and social—to produce poetry and games, but also to regulate courtly behavior in a playful manner. Its members were the legislators and arbiters of social conduct.

The historical importance of the Love Court's charter lies not only in the fact that it contains over 600 names, including those of some of the most powerful figures in France at the time, but also in the fact that it constitutes a virtual mirror of the estates of late medieval society, uniting as it does members of the upper and lower nobility with those of an increasingly powerful bourgeoisie, secular leaders with clergy, and, even within the clergy, bishops with simple priests. Undoubtedly inspired by the proliferation of chivalric orders in the 14th and 15th centuries, the Love Court combined the nobility of knighthood with the more bourgeois institution of the guild or literary *puy,* a word which originally meant "stage" and which referred to the literary circles—poetic clubs, self-help, and perhaps even burial societies—organized in northern France from the 13th century on.

Anticipating a *noblesse de robe* (a nonwarring nobility), the Love Court contained all the offices or functions of a royal court. Thus Pierre de Hauteville (1376–1448), a protégé of the duke of Burgundy and the drafter of the charter, was declared "prince." Charles VI, king of France; Philip the Bold, duke of Burgundy; and Louis, duke of Bourbon, were named sovereign conservators. Eleven lesser conservators, like a royal council, functioned as advisers. The conservators were in turn assisted by 24 ministers of the Love Court and 121 high church officials and great lords. To maintain the accounts—both economic and poetic—of the Love Court, 9 auditors were conscripted from the king's legal and financial services. Also appointed were 63 knights of honor, 24 knight treasurers, 8 keepers of love records and registers, 201 squires of love, 58 masters of requests, 32 recording secretaries, 8 alternates to the attorney general, 4 concierges of the gardens and orchards of love, 2 master gamekeepers, and 19 lesser hunters (*veneurs*) of the Love Court.

The double nature of the Love Court—at once poetic and legal, both playful and serious—as well as its mixed social composition no doubt reflects the ambiguous situation of France's aristocracy. In the midst of the Hundred Years' War royalty found itself less and less capable of controlling nobles, who themselves were growing increasingly alienated from the principles and practices of rule by force by which they had traditionally dominated their economic and military dependents. Aristocracy's hereditary function of rule by force had been superseded by rule according to the chivalric values of prestige and honor. At the same time, great feudal princes, who, as Daniel Poirion has shown, were increasingly given to sporting versions of traditional warlike practices, came to be seen as corrupt (*Le poète et le prince,* p. 33). Nobles were accused of cowardice, their tournaments of decadence, the most powerful among them of cupidity. From this perspective, then, the Love Court can be seen as an attempt to maintain values that were in fact on the decline, to construct an edifice beyond what seemed the inevitable collapse of the feudal aristocratic world. The search for order and probity was undoubtedly one of the reasons for the almost pathological scrupulousness with which the Love Court was both established and maintained. The charter itself simultaneously exalts the old noble values of joyous and prodigal expenditure and expresses the newer bourgeois materialist mentality in its detailed reckoning of the weight of the silver crowns to be offered to the victors of literary competitions, in the precision with which it specifies the salaries of the copyists who will record the ballads, and in its calculation even of who will pay for paper.

The Love Court's charter conceived of its members' songs and poetry as archives: "the record of arms, the papers of ballads, and other acts of rhetoric will be protected as soon as written, to be shown in time to come when it pleases those who will request and value it" (*La cour amoureuse,* p. 38). The poetic Love Court was, moreover, a meritocracy, or rather, an elite group accessible through nobility of heart and manners and in which the service of love, and not birth alone, would define social status. The names of members, stated the charter, would be written in the Love Court's register according to the function of its members, "without the slightest regard to more ancient nobility, authority, valor, renown, present power, or wealth" (pp. 38–39). Literary productions were to be judged according to their moral integrity, "without regard to high princely or noble rank" (p. 37), and also according to their rhetorical quality: exactitude of rhyme and meter, lack of redundancy. Love cases were to be addressed to the court in writing. Plaintiff and defendant were each to choose a color of ink (except black) and to use only that color. In this extremely specific material form the questions would then be submitted to the judges, who would render their sentences on St. Valentine's Day. Finally, if anyone should compose or have composed defamatory libels against present or past ladies, "his name and surname will remain written on his escutcheon, painted in the color of ashes, so that the glory of his renown will appear to the onlookers as tainted and generally accursed in all lands" (p. 42).

Despite the charter's prescribed ideal of a nobility of merit or soul, the Love Court's extensive internal hierarchy stratified princes, ministers, judges, lords, treasurers, gardeners, and scribes. Moreover, owing to the fact that its chief patron was Philip, duke of Burgundy, its membership was drawn exclusively from the Burgundian party: the political rivalries and divisions afflicting France at the turn of the 15th century promoted even literary factionalism. Thus in 1402 Christine de Pisan founded a rival amorous order for the benefit of the duke of Orléans, the Order of the Rose. The ideals of both orders were similar. Christine's goddess of loyalty, for example, claimed not "to recognize the scoundrel by base degree, but by lowly heart" ("Dit de la rose" {"Story of the Rose"}, lines 338–339). Their members, however, were drawn from opposing political camps.

These rival poetic courts are practically synonymous with the first literary quarrel of French literary history, a dispute that pitted the detractors of Jean de Meun against his defenders, feminists against antifeminists, over the question of how to interpret the second half of *Le roman de la rose* (ca. 1275; *The Romance of the Rose*). Certain members of the Love Court—Gontier Col, "notary and secretary to the king"; his brother Pierre Col, "canon of Paris and of Tournay"; and Jean de Montreuil, "provost of Saint-Pierre de Lille"—took Jean de Meun's side against women, which opposed them to Christine. The debate was symptomatic of late medieval discussions of literature, woman, and love in that it centered on the issue of fidelity in love, and thus of loyalty in general. The knight-poet Jean le Sénéchal, for example, asks repeatedly in *Les cent ballades* (1389; *The Hundred Ballads*) if "it is best in love to be loyal or not" (p. 195). Jean de Berry, a later member of the Love Court, declares in the refrain of his ballad: "One must say the one and do the other" (ibid., pp. 213–214). To the extent to which Jean expresses a heightened consciousness of the difference between the ideology of the Love Court and what is more a seduction than love, his cynicism underscores the degree to which this "game of love" contrasts with the ideal of the troubadours and trouvères, of the first romancers, and even of the theoretician of courtly love Andreas Capellanus. It reflects his awareness of belonging to a second generation of those writing about love, of being at a remove from the pretense of actually experiencing love as other than pretense. They were, in short, keenly aware of love as representation within the public space of the court. Love's theater is no longer the ladies' chamber, but the gallery, where it matters less whether one loves than what one says about loving. Christine de Pisan is quite conscious of this literary, fictive, and self-defining dimension. In *Le débat de deux amants* (1400; *The Debate of Two Lovers*), for example, she suggests that perhaps "once upon a time," "in bygone times," there had been true lovers who died of love for their ladies; but that is no longer the case today, nor was it even the case yesterday—which is to say, a hundred years before. Lovers reproduce literary practices. Their griefs are prescribed in romances (Christine cites *Le roman de la rose*) "and properly described in long prose" (lines 959–960).

The Love Court and Christine de Pisan's Order of the Rose were only two among the many *puys* of the 15th century. And the proliferation of such literary orders, themselves modeled on the orders of chivalry, was accompanied by a proliferation of parodies, such as Eustache Deschamps's "D'un beau dit de ceux qui controuvent nouvelles bourdes et mensonges" (1401; "A Lovely Tale of Those Who Imagine New Stupidities and Lies")—which tells of the creation of a parlement at Epernay for May festivals—and "Pour compte de ses bourdes rendre" ("To Account for One's Own Stupidities"). Even at the inception of the Love Court, the values it defended were undermined by derision. Their collapse can be seen in the contrast between Andreas Capellanus' proclamation that "any woman who wants to have the praises of the world must indulge in love" (*Art of Courtly Love*, p. 172) and Alain Chartier's *La belle dame sans merci* (1424), whose steadfast heroine not only refuses to love but also refuses even the homage of love. Chartier's poem provoked numerous indignant responses, many of them composed at the Tournai residence of Pierre de Hauteville. The game of courtly love was no longer playable according to the old rules, or playable at all. Antoine de La Sale's *Histoire du petit Jehan de Saintré* (ca. 1456; *History of the Little Jehan from Saintré*), also influenced by the Burgundian court, is the death certificate of aristocracy's traditional mode of courteous loving. In this work the Dame des Belles Cousines, who betrays the love of a young knight with a fat abbot who derides arms, embodies the impossibility of idealism where the passions are concerned. The Love Court's charter stands, then, as the last testament of the courtly myth.

By stressing ritual, the Love Court tried to maintain a doctrinal and social cohesion besieged on all sides by competing ideological and political currents. Nonetheless, to have attempted to slow the course of history by equating as it did life and art, by giving, in the phrase of Johan Huizinga, "a style to love," remains the hallmark of an epoch that struggled to write itself in order to survive.

See also 1225, 1277.

Bibliography: Andreas Capellanus, *The Art of Courtly Love,* trans. John Jay Parry (New York: Frederick Ungar, 1959). Carla Bozzolo and Hélène Loyau, eds., *La cour amoureuse dite de Charles VI,* vol. 1 (Paris: Léopard d'Or, 1982). Christine de Pisan, *Oeuvres poétiques,* ed. Maurice Roy, vol. 2 (Paris: Firmin-Didot, 1891). Eustache Deschamps, *Oeuvres complètes d'Eustache Deschamps,* ed. Gaston Raynaud, vol. 7 (Paris: Firmin-Didot, 1891). Johan Huizinga, *The Waning of the Middle Ages: A Study of the Forms of Life, Thought, and Art in France and the Netherlands in the XIVth and XVth Centuries,* trans. Frederick Hopman (1924; reprint, Garden City, N.Y.: Doubleday, 1954). Jean le Sénéchal et al., *Les cent ballades,* ed. Gaston Raynaud (Paris: Firmin-Didot, 1905). Arthur Piaget, "La cour amoureuse dite de Charles VI," *Romania,* 20 (1891), 417–454. Daniel Poirion, *Le poète et le prince: L'évolution du lyrisme courtois de Guillaume de Machaut à Charles d'Orléans* (Paris: Presses Universitaires de France, 1965).

Jacqueline Cerquiglini

ᘓᕲ 1456

François Villon Dates *Le lais*

"I the Scholar François Villon"

François Villon is one of the most famous poets of medieval literature, yet his poems lack the chivalric, courtly, moral, or religious emphases characteristic of most medieval lyric. They present neither a heroic figure from an exemplary past nor a timeless song of intimate desire, but the inner reflections of a marginal man at grips with the harsh present of an urban world. The body of works attributed to Villon is slim: sixteen short poems, mostly in the form of ballades, the conventional 14th- and 15th-century French lyric with three stanzas, envoi, and refrain; *Le lais* or *Petit testament* (wr. ca. 1456, pub. 1489; *The Legacy*), a 320-line mock legacy written in octosyllabic eight-line stanzas or *huitains;* and *Le testament,* also called *Grand testament* (wr. ca. 1461, pub. 1489; *The Testament*), a 2,023-line burlesque bequest in *huitains* among which are inserted sixteen ballades and three rondeaux.

Villon's few works were printed early and often, his popularity fed by comic stories and ballades composed in criminals' slang that portrayed him as a rascal hero. After a long eclipse by classicism, Villon's poems—and his legend—have been recovered in the 19th and 20th centuries not only through numerous editions, translations, imitations, and critical studies of his poetry, but also by an extraordinary number of plays, novels, and films representing the legendary character "Villon." Moreover, as archival research established the existence of

1. Woodcut from *Le grand testament Villon et le petit* (Paris: Pierre Levet, 1489). (Courtesy of the Bibliothèque Nationale, Paris.)

many named in *Le lais* and *Le testament,* critics sought to explain these allusions through biographical interpretation. Armed with the conviction that literary creation is grounded in and authenticated by an author's personal experience, they built biographies on the similarity in age, status, and experience between the speaker in the poems (characterized as a student, a lover, and a criminal recently released from prison) and documents showing the academic, police, and literary record of Master François de Montcorbier, also known as François Villon: Bachelor and Master of Arts (1448 and 1452), pardoned for murder (1456), guilty of burglary and theft (1456), condemned to hanging for participation in a street ruckus, then banished from Paris (1463). Finally the presence of three of his short poems, copied by the poet himself in the private album of Charles d'Orléans (1394–1465) (Bibliothèque Nationale Ms. fr. 25458), links Villon to the literary milieu of the court of Blois.

These records, coupled with the wrenching personal perspective of Villon's poetry and its many mentions of contemporary persons and places, have encouraged biographical interpretation of *Le lais* and *Le testament.* Such interpretation, however, has failed to resolve the tension between historical reference and poetic representation created by Villon's obscurely vindictive allusions, his derisive first-person commentary, and the startling discrepancy between the historical figures named and the grotesque roles and absurd bequests assigned them in the poems: old saddlebag linings are left to the magistrate Jehan Laurens, portrayed as the son of a drunk (*Testament,* lines 1222–29); an ague to Perrenet Marchant, constable of Paris, if he is caught farting (lines 1094–1101).

Although such incongruities spur biographical conjecture, it is essential to distinguish between the living poet of historical record and the persona he consistently represents as the speaker of his poems. Such a distinction between the living poet and his poetic "I," a literary construct, enables Villon's poetry to be read, not as autobiography (for true autobiographical writing remains scarce in France throughout the Middle Ages), but as the fictional representation of historical persons within the lyric genre, a practice popular in contemporary romances, allegories, and genre painting. Indeed, the poet's choice to represent "poor Villon" as a 15th-century man thrust into a complex social and economic world reflects the time's taste for literary effects of everyday realism.

Villon's historicized representation of poetic voice is unique, however, in medieval French literature. Although the lyric had from the first been the place where subjective expression developed, neither in courtly songs nor in poems of personal repentance is the speaking voice individually characterized in social or historical terms. In these lyrics as well as in *Le roman de la rose* (ca. 1225–1275; *The Romance of the Rose*) and other 13th-century first-person allegorical narratives, a paradoxically impersonal "I" speaks of inner feelings in a highly stylized, conventional diction but never claims any particular identity in an anecdotal world of history. This impersonal subjective mode still prevails, for example, in the verse of Villon's contemporary Charles d'Orléans, who nevertheless extends the thematic range of personal poetry far beyond love and repentance to the expression of melancholy, impotence, and old age. Unlike Villon, Charles does not clothe his speaker with a historical identity; he makes few allusions to his twenty-five-year imprisonment in England or to the dramatic events raging around him at the end of the Hundred Years' War. Such absence of historical references restrains any inclination to biographical interpretation. Instead Charles combines allegorical personifications with metaphors drawn from the world of chivalry, court life, nature, and everyday objects to "translate" a hidden, inner self into images such as the Well of Melancholy, the Forest of Long Waiting, the Hard Bed of Heavy Thought. Lyric debates between aspects of self—"I," Heart, Thought, Hope, and Melancholy—suggest inner complexity, but individual identity is diffused by a smoothly flowing tone, conventional figurative language, and stereotyped situations.

Villon's *Testament* does contain passages of elevated and relatively impersonal subjectivity comparable to that of Charles and to the ostentatious formal virtuosity of the *grands rhétoriqueurs,* the professional court poets such as Jean Molinet (1435–1507) who produced panegyric adorned with mythological figures to celebrate their princely patrons. An example is *Le testament*'s "Ballade des dames du temps jadis" ("Ballade of Dead Ladies"), which in the famous translation of the Pre-Raphaelite poet Dante Gabriel Rossetti reads (lines 329–336):

> Tell me now in what hidden way is
>   Lady Flora the lovely Roman?
> Where's Hipparchia, and where is Thais,
>   Neither of them the fairer woman?
>   Where is Echo, beheld of no man,
> Only heard on river and mere,—

She whose beauty was more than human? . . .
But where are the snows of yester-year?

Such instances of lofty style, so typical of 15th-century verse, are insistently
interrupted in *Le testament* by the abrupt shifts in tone and topic that characterize the voice of Villon's poetic "I." Indeed, unlike his predecessors Guillaume
de Machaut (ca. 1300–1377) and Alain Chartier (ca. 1385–ca. 1435), Villon
never represents his speaker as a poet but only as an ordinary man. He creates
an effect of immediacy and lively presence by interjecting familiar talk—
cursing, ellipsis, digression—into poetic diction. Everyday items such as socks,
saddlebags, and sausages abound along with transgressive word associations:
prophètes (prophets) rhymes with *fesses* (buttocks), *paix* (peace) with *pet* (fart).
There are few allegorical personifications and only a handful of metaphors (often
with obscene implications). Conventional figurative expressions are frequently
tilted toward literal meaning, as in the jeering legacy to his lady love, to whom
he leaves "neither heart nor liver" but rather "a big silk purse / Swollen with
coins thick and long" (*Testament*, in *Poems*, lines 911, 914–915). Grotesque
low words protrude through the elevated language of the rondeau that provides
the speaker's epitaph in *Le testament* (lines 1892–1903):

Rest eternal grant him
Lord and everlasting light
He didn't have the money for a plate or bowl
Or for a sprig of parsley
They shaved him, head, beard, and eyebrows
Like some turnip you scrape or peel
Rest eternal *etc.*

Harsh law exiled him
And whacked him on the ass with a shovel
Even though he cried out "I appeal!"
Which isn't too subtle a phrase
Rest eternal *etc.*

The speaker's coarse voice also intrudes in conventional set pieces such as the
"Double ballade," treating lofty victims of love with impertinent familiarity—Samson loses his spectacles (line 631), King David watches "shapely
thighs being washed" (line 647)—then joining their company: "Of my poor
self let me say / I was pummeled like laundry in a stream / Stark naked" (lines
657–659). The contentious tone and jolting, unpredictable shifts between
poetic and everyday diction create the illusion of direct access to the speaker's
embittered voice and experience, unmediated by art. "Villon is destitute of
imagination," said Ezra Pound; "he sings of things as they are" (*The Spirit of
Romance*, p. 171).

Villon's poetic "I" is dramatically plunged into a world of historical time,
space, and identity. *Le lais* begins: "In the year fourteen fifty-six / I the scholar
François Villon"; and *Le testament:* "In my thirtieth year of life / When I had
drunk down all my disgrace," a year soon identified as "the year sixty-one /

When the good king set me free / From the hard prison at Meun" (lines 81–83). The speaker is represented living in a hostile, rapacious city of taverns and tombs, a Paris peopled with policemen, thieves, judges, derelicts, financiers, and whores, all named in the legacy stanzas. In flashing vignettes "Villon" addresses the hustlers of Paris: "I mean you, comrades in revels / Healthy in body but sick in soul" (lines 1720–21); he invites the reader to join him in listening to the gossips at church, seen "by twos and threes sitting / With their skirts folded under them / In these monasteries, these churches" (lines 1543–45); he records the moans of ancient whores huddled against the cold (lines 525–530):

> "This is how we lament the good old days
> Among ourselves, poor silly crones
> Dumped down on our hunkers
> In little heaps like so many skeins
> Around a tiny hempstalk fire
> That's soon lit and soon gone out."

The somber realism of such lines, like the proper names of contemporaries, serves not history but the characterization of the speaker who overhears this lament that echoes his own.

Villon's poetic "I" is a composite of conventional character types. A few earlier medieval French poets had already attempted to represent a consistently individualized speaker sunk into the quotidian realities of mud, want, marriage, and decrepitude: Colin Muset, Rutebeuf, Adam de la Halle, and their goliard counterparts writing in Latin in the 13th century; Eustache Deschamps in the 14th. Their portraits, however, remain bound to single traditional types: the jolly hedonist, the poor fool, the victim of love and marriage, the ribald scholar, the criminal at the gallows. Motifs and forms associated with all these types are combined in Villon's poetry, where they both enrich his poetic persona and contribute significantly to its distinctive parodic manner and deep ambiguity in tone.

Villon uses his poetic voice to recast motifs associated with such character types in literature composed for both bourgeois and courtly audiences. He incorporates the types of *écolier* (student) and of *follâtre* (fool) associated with the poems and plays written respectively for youth associations of lawyers and administrators and for fool-societies such as the Parisian Basochiens and Enfants-sans-souci. Many dramatic monologues and farces staged for 15th-century city dwellers feature mock-testaments in which dramatic dialogue etches sharply individualized characters by using the rhythms of everyday speech: an example is the braggart's monologue in the anonymous *Le franc archer de Bagnolet* (ca. 1468; *The Conscript Soldier of Bagnolet*). The burlesque legal format of *Le lais* and *Le testament* had analogues in both realistic urban works such as the celebrated farce about a trickster lawyer, *La farce de maître Pierre Pathelin* (ca. 1460; *The Farce of Master Peter Pathelin*), and also in idealized courtly fictions such as Pierre de Hauteville's *La confession et testament de l'amant trépassé de deuil* (ca. 1441–1447; *The Confession and Testament of the Lover Who Died of Grief*).

Villon's "I," who cites Alain Chartier on his deathbed (line 1805), also incorporates the martyred lover type from that same courtly tradition.

In his *Testament* Villon revived a compositional structure favored by 14th- and early 15th-century court poets such as Machaut, Jean Froissart, and Christine de Pisan: musical or fixed-form lyrics inserted into a narrative frame and represented as sung or spoken by the characters. But whereas such earlier compilations of lyric and narrative constituted harmonious ensembles, coherent in theme and uniform in style, the testament format freed Villon to seek effects of dissonance and incongruity in his lyric insertions, subverting the language and ethos of his courtly models. Thus, although the five ballades of the initial "regrets" section of *Le testament* are smoothly integrated with the themes of the surrounding *huitains*—the three ballades of yesteryear, the "Ballade de la Belle Heaulmière aux filles de joie" ("Ballad of the Beautiful Helmet Seller to the Prostitutes"), and the "Double ballade" on unhappy lovers—the fourteen lyrics inserted as legacies often clash with the tone and topic of their setting and with each other. Two grave rondeaux—"Mort, j'appelle de ta rigueur" ("Death, I appeal your harshness," lines 978–989) and "Au retour de dure prison" ("On my return from the hard prison," lines 1784–95)—are prefaced by derisively obscene legacy stanzas. Even when the themes of the inserted pieces are conventional in themselves, they constitute a cacophonous medley when read in their larger context. Thus scattered among *huitains* 125–144 are a prayer cast as a drinking song: "Ballade et oraison de Jehan Cotart" ("Ballad and Prayer for Jean Cotart"); a nuptial poem: "Ballade pour Robert d'Estouteville" ("Ballad for Robert d'Estouteville"); a piece of ugly invective: "Ballade des langues ennuyeuses" ("Ballad of the Annoying Tongues"); and an antipastoral praising material comforts: "Les contredits de Franc Gontier" ("The Reply to Franc Gontier"). These poems are not anthologized to be read separately; instead the poetic "I" offers a repertoire of lyric modes—encomium, pastoral, parodic *sotte ballade*. It is the speaker who overhears the talk praised in the "Ballade des femmes de Paris" ("Ballad of Parisian Women"), who peers through a hole in the wall at scenes of the good life in "Les contredits de Franc Gontier," who groans under the fleshy whore in the "Ballade de la grosse Margot" ("Ballad of Fat Margot"). Villon's *Testament* is not what Charles Augustin Sainte-Beuve called it, an unpalatable "dungheap" from which "two or three pearls" can be lifted (*Causeries du lundi* {1859; *Monday Chats*}, 14:282), for the sense and effect of each piece are inseparable from the characterized poetic voice in all of them.

By means of his poetic voice, Villon not only took the world of experience into his poetry; he also preserved his poems as a cohesive whole. Although, unlike Machaut, Froissart, and Christine de Pisan, Villon did not arrange his poems within a written book, he did embed nineteen short pieces in the fictional frame of *Le testament* and linked *Le lais* and *Le testament* through a network of citations. Above all, he united his works by a fictive authorial identity. "Poor Villon" is an essential lyric element in the first and last stanzas of *Le lais* and in the eight short poems where the name appears in acrostic or refrain—"Better take things as they come, Villon," admonishes Fortune in the "Ballade de Fortune" ("Ballad of Fortune"). And at the end of *Le testament,* in the final ballade, the name of "the poor obscure scholar / Who was known as François Villon" chimes richly with thirteen rhymes including *carillon* (bell), *vermillon* (vermilion), and *couillon* (testicle) (lines 1996–2001). Villon's poetic identity thus encompasses a body of poems independently of their material arrangement in a single manuscript or book. His poetry can "live without life / As images do, by heart" (lines 987–988) within the artful creation of Villon's poetic voice, for he fused lyric feeling and expression of lived experience within the lyric itself by characterizing his poetic "I" fully in terms of historical experience and naming it "Villon."

See also 1225, 1342, 1493.

Bibliography: Pierre Demarolle, *Villon: Un testament ambigu* (Paris: Larousse Université, 1973). Jean Dufournet, *Recherches sur le "Testament" de François Villon,* 2 vols., 2d ed. (Paris: SEDES, 1971). John Fox, *The Poetry of Villon* (London: Thomas Nelson & Sons, 1962). Ezra Pound, "Montcorbier, *alias Villon,*" in *The Spirit of Romance* (Norfolk, Conn.: New Directions, James Laughlin, 1952). Nancy Freeman Regalado, *"Effet de réel, effet du réel:* Representation and Reference in Villon's *Testament," Yale French Studies,* 70 (1986), 63–77. Dante Gabriel Rossetti, "The Ballad of Dead Ladies," in *Poems & Translations, 1850–1870* (London: Oxford University Press, 1926), pp. 101–102. Charles Augustin Sainte-Beuve, *"François Villon, sa vie et ses oeuvres,* par M. Antoine Campaux," in *Causeries du lundi,* vol. 14, 3d ed. (Paris: Garnier, 1870). François Villon, *Le lais Villon et les poèmes variés,* ed. Jean Rychner and Albert Henry, 2 vols. (Geneva: Droz, 1977). Villon, *The Poems of François Villon,* trans. Galway Kinnell (Hanover, N.H.: University Press of New England, 1982). Villon, *Le Testament Villon,* ed. Jean Rychner and Albert Henry, 2 vols. (Geneva: Droz, 1974). Evelyn Birge Vitz, *The Crossroad of Intentions: A Study of Symbolic Expression in the Poetry of François Villon* (The Hague: Mouton, 1974).

Nancy Freeman Regalado

ᕗ 1460?

La farce de maître Pierre Pathelin Is Performed

Farces, Morality Plays, and Soties

Studies of French theater from 1400 to 1600 traditionally list together farces, morality plays, and *soties* (fools' plays), and there is some critical controversy about the extent to which they should be considered as separate genres. By "farce" we normally understand a short comedy in octosyllabic verse whose protagonists are real people: husband, wife, lawyer, student, shopkeeper; by *sotie,* a play of similar form though often more sophisticated versification, with anonymous or allegorical protagonists, such as First Fool, Second Fool, Mother Folly, Everyman, The World, The Pilgrim. Both farce and *sotie* aim primarily to amuse. A morality play, in contrast, is overtly didactic and seldom comic. It may be written in decasyllables or even alexandrines rather than octosyllables;

it may be much longer than the farce or *sotie;* and its action is usually allegorical, occasionally historical.

Examples of each genre have survived, either in manuscript or in printed form, but their texts are often corrupt, and we have regrettably little information about their authors, staging, or dates. Historians sometimes refer to them as "popular theater," to distinguish them from the humanist comedy of Etienne Jodelle and later authors.

Attempts to differentiate more precisely among the three genres immediately encounter difficulties: titles can be ambiguous and misleading, real and allegorical characters overlap; some *soties* are not satirical, but some farces are, and a number of plays are so mixed in character that they cannot be assigned to any one genre. Are the 16th-century plays of Margaret of Navarre, whose titles often begin *Comédie . . .* but which are profoundly religious, farces or morality plays? Critics disagree whether all this theater should be labeled "didactic," whether morality plays should be classified with religious theater (mysteries and miracle plays) rather than with comic theater, how to label other dramatic genres such as the *bergerie* (shepherd play) or the comic monologue, and whether all these are medieval or Renaissance genres.

Morality plays apparently were not as popular in France as in England, and few of them were printed. They vary in length from 200 to 30,000 lines. Most can be called exempla, staging the conflict between good and evil either morally or socially. A number dramatize historical or pseudohistorical anecdotes (the woman who tried to betray Rome and whose daughter fed her in prison with milk from her breast) or biblical episodes (Dives and Lazarus). Some, such as *Eglise, Noblesse et Pauvreté qui font la lessive* (*Church, Nobility, and Poverty Doing the Washing*), focus on the social plight of the poor, while others, such as *La condamnation de banquet* (*The Condemnation of Feasting*) and *Le coeur et les cinq sens* (*The Heart and the Five Senses*), are concerned with the moral health of the individual. A few of the best remind us of *Everyman:* of the two corrupt *Enfants de maintenant* (*Children of Nowadays*), one repents and amends while the other falls progressively a victim to Shame, Despair, and Perdition. Although some of these plays were written by competent poets whose personifications become lively characters, for modern readers they are literary curiosities rather than well-made plays.

So called because their characters are often *sots* (fools) in traditional fool costume, the *soties* delight both in contemporary reference and in assorted verbal pyrotechnics. Many were performed by semiprofessional *sociétés joyeuses* (merry societies) and have stock characters and situations (a disguised character turns out to be just another fool). The shortest, sometimes called *parades,* have no action but simply present two or three characters engaging in versified conversation or argument, often with satirical comment on the evils of "nowadays." Their authors were skillful poets who liked complex rhyme schemes and playful fragmentation of the octosyllabic line. In the longer plays the allegorical action is frequently based on untranslatable ambiguities: the New Men lead a wretched character called The World round the stage from a bad lodging to a worse one ("le logent de mal en pire"), or the Fools are *trompeurs* (both "deceivers" and "trumpet players"). The satirical emphasis is usually on the calamitous state of contemporary society. The best-known *sotie* is the *Jeu du prince des sots* (1511; *Play of the Prince of Fools*), by the well-known poet Pierre Gringore. It is a fierce satire (tolerated if not encouraged by the king) on the intrigues and corruption of the papacy, played by the stock character Mother Folly. It is preceded by a *cri*, a charming enumeration of all the varied fools (*sots* and *sottes*) who are summoned to watch the play.

Unlike the other two genres, farces are still considered "good theater" today. They are comic rather than satirical, involve characters drawn from real life in plausible situations, and frequently end with the deceiver deceived or the villain punished. The late 13th-century *Le garçon et l'aveugle* (after 1266; *The Boy and the Blind Man*) is sometimes claimed as the first farce, but most that can be dated are from the years 1450–1550. Like good farce of any age, they rely heavily on stock characters and plots, which are often reminiscent of the earlier fabliaux. Husband and wife argue and fight, merchant and customer cheat each other, teacher tries to instruct stupid pupil. Parish priests are seducers, soldiers are braggarts, and housewives, gossips. Action is fast-paced and lively, involving much disguise, hiding, urinating, beating, and hurling of fish, tripe, milk, or pitch. Peculiar to these plays is a delight in the ambiguities of language, often expressed in a title with an obscene double meaning: *Farce des femmes qui font récurer leurs chaudrons* (early 16th century; *Farce of the Women Who Ask the Tinker to Mend Their Cookingpots*), or a character who is comic because he is unaware that language can be ambiguous: Mahuet, told by his mother to give (sell) his eggs *au prix du marché* (*at* the market price), gives them away *to* a rogue who says that his name is Market Price.

As this last example implies, folly is an important theme in farces as in *soties*. Husbands unable to dominate their wives are fools, as are naïve servants, nitwitted pupils (who cannot answer the question "Who was the father of the Four Sons of Aymon?"), and absentminded shoemakers. Even shrewish wives can be portrayed as fools, as in *Le cuvier* (late 15th century; *The Tub*), in which the wife, after dictating to her weak husband a list of domestic duties he must perform, falls into the washtub and cannot get out. The husband reads carefully through his list, finds that "helping wife out of washtub" is not on it, and releases her only in exchange for a promise that in future she will be a submissive spouse. By far the best-known farce, and the only one that has been translated several times, is *La farce de maître Pierre Pathelin* (ca. 1460; *The Farce of Master Peter Pathelin*). It is considerably longer than most farces and has an elaborate plot. The rogue Pathelin cheats the foolish merchant Guillaume out of a length of cloth by flattering him and by feigning illness and delirium when Guillaume comes to his house to demand payment. Ably abetted by his wife, Guillemette, Pathelin puts on such a convincing performance that Guillaume is persuaded he must be mistaken. Pathelin then agrees to defend the merchant's shepherd, Aignelet, accused of killing and eating his master's sheep. He advises Aignelet to reply only "Baa!" to the judge's interrogation, and this tactic works perfectly; the judge assumes that Aignelet is half-witted and dismisses the case, but not before the unfortunate merchant has become hilariously entangled in his recollections of Pathelin's and Aignelet's dishonesty. Aignelet finally gets out of paying Pathelin by continuing to reply "Baa!" when Pathelin demands his fee, so that the rogue is finally himself vanquished by a "fool." It has been proposed that this neatly constructed play, which turns on a number of verbal ambiguities, is in fact France's first comedy.

Farces had more influence on later literature than did either morality plays or *soties*. The 16th-century playwright John Heywood translated several of them into English. Their precise relationship to the Italian commedia dell'arte, which uses many of the same dramatic devices, is still in dispute, but they unquestionably provided Molière and, through him, later comic authors with plots, characters, and farcical situations.

See also 1210, 1552, 1673.

Bibliography: Ancien théâtre français, vols. 1–3 (Paris: Jannet, 1854–1857). Heather Arden, Fools' Plays: A Study of Satire in the Sottie (Cambridge: Cambridge University Press, 1980). Jean-Claude Aubailly, ed., La farce de maistre Pathelin et ses continuations (Paris: SEDES, 1979). Barbara C. Bowen, "Metaphorical Obscenity in French Farce, 1460–1560," Comparative Drama, 2 (1977–78), 331–344. Gustave Cohen, ed., Recueil de farces françaises inédites du XVe siècle (Cambridge, Mass.: Medieval Academy of America, 1949). Joseph A. Dane, "Linguistic Trumpery: Notes on a French Sottie," Romanic Review, 71 (1980), 114–121. Eugénie Droz, ed., Le recueil Trepperel, vol. 1: Les sotties (Paris: Droz, 1935). Werner Helmich, ed., Moralités françaises: Réimpression facsimilé de 22 pièces . . . (Geneva: Slatkine, 1980). Alan Hindley, "Medieval French Drama: A Review of Recent Scholarship. Part II: Comic Drama," Research Opportunities in Renaissance Drama, 23 (1980), 93–126. Alan E. Knight, Aspects of Genre in Late Medieval French Drama (Manchester: Manchester University Press, 1983). Master Peter Pathelin, trans. Edwin Morgan (Glasgow: Third Eye Centre, 1983). Ian Maxwell, French Farce and John Heywood (Melbourne: Melbourne University Press, 1946).

Barbara C. Bowen

 1493

Jean Molinet, Poet at the Court of Burgundy, Publishes His
Art de rhétorique vulgaire

The Rhétoriqueurs

For a long time the poetic tradition mistakenly labeled *la grande rhétorique* was virtually eradicated from the French literary canon, and Charles Augustin Sainte-Beuve even ruled that, from about 1460 to 1520, between François Villon's *Testament* and Clément Marot's early works, France, Burgundy, and Flanders were a literary "waste land" ("terrain vague"). Early 20th-century literary historians, appalled by the "tastelessness" of the poets of this period, argued that the inability of the *rhétoriqueurs* to write "good literature" reflected the general crisis of a "waning" medieval society. Until the 1970s few scholars dared praise these literary pariahs. Fortunately, as a result of renewed scholarly interest in linguistics and in text-oriented criticism in the 1970s (the golden years of structuralism in France), fresh interpretative studies have acknowledged that this large group of writers in fact played a crucial role in a key transitional period of French literature.

The *rhétoriqueurs* include six major poets: Jean Meschinot (flourished 1450–1490), Jean Robertet (fl. 1460–1500), Jean Molinet (fl. 1460–1505), Jean Lemaire de Belges (fl. 1495–1515), Guillaume Crétin (fl. 1495–1525), and Jean Marot (fl. 1495–1525); secondary poets such as Henri Baude (fl. 1460–1495), André de la Vigne (fl. 1485–1515), Octavien de Saint-Gelais (fl. 1490–1505), Pierre Gringore (fl. 1500–1535), and Jean Parmentier (fl. 1515–1530); and the authors of anonymous works such as *L'abusé en cour* (ca. 1460; *The Court's Buffoon*) and *Le lion couronné* (1467; *The Crowned Lion*).

The *rhétoriqueurs'* discourse was fashioned by a double sociocultural alienation. Their ambiguous position, as both commoners and court poets, forced them to produce encomiastic poetry and chronicles to the glory of their patrons, and a strongly persistent medieval tradition constrained their literary themes, their formal poetic techniques, and their ritualized modes of speech. But despite these constraints, the *rhétoriqueurs* participated fully in the so-called first humanism of the 15th century. Their works, like those of the early humanists, are marked by ornate eloquence, moral preoccupations, and didactic fervor (although they lack the developing historical consciousness that made the humanists question the relevance of ancient and medieval exemplary literature). The *rhétoriqueurs* concentrated on generic, linguistic, and stylistic forms, disrupting conventional processes of meaning and reviving the two principal kinds of rhetoric that enabled the artist to persuade or dissuade by "beauteous and notable speech" (*Le jardin de plaisance et fleur de rhétorique,* 1501; *The Garden of Pleasure and the Flower of Rhetoric*).

The "first rhetoric," governing prose discourse, simply transposed the principles of Latin oratory (as contained, for instance, in the *Rhetorica ad Herennium*) into the vernacular, either directly or by way of medieval treatises (*artes poeticae*) transmitted by the scholastic tradition. That literary texts were so slow to assimilate the first rhetoric can be explained in part by the concurrent revival of belles-lettres in 14th-century Italy and by the rediscovery of ancient models with competing forms of eloquence. The revival of a Latin art of oratory (by, among others, Pierre d'Ailly, Jean de Gerson, Nicolas of Clémanges, and Jean de Montreuil) throughout the 15th century in the works of the great humanists (such as Giovanni Pico della Mirandola's discourse *Oratio de Dignitate Hominis* [1486; *Oration on the Dignity of Man*]) was accompanied by a slow but decisive assimilation of vernacular eloquence by the great French orators.

By ridding prose of its inevitable redundancies orators uncovered a formidable instrument of persuasion; it was one of the paradoxical consequences of the victory achieved by humanism over scholasticism. With formalist Aristotelianism under attack, the orator was viewed as the supreme human type.

Cicero took the place of Aristotle, and eloquence dethroned philosophy. Oratorical technique could not have made such progress without the rediscovery of Quintilian by Nicolas of Clémanges (ca. 1396) and by Poggio Bracciolini at the abbey of Saint-Gall (1416).

Fifteenth-century writers groped for rules as they shaped a new vernacular style, rewriting verse romances in prose, adapting or emulating the great classical orators, and slowly loosening the awkward and pompous style bequeathed by clerkly professionals. Such an evolution is obvious in Christine de Pisan's *La vision* (1405; *Christine's Vision*) and Alain Chartier's *Le quadrilogue invectif* (1422; *Four Accusatory Speeches*). In this movement, translations of Latin into the vernacular played a considerable role. At the court of Burgundy, Laurent de Premierfait translated Cicero's *De amicitia* (*On Friendship*) and *De senectute* (*On Old Age*) as well as the moralizing works of Boccaccio before producing the first French version of the *Decameron* (1414), in which the translator's learned and moralizing amplifications contrast curiously with the supple rhetoric and poetic refinement of the original.

Poetical theory about rhymed texts was generally considered to belong to a "second rhetoric" and was collected in manuals on versification. To defend and illustrate the art of versifying, theoreticians wrote an abundance of treatises, from the *Art de dicter* of Eustache Deschamps (1392; *The Art of Versifying*) to the *Grand et vrai art de rhétorique* of Pierre Fabri (1521; *The Great and True Art of Rhetoric*), enumerating the various categories of rhymes and of fixed forms to which poets, also called rhetoricians, had to adhere.

In the *rhétoriqueurs'* hands, however, poetics was never limited to the descriptive and normative aspect of versification. Quintilian's distinction between rhymers and poets is assiduously echoed by all manner of poetical theorists of the period, much before Joachim du Bellay's famous *La défense et illustration de la langue française* (1549; *The Defense and Enrichment of the French Language*). In his *Vita nuova* (1292; *The New Life*) Dante had explicitly drawn a distinction between the *poeta,* who employs Latin, and the *rimatore* (or *dicitore per rima*), who expresses himself in the *volgare.* The influence of Petrarch, who accorded the poet a sacred role and promised him laurels of glory even should he declaim in his native language, had been perceptible outside Italy as early as the 15th century. And even such self-admitted *rimeurs* as Jean Robertet expressed a strong belief in the immortality and divine inspiration of the poet.

After the "first" and "second rhetoric" (that of the orator and that of the rhymer-poet), writers also acknowledged the importance of what they called *poetria* or *poétrie.* According to Jacques Le Grand's *Archiloge sophie* (ca. 1410; *The Fair Speech of Wisdom*), *poétrie* was the "science that teaches feigning" and thus allowed the invention of fabulous things such as pagan myths, as long as they were presented "behind a beautiful exterior." "Feigning" did not then carry the pejorative sense that it has for us, nor even the ambiguous one it possessed for Pierre de Ronsard; to feign (*feindre*) was simply to create fictions, "subtiles inventions," which made the text "more fabulous than true" (Jean Bouchet, *Les renards traversant,* ca. 1520; *Foxes Traveling*). Similarly, Jean Bouchet introduced his *Epîtres morales et familières* (1545; *Moral and Familiar Letters*) as "fictions poétiques."

Practicing *poétrie* meant borrowing frequently from the fifteen books of Boccaccio's *De Genealogiis Deorum Gentilium* (1351–1360; *On the Genealogies of the Pagan Gods*), a vast storehouse of mythological tales with many allegorical and moral significations. However, *poétrie* was not simply a coupling of myths with a fanciful explanation of pagan cosmogony. As with Boccaccio, through its fables it attempted to reveal profound and universal truths, inviting readers to recognize those moral values that could help them to raise themselves closer to God.

Seen in this light, poetics had closer affinities to philosophy, indeed to theology, than to rhetoric. It aspired to be knowledge of the "real," that which goes beyond appearances (*fictions*) to seize the profound and hidden meaning of things. Recognizable here is the persistent medieval tendency to interpret everything allegorically. Thus it is not surprising that this search for a "higher meaning" (blood, sap, and marrow were the favorite images), which Rabelais later ridiculed, was coupled, at least in its most extreme forms, with an almost alchemistic experimentation with language: words themselves become in turn *fictions* concealing the mysteries of a higher reality.

Guillaume de Machaut (ca. 1300–1377) is often considered the last lyric poet for whom music and poetry went hand in glove. After him and in contrast to him, the *rhétoriqueurs*, even those such as Molinet who were in fact both writers and musicians, experimented with a language completely liberated from the tutelage of musical instruments. At the end of the 14th century Eustache Deschamps, in his *Art de dicter*, had first advanced the decidedly cautious hypothesis that "artificial" music (that of instruments) might be separated from "natural" music (that of unaccompanied voices). Even then, he conceded that "natural songs" were quite "delectable" when embellished by an artificial melody. If Machaut's poems are less colorful and expressive than those of Deschamps, it is partly because they are still meant to be sung, whereas Deschamps believed he could compensate for the absence of "artificial music" by painstakingly formal expression.

When Jean Molinet wrote that "rhetoric is a type of music" (*Art de rhétorique vulgaire*, 1493; *Art of Vernacular Rhetoric*), he was not making rhetoric a branch of music; rather, he was attempting to compete with music on its own terms and to create a rhythmic style that would be properly poetic. Dante's famous definition of poetry—a rhetorical fiction composed in music ("fictio rhetorica musice composita"; *De Vulgari Eloquentia* [1304; *On Vernacular Rhetoric*], chap. 4)—was thus to take on a new meaning. With the *rhétoriqueurs* the terms emerged in a new order: poetry was henceforth conceived as "rhetorical music fictitiously composed." The essence of poetry was no longer *fictio* (a feigning, forming), but *musica* (music).

In *La concorde des deux langages* (ca. 1511; *Harmony between French and Italian Cultures*), Jean Lemaire de Belges, the most talented of the *rhétoriqueurs*, proclaimed that sonorities of language are composed and orchestrated according to the laws of natural rhetoric and not according to the "artificial" sol-fa of instrumental music. "Rhetoric and music are one and the same," he wrote, meaning that poetic words, even emerging from the mouth of a pedagogue or a chronicler, could quite reasonably claim a status equal to that of music. The poetic muse was no longer a second-class citizen; and her emancipation paralleled that of a rejuvenated, defended vernacular language, whose virtues the 16th century proclaimed.

Yet for the *rhétoriqueurs* the text's spatial arrangement was just as important as its musicality. Textual space was beginning to be conceived as a canvas, according to the new laws of *perspectiva pingendi* illustrated by the school of Piero della Francesca. Great poets would be those who, through appropriate techniques, succeeded in striking the eye with a terrific clarity, in painting iridescent forms and composing rich illuminations. For theoreticians, words possessed a reality beyond the meaning they carried, one that was not only sonorous (syllables as musical notes) but also visual (syllables as the brushstrokes of a painter): writing was a visible object, meant to be spectacularly displayed.

Painters no longer enjoyed a monopoly on design and color. "Colored verbs" and the "colors of rhetoric" belonged to the poets who composed emblems (such as Andrea Alciato in Italy) and wove tapestries (such as Henri Baude in France and Enrique de Villena in Spain). In inscribing their art in the long tradition of the medieval figurative poems (*carmina figurata*), these poets sought every means of *figuring* writing, of describing its object in the act of representing it. This was especially true of the *rhétoriqueurs,* who, several centuries before Guillaume Apollinaire's *Calligrammes* (1918; *Calligrams*), pushed the taste for scriptural figuration to its extreme.

Transposing the litanies of the Virgin to vernacular verse, Jean Molinet combined anaphora and acrostic to proclaim the incantatory power of Mary's name (*Oraison sur Maria,* ca. 1490; *Prayer on Maria*). As a visual commentary on the tragic death of a friend, André de la Vigne reproduced the Latin words of the requiem in his French rhymed epitaphs. Jean Marot composed poems in the form of rebuses (fig. 1), and Jean Meschinot produced a rondeau that could be read in thirty-two different ways. Toward the end of the 16th century, Etienne Tabourot des Accords categorized almost all of these technical innovations in a vertiginous summa of literary gamesmanship (*Les bigarrures,* 1582 or 1583; *Miscellanies*).

The practical conditions of reading explain in part the technical refinements sought by poets to halt the observer's eye as if for the appreciation of a rich *enluminure,* a picturesque embroidery, a delightful miniature (*Heures de Rohan,* ca. 1435; *Rohan's Book of Hours*). For the new reading public, hearing was no longer the only sense appealed to, and the "sight lag" (as Lucien Febvre has called it) tended to disappear. Thus the illuminated manuscripts produced at the court of Burgundy were meant to cause the scholar to give himself up to the pleasure of a personal act of interpretation.

The writings of the *rhétoriqueurs* have long been considered as reflections of the end of a civilization. Their "artificial" language games were taken as the

L. RONDEAU.

L'homme dupé.

ryant   fuz   nagueres
  N   pris
E   Vᶜ.   D'une   Vᶜ.   affeᶜtée
                 tile
   efpoir   haittée
Que   vent
         j'ay
              de
Mais   fuz , quant   pr , s'amour , is
        japper   ris
Car   que fes mignars
  Traiᶜtz   a
Eftoyent   d'amour   mal   ée
                    ryant.
                 En
leil   de
Efcuz   &   moy a pris
     maniere ruzée
te , Me, nant
              veulx
Et quant je elle   é , faire, e
                que
Me dit , to , ys, us   mal apris
                    ryant.
                 En

E X P L I C A T I O N

D U

L. R O N D E A U.

EN fousryant fuz nagueres furpris
  D'une fubtile entre mille affeᶜtée
  Que fous efpoir j'ay fouvent foushaittée,
Mais fuz deceu quant s'amour entrepris :
  Car j'apperfus que fes mignars foufris
Très furs eftoyent d'amour mal affurée
      En fousryant.
Efcuz fouleil & fous de moy a pris
M'entretenant fous maniere ruzée
Et quant je veulx fur elle faire entrée
Me dit que fuys entre tous mal appris
      En fousryant.

1. Rondeau in the form of a rebus, by Jean Marot, with its transcription, in *Oeuvres de Clément Marot, avec les ouvrages de Jean Marot, son père,* ed. Nicolas Lenglet-Dufresnoy (The Hague: P. Gosse & J. Neaulme, 1731), pp. 291–292. (Courtesy of the Firestone Library, Princeton University.)

last twitches of an age wishing to regain control of itself and to undertake one last self-evaluation before dying. But today we can no longer regard the "waning years" of the Middle Ages, as Johan Huizinga called them, as a period of decline. The "monstrosities" of flamboyant art can no longer be interpreted solely as a culture's defiance of its imminent death. The age of the *rhétoriqueurs* is already fully a part of the historical phenomenon that we still confidently, though somewhat arbitrarily, call the Renaissance.

See also 1267, 1342, 1536, 1549, 1555 (13 September), 1913.

Bibliography: Eustache Deschamps, *Art de dictier,* in *Oeuvres complètes,* ed. Gaston Raynaud, vol. 7 (Paris: Didier, 1891). Pierre Fabri, *Le grand et vray art de rhetoricque,* ed. A. Héron, 2 vols. (1889–1890; reprint, Geneva: Slatkine, 1969). Johan Huizinga, *The Waning of the Middle Ages: A Study of the Forms of Life, Thought, and Art in France and the Netherlands in the XIVth and XVth Centuries,* trans. Frederick Hopman (1924; reprint, Garden City, N.Y.: Doubleday, 1954). Ernest Langlois, ed., *Recueil d'arts de seconde rhétorique* (1902; reprint, Geneva: Slatkine, 1974) (includes Jacques Le Grand's *Archiloge sophie* and Jean Molinet's *Art de rhétorique vulgaire*). Jean Lemaire de Belges, *Oeuvres,* ed. A. J. Stecher, 4 vols. (Louvain: J. Lefever, 1882–1891). Jean Marot, *Oeuvres de Clément Marot, avec les ouvrages de Jean Marot, son père,* ed. Nicolas Lenglet-Dufresnoy, 5 vols. (The Hague: P. Gosse & J. Neaulme, 1731). François Rigolot, *Poétique et onomastique: L'exemple de la Renaissance* (Geneva: Droz, 1977), pp. 11–79. Rigolot, *Le texte de la Renaissance: Des rhétoriqueurs à Montaigne* (Geneva: Droz, 1982), pp. 23–121. Paul Zumthor, *Le masque et la lumière: La poétique des grands rhétoriqueurs* (Paris: Seuil, 1978).

François Rigolot

 1512

Desiderius Erasmus of Rotterdam Publishes His Treatise on Style, *De Duplici Copia Verborum ac Rerum*

Writing without Reserve

Erasmus had begun to draft a treatise on *copia* (the rich or abundant style) before 1500, but the first official edition of his *De Duplici Copia Verborum ac Rerum* (*On Abundance of Words and Ideas*) was not published until 1512; it was dedicated to John Colet for use at St. Paul's School in London, which Colet had recently founded. Greatly expanded in later editions, the work was at once the most elementary and the most seminal of Erasmus' contributions to the humanist conception of style, and it became so popular that by 1532 the German humanist Philipp Melanchthon could claim that "everyone" had a copy. Medieval stylists had developed techniques of rhetorical expansion ("amplification"), and Erasmus was not the first to borrow from Cicero and Quintilian the notion of *copia;* but he made the term his own, and his prestige and influence guaranteed its currency among 16th-century writers.

The title itself signals the aesthetic preference of a whole era. The Renaissance taste for copiousness in style and subject matter prevailed throughout the 16th century in France and was definitively superseded only in the mid-17th century by the rise of a neoclassical doctrine based on diametrically opposite principles: thus, for example, Nicolas Boileau's famous dictum in *L'art poétique* (1674; *The Art of Poetry*), "He who cannot keep within bounds was never a writer."

The word *copia* means many things. As "plenty" or "abundance," it becomes a powerful metaphor for a way of writing that purports to imitate the variety and diversity of nature itself. As "fluency," it refers to the ability of the writer or orator who has thoroughly mastered his art and can develop his topic at will. And as "storehouse," it designates the resources a writer has to hand: Erasmus recommends in *De Copia* that the student work his way through that vast storehouse constituted by the writings of classical antiquity and compile an ordered notebook of materials—words, turns of phrase, figures of speech, anecdotes, maxims, and the like—which he will later use for his own purposes.

The many-sided notion of *copia* is central, then, to the humanist enterprise of assimilating the achievements and insights of the ancients and reissuing them in a clear and elegant style. The Latin word for this enterprise is *imitatio,* and theories of imitation of the ancients abounded in the Renaissance, in the vernaculars as well as in Latin. To anyone brought up on the modern preference

133

for "originality," the concept of imitation might sound unpromising. Renaissance humanists, however, were acutely aware—more acutely, perhaps, than any writers before or since—of the extent to which all writing depends on earlier models, on what has already been said. Faced with the overwhelming power and prestige of the great masters of antiquity, they felt impotent, like exiles piecing together the fragments of a culture forever lost, or like necromancers trying to resurrect the shades of the past. How could they aspire to write Latin like Cicero or Virgil, still less achieve comparable effects in what they regarded as impoverished or untried vernacular languages? Their writing might well be no more than a lifeless copy rather than a renewal of the true *copia* of the Greek and Roman golden age. The theories of Erasmus and others represent a sustained and serious attempt to face such problems precisely by accepting the fragmentation and "death" of antiquity and by proposing a process of digestion, of appropriation and transformation, whereby elements of past writing are selected and recombined to become a new living substance designed to serve the needs of a new age. To write like Cicero, one must learn to write differently—to write like oneself: such was Erasmus' argument in his polemical dialogue *Ciceronianus* (1528; *The Ciceronian*). And so, in this period, the first person singular begins increasingly to assert its power as a focus of style and, eventually, as an independent, authoritative voice.

Though conceived in the first instance in terms of a revival of Latin style, the Erasmian theory of *copia* undoubtedly served as a model for the vernacular writers of the French Renaissance, all of whom would have been taught to write and read Latin as a matter of course. Rabelais (1483?–1553) pays enthusiastic tribute to Erasmus; Joachim du Bellay (1522–1560) quotes some of his arguments without mentioning him (by the late 1540s, Erasmus' work was regarded as theologically suspect). Whether directly or indirectly, in fact, 16th-century French literature may be said to explore in depth the problems and stylistic preferences of Erasmian humanism. In Rabelais's comic novels, the primacy of the fragment is visible on almost every page: quotations, allusions, references authentic and spurious follow one another in bewildering succession; eventually the whole work becomes a quest for truth conducted amid such fragments of potential wisdom or knowledge. And Rabelais's style turns *copia* into a principle of comic inventiveness, generating endless lists of words and phrases by means of association, alliteration, or assonance: Rabelais himself calls his book a cornucopia.

The first book of du Bellay's *La défense et illustration de la langue française* (1549; *The Defense and Enrichment of the French Language*) addresses explicitly the problems of imitation, countering images of impoverishment and sterility with metaphors of grafting, digestion, transformation, and resuscitation. A similar sense of the poet's predicament in the face of the lost greatness of the past is expressed in figurative terms in du Bellay's sonnet cycle *Les antiquités de Rome* (1558; *The Antiquities of Rome*); in his longer and more celebrated sequence *Les regrets* (1558; *The Regrets*), the confrontation with Rome and its fall provokes a first-person meditation on the themes of exile and transience.

La défense was the manifesto of the group of young humanist poets, writing mainly but not exclusively in the vernacular, that became known as the Pléiade. Whereas du Bellay was hesitant about his own powers as a poet, opting for the less elevated genres and themes, his great contemporary Pierre de Ronsard (1524–1585) was notoriously ambitious, writing collection after collection in emulation of the great models of Greek and Roman antiquity. In an early preface he speaks of poetry as imitating the "copious diversity" of nature, and his own poetry blends materials from every possible source to create a sense of almost organic growth and profusion: in many poems, indeed, the heady exploitation of new stylistic domains by means of *imitatio* is combined with an evocation of natural plenitude as a metaphor of the poet's own creative energies. Yet the enterprise carried its risks for Ronsard too: he never completed *La Franciade,* his projected epic poem on the origins of the French nation, and a number of his later poems revert to themes of exhaustion, of failed inspiration, as if his poetic horn of plenty had become depleted.

Montaigne (1533–1592) represents a late stage in the development of 16th-century humanism. He was thoroughly familiar with the Latin poets, whom he frequently quotes, together with Seneca, the historians, and many others; he also read Greek works—notably those of Plutarch—in translation. He refers to his own relation to these models in terms of ironic self-deprecation, yet ultimately he affirms the value of his own judgment; whatever he may borrow from elsewhere has always, he claims, become part of his individual substance. In consequence, the first person singular in Montaigne's *Essais* (1st ed. 1580; expanded 1588 and 1595) develops into the thread that links all the fragments: the work is presented as a self-portrait, though an infinitely mobile and flexible one. And because the angle of vision is more important than the subject matter as such, the manner of composition, too, remains mobile, associative, open-ended. The *Essais* are not an ethical handbook or a mere compilation: they are an exploration of ways of understanding experience, and their title should be taken in its etymological sense ("trials," "samples," or "experiments").

Rabelais, Ronsard, and Montaigne are highly self-conscious writers whose work often reverts explicitly to problems of writing, primarily the problems of *copia* and *imitatio.* Characteristically, their works are also in an important sense unfinished: Rabelais's comic narrative, fragmentary in its very nature, breaks off in midstream; Ronsard writes a series of poetic experiments in preparation for a single complete work—the epic—that will never be realized; Montaigne's writing proliferates continuously until the moment of his death. Like Erasmus, they are aware that language is a treacherous instrument, that *copia* can be used to deceive, seduce, or subvert, that total knowledge and truth cannot reside in human words. They conceive of writing as a heuristic exercise, a constant process of discovery. If we read them with an open mind, resisting the desire for single coherent meanings, they provide not only aesthetic riches unparalleled in more orderly periods, but also a storehouse of insights into the nature of writing itself.

See also 1532, 1534 (Fall).

Bibliography: R. R. Bolgar, *The Classical Heritage and Its Beneficiaries* (Cambridge: Cambridge University Press, 1954). Terence Cave, *The Cornucopian Text: Problems of Writing in the French Renaissance* (Oxford: Clarendon Press, 1979). Erasmus, *"Copia": Foundations of the Abundant Style,* trans. Betty I. Knott, in *The Collected Works of Erasmus,* vol. 24, ed. Craig R. Thompson (Toronto: University of Toronto Press, 1978). Thomas M. Greene, *The Light in Troy: Imitation and Discovery in Renaissance Poetry* (New Haven: Yale University Press, 1982).

Terence Cave

✑ 1517

Guillaume Budé Addresses to Francis I the Manuscript of
Le livre de l'institution du prince

Humanist Models for Thought and Action

Guillaume Budé (1467–1540) was the dominant intellectual figure in the rise of French humanism under Francis I. Friend to Erasmus, Rabelais, and Juan Luis Vives, antiquarian, jurist, historiographer, and indisputably the greatest Hellenist of his day, Budé (or Budaeus, as he is known in Latin) embodies both the aspirations and the contradictions of French humanist culture. Though he is known today chiefly for his historical role in helping to found the institutions that became the Collège de France and the Bibliothèque Nationale, Budé's scholarly achievements were of signal importance for early 16th-century French culture: his treatise on Roman coinage, *De Asse et Partibus Eius* (1514; *The As and Its Parts*), is often regarded as the major philological achievement of the age; his *Commentarii Linguae Graecae* (1529; *Commentaries on the Greek Language*) sparked the vogue of Hellenism that was to culminate in Ronsard's *Odes* (1550); and his *Le livre de l'institution du prince* (wr. 1517, pub. 1547; *The Book of the Institution of the Prince*) stands as an influential example of humanist advice literature written in the vernacular.

The salient feature of Budé's humanism is its close connection with nascent French nationalism. In contrast to his friend Erasmus, for whom humanism was essentially Christ-centered, Budé conceived of humanism as a restoration of *bonae litterae* going hand in hand with a unified France's cultural and political ascendancy. The "Dark Ages," Budé argues in the *Institution,* were dark precisely because they lacked good historians and rhetoricians to sing the praises of royalty. And royalty in turn failed to execute heroic deeds worthy of praise. Budé proposes to rectify this situation by offering a book of practical advice to Francis, who will embark upon heroic undertakings to the greater glory of France. This in turn will provide material for future historians, who will praise Francis. This nationalism extends to Budé's choice of the vernacular instead of Latin. Budé apologizes for the clumsiness of his French ("the language that I have practiced the least"), but he makes it clear that by writing in it he is promoting a national literature and a nationalist politics.

Budé's *Institution* belongs to the popular late medieval and Renaissance genre of the advice tract or "mirror for princes" (*speculum principis*). And like its better-known contemporaries, Machiavelli's *Il principe* (1513; *The Prince*) and Erasmus' *Institutio Principis Christiani* (1516; *The Education of the Christian Prince*), it seeks to influence the monarch's behavior in the world by urging him to virtuous action in the governance of his state. The authority and direction for the prince's action are to be provided by history, which Cicero had called "the mistress of life" ("historia magistra vitae"). For Budé, as for all humanists, history is repetition; the past offers a reservoir of examples to be imitated by actors in the present. At the center of this model of history as repetition lies the cult of the illustrious exemplar or heroic personality, whose words and deeds are signs of a virtue to be emulated by the modern prince. The lives of the heroic ancients constitute a series of narratives against which modern readers are to measure and fashion themselves. Only by studying history and following the ancients, suggests Budé, can Francis achieve the glory that rightfully belongs to both him and his people.

This conception of ancient history as guide presumes that ancient virtue is universal, that the excellence of the ancients is relevant for modern actors. Yet when Budé actually attempts to apply historical models to action in the present, the problems that emerge underscore the contradictory nature of French humanism itself. The *Institution* consists of a series of anecdotes drawn from ancient history, interspersed with praise of Francis and allusions to Budé's other works, most particularly *De Asse*. At the beginning of his text Budé modestly claims that his intention has been merely to "collect" or "gather" the deeds of the ancients for the benefit of the prince. The prince, he points out, can read history for himself. Budé claims that the textual prototype for the *Institution* is Plutarch's *Apophthegmata*, a collection of anecdotes (recently translated into Latin by Erasmus) taken from the lives of the illustrious ancients. Yet whereas Plutarch merely lists the words and deeds of his exemplary figures, as if their meaning were obvious, Budé feels compelled to interpret them at every turn. This imposition of the pedagogue's voice upon the material of history is doubtless linked to Budé's position at the Valois court. Whereas Erasmus attempted to maintain his independence from all secular political authorities, Budé was a courtier. As such, his text had to demonstrate his own intellectual prowess and advertise the value of the humanist as adviser. Thus, although humanism proposes in theory that the prince can study history for himself, the practicalities of life at court impel the ambitious Budé to promote himself by constantly pointing to the lessons that history provides for his patron. The model of reading that Budé proposes is denied by his own rhetorical strategies. The humanist as courtier and the humanist as philologist stand at odds.

The history that Budé presents to his prince consists of a multitude of narratives from the past, some of which offer conflicting versions of the same heroic event or life. This discursive multiplicity is one reason why the *Institution* seems to lack any clear structure. Yet the very shapelessness of the book reflects the paradoxical nature of the humanist attempt to learn from the past. Budé seeks to define an exemplar for Francis; yet he is unable to settle upon a sufficiently virtuous model for the French king. He moves from exemplar to exemplar, first promoting a particular ancient, then qualifying that promotion, and finally moving on to another figure. Thus in the opening pages of the text Budé proposes Alexander the Great as the ideal model (which implicitly casts the author of the *Institution* as the modern counterpart to Alexander's tutor, Aristotle). Yet this attempt to appropriate Alexander soon fails. For Budé acknowledges that Alexander's virtue was imperfect, that his vices worked to "efface the luster of his renown and obscure the illustrious meaning of his marvelous deeds" (p. 132). Budé replaces Alexander with Pompey, whose glory was free of "cloudy shame or reproach" (p. 132). Yet Budé carefully stipulates *which* history of Pompey is applicable to the career of Francis (the version offered in Lucan's *Pharsalia*) and *which* moment of that life is appropriate material for his prince to study (the eulogy pronounced by Cato in book 9 of Lucan's poem). Still later Budé shifts focus again, to promote Hercules, whom he sees (as did contemporary mythographers) as an exemplar of both Gallic heroism (Francis) and Gallic rhetoric (Budé himself). In short, the voices of the past seem to be too varied and complex for Budé's humanist project of defining a definitive exemplar for his king. Historical distance and circumstance tarnish the great deeds of the past for the modern who seeks to appropriate or imitate them. Moreover, because some of the exemplar's deeds demonstrate vice instead of virtue, his personality cannot be understood as consistently virtuous, nor can the narrative of his life be seen as a story after which present action can be modeled without risk of error. The narrative of the heroic biography and the image of ancient heroism are both fragmented as the humanist seeks to overcome historical distance and use the past to guide the present.

The shapelessness of Budé's *Institution* sets in relief an important contradiction within humanist discourse generally. On the one hand, humanism draws its authority from history; it argues that history is moral philosophy and that the modern revival of *studia humanitatis* has ethical implications for action in the present. As the 16th century proceeded, however, humanist historiographers and moralists became increasingly conscious of what Budé's *Institution* already demonstrates: that the actions of the past may be too multivalent and fluid to interpret with any certainty. The words and deeds of the ancients, which humanism tries to read as signs of virtue, may simply be unreadable; their ambiguity may resist the moralizing structures of humanist hermeneutics. In Italy this skepticism first became explicit in the work of Budé's contemporaries Machiavelli and Francesco Guicciardini. In France it appeared only toward the end of the century: first, in a limited way, in the work of Jean Bodin, then, more extensively, in the *Essais* of Montaigne.

Budé, then, adopts in the *Institution* an array of frequently contradictory positions; he is moral philosopher, ambitious courtier, disinterested philologist, royal apologist. The variety in Budé's self-presentation combines with the frequent clumsiness and the contradictions in the *Institution* to demonstrate the fragility of French humanism itself. The alliance between the humanist appropriation of the past and the Gallic plan to dominate the future soon found itself in trouble, as Francis' projects for national unity and Gallic preeminence were increasingly hindered by military defeat and religious conflict. As the Reformation gained strength, the families of the high nobility, whose allegiance Francis had briefly marshaled, divided over the issue of religion. The resulting conflict split the country and ended all prospects of an easy alliance between the humanities and political power. Only twenty years later, at the height of the religious wars, the political and cultural optimism of figures such as Budé looked like naïve idealism. Indeed, the most trenchant irony regarding Budé's *Institution* may lie in the timing of its publication: though written in 1517, it was published only in 1547, after the death of both Budé and his patron. One of its first editions was dedicated to Claude I of Lorraine, duc de Guise—a member of a family destined to play an important role on the Catholic side in the religious wars that ravaged late 16th-century France and obliterated humanist idealism.

See also 1566.

Bibliography: Guillaume Budé, *Le livre de l'institution du prince,* in *Le prince dans la France des XVIe et XVIIe siècles,* ed. Claude Bontems (Paris: Presses Universitaires de France, 1965). Marie-Madeleine de la Garanderie, *Christianisme et lettres profanes* (Paris: Champion, 1976). Donald R. Kelley, *The Foundations of Modern Historical Scholarship: Language, Law, and History in the French Renaissance* (New York: Columbia University Press, 1970). David O. McNeil, *Guillaume Budé and Humanism in the Reign of Francis I* (Geneva: Droz, 1975).

Timothy Hampton

1526, *July*
Michel de Saint-Aignen, after Killing His Wife's Suitor,
Addresses a Letter of Remission to Francis I

Life-Saving Stories

In July 1526 Michel de Saint-Aignen, a notable resident of Alençon, asked King Francis I to pardon him for killing a young solicitor who, he claimed, had been seducing his wife and conspiring to murder him. His account, written down by a royal notary, reads like a Renaissance novella—and indeed, it was the inspiration for a tale in Margaret of Navarre's *L'heptaméron* (1559; *The Heptameron*). Sealed by the king's chancellor and reviewed by a royal court, Saint-Aignen's supplication is one of the thousands of letters of remission found in the French archives, each providing evidence not only for 16th-century patterns of violence, criminal justice, and reconciliation but also for habits and tastes in storytelling. They constitute a literary production beyond the pens of known authors and the output of the printing shops, one in which even the recitals of the unlearned do not seem unadorned.

Not long after his victim died, Saint-Aignen fled in order to avoid arrest and soon found his way to a royal notary, who had the right to draw up the king's letters. A man of the law himself, Saint-Aignen would not have needed to consult an attorney about what circumstances made a homicide remissible. These excuses were widely known even to villagers: homicide in self-defense, in vengeance for adultery, in sudden hot anger, in drunkenness, in the course of a game, by accident, by imprudence—to name the most important pardon plots. Saint-Aignen would also have known that he must portray himself as a man of good character, innocently going about his business with no sign of planning murder.

As for the royal notary, he could be counted on to supply all the formulas for the letter of remission, including the preamble, in which the king reports he has received a humble supplication from one of his subjects, and the conclusion, in which he orders his officers not to prosecute (or to cease prosecuting) the petitioner. He would also turn Saint-Aignen's "I" into the third person of the supplicant to whom the king is listening and would translate any regional dialects into French. But whatever shape he gave to the account, the notary ordinarily kept it quite colloquial and near enough to the supplicant's report so that he could repeat it later when examined on his letter of remission by the king's judges.

Saint-Aignen's letter (Archives Nationales JJ239, 48v–49r) opens by describing how his reputation and prosperity in the town of Alençon had aroused envy and ill will, especially on the part of a young man named Jacques du Mesnil. This was all the more unjust because Saint-Aignen had received du Mesnil with great favor in his house, even thinking to marry him to one of his relatives. Nonetheless, the iniquitous du Mesnil had tried to stir up division between Saint-Aignen and his wife, "with whom he had always lived in good, great, and perfect love." Du Mesnil told her that her frequently absent husband did not care for her and wished her dead; she forbade him to say such things and threatened to tell her spouse. He told her that if she would consent to her husband's death, he would marry her; she refused. Du Mesnil then bribed a servant girl to let him into the wife's bedroom, where he forced her to sleep with him. Through further gifts he tried to entice the servant to poison Saint-Aignen, but the maid confessed to her master at Easter. When news of the plot began to spread, du Mesnil spirited the servant out of the area, meanwhile skulking around the house and garden at night. "Seeing his wife so scandalized" and himself so wronged, Saint-Aignen ordered du Mesnil to stop coming to see his spouse. Du Mesnil responded that he would visit her even if he had to die in the attempt.

To avoid further trouble, Saint-Aignen moved his household to the town of Argentan, some ten leagues away, but the obstinate du Mesnil persisted. Finally, on 8 July, du Mesnil disguised himself in mask, plumed hat, and checkered garments quite different from those he wore for his post as solicitor, rode to an inn at Argentan where he concealed himself until late at night, and then stealthily entered Saint-Aignen's house and hid in a wardrobe. When a

140

manservant went to get Saint-Aignen's nightclothes from the wardrobe, out came the disguised du Mesnil with bared sword. A fight ensued in the court-yard, and, hearing the intruder shout "Help, murder, confession," Saint-Aignen ran down, sword in hand, and finally recognized du Mesnil in the dark. "Astounded to find his enemy in his house at such an hour . . . and remembering all the injuries he had done him, Saint-Aignen gave him two or three blows in hot anger and said, 'Ho, evil one, what brings you here? Haven't you wronged me enough already? I've done you no harm.' 'It's true,' du Mesnil said. 'I've wronged you too much, I've been too wicked. I ask your pardon.' Where-upon he fell as if dead to the ground."

Recommending his soul to God, Saint-Aignen went to bed with his wife, who had slept through everything. In the morning he had his servant bury the body "to avoid scandal," saw to it that du Mesnil's servants and horses left the inn, and absented himself from the country. Now he humbly asks the king for pardon.

Why did a request for pardon take the form of a story, rather than a mere verification of the person's good name and reputation and the essential facts of the case? The custom dates from the earliest preserved letters of remission in the 14th century, and by the 15th century their narrative style and motifs resemble those of the anonymous *Les cent nouvelles nouvelles* (ca. 1456–1461; *The Hundred New Novellas*). Here, where the king had the most room for discretion—and often wanted to enhance his majesty by increasing the range of his pardon beyond what was legally remissible—here, there was the most room for a supplicant to tell a story. Furthermore, the request for remission was supposed to evoke a personal exchange: a subject giving his recital directly to the king and the merciful king responding.

The resulting tales use some of the same techniques as the Renaissance novella, especially those to create *vraisemblance,* verisimilitude. The supplication had, of course, distinctive ends: precise names must be built into the account to provide a list of witnesses for the judicial hearing, along with precise events to which witnesses could attest. Thus during du Mesnil's entry, Saint-Aignen locates himself in the salon doing late-night business with a Master Thomas Guérin and describes the clothing, exclamations, and movements of the dis-guised lover erupting from the closet, which Guérin can then confirm.

But many homicides had no living witnesses, and still the supplicants' accounts are rich in concrete detail—in reality effects—going well beyond the bare narrative of the homicide. Here the verisimilitude has the same intention as that of the literary novella: to persuade the reader that the events recounted really happened and that their teller is a believable person. Of course, the sup-plicant takes this goal more seriously than the author: for the former the hope is to save one's neck, whereas for the latter the hope is merely to save one's reputation as a good or playful storyteller.

The concrete detail in the pardon tales also had another function. It could try to captivate the reader or listener so as to conceal certain gaps or mysterious elements in the narrative. The mysterious element in Saint-Aignen's tale is his wife, whose name he gallantly or prudently omits. Somehow she keeps receiving du Mesnil despite his threats to kill her husband and his bribing his way into her bed. Somehow she sleeps through a noisy fight that starts at a wardrobe not far from her door. Saint-Aignen describes his own feelings—"baffled, astonished, in wrath"—but says nothing of hers. The description of du Mesnil's disguise, the exact words he and the solicitor exchanged, Saint-Aignen's reflections to his servant about whether the body should be buried in holy ground or thrown into the street—these fill the silences in the story.

Verisimilitude and reality effects are found in almost all pardon tales, but letters of remission differ in many other respects, not only according to the storytelling skills of the supplicant (or the notary or attorney when they play a role in shaping the tale) but also according to the circumstances of the homicide and the estate or gender of the supplicant. For example, few letters of remission open with a preexisting feud or grievance the way Saint-Aignen's does, for this might suggest premeditation. Instead they start out with the blameless activities of everyday work or holiday festivity, then build to a climax of insult and injury, during which the victim is shown to have started the trouble. Saint-Aignen had little to fear from a narrative in which his husbandly honor was at stake, for French law found homicide "to avenge the adultery of a wife" especially excusable, according to one legal commentator, "because of the intolerable anguish to him offended" (Jean Papon, *Trias iudiciel du second notaire,* p. 456). What is distinctive about Saint-Aignen's adultery tale is that it focuses only on the lover, and the wife gets off scot-free.

Women's stories of homicide in defense of their sexual honor are a different matter. Most of them involve efforts to protect their own bodies against rapists or men who think them prostitutes; and they frame the events by their proper domestic activities whenever they can, for festive openings tend to cast women in the wrong. The case of a Gascon villager who killed her husband's lover in 1523 presents another contrast in the movement of a pardon tale. Whereas the husbands represent themselves as "angry" at the offense to their honor and at their wife's disobedience, Vidalle Bayonne was not merely "in hot anger" when she picked up the stones to throw at Catherine Bonnemate; she was also "jealous." Husbands did not admit to that demeaning sentiment, so mocked by Rabelais in his portrait of the obsessed old husband Hans Carvel in the *Tiers livre* (1546; *Third Book,* chap. 28).

Although letters of remission did not circulate in printed form, their contents were heard and debated by many people who had never seen the original parchment. Told to neighbors and patrons, to notaries and attorneys, to chancellery officers, judges, sergeants, and jailers; retold to the curious; and discussed sometimes by king, privy council, and courtiers, pardon tales moved throughout French society. Not surprisingly, Renaissance authors drew upon them for motifs, events, and narrative form and for commentary on the whole pardoning process. Should a pardon tale be believed? authors might ask, just as readers of their *contes* might ask whether the claims that their stories "really happened" were to be believed. When was a remission rightly given? In his *Propos rustiques* (1547; *Rustic Sayings*), Noël du Fail shows Breton peasants practicing swordblows while saying, "Friend, I'm not asking for trouble" ("Mon ami, je ne vous demande rien"), a statement that served as evidence that one had acted in self-defense; in the 111th tale of his *Nouvelles récréations et joyeux devis* (1558; *New Amusements and Pleasant Chats*), Bonaventure Des Périers tells of a crafty thief who got his remission "for having spat out some words in roasted Latin" (2:152) and then went on to steal as before. Guillaume Bouchet, in the fourteenth of his *Sérées* (1597; *Evenings*), describes a poor offender, on the way to be hanged, who obtains his grace from Louis XI by a trick: having got the king to swear to grant him a final gift so long as it is not a pardon, he says, "I pray you only, Sire, to kiss my ass after I am dead" (3:42).

The author making fullest use of letters of remission was Margaret of Navarre, herself often close to the pardoning process by virtue of her position as duchess of Alençon (from 1509 on), royal sister (after 1515), and then queen of Navarre (1527). The twenty-third novella of *L'heptaméron* is in part a remission tale on behalf of a young gentleman of Périgord who killed his brother-in-law, wrongly thinking he was avenging his sister's murder. The first novella is about the lies in a plea for pardon: it is Margaret's account of what "truly" happened to an attorney of Alençon named Saint-Aignan [*sic*], his well-born wife, "more beautiful than virtuous," and a handsome young judge's son named du Mesnil. Here it is the wife who is primarily at fault, not in killing du Mesnil herself, but in instigating her husband to do it out of injured vanity.

The story opens with the wife being maintained in an adulterous and profitable relation with the bishop of Sées, Saint-Aignan conniving in the affair because of the advantages the bishop brings him as well. The wife becomes infatuated with du Mesnil, however, and arranges trysts with him when her husband is busy with the bishop. Du Mesnil discovers his mistress's duplicity one night when he finds her in bed with the bishop. Stung and in despair, he rejects her the next time she approaches him, saying that "as she had been in contact with sacred things, she was too holy to speak to a sinner such as himself" (*Heptameron*, p. 72).

The wife then plots her revenge, telling her husband that they must move to Argentan because the judge's son has been attempting her honor. Established there, she summons du Mesnil with the false accusation that he has been spreading rumors about her and the bishop of Sées. Meeting her in church at vespers, he denies it, but she insists he must tell her husband this as well. She sends for him that night, her husband having hidden a hired murderer named Thomas Guérin and others in a wardrobe. They ambush du Mesnil, Guérin kills him with his sword, and he dies recommending his soul to God. Only then does Saint-Aignan dare to strike him with his dagger.

After having du Mesnil's body burned and his bones cast in mortar, Saint-Aignan plans what to do. The murder cannot be kept secret, for du Mesnil's servants and a chambermaid have fled with the news. Saint-Aignan pays Guérin

143

to leave the kingdom, compromises another chambermaid by having her taken off to be a prostitute in Paris, and sends to the king for his remission, saying that "he had several times forbidden his house to a suspicious person, who was seeking the dishonor of his wife; that nonetheless he had come to talk to her at night; and that finding him at the entrance to her room, he had killed him, more in anger than in reason" (*Heptameron*, p. 75; translation modified). At this point the duke and duchess of Alençon (that is, Margaret herself) intervene, and Margaret's novella diverges radically from the closing formulas of Michel de Saint-Aignen's letter of remission, in which Francis I pardons the supplicant. Apprised of the truth by du Mesnil's father, they prevent the remission from being granted, and Saint-Aignan and his wife flee to England. Condemned to death in their absence, they ingratiate themselves so effectively with Henry VIII that he persuades Francis to pardon them and allow them to return so long as they pay a large fine to their victim's family. Reluctant to do so, Saint-Aignan turns to a Parisian magician to win him the grace of the king and the chancellor and the death of those who have caused him all this trouble: du Mesnil's father, the duchess of Alençon, and his own wife. Denounced by his wife, Saint-Aignan is condemned to death, but at Margaret's intervention is sent off to the galleys for the rest of his life. His wife continues her sinful ways and dies miserably.

Margaret's novella is a counter letter of remission. It opens not with the king's voice, but in her court of Alençon, where the ducal attorney Saint-Aignan is shifting his loyalty to the bishop of Sées; it closes not with the king's grace and mercy but with hers, urging the commutation of Saint-Aignan's sentence. Every step in Michel de Saint-Aignen's pardon tale is here given a different twist, from the lovers' bed to the wardrobe to the burial; and the mysterious wife emerges only too clearly as the vindictive and manipulative figure "who does foul deeds to men" (p. 70).

But there are gaps and baffling elements in Margaret's tale, just as in a letter of remission, and doubts about its claim to "pure truthfulness." How does an Alençon attorney with a death sentence on his head rise so easily in the favor of the king of England? What are the duchess of Alençon's interests in a quarrel whose major actors are all judicial officers in her court, and what accounts for her final mercy toward Saint-Aignan? Margaret herself raises questions about the novella's true meaning at its end, in the discussion among the storytellers that follows every tale. The story of Saint-Aignan's wife has been recounted by the gentleman Simontault, who refers to women's ill-treatment of men since Eve, even while he tries to flirt with Parlamente before her husband's eyes. Simontault invites old Dame Oisille to tell the next story, sure she will agree with him about the cruelty of women. She responds that, on the contrary, she will search her past for an account that gives the lie to his misogynistic views.

The two tales of the attorney of Alençon and his wife suggest the multiple settings for storytelling in 16th-century France. Despite the application of legal rules to the pardon tale, similar literary conventions operate in both cases. Together they reveal that the tension between the true and the plausible, between the *vrai* and the *vraisemblable,* was not just a Renaissance game but could also be a matter of life and death.

See also 1527.

Bibliography: Guillaume Bouchet, *Les sérées,* ed. C. E. Roybet, 6 vols. (Paris: Lemerre, 1873–1882). Natalie Zemon Davis, *Fiction in the Archives: Pardon Tales and Their Tellers in Sixteenth-Century France* (Stanford: Stanford University Press, 1987). Bonaventure Des Périers, *Nouvelles récréations et joyeux devis,* ed. Louis Lacour, 2 vols. (Paris: Librairie des Bibliophiles, 1874). Noël du Fail, *Les propos rustiques,* ed. Arthur de La Borderie (Geneva: Slatkine, 1970). Margaret of Navarre, *L'heptaméron,* ed. Michel François (Paris: Garnier, 1967); translated by P. A. Chilton as *The Heptameron* (Harmondsworth: Penguin, 1984). Jean Papon, *Trias iudiciel du second notaire* (Lyons: Jean de Tournes, 1575). Gabriel A. Pérouse, *Nouvelles françaises du XVIe siècle: Images de la vie du temps* (Geneva: Droz, 1977).

Natalie Zemon Davis

ᗧᗡ 1527

Margaret of Angoulême, Sister of King Francis I, Is Married to Henri II d'Albret, King of Navarre

Margaret of Navarre

Of the many female writers known to us from the early period of French literature, only one, Margaret of Angoulême, better known as Margaret of Navarre (1492–1549), made her most significant contribution in prose. Her posthumous collection of seventy-two novellas, *L'heptaméron* (1559; *The Heptameron*), composed for the most part between 1542 and 1549 but begun as early as 1520, was left unfinished at her death. In imitation of Boccaccio's *Decameron* (1353), it begins with a fictive catastrophe (but a flood rather than a plague), spans seven days (instead of ten), and involves five male and five female storytellers. This equal division of the sexes (in the *Decameron* there are seven women and three men) emphasizes the thematic importance of gender difference and signals *L'heptaméron*'s polemical relation to Boccaccio's model.

The work is introduced by a general prologue, replete with geographic and historical detail, in which the narrator recounts how, after a great flood, the ten *devisants* (storytellers) took refuge in a monastery in the Pyrenees. Though seemingly naturalistic, the flood and the various dangers each character faces as he or she seeks refuge are also symbolically reminiscent of the biblical flood and its implication for Christian history. Despite the narrator's claim that, contrary to Boccaccio's, all the stories told by her ten *devisants* are "true" and unhampered by rhetoric, each tale is presented as an exemplum or parable whose symbolic value outweighs and even undermines its documentary value as a realistic story. A more specific frame-narrative opens and concludes each of the seven days (on each of which ten stories are told) and recounts the storytellers' discussions of each tale. These conversations bear little or no obvious relation to the stories that motivate them and contain narrative digressions that are themselves novellas in miniature. In this work, distinctions and boundaries (such as between story and commentary) seem to be constructed only to be undermined or altogether dissolved. The same indecision between history and allegory is reenacted in the endless critical debates concerning the meaning of the storytellers' proper names, which have been read either as anagrams of historical figures in Margaret's entourage or as personified allegories of spiritual attributes.

Margaret's extensive correspondence illuminates both this problematic relation between historical context and literary production and *L'heptaméron*'s concern with gender relations, especially when they involve tension between the "private" sphere of the family and the sociopolitical context.

In 1509, at age seventeen, Margaret was married to Charles, the duke of Alençon. This arrangement settled a long dispute between the houses of Angoulême and Alençon over the succession rights in Armagnac and guaranteed Margaret's renunciation of the succession rights to Angoulême. In 1515 Margaret's brother Francis became king of France. Charles died in 1525. Two years later Margaret was married to Henri II d'Albret, king of Navarre, and began an illustrious career as a lady of the court, a patron of the arts, and, shortly thereafter, a writer. The marriage marked an important stage in the long struggle between France and Spain. Most of Navarre belonged to Spain; by arranging for Margaret's marriage to Henri, Francis I secured French Navarre. At the same time he promised (in vain) to recapture the rest of Henri's kingdom from Charles V Hapsburg.

Jeanne, Margaret's daughter, later served as currency in the negotiation of another political alliance. In 1538, when she was ten years old, Francis I imprisoned her to ensure her marriage to the ally of his choice. Henri, her father, had been negotiating an alliance with Charles V that was to involve Jeanne's marriage to a Spanish ally. But, promising to recapture Navarre, Francis obtained Henri's consent in 1540 to marry Jeanne to the duke of Clèves, who had just defected from Spain to ally himself with France. In 1545 the duke was forced to serve Charles once again, and the marriage was annulled. Among the documents submitted as evidence that the marriage had never been consummated is the following protestation dated 1545 and signed by the then fifteen-year-old Jeanne d'Albret:

> I, Jeanne de Navarre . . . declare and protest again that the arranged marriage between myself and the duke of Clèves is against my will; that I have never and will never consent, and that anything I might do or say from here on in, from which one might say that I consented, will have been by force, against my pleasure and my will, and from fear of the king, of the king my father and the queen my mother, who menaced me and had me whipped by my governess, who several times urged me by commandment of the queen my mother, warning me that, if I did not agree to this marriage that the king wants, and if I did not consent, I would be beaten to death, and that I would

be the cause of the loss and destruction of my father and mother and of their house; of which I am so greatly fearful, also for the destruction of my parents, that I do not know to whom to have recourse except to God.   (*Nouvelles lettres*, pp. 291–292)

This powerful document, which tells us much about the relationship of marriage, maternity, and the state, is helpful in understanding portions of *L'heptaméron*. Much of *L'heptaméron* consists of a mother-daughter dialogue. Indeed, many of Margaret's stories focus on the social and political concerns addressed in this document. Dagoucin, one of the *devisants*, concludes the discussion of the fortieth tale with a remark about aristocratic marriages: "In order to maintain peace in the state, consideration is given only to the rank of families, the seniority of individuals and the provisions of the law, and not to men's love and virtue, in order that the monarchy should not be undermined" (*Heptameron*, p. 374). Several female protagonists of *L'heptaméron*'s novellas pit their wills against this sociopolitical order, struggling for self-determination in a world that regards women as currency on a political market. Two novellas in particular dramatize the question of matrimonial politics. Both are told by Parlamente (generally identified as Margaret's persona), who, along with Oisille, the oldest woman in the company, is the first to comment on the significance of the tale.

The twenty-first tale presents a conflict between a queen and her subject, Rolandine, who chooses her own mate ("a bastard") and is punished by being locked up in her father's tower. Rolandine's speech, in her confrontation with the queen, recalls the protest of Jeanne d'Albret in lamenting her lack of advocacy and claiming recourse to the divine. Rolandine's mate eventually proves unfaithful and dies, whereupon she is released from prison, marries a husband of her father's choosing, and lives happily ever after. The narrative thus resolves the impasse between Rolandine and authority (represented by the queen and her father) by rewriting political contingency as desire: although Rolandine's actions constitute an "offense," marriage is her goal. The resolution is signaled by the replacement of Rolandine's socially and politically unacceptable choice with a mate bearing "the same name and arms as her father" (*Heptameron*, p. 252). In commenting on the story, neither Parlamente nor Oisille refers to Rolandine's disobedience; both focus only on her constancy. Their silence can be seen as a narrative compromise between the dictates of the sociopolitical order (represented by the queen/mother) and feminine desire (Rolandine).

In the fortieth tale, a woman again disobeys her family and marries a man below her station. Parlamente concludes her story by condemning the unauthorized exercise of choice: "Ladies, I pray God . . . that none of you will wish to marry merely for your pleasure, without the consent of those to whom you owe obedience" (p. 370), and Oisille supports her point of view.

Thus unlike the *Decameron*, which aims through the art of storytelling to seduce its female readers (Boccaccio calls it a *galeotto*, the same word used by Dante to describe the book that led Francesca da Rimini to her adulterous downfall), Margaret's novellas mediate between the patriarchal structures that define the social order (including the maternal authority that serves that order) and the female subject, whose desires may run contrary to social norms. Margaret's text provides a space for sociopolitical debate in which women's voices and desires can be expressed.

Margaret's inclusion of this fragment of her own history and the mother-daughter dialogues throughout *L'heptaméron* connect the world of politics, with its social and personal implications for women, to the world of fiction, making literature operate as a vehicle for women's history. With her rewriting of the *Decameron* as a cautionary tale for mothers and daughters, she advanced a form of feminist polemics that finds its fullest expression in 20th-century novels by women. From her position on the margins of patriarchal literature and history, Margaret of Navarre quietly challenged the norms of male-dominated society and fiction by revealing the cultural politics of women's history.

See also 1526, 1534 (17–18 October).

Bibliography: Nancy Armstrong, "Literature as Women's History: A Necessary Transgression of Genres," *Genre,* 19 (1986), 347–369. Carla Freccero, "Rewriting the Rhetoric of Desire in Marguerite de Navarre's *Heptameron,*" in *Contending Kingdoms: Historical, Psychological, and Feminist Approaches to the Literature of Sixteenth-Century England and France,* ed. Marie-Rose Logan and Peter Rudnytsky (Detroit: Wayne State University Press, 1989). Jules Gelernt, *World of Many Loves: The "Heptameron" of Marguerite de Navarre* (Chapel Hill: University of North Carolina Press, 1966). Marguerite de Navarre, *L'heptaméron,* ed. Michel François (Paris: Garnier, 1967); translated by P. A. Chilton as *The Heptameron* (Harmondsworth: Penguin, 1984). Marguerite de Navarre, *Lettres de Marguerite d'Angoulême, soeur de François Ier, reine de Navarre,* ed. François Genin (Paris: Société de l'Histoire de France, 1841). Marguerite de Navarre, *Nouvelles lettres de la reine de Navarre adressées au roi François Ier, son frère,* ed. François Genin (Paris: Société de l'Histoire de France, 1842). Marcel Tetel, *Marguerite de Navarre's "Heptameron": Themes, Language, and Structure* (Durham, N.C.: Duke University Press, 1973).

Carla Freccero

∽ 1528
Francis I Commissions the Renovation of the Château at Fontainebleau

Manners and Mannerisms at Court

In the 16th-century section of his *Histoire de France* (*Renaissance et Réforme,* 1855; *Renaissance and Reformation*), Jules Michelet notes that Francis I (1515–1547), having lost his claim to Italy, set about creating Italy in France ("se fait une Italie française"; *Oeuvres complètes,* 7:434). This witty fiction of a monarch so generatively powerful that he reproduces nations alludes to both the military and the cultural exploits of the French king. Although Italy had already been (and would continue to be) both won and lost, the occasion to which Michelet obliquely refers is the battle of Pavia (1525), where the French were forced to cede not only their honor but also their leader to the troops of Hapsburg Holy

Roman emperor—and king of Spain—Charles V. For more than a year Francis was held hostage while his mother, Louise of Valois, and his sister, the future Margaret of Navarre, negotiated a suitable exchange (two royal sons for one royal father). Decidedly shaken at its foundation, the edifice of nascent French monarchy demanded reconstruction; upon his return, the militarily humiliated Francis would refigure himself as the culturally triumphant patron, as the "father of French arts and letters," through a massive building program centered in large part at Fontainebleau.

Although it may be correctly argued that Michelet's passing observation reveals more about the motives and strategies of 19th-century visions of "the Renaissance" than about 16th-century creative practice, his causal association of a military defeat and a cultural victory is telling. For its underlying assumption firmly locates the production of Renaissance "high art" not only in the aesthetic aspirations of the individual artist but also in the political aspirations of the Renaissance patron. Michelet's notion of a "French Italy" makes a broad definition of the term *conquest* critical to understanding early modern state formation, a definition that embraces the interconnected desires for colonized territory and colonized culture. Colonization moves, of course, in two directions: the outbound occupation of foreign states as well as the inbound appropriation of conquered riches. Even his contemporaries described Francis' agents, amply funded and specifically commissioned, as "pillaging" Italy in the name of France. In such a context artists and their works became collectible commodities, properties if not winnable at least purchasable in the highly competitive 16th-century art market. The French booty of Italian manuscripts, books, paintings, and sculptures thus constituted a crucial and enabling factor in Francis' expansive display of his own royal magnificence.

A castle site since the 12th century, Fontainebleau's medieval structure required serious modification if it was to become Francis' principal showplace. At the very least, his commissions included a monumental entrance—la Porte Dorée (1528; the Golden Doorway), a three-tiered Italianate gallery (library, ceremonial space, and baths), and a scheme of overall embellishment. When in 1539–40 Charles V passed through France, the king insisted that he be grandly received at what had then become the nation's principal site of artistic accomplishment, Fontainebleau. A year later Sir John Wallop, envoy from Francis' other rival, Henry VIII of England, met the court at Melun to resolve a small military dispute. Discussion of the overt political issue was, however, deferred when Francis asked "what maner of howse that Windsour was, and how it stode." When told that it stood on a river, the king persisted: "And Hampton Court . . . is it on the same river?" Moving to the relative merits of competing French and English decorative styles, Francis invited Wallop to pursue his mission several days later at Fontainebleau—"to th'entent," Wallop informed Henry, that "I myght advertis Your Majestie thereof." Francis planned a highly personalized visit that included the royal chamber (where the king hoisted Wallop onto a bench so that he might touch the "mattyer and stuff" the "borders was made of"), the gallery ("the most magnifique that ever I sawe"), and the baths (which "being warme, and reked so much, like as it had ben a myst, that the King went before to guyde me"). Wallop curiously makes no mention of Francis' exceptional collection of Italian paintings located in the baths; they were no doubt obscured by the "myst." He does, however, note that Fontaine-bleau's Italianate decor was about to be further enhanced by "divers mowldes of anticke personages that he [Francis] hathe nowe cummyng owte of Ytalye" (*State Papers*, 8:482–484).

Francesco Primaticcio, who after 1540 was charged with overseeing Fon-tainebleau's artistic program, attended to the production and translocation of those "anticke personages," a set of plaster casts from classical statues that were destined, once rendered in bronze, to decorate the palace. Primaticcio, a stu-dent of the painter Giulio Romano, had arrived in France in 1532, but he was neither the first nor the last of Francis' notable Italian imports. In 1516, well before Pavia, Leonardo da Vinci had moved to Amboise, where he died three years later; in 1531 a student of Michelangelo, Giovanni Battista Rosso, both conceived and initiated the decoration of the Fontainebleau gallery; in 1540 Benvenuto Cellini began a five-year French exile during which he produced not only exquisite goldsmith's work (*La salière de François Ier*, 1543; The Saltcellar of Francis I) but also monumental sculpture (*La nymphe de Fontainebleau*, 1543; The Nymph of Fontainebleau). As the fathers of French mannerism, these and other Italians transformed Francis' privileged place into a site of highly effective apprenticeship for local artists; the gallicized Italians of the 1530s and 1540s thus set in motion the vigorous native production that dominated the second half of the century.

Francis' program of cultural importation was by no means limited to the plastic arts. Before and after moving the royal library to Fontainebleau (1544), the king sought to augment the collection with manuscripts purchased pre-dominantly in Italy as well as with printed books. His court, moreover, not only encouraged but also enacted the early stages of the 16th-century fashion of Petrarchism. Triumphal entries, the extravagantly staged city pageants that celebrated the arrival of the king or members of his family, gradually assumed a more classical form through assimilating Italian practices as well as Petrarch's *Trionfi* (1374; *Triumphs*). In addition, poets and poetasters alike (Francis among them) gradually appropriated the lyric style and stance of Petrarch's *Canzoniere* (1374; *Songbook*); indeed, Petrarch's imitators, and the imitators of his imita-tors, reiterated his mode with such regularity that his devotional pose and ornate rhetoric eventually shaped court behavior as well as court literature. Petrarch's self-fashioned posture of eloquent service to his beloved Laura readily lent itself to the demeanor of courtiers flattering their beloved prince; his con-torted rhetorical figures and particularizing aesthetic effaced the obsessive repe-tition of his matter (Laura) by inspiring admiration for the virtuosic self-display of his manner. Mannerism and court manners went hand in hand in more than etymology—"mannerism," from Italian *maniera* (style), in turn from the Latin *manus* (hand). Privileging artful gestures over substance, the "stylish style" (as John Shearman called it) of the "anticke personages" that decorated Fontainebleau increasingly found its counterpart in the polished speech, the sumptuous dress, and the studied nonchalance of the court.

Anti-Petrarchan texts and anticourtier polemics of the period tellingly reveal this conflation of court poetics and court practices. Both critiques articulated disdain, the one poetical and the other political, for the mannered, feminizing Italianization of French culture. When, for example, Joachim du Bellay mounted his attack "Contre les Pétrarquistes" (1558; "Against the Petrarchans"), he specifically labeled the mode "courtly" and then characterized it in terms long associated with the seductive artifices of Italian women: it was cosmetic, bejeweled, counterfeit, flattering, deceptive, and notably Tuscan (in *Divers jeux rustiques,* pp. 70–82). When Pierre de Ronsard abandoned the Petrarchan praise of court lady Cassandra Salviati, the daughter of an Italian banker, he opted for a simpler woman and a simpler style, both without "ruses" or "makeup" ("Elégie à son livre" [1556; "Elegy to His Book"], in *Oeuvres complètes,* pp. 315–325). From a radically different perspective, the militant Protestant poet Agrippa d'Aubigné adopted identical terms to indict Italian contamination of the French court and, by extension, of his own youthful love poems. In *Les tragiques* (begun 1577, pub. 1616; *Tragic Stories*) he decried both the "ruses" of regent Catherine de Médicis, a Florentine imported in 1533 to marry Francis' son, the future Henri II, and the effeminacy of her courtiers: they were prostituted, frivolous, mannered, powdered, perfumed, made-up, and deceptive (*Les tragiques,* 2:92–93). By the end of the century George Puttenham's *Arte of English Poesie* (1589) made explicit the long implicit relation of literary to literal fashion; it compared refined, ornate rhetoric to the "courtly habillements" of ladies of honor, to "silkes or tysseues and costly embroideries [textiles imported from Italy] rather than plaine and simple apparell" (p. 137). From the court's perspective, cosmetics, jewels, and fancy dress—whether worn, spoken, or written—enhanced not only the splendor of the individual but also the magnificence of the entire royal company. Style for style's sake, then, was aesthetically and politically motivated; abundant embellishment was read, and resisted, as abundant control.

The Galerie François Ier (ca. 1528–1540; Gallery of Francis I), a composite and lavish mannerist masterpiece, allegorizes that putative control through a patently celebratory, though enigmatic, portrayal of Francis. At the center of its south wall, a Primaticcio evokes kingly power in terms of generative power by reworking a common classical myth, a "love (or rape) of Jupiter." Here, an elegant court lady—denuded of her "courtly habillements" but stylishly situated, draped, and coiffed—assumes the nonchalant pose of an "anticke personnage," Danaë. An oracle foretold that Danaë's father, King Acrisius, would die at the hands of his grandson; he therefore imprisoned his daughter in a guarded chamber to prevent her impregnation. But Jupiter, transforming himself into a shower of gold, poured through the roof, possessed Danaë, and fathered the fatal child, Perseus. Acrisius' plan was thus undone not by the projected storming of his fortifications, not by the manly valor of warrior suitors, but rather by a divine metamorphosis. At the center of the tale, then, is a drama of

power: a greater king artfully triumphs over a lesser one by cunningly appropriating a beautiful woman.

The embodiment of beauty itself within the mannerist aesthetic, the beautiful woman has traditionally emblematized Fontainebleau style. And Primaticcio's *Danaë* (ca. 1543) reveals the virtuosic manipulations that characterize the
mode: limbs are disproportionately elongated in relation to the body; torsion
permits multiple perspectives (one sees hands and feet from both top and
bottom, legs from front and back, frontal and profiled breasts); drapery isolates
parts from the whole (the right arm, the right leg above the thigh, the left leg
below the knee). Elizabeth Cropper has persuasively located a source of this
aesthetic of particularization, this preeminence accorded to detail at the expense
of proportion, in Petrarchan descriptive technique. Its extension, she then
argues, is developed in mannerist theoretical tracts and enacted in mannerist
practice. Petrarch, who defined his lyric purpose as "depicting and showing"
Laura to "whoever did not see her" (*Canzoniere,* 309, line 5), promoted a poetics
of display (from Latin *displicare*—"to scatter, to unfold to view") that in turn
readily, albeit partially, informed a politics of display: thus the patron collected
related but distinct beautiful objects (books, sculptures, paintings, court ladies)
in order to subject them to the gaze of intentionally impressed viewers (such as
Charles V or Wallop); thus the poet invented anatomical blazons, the anthology
of illustrated poems in praise of individual parts of the female anatomy, in order
(according to a 1536 verse letter by court poet Clément Marot) to "please
everyone and distract the King from the worries of war" (*Les épîtres* [*Epistles*],
no. 39, lines 83–85).

And yet the art of praise through display, when appropriated to the end of
poetic, painterly, or patronly self-display, is not without cost. When Shakespeare, for example, mounted his own assault "against the Petrarchans," he
strikingly identified a danger implicit in the mode: "I will not praise," he wrote
in Sonnet 21, "that purpose not to sell" (1609). By resisting the fashionable
"praise" of his day—public celebrations of ostensibly private loved ones—
Shakespeare refused to assume a lyric stance that seemed to work at counter-
purpose, that appeared more appropriate to a merchant who would sell his
riches than a lover who would win and keep them. Indeed, he interpreted the
excessiveness of Petrarchan corporeal metaphors (eyes are diamonds, lips are
rubies, hair is gold) not as innocent figurations of excellence but rather as com-
modifying and hyperbolic maneuvers better suited to advertising than to
courting. For beautiful bodies placed on display readily connoted beautiful
bodies for sale; deploying a court lady's "beauties" flirted with transforming her
into a courtesan. In Primaticcio's rendering of Danaë, for example, the virgin
girl of the myth is metamorphosed into the marketable woman of the court;
the irresistible shower is even made up of golden coins. When viewed within
the decorative scheme of the Gallery, moreover, that particular rain of gold
emanated from a doubled source—not only Jupiter's traditional cloud (shown
at the upper center of the engraving made after Primaticcio; fig. 1) but also
Francis' device (a triumphant, equally golden salamander poised atop the

1. "Danaë," engraving by Master L. D. (Léon Davent?) after Francesco Primaticcio, ca. 1543. (Courtesy of The Metropolitan Museum of Art, The Elisha Whittelsey Collection, The Elisha Whittelsey Fund, 1949 [49.95.379].)

image's architectural frame). Jupiterlike by design, Francis used whatever means necessary to overcome obstacles, to possess what he wanted.

Michelet describes Francis I, at the outset of the Fontainebleau project, as a "widower" bereft of his bride, Italy. Wedded instead to France, which Baldesar Castiglione noted "must always seem a petty realm to him" (*Il libro del cortegiano* [1528; *The Book of the Courtier*], p. 68), Francis sought to dress her in the image of the lost Other, to decorate her with the comely, collectible ornaments of Italianate culture. It is, of course, paradoxical that Castiglione, who wrote in praise of the tiny duchy of Urbino, should judge France a "petty realm." Indeed, as a highly particularized and thus indefensible territory, Italy was repeatedly forced to offer herself to powers beyond her control, to accede to the violent enactment of their rivalries upon her open, accessible body politic. Figured as a wounded and prostituted lady even by her most engaged admirers— Dante, Petrarch, Machiavelli—Italy was not, however, won by Francis I; she was purchased. For this early modern monarch participated in a new definition of patronage that went hand in hand with a new political phenomenon: the unprecedentedly rich nation-state. When in 1544 one of Fontainebleau's Italian "ornaments," a Florentine sculptor, threatened to return home, the king responded with an overpowering, albeit predictable, seduction. Francis, persisting in the reproduction of his own majestic image, proposed to continue

153

fathering "French Italies" by "drowning" Benvenuto Cellini in gold (*Vita* [begun 1558, pub. 1728; *Autobiography*], p. 304).

See also 1536 (Summer), 1553 (June), 1573, 1581, 1661.

Bibliography: Baldesar Castiglione, *The Book of the Courtier,* trans. Charles S. Singleton (Garden City, N.Y.: Doubleday, 1959). Benvenuto Cellini, *Autobiography,* trans. George Bull (Harmondsworth: Penguin, 1956). Elizabeth Cropper, "On Beautiful Women, Parmigianino, *Petrarchismo,* and the Vernacular Style," *Art Bulletin,* 58 (1976), 374–394. Théodore Agrippa d'Aubigné, *Les tragiques,* vol. 2, ed. Armand Garnier and Jean Plattard (Paris: Didier, 1967). Joachim du Bellay, *Divers jeux rustiques,* ed. V.-L. Saulnier (Geneva: Droz, 1965). Madlyn Millner Kahr, "Danaë: Virtuous, Voluptuous, Venal Woman," *Art Bulletin,* 58 (1978), 43–55. R. J. Knecht, *Francis I* (Cambridge: Cambridge University Press, 1982). Clément Marot, *Les épîtres,* ed. C. A. Mayer (London: University of London Press, 1958). Jules Michelet, *Histoire de France au seizième siècle: Renaissance et Réforme,* ed. Robert Casanova, in *Oeuvres complètes,* ed. Paul Vialaneix, vol. 7 (Paris: Flammarion, 1978). James Mirollo, *Mannerism and Renaissance Poetry: Concept, Mode, Inner Design* (New Haven: Yale University Press, 1984). *Petrarch's Lyric Poems: The "Rime Sparse" and Other Lyrics,* ed. and trans. Robert Durling (Cambridge, Mass.: Harvard University Press, 1976). George Puttenham, *The Arte of English Poesie,* ed. Gladys Doidge Willcock and Alice Walker (Cambridge: Cambridge University Press, 1936). Pierre de Ronsard, *Oeuvres complètes,* vol. 7, ed. Paul Laumonier (Paris: Droz, 1934). John Shearman, *Mannerism* (Harmondsworth: Penguin, 1967). Sir John Wallop, "To King Henry VIII, 17 November, 1540," in *State Papers of Henry VIII,* vol. 8, pt. 5 (London: Her Majesty's Commission, 1849). Henri Zerner, *The School of Fontainebleau: Etchings and Engravings,* trans. Stanley Baron (London: Thames and Hudson, 1969).

Nancy J. Vickers

✒ 1532

Pantagruel, by Alcofrybas Nasier, Is Published in Lyons

Rabelais and Textual Architecture

With the anonymous publication in 1532 of an unprepossessing little chapbook titled *Les horribles et épouvantables faits et prouesses du très renommé Pantagruel, roi des Dipsodes* (*The Horrible and Terrifying Deeds and Words of the Renowned Pantagruel, King of the Dipsodes*), François Rabelais, under the anagrammatic pseudonym Alcofrybas Nasier, offered to the citizens of Lyons the first volume of what was to become one of the great monuments of French literature. This comic sequel to *Les grandes et inestimables chroniques du grand et énorme géant Gargantua* (*The Great and Inestimable Chronicles of the Great and Enormous Giant Gargantua*), an anonymous and rather mediocre burlesque of chivalric romances published earlier the same year, narrates with apparent abandon the comical and sometimes obscene adventures of the giant hero and his trickster sidekick Panurge, from the grotesque birth of the hero in Utopia and his humanistic education in Paris to a burlesque epic victory over the Dipsodes (Thirsty Ones) who have invaded Utopia under the usurping King Anarche (Anarchy) and his general Loupgarou (Werewolf).

The success of this popular romance epic appears to have been enormous, for two or three years later (whether before or after the Affaire des Placards in October 1534 is an open question) Rabelais published, again anonymously, a second burlesque epic, *La vie inestimable du grand Gargantua* (*The Inestimable Life of the Great Gargantua*), which relates the life of Pantagruel's folkloric father and is designed to replace the *Grandes chroniques* as the "pre-text" for *Pantagruel*. This second book is so similar in its broad lines to the first that it has often been called a simple rewriting of *Pantagruel*. Like its predecessor, it traces the boisterous adventures of a giant hero from his birth and education to his exploits and final victory over an invading army. Gargantua replaces Pantagruel in the role of hero, the tireless and ribald monk Friar John replaces Panurge in the role of epic companion, and the mad Picrochole (Bitter Bile) replaces Anarche in the role of invading king. Despite its obvious similarities to *Pantagruel*, *Gargantua* is nevertheless quite distinct in its greater length and detail, in its relative realism (for example, the war takes place not in Utopia but in the region around Chinon), and in its partial elimination of the popular elements that predominate in *Pantagruel* (the romance culminates with the foundation of a utopian, exclusively aristocratic society in the abbey of Thélème).

After a twelve-year silence Rabelais published, this time in Paris and under his own name, a *Tiers livre des faits et dits héroïques du noble Pantagruel* (1546; *Third Book of the Heroic Deeds and Words of the Noble Pantagruel*), which begins where *Pantagruel* left off, with the peaceful colonization of Dipsodia. This new sequel is entirely different from the first two burlesque epics in subject, structure, style, tone, and even physical appearance (the gothic type of the earlier chapbooks having given way to the roman type of humanist publications). Now that the war against the Dipsodes is over, Pantagruel's companion Panurge wishes to marry and thus to avoid further military service and responsibility for himself. But at the same time he does not wish to be cuckolded. The greater part of the book is devoted to a kind of pseudo-Socratic quest in which Panurge consults various sources of divination and knowledge in the vain hope of learning his future in marriage, and thus of deciding whether or not to marry. All consultations are inconclusive, and the book ends as Panurge, still refusing to accept the contingencies of an unknown future, proposes to set off to the ends of the earth in search of an imaginary oracle, the Holy Bottle. Though comical, the book is less ebullient than its predecessors and abounds in classical erudition, making it by far the most difficult of all Rabelais's works.

The quest of the *Tiers livre* is continued in the *Quart livre des faits et dits héroïques du noble Pantagruel* (*Fourth Book of the Heroic Deeds and Words of the Noble Pantagruel*), which Rabelais published in complete form in 1552, a year before his death. (A fragment had already appeared in 1548, possibly without the author's permission.) This last completely authentic sequel to the original *Pantagruel* relates the long sea voyage in search of the Holy Bottle, Bacbuc, but the focus of the book shifts markedly from the purely moral, individual problem of the *Tiers livre* (Panurge's dilemma) to a more general, political one (the critical state of the world in 1552). Here the Pantagruelians encounter a series of islands and adventures at sea, most of which satirize the various religious or political forces responsible for the international crises and wars that were ravaging mid-16th-century Christendom.

A *Cinquième et dernier livre des faits et dits héroïques du bon Pantagruel* (1564; *Fifth and Last Book of the Heroic Deeds and Words of the Good Pantagruel*) continues the peregrinations of the *Quart livre* all the way to the Temple of the Bottle and its final, oracular "word": "Trink." But the authenticity of this last sequel, published eleven years after Rabelais's death, is subject to doubt. Although Rabelais may have written most of the episodes contained in it, he is definitely not responsible for their publication in a single, concluding volume. The final consultation with Bacbuc may in fact have been the original conclusion of an early draft of the *Tiers livre,* rejected by Rabelais but discovered among his papers and published posthumously as a spurious conclusion to the deliberately uncompleted odyssey of the *Quart livre.*

Rabelais's books are immensely appealing but notoriously difficult to interpret. One difficulty that has preoccupied modern readers is their curious mixture of the highest humanistic erudition and the basest "Rabelaisian" humor. But this difficulty is largely an anachronistic one, since the intellectual elite of Rabelais's day seem to have been perfectly at home in both humanistic and popular cultures. It is also a rather partial difficulty, since the qualities we generally think of as Rabelaisian (bibulous ebullience and spontaneity, gross physicality, popular coarseness, and obscene or scatological humor), though much in evidence in the first book, are gradually eliminated in the second and are virtually absent from the last two.

A far more constant aspect of Rabelais's works, and one that poses far greater difficulties for the exegete, is their episodic, fragmentary, and apparently random composition. Whether their subject is popular or aristocratic, whether their tone is burlesque or humanistic, each of Rabelais's four books gives an impression of disarticulation, directionlessness, and radical open-endedness. The importance of this formal idiosyncrasy is that it seems to allow, and even to entail, an unfocused, "Menippean" indeterminacy of meaning. In the absence of any obvious unifying principle or controlling design, readers have felt condemned (or free) to decide for themselves which episodes are important and which are not, to interpret each episode independently as an autonomous unit or in conjunction with any others they might choose, and to combine these various, variously interpreted parts as they see fit into some global interpretation of the whole. Such exegetical liberty has naturally led to widely divergent, indeed antithetical, views of what Rabelais is all about. Rabelais has been variously portrayed as a rationalistic atheist (Lefranc), a typical Franciscan monk (Febvre), and an antimonastic evangelical (Screech); as a royal propagandist (Lefranc) and an antiestablishment revolutionary (Bakhtin); as an antischolastic mystic (Defaux), a word-spinning mystifier (Rigolot), and a Derridean deferrer of meaning (Cave)—to mention only a few of the more influential and convincing readings. The most fundamental difficulty in Rabelais, then, is one of formal and ideological coherence, "form" and "ideology" being inextricably related aspects of the same underlying problem.

This exegetical difficulty vanishes once one puts aside anachronistic notions of literary form and considers each of Rabelais's books in terms of the two general types of compositional logic commonly found in classical, medieval, and early modern literature: the forward-moving, teleological design of the epic quest; and the static, symmetrical design of certain epic and lyric forms. Each of these two types of "textual architecture" helps to guide interpretation by focusing attention on a single, salient locus of meaning. But the "meaning" they reveal is of two rather different kinds. Whereas a teleological design naturally points to a revelation and a resolution at the end of the work, a symmetrical design points to a revelation—but not a final resolution—at the center. In the first case meaning is definitive and literally "final." In the second case meaning is less definitive, more provisional, but nevertheless somehow "central."

Each of the four books, however fragmentary or open-ended, conforms to one or both of these kinds of compositional logic, and is thus both coherent and comprehensible on some very basic level. With each successive book Rabelais moved further from the first type of textual architecture and closer to the second. To this evolution in compositional logic corresponds a profound change in meaning, and change in the nature of meaning.

Pantagruel conforms entirely to the first type. Not only are its episodes arranged in a strictly linear sequence, but their sequence is endowed from the beginning with a strong sense of direction and finality. The heroic exploit performed by Pantagruel at the epic climax fulfills a prophecy contained in the first two chapters and brings about the final resolution toward which the entire book has moved. This purely teleological design takes the form of a messianic, redemptive scheme involving an archetypal original sin of brother against brother (the murder of Abel by Cain) and the eventual establishment of a new reign of brotherly love in Utopia. The textual architecture of *Pantagruel* thus lends to an ostensibly freewheeling chronicle both a formal coherence and a stable meaning whose overtones are distinctly evangelical, and whose telos (both goal and fulfillment) is entirely utopian in the modern sense of the word.

In the successive sequels to *Pantagruel* Rabelais gradually subverts this strongly teleological, utopian scheme by mitigating and eventually even eliminating the telos toward which each book seems to point. This transformation begins slowly with *Gargantua*. Though culminating in Gargantua's victory over Picrochole's invading armies and the institution of the utopian society in the abbey of Thélème, *Gargantua* ends anticlimactically with an unresolved disagreement over the meaning of an obscurely prophetic text. The relative instability of this telos is compensated by a rudimentary symmetry consisting in a deliberate correspondence between the first and last episodes of the book, both of which relate the discovery of ancient texts found under slabs of bronze. Whatever the precise meaning of these enigmatic texts, they clearly work together as a kind of frame to create a sense of closure even within open-endedness while drawing attention to the problem of literary interpretation in general. Although the book itself is obviously complete, its meaning is not: the obscure prophecies with which it begins and ends will be fully comprehensible only in the fullness of time, sometime beyond the confines of the book. Once again, textual architecture appears in the service of meaning, but here meaning is presented as somehow more problematic and less definitive.

This tension between a forward-moving and a static structure is even more pronounced in the *Tiers livre*. The teleological thrust of the book is provided by Panurge's quest for a definitive answer. But far from leading to a final revelation, the quest ends in total failure, and the narrative itself ends aclimactically, not with a conclusion but with preparations for a new beginning. This radical open-endedness is compensated by a static architecture that develops to the extreme the framing device of *Gargantua*. The quest is framed by satirical eulogies, and the consultations themselves are arranged symmetrically around a central episode, chapter, passage, and word, in which the questing Panurge is made to function as his own oracle and to utter, in a moment of supreme dramatic and circumstantial irony, the only legitimate answer to his quest: "Know thyself." The symmetrical composition thus displaces the telos of the quest from the end of the book to the center, and from an outside authority to the quester himself. At the same time it reveals a stable, unequivocal meaning that is literally central to the entire book and allows us to interpret Panurge's open-ended quest without in any way resolving it.

A similar design governs the continuation of Panurge's quest in the *Quart livre*, whose odyssey ends even more inconclusively than the quest of the *Tiers livre*, as Panurge, far from the oracular "word" of his quest, utters a deluge of mendacious words to the effect that his own excrement is Irish saffron. As in the *Tiers livre*, however, this frustrated teleology is compensated by a static textual architecture that sends the reader not to a telos beyond the text but back to a crucial, highlighted locus within the text. As in the *Tiers livre*, a neatly framed central episode (that of the "physeter," or whale) contains a literally central revelation indispensable to understanding the book as a whole—namely, that Pantagruel, not Panurge, is the true hero of the quest, and that his role consists not in a definitive resolution of all conflicts, but in the never-ending practice of active *caritas* (brotherly love).

In each of Rabelais's episodic, fragmented, and increasingly open-ended books, textual architecture thus serves to guide and focus interpretation. Neither type reduces Rabelais's books to a single or univocal meaning, but each provides a stable perspective from which to circumscribe the possibilities of meaning and to understand what is truly at issue even in cases of deliberately irreducible polyvalence.

This last point is a crucial one. The issue of polyvalence in Rabelais has so often been simplified and polarized that the most profound meaning of Rabelais's work has tended to get lost. Not the least consequence of the evolution from a teleological to a symmetrical form is that in the very process of displacing the telos from the end to the center, Rabelais transformed that telos from the complete revelation and final solution of the 1532 *Pantagruel* into a provisional revelation and a solution of a decidedly less final kind. Gradually and systematically, he subverted the utopian idea of a definitive answer, along with its implications of completion, plenitude, and certainty. The result is an increasing sense of permanent and irremediable incompleteness, which is compensated only by some ethical principle, revealed at the center. This principle is not an *end* but a never-exhausted *means,* and a constantly renewed *beginning.* It is a stable principle of action that allows the hero to continue to act with assurance, even in a very un-utopian world characterized by unending contingency and violence. As such it also serves as a stable principle of interpretation that allows the reader to continue to read and to understand with some degree of certainty, even in the absence of a final, definitive revelation of meaning.

See also 1512, 1534 (Fall), 1534 (17–18 October), 1942.

Bibliography: Mikhail Bakhtin, *Rabelais and His World,* trans. Hélène Iswolsky (Cambridge, Mass.: MIT Press, 1968). Terence Cave, *The Cornucopian Text: Problems of Writing in the French Renaissance* (Oxford: Clarendon Press, 1979). Gérard Defaux, *Pantagruel et les sophistes: Contribution à l'histoire de l'humanisme chrétien au XVIe siècle* (The Hague: Nijhoff, 1973). Edwin M. Duval, "Panurge, Perplexity, and the Ironic Design of Rabelais's *Tiers Livre,*" *Renaissance Quarterly,* 35 (1982), 381–400. Lucien Febvre, *The Problem of Unbelief in the Sixteenth Century: The Religion of Rabelais,* trans. Beatrice Gottlieb (Cambridge, Mass.: Harvard University Press, 1982). Abel Lefranc, *Rabelais: Etudes sur Gargantua, Pantagruel, le Tiers livre* (Paris: Albin Michel, 1953). François Rabelais, *Gargantua and Pantagruel,* trans. J. M. Cohen (Baltimore: Penguin, 1955). Rabelais, *Oeuvres complètes,* ed. Pierre Jourda, 2 vols. (Paris: Garnier, 1962). François Rigolot, *Les langages de Rabelais* (Geneva: Droz, 1972). Michael A. Screech, *Rabelais* (Ithaca: Cornell University Press, 1979).

Edwin M. Duval

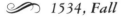 **1534, Fall**

Rabelais Publishes *Gargantua* Anonymously in Time for the Fair in Lyons That Follows the Harvest of the Grapes

Renaissance Orality and Literary Banquets

"As soon as he was born, he cried not as other babes use to do, miez, miez, miez, but with a high, sturdy and big voice shouted about, Some drink, some drink, some drink, as inviting all the world to drink with him" (*Gargantua,* p. 9). This is the first babble of the baby Gargantua; it has been taken for the voice of the Renaissance itself, thirsting for life and knowledge. We are at the beginning of the novel. The giant comes into the world during a feast in the country, where meats, wines, and enjoyment are overflowing. The hero's destiny and the whole book thus open on this note of joyous abundance. Rabelais's first novel, *Pantagruel* (1532), had also started as a story of a bout of overeating, during which the bodies of the first men, at the beginning of the world, had swollen up and given birth to the race of giants. The inaugural act, which creates life and appeals to the reader, is, then, the invitation to share copious nourishment.

Mikhail Bakhtin has decisively established the links between Rabelais's work and the ideology and images of the carnival. For people whose normal lot was famines and fastings, these overflowing menus symbolized nature's bounty, her fertility, and also the continuation of vital energies in a productive cycle renewed after the dead season. In this perspective, hunger and sexual impulses often go together, and to admit to, to satisfy, enormous appetites is also to claim that instincts are legitimate and that supposedly shameful organs are wholesome. When he sits down at table, man frees himself from moral embargoes and renews his harmonious relationship with nature and society. By praising good food in his first two novels, Rabelais expresses a naturalistic and vitalistic ideal and recreates rites and myths that are deeply rooted in folklore. Later, it is true, in the *Quart livre* (1552; *Fourth Book*), the feast becomes an orgy, and abundance turns into excess: the stomach (Messere Gaster) looks like a monster, and Rabelais makes gluttons (Andouilles, Papimanes, Gastrolâtres) violent and repulsive.

In the prologue to *Gargantua,* the author, in the guise of a happy fellow drinker—he claims to have dictated his book while drinking and eating— invites his readers not merely to drink and have fun with him, but also to break open the bone and to suck its "substantific" marrow. It is as if feasts and libations created a favorable framework for literary communication—a kind of literature that in this way emphasizes its solidarity with the basic gestures of everyday life.

Oral reciting, reading aloud, whether during the meal or afterward, was of course an old tradition, in courts as well as in cottages, and one that Rabelais was probably trying to keep alive despite the recent introduction of printing. But as a humanist, he also refers to classical examples. He could have claimed the *Odyssey* as a model: Ulysses tells of some of his adventures during a feast among the Phaeacians, with the meats roasting and the cups being passed around. But an allusion at the beginning of the same prologue to Plato's *Symposium* points to the Greek tradition of the philosophical banquet, where a group of friends, inspired by the wine (*syn-posion,* to drink together), talk freely about a subject that is both entertaining and serious. The confidence and well-being that prevail among the guests create the conditions for a quest unhampered by systems, a collective experimental search for truth. The complementary ideal of the gospels' Last Supper, where the communion of the apostles is consecrated by the sharing of bread and wine, reinforces for the humanists the symbolic value of the banquet. For Plutarch in his *Table-Talk* (in *Moralia*) and for Erasmus, an essential model for Rabelais, in the several banquets to be found in his *Colloquia* (1518, 1526; *Colloquies*), the friendly circle of eaters creates the image of a society giving itself up without restraint to the quest for wisdom and satisfying simultaneously the appetites of the body and the curiosity of the mind. The head does the thinking, the conversation stimulates reflection and helps ideas circulate, while mouth and stomach take pleasure in food. In the ideal integration of the banquet, man can satisfy all his faculties, intellectual, moral, and sensual. Montaigne (*Essais,* III, 13) agrees with many of his contemporaries when he explains that a good meal, seasoned with good conversation, creates for the individual a special occasion in which he can bring all his capacities into harmonious play, and thus realize an essential aim of humanistic ethics.

Literary banquets in late antiquity—after those of Plato and Xenophon—changed their character: the works of Plutarch (*Table-Talk* and *The Dinner of the Seven Wise Men*), Athenaeus (*The Deipnosophists,* or *Sophists at Dinner*), and Macrobius (*Saturnalia*) have an aim that is less philosophical than learned and encyclopedic. They are enormous catalogues designed to conserve knowledge. The fiction of a meal, with its desultory conversation, allowed these learned writers to accumulate literary memories, practical observations, philological remarks, and so on. The French humanists, who strove to store as vast a number of documents on ancient culture as possible, liked this sort of compilation. They published and translated those of antiquity and, especially in the second half of the 16th century, produced many miscellanies. Guillaume Bouchet's *Les sérées* (1584–1598; *Evenings*) illustrates how the genre had evolved. The structure of a meal permits the proliferation of anecdotes, bits of erudition, and serious or amusing subjects with the intention of collecting multifarious pieces of knowledge. A mere concern for quantity tends to overlay the pleasure in the story and the festive atmosphere that existed in Rabelais. Nevertheless, this reflex of encyclopedic accumulation is profoundly rooted in the mentality of the period. Whether in a symposium form or not, there are many examples of this gluttonous taste for miscellanies in which learning, wisdom, and science are heaped in profusion (see, for example, the works of Pierre Boaistuau, Pierre de La Primaudaye, François Béroalde de Verville, and Pierre Messie).

The literary device of conversation at a banquet shows up two important and closely related tendencies in 16th-century literature. As we have seen, the spontaneous and composite nature of table talk corresponds to a generalized emphasis on abundance: humanist texts are often prolix, heterogeneous, and apparently disordered; they are not bound by the principles of order, clarity, and sobriety that ruled in the following century. With this structural freedom comes a great license in the handling of the language, bestowing on Renaissance works—those of Rabelais and of such short story writers as Margaret of Navarre, Bonaventure Des Périers, Noël du Fail—an extraordinary charm: the syntax and the vocabulary are still elastic, words can be invented, and all sorts of special effects can be created by style, which the purism of the subsequent classical era forbade. In particular the fiction of a dialogue at table authorizes and encourages linguistic fantasy. When they joke, the guests like to play on words; they use vulgar terms; they parody noble or learned turns of phrase; they indulge in medleys of different languages and different genres, as if the proximity to food gave the words a flavor and a sonorous substance richer than in ordinary use. Béroalde de Verville's *Le moyen de parvenir* (ca. 1610; *The Way to Succeed*), a literary banquet of an extraordinarily free composition and inventive style, proves in virtuoso fashion that literature is also a matter of conviviality and that, when fable sits at table, good words are as palatable as good wine.

See also 1512, 1532.

Bibliography: Mikhail Bakhtin, *Rabelais and His World,* trans. Hélène Iswolsky (Cambridge, Mass.: MIT Press, 1968). Terence Cave, *The Cornucopian Text: Problems of Writing in the French Renaissance* (Oxford: Clarendon Press, 1979). Michel Jeanneret, *Des mets et des mots: Banquets et propos de table à la Renaissance* (Paris: José Corti, 1987). François Rabelais, *Gargantua and Pantagruel,* trans. Sir Thomas Urquhart and Peter Motteux (Chicago: W. Benton, 1952).

Michel Jeanneret

✑ *1534, 17–18 October*
The Posting of Violent Anti-Catholic Placards in France's Main Cities and on the Very Door of Francis I's Room Launches a Period of Systematic Repression

Evangelism

In his letter of 22 December 1521 to Margaret of Alençon, sister of King Francis I and future queen of Navarre, Guillaume Briçonnet, bishop of Meaux, echoed what Luther and others had said before, what Clément Marot, Rabelais, and Calvin would repeat soon thereafter: "The water that flows from the abyss of wisdom and of evangelical doctrine is not being supplied by those who are in charge of it, hence the sterility and drought of souls, and not because of a lack of water . . . The church is today arid and dry like a torrent during the high heat of summer. Everyone is looking out for his own welfare and advancement. No one is concerned about God anymore. We are completely given to terrestrial matters, when we should be all spirit. And this is because we lack of the water of wisdom and evangelical doctrine, which does not flow and is not supplied as it should" (*Correspondance,* 1:85).

The church was indeed ailing. Weakened by the sophistry and intellectual arrogance of its theologians, the immoral behavior of its prelates, the petty rivalries among its monastic orders, the ignorance and superstitions of the vast majority of its members, it was no longer able to meet the new spiritual needs of Christianity. Those whose responsibility it was to supply "the water of wisdom and of evangelical doctrine" had become slaves to their own appetites. Wholly "terrestrial" and corporeal beings, they resembled in every way the oxen of scripture condemned by St. Augustine, or the happy, smug and troubling "Papimanes" (Pope Lovers) whom Rabelais would soon satirize so brilliantly in his *Quart livre* (1552; *Fourth Book*). Fortunately, the remedy was simple; it was, for Briçonnet, inscribed in the very nature of the sickness itself. To slake the spiritual thirst of the early French Renaissance, to cure the "sterility and drought of souls," one needed only to set that miraculous water free, to make it flow once again everywhere on earth so that all might drink of it.

A few days later, in another letter, dated 31 December, Briçonnet did not hesitate to address the issue directly. Adroitly mixing criticism and compliment, he tried hard to marshal the energy of his correspondent. "I believe," he wrote Margaret, "that your heart is in the right place. But, to tell you the truth, your hands are still hidden in your gloves. I still do not see any faith and flame coming from your hands. Take off your gloves, Milady; it is not enough to feel, to know, and to desire; one must also act" (*Correspondance*, 1:128). Briçonnet knew that the evangelization he dreamed of and sought to carry out would encounter strong resistance. He knew that the humanists and theologians he had gathered around him—Jacques Lefèvre d'Etaples, Guillaume Farel, François Vatable, Gérard Roussel, Pierre Caroli, and others—would one day need help. And he understood that the king's sister, given both her own feelings and her position at court, would be of service to them. Margaret would be the instrument of God's Word, and through her the king himself would lend his support to the Reformation—a movement unquestionably founded by Erasmus, Luther, and Lorenzo Valla, but one that, in France, thanks to his initiative, had now acquired political leadership, structure and means of action.

French Evangelism was a phenomenon of great complexity. It combined the crudest and most biting satire with the most authentic mysticism. And faith, demanding and aroused, sought to manifest itself not only in words but also in deed, throughout social and political life. In this respect Rabelais's *Gargantua* (1534) is highly symbolic: in the war waged by the good against the bad for the establishment of a joyful republic, Grandgousier's prayers require the armed support of Frère Jean, with his "staff of the cross." To vanquish Picrochole and allow Christ's law of love to triumph, one needed to do more than believe and drop to one's knee; one had also to fight: "Take off your gloves, Milady . . ."

To this day, literary histories have emphasized the satiric aspect of Evangelism: Clément Marot's *Enfer* (1526; *Hell*), his famous *coq-à-l'âne* (cock-and-bull) stories (1531–1536), and some of his ballads and epigrams; Rabelais's *Pantagruel* (1532), *Gargantua*, and *Quart livre;* and even Margaret of Navarre's posthumous *L'heptaméron* (1559); *The Heptameron*). Like Erasmus' *Colloquia* (1518, 1526; *Colloquies*) and *Moriae Encomium* (1511; *Praise of Folly*), these works denounce the church's corruption and scandals; they spare neither the theologians nor the monks, describing mercilessly their boorishness and laziness, their ignorance, debauchery, and hypocrisy. In the early 16th-century evangelical literature, all clerics are always and necessarily either Friar Lubins or Jobelin Bridés, that is, people whose only God is their belly.

But the literature of Evangelism involved far more than this satiric aspect; the sap that nourished it and alone gave it meaning was faith and mysticism. It started with the work of printers, translators, commentators, and preachers of the Word of God who did not hesitate to risk and sometimes lose their lives for the dissemination of its letter. Besides the masterpieces that are now part of the canon, it includes catechisms and "almanacs," devotional manuals, hand-books, and treatises of religious instruction: Evangelism, by its very nature, transcended linguistic, geographic, and, for that matter, academic borders.

During the 1520s Luther's writings were widely circulated in France, some of them translated by Louis de Berquin and by the small group of Evangelicals gathered around the king's sister. In 1527 Margaret, who maintained close ties with the Reformed circles of Strasbourg, where she was known as "the most Evangelical" lady of France, translated in French verses Luther's 1518 commentary on the Lord's Prayer (1527; *Le Pater Noster, fait en translation et dialogue par la reine de Navarre*). From 1515 on, Erasmus and his "Philosophy of Christ" played an important role in the triumph and dissemination of the new ideas—despite a certain resistance among French Evangelicals to the Dutch humanist's lofty conceits, verbosity, and obvious penchant for Greek rationalism. Not only did Berquin translate several of his treatises around 1525 and Marot three of his *Colloquies* about a decade later; but Etienne Dolet, who had just published Marot's *Enfer* and in 1542 would reissue Lefèvre d'Etaples's *Epîtres et évangiles pour les cinquante et deux dimanches de l'an* (1526; *Epistles and Gospels for the Fifty-two Sundays of the Year*), printed also his *Manuel du chevalier chrétien* (1505; *Manual of the Christian Knight*) and Claude Chansonnette's translation of his treatise on confession. Rabelais, who revered Erasmus and publicly acclaimed him as his spiritual father, filled the four authentic books of *Pantagruel* with countless references to his works. Erasmus' Christocentrism was in fact so close to that of the French Evangelicals in the circle of Meaux that the School of Theology of the University of Paris—the Sorbonne and its formidable syndic, Noël Béda—always found it quite natural to associate his name with those of Luther and Lefèvre d'Etaples in the "determinations" it launched against "heretical" writings from 1521 on.

The main theological feature of Evangelism was its logocentrism: not only is God always and infinitely *present* in his Word; God and his Word are also one, identical to the point of being indistinguishable. For the Evangelical, the divine Word is the infallible source of salvation of souls and also of the social and political world, the "republic." To open one's heart to this Word, to receive and lodge it within oneself, to assimilate it and make it one's own, was, wrote Erasmus in his *Paraclesis* (1516; *Consolation*), to allow within oneself "the restoration of a nature originally created good." To listen to this Word resound within oneself to the exclusion of any other, to try humbly to understand it, to be content to believe it if one did not understand it, to serve it, and to disseminate it through publication, translation, preaching, paraphrase, or commentary—in effect to become its "instrument"—was to achieve the double possibility of acting and of being acted upon. The Word seized, ravished, transported, and transformed all that it touched. And he who, like David, John, or Paul, taken over by the Word, has first allowed It to transform him would contribute all the more effectively to saving and transforming the world. Both Erasmus and Lefèvre d'Etaples saw in this restoration and rebirth the inevitable and necessary consummation of all hermeneutical endeavor. Knowing was not enough: it did not constitute an end in itself. The only thing that mattered was the transformation, the interior revolution, that this knowledge brought about. By making himself *theodidaktos* (taught by God) and allowing the Logos to imprint itself upon him, man would finally become again—and render the world he lives in—Christiform.

This fundamental belief in the transformative power of the Word explains the pedagogical and militant dimension of Evangelism. Convinced that the Word, this divine *pharmakon* (drug), would infallibly "cleanse" all "the diseased and ill souls," the Christian humanist became its *fidus interpres*—its translator, commentator, propagator, and guardian all at the same time. Confronted with increased prosecutions, censorship, and interdicts, from the Sorbonne, he took on the task of "sowing" among all Christians "the precious pearls of holy scripture" (Lefèvre d'Etaples, *Prefatory Epistles,* p. 460). He taught both kings and the people to pray and to confess, to read the gospel correctly, to leave behind all "human traditions," and "to correct the errors of Christianity" (p. 450). As Lefèvre d'Etaples admonishes in the prefatory epistle to his *Commentarii Initiatorii in Quatuor Evangelia* (1522; *Initiatory Commentaries on the Four Gospels*): "God's Word suffices. It is enough to make man see that life is eternal. Everything that does not serve this Word is completely superfluous. May all have but one course of study, one consolation, one desire: to know the gospel, to follow the gospel, to proclaim it everywhere. Let everyone hold firmly to what our ancestors and the primitive church soaked in the blood of its martyrs believed: to know nothing outside the gospel, to know that it is all things; to remain ignorant of everything that lies outside its boundaries: for the Truth that is God's Word alone saves man; all that is not It condemns him" (pp. 435–436).

The urgency and energy animating these exhortations were pregnant with consequences. The program they defined, as Lefèvre's tone suggests, was highly subversive. It supposed a revolution, everything we understand by "the Reformation": to reclaim from the hands of the theologians, who had usurped it for centuries, the dual privilege of authority and exclusivity with respect to the Word and its interpretation. God, wrote Lefèvre, "wants his Law to apply to everyone." Those who "do not want the simple folk to see and read the gospel of God in their own language" were wrong (*Prefatory Epistles,* p. 454). No matter the pretext, one cannot forbid "children to have, see, and read their father's testament." The Word could live only in and through the people.

Briçonnet's desire to "put the divine text into the hands of the people," Berquin's eagerness to "return Christ and God's word to the heart of all Christians," Dolet's commitment to advance the public good by publishing everything that might be found "useful to Christian instruction and the edification of our faith," also explain the parallel linguistic revolution. Latin, which until then had been the sole vehicle of knowledge, was suddenly challenged by the vernacular, as part of the goal of providing "simple" and "unrefined" people with direct access to God's Word. Like the hearts it was supposed to move and to transform, this vernacular was to be simple and unrefined, humble, transparent, and sincere—even, says Lefèvre, "abject" and "gross," without any "theatrical pump," that is, free of all the ornaments and guiles of rhetoric. For this reason Marot, the greatest poet of his time, "rhymed in prose," and for this reason also Antoine Augereau prefaced his 1533 edition of Margaret's *Le miroir de l'âme pécheresse* (1531; *The Mirror of the Sinful Soul*) with a short treatise in which he praises the new printing signs (such as apostrophe, accents, and cedilla) he was using: like the translator and the poet, the printer of evangelical texts wanted above all, in Augereau's words, to make "the French language clearer, and easier to understand."

These changes demonstrate how closely the literary history of the period is tied to religious history. Evangelism was answering a spiritual need. Actively supported by the printing shops—mainly those of Simon du Bois, Simon de Colines, Geoffroy Tory, Pierre de Vingle, and Etienne Dolet—it could also count on the goodwill of the crown. Margaret followed Briçonnet's advice quickly: as soon as the Sorbonne became dangerous—that is, around 1525— she "took off her gloves" and protected the Evangelicals for the rest of her life, doing her best to keep Francis I sympathetic to them. On several occasions between 1526 and 1530 the king intervened personally with the Sorbonne or the Parlement to halt proceedings against Lefèvre d'Etaples, Briçonnet, Erasmus, Marot, and Berquin. As always, the Sorbonne played its hand. Its ambition was to remain the guardian of dogma. But its powers were limited. It could do nothing without the support of Parlement, and Parlement depended directly on the king. At times, however, its efforts were rewarded: the circle of Meaux was forced to break up in 1525; Briçonnet submitted; Lefèvre d'Etaples had to flee to Strasbourg; Berquin was finally burned at the stake in 1529; Marot was imprisoned twice and eventually, like so many others, forced into exile. Nevertheless, between 1526, when the king returned from captivity in Madrid, and 1534, the year of the famous Affaire des Placards, the Sorbonne's authority declined considerably. In 1530, despite legal proceedings, interdictions, and censures, Lefèvre managed to complete and publish his *Sainte Bible en français* (*The Holy Bible in French*); there were increasing numbers of commentaries on the gospels and handbooks of religious instruction; Margaret continued to have Luther's treatises translated into French; and in 1533 Marot published without incident his translations of Psalm 6, the Lord's Prayer, the Credo, and the Ave Maria. All this occurred with the approval of Francis I, who appointed Lefèvre tutor to his children in 1526, founded the College of Royal Readers in 1530, and in 1533—a year of triumph and optimism for Evangelism and the year *Gargantua* was written—exiled Noël Béda twenty leagues from Paris.

This series of successes came to an abrupt halt during the night of 17 October 1534, when, on the walls of the main cities of France and even on the king's bedroom door, overzealous militants hung up posters denouncing in violent terms "the horrible, great, and intolerable abuses of the papal mass." The scale and audacity of the plot frightened the king and impelled him to a policy of brutal repression. Proceedings against the "heretics" had already started in November 1533, after a speech by Calvin's friend Nicolas Cop at the University of Paris. But now they became systematic. With Jehan Morin, the criminal prosecutor, at the helm, searches, arrests, interrogations, and tortures increased. The first stakes were set up on 10 November 1534 and not taken down until spring of the following year. During this period, the king responded to a new provocation by Antoine Marcourt—author of the 1534 Placards—by promulgating an edict against the press and organizing in Paris, on 21 January 1535, a massive expiatory procession that sealed the definitive triumph in France of the most intransigent orthodoxy. Most French Evangelicals left the country. Those who were able to stay had to find refuge in silence. The Reformation they had tried to bring about was meant to be a peaceful one. They had sought love and peace, and they had found fanaticism, hatred, and violence. It was indeed the end of an era; for many, the end of one of the most beautiful dreams ever inspired by the gospel.

See also 1541 (September), 1555 (13 September), 1609.

Bibliography: Aspects de la propagande religieuse (Geneva: Droz, 1957). Gabrielle Berthoud, *Antoine Marcourt, réformateur et pamphlétaire: Du "Livre des marchans" aux Placards de 1534* (Geneva: Droz, 1973), pp. 157–281, 287–289. Guillaume Briçonnet and Marguerite d'Angoulême, *Correspondance,* ed. Christine Martineau, Michel Veissière, and Henri Heller, 2 vols. (Geneva: Droz, 1975–1979). Gérard Defaux, *L'Ecriture comme présence: Marot, Rabelais, Montaigne* (Paris: Champion, 1987), esp. pp. 11–144. Etienne Dolet, *Préfaces françaises,* ed. Claude Longeon (Geneva: Droz, 1979). Desiderius Erasmus, *The Colloquies,* trans. Craig R. Thompson (Chicago: University of Chicago Press, 1965). Francis M. Higman, *Censorship and the Sorbonne: A Bibliographical Study of Books in French Censured by the Faculty of Theology of the University of Paris, 1520–1551* (Geneva: Droz, 1979). Jacques Lefèvre d'Etaples, *The Prefatory Epistles of Jacques Lefèvre d'Etaples and Related Texts,* ed. Eugene F. Rice, Jr. (New York: Columbia University Press, 1972). Marguerite de Navarre, *Le miroir de l'âme pécheresse,* ed. Renja Salminen (Helsinki: Sijomaleinen Tiedeakatemia, 1979) (includes the translation made by the future Elizabeth I of England, *The Glasse of the Synnful Soule*). "La *Paraclesis* d'Erasme, traduite par Pierre Mesnard," *Bibliothèque d'humanisme et Renaissance,* 13 (1951), 26–42.

Gérard Defaux

 1536

Jehan Le Febvre Translates into French Andrea Alciato's
Emblematum Libellus

Emblems

The emblem "In Astrologos" ("On Astrologers"; see fig. 1), by Andrea Alciato (1492–1550), consists of three elements—a title, a picture, and a verse text—disposed in a regularly repeated format on a single page, with the French translation on the facing recto. The relationship between the title and the picture is not immediately apparent. But the text quickly identifies the mythical figure of Icarus and, in the last three lines, turns it into a lesson warning astrologers of the dangers of prediction.

Although emblems often functioned as neat little riddles like this one, they were taken very seriously and understood as a particularly potent means of communication, combining the discursiveness of text with a pictorial representation of the same message. This pictorial part of the composition was held in particular esteem because it was thought to resemble the earliest pictographic or ideogrammatic languages considered in the Renaissance to derive from the pre-Babel Adamic language, and hence to be a direct link with the sources of religion. Egyptian hieroglyphics, which we now know to have been phonetic signs, were understood in this way throughout the Renaissance.

This conception of the hieroglyphic signs, together with the notion that painting was supposed to be mute poetry, and poetry, speaking painting, was well known to Andrea Alciato, the Milanese jurist generally credited with the creation of the emblem. It certainly influenced his development of the emblem as a collaboration between the arts that would make the verbal visual in order to enhance the impact and universality of the message. But Alciato also capitalized on the Renaissance interest in epigrams, especially those of the Greek Anthology: about a third of the texts in the original edition of his emblems already figured in a Latin translation of Greek epigrams from the Planudean Anthology published in Basel in 1529. Most of these pieces described ancient monuments and works of art. Alciato also used epigrams to describe pictures, but in such a way as to infer a general moral lesson. That modification formed the basis for a hybrid genre in which a fusion of picture and text was intended to produce a new vehicle for communication.

Although his correspondence suggests that Alciato may have been composing emblems for friends as early as 1522, the first edition of 104 Latin emblems was not published until 1531, and then in an unauthorized Augsburg edition. The first Latin edition to have Alciato's blessing was issued in Paris by Christian Wechel in 1534, and Wechel published Jehan Le Febvre's French translation, *Livret des emblèmes de maître André Alciat en rime française et présenté à monseigneur l'amiral de France* (*Master Andrea Alciato's Little Book of Emblems in French Verse and Presented to Monsignor the Admiral of France*), two years later. Alciato expanded the collection during the 1540s, and it contained 212 emblems at the time of his death. The emblems were an immediate and immense success in France; nearly all editions of his emblems were published there, and between 1534 and 1565 some sixty editions in Latin, French, German, Italian, and Spanish were published in Paris and Lyons. In 1549 Barthélemy Aneau published a completely new French translation.

Although Alciato's three-part format of title, picture, and epigrammatic text has been taken as the generic standard, Alciato really used the term *emblema* as a title for his collection of illustrated epigrams, and the sense of the emblem as a genre did not emerge until his French epigones began to use the name to describe compositions sometimes quite different from his. Many French works described as collections of emblems predate the earliest imitations of Alciato outside France, including Guillaume de La Perrière's *Le théâtre des bons engins* (1536?; *The Theater of Fine Devices*) and *La morosophie* (1553; *The Morosophy*), Gilles Corrozet's *Hécatomgraphie* (1540), Guillaume Guéroult's *Le premier livre des*

In Aſtrologos.

Icare per ſuperos qui raptus & aëra,donec
  In mare præcipitem cera liquata daret.
Nunc te cera eadem feruensḿ; refuſcitat ignis,
  Exemplo ut doceas dogmata certa tuo,
Aſtrologus caueat quicquam prædicere,præceps
  Nam cadet impoſtor dumſuper aſtra uehit.

Liuret des Emblemes de
Andre Alciat.

¶ Contre Aſtrologues.

Icarus cheut dedans la mer
Par trop grand exaltation:
Cil qui veult le ciel entamer/
Eſt trop plain de preſumption:
Donques ſur ceſte fiction/
Doibuent garder les aſtrologues/
Que leur haulte diſcuſſion/
Les mette ou dieu reduit tous rogues.

H iii

1. "In Astrologos," in Jehan Le Febvre, *Livret des emblèmes de maître André Alciat en rime française et présenté à monseigneur l'amiral de France* (Paris: Christian Wechel, 1536), sig. Hii–iii. (Courtesy of the Houghton Library, Harvard University.)

emblèmes (1550; *The First Book of Emblems*), Barthélemy Aneau's *Picta Poesis* (1552; *Painted Poetry;* translated into French the same year as *Imagination poétique* [*Poetic Imagination*]), and Pierre Coustau's *Le pegme* (1555; *Pegma*).

In fact it is fair to say that the genre actually took shape in France between 1536 and 1560. Not only were the French the first to imitate Alciato, but it was in France, beginning with Wechel, that printers began to format emblems in regular patterns on a single page or on facing pages in such a way as to emphasize the organic unity of text and illustration. Emblems were anthologized in collections of poetry and influenced the poetry of Maurice Scève in ways that were essential to the economy of his *Délie* (1544). Later, in the mid-1560s, Georgette de Montenay composed the first collection of religious emblems, *Emblèmes ou devises chrétiennes* (*Christian Emblems or Devices*), first published in Lyons in 1571 with magnificent copperplate illustrations by Pierre Woeiriot.

The early development of the genre in France was related to indigenous traditions of illustrated moralizing literature dating from the 14th century. Teaching law in Avignon (1518–1522, 1527–1529) and then in Bourges (1529–1533), Alciato could well have known these traditions through tapestries and stained-glass windows illustrating proverbs, through the bizarre composite personifications of the virtues created in the second half of the 15th century, or even through moralizations of Ovid or Petrarch's *Triumphs*. Whether or not Alciato was directly influenced by such earlier traditions, the French surely saw his emblems in the light of these models.

The *devise* (Italian *impresa*), a related emblematic form, emerged in France in the last third of the 14th century at the Burgundian courts and developed into a highly articulated art form in Italy in the second half of the 15th century. Whereas emblems expressed universally valid moral rules, devices encapsulated the owner's personal ideal or intention in a closely related combination of visual sign and short motto. The device was a much more disciplined and theoretically self-conscious form than the emblem and expressed the concerns of individual members of noble families in ways that heraldic symbolism, belonging to and designating entire families, could not—a real attraction at a time of developing individualism.

Devices graced the reverse of medals and provided motifs for interior decoration and themes for poetry. Francis I's salamander device with its motto *Nutrisco et Extinguo* (I nourish and I extinguish) was inspired by one of Petrarch's sonnets and commonly served as a motif, with or without the motto, in decorating such royal, or simply noble, residences as Fontainebleau, Blois, and La Possonnière. Other devices and emblems inspired motifs for châteaux at Anet, Dampierre-sur-Boutonne, and, later, Saint-Cloud. Montaigne had a *jeton* (token) struck in 1576 with his device—a set of scales and the Socratic motto *Que sais-je?* (What do I know?)—on the reverse; this device continued to find a place on the frontispieces of editions of the *Essais* through the first half of the 17th century. Rémi Belleau, Amadis Jamyn, Jacques Hyver, Agrippa d'Aubigné, and several précieux poets and novelists composed emblems or designed literary texts in which emblems and devices played an explicit role.

Although the emblem and the device tended to be somewhat conflated as they spread throughout Europe after 1560, they remained largely distinct and very popular in France through the late 17th century. Beginning in the 1590s, Henri IV began to use devices composed by his minister the duc de Sully and others as a vehicle for political propaganda, and by the middle of the 17th century it was established practice to produce new devices each year for the different royal ministries. The task of producing these compositions often fell either to the Little Academy, later to become the Academy of Inscriptions and Letters, which Jean-Baptiste Colbert founded for this purpose in 1663, or to the historiographers of the king; and it is in that capacity that Racine and Nicolas Boileau composed devices for Louis XIV and members of his government.

During the 17th century the emblem was taken over in France mainly by the Catholic religious orders, especially the Jesuits. The emblematic forms met the Counter-Reformation requirement for a more incarnate presentation of religious doctrine; the emblem served as a rhetorical matrix in structuring sermons and was a highly prized pedagogical tool in religious schools. In fact the form was considered so useful in communication that the Jesuits taught the composition of emblems in the upper classes of their *collèges*. Jesuits such as Pierre Le Moyne, Claude-François Menestrier, and Dominique Bouhours were largely responsible for the theorizing about the emblem and device that took place in the middle years of the century, and they also helped develop a taxonomy of the forms and their functions. These writings relegated the device to the needs of courtly communication (messages of love, propaganda, the articulation of a personal ideal or project), whereas the emblem was regarded as a looser form intended for use in the instruction of the middle classes. The more fashionable devices played a small but not insignificant role in précieux society. And the dynamics of that society also produced satirical devices such as the ones Roger de Bussy-Rabutin used to decorate his country house. Their appeal can be gauged by the space accorded to reporting the annual official devices in the fashionable journal *Le Mercure galant* and elsewhere in the second half of the century. But French society began to lose interest in both forms around 1690, and they gradually ceased to exercise any important influence on French cultural or intellectual life.

Throughout their history in France the emblematic forms often provided the key to the program for courtly festivals as diverse as *entrées,* ballets, marriages, and funerals; and they served as identifying marks for individuals and their possessions. Taken together with the impact of the emblematic forms on rhetorical and literary structure and interior decoration, such activity suggests that the emblematic forms are the most visible symptoms of a symbolic mentality that lies somewhere between medieval allegory and Romantic metaphor.

See also 1493, 1544, 1555 (13 September), 1634, 1640, 1654, 1770.

Bibliography: Andreas Alciatus, *The Latin Emblems* (vol. 1) and *Emblems in Translation* (vol. 2), ed. Peter M. Daly, Virginia W. Callahan, and Simon Cuttler (Toronto: University of Toronto Press, 1985). Barthélemy Aneau, *Imagination poétique* (Lyons: Macé Bonhomme, 1552). Gilles Corrozet, *Hecatomgraphie* (1540; reprint, London: Scolar Press, 1974). Peter M. Daly, *Literature in the Light of the Emblem* (Toronto: University of Toronto Press, 1979). Guillaume de La Perrière, *La morosophie* (Lyons: Macé Bonhomme, 1553). La Perrière, *Le théâtre des bons engins* (1539; reprint, Gainesville, Fla.: Scholars' Facsimiles & Reprints, 1964). Georgette de Montenay, *Emblèmes ou devises chrestiennes* (1571; reprint, London: Scolar Press, 1973). Mario Praz, *Studies in Seventeenth-Century Imagery,* 2d ed. (Rome: Edizioni di Storia e Letteratura, 1964). Daniel S. Russell, *The Emblem and Device in France* (Lexington, Ky.: French Forum, 1985). Maurice Scève, *Délie,* ed. I. D. McFarlane (Cambridge: Cambridge University Press, 1966).

Daniel S. Russell

∽ 1536, Summer
Clément Marot Imports into French the Petrarchan Sonnet

The Sonnet

Since the beginning of this century, and particularly in the last fifteen years, most contributions to the debate on the origins of the sonnet in France have centered on the questions of dating and authorship and, secondarily, of the definition and designation of poetic forms. According to the prevailing view,

the first French sonnet was written in Venice during the summer of 1536 by
Clément Marot ("Sonnet à Madame de Ferrare"). Its fourteen lines, divided into
two quatrains and two tercets, follow a "feminine" *abba abba ccd ccd* rhyme
scheme, each line ending with a mute *e*.

Michel d'Amboise, Jean Bouchet, and Mellin de Saint-Gelais have occasionally been mentioned as possible predecessors. But their fourteen-line poems
have neither the strophic form (the *abba* rhyme scheme) nor the rhetorical structure (the contrastive movement between quatrains and tercets) of Marot's first
sonnets. They are simply *quatorzains,* fourteen-line poems that follow the rules
of composition and take the name and form of the epigram, a genre much in
favor in France around 1536. The paternity of the first French sonnet seems
thus to lie with Clément Marot.

What is remarkable about this quest for origins is the failure of modern
specialists to talk of a "sonnet" in anything but the precise technical sense
that defines it today, as if the term had taken from the beginning a single
unequivocal signification at a specific identifiable moment. None of the pioneers
in the investigation of the sonnet entertained, however briefly, the possibility
that the semantics of the word *sonnet* could extend beyond the formal boundaries
of an Italian importation. None of their successors deemed it necessary to depart
from the narrow considerations of literary history (that is, dates and authorship)
or of formal techniques (that is, the definition of poetic forms) to formulate the
problem in terms of historical semantics.

The word *sonnet* was part of the French language well before it came to designate a new poetic form. With orthographic variations, it was used without
interruption until the 16th century as a diminutive of the French word *son* in
the sense of *chanson,* or lyrical song. During the reign of Francis I (1515–
1547), the sonnet designated a relatively unpopular type of epigram derived
from the Italian. Its use was generally limited to dedicatory poems and translations. In 1544 Marot published a translation of six sonnets by Petrarch; in the
same year, Maurice Scève published his major work, *Délie,* consisting not of
sonnets but of 449 ten-line poems. And if Francis I is to be judged by his own
poetic works, he was not interested in the sonnet; it is even possible that he felt
some aversion to a poetic form whose Italian origins were all too evident.
Despite her efforts, the dauphine, Catherine de Médicis had not persuaded
French courtly circles to adopt the new form. Yet all this would change after
Francis I's death in 1547.

Suddenly, with the accession of Francis' son, Henri II, the sonnet seemed
endowed with some reflection of the royal luster. In the first year of his reign,
poets, probably eager to please the new Italian queen, hastened to publish their
works. Among them were Mellin de Saint-Gelais and Jacques Peletier du Mans,
who, after Clément Marot, was instrumental in introducing the new form into
French literature. Whereas in the two quatrains the *embrassé* rhyme scheme
(*abba*) had been the rule from the beginning, Marot and Peletier du Mans initiated two different arrangements for the tercets (*deed* and *dede,* respectively),
which were almost universally adopted by later French poets.

Still in the first year of Henri's reign (1547), Vasquin Philieul published a translation of the first 196 sonnets of Petrarch and Thomas Sébillet wrote in his *Art poétique français* (1548; *French Poetic Art*) the first theoretical chapter ever devoted to the sonnet. In 1549 Pontus de Tyard published *Les erreurs amoureuses* (*Love's Strayings*), a collection of 168 poems that included 142 sonnets. In the same year, Joachim du Bellay's *La défense et illustration de la langue française* (*The Defense and Enrichment of the French Language*) was accompanied by a collection of neo-Petrarchan sonnets, *L'Olive, Vers lyriques* (*Olive, and Lyric Verses*). Significantly, when a new edition of *L'Olive* was published in 1550, the number of sonnets increased from 50 to 115. Soon du Bellay's friend Pierre de Ronsard gave the new form its finest luster in his famous collections of love sonnets: *Les amours* (1552 and 1553; *Love Poems*), the *Continuation des Amours* (1555) and *Nouvelle continuation* (1556; *New Continuation*), and, later, the two books of *Sonnets pour Hélène* (1578; *Sonnets for Hélène*). By the end of the century, mannerist and baroque poets were still composing many collections of sonnets on love and death, even though the new, competing longer form of multiple-stanza poems, the *stances,* became increasingly popular as an expressive medium for lyric poetry.

In the Pléiade's theoretical manifesto, du Bellay sought to affirm the essentially lyrical character of the sonnet by opposing it to the epigram and linking it to the ode. French lyric poetry would henceforth be written in the new form because, though borrowed from Italy, it conformed to the ancestral sense of the old French lyric ode. Hence his famous apostrophe to the French apprentice poet: "Sonne-moy ces beaux sonnets," an injunction that means both "Write those fair sonnets" (the Italian new form) and "Sing those fair (French) songs."

At the beginning of the 17th century, dictionaries continued to record the same duplicitous meaning of the word *sonnet.* Thus Randall Cotgrave, in his *Dictionarie of the French and English Tongues* (London, 1611), gives the following definition: "*Sonnet:* m. A Sonnet or canzonet, a song (most commonly) of 14 verses." One could hardly hope for a better example of a "floating signifier." Cotgrave's alternative "Sonnet *or* canzonet" refers, even as it reproduces the rhyme, to the associative double of *son* and *chanson,* rendering it in an anglicized and diminutive expression. The word *song* serves to recall the correct, yet paradoxically French, etymology of the Italian form. As for Cotgrave's approximate parenthesis—"(most commonly)"—it casts doubt on the very definition of the sonnet as composed of fourteen lines, and thus as a fixed form: we are far from the "uniformity" of "structure" advocated by Sébillet, for whom the "fourteen verses" must be "perpétuels" (in the sense of *perpetuus, sempiternis,* "always the same," as Robert Estienne informs us in his *Dictionnaire français-latin,* 1539).

Not until the so-called classic age did the semantics of *sonnet,* like that of so many other concepts, finally stabilize. By then Oronte's famous remark in Molière's *Le misanthrope* appeared comic to all concerned because it had become a pure tautology: "*Sonnet*—it's a sonnet."

See also 1549, 1555 (July).

173

Bibliography: Max Jasinski, *Histoire du sonnet en France* (Douai: Brugère, 1903). François Rigolot, "Qu'est-ce qu'un sonnet? Perspectives sur les origines d'une forme poétique," *Revue d'histoire littéraire de la France,* 84 (1984), 3–18. Hughes Vaganay, *Le sonnet en Italie et en France au XVIe siècle* (1902; reprint, Geneva: Slatkine, 1966). Pierre Villey, "Marot et le premier sonnet français," *Revue d'histoire littéraire de la France,* 20 (1920), 538–547.

François Rigolot

✒ *1538, 6 March*

The Printer Jean Morin Is Jailed for Having Published the Anonymous *Cymbalum Mundi*

Dialogue

On Wednesday, 6 March 1538, a young Parisian printer named Jean Morin was jailed for having published an anonymous forty-page French text bearing the mysterious title *Cymbalum Mundi,* a misleading Latin tag that could be translated as "worldly din." The subtitle announced *Quatre dialogues poétiques, fort antiques, joyeux et facétieux en français (Four Poetical Dialogues, Very Ancient, Merry and Facetious, in French).* But Francis I's censors had declared the seemingly innocuous text to be "full of abuses and heresies" and had requested an investigation. Morin was arrested, caught up in the religious controversy that had reached a climax in France with the 1536 publication of Calvin's *Christianae Religionis Institutio (Institutes of the Christian Religion).*

In a letter of appeal written from his cell, Morin proclaimed his innocence and is said to have given away the name of the author, definitively accepted by scholars as Bonaventure Des Périers. Born around 1510, a poet, translator of Plato, collaborator on the Calvinist translation of the Bible, and close friend of the poet Clément Marot, suspected of heresy and recently returned from self-imposed exile in Italy, Des Périers was a protégé of the king's sister, the influential Margaret of Navarre. Apparently he was never pursued by the authorities.

On 10 June the court decided that the *Cymbalum Mundi* contained "many errors and scandalous words against the Catholic faith" and condemned Morin to exile. However, the judgment was overturned by the theologians of the Sorbonne, who ruled that no "open errors against the faith" were contained in the text. The Sorbonne may thus have hoped to settle the controversy surrounding the *Cymbalum,* although it did call for its destruction as a "pernicious" book. Consequently, there is only one known extant copy of the first 1537 Parisian edition, preserved at the Versailles Municipal Library.

What was the content of this book that allowed such different readings? In the first dialogue, Jupiter's Book of Destiny is stolen from Mercury, who has been sent to earth to have it bound. In the second dialogue, Mercury makes fun of philosophers claiming to possess the Philosopher's Stone, which he has broken and scattered in the sand. In the third dialogue, Mercury anxiously tries to find the Book of Destiny, which Jupiter needs to command the weather. Cupid reports that two mortals are using a book to foretell the future, but he is more concerned with instilling love in a young girl's heart. The dialogue ends with an apparent digression in which a horse, under the spell of magic words pronounced by Mercury, complains about the poor treatment he receives from his master. In the last dialogue, two dogs debate the danger of letting mortals know that they can speak. The court read these whimsical and apparently innocuous stories as an allegorical attack against the faith, and in fact the stories do allow ample margins for differing interpretations, depending on the religious or political predisposition of the reader, as the history of the reception of the text shows.

The *Cymbalum Mundi* was published again in 1711 by Prosper Marchand, and an English translation appeared the following year. Marchand dismissed the previous interpretations that denounced Des Périers's impiety, and presented him as a candid and open Christian spirit who had fallen victim, according to the English preface, to the dogmatism of the *"Romish* Clergy." With the Enlightenment, however, Des Périers's putative impiety resurfaced, and for the next two centuries he was regarded as a modern freethinker: allegorical readings of the text suggested keys for each character and saw antireligious meaning behind each episode. In 1951 V.-L. Saulnier questioned this tradition and showed how the dialogues, when seen in the context of the religious debate, might be read as an allegorical apology for mystical and evangelical silence, in the antidogmatic tradition of *contemptu mundi* (contempt for the world). Thus the "Noisemaker," as one possible translation of *cymbalum mundi* suggests, continued to provoke dissension "throughout the world."

Along with other contemporary French dialogues, such as those by Jacques Tahureau, the *Cymbalum* was modeled upon the Greek dialogues of Lucian, which were revived by the Dutch humanist Erasmus in his *Colloquia* (1518, 1526; *Colloquies*). Almost invariably, the playful antidogmatism of their social and religious satire was regarded with suspicion. In these years of political and religious turmoil, although the protection of the king's sister might have saved the author of the *Cymbalum,* the claim of innocence could not help Jean Morin.

But the most prolific period for the French dialogue in the 16th century was still to come. Its development after the middle of the 16th century coincided with the dissemination, through translations and vernacular adaptations, of Neoplatonic texts such as Baldesar Castiglione's *Il libro del cortegiano* (1528; *The Book of the Courtier*), a textbook on Renaissance ethics and social behavior based on tolerance, published in French in 1537, the same year as the *Cymbalum.* In 1551 the translation of Judah Leon Abrabanel's *Dialoghi d'amore* (1535; *Dialogues of Love*) by Pontus de Tyard (*De l'amour*), himself an author of numerous Neoplatonic dialogues, launched a fashion for dialogues written in French and celebrating intellectual tolerance.

The new form of literary dialogue became known as the "philosophical" dialogue. In contrast to its allegorical and satirical predecessors, such as the *Cymbalum,* it represented a friendly exchange between open and curious amateurs eager to learn or to enter into debate on such various matters of opinion as truth, moral principles, law, love, and poetry. The verbal exchange now served as an effective method for the exposition of new knowledge and discussion of various points of view: in didactic dialogues, a teacher imparts "science" to an inquiring student eager to learn and to understand. Bernard Palissy names the protagonists of his pragmatic treatises on natural sciences (1563–1580) Theory and Practice, Question and Answer. But most often a master and a pupil, usually a man and a woman, enter into a philosophical inquiry, overcoming doubts or objections and reaching for a common truth.

When a real debate is staged, a final consensus is usually reached. An exception is Jacques Peletier du Mans's *Dialogue de l'orthographe et prononciation française* (1550; *Dialogue on French Orthography and Pronunciation*), in which the opponents are allowed to disagree openly with the leading opinion. More often, different positions are expressed as an exercise in contradiction. A protagonist may strategically sustain an argument independently of his own opinion. In the ensuing dispute, the proponent of the position that is held to be correct wins over the playful devil's advocate: the reader is seduced rather than persuaded by another person's acquiescence in an exemplary opinion. But sometimes, when a supposedly discredited position is represented truly and fairly, it may win over the attentive reader. In Guy de Bruès' *Dialogues* (1557), although the apparent skeptics emphatically proclaim the inevitable defeat of their assumed positions, Montaigne finds that their arguments support his own kind of skepticism. In different ways, the philosophical dialogue truly presents the intellectual qualities it claims for itself as a literary genre.

A formal and essential characteristic of the Renaissance dialogue is the constant attention given to the staging of the exchange. In the philosophical as well as the satirical dialogue, the interrelation between the participants is characterized by the spatial, temporal, and social decorum. Dialogues are structured by everyday life events: times of day, meals, games, and various social or private functions. The circumstantial, often sensory aspects of the exchange play a constant role: salons, gardens, promenades, summer shade, food, music, poetry, and friendship. Love between master and pupil interferes with, even undermines, abstract and intellectual treatment of the topics. Dialogues appear to testify to the hedonistic and aesthetic Renaissance enjoyment of the physical setting and of an intellectual exchange that is both a metaphor of and an exercise in human love.

The silencing of the exuberant allegories of the *Cymbalum* reflected the religious and political intolerance of the period. In opposition to this trend, a privileged society of humanists claimed openness, tolerance, and civility as the cardinal virtues of social intercourse and human communication. For them, difference should not lead to exclusion. The Other ought not to be seen as an enemy, but as a person with whom one should be eager to enter into a dialogue, in a gesture of reciprocal seduction.

See also 1534 (17–18 October).

Bibliography: Judah Abravanel (Abrabanel, called Leone Hebreo), *The Philosophy of Love,* trans. F. Friedeberg-Seely and Jean H. Barnes (London: Soncino Press, 1937). K. Mustapha Bénouis, *Le dialogue philosophique dans la littérature française du seizième siècle* (The Hague: Mouton, 1976). Guy de Bruès, *The Dialogues of Guy de Bruès,* ed. Panos Paul Morphos (Baltimore: Johns Hopkins Press, 1953). Baldesar Castiglione, *The Book of the Courtier,* trans. George Bull (Baltimore: Penguin, 1976). Desiderius Erasmus, *The Colloquies of Erasmus,* trans. Craig R. Thompson (Chicago: University of Chicago Press, 1965). Eva Kushner, "Réflexions sur le dialogue en France au XVIème siècle," *Revue des sciences humaines,* 148 (1972), 485–501. Bernard Palissy, *Oeuvres complètes,* ed. P.-A. Cap (Paris: A. Blanchard, 1961). Jacques Peletier du Mans, *Dialogue de l'ortografe e prononciation françoese* (1550; facsimile ed., Geneva: Slatkine, 1964). Bonaventure Des Périers, *Cymbalum Mundi,* ed. Peter H. Nurse (Geneva: Droz, 1983); translated as *Cymbalum Mundi or Satyrical Dialogues upon Several Subjects* (London, 1712). V.-L. Saulnier, "Le sens du *Cymbalum Mundi,*" *Bibliothèque d'humanisme et Renaissance,* 13 (1951), 43–69, 137–171. Jacques Tahureau, *Les dialogues non moins profitables que facétieux,* ed. Max Gauna (Geneva: Droz, 1981). Pontus de Tyard, *Léon Hébreu: Dialogues d'amour,* ed. T. Anthony Perry (Chapel Hill: University of North Carolina Press, 1974).

Jean-Claude Carron

 1539

Robert Estienne, a Humanist and the King's Printer, Publishes His
Dictionnaire français-latin, and the Edict of Villers-Cotterêts
Makes French the Official Language of Justice

The Birth of French Lexicography

In 1539 appeared for the first time, in one and the same object—Robert Estienne's *Dictionnaire français-latin*—the French word *dictionnaire* (spelled *dictionaire*) and an alphabetically ordered compilation of general French vocabulary. Estienne's French-Latin dictionary, produced to help young French scholars learn classical Latin, had the simultaneous effect of promoting the mastery of French.

A principal agent of the renaissance of humanist studies through his exemplary editing of classical Latin and Greek authors, the Paris printer-publisher Estienne had, some eleven years earlier, been asked to reedit Ambrogio Calepino's multilingual *Dictionarium,* published at the beginning of the century. Confronted with the chaotic contents and corrupt Latin of this work, Estienne decided to compose an ordered dictionary of classical Latin exemplified by the best writers and glossed by the most authoritative commentators. The resulting *Dictionarium seu Latinae Linguae Thesaurus* (1531; *Dictionary or Thesaurus of the Latin Tongue*) contained a number of French equivalents in its first two editions: thereafter it became strictly monolingual and founded modern classical Latin lexicography.

While he was revising his *Thesaurus* to make it better suited to the requirements of his erudite readers, Estienne was working on an abridged version with French equivalents appropriate to the needs of young students of Latin. The *Dictionarium Latinogallicum* (*Latin-French Dictionary*) was published in 1538; its contents were then turned round so that French became the entry language, and the *Dictionnaire français-latin* appeared a year later.

The French of the *Dictionnaire français-latin* is that of Estienne and several men of letters whose collaboration he sought. The entries—translations of Latin words, expressions, and illustrative examples in the Latin-French version—are assembled, with Latin equivalents, in articles under a headword; the headwords are in turn grouped in functional word families—root word plus derivatives, separation of homonyms—and the families ordered alphabetically by root word. This form of lexical organization continued to be used as a basis of French dictionaries for the next century and was adopted as a model for the first edition of the *Dictionnaire de l'Académie Française* (1694). After a long surrender to a strict alphabetical ordering, its linguistic merits were again recognized in such compilations as the *Dictionnaire du français contemporain* (1967), *Micro Robert* (1971), *Lexis* (1975), and *Robert méthodique* (1982). In the first edition of Estienne's French-Latin dictionary, each "macro-article" (root word and derivatives) is prefaced by a list of the words it contains; there are 4,882 such macro-articles containing a total of 8,811 listed words (including some 100 variants given as such). The *Dictionnaire français-latin* of 1539 is thus a dictionary of basic 16th-century French.

Estienne explicitly recognized this last fact in the second edition, published in 1549. On the one hand, his readers had appreciated the reference and learning value of the sizable inventory of French lexical items offered by the first edition; on the other hand, he was responding to the growing importance of French as a language of communication and the need to codify it. The previous twenty years had seen the publication of major works of French prose such as Rabelais's *Pantagruel* (1532) and *Gargantua* (1534) and Calvin's 1541 translation into French of his *Christianae Religionis Institutio* (1536; *Institutes of the Christian Religion*); the French grammars of Geoffroy Tory, John Palsgrave, and Jacques Dubois; the orthographic treatises of Montflory, Etienne Dolet, and Louis Meigret; and some of the first French translations of classical writers. As king's printer, Estienne could not help but be fully aware of the significance of the Edict of Villers-Cotterêts issued by Francis I in 1539; this decree, following similar though less comprehensive royal edicts of the previous fifty years and the publication in French at the beginning of the century of the body of local customs, stated that thenceforth, in the exercise of justice, all judgments and other procedures were to be pronounced, recorded, and delivered to the parties in French only. Estienne made an important contribution to the understanding, and perhaps the drafting, of these texts by incorporating into his second edition several thousand procedural expressions—French with Latin equivalents—taken from Guillaume Budé's *Forensia* (*Forensic Terms*), with a French-Latin index, which he had published in 1545. Specialized vocabularies needed to be developed in French in many domains of knowledge and practice; thus Estienne included in his dictionary many items taken from the works of such writers as Pliny (natural history) and Vitruvius (architecture), himself (or his collaborators) providing the French where none yet existed in published form. Many other items were added, including a more comprehensive range of derivatives, words without Latin equivalence, a number of glosses and etymological explanations for difficult words, and an appendix of hunting and falconry terms.

Estienne died in 1559 in voluntary exile in Protestant Geneva. The third edition of the *Dictionnaire français-latin,* published in Paris in 1564, contained some 3,000 additions contributed by one of Estienne's principal associates, Jean Thierry. The dictionary had by this time reached an international audience, being particularly appreciated in, and starting to influence the indigenous bilingual lexicography of, Germany, Flanders, and England. The third edition included still more technical and natural-history terms; literary French was represented by about 200 references to the vocabulary of the Pléiade and of medieval romances and *chansons de geste.*

Two more major editions followed, almost entirely as a result of the efforts of the jurist-diplomat-scholar Jean Nicot. The printer-publisher of the third edition, Estienne's brother-in-law, Jacques Dupuys, published a fourth edition in 1573, using material provided by Nicot. The latter subsequently devoted himself to expanding the text with definitions; examples; descriptive and normative remarks on orthography, pronunciation, and usage; and etymological, historical, and encyclopedic commentaries. The bilingual dictionary had become, in the mind of its reviser, a historical treasury of the French language: the work was published in 1606 by the Paris bookseller David Douceur with the title *Trésor de la langue française, tant ancienne que moderne (Treasury of the French Tongue, Both Ancient and Modern).* In the preface to the fourth edition, Dupuys had already expressed his ambition to make the dictionary, through the contributions of Nicot, the equal of the Latin and Greek thesauruses (Estienne's son, Henri, had published a Greek thesaurus the previous year). New lexical items in the Nicot editions—bringing the total number of headwords (root words and derivatives) to some 18,000 in the *Trésor*—consisted of nautical, legal, political-history, natural-history, geographic, architectural, military, chivalric, hunting, and falconry terms, as well as general and poetical vocabulary, both archaic and current; this vocabulary and the accompanying commentaries were illustrated by references to over 200 sources of all periods (from Homer on) and of various linguistic origins besides French, and to analogous words in French dialects and other European languages.

Sixteenth-century France was unable to produce a true monolingual French dictionary. The erudite *Trésor* was used as a source by French lexicographers of the next two centuries but, because of its heterogeneous nature—five editions in one (Estienne plus Thierry plus Nicot), resulting in a mixture of the bilingual, monolingual, and multilingual, of dictionary and encyclopedia—was not reedited. The *Dictionnaire français-latin* of 1573 was reedited several times, between 1593 and 1628, as a desk dictionary, titled the *Grand dictionnaire français-latin* (familiarly known, like the *Trésor,* as "Nicot's Dictionary"), with the addition of many new items taken from a variety of 16th-century writers, in Geneva, Lyons, Paris, and Rouen. It was to take the efforts of the Académie Française, Pierre Richelet, and Antoine Furetière to transform the French dictionary—created by Robert Estienne and given its first, imperfect, monolingual form by Jean Nicot—into the organized, unilingual dictionary we recognize today.

See also 1634, 1697, 1751.

Bibliography: E. E. Brandon, *Robert Estienne et le dictionnaire français au XVIe siècle* (1904; reprint, Geneva: Slatkine, 1967). Bernard Quemada, *Les dictionnaires du français moderne, 1539–1863* (Paris: Didier, 1968). T. R. Wooldridge, *Les débuts de la lexicographie française: Estienne, Nicot et le Thresor de la langue françoyse (1606)* (Toronto: University of Toronto Press, 1977).

Terence R. Wooldridge

✐ *1541, July*
Jacques Peletier du Mans Translates Horace's *Ars poetica*

Translation as Literature

First published anonymously in 1541, and reprinted in 1545 with the translator's name, Jacques Peletier du Mans's *L'art poétique d'Horace traduit en vers français* (*Horace's Ars Poetica Translated into French Verse*) came at the end of an intensely fertile period of translation activity. From 1475 to 1540 some 362 texts, 98 of them by classical authors, were published, translated into French from another language, attesting the growing importance of the vernacular in the literary culture of the early French Renaissance. This period also coincided with renewed scholarly interest in Horace: the *princeps* edition of his complete works in about 1470 was supplemented by commentaries by Cristoforo Landino (1482), Josse Bade (1503), Giovanni Britannico (1518), Aulo Giano Parrasio (1531), and Henricus Glareanus (1543). Peletier, a polymath whose interests embraced both the arts and the sciences, was undoubtedly aware of his role within this emerging scholarly tradition.

As a translator and humanist, Peletier was also profoundly affected by Francis I's creation of royal readerships in Latin and Greek eloquence in 1530, which had far-reaching implications for Renaissance translation theory. The ensuing study of classical treatises on rhetoric, especially those of Cicero and Quintilian, restored translation as a part of rhetorical training. Antoine Macault's, Jean Colin's, and Etienne Le Blanc's French translations of works by Cicero were in the 1530s a significant contribution to this trend. In 1534, with the appointment of Barthélémy Latomus to the Chair of Latin Eloquence at the Collège des Lecteurs Royaux (College of Royal Readers), humanist rhetorical scholarship received a vital stimulus. Inevitably, the readers' commitment to textual editing, interpretation, and commentary brought them into open conflict with the entrenched authority of the Sorbonne theologians, especially when this commitment extended to biblical translation. The long-standing conflict culminated in June 1551 with the repressive parliamentary Edict of Chateaubriant, asserting the Sorbonne's authority to approve or censor all books purporting to interpret or translate holy scripture. In the humanists' view, the right to translate was absolute; to the Sorbonne, in the theologians' view, it was subject to statutory regulation. Even in theoretical terms the breach between the two camps was unbridgeable. Rhetoricians such as Etienne Dolet, on the ancient authority of Cicero and Quintilian, saw language and translation as the most powerful means of grasping the style and meaning of an original text; theologians such as Noël Béda saw translation as a scriptural and theological mystery. Joachim Périon's 1540 commentary on Cicero described translation as a process of internalizing and thereby of recreating the source text. In the same year, Dolet's treatise *La manière de bien traduire d'une langue en autre* (*The Technique of Translating Well from One Language to the Other*) developed the point by showing how translation would contribute to the genesis of a "French Orator," a French Cicero, whose being would be shaped by his ability to absorb the discourse of a temporally distant culture. By placing that discourse in a new cultural and linguistic environment, translation, Dolet claimed, would bring a new assertiveness to a vernacular language still in the process of formation.

Horace's *Ars poetica,* widely known and quoted by humanist rhetoricians, comments on the art of translation in connection with fidelity to the original: "In ground open to all you will win private rights . . . if you do not seek to render word for word as a slavish translator" ("publica materies privati iuris erit, si . . . nec verbo verbum curabis reddere fidus / interpres"; lines 131–134). On 10 January 1534 the Sorbonne theologians filed a complaint against the Royal Readers not only misquoting Horace's text but separating it from its rich poetic context. Horace—himself a rewriter—is not attacking such translation, but describing how a poet should not proceed. In citing Horace's Latin text, however, the Sorbonne complaint substituted a third-person ending (*curabit*) for the original *curabis* ("you seek to"), linked it erroneously to *interpres,* and produced: "A faithful translator does not seek to render word for word" ("Nec verbo verbum *curabit* reddere fidus interpres"). Ten years later the Royal Reader Glareanus, correcting this error, would point out that Horace is talking not about translation proper but about poetic imitation, the reworking of another text through internal adaptation of themes and material rather than through external fidelity to wording or diction. Contrary to the Sorbonne's reading, he showed Horace to be advocating relative fidelity to diction as the proper concern of the faithful translator, whose duty is "to render word for word insofar as he is able and as the peculiarity [or property: *proprietas*] of the language may allow" (*Annotationes,* sig. Bbiiiiv). Horace is thus championing a cautious literalism of the translator/philologist, attentive to the respective differences of source and target language.

Peletier may well have had Glareanus' cogent reading of Horace in mind when he took up the issue again in his own *Art poétique* (1555) which somehow crystallizes the relationship between a proper reading of Horace and the abstract notion of fidelity. Recalling, perhaps, Glareanus' reference to the *proprietas* of a language, Peletier focuses on the humanist correlation between correct philology and faithful translation. He sees translation as a problem of identity: books and languages having, like people, certain identifying features, the assimilation of one book by another, of one language by another, implied by translation, depends primarily on the translator's perception of what Peletier calls the *efficace* (power) and *phrase* (style) of the original text revealed by philology or textual analysis. As a consequence, Peletier's attempt to correct the prevailing misreading of lines 133–134 of *Ars poetica* becomes in itself a statement on what "faithful" translation can accomplish when it strives to get at the words through the application of correct philology. At the heart of the process lies a paradox. For Peletier, the more the translation and vernacular language try to restore the original text, the more they commit themselves to expressing their own identity and estrangement from that original. They become literature.

Peletier's summary of these theoretical issues in his *Art poétique* stems not only from his understanding of humanist rhetorical scholarship but also from his earlier translation of the *Ars poetica*, a translation that embodies more than Horace's tenet of fidelity: it demonstrates, by its own performance, how the translator comes to transform and to appropriate an earlier poetic discourse through converting traditional subjects ("public" material) to the poet's own ("private" material). In Horace's words: "In ground open to all [*publica materies*] you will win private rights [*privati iuris*]." Accordingly, Peletier's translation fulfills the principal aims of rhetorical theory as they were known to the generation of the 1530s.

Many of these issues, shortly taken up by the Pléiade poets, notably by Joachim du Bellay in *La défense et illustration de la langue française* (1549; *The Defense and Enrichment of the French Language*), are explicit both in Peletier's preface and in his verse translation of the *Ars poetica*. In his preface he defends a French vernacular enriched by contact with the rhetoric and the terminology of Greek and Latin and thus able to function artistically as a medium of translation. The ancients themselves have set the precedent for such enrichment. Faced with the prestige of the Greek language, the Romans set out to "make illustrious" and "enrich" their own tongue by founding a national literature. In turn, Dante, Petrarch, Boccaccio, and Jacopo Sannazaro, great Latinists all, reduplicated these efforts for the Tuscan language. Now the process of emulation has been further extended: the reign of Francis I promises to usher in a new Augustan age, highlighted by new levels of poetic achievement in the French vernacular.

Having recognized that Horace's *Ars poetica* promotes a new poetic Latin grafted onto the Greek tradition, Peletier performs analogous transformations in his translation of Horace's text. Though adhering closely to the original in 356 of its 476 lines, he also seeks to make it more accessible to contemporary readers. Where he considers certain terms or allusions either too obscure or too

Roman, he changes the situational framework, giving modern equivalents for ancient place-names, social relationships, and even historical figures. Antithetical types such as Colchis/Assyria and Thebes/Argos (line 118) are replaced by more familiar sets of rivals (the Lombard/the Frenchman; the German/the Scot); allusions to the orator Massala and the lawyer Aulus Cascellius (line 371) give way to the contemporary jurists Guillaume Poyet and Pierre Liset. Still other Horatian allusions are either deleted altogether or explained at length. Where Horace talks about vocabulary and the way usage, new coinage of words, and the tendency of language to change enhance the poet's creativity (lines 52–58), Peletier seizes the opportunity to dramatize the message for his vernacular audience. For the Latin poets Virgil, Varius Rufus, Plautus, Caecilius Statius, and even Horace himself, who look back derivatively on Greek sources, Peletier substitutes the French Parnassus consisting of Jean de Meun, Alain Chartier, Jean Lemaire de Belges, Guillaume Crétin, Clément Marot, and Mellin de Saint-Gelais, who themselves look back to Latin sources. As a result, the first-person speaker in Horace's text takes on a wholly new poetic and rhetorical status; Peletier becomes Horace's stand-in, similarly engaged in the enrichment of his national tongue ("sermonem patrium," line 57).

When Peletier's translation of the *Ars poetica* first appeared in 1541 (the only surviving copy of this edition is in the Musée Condé, Chantilly), his transformative approach to the problem of faithful translation connected with two literary movements: humanist rhetoric and Pléiade poetics. To the extent that the ancients viewed rhetoric, of which translation was a part, as a tool for interpreting the world, it was natural that the rhetorical upsurge of the 1530s would subsume translation within the larger enterprise of scholarly interpretation. As interpreters, the rhetorician and translator were both seen to operate within the particularity of their own time, place, culture, and language. To translate a text meant, quite literally, to bring it into a new context, to make it contemporaneous both linguistically and culturally. In the sphere of poetics, the Pléiade later amplified these notions by showing how translation and imitation helped the would-be poet to bring new life and energy to ancient themes and sources. The Odyssean sonnets of du Bellay's *Les regrets* (1558; *The Regrets*) are striking examples of the way Pléiade poets reworked and adapted classical myth to current lyric discourse. Du Bellay's own views of translation were compatible with this practice in that they stressed the need to give a new cultural and linguistic identity to a textual source, to make it, as he and his contemporaries often put it, "speak French." Thus translation came to serve the wider purpose of linguistic enrichment, taking its place in the evolution of spoken and written language. This evolutionary role led du Bellay to view translations as fragile linguistic records that chart and measure discourse at fixed instants of time. They transform a textual past, only to be transformed themselves by later generations seeking to update the record.

During the second half of the 16th century, a period of decline in translation activity, only Blaise de Vigenère, Louis Le Roy, and especially Jacques Amyot would meet the creative challenge envisioned by Peletier and his contemporaries. The infrequency of verse translation signaled a narrowing of French Renaissance translation's sphere of influence; its contribution to the 17th-century neoclassicism of, say, Nicolas Perrot d'Ablancourt and Jean Louis Guez de Balzac would be limited largely to its stake in the development of literary prose.

See also 1517, 1534 (17–18 October).

Bibliography: Paul Chavy, "Les traductions humanistes du début de la Renaissance française: Traductions médiévales, traductions modernes," *Canadian Review of Comparative Literature,* 7 (1981), 284–306. R. J. Fink, "Une 'Deffence et illustration de la langue française' avant la lettre: La traduction par Jacques Peletier du Mans de l'*Art poétique* d'Horace (1541)," ibid., pp. 342–363. Henricus Glareanus, *Annotationes,* in *Q. Horatii Flacci opera cum quatuor commentariis . . . Adiectae in calce libri eundem in authorem Henrici Glareani Helvetii* (1543). Horace, *Satires, Epistles, and Ars Poetica,* trans. H. R. Fairclough (1926; reprint, Cambridge, Mass.: Harvard University Press, 1955). G. P. Norton, "*Fidus Interpres:* A Philological Contribution to the Philosophy of Translation in Renaissance France," in *Neo-Latin and the Vernacular in Renaissance France,* ed. Terence Cave and Grahame Castor (Oxford: Clarendon Press, 1984), pp. 227–251. Norton, *The Ideology and Language of Translation in Renaissance France and Their Humanist Antecedents* (Geneva: Droz, 1984). Norton, "The Politics of Translation in Early Renaissance France: Confrontations of Policy and Theory during the Reign of Francis I," in *Die literarische Übersetzung: Fallstudien zu ihrer Kulturgeschichte,* ed. Brigitte Schultze and A. P. Frank (Berlin: Erich Schmidt, 1987), pp. 1–13. Jacques Peletier du Mans, *L'art poétique d'Horace traduit en vers français par Jacques Peletier du Mans, recognu par l'auteur depuis la première impression* (1545; facsimile ed., Paris: Aquila, 1970).

Glyn P. Norton

✍ 1541, September

Before Returning to Geneva, Jean Calvin, the French Reformer, Translates His *Christianae Religionis Institutio* into French

Calvin the Writer

Jean Calvin (1509–1564), frail and retiring scholar catapulted to the forefront of the Reformation battle, made his mark on the history of French literature in 1541. Six years earlier he had published *Christianae Religionis Institutio,* a six-chapter summary of theological doctrine in Latin that had led Guillaume Farel to dragoon him into consolidating the Reformation in Geneva. From the less turbulent Strasbourg, to which Calvin had withdrawn after being driven out of Geneva in 1537, he first enlarged his *Institutio* to seventeen chapters (1539) and then took the momentous step of translating it into French, thus creating what is considered to be the first monument of French eloquence.

The *Institution de la religion chrétienne (Institutes of the Christian Religion)* was not the first exposition in French of Reformation doctrines. Summaries had already been written by Farel, Franz Lambert, and others, often in the form of commentaries on the Apostles' Creed, the Lord's Prayer, and the Ten Commandments; and some of Luther's writings had been translated into French during the 1520s and 1530s. Nor was the *Institution* a new exposition of radical thinking comparable to Martin Luther's or Huldreich Zwingli's a generation earlier. In essence, it presented the doctrines already defined by the earlier reformers (though with new emphases in eucharistic doctrine and in church-state relations): man is acceptable to God not because of his actions, but because God chooses to accept him despite his sinfulness; all man needs do is believe in that free promise. This doctrine, of justification by faith alone, claimed the Bible as its sole source of authority and swept aside much of the traditional teaching and practice of the Catholic church.

So what was new in Calvin? Two qualities, closely related: firmness of thought and clarity of language. Luther and Zwingli never assembled their doctrines into comprehensive statements; they were expressed in a series of occasional individual pamphlets, sermons, and commentaries. Calvin gave the Reformation an answer to Thomas Aquinas' *Summa Theologica* (1267–1273): a systematic exposition of the essentials of Christian doctrine (which he continually refined and augmented; the final version—Latin, 1559; French, 1560—ran to four books and eighty chapters). The abstraction and the structure of Calvin's theology rendered it particularly apt for exportation to other, and diverse, cultures. Whereas the Lutheran Reformation remained mainly within the German-speaking world, Calvinism spread to central Europe, Scotland, England, Holland, and thence to America and South Africa.

Though translating from Latin, Calvin avoided the heaviness and overcomplexity that plagued most of his contemporaries who sought to express abstract thought in French. His model was the unadorned simplicity of the gospels. He discovered the secrets of the short sentence, ordered linear thought, and a precise choice of vocabulary. He repeatedly stressed the need for brevity and practicality. His friends praised the work warmly; even his enemies, while legislating to ban it, admired its seductive style. Through Calvin, the French language acquired the capability of conveying complex abstract thought with precision and elegance. Calvin also communicated his religious message in a host of other writings: for the simple faithful, short expository and teaching tracts (*Petit traité de la sainte Cène* [1541; *Short Treatise on the Lord's Supper*], *Catéchisme* [1542; *Catechism*]); for the Reformation battle, colorful, forceful, sometimes vulgar polemics (*Traité des reliques* [1543; *Treatise on Relics*], *Excuse aux Nicodémites* [1544; *Excuse to the Nicodemites*], *Avertissement contre l'astrologie* [1548; *Warning concerning Judicial Astrology*]); he attacked the radical sects in *Brève instruction pour armer tous bons fidèles contre les erreurs de la secte des Anabaptistes* (1544; *Brief Instruction to Warn All the Faithful against the Errors of the Anabaptists*), and *Contre la secte fantastique et furieuse des libertins qui se nomment spirituels* (1545; *Against the Fantastical and Demented Sect of the Libertines Who Call Themselves Spiritual*); and, for the learned, numerous Latin treatises, and commentaries on most books of the Bible. He corresponded with people of high and low station throughout Europe. To the Genevans he preached regularly on the

Bible (over 2,000 sermons are known to have been taken down in shorthand, although three-quarters of these have been lost). In all, the edition of Calvin's works amounts to sixty-nine large volumes, including ten volumes of the surviving sermons.

Calvin's work in Geneva lasted from 1541 (when he returned from Strasbourg) until his death in 1564. During most of that period the city was wracked by an internal power struggle and by threats from hostile countries such as France. Although he never held political office in Geneva, Calvin's moral influence was enormous. Under his leadership, and thanks to the city's prolific printing industry from 1540 on, Geneva became the powerhouse of the Reformation in France. Thousands of French refugees fled there during the persecutions of the 1550s. From the city hundreds of missionaries were sent into France (the University of Geneva was founded as a training school for them). Genevan publications were the chief single target of censorship decrees by the French authorities (from 1544 to 1556, four major lists of condemned works were published; in each, three-quarters of the French works listed had been printed in Geneva). Above all, from 1550 on, these Genevan books stimulated Catholic writers—such as Edmond Auger, Gentian Hervet, René Benoist, and Francis of Sales—to respond, for the first time, with theological arguments in French. These writers, most of whom are now forgotten, adapted the use of French for the communication of abstract thought to a nonspecialist audience. Of equal importance, because most of these Catholic writings were responses to Genevan compositions—often Calvin's own—they adopted the structures and the language of the works they were refuting.

When the Wars of Religion broke out in 1562, the religious pamphleteering of the previous forty years was superseded by political pamphleteering (advice from all sides to the king of France, violent diatribes from both camps after the St. Bartholomew's Day Massacre in 1572, and increasingly vicious and hate-filled condemnations of Henri III by Catholic extremists after the assassination of the duc de Guise in 1588). The *Satire ménippée de la vertu du catholicon d'Espagne* (1594; *Menippean Satire about the Powers of Spanish Catholicon*) is the outstanding example of these political pamphlets: burlesque satire of the ambitions of Spain and the ultra-Catholic League is juxtaposed with an eloquent defense of the rights of Henri de Navarre to the throne of France. Many of these pamphleteers, including Pierre Pithou, the central figure in the group that collaborated in the *Satire ménippée,* were nourished on Calvin's texts and adopted his techniques of writing.

This clear, lucid, and concise style, avoiding rhetorical flourishes or showy images for their own sake, constituted a certain sober literary aesthetic much closer to that of the next century than to the rich wordplay of Calvin's contemporary Rabelais or the fabulous mantle of Ronsard's poetry. Calvin was the chief, but not the only, practitioner. Clément Marot's metrical translations of the Psalms, completed in 1561 by Théodore de Bèze, were also characterized by accessible simplicity, as was Bèze's *Abraham sacrifiant* (1550; *The Sacrifice of Abraham*), the first French tragedy. Other genres were pressed also into the service of Reformation proselytizing: short stories, pastiches of Catholic texts, comedy, popular songs—and, especially from the reformer Pierre Viret, a series of relaxed, witty dialogues presenting theological arguments in popular form.

It is often noted that French literature, more than that of any other nation, is a "literature of ideas." The language used by Montaigne, Descartes, Pascal, and the 18th-century philosophes is certainly not the archaic, cornucopian, linguistically self-indulgent language of Rabelais: it is a disciplined, linear idiom that places high value on simplicity and sobriety, definition and clarity. The French themselves often attribute these qualities to Descartes, but the essential intellectual characteristics that they call the "Cartesian spirit" originated a century earlier, in the writings of Jean Calvin.

See also 1534 (17–18 October), 1609.

Bibliography: Théodore de Bèze, *Abraham sacrifiant, tragédie françoise* (Geneva: C. Badius, 1550). John Calvin, *Institutes of the Christian Religion,* ed. John T. McNeill, trans. F. L. Battles (Philadelphia: Westminster Press, 1960). F. M. Higman, *The Style of John Calvin in his French Polemical Treatises* (London: Oxford University Press, 1967). T. H. L. Parker, *John Calvin: A Biography* (London: Dent, 1975). *Satyre ménippée de la vertu du catholicon d'Espagne, et de la tenue des estatz de Paris* (1594; reprint, Geneva: Slatkine, 1971). François Wendel, *Calvin: The Origins and Development of His Religious Thought* (New York: Harper & Row, 1963).

Francis M. Higman

◈ 1542

Three Poets Debate on Women and Love

The Neoplatonic Debate

The *querelle des femmes,* a literary debate on the status of women, began in the early 15th century when Christine de Pisan (1363?–1431) refocused the discussion of the institution of marriage by questioning the misogyny in romances such as Jean de Meun's *Le roman de la rose* (ca. 1275; *The Romance of the Rose*), in fabliaux such as Gautier Le Leu's *La veuve* (1248; *The Widow*), and in satirical clerical literature such as Matheolus' *Lamentations* (ca. 1286), which caustically ridiculed women and the female body. In *Le livre de la cité des dames* (1404; *The Book of the City of Ladies*) Christine urged women to reject the depiction of themselves as inferior to men on physiological and theological grounds and to seek the truth of their condition in the reality of personal experience. She challenged the authority of traditional texts and offered an alternative cultural history of women that demythologized the male conception of the inequality of the sexes.

In the 1530s the *querelle* took on a new focus, the nature of love and the behavior of women at court. Two successive French editions of Baldesar Castiglione's *Il libro del cortegiano* (1528; *The Book of the Courtier*) in 1537 and 1538,

translated by Jacques Colin at the request of Francis I, gave cultural accepta-
bility to the idealized portrait of the civilized female. Castiglione portrayed the
ideal woman as primarily a public creature, displaying learning and discrimination in food, music, and dancing. Her virtue, he suggested, lay in her ability
to mediate between reason and passion. The essentially Neoplatonic figure of *Il
cortegiano* is an asexual noble being capable of inspiring desire for a spiritual life.
But the love that she generates can be realized only within matrimony, a union
that enables the man who loves her to transcend the particular beauty of the
beloved and gain access to the source of universal ideal beauty. Thus the patriarchal need to maintain the fabric of society by confining women to the family
and procreation is given a "higher" purpose through its promotion of feminine
virtue. Though idealized as the mediator of spiritual transcendence, woman is
in fact the passive target of the courtier's desexualized desire.

In the 1540s Castiglione's book prompted an exchange of poems among
Bertrand de La Borderie, Charles Fontaine, and Antoine Héroët, known as the
querelle des Amies, because the female figures of the poems were called, respectively, Amie, Contr'Amie, and Parfaite Amie. This literary debate concerned a
major topos of pre-Pléiade poetry, love at court and in society and the respect
or disrespect for woman that it implied.

La Borderie's aggressively satirical *Amie de Cour* (1541; *Courtly Friend*) implicitly attacked the divine power of platonic love and the honor of women. The
voice of the poem is that of a young woman, Amie (Friend), who turns the
court into an arena for unscrupulous behavior. Her discourse is an elegant
parody of the contemporary cult of virtue and the conventions of courtly
exchange. Representing herself as an advocate of free will who refuses love but
nevertheless engages in verbal flirting, Amie de Cour opts for mercenary love.
Taking great pleasure in her ability to dominate men, she secretly allows herself
to be seduced and ironically justifies her behavior as a quest for virtue. This
cynical coquette is scornful of matrimony based on love and achieves glory by
undercutting the vain idolatry of courtly love.

Fontaine quickly responded to this satirical attack on Castiglione's code of
womanly conduct with the poem *Contr'Amie de Cour* (1541). Drawing on Plato's
Symposium and *Phaedrus* as well as on Neoplatonism, he defended the power of
ideal love through the figure of a young bourgeoise who consciously resists the
vanity of self-interest and the corruption of court manners, opts for reconciliation of love in marriage, and distances herself from physical desire. Fontaine's
Contr'Amie (Anti-Friend) becomes a kind of moral crusader devoted not only
to rejecting passionate love's opposition to reason but also to discrediting Amie
de Cour's cynical egotism. Love creates the harmonious order of the universe;
it enables the conventionally moral woman to become an exemplar of virtue by
staving off physical satisfaction.

Héroët responded to the texts of La Borderie and Fontaine with *La Parfaite
Amie* (1542). Loosely based on Castiglione and Neoplatonism, it became a best-
seller, with almost twenty 16th-century editions. In a long (1,662-decasyllable)
monologue the aristocratic paragon Parfaite Amie (Perfect Friend) analyzes the

feelings aroused by her lover, now dead, then articulates a philosophy of pure but sensual love. Although Parfaite Amie suffers emotional anguish, like many medieval heroines awaiting the return of their lovers, she attempts to subscribe to a higher form of love, which she elaborates as a predestined passion free of suffering. For her, true love is the result of mutual recognition emanating from a divine source and yields the gift of eternal happiness.

Parfaite Amie's ideal love has much in common with the Androgyne myth presented by Aristophanes in Plato's *Symposium,* in which the incomplete soul finds satisfaction through union with its double, or other half. The union of souls that she celebrates is merely the earthly reenactment of a harmony that existed previously in heaven. But the consummation of that love involves more than abstract reason: true love also involves sensual delights such as the pleasure of kissing. This praise of *volupté* challenges the purity associated with a divine contemplative philosophy. Like Aristophanes, Héroët's Parfaite Amie shows the soul as content to remain in the body. Love outside marriage is acceptable, and marriage becomes praiseworthy when it is rooted in amorous delight. Thus Héroët's image of woman reconciles the spiritual quest with joys of the body. She achieves her own fulfillment or perfection through her consciousness of the philosophical implications of her own complex and intensely personal experience.

See also 1277, 1401, 1555 (July).

Bibliography: Joan Kelly, "Early Feminist Theory and the *Querelle des Femmes,"* in *Women, History, and Theory* (Chicago: University of Chicago Press, 1984), pp. 65–109. Madeleine Lazard, *Images littéraires de la femme à la Renaissance* (Paris: Presses Universitaires de France, 1985). Michael A. Screech, "An Interpretation of the Querelle des Amyes," *Bibliothèque d'humanisme et Renaissance,* 39 (1959), 103–130. Emile V. Telle, *L'oeuvre de Marguerite d'Angoulême reine de Navarre et la querelle des femmes* (Toulouse: Imprimerie Toulousaine Lion et Fils, 1937).

Lawrence D. Kritzman

✐ 1544

Maurice Scève Publishes *Délie* in Lyons

The Architecture of Poetic Sequences

The largest city on the route that linked Paris and the north of France to Italy, not far from the Swiss border and lying at the juncture of the Rhône and the Saône rivers, Lyons was, in the first half of the 16th century, a dynamic center of trade, manufacturing, publishing, and cultural activity. It was here that Italian literature made its first significant impact on French letters. The publication in Lyons of Maurice Scève's *Délie, objet de plus haute vertu* (1544; *Delie, Object of Highest Virtue*) marks the full-scale introduction into French of love poetry based on the Italian tradition stemming from Petrarch's collection of lyric poems, the *Rerum Vulgarium Fragmenta* (1374), better known as the *Canzoniere* (*Songbook*) or *Rime sparse* (*Scattered Rhymes*). This immensely influential work, composed two centuries earlier, celebrates the poet's love for Laura de Noves, who lived in Avignon, a city south of Lyons, downstream on the Rhône, to which the poet followed the exiled papal court. Petrarch's collection of vernacular lyrics is devoted to the poet's unrequited love for this unattainable lady, and in 366 poems of various forms but dominated by the sonnet, it details the lover's adoration and suffering, his psychological and spiritual responses to love.

Petrarch's work provided subsequent poets with a rich corpus of themes, images, rhetorical devices, and lyric forms, which they imitated and varied ad infinitum. Its impact in France began to be strongly felt in the early 16th century, when the very idea of a poetic sequence as a coherent body of work ordered around a thematic center was still relatively new. In addition, it provided a model of elaborate textual organization for a new group of poets, imbued with Renaissance humanism, who sought to elevate their art from the often playful entertainment supplied by court verse to that of a noble humanist endeavor. To such readers, trained to read allegorically, Petrarch's carefully composed work implied that a higher order—religious, moral, cosmic, intellectual—underlay and regulated the varied expressions of the lover's plight. The combination of the disorder of passion, expressed in the lyrics, with the tantalizing suggestion of an encompassing order (which commentators of the work sought to define, often by proposing new arrangements) provided a means of representing the complex and contradictory emotions and the life of the senses essential to love poetry while implying an extension of its significance to other, more intellectually elevated domains.

In *Délie*, Scève adapted these aspects of the Petrarchan model in ways that heightened the impression of both disorder and order and augmented the contrast between them. The tormented emotions expressed in the poems are fragmented and fragmentary, beset by incoherence and obscurity, and, so far as one can tell, inconclusive. This largely painful and chaotic experience is set in an obtrusive formal framework provided by a series of fifty woodcut emblems (see fig. 1), formed of an image, a motto, and a title, for the most part unrelated to the theme of love. The emblems are disposed at regular intervals throughout the work (every nine poems) and tend to suggest the order, symmetry, and regularity that are the purview of the mind. In addition, the poetic form used suggests rigor: each of the 449 poems consists of ten decasyllabic lines (10×10). Close examination of the work has suggested a number of other patterns, some arising from the emblems, others tied to proportion, various properties and associations of number, and symmetry. As a result, the work powerfully represents both the physical passions of love and the effort to dominate the experience through intellectually imposed order. This combination, together with the tension between order and disorder, has found succinct expression, in the eyes of many readers, in the anagram of the beloved's name: *Délie* $=$ *l'idée* (Délie $=$ the idea).

Although the formal architecture of the work is evident, its implications have

1. Maurice Scève, *Délie, objet de plus haute vertu* (Lyons: Sulpice Sabon, 1544):
"Entre toutes une parfaite," p. 12; "A tous clarté à moi ténèbres," p. 27; "Assez
meurt qui en vain aime," p. 31; "De mort à vie," p. 47; "Douce la mort qui de
deuil me délivre," p. 55; "J'ai tendu le lacs où je meurs," p. 187. (Courtesy of
the Bibliothèque Nationale, Paris.)

proved extremely difficult to assess. The presence of an articulated and complex
structure, allied with Scève's reputation as an erudite Renaissance humanist,
has led scholars to examine the work in the light of scientific and philosophical
thought. They have perceived the influence of late 15th-century Florentine
Neoplatonism, of a Hermetic tradition with esoteric Pythagorean or Cabalist

implications, of numerological design, of astronomical patterns (Délie, a mythological variant of the goddess Diana, is identified with the moon, in a suggestive opposition to Petrarch's Laura, identified with the sun), and of biblical number symbolism. And whether or not the more arcane numerical or numerological descriptions that have been advanced are in some sense "correct," one of the effects of the textual architecture clearly is to open the text to these broader considerations. At the same time, the obscurity of expression, the apparent superposition of a number of patterns, and the possibility thus presented of reference to a variety of domains ultimately lead, if not to confusion, at least to a perception of extreme complexity. On the one hand, the architecture exerts a stabilizing influence on the textual expression of the lover's disorder by suggesting Renaissance notions of the harmonic proportions of the universe, the capacity of art to reflect intellectual design, and the value of an architectural form that corresponds to a divine cosmic order. On the other hand, the apparent impossibility of defining that order and ascertaining its meaning has a destabilizing effect, which helps to reinforce the impression of opacity, even of obscurity. The architecture that at first appears to provide signposts eventually leads into a labyrinth.

This difficult poetic text with its ultimately mysterious architecture makes it clear that Scève's public, even more than Petrarch's, consists not of *le vulgaire* (the common herd) but of those who share his learning, his philosophical and even esoteric concerns, and his taste for difficulty and complexity. In *Délie,* the expression of the lover's torment is formulated largely through a sophisticated poetic language based to a considerable extent on Petrarch's *Rime.* In addition, the concept of love it develops appears enriched by echoes of the philosophical thought of the late 15th-century Florentine Academy, which sought to revive Plato's Athenian school. Its influence was largely felt through the publications of Marsilio Ficino, whose interpretations of Plato's dialogues synthesized the ancient philosopher's thought and Christian doctrine. His Neoplatonism, which viewed love as a means of access to higher wisdom, even to a union with the divine, was later translated into more worldly terms, notably in Baldesar Castiglione's *Il libro del cortegiano* (1528; *The Book of the Courtier*). It furnished a means of exploring the movements of the soul between body and mind and of viewing the human condition in the context of a superior ideal or knowledge attained only in the desire for it or at best in rare and fleeting moments.

In this context, poetry—and love poetry in particular—could become a vehicle for expressing the full range of desire. In Scève's *Délie,* the textual architecture, with its mysterious resonances, extends the boundaries of its theme to include such less specific and less readily definable objects. And although this textual architecture raises more questions than it answers, the effort to represent the complexity of emotional and intellectual experience in a love sequence helps redefine the scope of love as a poetic theme. *Délie* contrasted dramatically with the lighter tone of earlier love poetry written at the French court, such as that of Clément Marot (1496–1544) and Mellin de Saint-Gelais (1491–1558), and it prepared the way for the elevated poetry that Joachim du Bellay and Pierre de Ronsard more stridently called for some five years later.

But *Délie's* obscurity severely limited its success. Scève's use of explicit structure found no followers, and architectonic design in subsequent Renaissance poetic sequences is generally less obtrusive, apparently less complex, and thus less problematic. Even Scève's own *Microcosme (Microcosm)* of 1562 is more subtly patterned; it contains 3,003 verses—divided into three sections of 1,000 verses (10 × 10), plus 3—a number evidently appropriate to the poetic presentation of human history in relation to a divine plan, as three is the number of the Trinity. Ronsard's early *Odes* (1550) are disposed in a symmetrical plan reinforced by number, a poetic monument reminiscent of those made by the poets of Augustan Rome, but they have no overt structure such as that created by Scève's emblems. Other collections are defined by round numbers (such as 50 or 100, sometimes "hidden" by the presence of introductory or final poems) or simple symmetries.

Poetic architecture, however simple or complex, entered Renaissance poetic design by furnishing an element of order dependent on the intellect, a presence then considered appropriate to all high endeavor. Readers today may find it simplistic or even irrelevant to an appreciation of the poetry. It is nonetheless true that the effects of metaphor, allegory, and symbol—three important elements of Renaissance poetic expression—are enhanced by the presence of a formal structure that implies the inclusion of the analogical relationships they imply within a conceptual whole. Architectural design suggested that the work was modeled on the heavenly architecture that God, the first Poet (or Maker), created; it allowed the poet to reflect the world as the 16th century saw it, with its rich variety and the implicit unity of its overall conceptual form, as well as the fundamental dichotomies of body and mind, of sense perception and intellect. Scève's *Délie,* in introducing architectonic form to the French lyric sequence, exploited these possibilities in extraordinarily complex and infinitely compelling ways.

See also 1532, 1555 (13 September), 1562.

Bibliography: Dorothy G. Coleman, *Maurice Scève, Poet of Love: Tradition and Originality* (Cambridge: Cambridge University Press, 1975). Jo Ann Della Neva, *Song and Counter-Song: Scève's Délie and Petrarch's Rime* (Lexington, Ky.: French Forum, 1983). Doranne Fenoaltea, *"Si haulte Architecture": The Design of Scève's Délie* (Lexington, Ky.: French Forum, 1982). Ruth G. Mulhauser, *Maurice Scève* (Boston: Twayne, 1977). Francesco Petrarch, *Petrarch's Lyric Poems: The Rime Sparse and Other Lyrics,* ed. and trans. Robert Durling (Cambridge, Mass.: Harvard University Press, 1976). Maurice Scève, *Délie,* ed. Françoise Charpentier (Paris: Gallimard, 1984). Scève, *The "Délie" of Maurice Scève,* ed. I. D. McFarlane (Cambridge: Cambridge University Press, 1966).

Doranne Fenoaltea

Joachim du Bellay Publishes *La défense et illustration de la langue française*

An Offensive Defense for a New Intellectual Elite

Joachim du Bellay's *La défense et illustration de la langue française* (1549; *The Defense and Enrichment of the French Language*) is a polemical, often paradoxical treatise that offers both more and less than its title suggests: more, because under the guise of a discussion of the French language it addresses a number of important issues in literary theory, such as the nature of imitation, its relation to translation, and the features and relative value of poetic genres; less, because the defense of French promised by the title is highly ambivalent, articulating contradictory views on the social and aesthetic value of the vernacular. Contemporaries were quick to see the contradictions. Barthélemy Aneau, principal of the Collège de la Trinité in Lyons, asked in his anonymous *Quintil Horatian* (1550; *Horace's Quintilius*): "Is this a defense and illustration, or rather an offense and denigration?" (*Quintil Horatian*, p. 28).

Soon after arguing that French is *by nature* equal to Latin and Greek, du Bellay blames "the ignorance of our ancestors" for its *present* inferiority (*Defence*, bk. 1, chap. 3, p. 26). As a remedy, he urges the modern poet to emulate foreign models—not only the ancient Greeks and Romans but also Italians such as Petrarch—rather than French predecessors. He labels medieval forms such as the rondelet, the ballade, the *coq-à-l'âne* or satire, and the *chant-royal* vulgar—that is, ignoble—cowardly, and effeminate (bk. 2, chap. 4); and in a violent figure he urges those who have "knowledge and judgment" to cut and cauterize the corrupted flesh that bad poetry has created in the French tongue (bk. 2, chap. 11, p. 98). The chief target of this attack is Clément Marot (1496–1544), a popular court poet of self-acknowledged humble birth. Sometimes directly, sometimes by innuendo, du Bellay repeatedly condemns Marot and his fellows (such as Mellin de Saint-Gelais and Charles Fontaine) for being "unlearned": they "translate on credit those languages of which they never understood the first elements, like Hebrew and Greek" (bk. 1, chap. 6, p. 35). Yet soon afterward he vehemently laments the time wasted in learning Greek, Hebrew, and Latin: servitude to the ancient languages, here portrayed as harsh schoolmasters, keeps the French writer in a state of regrettable "infancy" (from Latin *infans*, speechless; bk. 1, chap. 10, p. 48). With a similar shift in attitudes at times he describes classical learning as a domain reserved for an elite and to be entered only by a difficult process of initiation, but elsewhere he decries the conservative Catholics and strict humanists who oppose vernacular translation for nonelite readers.

The attacks on Marot highlight the complexity of du Bellay's concept of the vulgar and his ambivalent feelings about his potential readers. Most of Marot's initial readers had been members of the court during the reign of Francis I (1515–1547), the patron of art and literature. To blame Marot's idiom for being vulgar, capable of pleasing because it was "easy," close to "the common manner of speaking" (bk. 2, chap. 1, p. 62), was therefore a challenge to elite readers of the new reign of Henri II: they would betray a lack of cultivation if they failed to alter their taste.

There were in fact fewer differences between du Bellay and Marot than the rhetoric of *La défense* suggests. In addition to French medieval genres, Marot had imitated Italian and classical models with considerable versatility—not only the elegy, eclogue, and epigram, but most especially the Petrarchan sonnet, which he introduced in France. Several of Marot's *Epîtres* (1532; *Epistles*), written during a period of exile in Ferrara, subtly rework Ovid's elegiac epistles, in the *Tristia* and *Ex Ponto,* lamenting his exile from Rome and his beloved Latin language. Du Bellay imitated the same models later, in *Les regrets (The Regrets)* and in his Latin *Poemata (Poems)*, both published in 1558 after du Bellay's four-year sojourn in Rome. Yet in *La défense* he had denigrated the verse epistle, and done so in the very chapter in which he urged the French poet to imitate Horace and Ovid, both of whom had written much in that genre.

True, Marot's work was less replete with classical allusions and mythological periphrases than du Bellay's. He had written in the forms *La défense* excoriates, never considered writing an epic—the highest genre in du Bellay's pantheon—and, not knowing Greek, never thought about imitating the Pindaric ode as did du Bellay's friend (and rival) Pierre de Ronsard. But du Bellay himself came relatively late to the study of that language. Like Marot, he had an impoverished youth: the autobiographical "Complainte du désespéré" (1552; "Complaint of the Despairing One") presents him as the orphaned younger son of a minor branch of a noble family whose gifts were left uncultivated by his relatives during his childhood. Anxiety about the adequacy of his own learning may well underlie his attacks on Marot, his ambivalence about whether education should be reserved to an elite or made available to all, and his insistence on the need to enrich the vernacular.

Nature, personified as a mother or a stepmother in the opening paragraph of *La défense,* is linked to the notion of the vernacular as a mother tongue, something one can learn without effort. Many of the paradoxes of du Bellay's insistence on the use of foreign rather than native models reflect the humanist's sense of exile from a time and place in which Latin and Greek were living vernaculars. Du Bellay implicitly contradicts his assertion that all languages are equal when he envies the ancients for having learned theirs by sucking them in with the "milk of their nurse" (bk. 1, chap. 11, p. 56). But, like other Renaissance humanists, he at the same time values active learning and industry over natural acquisition. Latin, the model "paternal" language that the modern poet must emulate in order to develop a desirable vernacular style, is presented as the prime example of a literary language made great by art and labor. The Romans enriched their language by imitating the Greeks; so, du Bellay argues, the French should enrich theirs by imitating the Romans. At its most general level, this argument urges one culture to appropriate another's habits of appropriation.

Du Bellay connects his ideal of imitation with the belief in *translatio studii,* the notion that culture (and imperial power) moves inexorably westward. Cultural "translation" (in the root sense of a "bearing across") is most fully articulated, for du Bellay, in Virgil's *Aeneid,* an epic that presents the translation of Trojan civilization to Rome as a heroic male performance. Du Bellay's denigration of the vernacular as effeminate and natural must be understood in the light of an ambition to prepare France and her poets for a new kind of epic achievement. Thus imitation is a means of transporting the riches of the classical poets (and empires) to France. Yet even this concept is conflicted: Rome and France are figured as female in the treatise, and both places are represented as objects of an as yet unfulfilled desire. The rivalry inherent in admiration is discernible in du Bellay's ambivalent attitude toward the Romans and transforms imitation into a locus of theoretical and rhetorical tension. On the one hand, he accuses those who "profane" the "sacred relics of antiquity" (bk. 1, chap. 6, p. 36) of failing to approach the ancient texts with sufficient reverence; on the other hand, he urges his fellow countrymen to "march courageously" on Rome to rape and pillage the treasures she contains (Conclusion, p. 107).

The related concepts of translation and of imitation in the same language are also riddled with contradictions in *La défense,* where du Bellay shifts from encouraging translation as a means of enriching the general store of knowledge to inveighing against translators as traitors to the spirit of great poetry. One way to resolve the problem is to conclude that du Bellay approves of the translation of prose works but opposes translation of poetry, on the grounds that poetry has a stylistic "spirit" or "genius" that cannot be successfully transported from one language to another. But this distinction does not fully explain the fact that du Bellay published his own translation of the fourth (1552) and sixth (1556) books of the *Aeneid.* Nor does it explain his close imitation—not only of Petrarch, Horace, and Virgil but also of Marot—in his first volume of poems, *L'Olive, Vers lyriques* (*Olive, and Lyric Verses*), published only three weeks after *La défense.* These imitations, some of which modern critics would classify as translations, were immediately attacked as thefts.

Written when the new nation-states of Europe were continually waging wars for territory and gold, *La défense* depicts a related arena of struggle for intellectual property: to whom does a text belong? But du Bellay's tenuous distinctions in attempting to delimit a "good" imitation from "bad" are also deeply colored by his personal circumstances in 1549—by his economic situation, his social and literary ambition, and, most immediately, by his membership in a coterie of young poets studying classical literature at the Collège de Coqueret in Paris under the humanist scholar Jean Dorat. In 1549 du Bellay, his friend Ronsard, and others in the group that would later be known as the Pléiade were not yet visible as stars. They had given themselves a military rather than an astral name—the Brigade—and chose du Bellay to take up his pen to defend French, or rather, the Brigade's vision of a glorious future for French poetry and a new group of poets.

The immediate provocation for *La défense* was the publication in 1548 of Thomas Sébillet's *Art poétique français* (*French Poetic Art*). This pamphlet by an obscure Parisian lawyer seemed to anticipate many features of the Brigade's new poetics, in particular the Neoplatonic notion of the divinely inspired poet and the advocacy of French as a literary language capable of rivaling the classical tongues. Sébillet appears to have irritated the Brigade less by stealing its theoretical thunder than by praising Marot as an innovator in both native and classical forms and as a herald of a new glorious age in French arts and letters. Many of the Brigade's key theoretical notions had also been anticipated by Jacques Peletier du Mans in his introduction to his translation of Horace's *Ars poetica* (1541; *Art of Poetry*). However, Sébillet's treatise was more of a threat: its praise of Marot suggested that the work of cultural renaissance had already been done. Du Bellay's reply was as much a defense and illustration of his and his peers' projects as of literary French.

Nobly born, like most of the other members of the Brigade, du Bellay became, by education and economic necessity, a member of the new Renaissance class known to historians as the *noblesse de robe*—men from various levels of society who became courtiers or state bureaucrats by virtue of their verbal skills. Anxious lest the profession of letters might be considered unfit for the strict requirements of noble estate, du Bellay endeavored to ennoble the status of poet. This project shapes many aspects of *La défense*. Its preface is a fulsome dedication to du Bellay's noble and wealthy kinsman Jean Cardinal du Bellay. Though temporarily out of favor at court in 1549 (Henri was not prone to favor his father's servants), the cardinal was his young relative's most likely source of patronage and in fact employed him as a secretary while serving as Henri II's emissary to the papal court in Rome from 1553 to 1557. Both du Bellay's emphasis on imitation as a means of enriching the vernacular and his general conception of poetry as a form of heroic labor owe much to his situation as an aristocrat in need of a job. His lower-born contemporary Aneau, irritated by du Bellay's aspirations to a grand social and literary style, characterized *La défense* as the work of a "little foolish person who mounts on [rhetorical] stilts in order to attain a high position" (*Quintil Horatian,* p. 3). This critique signals the importance of class rivalry and resentment both in the treatise and in society.

These serious contradictions are only partially resolved by construing du Bellay's *Défense* as an attempt to "ennoble" the vernacular by making it both illustrious, like a famous man, and, like a woman, a worthy object of desire. Du Bellay's defense of imitation reflects contradictory forces at work in mid-16th-century France: the writer's intense awareness of being the heir to both a distant (noble, classical) past and a near ("dark," vernacular) one, and his membership in an emerging class of intellectuals who grafted classical notions of poetry as an elite vocation onto feudal aristocratic attitudes. The humanist intellectual, unlike the typical aristocrat of earlier times, had to earn his noble identity by his pen. The potential to be ennobled by one's pen, however, suggested that anyone with sufficient talent and energy could do the same. And therein lay a threat to the self-fashioned noble identity: it would lose its illustrious character if it were possessed by many.

This paradox of a nobility endangered by its relativization is at the heart of du Bellay's defensive project and of the Pléiade's aesthetic theory in general, with its precociously neoclassical insistence on enriching the literary language by purifying it of vulgar elements.

See also 1541 (July), 1550, 1553 (June).

Bibliography: Barthélemy Aneau, *Quintil Horatian*, in Joachim du Bellay, *La deffense et illustration de la langue françoyse*, ed. Henri Chamard (Paris: Didier, 1948). Ferdinand Brunot, *Histoire de la langue française des origines à nos jours*, vol. 2: *Le XVIe siècle* (Paris: Armand Colin, 1967). Grahame Castor, *Pléiade Poetics: A Study in Sixteenth Century Thought and Terminology* (Cambridge: Cambridge University Press, 1964). Dorothy Gabe Coleman, *The Chaste Muse: A Study of du Bellay's Poetry* (Leiden: E.J. Brill, 1980). Joachim du Bellay, *The Defence and Illustration of the French Language*, trans. Gladys M. Turquet (London: J. M. Dent & Sons, 1939). Margaret W. Ferguson, *Trials of Desire: Renaissance Defenses of Poetry* (New Haven: Yale University Press, 1983). P. M. Smith, "Marot and the Pléiade," in *Clément Marot: Poet of the French Renaissance* (London: Athlone Press, 1970).

Margaret Ferguson

∾ 1550

Pierre de Ronsard Publishes His *Quatre premiers livres des odes*

Inspiration and Poetic Glory

The second quarter of the 16th century marked a transition between the late medieval poetics of the *rhétoriqueurs* and the neoclassical doctrine of the group of poets known as the Pléiade (Ronsard himself, Jean-Antoine de Baïf, Rémi Belleau, Joachim du Bellay, Etienne Jodelle, Olivier de Magny, Jacques Peletier du Mans, Pontus de Tyard), whose coming of age at midcentury was heralded by Joachim du Bellay's manifesto *La défense et illustration de la langue française* (1549; *The Defense and Enrichment of the French Language*) and his sonnet sequence *L'Olive* (1549; *Olive*), soon followed by Pierre de Ronsard's *Quatre premiers livres des odes* (1550; *The First Four Books of Odes*). During this period, traditional poetic forms such as the ballade, the *chant-royal,* and the courtly rondeau were replaced by somewhat less constraining lyric forms: the *chanson,* rendered amorous and folksy by Clément Marot, became, with Margaret of Navarre, a vehicle for spiritual exaltation. Maurice Scève brought the sequence of love *dizains* to such dark perfection in *Délie* (1544) that he had no followers. By far, the most successful lyrical form was the Petrarchan sonnet, which soon threatened to supersede the now obsolete medieval forms. In the early 1550s, after du Bellay, poets associated with the Pléiade as well as others (Louise Labé), hastened to publish collections of Petrarchan sonnets.

Having discarded old forms and such traditional topics as princely eulogies, celebration of military victories and lamentation of defeats, vituperation of enemies, and glorification of cosmic harmony, most French poets had drastically narrowed the range of occasions and emotions deemed capable of stirring and sustaining the lyric impulse. In keeping with their limited understanding of the triumphant Petrarchan model, the new lyric poets set out to modulate endlessly the pangs of unrequited love and to sublimate sexual desire in accordance with Neoplatonic thought.

In *La défense,* du Bellay attempted to justify the surrender to Italian models with a clever philological argument, as he exhorted his readers to "sound those fine sonnets, no less learned than pleasant Italian invention, conforming in name to the ode [ode comes from Greek *aedein,* which means to sing, as does Latin *sonare,* from which comes sonnet] and differing from the latter only in that the sonnet has certain regular and limited verse, while the ode may run freely on through all kinds of verse and even invent some at will" (*Défense,* bk. 2, chap. 4).

Although the French sonnet was soon used to deal with topics other than love (du Bellay's *Les regrets* of 1558 was in turn elegiac and satirical), and although classical odes had occasionally expressed erotic yearning (as in Horace, *Odes* 1.13 and 3.10), much more than mere formal differences separated the two forms. Ronsard early realized that the ode's metrical, thematic, and tonal versatility offered a magnificent array of lyrical postures and appropriate settings for displays of the vast classical learning he had acquired during the late 1540s at the Collège de Coqueret in Paris, under the charismatic guidance of Jean Dorat, an outstanding classical scholar and an honorable poet in his own right. Having learned to read, interpret, and imitate the masterpieces of ancient lyric, especially the odes of Pindar and Horace, Ronsard was as eager to emulate them in French as he was loath to limit himself to writing "small Petrarchized sonnets" (*Oeuvres,* 2:973), which in the 1550 preface to his *Odes* he contemptuously relegated to poetasters and courtiers. Despite his extraordinarily successful use of the genre as late as 1578 (*Sonnets pour Hélène; Sonnets for Hélène*), in a letter to Scévole de Sainte-Marthe, in 1577, he referred to a sonnet sequence as a "small and puny hodgepodge" (ibid., p. 1047).

Ronsard found the classical ode the supreme medium for serious lyricism. Distancing himself from immediate predecessors and contemporaries, he acknowledged Clément Marot as his only French model, for Marot's recent translations of the Hebrew Psalms had placed a startling variety of new stanzaic forms in the service of divinely inspired song. With the *Odes,* Ronsard boldly claimed to be the only French lyric poet capable of matching the powers of pagan song and the biblical majesty of the Psalms. He audaciously wrote in his preface: "When you call me the first French lyric author, and the one who guided others upon the path of such honest labor, then you will give me my due, and I shall endeavor to show I did not receive it in vain" (p. 971). And indeed the *Odes* do mark a turning point in French lyric poetry.

The 1550 *Odes* present a striking diversity of forms, themes, and modes. Thirteen odes patterned on Pindar praise the king, the queen, victorious princes, and fellow poets such as du Bellay, Baïf, and Dorat; shorter odes, modeled on Horace and Anacreon, evoke a multitude of moods as they celebrate places, fleeting moments, and mortal creatures to preserve them, lifted out of time, from human forgetfulness.

Whether of the large, ritualized, Pindaric kind, or the small, informal Horatian one that mimics spontaneous utterance, the ode contrasts sharply with heroic and dramatic poems in that it is not a narrative. Unlike epic and tragedy, it has no plot. In the ode, narrative and descriptive elements are either subservient to praise or blame or are used to confer energy upon speech acts such as requesting, entreating, admonishing, wishing, and praying. The dominant feature, embodied in frequent verbal imperatives, is the fiction of a face-to-face encounter between the poet, who is the sole "speaker," and an addressee. The ode thus sets forth the presence of voice, a voice seemingly singing to the inscribed recipient of the utterance. Usually, the ode names a human or divine addressee, but in many instances, such as Ronsard's "O fontaine Bellerie" (bk. 2, ode 9), an imitation of Horace's famous "O fons Bandusiae" (3.13), the singer addresses inanimate entities to which he attributes an immanent spirit.

Ronsard's 1550 *Odes* have no other ordering principle than the genre itself and the ideological contexts provided by allusions to Pindar and Horace. The ancient poets' fame supplies the collateral that enables the modern poet to confer immortality upon contemporaries. From the same fund Ronsard borrows not only the attributes of his own poetic persona but also the pagan elements that give a mythic dimension to his birthplace, his life, and the very process of poetic production. Each ode is two-faced, at once translated from ancient Greek or Latin and bearing the trace of a recent performance.

Ronsard understood that the ode attempts to confer enduring fame not only upon the mortal participants in time-bound events and upon ephemeral things, but also upon praise and the praiser themselves. Lasting glory accrues to the poet who has been moved to song by an overwhelming transcendent force; for only so long as the poet is remembered will his voice "sing" to readers of his verse. Hence the fiction of a timeless voice breaking through the poet's time-bound utterance and violating his mortal body with its superhuman spirit.

Poetic possession or "madness" (*furor poeticus*), a gift granted by immortal deities, not only lifted production above mere rhyming; it also made the ode unique, in that each lyrical outburst supposedly stemmed from an irresistible frenzy suddenly overwhelming the poet. Poetic furor accounted for the ode's syntactic disorders and semantic obscurity. The first strophe of Ronsard's great Pindaric ode to Henri II's wife, Catherine de Médicis (bk. 1, ode 3), enumerates the symptoms of poetic delirium. Given the royal status of the addressee, such a catalogue is appropriate only because the physical effects of divine possession legitimate the poet's claim to be able to bestow immortal glory upon the august recipient of the ode:

> Furor is perturbing me
> My body shakes with horror
> Dread fills my soul
> The panting of my breast
> Stops the gullet through which
> My voice strains to break out.
> A deity pulls me away:

O people, let go of me!
The Goddess is coming near!
Flee, O people, I see her!
Happy he upon whom she glances
Happier still he who retains her
In his breast, as I do.

By reviving this fiction, Ronsard presents himself, not as an empty-handed rhymer beseeching royal favor, but as a divinely possessed giver of glory. This fiction also renders plausible a bargain proposed in antistrophe 8 of "Au roi Henri II" ("To King Henri II"), the magnificent Pindaric ode first published separately a few months before it became the opening piece of the 1550 collection:

Prince, I send you this ode
Trading my verse in the very fashion
A merchant deals his goods,
Quid pro quo: You, who are rich,
You, the king of goods, be not chary
Of exchanging your gift for mine
And you shall see how I accord
The honor I pledge to sound
When a present gilds my chord.

Ronsard—attempting to renegotiate the unequal contract traditionally binding the court poet to his lord whereby, in return for entertainment and propaganda, the poet might receive small favors and capricious stipends—further ventured to remind the king that the glory of his royal ancestors (with the exception of his father, Francis I the great, protector of the arts) had become dim for lack of adequate poetic praise; the mercantile simile underlying the proposed quid pro quo implies a parity between the radiance of fame and the effulgence of gold. The poet also thereby maneuvered himself into a position that would increase his chances of receiving royal support for his projected national epic *La Franciade,* a revision of Virgil's *Aeneid* that was going to provide Trojan origins to the French dynasty and illustrate the present king's unsung ancestors. Although Ronsard may not have started the epic in earnest before 1555, it already served as a permanent alibi for the many shorter poems Ronsard wrote and kept revising. Four books of *La Franciade* were eventually published in 1572, but Ronsard had given up on his glorification of obscure French monarchs before reaching the reign of Charlemagne.

Nor was Ronsard able to raise his own status from that of court rhymer to that of a royal poet. Several kings came and died. Increasingly beset with factional dissent and religious strife, Francis I's successors were unable to pursue his ambitious cultural policy. Ronsard's powerful cosmic hymns (*Hymnes,* 1555; *Le second livre des hymnes,* 1556), rivaling Hesiod's, and his great elegies (*Les élégies,* 1567) found less favor at court—and with contrary posterity—than did his love sonnets (*Les amours* [1552; *Love Poems*]; *Continuation des Amours,*

1555; *Nouvelle continuation* [1556; *New Continuation*]). With the outbreak of the Wars of Religion (1562–1598), Ronsard dedicated his poetic voice to the Catholic cause; the giver of timeless glory became an acerbic satirist (*Discours des misères de ce temps,* 1562; *Discursive Poems on the Terrible Events of These Days*).

In 1550 or thereabout, Ronsard had devised a new poetics in order to justify his claim that he was at once the first French lyric poet and the legitimate heir to ancient poetry. Since the odes were a resurgence of Greek and Latin lyricism, the myth-making gift of the old poets had devolved upon Ronsard. French poetry would not be a mere repetition of the old poems. Imitation meant invention as well as translation and transposition. Ronsard kept insisting on his Frenchness, on his rootedness in French places which it was his task to raise to the level of poetic universality achieved for Thebes and Mantua by Pindar and Virgil. This endeavor induced a poetic double vision, an allegorization of French things, which though transported into the context of ancient fables, yet retained their grounding in the here and now. The fiction of a possession by ancient spirits operated a mediation between two planes of poetic experience: between the past and present, it opened up timelessness. As the empirical person of the poet was eliminated from his poetic performance, his living body became a proxy for voices emanating from classical culture. The 1550 *Odes* combined imitation and inspiration in such a way that hard-won knowledge became poetic power. Writing under the influence of ancient spirits, Ronsard put into practice a kind of poetics that would remain paradigmatic until the waning of French classicism.

See also 1536 (Summer), 1541 (July), 1549, 1553 (March), 1553 (June), 1555 (July), 1572, 1820, 1827 (February).

Bibliography: Grahame Castor, *Pléiade Poetics: A Study in Sixteenth Century Thought and Terminology* (Cambridge: Cambridge University Press, 1964). Terence Cave, *Ronsard the Poet* (London: Methuen, 1973). Joachim du Bellay, *La deffense et illustration de la langue françoyse,* ed. Henri Chamard (Paris: Didier, 1948). Pierre de Ronsard, *Oeuvres complètes,* ed. Gustave Cohen, 2 vols. (Paris: Gallimard, 1950).

Michel Beaujour

◈ 1552
Etienne Jodelle's *Eugène* Is Performed

Renaissance Comedy

When Joachim du Bellay published *La défense et illustration de la langue française* (1549; *The Defense and Enrichment of the French Language*), he included in his call for a transformation of French letters a specific reference to the need for a new theater. Farces and morality plays had "usurped" the dignity of ancient comedy and tragedy, he said, intimating that the time had come to restore these genres to their former grandeur. And almost immediately du Bellay's fellow Pléiade poets began to produce comedies in the classical style.

Some wrote only translations or adaptations of Latin plays. Jean-Antoine de Baïf's *L'eunuque* (wr. 1565? *The Eunuch*) translates Terence's comedy of the same name. His *Le brave* (1567; *The Braggart*) adapts Plautus' *Miles Gloriosus*. Etienne Jodelle's *Eugène* (wr. 1552, pub. 1574), however, signals the beginning of a sustained effort to create original works as well. It was followed by Jacques Grévin's *La trésorière* (performed 1559, pub. 1561; *The Treasurer's Wife*) and *Les ébahis* (1561; *Taken by Surprise*), Rémi Belleau's *La reconnue* (composed 1563? pub. 1578; *The Rediscovered Daughter*), and Jean de La Taille's *Les corrivaux* (composed 1562? pub. 1573; *The Rivals*).

The next generation continued this work but drew more strongly on the Italian comic tradition. Prominent among the French playwrights who began writing in the late 1570s were Pierre de Larivey, François d'Amboise, and Odet de Turnèbe. Turnèbe has left us only *Les contents* (1584; *Satisfaction All Around*), but it is one of the finest achievements of the genre. Although the plot relies heavily upon traditional features of comedy, such as mistaken identity and servants' tricks, Turnèbe also infuses his work with the attitudes and reality of contemporary bourgeois life. The result is a vigorous comedy that at the same time gives unusual depth to the situations depicted. D'Amboise's *Les Napolitaines* (1584; *The Women of Naples*) is his only work to survive, although in the preface the author claims to have written other comedies. Larivey dedicated to d'Amboise his nine comedies, most of which were published in *Les six premières comédies facétieuses* (1579; *The First Six Merry Comedies*), to be followed by *Trois nouvelles comédies de Pierre de Larivey* (1611; *Three New Comedies by Pierre de Larivey*). All, including *Les esprits* (*The Spirits*), perhaps his most interesting play, are taken from specific Italian models.

A dearth of surviving texts makes it difficult to chart the fate of this genre in the closing years of the 16th century and in the decades before Pierre Corneille wrote his first comedy (*Mélite*, 1629). What does remain (carefully reviewed in Brian Jeffery's general study) suggests that the shape and content of 16th-century comedy persisted well into the 1620s. In particular, the figure of the braggart keeps reappearing, as do the use of disguise and the portrayal of tensions between parents and their children with regard to proposed marriages.

Early literary historians emphasized so strongly a Pléiade revolt against the farce that they promoted a devaluation of the works produced by this reaction. Recognizing that the Pléiade's effort signaled a movement away from France's literary heritage and toward the classical form that Molière later perfected, these historians believed that 16th-century comedies could be analyzed in the same way that a critic approached the theater of the 17th century. When they applied this principle, however, the Renaissance works were always found wanting. Not only, it seemed, did their authors lack the genius of Molière, but also, mere fledglings in a new art, they were said to have relied too heavily upon their sources for inspiration.

Since the 1960s the evidence for and against the Pléiade's supposed break with the past has been carefully reassessed, with the result that we are more willing today to appreciate to what extent the period did not distinguish firmly between farce and Roman comedy. Although *Eugène* and *Les ébahis* employ the classical five-act structure, they are written in octosyllabic verse, the form used regularly in farce. The content of *Eugène*—a husband's infidelity, a clergyman's philandering—is even more reminiscent of the farce.

The playwrights' alleged dependence on their sources has also been reevaluated. Much Italian material once cited as the inspiration for French comedy has proved to contain only analogous plot lines. Even in cases in which a French play possesses a distinct Italian model, such as Larivey's use of Lorenzino de' Medici's *Aridosio* (1548) in *Les esprits,* it is clear that the writers attempted to adapt their borrowings to a French audience. Paris streets and churches are referred to, as are significant events in recent French history. Even religious and moral issues are revamped. The imitation that critics used to decry has in reality become a valuable tool for defining the particularity of the genre.

The playwrights' so-called ineptness, too, can be related to special features of the period. Comic theory as it was known did not go beyond the very rudimentary remarks on the subject penned by Donatus and Horace. Writers understood their craft in the light of the broad precepts of ancient rhetoric, which left untouched the subtleties about structure and characterization that fascinated the 17th century. Although the overlap in technique among the farce, the commedia dell'arte, and printed Italian comedies has to date defied modern attempts to make definitive statements about the role of each in the creation of their French counterparts, the classical form used in the 16th century can no longer be confused with the aesthetic of French classicism yet to come.

Bibliography: François d'Amboise, *Les Napolitaines,* ed. Hilde Spiegel (Heidelberg: Carl Winter, 1977). Jacques Grévin, *La trésorière, Les esbahis,* ed. Elizabeth Lapeyre (Paris: Champion, 1980). Grévin, *Taken by Surprise,* trans. Leanore Lieblein and Russell McGillivray (Ottawa: Dovehouse, 1985). Brian Jeffery, *French Renaissance Comedy, 1552–1630* (Oxford: Clarendon Press, 1969). Etienne Jodelle, *L'Eugène,* ed. E. H. Balmas (Milan: Cisalpino, 1955). Pierre de Larivey, *Les esprits,* ed. Donald Stone (Cambridge, Mass., 1978). Jean de La Taille, *Les corrivaus,* ed. Denis Drysdall (Paris: Didier, 1974). R. C. D. Perman, "The Influence of the commedia dell'arte on the French Theatre before 1640," *French Studies,* 9 (1955), 293–303. Donald Stone, "Anatomy of a Moral: Seduction in Sixteenth-Century French Comedy," in *Essays in Early French Literature Presented to Barbara M. Craig,* ed. Norris J. Lacy and Jerry C. Nash (York, S.C.: French Literature Publications, 1982), pp. 147–161. Odet de Turnèbe, *Les contens,* ed. Norman B. Spector (Paris: Didier, 1961). Turnèbe, *Satisfaction All Around,* trans. Donald Beecher (Ottawa: Carleton University Centre, 1979).

Donald Stone, Jr.

ᕲᕲ *1553, March*

Etienne Jodelle's Tragedy *Cléopâtre captive* Is Performed in the
Presence of Henri II

The Origin and Development of French Tragedy

Practically, if not chronologically, Etienne Jodelle's *Cléopâtre captive* (*Cleopatra in Captivity*) may be considered the first original tragedy written in French. Though not published until 1574, it was first performed at the Hôtel de Reims, the Paris residence of Charles de Guise, cardinal of Lorraine, probably at the beginning of 1553 (new style). This dating makes it clear that the performance occurred before the royal court, celebrating the return to Paris of the cardinal's brother, Francis I of Lorraine, duc de Guise, after his victory in raising the siege of Metz against Holy Roman Emperor Charles V.

The king's presence at the performance acquired particular political and cultural significance. Indeed, Jodelle placed Henri II at the very center of events. The prologue addressed the king, setting him in a Roman mythology, making him mightiest among monarchs, ruler of earth, sea, and sky, and the man responsible for returning the muses to France. He was applauding not so much a king, said Jodelle, as "a god whose place is already designated in the skies." His tragedy was to become the ordered sign of the king's majesty, at once caused by him and staging his sovereign authority.

Physically present in the performing space, the king was also the play's central reference and point of origin. He was doubly its reference. The tragedy was directed at him, but he was also represented in it as Octavian: "Here you will sound the depths of the desires and ardor of the two lovers [Antony and Cleopatra]: and of Octavian, too, the pride, courage, and daily care for victory, and you will set yours even above his; since his very successors must yield to the supreme wills in your favor, who are already ordaining the world to your dominion, and admitting you as representative of all the gods" (act 2, line 94). The king was the play's origin because it was his "triumph and name" that brought about the writing of the play, whose concern was then to follow the catastrophic dissolution provoked by the fabled love affair. The tragic outcome was circumscribed by an inescapable destiny. Octavian embodied that destiny, as he did the hope of a new, national, and centralized political order.

The play was probably first written, however, more as a scholarly exercise than as a deliberate political commentary. Jodelle was one of the Brigade, soon better known as the Pléiade, the squad of young humanist poets most of whom were studying at two Parisian colleges, Coqueret and Boncourt. Indeed, *Cléopâtre* was quickly produced again at Boncourt for its members. Among them was the renowned humanist teacher Marc Antoine Muret, himself the author of a Latin *Julius Caesar*—the first known original tragedy on a secular theme composed in France, played in Bordeaux in the 1540s. Montaigne relates his pride at having played in the tragedies of George Buchanan, Guillaume Guérente, and Muret while a pupil at the Collège de Guyenne in Bordeaux (*Essais*, I, 26).

The experience of these scholars highlights a second important aspect of humanist tragedy. Before it was appropriated for overtly political and ideological ends, it played a fundamental role in the new pedagogy and in the revival of learning. Tragedy signaled the discovery of Greek and Latin drama and their reworking for a new audience and a different culture. At the same time, it was a very self-conscious effort to create two new "languages"—that of the genre tragedy and that of a French literary vernacular. It provided an experience of translation and also served as a rhetorical and stylistic teaching device. Seneca's tragedies had been available for such purposes from the earliest days of printing, but the Greeks became accessible only slowly during the first half of the 16th century (although Aeschylus remained virtually unknown). Senecan tragedy was certainly the most stylistically and thematically influential (probably in part because of the entire familiarity of Latin), but it was in Greek tragedy that formal perfection was sought, perhaps because of a belief in that language's expressive superiority.

In 1506 Erasmus published in Paris Latin translations of Euripides' *Hecuba* and *Iphigenia at Tauris,* and from then on many translations, first Latin and then French, were made of Euripides and Sophocles, culminating in the 1540s—a decade that also saw the first two original tragedies written and performed in France: *Baptistes sive Calumnia* (*John the Baptist, or Calumny*) and *Jephthes sive Votum* (*Jephthah, or the Vow*), by the Scots humanist George Buchanan. Their importance for the rising generation of poets cannot be exaggerated. In the plot of both tragedies, an important part was played by the discovery of a language able to express a communal truth adequate to facts, events, and human relations. But in neither, ultimately, could any version of truth or human freedom win (or even be established). Both seemed to express an ever-more-anguished sense that language not only could form an obstacle to understanding, but indeed might be quite unable to express any communal meaning at all. At another level, this theme perhaps offered an implicit critique of Latin, incapable of expressing a new human view of the world.

This new view increasingly involved the supposed effacing of the human instrument before its "object." Latin, however familiar, yet remained an alien language, whose very foreignness made it impossible for its mediating presence to disappear before what it claimed to express. This concurrence of concerns was no doubt the reason why tragedies came to contribute centrally to a more general cultural change and occupied a special place in the creation of what was called a "precellent" national language (one capable of expressing whatever thought one wished, in as various a form as would make that expression agreeable, and above all able to rival Greek and Latin in such accomplishments). They should be written, wrote du Bellay, "for the embellishment of the language" (*La défense et illustration de la langue française* [1549; *The Defense and Enrichment of the French Language*], p. 126). Later on, most authors of the liminary poems placed before Robert Garnier's published tragedies praised him for surpassing Greek theater and above all the classical languages. Then as now, Garnier was held to be the finest 16th-century writer of tragedy. In his 1605

L'art poétique (*The Art of Poetry*), Jean Vauquelin de la Fresnaye summed up this achievement by asserting that as its result "our language now surpasses the very finest" (p. 121). Such claims on behalf of a national vernacular had profound political significance.

The political and linguistic aspects of humanist tragedy are bound inseparably with the final strand in its development. *Cléopâtre* was not in fact the first original French-language tragedy: this honor belonged to the Calvinist leader Théodore de Bèze's *Abraham sacrifiant* (*The Sacrifice of Abraham*), performed in Lausanne in 1550. The use of the genre to further the Protestant (or Catholic) cause was an integral part of tragedy's evolution: Protestant tragedy's emphasis on the vernacular was closely related to general arguments about biblical interpretation (to the effect that every individual, given the analytical instrument, was capable of understanding the Bible without the guidance of Latinate ecclesiastical authority). A play such as the anonymous *Tragédie du sac de Cabrières* (ca. 1566), whose chief object was the horror of the Catholic massacre of Cabrières but which gave more space to discussing the power of language, combined these two aims.

Bèze's play revealed the evident ties of this entire development to a native Christian tradition, as well as to a Greek and Latin past. The story of Abraham's preparation to sacrifice his son at Jehovah's command had been a common episode in mystery plays. Though banned in Paris by the Parlement in 1548, they only gradually disappeared from the provinces, and anyway episodes from the mysteries often differed little from the always popular morality plays. Indeed, the majority of early tragic authors, Protestant or Catholic, saw the genre as having indigenous as well as foreign roots, closely linked with a late medieval tradition: "Tragedy," wrote Lazare de Baïf in the preface to his translation of Sophocles' *Electra* (*Electre*, 1537), "is a morality composed of great calamities, murders, and adversities inflicted on noble and excellent personages." In his 1548 *Art poétique français* (*French Poetic Art*), Thomas Sébillet wrote: "The French morality somehow takes the place of Greek or Latin tragedy, especially in its treatment of serious and princely deeds. And if the French had agreed that morality should always end in unhappiness and grief, morality would be tragedy" (p. 161). Like Bèze's *Abraham,* Louis des Masures's Protestant trilogy *Tragédies saintes* (1563; *Holy Tragedies*), published in Geneva, also fell into this tradition.

In his *De l'art de la tragédie* (1572; *On the Art of Tragedy*), Jean de La Taille criticized not only "farces and moralities" but also tragedies like those of Bèze and des Masures as being "cold and unworthy of the name of tragedy," having "neither sense nor reason," and often composed of "ridiculous words {mixed} with badinage" (pp. 4, 8). These dramas, he wrote, failed to follow the rules of Aristotle and Horace, to adopt the three unities, to deal with great, if imperfect, secular personages, or to end in catastrophe. By the 1570s the feeling was general not only that French had achieved parity with Greek and Latin, but also that the medieval past must be rejected as primitive. At one level, of course, the criticism of Protestant tragedy simply echoed the twenty years of religious and civil conflicts that reached their climax in the St. Bartholomew's Day Massacre the very year of La Taille's aesthetic complaint. Tragedy was considered the literary genre best able to represent those "horrible disasters once brought upon France by our civil wars" (p. 2), as La Taille wrote optimistically (the Wars of Religion would continue for more than two decades).

Most of the plays mentioned, like those of the Protestant André de Rivaudeau (*Aman,* 1566) or the Catholic Nicolas de Filleul (*Achille,* 1563, and *Lucrèce,* 1566), were readily understood in terms of the wars and their horrors. Garnier's whole output was so interpreted. This most important of the dramatists published a series of tragedies on Greek, Roman, and biblical topics, from *Porcie* in 1568 to *Les Juives* in 1583, including *Hippolyte* (1573), *Cornélie* (1574), *Marc-Antoine* (1578), *La Troade* (1579), and *Antigone* (1580). Garnier was *lieutenant criminel,* the principal criminal judge of the Maine province by 1574 and a member of the Great Council in 1586: he thus was really involved in political issues at the very highest levels. (He joined the Catholic League at the end of the 1580s, and died poor and disgraced in 1590.) His involvement was reflected in his tragedies, both by their subjects and by the constant generalizations of political themes and theoretical commonplaces.

The twenty or so years of Garnier's output formed the heyday of French humanist tragedy, although there was a considerable and diversified production from 1580 to the 1610s. Authors of tragedies by no means limited themselves to Greek, Roman, or biblical topics. They also drew on French history, legendary, medieval, and recent; on literary romance (Garnier's *Bradamante* [1582] used a heroine from Ludovico Ariosto's *Orlando furioso* [1532]); and on exotic material (Gabriel Bounin's *La sultane* [*The Sultana*] of 1561 was the earliest of these). Most of these efforts were produced by individuals working alone and away from Paris (already the cultural center of the nation). They were performed by itinerant professionals and local amateurs in châteaux and elsewhere, before audiences of provincial aristocrats, lawyers, merchants, and other bourgeois, as well as artisans and peasants. There were also "private" performances in schools and colleges.

The provinces certainly enjoyed more such performances than the capital, where a serious professional theater was long in gaining acceptance. The growth of a popular public theater in France was much slower than in Italy, England, and Spain. The civil wars were no doubt partly responsible for the delay. Tensions did not really relax until the end of the 16th century, and then most energy went toward social and political reconstruction. Even then, however, the assassination of Henri IV in 1610 threw everything back into confusion. This decade saw the publication of six tragedies each by two belated but important authors of humanist tragedy, Antoine de Montchrétien and Claude Billard.

Only in the late 1620s, after Marie de Médicis' deeply troubled regency, was a cohesive public audience constituted (as opposed to a courtly or scholarly one). By then two theatrical troupes were competing in two permanent Paris theaters. Only then did France see a new generation of authors of tragedy: Théophile de Viau, Jean Mairet, François Tristan l'Hermite, Pierre Du Ryer, Georges de

Scudéry, Jean Rotrou, Pierre Corneille, and others. They created a tragedy showing a confidence in human power and authority quite absent from that of their humanist predecessors, even though they often used the same subjects. A new sense of "psychological" characterization and individual responsibility and a wholly new emphasis on relations between such individuals marked the change. The importance of language as such was almost entirely abrogated, and tragedy's political concerns became internal to the drama rather than an element of the genre's broader social role.

See also 1637, 1651, 1664.

Bibliography: Lazare de Baïf, *Tragédie de Sophocles, intitulée, Electra . . . traduicte . . . en rythme françoyse* (Paris: Etienne Roffet, 1537). Geoffrey Brereton, *French Tragic Drama in the Sixteenth and Seventeenth Centuries* (London: Methuen, 1973). Joachim du Bellay, *La deffense et illustration de la langue françoyse,* ed. Henri Chamard (Paris: Didier, 1948). Etienne Jodelle, *Oeuvres complètes,* ed. Enea Balmas, 2 vols. (Paris: Gallimard, 1965–1968). Jean de La Taille, "De l'art de la tragédie," in *Saül le furieux: La famine, ou les Gabéonites: Tragédies,* ed. Elliott Forsyth (Paris: Didier, 1968). Timothy J. Reiss, *Toward Dramatic Illusion: Theatrical Technique and Meaning from Hardy to "Horace"* (New Haven: Yale University Press, 1971). Reiss, *Tragedy and Truth: Studies in the Development of a Renaissance and Neoclassical Discourse* (New Haven: Yale University Press, 1980). Thomas Sébillet, *Art poétique françoys,* ed. Félix Gaiffe (Paris: Cornély, 1910). Donald Stone, Jr., *French Humanist Tragedy: A Reassessment* (Manchester: Manchester University Press, 1974). Jean Vauquelin de la Fresnaye, *L'art poétique,* ed. G. J. M. Pelissier (Geneva: Slatkine, 1970).

Timothy J. Reiss

⤳ 1553, June

Four Years after Writing the Pléiade's Manifesto, Joachim du Bellay Goes to Rome and Repines

Antiquities and Antiquaries

"Go for it, Frenchmen! March on that arrogant Roman city and with its sub-servient spoils (as you have done more than once) adorn your temples and altars!" With this patriotic exhortation, Joachim du Bellay concludes his famous treatise, *La défense et illustration de la langue française* (1549; *The Defense and Enrichment of the French Language*). In *La défense,* the march on Rome functions primarily as a metaphor for the imitation of classical literature conceived of as a sort of looting of ancient ruins, but the highly evocative image of sacking Rome suggests many other important themes of French Renaissance writing. To begin with, the martial aspect of du Bellay's metaphor evokes the wars in Italy that began under Charles VIII in 1494 and continued through the reign of Henri II (1547–1559). During this period numerous French soldiers marched on Rome, Naples, Milan, and other Italian cities in pursuit of the illusory dream of French imperial conquest. More specifically, the imagery of pillaging recalls the sack of Rome in 1527, which resulted from French and Spanish rivalry for hegemony in Italy. While French monarchs pursued their ambitions of territorial conquest in Italy, nationalistic French writers mounted a serious challenge to Italy for cultural primacy in Europe. Thus du Bellay's idea of adorning French building with Roman ruins reflects his and his compatriots' obsession with *translatio,* the transfer of cultural and political preeminence from ancient Rome to modern France. All these political and poetic ideals underlie the literal import of the passage, which is that French writers must go to Rome and see the ruins in order better to appreciate and to appropriate the splendors of antiquity.

In the forefront of the march on Rome were the antiquarians, those art collectors and students of antiquity who visited the city in the hopes of discovering some material remnant of Roman grandeur that could be restored and preserved in France. One of the pioneers of French antiquarianism was Joachim's patron and uncle, Jean Cardinal du Bellay, whose duties as prelate and diplomat frequently brought him to his estate in Rome near the ruins of the baths of Diocletian. From his estate the cardinal excavated numerous ancient inscriptions and statuary pieces, transported them to France, and installed them either in his gardens at Saint-Maur or in the king's collection at Fontainebleau. In this way he helped to enact the type of cultural pillaging that Joachim advocated in *La défense.*

Often in the course of such learned looting Jean du Bellay would consult with his private physician, François Rabelais, who accompanied the prelate to Rome in the spring of 1534. While in Rome Rabelais conducted topographical researches and visited various excavation sites, including his patron's estate. He recounted these antiquarian experiences in the dedicatory epistle he composed for his edition of Bartolommeo Marliani's treatise, *Topographia Romae Antiquae* (*The Topography of Ancient Rome*), which first appeared in Rome in 1534 and which Rabelais published in Lyons later in the same year. Rabelais's publication along with Jean du Bellay's excavations laid the foundation for antiquarian studies in France.

The chief antiquarian during the reign of Francis I was the king himself. To adorn his residence at Fontainebleau, he enlisted the services of many Italian artists, including Francesco Primaticcio, whom the king sent to Rome in 1540 with a commission to collect antiquities. According to the contemporary biographer Giorgio Vasari, Primaticcio quickly located and bought 125 miscellaneous pieces, including heads, torsos, and other figures. He also had plaster casts made of the statues in the pope's Villa Belvedere, including those of Venus and of Laocoön, which he cast in bronze upon his return to France. The installation of these statues in the queen's garden at Fontainebleau transformed the royal residence, in Vasari's eulogistic view, into a new Rome. The king could not have asked for a more eloquent tribute to his success in transferring the prestige of classical culture from Rome to France.

The artistic and political ambitions of French antiquarianism inform much of the poetry composed by du Bellay during the four years he spent in Rome with his uncle. His poetic output from 1553 to 1558 includes his two master-pieces *Les antiquités de Rome* (*The Antiquities of Rome*) and *Les regrets* (*The Regrets*), as well as a collection of neo-Latin verse titled *Poemata*, all of which were published in Paris in 1558. In *Les antiquités* du Bellay enacts an alternative antiquarianism: through literary imitation he attempts to recover not the material remains of ancient Rome, but its poetic forms, which he deems much more valuable and more enduring. Through such imitative renewal, he hopes to contribute to the *translatio* that lies at the heart of French antiquarianism.

One of the most prominent themes of classical poetry that du Bellay imitates in *Les antiquités* is that of *exegi monumentum*, drawn from a Horatian ode in which the poet boasts of having raised a monument that will outlast all other human endeavors. Although the theme of poetic immortality also assumes an important role in du Bellay's early poetry, such as the *Vers lyriques* (*Lyric Verses*) of 1549, these early versions do not achieve the complexity of *Les antiquités*, where poetic ambition constantly confronts the admonitory spectacle of the collapse of classical civilization. At the beginning of *Les antiquités*, du Bellay confidently opposes the impermanence of Roman architecture to the immortality of Latin literature, but in the course of his sonnet sequence the general ruination of Rome begins to implicate all aspects of classical civilization, so that in the concluding sonnet the poet is forced to inquire plaintively of his own verses whether they hope to outlast Rome's marble monuments. Although their tone often conveys a sense of humanist despair over the impermanence of art and the absence of antiquity, the poems of this collection achieve a grandeur worthy of their poet's lofty ambitions.

Not all of du Bellay's Roman poetry sustains the solemn, monumental voice articulated so brilliantly and paradoxically in *Les antiquités*. His greatest collection, *Les regrets*, employs a wide variety of styles and genres, ranging from elegy to satire to court encomium. The most memorable verses, at the beginning of the collection, express the poet's longing for his homeland and his eloquent estrangement from poetic inspiration. Interweaving poignant memories of distant hearth and home with literary allusions to Ulysses and Ovid, these elegiac sonnets develop the theme of exile that becomes the distinguishing characteristic of du Bellay's Roman experience. The poems that deal most directly with Rome are the satiric verses from the central section of *Les regrets*, where du Bellay indicts the corruption of the papal curia. Rather than meditating on the relics of ancient Rome, these sonnets ridicule the customs of modern Rome, the Rome of Popes Julius III and Paul IV. In effect these satiric sonnets enact a subversive form of antiquarianism by digging up the vices of the papal city and exposing them to public scorn.

The most striking portrait of Roman decadence comes in sonnet 80 of *Les regrets*. Here the poet makes a tour of the city, pausing to observe the arrogance and hypocrisy of the prelates, the greed of the moneylenders, and the boldness of the prostitutes, who, as he remarks elsewhere, outnumber the monks in Rome. When he passes from the new city to the old he finds nothing but "de vieux monuments un grand monceau pierreux" ("a stony heap of old monu-

1. Woodcut attributed to Jean Goujon, in Francesco Colonna, *Hypnérotomachie, ou discours du songe de Poliphile nouvellement traduit de langage italien en français* (Paris: Jacques Kerver, 1546), p. 83 verso. (Courtesy of the Beinecke Rare Book and Manuscript Library, Yale University.)

ments," p. 151) (fig. 1). This clever juxtaposition of old and new deflates some of the grandiloquent humanism of *Les antiquités*. Here, far from deploring the discontinuity between the present and the past, du Bellay stresses an ironic continuity between ancient and modern Rome. Now, the passage from old to new is only too easy to make. Rome's monuments no longer represent an enduring cultural achievement worthy of imitation: they are merely another regrettable symptom of Rome's decline. Thus, in *Les regrets,* the humanist ambition to revive antiquity yields to a sense of disillusionment and alienation, which, paradoxically, constitutes du Bellay's most effective and most engaging poetic voice.

When du Bellay left Italy in the fall of 1557, Rome was under siege from the Spanish forces, and its inhabitants feared another sack like that of 1527, as several of *Les regrets* testify. Thus from an advocate of siege du Bellay became a victim, and this transformation reflects the change in France's political fortunes at the end of the decade. For du Bellay's departure from Italy coincided fairly closely with the withdrawal of the French forces under the command of Francis I of Lorraine, duc de Guise, whose services were needed in France to protect Paris against the incursion of Spanish troops advancing from the Low Countries after their victory at Saint-Quentin in Picardy. The march on Rome thus yielded to a retreat from Rome as France abandoned its Italian campaigns and prepared to enter a period of civil war in which antiquarian fervor and imperial ambition seemed obsolete. Yet, while it lasted, the antiquarian impulse inspired some enduring monuments of French literature.

See also 1528, 1549, 1550.

Bibliography: Joachim du Bellay, *Les regrets et autres oeuvres poétiques,* ed. M. A. Screech (Geneva: Droz, 1979). Gilbert Gadoffre, *Du Bellay et le sacré* (Paris: Gallimard, 1978). Thomas Greene, "Du Bellay and the Disinterment of Rome," in *The Light in Troy* (New Haven: Yale University Press, 1982). K. Lloyd-Jones, "Du Bellay's Journey from 'Roma vetus' to 'La Rome neuve,' " in *Rome in the Renaissance: The City and the Myth*, ed. P. A. Ramsey (Binghamton, N.Y.: Center for Medieval and Early Renaissance Studies, 1982). Eric MacPhail, "The Roman Tomb or the Image of the Tomb in du Bellay's *Antiquitez*," *Bibliothèque d'humanisme et Renaissance*, 48 (1986), 359–372. Edmund Spenser, "The Ruines of Rome" (a translation of *Les antiquités de Rome*), in *The Shepherd's Calendar and Other Poems*, ed. Philip Henderson (London: Dent, 1975).

Eric MacPhail

✑ 1555, *July*
Louise Labé, from Lyons, Publishes Her *Oeuvres*

Petrarchism with a Difference

Louise Labé (1526–1566), the daughter and wife of wealthy ropemakers in Lyons, inhabited a social and literary milieu typical of female poets in early modern France. She lived in a culturally energetic city relatively independent of the court and the theological scrutiny of the Sorbonne; she belonged by birth and marriage to the rising bourgeoisie, who valued belletristic education for their daughters as a sign of high social status; and, by participating in the circulation of friendships and texts that occurred in the socially open, mixed-sex salons of her town, she learned how to use the dominant lyric traditions of the 16th century, Petrarchism and Neoplatonism. Labé's twenty-four sonnets, the epigrams of her fellow Lyonnaise Pernette du Guillet, and the sonnet dialogue composed by Catherine des Roches of Poitiers simultaneously adopt and challenge these literary modes. In each text the poet demonstrates her control of the rhetoric of Petrarchan loss and Neoplatonic sublimation, but she also calls into question assumptions built into the love discourses elaborated by her male predecessors. The ostensibly solitary "I" of each of the three poets is addressed to a sophisticated reader whom she expects to be aware of the dialogue she is carrying out with the poetic practices of her time.

Pernette du Guillet, born in Lyons in about 1520, trained in music and languages, and married to a gentleman of the same city in 1537 or 1538, died of the plague at twenty-five. But by 1540 her songs and poems were known in Paris as well as in Lyons. Her *Rimes*, published the year of her death, in 1545, includes about seventy poems, written mainly in the Neoplatonic vocabulary and the epigram form used by her fellow Lyonnais Maurice Scève, whom she met in 1536 and who celebrated her as the heroine of his massive sequence of ten-line poems, *Délie* (1544). In her early poems Pernette presents herself as a humble disciple to Scève, whom she praises as her "Jour" (Sun, Daylight), the man who has brought her spiritual illumination and poetic ambition. But in contrast to the glimpses of erotic frustration that disrupt the prevailing Neoplatonism of *Délie*, Pernette's Neoplatonism is rigorously pure. Where Scève speaks of his jealous torment as he imagines Délie's sexual relationship with her husband (dizain 161) or celebrates the "sweet death" of amorous union (dizain

136), Pernette echoes but transforms Scève's words by stressing duty and honor as the pleasures of love (epigram 13). She alludes to Plato's *Lysis* (recently published in Lyons in a French translation by Bonaventure Des Périers), cites the love theory of contemporary Italian dialogues by Judah Leon Abrabanel and Sperone Speroni, and insists that the lovers' goal is a transcendent spirituality. In her opening epigrams she adopts an artfully simple language to declare her transformation by love, to trace out the intellectual ascent stimulated in her by her beloved, and to assert the equality and stability built into "vraie amitié" (true affection). In poems written in response to specific *dizains* (ten-line stanzas) by Scève, she corrects his "erreurs amoureuses" (lover's strayings) by reminding him of the primacy of reason and spirit in ideal love (epigrams 13, 16, 48). Pernette's use of a hypercorrect Neoplatonism is a strategy for justifying her performance as a female poet. By demonstrating that she fulfills Neoplatonic ideals of humility and chastity, she makes a convincing claim to the enlightenment promised to the accomplished philosopher-lover; and because humility and chastity were virtues that corresponded to 16th-century ideologies of proper feminine behavior, she can redeem herself for daring to enter masculine poetic terrain by insisting on the purity of her method and motives. Her exemplary compliance with Neoplatonic ideals is a technique of compensatory assimilation: through fidelity to the love theory of the philosophers and careful use of their poetic vocabulary, she circumvents social demands for women's silence and invisibility.

Louise Labé was equally accomplished in music and languages, according to the authors of the twenty-four sonnets that accompany the same number of her own in her *Oeuvres* (1555). It is possible that her poems were written to Olivier de Magny, a nobleman passing through Lyons on his way to Rome as a companion to papal envoys, who quoted passages from her lyrics in his *Soupirs* (1556; *Sighs*). Labé writes from a typically Petrarchan position: separated from her beloved, she praises his virtues and reproaches him for his indifference, pleads with him to return her love, and analyzes the violently opposed emotions of love's "martyrdom." But her adoption of this discourse is more mixed and more critical than Pernette's adoption of Neoplatonism. In her famous eighteenth sonnet, for example, Labé intensifies the physical eroticism of Roman love poetry; she builds on Catullus' request for kisses from his Lesbia by making a passionate demand for kisses from her beloved, promising to return four for his one. Her recognition of the startling frankness of such a request in the context of Petrarchism, which is structured around the lady's inaccessibility, is marked in her conclusion, where she excuses her code-breaking outspokenness by claiming that only the long misery of separation has forced her to "think such madness." A similar consciousness of her problematic relationship to poetic convention produces the list of theoretical questions in her *blason* poem, traditionally a list of the bodily attractions of the female beloved. In sonnet 21, rather than describing her beloved according to standard criteria, as male poets following Petrarch's enumeration of Laura's charms had done, Labé asks instead what the standards of masculine beauty are (what build? what sort of hair? what coloring?), thus calling attention to the lack of a parallel system of desiderata for a beloved man. She questions the traditional *blason* again in a late sonnet (23) by reproaching her beloved for the insincerity of his conventional praise: her golden hair, her eyes from which Love drew fatal arrows. Labé rejects such language as hypocrisy; unaccompanied by lasting devotion, Petrarchan compliment deserves only contemptuous citation. Here, too, she mitigates her critique by explaining that "spite and fury" inspired it. But her measuring of such topoi against the actual behavior of the poet-lover brings a new feminine skepticism to bear upon the long-standing conventions established by Petrarch's first *Canzoniere* (1374; *Songbook*). Labé's relationship to Petrarchism is one of explosive appropriation: disturbing the lyric mode with erotic counterconvention, she points out the gender asymmetry that has shaped its evolution and the undependability of its laudatory rhetoric.

In Poitiers twenty years later, Catherine des Roches published *Les oeuvres de Mesdames des Roches de Poitiers, mère et fille* (1578; *The Works of Mesdames des Roches from Poitiers, Mother and Daughter*). This joint collection included a set of twenty-six sonnets in which Catherine combined Neoplatonism and Petrarchism in speeches attributed to an ideal couple, Sincero and Charite. Charite was the salon nickname (and a near anagram) for Catherine, the daughter of a lawyer and of Madeleine des Roches. Together they presided over a literary coterie joined by Parisian magistrats during "Les Grands Jours," the special law sessions held in Poitiers in 1579. In *La puce* (*The Flea*), a collection of poems edited by one such visitor, Etienne Pasquier, and published in Paris in 1583, Catherine uses Neoplatonism as a counterdiscourse to the salacious *blasons* dedicated to the flea that Pasquier claimed to have seen upon her breast. For example, in response to Claude Binet's fantasy of following the flea on its voyage into the depths of her gown, she takes up only his closing reference to Minerva as the inventor of a celestial ideal. In the poems of her own collection, too, a striking aspect of Catherine's use of amorous discourses is her exploratory rather than confessional use of the literary modes she puts into circulation. Rather than speaking in the voice of a poet in love, she announces in her preface that she is constructing "a perfect lover" in the figure of Sincero, a procedure she links to exemplary portraits of the orator and courtier. Charite, similarly, is represented as an ideal mistress, dispensing moral guidance and witty correction to Sincero. Through their lyrical dialogue, Catherine neoplatonizes Petrarchism. Sincero describes his early years in a version of the storm-tossed-ship metaphor that Petrarch initiated as an emblem for the lover's endurance of passionate extremes (sonnet 9), but he grafts a Neoplatonic compliment onto this convention: the "holy honor" of Charite's perfection has grounded his youthful errors in wisdom. Through Charite, Catherine transforms the Petrarchan *blason* by listing Sincero's "wondrous spirit and divine knowledge" among his other perfections (sonnet 1). Furthermore, she regenders the male poet's claim to eternalize his beloved by assigning Sincero praise for Charite's "learned writing," through which he emphasizes that the woman poet is preserving the man's fame (sonnet 12). Des Roches's Neoplatonic revision of Petrarchism is a feminine transvocalization of both discourses: by writing lyrics in the voice of a perfect male lover, she affirms the moral and poetic authority of a heroine constructed in her own image.

Contemporary commentators on all three poets fixated on the sexual dangers assumed to accompany the appearance of women in public—or in print. Pernette's editor, Antoine du Moulin, insisted on her virtue and spirituality in his introduction to her *Rimes;* Labé was condemned for unbridled promiscuity by a variety of writers, including Jean Calvin, in an attack on a liberal churchman of Lyons; Claude de Rubys, a reactionary historian of the city, dismissed both Labé and Pernette as "infamous courtesans." Pasquier's comment that Catherine des Roches uniquely combined wit with propriety typifies Renaissance ambivalence toward female poets. Later critics attempted to reconstruct romantic biographies for them, focusing on the identity of their lovers to the exclusion of the social and linguistic maneuvers through which they made a place for themselves in the libraries of "honest readers." Since Verdun-Louis Saulnier's study of Pernette in 1944, however, analysis of female poets' texts as responses to their social and literary milieus has replaced conjecture about their private lives, and studies of urban history and culture such as those by Natalie Zemon Davis and Jacqueline Risset have provided valuable contexts for understanding women's lyric as engagement and contestation with the male-authored poetic system of 16th-century Europe.

Bibliography: Karine Berriot, *Louise Labé: La belle rebelle et le françois nouveau* (Paris: Seuil, 1985). Madeleine and Catherine des Roches, *Les oeuvres de Mes-dames des Roches de Poetiers, mère et fille* (Paris: Abel L'Angelier, 1578). Georges Diller, *Les dames Des Roches: Etude sur la vie littéraire à Poitiers dans la deuxième moitié du XVIe siècle* (Paris: Droz, 1936). Pernette du Guillet, *Les rymes de Pernette du Guillet,* ed. Victor Graham (Geneva: Droz, 1968). Louise Labé, *Oeuvres complètes,* ed. François Rigolot (Paris: Flammarion, 1986). Jacqueline Risset, *L'anagramme du désir: Essai sur "La Délie" de Scève* (Rome: M. Bulzoni, 1971). V.-L. Saulnier, "Etude sur Pernette du Guillet et ses *Rymes,*" *Bibliothèque d'humanisme et Renaissance,* 4 (1944), 7–119.

Ann Rosalind Jones

✎ *1555, 13 September*

Pierre de la Ramée Receives the Privilege for Publishing His *Dialectique,* the First Philosophical Work to Appear in French

Books in Print

The invention of printing transformed Renaissance writing by toppling the systems of *auctoritas* (authority) and tradition that controlled the medieval patristic and scholastic texts. Montaigne was the privileged witness of this age of transition, and, ultimately, through the severe criticism of his *Essais* by Antoine Arnauld and Pierre Nicole, by Blaise Pascal, and by Nicolas de Malebranche, a new system of control, a new ethics of writing, emerged in the 17th century. But the philosopher and logician Pierre de la Ramée, better known as Petrus Ramus (1515–1572), was more central yet in the elaboration of a new textual model.

Ramus earned a reputation as an iconoclast when in 1536 he defended a thesis at the Sorbonne that harshly contested the domination of the Aristotelian tradition in philosophy and theology: he claimed that "everything that Aristotle said is *commentitia,*" that is, an invention or falsification, perpetrated either by Aristotle himself or by his commentators. But Ramus clearly intended less to condemn Aristotle than to denounce the role the university forced him to play in presenting him as the supreme *auctoritas.* In the preface to his *Dialectique* (1555; *Dialectic*) Ramus declares his intention of reviving dialectic, a discipline abandoned since Galen imposed Aristotelianism. Beyond Aristotle, it is the argument based on authority that Ramus condemns irrevocably in the name of reason, in a clear anticipation of Descartes.

Ramus' *Dialectique* was the first philosophical work written in French. His choice of the vernacular went in tandem with the rejection of *auctoritas*— identified with Greek and Latin—and with his insistence upon bypassing commentaries and returning to the text itself. Ramus' oeuvre is contemporaneous with the Reformation. He himself converted to Protestantism in 1561, went into exile in Switzerland and Germany from 1568 to 1571, and was assassinated during the St. Bartholomew's Day Massacre. Although the influence of Ramus, under the name Ramism, was apparently stronger in lands won by the Reformation, and his *tabula rasa* was overshadowed in France by Descartes's methodical doubt, his contribution to the history of the text was crucial.

Ramus condemned commentaries as inseparable from their mode of textual transmission: the manuscript copy, which, through its introduction of distortions and errors, was inherently corrupt. The development of printing had a profound influence on the intellectual course of the Renaissance, one that went far beyond the consequences of mass diffusion. Even before printed copies significantly exceeded the production of the largest transcription workshops, the models of reading and writing were transformed, and the theory of language was altered.

Ramus' *Dialecticae Partitiones* (*Divisions of Dialectics*) of 1543 is printed entirely in roman type, except the preface, which is entirely in italics. But in his French *Dialectique* all citations of foreign texts are distinguished by typography: italics are used for poetry, inverted commas enclose prose. These indicators, forerunners of the quotation marks that became standard in the following century, were among the first to appear in any book. Ramus used these devices in all his later works, thus rigorously distinguishing the main body of the discussion from other texts, preventing the citations from becoming arguments based upon authority, and underscoring their new status as reasoned examples or illustrations. The innovation was decisive: it was only with the introduction of printed books, and then for one of the first times in the works of Ramus, that a text clearly marked its citations.

Before printing, the materials of a book were not indicated precisely. The text, whether preceded by a title or not, ran continuously, without interruption, unfolding itself like *flumen orationis,* a stream of discourse, on the model of the voice. The form of the text, its physical appearance, gave readers no indication of its internal organization. The content of the text had to express its own structure, following, for example, the rules of *dispositio* (the second part of rhetoric, after *inventio* or invention), which taught how to "dispose" ideas rigorously. This internal disposition made it possible to divide classical texts into paragraphs and subheadings when reproducing them for modern readers. But such a division presupposed the substitution of a *spatial model* of the text, the printed book, for a *linear model,* that of the manuscript. They are as different as sight and voice. The new printed page, with its spatial disposition, is not read aloud without the loss of some information (some printed signs—such as punctuation—as well as most of the peculiarities of the layout are not translated into sounds); it requires a visual reading, because the typography makes the text's structure immediately apparent.

Two elements without which we can now scarcely imagine a book—the title page and the table of contents—came into existence with printing and confirmed the transformation of the model of the text. The first printed books began directly with the first sentence of the text and concluded with a colophon, after the fashion of manuscripts. Soon, though, a richly decorated first page gave the title of the book, the name of the author and the printer, the date and place of publication, and, at the bottom, the printer's mark. The title given by the author became the name of the book; it was no longer taken from the book's general content, as did the Latin manuscript designations beginning with the preposition *de,* "about, on the subject of." The printer's mark was another new type of sign, an emblem chosen by the individual to represent himself and accompanied by a motto. The title page, with its different elements and its combination of text and image, resembled the typical disposition of the emblem books, books meant to be looked at more than to be read, which became fashionable during the Renaissance.

The table of contents came at the other end of the book. Originally called an *index locorum,* or "index of places," it was the directory of the *loci,* places or sites, specific to any book, as opposed to the topics, that is, the list of topoi or commonplaces, which in the old rhetorical practice were transferable in each discourse. Thus the *index locorum* signaled the shift toward the conception of the book as individual and original. It listed in order chapter titles and subtitles and their page numbers. Ramus pushed this spatial or diagrammatic representation of the book further than anyone else. He concluded his books not with a simple inventory or catalogue, but with a projection of the volume on a plan, a true map, which he called a "table." With this word he designated an organic diagram, a tree displaying the structure of the work on a large page that had to be unfolded. Thus, in the *Dialectique* the table began by dividing the title into its constituents: "dialectic comprises two parts, invention and judgment"; and so on (fig. 1). Ramus' table exploited to the limit the technical possibilities offered by the printed page. Nothing has been invented since to indicate more directly a book's contents.

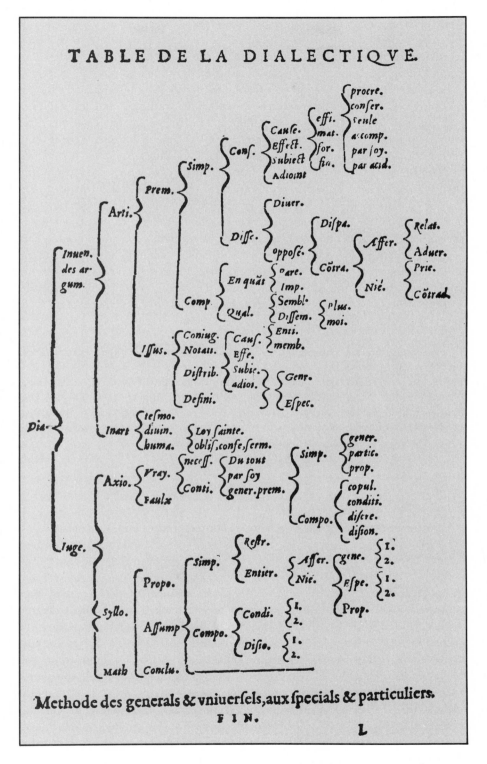

1. "La table de la dialectique," in Pierre de La Ramée, *Dialectique* (Paris: André Wechel, 1555), p. l. (Courtesy of the Bibliothèque Nationale, Paris.)

In both versions of his later *Grammaire* (1562, 1572), Ramus showed his continued concern with printing. Typically, he substituted the term *character*, related to printing, for *letter*, to designate the basic element of written language. *Letter* was ambiguous, because traditionally it referred more to the sound than to the visual symbol. In accordance with this shift of emphasis, Ramus invented new typographic characters to render the multiple phonetic values of each ancient letter. He proposed a reform of writing so that each character would correspond to one single specific phonetic value. Antoine Arnauld and Pierre Nicole condemned such reforms in the Port-Royal *Logique* (1662; *Logic*) because they would cut off language from its history, to which the old spelling bore witness: what one would gain in clarity, one would lose in history. But Ramus' dream of perfect writing and transparent signs clearly belongs to a Renaissance ideal. The Renaissance text sought to achieve the transparency of the sign and the self-evidence of the page. The emblem supplanted the allegory of the Middle Ages, which implied an esoteric relationship to hidden meanings. The *Adagia* (1500; *Adages*) of Erasmus and the *Essais* (1580) of Montaigne are based on the same notions. But nowhere will we find more clearly than in the works of Ramus the effects of the printed model on the Renaissance text.

See also 1123, 1267, 1534 (17–18 October), 1536.

Bibliography: Antoine Compagnon, *La seconde main, ou le travail de la citation* (Paris: Seuil, 1979). Lucien Febvre and H. J. Martin, *The Coming of the Book: The Impact of Printing (1500–1800)*, ed. Geoffrey Novell-Smith and David Wooton, trans. David Gerard (London: NLB, 1976). Walter Ong, S.J., *Ramus: Method and the Decay of Dialogue* (Cambridge, Mass.: Harvard University Press, 1958). Petrus Ramus, *Dialectique*, ed. Michel Dassonville (Geneva: Droz, 1964).

Antoine Compagnon

❧ 1562

Maurice Scève Rewrites the Story of Humankind in His *Microcosme*

Scientific Poetry

When Adam and Eve fled from Eden under a storm of pelting rain, they mustered their courage, built a makeshift shelter, racked their brains to design a plow, and tilled the soil until they could produce food good enough to be named in human language. These were, according to Maurice Scève, the first signs of our first parents' deep-seated self-interest, thirst for innovation, and relentless imaginative spirit that gradually led their offspring to rule the world. In his 3,003-line encyclopedic poem, *Microcosme* (1562), Scève thus dramatically moved to reverse the traditional (biblical and medieval) curse on our earliest ancestors' insane inquisitiveness (*curiosité*) and promoted human ingeniousness and resourcefulness beyond any previous expectations, though warning at the same time against the potential risks involved, for (lines 1099–1100):

In experimenting with things man may deceive himself
By his ever-insatiable curious desire.

Scève was not alone in his fascination with the ambiguous nature of human desire. Two decades later, in a more religious vein, Guillaume de Salluste du Bartas, a prolific Protestant poet with an epic vision, produced a series of remarkably picturesque vignettes of the biblical Creation narrative, *Première semaine* (1578; *The First Week of Creation*) and *Seconde semaine* (1584; *The Second Week of Creation*). His enthusiasm for the dignity of man and his irrepressible spirit in the face of cosmic adversity must account for the many editions of and learned commentaries on his work, and for his influence in England, where through Josuah Sylvester's translation he had considerable influence on John Milton's *Paradise Lost*.

Renaissance "scientific poetry" stemmed from a lyrical impulse both to praise and to caution against the awesome potentialities of human desire (*curiosité*) and thirst for knowledge (*science*). It lavishly displays an extraordinary variety of themes and styles, bringing together apparently unrelated ways of envisaging the universe: the scientific, the religious, and the magical, seen later as being at odds. Science, in its 19th-century mode, was scarcely conceivable in a period whose cosmology was geocentric.

Scientific poets such as Jacques Peletier du Mans (*L'amour des amours*, 1555; *Love for Loves*), Jean-Antoine de Baïf (*Le premier livre des météores*, 1567; *The First Book of Meteors*), and Isaac Habert (*Les trois livres des météores*, 1585; *The Three Books of Meteors*) felt compelled to sing the complex world of astronomical and meteorological phenomena, from the weather to the comets and their portents. Rather than turning to explanatory models traditionally provided by the medieval quadrivium (arithmetic, geometry, astronomy, and music), they turned instead to great philosophic encyclopedias, such as Georg Reisch's *Margarita Philosophica* (1496; *The Precious Stone of Wisdom*), and reveled in a strange mix of empirical observations and the most arcane interpretations of the magical and the occult. As a result, each poet was able to promote himself as a magus, an enlightened prophet who could go beyond the mechanical phenomena and interpret, in eloquent and often mystical verse, his vision of the intricate relationships between the cosmos and the human creature, the microcosm.

As early as 1555 Pierre de Ronsard, the leader of the Pléiade poets, had published his *Hymnes*, a series of visionary poems whose sheer attractiveness comes from the sensual beauty of its scientific allegories. The glorious cosmos he describes elicits both a sense of awe and a feeling of disquietude in the face of its uncanniness. How can one not be frightened at the mysterious presence of fantastic *daimons* (good or bad spirits in the Neoplatonic sense) influencing the dance of the stars and the moods of human creatures ("Hymne des démons"; "Hymn of Demons")?

In a different mode, Peletier sought to represent the jarring yet awe-inspiring "noises" of the universe (as in his poem on thunder) through the incantatory rhythm of imitative harmony (*L'amour des amours*). Later, in his *Louange de la science* (1581; *Praise of Knowledge*), he was to describe the universe as an abstract, purified machine relying on a vast, unified system of signs to be deciphered only through an arcane knowledge of numbers.

Indeed, around 1570 scientific poetry had taken on a new aspect with the poetry of Guy Lefèvre de la Boderie, probably the greatest scientific poet of the century and a translator of Marsilio Ficino and Giovanni Pico della Mirandola (*Encyclie des secrets de l'éternité* [1571; *The Circle of Eternity's Secrets*]; *La Galliade, ou de la révolution des arts et sciences* [1578; *The Galliad, or on the Revolution of Arts and Sciences*]). As cabalism reentered the elitist domain of late humanistic thought, more technical references to mathematics and the whole idea of numbers and proportion came together in long occult poems starred with superb passages of magical evocation. Combining elements of Christianity, Neoplatonism, and Judaism, Lefèvre meant to lead his readers through the intricate maze of multiple truths to a poetic sense of eternal unity. But his poetry's attractiveness derives from the uncontrolled, freewheeling virtuosity with which he draws upon the Hermetic tradition to express the mysterious, paradoxical truths of the universe.

Alchemy was also a favorite topic for scientific poetry, especially late in the century. The case of François Béroalde de Verville is typical. Although *De l'âme et de ses facultés* (1583; *On the Soul and Its Faculties*) appears to be a versified vestige of medieval philosophy, it dwells insidiously on the occult properties of the *pneuma* (living breath) in a way meant to be suggestive to the enlightened alchemist who seeks out "the ultimate form of all things" (*Sérodokimasie*, 1600; *On Silkmaking*).

As a specifically recognizable genre, scientific poetry died out around the beginning of the 17th century, and no doubt partly as a result of the growing acceptance of Copernican theories. In becoming less motivated and more rational, the learned gaze tended to concentrate on fragmented phenomena, detached from any vision of wholeness or harmony. Science became less expressible in poetic terms as it sought out a methodical discourse suspicious of the trappings of a lyrical voice.

See also 1647, 1753, 1942.

Bibliography: Guillaume de Salluste du Bartas, *The Divine Weeks and Works of . . . Du Bartas,* ed. Susan Snyder, trans. Josuah Sylvester, 2 vols. (Oxford: Clarendon Press, 1979). Du Bartas, "Scientific Poetry," in *A Critical Bibliography of French Literature,* ed. Raymond C. La Charité (Syracuse: Syracuse University Press, 1985), pp. 331–346. Maurice Scève, *Microcosme,* ed. Enzo Giudici (Paris: Vrin, 1976). Albert-Marie Schmidt, *La poésie scientifique en France au seizième siècle* (1938; reprint, Lausanne: Rencontre, 1970). Hans Staub, *Le curieux désir: Scève et Peletier du Mans poètes de la connaissance* (Geneva: Droz, 1967). Frank Warnke, *European Metaphysical Poetry* (New Haven: Yale University Press, 1961). Dudley B. Wilson, *French Renaissance Scientific Poetry* (London: Athlone Press, 1974).

Dudley B. Wilson

✍ 1563, 18 August
Montaigne Witnesses the Death of His Friend Etienne de La Boétie

Anti-Dictator

In August 1563 Montaigne's friend Etienne de La Boétie lay dying. Doctors prescribed various remedies for the violent stomach cramps and diarrhea that afflicted the thirty-two-year-old Bordeaux magistrate, but the symptoms only increased in intensity, and soon the patient and those around him began to lose hope of a recovery. A serious illness in the Renaissance was regarded only in part as a medical event; pain, fear, and dying transcended the medical and became for observers and sufferers alike moral events. Hence in the midst of his intense anxiety and grief Montaigne began to read what transpired before his eyes as a series of signs, a succession of scenes that confirmed, in a manner at once consoling and painful, his own expectations. "I readily foresaw," Montaigne wrote to his father, "that if illness left him the power to express himself, nothing would escape him in such a necessity but what was great and full of good example" ("Extrait d'une lettre que Monsieur le Conseiller de Montaigne écrit à Monseigneur de Montaigne son père, concernant quelques particularités qu'il remarqua en la maladie & mort de feu Monsieur de La Boétie" [1563? "To His Father: On the Death of La Boétie"], in *Montaigne,* p. 1046). It was always possible for circumstances to block the performance by rendering expression impossible, but if there were no such hindrance, the living and the dying would be conjoined in an intense mutual compact of admiration and example. "Thus I was attentive as I could be."

In Montaigne's account this compact was extraordinarily explicit and self-conscious. He wished there to be a larger audience for his friend's courage at the point of death; that courage, he told La Boétie, "would serve me as an example, to play this same part in my turn" (p. 1050). Not only does La Boétie's behavior serve as a theatrical performance on which future performances of death can be modeled, but it also is the enactment of a script that the two friends had fashioned in their conversations and their humanistic studies. A good death—in a world without any of the means we now deploy to protect ourselves from the full agony of parting—would reveal the authentic presence of humane philosophy in the secret recesses of the individual. And correspondingly, it would give that philosophy an authentic presence in the world, a place of honor that would at the same time confer glory upon the individual. Montaigne excerpted parts of the letter describing La Boétie's last days and published it in 1570 at the end of his edition of his friend's *Oeuvres:* in effect, dying has become the last and perhaps the best of La Boétie's works.

For, as the days of excruciating pain wore on, La Boétie performed his part as brilliantly as Montaigne could have hoped: that is, he performed according to the ideal text that the two friends had constructed. Yet at the very end, Montaigne records something strange: utterly enfeebled, La Boétie surprised everyone by writhing in his bed with sudden violence and raising his voice in a final, desperate appeal to his friend. Again and again "with extreme affection" the dying man entreated Montaigne "to give him a place." Montaigne gently replied that "these were not the words of a man in his sound mind," but La Boétie persisted: "My brother, my brother, do *you* refuse me a place?" (p. 1055). These unsettling, anxious words, with their undertone of shocked reproach, were obviously not in the script that the two friends had imagined for themselves, and they elicited a philosophical argument at the brink of the grave: "He forced me to convince him by reason and tell him that since he was breathing and speaking and had a body, consequently he had his place." The material basis for the human possession of a place is the body; La Boétie's friend cannot either grant or refuse this body—it is La Boétie's by virtue of life itself. But that life was ebbing—"When all is said," the dying man declared, "I have no being left"; and hence the place it conferred was "not the one I need." In response, Montaigne led La Boétie to direct his longings toward a "place" beyond this world, a place only God could give him. "Would that I were there already," La Boétie replied. "For three days now I have been straining to leave" (pp. 1055–56). In a few hours he was dead.

Montaigne thus succeeds in transforming La Boétie's last moments from an irrational expression of fraternal reproach to an impatient craving for release from the very breathing and speaking body that secures his place in the world. The transformation confers upon the close of La Boétie's life that exemplary status to which both the dying man and his friend aspired, yet there is a lingering sense of something like betrayal. Montaigne could scarcely be accused of a failure of friendship, but La Boétie's words oddly impute to his friend a power to confer a place in the world, and they suggest, however briefly and wildly, that Montaigne might refuse to give that place to the man he most loved.

Montaigne well understood that the choice was not his to make, but in the almost thirty years that followed, until his own death in 1592, his life was strangely haunted by his responsibility for the posthumous "place" of Etienne de La Boétie. The dying man had bequeathed to him his books and manuscripts. The former became the core of the famous library that Montaigne assembled in his study: that is, they found their place at the center of the personal world that Montaigne constructed for himself and out of which he embarked on his great meditative enterprise. The latter—the manuscripts—Montaigne undertook to publish. "I am prodigiously eager," he wrote in 1570, "that at least his memory after him, to which alone from now on I owe the good offices of our friendship, should receive the reward of his merit and be well lodged in the good opinion of honorable and virtuous persons" ("A Monseigneur de L'Hôpital," in *Montaigne*, p. 1059). These words, in the dedicatory epistle to an edition of his friend's Latin poems, were echoed in other editions that Montaigne lovingly saw through the press: La Boétie's French poems and his translation of works by Plutarch and Xenophon. And they were echoed more intimately, more deeply, throughout Montaigne's own essays, above all in the famous essay "De l'amitié" ("On Friendship").

What most readers remember from that essay is the extraordinary absoluteness of its vision of spiritual oneness. But paradoxically Montaigne originally conceived this expression of perfect fusion—the commingling of both identities so that the autonomous existence of either is entirely lost—as the introduction to a text written by La Boétie years before the two had met. "De l'amitié" was to serve as a preface to the most important of La Boétie's manuscripts, *Discours de la servitude volontaire* (*Discourse on Voluntary Servitude*), also known as *Le contr'un* (*Against One Man*). (An English translation was published in 1942 as an antifascist tract: *Anti-Dictator*.) This meditation, undertaken perhaps as a rhetorical exercise when La Boétie was only sixteen or eighteen, functioned, Montaigne writes, as the "medium" of their first acquaintance, for Montaigne had read a copy before he met its author. Now, in its proposed position directly following the essay on friendship, the *Discours* would have a place of honor in Montaigne's own text and would at the same time confer honor upon that text.

The voice Montaigne contemplated coupling in this way with his own was that of a severe and uncompromisingly radical champion of liberty. In the *Discours* La Boétie sets out to ask why the men and women of his time allow themselves to be cheated and oppressed, why they meekly turn over the fruits of their labor to worthless overlords, why they are everywhere in subjection. That such questions should be asked at all is a remarkable achievement: they depend upon a willed estrangement from both the piety and the cynicism of the everyday, a refusal to assent without surprise to all-too-familiar arrangements. Humanist education, though by no means always a radical intellectual force in the period, evidently led La Boétie to challenge the prevailing religious and political justifications for obedience and to regard the social order of his times with studied amazement: "Who would credit such a report if he merely heard it, without being present to witness the event? . . . A people enslaves itself, cuts its own throat, when, having a choice between being vassals and being free men, it deserts its liberties and takes on the yoke" (*Anti-Dictator*, p. 9).

La Boétie's text is sometimes described as an argument against tyrants—there were a number of such arguments, modeled on classical precedents, in circulation in his time—but it seems to go beyond the usual castigation of wicked princes. There are, La Boétie writes coolly, three types of tyrants: those who are elected to their position of power, those who conquer it, and those who inherit it. By this account, even so-called legitimate monarchs are actually tyrants, and they remain tyrants even if their subjects quietly acquiesce in their rule and convince themselves that they are merely acting according to time-honored custom or law. Such acquiescence, the willingness of potentially free men to live on their knees, is precisely what fascinates and appalls La Boétie.

Whereas Montaigne is characteristically intrigued by social plenitude, the inexhaustible variety of customs and beliefs, La Boétie is characteristically concerned to demystify this plenitude, to strip away the surface diversity of legitimating practices and reveal the shameful truth of almost universal submission to ruthless exploitation. Like the Roman emperors, modern rulers "never undertake an unjust policy, even one of some importance, without prefacing it with some pretty speech concerning public welfare and common good" (*Anti-Dictator*, pp. 35–36). Some subjects are foolish enough to believe this hypo-critical nonsense, but the will to serve may be fashioned by less high-minded means than such rhetorical invocations of the common good. "Plays, farces, spectacles, gladiators, strange beasts, medals, pictures, and other such opiates, these were for ancient peoples the bait toward slavery" (p. 33), and comparable baits lure the vulgar crowd of La Boétie's own time toward their subjugation.

For La Boétie, the sparks of liberty are altogether extinguished in the mul-titude, the *canaille* who would rather give up their freedom than a bowl of soup. They have neither individual nor collective memories of an independent existence; hopelessly sunk into servitude, they are pathetically grateful to the scoundrels who exploit them. What they, and even their social superiors, alto-gether lack is what we might call the spirit of negation—the spark of the *Discours,* Montaigne writes, may have been Plutarch's remark that "the inhabi-tants of Asia served one single man because they could not pronounce one single syllable, which is 'No'" ("De l'institution des enfants" ["On the Education of Children"], in *Montaigne,* p. 115). That negation might, at its most heroic, find expression in an act of violence; classical history provided several stirring examples of honorable tyrannicides. But, according to La Boétie, the recovery of liberty does not necessarily entail violence; it can be achieved simply by a refusal any longer to serve. If servitude is voluntary, it can be annulled by a withholding of the act of will that invents and sustains the tyrant: "It is not necessary to deprive him of anything, but simply to give him nothing; there is no need that the country make an effort to do anything for itself provided it does nothing against itself" (*Anti-Dictator,* p. 9).

In a breathtaking leap of insight and indignation, the young La Boétie has in effect conceived the idea of nonviolent resistance. The effect of this resistance would, he suggests, be devastating to tyrants precisely because in themselves they do not possess either power or property: "If not one thing is yielded to them, if, without any violence they are simply not obeyed, they become naked and undone and as nothing, just as, when the root receives no nourishment, the branch withers and dies" (*Anti-Dictator,* p. 10). The people need only reclaim what is theirs, and they will be free. The imposing structures under which men groan, the dazzling images they worship, the immense figures before whom they kneel—all are the creations of the oppressed themselves. "I do not ask that you place hands upon the tyrant to topple him over, but simply that you support him no longer; then you will behold him, like a great Colossus whose pedestal has been pulled away, fall of his own weight and break in pieces" (pp. 12–13).

If liberation is so easy to achieve, why does it not occur? La Boétie offers a structural explanation: the tyrant is supported by 5 or 6 key figures who in turn have 600 who profit hugely under them; the 600 maintain a network of 6,000 whom they reward with rank and property; and so on. Eventually, the network of clientage and dependence extends to hundreds of thousands and even millions who are persuaded that their well-being depends upon their place in a pyramid of dependence. A majority of the country can come to believe that they are better off without liberty and that their interest lies in satisfying the desires of the tyrant.

This malignant structure is sustained by a systematic extirpation of the memory of liberty. The ruling elite typically encourages a servile adherence to custom, for custom legitimates oppression, transforming the contingent into the seemingly eternal, muting a rational detestation of tyranny, and paralyzing the will to be free. In an enslaved world, hope of reawakening this will lies in the possibility of imagining freedom, a possibility that for La Boétie is bound up with education. But tyrants see to it that a liberating education is difficult to attain, and the few who have managed to achieve it feel themselves solitary in their longings, uncertain as to possible comrades. "Indeed Momus, god of mockery," La Boétie writes, "was not merely joking when he found this to criticize in the man fashioned by Vulcan, namely, that the maker had not set a little window in his creature's heart to render his thoughts visible" (*Anti-Dictator*, p. 25). To a modern reader, familiar with the surveillance techniques of the tyrant-states of our own time, this playful fantasy of the "little window" strikes a chilling note, for the visibility it projects could serve so easily as the tyrant's instrument. But it suggests how anxious La Boétie was to escape from the isolation, the loneliness, of his radicalism.

In the openness of its clear, hard outrage, the *Discours* was itself a powerful instrument for the awakening of a common will to liberty. But the effectiveness of this instrument would obviously depend upon wide circulation, the circulation Montaigne originally intended to confer upon it. His belated decision to suppress publication of the *Discours* at the center of the first book of his own *Essais* (1st ed. 1580) is a move to restrict its readership. Montaigne characteristically does not efface the traces of his altered intention: he has changed his mind, he writes, because he found that the *Discours* had already been published by seditious Protestants, "those who seek to disturb and change the state of our government without worrying whether they will improve it" ("De l'amitié," in *Montaigne*, p. 144). In the embittered climate of France's religious wars, La Boétie's work seems to Montaigne less liberating than dangerous; in the place that was meant for the heroic critique of voluntary servitude, Montaigne decides to print twenty-nine love sonnets by La Boétie.

"My brother, my brother, do *you* refuse me a place?" Montaigne does refuse a place in his own writing to his friend's most significant and enduring work. But as if in recompense for this refusal, with its trace of political difference and even of betrayal, Montaigne spends his whole life trying to do what La Boétie only dreamed of: to open a little window in his heart and to make his thoughts visible.

Bibliography: Etienne de La Boétie, *Discours de la servitude volontaire,* ed. Miguel Abensour, Pierre Clastres, and Claude Lefort (Paris: Payot, 1976); translated by Harry Kurz as *Anti-Dictator* (New York: Columbia University Press, 1942). La Boétie, *Oeuvres complètes,* ed. Paul Bonnefon (1892; reprint, Geneva: Slatkine, 1967). Jeffrey Mehlman,

"La Boétie's Montaigne," *Oxford Literary Review*, 4 (1979), 45–61. Michel de Montaigne, *Oeuvres complètes*, ed. Robert Barral and Pierre Michel (Paris: Seuil, 1967); translated by Donald M. Frame as *Montaigne: Essays, Travel Journal, Letters* (Stanford: Stanford University Press, 1948). François Rigolot, "Montaigne's Purloined Letters," *Yale French Studies*, 64 (1983), 145–166. Jean Starobinski, *Montaigne in Motion*, trans. Arthur Goldhammer (Chicago: University of Chicago Press, 1985).

Stephen Greenblatt

✒ 1566

In *Methodus ad Facilem Historiarum Cognitionem* Jean Bodin Emphasizes a Nationalist and Pragmatic View of History

History and Vernacular Humanism

Jean Bodin's *Methodus ad Facilem Historiarum Cognitionem* (1566; *Method for the Easy Comprehension of History*) marks the beginning of a new genre, the treatise on historical method and criticism. Building on the Italian "arts of history" (*artes historicae*), Bodin's book shifted emphasis from the writing to the reading of history, in effect from an aesthetic to a utilitarian view, and implicitly from narrative to analytical (problem-oriented) form. His aim was not to recreate the past but rather to pluck the "flowers" of history and, in much the same spirit as the "method" of Petrus Ramus, to arrange material topically for the use (in Bodin's case) of legal and political philosophy. Indeed, Bodin's more famous *Les six livres de la République* (1576; *The Six Books of a Commonweale*), published a decade later, was essentially an expansion of chapter 6 of the *Methodus* on "the type of government in states."

"What is history?" Bodin asked, and "how many kinds of history are there?" (*quid et quotuplex*, a standard scholastic beginning). The standard answers to these questions for French Renaissance historians were based on classical commonplaces. According to the frequently invoked Ciceronian formula, history was "the witness of time, the light of truth, the life of memory, the mistress of life, and the messenger of antiquity" (*De oratore* 2.9). It was commemorative, accurate, restorative, and useful; and its "first law" was to tell the truth and the whole truth. History also possessed the rhetorical virtues of explanatory and persuasive power, and on such literary grounds it was distinguished from simple annals and chronicles as well as from poetry.

To these questions Bodin's answers were at once more philosophical, more political, and more "pragmatic." Like Roman law, history was of three sorts— human, natural, and divine. Bodin's concern was with the first sort, "civil history," a category (along with "sacred" and "natural" history) preserved in Francis Bacon's influential scheme of learning. Like his one major predecessor, François Baudouin, in *De Institutione Historiae Universae et Eius cum Jurisprudentia Conjunctione* (1561; *Institution of Universal History and Its Conjunction with Jurisprudence*), Bodin distinguished the human from the natural (and the divine) order on the basis of free will, sin, instability, and other attributes of humanity. Such a distinction was a basic premise of historical thought and writing in Renaissance France (following, as usual, Italian humanist models).

Bodin also distinguished between universal and particular history. The former included not only modern world histories, such as Jacques-Auguste de Thou's *Historiae Sui Temporis* (1604–1608; *History of His Time*), which presented a panoramic survey of 16th-century Europe, but also universal chronicles, a medieval genre with modern descendants such as Nicolas Vignier's *La bibliothèque historiale* (1587; *Historical Library*), which treated world history from the Creation but also promoted the use of the French language. Bodin himself was suspicious of the universalist (and "imperialist") bias of universal chronicles and devoted chapter 7 of his *Methodus* to refuting the old thesis of Four World Monarchies, which established the Hapsburg Holy Roman Empire, France's rival, as the legitimate descendant of the Roman, Greek, Persian, and Median empires of old.

One major historiographic novelty, celebrated and encouraged by Bodin, was a view of the past that, following the "encyclopedic" and cultural thrust of French humanism, treated not only political and military affairs but also the "arts of peace." Louis Le Roy's *De la vicissitude ou variété des choses en l'univers* (1575; *On Vicissitude or Variety of Things in the Universe*), which attempted a comparative and global survey of this sort, has been regarded as the first history of civilization and, arguably, as an anticipation of the modern idea of progress. Similarly, Bodin's disciple Pierre Droit de Gaillard argued in his own treatise, *La méthode qu'on doit tenir en la lecture de l'histoire* (1579; *Method for the Reading of History*), that the aim of the study of history, whether particular or universal, was self-knowledge; and at best this involved study of human and "civilized" arts and sciences—which proceeded, Gaillard added, "as from an overflowing fountain." Finally, Henri Voisin de La Popelinière, another of Bodin's followers, proposed a "new history" that was to include "the origin . . . , progress, and change of all the arts and sciences." Following Bodin's *Methodus*, La Popelinière's vast history of historiography, *L'histoire des histoires, avec L'idée de l'histoire accomplie* (1599; *History of Histories and The Idea of Perfect History*), likewise recommended study of all the arts of civilization on which the presumed superiority of the Moderns to the Ancients was based.

For Bodin, particular history included biographies and especially studies of specific nations, either from their origins or in particular periods. In 16th-century France the major national histories all followed the form and style established by Italian humanism and commended by Bodin, beginning with the seminal work of Paolo Emilio, *De Rebus Gestis Francorum* (1517; *On the Deeds of the French*), published many times, translated into French in 1556, and emulated by later generations of historiographers, including even Pierre de Ronsard's poetic celebration of the national past in *La Franciade* (1572).

In general the impulse behind the writing of history in the 16th century was national pride—"vernacular humanism" being the literary form—and a feeling that the French past had been neglected, especially in comparison with that of the Italians. Frenchmen had been too busy with deeds to attend to words—too busy fighting, that is, to be concerned much with writing and recording their history—and 16th-century scholars such as Etienne Pasquier and Le Roy hoped to remedy this. The question of national "origins" (taken up critically in Bodin's chapter 9) continued to fascinate historians, but their conclusions were tempered by the new methods of criticism and evaluation associated with historical method and humanist philology, and they began to reject such time-honored myths as the Trojan origins of the Franks and the founding of the University of Paris by Charlemagne—although they went on to substitute other, more modern myths of national or religious character and cultural superiority.

The study of history was deeply involved, too, in 16th-century partisan controversy, both political and religious, and indeed was a major form of propaganda. Martyrological works, such as the Genevan *Histoire ecclésiastique des églises réformées* (1580; *Ecclesiastical History of the Reformed Churches*), often attributed to Théodore de Bèze but in fact a collaborative work, and Jean Crespin's *Histoire des martyrs* (1564; *History of the Martyrs*), not only celebrated evangelical heroes and ideals but also expressed a new vision of history derived from Luther's and Calvin's view of spiritual tradition and "papist" degeneration. The Reformation view of the "primitive church" and of its subsequent corruption had political parallels, including François Hotman's *Francogallia* (1573), which portrayed a similarly idealized "ancient constitution" of the French monarchy.

In general the French theory and practice of history in the later 16th century was rich and eclectic—a blend of the old and the new, the ornamental and the useful, the barbarian and the classical. On the one hand, ancient ideals persisted; yet champions of the Moderns and of national culture realized that it was, as Le Roy wrote in his *Vicissitude* (fol. 255), "necessary to do . . . what antiquity has done for us," this time in vernacular terms. The study of history continued both along popular and literary and along antiquarian, "scientific" lines. Besides providing entertainment and edification, history assumed an essential legitimating function in various partisan, national, and confessional contexts. It was taught in universities and written by professional historiographers; and, more broadly, it emerged as a way of organizing knowledge and understanding culture. As Bodin put it, history was placed "above all other disciplines"; and this judgment was endorsed by many of his 17th- and 18th-century followers, who imitated and elaborated on his "method of history."

See also 1202, 1214, 1517, 1677, 1823.

Bibliography: Jean Bodin, *Method for the Easy Comprehension of History,* trans. Beatrice Reynolds (New York: Columbia University Press, 1945). Claude-Gilbert Dubois, *La conception de l'histoire en France au XVI siècle* (Paris: Nizet, 1977). George Huppert, *The Idea of Perfect History: Historical Erudition and Historical Philosophy in Renaissance France* (Urbana: University of Illinois Press, 1970). Donald R. Kelley, *Foundations of Modern Historical Scholarship: Language, Law and History in the French Renaissance* (New York: Columbia University Press, 1970).

Donald R. Kelley

✍ *1572, 24 August*

In the St. Bartholomew's Day Massacre, Thousands of Protestants
Are Killed in Paris and throughout France

Poetry and Action

In the unusually torrid summer of 1572, after more than a decade of religious
strife and uneasy truces between Catholics and the ineradicable Protestants,
a conciliatory wedding took place in Paris: on 18 August Henri de Navarre,
one of the Huguenot leaders, was married to Margaret of Valois, daughter of
Catherine de Médicis and Henri II and sister of King Charles IX. Huguenot
noblemen poured into the city for the ceremony, having been reassured by
Gaspard de Coligny, the Protestants' most influential spokesman, military
leader, and close (in the view of some, too close) adviser to the king. A worse
site for the ceremony could not have been chosen. The Parisian populace was
outraged by this enormous concession to the Huguenots. It was further outraged by the perceived haughtiness of the Huguenot noblemen in the city and
inflamed by fanatic preachers, monks, and even bishops who publicly attacked
the marriage as a symbol of the monarchy's weakness. On 22 August, the
morning after the end of the wedding festivities, an assassin (probably hired by
Catherine de Médicis) fired two shots from his harquebus and wounded Coligny.
From that point on an inexorable chain of events unfolded: guards were placed
around the Huguenot living quarters, militia were armed, and rumors ran wild.
The next day, Catherine and her advisers decided to order the execution of the
leaders of the Huguenot party. The king, despite his personal admiration and
affection for Coligny, was persuaded to go along with the plan. Toward midnight, before the king could change his mind, Catherine ordered the tocsin to
be sounded, and the massacre began. Instead of a few dozen noblemen, hundreds of Protestants were killed, as a feverish thirst for blood swept the city.
The killing and looting continued for days. In the provinces similar massacres
occurred, the last one as late as October. Estimates of the total number of
victims range between 12,000 and 100,000.

Among the various anecdotes relating examples of cruelty, martyrdom, and
compassion, one in particular symbolizes a loss of innocence that the St. Bartholomew's Day slaughter came to stand for in general. A young Huguenot
friend of Charles IX, Comte François de La Rochefoucauld, spent most of the
night of 23 August playing games with the king. When, exhausted, he asked
to leave, Charles insisted that he stay and spend the night in the royal chambers, intending to save his friend's life. However, La Rochefoucauld refused.
When his masked killers knocked at his door later that morning, he believed
them to be pranksters sent by the king. As Jules Michelet phrased it in his
Histoire de France: "Il riait quand on l'égorgea" ("He was laughing as they murdered him") (vol. 7, chap. 25).

Much of Renaissance literature is written as an aesthetic *game,* as a disposition
of pleasing conventions, often in the context of a court. The most telling exam-

ples of this conventionality are found in poetry, especially in the lyric oeuvre of the Pléiade, the best-known group of poets writing toward the middle of the 16th century. This literary and courtly aesthetic, which combined and rearranged motifs and rhetorical devices culled from classical and Italian literature, was by its nature limited to a small, cultivated elite and little concerned with the relationship between its language and immediate reality. The court provided a social, aesthetic, and economic space in which the referential aspect of literature—that is, its designation of real situations—was suspended or at least unimportant. Literature was in this sense a pleasing game. That game could contain a moral truth, but it was often nonspecific; the message was a celebration of the continuity of culture, an imitation of exemplary Greeks and Romans, as well as a praise of noble or royal patrons.

When La Rochefoucauld mistook his masked killers for pranksters sent by the king, his mistake involved the kind of suspension of reality demanded by courtly literature and behavior. The tragic inappropriateness of his laughter is emblematic of the inappropriateness—because of the anachronism—of that literature. In the violent context of the religious struggles in France, games had become serious; there was no longer a place where religious differences did not matter, in which weapons could also be mere ornaments.

In Agrippa d'Aubigné's *Les tragiques* (1616), the greatest literary product of the Wars of Religion (1562–1598), there is a pervasive sense of the compelling connection between literature and reality. The title is difficult to translate, as it can be understood several different ways: perhaps "Tragic Stories," depicting the tragic fates of the Protestant martyrs, comes closest, but it does not convey the epic force and urgency of his poem. The author himself escaped the massacre only by chance: he attended the royal wedding but was forced to leave Paris on 21 August because he had wounded a sergeant who had attempted to prevent a duel in which d'Aubigné served as second. D'Aubigné, who was only eight when his father showed him the corpses of the Huguenots executed as a result of the Amboise conspiracy of 1560, devoted his life (1552–1630) to the Protestant cause, as soldier and military engineer, as envoy, as pamphleteer and satirist (*Confession catholique du sieur de Sancy* [wr. 1598–1600; *The Catholic Confession of Monsieur de Sancy*]; *Les aventures du baron de Faeneste* [1617–1630; *The Adventures of the Baron de Faeneste*]), and as historian (*L'histoire universelle*, 1618–1626; *The Universal History*). His poetic production is no less abundant: in addition to *Les tragiques*, he wrote a collection of love sonnets and longer poems, *Le printemps* (wr. 1571–1573; *Springtime*), religious poetry (*La création; The Creation*), and the more personal and meditative *L'hiver* (*Winter*). His autobiography, *Sa vie à ses enfants* (1729; *His Life Written for His Children*), circulated in manuscript in the 17th century.

Les tragiques is an epic poem written in alexandrines and divided into seven books: "Misères," "Princes," "La chambre dorée," "Les feux," "Les fers," "Vengeances," and "Jugement" ("Misery," "Princes," "The Golden Chamber," "Pyres," "Irons," "Vengeance," "Judgment" are approximate translations). Its subject is the Wars of Religion: the horrors visited upon France and its people, the corruption of court life under Catherine de Médicis, the martyrdom and military struggles of the Huguenots, and appeals to God for revenge and judgment. The poem ends as the poet experiences a mystic reunion with God. Throughout the poem the figure of the poet is inspired by the Holy Spirit, possessed by near-prophetic visions, and capable of distinguishing the elect from the reprobate. D'Aubigné owes many of his themes, rhetorical devices, and language to the Old and New Testaments, Lucan's *Pharsalia,* Juvenal's *Satires,* and the works of Protestant contemporaries, including the theological works and polemics of Calvin's successor in Geneva, Théodore de Bèze, the sermons of Heinrich Bullinger, the philosophical and theological writings of Philippe Duplessis-Mornay, and the poetry of Guillaume de Salluste du Bartas. At about the same time, poets, satirists, and polemicists such as Jean de La Taille, Etienne de Maisonfleur, and Antoine de Chandieu published separate pieces or collections of militant poetry attacking the papacy and the ultra-Catholic Guise family, forming a whole corpus of *littérature de combat.* D'Aubigné also derived material from martyrologists such as Jean Crespin, whose *Histoire des martyrs* (first published in 1554, amplified during the Wars of Religion, and published in its final version in 1619 by Simon Goulart) provided gruesome accounts of Protestant victims' deaths and their inspiring professions of faith.

Les tragiques is an accumulation of tales of suffering, martyrdom, and vengeance. The St. Bartholomew's Day Massacre, "the tragedy that effaces all the rest" ("Fers," lines 702–703), constitutes a central episode in the bloody epic (see especially "Fers," lines 705–1564). An often detailed description of individual scenes of slaughter is combined with scathing invective against the king, his mother, and the court. D'Aubigné ends his furious diatribe with an allegory of Ocean recoiling in horror as the rivers of France turn to blood (the Huguenots were often stabbed and then thrown into rivers from city bridges). The tone is relentlessly urgent and indignant: driven by the excess of horrors, the poet can never do justice to his material, cannot modulate his energy, and cannot stop. Violent scenes are presented as if by an eyewitness: *Voici, Vois encore, Voilà, Je vois, Vois-tu* (Here! See here! Look at this! I see! Do you see?) punctuate the breathless litany. D'Aubigné also interjects long apostrophes to protagonists and direct appeals to God. The reader is, as it were, forced to watch; there is no room for hesitation, play, or suspension of judgment.

The poem's opening lines clearly refuse to engage in any of the rhetorical preambles designed to recall epic conventions and please the reader. They are an explicit call to action, a response to the tocsin: "Puisqu'il faut s'attaquer aux légions de Rome . . ." ("Since we must attack the legions of Rome . . ."). The allusion to ancient Rome in no way detracts from the contemporary situation, for in the language of Huguenot polemics Rome was immediately identifiable as the seat of all vices, the scourge of the true, original church. Persuasion is no longer needed, since the facts are obvious, and they call for a response. The poem is that response.

D'Aubigné likes to underline the relative novelty of his writing: he is teaching his pen "a different fire," a fire that is consuming France. Unlike pastoral poetry set in the fields of Thessaly, his songs are born (d'Aubigné frequently uses *avorter*—to be born in difficult circumstances, or with great difficulty) in the midst of armies, as the poet's arms pause during battle: "Blood is not feigned, murder is everywhere, / Death plays herself on this sad stage" ("Misères," lines 75–76). Fiction is redirected to the representation of contemporary events; it pictures itself as inseparable from the circumstances of its physical birth. The writer does not think of writing as primarily rising out of tradition; instead, literature is directly determined by experience.

D'Aubigné and other Protestant writers were reacting against the type of literature best exemplified by court poetry and best represented by Pierre de Ronsard (1524–1585), the most famous and prolific of the Pléiade poets. Ronsard contributed to the religious controversy with polemical pieces of his own, most of which were written in 1562 and 1563, that is, after the Amboise conspiracy (1560) and the massacre at Wassy (1562) but well before St. Bartholomew's Day, on which he remained silent. First published separately, these poems were later grouped together, in the 1567 edition of Ronsard's collected works, under the title *Discours* (*Discursive Poems*). They are commonly referred to as the *Discours des misères de ce temps* ("Discursive Poems on the Terrible Events of These Days" is an approximate albeit awkward rendering), after the title of the first major piece. In this poem, addressed to Catherine de Médicis, Ronsard decries the calamities of the civil war, expresses his confidence in the queen's ability to mollify opposing parties, and, in the event of her failure, calls upon God to punish the rebels. The next poem, the "Continuation des misères de ce temps," a more specific attack on the Huguenots and Calvinist theology, includes a personal appeal to Théodore de Bèze. The "Remontrance au peuple de France" ("Warning to the French People") continues theological argumentation and vehemently criticizes Protestant reliance on individual interpretation of the Bible and the attendant supplanting of knowledge by Opinion, who is personified as the daughter of Fantasie (*Imagination:* usually a pejorative term, and especially so in this context). Opinion visits Luther and persuades him to undertake his campaign against the pope and the church, causing bloodshed, discord, and fratricide.

The most interesting piece in the collection is the "Réponse de P. de Ronsard, gentilhomme Vendômois, aux injures et calomnies de je ne sais quels prédicants, & ministres de Genève" ("Response by P. de Ronsard, Nobleman from the Vendôme, to the Insults and Calumnies of Some Preachers and Ministers of Geneva"), Ronsard's last substantial political poem. The "Réponse" is a reply to invectives by the Protestants Antoine de Chandieu and Bernard de Montméja, who accused the court poet of being a priest, of believing in evil demons, of having contracted syphilis, of not being a Christian, of having staged a pagan sacrifice, of leading a disorderly and lascivious life, of being a base flatterer of the powerful, and of writing meaningless, chaotic poetry. Ronsard replies to each of these accusations, sometimes in a playful, sometimes in a virulent tone, using many of the devices that characterize his poetic oeuvre. He defends his (relatively modest) ecclesiastical income and his faith, gives an account of his daily activities, and reaffirms the value of poetry as opposed to oratory. The former is not obliged to follow the "natural" disposition of a speech, but can move here and there freely, guided only by the muse. Overall meaning and order do not have to be obvious, but can be hidden by pleasing and diverse digression. The sense of playful movement is captured by the Horatian simile of the bee collecting nectar. This slightly detached and superior display of lyrical powers is in distinct contrast to the relentless exclusion of play and disengagement in *Les tragiques,* although d'Aubigné much admired Ronsard's literary talent.

Whereas the Huguenot poet refuses all discussion and reasonable argument as patently unnecessary ("Puisqu'*il faut* s'attaquer aux légions de Rome"—we *must* act), logical argument occupies a good deal of Ronsard's *Discours.* The poet takes pains to refute Protestant positions on biblical interpretation, the eucharist, justification, and the like. In part this difference is explained by the different models imitated (Erasmus and Horace versus Lucan and Juvenal), in part by the different readership envisaged. Ronsard at the outset feels the need to convince Catherine to proceed firmly against the Huguenots, and later he attempts to argue with the Huguenots themselves. D'Aubigné offers encouragement to the Protestants still faithful to the cause and assumes the role of an apocalyptic witness to God's revenge. Nowhere is the sense that Ronsard's poetry belongs to an earlier type of writing clearer than in the opening lines of the *Discours,* addressed to the queen. Here he accumulates syllogisms to show that the sum total of virtues and vices has always remained the same in any one period of history; he concludes by advocating prudence and defense of the Catholic faith, in a sort of skeptical conservatism, although later in the poem he comes out much more strongly against the "foreign" religion of the Huguenots. The emphasis on rational discussion and persuasion makes his polemical stance much weaker than that of his virulent successors. This weakness, however, was less obvious to Ronsard's contemporary readers, for many of whom such argumentation became the basis for their faith. But in a sense the St. Bartholomew's Day Massacre marked a symbolic, though not historical, dividing line between the possibility of reasonable argument in a space separate from action, and its impossibility. In literary terms, the massacre divides the conventional court poetry of Ronsard from the hyperbolic, self-consciously transgressive battle cries of d'Aubigné.

Ronsard was not the only Catholic poet writing against the Huguenots; during the second half of the 16th century several *recueils,* collections or anthologies, presented "Christian" poems from the works of such notable poets as Joachim du Bellay, Philippe Desportes, Etienne Jodelle, Rémi Belleau, Jean-Antoine de Baïf, and Robert Garnier. These collections, with titles such as *Muse chrétienne* (1582; *Christian Muse*), were then used as polemical material. Satirical and polemical pamphlets abounded on both sides. The best known is a satire written by moderate humanist Catholics (Pierre Le Roy, Pierre Pithou, Nicolas Rapin, Florent Chrestien, and Jean Passerat) against the ultra-Catholic League in 1593 and published in enlarged form in 1594 as the *Satire ménippée de la vertu du catholicon d'Espagne* (*Menippean Satire about the Powers of Spanish Catholicon*). As the prologue points out, this book was a deliberate imitation of Greek satire, a mixture of prose and verse deriding society's faults, performed onstage by satyrs (an erroneous etymological association) and actors, and attributed to the Cynic philosopher Menippus. The pamphlet accused the League of being paid with Spanish gold and presented various parodic speeches by its leaders, exposing their hypocrisy and greed. The final speech, by d'Aubray, representing the Third Estate, criticizes his predecessors and urges acceptance of Henri de Navarre as king of France. The *Satire ménippée* seems simultaneously an unusual throwback to humanist culture before the Wars of Religion and a symptom of the weariness stemming from thirty years of strife and polemics.

Weariness was also what the violent polemical poetry of this period provoked in 17th- and 18th-century readers. Classical taste and political prudence caused d'Aubigné's long eclipse, although, curiously, the very Catholic and devout Françoise de Maintenon, Louis XIV's companion in his old age, owned a manuscript of d'Aubigné's *Le printemps*. She was the Huguenot poet's granddaughter. D'Aubigné, and baroque poets in general, were in vogue again in the 19th century. Victor Hugo found in him a kindred spirit, and in 1857 Baudelaire used six lines of *Les tragiques* as an epigraph to the first edition of *Les fleurs du mal* (1857; *The Flowers of Evil*), a misreading that nevertheless demonstrates the appeal of d'Aubigné's hyperbolic, urgent, and apocalyptic language to Romantic sensibility.

The wrenching religious wars pushed literature to extremes: they made courtly literature appear inappropriate at best, cynical at worst. They provoked the use of literature to influence contemporary hearts and minds, and, finally, they helped produce France's only truly powerful epic since the Middle Ages.

See also 1534 (17–18 October), 1573.

Bibliography: Théodore Agrippa d'Aubigné, *Les tragiques,* in *Oeuvres,* ed. Henri Weber (Paris: Gallimard, 1969). Terence Cave, ed., *Ronsard the Poet* (London: Methuen, 1973). Robert M. Kingdon, *Myth and Massacre in 16th-Century Europe: Reactions to St. Bartholomew's Massacres of 1572* (Cambridge, Mass.: Harvard University Press, 1988). Frank Lestringant, *Agrippa d'Aubigné: Les tragiques* (Paris: Presses Universitaires de France, 1986). Jacques Pineaux, *La poésie des protestants de langue française (1559–1598)* (Paris: Klincksieck, 1971). Pierre de Ronsard, *Discours des misères de ce temps,* in *Oeuvres complètes,* ed. Paul Laumonier, Raymond Lebègue and Isidore Silver, vol. 11 (Paris: Didier, 1946). *Satyre ménippée de la vertu du catholicon d'Espagne . . .* (1594; reprint, Geneva: Slatkine, 1971).

Ullrich Langer

ᘓᘓ 1573

Philippe Desportes, Court Poet, Collects His *Premières oeuvres;*
Agrippa d'Aubigné Completes *Le printemps*

From Mannerist to Baroque Poetry

"When *I* use a word, it means just what I choose it to mean." Humpty Dumpty's famous words to Alice provide a wonderfully appropriate epigraph to any discussion of what has been called the "baroque problem" in literature. To use "baroque" or not to use "baroque": that is the question that has perhaps been more hotly debated than any other by 20th-century literary historians. One critic after another has proposed a "new" definition of that protean term, often totally overturning previous definitions in the process of trying to discover what, if anything, constitutes the baroque.

The word *baroque*, which perhaps derives from a Portuguese word meaning an irregularly shaped pearl, or most likely (according to René Wellek) from the name of a particularly strained scholastic syllogism, was originally popularized by the German art historian Heinrich Wölfflin. He established five criteria for distinguishing a baroque from a Renaissance work of art: closed versus open form, linear versus painterly representation, multiplicity versus organic unity, absolute versus relative clarity, plane versus recession. These criteria were subsequently seized upon by literary critics and applied to works of the 16th and 17th centuries, even though there was some question as to the appropriateness of such a transfer from one artistic medium to another. The waters were further muddied when art historians postulated another, intermediate artistic style intervening between Renaissance and baroque, mannerism. Literary critics were also quick to embrace this new term, which some used to describe characteristics of literary works previously labeled baroque.

Despite this chaos and confusion, the mannerist/baroque distinction is a useful one, provided we can agree on some basic definitions. "Mannerism" refers to an artistic and literary style that began in Italy in the early 16th century, was quickly imported into France by Francis I, and influenced the poetry of Clément Marot, Maurice Scève, Pierre de Ronsard, Joachim du Bellay, and Philippe Desportes, among many others, finally disappearing in the last years of the century. A mannerist work, to follow the definition of John Shearman, is one that is polished, refined, sophisticated, and stylized, a work that places greater emphasis on formal elegance than on the intellectual and metaphysical. Baroque describes the style that succeeded mannerism and was predominant in France from around 1570 until about 1630. According to the art historian John R. Martin, the baroque is characterized by a return to a naturalistic representation of the world (as opposed to the stylized representation associated with mannerism) and by an emphasis on violence, metamorphosis, and movement. Baroque art tends to restore metaphysical concerns to a central position, stresses the importance of emotion and the senses, and, particularly in its later phases, indulges in extravagant and sometimes excessive opulence. Its purpose is not primarily to amaze and delight (a mannerist goal), although it does both, but above all to persuade.

Like definitions, dates are often the results of arbitrary choices. But if one had to choose a specific date to mark the beginning of the baroque style in French literature, 1573 would be less arbitrary than most, for it was then that two major poets were writing or editing their youthful work. The first, Philippe Desportes (1546–1606), was both the rival and the emulator of Ronsard and represented the ultimate extension of the Petrarchan poetic tradition of the

French Renaissance. He was the last great representative of the mannerist style. The other, Agrippa d'Aubigné (1552–1630), the fiery Protestant polemicist and poet, was also influenced by Ronsard. However, he was already manifesting signs of a new poetic sensibility, which he expressed in his love poetry (dedicated to Diane Salviati, niece of Ronsard's Cassandra), and which is already marked by the violent and graphic imagery associated with the baroque. Desportes's love poetry, imitated from minor Italian Petrarchans, finally appeared in print, after circulating in manuscript for many years, in the *Premières oeuvres* (1573; *Early Works*) and was an immediate and continuing success until his death. His amatory verse is characterized by formal perfection and lack of overt emotion, hallmarks of mannerism, according to Shearman. His religious verse and psalm paraphrases, however, dating from about 1587, lack a mannerist veneer, and their rougher texture and sometimes violent imagery are much closer to the emotional impact associated with the baroque.

Despite Desportes's popularity and influence during his lifetime, he is now read little. D'Aubigné, on the other hand, started writing his love poetry around 1573, but, because he came to consider profane love a frivolous subject, his *Printemps* (*Springtime*) did not appear in print until the middle of the 19th century. Ironically, d'Aubigné is today much more widely read than Desportes.

Le printemps, a reconfiguration of the Petrarchan material favored by mannerist poets, shocks the reader with its surprising and often violent metaphors. These images, together with an unusually abundant use of antithesis, give new vigor and force to the traditional clichés of love and death, as here: "I open up my bosom, a bloody tomb of hidden troubles; in God's name, turn your gaze, Diane, and look in the depths at my heart split in two and my lungs marked by violent passion" (Cameron, *D'Aubigné,* p. 34).

One of the principal benefits of the mannerist/baroque controversy has been the rediscovery of many poets whose work had been ignored or forgotten since the 16th century. Three of the most important are Jean de Sponde (1557–1595), Jean-Baptiste Chassignet (ca. 1571–ca. 1635), and Jean de La Ceppède (ca. 1550–1623). All three are part of a tremendous wave of devotional poetry that flooded Europe in the wake of the Reformation and Counter-Reformation and was influenced by techniques of religious meditation practiced by Catholics and Protestants alike. Sponde, a Protestant who later converted to Catholicism, published a number of love poems (twenty-six sonnets and ten other pieces) whose intellectual quality is reminiscent of the English metaphysical poets. He also wrote some striking religious verse (twelve sonnets and two longer poems) focusing on the vanity of life, the inevitability of death, and the necessity of preparing for it. Although Sponde's verse lacks the level of violence found in d'Aubigné's, his poetry is dynamic and restless, exemplifying the baroque desire to persuade the reader of some important moral or religious truth while demonstrating the type of tightly knit, formal control typical of mannerist verse.

The second poet of this trio, Chassignet, influenced by the Christian neo-stoicism of the later 16th century (and not a little by Montaigne), writes in a similar vein. His principal work is *Le mépris de la vie et consolation contre la*

238

mort (1594; *The Vanity of Life and Consolation against Death*). His poems are on the whole less striking than Sponde's, perhaps because of their sheer number (almost 300 sonnets), although the best produce the same emotional impact as a baroque crucifixion painting. One of his most grisly poems (sonnet 125) describes with clinical precision the decomposition of the body after death in order to persuade the reader that the only hope for mankind is to turn to God. Others deal with the theme of metamorphosis and the shifting nature of reality in order to convince the reader that stability can be found in God alone.

Jean de La Ceppède, a magistrate from Aix-en-Provence, is perhaps the most ambitious of this group of religious poets. His devotional sequence of over 500 sonnets, published in two parts (*Les théorèmes sur le sacré mystère de notre rédemption,* 1613 and 1622; *Theorems on the Holy Mystery of Our Redemption*), recounts the life of Christ from the Last Supper to the Ascension. His poems are remarkable for their lyrical intensity, their unflinchingly naturalistic representation of the sufferings inflicted upon Christ, and their spirituality. La Ceppède's poetry clearly shows the influence of the theory and practice of meditation upon poetic composition. The often violent and dynamic narrative thread linking the sonnets is constantly broken by poems that stress inward reflection and invite the reader to look beneath the surface texture of the narrative to discover and meditate upon the theological mysteries hidden in the biblical source material.

The last major writer to be considered as at least a partial baroque poet was a friend of La Ceppède, François de Malherbe (1555–1628). One of the most influential writers of his age, he is generally regarded as the father of French classicism. However, his early religious poetry, particularly "Les larmes de saint Pierre" (1587; "The Tears of Saint Peter"), an imitation of Luigi Tansillo, enriches the Venetian poem with a plethora of antitheses, amplifications, and unusual images, imparting a vigorous, dynamic quality lacking in the original. Malherbe later regretted what he considered to be the stylistic excesses of this poem and attempted to dissociate himself from it; the vast majority of his poetry is characterized by the measured, unornamented style typical of French classicism, which the older Malherbe saw above all as a reaction against mannerism and the baroque. Ironically, some modern literary critics (such as Leo Spitzer) and art historians (such as John R. Martin) now see this style as the final metamorphosis of the volatile baroque.

If we can say that the first manifestations of the baroque began around 1573, by 1630 most of its best-known lyrical poetry had been published, or at least written, and the taming of the baroque had begun, as it moved into its classicist phase.

Bibliography: Terence Cave, *Devotional Poetry in France c. 1570–1613* (Cambridge: Cambridge University Press, 1969). Jean-Baptiste Chassignet, *Le mespris de la vie et consolation contre la mort,* ed. Hans-Joachim Lope (Geneva: Droz, 1967). Philippe Desportes, *Oeuvres,* ed. Alfred Michiels (Paris: Delahays, 1858). Théodore Agrippa d'Aubigné, *Le printemps, l'hécatombe à Diane,* ed. Bernard Gagnebin (Geneva: Droz, 1948). Keith Cameron, *Agrippa d'Aubigné* (Boston: Twayne, 1977). Jean de La Ceppède, *Les théorèmes sur le sacré mystère de notre rédemption* (1613–1622; reprint, Geneva: Droz, 1966). La Ceppède, *From the "Theorems" of Master Jean de La Ceppède,* ed. and trans. Keith Bosley (Manchester: Carcanet New Press, 1983). François de Malherbe, *Oeuvres,* ed. Antoine Adam (Paris: Gallimard, 1971). John Rupert Martin, *Baroque* (New York: Harper & Row, 1977). Harold Segel, *The Baroque Poem* (New York: Dutton, 1974). John Shearman, *Mannerism* (Harmondsworth: Penguin, 1967). Jean de Sponde, *Oeuvres littéraires,* ed. Alan Boase (Geneva: Droz, 1978). Frank Warnke, *European Metaphysical Poetry* (New Haven: Yale University Press, 1961). René Wellek, *Concepts of Criticism,* ed. Stephen G. Nichols (New Haven: Yale University Press, 1963). Brian Woledge, Geoffrey Brereton, and Anthony Hartley, eds., *The Penguin Book of French Verse* (Harmondsworth: Penguin, 1975).

Lance K. Donaldson-Evans

✐ 1578

Twenty Years after His Return, Jean de Léry Publishes His Account of the Villegagnon Expedition to the Bay of Rio de Janeiro

Antarctic France

In the 16th century the face of the world changed completely. In particular, the colonization of America extended the limits of the territories known to man. Why, then, does the New World occupy only a rather modest place in the French literature of the Renaissance? Essentially there are two reasons.

First was the lack of an effective colonial policy. There were three French attempts to found colonies—Jacques Cartier's expeditions to Canada (1534–1540), of which he left personal accounts; Admiral Nicolas Durand de Villegagnon's three-year sojourn in the bay of Rio de Janeiro (1555–1558) to create an overseas settlement for Protestants persecuted in France; and the journey to Florida by Jean Ribault and René de Laudonnière (1562–1564) for the same purpose—and all three failed. From these abortive attempts the French acquired, not a share in the wealth gained by the Spanish and Portuguese, but only stories and myths—such as the myth of the Noble Savage, which Montaigne (*Essais,* I, 31, and III, 6) and others were to use to criticize European institutions, contrasting them with the "natural" goodness of the American Indians.

The other reason why the New World seeped only slowly into French consciousness was the resistance of people's minds. Those travelers and scholars—there were not many—who took an interest in distant lands preferred to turn to the East, whose history and geography were less radically new. To look in that direction was to turn to the cradle of religion, science, and the arts: the land of origins. And it is easier to hang on to what is already known—the past—than to face the unknown—the future. The Far East, described more than two centuries earlier by Marco Polo (1298) and John Mandeville (1327), was known essentially through legends and fantastic rumors. Yet the Ottoman

Empire, which spanned the entire eastern Mediterranean, attracted many explorers and inspired several narratives. Guillaume Postel (*De la république des Turcs,* 1560; *On the Turkish Republic*), one of the most learned orientalists of his time, was mainly interested in the languages, the religious ideas, and the occult traditions, whether they came from the cabala, the Koran, or magical sects. Other travelers preferred to bring back "singularities"—strange spectacles, picturesque phenomena that they had collected themselves or had, with credulous eclecticism, borrowed from oral or written sources; examples are André Thevet's *Cosmographie du Levant* (1555; *Cosmography of the Levant*) and compilations by Pierre Belon and Nicolas de Nicolay. But this attraction for the Near East was not due only to the desire for knowledge, tales, curiosities, or erotic dreams. At that time the Ottoman Empire was at the gates of Western Europe, threatening Christendom, and its military might and political system fascinated as much as they repelled.

Despite these political, intellectual, and emotional barriers and the failure of Villegagnon's short expedition to Brazil, two remarkable accounts, *Les singularités de la France antarctique* (1557; *The Singularities of Antarctic France*), by the monk André Thevet, and *Histoire d'un voyage fait en la terre du Brésil* (1578; *History of a Voyage Made to the Land of Brazil*), by the Protestant Jean de Léry, are worth remembering. They represent the beginnings of anthropological writing in France. Not only do these two texts have great value as documents, but their differences in method illustrate some of the fundamental problems of Renaissance epistemology: How is an unknown reality to be interpreted? How can one speak of a world that no one has ever spoken of?

Thevet supplies considerable anthropological documentation; his chapters on cannibalistic ritual and on the religion, the magic, and the myths of the Tupinamba Indians demonstrate a remarkable curiosity about the "singularities" of America. But the man who was to become the "king's cosmographer" had a more ambitious project: he wanted to survey the whole world. The Brazilian journey was to be only one stage in an account that on the outward journey would include Africa and bits of Asia and on the return journey, the rest of America. Now no traveler at that period had been able to visit all these countries. Thevet's account is a composite of what he has seen, heard, and read; he mixes together plausible reports and imaginary constructions, endowing direct experience and borrowed learning with the same status. He exploits all the possible sources—legends, accounts by Spanish conquerors, Greek and Latin authors—without distinguishing among them, so that his book takes on the character of a collective and impersonal work, a medley of disparate documents.

The method is typical of humanist culture: one observation in itself is meaningless; absolute novelty is incomprehensible and must be related to a network of familiar references (see fig. 1). The nakedness of the Brazilians is shocking? Then it is compared to ancient statues. A tribe of female warriors is found disturbing? Then they are assimilated to the Amazons of Greek mythology. These analogies are founded on an almost magical belief in the unity and order of the universe. Throughout time and space, all things are in correspondence

1. Jean de Léry, *Histoire d'un voyage fait en la terre du Brésil, autrement dite Amérique* (Geneva: Antoine Chuppin, 1578), p. 235. (Courtesy of the Bibliothèque Nationale, Paris.)

with, and consequently explain, each other. The epistemological shock of the discovery of America was attenuated in this way; the strangeness of the New World was integrated without upsets into the system of traditional knowledge. This method, typical of cosmographers, was developed by Thevet in *La cosmographie universelle* (1575; *Universal Cosmography*) and by François de Belleforest in *La cosmographie universelle de tout le monde* (1575; *Universal Cosmography of the Whole World*).

The publication of Jean de Léry's book is an important event, as Claude Lévi-Strauss acknowledges in *Tristes tropiques,* because he adopts a different formula in the face of the American challenge. Léry discards the theory of a harmonious world unified by secret sympathy and thus no longer attempts to construct a system of global knowledge. There are no extrapolations, analogies, or learned quotations; instead there is a kind of reporting that claims to be based exclusively on the author's experience during the few months that he spent with the Indians. Instead of looking for resemblances and explanations that mitigate the surprise of discovery, Léry makes an effort to respect the uniqueness of things and to reveal their difference and specific quality.

In this way ethnographic investigation breaks loose from the world of books and moves out to the field. Its only guarantee now is the careful gaze of the unprejudiced traveler, who observes, tries to understand, and then relates what he has seen and lived through. Instead of an anonymous compilation of oddities, Léry constructs a personal tale, in which he talks about himself and recalls his memories, occasionally with emotion. The splendor of the tropical landscape, with the multicolored feathers of the parrots and the red bark of the trees, the strangeness of cannibal feasts, the painted bodies of the savages—all these are narrated as marvels that require no justification beyond the pleasure of seeing them. Not that Léry, a Protestant and a pessimist, yields to the illusion of having found the golden age; these Indians are pagans and bear the curse of the Fall just as much as the Europeans. His attention to them is thus all the more open and brotherly. Whether he is talking about their food or their ceremonies, about the variety of fish or the different species of plants, his descriptions are extraordinarily vivid and precise.

From the moment of its discovery, America posed a serious methodological problem to the humanists. What course should one follow: submission to the authority of the ancients or recognition of newly acquired experience? The New World was challenging the Old to bring itself up to date. Not for the last time!

See also 1721, 1847.

Bibliography: Geoffrey Atkinson, *Les nouveaux horizons de la Renaissance française* (Paris: Droz, 1935). Jean de Léry, *Histoire d'un voyage fait en la terre du Brésil,* ed. A.-M. Chartier (Paris: Epi, 1972). Frank Lestringant, "Fictions de l'espace brésilien à la Renaissance: L'exemple de Ganabara," in *Arts et légendes d'espaces* (Paris: Presses de l'Ecole Normale Supérieure, 1981). Tzvetan Todorov, *The Conquest of America,* trans. Richard Howard (New York: Harper & Row, 1984).

Michel Jeanneret

✑ 1581

Balthazar de Beaujoyeux Presents His *Ballet comique de la reine* at the Louvre before Henri III and His Court

The Spectacle of Power

On 15 October 1581 the *Ballet comique de la reine* (*Queen's Ballet*) was played before Henri III and his court in the Louvre palace (fig. 1). The five-and-a-half-hour performance constituted the high point of an elaborate series of *magnificences* celebrating the marriage of the king's favorite, Anne d'Arques (later duc de Joyeuse), to the queen's sister.

In tacit recognition of the constant threat of civil and religious strife in France, the *Ballet*'s creator, the Italian violinist and choreographer Balthazar de Beaujoyeux, explicitly sought to inspire a sense of harmony whose effects could be felt beyond the confines of the Great Hall of the Louvre. The production was a dramatic demonstration that the powers of evil—represented by the enchantress Circe—could be overcome by manifestations of good—embodied principally in the French king. His very presence promotes a return to order, inspiring the support of the gods, who appear in a sequence of sung and danced episodes: sea creatures sing the praises of Henri III; Mercury unlocks the charms of Circe; Minerva (Reason) and the cardinal virtues with Pan and his wood spirits bring their aid; and finally, Jupiter descends to lead the advance on

1. "Figure de la salle," engraving after a design by Jacques Patin, in Balthazar de Beaujoyeux, *Ballet comique de la reine, fait au noces de Monsieur le duc de Joyeuse & Mademoiselle de Vaudemont sa soeur* (Paris: Le Roy, Ballard et Patisson, 1582), folio 4. (Courtesy of the Bibliothèque Nationale, Paris.)

Circe's garden. The powers of good quickly triumph, and the performance concludes with homage paid to the king, the queen mother, and other significant members of the court. As tradition decreed, the entertainment ended with a ball.

No spectacle at the French court had ever before been conceived or presented on such a lavish scale. The long preparations, requiring the skills of many experts; the numbers of dancers and musicians; and the cost of the rich costumes, machines, and décor were unprecedented. The collaborators were well aware of the unique nature of their achievement. In his printed account of the performance (published in 1582) Beaujoyeux pointed to the work's novelty, beauty, and variety, especially the preeminent role given to dancing; and he included the poems subsequently dedicated to him, which praised the immense learning and the familiarity with Greek forms of music, dancing, and poetry that informed the *Ballet*. In the *Ballet comique,* Beaujoyeux had tried to fashion a work of art that would interweave music, dance, and poetry within a spectacular décor so that the expressive power of each medium, enhanced by artful combination, might rival the therapeutic effects ascribed to Greek drama. His admiring supporters, convinced that cosmic influences could actually be shown to affect human affairs, praised Beaujoyeux's revival of that ancient skill of fusing the arts, which in a mystical way revealed the harmonies organizing the heavenly spheres. At the Academy of Poetry and Music, instituted in the early 1570s, Jean-Antoine de Baïf and Thibaud de Courville had calculated the modes and intervals required for measured music—the essential starting point for the revival of "effects." Ronsard enthusiastically praised such experiments in linking the arts. When one observer wrote that the performance of the *Ballet comique* "bewitched his soul," he was not offering conventional praise but indicating that years of artistic endeavor had finally found their full expression in this work.

The *Ballet comique* had shown that poets, musicians, and choreographers could cooperate effectively in the creation of a coherent and spectacular theatrical form. But it was not the first intensive cooperative effort among artists. Composite art forms were familiar features of 16th-century European courts, where the verses of poets often heralded a tournament whose staging depended on the ingenuity of an army of painters and architects; where musical and poetic dramas accompanied the entry of courses in banquets, for which artists such as Germain Pilon devised sweetmeats in the form of graces, virtues, gods and goddesses; and where masquerades brought together courtier, poet, musician, and ballet master. Such collaborations obviously influenced the ways in which poets and artists saw their role. Necessarily, they had the same objectives, and they also used the same aesthetic criteria: the concept of grace, the natural (composed of elements of artifice rendered to perfection), decorum, and variety. Many forces contributed to this convergence of artistic disciplines; chief among them were political practicalities that linked display with power, and social and educational trends that required patron, poet, and artist to speak the same normative language.

These lines of convergence would not have produced the brilliant literature of the French court had they not occurred at a time of technical advances. Consider the décor of the *Ballet comique*. Dispersed throughout the Great Hall of the Louvre, it ensured that the spectators participated in the performance; but it also illustrated how French machinists had begun to absorb the lessons and techniques of their Italian counterparts. Although French technicians had yet to build the permanent theaters with elaborate stage machines that were being erected in the 1580s in Vicenza and Florence, they contrived to mount the same kind of obligatory scenes. Circe's magical garden, situated at the end of the hall, showed through a triple trellis of leaves and flowers the enchantress's palace, and in the foreground roamed her victims (Ulysses' companions turned into swine). On opposite sides of the hall were Pan's wood, filled with dancers and musicmakers, and the heavenly vault that housed many of the musicians

245

from the king's chapel. Mobile structures—chariots and fountains—and cloud machines brought sea creatures and gods into the court's midst. The capacity to astonish by manipulation of stage machines was an important factor in achieving the "effects" that poets and artists had striven for more than a decade to reproduce.

Above all, the *Ballet comique* demonstrated a prevailing conviction among artists and princes that power and display were synonymous. Praising the monarch, celebrating his power, and providing a spectacular setting in which (with the ready complicity of an audience whose applause was part of the performance) members of the French court might project enhanced images of themselves were familiar modes of behavior; they were simply made more compelling through the artistic control of Beaujoyeux and his collaborators. During the Renaissance, poets, artists, and patrons developed a close and mutually reinforcing relationship. Princes needed the expressive power of the creative artist to promote their lofty notions of themselves and of their function, while poets and painters relied on the wealth of noble patrons as a means of giving adequate expression to their elevated ideas. It became customary for official court poets and artists to depict French kings and their courts as inhabitants of Olympus, as in Mellin de Saint-Gelais's "Chanson des astres" (1544; "Song of the Stars") and Pierre de Ronsard's "Hymne de Henri II" (1555), on the ceiling of the guard room at Tanlay castle, or on the enameled dish designed by Léonard Limosin in 1555. Similarly, the poet was increasingly associated with the activities of Apollo and the muses and with their portrayal on Parnassus, as in Francesco Primaticcio's design for the ceiling of the Galerie d'Ulysse at Fontainebleau or in Ronsard's 1560 *Discours* addressed to Pierre Lescot, the architect of the new Louvre palace. Thus, although poets were rarely princes, the same rich, decorative techniques were used to describe both. Olympus and Parnassus were far more than conventional status symbols: their insistent elaboration reveals not only a belief in the value of such self-representation but also a preoccupation with the aesthetic challenge of visualizing power.

The display of power had a long history, and humanist scholars approved its many forms. Erasmus, for instance, had praised the panegyric (eulogy) and its serious purposes: to elevate the minds of princes and to encourage them to attempt great deeds and to exercise power wisely. An extensive tradition of panegyric, in texts titled *Miroirs des princes* (*Mirrors of Princes*), had offered perfect models of kingship since antiquity. But in 16th-century France technical developments in all the arts had provided princes with unparalleled means of exhibiting their magnificence. For Guillaume Budé and Michel de L'Hôpital, the French court itself became the mirror of the prince, a spectacle and the theater of majesty. The metaphor aptly caught the display and the ritual inherent in any court occasion: banquet, coronation, tournament, or funeral.

Many other metaphors and images were also available to convey the sense of splendor and awe that the sight of the king and his entourage always seemed to provoke in the approving onlooker. Poets and painters alike exploited the vast corpus of myths gleaned by Renaissance compilers from Greek and Latin poets, legends and histories from the ancient world, and the powerfully evocative imagery bequeathed by imperial Rome. Thus Ronsard and Titian recreated the stories of Jupiter, Bacchus, and Venus; the journeys of Ulysses or of the Argonauts appeared on the walls of royal palaces (Fontainebleau), on arches decorated for royal entries (Paris, 1571), and in poems; the deeds of Hercules, Alexander, Achilles, or Godfrey of Bouillon were juxtaposed with the martial prowess of a duc de Guise or a Henri II. Their portraits were enhanced with visual allusions to great commanders from the past: Ronsard's depiction of Francis I of Lorraine, second duc de Guise, at the siege of Metz (1553) in *Le bocage royal* (1565; *The Royal Grove*) mingled the deeds of his ancestor Godfrey with those of Hercules; the parade armor of the king showed scenes of the rivalry between Caesar and Pompey.

Although images created with words required different techniques from those formed in paint, marble, or steel, their themes and objectives were identical. Admiration and appreciation dominated social intercourse and regulated taste. Patrons and artists alike were connoisseurs: princes became great collectors, sending agents far and wide to bring back the artistic remains of the Roman Empire; and they rewarded artists and poets who, competing with one another, challenged those ancient incarnations of glory. Joachim du Bellay in *La défense et illustration de la langue française* (1549; *The Defense and Enrichment of the French Language*) exhorted poets to renew their art by imitating Greek and Roman models; Ronsard responded by reviving the spirit of Pindar in his *Odes* (1550) and striving to incorporate into his *Hymnes* (1555) and *La Franciade* (1572) the decorative set pieces—shields and painted temples—that he had admired in Homer and Virgil; at the same time, artists depicted almost side by side heroic scenes from the Trojan War and the inspiring dwellers of Parnassus.

Charm, simplicity, and simulated naïveté, the hallmarks of Clément Marot (1496–1544), had passed out of fashion. Poets now copied artists; a wealth of ornamental description characterized the elaborate tapestries they wove in the cause of praise. There was, of course, a danger that this emphasis on exaltation, which entailed an elaborate and copious style, would produce works that were static and remote, elevated but alien and emotionless. For Ronsard, however, the conditions of praise, far from being a constraint, proved a liberation, sparkling in triumphal odes recording the achievements of French princes (such as the "Ode à monseigneur le dauphin," reenacting a Roman triumph (in *Odes*) and in poems exalting the beauty of a beloved woman (*Les amours,* 1552, 1555, 1556).

This exhilaration involved its audience, whether reader or spectator, in the process of transformation. Thus for Beaujoyeux, the geometric patterns traced on the floor by the *Ballet*'s dancers, repeating (as it was then thought) similar patterns shaped by the planets in the heavens, had the power to produce order out of disorder and to imprint beneficent influences in the minds of those who danced and those who watched. The earthly ballet became a dance of the spheres. The same process of transformation is at work in Ronsard's poems. In book 2, sonnet 30 of *Sonnets pour Hélène* (1578), Helen performs similar complicated steps until, through the act of dancing, she is made divine; and, in *La Charite* (1578; *The Grace*), which captures the intoxication and dazzling atmosphere of a court ball, the Volta danced by Charles IX and his sister Margaret of Valois changes them into supernatural beings. Ronsard often recreates the feeling of being transported out of earthbound bodies by the sight or activity of dancing, especially when he evokes poetic inspiration.

Elevation and transformation were crucial both for celebrating the prince and for performing as a poet. The demands of praise frequently involved a blurring of distinctions between the natural and the artificial, and between the real and the imagined. Through the universally accepted aesthetic language, distinctions were equally fused with respect to the differing forms of artistic expression. Thus Ronsard's vast poetic production can be clearly understood only in the context of competition and cooperation with painters, sculptors, architects, and musicians. A poem was illuminated by a picture or a building and was intended to be "read" in the same way: unraveling the complex fictions, studying the shape and the interrelations of the figures, identifying their appropriateness, and appreciating their grace and rich variety. It is tempting to see the *Ballet comique* as the culmination of years of trial and experiment in a particular tradition of court literature. Yet court festivals were essentially ephemeral, and the fact that a detailed account of the performance survived intact mostly by chance provides more eloquent testimony to the artistic preoccupations of the French court toward the end of the 16th century. Poets, painters, musicians, and choreographers had encyclopedic minds; they thought beyond their immediate craft. From the extension and integration of their knowledge came the creations of composite art forms such as the *Ballet comique,* which shone out brightly against the gathering gloom of war and collapse that ended the Valois dynasty.

See also 1528, 1661.

Bibliography: Balthazar de Beaujoyeulx, *Balet comique de la reyne* (1582; facsimile ed., Binghamton, N.Y.: Medieval and Renaissance Texts and Studies, 1982); translated by Carol and Lander MacClintock as *Balet comique de la reyne* (Dallas: American Institute of Musicology, 1971). Terence Cave, *The Cornucopian Text: Problems of Writing in the French Renaissance* (Oxford: Oxford University Press, 1979). Margaret M. McGowan, *Ideal Forms in the Age of Ronsard* (Berkeley: University of California Press, 1985). Frances A. Yates, *French Academies in the Sixteenth Century* (London: University of London, Warburg Institute, 1947).

Margaret M. McGowan

꿍꿍 *1595*

Marie de Gournay Publishes the Posthumous Edition of Montaigne's *Essais*

Montaigne and His Readers

In 1571, after thirteen years as a counselor in the Chambre des Enquêtes (Chamber of Hearings) of the Bordeaux parlement, Michel de Montaigne, having resigned his position, returned home to care full time for his estate. On the wall of the study next to his library he had inscribed in Latin the official statement of his retirement:

> In the year of Christ 1571, at the age of thirty-eight, on the last day of February, his birthday, Michel de Montaigne, long weary of the servitude of the court and of public employments, while still entire, retired to the bosom of the learned virgins, where in calm and freedom from all cares he will spend what little remains of his life, now more than half run out. If the fates permit, he will complete this abode, this sweet ancestral retreat; and he has consecrated it to his freedom, tranquillity, and leisure. (*Complete Essays,* p. ix)

But Montaigne's years of retirement until his death in 1592 were not spent entirely in domestic quiet and leisure. During those two decades he received the Order of Saint Michel, was made a gentleman-in-ordinary of the king's chamber by three kings of France, traveled through Italy, was twice elected mayor of Bordeaux, and on numerous occasions played a role in national political affairs on behalf of Henri de Navarre, the future King Henri IV. And in the bosom of the muses, which we might think of as his library in the tower where he worked surrounded by his books, Montaigne wrote and rewrote what he called the trials or tests of his judgment, his *Essais* (from *essayer,* to test, try out).

The first two books of Montaigne's *Essais* were published in 1580. Eight years later a new edition incorporated a third book with thirteen new essays and over 600 additions to the earlier books. At his death Montaigne was again reworking his text for republication; he left a copy of the 1588 edition with instructions to the printer and with over 1,000 additions handwritten in the margins and, where he ran out of space, continued on loose pages inserted into the book. No new essays were composed during these last four years of his life; Montaigne continued the process begun earlier of interacting with his own previously written text. In 1595 Montaigne's adopted daughter and literary executrix, Marie de Gournay, in collaboration with his friend Pierre de Brach, published a posthumous edition of the *Essais* based on Montaigne's own copy of the 1588 edition with its handwritten additions. The edition of these two devoted admirers, who had all the essayist's papers at their disposal and who asserted their own diligence, long stood as the definitive expression of Montaigne's thought.

Modern scholarship has modified this view by revealing that the posthumous edition is based not on Montaigne's actual manuscript, but probably on a copy that Marie de Gournay had made and sent to Paris, where she supervised its publication. Besides the occasional copying errors that were inadvertently reproduced, she and Pierre de Brach made numerous editorial changes, toning down forceful passages, correcting provincialisms and archaisms, making the style conform to Parisian norms. And the original text in Montaigne's hand, the "Bordeaux exemplar," has been mutilated. Sometime after Marie de Gournay's copy was made, a careless rebinding of the text cut the ends of numerous sentences, and the loose sheets on which Montaigne continued his additions have been lost. Those who seek to reconstruct an "original" Montaigne must read and interpret the Marie de Gournay edition and the "Bordeaux exemplar" side by side. In the 20th century, scholarly readers of the *Essais* have been particularly fascinated with Montaigne's mode of composition, with his inclination and his need to reread and to rework his text, as a reflection of this mind and its evolution. Since Pierre Villey's magisterial edition (1922–23), all modern editions have included indications in the text that permit readers to distinguish the three major stages of the composition of the *Essais* (1580, 1588, 1595).

Although Pascal objected to Montaigne's secular perspective and to what he called the essayist's nonchalance about salvation, and although Rousseau criticized Montaigne's modesty as self-serving, generations of readers have venerated Montaigne for the generous and compassionate wisdom of his insights into the human condition, the understanding and moderation of his comments on social and political affairs, and the gentle and sympathetic irony with which he viewed the world and himself. In the personal, conversational essays of the learned humanist, readers have identified a voice whose naturalness, sincerity, and spontaneity guarantee the truth and validity of its words. The text's frequent humble proclamations of its own vanity, and the writer's insistence on his own ignorance—the writer who took as his model Socrates and as his motto the words "What do I know?"—notwithstanding, a figure of towering authority, an imposing authorial presence has dominated the traditional reading of the *Essais*. Though not a chronological life history, the text has been treated as autobiographical writing, as the unfolding of a mind of genius in dialogue with itself and with the world, a Renaissance humanist speaking to all humanity.

Montaigne himself fosters this view that he and his work are one. In the prefatory note "To the Reader," he offers his writings as a faithful and sincere portrait of his natural self and claims that he himself is the matter of his book. The diverse subjects on which Montaigne writes—on sadness, liars, education, friendship, cannibals, names, practice, presumption, repentance, vanity, and experience, to name just a few—appear to provide him the opportunity to try out his judgment and to measure the quality of his mind. The essay "De Démocrite et Héraclite" ("On Democritus and Heraclitus"; I, 50) explicitly makes this "trial" the essential subject of the writing:

> Judgment is a tool to use on all subjects, and comes in everywhere. Therefore in the tests that I make of it here, I use every sort of occasion. If it is a subject I do not understand at all, even on that I essay my judgment, sounding the ford from a good distance; and then, finding it too deep for my height, I stick to the bank . . . Sometimes in a vain and nonexistent subject I try to see if it will find the wherewithal to give it body . . . Sometimes I lead it to a noble and well-worn subject in which it has nothing original to discover . . . There it plays its part by choosing the way that seems best to it . . . I take the first subject that chance offers. They are all equally good to me. (*Complete Essays*, p. 219)

250

Although the essays are imbued with Montaigne's wide reading of classical literature (both in the original and in contemporary translations and compilations, from all of which he quotes both impressively and with seeming abandon), and although they speak both to issues treated in that literature and to contemporary issues, the ideas expounded and the commentary on that exposition point not primarily to themselves but to the judgment at work thinking them through. Each time Montaigne returned to his text to add or emend, his judgment would reveal itself in the moment of reflective activity. The textual indicators that mark the stages of the composition of the *Essais* appear to mark as well the stages of the evolution of Montaigne's mind and to give the reader access to the self-portrait and to the process by which the essayist gained self-knowledge over time.

In recent years scholars have begun to challenge the bases of the autobiographical and evolutionary readings of the *Essais* and to address issues that these approaches have ignored. Following the reflections on subjectivity and language by Nietzsche, Freud, Saussure, Heidegger, and Derrida, readers have questioned both the traditional notion of the integral and self-sufficient subject who exists prior to and outside of any signifying system and the accepted status of language as the authentic representation of truths that lie beyond it in the physical world, in things and in ideas. Instead of considering the writing as the faithful and trustworthy mirror of Montaigne and the untrammeled expression of his ideas, modern readers have turned to the writing itself, to its internal working and mechanisms, its rhetorical devices and arguments, to consider the "self" Montaigne portrays. Form, subjectivity, and history are considered as part of a dynamic and multilayered textual system, with no one term given absolute priority. The historical context of the essays has been reformulated to include not only Renaissance ideas about humanity and human experience but also contemporaneous attitudes toward the nature and function of language, notions of current writing practice, and the conception of traditional rhetoric in 16th-century France. Montaigne's own preoccupation in the *Essais* with language, with the act of writing, and with books has been taken to indicate his own desire that existential life both generate his writing and be its ultimate creation. The essayist appears to invite us to accept his art as self-portraiture and at the same time directs our attention to the distinctions between life and literature and to the problematic nature of the interplay itself.

Montaigne's education and his reading habits reflected the 16th-century French reverence for Greek and Roman letters and its interest in the intellectual and artistic expression of Renaissance Italy. According to his own testimony, his library contained over 1,000 volumes of classical, Italian, and French literature, philosophy, and history. Those who have treated the *Essais* as autobiography have used this reading to explain the evolution of the essays in two ways: they have imagined a movement in Montaigne's writing from stoic to skeptic to a broadly humanistic posture and from less personal, derivative essays to more personal ones as the essayist discovered successively the writers representing these attitudes (such as Seneca the Stoic, Sextus Empiricus the Skeptic, and the personal and intimate Plutarch). But the relation between Montaigne's. reading and his writing is more complex than this clear-cut schema allows. Recent scholarship has demonstrated convincingly that the early essays, though on the whole not as richly developed as the later ones, express the personal voice of their author and his pursuit of self-knowledge and that, rather than simply mirroring his reading in some evolutionary way, Montaigne's writing at all periods of his intellectual life engages in dialogue with a spectrum of thinkers and ideas. Accordingly, scholarly concern has turned from the "man" to inquire about the textual function of this reading, both in terms of how an individual "self" might be formed through interaction with reading as the embodiment of tradition, of the past, and of culture itself, and in terms of how its specific presence as quotation operates in Montaigne's writing.

The sheer volume of borrowed ideas and borrowed writing in Montaigne's text reflects the authority of tradition and might imply as well that a "self" can indeed be conceived out of that which was originally foreign to it. Renaissance culture—and Montaigne himself—used the metaphor of the bee gathering pollen to make its own honey as a commonplace to suggest that this process was in fact an aspect of the organic nature of things. But Montaigne's text does not only claim that it appropriates the past through the workings of judgment; it also turns in a self-reflexive gesture to question its own basic assumption. More than once Montaigne denounces the practice of quotation, challenges and contests tradition, belittles his quotations as pilferings, and claims that his book is little more than borrowed flowers. In the interest of coherence, past readers tended to underplay this inclination. More recent readers have directly confronted this tendency of the text to undermine its own project, interpreting it as a sign of the unavoidable tension between the writer's desire to constitute an integral, personal self and his realization that the self is always constituted out of what is borrowed. The status of quotation, like that of language generally in the 16th century, emerges as relative and unstable, like the status of the subject itself.

Montaigne writes about himself and his experience in the world, giving opinions, discussing moral themes, citing examples, seeking to have his text mirror himself, be "consubstantial" with him, as he puts it in the essay "Du démentir" ("On Giving the Lie"; II, 18). But as was clear as early as 1571 in the inscription of his retirement, Montaigne also projects himself self-consciously *through* his writing as "Michel de Montaigne," and in the self-performance of the *Essais* this textual figure emerges as a metaphor of self, a function of the language—its vocabulary, syntax, topoi—in which it articulates itself. The risks of conceiving of one's "self" in language and its figures are real, but there is no other way to give birth to oneself. The metaphor always risks taking the place of the "living" author, because he is absent when the text speaks for him; but, just as significantly, it risks revealing itself in all its factitiousness. Alongside his claims of being present in his text, Montaigne affirms the vanity and emptiness of the self and of the discourse into which it casts itself. The unresolved dualities of Montaigne's *Essais* admit neither of unitary resolution nor of simple opposition, but in dynamic relationship compose a figure built up—like the endless digressions and parentheses that characterize the text—of supplements and deferments of wholeness and closure. "Who does not see," Montaigne writes in "De la vanité" ("On Vanity"; III, 9), near the end of his *Essais,* "that I have taken a road along which I shall go, without stopping and without effort, as long as there is ink and paper in the world?"

Bibliography: Terence Cave, *The Cornucopian Text: Problems of Writing in the French Renaissance* (Oxford: Oxford University Press, 1979). Gérard Defaux, ed., *Montaigne: Essays in Reading* (New Haven: Yale University Press, 1983). Hugo Friedrich, *Montaigne,* trans. Robert Rovini (Paris: Gallimard, 1968). Michel de Montaigne, *The Complete Essays of Montaigne,* trans. Donald M. Frame (Stanford: Stanford University Press, 1965). Montaigne, *Les essais de Michel de Montaigne,* ed. Pierre Villey and V.-L. Saulnier (Paris: Presses Universitaires de France, 1965). Richard Regosin, *The Matter of My Book: Montaigne's Essais as the Book of the Self* (Berkeley: University of California Press, 1977). Jean Starobinski, *Montaigne in Motion,* trans. Arthur Goldhammer (Chicago: University of Chicago Press, 1987).

Richard L. Regosin

✎ 1609

François de Sales Publishes His *Introduction à la vie dévote*

Devout Humanism

The first edition of the *Introduction à la vie dévote* (*Introduction to the Devout Life*), by François de Sales (better known to English speakers as Francis of Sales; 1567–1622), was published in the last year of the reign of Henri IV, whose formal renunciation of Protestantism (1593) and promulgation of the Edict of Nantes (1598) had promoted the reintegration of the French body politic after thirty years of bloody religious wars. The second edition appeared late in the same year, with additional chapters for well-born laypeople, principally women. In 1610 Henri's assassination by a Jesuit renewed the religious and political conflict, and the increasingly popular *Introduction* came out in a third, corrected, edition. By 1616, the year of a pocket-sized revised edition, the Huguenots were threatening Louis XIII with rebellion. In 1619, when the canonical edition appeared, Louis XIII had crushed the Protestant uprising and restored royal authority. The *Introduction's* numerous reprintings thereafter attest to its continued profound influence on French religious life.

The *Introduction* is the principal elaboration of devout humanism. Humanism, which had begun as an educational reform movement in the 16th century, promoted the works of classical Greece and Rome as part of a new evaluation of human nature. Giovanni Pico della Mirandola's *Oratio de Dignitate Hominis* (1486; *Oration on the Dignity of Man*) incorporated numerous concepts from Platonism in representing humanity as the highest point in a harmonious chain of creation. Throughout the 16th century, Platonist humanism sought to harmonize Christian doctrine and pagan culture by interpreting the latter symbolically. In their writings, clerics such as Erasmus increasingly emphasized practical ways for humans to achieve harmony with God, and correspondingly deemphasized original sin and the sacramental and ritual aspects of religion.

Devout humanism was less restricted to a Latin-speaking elite and more committed to vernacular popularization, less intellectual and more emotional, less speculative and more practical. It became also more politically astute, more socially invasive. In France, 16th-century evangelical humanists such as François Rabelais, Margaret of Navarre, Jacques Lefèvre d'Etaples, and the moderate reforming bishop of Meaux, Guillaume Briçonnet, promoted this synthesis of the sacred and profane, which came to dominate 17th-century religious life. The lay devotional movement, humanist learning, and royal power coalesced in the 1520s in the circle of Margaret of Navarre and developed with the Pléiade (1550), the Academy of Jean-Antoine de Baïf (1570–1585), and especially the Palace Academy at Vincennes, where Henri III brought together lay confraternities, religious orders, poets, and scholars hoping for spiritual refuge and political resolutions. The humanist theologians at the Council of Trent (1545–1563) sanctioned the private life of the soul as an avenue to salvation. The Society of Jesus, founded in 1540 by Ignatius Loyola, promoted the establishment of new religious orders to spread and maintain the faith and produced a vast number of devotional books for laypeople in the late 16th century. Despite fierce opposition and repeated expulsions, the Jesuits played an influential role in France, especially under Louis XIII (1610–1643). Francis of Sales studied rhetoric and human letters at their Paris Collège de Clermont from 1583 to 1588, and then studied law at Padua in 1588 under the Jesuit jurist Antonio Possevino. Other key religious, political, and literary figures were similarly trained—Louis Richeome, Pierre de Bérulle, Jean-Jacques Olier, and Pierre Corneille, as well as Pierre Coton, the confessor to both Henri IV and Louis XIII. Coton's *Intérieure occupation d'une âme dévote* (1609; *Interior Occupation of a Devout Soul*) promoted methodical lay devotion at court.

Francis of Sales and his devotional works played an interesting part in Henri IV's attempts to unify a religiously dismembered France. Francis was a subject of the Catholic duchy of Savoy, whose duke, allied by marriage to Spain, had invaded French territory in 1590, soon after Henri III's assassination, and had ambitions toward Calvinist Geneva. Francis himself was provost (1592), then bishop (1602) of Geneva; in that capacity, with the support of Antoine Favre, a member of the Savoy senate, he sought to convert Calvin's successor Théodore de Bèze and, with somewhat greater success, to "evangelize" the Protestants of the Chablais region, newly reunited to Savoy. His *Controverses* (1672; *Controversies*) and *Défense de l'étendard de la sainte croix* (1600; *Defense of the Standard of the Holy Cross*), collections of propaganda pamphlets and sermons shot through with military metaphors, were the result of this militant missionary campaign. In 1598 Francis led diplomatic missions to Rome to thwart French recognition of Protestant Geneva and to seek the reversion of revenues to reconverted Catholic parishes. In 1601 part of his diocese was ceded to France; the next year the duke of Savoy sent him to negotiate with Henri IV. The king, seeking to balance power in his realm, gave no ground on this matter but was very interested in Francis' devotional enterprise, which coincided with the royal policies of pacification and order. He had him preach at Fontainebleau and tried to attract him to France with a diocese. While in Paris, Francis was confessor to Mme. Acarie (Barbe Avrillot), who established St. Theresa's Carmelites in France (1604), and attended the spiritual salon of Louise Séguier, whose son, Pierre Cardinal de Bérulle, founded the French Oratory (1611).

During this period many new religious orders were founded in France, including a large number by and for women, who joined the vanguard of the Counter-Reformation as they had that of the Reformation. At this time, too, Francis of Sales began to serve as spiritual director to both lay and religious aristocratic women in Savoy and France. In many cases he performed his function through personal letters, which formed the basis of the *Introduction,* the *Traité de l'amour de Dieu* (1616; *A Treatise of the Love of God*), and the *Entretiens spirituels* (1628; *Spiritual Conversations*). Francis founded an order for visiting the poor and sick at Annecy with the assistance of Jeanne Françoise Frémiot, baronne de Chantal, the daughter of Antoine Favre, and others. It was intended to be an order for widows and virgins, but stripped of physical monastic rigors.

The *Introduction* defines devotion and prescribes a meditative cycle and a code of personal conduct for wealthy married women in letters to a fictive "Philothea." Marriage had traditionally been represented as a spiritually inferior condition, woman as a spiritually inferior creature. But the *Introduction* turns the closed contemplative life inside out, through the humanist bridging concept—fostered by the Jesuits and adopted by the Protestants—of the *devoir d'état,* the duty to one's estate in life. The social order, worldly as well as religious, is taken as given, as good, and one's place in it as a space for personal sanctification. True devotion, Philothea is told, is "spiritual sugar," "honey," the "cream of the milk," "suavity," "the sweetness of sweetnesses." These cloying recurrent images transport devotion from the ascetic cloister to the worldly court, and more specifically, to the boudoir. Although the exercises prescribed are vigorous, divine clemency permits Philothea white lies, fashionable dresses, and dancing, provided the spiritual honeybees of the conscience chase out the corporeal spiders of affection for the sinful world.

The worldly woman can practice aspects of monastic obedience (through political loyalty to magistrates and one's ruler and, above all, obedience to one's husband) and poverty (through inward detachment from one's wealth and privilege). But the most fundamental feature is Francis' transformation of monastic chastity into an ideology of marriage and reproduction. For the church, marriage is "the nursery of christianity that supplies the earth with fruitful souls"; for the state it is "the origin and source of all its streams" (*Introduction to the Devout Life,* p. 378).

This transposition of the spiritual life from the cloister to the bedchamber had far-reaching implications for fertility in French society. Part 3 of the *Introduction* contains one of the earliest-known French diatribes against coitus interruptus, with a detailed metaphoric equation between sexual intercourse and socially acceptable table manners. Sex, like social eating, is a duty, with no excuses for women, no exemptions even for spiritual commitments; it should be performed with good grace, without gluttony, primarily for nourishment, and without spilling. The rule of procreative sex as a spiritual duty inverts the rule of monastic abstinence and coincides with secular political concerns: Jean-Baptiste Colbert was soon to condemn coitus interruptus as contrary to the interests of the state. Francis' discussion of the practice may have reflected its prevalence among aristocratic women. Perhaps his propaganda and that of other Counter-Reformation preachers contributed to its temporary decline and to the population rise evident in some parts of France toward the end of the 17th century. Perhaps, too, preaching against contraception led eventually to a contrary effect, for it was accompanied by an increased emphasis on maternal duties to offspring, which may have led to a desire to limit births and thus contributed to the aristocratic population's decline in the early 18th century. The Counter-Reformation's tendency to intervene in sexuality and fertility is evident at all social levels. In 1609 the peasant courtship custom of *albergement,* which permitted a boy to spend the night with a girl in her parents' house, fostering noncoital lovemaking, became grounds for excommunication in the duchy of Savoy.

The *Introduction's* feminization of devotional discourse also legitimated a trend to devotional poetry begun in the previous century by Francis I's sister, Margaret of Navarre (*Le miroir de l'âme pécheresse* [1531; *The Mirror of the Sinful Soul*]; *Chansons spirituelles* [1547; *Spiritual Songs*]); the nun and poet Anne de Marquets, who had published devotional verse in the 1560s and whose *Sonnets spirituels* (*Spiritual Sonnets*) was published in 1605; and Gabrielle de Coignard (*Oeuvres chrétiennes,* 1595; *Christian Works*). Later, male poets in Francis' orbit adopted the meditative pattern, emotional effusiveness, and vocabulary of spiritual pleasure that characterized this poetry. Antoine Favre acknowledged his debt to Francis in his *Centurie première de sonnets spirituels de l'amour divin et de la pénitence* (1595; *First Century of Spiritual Sonnets on Divine Love and Penitence*); Francis sent Jean de La Ceppède a letter praising his *Théorèmes sur le sacré mystère de notre rédemption* (1613; *Theorems on the Sacred Mystery of Our Redemption*). And in the same year as the *Introduction,* Henry Humbert's *Semaine sainte* (*Holy Week*) combined emotionally charged prose and poetry clearly influenced by the genre of the devotional treatise. These poets' major stylistic aim was to convert to Counter-Reformation sensibility the profane, even pagan, styles fostered earlier by the Pléiade.

Francis' own purpose, consciously or otherwise, in coopting feminized discourse is illuminated by a letter he wrote to the abbess of Montmartre in January 1603: "Your sex wishes to be led, and never in any project will it succeed except by submission; not that often it does not have as much intelligence as the opposite sex, but because God has so established it" (*Oeuvres,* 12:173). Clearly, Francis not only admired but perhaps also envied and feared women's creative energies; certainly one of his aims was to place them under priestly male mentorship. If this is so, then the effusive sweetness of the *Intro-duction* is not just a concession to the supposed characteristics of female readers, but a demonstration of the mastery of a feminine mode, an appropriation of creative powers.

As for the *Introduction*'s significance in the context of reproductivity, in the "feminized" devotional style there is a kind of metaphorical logic that links the proscription of the sin of Onan with a prescription for fertility, and in turn with the characteristic imagery of devotion. Two images of female sweetness pervade devotional poetry of the period: the penitent lover, Mary Magdalene, erotically portrayed as turning from adulterous pleasure to the deeper fulfillment of sub-missive ecstasy in union with the divine bridegroom; and Mary, the archetypal nurturing mother of the Pietà and of the many verse paraphrases of the Stabat Mater. "Sweetness," "honey," "sugar" in the *Introduction* are associated with the same twin poles of sexual union and maternal nurture. The imagery, derived from the celibate mysticism of the cloister, takes on a quite material significance when projected into the worldly context. On the one hand, there is the imagery of emotional release, the sweet receptivity of the (female) soul, the inpouring of grace, and the ecstatic climax of divine congress. On the other hand, sweet-ness is also associated with the outpouring of maternal nourishment and maternal care. "Honey" in Francis' text is frequently the "honey" of a mother's milk, an image sometimes applied also to God the father. All this translates almost too obviously into Francis' advocacy of a sexual relationship in which orgasmic coition, conception, and maternity should not, any more than spiri-tual climax, be resisted or withheld. The obverse of the liquid imagery of sweet-ness is the equally long-established and equally ambivalent imagery of spiritual restraint, withdrawal, dryness, and barrenness. And this powerful mode of dis-course is directed at aristocratic women, who in all likelihood sought to control their own fertility by abstention or coitus interruptus.

The interactions between church, devotionalism, and state in 17th-century France are clearly complex, but there is an arguable compatibility between Francis' endeavors and ancien régime society. No monarch would need to reject his essentially conservative and persuasive discourse rooted in humanist cul-ture. Devout humanism, in contradiction to Jansenism, implied acceptance of human nature and of the social order. It represented for Molière the *honnête* devotion whose antithesis was the antisocial Tartuffe. The *Introduction*'s ambig-uous mixture of rigor and leniency meant that it could be invoked by Jacques Bénigne Bossuet as well as by François de La Mothe–Fénelon. In 1696 Louis XIV protected with an ordinance the doctrine and letter of this authoritative and seductive text.

See also 1215, 1534 (17–18 October), 1685.

Bibliography: Henri Bremond, *Histoire littéraire du sentiment religieux en France,* vol. 1: *L'humanisme dévot (1580–1660)* (Paris: Librairie Bloud et Gay, 1935). Terence Cave, *Devotional Poetry in France, c. 1570–1613* (Cambridge: Cambridge University Press, 1969), pp. 1–93. J.-L. Flandrin, "Repression and Change in the Sexual Life of Young

People in Medieval and Early Modern Times," in *Family and Sexuality in French History,* ed. Robert Wheaton and T. K. Hareven (Philadelphia: University of Philadelphia Press, 1980), pp. 27–48. Francis of Sales, *An Introduction to a Devout Life,* trans. J. K. Ryan (Baltimore: Bernard Dornin, 1816). Francis of Sales, *Oeuvres de Saint François de Sales,* ed. André Ravier and Roger Devos (Paris: Gallimard, 1969). Pierre Janelle, *The Catholic Reformation* (Milwaukee: Bruce Publishing, 1963), pp. 28–32, 183–205, 226–249.

Paul A. Chilton

ᘒᕔᕽᕽᕽᕽᕽ 1619

Honoré d'Urfé Finally Publishes the Third Part of *L'Astrée*

Pastoral Fiction

By 1619, when its third part appeared, *L'Astrée* was a monumentally famous work, coveted eagerly by the literate public. But they surely had to wait, the aristocratic readers who so favored Honoré d'Urfé's novel: twenty years elapsed between the appearance of Part I (1607) and the posthumous publication of Part IV (1627) (Part II was published in 1610). While waiting, they acted out the best passages of the work, dressing up and mimicking the shepherds and shepherdesses who people *L'Astrée*. D'Urfé, however, rewarded them for their patience with length and mass: each part comprised in turn several books and ran to several hundred pages. *L'Astrée* represents an important tradition of preclassical France: the extremely—even interminably—long multivolume novel, which predominated in the early and middle 17th century.

Honoré d'Urfé (1567–1625) was the product of the French literary Renaissance in the area around Lyons. The d'Urfé family château, La Bastie, in the Forez region of southeastern France, was an important center of learning. D'Urfé received advanced instruction from the Jesuits at the Collège de Tournon. *L'Astrée* incorporates what he learned at both La Bastie and Tournon; although it is above all a romance, its pages also demonstrate vast historical and philosophical erudition. Astraea was the mythological virgin goddess of justice and the last deity to leave earth at the end of the golden age. For d'Urfé and his readers her name perhaps evoked the end of the Wars of Religion (Henri IV signed the Edict of Nantes in 1598) and the vision of a newfound terrestrial harmony. Pastoral literature, the category to which *L'Astrée* is traditionally assigned, depicts a mythical era of contentment and fulfillment, a golden age free of the problems of everyday existence. D'Urfé began his opus at that moment when the aristocratic public, weary of the long years of warfare between Catholics and Huguenots, was ready to indulge a taste for the subtle portrayal and analysis of the passions.

France, however, offered little in the way of this "new" fiction. For nuanced analysis of the emotions, and particularly of love, the French had turned to Italy and Spain, where a more "sentimental" tradition had developed during the second half of the 16th century, particularly under the guise of pastoral fiction. This body of literature—in combination with the chivalric tale, the ancient

Greek romances, and the Renaissance *nouvelle* tradition, best represented by Margaret of Navarre's *L'heptaméron* (1559; *The Heptameron*)—served as the base for *L'Astrée,* although d'Urfé ultimately subverted the pastoral genre for his own purposes.

The principal conventions are remarkably constant throughout pastoral fiction. All are love stories involving a shepherd and shepherdess in a magnificent natural setting. Nonconsummation of their love provides both the principal theme and the fundamental narrative structure that prolongs the story. Obstacles to the satisfactory conclusion of the romance are everywhere, forcing the lovers to adopt various subterfuges. Episodes incorporating Arthurian, chivalric tones allow the hero (who is very often a knight *disguised* as a shepherd) to demonstrate his prowess. Scores of additional characters inhabit the pastoral: other shepherds and shepherdesses, both rivals and friends; aggressive and predatory strangers; priests, magicians, and wise hermits. Frequently their stories are intercalated, interrupting the progress of the primary tale. The wide variety of narrators provides the *illusion* of polyphony, another conventional element of pastoral fiction, although in *L'Astrée* these voices are ultimately indistinguishable from one another. To advance the plot, and to vary the monotony of the basic narration, writers of pastoral fiction used letters, poems, and songs, whose themes echoed those of the primary prose text. D'Urfé, in particular, made extensive use of the letter format, establishing *L'Astrée* as an early example of French epistolary fiction.

The naturally beautiful setting, the themes, and the formal structure of *L'Astrée* all adhere closely to the basic conventions of pastoral literature. The setting is 5th-century Forez, at once the conventional paradise in its Arcadian, Edenic splendor, but also historically and geographically focused. As is the case in much pastoral fiction, the shepherds and shepherdesses are in fact of high birth: their noble ancestors, seeking a haven, had quit the life of the court to retreat to the gentler countryside.

L'Astrée's strong unifying symbol, adopted from the tradition of courtly literature, is the magical "Fountain of Love's Truth." If one is reciprocally loved, one will see the beloved's image reflected in the water along with one's own. Throughout the story, however, the fountain's extraordinary powers have been suspended as a result of a spell cast on it by one unfortunate lover. When the fountain may once again display its magical charm, the characters will finally learn their true amorous fate. Such revelations will occur, however, only with the sacrificial death of Forez' two most exemplary lovers.

Although such a sacrifice never actually occurs, the two most exemplary characters may be assumed to be Astrée and Céladon, starcrossed adolescent lovers who cannot wed because their families detest each other. But their love story occupies only a section of the work. Just as important are the tales of Diane and Silvandre, of Phillis and Lycidas, of the "free love" womanizer Hylas, and of the nymph Galathée. Each of these stories penetrates, and is penetrated by, the others, forming a fantastic hymn to the tribulations of love. Moreover, these tales are reinforced by a host of secondary ones, some of which mesh directly with the principal stories. Yet despite the proliferation of characters, of names, of situations, there is paradoxically almost no sense of differentiation. Ultimately the plots are remarkably alike, the names strikingly similar. D'Urfé's work is a curious trap, a literary fresco of redundant patterns designed to convey the eternal predicament of man and woman in love.

In fact two different, even opposing, views of the nature of love coexist in *L'Astrée*. On the first level, d'Urfé offers an exaltation of spiritual, desexualized love, reflecting a long-standing Western tradition of intellectualizing coupling, along with a retreat from erotic love typifying much of 17th-century literature and philosophy. A preoccupation with the passions, and particularly with the powers of erotic desire, is one hallmark of preclassical and classical writing. Descartes's important *Les passions de l'âme* (1649; *The Passions of the Soul*), for example, repeatedly calls on self-control through reason to temper excessive emotion and its resulting sense of self-alienation, recalling in many instances the shepherd Silvandre's similar pronouncements in *L'Astrée*. During the second half of the century, psychological analysis of passionate love reaches a new level, in the theater of Racine, in the novels of Marie-Madeleine de La Fayette, and in the works of the moralists (Pascal, La Rochefoucauld), which explore love and sexuality in terms that suggest a strong understanding of what modern psychology labels the unconscious. In *L'Astrée,* retreat from passionate involvement coexists with fantasized enactment. Romance remains intact as both message and medium; the story of the characters' artifices is the story of their recourse to fantasy whenever they are unable to meet realistically the demands of their desire.

In *L'Astrée* the retreat from love is enacted in three different ways: in the female characters' reluctance to engage in heterosexual courtship rites, though permitting the freest expression of bonding between females—a practice sanctioned by both Neoplatonism and the traditions of pastoral literature; in solitary and solipsistic wanderings by passive male characters afraid to declare their ardor openly; and in the spiritualized idealization of love by the two philosopher "intellectuals," the druidic priest Adamas and the shepherd Silvandre. Their metaphysical claims occupy much space in *L'Astrée,* forming an elaborate dissertation on the preeminence of spiritually conceived love. Their code evolves from principles inherited from medieval courtly literature, in combination with Renaissance Platonism. Such idealism had flourished during the reign of Henri IV (1589–1610), whose court made a determined effort to purify sexual customs and expression. *L'Astrée* portrays males who are submissive to females, and, in accordance with its pastoral conventions, the relationships (unlike those in courtly literature) are "naive," rarely adulterous.

The courtly tenets harmonized easily with the precepts of Renaissance Platonism, whose metaphysics govern the "high" tone of *L'Astrée*. Neoplatonism postulated a positive view of women as superior beings with a link to God; a belief in love as a source of all goodness, and of beauty as the reflection of that good; a spiritual transformation of true lovers' souls; and happiness as belonging to those whose love was mutual and perfect. D'Urfé devotes page after page to a detailed explanation of such spiritually conceived love, and these tenets are then reinforced by the ascetic ones of Christianity (the druidism of *L'Astrée* is essentially a thinly disguised Catholicism).

260

Were such didactic writing all that d'Urfé offered, *L'Astrée* would no doubt have been discarded long ago as a verbose fossil. Without ever destroying these abstract codes, however, he builds a second structure, one that portrays love in its most passionate, troublesome, and fantastic forms. In *L'Astrée,* as elsewhere in the Western literary tradition, the romance and the compendium of morally uplifting thought are separate and distinct modes, beyond harmonizing, and thus create continual tension and discord.

In fact the narratives tend to move away dramatically from doctrine. Brutal aggression, unbridled sexuality, and victimization of women are all obviously present, particularly in the secondary tales, thereby unsettling the Neoplatonic, courtly, and pastoral base. The primary episodes, though usually lacking in flagrantly aggressive behavior, move toward elaborately conceived fantasy dramas. Not only are the male figures—especially Céladon and Silvandre— portrayed as excessively timid and passive, but the element of disguise, traditionally associated with pastoral and Renaissance literature, is raised to new heights. Travesty turns toward transvestism in a massive accumulation of disguise episodes. Céladon, for example, is costumed as a woman for a huge portion of the novel. These fantasies of libidinal projection form the liveliest and most titillating sections of *L'Astrée.* Some scholars see a purely androgynous motif in these episodes, which would clearly connect them to Neoplatonic doctrine. However, it may also be that the passages in which Céladon is disguised as a woman, wooing an "unknowing" Astrée who readily accepts "her" overtures (and d'Urfé carefully manipulates his pronouns and possessive adjectives, so that the grammar also promotes the fantasy), is the author's exploration of ultimate romance. In *L'Astrée,* characters simultaneously love heterosexually and homosexually (within the same episode), reflecting the freest moves of the imagination: the author's, the characters', our own.

Ultimately neither heterosexuality nor homosexuality predominates in d'Urfé's work. Rather, *L'Astrée* is the textual embodiment of a gender-free sexuality: identity is lost in a maze of pure eroticism, and desire is experienced as independent of a clearly delineated object. Céladon desires Astrée as a man and, simultaneously, as a woman. Moreover, after disguising himself as the female "Alexis," he dons Astrée's own clothing, surrendering his identity for hers, as the fantasy turns autoerotic, liberated from the need for any partner other than the self, and thereby revealing a multilayered desire.

Traditionally, we may read *L'Astrée* in five parts: the four composed by d'Urfé, and a fifth part, a conclusion, written by his secretary, Balthazar Baro. (Another conclusion was written by the novelist Marin Le Roy de Gomberville, whose ending is now known as "Gomberville's sequel" or Part VI of *L'Astrée.)* D'Urfé's untimely death does little to explain why, in the course of so many years, he did not finish his opus. Perhaps the explanation lies in the fact that Honoré d'Urfé had successfully created a work sustaining diverse levels of sexual tension. He avoided conclusions, delayed consummation (although marriage is the traditionally envisioned conclusion of pastoral fiction), because his mastery lay precisely in the concept of infinite suspension.

The mood, however, was to shift. Before *L'Astrée,* the pastoral novel in

France was a mediocre production, nor, despite (or perhaps because of) d'Urfé's enormously popular work, was the genre very successful afterward. Pastoral literature developed instead primarily as a dramatic form in France. The very long, multivolume novel continued to enjoy great favor, but in other formats (adventure, historical, psychological) that d'Urfé had included within his own large framework. Writers such as Gomberville, Gautier de Costes de La Calprenède, and Madeleine de Scudéry, who abandoned the bucolic setting preferred by d'Urfé, became the favorite authors of the literate public. A vein of satiric literature had also developed in the early decades of the century, a challenge to d'Urfé's pastoral prose. In 1627 Charles Sorel had produced *Le berger extravagant* (*The Extravagant Shepherd*), a direct parody of pastoral fiction. By midcentury Paul Scarron and Savinien de Cyrano de Bergerac offered satirical, burlesque challenges to the lyrical mode of *L'Astrée*. And finally, new concise fictional works emerged, which emptied the romance medium of almost all secondary material, as well as of the entire doctrinal apparatus so evident in *L'Astrée*. *La princesse de Clèves* (1678; *The Princess of Clèves*, published anonymously but attributed to La Fayette) stands out as the decisive novel of the classical age, not only for its tight and centrally focused story, but especially for its presentation of the repression of sexual fantasy. So, too, the *Lettres portugaises* (1669; *Letters from a Portuguese Nun*, traditionally attributed to Gabriel-Joseph de Lavergne de Guilleragues) moves toward a minimal, centralized story, using the epistolary format to create a short, tightly focused tale. These works, which represent the dominant development in French fiction, stand in stark contrast to *L'Astrée*, whose power resides in its intensely encyclopedic nature.

See also 1165, 1527, 1654.

Bibliography: Honoré d'Urfé, *L'Astrée*, ed. Hugues Vaganay, 5 vols. (1925; reprint, Geneva: Slatkine, 1966). Jacques Ehrmann, *Un paradis désespéré: L'amour et l'illusion dans "L'Astrée"* (New Haven: Yale University Press, 1963). Louise K. Horowitz, *Honoré d'Urfé* (Boston: G.K. Hall, 1984). Myriam Yvonne Jehenson, *The Golden World of the Pastoral: A Comparative Study of Sidney's "New Arcadia" and d'Urfé's "L'Astrée"* (Ravenna: A. Longo, 1981).

Louise K. Horowitz

✒ 1627

One Year before His Death, François de Malherbe Publishes an Anthology of Sixty-two Poems Representative of His School

The Age of the Technician

Early 17th-century French poetry wavered between baroque and classical poles. One year before his death, François de Malherbe (1555–1628), champion of the classical style, triumphantly published a definitive anthology of his poems, the *Recueil des plus beaux vers de Messieurs de Malherbe, Racan, etc. (Collection of the Most Beautiful Verses of Messieurs de Malherbe, Racan, etc.).* Pointedly omitting his major early baroque poem, "Les larmes de saint Pierre" (1587; "Saint Peter's Tears"), Malherbe selected the sixty-two texts he wished to preserve as founder of the modern poetic style, now known as French classicism. Also included were lyrics by Honorat de Bueil de Racan, Jean-Nicolas Garnier de Monfuron, François Maynard, François Le Métel de Boisrobert, and others who wanted to be recognized as Malherbe's disciples and to share in his success. In this moment of classical victory Malherbe's school showed that it had broken with the Renaissance humanist tradition derived from Pierre de Ronsard and Joachim du Bellay; yet only two years later the great late baroque poet Antoine Girard de Saint-Amant (1594–1661) published his own successful challenge to Malherbian lyric, the first volume of his *Oeuvres,* including the celebrated "La solitude," "L'Arion," and "Le fromage" ("The Cheese"). Saint-Amant's success owed a good deal to Malherbe's reform of French lyric, and both in turn contributed to forming the verse style of the lyric in the second half of the century.

The arrival of the classical style was a social and political event, engineered by Malherbe to coincide with his move to Paris from Provence in 1605. Malherbe was not only a poet but also a clever court politician who sensed that a new poetics was in the air of the increasingly important royal court in Paris. By adopting and then articulating the new taste for a more accessible poetry, Malherbe knew that he could win royal favor and attach his name to poetic values in tune with the more authoritarian culture of France after its many years of civil war. Malherbe attracted the attention of Paris literary circles by his outspoken disrespect for the established poets of the older school. His flair for the dramatic, his celebrated outbursts against all that was obscure, excessively imaginative, or archaic in the verse of his predecessors and his contemporaries marked him as an advocate of reform. The provincial poet soon gained notoriety, patrons, and disciples. Poets and would-be poets came to ask his advice and saw the handwritten notes on his edition of the works of Philippe Desportes, the latest exponent of the Renaissance tradition. These marginalia and Malherbe's own conversation, rather than any formal treatise, were the vehicle for the Malherbian poetic doctrine. Anecdotes of his everyday habits came to embody his literary values. Malherbe had seven chairs in his room, wrote his disciple Racan. If an eighth visitor arrived he had to wait for one of the chairs to be vacated. Racan told the story to illustrate Malherbe's use of metaphor: the poet would leave out an idea for which his stock of metaphors was insufficient.

Racan's anecdote of the chairs conveys the major difference between Malherbian classicism and the Renaissance tradition against which the 17th-century poetic reform was aimed. In an important shift from emphasis on semantic and lexical enrichment to a stress on metric form, Malherbe's "new poetry," as it was called by such traditionalists as Marie de Gournay, aimed at using simple concepts and fitting them to a very regular, carefully crafted verse form. Confronted with a complex idea that seemed to require a novel and witty image to convey it, Malherbe would rather drop the idea than risk an unusual metaphor.

If some expression was appropriate to his thought but would spoil a beautiful rhyme, he would choose the rhyme. Malherbe presented the poet as a technician of language. Clarity, use of standard French grammar and vocabulary, perfect mastery of rhythm through rigorous care in counting the syllables of each verse, and patient construction of rhymes that followed elaborate rules were the marks of the poetic craftsman.

Much of the detail of this craft appears quite arid to modern readers. Malherbe disapproved of the more elaborate traditional verse forms, such as the rondeau and triolet—short forms that displayed a rather contrived but playful virtuosity—and the longer ballad and "verse letter," which lacked the elegance and majesty he preferred. He denounced rhymes based on a compound word and the root from which it was derived (*armes* and *alarmes*) and insisted that not only vowels but also preceding consonants rhyme (such as *fleurs* and *pleurs* but not *fleurs* and *donneurs*). He disliked cases of enjambment, the running over of a natural spoken phrase from one verse to the next. He condemned the use of superfluous words serving as metric stuffing without adding to the meaning.

Malherbe primarily wrote sequences of four-, six-, or ten-line stanzas, in poems ranging from 40 to 200 lines. He increasingly favored heterometric stanzas made up of lines of different lengths (such as 12–6–12–6 syllables). The technical difficulty of sustaining these forms over more than 100 lines was the kind of challenge pleasing to Malherbe the technician.

This approach to poetry collided head-on with the Renaissance tradition of Ronsard and his associates in the humanist Pléiade, for whom erudition and inspiration were the two great marks of a poet. The humanist poet was expected to amass and display a learned acquaintance with the ancient languages and literatures. The poet was also expected to convey a sense of a transcendent mission. With Malherbe, inspiration fell into a disfavor from which it did not fully recover for at least a century and a half with Romanticism. Poetry was not to be judged on the basis of the richness of its metaphorical invention, the suggestive hermeticism of its mythological or theological allusion, or the idiosyncratic diction of an inspired individualism. Poetry began to follow the general rules of clear, grammatical speech embodying common sense. The poet was not very different from a competent public speaker, except that he could fit his speeches into verse and rhyme. Local color, regionalisms, neologisms, and archaic and foreign words were rigorously proscribed in favor of standard French. A display of unusual learning became a defect; the Malherbian classical poet was taught to avoid any reference beyond the domain of ordinary knowledge.

The Malherbian poetic was exclusive, formalist, and reductive. It aimed at reducing the lexical materials available to the poet to the plain Parisian French of polite urban and court society. Skill in the arrangement of this limited lexicon could be judged according to rules of organization and clarity. The promotion of poetry as a technique thus coincided with one form of literary criticism, what we now recognize as the criticism of the reviewer, the person who judges success or failure of new works on the current market. By restricting the variables, the Malherbian reform made the writing and reading of poetry available to a wider public. A rising middle class and a nobility coming from the provinces to take up residence near the court could use Malherbe as a "consumer's guide" to contemporary poetry. Following him, they could judge and talk about poetry without fear of embarrassment. They could even aspire to become poets. Learning how to write poetry did not require learning a great deal about classical and Renaissance literature or learning another vocabulary more appropriate to poetry than everyday speech. Du Bellay and Ronsard had advocated the enlargement of poetic language, seeing it as the model for the written language as a whole, enriching French and making it better able to render nuances of meaning, even taking over terms from outside what had been recognized as the limits of French.

In its content as well, Malherbe's poetry is not expansive or centrifugal but limiting or centripetal. It exalts rationalism and authority and denounces the sentimental, the eccentric or individualist, and deviations from the laws of the monarch and of the established Catholic church. His "Consolation à monsieur le premier président, sur la mort de madame sa femme" (1626; "Consolation of Monsieur the Presiding Judge [of Verdun] on the Death of His Wife") is one of many poems written on the occasion of the death of relatives of a friend or protector. It uses a series of commonplaces and well-known mythological references to exhort the receiver to abandon grief and to return to civic duties. Praise of Henri IV, Louis XIII, and the regent Marie de Médicis is a constant in Malherbe's work, from "Prière pour le roi allant en Limousin" (1605; "Prayer for the King, Going to Limousin") to the ode "Pour le roi allant châtier la rébellion des Rochelais" (1628; "For the King, Going to Punish the Rebellion of La Rochelle"). Love poetry is reduced to a fairly self-interested argument for physical satisfaction. In short, Malherbe's poetry, like the philosophy of his contemporary Descartes, is consonant with an age of reason directed toward useful achievement.

The publication of the 1627 anthology of Malherbe and his disciples was a high-water point for classicism in the first half of the century, but it did not mark the definitive establishment of French classical poetry. Although the styles of Molière, Racine, Nicolas Boileau, and La Fontaine—the great classical writers of verse—manifest a long-term trend toward simpler vocabulary, modern grammar, and avoidance of erudite reference, between 1627 and Boileau's classical *L'art poétique* (1674; *The Art of Poetry*), other poetic styles flourished while rejecting much of Malherbe's model. The *précieux* poetry, typified by the work of Vincent Voiture (1597–1648), represents one current of deviation from Malherbe: the other major current is the late baroque of Saint-Amant.

Voiture retrieved some of the traditional verse forms condemned by Malherbe but did not return to the model of the inspired, learned poet. Rather, he struck an ostentatious pose of amusing virtuosity. Instead of addressing high political and religious commonplaces, he preferred to amaze with the brilliant manipulation of very limited material, drawn primarily from the contemporary

Parisian scene. Voiture's best-known work is the 1636 rondeau for Ysabeau, in which he creates a perfect metrical and rhyme structure without presenting any content other than an account of the writing of the poem itself.

The late baroque current in the works of Saint-Amant is a reminder of what Malherbe suppressed from the 1627 collection: his connection with the Renaissance through the early baroque. The baroque had appeared in French literature at the end of the 16th century as a reduction of humanist culture to vivid and less subtle thematic and descriptive formulas. One of its themes was illusion, which it laid bare and attempted to cure. "Les larmes de saint Pierre" illustrates the reduction of humanist culture to recognizably codified series, antitheses, and allusions that allowed a moderately literate public to appreciate its message of rather commonplace stoicism. Malherbe's later classicizing simply carried this reduction further on the semantic level while shifting emphasis to verse form.

Saint-Amant showed nostalgia for the language, the repertoire of cultural allusions, and the formal freedom of 16th-century poetry. He accentuated the bizarre, the vulgar, erudition in vocabulary and metaphor, and originality in the overall conceptual plan of his varied works, many of which specifically allude to the Renaissance poets, to Rabelais, and to Ovid. In response to the Malherbian reductionist aesthetic, Saint-Amant aggressively practiced inclusiveness and excess. Yet his awareness of responding to the challenge of the "new poetry" revealed the difference between his use of language and literary allusion and the 16th-century excitement in the rediscovery of antiquity. For the 16th century the old was the height of modernity; antiquity was at the extreme point of the new fashion. The Pléiade was conscious of assimilating the past and seriously intent on enriching French language and literature with Greek, Latin, and even Hebrew words. For Saint-Amant that consciousness became a self-consciousness; Malherbe's condemnation of pedantry and the new fashion of conceiving the public as lacking in humanist culture and interests made antiquity reemerge as the old, the quaint, the ironically humorous. In numerous works Saint-Amant uses a burlesque mode—the humorous rewriting of classical works in fragmented form with vocabulary that is both deliberately anachronistic and inappropriate in tone and level. "Le melon" (1631) traces the history of the fruit back to an orgiastic dinner of the Olympian gods. "Epître héroï-comique" (1644; "Heroic-Comic Epistle") and "Le passage de Gibraltar" (1636–1638; "The Passage of Gibraltar") describe military and naval battles in a mixture of scatology and humorous mythology. And "Le contemplateur" (1628; "The Contemplator") fuses Christian iconology, ancient mythology, and amusingly sensationalist scenes of horror. Throughout these works both the events reported and the poetic text are distanced and undercut by a permanent irony. By the mid-17th century, Saint-Amant could maintain the Renaissance tradition only by holding it forth at arm's length, as an object of some curiosity. Removed from the mainstream of contemporary poetry, humanist vocabulary and themes could become objects of interest and pleasure in their own right. By recycling this language, Saint-Amant showed that 17th-century poetry could make use of Pléiade materials without accepting Pléiade ideals.

Bibliography: Claude K. Abraham, *Enfin Malherbe: The Influence of Malherbe on French Lyric Prosody, 1605–1674* (Lexington: University Press of Kentucky, 1971). Edwin M. Duval, *Poesis and Poetic Tradition in Early Works of Saint-Amant* (York, S.C.: French Literature Publications, 1980). David L. Rubin, *The Knot of Artifice: A Poetic of the French Lyric in the Early 17th Century* (Columbus: Ohio State University Press, 1981). Frank Warnke, *Versions of Baroque* (New Haven: Yale University Press, 1972).

John D. Lyons

✍ 1634, 13 March

The Académie Française, Created by Cardinal Richelieu,
Holds Its First Meeting

The Académie Française

In February 1634 Louis XIII's minister of state, Cardinal Richelieu, learned from his informant François Le Métel de Boisrobert, abbé de Châtillon, that a group of literary figures had been holding secret social meetings in Paris, usually at the residence of Valentin Conrart. Since 1629 these gatherings, in the tradition of Jean-Antoine de Baïf's 16th-century Academy of Poetry and Music, had provided occasions for the twelve members, Catholics and Protestants, to discuss books, authors, and general topics in philosophy and music. This body included such influential figures as Jean Chapelain, Jean Desmarets de Saint-Sorlin, and Boisrobert himself. Richelieu immediately proposed to Boisrobert that they become an official literary association under state sponsorship, and thus seized the opportunity to use these intellectuals in his overall program to consolidate sovereign power by centralizing the standards of literature and language. The members' private response to the proposal may have been less than lukewarm, given some of their political differences with Richelieu and a general desire to preserve the autonomy, informality, and tradition of the proceedings. Yet the company, sensitive to the danger of offending the powerful minister of state, reluctantly instructed Boisrobert to accept the privilege on its behalf. The intimate group was then expanded to include forty members and named the Académie Française.

Richelieu, however, did experience weak but prolonged opposition to his official sponsorship: the Parlement of Paris refused for two and a half years to verify the Académie's letters of patent, signed by Louis XIII on 29 January 1635. This resistance was explained by Paul Pellisson-Fontanier, the Académie's 17th-century historian, as a symbolic attempt to prevent further erosion of the Parlement's authority, already sharply curtailed by Richelieu's efforts to strengthen his own influence over both government and culture. The formal establishment of the Académie Française to oversee "the exact rules" of the French language and "to render it capable of treating the arts and sciences" (quoted in Robertson, *History,* p. 13) paved the way for further centralization of the arts, first by Richelieu and later by the Académie's most influential sponsor, Louis XIV. Indeed, it was the initial success of the Académie Française and its artistic counterpart, the Royal Academy of Painting and Sculpture (1648), that inspired the later efforts by Jean-Baptiste Colbert and Louis XIV to organize the Academy of Dance (1661), the Academy of Inscriptions and Letters (1663), the Academy of Sciences (1666), the Academy of Music (1669), and the Academy of Architecture (1671). All of these selective bodies were administered by their sovereign patron to propagate an ideology of uniform cultural production. In fact the intellectual academies so symbolized royal centralization that they were targeted for suppression by the French Revolution in 1793 and replaced in 1795 by the more democratic Institut de France (the Académie Française was reestablished in 1815).

The fifty Statutes and Regulations drawn up by the Academicians for Richelieu's approval in 1634 make clear the extent of the cardinal's early hold on the Académie Française. Although Statute 22 decrees that "matters political and moral shall be treated in the Académie in conformity with the authority of the Prince, the state of the government, and the laws of the realm," Statute 2 requires that the Académie have a seal bearing "the face of His Eminence, the Cardinal Duke of Richelieu . . . with the words roundabout: Armand, Cardinal Duc de Richelieu, Protecteur de l'Académie Française . . . and a counter-seal, on which shall be represented a crown of laurel, with this legend: A L'IMMORTALITE" (Robertson, *History,* pp. 12, 10) (fig. 1). Given that the Académie was founded to represent the intellectual interests of the state, it is significant that Cardinal Richelieu, not his ineffectual king, Louis XIII, is represented on the seal as its protector, or "immortal Prince."

Richelieu's complex influence over this "independent" group of intellectuals is made most boldly manifest in the very first statute, which prescribes that "no person shall be received into the Académie who shall not be agreeable to Monseigneur the Protector, and of good morals, good reputation, good intelligence, and fitted for academic functions" (Robertson, *History,* p. 10). Although all the Académie's nominees were to be elected by the members on the basis of merit, this statute set the precedent not only that they should be acceptable to the body's protector but also that a candidate's qualifications must be grounded in more than learning and literary production. Most important were the abstract factors of morals and reputation promoted by Richelieu and associated with membership in the Académie Française. As explained by the 20th-century Academician Jean Guitton in his preface to Choucri Cardahi's history *Regards sous la coupole* (*Looking in on the Académie*), "The Académie Française knows full well that its members are elected not according to measurable merits, books, works, success, but on the basis of a something [*un je ne sais quoi*] that resembles predestination." Indeed, this reference to the predestination of "the chosen" (*les élus*) typifies the promotion of the intangibles of "genius" as attributes of the ideal Academician.

But if the interwoven threads of genius, reputation, and morals constituted the fabric of the ideal Academician, what should be made of the fact that some of the 17th century's brightest intellectual stars are missing from the roster of the Académie? In view of the stress on "genius" and the *je ne sais quoi,* how are

1. "Arm[and] Card[inal] de Richelieu. Protec[teur] de l'Acad[émie] Franç[aise].
1635"; "A l'Immortalité." Matrix of the seal and counterseal of the Académie Française, copper engraving after Varin (Archives de l'Académie Française). (Photo courtesy of Patrick Robert.)

we to understand the Académie's failure to include such significant figures as
Descartes, Molière, Pascal, La Rochefoucauld, Madeleine de Scudéry, and Pierre
Nicole? The answer has more to do with the influences of patronage than with
the predestination of genius. It was common for significant literary figures to
be excluded from the Académie as a result of their political or aesthetic differences with the Académie's most influential patrons, Richelieu, Colbert, and
Louis XIV. Another significant factor—one applicable to all periods of the
Académie's history—was the biological matter of gender. The Académie Française purposefully excluded women from its membership until it elected Marguerite Yourcenar in 1980. Although the Académie's most famous debates on
the issue of gender took place in the late 19th and early 20th centuries, female
participation in Académie functions was always a delicate issue among the
members. Very early in its history, the Académie apparently did discuss the
specific nominations of two esteemed females, Antoinette Deshoulières and
Madeleine de Scudéry. Its failure to elect them diminished the significance of
Scudéry's receipt of the Académie's first award of the Prize of Eloquence in
1671. In 1673 women were barred even from the public receptions for new
Academicians initiated by Louis XIV (although the ban was lifted in 1702).
These events initiated the Académie's tradition of purposeful exclusion of female
members (women were also excluded from the republican Institut). This long-
standing misogynist position was justified over the years by reference to France's

269

16th-century endorsement of the Salic Law, which excluded females from the line of succession to the throne.

By so abandoning the earlier French model of mixed-gender meetings treating interdisciplinary issues in the human sciences, the Académie Française closely resembled its highly esteemed precursor, the Accademia della Crusca of Florence, which produced the first Italian dictionary. Like its Italian predecessor, the Académie was an exclusively male "linguistic" body working toward the establishment of the "exact rules of our language." The Académie initially set out to honor Richelieu's wish that it compose a French dictionary, a grammar, and treatises on rhetoric and poetry that would establish rules for the valid practice of these arts. Although the first part of a grammar was published with the Académie's approval by Abbé François-Séraphin Régnier-Desmarais, the Académie's secretary from 1684 to 1713, the Académie was unable to produce a "rhetoric" or a "poetry." Still, its interest in establishing strict rules of language set a crucial precedent for the study of French literature. For writing published under the aegis of the Académie, the body's Statute 23 proscribed "any loose or licentious term, open to equivocal or evil interpretation" (Robertson, *History,* p. 12). Such exclusion of ambiguous or loose language endorsed the beliefs that words could be defined unequivocally and that readers could know exactly what an author meant by the use of any particular phrase. In sum, the Académie promoted the standard of arriving at an "exact" or "true" interpretation of literary intent—a false notion depending on the repression of illegitimate terms and interpretations. This unnatural formula of linguistic "truth" reflected Richelieu's politically motivated desire to promote an "official" language and a legitimate code of interpretation, both answerable to a uniform seat of judgment, his patriarchal Académie Française. Indeed, the strict standards of French language and literature established by the early Académie best embody the legacy of Richelieu's program of politicized aesthetics: a writer's loyalty to state-sponsored poetic and linguistic conventions takes precedence over artistic and interpretational freedom.

The extent of the Académie's authority to establish "exact" literary meaning and rules is illustrated by two significant 17th-century documents: the Académie's infamous 1637 judgment against Corneille's *Le Cid* and its dictionary of the French language (1694). *Les sentiments de l'Académie sur Le Cid* (*The Opinions of the Académie on Le Cid*) both established a precedent in literary law and exemplified Richelieu's successful manipulation of the young organization to review the dispute between Corneille and Georges de Scudéry (who were not elected to the Académie until 1647 and 1650, respectively, after Corneille had been rejected twice). Scudéry claimed both that Corneille had plagiarized an earlier Spanish play and that the result was disloyal to the dramatic unities and the acceptable standards of decency. The charge of "looseness" and "licentiousness," however, was leveled not so much at the language of *Le Cid* as at its central female character, Chimène, for marrying (for desiring) the man who killed her father. The Académie's judgment was mixed; it exonerated Corneille of plagiarism but insisted on the importance of preserving the dramatic unities and also blamed the author for Chimène's licentious behavior, which left her character open to "equivocal or evil interpretation." The Académie's particular justification for defending patriarchy against the paradoxes of female desire had a lasting impact on the ideological codes of literary study. Not only did it hint at the patriarchal bias of the literary and linguistic conventions being established—in decrying the licentiousness associated with women—but it hypocritically cast aside the standards of fact and truth that legitimated its judgment of *Le Cid*. *Les sentiments de l'Académie* foreshadowed François Hédelin, abbé d'Aubignac's treatise *Pratique du théâtre* (1657; *Theatrical Practice*) by ruling that not all truths are necessarily appropriate for literary representation. In the language of the *Sentiments*, "monstrous truths . . . must be suppressed for the good of society. It is primarily in such cases that the poet has the right to favor the verisimilar [*le vraisemblable*] over the real [*au vrai*]" (*Sentiments*, p. 32). In other words, the poet must suppress representation of the monstrous, the evil, or the abject—in this case, the desiring woman—to lend credibility to the ideology of social and literary unification being nurtured by His Eminence Cardinal Richelieu.

The suppression of "monstrous truths" took on even greater proportions in the Académie's work on the first French dictionary. In a letter on 22 March 1634 accepting the cardinal's offer of patronage, Jacques de Serizay, a member of Conrart's circle, promised on behalf of his colleagues that the new Académie would seek foremost "to cleanse the language of the filth it has acquired" (Pellisson-Fontanier, *Relation*, p. 23). Jean Chapelain restated this position by declaring in 1635 that the group's purpose "should be to work toward the purification of our language and to make it capable of the highest eloquence" (ibid., p. 28). From its earliest conception, the Académie's dictionary was understood by Richelieu and his Academicians as a means of restoring control over a language whose free and infectious usage by courtesans and plebeians alike had acquired "monstrous proportions."

The Academicians agreed to follow two general rules in assembling their version of French language. They decided, first, to exclude purely technical and scientific terms as well as entirely obsolete words, vulgar expletives, and "words offensive to modesty" and, second, to include citations from notable French authors to justify or illustrate particular definitions, following a precedent set by the dictionary of the Accademia della Crusca. For this purpose the Académie assembled a catalogue of "the most celebrated books" written in French, an effort that represented an official compilation of a French literary canon. An abbreviated version, by Pellisson-Fontanier, includes poets such as Clément Marot, Ronsard, Joachim du Bellay, François de Malherbe, and Nicolas Rapin, in addition to esteemed prose authors such as Montaigne, Antoine Arnauld, Francis of Sales, and Honoré d'Urfé. Although the Academicians abandoned the project of cross-referencing, the provisional list of "the most celebrated books" illustrates the Académie's complex relation to the French literary tradition, since it includes, for instance, the name of Théophile de Viau, who was incarcerated in 1623 while awaiting trial for his alleged part in the obscene collection *Le Parnasse des poètes satiriques* (1622; *Satirical Parnassus*). Although

Viau was cleared of these charges launched by the Jesuits, he enjoyed wide recognition for his passionate sonnets, which neglected the tradition of *galant* (morally acceptable) poetic form and content. In contrast to the unexpected inclusion of Viau, the name of Rabelais, whom Montaigne half a century earlier had praised so highly for the literary quality of his ribald tales, is conspicuous by its absence from the list. The omission reflects the Académie's determination to exclude from its dictionary the sort of "monstrous" discourse that provided Rabelais's wide readership with indecorous delight. As in the pronouncement against Chimène's desires in *Le Cid,* the Académie was bent on excluding the more glaring examples of carnivalesque or sexual discourse. In the dedication of the first edition of the dictionary (1694) to Louis XIV; such claims to moral and literary purity stand together with an ideology of untarnished and absolute sovereignty: "If there has ever been the promise that a living Language may come to be fixed, and no longer to depend on the caprice and the tyranny of Usage, we have reason to believe that ours has reached in our days to that glorious point of immutability, since the books and the other monuments that will speak of YOUR MAJESTY, will always be regarded as made in the golden age of France" (Robertson, *History,* p. 240).

Despite its many flagrantly tyrannical manipulations of discourse and membership, the chief legacy of the 17th-century Académie Française is a tradition of honor, genius, and *je ne sais quoi* that has provided France with a fixed set of "laws" for language and literature. The credit for this surprisingly consistent tradition might be argued to rest with the Académie's two most dominant 17th-century patrons, Richelieu and Louis XIV, both of whom manipulated the Académie to serve the ideological needs of royal centralization. But it was Jean Chapelain who left the deepest internal imprint, for which he is called *"the* Académie." His quiet impact on the propaganda of French literary and artistic patronage cannot be overstated. Serving under Richelieu, Chapelain worked diligently behind the scenes to engineer both the Académie's fifty Statutes and its method of compiling the dictionary. He was also the direct link to Richelieu on the three-person review board of *Le Cid.* Later, when Louis XIV assumed the role of the Académie's protector, Chapelain not only joined Colbert in overseeing the activities of the artistic and literary academies but was also responsible for composing an official "Liste de quelques gens de lettres" ("List of Some Men of Letters"), which entitled select writers to handsome governmental stipends and the accompanying prestige of the sovereign's patronage. Displaying his special allegiance to the Academicians, Chapelain entitled even its amateur writers to these benefits by adding a special category for "autres écrivains français" ("other French writers"). Further ensuring Chapelain's role in guaranteeing the ideological allegiance of the Académie, Louis XIV appointed him in 1663 as one of four Academicians to sit as the founding members of the Academy of Inscriptions and Letters, the group charged with the creation of a series of medals commemorating the history of Louis XIV's reign. Chapelain's influence over all the significant activities of the 17th-century Académie identifies him as the source of the Académie's genius. Chapelain, *"the* Académie," remains today both the prototypical patriarch of the Académie Française and the architect of its *je ne sais quoi*—in all its monstrously exclusive forms.

See also 1536, 1627, 1694, 1791 (13 January).

Bibliography: Académie Française, *Les sentiments de l'Académie sur Le Cid* (1637), ed. Colbert Searles, *University of Minnesota Studies in Language and Literature*, 3 (March 1916). Choucri Cardahi, *Regards sous la coupole: Histoire et petite histoire de l'Académie Française* (Paris: Mame, 1966). Louis Marin, *Portrait of the King*, trans. Martha M. Houle (Minneapolis: University of Minnesota Press, 1988). Timothy Murray, *Theatrical Legitimation: Allegories of Genius in Seventeenth-Century England and France* (New York: Oxford University Press, 1987). Paul Pellisson-Fontanier, *Relation contenant l'histoire de l'Académie Françoise* (Paris: Augustin Courbé, 1653). Duncan Maclaren Robertson, *A History of the French Academy, 1635–1910* (New York: G.W. Dillingham, 1910).

Timothy Murray

❧ *1637*

The Académie Française Disapproves of Various Liberties Taken by Corneille in *Le Cid*

Toward French Classical Tragedy

The most significant political event of 1637 was neither military nor diplomatic, but theatrical. Pierre Corneille (1606–1684), after writing *Le Cid* and having it produced on the Parisian stage, became the center of a major controversy, which Cardinal Richelieu eventually quieted by securing a ruling on the issue by the Académie Française. Though suddenly a celebrity, the author of *Le Cid* was by no means a newcomer to the theater. Several comedies by this young playwright from Rouen had been performed in Paris, beginning with *Mélite* in 1630: *La galerie du palais* (1631–32; *The Palace Arcades*), *La suivante* (1634; *The Lady-in-Waiting*), *La place royale* (1634; *The Royal Square*), and *L'illusion comique* (1645; *The Dramatic Illusion*). Corneille's comedies introduced into the traditionally implausible plots of the 16th-century Italian theater characters whose comic dilemmas were the result of their own inner psychological conflicts. The shift from comedy of circumstance to comedy of character, anchored in situations produced by strongly differentiated personalities, had profound consequences not only for the subsequent development of comedy in the 17th century but also for Corneille's titanic career as a dramatist, which spanned nearly half a century and includes, in addition to plays—comedies, tragedies, tragicomedies, as well as *pièces à spectacles* plays containing spectacles—decisive contributions to theoretical debates about the theater (the three "Discourses" he wrote for the 1660 edition of his plays). In retrospect the comedies appear to be the arena of human conflict in which Corneille worked out the psychological model for a new kind of hero, beset by internal struggles yet capable of pursuing noble ideals and rising to surpassing acts of will. From such heroic figures, whose depth and complexity were unprecedented in comedy, he went on to construct his revolutionary tragedies.

According to the dramaturgical criteria that were emerging in the 1630s, *Le Cid* is, properly speaking, really a tragicomedy. The play does not strictly apply the newly formulated laws of the three unities (time, place, and action), and it concludes, not with a bloodletting, but with a conciliatory dialogue that predicts a conventional comic ending, the marriage of hero and heroine. Nevertheless, the main characters' psychological conflict turns upon the stringent conception of heroism that, with its elevated tone and aristocratic values, carried over into Corneille's authentically tragic dramas.

Le Cid's dramatic conflict centers upon two young lovers, Rodrigue and Chimène, caught up in the changing political structures of the newly consolidated Castilian monarchy. Her father, Don Gomès, insults his father, Don Diègue, who calls upon Rodrigue to avenge him. Rodrigue slays Don Gomès in a duel and thus saves his family's honor, but now Chimène must seek his death to avenge her father. The lovers are torn apart because both are faithful to a feudal, family-centered sense of justice that conflicts with their inner desires. This situation exemplifies the essential dilemma of Corneille's universe: "duty"—an obligation to one's family, or to the state, or to a certain sense of one's worth that requires a search for honor and glory in that family/state—is never able to find a harmonious compromise with "love," with personal desire. Although Rodrigue achieves a decisive victory over the Moorish invaders and becomes a national hero ("The Cid"), this dilemma remains irresolvable. It persists because in the end Chimène, still resisting her love and the interests of the state, will not abandon her duty. The play ends on a note of resolution that is purely rhetorical: confronted with Chimène's obstinate refusal either to forgive Rodrigue or to have him punished, King Fernand steps in and predicts that the two will eventually be married. This intervention is an assertion of the king's newly enhanced authority, and it attempts to paper over the rift between the state and its subjects that Chimène's recalcitrance occasions.

Le Cid became the object of intense public debates that were followed in the highest circles of government. In dealing with the controversy, the Académie Française exonerated Corneille from charges of plagiarism that his enemies had brought against him claiming he had merely translated a Spanish play of the same subject, but expressed indignation at Chimène's scandalous behavior, which Jean Chapelain, the author of the judgment, qualified as "unnatural" if not "perverse." The Académie's opinion reflected a deep-seated sexual bias inherent in the 17th century. It is the sexual and political ambivalences of this patriarchal monarchy that Corneille's tragedies seem both to uphold and subtly to undermine.

Between his first tragedy, *Médée* (1631; *Medea*), and *Le Cid,* Corneille turned away from the world of classical myth, which in *Médée* is associated with the terrifying power of the female, and specifically with the threatening mother.

Corneille's new focus became the world of history. This shift mirrored the contemporary political evolution from late feudalism toward nascent absolutism. Whereas *Médée* shows civilization being defeated by chaotic forces of nature associated with the feminine, *Le Cid* represents an established patriarchal/monarchical society. Here and in the plays of the early 1640s, there is no mother; the self-assertive heroine—always acting as a wife, sister, or daughter—incarnates a regressive tendency: she is unable or unwilling to make the "right" historical choice (typically marriage). Her dilemma within the family is analogous to the political tensions confronting emergent absolutism. Chimène's unwavering refusal to marry Rodrigue, upheld at the end of *Le Cid,* is a refusal to break with the feudal values of her father and accede to the new, progressive monarchical order.

Corneille responded indirectly to the attacks made on *Le Cid* in the next play he sent to Paris, *Horace* (1640; *Horatius*), his first great Roman tragedy. Respecting the unities of time, place, and action, the tragedy is situated in the historical period and place in which Corneille will achieve his greatest distinction. The drama contrasts Horace, the unflinching Roman patriot, with his less single-minded brother-in-law, the Alban Curiace, who is also the fiancé of Horace's sister, Camille. Whereas Horace readily dismisses personal attachments in favor of absolute devotion to Rome, Curiace and Camille are torn between their feelings of affection and their patriotic duty. Horace and his two brothers are pitted against Curiace and his brothers in a duel that resolves a long-standing struggle between Rome and Alba. Of the six combatants, Horace alone survives; he thus becomes the hero responsible for Rome's victory over a rival city-state, but, more important, this victory is the origin of Rome's imperial grandeur. Yet his triumph is tarnished; for his bitterly grieving sister responds to the debacle by cursing Rome, thus provoking Horace to slay her. He must then be cleansed of his fratricide. In the dénouement, the king of Rome, Tulle (Tullus), absolves Horace of his crime, justifying his pardon by invoking Horace's value to the state. Although this act of kingly self-interest ushers in a new order of "manly" prerogatives and political expediency that outweighs or overshadows the specter of Camille's murder, it also acknowledges the compromise with wrongdoing that is vital to an absolutist regime.

In contrast to *Horace,* with its intensely combative dialogues and fratricidal violence, *Cinna ou la clémence d'Auguste* (1640; *Cinna, or Augustus' Clemency*), Corneille's second great Roman tragedy, is curiously pallid. The play continues to probe the role of absolute monarchy and its conflict with recalcitrant femininity, deploying more subtle and corrosive scenarios than either *Le Cid* or *Horace.* The action, set in the court of the Roman emperor Auguste, is devoid of bloodshed, although a bloody past—Auguste won his throne after a series of civil wars and murderous power struggles—is a central motive in the continuing power struggle. Now elderly and tempted to abdicate, the emperor confronts a conspiracy that seeks revenge against him. The two leaders of the conspiracy are discovered to be Cinna, his confidant, and Emilie, whom Auguste adopted. After an inner struggle, Auguste opts to pardon rather than punish the conspirators, and to rule as an enlightened, exemplary monarch rather than abdicate. They, in turn, are won over by his magnanimity, give up their desire for revenge, and accept the benevolent protection of the emperor.

The dénouement of *Cinna* thus records a historical advance, more successful than the one represented in *Le Cid*. Auguste's heroic act of pardoning rather than seeking revenge entails breaking away from an outmoded cycle of endless vendetta in favor of a progressive vision of social behavior. The play's most recalcitrant character, Emilie, whose long monologue in the play's opening scene sets off in strong relief her desire to avenge Auguste's killing of her father, is the driving force behind this scenario. Both her power and her failure are effects of her position in a love triangle that includes Cinna and a fellow conspirator, Maxime. Emilie uses Cinna's love to force his remorseful cooperation. Yet her plot is foiled by the unrequited love and jealousy of Maxime, who betrays Cinna to Auguste and abjectly pleads with the appalled Emilie to flee with him from Rome and from the emperor's wrath. Emilie's aggressive role reproduces the symmetrical opposition between subversive femininity, a source of division and strife, and dominant masculinity, which *Cinna* concentrates and consummates by amalgamating the functions of tragic hero and adjudicating ruler in the single, sublime figure of Auguste. After a taxing trial and illumination, the emperor proceeds to a reckoning with Emilie that she in turn experiences as an illumination, accompanied by repentance and rebirth. Unlike her stubbornly reserved predecessor, Chimène, she finds pleasure and pride in joining the chorus of submission to a divinely sanctioned royalty.

Through this act of clemency Auguste constitutes a new order of history and enlightened politics. By winning the hearts of the rebels, he enables them willingly to sacrifice their republican values to the monarchy. At the end of the play the emperor's wife, Livie, explicitly traces Rome's newfound preference for monarchy to his "art of mastering hearts" and making his subjects happy (lines 1764–70). Yet is this not precisely the ultimate ploy of the tyrant, impressing his own supremacy onto his subjects' minds and hearts as the source of their pleasure and sense of self? *Cinna* can present its exaltation of monarchy only at the price of exposing this troubling display of the workings of power. In Corneille's last great Roman tragedy, *Polyeucte, martyr* (1643; *Saint Polyeuctus, Martyr*), a similarly critical perspective on the very values that are exalted is not far from the surface. *Polyeucte* returns to *Cinna*'s questioning of the relations of pleasure and power while adding its own pointed insight on the tensions between sexual desire and religious duty.

Polyeucte, a "Christian tragedy," is both the apogee of Corneille's classical construction and, paradoxically, the sign of its exhaustion. The drama enacts the sacrifice of human ties—Polyeucte's love for his wife, Pauline, and eventually Pauline's abandonment of her love for the military hero, Sévère—for a more fulfilling love, that of a Christian for his God. For the Christian characters the tragedy is played out in the tension between spiritual love and carnal desire, as one after another all the individuals touched by the grace of Polyeucte's example abandon the illusions of earthly existence for what appear to them to be the greater rewards offered by his religion. But his "higher love" introduces another conflict: the conversion to Christianity is a crime against the Roman state, a rebellion that impels Félix, the Roman governor and Polyeucte's father-in-law, to have Polyeucte executed, making him a Christian martyr.

Far from leaving a chasm between Christianity and the Roman state, however, *Polyeucte* establishes its hero's example as the basis for a far-reaching compromise. The play ends with the double conversion of Pauline and her father, and with Sévère's call for religious freedom and tolerance under the Roman Empire. Thus the martyr's example has become the ground for an accommodation that reconciles the temporal and spiritual realms by allowing the Christian to serve both religion and the state. The ascendancy accorded to martyrdom establishes the Christian's relation to his almighty God as the determining model for the patriarchal vision that informs French classical theater's vision of both family and state. God becomes the transcendent origin of all personal and social values; and the Christian's blissful love for God becomes the consummate order of felicity, the mystical end that reduces the adventures and pleasures of carnal love to relative triviality.

The compromise with religion achieved in *Polyeucte* thus harbors an uneasy paradox: the viability of Christianity in the social world rests upon the exaltation of the martyr's otherworldly experience. Polyeucte's heroic apotheosis lifts him above sexuality and politics, above individual desire and *Realpolitik;* his uncompromising stand takes him out of the realm of history in which Cornelian tragedy has constructed its personal and political dramas and into a transcendent, absolutist realm in which the tragic event, converted into the hero's salvific ascension, transforms temporal drama into timeless ecstasy.

Polyeucte, then, brought Corneille to the outer limit of his historical sense of the tragic—a limit from which he could only recoil. None of his tragedies after 1642 equaled the four early masterpieces in power and grace. The remainder of Corneille's long and illustrious career divides into two periods. In the first, in plays such as *La mort de Pompée* (1643; *The Death of Pompey*), *Rodogune* (1644), and *Nicomède* (1651), Corneille brought the mother back onstage. In this world of patriarchal dominance, however, the mother is not a nurturing, loving, protective force, but a "hysteric." Her presence reenacts, in exaggeratedly complicated plots, the struggle with the forces of chaos and dispersion that Corneille had put aside in his great plays.

In the second period, the elderly dramatist confronted a new artistic era—the high classicism of the 1660s—and a changing public. In plays such as *Sertorius* (1662), *Attila* (1665), and *Suréna* (1674), Corneille focused instead on dramas that revealed the weaknesses and dangers of absolute monarchy. Although these works continued to appeal to the aristocrats who participated in the political upheavals of the 1630s and 1640s, the younger members of Louis XIV's brilliant court preferred the new tragedy of Racine, less sympathetic to larger-than-life heroism and its code of duty and honor, and more intrigued by the labyrinthine twists of amorous passion. Corneille, however, remained a pre-eminent force in French theater. Racine had to contend less with rivals of his own generation than with the theatrical legacy of his predecessor.

See also 1552, 1553 (March), 1634, 1660, 1661, 1664.

Bibliography: Serge Doubrovsky, *Corneille, ou la dialectique du héros* (Paris: Gallimard, 1963). Mitchell Greenberg, *Corneille, Classicism and the Ruses of Symmetry* (Cambridge: Cambridge University Press, 1986). Robert J. Nelson, *Corneille, His Heroes and Their Worlds* (Philadelphia: University of Pennsylvania Press, 1963).

Mitchell Greenberg

✍ 1640

The Jesuit Pedagogue Pierre Le Moyne Publishes *Les peintures morales*

Problems in Logic and Rhetoric

The little-known Pierre Le Moyne (1602–1671) and his treatise *Les peintures morales, où les passions sont représentées par tableaux, par caractères, et par questions nouvelles et curieuses* (1640; *Moral Paintings in Which the Passions Are Represented by Means of Pictures, Characters, and New and Curious Questions*) mark an important transition in the development of modern ideas about language, communication, and epistemology: a transition from an emphasis on the power and authority of language to a reliance upon visual representation. This dramatic reorientation of human thought and action had a profound influence on subsequent culture.

Le Moyne lived through the perilous years of France's rise to European leadership and died at the apogee of that growth. He was an energetic and prolific participant in many of the cultural struggles of the period, on what we would now think of as the "liberal" side. In 1647 he contributed to the continuing debate about the relative status of the sexes with *La galerie des femmes fortes* (*The Gallery of Strong Women*). He published an epic (*Saint Louis*, 1651–1653) at a time when the pertinence of that genre was much in dispute. He participated in political and historical discussion with *De l'art de régner* (1665; *On the Art of Ruling*), *Mémoires d'état* (1666; *Memoirs of State*, a work on Marie de Médicis' regency), an equally topical work on the nature and purpose of historiography (*De l'histoire*, 1670; *On History*), and an unpublished *Histoire du Cardinal Richelieu*. As a Jesuit, he joined wholeheartedly in the anti-Jansenist campaign, with his *Manifeste apologétique pour la doctrine de la Compagnie de Jésus* (1644; *Apologetic Manifesto on behalf of Jesuit Doctrine*) and *Véritables sentiments de saint Augustin et de l'église, touchant la grâce* (1650; *True Opinions of St. Augustine and the Church, concerning Grace*). He is probably best known today for his *Dévotion aisée* (1652; *Comfortable and Easy Piety*), a work presenting the ethical views of his order, for which he was mightily taken to task by Pascal in the eleventh *Lettre provinciale* (*Provincial Letter*). He contributed to more general ethical debates in *Entretiens et lettres morales* (1665; *Moral Conversations and Letters*). In addition he produced many shorter pamphlets and poems.

Unlike these works, Le Moyne's 802-page *Les peintures morales* was probably more important for its mode of presentation than for its matter. Its author sought to discover the universal principles beneath the human passions by presenting them as more or less traditional rhetorical topoi (fig. 1). Indeed, in his preface Le Moyne asserted that his work was Aristotelian and scholastic in intent and orientation. Yet he departed from that purely rhetorical tradition in making a pictorial dimension central to his analysis. His book's explanatory subtitle implied that "representation" of the passions "by means of pictures" was a major expository device, more essential than either of the other two techniques mentioned, "characters" and "curious questions."

Each of seven pictures scattered throughout the two volumes of the work composed a kind of emblem or allegorical picture, followed by explanatory poems and "discourses." Thus the presentation was similar to that of the emblem books' threefold device of maxim, picture, and epigram/poem. Indeed, in 1649 Le Moyne produced such an emblem book (*Devises héroïques et morales; Heroic and Moral Emblems*) and later wrote a theoretical work on the subject, *De l'art des devises* (1666; *On the Art of Emblems*). In *Les peintures morales,* the "ques-

1. "Actéon: Quatrième peinture où sont représentés les mauvais effets des principales passions," engraving by Grégoire Huret, in Pierre Le Moyne, *Les peintures morales, où les passions sont représentées par tableaux, par caractères, et par questions nouvelles et curieuses,* vol. 1 (Paris: Cramoisy, 1645), p. 488. (Courtesy of the Beinecke Rare Book and Manuscript Library, Yale University.)

279

tions" (a term taken over from the Aristotelian and scholastic *quaestiones*) were prose disquisitions on the various passions, but the "characters," Le Moyne asserted in his preface, were themselves a kind of verbal "picture": "colorless Paintings, in which the Nature of each Passion is expressed by the marks proper to it." That is, they were versions of those Theophrastian "Characteristicks" (as they were called in contemporary English) that became so popular during the 17th century and whose most celebrated producer was Jean de La Bruyère. Le Moyne justified his use of them by referring to Seneca and, more important, to the pseudo-Ciceronian *Rhetorica ad Herennium:* "A description made of some Nature [temperament], by certain signs that may be considered its properties and attributes" (*Peintures,* preface).

Le Moyne thus chose to emphasize and to reconcile two different notions of reason. One worked through language and rhetoric, relying upon accepted authorities and familiar tradition. The other worked through what was increasingly understood as the direct evidence of the senses, especially vision. Indeed, vision very soon became the standard metaphor for reason, to the extent that the terms were soon generally used almost synonymously.

These two notions of reason may not appear contradictory, as Le Moyne's effort to combine them suggests. Yet their simultaneous presence also signaled a deeper change. Le Moyne's use of an Aristotelian orientation itself challenged a new scientific philosophy for which Aristotle's name stood for everything retrograde. The Jesuit's assumption that the worldly was embedded in the divine and that the end of all human action was divine love, conflicted with ever more widespread arguments favoring human autonomy, a morality whose validity did not require divine sanction, and political action whose surety was provided by the reliable order of universal human reason alone. These arguments required an assumption that the very passions Le Moyne himself was discussing could be ordered without divine intervention, that they could be controlled by humans themselves. Le Moyne's claim to present the universal principles underlying human passions necessarily implied their ultimate rationality, a view shared by Descartes in *Les passions de l'âme* (1649; *The Passions of the Soul*). Indeed, Le Moyne argued at length that the passions were subject to reason, and that, were this not the case, it would spell the end of civil society, of morality and of all knowledge—reason, he wrote, was always sovereign (*Peintures,* pp. 356–451).

This mid-17th-century development reflected a quarrel that had begun more than a century earlier over the proper function—indeed the very nature—of rhetoric. Two forms of Ciceronianism struggled with Ramism for epistemological and cultural dominance. Rhetoric in general continued to be the chief instrument for the communication of knowledge and the exposition and direction of human action well into the 18th century, even though the changes occurring in Le Moyne's time had already had profound effects by then.

Since antiquity, three forms of communication had been described. Logic addressed the problem of valid and invalid statements about reality and involved a learned communication whose main propositional device was the syllogism. (The once separate discipline of dialectic dealt with generally accepted opinion, not with things real.) Rhetoric concerned itself with the nature of communication between expert and layperson. Poetry fell between the two, but closer to the second (the late Middle Ages and early Renaissance knew it as the "second rhetoric"). In the 16th century, logic was trimmed to the discussion of invention and of judgment or disposition. It did not consider discovery in any modern sense, but rather the analysis of debatable propositions (invention) and the method of arranging appropriate arguments (*dispositio* or judgment). Rhetoric discussed all other matters. Indeed, since the original notion of logic essentially concerned the communication of received and recognized authority, it might easily have been subsumed in its virtual entirety under rhetoric.

In the 16th and much of the 17th centuries Cicero's rhetoric (and Quintilian's *De institutione oratoria*) underlay all schemes of knowledge and civic action. The early 16th-century Ciceronians held that rhetoric as a whole provided the essential instrument for the good life and civic order, combining eloquence and wisdom, "copious" expression, and exposition of true knowledge and experience. This ideal provoked a quarrel lasting well into the next century; for pleasant words could readily conceal truth or even make falsehood attractive. At the same time, it could be argued that truth did not require artifice to be persuasive. Two opposing schools thus appeared. One, the "civic humanists," claimed rhetoric as the foundation of social stability, as the only proper means of presenting the truths of knowledge and experience vital to persuade humans toward political and civic improvement. The other, a "courtly" tradition, emphasized eloquence and style as the strongest enabling instrument of social order and indeed of political power itself.

Both schools claimed Cicero as their model. The first included scholars, lawyers, and clergy such as Erasmus, Thomas More, Guillaume Budé, and Montaigne. The other school focused on princely courts, affirming the virtues of affable social intercourse, noble friendship, and *sprezzatura* (the difficult art of making the hard look easy in all social behavior): its standard-bearers were Baldesar Castiglione and Pietro Bembo. Not only Cicero's rhetorical writings (and those attributed to him) but also texts such as his *De officiis* readily supported both views. But the disagreement did not touch fundamentals. Both sides insisted that language in and of itself embodied the persuasive means necessary for right action and understanding, as well as the knowledge enabling them—hence the considerable interest of Le Moyne's later use of Cicero to support his use of *pictorially* oriented "characters."

The second important strand in the history of logic and rhetoric throughout this roughly two-century period was Ramism and the rejection of Aristotle. Pierre de la Ramée (better known as Petrus Ramus, 1515–1572) was troubled by the evident redundancy in the several Ciceronian theories. He did not doubt that one ought to learn how to find subject matter and set it in order (*inventio* and *dispositio*), but he saw no reason why both logic and rhetoric should teach them. Rhetoric could handle style and delivery, while knowledge of fact, knowledge of opinion, and the needs of scientific and social communication were the proper objects of a single rational logic. Ramus adapted the Aristotelian laws *du tout, par soi,* and of *universalité,* known in English as the laws of truth, justice, and wisdom. The first concerned the real and constant nature of a thing (or its statement). The second applied to the internal homogeneity of statements. The third described a necessary reciprocity between the elements of a proposition. In extending this third law to demand that subject and predicate be in proximate association, Ramus formulated his celebrated method, requiring things to be classed in "descending" order as they were of decreasing generality. This demand in turn produced the familiar Ramist "trees," depicting epistemological relations in genealogical form. Knowledge itself was now presented in pictorial shape, and a *visualization* of conceptual relations became essential to reason.

These two strands, Ciceronianism and Ramism, are essential to any understanding of logic, rhetoric, and epistemology in the 17th century. In France the first form of Ciceronianism gradually lost its prestige. The civic humanists' interpretation of rhetoric had remained close to the older understanding of logic, though dealing with social behavior and civic experience rather than with philosophical knowledge. Both emphasized invention and disposition of statement. This affinity between the ancient tradition and civic Ciceronianism lingered in the judicial rhetoric of a Guillaume du Vair at the turn of the 16th century, and later, to a degree, in that of Antoine Arnauld and the Port-Royal group (although there it was soon replaced by a Cartesian rationalism). Courtly or stylistic Ciceronianism enjoyed a different destiny. Jean Louis Guez de Balzac and the Académie Française, with an impetus provided by Richelieu, put it to the service of the new centralized monarchical authority, where it eventually gave rise to what were increasingly known as belles-lettres. It flourished in the salons of Catherine Vivonne de Rambouillet and others, whose social manners created a new ideal of relations between autonomous individuals placing self-interest before that of society as a whole (the humanist ideal).

This ideal depended as well upon a new view of humankind emphasizing a rationality in which Ramism was no less significant than Cartesianism. Ramus' visual taxonomies rested upon assumptions more familiar to us from Descartes's theories. They assumed an identity of logical form between natural reality and the rational order of human judgment (Ramus' law of truth). They also presupposed that the linguistic form taken by correct and true propositions echoed those of both the mind and the world (Ramus' laws of homogeneity and reciprocity). Ramus himself did not extend what he saw as an internal matter of logic and "universal method" to any referential relation between mind and world; but that refusal has little to do with the underlying implications of his arguments.

Such views meant that right thought was *always* visually representable, because it necessarily reflected the order of things. They also meant that a logic of communication (traditional logic, as well as rhetoric) could be replaced by a logic of inquiry, since true and correct knowledge of things was obtained by such right use of reason. The clarity and distinctness of such knowledge, as Descartes had it, depended upon a kind of visual scanning of ideas. These views marked the advent of experimental science and its justification. Finally, they implied that humans had full control over the means and ends of this knowledge, because the mind's rational order and process exactly reflected the world's mechanism and could express and communicate it in language by means of correctly formulated propositions.

These views on the relation between language, mind, and world were already apparent in Le Moyne's *Peintures morales*. They were clear as well in Claude Favre de Vaugelas's *Remarques sur la langue française* (1647; *Remarks on the French Language*), which aimed to show its reader how best to use language to reflect right judgment: "Speech," wrote Vaugelas, "is an image not only of thought, but also of the thing itself we want to represent" (p. 160). Still, Vaugelas's aim remained the mastery of language, not of nature. The clearest expression of the new relation between mind, language, and world, and of the human authority accompanying it, had to await the Arnauld and Lancelot *Grammaire générale et raisonnée* (1660; *General and Reasoned Grammar*) and the Arnauld and Nicole *Logique, ou l'art de penser* (1662; *Logic, or the Art of Thinking*). The *Logique* discussed, first, the storing of images of the world in the mind in the shape of ideas. "Conception" was "the simple view we have of things as they present themselves to the mind," and "ideas" were "the form in which we represent these things to ourselves" (*The Art of Thinking*, p. 59). Next it discussed the rational processes that succeeded upon such storing: judgment, reasoning, and order. The *Grammaire* taught how to set these things in a language that was the very representation of thought and its object. In 1672 Bernard Lamy brought the process full circle, writing his Port-Royalist rhetoric, *De l'art de parler* (*On the Art of Speaking*), on the same principles.

How very far we are from the quarrels of Ciceronianism and the rejection of Artistotle is clear. The remnants of the old rhetorical concerns passed over into literature and its criticism. The new logic eventually became the theoretical foundation of the new experimental sciences. Within this development Le Moyne's *Peintures*—and this may well be why that text is now so unfamiliar even to specialists—marked the transitional moment.

See also 1267, 1493, 1536, 1555 (13 September), 1657, 1689.

Bibliography: Antoine Arnauld and Claude Lancelot, *Grammaire générale et raisonnée* (Paris: Paulet, 1969). Antoine Arnauld and Pierre Nicole, *La logique, ou l'art de penser,* ed. Louis Marin (Paris: Flammarion, 1970); translated by James Dickoff and Patricia James as *The Art of Thinking* (Indianapolis: Bobbs-Merrill, 1964). Noam Chomsky, *Cartesian Linguistics: A Chapter in the History of Rationalist Thought* (New York: Harper & Row, 1966). Marc Fumaroli, *L'âge de l'éloquence: Rhétorique et "res literaria" de la Renaissance au seuil de l'époque classique* (Geneva: Droz, 1980). Wilbur S. Howell, *Logic and Rhetoric in England, 1500–1700* (Princeton: Princeton University Press, 1956). Pierre Le Moyne, *Les peintures morales, où les passions sont représentées par tableaux, par charactères, & par questions nouvelles & curieuses* (Paris: Cramoisy, 1640). Walter Ong, S.J., *Ramus, Method, and the Decay of Dialogue* (Cambridge, Mass.: Harvard University Press, 1958). Timothy J. Reiss, *The Discourse of Modernism* (Ithaca: Cornell University Press,

1982). Claude Favre de Vaugelas, *Remarques sur la langue françoise,* ed. Jeanne Streicher (Paris: Droz, 1934).

Timothy J. Reiss

✍ 1647

The Duc de Luynes and René Descartes Translate the Latter's
Meditationes de Prima Philosophia into French

The Subject of Modern Discourse

In 1647, at the publication of *Méditations sur la philosophie première* (*Meditations on First Philosophy*), the French translation of René Descartes's *Meditationes de Prima Philosophia* (1641) undertaken by the duc de Luynes and revised by Descartes himself, the fifty-one-year-old author was one of the most respected philosophers of the time, sought equally by intellectuals, aristocrats, and monarchs. Yet since 1628 he had led a semisecluded existence in Holland, remote from the religious controversies and wars in France and from the close supervision of the Catholic church.

Descartes had been educated at the Jesuit collège of La Flèche and at the University of Poitiers. A memorable event of these years was Galileo's discovery of Jupiter's satellites in 1611, an important piece of evidence for the validity of the Copernican theory. While serving in the army of Maurice of Nassau, in 1619 Descartes experienced a quasi-mystical revelation, which led to his decision to devote his life to study. After a period of travels (1620–1625), followed by a short stay in Paris (1626–1628), he settled in Holland. There he wrote a treatise, *Le monde* (1664; *The World*), a comprehensive view of the universe at odds with the prevalent Aristotelian physics. Galileo's condemnation by the church in 1633 made him decide not to publish it.

Like Galileo, Descartes based his physics on mathematics and observation. The severity with which Catholic theologians met Galileo's theories convinced Descartes that the scientific description of the world had to be backed up by unimpeachable philosophical legitimation. The *Discours de la méthode* (*Discourse on Method*), first published in French in Holland in 1637 as an introduction to three fragments of his earlier treatise, is a philosophical manifesto advocating systematic and rational scientific inquiry against both the Aristotelian physics of late scholasticism and the materialist philosophy and Epicurean ethics of Pierre Gassendi (1592–1655), who stressed the importance of experience and mistrusted speculative systems. The first, autobiographical chapter asserts the writer's honesty of purpose. The second focuses on the author's solitude while he conceived the project of universal knowledge, an analogy to monastic isolation. The third chapter defends morality and tradition; the fourth includes a proof of God's existence. Only the last two chapters deal with science proper and with the project of rational knowledge—and mastery—of the universe.

The *Discours* went unnoticed. Soon, in 1641, after circulating it among philosophers and theologians, Descartes published his *Meditationes de Prima Philo-*

sophia, an expanded philosophical defense of rationalism followed by objections from important writers and the author's answers. For a revolutionary doctrine to acknowledge its adversaries was a particularly apt way of preempting condemnation. The success of the work was considerable; it led not only to the preparation of a French translation, but also to a pressing invitation from Queen Christina of Sweden to come to Stockholm, where Descartes died in 1650.

Descartes's work has been acclaimed as a turning point in modern philosophy. But his achievements cannot be described as the result of a single-purpose mind. There are several different Descartes. The first, best known, and most often referred to is the modern scientist and philosopher of knowledge, who created analytical geometry, made invaluable contributions to mathematics, physics, astronomy, anatomy, physiology, and medicine, and felt confident enough about his knowledge to write a full description of the world. This is how the mature Descartes must have perceived himself: as the conceptual master of a vast and complete empirical universe, swarming with a multitude of terrestrial and celestial bodies, all existing by virtue of purely spatial extension and obeying the immutable mathematical laws that God created together with the world.

In the wake of Galilean mechanics, Descartes changed the mode of philosophical speculation. Scholastic ratiocination gave way to a method borrowed from mathematical thought, in which maximal concentration of attention is deemed sufficient for discovery of evident truths. Hence the central place of the conscious subject who, through mastery of the power of attention, methodically finds the first principles and combines them into a perfect doctrine. The *Discours de la méthode* teaches that, like mathematical notions, philosophical concepts and propositions should be clear—that is, accessible to intuition and distinct from one another, and thus susceptible to rational manipulation. Difficulties are better handled by division into smaller problems. Thought should proceed in orderly fashion from simple to complex questions, and all cases should be covered. In a first stage, these requirements lead to universal doubt, since, in the world of common sense and tradition, nothing qualifies as certain knowledge, and our present certitudes, including those originating with the senses, might be illusions triggered by the deceptive powers of an evil genius. Doubt has a limit, however; one cannot doubt that one doubts: I think, therefore I exist. And whereas I exist as a finite thinking substance, God must exist by virtue of my possessing the idea of an infinite perfect being. Indeed, because such an idea is beyond the generative power of a finite intellect, it must have been sown there by the infinite being itself. Moreover, since a perfect, infinite being cannot be suspected of deceiving us, empirical and mathematical truths cannot be doubted either.

Descartes's science is thus rooted in theology. Behind the standard image of Descartes—the heroic founder of modern epistemology—there lurks a second Descartes, a maverick late-scholastic thinker, tormented by the philosophical consequences of the recent alliance between mathematics and physics. This is the Descartes who, on the one hand, fought hard against the skeptics and, on the other, attempted to infuse new life into the Aristotelian and medieval doctrine of the analogy of being, according to which, despite the radical difference that separates God from his creatures, they share being and other properties in an analogical way. Descartes's purpose was at once to build a solid foundation for the newly created nonspeculative physics and to construct an irrefutable theology. For, like all his contemporaries, Descartes, though a revolutionary by virtue of his interest in mathematical certainty, reflected at length on the analogies and differences between man and God.

One step further behind Descartes's philosophical mask is a third Descartes—the Rosicrucian and mystic. At the beginning of the 17th century, only a few thinkers interested in the natural sciences and medicine had fully detached themselves from the magic ties of the Renaissance and from the pantheistic vision of the world as a great occult whole, governed by the laws of universal sympathy. The third Descartes still believed in the secret marriage of heaven and earth: he was the dreamer who discovered his intellectual call through three confusing visions and chose to become a philosopher only after experiencing an overpowering revelation. It is this third Descartes who, according to some, was indirectly influenced by the Rosicrucian sect.

A fourth, less often noticed, Descartes is the· lonely wanderer. Both the young mercenary soldier crossing Europe and the thinker searching for truth through the maze of doubt are heroes of quest romances. Recent critics and philosophers have analyzed the literary aspects of the *Discours* and the *Méditations*, noting the influence of the genre of spiritual meditations and the use of rhetoric. Seen as narratives, they tell the story of the quest for knowledge; yet, lacking a strong conflict, they display no genuine plot. Descartes's lonely journey toward truth lacks theatrical tension and, above all, an adversary. Amélie Oksenberg Rorty observes that the *Meditations* follows the model of spiritual literature: the steps by which the mind advances toward knowledge are similar to those in the soul's journey to God. Most religious meditations, however, emphasize the spiritual struggle of the soul against its mortal enemy, the devil, whose reality and power are never questioned. In Descartes's *Méditations*, the mind lacks a real adversary; therefore it must concoct "un malin génie," some evil genius "of utmost power and cunning," who "has employed all his energies in order to deceive me" (*Meditations*, p. 15). But the struggle is soon over: in spite of "the delusions of dreams which he has devised to ensnare my judgment," the imaginary adversary vanishes as soon as the narrator finds his first single certitude: that, since he thinks, he exists. The antagonist is not defeated; rather, it turns out that he never existed.

Traditional quest narratives, set in a world governed by stable norms, gradually lead the hero through increasingly difficult tests toward a final state of integration. But in Descartes's narrative the quest does not depend on an external normative authority that decides on the ordeals, administers them, and judges how well the hero has fared. All doubts, antagonists, and temptations in the *Méditations* are set by the narrator-hero himself. All ordeals are self-inflicted. The final decision is made by the epistemological hero, who is at once judge and judged, master and subject.

There is, then, a feature common to Descartes the adventurer, Descartes the founder of modern epistemology, and Descartes the late scholastic: to deploy their arguments, they all displace the rules of the game: Descartes the epistemologist discards Aristotelian physics without examining it; Descartes the scholastic takes a provocative stand on the question of the analogy of being, without ever mentioning the complex discussions that his own theology strives to make obsolete. As in the Cartesian quest, these philosophical assertions dispense with the accepted forms of legitimation, replacing them with a new, self-legitimating mastery over thought.

Indeed, the *Conversation avec Burman* (1648; *Conversation with Burman*) makes clear that, for Descartes, the mind is endowed with a faculty of self-control that recalls the aristocratic command of the self. Replying to Burman, a young Dutch admirer who emphasized the fleeting character of our mental operations, their independence from our will, and their radical temporality, Descartes stresses that thoughts are neither instantaneous nor isolated; like the passions of Corneille's heroes, they are fully governed by the ego.

Descartes's self-legitimating rationalism transformed 17th-century thought. Not only the Cartesians proper (the best known being Louis Géraud de Cordemoy), but also independent thinkers such as Antoine Arnauld (1612–1694), Blaise Pascal, Nicolas de Malebranche, Baruch Spinoza, and Gottfried Wilhelm von Leibniz were indebted to the Cartesian project.

One of Descartes's greatest innovations was to dispense with traditional Aristotelian concerns about the tensions between language and thought. Both Aristotelian and medieval logic were highly sensitive to the discrepancies between language and thought and their negative effects on the search for truth. Descartes's approach, modeled after mathematical reasoning, paid little attention to language, including the language of philosophy itself. Antoine Arnauld, the foremost theologian of the Jansenist group, who was strongly critical of Descartes's proofs for God's existence but admired his critique of skepticism and recognized "the third Descartes's" proximity to the traditions of St. Augustine and St. Anselm, attempted to render explicit the relations of the new philosophy with human language. Hence the Port-Royal *Logique* (1662) and *Grammaire* (1660), the first written in collaboration with Pierre Nicole, the second with Claude Lancelot. By stressing the closeness of language and thought, Arnauld and Nicole's *Logique* started from the Cartesian theory of clear and distinct ideas and developed an influential technique of rendering language as transparent and faithful to thought as possible.

Pascal's posthumous *Pensées* (1670), fragments of an unfinished apology for the Christian religion, express a more radical view of reason than Descartes's. A mathematician himself who, before his religious conversion in 1654, made important contributions to science, Pascal believed that rooting Christian theology in reason and transparency of language amounted to relinquishing revelation. Symptomatically, the *Pensées* are directed at the nonbeliever, who by definition does not accept the truth of the Bible. But instead of defending religion through rational arguments, Pascal starts by denouncing rational discourse. He uses skeptical arguments to demonstrate the instability and cultural relativity of human beliefs, thus undermining the rationalist claim to universality. Ironically, Pascal's views imply a double move related to language. On the one hand, he realizes that Descartes's ideal of complete linguistic clarity is impossible to attain, since any attempt to define all our words must necessarily rest on a few undefined primitive terms. On the other hand, as a representative of the classical tradition, Pascal writes as if language unproblematically reflected thought. His confidence in language is perhaps related to the tempered nature of his skepticism. Although mistrust of reason leads him to rely on the heart, he nevertheless avoids complete incertitude, since the dictates of the heart teach us to listen to some extent to reason, feeble as it is. Pascal does not reject the validity of scientific discourse at its own level; he only aims at subordinating the order of truth to a more complete view of the human condition. We are at once great, by virtue of our intellect, and miserable, by virtue of its fragility. "It is dangerous to explain too clearly to man how like he is to animals without pointing out his greatness. It is also dangerous to make too much of his greatness without his vileness" (*Pensées*, p. 60). No philosophy, Pascal claims, draws an accurate picture of our paradoxical nature. The closest approximation to it Pascal finds in the Augustinian doctrine of original sin, which explains the feeble greatness of humans as a vestige of God's original purpose in creating them, and their wretchedness as resulting from the Fall. Philosophical reflection inevitably leads to religion.

The persecution of Port-Royal and the Jansenists during the second half of the century weakened the chance for Pascal's critique to be heard. The dominant forces of French Catholicism were more ready to compromise with a watered-down version of Cartesian rationalism that was also palatable to monarchy, than with the extreme vision of Pascal, with its sharp distinction between scientific knowledge and religion. Later, Romanticism and existentialism would take up Pascal's themes.

See also 1555 (13 September), 1640, 1668, 1761 (December).

Bibliography: Jean-Marie Beyssade, *La philosophie première de Descartes* (Paris: Flammarion, 1979). René Descartes, *Meditations on First Philosophy,* trans. John Cottingham (Cambridge: Cambridge University Press, 1986). Marjorie Greene, *Descartes* (Minneapolis: University of Minnesota Press, 1979). Jean-Luc Marion, *Sur le prisme métaphysique de Descartes* (Paris: Presses Universitaires de France, 1986). Blaise Pascal, *Pensées,* trans. A. J. Krailsheimer (New York: Penguin, 1966). Amélie Oksenberg Rorty, *Essays on Descartes's Meditations* (Berkeley: University of California Press, 1986).

Thomas G. Pavel

✑ 1648, 26–28 August
Barricades Are Built in the Center of Paris

The Sound of the Fury

Historical texts are commonly taken to be reflections of events and are read as such. But certain writings about current events do not stop at distorting the facts or twisting their meaning; when they also function as catalyst of events, they become events themselves. This is the case with incendiary accounts whose violence supersedes the political clashes they claim to describe.

The period of civil war known as the Fronde began in Paris in May 1648, when the Parlement opposed measures announced by Jules Cardinal Mazarin to increase revenues and further consolidate the growing power of the monarchy; it ended in February 1653, when Mazarin returned to Paris from Saint-Germain, where the court had taken refuge. During these five years three heterogeneous groups formed a tenuous alliance against the crown: members of the Parlement, who had been humiliated by Richelieu; the great aristocrats, deprived of their powers by the absolutist centralization; and the ordinary people, who felt most acutely the effects of excessive taxation and the economic declines caused by foreign wars, and who also resented the foreign prime minister, Mazarin. During the insurrection, the slingshot (*fronde*) used was often a printed one. Official newspapers and private gazettes, memoirs and biographical writings, pamphlets and political tracts proliferated to press the representation of historical reality into the battle for opinion. In this first form of a now-familiar struggle to capture public opinion, information, disinformation, and polemic rubbed elbows in the turmoil of political crisis.

Two types of text bore witness to the struggles of the Fronde: journals and memoirs that purported to present an objective view and the overtly inflammatory pamphlets generally referred to as *les Mazarinades,* after the title of Paul Scarron's 1651 contribution to the genre. But the distinction is not always easy to make. Even accounts claiming to be objective contain distortions reflecting the witness's proximity to events, degree of involvement, or allegiance to one camp or the other. With the relation between historical account and historical referent thus blurred, we must wonder which one really created the other and shaped posterity's perceptions of them. In the case of the Mazarinades' polemical texts, it is clear that writing incited political event.

The Parlement had just refused to approve Mazarin's latest tax. On 26 August 1648 at about one o'clock in the afternoon, after a *Te Deum* was sung at Notre-Dame in celebration of the prince de Condé's victory over the Spanish at Lens, Anne of Austria, the regent queen since Louis XIII's death in 1643, had the aging counselor Pierre Broussel and several members of the Parlement arrested. Rumor of the arrests spread throughout the city, shops closed, groups formed, vagabonds pillaged. In the center of Paris, bourgeois drew chains tightly across the streets for fear of the growing popular rabble, blocking the way of about fifty soldiers commanded by the maréchal Charles de La Meilleraye. Accompanying them was Jean-François Paul de Gondi, the future cardinal de Retz, at the time coadjutor of Paris' archbishop, who had tried in vain to calm the crowd. All were forced to withdraw toward the Palais-Royal under a hail of stones. On the following night the barricades were raised.

These few hours were recorded by clerks close to the members of the Parlement. Their accounts, published in the official *Registres de l'Hôtel de Ville de Paris,* clearly overstate the events. Reading almost like tape-recorded journalism, the document reports: "None of that could have happened without a lot of noise and commotion . . . someone was ringing the alarm . . . the fer-rymen were armed and crying, 'Kill! Kill!'" (*Registres*, 1:447). Yet, as soon afterward as 29 August the *Gazette du Parlement*, playing the card of reconcilia-tion, refers to the same scene as merely a "rumor that was hardly stirred up before being calmed," one that "did not prevent cries of 'long live the king!'" (The latter account, though possibly true, muffles the "sound" of events.) And, in a report addressed on 28 August 1648 to the governor of Provence by Henri-Auguste Loménie de Brienne, the secretary of state, a few echoes of pillage are all that remain against a backdrop of general calm. The role of Retz goes unmentioned.

In the retrospective accounts in memoirs, the manipulation of sound is even more pronounced. Bussy-Rabutin (Roger de Rabutin de Bussy), in Calais with Condé's victorious army, notes rather flatly on 30 August: "Everywhere they made barricades" (*Mémoires*, 1:170). Nor does La Rochefoucauld, who was staying in his domain in Guyenne, comment at length. Meanwhile, the accounts of those close to the scene vary on their interpretation of what was to be heard. Dubuisson-Aubenay (François-Nicolas Baudot) registers the cobble-stones, the guns, and the dead in his *Journal des guerres civiles* and notes that people were yelling simultaneously "Long live the king!" and "Free the pris-oners!" (*Journal*, pp. 50–56). Mathieu Molé, instead of a panoramic view of the riot, offers a close-up of "an unfortunate girl who, pretending to cry, was shouting 'Give me back M. de Broussel!'" (*Mémoires*, 3:26 August).

But the most partisan memoirs stage fully orchestrated productions. Fran-çoise Bertaut de Motteville, the queen's confidante, expressing the fear of the court, turns up the volume of popular tumult: "An old woman began to shout from her house . . . they began to shout . . . they were all there shouting in the streets like maniacs that they were done for" (*Mémoires*, 2:153). Retz, the darling of the insurgents, transforms the vociferous cries into a silence dumb-founded by his eloquence; and the tragic scramble, into a procession directed by himself. An incoherent and collective cacophony turns into symbolic self-promotion. At first, "The people exploded all at once: they were aroused, they yelled, they closed the shops" (*Mémoires*, p. 215). All is sound and fury. But Retz, having donned his ecclesiastical dress, penetrates the tempest: "I was overwhelmed by a crowd of people who were roaring more than they were shouting." In the midst of this clamor, his voice alone carries the day: "I extri-cated myself by telling them that the queen would do them justice." And after having freed La Meilleraye (oratory rescuing armed force), he leaves followed "by an infinite number of people" (p. 216). His elocutionary magic transforms the roaring tide into an orderly procession. In contrast, his adversary Motteville portrays the populace ceaselessly uttering "horrible curses" and refusing to listen to the coadjutor. Guy Joly, Retz's secretary, also observes that the people "would not refrain from shouting" and reveals that they threw stones at the coadjutor (*Mémoires*, 1:21).

Thus in texts in which some kind of pact of truth is implied between author and reader, the narrative tonalities can differ widely for a single event. Nor are polemical texts any more uniform. Whether amplified or silenced, the shouts betray a *lack:* the absence of a discourse that would capture the "sounds" of real facts—insignificant events by themselves—in order to call forth in response other words that would convey, if not an ideology or even an opinion, at least a meaning for these events and would thus orient future movements and rumors. Among these future manifestations were the Mazarinades.

The word *pamphlet* (libel) appeared in French in 1653, in response to the need for a new generic designation that would encompass the mass of small-format lampoons published during the years of the Fronde. The title of one of them, a satirical epic, *La Mazarinade* (1651), attributed to Paul Scarron, became the generic name for the more than 5,000 polemical works for and against Mazarin that flooded Paris during the troubles. These pamphlets ranged from one to 400 pages (although most were brief) and had press runs of from 500 to 1,000 copies, with uneven levels of production from year to year (2,000 in 1649; 500 in 1650; 1,500 in 1652). Published by hired professionals (Condé had presses in his townhouse; Retz used the diocesan printing house; and the court, that of Théophraste Renaudot), written by pamphleteers recruited from influential coteries (Claude Du Bosc de Montandré, Isaac Laffemas, Claude de Verderonne) or from among the literati (Scarron, Cyrano de Bergerac, Jean-François Sarasin, Olivier Patru, Jacques Carpentier de Marigny), they were distributed by venders who hawked their headlines on the Pont-Neuf. Such was their success that *L'adieu et le désespoir des auteurs et écrivains de la guerre civile* (1649; *The Farewell and Despair of the Authors and Writers of the Civil War*) could suggest: "Half of Paris prints and sells printed matter; the other half consumes it" (Moreau, *Choix de Mazarinades,* 1:520). Notwithstanding an element of ironic and nostalgic exaggeration in such a statement of sympathy for those writers whose job it had been to fuel the fight to which the treaty of Saint-Germain threatened to bring an end, an immense output and an impassioned reception did occur, tied to a sudden cultural fashion as much as to the political context.

The riot of August 1648 is an important rallying point of this literature. *Agréables conférences de deux paysans de Saint-Ouen et de Montmorency* (*Pleasing Lectures by Two Peasants from Saint-Ouen and Montmorency*) relates it in a pseudorustic patois, with effective use of wordplay (Retz, the coadjutor, is "le couarjuteux," the "juicy coward"). Saint-Julien's *Les courriers de la Fronde en vers burlesques* (1650; *Correspondence of the Fronde in Burlesque Verse*), though burlesque, attempts to make the rebels honorable: "There is nearly no more rabble / 'Mongst this people prone to babble" (but "plenty decent folk") (*Courriers,* 1:71). Other Mazarinades used the weapon of laughter against the uprising. Verderonne, in his *Agréable récit* (1649; *Pleasing Narration*), discredits in succession the rivals of his master, the duc d'Orléans. In a parody of epic, he brags that he plans to "sing the barricades," but he transforms them grotesquely: "At market and in the vicinity / People take refuge behind chestnuts / Behind pumpkins and rotten apples / Behind artichokes, brie cheese," and "quite foul-smelling shallots" (Moreau, *Choix,* 1:16). There were also "serious" Mazarinades. But all had the same objective: to manipulate the public. There is no real argumentation, no theoretical justification, no empirical evidence: all is reiteration of affirmations for or against. The terrain of the Mazarinades is one of propaganda and polemic.

Subsequent literature bore traces of this sonorous and often grotesque battle of books. Some allusions are direct: Aeneas' opponents are called *frondeurs* in Scarron's *Virgile travesti* (1648–1652; *Virgil Disguised*); a "state criminal" entrusts to Orgon his compromising casket in Molière's *Tartuffe* (1664–1669); political reflections are transposed in the context of dramatic works, such as Corneille's *Nicomède* (1651) and *Pertharite* (1653). There are also indirect traces: stylistic (through the continued popularity of burlesque), thematic (La Roche-foucauld's emphasis, in the *Maximes* [1665], on the ambiguous nature of com-mitments, or Scarron's and Antoine Furetière's challenges of the heroic values in their parodic novels *Le roman comique* [1651, 1657; *The Comic Novel*] and *Le roman bourgeois* [1666; *The Bourgeois Novel*]), economic (with the slowing down of private patronage and the stagnation of theater), and, above all, ideological (through the discovery of the polemical might of the printed word, a lesson not lost on Pascal, the polemicist of *Les lettres provinciales;* 1656–57; *Provincial Let-ters*). Finally, in revealing the lack of a true instrument for the people's voice, the Mazarinades manifested an issue still unresolved in 1789, and in doing so disclosed the fundamental role of discourse in the construction of the event.

Bibliography: Henri-Auguste de Loménie de Brienne, *Mémoires du comte de Brienne,* vol. 27 of *Nouvelle collection des Mémoires relatifs à l'histoire de France depuis le XIII siècle jusqu'à la fin du XVIII siècle,* ed. Michaud et Poujoulat (Paris: Didier, 1857). Bussy-Rabutin, *Mémoires,* vol. 1. (Amsterdam: Vacquerie Châtelain, 1731). Dubuisson-Aubenay, *Journal des guerres civiles,* ed. G. Saige, vol. 1 (Paris: Champion, 1883–1885). Guy Joly, *Mémoires,* vol. 1 (Rotterdam: De Leers, 1718). Christian Jouhaud, *Mazari-nades: La Fronde des mots* (Paris: Aubier, 1985). Mathieu Molé, *Mémoires,* vol. 3 (Paris: Société de l'Histoire de France, 1856). Célestin Moreau, ed., *Choix de Mazarinades,* 2 vols. (Paris: J. Renouard, 1853). Madame de Motteville, *Mémoires,* ed. Francis Riaux, vol. 2 (Paris: G. Charpentier, 1891). Roland Mousnier, *La plume, la faucille et le marteau* (Paris: Presses Universitaires de France, 1970). *Registres de l'Hôtel de Ville de Paris pendant la Fronde,* 3 vols. (1846–1848; reprint, Paris: Johnson, 1966). Cardinal de Retz, *Mémoires et Mazarinades,* ed. Marie-Thérèse Hipp and Michel Pernot (Paris: Gallimard, 1984). Saint-Julien, *Les courriers de la Fronde en vers burlesques,* ed. Célestin Moreau, 2 vols. (Paris: Jannet, 1857).

Pierre Ronzeaud

 1651

In *Le roman comique* Paul Scarron Describes the Misadventures of a Theatrical Company Traveling through Maine

Cultural Life outside Paris

When Antoine Furetière, in his *Dictionnaire universel* (1690; *Universal Diction-ary*), defined the provincial as a "man who does not have the looks and life-style of people at court or in the capital," he confirmed a distinction and a derogation already discernible in *Les caractères, ou les moeurs de ce siècle* (1688–1696; *Characters*) of the moralist Jean de La Bruyère, as well as in certain plays of Molière: *Les précieuses ridicules* (1659; *The Precious Damsels*), for example, asserts that "outside Paris there is no refuge for polite people" (scene 9); and in *La comtesse d'Escarbagnas* (1672), the provincials are mimics of polite society and unwitting parodists of gallant style whose only resources are their "stupidity" and "foolishness."

The Parisian hegemony arose from the convergence of several factors. Undoubtedly foremost among them was the political centralization reinforced by Cardinal Richelieu, which under Louis XIV would find its symbolic expression in the myth of the Sun King. The effects of centralization were reinforced in turn by the illiteracy of a large majority of the French population and by the incomplete linguistic unification of the kingdom (a situation compounded during Louis XIV's reign by the annexation of new provinces: Alsace in 1648, Roussillon and Artois in 1659, Franche-Comté in 1678). The regions near Paris that had, since the 16th century, contributed so significantly to the national heritage (Ile-de-France, Touraine, Normandy, and Champagne) still benefited from being in the capital's orbit, but the Loire River traced a physical and cultural frontier between the north, with its preponderant cultural authority, and a south pejoratively designated the land of *galimatias* (gibberish) and of *adiousas* (*adieu* in *langue d'oc*). Finally, the system of *privilèges*—the exclusive rights of publication granted to printer/booksellers by the king's council—worked to the advantage of the capital, especially after 1665, when Louis XIV's minister, Jean-Baptiste Colbert, tightened the procedures. The provincial presses survived on the reprinting of traditionally popular standard works, such as devotional books, and Parisian works currently in vogue. The centralized control of printing accounts for the decline of the publishing industry even in Lyons, which, located on a main axis of communication, the valley of the Rhône, had been, with Rouen and Paris, among the most active publishing centers since the beginning of printing.

However, Paris and the provinces did not constitute two independent spheres. The social mobility of writers makes their place of origin or residence a fragile criterion of identification. Although it might have been legitimate for a province to claim for its own the son who made a name for himself in the capital's salons, nobody in Paris would have associated Gilles Ménage's work with Anjou, where he was born; considered Madeleine de Scudéry and Pierre Corneille simply as Normans, Jean de La Fontaine as Champenois; or characterized the marquise de Sévigné as a Breton because of her frequent stays in Rochers. Contemporary correspondences—so numerous that many are still unpublished—attest to a widespread and intense interest for recent publications throughout Europe: clerics, scholars, and men of culture watched impatiently for the new arrivals. The uninterrupted proliferation of periodicals attests to the wide dissemination of "literary" information—in the 17th century, literature included everything grounded in textual erudition, including, according to Furetière, physics, geology, and the physical sciences—outward from Paris and the few other intellectual centers to the remote provinces as well as to foreign countries; their diffusion and circulation modernized the flow of information that had been sustained, during the era of humanism, by young scholars' pilgrimages from library to library.

The influence of the Parisian model was visible in the institutions established in several provincial cities, and subsequently in their activities. Societies and reading or discussion groups often served as seedbeds for later academies that received letters patent and charters approved by the Académie Française. An Academy of Wit and Gallantry, founded in Arles in 1622, became the Academy of the Poem in Set Rhymes in 1661, and seven years later a royal academy. In Caen in 1652 Moisant des Brieux formed a group to "read the gazette and see the new books." In Toulouse, beginning in 1642, Paul Pellisson-Fontanier, future historian of the Académie Française, joined the group of local literati called—probably because of their late meetings—the Lanternistes. A useful tool of cultural unification and ideological control, the network of provincial academies expanded with Parisian backing: academies were established in Castres (by Pellisson, in 1648), Soissons (1673–1675), Angers (1685). Their few members consisted of nobles, clerics, and, above all, "men of the robe," that is, members of the Third Estate, such as lawyers and members of parlement. (Booksellers and printers often set up shop near houses of parlement.) The academies' activities consisted largely of speeches and eulogies, readings of local literary pieces, discussions of works from Paris, debates about questions of language and style. Religious, political, or philosophical controversies were carefully excluded as divisive topics.

Paul Scarron's *Le roman comique* (1651, 1657; *The Comic Novel*) illustrates the ambiguities attending Parisian dominance and provincial intellectual life. The son of a counselor in Paris' Parlement, a writer of burlesque and political poetry (including numerous lampoons attacking Jules Cardinal Mazarin, such as *La Mazarinade,* 1651) who spent some time in the service of the bishop of Le Mans, Scarron follows the misadventures of a traveling theatrical company in the Maine region, with a picturesque flair that Théophile Gautier recalled in *Le capitaine Fracasse* (1863; *Captain Fracasse*). In Scarron's human comedy actors named Le Destin (Destiny) and L'Etoile (Star) rub shoulders with diverse social types (the hack-writer Ragotin, an innkeeper, a groom, a provincial wit who imitates Parisian gallantries). To the vogue of the pastoral novel, with its fiction of an idealized world, Scarron's narrative, with its choice of characters and setting, opposed an exercise in social realism that served simultaneously as a tool for mockery: the adjective *comique,* which Furetière defined, referring to *Le roman comique,* as "joking and amusing," underscores the change in tone and its demystifying purpose.

But, unlike Benech de Cantenac's *Mercure dolent* (1678; *Mercury Whining*), which depicts daily life in Bordeaux, *Le roman comique* is concerned less with offering a picture of provincial life than with providing a devalued and ridiculous image of it to its Parisian audience. Every detail of dress or material existence, with special emphasis on the ridiculous and ugly, is described with all the stylistic refinements that indicate a cultural and literary complicity between the author and his readers. Modern critics have focused on Scarron's virtuosic handling of multiple genres and techniques: Spanish short stories interspersed in the narration; parodies and pastiches of heroic or gallant style; direct authorial interventions to underscore an effect, to remark on an attitude, or to display the flippancy of a transition. These diverse signs of an ever-alert aesthetic consciousness mark the contrast between subject matter and artistic manner that defines the burlesque—a style very much in vogue from 1643 to 1650, and which Scarron, with the poet Antoine de Saint-Amant, initiated. The same contrast or disunity is discernible in the relations between Paris and the provinces.

But although the provinces lived in the shadow of Paris, they did not always keep to its rhythm. They imprinted a cultural style of their own on their activities. The itinerant theatrical troupes, for example, whose repertoires included mimes and farces as well as comedies and tragedies, attracted an audience drawn from all social spheres. Such was the troupe the young Molière organized after the failure of L'Illustre-Théâtre. From 1645 to 1658 the company traveled from Toulouse to Agen, Pézenas, and Montpellier, while Molière performed his apprenticeship as an actor, dramatic author, and company director before returning to Paris.

Whatever their region, provincial writers were less sensitive to the hierarchy of genres established by Parisian theorists. The result was more diversified literary activity. Celebrations of public events (royal entrances, eulogies, funeral orations), local history, works of jurisprudence or devotion, versified complaints about the woes of the age appeared alongside plays, poetry, or novels that often reflected Parisian models. With *Chevilles* (1644; *Pegs*) and *Villebrequin* (1633; *Brace*), Adam Billaut, poet and carpenter from Nevers—known as "the Virgil of the plane"—achieved a success that reached all the way to the capital.

The slower rhythm of provincial life rather than the relative slowness of communications probably accounts for the persistence in the provinces of Latin as a literary language and of a taste for erudition at a time when, in Paris, scholarship was becoming confined to the universities and when the emergence of new social types—the *galant homme* (gentleman), the *honnête homme* (honorable man), the *bel esprit* (wit)—was eclipsing and discrediting pedants such as Hortensius in Charles Sorel's *Histoire comique de Francion* (1623–1633; *Comic History of Francion*) or Vadius and Trissotin in Molière's *Les femmes savantes* (1672; *The Learned Ladies*). As individual taste (even if it was entirely a product of culture) predominated over "the encrusted knowledge of pedants" (Molière), Parisians relegated these outdated forms and genres to the provinces: "Farce diverts still more than comedy, as one can generally see everywhere except in Paris . . . Comedy is completely purged today, at least in Paris, of its licentious side" (*Le roman comique*, pp. 224, 249). Furetière, in his tableau of literary France, *Nouvelle allégorique* (1658; *Allegorical Novella*), makes Galimatias, "an obscure man, born of the dregs of the people" (p. 11), the captain of provincials and prince of the outmoded.

Finally, provincial writers produced works in dialect, reflecting a popular culture on the fringes of the literary. The regional languages sustained their vitality in Normandy, the Basque region, and Burgundy. Racine, during his sojourn in the southern town of Uzès in 1661–62, surprised by the strength of this phenomenon, comments on it in his letters: "I do not understand the French of this region and they do not understand mine . . . I am in danger of soon forgetting the little French I know; I unlearn it every day, and I hardly speak anything but the language of this country which is no more French than 'low Breton' " (*Oeuvres complètes,* 2 : 405, 410). Popular provincial literature was promoted by the Bibliothèque Bleue (Blue Library), little volumes with blue paper covers published in Troyes by Nicolas Oudot and disseminated by peddlers: medieval legends, almanacs, brochures expressing the misery of the people in times of famine. This was an authorless literature, in Geneviève Bollème's words a "lost literature," and in terms of quantity it was the most important sector of provincial literature. Charles Perrault, author of *Histoires, ou contes du temps passé, avec des moralités* (1697; *Stories, or Tales from Olden Days, together with Moralities*), even found in it a chance to poke fun at his enemy Nicolas Boileau, author of *L'art poétique* (1674; *The Art of Poetry*): "It is in vain that he glories in the market for his satires; their dissemination will never come close to that of the least important almanac printed in Troyes" (*L'apologie des femmes* [1694; *The Apology to Women*], p. 8).

Away from the society of Paris and Versailles, whether through choice, resignation, financial need, failure of a career, or political disgrace, some scholars, philosophers, and men of letters still produced distinctive works. After traveling in Italy and England, Claude Fabri de Peiresc (1580–1637) settled in his native Provence and gathered together in his residence at Belgentier, which was both a library and a museum, scientific and literary information and cultural artifacts from all over Europe. He left behind unpublished notes, essays, innumerable letters, and a European reputation. Jean Louis Guez de Balzac (1595?–1654), dubbed "the hermit of Charente" or "the great letter-writer of France" by his contemporaries, repaired to his manor near Angoulême when his Parisian ambitions were disappointed, and from there he sent to Paris and throughout Europe eloquent letters in which the models of modern prose were forged, as well as political (*Le prince,* 1631), moral (*Socrate chrétien,* 1652; *Christian Socrates*), and literary treatises (*Oeuvres diverses* [1644; *Miscellanies*]; *Entretiens* [1657; *Conversations*]); Guez de Balzac, heir to all the philosophical knowledge of the humanist age, kept strong ties with the salon of the Hôtel de Rambouillet and the poet Vincent Voiture, and through his correspondence his opinions influenced the formation of French classical style in Paris. François Maynard (1582–1646), a disciple of François de Malherbe and an Academician, composed at Aurillac and Saint-Céré, not far from Guez de Balzac's Charente, the main body of his letters and his poetry, love stanzas, and eulogies of his protectors or of pastoral life, while his hopes for a career vanished.

But, on the whole, in contrast to the 16th century, when Joachim du Bellay brought fame to Anjou, Rabelais to Chinonais, Ronsard to Vendômois, Maurice

Scève and Louise Labé to Lyons, Montaigne to Guyenne, the 17th century is marked by the fecundity of Parisian literature. Through the multiple splits and oppositions then operative in France (city/country; elite/common people; written culture/oral culture; Latin/French; Ancients/Moderns), Paris became the fulcrum of literary fortune.

The triumph of worldliness simultaneously vanquished Latin and the republic of letters, which was henceforth confined to erudite circles and to the provinces. Voltaire's canonization of the "Century of Louis XIV," the Versailles myth, and the conception of Enlightenment Europe as centered in France, all contributed to the neglect of literary life outside Paris. But the development of a national educational system and erudite research by local archaeological societies in the 19th century, the Romantics' interest in history and in the common people, Gustave Lanson's groundbreaking 1903 article on provincial literary history, the new materials gathered by "neohistorical" researchers, and recent attempts to revive regional elements that resisted the traditional Paris-centered patterns have restored balance to the portrayal of 17th-century literary life.

See also 1657, 1673.

Bibliography: André Berry, "Les littératures du domaine d'oc," in *Histoire des littératures,* ed. Raymond Queneau, vol. 3 (Paris: Gallimard, 1967), 1504–1564. Geneviève Bollème, *La bibliothèque bleue* (Paris: Julliard, 1971). Antoine Furetière, *Nouvelle allégorique* (1658; reprint, Geneva: Van Gineken, 1967). Gustave Lanson, "Programme d'études sur l'histoire provinciale de la vie littéraire en France," *Revue d'histoire moderne et contemporaine,* 4 (1903), 445–464; reprinted in *Essais de méthode, de critique et d'histoire littéraire,* ed. Henri Peyre (Paris: Hachette, 1965). H. J. Martin, *Livre, pouvoirs et société à Paris au XVIIe siècle* (Geneva: Droz, 1969). Charles Perrault, *L'apologie des femmes* (Paris: Jean-Baptiste Coignard, 1694). Maurice Piron, "Les littératures dialectales du domaine d'oïl," in Queneau, *Histoire des littératures,* 3:1455–1503. Jean Racine, *Oeuvres complètes,* vol. 2 (Paris: Gallimard, 1966). Paul Scarron, *Le roman comique* (Paris: Garnier-Flammarion, 1981). Alain Viala, *Naissance de l'écrivain* (Paris: Minuit, 1985). Chantal Vieuille, *Histoire régionale de la littérature en France,* vol. 1 (Paris: Plon, 1986).

Bernard Beugnot

 1654

In Her Novel, *Clélie,* Madeleine de Scudéry Inserts a Map That Will Chart Seduction Strategies among the Elite for Years to Come

The Salons, "Preciosity," and the Sphere of Women's Influence

Among the hits of the 1986–87 theater season in Paris was *Les salons,* a montage of the letters of two 18th-century leaders of salons, Marie Anne du Deffand and Julie de Lespinasse. A recent episode of "Apostrophes"—the amazingly popular weekly television program whose moderator, Bernard Pivot, gathers a group of authors together for a two-hour-long discussion of their works—was devoted to biographies of women who rose to prominence in the salons.

This mass marketing of illustrious literary women is not simply the product of recent feminist consciousness raising. In France, the notion that women played a crucial, perhaps even dominant, role in the development of modern French literary culture is a familiar one. It has been revived at regular intervals over the last three centuries whenever the integrity of the French state has been threatened. For example, perhaps the most sweeping claims about the role of literary women during the ancien régime were formulated in the darkest days of World War II. From his voluntary exile in America during the German occupation of France, Roger Picard, a prominent French political and economic historian, proclaimed the centrality of the salons to the development and the dissemination of French culture and civilization and predicted a parallel future role for this long-vanished women's movement: "Tomorrow, when France is delivered from the profaning presences that defile it, it will reconstitute itself . . . The salons will contribute to [this national reconstitution]" (*Les salons littéraires,* p. 14). However, this view of the salons as defenders of French nationalistic spirit in no way corresponds to the often subversive role the most prominent of these female assemblies played in the political life of the ancien régime.

The movement portrayed as paradise lost by Picard began around 1610 when a young noblewoman decided to stop frequenting Henry IV's still quite rustic court. Esteeming the level of politeness and wit there unacceptable, the marquise de Rambouillet (née Catherine de Vivonne de Savelli) simply created an alternative space. She served as her own architect for the reconstruction of a house near the Louvre: her crowning innovation was a suite of salons, leading one into the next, a style that would be much copied in the next decades. She thereby set the tone for French classical architecture, in which privacy is continually sacrificed for effect, in this case for drawing attention to the ultimate salon, a sort of inner sanctum. This room, known to all as the *chambre bleue,* became for decades one of the most important spaces in France: the marquise de Sévigné (née Marie de Rabutin-Chantal) claimed that for a time "the Hôtel de Rambouillet was the Louvre" (letter dated 12 January 1680). Within her blue room, the marquise de Rambouillet created an alternative court, a new center of power, a place where power was exercised through conversation. If conversation was not "born" in the salons, as has often been said, it did become in these assemblies a fine art, one that for centuries was discussed by foreign visitors like a monument worthy of the tourist's admiration. Good manners, wit, and, above all, conversational brilliance became the highest values. The *chambre bleue* and its habitués set the pattern for a style, both social and literary, that many have considered ever since the essence of the French style.

But the Hôtel de Rambouillet was a center of more than social refinement. For decades, many of the finest minds in France met there not only to discuss literature but also to set themselves up as arbiters of literary taste. With the marquise de Rambouillet acting as a moderator, the discussions were free-ranging, touching on the latest mode, whether linguistic, sartorial, or literary. The absolute distinction we make today between high and popular culture was not operative. The influence these informal debates had on the literary life of the age was immense: authors came there to read their works and await judgment. Corneille, for example, after reading *Polyeucte, martyr* (1643; *Saint Polyeuctus*) to the regulars, was unable to convince them that Christian tragedy had a future in France; young authors, such as La Rochefoucauld in 1631, received their first ideas of literary society there.

The salon was not the invention of the marquise de Rambouillet—similar assemblies had existed in the 16th century both in her native Italy and at the French court—nor was her blue room the uncontested literary control center of the day. But whereas the Académie Française, founded in 1634, was the first intellectual assembly created by the crown and invested with increasingly diversified powers—to act as a semiofficial court in literary quarrels, to edit a dictionary—in the republic of letters, the *chambre bleue* was the beginning of a salon tradition never equaled in any other country. Contemporary commentators reveal that the salons, which first proliferated in Paris, then spread to the provinces throughout the 17th century, were considered the private sector equivalent of the state-sponsored academies.

The official academies were visibly different because of their all-male membership. (Women are not banned in the charter of the Académie Française; we know that in the 1650s female members were proposed; we do not know the grounds on which they were excluded.) The salons, on the other hand, were a world presided over by women; each salon leader set the tone and determined the membership and, in large part, the subjects for discussion. Thus each salon had its own character and generally also its own designation. Their members referred to these gatherings either by the day of the week on which they met—thus "the Saturday" meant the weekly gathering at Madeleine de Scudéry's home in the Marais—or by an architectural term, such as *ruelle*, literally the space between the bed and the wall where the marquise de Rambouillet seated her regulars, whom she received lying in bed. *Ruelle* came to signify metonymically any salon assembly. The word *salon* itself entered the French language only after the Revolution had brought the assemblies of the ancien régime to an end. (The word seems to have first appeared in the 1807 novel *Corinne*, by Germaine de Staël, the last woman to preside over a true salon.)

It is fitting that these private academies were designated by temporal and spatial terms, for the essence of the salon's importance in literary life was bound up with its status as a world apart, a parallel sphere with its own rules, activities, and schedule. This is the only time in the history of the French literary tradition that a powerful phenomenon, a movement with important literary, social, often even political implications, was initiated by women. It remained under female control for nearly two centuries.

During their early years, the salons' impact was largely literary. Two genres—light, witty, occasional poetry associated with house poets such as Vincent Voiture, and letters created more as literary artifacts than as private documents—first really came into their own then and flourished for the remainder of the ancien régime. Many salons also became centers for a kind of linguistic

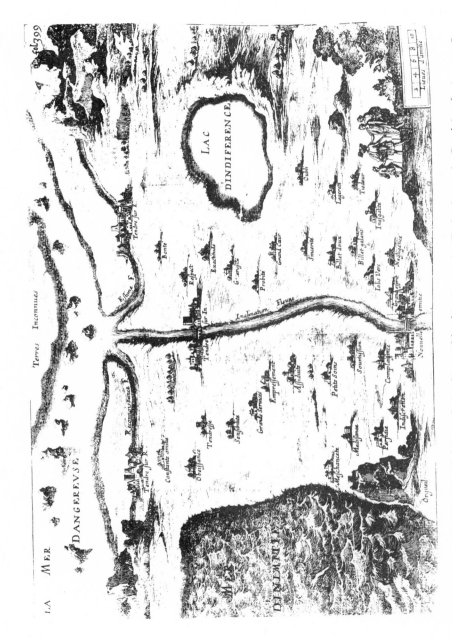

1. "La carte de Tendre," in Madeleine de Scudéry, *Clélie, histoire romaine* (Paris: Augustin Courbé, 1654), p. 398. (Courtesy of the Princeton University Library, Department of Rare Books and Special Collections.)

arbitration. Members debated correct usage in French, for the language was still far from codified. This is the origin of the assertion by the scholar Claude Favre de Vaugelas, in his *Remarques sur la langue française* (1647; *Remarks on the French Language*), that "in cases of doubt about language, it is ordinarily best to consult women" (p. 503). At several points in the salons' history, these debates turned into displays of linguistic invention that approximated attempts at creating private languages comprehensible only to the initiate.

To this blend of brilliant conversation, social refinement, and literary and linguistic deliberation was soon added the fourth component of the salon movement: political fermentation. From Cardinal Mazarin's secret notebooks we know that the prime minister, during the regency of Louis XIII's widow, Anne of Austria, used spies to infiltrate the salons. His strategy was justified, for the sedition that culminated in the Fronde (1648–1653), the uprising against Cardinal Mazarin during the early years of Louis XIV's reign, led, in its last stage, by members of the highest nobility, was fermented in drawing rooms and *ruelles*. These assemblies foreshadow the last great pre-Revolutionary salons, especially that of Staël's mother, Suzanne Necker, which beginning in the late 1760s was a center for the political opposition. During the Fronde French women—especially two noted salon figures, the Great Mademoiselle and the duchess of Longueville—had a military role unsurpassed since. They led battles and armies, defended strongholds, and, when Paris was under rebel control, even ordered the canon of the Bastille to be used against the royal army. Once the nobles were defeated and the king's administration was in control of the kingdom, salon activity had to be radically redefined. That redefinition has often been mistaken for a lapse into frivolity.

In August 1654, eighteen months after Mazarin had returned to Paris at the end of the Fronde, there appeared the first volume of a novel impatiently awaited by the salon public largely composed of ex-Frondeurs. During the last years of the civil war, while salon activity was in suspension, Madeleine de Scudéry had become the official novelist of the rebel camp, whose military and amorous exploits she fictionalized in *Artamène, ou le grand Cyrus* (1649–1653; *Artamenes, or the Great Cyrus*). The first volume of her new novel, *Clélie, histoire romaine* (*Clelia, a Roman Story*), had as its centerpiece the most celebrated document in salon literature, "La carte de Tendre," the map of the land of Tenderness (fig. 1).

"La carte de Tendre" functions on a number of levels. Allegorically it is the map of an imaginary land called Tenderness. As the novel's heroine teaches her audience how to read it, the map is revealed to be a course in gallantry, giving men the woman's perspective on both the ways to win her heart (for example, a stop in Pretty Verse and a visit to Sincerity eventually lead to the town of Tenderness-on-the-Esteem) and the ways to lose it (a wrong turn at Negligence puts a suitor on the road to Obliteration). Scudéry's map is an ancestor of board games such as Monopoly, and it was just as successful in its day: at least fifteen imitations and parodies appeared in the next decade to capitalize on the success of the game of love.

"La carte de Tendre" also represents more concrete territories under female control. *Clélie* heralds the renaissance of salon activity after the unrest of the Fronde, the beginnings of what Dorothy Backer terms "the precious decade" (1654–1661), a prolonged last fling before the increasingly rigid formality that gradually overtook the French court after Louis XIV's marriage in 1660. The salons were perhaps never more influential than during those years, when France for once was not at war and creative energies were high. *Clélie* is the ultimate in salon literature: in it, Scudéry replaces whenever possible action and exteriority with the recounting of action. In particular, she highlights a novelistic set piece of her invention, the conversation, a fictional recreation of salon assemblies in which characters weigh the merits of different responses to a given situation, much as characters in recent experimental theater talk about how the play might end rather than ending it.

This radical shift in the focus of fiction, from action to collective commentary on event, reflects Scudéry's awareness that the time for women's political activism had passed with the Fronde and that its future lay in less openly subversive domains such as the salon and the novel. Her realignment of prose fiction is the first clear indication of what would prove to be the great tradition of the French novel, a tradition that, in the hands of novelists such as Marie-Madeleine de La Fayette and Marie-Catherine Desjardins (Mme. de Villedieu), would initially be as much under female control as the salons. Conversation instead of action and an ever more intricate analysis of the human heart: as Ferdinand Brunetière remarked in 1889, French "novelists have never ceased traversing the *carte de Tendre*" (*Questions de critique*, p. 56).

Seventeenth-century detractors dismissed all salon art—"La carte de Tendre" and especially the explosions of linguistic creativity that critics named *préciosité* (or, in the 18th century, *marivaudage*)—as frivolous affectation. Certainly the digressive, conversational style was at odds with the more sober manner of classicism, the yardstick of French literary greatness until the Revolution. Ultimately, however, these scornful attacks on the production of the private academies have served—as have the eulogies by Picard and others of the salons as the guardians of true French culture, that is, the aristocratic culture of the ancien régime—to distract attention from the multifaceted social fermentation generated by these assemblies.

Préciosité was much more than a literary movement of minor importance. It began as a feminist movement, inspired by early 17th-century projects for women's education. In addition to formal education and increased participation in the choice of a marriage partner, the précieuses made demands of striking actuality: they sought for women what would today be termed control over their bodies (for example, the right to decide when they would have children). Although this early "vindication of the rights of women" did not achieve any long-term gains in marital or reproductive freedom, it did effect major changes in the fabric of the French class system. Inside the *chambre* and the *ruelle*, all were equal: the much-praised dissemination of French culture associated with the salons initially involved the spread of aristocratic behavior to those of lower birth. Carolyn Lougee traces the link between the feminist demand that merit rather than rank determine the choice of a husband and the rise of a new aristocracy, the self-made nobles. Far from being guarantors of the old order, the women of the salons worked to infiltrate and democratize the aristocracy.

The leaders of salons tended to have long lives and thus assured the survival of styles and values from one age to the next. The marquise de Rambouillet's direct heirs—those who began their careers in her salon, such as Madeleine de Souvré, marquise de Sablé, and those who knew firsthand the gatherings of the "precious decade," such as Marguerite Hessein, dame de La Sablière—carried the torch until the end of the 17th century and, in the case of Anne Thérèse de Lambert, formed a bridge to the next. Throughout that century, salon leaders inherited (or stole, as did Lespinasse from du Deffand) guests and time slots: from Lambert to Claudine Guérin de Tencin, from Tencin to Marie-Thérèse Geoffrin, the genealogy unfolds. Eighteenth-century salons became, like the century in general, more philosophical. They were also increasingly dominated by the great male writers, who used them to showcase their talents and who, in some salons, outnumbered and outshone the female members. To the end, however, the ceremonies in these assemblies that kept the republic of letters under the reign of conversation were always directed by women. If "Apostrophes" had been a phenomenon of the ancien régime, Bernard Pivot's role would never have been played by a man.

See also 1627, 1725, 1735, 1787, 1816.

Bibliography: Dorothy Backer, *Precious Women* (New York: Basic Books, 1974). Ferdinand Brunetière, *Questions de critique* (Paris: Calmann-Lévy, 1899). Carolyn Lougee, *Le Paradis des Femmes: Women, Salons, and Social Stratification in 17th-Century France* (Princeton: Princeton University Press, 1976). Roger Picard, *Les salons littéraires et la société française, 1610–1789* (New York: Brentano's, 1943). Claude Favre de Vaugelas, *Remarques sur la langue française,* ed. Jeanne Streicher (Paris: Droz, 1934).

Joan DeJean

⁓ 1657

Cyrano de Bergerac's Posthumously Published *Histoire comique des états et empires de la lune* Inaugurates Science Fiction

Figures of Social and Semiotic Dissent

The real Cyrano de Bergerac (1619–1655) was neither the romantic character of Edmond Rostand's play (1897) nor the much-admired author he is today. He was known as a writer, but his output was small: a few public letters, a couple of plays. He was working on his libertine masterpiece, *L'autre monde* (*The Other World*), a narrative of a trip to the moon, but it did not appear until two years after his death, in a bowdlerized edition, as *Histoire comique des états et empires de la lune* (1657; *Comic History of the States and Empires of the Moon*). He had some notoriety as an associate of the libertines, as a suspected atheist, as an aggressive wit. His prowess with the sword was legendary, but he also took dancing and philosophy lessons. Fickle in politics, he supported the Fronde, then Cardinal Mazarin and absolutism. With ideas still steeped in bourgeois traditions, he displayed outward signs of nobility. What can one make of this man of many signatures (Hercule de Bergerac, Alexandre de Cyrano Bergerac, Savinien de Cyrano, and so on)? In his elusiveness, he was exemplary of a vast group of people without clear identity.

Indeed, Cyrano's milieu developed on the margin of formal divisions of 17th-century society, somewhere at the interface of nobility and bourgeoisie: an open, fluctuating, heterogeneous, and often warring crowd of writers, scholars, magistrates, courtiers, patrons and patronesses, nobles about town, sons of wealthy merchants, and various fringe types; a busy world already reflected in Charles Sorel's novel *Histoire comique de Francion* (1623–1633; *Comic History of Francion*). It was a *protointelligentsia:* intelligentsia, because its leading figures, not unlike modern intellectuals, were men and women of ideas, either playing with them in their field of interest or exchanging them in the framework of conviviality; but proto-, because they were not yet a recognized group that could provide a distinct identification. In a society that valued social identity and denoted it with fixed status and signs, protointellectuals could find no appropriate roles. The traditional discourse was driving them to marginality; and while many clung to safe social categories, suppressing the need to affirm a difference, many others reacted with an instinctive distrust of the discourse that threatened to alienate them. They challenged the authority of concepts and the adequacy of a language that could not offer them self-definition. And their frustration, meeting other forms of a semiotic malaise resulting from a general failure of signs to keep up with social changes, fueled a steady dissent among protointellectuals throughout the ancien régime. The intensity and scope of that dissent varied with the degree of marginality, its forms and targets with contingencies of personal and cultural history. The libertine movement was no doubt the most daring of its protean manifestations, but it also inspired Jansenist tracts and anticanonical literature.

Much has been written about the libertines, their humanist and scientific background, their skepticism, naturalism, even atheism. Whether poets such as Théophile de Viau, learned scholars such as François de La Mothe Le Vayer, or philosophers such as Pierre Gassendi, their main target was religious dogmatism. *L'autre monde*'s rejection of God and promotion of reason, Lucretian atomism, and universal Eros as the law of nature are not especially original, but in style and tone they are exceptionally bold. Also bold is the book's impertinent parody of the scriptures. As a rule, however, Cyrano, like the other libertines of his generation, avoided an open confrontation with the authorities.

L'autre monde's uniqueness lies instead in a visionary use of fantasy that, in order to subvert the very language of authority, turns upside down the relation between signs and reality. On Cyrano's moon, there are only relative signs. Instead of a single language, two idioms, both arbitrary, coexist: musical sounds for the nobility, body movements for lower classes. More radically, lunar people endow some signs with instrumental functions, substituting them for objective reality: they nourish their bodies with aromatic signs of food and their minds with acoustic signs of writing; poetic signs replace hard currency; wars are won with words. As a mirror of earth, the moon thus appears to offer a semiotically aberrant image, and its apelike inhabitants, by dint of a graphic pun, seem to be both *signes* and *singes* (signs and apes), a grotesque representation of humankind. But, on the moon, humans in turn are viewed as apes of lunar people, and accounts of earth as distorted versions of reality. Both worlds are thus reduced to mutually misleading specular images, the signs of one relating to the signs of the other rather than to any objective reality. Social identities and roles, fixed by signs, are destabilized by this double relativity. When swords on earth, but phalluses on the moon, serve as equally ludic signs of nobility, their reciprocal subversion undermines not only their own semiotic validity but also the credibility of any language that defines concepts by their signs. And when family authority, vested in fathers on earth, is entrusted by specular logic to sons on the moon, then the very notion of a natural authority becomes subverted, and with it the entire discourse on social organization. Yet, beyond the illusionary screen of signs, Cyrano perceives only a universal and anarchic *être* (being) of nature, which affords no better chances for stable identity. Although it entertains as science fiction, playing imaginatively with the marks of semiotic malaise, *L'autre monde* opens up no possibilities for meaningful behavior in the real world. At best, humankind can learn only how to *dream to live freely*.

A few decades earlier, first generation libertines had shown more optimism. In *Histoire comique de Francion,* a young Charles Sorel promised to teach men how to "live like Gods" (p. 254). True, he did not sign his book, and he encoded his most provocative ideas in a hermetic dream sequence packed with delirious erotic phantasms. But his message was hopeful: like Francion, individuals in search of inner truth could achieve philosophical freedom, discard dogma, break taboos, and satisfy natural appetites as well as an innate sense of beauty. Francion's adventures among students and prostitutes illustrate a coarse hedonism rather than aesthetic refinement, but for that very reason they appeared all the more realistic to contemporary readers. Sorel's libertine program benefited from the credibility of a familiar world; it seemed to demand only a minimal adjustment of society. *Francion* was very popular. Cyrano had read it, borrowed from it. But he turned its pragmatic proposals into a fantastic vision. And Sorel himself, in his later works, abandoned libertine ideals.

It is doubtful that fear of censorship caused this loss of faith. Libertine ideas survived, notably in Charles de Saint-Evremond's *Conversation avec le maréchal d'Hocquincourt* (1654; *Conversation with the Marshal of Hocquincourt*). Nor could age alone have changed Sorel's convictions; it did not silence his dissenting voice. With *Le berger extravagant* (1627; *The Extravagant Shepherd*), the first French *anti roman,* he merely switched targets, striking at literary conventions. His belief in individual self-affirmation expressed in *Francion* was more likely undermined by the growing general uncertainty about ways of defining and affirming identity. The nobility was particularly affected by the widening gap between the meaning of signs and social reality: thousands of "new nobles," in fact wealthy bourgeois, openly paraded titles, swords, and other marks that were still coded as signs of noble birth or high office. The prestige of nobility was not in question; the rigid social discourse and the general opinion concurred that a noble had merit. But how to identify a noble when signs were misleading? and how could nobles affirm their status? Was there any real identity behind the appearances? The tension between *être* (being) and *paraître* (seeming), a major topos in 17th-century literature, grew from a form of semiotic malaise that, though not yet questioning codes nor destabilizing signs, manifested an awareness of their unreliability. In the 1623 version, Francion manages at the very end to appear what he is, a noble *and* a libertine. But in later added sections, he dons new masks, and his identity dissolves into new roles. Surrounded by obsolete codes and unreliable signs, even a libertine cannot affirm what he is. Hence Cyrano's more radical mistrust of all semiosis. Hence also, if differently, Pascal's.

Pascal was no stranger to the dissent of the libertines. He argued vigorously against them in the posthumous *Pensées* (1670) but he knew them well, sharing their protointelligentsia background and appreciation of scientific progress. Like Cyrano, he drew on mathematical concepts in his images; in addition, he followed several strategies traced by Joan DeJean in libertine writings: use of pseudonyms, mixture of genres, fragmented organization, irony. His own dissent and distrust of signs were most militantly expressed in *Les lettres provinciales* (1656–57; *Provincial Letters*), a series of satirical letters in defense of Jansenism, an almost heretical religious movement that was perceived by both civil and ecclesiastical authorities as perhaps more dangerous than free thought.

First anonymous, then signed Louis de Montalte, these public letters were written initially in support of Antoine Arnauld, an outspoken Jansenist accused of denying man's ability to act rightly without a special grace from God. But they deal little with theological questions, exposing instead the duplicity of Arnauld's adversaries and, after his expulsion from the Sorbonne, the casuistry of Jesuits who justified crimes for the sake of their own popularity. By castigating the Jesuits' excesses, Pascal challenges the church and even the king, whose Jesuit confessor is the target of the last letters. More generally, however, Pascal denounces the dominant discourse that unscrupulously manipulates its own signs.

With a modern insight he thus unveils, at the source of various impostures, the *arbitrary* relation between two parts of a sign, noting that in each word "there is the sound, which is only so much breath; and there is the thing which it signifies, which is real and effectual" (*Provincial Letters*, no. 2, p. 340). When Arnauld's enemies split the two parts, they can agree to pronounce the same words while assigning them different meanings. They also pervert the referential function of language, invoking *probability* or *intentionality*—what may occur or what someone intends—instead of referring directly to real actions. Such a semiotic manipulation of truth, Pascal claims, is then enforced with violence by authority; and since truth and violence have no common language, only God will ultimately resolve their conflict in favor of his own truth. Meanwhile, society must remain in a state of semiotic malaise, with reality slipping from under the signs of the discourse. In 1660, the king's council ordered the *Provinciales* burned.

The divergence between ideology and reality increased under Louis XIV. A stronger central authority hardened traditional concepts and signs. But social reality moved further away from the ideological model. The power of the bourgeoisie grew tremendously but did not generate new values or revisions of semiotic codes. Some successful bourgeois swelled the ranks of nobility; others, less fortunate, indirectly sustained nobility's coded signs by trying to speak, dress, and behave like nobles. The dominant discourse ridiculed their aspiration to appear what they were not, as in Molière's *Le bourgeois gentilhomme* (1670; *The Would-be Gentleman*). It also censured subversive displays of bourgeois wealth. Antibourgeois satires multiplied. Even legally ennobled bourgeois were accused of usurping a status and signs for which they had not true *qualité*. The *être/paraître* conflict pervaded literature.

By 1688, with Jean de La Bruyère's *Les caractères* (*Characters*), the conflict reached the realm of stylistics, inspiring a recurrent alternation of forms stating what *is* and what only *appears,* always competing, often without resolution, and producing ambiguity in rare cases of convergence. Thus, in the celebrated portrait of Giton, a long list of external traits culminates in one essential quality: *he is rich.* But although wealth does explain Giton's appearance and behavior, it is not innate and requires marks to be acknowledged; unlike birth and merit, it lacks a fixed ideological value. Ironically, La Bruyère exhibits here and elsewhere the same semiotic confusion that he uncovers in his society, the same inability to distinguish between "real things" and signs. His portraits, stories, group tableaux, essays—for he too mixes media like libertine dissenters—thus evoke personalities defined by the absence of a true personality, fashions and games as role models, discrete idioms and meaningless formulas, and all manner of deceit by which real power corrupts the social system without disturbing its surface order.

A few figures shine; they are exceptions. Even the king is not spared: in one of La Bruyère's portraits, Louis XIV might have recognized himself as the ideal monarch; the rest of the text proves that no such king rules France. Yet La Bruyère does not question the ideology of his time. Half-bourgeois and half-noble, like Cyrano and Sorel, he protects his ambiguous status. A radical adjustment of signs to reality could have exposed the fragility of a dominant discourse contingent on conventions; and in the resulting upheaval, there might be no signs for hybrid identities, no place for a writer depending on the patronage of the establishment. In contrast, dissent limited to literary forms and a mere observation of semiotic disorder could and did open for La Bruyère the doors to the Académie Française.

The same Académie had previously elected Antoine Furetière, who, like La

Bruyère and the mature Sorel, also restricted subversion to literature and language. True, with his magnum opus the *Dictionnaire universel* (1690; *Universal Dictionary*) he eventually challenged the authority of the Académie, which expelled him; and the *Dictionnaire* was published posthumously, like Cyrano's and Pascal's great works. Unlike the other dissenters, however, though born in the same bourgeois milieu, Furetière was satisfied with his role as a bourgeois, securely grounding his social identity in bourgeois reality. He welcomed the advance of the bourgeoisie but within the framework of traditions; and in his early satires he denounced excessive flaunting of bourgeois wealth and power. In short, he was an establishment man on all issues except those that involved his professional identity as a writer.

For the same sense of reality that made Furetière a bourgeois led him, in literature, to dissent from any fashion, old or new, that relied on arbitrary conventions. His *Roman bourgeois* (1666; *The Bourgeois Novel*), advocating fictional realism, was overtly intended as a break with all contemporary canons, including that of the *histoires comiques,* at one time dissenting parodies of orthodox fiction but subsequently formularized by Sorel and Paul Scarron (*Le roman comique,* 1651, 1657). By the same token, it revealed the presence of a distinctly bourgeois inspiration within the protean protointelligentsia. *Le roman bourgeois* displeased everybody.

To an extent, *Le roman bourgeois* remains disconcerting. Not by choice of topic, the middle bourgeoisie, which has been since widely exploited. Nor by games played by the narrative voice, both telling a story and the story of its own storytelling: Scarron and, more recently, the New Novelists made them familiar practices. Together with gaps in the plot, these strategies were to bring fiction closer to reality; they are no longer surprising. To this day, however, we have problems with challenging, like Furetière, the rational principle of coherence. And incoherences abound in *Le roman bourgeois.* Many reflect contradictions between what Furetière says and does. More disturbing is his injection of alien material into the novel—a marriage tariff, a library's inventory, a summarized essay on book dedication, a court sentence, fables, and so on. Applied to a *single* genre, such mixing of media undermines the very definition of the genre. Also, can a novel, as this one does, have two unrelated parts? Furetière suggests not calling it a novel, subtitling it "ouvrage comique" ("comic work"). But there is *roman* in the title. Besides, what else could it be? By pointing to the failure of signs to identify and direct his incoherent practice, Furetière thus destabilizes not only one genre but literary discourse itself and, by implication, any discourse articulated within a fixed semiotic system. No wonder, then, that *Le roman bourgeois* is still not readable today.

To that extent, it is exemplary of forms of literary dissent that, generated by social malaise but experienced as a semiotic malaise, limit to literature the subversion of the dominant discourse. Like Sorel in *Le berger extravagant,* also hard to read today, Furetière does not question the signs of an obsolete ideology that has no place for the writer as an intellectual; he concentrates his frustration on a radical deconstruction of signs of his own—literary—discourse. In contrast with earlier libertine writings, which subverted the social discourse, such a solipsistic dissent could have but little effect either on society or on literature.

See also 1668.

Bibliography: Savinien de Cyrano de Bergerac, *Other Worlds; the Comical History of the States and Empires of the Moon and the Sun,* trans. Geoffrey Strachan (New York: Oxford University Press, 1965). Joan DeJean, *Libertine Strategies: Freedom and the Novel in Seventeenth-Century France* (Columbus: Ohio State University Press, 1981). Antoine Furetière, *Le roman bourgeois* (Paris: Gallimard, 1981). Jean de La Bruyère, *Characters,* trans. Jean Stewart (Harmondsworth: Penguin, 1970). Blaise Pascal, *The Provincial Letters,* in *Pensées. The Provincial Letters,* trans. Thomas M'Crie (New York: Modern Library, 1941). Claude Reichler, *L'âge libertin* (Paris: Minuit, 1987). Jean Serroy, *Roman et réalité: Les histoires comiques au 17e siècle* (Paris: Minard, 1981). Charles Sorel, *Histoire comique de Francion* (Paris: Garnier-Flammarion, 1979).

Jean Alter

✍🏻 1660

Pierre Corneille, at the Peak of His Career as a Dramatist, Publishes His Collected Plays along with a Series of "Discourses" on the Art of Theater

The Autocritical Dramaturgy of Classicism

In 1660 Pierre Corneille, then acknowledged the foremost playwright of his nation, brought out a monumental three-volume edition of his *Théâtre complet.* Three discourses prefaced the collection, forming a kind of retrospective theoretical justification of his oeuvre: "Discours de l'utilité et des parties du poème dramatique" ("On the Utility and the Parts of the Dramatic Poem"), "Discours de la tragédie—et des moyens de la traiter selon le vraisemblable et le nécessaire" ("On Tragedy—and on the Means of Treating It according to the Probable and the Necessary"), "Discours des trois unités—d'action, de jour et de lieu" ("On the Three Unities—of Action, of Time, and of Place"). Each play was fitted, in addition, with an "Examen" ("Examination") that set out the ways in which it fulfilled, exceeded, or fell short of the norms established by classical doctrine. The views expressed in those pages were not unexampled: there had developed over the previous three decades a body of theory and practice designed to tame the wild exuberance of baroque taste in the theater—its heedlessness of probability, its excessive delight in spectacle, its love of the rhetorical flourish. Only three years before, in 1657, François Hédelin, abbé d'Aubignac, had penned a *Pratique du théâtre* (*Theatrical Practice*) that, although it lent itself to bad jokes at the expense of the good abbé's own practice as a playwright manqué, covered much of the ground that Corneille, who deigned not to allude to it even where they differed, was to make his own. D'Aubignac harped on the importance of probability in the theater, that centerpiece of classical doctrine, albeit he took it to such trifling lengths as to wax indignant at a prince represented onstage without his proper retinue. It was to dispel this kind of silliness that Corneille, at the height of his fame as a successful playwright, took up the pen as theoretician.

The resolve to measure in retrospect the playwright's considerable theatrical accomplishment against undeviating standards drawn from what looked like eternal laws of the theater was an exercise in Olympian detachment that did not lend itself to easy emulation. It nevertheless set a style and established a manner: classical drama was to be marked by high seriousness; it took a view of the art that acknowledged principle, and it held itself indebted to theory.

A keystone of that theory was the pride of place granted to classical antiquity. The writers who, like Corneille, accepted the authority of ancient example would themselves be dubbed *les anciens* (the term *classicism* itself did not come into use until the next century, with Voltaire's backward look at what he called the Age of Louis XIV). Clear as it was to Corneille that a mastery of his craft required attentive study of the practice of those ancient forebears, Sophocles in particular, it is no less clear that he gave them a reading that conformed above all with his own practice. No less vivid than the sense that the roots of drama lay in antiquity was the consciousness that the recovery of both comedy and tragedy was an achievement of modernity. Corneille was in no doubt that in *Le Cid* (1637), by pitting lover against lover tragically, he had invented a form of tragedy undreamed of by Aristotle. Antiquity was there to be as decisively "modernized"—although the term was never used—as it was to be "imitated." Where Corneille was concerned, the imitation would take the form of a reinvention of Roman identity. Roman republican virtues, Roman imperial majesty were to serve as a model of the *gloire,* the warrior caste's pride of place, out of which he was to fashion heroic tragedy.

The same boldness that led Corneille to derive classical doctrine from his own practice—no other living playwright rises to the dignity of citation in the three discourses—appears in his cavalier treatment of Aristotle's *Poetics.* All dramaturgical theory then resided in the exegesis of that capital text. D'Aubignac had already posited that the sacrosanct *rules* of the theater derived from learned interpretation of Aristotle's text were founded, not in authority, but in reason. Aristotle had done no more, as Corneille then saw it, than derive the principles of dramaturgy embedded in the practice of the Greek theater at its 5th-century apogee. Nor did he hand out his precepts so unambiguously that there was not a call for their interpretation (read: their retranslation into the terms suited to modern conditions, to present-day expectations of decorum— *les bienséances*). Crisply put: "There are precepts beyond a doubt; but it is not beyond doubt *what* these precepts may be" ("Discours de l'utilité," p. 51).

Playing the authority of Horace against that of Aristotle, stating moreover that, whereas he read Aristotle in his own fashion, he saw no objection to others' reading him in theirs, Corneille set an example that Racine and Molière were to follow each in his own fashion, of tempering a respect for the rules with a healthy regard for their own freedom of action—freedom under law, so to speak.

With regard to the celebrated unities, ancient authority was made more binding by "strict construction" of the moderns, Corneille tagging along somewhat reluctantly. Aristotle's assertion that a drama should possess a beginning, a middle, and an end was read as an injunction to keep the plot unified, to respect unity of peril in tragedy, unity of interest in comedy. The mild desideratum that the drama encompass, if possible, no more than what could occur within a single revolution of the sun was turned into the rule of twenty-four hours, Corneille granting himself a latitude of thirty. Thus corseted, the plot dared not convey the action beyond the walls of a single city, a single palace, a single room! That last of the unities, nowhere attested in Aristotle, may well have been the first in the minds of the dramatists who wished to compose in accordance with rule, *les réguliers.* In the first place, the physical layout of the theater (laborious curtain action, narrow stage) rendered that rule a staging necessity, if any sort of verisimilitude was to be observed. Second, the wild practice of playwrights in the early part of the century, whose plays crossed oceans and spanned continents, inspired the wish for a more acceptable ratio of represented time and space to the time and space of representation.

Other rules, such as the *liaison des scènes* (ensuring that the stage never stood deserted) and the stipulated length of play or of its component acts, also fell under the logic of representation covered by the term *vraisemblance,* whose intrinsically elastic character was only fitfully recognized. Together with *les bienséances*—decorum or, more generally, suitability (characters must act their age, live up to the requirements of their station)—*le vraisemblable,* the public's sense of what was appropriate or likely, ruled the day.

The rule of rules, in the theater, is indeed to please the public. Molière was to put these very words in the mouth of a straight man in *La critique de L'école des femmes* (scene 6, line 505) (1663; *The School for Wives Criticized*). That the purpose of drama is to please the spectators is also the opening statement of Corneille's first discourse. Racine likewise was to raise the shield of massive public approval against the cavils of the few. In the minds of its practitioners the classical theater was above all successful theater. They aimed to move, astound, take by storm. An art that concentrated on the inner drama of tangled motives and clash of wills conveyed in elevated language met a public that rose to the challenge of such exacting fare. Martin Turnell has aptly called the conjunction "the classical moment."

Another point of agreement among the three classical dramatists was supplied by Horace's dictum that art must mix the useful with the pleasant, that it should instruct as well as delight. In an age in which the theater was required to justify its existence in the face of ecclesiastical reprobation fueled by Counter-Reformation zeal, classical doctrine sought to secure for itself the highest possible moral ground. Molière was to paraphrase the Latin tag "Comedy rebukes our manners laughingly" in defense of his *Tartuffe* (1664–1669; *Théâtre complet,* 1:632). "Vice," Racine's preface urges in behalf of his *Phèdre* (1677; *Phaedra*), "in this play is shown for what it is: hateful and misshapen" (*Théâtre-poésies,* p. 765). In this matter too Corneille had taken the boldest stand. The moral utility he claimed for drama lay in the uncompromising depiction of the passions. Virtue convincingly portrayed could not fail to win our love and approval even in misfortune, vice to draw our hate and contempt all the while it prospered. Morality's best safeguard lay in artistic truth.

In the 1660s Corneille's star began to wane. Louis XIV had firmly taken in hand the reins of power in 1661, at the death of his mentor Cardinal Mazarin. The queen mother's straitlaced "old court," steeped in the romance and the heroics of the Cornelian style, had to make way for Louis's own pleasure-loving "young court." Racine and Molière were to give a new cast to the ideas of tragedy and of comedy, respectively, the one focused on the corrosiveness of unrequited passion, the other giving full play to the petty meannesses and large fraudulences of humankind as perceived in the manners of the day (apes of fashion, medical humbugs, pious frauds). No longer did the thinking on the nature and function of the theater take the form of stately discourse and searching self-scrutiny. Racine, in preface after preface, gave notice that he was prepared to justify his every move on the authority either of ancient precedent or of the public's sovereign endorsement. Molière cheerfully held up the opposition to scorn in a couple of fighting one-acters, *La critique de L'école des femmes* and *L'impromptu de Versailles* (1663; *The Versailles Impromptu*), in the polemic that arose from the huge success of *L'école des femmes* (1662; *The School for Wives*).

Corneille had taken a characteristically broad view of tragedy, defining it not by its dire outcome nor yet by the princely status of its personnel, but by the jeopardy in which it placed its heroes and by the grandeur of the issues involved. Racine's aesthetic was more attuned to the virulence of thwarted passion than to the heroics of noble souls caught in predicaments that matched their stature. The infamous Nero was more his game than the glorious Augustus. The shift from the heroic to the grim was unsettling to many, as the preface to his *Britannicus* (1668) testifies. Some felt he had painted too dark a picture of the young Nero; others reproached him for making him too human. His defense: Nero in his play is a monster still in the making—*un monstre naissant.* No better account could be given of his aesthetic: in the depiction of evil it sought that exact degree of helplessness that balanced terror with pity. Thus his Phaedra, as he pointed out in his preface to the play, matched Aristotle's definition of a tragic hero neither wholly good nor wholly evil, having fallen into a criminal passion against her will, pitting all her strength against that fate, but in vain.

In the preface to *Andromaque* (1667; *Andromache*), on the other hand, Racine reminded his critics that "Pyrrhus had not read our romances" (*Théâtre-poésies,* p. 260). This in answer to the charge that the Achaean princeling dealt with his slave woman too ungallantly! The retort is noteworthy for the light it casts on Racine's almost fanatical insistence on the fidelity of his plays to his ancient models. Whatever the considerable liberties he took with ancient legend (his Pyrrhus woos the slave Andromache in a manner that would have surprised Homer) or ancient history (Nero in love), his characters were faithful to their originals in spirit and in tone. Pyrrhus, in Virgil's *Aeneid,* slaughters old Priam and young Polyxena. His vacillations in *Andromaque* are of a piece with this unheroic image. Achilles, in *Iphigénie* (1674; *Iphigenia*), rants and raves at Agamemnon quite as he had in the *Iliad*. The portrayal of Nero, by Racine's own avowal, is right out of Tacitus. Racine's fidelity is a fidelity to the ambiance and the style of his sources. His biblical characters thunder convincingly in the language of the prophets. In his portrayal of Hippolytus, the virginal servant of Artemis in the tragedy of Euripides merges convincingly with the features of a youth in the blush of first love, which Racine invented in deference to the interests of his own public. The seamless weave of legendary theme with modern sensibility, so tight that one could not easily tell where the one began and the other left off, thus achieved what had been the unspoken aim of classical theory: to naturalize upon the French stage a genre grown in another land at another time.

Comedy was a case fought out under other rules. The immense box-office success of *L'école des femmes* set into motion a free-for-all of tracts and counterplays to which Molière replied in kind with a couple of counter-counterplays of his own. The issues were, in a nutshell: is it licit to laugh at what some deem both lewd and offensive? and is the laughter of playgoers authoritative, does it guarantee the worth of a play?

Molière had no trouble disposing of a preliminary charge of a more technical nature: that the play lacked action, that it relied too exclusively on narrative (Horace, mistaking his rival for a friendly party, faithfully reports to him act by act the miserable outcome of his every countermove). D'Aubignac already, though his authority was not invoked, had declared legitimate a recital of events offstage that advanced the action. Laughter, on the other hand, was an outcome as definitional of classical comedy as pity and terror were of tragedy. Molière began by disqualifying those who professed themselves shocked rather than amused. The suspense created by the famous *le . . . ,* in the scene in which the ingénue could not bring herself to complete the sentence "He grabbed my . . . ," was an invitation to the prudes to let their minds wander into a gutter strictly of their own choosing. So much for *their* indignant outcry. As to the laughing public, it fell into three classes: the pit, which itself divided into a minority who judged a play by the rules and a majority who reacted instinctively to what they liked; and the court, whose easy manner concealed a finesse greater "than all the rusty science of the pedants" (*Théâtre complet,* 1 : 504). The body politic, in a word, from top to bottom. But the trick was to provoke laughter among the better sort—*faire rire les honnêtes gens*—in whose ranks the king sat conspicuous: an achievement that set comedy ahead of tragedy in the ranks of dramatic accomplishment.

Molière was to do battle again, this time for the freedom of his pen, in the five-year-long struggle to lift the ban on *Tartuffe*. In the preface to the five-act definitive version, he mounted a full dress defense of the theater. Pointing to its origins in religion, he distanced classical comedy from its scurrilous antecedents, which had called down upon themselves the anathemas of the church fathers. He staked out comedy's claim, in the words of the first petition for the then-banned *Tartuffe,* "to reprove our follies while diverting us" (*Théâtre complet,* p. 632). Infringing on the church's monopoly of moral instruction, the classical theater thus vaulted itself to the highest ground of social utility in behalf of a comedy that derided the antics of the piously fraudulent and the piously deluded. Its freedom, it would seem, had been won.

Relentlessly theatrical, reaching back to ancient precept the better to espouse the present day, classical drama achieved a balance that was fated not to outlast the fragile union of playwright and public, remote past and stylized present, that it had occasioned. The French stage was to pay for that improbable achievement with more than a century of vain endeavor to recapture its magic.

See also 1637, 1673, 1699.

Bibliography: René Bray, *La formation de la doctrine classique en France* (Paris: Nizet, 1951). Pierre Corneille, *The Chief Plays,* trans. Lacy Lockert (Princeton: Princeton University Press, 1957). Corneille, *Théâtre complet,* vol. 1 (Rouen: Publications de l'Université de Rouen, 1984). H. C. Lancaster, *A History of French Dramatic Literature in the Seventeenth Century* (Baltimore: Johns Hopkins Press, 1929–1942). Molière, *Théâtre complet,* vol. 1 (Paris: Garnier, n.d.). Henri Peyre, *Le classicisme français* (New York: La Maison Française, 1942). Jean Racine, *Théâtre-poésies* (Paris: Gallimard, 1950). Jacques Schérer, *La dramaturgie classique en France* (Paris: Nizet, n.d.). Martin Turnell, *The Classical Moment: Studies in Corneille, Molière, and Racine* (New York: New Directions, 1948).

Marcel Gutwirth

✌ 1661

After the Death of Cardinal Mazarin, Louis XIV Decides to Govern France Himself

From Roi Soleil to Louis le Grand

When Jules Cardinal Mazarin died in 1661, Louis XIV, then twenty-three years old, made the decision to govern alone. He not only defined the major political orientations of the kingdom but also supervised the work of his ministers. The beginning of his personal reign was marked by an unprecedented proliferation of intellectual and artistic activity, whose prime consequence was to transform the king into a living myth.

Since the reign of Francis I (1515–1547), French sovereigns had traditionally been patrons of the arts, but the young Louis XIV was probably more motivated by the example of Nicolas Fouquet than by that of his own ancestors. Fouquet, the superintendent of finances, had amassed a prodigious personal fortune and become a state within the state. On the island Belle-Ile-en-Mer, off the coast of Brittany, he maintained a military force for his own private use. Most important, he had created around himself a veritable court that eclipsed the king's in numbers and brilliance. At Vaux-le-Vicomte, the château that he had built near Paris, he surrounded himself with some of the most prestigious writers and artists of the time: La Fontaine, Molière, Louis Le Vau, Nicolas Poussin, Charles Le Brun. Jean-Baptiste Colbert, who coveted the superintendency, denounced Fouquet's malversations to the king. Fouquet was arrested the day after an overly sumptuous feast at Vaux to which the king had been invited, and was imprisoned in the fortress of Pignerol, in Piedmont. His arrest constituted the first political act of Louis XIV. The king then took over the cultural projects of the fallen superintendent, but on a larger scale. Versailles was to supersede Vaux-le-Vicomte.

Named superintendent of finances in his turn in 1661, Colbert enlisted individuals he considered to be key intellectual figures: Jean Chapelain in literature, Le Brun in the plastic arts. Chapelain, largely forgotten today, was the author of a twenty-four-canto epic poem about Joan of Arc, *La Pucelle, ou la France délivrée* (1656; *The Maid of Orléans, or France Delivered*). Most important, he had been instrumental in the creation of the Académie Française and had long promoted the literary ambitions of its patron, Cardinal Richelieu. He was the perfect choice to serve as a liaison between the worlds of politics and literature. Le Brun played a major role in establishing the Royal Academy of Painting and Sculpture, of which he was named chairman in 1661. The following year he was appointed the King's First Painter. The meeting of minds between Chapelain and Colbert was spelled out in a letter-prospectus from the writer to the minister dated 18 November 1662, in which Chapelain surveyed all the arts, explaining how each could be put to the service of the state (*Lettres*, 2:272). The concept of appropriating the services of poets was reconceived within the framework of absolute monarchy. Whereas Clément Marot and Pierre de Ronsard often focused on Francis I and Henri II as private individuals, the official poets would henceforth celebrate Louis XIV as a political personage, transforming him into a demigod. Moreover, an official institution would concern itself with the royal mythology: the five members of the Academy of Inscriptions and Letters (or Little Academy), founded in 1663, were charged with overseeing the ensemble of intellectual productions to the glory of the king. They would supervise successively a book of official eulogies of the monarch, a history of the king told through medals, and proposals of subjects for operas in his praise.

It was especially through the court festivals that Louis XIV aspired to transcend ordinary humanity and to become a god. The Abbé Charles Cotin attested to his success: "He is the living image of God himself; he is not the simulacrum and the idol of royalty. He is one of those divinities who, from time to time, descend from heaven to testify upon the earth to the truth of all that is said, all that is believed, about Providence" (*Réflexions sur la conduite du roi* [1663; *Reflections on the King's Conduct*], p. 28). Of the many court festivals of Louis's reign, the most profusely commemorated were the three great ones given at Versailles in 1664, 1668, and 1672. The night-long festival of 18 July 1668, for example, celebrated the first military victories of Louis XIV, ratified by the Treaty of Aix-la-Chapelle on 2 May of that year. It offered all the pleasures accessible to the privileged class: a sumptuous dinner, a ball, a comedy

(Molière's *George Dandin*), illumination of the park by fireworks. The king did not allow a moment's rest to his some 600 guests, who discovered a new Versailles, transformed by the magic of art. The painter Henri Gissey had populated the fountains, the groves, and the façade of the château with luminous transparencies that stood out in the night like magical presences. The cost of these expenditures was scrupulously recorded: 98,108 livres and 19 sols for the constructions, decorations, and illuminations; 44,148 livres and 14 sols for the actors' and dancers' costumes and the wages and lodging expenses of the artists (Marie, *Naissance de Versailles*, p. 334). Fouquet had never dared to dream of conspicuous consumption on such a grandiose scale. The most important distinction between the festival at Vaux in 1661 and the one at Versailles in 1668 was that, in the latter, each aspect of the decoration constituted an allegory of royal power.

The court festival in effect inaugurated a new bond between the monarch and his subjects. The king recovered to his own advantage certain feudal practices such as the exchange of gifts. He invited the principal members of the aristocracy to his château; he offered them entertainments that none of them could offer themselves without financial ruin. Because of its extraordinary sumptuousness, the king's gift precluded reciprocity. The festival was thus an opportunity to bedazzle the participants and to emphasize their distance from the monarch. He and his subjects no longer shared a common nature; he was placed above men, a veritable demigod.

The court festival effected an equally important metamorphosis in the members of the second order, the nobility: it transformed them into courtiers. It also transformed while representing them in spectacle the traditional pastimes of the nobility: the tournament became a carousel, the dance a court ballet, the military review a parade of theatrical costumes; and risk-taking was limited to lotteries and games of chance in which the lives of the players were no longer at stake. In fact, since the prizes were distributed in advance, chance no longer played any role at all in the lotteries. As for gambling, to which the aristocracy was passionately devoted, in the case of total ruin the king intervened to pay the debts of the unlucky player in exchange for his promise to leave the game. The coat of arms, a visual code of alliances and affiliation, was gradually replaced by the heraldic device, with a maxim inscribed below the escutcheon expressing the moral qualities of its bearer. The written thus came to take precedence over the visual. The coat of arms itself, in the court festivals in which it appeared (as in the carousel of 1662 or the one at Versailles in 1664), tended to become an allegory. It no longer signified affiliation with a clan or attachment to a territory; rather, through its *devise* (device), it attested to the privileged bond between each courtier and his king.

From 1660 to 1674 the festival and the festival mentality characterized life at the court. During these years the royal mythology was created and sustained by all aspects of the arts at court—ballet, music, occasional verse (especially that of Isaac de Benserade), and the ballet-comedy invented by Molière. This mythology portrayed Louis XIV as a figure of classical antiquity. He was

Apollo, or the Sun King. Thus in 1662, in the *Ballet des origines et de la grandeur de la maison de France* (*Ballet of the Origin and the Grandeur of the House of France*), Louis XIV danced as the image of the sun, accompanied by the twelve hours of the day. Adorned with sparkling jewels, he descended upon the scene in a dazzling machine of light. The golden hairpiece conceived for the occasion transformed the royal visage into the very image of the mythical Apollo. During this period Versailles was not continuously inhabited; the court moved there principally for hunts and festivals. The château, though of modest dimensions, was conceived on the model of the Sun Palace described in book 2 of Ovid's *Metamorphoses*. All its figures and ornaments were related either to the sun or to their specific sites on the grounds, promoting the conflation of the king with Apollo and the sun (Félibien, *Description du château,* p. 72).

In his effort to found the new values of the reign, to assure a consensus less in terms of political issues than in terms of an art of living, Louis established and promoted the qualities of the "good courtier," a paradigm that evolved into the model of *l'honnête homme* (the "perfect gentleman"). The type of human thus elaborated was capable both of permanent self-control and of giving the impression of perfect naturalness. *L'homme de cour* (the "perfect courtier") invented his own personage, using his body as the starting point. He limited himself to socially approved gestures, carried himself lightly, smiled at everyone, and spoke according to the canons of correct usage codified by Claude Favre de Vaugelas (1585–1650). According to Jean de La Bruyère's cruel portrait of this figure some years later, in *Les caractères, ou les moeurs de ce siècle* (1688–1696; *Characters*), the perfect courtier was a mechanism: "A perfect courtier can command his gestures, his eyes, and his countenance; he is profound and impenetrable; he seems to overlook every injury; he smiles on his enemies, controls his temper, disguises his passions, belies his inclinations, and both speaks and acts against his opinions" (*Characters,* pp. 183–184). He never displayed direct aggression in his dealings with inferiors or with women. The notion of virility was yielding to that of *politesse*. The perfect gentleman was a new man. Mastering his aggressive and sexual drives, he developed an interiorized, imaginary life that in fact became his true life. This interior space of freedom, already opened up at the end of the Wars of Religion (1562–1598) by freedom of worship, was the origin of a new sensibility that in the next century would give rise to a different, autonomous type of literature—psychological novels and dramas, philosophical essays. These genres are all characterized by an internal liberty that was the very condition of their birth.

After 1675 the king's palace, formerly the site of festivals, became a place of residence. Although the court did not move permanently to Versailles until 1682, a transformation of the monarchical ideology began seven years earlier, reflected in the evolution of the aesthetics of the château and of its gardens. Initially, Le Brun was in charge of construction at the palace. In 1674 he submitted three great plans whose common aim was to transform the domain into a gigantic allegory to the glory of the king. But Louis XIV rejected the projects. The statues that Le Brun had ordered were executed, but they were placed in sites other than those for which they were conceived and thus lost all their significance. As a result of François Mansart's gradual ascendancy over his rival Le Brun, the intellectual coherence of Versailles was destroyed in favor of its aesthetic arrangement. In architecture, as in painting and literature, the images of antiquity no longer served to celebrate the glory of Louis XIV.

The time of allegories was over; the great festivals were finished; the artistic activity of the reign seemed to have lost its impetus. The time for reflection had come: rules were elaborated, precepts drawn up, the literary and artistic patrimony was administered. The dominant impression, stated by La Bruyère, was that everything had already been said: "After above seven thousand years, during which there have been men who have thought, we come too late to say anything that has not been said already" (*Characters,* p. 7). The theories of classicism were elaborated during the Quarrel of the Ancients and the Moderns. In the political domain, Louis XIV was no longer *le Roi Soleil* (the Sun King); since his military victories (the second Flanders campaign, 1678) he had become *le Grand Roi* (the Great King). The mythologization of the monarch gave way to incessant propaganda: the sovereign was eulogized on every public occasion, in the academies and even, after the Revocation of the Edict of Nantes (1685), in the churches.

Artistically, the first fifteen years of the king's personal reign appeared to be an unsurpassable model requiring only attempts at imitation: through analysis of the earlier period's masterpieces of literature or painting, artists sought to discover the formula that would permit their eternal reproduction. Everywhere precepts were set forth that froze creativity in literature, painting, architecture, and even the arts of heraldry and pyrotechnics. Artists repeated themselves under the vigilant eyes of theorists who verified the conformity of products of the mind. Classical canons prevailed, and a formal, autonomous aesthetic took the place of the previous ideological inspiration. How one spoke would be henceforth more important than what one said.

Only two genres managed to flourish in this closely monitored cultural life. One was the opera, which concentrated all artistic techniques in a single representation at the same time that it became the primary vehicle of the royal ideology. Whereas traditional literary genres were polysemous, allowing for different interpretations, the opera conveyed a clear and unequivocal message. It derived its power to fascinate from its capacity to concentrate in a single representation the totality of the arts, all tied together by music. However, what had been history in the other dramatic genres became propaganda in the opera. The performances took place in Paris; they were addressed to spectators nostalgic for the splendors of the beginning of the reign. This explains why they seemed to revive the ancient allegories that elsewhere had passed from fashion. In Corneille's or Racine's theater, the monarch represented onstage was never the double of the actual monarch; on the contrary, he represented the sacred monarch the latter could no longer be, should no longer be, ever since he had taken charge of the administration of the kingdom. But, in the opera, this sacred monarch was not even represented; he was commented upon: representation was transformed into recitation. The performance evoked the sacred, but a sacred without tragedy, without sacrifice. Everything was played out in advance; everything unfolded according to an accepted ceremonial that began with the apotheosis of Louis XIV. The glory of the king was celebrated in the prologue, as in Philippe Quinault's and Jean-Baptiste Lully's *Alceste* (1674; *Alcestis*) and *Isis* (1677). However, the characters of the drama, Hercules or Jupiter, no longer served as models for the king; on the contrary, they followed the king's example. Whereas in the first part of the reign the images of antiquity had supported the glorious figure of the sovereign, the relationship was now inverted: in the opera, the heroic image of Louis XIV served as an example to the ancient gods, who were reduced to the condition of mortals fallen prey to their passions.

Under the direction of Lully, whom Louis XIV protected against prospective rivals, the opera gradually came to influence the other arts, when it did not simply seek to absorb them. The ballet-comedy, a kind of opera dominated by speech, disappeared upon the death of Molière. Corneille participated with Molière, Quinault, and Lully in *Psyché* (1671); he wrote *Andromède* (1650) and *La conquête de la toison d'or* (1681; *The Conquest of the Golden Fleece*). Racine ended his theatrical career by composing tragedies with choruses (*Esther*, 1689; *Athalie*, 1691); he also supposedly composed, with Nicolas Boileau, an opera that has been lost. Even the great authors had to adapt themselves to the new genre or disappear.

The second genre to flourish at the court after 1675 was the fairy tale. These stories, even when they had their origin in an oral popular tradition, were aimed at a fashionable audience. Written either by the courtiers themselves or by writers who frequented the same circles, they permitted the evocation, through allegory, of the values of the court of *le Grand Roi*. This was the purpose of Henriette-Julie de Castelnau, comtesse de Murat, in her *Histoires sublimes et allégoriques, dédiées aux fées modernes* (1699; *Sublime and Allegorical Stories*), whose settings are almost always reminiscent of Versailles. Louis XIV was himself the hero of Jean de Préchac's *Sans-parangon* (1698; *Nonpareil*), a fairy play that allegorizes his reign and celebrates the extraordinary character of the monarch.

The mythologization of Louis XIV spanned his entire reign, although its content changed. What began as an imitation of the Ancients became a model for the Moderns. Starting from Versailles, this image spread outward everywhere, in concentric circles, relayed in the provinces by the local academies, the clergy, and the pervasive bureaucratization of artistic and intellectual endeavor through the system of *privilèges* and the creation of numerous academies, so that it became a national ideology. Although the encroachment of the political upon the cultural was not a new phenomenon, it did assume an exceptional character and unprecedented proportions during the reign of Louis XIV. The monarch wished for a country ruled by "une loi, une foi, un roi" (one law, one faith, one king). At a time when religious faith was declining, he attempted to recreate a lost unity around his personage, around an ideology

319

that made the monarch the heart of the nation. He thus created a mirror in which the nation could read a glorious image of itself.

See also 1673, 1694, 1700, 1707, 1774.

Bibliography: Jean Chapelain, *Lettres de Jean Chapelain,* ed. Philippe Tamizey de Larroque, 2 vols. (Paris: Imprimerie Nationale, 1880–1883). Charles Cotin, *Réflexions sur la conduite du roi* (Paris: P. Le Petit, 1663). André Félibien, *Description du château de Versailles* (Paris: D. Mariette, 1696). Jean de La Bruyère, *Characters,* trans. Jean Stewart (Harmondsworth: Penguin, 1970). Alfred Marie, *Versailles et son histoire,* vol. 1: *Naissance de Versailles* (Paris: J. Fréal, 1968).

Jean-Marie Apostolidès

✍ 1664

Molière Stages Jean Racine's First Play, *La Thébaïde, ou les frères ennemis,* at the Palais-Royal Theater

Jansenist Tragedy

Like Blaise Pascal (1623–1662), Jean Racine (1639–1699) was immensely indebted to the Jansenists, the deeply pious advocates of strict Christian morality and doctrinal integrity whose work was centered at the Port-Royal-des-Champs abbey. Orphaned at the age of two, the young Racine received a remarkable classical education from mentors such as Antoine Arnauld, Claude Lancelot, Antoine LeMaître, and Pierre Nicole, who made Port-Royal a center of rationalist inquiry as well as a bastion of religious rigor. Racine commemorated the Jansenists in his last work, the unfinished *Abrégé de l'histoire de Port-Royal* (1697; *Short History of Port-Royal*).

Port-Royal acquainted the young Racine with the theological horizon of Jansenism that Pascal would reappropriate in his apology for Christianity (*Pensées,* 1670). Within French Catholicism, Jansenism was a reformist movement opposed to devout humanism and to the doctrinal compromises allowed by the Jesuits. For the educated public, Port-Royal's considerable appeal doubtless lay primarily in its defense of individual freedom of thought and conscience against the absolutist authorities of church and state. Jansenism owed its name to a Dutch theologian, Cornelius Jansen (1585–1638), whose posthumous apology for Augustinian theology (*Augustinus,* 1640), was censured by a papal bull in 1653. It elaborated a pessimistic vision of human nature ravaged by egocentric lust. Augustinian doctrine afforded salvation—through an experience of conversion from love of self to love of God—only to those predestined by God to receive the special grace of Christ. In articulating the radical consequences of the Jansenist theology of grace, Pascal stressed the mystery of original sin and the Old Testament account of God's withdrawal from an intimate relation with humanity. The paradox of the hidden God, both present and absent, inaccessible to intellectual faculties yet knowable through faith, underlies Pascal's resistance to the Cartesian rationalism sustained by Arnauld and Nicole. Lucien Goldmann connects Pascal's stern critique of human reason and will to a tragic scenario that Phèdre, the last and most deeply passionate heroine of Racine's secular tragedies, plays out: the possibility that victims of the Fall—even those striving to be just—could be doomed to die, without grace, in unremitted sin.

Arnauld and Nicole, the chief Jansenist spokesmen, generally stood for a skeptical detachment from the world of letters and polite culture. Their severity was disdained by the young Racine as he rose to unrivaled preeminence as an author of secular tragedy. Thus his biography reflects the same sharp split between religion and the world that marks the career of Pascal. But after his departure from the theater in 1677, when he and his artistic ally, Nicolas Boileau-Despréaux, were named historiographers of the king, Racine's life and his dramatic works—the biblical plays *Esther* (1689) and *Athalie* (1691)—evince a reconciliation with Port-Royal. For Pascal, time spent in the world—whether in pursuing scientific work or the pleasure of polite society—ultimately was not divorced from religion. Indeed, for the many readers of the *Pensées* who stress the work's account of fallen humanity's tragic condition, the Christian apologist was above all a penetrating *moraliste* whose sphere of observation was his own worldly experience. In the case of Racine the artist, however, the time spent in the theatrical world seems largely disconnected from his earlier and later spiritual life: except for the predestined and irreparable entrenchment of certain formidable characters (Néron, Bajazet, Eriphile, Phèdre) in evil, Jansenism rarely seems to penetrate the rigorously pagan universe of Racine's tragedies. But in the preface to *Phèdre* (1677; *Phaedra*), his last secular play, he took pains to qualify his tragedy as morally edifying and worthy of sympathy from his Jansenist friends.

In addition to the two late religious plays (*Esther* and *Athalie*) and one acerbic comedy, *Les plaideurs* (1668; *The Litigants*), Racine's dramatic corpus comprises nine tragedies. Except for *Bajazet* (1672), which is set in contemporary Turkey, the tragedies rework material either from Greek mythology—*La Thébaïde, ou les frères ennemis* (1664; *The Thebans, or the Enemy Brothers*), *Andromaque* (1667; *Andromache*), *Iphigénie* (1674; *Iphigenia*), and *Phèdre*—or from the history of Greece (*Alexandre le Grand*, 1665) and Rome (*Britannicus*, 1669; *Bérénice*, 1670; *Mithridate*, 1673). The immense success of his second play, *Alexandre*, made Racine a celebrated playwright.

When Racine's inaugural work, *La Thébaïde*, was produced by Molière's troupe, it met with a lukewarm reception and quickly fell into neglect. The dramaturgical problem is its dual plot. The principal action develops in the conflict of the twin brothers, Etéocle and Polynice, born of the incestuous union of Oedipe and Jocaste; the tragic crisis culminates in act 4, when the fraternal enemies kill each other. But a second drama ensues in act 5, when their mourning sister, Antigone, confronts Créon, her power-craving uncle, whose loss of his two sons and his nephews frees him to express his incestuous desire for her. The dénouement moves icily through the suicides of Jocaste, Antigone, and Créon.

By stringing out the family's self-extermination into this second series of catastrophes, the play fails to achieve the tightly wrought unity and finality of impact that typify Racinian tragedy. Yet *La Thébaïde* most incisively delineates the mythic and psychodramatic horizon of Racine's tragic universe. On the one hand, fraternal rivalry, in its various permutations and displacements, is crucial to the plots of his historical plays (*Bérénice* excepted). On the other hand, Antigone's tragic experience and insight expose the workings of genealogical perversion and illicit sexuality that imbue the great ceremonial masterpieces of Euripidean extraction—*Andromaque, Iphigénie,* and *Phèdre.*

In *La Thébaïde* the enmity of the brothers is primary, congenital, intractable. Their obsessive struggle suspends them in a prenatal (line 930) competition for their mother's affection. Oedipe's vengeful command that they share the throne has merely locked them more tightly in their conflict, blocking them from a conventional rivalry with the father. In Racine's historical tragedies, however, the dynamics of fraternal rivalry are more complex and less settled. To the struggle for familial or political authority a crucial Racinian motif is added: the clash of erotic desires. The intensification of dramatic crisis and vengeful violence that occurs when sensuality and jealousy fuel the fraternal power struggle is central to *Bajazet, Britannicus,* and the less calamitous *Alexandre* and *Mithridate.* In the latter plays, the conflicts generated by passion are resolved, after heroic struggles, under the paternalistic eye of monarchical authority. Thus Racine's evocations of the tragic order in history leave at least an episodic place for Corneille's treatment of death or catastrophe as an occasion for transcendent heroism. To such a muted vision of the tragic, however, the great mythological plays oppose a firm denial.

While *Andromaque, Iphigénie,* and *Phèdre* share with *La Thébaïde* a pagan sense of the sacred that places humans at the mercy of the gods, they go beyond *La Thébaïde* by making the place of the sacred—the altar—the pivotal dramatic site. Yet these three masterworks partake of the oedipal perversion that unfolds in the Antigonian dimension of *La Thébaïde,* in which illicit love or thirst for power is the driving force behind infanticidal impulses. *Andromaque, Iphigénie,* and *Phèdre* also renew Antigone's association of a violent, bloody, heroic death (that of Hémon) with sacrifice; and in deepening the bond evoked by Antigone between the acts of sacrifice and suicide, they rely upon the spellbinding figure of the suicidal woman.

Drawing on Homer, Plutarch, and above all Euripides, Racine weaves elaborate intertextual threads into his mythological tragedies by connecting them genealogically and situating them in relation to the Trojan War. *Andromaque,* a postwar drama set in Epirus, stages the rise to power of the widow of the Trojan Hector, held captive with her son, Astyanax, by Pyrrhus, the son of Achille. Her Spartan enemies, Oreste and Hermione, are, like Pyrrhus, relatives of the characters whose prewar drama—that of the Greek army trapped in port at Aulis by the lack of wind—is enacted in *Iphigénie.* In the latter play's dénouement, Iphigénie, the daughter of Agamemnon and Clytemnestre, is saved from sacrifice when her place as victim is taken by her mysterious rival for the love

of Achille, Eriphile. The identification of this "other Iphigénie" as the child of
an illicit union between Hélène and her earliest captor, Thésée, places *Phèdre*
prior to *Iphigénie* in the mythohistorical continuum: Thésée is the tragically
illuminated king who, at the end of *Phèdre,* must live on after the deaths of his
son, Hippolyte, and his wife, Phèdre. Hélène, whose kidnapping by Paris led
to the Trojan War, is as vital as Thésée to this genealogical labyrinth: the
daughter she bore to Ménélas, Hermione, incites Oreste (Iphigénie's brother) to
avenge Pyrrhus' infidelity to her in *Andromaque.*

A now proverbial formula underscores the dominance of love in *Andromaque:*
Oreste loves Hermione, who loves Pyrrhus, who loves Andromaque, who loves
Hector, who is dead. The play's political drama opposes a menacingly independent Epirus to Sparta and the newly consolidated Greek nation. In a move
characteristic of frustrated lovers in Racine's universe, Pyrrhus attempts to use
his power to win over Andromaque: unless she marries him, he will marry
Hermione and turn Astyanax over to Oreste and the Greeks. Andromaque
settles on a desperately tragic response: to give her son an adoptive father committed to protecting him by marrying Pyrrhus, then immediately to absolve
herself of infidelity to Hector by taking her own life, transforming the marriage
ritual into a binding maternal sacrifice.

The supreme tragic irony of *Andromaque* stems from the substitution of Pyrrhus for Andromaque in this scenario of bloody sacrifice at the marriage altar.
His marital vow, crowning the Trojan Andromaque queen of Epirus and recognizing Astyanax as king of the Trojans, exerts a perlocutionary force that
extends beyond its realization of an incomparable *gift;* Pyrrhus' vow—"I give
you my crown and my faith, Andromaque; reign over me" (lines 1507–08)—
effectively bespeaks his abdication or demise as king. For his defiant allegiance
to the Trojan enemy provokes Oreste and his Greek compatriots to instant
reprisal. By wedding Andromaque, Pyrrhus has married into her suicidal project; giving over his identity and power even while understanding that she will
never love him, he assumes her desperation and expends his love in a passionate
gift of life. In a sacramental setting before the Epirean people, his act of dying
at the hands of his adopted (son's) enemies ("I here proclaim his enemies my
own"; line 1511) sanctifies—seals with his blood shed at the altar—the new
order he has proclaimed. Suicidal and sacrificial, his marriage and his adoption
commit his people, even as they express the all-consuming ardor and pathos of
the Racinian hero's passion. The fulfillment of passion in death is consummated
by Hermione. Hearing that Oreste and his men have carried out her vengeful
command to murder Pyrrhus, she flees in frenzy from Oreste and, stabbing
herself, falls lifeless upon Pyrrhus' corpse. The conjoined corpses bind the parallel spectacles of suicidal violence in a single, stark representation of the passion that is proper to Racinian tragedy: passion that subjects its victims no less
to eros—the incriminating violence of libidinal drives—than to *thanatos*—a
nobler compulsion expressed in their tragic will to die.

That same coincidence of the tragic and predestination emerges in the stunning death scene recounted by Ulysse at the end of *Iphigénie.* To *Andromaque's*

substitution of one victim for another, *Iphigénie* adds the drama of the sacrificing father, Agamemnon, king of the nascent Greek nation. His hesitant decision to heed the gods' call to sacrifice his beloved Iphigénie resonates with the biblical drama of Abraham, whose willingness to sacrifice Isaac consecrates his calling by Yahweh to be the founding father of the Hebrew nation (Genesis 22). But whereas Yahweh's providence allows for Isaac to be replaced on the altar by a ram, and thus for conversion of the filial sacrifice into a symbolic rite, the victim fated to substitute for Iphigénie is her bitterly jealous rival, the suffering captive Eriphile; and whereas the biblical drama preserves and sanctifies the son's right to rival and displace the father, Racine's drama binds the consecration of the Greek national alliance to the violent, bloodletting self-sacrifice of the suicidal woman.

No sooner does the high priest Calchas identify Eriphile as the Iphigénie designated by the gods for sacrifice than, vehemently assuming this identity, she moves to preempt the priest's authority: she orders him back just as he raises his hand in a gesture that evokes Clytemnestre's vision of her daughter's violation at the hands of a priestly castrator. The mother had imagined him melding his sacramental offices with a public display of phallic aggression: he would "tear out her breast and with a curious eye read in her fluttering heart the gods' decree" (lines 1303–04). But the violent sacrifice is enacted by the "other" Iphigénie, who seizes the sacred knife, cuts open her chest, and fulfills her tragic identity with the shedding of the maternal blood of Hélène, evoked a few lines earlier (1749) by Calchas. Ulysse reports that her blood had hardly reddened the ground before thunder, wind, and fire confirmed the satisfaction of the gods (lines 1777–80).

Iphigénie-Eriphile's death is caught up in multiple determinations emanating from herself (her jealousy), her father (her illicit birth), the gods (their vengeance), the high priest (his powermongering), the soldiers (scapegoating her). Yet with all these forces driving her to death in guilt and victimage, the Iphigénie born of Hélène and Thésée makes the sacrifice that cements the Greeks in their collective solidarity *her own act*. Her imperious imperatives, repelling the rapacious priest's aggression, deny Calchas' hold over her destiny; moreover, asserting her power in his domain, they place the tragic virgin in the realm of the sacred and exclude the priest, with his "profane hands" (line 1774), from that realm. In committing suicide she performs on herself the expiatory rite of spreading her family's blood; she assumes responsibility for an act of reparative infanticide prepared by Agamemnon for his Iphigénie, yet ultimately atones instead for her own father's (Thésée's) licentious past. Thus in this portentous ritual consolidation of the emerging Greek nation, Thésée's Iphigénie's self-destruction, staining the earth with the blood of the virgin woman, figures her symbolic castration at the hands of a distant father. When that same awesome spectacle of a genetically determined infanticide, willfully assumed and carried out by the victim of tragic passion, recurs in *Phèdre*, a providential grace is accorded to the incriminated father—again Thésée, but this time placed at the center of the drama—who survives to reckon with the filial sacrifice he has unwittingly fostered.

In *Phèdre* the profane hands ("my homicidal hands"; line 1271) belong to Phèdre, who consummates her debasing confession of incestuous love to her stepson Hippolyte by seizing the sword he had received from his father. The young man, stunned by this act of symbolic castration, is unable to reclaim the instrument that symbolizes his manhood and his identity as Thésée's son because, Phèdre observes, it has been sullied by her hands. The drama unfolds the repercussions of her assault on Hippolyte's identity: first, when her confidante Oenone falsely accuses Hippolyte of expressing an incestuous desire for Phèdre; then, when Thésée responds to this accusation by declaring Hippolyte a monster and calling on his patron god, Neptune, to avenge him; and finally, when the sea monster sent by Neptune causes the horses that are integral to Hippolyte's identity (Greek *hippos* = horse) to drag their master to a mutilating death. This unspeakably violent scene is recounted by Hippolyte's mentor, Théramène. His celebrated narrative, marked by mammoth proportions (nearly 100 lines) and graphic images, works the surging power and complexity of baroque style into the climax of Racine's neoclassical masterpiece. Hippolyte's destruction, like that of Eriphile-Iphigénie, is represented as an effect of over-determination: the monstrosities figuratively packed into the murderous sea monster include the gods (Neptune and Vénus), Thésée, Phèdre, and Hippolyte himself. Yet Hippolyte willfully assumes his heroic destiny as he attacks and defeats the sea monster before, in an ending bathed with irony, he comes to rest, emasculated, near the tombs and temple of his maternal ancestors. In this sacred place the rebelling son had intended to conduct his own, self-contrived and self-executed marriage with Aricie, the woman he loved despite his father's prohibition denying her the right to matrimony. Instead he expires there, imploring Théramène to seek Thésée's beneficence for Aricie.

Phèdre's suicide by poison completes the catastrophic spectacle Thésée is forced to confront. Reappearing in time to declare Hippolyte's innocence and her guilt, the victim of desire and jealousy offers her death for Thésée—the celebrated champion of amorous exploits—to hear and see. Crowning a powerfully suggestive scene that violated French classicism's prohibition against dying onstage, Phèdre's death speech deploys a visual dynamics—the play of light and darkness, the action of the eyes as communicating channels of desire—that is always pivotal in Racine's dramatic poetry. Her descent into the underworld, where her father passes judgment on the dead, is, she asserts, an act of purgation: withdrawing her "profaning, incestuous eye" (line 1624), she is restoring light and purity to the world that her eyes defiled (lines 1643–44). For Thésée her corpse collects and conceals the darkness of a monstrous past; ensconced in death, the inert wife whom the chastened husband immediately wills himself to *forget* signifies his release from the poisoning gaze of illicit passion and from bondage to a debilitating divine ancestry. Phèdre thus leaves Thésée in the position of the penitent father; his expiatory response to his son's sacrifice ends in the assertion of a new, adoptive relation with Aricie. In this belated act of identification with his emasculated son, Thésée denounces his recourse to Neptune and takes his place in a decisively human order.

Thus Racine's secular tragedies culminate in the myth-based sacrifices of Thésée's daughter, in *Iphigénie,* and of his son and his wife, in *Phèdre.* In the dénouement of each play, heroic—yet passionate and guilty—human victims confront the intervention of a vengeful divine justice and enact a sacrificial spectacle of passion violently fulfilled. Among the allegories inhabiting this fateful scenario that combines victimage with self-destruction is one that stems from the survivor's recognition of a paradoxical triumph in the tragic character's passion. Against the malevolence of gods who prey upon human descendants, Thésée's children affirm their self-sufficient identity, dignity, and authority; his wife, the cathartic, epoch-ending sense of the tragic victim's self-sacrifice. For the surviving rulers the catastrophes at the altar—in *Andromaque* as well as in *Iphigénie* and in *Phèdre*—entail a reversal that brings a new order of human solidarity and responsibility into view. Whereas the tragic dénouements of *Andromaque* and *Iphigénie* still reserve a comic escape for the absent Andromaque and Agamemnon, in *Phèdre,* the ultimate and radical case, the tragic is unmitigated. Although Thésée's vision of the future can hardly entail a denial of the gods, his withdrawal from a nefarious alliance with them allows him to glimpse a fully human history, left to those who take charge of their own, passion-driven destiny. Phèdre, the granddaughter of Zeus, burned incessantly with the contradiction of the divine mixing with the human. Thus the purgation she invokes in her death speech can be construed as a removal of that contamination, and her death itself as figuring the gods' initial retreat from an earth left to Thésée and his human lineage.

The farthest-reaching Jansenist motif in *Phèdre* lies, then, not in the deeply tragic heroine's tortured conscience, but in the play's anguished revelation, communicated to Thésée by both Phèdre and Hippolyte, of a receding divinity—emblematized by the defeated sea monster—that will not reappear, that will remain concealed and ineffable. Anticipating the efforts of modern playwrights to recover the awesome gravity and austere intensity of ancient Greek tragedians, the closure of Racine's masterpiece depicts the extreme isolation, the brutally enforced in-dependence, the fatal sentence to mortality and responsibility imposed without reason on the victim of irreversible tragedy. Pascal, too, approaches this uncompromising sense of the tragic with his insistence on fallen humanity's estrangement from a hidden deity. But since the apologist's aim is to prepare his interlocutor for salvation through a redemptive grace that restores a sacred relation between the human and the divine, his vision renews the ultimately providential horizon that reappears in the dénouements of *Andromaque* and *Iphigénie.* By contrast, *Phèdre* presents an anguishing resistance to such a redemption. Thésée's final speech of tragic illumination articulates the sense of his unwitting descent into filial sacrifice: the monstrous act that alienated him from the gods will compel him to sanctify his irreducibly human relation with his son. *Phèdre* thus withholds the providential framing of sacrifice that Racine retained in his earlier works and resurrected in his didactic plays a decade later. Its implacable rigor in consigning the meaning of heroic passion to human history takes the tragic to an irrecuperable extreme from which the Christian Racine could only recoil.

See also 1609, 1637, 1640, 1657, 1660, 1668, 1677, 1689, 1699.

Bibliography: Lucien Goldmann, *The Hidden God: A Study of Tragic Vision in the Pensées of Pascal and in the Tragedies of Racine,* trans. Philip Thody (New York: Humanities Press, 1964). J. D. Hubert, *Essai d'exégèse racinienne* (Paris: Nizet, 1956). R. C. Knight, *Racine et la Grèce* (Paris: Didier-Boivin, 1951). John Lapp, *Aspects of Racinian Tragedy* (Toronto: University of Toronto Press, 1955). Raymond Picard, *La carrière de Jean Racine* (Paris: Gallimard, 1961). Jean Racine, *The Complete Plays of Jean Racine,* trans. Samuel Solomon, 2 vols. (New York: Random House, 1967).

Philip E. Lewis

✍ 1668

Jean de La Fontaine Publishes His First Book of *Fables choisies mises en vers*

Moralists and the Legacy of Cartesianism

By some accounts, every classical French author is a moralist. Since the aesthetics of French classicism prescribed the conjoining of the useful with the pleasant, this generalization is valid to the extent that the literature of the mid-17th century accordingly legitimated aesthetic pleasure by a didactic focus on "moral" issues such as hypocrisy, misanthropy, or the conflict between duty and passion. A moralist writer, however, was not simply a moralistic one, but one who studied "morals" in the sense of customs or manners (*moeurs*). Although the noun *moraliste* appears with this particular sense in Antoine Furetière's *Dictionnaire universel* (1690; *Universal Dictionary*), the writers who have come to be called by that name were not so designated until Germaine de Staël's *De la littérature considérée dans ses rapports avec les institutions sociales* (1800; *The Influence of Literature upon Society*). Before that, the term was applied to either religious writers or "bad" philosophers, while the "moralist" writers were most often called simply *philosophes*. Insofar as their descriptions of human foibles drew upon abstract moral qualities as agents of behavior, the moralists anticipated the distinction between psychology and sociology and conceptually occupied a terrain in between. More specifically, the French moralists of the 17th century undertook a critique of humankind that drew upon Montaigne's brand of humanism, the Jansenist revival of St. Augustine, and, more paradoxically, the legacy of Descartes.

While the scholarly community questioned the validity of Descartes's metaphysically grounded system and the logic of his chains of reasoning by measuring them against other bona fide philosophers (and in the 17th century, this meant Aristotle), a more "popular" appropriation of Cartesian thought crystallized amid the urbane intelligentsia of wealthy bourgeois and disfranchised nobility, who enthusiastically discussed Descartes's ideas in the salon world, a space where church and university censors held no jurisdiction and were of little consequence, except perhaps to ensure a *succès de scandale*, to judge by the inclusion of the Cartesian opus in the Index of Forbidden Books in 1663. To a great extent, this popularity stemmed from Descartes's heuristic espousal of radical doubt as stated most notoriously in his *Discours de la méthode* (1637; *Discourse on Method*), a book explicitly addressed to a general audience and cautiously couched in the form of what he calls a "fable." Disregarding Descartes's own injunctions to his readers against a generalized practice of critical self-authorization, this worldly public empowered itself intellectually by extending the philosopher's "geometric method" of discovering truth by progressive, rational deduction to that area of greatest interest to itself but least developed by Descartes, namely, human ethics, psychology, and "morals." The latter were only briefly adumbrated in Descartes's "provisional ethics" of submission to the laws within which one is born (one of the moves he made in the *Discours* precisely to limit the extension of radical doubt to social and political issues) and in the voluntaristic psychology outlined in *Les passions de l'âme* (1649; *The Passions of the Soul*). An ambiguous situation resulted. On the one hand, the application of the new scientific vocabulary provided a ready fund of metaphor; for example, Pierre Nicole, in his *Essais de morale* (1671–1682; *Moral Essays*), analyzed desire in terms of the refracted coloration that the human heart exerts, like a prism, upon objects of perception, and discussed ambition in terms of the hemispheric limitation our eyes impose on sight. On the other hand, there remained the difficult if not unanswerable question of ascertaining what was the true "perspective" (a term that refers to painting as well as to the science of optics) from which to view the human animal as a moral creature.

The question of perspective is explicitly raised by Blaise Pascal in his *Pensées sur la religion et sur quelques autres sujets* (1670). After noting that "there is just one indivisible point which is the right place" from which to view a painting, a point assigned by the "rules of perspective," he asks: "but who will assign [this point] when it comes to truth and morality?" (p. 35). Pascal challenges the extension of Descartes's geometric method even as he appropriates its language. Within the general framework of the unfinished apology for the Christian religion which Pascal was writing until his death in 1662, and which we know today as that collection of nearly 1,000 fragments edited under the title *Pensées*, the only satisfactory answer is in the positing of a theological "point": the point of view of God. Without God, man remains lost, blinded by the concupiscence that defines his fallen state and caught between the infinitely large and the infinitely small so eloquently described in the famous fragment "Disproportion de l'homme" ("Disproportion of Man"). Not only does Pascal bring St. Anselm's proof of God up to date in this fragment by exploiting the new scientific cosmology enabled by the telescope and the microscope, but he also intensifies the Augustinian apology by radicalizing Montaigne's skepticism and Descartes's doubt until all human knowledge, even the putatively firm foundation and indubitable truth of Descartes's *cogito,* is shown to be vain: "We burn with desire to find a firm footing, an ultimate, lasting base on which to build a tower rising up to infinity, but our whole foundation cracks and the earth opens up into the depth of the abyss" (p. 92). The pivotal concept of infinity turns out to be as theological as it is mathematical, and overturns the rational basis of the mathematical by its very prolongation. For instance, in the fragment commonly known as the *pari,* or "Pascal's Wager" (pp. 149–153), the odds for God's existence are considered and meticulously calculated with all the ratiocinative skill of a seasoned gambler. These betting odds are positively concluded in favor of God *once* the possibility of *infinite* and eternal happiness is weighed into the balance against the merely finite blessings of temporal existence.

But rather than the theological Pascal who further pursues his apology through scriptural analysis and the "evidence" of miracles, it is the moralist or anthropological Pascal who has seized the imagination of generations of French readers with his debunking of Cartesian rationalism and implicit secularization of the Augustinian moral critique, as in his discussion of *divertissement* (diversion): the frenetic human engagement in activity of any kind so as not to have to confront the dread solitude of humanity's metaphysical plight. Insofar as the manuscript was left unfinished, the relation between the uncompromisingly bleak lucidity of the critical Pascal and the mysticism of his apologetic counterpart becomes an affair of interpretation, marked most manifestly by the long history of editions of the *Pensées,* in the course of which different Pascals have emerged from the mere regrouping, consolidation, splitting, addition, or suppression of fragments. In the aftermath of the reprieve granted Jansenism by the Church Peace of 1668, the initial editors at Port-Royal had few compunctions about aggressively editing the text to fit their own dogma. Modern editors tend to respect the provisional classification suggested by the order of the manuscript copies (Louis Lafuma) or to reject any pretension to a "true" ordering of fragments by rearranging them under thematic rubrics (Léon Brunschvicg). *Pensées* is less a work forming a "whole" than an ensemble of parts that are wholes, discrete units that mark an internal plurality separated by blank spaces, hence given to be read noncontinuously and open to the most heterogeneous interpretations.

By its form, then, as well as by its anthropologically critical content, *Pensées* bears less resemblance to the immensely popular strain of contemporary religious literature in a moralizing vein than to the works of other moralist writers, including François de La Rochefoucauld's *Réflexions, ou sentences et maximes morales* (1665–1678; *Maxims*), La Fontaine's *Fables choisies mises en vers* (1668–1693; *Fables*), and Jean de La Bruyère's *Les caractères, ou les moeurs de ce siècle* (1668–1696; *Characters*). All these works are more colloquially known by shorter, generic titles (*Maximes, Fables, Pensées, Caractères*) that have become inextricably linked to the author's name and have acquired a literally sui generis character, to the point that the late 18th-century moralist Nicolas Chamfort could embrace the tradition with the title *Maximes et pensées, caractères et anecdotes*

(1795; *Maxims and Thoughts, Characters and Anecdotes*). The strength of the identification between author's name and quasi-eponymous genre inevitably made
subsequent practitioners appear derivative. La Bruyère's *Caractères,* written
slightly after the other great 17th-century moralists' texts, already displayed
the intertextual process: alongside the satirical portraits that gave the collection
its name and fame, the book offered a compendium of short bits of prose,
reflections, maxims, and so forth, many of which were obvious adaptations,
amplifications, or retranscriptions of fragments from Descartes, Pascal, and La
Rochefoucauld.

Notwithstanding the moralist writers' status as originators of a genre,
explicit rewriting is a key dimension of their literary output. Pascal and La
Rochefoucauld often rephrase the texts of their intellectual forebears, especially
those of Montaigne and St. Augustine. La Fontaine and La Bruyère legitimate
their genres by citing the precedent of ancient authors. La Fontaine presented his
first collection of fables in 1668 as a versified translation of Aesop; La Bruyère
claimed to derive his practice of character portraits from Theophrastus. A
second kind of rewriting is evidenced by the proliferation of editions and variants, and by the circulation of selections among salon publics or other notables
before publication. La Rochefoucauld's maxims are perhaps the most notorious
in this regard, although La Bruyère's debt to his public and his expansion of his
work over numerous editions are equally pronounced. And, if La Fontaine's
Fables did not undergo substantial textual modification, the number of fables
increased to double their original number fifteen years after the first edition.
Some of his fables were also circulated privately for comments and many were
first printed singly or in small groups. *Pensées* does not fit the same pattern,
given its fragmented state at the author's death, but Pascal had already read
portions of the manuscript at Port-Royal and consulted Jansenist scholars such
as Antoine Arnauld and Pierre Nicole. More to the point, the text that appeared
in 1670 resulted from the *collective* labors of an entire team of editors.

The complex interplay of (re)writing, (re)reading, and (re)editing that marks
these texts implicates a wider community in their production; indeed, that
community is drawn into the texts in such a way as to justify the curious
impersonality of their authorial personae. For the crucial pronoun in these
works (whether stated or not) is a vertiginously self-implicating *nous* (we), when
it is not an indefinitely extensible and substitutable *on* (one). The provocative,
even intimidating, quality of the moralist critique comes from the inclusion of
its addressor and addressee within the community to which the moralist's dis-
abusing critique pertains. Upon reading Pascal's claim that "we run heedlessly
into the abyss after putting something in front of us to stop us seeing it"
(*Pensées,* p. 82), we can deny that the "us" refers to *us* only at the price of
confirming what the moralist observes, of demonstrating our own unwitting
entrapment by the ruses of egotism and self-delusion that the Pascalian critique
·explores. Similar cases of psychomoral debunking abound in La Rochefoucauld—"We get so much in the habit of wearing a disguise before others that
we finally appear disguised before ourselves" (*Maxims,* no. 119)—and in La

1. "L'homme et son image. Pour M. le duc de La Roche-foucauld. Fable XI," plate designed by Jean-Baptiste Oudry, engraved by Jean-Jacques Flipart, in Jean de La Fontaine, *Fables choisies mises en vers* (Paris: Desaint & Saillant, 1755), facing p. 22. (Courtesy of the Beinecke Rare Book and Manuscript Library, Yale University.)

Fontaine, who endows many of his didactic tales in verse with lessons (*moralités*) that are all-inclusive in scope.

One fable in which La Fontaine asserts his universalist reach—"Je parle à tous" (I preach to everyone; line 21)—invokes in its title, "L'homme et son image" ("Man and His Reflection"), the very object of the moralist's criticism. Dedicated to La Rochefoucauld (fig. 1), its brief narration allegorizes the predicament of the reader of the *Maximes* seeking to escape the moralist's indictment. The protagonist, a Narcissus type, obstinate in his self-love, flees society, where he is constantly confronted by the ego-deflating power of mirrors that reveal his shortcomings to himself. Out in the wilderness, he nonetheless comes upon a canal so beautiful that he cannot help but contemplate the true image of himself reflected within it. The subsequent moral explicates the allegory: the narcissistic man is "*our* soul"; the mirrors are "all the follies of *our* kin, / Held up for *us* to see *our* frailties in" (*Fables,* p. 17; emphasis added); and the canal is La Rochefoucauld's book of maxims. The moralist text thus serves as a diagnostic mirror, one that probes the ego's duplicities, defects, and disguises.

No less dignified (as the perceiving, self-critical subject) than vilified (as the egocentric object of the critique), the "we" of moralist discourse is dissected with the aid of a highly abstract vocabulary: self-love (*amour-propre*), vanity, taste, passion, merit, ambition, and so on. Self-love is the most celebrated moralist concept. Derived from the Augustinian category of concupiscence, in the hands of La Rochefoucauld it becomes, more than the sin of denying God the love owed him, the autonomy of a fundamental narcissism underlying and motivating the near totality of human behavior. For Pascal, it is an ego-preservative force that deflects or denies criticism from others. As such, the resistance one faces in trying to show others their defects not only makes sincere friendship impossible but also defines social interaction as "nothing but mutual deception and flattery" (*Pensées*, p. 349). The desire not to know the truth about oneself is thus socially reinforced; whence the recourse in moralist discourse to edifying fictions intended to defuse or circumvent ego resistance. La Rochefoucauld represents merely the most abstract variant in this personification of moral attributes: "Self-love is the greatest of all flatterers"; "The mind is always the dupe of the heart" (*Maxims*, nos. 2, 102). La Fontaine's animals incarnate similar qualities (the crafty fox, the industrious ant, the rapacious wolf, the kingly lion), as do La Bruyère's "characters" (the portrait of Ménalque represents distractedness, Giton wealth, Phédon poverty, Gnathon gluttony, Onuphre religious hypocrisy). Whereas Descartes's fundamental insight is the innate self-*evidence* of *my* self as thinking being, moralist cynicism insists upon *our* mutually blinding self-*delusions*. Says Pascal, "We like being deceived and we are deceived" (*Pensées*, p. 349).

Although the moralists' "we" appears generally as coextensive with human-kind in general, a particular kind of man does seem to be targeted, what the moralists call the *honnête homme* (honorable man), an abstract compromise figure in an age marked by a limited but perceptible blurring of class distinctions. Vacillating unstably between its moral definition (an honest man) and its class definition (a gentleman), and implicitly connoting one by the other (honest men are gentlemen, or gentlemen are honest men), the term could be applied discriminately as a sign of social distinction according to a particular group's need either to defend its privileges or to claim entry into an elite category. Even the chief *sign* of *honnêteté*, one's "taste," was equally vague and shifty, conceptually undefinable but socially palpable. The term *honnête homme* was first coined by Nicolas Faret in *L'honnête homme, ou l'art de plaire à la cour* (1630; *The Art of Pleasing at Court*), and the concept was extensively theorized by the chevalier de Méré (Antoine Gombaud) in such works as *Les conversations* (1668) and the post-humously published "De la vraie honnêteté" (1700; "On True *Honnêteté*"). In the tradition of Baldesar Castiglione and Baltasar Gracián, the notion of the *honnête homme* expounds a social ethic and etiquette of polite, pleasing behavior. Its conversion of social being into aesthetic practice reaches its peak in the requirement that such artful behavior *appear* artless: a certain *finesse* appears as the sign of the *honnête homme*'s innate *honnêteté*. Pascal contrasts such finesse to the "geometric spirit" of principled deduction, a quality displayed in caricature by the *honnête homme*'s artless opposite, the pedant, who gauchely exposes the artifice behind his discourse. Although Descartes is certainly no stranger to deductive chains of reasoning, his famous first principle ("I think; therefore, I am") cannot itself be deduced and is capable of no greater argument than that of its innate or self-evident "clarity" and "distinctness." This visual criterion recurs in Pascal's discussion of the *honnête homme*'s spirit of finesse, which *imme-*

diately perceives the heart of the matter by dint of an inexplicably innate "good sight." In fact Pascal's entire antinomy can be read against Descartes's curious combination of both kinds of spirit. Or perhaps it is testimony yet again to the two Cartesian traditions: the philosophical (geometric) and the worldly (self-evidential).

Although this tension between logic and intuition is generally resolved by valuing the latter at the expense of the former, the recourse to *honnêteté* is not simply dismissive of science and learning. Rather, the accommodation it promotes by the value put on aesthetic experience—taste, judgment, artfulness, culture, the *naturel,* the *je ne sais quoi*—depends upon preserving abstractions that leave unelaborated or unthought the particularities they gloss. If the abstraction *honnête homme* allows for a certain accommodation with the social contradiction whose class distinctions it both occludes and maintains, then it is because its applicability is indeterminate: both limited to a "moral elite" *and* extensible to the entire reading public. At its best, it is potentially open to whoever flatters oneself into believing in his or her own *honnêteté;* to whoever is willing to be perceived in the unflattering mirror of moralist discourse (whose intimidating self-evidence is underscored by its formal brevity, typified in the fragment or maxim, which disdains the tedious geometry of discursive reasoning). Finally, the discourse of abstraction is a compromise formation that also by its very nature makes a claim to timelessness as well as to universality. The same inclusive qualities that give the moralist critique its virulence also define and limit it as "classical."

It is interesting, then, that the least classical among the moralists, La Bruyère, is also the most Cartesian when classifying his observations under thematic rubrics: Man, Town, Court, Women, Personal Merit, Fashion, and so on. Writing a generation later than Pascal, La Rochefoucauld, and La Fontaine, La Bruyère is more particular in his representation of specific characters—often recognizable as contemporary individuals—and more insistent on the economic determinants behind the masquerade of social appearances. In addition to his (still timid) gesturing beyond classicism's exclusivist notion of "humanity" in his famous description of peasants, his work further debunks the notion of the *honnête homme:* "The well-bred man [*honnête homme*] is one who commits neither highway robbery nor murder, whose vices, in short, cause no scandal. Everyone knows that a good man is well bred, but it is amusing to reflect that not every well-bred man is good" (*Characters,* p. 229). As has often been remarked, La Bruyère's portraits often empty or hollow out the characters described, marking them with a progressively disturbing vacuity and insubstantiality. Cartesian optimism, founded upon the indubitable bedrock of human subjectivity and carried over into the tentative composite of *honnêteté,* thus gives way to the pessimism of one's preinscription within a cultural and economic system, a pessimism whose inaugural insight is the negative one that *tout est dit,* "everything has been said" (*Characters,* p. 25). La Bruyère's belatedness is also the sign of his modernity.

See also 1647, 1657.

Bibliography: Roland Barthes, "La Bruyère," in *Critical Essays,* trans. Richard Howard (Evanston: Northwestern University Press, 1972). Barthes, "La Rochefoucauld: 'Reflections or Sentences and Maxims,'" in *New Critical Essays,* trans. Richard Howard (New York: Hill and Wang, 1980). Paul Bénichou, *Man and Ethics: Studies in French Classicism,* trans. Elizabeth Hughes (Garden City, N.Y.: Doubleday, 1971). René Descartes, *Discourse on Method* and *The Passions of the Soul,* trans. Robert Stoothof, in *The Philosophical Writings of Descartes,* ed. John Cottingham, Robert Stoothof, and Dugald Murdoch, vol. 1 (Cambridge: Cambridge University Press, 1985). Jean de La Bruyère, *Characters,* trans. Jean Stewart (Harmondsworth: Penguin, 1970). Jean de La Fontaine, *The Fables of Jean de La Fontaine,* trans. Edward Marsh (London: Heinemann, 1933). François de La Rochefoucauld, *The Maxims of La Rochefoucauld,* trans. Louis Kronenberger (New York: Random House, 1959). Blaise Pascal, *Pensées,* ed. Louis Lafuma, trans. A. J. Krailsheimer (Harmondsworth: Penguin, 1966). Pascal, *Pensées et opuscules,* ed. Léon Brunschvicg (Paris: Hachette, 1897). Louis Van Delft, *Le moraliste classique: Essai de définition et de typologie* (Geneva: Droz, 1982).

Georges Van Den Abbeele

✐ 1673, 17 February

Molière Is Stricken Onstage during the Fourth Performance of
Le malade imaginaire

The Comic at Its Limits

Molière died late in the evening of 17 February 1673, only hours after having played the title role in his last play, *Le malade imaginaire* (1673; *The Imaginary Invalid*). Some contemporary accounts declare that he felt the first twinges of the fatal attack onstage, during the burlesque and satirical coronation of Argan as "novus Doctor." What his life of endless trials, tribulations, mournings, failures, and betrayals had been unable to do, his death—cast by circumstances into a symbolic and legendary dimension—accomplished. It took the convulsions of agony to smother the laughter in Molière's throat.

Until the very end Molière remained passionately committed to the theater. Refusing to cancel the final performance lest he deprive "fifty poor workers who have only their daily wages on which to live" (Grimarest, *Vie de Molière,* p. 119), he carried his concern for his art to the point of making himself the director of and actor in his own death scene. Like his tricksters Mascarille and Scapin, he was such a "clever handler of motive and plot" that he wanted to be certain not to flub his exit. When he wrote *Le malade imaginaire,* Molière knew that his own illness was not at all imaginary, that his days were numbered. Openly constructing his ballet-comedy on the model of his previous works, he reused the fundamental structures and mechanisms of *Tartuffe* (1664–1669), *Les femmes savantes* (1672; *The Learned Ladies*), and *Le bourgeois gentilhomme* (1670; *The Would-be Gentleman*) and borrowed dialogues and themes from *Dom Juan* (1665), *L'amour médecin* (1665; *Love Is the Best Doctor*), and *Les fourberies de Scapin* (1671; *That Scoundrel Scapin*). Thus *Le malade imaginaire,* with its therapeutic profession of faith—only laughter allows man to accept his mortal condition, cures him from the fear and anxiety of dying—sums up Molière's thought and art; as his comic will and testament, the play worthily crowns his exemplary career as an apologist, poet, and theoretician of theater.

In the 17th century only Pierre Corneille, the jealous and influential father of French "classical theater," had a longer career than Molière. After the miseries and financial ruin of his first troupe, the Illustre-Théâtre (1643–1645), Molière and his associates, the Béjart family, left Paris and spent a dozen arduous years traveling the roads of Languedoc and southern France. In 1658 they returned to the capital, where they competed with the established theatrical companies of the Marais and the Hôtel de Bourgogne. By then Molière was already a complete athlete of the theater, an actor, director, and manager who had also composed some farces and two large-scale comedies of intrigue, *L'étourdi, ou les contre-temps* (1654; *The Blunderer, or the Mishaps*) and *Dépit amoureux* (1656; *The Amorous Quarrel*). But it was during the years in Paris (1658–1673), with his troupe solidly installed in the Palais-Royal theater, that, as "court jester," protégé of the king, and popular author, Molière wrote, staged, and performed his masterpieces.

This lifelong total involvement with the theater undoubtedly provides the best explanation for the riches and diversity of Molière's work, for its astonishing powers of metamorphosis and renewal. He deliberately exploited all existing forms and genres, giving them a soul, a meaning, and a vigor they had previously lacked: farce, with *La jalousie du Barbouillé, Le docteur amoureux, Le médecin volant* (before 1658; *The Jealousy of Barbouillé, The Amorous Doctor, The Flying Physician*), *Les précieuses ridicules* (1659; *The Precious Damsels*), and *Le médecin malgré lui* (1666; *The Physician in spite of Himself*); three-act comedy, with *L'école des maris* (1661; *The School for Husbands*), *George Dandin* (1668), and *Les fourberies de Scapin;* tragicomedy, with *Dom Garcie de Navarre* (1661); mythological fantasy with stage machinery in *Amphitryon* (1668); the court *divertissement,* with *La princesse d'Elide* (1664; *The Princess of Elis*), *Mélicerte* (1666), *La pastorale comique* (1666; *The Comic Pastoral*), *Les amants magnifiques* (1670; *The Magnificent Lovers*), and *Psyché* (1671)—this last written in collaboration with Corneille and Philippe Quinault, with music by Jean-Baptiste Lully—and, above all, the great five-act classical comedy in verse, as well as its variant in prose, a brilliant list of masterpieces including *L'école des femmes* (1662; *The School for Wives*), *Tartuffe, Dom Juan, Le misanthrope* (1666; *The Misanthrope*), *L'avare* (1668; *The Miser*), and *Les femmes savantes.* Thanks to the unequaled splendors of *Psyché,* Molière also contributed significantly to the birth of the French opera. Finally, after an apparently fortuitous experiment with *Les fâcheux* (1661; *The Bores*), he created an entirely new type of spectacle, the ballet-comedy—a hybrid that, according to Hali, a character in *Le Sicilien, ou l'amour peintre* (1667; *The Sicilian, or Love Makes the Painter*), "dabbles a bit in music and in dance," adding the pleasures of the senses to those of the text. Of these Molière offered to the king, in his châteaux at Chambord and at Saint-Germain, or to his Paris public at the Palais-Royal, such dazzling masterpieces as *Monsieur de Pourceaugnac* (1669), *Le bourgeois gentilhomme, La comtesse d'Escarbagnas* (1672), and *Le malade imaginaire.*

Overall, then, a corpus of more than thirty plays, twenty-nine of them written after the troupe settled in Paris. Between 1658 and 1673, for fourteen full theatrical seasons, Molière wrote an average of two plays per year (three in 1661, 1664, 1666, 1668, and 1671). This productivity is even more remarkable given the difficulties that ceaselessly battered him throughout the years, suffering and disappointment in his private life mingling with every sort of professional problem to undermine his ever more fragile health: in 1663 Corneille and the rival troupe of actors at the Hôtel de Bourgogne dragged him into a public quarrel over the merits of *L'école des femmes;* the following year the church and the "devout faction" obtained a prohibition of public performances of *Tartuffe* that would last five years; his wife deceived him; Racine betrayed him; in 1667 he was so ill that he had to close his theater for a while, and rumors of his death circulated through Paris; and in 1672, a final test, the king abandoned him, granting Lully the directorship of the Royal Academy of Music and the monopoly of all musical productions in the kingdom. In each case Molière fought back with verve and wit, knowing that his best response to jealous rivals was to continue to please his public with new plays; knowing that his dependency on subsidies from the crown required him to honor the commissions he received from the king for the Carnival or for nuptial, military, or holiday celebrations; and knowing, above all, that he must continue to produce for his actors, who depended on him for their livelihood.

These constraints, considered with the amazing diversity of Molière's works, give the impression of an author driven by obligation, who produced his work in haste under multiple pressures. This image led interpreters to envisage each of his comedies as a discrete unit, and the corpus as a random succession of forms, lacking cohesion as well as spirit. Molière was taken to be a writer under too much pressure to think, to meditate on his art and on humanity, a creator whose only concern was to make us laugh. No more.

In the 1960s American critics overturned this interpretation. A series of brilliant analyses of the great trilogy, *Tartuffe, Dom Juan,* and *Le misanthrope,* returned Molière to his proper place as a "highly conscious literary artist" (Judd Hubert), as a dramatist for whom creation constantly "moves beyond itself into self-consciousness" (Jacques Guicharnaud). He was recognized not only as a great comic poet—certainly, with Rabelais, the greatest in French literature—but also as a strong theoretician of the comic who was in perfect control of his work from beginning to end and who never conceded to circumstances any more than he had to. Viewed in this light, Molière's creation regained its coherence and internal dynamism. It was at last considered, not as a fortuitous succession of discrete moments, but as a living and continuous fabric in which "no individual work, perhaps, can be properly understood in isolation from the whole, any more than one movement of a sonata can stand apart from the whole sonata" (Lionel Gossman, *Men and Masks,* p. vii). Critics perceived that Molière's work conformed to an evolutionary process that was both necessary and deliberate—a movement, a temporal and organic metamorphosis, that, passing through the deep and decisive crisis caused by the prohibition of *Tartuffe* in 1664, led him from classical humanist comedy to the total spectacle of the ballet-comedy.

In a first major period, running from *Les précieuses* to *Tartuffe* and *Le misanthrope,* Molière fashioned a kind of comedy modeled essentially on Terence and the dramatic theories nurtured on Aristotle's *Poetics.* He himself sketched out the theory of this genre in two little one-act plays in prose, both produced in 1663 as a reply to those who were criticizing *L'école des femmes: La critique de L'école des femmes* (*The School for Wives Cricitized*) and *L'impromptu de Versailles* (*The Versailles Impromptu*). During this period Molière was following prevailing classical tastes, rules, and prejudices. Although Corneille's tragic heroes were beginning to show signs of fatigue around 1660—the dramatist had by then reigned supreme for more than twenty years—tragedy remained the noble genre, the only genre, along with epic, able to elevate the writer to the level of the ancients; comedy, though it could make the king and the Paris bourgeoisie laugh heartily, was still considered a bagatelle, unworthy of an author's primary attention. In fact it was not as a writer of farces or as a "mocker of mores" but as a hero of tragedy that Molière set out in 1658 to win over the king and Paris; Pierre Mignard's famous portrait shows him dressed as a Roman emperor. All the work of his early years, from *Sganarelle, ou le cocu imaginaire* (1660; *Sganarelle, or the Imaginary Cuckold*) to *Dom Juan,* and including *Dom Garcie de Navarre* (1661) and *L'école des femmes* (a "burlesque tragedy"), reflects a deep nostalgia for the tragic. Unable to satisfy his desire to be Alexander the Great, Sertorius, or Pompey, because his fate was laughter, Molière became Sganarelle and Arnolphe. Yet his purpose remained lofty: he aimed to achieve in and for comedy the dignity and respectability that it still lacked, to have it recognized as a genre that was, if not superior, at least equal to tragedy. This is why Corneille, still more than Terence, can be considered the true father of classical comedy: a comedy modeled on tragedy—with five acts, alexandrine lines, respect for the *bienséances* (decorum) and the rules of dramatic composition—that would lead Molière to the incomparable greatness of *Le misanthrope.*

As a sister of Cornelian tragedy, classical comedy rapidly assumed the somewhat affected posture of an irreproachable, upright lady. Primarily a woman of the world, she aimed to please by her virtues, her reason, and her conservatism. Steeped in *honnêteté* (honorability), in perfect harmony with the dominant social ideology, she presented herself as strictly orthodox, as conforming in all respects with the expectations of the day. Her greatest quality was perhaps an elaborate "naturalness." In her urbanity and proper modesty, she made only the most traditional of claims: to be a mirror, an image or representation, an imitation of everyday life. Unlike tragedy, which too often veered into the extraordinary and the marvelous, her concern for truth led her to paint "according to nature," to show humanity "as it is," to put onstage portraits that resembled the originals so closely that the latter could not but recognize themselves. This commitment to "realism" allowed comedy to proclaim its utility, to recall that "the theater is the school for man," that it had "a great capacity for correction" (preface to *Tartuffe,* 1669). If comedy was, as the church claimed, a vivid and therefore dangerous description of the passions, it was also "a severe lesson in keeping them in check" (ibid.). Hence Molière's proud declarations to vindicate himself, especially with regard to *Tartuffe:* the responsibility of comedy, its duty, was to correct humanity while entertaining it. Nothing improves humanity better than the depiction of its faults. Vices are hit hard when exposed to universal laughter. People put up readily with remonstrances, but not with mockery. They are willing to be wicked, but not to be ridiculous.

This realist and moral comedy, which showed people their vices and their follies in order to cure them, was imbued with the optimistic humanism of the Counter-Reformation. As Molière's mouthpiece—presumably Jean Donneau de Visé—remarks in the *Lettre sur la comédie de L'imposteur* (1667; *Letter on the Comedy of The Impostor*), comedy treats human beings as *naturally* sensitive to reason, and thus as capable of seeing their errors and correcting them; it places this rational being in an eminently comfortable and reassuring world, a world in which common sense and *honnêteté* rule, in which laughter is the collective expression of reason and moral health, a legitimate weapon serving a triumphant justice and welfare. The ridiculous characters of these comedies—from Cathos and Magdelon through Sganarelle, Arnolphe, and Orgon, to Tartuffe—all amply deserve the public correction that is inflicted on them; they all appear, in the light of the social norm that, through the complicity of comedy, judges and condemns them, as laughable aberrations. Their singularity isolates them irremediably. It excludes them from the polite and conformist world of *honnêteté*—from a world watched over by the king, with his benevolent, just, and lucid gaze.

This poetics enabled Molière to rise to the rank of Secretary of State for the Ridiculous, and comedy to take its place alongside tragedy as an estimable genre—a "respectable woman," as Molière dubbed her in the preface to *Tartuffe.* But no theoretical statement accounts satisfactorily for Molière's actual practice. And his conformist outlook and praise of orthodoxy were only a façade. From the beginning, Molière's supposedly "respectable woman" was in fact an irreverent soubrette who took unacceptable liberties. Her "natural" demeanor was often condemned for tending toward grotesque caricature and sinking into the obscene, the improbable, or the ludicrous. It was no longer Terence's urbanity—his *sermo moratus*—that controlled comedy, but Plautus' *vis comica* (comic force) and buffoonery. *L'école des femmes* already possessed all the elements necessary to make clergymen wonder just how far this daring newcomer would go. Molière's comedy had a provocative tendency to pry into everything and respect nothing. When it went so far as to strip Tartuffe of his mask of false piety, Molière's laughter crossed into the realm of public scandal: comedy assumed the dimensions of an affair of state. Aristotle and Cicero had confined the domain of ridicule to the narrow limits of *deformitas* and *turpitudo sine dolore,* physical deformity and moral ugliness, allowing no feelings of horror, misery, or pity. Molière, in contrast, exposed the most unbearable defects, the most monstrous vices; with Tartuffe and Dom Juan, he invited his audience to laugh at a hypocrite and at an "evil lord"; with Harpagon, he put onstage a character who was indeed, "of all humans, the least humane" (act 2, scene 4). With Molière, the comic no longer had any limits; it became something universal, a point of view on the entire human condition.

The magnitude of the *Tartuffe* affair prompted Molière to question systematically the principles and the comic mechanisms on which he had been relying. *Dom Juan,* his following play, reflects the first stage of this process: through the libertine's ironic gaze, Molière puts society, its language, its hypocrisy, and its false values, on trial. A year later *Le misanthrope* goes a step further, staging the trial of laughter and moral comedy—his own trial. Alceste's incurable "illness" is his desire to "correct the world" (line 158), his belief that people are receptive to and capable of correction, and his presumptuous righteousness in judging and censuring the vices of his century. If society has no right to laugh, then comedy has no right either to blame or to pass judgment. In this world, justice and reason simply do not exist. There is no norm, and no truth. We are all fools to some degree, and all equally incorrigible. Rediscovering Erasmus' vision in *Moriae Encomium* (1511; *Praise of Folly*), comedy here abandons its educative and moral claims: as Alceste's friend Philinte says to him, "the world will not be changed by your efforts, you know" (line 102). The only option, then, is to adjust, to make accommodation with this universal folly that no one can avoid, to transform it into a spectacle, to make it a pleasure, a pretext for the triumph of festivity and amusement. Far from wishing to "cure" the would-be gentleman and the imaginary invalid of their errors, of their blindness and folly, Molière's late comedies make them kings of the Carnival—blossoming, euphoric, happy fools, living in a world of fantasy. Whereas moral comedy had treated human vice and virtue from a social perspective, Molière's new comedies do not envision humanity's weak and barren nature in terms of moral value, but in terms of *being* or *existence.* Their perspective is less ethical than both aesthetic and metaphysical. The alternation, in *Le malade imaginaire,* of Argan's somber mania with the various onstage *divertissements* is emblematic of this new trend. Molière's simultaneous shift, after the crisis of *Tartuffe,* toward a pessimistic vision of humanity and a comic wisdom made up entirely of lucid awareness and acceptance, did not impose a dampening, prudential mark on his dramaturgy. On the contrary, his new, disabused conception of comedy proved to be amenable to this renewed theatrical experimentation in the ballet-comedy after 1666. With this charitable sister whose laughter, far from seeking to punish, was primarily benevolent and consoling, he was able to expand the theater's resources, anticipating the search for a total spectacle that Pierre Caron de Beaumarchais would pursue a century later.

In 1673, when Molière expired, the great classical genres were also dying. After Racine's *Phèdre* (1677; *Phaedra*) tragedy would fade away. As for comedy, it survived in the works of a few imitators of varying talent: Charles Dufresny (1648–1724), Jean-François Regnard (1655–1709), Florent Dancourt (1661–1725), and Alain-René Lesage (1668–1747). But none of them, not even

Lesage, managed to revitalize a genre that Molière had brought to perfection. Not until Pierre Carlet de Marivaux, Pierre Caron de Beaumarchais, and Denis Diderot would Molière have successors worthy of his genius. The end of the "great century" was instead marked by the success of Lully and the opera. On the fate of comedy after Molière, then, we can hardly differ with the judgment of Nicolas Boileau, who in 1677 evoked the departed Molière in his seventh *Epître* (*Epistle*) addressed to Racine (lines 36–39):

> With Molière lovable comedy was laid low,
> Sought in vain to recover from such a rude blow,
> For to stand in his shoes she was now too late.
> Such was our classical theater's fate.

See also 1581, 1637, 1651, 1660, 1661, 1680.

Bibliography: Nicolas Boileau-Despréaux, *Satires. Epîtres. Art Poétique,* ed. Jean-Pierre Collinet (Paris: Gallimard, 1985). Gérard Defaux, *Molière ou les métamorphoses du comique: De la comédie morale au triomphe de la folie* (Lexington, Ky.: French Forum, 1980). Lionel Gossman, *Men and Masks: A Study of Molière* (Baltimore: Johns Hopkins Press, 1963). Jean Léonor Le Gallois, sieur de Grimarest, *La vie de M. de Molière,* ed. Georges Mongrédien (Paris: Michel Brient, 1955). Jacques Guicharnaud, *Molière. Une aventure théâtrale: Tartuffe, Dom Juan, Le misanthrope* (Paris: Gallimard, 1963). Judd D. Hubert, *Molière and the Comedy of Intellect* (Berkeley: University of California Press, 1962). Molière, *The Misanthrope and Other Plays,* trans. Donald M. Frame (New York: New American Library, 1968). Molière, *Tartuffe and Other Plays,* trans. Donald M. Frame (New York: New American Library, 1967).

Gérard Defaux

༄ 1674

Nicolas Boileau-Despréaux Translates from the Greek Longinus' Treatise *On the Sublime*

On the Sublime, Infinity, Je Ne Sais Quoi

The mordant four-canto poem in alexandrine verse, *L'art poétique* (*The Art of Poetry*), which Nicolas Boileau started to read in Paris salons in 1673, gained him the title "Législateur du Parnasse" (Lawmaker of Parnassus), acknowledging him as the preeminent spokesman for the neoclassical aesthetic doctrine that canonized values such as truthfulness, decency, measure, and moral nobility. This common-sense, at times almost prosaic aesthetic was condensed into the famous verse: "What has been clearly conceived can be clearly stated" (*L'art poétique,* canto 1, line 154). Yet in the same volume with the work asserting these values, Boileau also introduced to France the *je ne sais quoi,* the ineffable, indescribable "I-know-not-what" of the aesthetic sublime. For Boileau's 1674 *Oeuvres diverses* (*Collected Works*) included also his translation, the first one into French, of Longinus' *Peri Hypsos* (*On the Sublime*), followed by

Réflexions critiques sur quelques passages du rhéteur Longin (*Critical Reflections on Some Passages of the Rhetorician Longinus*).

This ineffability announces itself in Boileau's own attempts, in his preface, to characterize the historical Longinus, for part of Boileau's argument is that the special value of the *Traité du sublime* lies in its author's capacity not simply to analyze but also to exemplify the sublime. Interpreting the sublime *work* as inextricably fused with a sublime *life,* Boileau emphasizes the elevated and powerful status of Longinus as orator, critic, minister of state, and philosopher, seeing him as a figure "worthy of being compared with a Socrates or a Cato" (*Oeuvres,* p. 336). Sensing the author's intimate presence in his text, Boileau then declares: "His feelings have a certain *je ne sais quoi* that characterizes not only a sublime mind, but a soul far above the ordinary." And in this, the master of neoclassical order confronts an intangible, indefinable trait, a *je ne sais quoi* that points, not to the sublime it announces, but to the critic's inability to describe it positively.

In chapter 15 of his treatise, Longinus characterizes the sublime as the effect resulting from an invisible trope, from a trope's becoming invisible, asking, "How did the Orator manage to conceal the trope he is using? How can we fail to see that it is through the very brightness of his thought? For, the same way lesser lights fade when the sun starts to shine, rhetorical subtleties disappear when surrounded by such grandeur" (p. 370). Like the sun, the sublime is neither directly visible nor directly expressible and frustrates all attempts to define it. Thus the sublime escapes qualification.

For Boileau, the crucial distinction is between *the sublime* and *sublime style.* The sublime is an effect of style, not a style in itself. And the sublime effect is never achieved by "high," "elevated," or even "sublime" discourse: stylistic simplicity and restraint characterize the sublime. The sublime can occur in any genre, being proper to none. Neither trope nor figure, and belonging to no class in rhetorical taxonomy, it is rather a function of the multiple factors at work in a given discourse's utterance. Induced by an act of enunciation, the sublime occurs in semantic effects linked to the circumstantial. "It is not, properly speaking," says Boileau in the *Réflexions critiques,* "something that one proves or demonstrates; but it is a marvel that grips, that hits, that makes itself felt" (p. 546).

Lefèvre Tanneguy, in the preface to his Latin translation of Longinus (1663), discusses at length the translation of *hypsos:* grandeur, magnificence, dignity, weight, intensity, *sublimitas* . . . Boileau, for his part, proposes what is extraordinary, or surprising, or, "as I chose to translate it, what in discourse is marvelous [*merveilleux*]" (p. 338). The marvelous is what delights, enraptures, ravishes, what strikes, seizes, surprises, bewitches, excites. "Primarily, it produces an effect on us that is very hard, if not impossible, to resist" (p. 349). It is definable primarily through its effects—but these effects in turn are definable only through reference to the defining proposition: the sublime is what produces the feeling of the sublime, the sublime as pathos. The presentation of the sublime is thus itself sublime insofar as it performs an "affect-effect" with no objectively identifiable distinctive feature: it is not a single passion, but the pathos of all the passions; it is not one emotion, but the motion of all emotions.

Boileau discusses an example of sublimity quoted by Longinus from Herodotus and shows that its grandeur does not result from the use of big words; rather, the *petitesse énergique* (energetic smallness) of the words produces "a certain energizing force, which, accounting for the horror of the thing that is said, has *je ne sais quoi* sublime" (p. 550). The indefinable, unrepresentable presence of the sublime affects the position of the speaker as well as the act of enunciation. For both the author and the audience, the sublime affect-effect always entails a deprivation, a weakening of the subject's identity, a dispossession of the subject from himself or herself (whether through rapture, transport, ecstasy, stupefaction, astonishment, or bedazzlement).

The sublime is thus the elusive *je ne sais quoi* not only of the rhetoric and poetics of genres and styles, of their rules and figures, but also of all aesthetic response, of value judgment based on taste, of art theory in general. So construed, the sublime indicates a gap within the theory itself. What the theory approaches but cannot grasp, it positions as the "end" of art—both its ultimate goal and its cessation. Whether the sublime is the endpoint in an ascending hierarchy of values, as it is for Lefèvre, or the ultimate feature of beauty, as for Boileau and Dominique Bouhours, it paradoxically both completes and supplements: it lies on the borderline of the beautiful form, at the threshold of the undefinable aspect of beauty; yet this threshold of indefinition is also the place where the form encounters the limit that makes it a beautiful form.

The same ambiguous position characterizes Boileau's marvelous. For the author of *L'art poétique,* the marvelous is not a characteristic of the epic genre, and even less of the Christian epic, although the epic genre is potentially more open to the sublime than is tragedy. Rather, Boileau's marvelous is caught up in a major confrontation within aesthetics: on the one side, *mimetic* representation, governed by the imitation of either nature or its ideal order (in Kant's terms, the mechanism of *reproductive* imagination); and on the opposite side, a notion of *phantasia* or image-making (Kant's *productive* imagination). In Longinus' *On the Sublime* the motifs of the marvelous emanate from this latter tradition, a Platonic one that can be traced through Plotinus, Aristotle, Seneca, the Stoics, and the Second Sophistic movement, a tradition that links poetry to enthusiasm and inspiration, to states that, at their origin, were induced by divine or demonic powers. The poetic theory of the marvelous has the same relation to mimetic representation as the philosophical theory of *phantasia* does: by marking the internal fissure in the relation of language to things and to essences, and thereby exposing the immanent lapsing of the ontological power of language, the theory of the marvelous brings the challenge of the sublime inside the mechanism of representation.

What marks the pivotal decade of the 1660s is, however, not a simple confrontation in which the sublime directs its challenge or resistance against the system of classical representation, but an attempt to integrate the theory of the marvelous and *phantasia* into the very order of representation. Such an inclusion would complete the expansion of the representational system while still allowing it to be questioned from within. The key stratagem in this effort is probably the granting of noun status to the *je ne sais quoi*. It allows it to retain, while acting as an agent of integration, the questioning force of the sublime: it remains an aesthetic motif while calling into question aesthetics itself and suggests at the same time the fulfillment and the evanescence of art.

A linguistic articulation of the sublime had already occurred not long before Lefèvre's Latin translation of Longinus, in sections of Pascal's *Pensées sur la religion et sur quelques autres sujets* (1670; *Pensées*) such as the following fragment from "Diversité" ("Diversity"): "A city, a plain, seen from a distance, is a city and a plain; but as one draws nearer, there are houses, trees, tiles, leaves, grass, ants, ants' legs, and so on indefinitely [*à l'infini*]. All are included in the word 'plain'" (*Pensées,* pp. 37–38). Here, more than a century before Immanuel Kant's *Critique of Judgment* (1794), Pascal describes the mind's encounter with the infinite in terms that announce the sublime, pointing out how following the subject's mobile viewpoint brings a sense of the infinite into our conventional ideas—apparently stable and closed—of the objects we encounter. In principle, just as the noun *countryside* tames an unimaginably diverse expanse, every other name also envelops the infinite. That is, underlying every "noun" is the double-edged conditioning of thought that Pascal discloses: first, our *finite* capacity to conceive (we can never embrace every perspective on or component of an object; there is a fundamental gap between our image and an exhaustive perception of the object) and, concomitantly, the *infinity* of differences (we can always produce additional differences by moving to another viewpoint) from which each being draws its particular (self-)conception. This vision of an ever-expanding field of differences works in language just as it does in perspective. Language functions as an open-ended field of differences in which man's being is articulated in acts of meaning, in relations formed by discourse among discrete units in that field. Since the number of potential distinctions and propositions is limitless, the full range of semantic possibility can never be circumscribed. Thus language bears the mark of the same constitutive gap that structures perception—that of the sublime, the infinite.

Pascal's celebrated fragment "Disproportion de l'homme" ("Disproportion of Man"), with its famous passage on the two infinities, is perhaps the most telling illustration of his remarkable anticipation of Kant's thought on the sublime. In effect Pascal opposes reproductive imagination, a "mistress of error and falsehood," to productive imagination. The latter, although it pursues knowledge that is ordered by the geometric schemes of proportion, carries the knowing subject infinitely beyond itself, into an existential disproportion:

> Let man then contemplate the whole of nature in her lofty and abundant majesty; let him withdraw his gaze from the worthless objects that surround him. Let him behold that blazing light, set like an eternal lamp to illumine the universe; let him see the earth as a mere point in comparison with the vast orbit described by the sun; let him wonder at the fact that that vast orbit is

itself but a very faint speck compared with that described by the stars in their journey through the firmament. But if our view is to stop short there, let the imagination pass beyond; it will sooner cease to function than will nature to supply him material . . . try as we may to enlarge our notions beyond all imaginable space, and yet be conceiving mere atoms in comparison with the reality . . . In short, the greatest sensible indication of God's omnipotence is the fact that our imagination loses itself in that thought. (*Pensées*, p. 106)

The dynamic that transgresses every perceptual limit of the imagination produces new conceptions, but repeats indefinitely the same proportionality: hence the effect of lassitude, the affect of monotony. Here theoretical consciousness encounters its pathos, which is melancholy, and, inversely, the melancholy pathos of the indefinite discovers itself to be geometric knowledge. To "the art hidden in the depths of the human soul" responds a nature that, enshrouding itself in its depths, never relents as it develops indefinitely its present, yet unrepresentable, infinity: its totality.

Therefore, the unbridgeable gap between the product of the theoretical imagination and the inexhaustible production of nature is none other than the sublime thought of the infinite as a melancholy geometry. And it is at precisely this moment that the term *God* appears. It is not, however, an epiphany of God in nature or an ontological positioning of divinity. The perceptible mark, the tangible sign of divine omnipotence is that the imagination gets lost in the thought of the infinite: the impossibility of perceiving the infinite dynamics of nature occasions a "properly" sublime sensation. God is made manifest through the infinite regress or retreat of all manifest signs, through the encounter with the impossibility of representing the totality of nature. Manifested when the (productive) imagination becomes lost *in* the idea, the unrepresentable presence is the presentation of the unrepresentable itself.

The notion of the sublime in Pascal is thus part of the epistemological foundation of the study of humanity. The paradoxical nature of this foundation is that it "unfounds" or confounds all theoretical knowledge. But far from surrendering knowledge to skepticism, the notion of the sublime, by virtue of this very unfounding, at once opens up and bridges the gulf between the speculative and the ethical, the rational and the religious. The very appearance of the "marvel" is what triggers the transcendental movement of the speculative in to the ethical, as Pascal suggests in his pamphlet "De l'esprit géométrique et de l'art de persuader" ("On the Geometrical Mind and the Art of Persuasion"): "those who clearly see these truths can admire the grandeur and the power of nature in this double infinity which surrounds us on all sides. And by the consideration of these wonders they may learn to know themselves . . . As a result we may learn to estimate our own value and to make reflections which are worth more than all the rest of geometry" (*Shorter Works*, p. 202).

Whereas the theoreticians of classicism from Boileau to René Rapin (who translated Longinus in 1686) sought to integrate the conception of the sublime into an aesthetics of representation (such was, in particular, the function of the *je ne sais quoi* in Bouhours's work), the theory of the infinite in Pascal—who was nevertheless in many respects a classical thinker—was linked to an effort to destabilize the mechanisms of mimesis and the philosophy underlying them. Unlike Gottfried Wilhelm von Leibniz (1646–1716), who would master the challenges of the infinite in the domains of knowledge, ethics, and metaphysics, Pascal made the infinite both the distinctive feature of human experience and the decisive basis for questioning the conditions of knowledge, the imperatives of ethics, and the requirements of faith. Pascal's treatment of the infinite subsequently provided the Romantics with an aesthetic model, that of the fragment, for sublime writing.

From this point of view it clearly anticipated the notion of the sublime elaborated in Kant's third *Critique*. Does not the feeling of the sublime, like the "disproportionate" feeling of the infinite in Pascal, manifest itself when the imagination fails to present the mind with an object that corresponds with a concept? Does the value of Kant's idea of the infinite not lie, like "the mark and utterly empty trace" invoked by Pascal (*Pensées*, no. 148/425) even as he stresses the pain of the imagination seeking after an object capable of filling in this emptiness, in its *negative* presentation and in that strange ecstasy in which it is revealed that "man surpasses man infinitely" (*Pensées*, no. 131/434)?

See also 1750.

Bibliography: Nicolas Boileau, *Oeuvres complètes*, ed. Antoine Adam and Françoise Escal (Paris: Gallimard, 1966). Jules Brody, *Boileau and Longinus* (Geneva: Droz, 1958). Neil Hertz, "A Reading of Longinus," in *The End of the Line: Essays on Psychoanalysis and the Sublime* (New York: Columbia University Press, 1985). Théodore A. Litman, *Le sublime en France (1660–1714)* (Paris: Nizet, 1971). Louis Marin, "Le sublime dans les années 1670," *Papers on French XVIIth-Century Literature*, 25 (1986), 185–201. Blaise Pascal, *Great Shorter Works of Pascal*, ed. Emile Cailliet and John C. Blankenagel (Philadelphia: Westminster Press, n.d.). Pascal, *Pensées*, ed. Louis Lafuma, trans. John Warrington (London: Dent, 1973). Theodore E. B. Wood, *The Word "Sublime" and Its Context (1650–1760)* (The Hague: Mouton, 1972).

Louis Marin

∾ 1677

Louis XIV Asks Jean Racine and Nicolas Boileau to Write
a History of His Reign

Historiography in the Age of Absolutism

In the fall of 1677 Jean Racine and Nicolas Boileau-Despréaux seemed to have reached the peak of their literary careers: Racine had enjoyed the triumph of *Phèdre* that spring, and Boileau had already published in 1674 his one-volume *Oeuvres diverses* (*Collected Works*), containing the major texts on which his literary reputation is founded. Then, in September, Louis XIV, in the marquise de Sévigné's words, "ordered them to give up everything in order to work on his history" (letter, 13 October 1677, *Correspondance*, 2:572). They were named royal historiographers as a result of the influence of the current royal favorite, Françoise de Montespan, and of Jean-Baptiste Colbert, to whom Louis XIV had given financial control over literary and architectural projects. Boileau and Racine supplanted Paul Pellisson-Fontanier, whose patron, Nicolas Fouquet, had formerly exercised the duties now assigned Colbert. Louis XIV's choice was widely criticized on the grounds that these bourgeois writers who excelled in poetry rather than in prose were not up to the task of chronicling royal glory. But this choice and the poets' willingness to give up virtually all other literary activity nevertheless say a great deal about the prestige historiography enjoyed in the Versailles era.

During the triumph of absolutism, the writing of history was preeminently concerned with the reigning monarch and was entrusted to appointees with titles such as "historiographer of the king," "historiographer of France," and "historiographer of the buildings of the king." At the beginning of his personal reign, from 1661 to 1666, Louis XIV, following the policy of Jules Cardinal Mazarin and Colbert, had appointed seven historiographers of the king, two of France, and one (André Félibien) of buildings, paintings, and sculpture. The appointments were then interrupted until Pellisson's nomination in 1670. After the appointment of Racine and Boileau, only five historiographers of the king (among them Louis Géraud de Cordemoy in 1683, Jean Donneau de Visé in 1691, and Jean-Baptiste-Henri de Valincour in 1699) and one historiographer of France were appointed.

The office of historiographer remained ill defined. Only a larger stipend and greater prestige clearly distinguished historiographers of France from historiographers of the king. Nor did there appear to be a consistent policy behind the granting of the position. The extreme diversity in the writers selected, in the duration of the appointments, and in the amount of the pensions (which changed from one year to the next) made it difficult to regard the office of historiographer as genuine. The title appeared to be a means of rewarding those who served the glory of the reign and of the dynasty by writing history.

Sometimes it represented a reward for a book already written, as in 1685 in the case of Claude-Charles Guyonnet de Vertron, who had completed that year a *Parallèle de Louis le Grand avec tous les princes qui ont été surnommés Grands* (*Comparison of Louis the Great with All Other Sovereigns Who Have Been Called Great*), or in that of the Jesuit Gabriel Daniel in 1706, ten years after he had written his *Histoire de France depuis l'établissement de la monarchie française* (*History of France since the Foundation of the French Monarchy*). Usually, however, the post was granted for a projected history. In 1670 Pellisson received an appointment after having presented Colbert with a "Projet de l'histoire de Louis XIV" (Plan for a history of Louis XIV), described as "a great history in the style of Livy, Polybius, and other classical historians," a work that would have been neither history, chronicle, or memoir nor defense or panegyric. But neither this nor similar projects were ever realized. Accompanying the monarch in his campaigns and battles, the historiographers of the king produced only fragmentary accounts, dedicated to Louis alone or to his intimates (such as Pellisson's letters to Madeleine de Scudéry). These accounts were sometimes published as works of propaganda, such as Racine's *Relation de ce qui s'est passé au siège de Namur* (1692; *Account of the Events at the Siege of Namur*) and Racine and Boileau's collaborative *Eloge historique du roi en ses conquêtes* (1678; *Encomium of the King's Conquests*). The list of accomplishments of Louis XIV's historiographers is thus rather short, marked by aborted projects, occasional pieces, and material collected but never organized into a formal history of the reign (such as Donneau de Visé's *Mémoires pour servir à l'histoire de Louis le Grand*, 1697–1703; *Memoirs to Serve in the History of Louis the Great*).

There are several reasons for this deficiency. One is that Louis XIV wanted to be his own historian, an ambition that would have established a perfect coincidence between action and its representation, between the king who enacted history and the historian who narrated it. This aspiration accounts for Louis XIV's concern, from 1666 to 1670, over his *Mémoires,* which were to serve as instruction for the dauphin. Starting in 1666, he participated in the production of various texts, particularly his memoirs for the years 1661, 1662, 1666, 1667, and 1668: he wrote with his own hand notes and fragments of drafts; he dictated, corrected, and annotated the account composed by Octave de Périgny, the reader for the king and instructor to the dauphin; and, finally, he revised the two, three, or four successive versions of the final text. Not until 1672, with the beginning of the war against Holland and perhaps also because the project lost its pedagogical purpose when the dauphin attained his majority—did Louis cease this direct involvement.

Another reason the project remained unfinished may have been the fact that writing was not the most important medium for the history of the reign. Visual representations were better suited than printed ones to present history to those who could not read. Hence the production of medals (by the Little Academy, which in 1702 published the *Médailles sur les principaux événements du règne de Louis le Grand; Medals of the Principal Events of the Reign of Louis the Great*), historical engravings, and mural almanacs. Hence also, in the 1670s, the abandonment of solar or Apollonian symbolism in favor of more accessible representations, showing the king with his own features on monuments dedicated to his personal glory.

But although the history of Louis's reign remained unwritten, from the mid-17th century to the early 18th century history accounted for more than 20 percent of titles published in Paris. After 1670, history ranked behind religious books but before literature in popularity. Readers of history formed a faithful clientele, eager for new texts and new editions. These texts covered a wide range of subjects—histories of France; histories of Christian heresies; universal histories; fictionalized histories (whose best-known practitioners were Antoine Varillas and César de Saint-Réal); and the sought-after memoirs of important individuals of the preceding two centuries—and included both scholarly and popular accounts. Best-sellers were primarily histories of France, compilations and sequels offering simple variations on a fixed pattern. From Michel de Marolles's *Histoire des rois de France* (1663; *History of the Kings of France*) to

Daniel's complete *Histoire de France* (1713), eighteen elementary histories were published. Their purpose was above all ethical: they appraised monarchs as good or bad, starting with a list of the most necessary virtues and the most abhorrent vices. Throughout the century, piety took precedence over all other monarchical virtues, followed by justice and valor. In the ranking of sovereigns, St. Louis (Louis IX) gradually outshone Philip II Augustus, becoming the founding hero of the dynasty and the model of a good king. At least four biographies of the saint king were published from 1666 to 1689. In the histories written after 1680, other qualities, such as prudence, liberality, and love of letters, became more prominent, as if the concept of royalty had been somewhat emancipated from traditional definitions.

On the side of scholarly history, the Benedictines of Saint-Maur, especially those of the abbey of Saint-Germain-des-Prés, spearheaded a revival of erudition, initially in the form of ecclesiastical history. Jean Mabillon, in his *De Re Diplomatica* (1681; *Concerning Official Documents*), gave the new erudition its discourse on method and illustrated that method in his editions of the *Acta* (1669–1701; *Acts*) and then the *Annales* (1703–1739; *Annals*) of the Order of St. Benoît. Several lay scholars followed this lead: Etienne Baluze, Charles Du Cange, and the Jansenist Sébastien Le Nain de Tillemont. This meticulous antiquarian erudition also characterized secular genres unrelated to religious history: numismatic research, genealogy (with its important social consequences), and heraldry.

Antoine Furetière's definition of history in his *Dictionnaire universel* (1690; *Universal Dictionary*) as "description, narration of things as they are, or of actions as they have occurred or as they might have occurred" embraced both "real narration connecting many memorable events that have occurred in one or more nations, in one or more centuries" and "fictitious but probable narrations, which are invented by an author." For Furetière and most of his contemporaries, the split was not between history and fiction, but between stories whose plots lacked verisimilitude (stories and novels) and stories, real or imagined, that were verisimilar, belonging to the order of what could have been or might be. Thus understood, history could be approached as if it were a realistic fable. Furetière's definition sheds a striking light on the distance between the two main axes of historiographical writing in the age of Louis XIV—between the Benedictines' exacting erudition, collecting memorials of the past without arranging them in a narrative form, and the forms of writing that were barely affected by the accumulation of new knowledge.

This split between narration and erudition put an end to the "new" or "perfect" history, which developed during the last third of the 16th century, beginning with Etienne Pasquier's *Recherches de la France* (1560; *Studies of France*) and culminating in Henri Voisin de La Popelinière's *Idée de l'histoire accomplie* (1599; *The Notion of History Perfected*) and *Histoire des histoires* (1604; *History of Histories*). At this time the discovery of archives, the passion for philology and documentary criticism, together with an interpretation of the history of the law intended to legitimate absolute monarchy, merged harmoniously with a demand for erudition and linked it to the idea of a history whose goal was the rational comprehension of human activity—what La Popelinière called "the representation of everything" (*Idée de l'histoire accomplie*, p. 85). The erudite lawyers of the beginning of the 17th century, and then the Benedictines of Saint-Maur, inherited the archival project and made it thrive, but in doing so abandoned the writing to compilers and men of letters who limited their work to praising the monarch and the dynasty in morally freighted stories. "The history of a kingdom or of a nation has for its object the Prince and the State; this is the center where everything must converge," declared Daniel (*Histoire de France*, p. xxiii). The "representation of everything" was less important than the glory of the prince and the greatness of his lineage.

With certain historians, however, something remained of the old project of "perfect" history. Thus François de Mézeray, in his three-volume *Histoire de France depuis Faramond jusqu'à maintenant* (1643, 1646, 1651; *History of France from Faramond to the Present*), dedicated a part of each chapter to the manners and customs of the period under discussion; his organization of the account by reign and his exaltation of the dynasty did not prevent him from including details of antiquarian and erudite curiosity. In the same way, in *Moeurs et coutumes des Français* (1712; *Manners and Customs of the French*) Louis Le Gendre displaced attention from the history of sovereigns to that of the nation, its institutions, and its culture, using history to criticize absolutism.

Mézeray's fall from favor demonstrates the historian's dependence at the time of Louis XIV. In the *Abrégé* (1668; *Summary*) of his *Histoire de France* he described the origin of royal taxes in a manner that strongly displeased his patron, Colbert, and was severely reprimanded: "The king had not given him a pension of 4,000 livres so that he might write with so little circumspection" (letter from Colbert to Charles Perrault, 1668, quoted in Larroque, *Vie*, p. 37). The pension was first reduced by half, then cut off, and finally Mézeray was removed from his position as historiographer of the king, which he had held since 1661. Torn between royal patronage, which required submission, and the reading public, who expected the writer to be independent, between the rules of narrative eloquence and the achievements of erudition, historiography in the age of absolutism was always the result of an unstable, fragile compromise between contradictory demands.

See also 1566, 1661.

Bibliography: Philippe Ariès, *Le temps de l'histoire* (Paris: Seuil, 1986). Père Gabriel Daniel, *Histoire de France* (Paris: Mariette, 1713). Blandine Barret-Kriegel, *Les historiens et la monarchie*, 4 vols. (Paris: Presses Universitaires de France, 1988). Henri Voisin de La Popelinière, *L'histoire des histoires, avec L'idée de l'histoire accomplie* (Paris, 1559). Daniel de Larroque, *La vie de François Eudes de Mézerai* (Amsterdam: Pierre Brunel, 1726). Louis XIV, *Memoirs for the Instruction of the Dauphin,* trans. Paul Sonnino (New York: Free Press, 1970). Louis Marin, *Portrait of the King,* trans. Martha M. Houle (Minneapolis: University of Minnesota Press, 1988). Paul Pellisson-Fontanier, *Oeuvres diverses,* 3 vols. (1753; reprint, Geneva: Slatkine, 1971). Marie de Rabutin-Chantal, marquise de

Sévigné, *Correspondance,* ed. Roger Duchêne, 3 vols. (Paris: Gallimard, 1972–1978).
Orest Ranum, *Artisans of Glory: Writers and Historical Thought in 17th-Century France*
(Chapel Hill: University of North Carolina Press, 1980).

Roger Chartier

✍ 1678

La princesse de Clèves Is Published Anonymously

The Emergence of the Novel

The great literary scandal and debate provoked by the anonymous publication
of *La princesse de Clèves* in 1678 marks a major renewal in the prose narrative
tradition, a milestone in the history of the novel. There are many indications
that Marie-Madeleine de La Fayette (1634–1693), the accepted author of the
book, meant to create a literary sensation and especially to raise questions about
what kind of book she had written. La Fayette was not alone in accomplishing
the transformation of narrative prose that took place in the 1670s. *Les désordres
de l'amour* (1675–76; *The Turmoils of Love*), by Mme. de Villedieu (Marie
Catherine Desjardins), and *Don Carlos* (1672), by César Vichard, abbé de Saint-
Réal, are similar to La Fayette's work in their brevity, their modern historical
settings, and their emphasis on using narrative to raise important questions
about the norms of human conduct. But *La princesse de Clèves* was the catalyst
of public recognition that a new kind of narrative genre was becoming dominant. Twentieth-century readers often have trouble understanding why this
story of an unfulfilled love should have generated the several volumes of criticism published about it within a year of its printing. The intense and introspective story of a young married woman who falls in love with another man
fits a pattern with which we are familiar. But our calm acceptance of its characters, its style, and its plot is possible because we view it as belonging to a
generic category unfamiliar to La Fayette's contemporaries and for which they
lacked both a name and a theory. The novel, as we know it after La Fayette,
fills the gap created by the juxtaposition of two previously dominant genres,
the romance and the novella. La Fayette's text combines key elements of these
genres.

In modern French a novel is called a *roman,* which is also the term used in
17th-century French for romances: the loves and exploits of Arthurian knights
seeking the grail, pastoral fictions of princes disguised as shepherds, and tales
of shipwreck, piracy, and rediscovery of long-lost family. Generally set in
epochs or places distant from the author's and original readers', romances
enjoyed considerable latitude in their characters' conduct and even in the order
of possible natural occurrence. Magic and supernatural interventions were
common, and the characters were likely to wrestle with problems of illusion,
whether induced by magic or by human misperception. Although 17th-century
French romances (such as Honoré d'Urfé's *L'Astrée,* 1607–1627, and Madeleine

de Scudéry's *Clélie*, 1654–1660) incorporated discussions of human nature and psychology, they traditionally involved the subjective confusions of a multitude of individual characters faced with the challenge of distinguishing illusion from reality. The narrative of each character's confusion provided many subplots harmonized into a complex polyphony.

The English term *novel* descends from the French *nouvelle* or Italian novella, a genre distinguished from the romance not only by its relative shortness but also by a host of other features, including the representation of the narrator as storyteller and the attitudes portrayed toward standards of conduct and truth. The novella was generally set in a location and period closer to those of the author and original readers. Its characters generally behaved in accordance with prevailing social conventions. Its plots were usually dominated by a single character. Whereas the romance emphasized subjective emotional quests and the problem of illusion and reality, the novella stressed the objective qualities of the world and the demonstration of certain laws of human conduct. The novella hero was often a trickster who had obtained a knowledge of such laws and used them to gain an advantage over others.

This generic background explains the perplexity of many of La Fayette's contemporaries when *La princesse de Clèves* appeared. The contemporary critics Jean-Baptiste-Henri de Valincour and Roger de Bussy-Rabutin argued that its historical inaccuracies, the exceptional events of the plot, and the nature of the heroine would have been acceptable in the exotic world of the romance but were not tolerable in a fictive representation of a world like our own. The story is set in the court of Henri II (1547–1559), little over a century earlier. Thus the proximity of the events seemed to favor realism and to invite readers to assume that the characters' behavior would be close to contemporary norms. This assumption would lead toward the logic of the novella. However, the text of *La princesse de Clèves*—including plot and characters—is not *normal:* that is, it does not confirm expectations about the way men and women did or should behave. For example, the heroine's admission to her husband that she loves another man but that she remains faithful as a wife seemed to many readers atypical of marital conduct; according to such readers, La Fayette's plot diverged on this point from the way things *were,* from the way people really behaved. As Bussy-Rabutin argued, such behavior on the part of a wife might appear in a *true* story (of some eccentric individual) or in a romance, but not in the kind of in-between, lifelike fiction that the author of *La princesse de Clèves* seemed to present. The heroine's confession also led to a discussion of whether a wife *should* make such a statement to her husband. These two concerns are among the most powerful indications of how the novel, as a genre, calls into question the ideology—that is, both its view of objective reality and the social values imposed on that reality—of the society that produced the text. In the 17th century the terms *verisimilitude (vraisemblance)*—"how we act"—and *propriety (bienséance)*—"how we should act"—converged in discussions of the heroine's conduct. It was not believable (or verisimilar), thought some, that the heroine would so depart from what was proper.

351

La Fayette herself participated directly in the critical debate. In a letter to the secretary of the duchess of Savoy, she denied being the author of the text, affirmed the overall accuracy of the book's representation of life at the French court, and claimed that *La princesse de Clèves* was not a *roman* or romance but a historical memoir. Yet the clearly nonhistorical character of the book—the "princess" herself did not really exist—prevents us from taking literally La Fayette's claim that the book is nonfiction. Perhaps she meant that the story was an accurate model of relationships in the royal court. By rejecting the term *roman* she pointed toward a stricter standard of accuracy than that of romance.

La Fayette also seems to have anticipated the critical debate through the deliberate emphasis on the unlikely and unverisimilar in the book itself, particularly through the characteristics and actions of the heroine, a young noblewoman recently arrived at the court and therefore without direct experience of amorous and political intrigue. The heroine (after her marriage, the princess of the novel's title) is repeatedly described as exceptional and even describes herself as unique. She is contrasted with several other female characters who fit the thematically central norms of fidelity and infidelity. The heroine's departure from these courtly patterns, together with other "unrealistic" behavior (for example, her suitor, Nemours, takes outlandish risks), seemed to contemporary readers to accord with the exotic realms of romance.

From a 19th- or 20th-century perspective, *La princesse de Clèves* appears to be a prototype of the *Bildungsroman,* the novel of education or development, centered on a young person's move out of the sheltered world of childhood. Education is an explicit theme of La Fayette's book, for the heroine's mother adopts an unusual approach, warning her daughter in advance about the conduct of courtiers, and especially about the untrustworthy nature of suitors. Thus La Fayette creates an important distinction between innocence and inexperience. The mother's lesson not only provides the heroine with a series of concepts of what constitutes reality, or verisimilar conduct in courtiers, but also provides a particular structure of learning, which consists in placing a rule next to narrative accounts based on experience. Throughout the text the heroine hears other stories about the outcome of love affairs and compares her own experience with these narratives.

The princess's comparison of her own experience with others' illustrates an inductive approach to learning, the search for a single unifying pattern. Her introspection is thus not merely psychological, although *La princesse de Clèves* has long been recognized as the first narrative of psychological analysis: many passages seem to be an account of the thoughts of the heroine herself, mediated by the narrator only to the extent that these thoughts are stated in the third person as indirect discourse. For instance, "How could she not but recognize this nameless lady?" (p. 84) seems to be a transposition of the princess's own agitated question to herself, along the line, "How could that be anyone but . . . ?" This internal narrative is commented on by a nameless omniscient narrator who knows not only what the heroine thinks but also when she is wrong about her own feelings ("She was quite mistaken, since the unbearable pain she was suffering was nothing more nor less than jealousy"; p. 105).

As both *Bildungsroman* and psychological discourse *La princesse de Clèves* anticipated directions taken by the novel in the 18th and 19th centuries. But La Fayette was also modulating the genres available in her own day. The heroine's internal search for a norm in the stories she hears is also related to a major preoccupation of the novella. The internal narrators of novella collections try incessantly to detect a pattern in the series of short stories they recount to one another. Significantly, the only explicit reference to another literary work in the course of *La princesse de Clèves* is to Margaret of Navarre's 16th-century collection of novellas, *L'heptaméron* (1559; *The Heptameron*), which the princess is said to have read. By this literary allusion La Fayette strengthens the parallel between the heroine's activity of listening to the stories told about the court and the generic structure of the novella collection. In *L'heptaméron,* as in other classic examples of novella collections, such as Boccaccio's *Decameron* (1353) and Jean Regnault de Segrais's *Nouvelles françaises* (1657), a group of characters tell one another stories and discuss the "truths" about men and women that appear to be demonstrated therein. The discovery of a recurrent pattern on the novella model is important to La Fayette's heroine, because the single most important decision she faces, whether or not to marry Nemours after her husband's death, depends in large part on a judgment whether or not there are exceptions to the demonstrated norm that men are generally unfaithful once they have been assured of a woman's love. The typical novella response to questions of this sort is a proliferation of further stories both proving and disproving the possibility of male fidelity. *La princesse de Clèves* separates itself from the novella by bringing the narrative to an abrupt halt, as the heroine chooses independence from men and from the court and a life of retreat and monastic community. The narrative and the heroine refuse to answer the question of male fidelity either affirmatively or negatively and thus also refuse a typical novella dichotomy.

La Fayette's text also takes elements of romance and turns them to new purposes. The court of Henri II is described as a place where appearance and reality are radically distinguished—her mother tells the newly arrived heroine, "If you judge by appearances in this place, you will go on making mistakes, for things here are seldom what they seem" (p. 55)—an important feature of the romance. But whereas romance attributes illusion either to magic or to obsessive individual desire, *La princesse de Clèves* attributes illusion to the systematic workings of the ceaseless political maneuverings of court society. When Nemours spies on the princess in a pavilion at her country estate, the whole episode is reminiscent of romance, and the highly unreal, dreamlike quality reinforces the sense of a movement into a different genre. But the traditional expectation that Nemours's desire will ultimately be satisfied is aborted by the heroine's preference to transcend the whole amorous pursuit. When she chooses to depart both from the court and from her relationship with Nemours, the novel ends by stressing once again the exceptional quality of the heroine's conduct: "Her life,

353

which was not a long one, provided an example of inimitable goodness." This inimitable example opens the epoch dominated by the novel, whose "birth-place," as Walter Benjamin observed in 1936, "is the solitary individual" ("The Storyteller," p. 87). Who better fits that description than the princess of Clèves, setting her own course outside the dominant patterns?

See also 1527, 1619, 1654, 1704, 1735.

Bibliography: Walter Benjamin, "The Storyteller," in *Illuminations,* trans. Harry Zohn (New York: Schocken, 1969). Henri Coulet, *Le roman jusqu'à la Révolution,* vol. 1 (Paris: Armand Colin, 1967). Joan DeJean, *Libertine Strategies: Freedom and the Novel in Seventeenth-Century France* (Columbus: Ohio State University Press, 1981). Jean Fabre, *Idées sur le roman de Madame de La Fayette au Marquis de Sade* (Paris: Klincksieck, 1979). Marie-Madeleine Pioche de la Vergne, countess de La Fayette, *The Princess of Clèves,* trans. Nancy Mitford, rev. Leonard Tancock (1950; reprint, Harmondsworth: Penguin, 1978). Maurice Lever, *Le roman français au XVIIe siècle* (Paris: Presses Universitaires de France, 1981).

John D. Lyons

◢◣ 1680, 21 October

Seven Years after Molière's Death, Louis XIV Grants His Players the Monopoly on Theatrical Performances in Paris

The Comédie-Française

The establishment of the Comédie-Française was, after that of the Académie Française in 1634, the most powerful and enduring feature of the policy of cultural centralization developed by the French monarchy in its transition from feudalism to absolutism. One law, one faith, one king . . . one theater.

On 21 October 1680 an order signed by Louis XIV and his minister Jean-Baptiste Colbert under the king's private seal directed that the two French theatrical troupes in Paris merge, becoming the only group authorized to perform "comedies"—that is, plays—in Paris. Thus an establishment monopoly was founded. Actors in the temporary fairground theaters and the Comédie-Italienne continued to perform, but they were not allowed to present the works of established writers and the "great genres."

The consequences of the measure were manifold and immediately apparent. For the actors—the *comédiens français*—it meant both privilege and constraint. Subjected to the authority of his majesty, their contracts and regulations depended upon the whims of his representatives, the "gentlemen of the king's bedchamber." Moreover, the king "decided on the actors' and actresses' inclusion in the troupe." On the other hand, the monopoly guaranteed exclusive rights to the most prestigious texts—and therefore roles—in the French theater. For contemporary writers the results were also dual. Because the "great genres" had only one outlet, rejection could mean an aborted career. However, an accepted and successfully performed play meant glory (if not, until Pierre Caron de Beaumarchais's time, much material reward) and, it was thought, immortality: what more could one hope for than to be included in a repertory that had the monopoly on Corneille, Racine, and Molière?

The concept of a permanent association was already fundamental to the French medieval theater companies, whose organization paralleled that of the medieval corporations and *compagnonnages*. (As late as the 17th century the role in which an actor had excelled was still called his "masterpiece," just like an artisan's masterpiece.) But the creation of the Comédie-Française firmly established the concept of the permanent repertory company. In the second half of the 17th century, aside from the fairground theaters and the Comédie-Italienne, there were only three large theatrical troupes in Paris. The oldest was that of the Hôtel de Bourgogne, called "les grands comédiens" (the great players), at which Molière poked fun in *L'impromptu de Versailles* (1663; *The Versailles Impromptu*) and to which Racine entrusted most of his profane tragedies. The Théâtre du Marais, established in Paris since 1634, presented the first performances of many plays by Corneille. Finally, there was Molière's troupe, which became the basis for the Comédie-Française. During the brief and chaotic existence of the Illustre-Théâtre (1643–1645), before being exiled to the provinces, Molière (an amateur) and his associates (professionals) had established and signed an *acte d'association*, a contract by which they committed themselves to divide the profits—if any. Returning to Paris in 1658, thanks to a spectacle that had pleased the king and especially to Molière's authority—as writer, actor, director, and administrator—over his associates, the new troupe was accepted. In June 1673, a few months after Molière's death, the Théâtre du Marais, deprived of its building by the king's order, was absorbed by the so-called Troupe de l'Hôtel Guénégaud—that of Molière's widow and members of Molière's old company. Finally, in 1680, the old troupe of the Hôtel de Bourgogne was swallowed up by what was and is still called the Maison de Molière, reduced to one troupe only in order, in the words of the king and his minister, "to make the performance of plays more perfect." Thus quality was to come not from competition but from a concentration of talents. Louis XIV had once again used the collective feudal franchises, and their rigorous organization, to reinforce autocratic centralization.

The most influential period was 1680–1790—the period of the monopoly. Sustained by the prestige of the three great playwrights (Corneille, Molière, Racine), the members of the Comédie-Française, naturally eager for the success guaranteed by famous roles, accepted tragedies derived more or less from the classical repertoire, certified by Nicolas Boileau's *L'art poétique* (1674; *The Art of Poetry*), and canonized by Voltaire in *Le siècle de Louis XIV* (1751; *The Century of Louis XIV*). Thus several generations of playwrights, anxious to be performed, wrote with an eye to the past. What innovations there were at the Comédie-Française were mostly in the realm of comedy. In addition to works modeled largely on Molière's the company accepted broadly humorous comedies by Jean-François Regnard (1655–1709), satires of contemporary mores by

1. "Coupe de la salle de spectacle de la Comédie-Française vue du côté du théâtre et prise dans les plans sur la ligne C. D.," plate designed by Pierre-Joachim Bibault, engraved by Pierre-Edme Babel, in Jacques-François Blondel, *Architecture française, ou recueil des plans, élévations, coupes et profils des églises, maisons royales, palais, hôtels et édifices considérables de Paris,* vol. 2 (Paris: C. A. Jombert, 1752), plate 5. (Courtesy of the Art and Architecture Library, Yale University.)

Florent Carton Dancourt (1661–1725) and Alain-René Lesage (1668–1747), "serious" comedy marked by sermonizing and tearful sentimentality, and, finally, the *drame bourgeois,* including works by Michel Jean Sedaine (1719–1797) and Denis Diderot (1713–1784). Regnard's *Le légataire universel* (1708; *The Residual Legatee*) and *Les folies amoureuses* (1704; *Love's Follies*) have remained among the most popular: together eleven comedies by Regnard had been performed about 6,000 times by 1967. The most innovative works to be accepted were Beaumarchais's two triumphs—*Le barbier de Séville* (1775) and *Le mariage de Figaro* (1784).

Outside the Comédie-Française the existence of the monopoly actually promoted a diversification and enrichment of the theatrical genres considered unworthy of the royal stage for reasons of taste and literary quality. Although Lesage's social comedy *Turcaret* (1709) was accepted by the Comédie-Française, Lesage was rejected by the Maison de Molière for most of his career and was reduced to writing farces for the fairground theaters. Thus farce, excluded from the great stage, survived more freely and more vigorously in popular theaters.

Pierre Carlet de Marivaux (1688–1763), occasionally performed on the royal stage but not greatly valued by his contemporaries (Voltaire found him too "metaphysical"), was adopted by the Comédie-Italienne, which was allowed to perform comedies in French prose. Marivaux's close collaboration with the Parisian heirs of the commedia dell'arte resulted in a unique body of dramatic works on the fringe of the "French" tradition maintained by the Comédie-Française. If Marivaux had not thus been excluded from the repertory, what would he have become as a playwright? His comedies were finally included in the repertory in the 19th century, and as of 1967 his most famous play, *Le jeu de l'amour et du hasard* (1730; *The Game of Love and Chance*), produced by the Comédie-Française only in 1802, was the tenth most performed play on that stage. The field was also open to theater from which language was excluded (pantomime) or in which language reduced to a schematic prose with no "literary" style was reinforced by musical leitmotifs (melodrama) to enhance emotional nuances or the delineation of characters. Above all, the field was open to the great stage spectacles, in which the action was shown, not recounted. This renewal of marginal and popular theaters finally led to the creation of the French *drame romantique.*

The transformation of the Maison de Molière into the modern Comédie-Française took place during the Revolution (1789–1794) and the Empire (1804–1814). Partly because of controversies provoked by Marie-Joseph Chénier's tragedy *Charles IX, ou l'école des rois* (1788) and by the flamboyant behavior of the actor Talma, the Comédie-Française was in a state of upheaval at the beginning of the Revolution. In August 1790 the Constituent Assembly called for the freedom of all theaters—and the company thus lost its monopoly. In September 1793 Robespierre delivered the coup de grâce, asking the Committee of Public Safety to arrest the actors of the company, then called the Théâtre de la Nation. The Comédie-Française ceased to exist. But the actors survived the Terror, formed a new group called the Théâtre de la République, and in 1804, with the approval of First Consul Napoleon Bonaparte, again incorporated by signing an *acte de société*. Finally the constitution of the new Théâtre Français was approved and signed in 1812 by Napoleon, then emperor, during the Russian campaign. That "Moscow decree," with many amendments, has remained the basis for today's relationship among the *sociétaires* (as members of the company are called) as well as between the company and the authorities.

"I was alone at the Théâtre-Français last night," wrote Alfred de Musset in "Une soirée perdue" (1840; "A Wasted Evening"). Indeed, the Comédie-Française sometimes became a place of boredom, comparable to a dusty museum, but its function was essentially to preserve the integrity of acknowledged masterpieces despite shifts in taste, fashion, and ideology. Also, for three centuries it has accepted and given official recognition to new theatrical concepts such as those of the Romantic drama, which made a brief but historical and triumphant appearance on the national stage with plays by Alexandre Dumas (*Henri III et sa cour,* 1829; *Henri III and His Court*), Victor Hugo (*Hernani,* 1830), and Alfred de Vigny (*Chatterton,* 1835). In the 20th century, from Jacques Copeau, to the Cartel, to Jean-Louis Barrault—who was responsible for the epoch-making production of Paul Claudel's *Le soulier de satin* (1924; *The Satin Slipper*) in 1943—the most innovative French directors have been called upon to enliven the institution. Most recently, Jean Le Poulain in 1987 managed to get included in the repertory the masterpiece of French baroque theater, Jean Rotrou's *Le véritable saint Genest* (1646; *The True Saint Genest*). Since World War II, cultural decentralization and the increase in subsidized theaters have created dangerous competition for the Comédie-Française. Yet it has survived and absorbed many avant-garde works—not only by the established playwrights of the 1930s such as Jean Cocteau, Jean Giraudoux, and Armand Salacrou, but also by Samuel Beckett, Jean Genet, and Eugène Ionesco. The Comédie-Française, necessarily a museum, is a bastion of the French cultural tradition, to which modern wings are continually being added.

See also 1673, 1707, 1800, 1827 (December).

Bibliography: Emile Fabre, *La Comédie-Française* (Paris: La Nouvelle Critique, [1942]). Sylvie Chevalley, *La Comédie-Française* (Paris: La Comédie-Française, [1967]).

Jacques Guicharnaud

⟣ 1685

Louis XIV Signs the Edict of Fontainebleau, Revoking the Edict of Nantes

Religious Controversies

On 26 January 1686, before the throng of prelates, magistrates, and cabinet ministers gathered to hear his funeral oration for Michel Le Tellier, Jacques Bénigne Bossuet, the powerful bishop of Meaux who enjoyed the stature of a national orator, extolled this chief justice for writing, in the throes of a fatal illness, "the pious edict that delivered the final blow to heresy" (*Oeuvres oratoires*, 6:322). The Edict of Fontainebleau (17 October 1685), to which Bossuet was referring, abrogated the religious and civil rights of Huguenots (then about one million in France, or 5 to 6 percent of the population), which Henri IV had "permanently" guaranteed in the Edict of Nantes (13 April 1598) for the sole purpose of ending the Wars of Religion (1562–1598). The Edict of Fontainebleau in fact denied all forms of assembly to members of the Religion Réformée, disparagingly dubbed Religion Prétendue Réformée (So-Called Reform Religion); ordered its churches and schools demolished; and, while banishing its ministers into exile if they did not convert to Catholicism, prohibited all other Huguenots from emigrating, enjoining them to attend church. As Bossuet recognized, the Revocation aimed to annihilate, to achieve a "final solution" to, Protestantism in France. By its promulgation, he intoned in his oration, Louis XIV, the manifest instrument of God's miracles, had accomplished far more than Christian emperors such as Constantine, Theodosius, Marcianus, or Charlemagne, all of whom had instituted prohibitive laws to ensure that most of the "obstinate" eventually rejoined the church. But now "an inveterate heresy" had instantly disappeared; the erring flocks had returned in droves as their "false pastors" abandoned them; and in the sudden calm, "a stunned universe had seen . . . the clearest sign and best use of authority" (pp. 321–322).

Bossuet's mythopoeic enthusiasm for the "extraordinary event" that crowned the French church's efforts to combat the Reformation was widely shared by his contemporaries. "No king has ever done or will ever do anything more memorable," wrote Marie de Rabutin-Chantal, marquise de Sévigné, on 28 October 1685 (*Correspondance*, 3:239). The Revocation prompted an outpouring of personal feeling for Louis XIV that François-Timoléon, abbé de Choisy, described in his *Mémoires* (published posthumously in 1727): "never had the people shown such joy"; in the streets, "100,000 voices shouted: Long live the king" (p. 31). Spurred by the monarchy's propaganda machine, the universal acclaim for the "herculean" triumph over the "python of heresy" led the Protestant Pierre Bayle to exclaim, in *Ce que c'est que la France toute catholique sous le règne de Louis le Grand* (1686; *What a Wholly Catholic France Represents in the Reign of Louis the Great*), that not a single *honnête homme* (honorable man) was left in France to protest. But there were powerful pressures to silence protest. To his later expression of regret, Bernard Le Bovier de Fontenelle entered and won the Académie Française's competition in 1686 for the best poem on "the destruction of heresy" in order to dispel suspicions raised by his earlier *Relation de l'île de Bornéo* (1684; *Report on the Isle of Borneo*); that two-page allegory described the feud between two queens, Mréo (an anagram for Rome) and Eénegu (Geneva), both claiming the succession of their mother Mliseo (Isolem [= Jerusalem?]), the former in the name of historical continuity, the latter in the name of physical resemblance. The vast correspondence of Charlotte Elisabeth of Bavaria, the German princess of the Palatinate who had to convert when she married Louis XIV's brother in 1671, was even more closely policed; not until 1698 does she mention the conspiracy of silence about the Protestants' persecution, and only in 1715, when her son became regent, could she openly plead their cause. By then Choisy could criticize the excessive "zeal" of Louis XIV and his advisers in his private memoirs; he could see both the impact of the Revocation abroad (on the revolution that placed William of Orange on England's throne in 1688; on the resolve of Protestant states to attack France) and, as Jean-Baptiste Colbert and Sébastien Le Prestre, marquis de Vauban, had predicted in the 1680s, the domestic economic disaster caused by the diaspora of 200,000 Protestants—in Choisy's words, the loss of "more than two hundred million in cash" (*Mémoires*, p. 119).

Whereas Bossuet avoided mentioning the complex factors leading to the "miraculous" Revocation, Choisy noted that Louis XIV "had planned it since the beginning of his reign" (*Mémoires*, p. 117). The king's memoirs for the years 1661 and 1662 (written ca. 1669–70) confirm his early determination to let the "disease" die gradually by restricting to the "narrowest limits" the Huguenot "privileges," the separate politicoreligious constitution effectively granted them by the Edict of Nantes. Viewing that edict as inimical to the ideal of "one law, one faith, one king," Louis issued a flood of decrees—ranging from twelve in 1661 to eighty-five in the crucial period 1679–1685, when the court became markedly pietistic under the influence of Françoise de Maintenon, Louis's morganatic wife and the granddaughter of the Huguenot writer Agrippa d'Aubigné—that essentially rescinded it. A formal revocation, however, could realize Louis's desire for greater power and glory than those of his predecessors, who had had to compromise with the Religion Réformée; it would also provide a more spectacular victory over heretics than the defeat of the Turks in 1683 by the Holy Roman emperor Leopold I; and by exacting the gratitude of Innocent XI, it would end conflicts with Rome that had reached schismatic levels after the promulgation of the Four Articles of the Gallican Church (1682). In the belief that everything was to be gained, now that reports listed as many as 30,000 abjurations a day and that the "greatest part of our subjects have embraced Catholicism," as the Edict of Fontainebleau would state, Louis XIV committed what a half-century later Louis de Rouvroy, duc de Saint-Simon, termed "our madness" (*Mémoires*, 2:555). Seduced by sycophants, ambitious prelates, and, most of all, the "poison" of his own greatness, Louis had perpetrated horrors, Saint-Simon asserted in contrast to Bossuet, that rivaled those of "heretical and pagan tyrants" against the early Christians.

Yet until 1685, Protestant leaders regarded Bossuet as a moderate. Unlike the Jesuit Compagnie du Saint Sacrement, which from 1626 to 1666 thwarted and denounced Huguenots at every opportunity, Bossuet first joined the liberal effort, which verged on success in the 1670s, to reach a theological accommodation with Protestantism. His widely disseminated *Exposition de la doctrine de l'église catholique* (1671; *Exposition of the Doctrine of the Catholic Church*) showed that Protestant principles did not offend the foundations of the faith, and that the doctrine of transubstantiation constituted the only real, but not insoluble, obstacle to reconciliation. In addition to this effort toward reunification, which he pursued in his correspondence with the Protestant philosopher Gottfried Wilhelm von Leibniz in the 1690s, Bossuet favored "gentle" means of reconverting "the separated brothers," which in fact led to highly publicized defections among the nobility. However the clergy's failure to convert the masses prompted the doling out of "gentle" but very powerful economic incentives for new converts, which Huguenots excoriated as the "buying of souls." Sensitive to these charges, Bossuet urged the clergy to explain "the holy word to this new people" unceasingly and fostered the nationwide campaign to disseminate one million religious texts and to send on "missions" to the provinces the leading orators of this "golden age of the sermon," including his most famous disciple, François de Salignac de La Mothe–Fénelon, and the incomparably successful Louis Bourdaloue. But the years immediately before and after the Revocation witnessed unrestrained violence by dragoons quartered in resistant Protestant homes by order of Michel de Louvois, the minister of war and Le Tellier's oldest son. In keeping with the fanatical tenor of the times and his own obsession with authority, Bossuet's Fontainebleau sermon of 21 October 1685 invoked the doctrine of *compelle remanere* (force them to remain) propounded by

St. Augustine to fight heresy, and legitimated all forms of "secular pressure" short of death. Even so, his post-Revocation texts display a symptomatic ambivalence, rejecting forced Communion as idolatrous while upholding the monarch's right to enforce observance of the one true religion, which was unerring *because* it was unchanging and inflexible. Thus his *Histoire des variations des églises protestantes* (1688; *History of the Variations of the Protestant Churches*) pointed to the proliferation of new sects as proof of error and depravity, of a spirit of "satanic" individualism and division.

In a flood of religious tracts and letters, published chiefly in Holland, the seat of "The Refuge," and sent throughout Europe to mobilize public opinion, Protestants refuted texts such as Bossuet's *Histoire des variations* and denounced the practices of church and state. Drawing upon the detailed descriptions of barbaric torture, pillage, and abductions of women and children in works such as Pierre Claude's *Les plaintes des protestants cruellement opprimés dans le royaume de France* (1686; *Complaints of Protestants Cruelly Oppressed in the French Kingdom*), Pierre Bayle exposed the official policy of "gentle persuasion" as a massive Catholic and monarchical deception. More broadly, in showing that every religion believes it possesses the truth, Bayle's seminal *Commentaire philosophique sur ces paroles de Jésus-Christ: Contrains-les d'entrer* (1686–87; *A Philosophical Commentary on Luke XIV : 23*) argued for a transcendent natural law against persecution. He affirmed the beliefs of the individual conscience, even when in error, as an absolute whose violation constitutes a sin against God.

Such radical notions, which championed religious and civil tolerance and challenged the power of institutions, created deep divisions among Protestants. The intransigently Calvinistic Pierre Jurieu responded that a magistrate could use all means to combat idolatry—an attitude that in Bayle's view heralded "a Protestant inquisition." Jurieu's passionate tracts and pastoral letters called for a holy war against the Catholic "heretics," which his *Accomplissement des prophéties* (1686; *Fulfillment of Prophecies*) proclaimed would be won in 1689. His fervor was emulated by male and female prophets who arose in the rural areas, in proportion to the repression exerted against Protestants, advocating open defiance of the edict. Indeed, in addition to widespread acts of passive resistance, the decades following the Revocation witnessed the popular revolt of the Camisards (1702–1704), and before Louis's death in 1715 the establishment of the Assemblées du Désert. As Bayle had foreseen, however, the "crossing of the desert" and the persecution ended only with the Edict of Tolerance (1787), repudiating the Edict of Fontainebleau a century after Bossuet had hailed its universal success.

Aside from his efforts to stamp out Protestantism, Bossuet devoted the last decade of his life to combating the mystical "heresy" within the church known as Quietism, which upheld absolute "quiet" or a passive and permanent state of contemplation as "pure love" of God. Innocent XI's denunciation in 1687 of its exponent, Miguel de Molinos, and of other mystical writers set the stage for Bossuet's theological and personal struggle with Fénelon, his "seductive and enchanting" disciple as Saint-Simon dubbed him, who became preceptor to

Louis XIV's grandson from 1689 to 1694 and archbishop of Cambrai in 1695. The ostensible cause of the conflict was Fénelon's unrelenting defense of Mme. Guyon (Jeanne-Marie Bouvier de La Motte), a charismatic disseminator of mystical doctrine who, as their correspondence confirms, uncovered Fénelon's latent spiritualist tendencies. When Françoise de Maintenon expelled her from Saint-Cyr for indoctrinating its young women, Guyon requested that her teaching and many works—such as *Le cantique des cantiques de Salomon interprété selon le sens mystique et la vraie représentation des états intérieurs* (1688; *Salomon's Song of Songs Interpreted According to Mystical Meaning and the True Representation of Inward States*)—be evaluated for their orthodoxy by a church commission that included Fénelon and Bossuet. Unfamiliar with mystical writings, Bossuet chastised the "new prophetess" as a disciple of Molinos. He did not perceive the influence of St. John of the Cross and St. Theresa d'Avila, Benoît de Canfeld and Barbe Avrillot Acarie (Marie de l'Incarnation), Francis of Sales and Jeanne de Chantal in Guyon's metaphorical description of the "interior ways" by which the soul is swept into passivity to become one with God's will. In *Torrents spirituels* (1682; *Spiritual Torrents*), Guyon had dramatized the process of "abjection," the annihilation of all thought and desires for self that leads to "holy indifference" and culminates in a return to the divine source, a state of "invariable, inalterable" peace and plenitude. As Bossuet argued in his *Ordonnance et instructions pastorales* (1695; *Ordinance and Pastoral Instructions*), this quietist doctrine was fundamentally indifferent to the notions of sin, of striving for virtue, and of hope for salvation; it ignored the mediation of Christ and the church and sought extraordinary states that deified the individual. The perfect Christian life lay in following "ordinary channels," not the "false sublimities" and "outrageous elevations" of these "false" or "new mystics."

In 1695 Bossuet had Guyon incarcerated for refusing to sign a confession of heresy, and Fénelon rose to defend both a "saintly" woman and mystical doctrine against further, perhaps fatal, attack. His technical and dogmatic treatise, *Explication des maximes des saints sur la vie intérieure* (1697; *Explanation of the Maxims of the Saints on the Inner Life*), drew the "precise limits" of the true doctrine of "pure love" as a safeguard against the "illusions" of certain mystics, including Molinos. Citing the writings of church fathers, but above all, Francis of Sales' *Traité de l'amour de Dieu* (1616; *Treatise on the Love of God*), Fénelon strove to prove the perpetuity and thus the orthodoxy of a love of God so wholly disinterested in the self that it constitutes "perfect charity." Instead of a theological rebuttal, Bossuet mounted a brilliant but cruel personal attack, which won public opinion. His *Relation sur le quiétisme* (1698; *Report on Quietism*) ridiculed the passages on "torrential plenitude" in Guyon's *Torrents spirituels;* her self-representation as the pregnant woman of the Apocalypse in her autobiography (published posthumously in 1720), which she had given him in strictest confidence; and, more broadly, the maternal imagery that was her original contribution to mystical discourse. Moreover, in a classic gesture, Bossuet attacked Fénelon's "intimate liaison" with the Molinist "seductress" as the cause of his alienation from his brother(s) and his defense of heresy. Fénelon's no less personal *Réponse à la Relation sur le quiétisme* (1698) insisted that the autocratic Bossuet was using "an ignorant woman"—whose genuine piety and spiritual intentions should be distinguished from expressions in her work that would be "madly impious" if read literally—only to discredit him and the doctrine of "pure love."

In what proved to be a fatal error, Fénelon went beyond Bossuet to ask Innocent XII for a judgment of his *Explication*. The ambiguous papal brief censured twenty-three propositions as scandalous but not heretical. Although he immediately expressed submission to papal authority, Fénelon was disgraced, banished from court and confined for life to his archbishopric at Cambrai, where he continued to write works critical of absolute monarchy, such as *Télémaque* (1699–1717; *Telemachus*) and his *Lettre à Louis XIV* (1785; *Letter to Louis XIV*). Not surprisingly, Fénelon was depicted during the Enlightenment as a martyr to liberalism, Bossuet as tyranny's servant. This view, however, ignored Fénelon's opposition to Jansenism, the source of renewed controversy at the end of the century, which had first erupted in 1640 with the publication of the *Augustinus* of Cornelius Jansen, bishop of Ypres. Fénelon continued to denounce Jansenism as a form of Calvinism even after Louis XIV had its seat at Port-Royal razed in 1712 and Pope Clement XI had condemned its doctrine in 1713. Notwithstanding the preeminent role of individual experience in his mystical doctrine, in the case of Jansenism and, of course, of Protestantism, Fénelon shared Bossuet's aversion to "indocility and independence," as he wrote in his *Lettres sur l'autorité de l'église* (1767–68; *Letters on the Authority of the Church*), and affirmed the infallibility of the church.

Despite their differences, Bossuet and Fénelon were products of a time that equated tolerance for opposing beliefs with "indulgence for abuses," as the *Dictionnaire de l'Académie Française* defined the term in 1694. Like Jurieu, they regarded tolerance as a gangrene that would undermine all authority, civil and religious. Even worse, as Bossuet argued when he sided with Jurieu against Bayle in his *Sixième avertissement aux protestants* (1691; *Sixth Warning to Protestants*), tolerance would generate widespread indifference to religious truth. Whereas Bayle reacted to the Huguenot persecution by propounding the Enlightenment ideals of pluralism, relativism, and the rights of the individual conscience, Bossuet, Fénelon, and Jurieu rejected variant beliefs as signs of resistance to the truth and damned them as heretical. Through the power of the predicatory (s)word, they strove to suppress deviance and to impose the authority of what each upheld as orthodoxy. As Bossuet had emblematically warned in his "Sermon sur la parole de Dieu" (1671; "Sermon on the Word of God"), "those whom . . . the divine word . . . does not convert, it condemns; those whom it does not nourish it kills" (*Oeuvres oratoires*, 3:641). The violence of the Word is a vivid image for religious controversies in the absolutist era of Louis XIV.

See also 1534 (17–18 October), 1541 (September), 1572, 1609, 1678, 1697.

Bibliography: Jean Robert Armogathe, *Le Quiétisme* (Paris: Presses Universitaires de France, 1973). Pierre Bayle, *Philosophical Commentary*, trans. Amie Godman Tannenbaum (New York: Peter Lang, 1987). Jacques Bénigne Bossuet, *Oeuvres oratoires,* ed. Abbé J. Lebarq, 7 vols. (Paris: Desclée De Brouwer, 1926). François-Timoléon, abbé de Choisy, *Mémoires,* ed. Georges Mongrédien (Paris: Mercure de France, 1966). James Herbert Davis, Jr., *Fénelon* (Boston: Twayne, 1979). Elizabeth Labrousse, *La révocation de l'Edit de Nantes* (Paris: Payot, 1985). François de Salignac de La Mothe–Fénelon, *Oeuvres,* ed. Jacques Le Brun, 2 vols. (Paris: Gallimard, 1983). Jeanne-Marie Bouvier de la Motte (Mme. Guyon), *Song of Songs* (no translator named) (Maine: Christian Books, 1983). Louis XIV, *Memoirs for the Instruction of the Dauphin,* trans. Paul Sonnino (New York: Free Press, 1970). Louis de Rouvroy, duc de Saint-Simon, *Mémoires,* ed. Yves Coirault, 7 vols. (Paris: Gallimard, 1983). Marie de Rabutin-Chantal, marquise de Sévigné, *Correspondance,* ed. Roger Duchêne, 3 vols. (Paris: Gallimard, 1972–1978). Jacques Truchet, *La prédication de Bossuet,* 2 vols. (Paris: Cerf, 1960).

Domna C. Stanton

✑ 1687

Charles Perrault Reads His Poem "Le siècle de Louis le Grand" before the Académie Française

The Quarrel of the Ancients and the Moderns

> Antiquity, 'tis own'd, does well deserve
> Profound Respect, yet not to be adored.
> The Ancients I with unbent Knee behold,
> For they, tho' great, were Men as well as we,
> And justly one may venture to compare
> The Age of Louis to th'Augustus' Days.

Thus begins Charles Perrault's "Le siècle de Louis le Grand" ("The Age of Louis the Great"), the loudest "Modernist" salvo in the Quarrel of the Ancients and the Moderns, which raged in France from the heyday of "the classical generation" (1660–1680), with its decidedly "Ancient" stamp, until the third decade of the next century. Read by the author at a meeting of the Académie Française, of which he had been a member since 1671, the poem is one of the manipulative court favorite's many rejoinders to an old adversary, the feisty poet-critic Nicolas Boileau-Despréaux, the leader of the Ancients (as the defenders of the Greek and Latin authors of antiquity came to be called in their attack upon the Moderns). Boileau had been elected to the Académie in 1684, thereby gaining greater authority to maintain the brief for the Ancients presented earlier in *L'art poétique* (1674; *The Art of Poetry*), which held up the model of Greco-Roman antiquity while wittily attacking the Moderns, whom Perrault defended somewhat summarily in his poem here. Over the next decade (1688–1697), Perrault more fully probed the theses of his poem in his four-volume *Parallèle des anciens et des modernes en ce qui regarde les arts et les sciences* (1688–1692; *A Parallel between the Ancients and the Moderns concerning the Arts and Sciences*), dialogues between a provincial ("le Président") partial to the Ancients and a courtly partisan of the Moderns ("l'Abbé") as the two vie on aesthetic and other intellectual issues in the presence of a Chevalier representing the "average reader" from a newly enfranchised leisure class respectful enough of the ancients but predisposed by its economic and social status to the moderns.

Perrault and Boileau had long been personal as well as literary adversaries. The leader of the Ancients had long held a poor opinion of his medical care as the child-patient of Perrault's older brother, Claude, a physician better known to history as a distinguished architect. This memory was perhaps even more personally embittered by the death at eighteen of Anne Dongois, Boileau's niece, with whom he may have been in love, when she, too, had been under the care of the physician-architect. The "literary" grounds of resentment between the opposing poets were also of long standing. In his *Satire VII* of 1663, subsequent to his not having been included in Jean Chapelain's list of those to receive royal support, in the form of a pension, Boileau attacked the style of Chapelain's *modern* epic about Joan of Arc, *La Pucelle, ou la France délivrée* (1656; *The Maid of Orléans, or France Delivered*); in his *Satire IX* of 1668 he renewed the attack, extending it to other Moderns without naming Perrault directly. In 1671 Chapelain and Perrault prevailed on Jean-Baptiste Colbert, one of the king's most powerful ministers, to refuse permission to print a new edition of Boileau's *Satires* and of his recently completed *L'art poétique,* which, with its somewhat aesthetically irrelevant attack on Claude Perrault in the fourth canto, would thus not be published until 1674.

The enduring professional quarrels between Boileau and Perrault should not obscure the longer-standing, broader issues of the Quarrel of the Ancients and the Moderns. In this first round, the Quarrel was primarily a literary debate. However, it brought to the fore philosophical, linguistic, and political tensions nascent in French culture since Joachim du Bellay's *La défense et illustration de la langue française* (1549; *The Defense and Enrichment of the French Language*) and emerging more directly in Corneille's *Le Cid* (1637). Despite its reputation since as the founding work of French classical tragedy, upon its first production the play gave rise to a polemic (the "Quarrel of *Le Cid*") in which it was attacked for "irregularities" in values rooted in early 17th-century interpretations of Aristotle's *Poetics:* the rhetorical concept of verisimilitude and the ethical-religious concept of proprieties. More broadly, the Quarrel was the polemical apogee of a tension inherent in Renaissance humanism. The Ancients identified humanism with the uncritical and adulatory transmission of antiquity within fairly delimited literary bounds—humanism with an authoritarian and, largely, aristocratic face. The Moderns identified it as the springboard for critical examination of ancient or modern literature *and* life—humanism with a libertarian and, potentially, democratic face.

Perrault's thesis about nature's evenhanded distribution of talent had been posited earlier by another Modern, Bernard Le Bovier de Fontenelle. In his *Nouveaux dialogues des morts* (1683; *New Dialogues of the Dead*), in the dialogue between Socrates and Montaigne, the modern, leading the ancient to see that men are as unwise now as they were in the old days, slyly deprives the ancients of their vaunted superiority. In his *Digression sur les anciens et les modernes* (1688; *A Digression on the Ancients and the Moderns*), Fontenelle more forthrightly highlighted an epistemological advantage of the Moderns by noting "a precision and an exactness . . . scarcely known until now" (*Digression,* in *The Continental Model,* p. 363). Finding this advantage in all domains of discourse, Fontenelle posited a key tenet of the Moderns: the shift from a deductive, authoritarian concept of history to an inductive, libertarian one. For him, as for other Moderns, the great agent of this new outlook was René Descartes, the 17th-century philosopher of liberating doubt, whose critical spirit freed the new age from the authority of the ancients. For the Moderns, *criticism* took on the sense of its Greek root (to decide, to judge), thereby permitting more humane and useful responses to literature and life. Though congratulating the Ancients for useful models in eloquence, Fontenelle asserted that, on the other hand, their "poetry . . . was good for nothing, as it always has been under all kinds of government; that failing is of the essence of poetry" (p. 364). However, he also found versification in much contemporary poetry "just as noble today as it ever was" and left little doubt about the progressive character of this nobility as he added: "and at the same time more precise and exact" (p. 369).

For other Moderns, progress in poetry was substantive as well as technical. Thus Boileau presented a key tenet of the Ancients in his proscription of Christianity as a subject in poetry (*L'art poétique,* III), while Chapelain in *La Pucelle* and Jean Desmarets de Saint-Sorlin in *Clovis, ou la France chrétienne* (1657; *Clovis, or Christian France*) presented the opposite tenet, which Desmarets in his critical writings justified on intellectual rather than religious grounds. In his *Les délices de l'esprit* (1658; *The Mind's Pleasures*), a dialogue between Philédon, an initiate in learning, and his mentor, Eusèbe, *esprit* has Cartesian overtones. The mentor acknowledges that, in its address to the "sensual and the corporeal as well as the spiritual and the inner [man]," poetry differs from other discourses. Nevertheless, in poetry, too, only by *l'esprit* can we know the thoughts in a work as well as decide whether the work as a whole is excellent or not. Moreover, the progress of Christianity over the paganism of the Ancients being self-evident for Desmarets, the language in which to express or read of this progress is, for modern French Christians, their own *modern* language.

The progressive linkage of religion, poetry, and language informs the writings of Charles de Saint-Evremond, a more humanistic Modern convinced, on wider grounds than Fontenelle, of the value of poetry but no less convinced than he of the paramount role of reason in all domains. In *Sur le merveilleux qui se trouve dans les poèmes des anciens* (1685; *Of the Wonderful That Is Found in the Works of the Ancients*) he reflected on the prevalence of *le merveilleux* in so much ancient literature, wondered how "good sense" could be excluded from all art and science, and found "abominable" the extent to which "probability in the actions of men" was violated by ancient poets depicting the "actions of the gods" (*Of the Wonderful,* p. 183). Here, as in his *Dissertation sur la tragédie de Racine intitulée Alexandre le Grand* (1666; *Dissertation on Racine's Tragedy Called Alexander the Great*), Saint-Evremond called for greater historical knowledge of content as well as of form in ancient and modern texts. In basing verisimilitude on *probabilities* provided by *historical* understanding rather than by *modern* proprieties, Saint-Evremond anticipated the historical approach to scholarship that emerged over the next two centuries.

"Probabilities" were more mysteriously grounded for the Ancients. Boileau's notion of the "sublime" as the rarely realized expression of "the beautiful," the mysterious essence of great literature (*Réflexions sur Longin,* 1694; *Reflections on Longinus*), showed affinities with the notion of grace as the incomprehensible, arbitrary gift of "the hidden God" posited in his contemporary Pascal's post-humous *Pensées sur la religion et sur quelques autres sujets* (1670; *Pensées*). As with other partisans of the Ancients—such as Jean Racine and Jean de La Fontaine—this quasi-religious axis of the thought of Boileau, celebrated chiefly for his quasi-Aristotelian *L'art poétique,* shows that the poet-critic's theoretical position was more complicated than literary history has suggested. Nevertheless, his conception of language differed from that of the Moderns: for him language was not a secondary, transparent signifier of *present* signifieds, but the primary if paradoxical site of *eternal* truths transcending language and other signifying systems. Although, like other "modern Ancients," Boileau wrote in French, he sought an irreducible simplicity of expression as close as possible to that of the (for him) unsurpassable authors of antiquity. This "rule" of language underlay his orthodox "imitation" of the ancients.

Perrault's call for simplicity was as insistent, but it aimed at a more secular imitation. In the preface to *Les hommes illustres qui ont paru en France pendant ce siècle* (1696–1700; *Illustrious Men Who Appeared in France during This Century*), the emphasis shifted from author to reader, from producer to consumer, from the hieratic to the demotic. Not the arbitrary authority of the model but the critical judgment of the reader became the guide; the "rule" of imitation disappeared for readers and authors.

The gulf between the sides is epitomized in the confrontation between Boileau and Perrault on one class of "literary consumers" increasingly prominent by the late 17th century: women. In 1694 Boileau's "Satire contre les femmes" ("Satire against Women") and Perrault's *L'apologie des femmes* (*The Vindication of Wives*) were published back to back. In his preface, Boileau sought to preclude possible criticism from women: his poem is anodyne by its very generality; moreover, he has not used "a single word that could in the least offend modesty" (*Satire,* unpaginated). In his preface, Perrault did not let the satirist off so easily, blaming the faults in the "Satire" on Boileau's "scandalous" models, Horace and Juvenal. The latter excusably declaimed against "modesty" because, as ancients, they "had, as they say, diverse means for doing without marriage, means which were for them mere gallantries, but which are crimes among Christians, abominable crimes" (ibid.). Feminists may find that, in its terms, Perrault's defense of women is as ancient as Boileau's attack, but there is little doubt about the modernity of his further reproach to Boileau for "not thinking that all languages have their particular genius, and that often what is elegant in Latin is barbarous in French" (ibid.).

That Perrault could not speak for all women as victims of the ancients is clear from Anne Dacier's defense of the ancients in the second round of the Quarrel, some two decades later, centering on Homer. In 1711 Dacier brought out her translation of the *Iliad* only to find it challenged in a translation—with commentary (1714)—by Antoine Houdar de La Motte that reduced the divisions of the epic from twenty-four books to twelve and justified the removal of moral and poetic "faults" in the original. Dacier riposted in a lengthy treatise, *Des causes de la corruption du goût* (1714; *What Causes Good Taste to Be Corrupted*), exalting classical studies for removing us from the grossness of modern times and warning that neglect and disdain of these studies could only return us to that grossness. Later, Dacier testified for the Ancients in the "Battle of the Books" (the English phase of the Quarrel) by reproaching Alexander Pope for "pruning" Homer's text in translating the *Iliad* (1720) and for characterizing Homer as a "Wild Paradise" whose ancient spirit of "Revenge and Cruelty" offended modern taste. In *Madame Dacier's Remarks upon Mr. Pope's Account of Homer* (London, 1724), she retorted that the Christian era is itself marked by these traits, but that it is also the era of their redemption, even as Homer's reliance on nature as guide preserved his era from such corrupting modern traits as luxury and effeminacy.

By the third decade of the 18th century the issues raised in the Quarrel had gone well beyond the literary framework in which the Ancients had sought to maintain the debate. The Moderns would thus appear to have "won." However, as Rémy Saisselin argues, a standoff characterizes 18th-century French culture: the "critical" outlook of the Enlightenment informed most cultural activity *and* the ancient models continued to be respected, including those provided in their own work by defenders of the ancients. This dichotomy has since taken a curious turn in French culture. Racine's elevation above Corneille as the emblematic figure of the Age of Louis XIV, in Voltaire's *Commentaires sur Corneille* (1764), reflects the canonical identification of the highpoint of French Literature with French classicism, represented primarily by partisans of the Ancients in the Quarrel. This Racinocentric model has been consecrated not only by French literary historians but also, paradoxically, by major French writers from Stendhal (*Racine et Shakespeare*, 1823, 1825) to Roland Barthes (*Sur Racine*, 1963; *On Racine*). For more than two centuries now, partisans on both sides of French literary "quarrels" have assimilated *les grands classiques* into widely varying conceptions of literature and life. In their own day, the Moderns won a fair share of the battles, gaining at least a truce with the Ancients; in the three centuries since, they appear to have lost the war.

See also 1549, 1634, 1661, 1674, 1700.

Bibliography: Roland Barthes, *On Racine,* trans. Richard Howard (New York: Hill and Wang, 1964). Nicolas Boileau-Despréaux, *Oeuvres complètes,* ed. Charles Boudhours, vols. 1 (*L'art poétique, Satires*) and 5 (*Réflexions sur Longin*) (Paris: Société des Belles Lettres, 1939–1942). Boileau, *Satire du Sr. Despréaux contre les femmes avec l'Apologie des femmes par M. Perrault* (Amsterdam: Adrian Braakman, 1694). Anne Dacier, *Madame Dacier's Remarks upon Mr. Pope's Account of Homer, Prefixed to His Translation of the Iliad,* trans. Mr. Parnell (London: E. Curll, 1724). Scott Elledge and Donald Schier, eds.,

The Continental Model: Selected French Critical Essays of the Seventeenth Century in English Translation (Minneapolis: Carleton College and the University of Minnesota Press, 1960). Bernard Le Bovier de Fontenelle, *A Digression on the Ancients and Moderns,* in Elledge and Schier, *The Continental Model,* pp. 358–370. Fontenelle, *Nouveaux dialogues des morts,* ed. Jean Dagen (Paris: Didier, 1971). Gilbert Highet, "The Battle of the Books," in *The Classical Tradition: Greek and Roman Influences on Western Literature* (New York: Oxford University Press, 1949), pp. 188–261. Charles Perrault, *Parallèle des anciens et des modernes en ce qui regarde les arts et les sciences: Dialogues; avec le poème du Siècle de Louis le Grand et une épître en vers sur le génie* (1692; reprint, Geneva: Slatkine, 1971). Perrault, *The Vindication of Wives,* trans. Roland Grant (London: Rodale Press, 1954). Charles de Marguetel de Saint Denis de Saint-Evremond, *A Dissertation on Racine's Tragedy Called "The Grand Alexander,"* in Elledge and Schier, *The Continental Model,* pp. 132–140. Saint-Evremond, *Sur le merveilleux qui se trouve dans les poèmes des anciens,* in *Oeuvres en prose,* ed. René Ternois, vol. 4 (Paris: Didier, 1969), 185–195; translated as *Of the Wonderful That Is Found in the Works of the Ancients,* in Elledge and Schier, *The Continental Model,* pp. 181–185. Rémy Saisselin, *The Rule of Reason and the Ruses of the Heart: A Philosophical Dictionary of Classical French Criticism, Critics, and Aesthetic Issues* (Cleveland: Press of Case Western Reserve University, 1970). Stendhal, *Racine et Shakespeare* (1823 and 1825), ed. Pierre Martino, in *Oeuvres complètes,* ed. Victor del Litto and Ernest Abravanel, vol. 37 (Geneva: Cercle du Bibliophile, 1970); translated by Guy Daniels as *Racine and Shakespeare* (New York: Crowell Collier, 1962).

Robert J. Nelson

✐ 1689

Racine's Biblical Tragedy *Esther* Is Performed at Saint-Cyr, the School Established by the Marquise de Maintenon for Young Noblewomen

Pedagogy

When Racine's biblical tragedy *Esther* was first performed at the school for young noblewomen established by Françoise de Maintenon, the second wife of Louis XIV, a significant union between schools and the theater reached its peak. This performance at Saint-Cyr, located not far from Versailles in the area just southwest of Paris, united the efforts of France's most brilliant tragic playwright with those of one of the most determined educational reformers of the century. It was a lavish production, attended by the king and the most distinguished members of his court. Yet only a month and a half before the premiere performance, the superintendent of Saint-Cyr, Marie de Brinon, who had arranged for Racine to write and produce the play, was expelled from the school under a royal warrant, apparently because Maintenon began to see dangers in the increased contact between the pupils and the court. In 1691 Racine's second biblical tragedy, *Athalie,* was given only three performances in ordinary dress before a private audience. No further dramatic works at Saint-Cyr were performed for outsiders. The "crisis of *Esther*" tells much about the ambivalence of an educational system straining between a closed ideal world artificially constructed within the school and the practical needs of modern life and openness to social reality.

Esther is also a convenient reminder of the career of Françoise de Maintenon, founder of Saint-Cyr. Her own biography alternates between constraining walls and the world outside. Born in prison to Jeanne de Cardilhac, who had married the turbulent and impoverished Constant d'Aubigné (son of the great Protestant poet and military officer Agrippa d'Aubigné), Françoise d'Aubigné was raised by relatives, very much like the biblical Esther of Racine's play, a Jewish orphan. Like Esther, who married Ahasuerus, king of Persia, and influenced him to save the Jews from a genocidal plot, Françoise married Louis XIV in 1683 and influenced him to favor the conservative wing of the Catholic church. On the way to this eminence, Françoise, widow of the comic author Paul Scarron, had purchased the domain of Maintenon in 1674. Having been governess of children of the nobility, including the illegitimate children of Louis XIV himself, Maintenon planned Saint-Cyr to provide for the daughters of impoverished nobles a kind of subsidized education that she had not had, an education with a real intellectual basis that was not oriented to convent life.

In the prologue to *Esther* the allegorical figure of Piety says, "Here, far from turmoil, following God's commands, / A budding nation is formed by my hands." Racine's emphasis on the separateness of the school from the busy outside world displays an important characteristic of education in 17th-century France: the concept of enclosure and control of the scholastic space. Saint-Cyr was a doubly controlled space. Not only did Saint-Cyr, like other schools, limit the pupils' daily access to the world outside, but Maintenon's institution also limited admission to a small number of young women according to standards of birth, financial need, and a family history of service to the king.

One of the chief goals of the educational reformers of the late 16th and early 17th centuries was to get the pupils off the streets and into strictly controlled places, generally called "colleges." The most dramatic and systematic educational reforms in this direction were the work of the Jesuits, whose determination to separate pupils from everyday life and hold them in a structured environment set a model followed by most other teaching groups. Although there were some day pupils, or "externs," educators strongly preferred to have pupils live as "interns," or boarding pupils in the school. The interns were never unsupervised; even at night they were watched. Within the college only Latin was to be spoken, and all games were organized for educational purposes. Even parents could have only limited visits with pupils at holidays. Far from conceiving school as an apprenticeship for the world of daily life, the Jesuits believed in creating a substitute for that ordinary life, a substitute world with its own coherence, ranks—pupils were divided into little groups with their own pupil leaders—games, and rewards.

The world of "innocence"—the outcome of a long evolution that began with the founding of boarding colleges at the University of Paris in the 13th century—thus became an educational arrangement or device for the education of boys. Because society was also, for somewhat different reasons, preoccupied with the "innocence" of girls, destined to be wives, the education of men and women converged in the debate about the wisdom of teaching children and adolescents in an artificial world. Molière's mordant attack on the education of innocence hit a nerve in French society. In his comedy *L'école des femmes* (1662; *The School for Wives*), old man Arnolphe plans long in advance the education of a perfect wife in accordance with the doctrine of innocence. Imagining himself in complete control of a woman raised to be as idiotic as possible, he adopts the four-year-old daughter of a poor woman and has her raised in a convent strictly according to his specifications: "I told the nuns what means must be employed / To keep her growing mind a perfect void" (act 1, scene 1). Arnolphe soon discovers that innocence, far from ensuring his control over Agnès, protects Agnès from all the hypocrisies through which women submit to men like himself. Molière shows how Agnès' education is carried out by means of hermetic enclosure. Even after her release from the convent into Arnolphe's direct custody, Agnès is kept under lock and key while her guardian completes her education. He has her memorize absurd and repressive maxims about the duty of a married woman—one starts "She has no need, whatever she may think, / Of writing table, paper, pen, or ink" (act 3, scene 2). Molière reduces the whole pedagogy of enclosure to a shambles by pointing to the persistence of natural desire and its awakening upon the first contact with the outside world.

Voices were raised in criticism of the tactic of enclosure and cultivated innocence both before and after Molière. One of the pupils of the elite Jesuit school founded early in the century at La Flèche, in the Loire valley, was René Descartes, the "gentleman philosopher." In his *Discours de la méthode* (1637; *Discourse on Method*), Descartes claimed that reading too many classical books made readers lose touch with their own world. But he found that his later attempt to counter the school's artificial closed world by traveling, which he called studying in the "great book of the world," led to equally great disappointment: "When one spends too much time traveling, one becomes at last a stranger at home; and those who are too interested in things which occurred in past centuries are often remarkably ignorant of what is going on today" (*Discourse*, p. 4). As a result, Descartes rejected both the college education of books and the worldly education of experience in favor of withdrawal into his own reason.

At the beginning of the 17th century the language of the school was an important barrier against the contemporary world, for all instruction took place in Latin. Young boys who did not yet read were taught in Latin how to read Latin. Grammar and rhetoric were also taught in Latin. Toward midcentury the Port-Royal reformers, or Jansenists, challenged this way of making school an artificial world by using French as the beginning language in their little schools (*petites écoles*—the term is often associated with the schools of Port-Royal, although in fact it was used universally to mean any primary school). Bitter opponents of the theologically optimistic Jesuits, the Jansenists taught that not all believers would be saved, despite good works. Their teaching was oriented toward exposing the imperfect real world rather than toward creating fictive ideal worlds for the school as the Jesuits did.

In founding her school at Saint-Cyr, Maintenon took into account the tension between closed and open forms of schooling. Rejecting, at least initially, the model of the convent, she aimed at forming women for secular life. Yet preparing women for life outside the walls of a convent did not mean abandoning closure and artifice for free observation of the world. One of Maintenon's advisers was a clergyman with strong ideas on education in general and on the education of girls in particular, François de Salignac de La Mothe–Fénelon. In his treatise *De l'éducation des filles* (1687; *On the Education of Girls*) Fénelon emphasized the desirability of preparing women for activities carried out entirely in the home. He contrasted the good domestic woman with the fashionable and "public" woman of the salon.

Fénelon presented himself as the enemy of the artificial and the affected; for him, the domestic woman was the woman returned to her supposedly natural state. He decried women's tendency to put on appearances: "They have a pliable nature which enables them to play easily all sorts of parts. Tears cost them nothing" (*Education,* p. 66). Yet the means used for instructing them were deeply theatrical. Given that the nature of children is to imitate, how could one tell the actor or actress from the role? In other words, was there still a "nature" underlying the spectacle that children were constantly performing? Helping a pupil to acquire the highly praised natural style (*le naturel*) of the 17th century turned out to be more difficult than allowing the child to be affected. Although there was a widespread belief that a human nature existed, Fénelon realized that from their very first moments children were already adapting to the society around them. Consequently, being "natural" could only be an ideal toward which children could be guided by adults who put on a performance of naturalness. Fénelon noted that children's penchant for miming must often be curbed: "You should also prevent them from imitating silly people, for their mocking and farcical ways have in them something vulgar" (p. 14). Adults chosen to be around children must constantly put on a false front before the child audience (for example, "It is necessary therefore to take care of children without letting them realise that we are thinking much about them"; pp. 10–11). Even more active histrionics are suggested for instructing very young children: "Thus you can give them by words, aided by the tone of your voice or by gestures, the desire to be with the good and virtuous people . . . Thus by the different expressions of your face or by the tone of your voice you can express your horror at people whom they have seen giving way to anger" (p. 7). The wrong kind of adults, those who "scarcely restrain themselves" (p. 14), should be kept away. Adult "restraint" or role-playing will limit the scope of children's role-playing and produce the "natural" style.

Drama had been a prominent classroom technique at least since the 16th century, when the Jesuits had their pupils perform Latin plays as a way of making spoken Latin attractive. The consciousness of drama and acting in the schools at the end of the 17th century was of a different degree. The pedagogy described by Fénelon no longer separated acting from life. Racine's *Esther,* performed in the context of this exquisitely self-conscious theatrical view of life, is a form of theater within a theater. Because the ordinary educational process was based on performance, *Esther* was merely theater in which the role-playing was openly acknowledged.

In the crisis of *Esther* the convergence of school, court, and theater undermined the educational project of Maintenon and Fénelon. By marrying members of the court audience, several pupil-actresses moved beyond the humble state to which they were destined by Maintenon: the impoverished nobility from which the pupils were drawn was meant to form a stable base for the monarchy and was not meant to move upward. Through Marie de Brinon's program of producing Racine's biblical plays for the royal court, the strict control of the school and its pupils' ultimate vocation were being sacrificed to the seductions and prestige of Versailles. Maintenon's expulsion of Brinon and her refusal to permit further open performances at Saint-Cyr mark an attempt to prevent the theatricality of politics from merging with the theatricality of the school.

See also 1673, 1808.

Bibliography: Roger Chartier, Dominique Julia, and Marie-Madeleine Compère, *L'éducation en France du XVIe au XVIIe siècle* (Paris: Société d'Edition d'Enseignement Supérieur, 1976). René Descartes, *Discourse on Method,* trans. Laurence J. Lafleur (Indianapolis: Bobbs-Merrill, 1960). François de Salignac de La Mothe–Fénelon, *De l'éducation des filles,* in *Oeuvres,* ed. Jacques Le Brun (Paris: Gallimard, 1983); translated by H. C. Barnard as *The Education of Girls,* in *Fénelon on Education* (Cambridge: Cambridge University Press, 1966). Molière, *L'école des femmes,* in *Oeuvres complètes,* ed. Pierre-Aimé Touchard (Paris: Seuil, 1962); translated by Richard Wilbur as *The School for Wives* (New York: Harcourt Brace Jovanovich, 1971). Jacques Prévot, *La première institutrice de France: Madame de Maintenon* (Paris: Belin, 1981). Jean Racine, *Complete Plays,* trans. Samuel Solomon (New York: Random House, 1967). Racine, *Esther,* in *Théâtre complet,* ed. Jacques Morel and Alain Viala (Paris: Garnier, 1980). Georges Snyders, *La pédagogie en France aux XVIIe et XVIIIe siècles* (Paris: Presses Universitaires de France, 1965).

John D. Lyons

 1694

The Académie Française Presents Louis XIV with the First Copy of Its Long-Awaited *Dictionnaire*

Linguistic Absolutism

At Versailles on 24 August 1694 a delegation from the Académie Française presented the Sun King with two fine morocco-bound folios, the first printed copies of a long-awaited work, a dictionary of the French language (fig. 1). Fifty-nine years before, an edict by Louis XIV's father had provided for the organization of a private group of literary figures into the Académie Française. That organization had been rigorously implemented by Cardinal Richelieu. And one of the first tasks assigned the new Académie, conceived as the absolute monarchy's literary arm, was the preparation of the first dictionary of the French

AU ROY.

IRE,

L'ACADÉMIE FRANÇOISE *ne peut se refu-*
ser la gloire de publier son Dictionnaire sous les auspi-
ces de son auguste Protecteur.   Cet Ouvrage est un
Recueil fidelle de tous les termes & de toutes les phrases
                                                           ā ij

1. "Epître au roi," plate designed by Jean-Baptiste Corneille, engraved by Jean Mariette, *Dictionnaire de l'Académie Française,* vol. 1 (Paris: Jean-Baptiste Coignard, 1694).
(Courtesy of the Beinecke Rare Book and Manuscript Library, Yale University.)

language. By the time of its completion in 1694, French political absolutism had reached heights that even Richelieu could not have foreseen.

But when the official dictionary of the French language finally was delivered, its reception was hardly glorious. Louis XIV answered the presentation speech by Jacques de Tourreil by declaring that since the lengthy efforts of so many Academicians had been necessary, he was certain that "the book must be very beautiful indeed and useful for the language" (*Le Mercure galant,* August 1694), a remark that could have been seen less as praise for the result than as an ironic reference to the snail's pace at which it had been achieved. On the very same day, by a strange coincidence, the Dutch publisher Leers presented the king with a French dictionary that had had to be published in Holland because in France the Académie had been granted the exclusive privilege of producing one. Its author, already dead, had been ejected from the Académie because of his persistence in his project. His name was Antoine Furetière, and his *Dictionnaire universel des arts et des sciences* (*Universal Dictionary of the Arts and Sciences*), first published in 1690, then reprinted, received a warm welcome from the monarch. As Racine wrote on 28 September to his fellow royal historiographer Nicolas Boileau, the simultaneous presentation "was seen as a rather bizarre contretemps for the Académie's Dictionary, which to me does not seem to have as many supporters as the other one" (*Oeuvres,* 2:548).

A third major dictionary of the French language, compiled under the guidance of influential writers, had already been published by the teacher Pierre Richelet in Geneva (1680) and had met great success. Linguistic absolutism had hardly been as successfully imposed as its political counterpart.

Although these three dictionaries differ on many counts, they share one feature so obvious that it is not often noticed: they are entirely in French and contain no Latin. In the Western world, language dictionaries first appeared in bilingual or multilingual form. In France, Robert Estienne's *Dictionnaire français-latin* (1539; *French-Latin Dictionary*) provided the first expanded lexicographic description of French; Jean Nicot's *Trésor* (1606; *Thesaurus*), however, still included Latin translations. Before 1680, information about French had to be located in works such as Randall Cotgrave's *Dictionarie of the French and English Tongues* (London, 1611) and César Oudin's *Le trésor des deux langues espagnole et française* (Paris, 1607; *Thesaurus of the French and Spanish Tongues*). The suppression of Latin references from modern language descriptions was no simple matter, since most dictionaries were intended to serve as an introduction to Latin, the scholarly language still seen as the ultimate semantic reference. This was true of most dictionaries used in schools. An all-French dictionary was a radically new concept, analogous to the Edict of Villers-Cotterêts (10 August 1539), by which Francis I decreed that every legal decision must henceforth be handed down, not in Latin, but in French. The social and political struggle between Latin and French was mainly a 16th-century phenomenon: at that time, the Catholic church and the educational establishment pronounced in favor of Latin, whereas the king, Protestants, writers, and humanists backed a freer use of French. At the end of the 17th century the question was still unresolved:

it was revived in other guises during the Quarrel of the Ancients and the Moderns.

Like the decision to impose French as the official legal language, the systematic word-by-word description of the French language was a political and an ideological undertaking. Claude Favre de Vaugelas, Academician and author of the influential *Remarques sur la langue française* (1647; *Remarks on the French Language*), remained until his death the moving force behind the Académie's dictionary. Vaugelas, following the poet François de Malherbe, proposed usage as "the only true ruler of language," its "king and tyrant"—an evidently far-from-democratic conception. Correct linguistic usage was understood to be defined and legislated by a handful of wealthy, powerful individuals in possession of good taste, for the most part courtiers, especially after Louis XIV had moved his court from Paris to Versailles. Malherbe's often-quoted remark that his linguistic models were the "longshoremen of the Port-au-Foin [Paris' dockyard for hay]" (Racan, *Mémoires,* p. 223) probably signified no more than a belief that written French should be clear and simple enough to be understood even by the uneducated. Malherbe always argued for simplicity against the pedantic humanists who wanted to imitate Greek and Latin patterns. Vaugelas and Dominique Bouhours followed his lead, with the political support of Richelieu and, later, Louis XIV and his minister Jean-Baptiste Colbert, in order to impose a state-controlled linguistic nationalism. An inherently French tradition, based on aristocratic linguistic authority, was then established. The best writers accepted it: Racine, for example, asked for emendations from Bouhours. However, questions of linguistic politics were always debated in the name of abstractions: logic, the imitation (*mimesis*) of nature, elegance, and clarity.

Not everyone agreed with the Académie's policy. Among the dissenters were the heirs of the 16th-century linguistic flowering, such as Montaigne's adoptive daughter, Marie de Gournay, or the skeptic philosopher François de La Mothe Le Vayer, who opposed both absolute authority and the deliberate impoverishment of language. Until 1650, the impoverishment that resulted from classical rules and prohibitions was countered by baroque writers; after this, by members of the précieux school. But the most important dissent was not purely literary.

In all the earliest French dictionaries we can find strong evidence of the quiet struggle between state authority, the spirit of the court, and aristocratic taste (all linked to religious and civic absolutism), on the one hand; and, on the other, the powerful force of early capitalism, itself linked to the rise of a new bourgeois elite that was to lead the philosophical trends of the 18th century. For example, Richelet's dictionary, which appeared in 1680, while the Academicians were struggling to carry out the wishes of Colbert, was different from the Académie's project. Like the lexicographer Oudin, Richelet was well aware of pragmatic pressure: his dictionary does not strive for the purity and elegance of Vaugelas's ideal vision. Instead, it is a reflection of his belief that, in order to remain useful, dictionaries cannot be made only of strict rules on grammar and style. They must describe language and its products as social facts, reflecting contradictions between different types of usage. Even if Richelet, no more than Furetière, did not dare criticize the notion of "good usage," their dictionaries indicate that such an arbitrary social concept cannot be the only aim of a sensible linguistic tool.

New descriptive trends then began to loom large in French linguistics: objective historical description and a theoretical view of language. After much tentative exploration during the 16th and the early 17th centuries, the former trend paved the way for Charles Du Cange's admirable research on late Latin and Gilles Ménage's French etymologies. Imperfect though they were, Ménage's conjectures showed a new awareness of historical, hence social, linguistic laws (*Les origines de la langue française*, 1650; *Origins of the French Language*). Theoretical research, derived from the philosophies of Descartes and Nicolas de Malebranche, asserted itself brilliantly with the Jansenist fathers of Port-Royal, especially Claude Lancelot, Pierre Nicole, and Antoine Arnauld (*Grammaire générale et raisonnée*, 1660; *General and Reasoned Grammar*). This logical, universalist semantic trend in linguistics continued to develop in France throughout the 18th century and was reinforced by Gottfried Wilhelm von Leibniz and the British philosophers; it is still active in French thought today. Of course, the new theories could be used to support Vaugelas, Bouhours, and Boileau. For instance, the concept of an analytic structure of language was supposed to be ideally embodied in French. However, the emphasis on the formal structures and semantic rules found in any natural language could not coexist with the prescriptive attitude that royal authority required from the Académie Française. In short, logic (Port-Royal) and usage (Vaugelas) were bound to remain in conflict.

Seventeenth-century French language dictionaries were founded on other contradictions, in particular the unresolved opposition between selection for the sake of good taste and the inclusiveness indispensable to the new demands of knowledge. Nowhere is this contradiction more evident than in a comparison between the two dictionaries presented to the Sun King in late August 1694. The Académie is the champion of good usage, good taste, and the kind of speech used at Versailles by the court on formal occasions. Good usage was defined by Vaugelas himself as the usage of "the soundest part of the court" as far as spoken language was concerned and, for written language, the usage best in conformity with "the soundest authors" (*Dictionnaire de l'Académie Française*, p. ii)—undeniably an elitist social theory of language. "Soundness" was identified with the usage and the taste of the small circle close to the king, who was thus invested as a sort of shaman, embodying the strength and the health of the French language, society, and nation.

Furetière was not convinced that soundness and reason resided at Versailles rather than in the secluded studies of scientists and thinkers scattered throughout the kingdom. His dictionary was meant to reflect the rise of the sciences and arts (meaning both the development of craftsmanship and the fine arts). Furetière felt a greater need for rich, precise terminology than for severe exclusions in the name of good taste. This same need was obvious to the Academicians, for (also in 1694) they asked Pierre Corneille's younger brother Thomas, himself a well-known dramatist, to compile a dictionary of "arts and sciences" as a complement to their "good usage" compendium. When describing everyday language, Furetière often made use of the same material as the Académie, and this was one of the main objections made against him. Thomas Corneille used Furetière's sources but did not always put them to the same efficient use. Because he was less constrained by the good usage–good taste doctrine, Furetière gave a more comprehensive and more objective image of spoken and written French around 1650–1690 than did the Academicians. The Académie was criticized on two fronts: the elite found the dictionary incomplete and hard to use (its entries are grouped half etymologically, half morphologically) and the purists found in it far too many phrases they considered vulgar and common. It was even dubbed "le dictionnaire des halles" ("the Billingsgate dictionary").

From a modern standpoint, the three major French-language dictionaries of the 17th century afford excellent linguistic material, as well as further evidence of social rhetoric in the age of Louis XIV. They can also be seen as the beginning of the twofold French tradition. A dictionary can have two goals: to unveil the social truth of language (that is, the norm); and, through an appropriate use of words and terms, to reveal the scientific, philosophical, and cultural achievements of society at large. The Académie's dictionaries—eight editions in three centuries—pursued the social goal, as did Emile Littré's *Dictionnaire de la langue française* (1863–1872) and the remarkable *Dictionnaire général de la langue française,* by Adolphe Hatzfeld, Arsène Darmesteter, and André Antoine Thomas (1900). With the exception of the Académie dictionary, rather outdated after the 18th century, works in this tradition provide copious literary quotations. In many ways, they cling to 17th-century tradition. For example, around 1860 Littré reflected the influence of 19th-century German philology on the development of linguistics, but his philosophy of language was clearly still the Cartesian view of Port-Royal. In addition, he held a historical view of good usage. Even if this correct usage was no longer determined by a social group or imposed by an absolute political vision, it was still embodied in the classical literature of the age of political absolutism, in the styles of writers whom Littré still considered authoritative, from Malherbe to Chateaubriand (almost never his contemporaries).

The scientific approach considered words as tools for thought and knowledge. Furetière's work was continued by the Trévoux Jesuits' dictionaries, the conservative 18th-century counterpart of Denis Diderot and Jean d'Alembert's "reasoned dictionary," the *Encyclopédie* (1751–1772). The history of French lexicography is made of such complementary trends: in the second half of the 19th century, the social philologist Littré was complemented by Pierre Larousse, a pedagogue intent on democratically teaching the people about words and things. Both Littré and Larousse supported democracy and the Republic; both admired such figures as Victor Hugo, Emile Zola, Pierre Joseph Proudhon, and Léon Gambetta; however, they created very different lexicographic programs in the service of the same ideal. Like their 17th-century predecessors, they embodied the opposition between the theory of language as the highest cultural value, as thought or reason (*logos*), and the theory of language as an instrument for knowledge (terminology) and action (rhetoric): on the one hand, a refined, more or less purist view of language as a normative and social force (Littré); and on the other hand, language considered as a pragmatic and utilitarian tool (Larousse). This linguistic opposition can even be linked to the conflict between elite power and democratic education.

Thus the opposition between the Académie Française and Antoine Furetière was not just personal, or even institutional. It was in fact social and cultural in the profoundest sense of those terms. In France, the different ways in which social groups consider their own language are more or less faithfully reflected in the major dictionaries. This habit should not be deemed surprising in a country where some rulers or presidents have edited anthologies of poetry (as did Georges Pompidou) or written literary and musical criticism (as did Edouard Herriot, himself an Academician), and where governments sometimes make decisions on words, as well as on the citizens who use them.

See also 1539, 1627, 1661, 1687, 1697, 1751, 1791 (13 January).

Bibliography: Dictionnaire de l'Académie Française (Paris: Coignard, 1694). Ferdinand Brunot, *Histoire de la langue française, des origines à 1900,* vols. 3 and 4 (1909; reprint, Paris: Armand Colin, 1966–1968). Bernard Quémada, *Histoire des dictionnaires français* (Paris: Didier, 1968). Honorat de Racan, *Mémoires de la vie de M. de Malherbe,* in *Oeuvres complètes* (Paris: Bibliothèque Elzévirienne, 1857). Jean Racine, *Oeuvres complètes,* ed. Raymond Picard, vol. 2 (Paris: Gallimard, 1966). Alain Rey, introduction to *Le dictionnaire d'Antoine Furetière* (Paris: Le Robert, 1978).

Alain Rey

✑ 1697

The Philosopher Pierre Bayle Publishes His *Dictionnaire historique et critique* in Holland

Marginal Writing

Many of the shapers of modern culture have been marginal figures—Descartes, Spinoza, Rousseau, even Montesquieu ("a great provincial," as Pierre Barrière, one of his modern biographers, dubbed him)—critical outsiders who have questioned received ideas and thus stimulated the renaissances and innovations that have characterized Western history since the 15th century. Marginality seems paradoxically central to the entire culture of modernity. The relation of center and periphery may well be more symbiotic, less starkly oppositional, than one might be led to believe from the repressions, persecutions, and trials to which dissidents, nonconformists, and bohemian or avant-garde artists have been subject. Even in the heyday of Louis XIV there was an important marginal culture:

fictional social commentary, such as Giovanni Paolo Marana's *Lettres d'un espion turc* (1684; *Letters Writ by a Turkish Spy,* 1691–1694); utopian narratives, such as Gabriel de Foigny's *Terre australe* (1676; *A New Discovery of Terra Incognita Australis,* 1693) or Denis Veiras's *Histoire des Sévarambes* (1677; *A Voyage in Sevarambia,* 1727); more or less fanciful speculations about the origin of religion, such as the anonymous *Lettre d'Hippocrate à Demagette* (ca. 1700; *Letter from Hippocrates to Demagette*); and travel accounts, such as Jean-Baptiste Tavernier's *Voyages en Turquie* (1676; *Voyages through Turkey,* 1678) or Louis Armand de Lahontan's *Nouveaux voyages* (1703; *New Voyages to North America*). Some of these texts were produced in France, some by expatriates such as Jean (Sir John) Chardin (*Voyages en Perse,* 1686; *Travels into Persia*); some circulated freely, others clandestinely. Pierre Bayle (1647–1706) was one of the expatriates. His feisty, independent, deliberately unsystematic works, all published in Holland, turned out to be central to the writers of the Enlightenment. Bayle's *Dictionnaire historique et critique* (1697; *An Historical and Critical Dictionary,* 1710) was more popular among educated 18th-century laypeople than any other single work, and it served as a source of ideas and examples for all the philosophes.

Bayle himself led a thoroughly marginal existence. The son of a poor Protestant minister in a small town in the remote southwest of France, he lost his modest teaching post at the Protestant Académie de Sedan when the college was closed down by royal command in 1681, and spent the rest of his life in exile in Holland. Even here, however, he fell foul of the Huguenot establishment and was dismissed from the chair of philosophy that had been created for him on his arrival in Rotterdam. From 1693 until his death in 1706 he subsisted on a modest pension from his Dutch publisher, Leers. Enjoying the support of no noble patron, court, or church, he was one of the first professional intellectuals, as well as one of the glories of the Huguenot diaspora of the 17th century. Louis XIV's policy of persecution and banishment had catapulted many French Protestants from a ghetto existence in the French provinces to the center of the European intellectual scene. Huguenots from France exercised an influence disproportionate to their numbers in Rotterdam, Amsterdam, London, Berlin, Hamburg, Geneva, Bern, and as far afield as the Dutch settlements in South Africa. It was through them that ideas passed from England to France and vice versa (Pierre Coste, for example, Locke's French translator, was a Huguenot exile), and they helped to win acceptance for French as the language of Enlightenment, of *philosophie.* The exiles thus turned out to be central, mediating figures. The audience that Bayle addressed, in French, from Rotterdam included large numbers of his compatriots, despite the best efforts of the French censorship, but it was also a European audience.

At the very center of his work Bayle placed forms considered peripheral and subordinate: the review, the commentary, the occasional letter on a subject of current interest. His *Pensées diverses sur la comète* (1682; *Miscellaneous Reflections Occasion'd by the Comet,* 1708), *Critique de l'Histoire du Calvinisme du P. Maimbourg* (1682; *Criticism of Father Maimbourg's History of Calvinism*), *Commentaire philosophique sur ces paroles de Jésus-Christ: Contrains-les d'entrer, ou traité de la tolé-*

rance universelle (1686–87; *A Philosophical Commentary on Luke XIV:23*, 1708); his *Nouvelles de la république des lettres,* one of the earliest European learned journals, edited and largely written by Bayle between 1684 and 1687; and his great *Dictionnaire historique et critique* prepared the way for 18th-century classics such as the *Encyclopédie* (1751–1772) of Denis Diderot and Jean d'Alembert, Voltaire's *Dictionnaire philosophique* (1764; *Philosophical Dictionary,* 1765), and Diderot's *Lettre sur les aveugles* (1749; *An Essay on Blindness,* 1750) and *Supplément au Voyage de Bougainville* (wr. 1772, pub. 1796; *Supplement to the Voyage of Bougainville*) and for a literary culture focused not on the production of "great works" but on rapid exchange, on provocation and response. Bayle's writing challenged classical notions of literature and of the appropriate content and form of literature. It liberated religion and scholarship, science and philosophy, from their special spheres and made them the affair of the general reader. At the same time, it expanded the range of literature beyond the imitation of consecrated models and themes. There was a politically portentous blurring of the boundaries separating center and periphery, the writer of genius—as Pierre Carlet de Marivaux later ironically dubbed the "classical" writer—and the publicist, "noble" forms and subject matter ("eternal" epic and tragic themes) and "common" ones ("transitory" topics of scientific, scholarly, or practical interest).

In the 17th-century context it was an original view of the relation of center and margin that was inscribed in the format of Bayle's influential *Dictionnaire.* The usually "subordinate" part of the page—the space reserved for the footnotes below the "main" text—assumes an importance here at least equal to that of the main text and has considerably greater dimensions. There is no hierarchy of textual spaces. The annotated text is no more essential than the text of the annotations—in contrast to the traditional commentary, where the "original" text (invariably an "ancient" text, such as the Bible or Aristotle) had a sacred character, in virtue of which, even when not physically present, it enjoyed a prestige and authority that placed it above any "modern" commentary. Bayle's text also invades the margins, dotting them with last-minute but by no means incidental reflections and references. Reading the *Dictionnaire* requires equal attention to all areas of the text.

An influential body of critics has defended the view that Bayle remained a fundamentally Christian thinker in the fideistic tradition and was misread by Enlightenment writers such as Voltaire and Hume. Probably we shall never know what he himself thought and believed. Even the assumption that he held a single identifiable set of beliefs and convictions is questionable, as Ludwig Feuerbach suggested in 1839 (*Werke,* 5:267–285). But the position in which we consequently find ourselves—having to interpret without ever achieving certainty—is at least consistent with the recurrent message of Bayle's own text.

The essence of Bayle lies in his simultaneous practice of rational criticism and criticism of reason. Marginality reappears here as a central notion. Like Pascal, Bayle recalls that human beings are not located at the center of the universe; like Voltaire later, he finds no evidence that they are more than incidental to any divine plan there may be (*Pensées diverses sur la comète,* sec. 83). They have no direct contact—by reason, illumination, or any other means—with the origin and center of things. Exiles in a marginal situation, they can receive only skewed and imperfect data about the universe, and their only recourse is to bear this fact in mind and to interpret and correct these data to the best of their ability. All their speculations about how things "truly" are—that is, how they would be represented if they could be seen from the center, as God sees them, assuming there is such a center—are therefore only that: speculations that are always uncertain and subject to criticism (that is the bad news) but at the same time, and for the same reason, subject to correction and revision (that is the good news). If the "truth" were knowable, Bayle seems to be saying, there would be no need for scientific study: it is only because all our knowledge is inevitably hypothetical that we keep on trying to improve it. The point is not that all knowledge is declared to be interpretation. It is rather the emphasis on knowledge as *process,* as a kind of investment capital rather than as a fixed property—an emphasis confirmed half a century later for the entire Enlightenment by Gotthold Ephraim Lessing's comment that if he had to choose between the truth in the right hand of God and the mere desire to discover it in His left, he would not hesitate: he would choose the left hand. The conception of knowledge as a continuous process of discovery, hypothesis, criticism, and correction is vividly conveyed in the *Dictionnaire* through the constant generation of notes and commentary, the insertion of "last-minute" observations in the margins, and the addition of new material, including replies to critics, in successive editions (1702, 1715).

Bayle's "heroes" anticipate the 18th-century figure of the philosophe, of Candide or Zadig. Thus the Marrano Uriel da Costa (*Dictionnaire,* s.v. "Acosta"), a near-contemporary of Spinoza, because he asks questions and seeks the "true" religion, suffers exile, persecution, and abuse from everyone, Christian and Jew alike, and finally takes his own life in despair. His career bears an uncanny resemblance to Bayle's. Yet even the philosopher-hero is treated with a mixture of compassion and ironical detachment. As we cannot have absolute truth, we cannot have pure heroes.

The work of reason, for Bayle, is a constant unraveling. Just as it is a "silly vanity" of humankind to imagine that the birth of a prince is an event of cosmic importance, which might be marked, say, by the passage of a comet, it is ingenuous to believe that a statement is true simply because it has been accepted by tradition or carries some other mark of authority. Narratives are as full of holes and imperfections as princes, and neither deserves to impose on us. "A narrative full of the crassest ignorance is just as capable of exciting the passions and carrying conviction as one marked by historical accuracy" (*Dictionnaire,* preface). Understandably, all Bayle's work is critical—from the reviews in the *Nouvelles de la république des lettres* and the *Critique de Maimbourg* to the articles of the *Dictionnaire* itself, which were intended to "supplement" and where necessary "correct" Louis Moreri's *Grand dictionnaire historique, ou mélange curieux de l'histoire sacrée et profane* (1674; *Grand Historical Dictionary, or Curious Miscellany of Sacred and Profane History*).

One of the most paradoxical works ever written, since it is a tissue of unravelings, the *Dictionnaire* is Bayle's supreme achievement. The reason that operates in it is critical. It destroys error; it does not generate "truth." It is not like Cartesian reason, in which an incontrovertible original and immediately intuited truth gives rise to further truths until ultimately a complete system of true knowledge is derived from it. On the contrary, Bayle's reason turns on itself and attacks its own foundations. "Philosophy," he declares, "can be compared to one of those apothecary's powders that, after consuming the oozing flesh of a wound, begins to eat away the healthy flesh, and then rots the bones all the way through to the marrow" ("Acosta," note F). Reason, he says in another place, "is a veritable Penelope; she undoes at night what she wove during the day" ("Bunel, Pierre," note E). Inevitably, Bayle's work never assumes a systematic form. It is not offered as a comprehensive account of man and nature, but presents itself instead as continuing dialogue and debate. It never initiates; it always responds, most often in the form of reviews or rebuttals. It is fragmentary, critical, and unsystematic. The dictionary format, together with the more or less arbitrary selection of entries, constitutes a rejection of all claims to systematicity. It can therefore be only the *operation* of reason, not its structure, that Bayle's readers are invited to observe and acquire for themselves.

In each entry in the *Dictionnaire,* almost every word of the shallow narrative text at the top of the page is the occasion of a critical note that quickly spreads out over the space below and occasions in turn further notes, questions, and references. Every statement, every sentence, every word turns out to be a trap for the unwary, an abyss of undemonstrated assumptions and unwarranted connections. At every step the illusion of continuity disintegrates under critical scrutiny. The most minute erudition was justified, for Bayle, to the extent that it helped to demonstrate "through concrete examples how important it is to be constantly vigilant and suspicious of what one reads and to apply one's talent to discriminating among the facts brought before one" ("Cappadoce," note K). It is no accident that Bayle was not only one of the founders of modern historical scholarship, for which he provided basic rules of evidence and critical procedures that are still largely adhered to, but also a favorite of the historical scholars of the end of the 17th century in their running battle with the practitioners of rhetorical and narrative (that is, classical) historiography. The latter were often princely panegyrists; not surprisingly, those who aimed to pick holes in their narratives were for the most part bourgeois lawyers. The attitude Bayle promoted was obviously unlikely to appeal to those associated with the center of power.

The question remains whether Bayle goes "beyond" skepticism. This is not an easy question to answer, especially if one bears in mind that the original meaning of the Greek *skepsis* was neither methodical doubt in the Cartesian sense nor the cultivation of uncertainty, but a cautious and continuous peering, prying, investigating. Bayle's chief aim was almost certainly, in the heyday of that political absolutism from which he and his coreligionists in France suffered so much, critical and negative. A structure of oppression had to be torn down before thought could be given to what might replace it. Still, Bayle does more than show that reason corrodes everything it touches. Although it must be acknowledged that in matters of fact—as distinct from the tautological truths of logic and mathematics—human beings have no sure means of distinguishing true belief from false belief, as rational creatures they have an obligation to do their best to discover what seems most plausible. "One should never refuse to seek enlightenment in discussion with those who have something new to tell" (*Commentaire philosophique,* pt. 2, chaps. 5 and 10). Bayle often remarked on his own insatiable appetite for *nouvelles*—facts and information of all kinds. In the end, he claims, his form of skepticism is incompatible only with theology, described ironically as "that divine science." The theologian alone will find it dangerous, "for it is not clear why it should seem so to the natural scientist or to the statesman . . . We need not allow ourselves to be discouraged by the argument that the human mind is too limited to discover anything about the truths of nature, the causes that produce heat, cold, the tides, etc. We can be content to gather data from experiments and seek probable hypotheses" (*Dictionnaire,* "Pyrrhon," note B) (fig. 1).

In other words, knowledge is not worthless or invalid because it is uncertain. Nor is it impossible to discriminate among explanations and hypotheses and to reach a measure of (provisional) agreement about which are more and which less plausible. But it is of the very nature of human and scientific knowledge, as opposed to supernatural knowledge, that it is always subject to review. In both the natural sciences and history—Bayle does not distinguish epistemologically between the two—knowledge is constantly changing, and it is defined more by the criteria and procedures according to which it is produced and evaluated than by its content, more as a process than as a doctrine. Bayle's model of knowledge, one could say, is borrowed from history or law rather than from metaphysics and theology.

Bayle made the reading of his work itself a demonstration of the exercise of reason as he expounded it. Readers of the *Dictionnaire* are not securely guided by a master hand along a clear and straight avenue toward the possession of the truth. On the contrary, they stumble from digression to digression, disconcerted and thrown off balance by statements that appear to undermine what they thought was established or that lead them to intellectual dead ends, never enjoying the assurance that they have attained absolute truth about anything, including the author's own "final" meaning.

In the declining years of Louis XIV's reign, as financial and economic difficulties multiplied and military reverses followed one upon another, more and more individuals and groups—including even loyal servants of the throne, such as Marshal Vauban (*Projet de dîme royale,* 1707; *Project for a Royal Tax*)—began publicly to question established policies and to propose changes. More and more dissenters within France itself aired in writing opinions previously concealed. Literature, which, if Louis XIV had had his way, would have been a ceremonious and highly regulated activity, became increasingly a forum for public discussion and debate. Whereas classicism had recognized the existence only of high and low, tragedy and comedy, epic and burlesque, a new middle

en pourra justement conclure qu'il avoit beaucoup de capacité, & beaucoup de réputation. Il fut Bâtonnier de la Communauté des Avocats & des Procureurs du Parlement en 1682 (B), & il fut reçu l'un des vingt quatre Docteurs honoraires de la Faculté des Droits de Paris à la place de Mr. Boscager le 25 de Février 1688. Il mourut Doien de la Compagnie des Avocats le 10 d'Octobre 1691, à l'âge de plus de soixante & dix neuf ans, & fut enterré à saint Etienne du Mont. Il a laissé plusieurs enfans (a), & entre autres Mr. PINSSON des Riolles Avocat au Parlement de Paris, homme de mérite, & fort conu des Savans, & l'un des plus officieux amis que l'on puisse voir. Il travaille entre autres choses à la Vie des Professeurs de Bourges.

(a) Tiré d'un Memoire manuscrit.

(*) Tiré d'un Memoire manuscrit.

„ Bois Avocat au Parlement, intitulé *Maximes du Droit* „ *Canonique*, qui ont été publiées avec ce livre plusieurs „ fois, chez Jean Guignard en deux volumes *in* 12. en „ 1678, 1684. &c. par Maitre Denis Simon, Conseiller „ au Presidial & Assesseur en la Marechaussée de Beau-„ vais (7).„

(B) *Il fut Bâtonnier de la Communauté des Avocats & des Procureurs du Parlement en 1682.*] En faveur de ceux qui pourront lire ceci sans avoir le Dictionaire de Furetie-

re, je donnerai l'explication du mot *Bâtonnier*. „ Bâton-„ nier, en termes de Palais, est un ancien Avocat qui on „ choisit tous les ans selon l'ordre du tableau, pour être „ le Chef de la Communauté des Avocats & Procureurs, „ pour être maitre de leur Chapelle & de leur Confrairie, „ & presider au siege qui les tiennent pour l'entretenement „ de la discipline du Palais & des reglemens. C'est à lui „ aussi qu'appartient la comission des charges des Juges „ inferieurs pendant leur interdiction (8).„

(8) Dictio-naire de Fureticre, au Mot Bâtonnier.

PYRRHON, Philosophe Grec, nâtif d'Elide au Peloponnese, fut Disciple d'Anaxarque, & l'accompagna jusques aux Indes (a). Ce fut sans doute à la suite d'Alexandre le Grand, d'où l'on peut conoître en quel tems il a fleuri. Il avoit exercé le métier de Peintre (b) avant que de s'attacher à l'étude de la Philosophie. Ses sentimens ne différoient guere des opinions d'Arcesilas (A); car il s'en faloit bien peu qu'aussi bien que lui il n'enseignât l'incompréhensibilité de toutes choses. Il trouvoit par tout, & des raisons d'affirmer, & des raisons de nier: & c'est pour cela qu'il retenoit son consentement après avoir bien examiné le pour & le contre, & qu'il réduisoit tous ses Arrêts à un *non liquet*, soit plus amplement enquis. Il cherchoit donc toute sa vie la vérité; mais il se ménageoit toujours des ressources pour ne tomber pas d'accord qu'il l'eût trouvée. Quoi qu'il ne soit pas l'Inventeur de cette méthode de philosopher, elle ne laisse pas de porter son nom: l'Art de disputer sur toutes choses, sans prendre jamais d'autre parti que de suspendre son jugement, s'apelle le *Pyrrhonisme*: c'est son titre le plus commun. C'est avec raison qu'on le déteste dans les Ecoles de Théologie (B), où il tâche de puiser de nouvelles forces, qui

(a) Diog. Laërtius, in Pyrrhone, Libr. IX, init. num.61.

(b) Idem, ibidem.

(A) *Ses sentimens ne différoient guere des opinions d'Arcesilas.*] Si je suivis ponctuellement Ascagne d'Abdere, je dirois qu'il n'y avoit nulle différence entre ces deux Philosophes. Γενναίοτατα δοξεῖ φιλοσοφῆσαι τὰ τῆς ἀκαταληψίας καὶ ἐποχῆς εἴδη· εἰσαγαγὼν, ὥς Ἀσκάνιος ὁ Ἀβδηρίτης φησί. *Nobilissime Philosophiam tractasse videtur, commentus modum quo de omnibus nihil decerneret, neque quidquam comprehendi posse diceret, ut Ascanius Abderites auctor est* (1). C'est assurer nettement que selon Pyrrhon la nature des choses étoit incomprehensible: or c'étoit le dogme d'Arcesilas. Néanmoins j'ai mieux aimé laisser entre eux quelque différence, parce que l'esprit des Pyrrhoniens ne supose pas formellement l'incomprehensibilité. On les a nommez Sceptiques, Zetetiques, Ephectiques, Aporetiques (2), c'est-à-dire examinateurs, inquisiteurs, suspendans, doutans. Tout cela montre qu'ils suposoient qu'il étoit possible de trouver la vérité, & qu'ils ne décidoient pas qu'elle étoit incomprehensible. Vous trouverez dans Aulugelle qu'ils condamnoient ceux qui assurent qu'elle est, & voilà, selon cet Auteur, la différence des Pyrrhoniens & des Académiciens (3): en tout le reste ils se ressembloient parfaitement, & se donnoient les uns & les autres les noms que j'ai raportez (4). *Cum hac autem consimiliter tam Pyrrhonii dicant quàm Academici, differre tamen inter sese & propter alia quædam, & vel maximé propterea existimati sunt, quòd Academici quidem ipsum illud nihil posse comprehendi, quasi comprehendunt; & nihil posse discerni, quasi discernunt: Pyrrhonii ne id quidem ulla pacto videri verum dicunt, quòd nihil esse verum videtur* (5). Sextus Empiricus a trouvé une autre différence (6): Arcesilas prétendoit que la suspension fût bonne naturellement, & que l'affirmation fût mauvaise naturellement; mais selon Pyrrhon elles ne l'étoient qu'en aparence, ὁ κατὰ φύσιν ἀλλὰ κατὰ φαινόμενα, *non secundum naturam sed secundum id quod apparet*. Dans le fond l'un n'étoit pas pour le doute avec plus d'ardeur que l'autre; & rien n'étoit plus facile que de les mettre d'accord. Il ne faloit que leur demander qu'ils s'expliquassent nettement & sincerement (7).

(1) Diog. Laërtius, Libr. IX, num. 61.

(2) Voir. Gassendi, in Libro præamiali de Philosophia universæ, Cap. VIII, pag. m. 24. Voir. aussi Aulugelle, Libr. XI, Cap. V.

(3) Il faut entendre ceux de la 2 Académie fondée par Arcesilas.

(4) Aulus Gellius, Libr. XI, Cap. V.

(5) Idem, ibidem.

(B) *C'est avec raison qu'on déteste le Pyrrhonisme dans les Ecoles de Théologie.*] C'est par raport à cette divine Science que le Pyrrhonisme est dangereux; car on ne voit pas qu'il le soit guere, ni par raport à la Physique, ni par raport à l'Etat. Il importe peu qu'on dise que l'esprit de l'homme est trop borné, pour rien découvrir dans les véritez naturelles, dans les causes qui produisent la chaleur, le froid, le flux de la mer, &c. Il nous doit suffire qu'on s'exerce à chercher des Hypotheses probables, & à recueillir des Expériences; & je suis fort assuré qu'il y a très peu de bons Physiciens dans notre Siecle, qui ne se foient convaincus que la nature est un abime impénétrable, & que ses ressorts ne sont conus qu'à celui qui les a faits, & qui les dirige. Ainsi tous ces Philosophes sont à cet égard Académiciens & Pyrrhoniens. La vie civile n'a rien à craindre de cet esprit-là; car les Sceptiques ne nioient pas qu'il ne se falut conformer aux coutumes de son pais, & pratiquer les devoirs de la Morale, & prendre parti en ces choses-là sur des probabilitez, sans attendre la certitude &. Ils pouvoient suspendre leur jugement sur la question, si un tel devoir est naturellement & absolument legitime; mais ils ne suspendoient pas sur la question, s'il le faloit

pratiquer en telles & telles rencontres. Il n'y a donc que la Religion qui ait à craindre le Pyrrhonisme: elle doit être apuiée sur la certitude; son but, ses effets, ses usages, tombent dès que la ferme persuasion de ses véritez est effacée de l'ame. Mais d'ailleurs on a sujet de se tirer d'inquiétude; il n'y a jamais eu, & il n'y aura jamais, qu'un petit nombre de gens, qui soient capables d'être trompez par les raisons des Sceptiques. La grace de Dieu dans les fidelles, la force de l'Education dans les autres hommes; & si vous voulez même, l'ignorance (9), & le panchant naturel à décider; font un bouclier impénétrable aux traits des Pyrrhoniens, quoi que cette Secte s'imagine qu'elle est aujourd'hui plus redoutable qu'elle n'étoit anciennement. On va voir sur quoi elle fonde cette étrange prétention.

Il y a environ deux mois qu'un habile homme me parla fort amplement d'une Conference où il avoit assisté. Deux Abbez, dont l'un ne sçavoit que sa routine, l'autre étoit bon Philosophe, s'échaufferent peu-à-peu de telle forte dans la dispute, qu'ils penserent se quereller tout de bon. Le premier avoit dit assez froidement, qu'il pardonnoit aux Philosophes du Paganisme d'avoir flotté dans l'incertitude des opinions; mais qu'il ne pouvoit comprendre que sous la lumiere de l'Evangile il se trouvât encore de misérables Pyrrhoniens. Vous avez tort, lui répondit l'autre, de raisonner de cette façon. Arcesilas s'il revenoit dans le monde, & s'il avoit à combattre nos Théologiens, seroit mille fois plus terrible qu'il ne l'étoit aux Dogmatiques de l'ancienne Grece: la Théologie Chrétienne lui fourniroit des Argumens insolubles. Tous les assistans ouïrent cela avec beaucoup de surprise, & prierent cet Abbé de s'expliquer davantage; & ne doutérent pas qu'il ne fût échapé un Paradoxe qui ne tourneroit qu'à sa confusion. Voici ce qu'il répondit en s'adressant au prémier Abbé. Je renonce aux avantages que la nouvelle Philosophie vient de procurer aux Pyrrhoniens. A peine conoissoit-on dans nos Ecoles le nom de Sextus Empiricus; les moiens de l'époque qu'il a proposez si subtilement n'y étoient pas moins inconus que la terre Auftrale, lors que Gassendi (10) en a donné un Abrégé qui nous a ouvert les yeux. Le Cartésianisme a mis la derniere main à l'œuvre; & personne parmi les bons Philosophes ne doute plus, que les Sceptiques n'aient raison de soutenir que les qualitez des corps, qui frapent nos sens, ne sont que des aparences. Chacun de nous peut bien dire, *je sens de la chaleur à la présence du feu*, mais non pas *je sai que le feu est tel en lui-même qu'il me paroit*. Voilà quel étoit le style des anciens Pyrrhoniens. Aujourd'hui la nouvelle Philosophie tient un langage plus positif: la chaleur, l'odeur, les coleurs, &c., ne sont point dans les objets de nos sens; ce sont des modifications de mon ame; je sçai que les corps ne sont point tels qu'ils me paroissent. On auroit bien voulu en excepter l'étendue & le mouvement; mais on n'a pu; car si les objets des sens nous paroissent colorez, chauds, froids, odorans, encore qu'ils ne le soient pas, pourquoi ne pouroient-ils point paroitre étendus & figurez, en repos & en mouvement, quoi qu'ils n'eussent rien de tel (11)? Bien plus; les objets des sens ne sçauroient être la cause de mes sensations: je pourrois donc sentir le froid & le chaud; voir des couleurs, des figures, de l'étendue, du mouvement, quoi qu'il n'y eut aucun corps dans l'Univers. Je

(9) C'est le Mot de Simonide, ces gens-là font pour la plus part sans être trompez, par un homme comme moi. Balzac dit la même chose de filles de son village. Aqueslaus se plaignoit d'avoir à faire à des ennemis qui s'entendoient point la Guerre, ses russes étoient inutiles (9). Voir. Plutarque, dans la Vie vers la fin.

(10) Dans son Livre de Vita Logica, Cap. III, à la page 72, & suiv. du I. Volume de son Oeuvres d'Edition de Lion, 1658.

(11) L'Abbé Fouchet proposa cette Objection dans sa Critique de la Recherche de la Vérité: le Pere Malebranche n'y répondit pas. Il en sentit bien la force. Voici la Citation suivante.

ground began to be cultivated, and a middle register, elegant but not pompous, dignified but light and supple, was developed to bring issues that had been considered the prerogative of specialists and professionals and thus marginal to literature and inappropriate to gentlemen or ladies—trade and taxation, physics and theology, political organization and education—before a wide general public in the form of essays, letters, dialogues, and reviews.

As a provincial and an exile, Bayle lacked the courtly polish of his contemporaries in France. He wrote an earthy and forceful French closer to the language of Montaigne than to that of Versailles or the salons of Paris. The new dissenters within France were more urbane. François de Salignac de La Mothe-Fénelon, for example, wrote about political or educational questions in the unctuous language of a Ludovician bishop, albeit one more often out of favor than in favor. Bernard Le Bovier de Fontenelle—the nephew of the great Corneille, the product both of the rationalist legal culture of his native Normandy and of the literary circles of the capital—took over the language of the salons, to which a century of courtliness and urbanity had imparted unprecedented polish and refinement, and made it capable of expressing with elegance and clarity the most abstruse ideas, the most technical arguments. Physics, mathematics, economics, natural history, linguistics, politics entered the purview of literature and became matter for some of the classic texts of a new age. Thanks to Fontenelle's ingratiating facility, seductive wit, and skill at maneuvering himself into official positions (he was a member of three royal academies and permanent secretary of the Royal Academy of Science), the marginal took its place at the center.

See also 1685, 1694, 1751.

Bibliography: Pierre Bayle, *Dictionnaire historique et critique,* ed. Alain Niderst (Paris: Editions Sociales, 1974). Ludwig Feuerbach, *Pierre Bayle. Ein Beitrag zur Geschichte der Philosophie und der Menschheit* (1839), in his *Sämmtliche Werke,* ed. Wilhelm Bolin and Friedrich Jodl, vol. 5 (Stuttgart: Frommann Verlag, Günther Holzboog, 1905). Elisabeth Labrousse, *Pierre Bayle* (Oxford: Clarendon Press, 1983). Luc Weibel, *Le savoir et le corps: Essai sur le Dictionnaire de Pierre Bayle* (Lausanne: L'Age d'Homme, 1975).

Lionel Gossman

✑ 1699

Death of Racine

Racine and the French New Criticism

When, a few months before the end of his century, the fifty-nine-year-old Racine met his death in a most devout spirit, fostered by an upturn in his Jansenist convictions, he may have expected that, among all his secular achievements, at least his theater would survive undisturbed. True, for several years, perhaps since his alleged conversion of 1677, he had distanced himself from his profane tragedies, either on moral grounds or for the sake of his career at the court. Yet, as late as 1697, in a new edition of his writings, he took care to make several changes in their text, as if by a premonitory will to give them a final form. And he had good reasons to believe that his prefaces, clarifying his aims, would protect them against future interpretations. For those were authoritarian times when God's, king's, and author's intentions were taken to be the source of truth. Besides, Racine's stature as dramatic author had achieved monumental dimensions. His old rivalry with Corneille had been finally settled by a series of "parallels" that granted them equal, if different, genius; and the Quarrel of the Ancients and the Moderns had ground to a stop on the agreement that the best French were worth the best Greeks and Romans. Acknowledged as a classic, Racine could lay himself to rest without worries about the fate of his literary work and reputation.

And for well over two centuries they were little disturbed. No doubt Racine was challenged now and then, most dramatically by the Romantics, who, with Stendhal's *Racine et Shakespeare* (1823, 1825) and Hugo's *Préface de Cromwell* (1827), questioned the classical form of tragedy, introducing in France the more flexible *drame*. No doubt also the changing styles of acting and new conditions of production generated performances of Racine's tragedies that departed increasingly from the stage practices of his time. But whether attacked or extolled, the *written* text of his theater maintained its canonical prestige. Even by mid-20th century the best Racine scholars, such as Jean Starobinski, Judd Hubert, and Odette de Mourgues, rarely expanded their interpretations beyond recovery or discovery of meanings that were assumed to be inherent in the text and only needed to be highlighted. Their insights produced complementary rather than competing readings, original but carefully situated within Racine's textual enclosure. About that time, new Pléiade editions of Racine's works by Raymond Picard (1951, 1960), with variants and erudite commentary, offered a most convenient, reliable, and inspiring source for Racine criticism, while the same Picard's *La carrière de Jean Racine* (1956; *The Career of Jean Racine*) provided a definite account of the poet's public life. Both author and his works appeared unassailable in their fixed status as emblems of the French classical heritage.

Or so it might have seemed around 1960 when, with the exception of the *nouveau roman*, already in the process of growing old, there were few telling signs of the forthcoming intellectual and political unrest. No doubt, looking backward, one can now point to slow social changes that culminated in the events of 1968; yet that revolt against the establishment took even the French youth by surprise. Similarly, back in the 1950s, it was hard to guess that a couple of new works in literary theory or criticism, and some new accents in more traditional ones, were already breaking the ground for the structuralist and poststructuralist explosion during the next two decades. Thus, as far as Racine is concerned, Lucien Goldmann's *Le dieu caché* (1955; *The Hidden God*) and Charles Mauron's *L'inconscient dans l'oeuvre et la vie de Racine* (1957; *The*

Unconscious in the Work and Life of Racine), despite their controversial theses, were quietly filed with other Racinian scholarship. Even Roland Barthes's *Sur Racine* (1963; *On Racine*), innovative to the point of provocation, raised only a few eyebrows. Yet all three, and especially the last, led to the sudden shattering, only two years later, of the calm of the French republic of letters, and to the dignified Racine's removal from the pantheon and his installation at the center of controversy.

For it was in the defense of Racine that the first shot was fired in what came to be called the "New Quarrel of the Ancients and the Moderns." In 1965, outraged by Barthes's treatment of the most classic of French classics, Raymond Picard vented his anger in a pamphlet titled *Nouvelle critique ou nouvelle imposture?* (*New Criticism or New Fraud?*). With Barthes, he lumped Goldmann and Mauron, but also Jean-Paul Weber on Alfred de Vigny and Jean-Pierre Richard on Flaubert, as a gang of "New Critics," irrational in their search for unconscious meanings and irresponsible in their subversion of "academic criticism." The notion of a "New Criticism" appealed to everybody, including the accused. In the ensuing polemics, many young critics rallied to the new flag. The most influential of their statements, *Pourquoi la nouvelle critique?* (1966; *The New Criticism in France*), came from Serge Doubrovsky, previously known for an existentialist study of Corneille. In fact the New Critics had little in common besides their rejection of orthodoxy. All wanted to read beneath the surface of the text, but by various methods: structuralist, neo-Marxist, psychoanalytical. As their theories spread through the mainstream of French criticism, polemics abated and the New Quarrel fizzled out. Like the original 17th-century quarrel anticipating the Enlightenment, it announced, prepared for, and was superseded by a much ampler intellectual upheaval. But it had at least one lasting direct effect: it changed the ways of reading Racine's tragedies, brought Racine up to the present.

No doubt New Critics openly handled Racine's texts as pretexts for a demonstration of their own theories, namely, as texts for contemporary readings. Yet they did not want to "betray" Racine, as traditionalists claimed, but to pay him a tribute, testifying to their confidence that his text could both stand and generate new meanings after centuries of mummification. Their interpretations, though obviously self-serving, also served Racine in two ways: directly, by rejuvenating his text and readying it for a new generation of readers; and indirectly, by establishing Racine as the touchstone of critical readings, the author to be tackled by new theories. In that sense he came to play the same central role as Shakespeare in the English tradition, eclipsing as focus of inquiry both Corneille and Molière, competing only with Flaubert. Today any study of New Criticism and the sources of postmodernism in France must involve a rereading of Racine's tragedies; and, conversely, a study of Racine's tragedies must include their readings by the New Critics. At this interface of text and critical theory one encounters the elusive figure of the intellectual concerns of the 1960s.

Within that perspective, Goldmann's *Le dieu caché* exemplifies the then-fashionable marriage between respect for classics and neo-Marxist ideology. His "genetic structuralism," inspired by Georg Lukács, Marx, and Hegel, postulates that social conditions define various groups in society, and that each group generates its own literature, if any, as a response to these conditions. To this basically Marxist schema Goldmann brings his own notion of three types of homologous structures: structures of social conditions, structures of literature, and, mediating between them, structures of a worldview produced by the social conditions of a given group and in turn informing its literature. He roughly identifies Racine's social group as that of French magistrates who, largely superseded by Louis XIV's centralized administration, saw their privileges survive only by the goodwill of the same king who had eroded their functional basis. Their social group structure thus combined negation and affirmation by a superior power. The resulting homologous structure of their worldview, according to Goldmann, was that of Jansenism. Attempting to find a compromise between the Roman Catholic belief in the individual's free will and the Calvinist notion of predestination, Jansenists held that God simultaneously hides and reveals himself, helping those who are destined *and* want to seek him. The relation between Christians and God thus structurally reproduced the relation between magistrates and the king. But Jansenism was condemned, and Jansenists were forced either to accept or to reject a judgment that they perceived to be wrong. Because Racine was born in a magistrate family and educated by Jansenists, this dilemma in turn generated, by Goldmann's system, a homologous literary structure in his theater: his tragic heroes must choose either to live in a corrupted world or to withdraw from it to the ideal realm of the gods.

There are two problems with Goldmann's interpretation. First, he fails to distinguish between two groups of magistrates: the parliamentarians, who did suffer from Louis XIV's policies but were not particularly taken with Jansenism; and lower magistrates, who did promote Jansenism but were not affected by administrative reforms. Goldmann's homology between social and worldview structures is thus largely arbitrary. Second, several tragedies by Racine do not conform well to his literary structure. For some cases, Goldmann invokes a corruption by the nascent bourgeois drama; elsewhere, he is forced to attribute heroic dimensions to relatively weak characters. However, he is quite persuasive on *Phèdre* (1677; *Phaedra*). Yet his is not a Phèdre moved by a criminal passion, wracked by guilt. She incarnates idealism, almost a revolutionary fervor; facing a corrupt society, she tries for a time to compromise with it (as a "reformist" would), but finally she chooses death to preserve her integrity. She is not a traditional Phèdre, but in some regards she can be said to anticipate the mood of May 1968. Paradoxically, Goldmann's plunge into the 17th century to retrieve a historical Racine brought him to the leading edge of political concerns of his time, offering Racine as a text for left-wing ideology. Applying Goldmann's structuralism to his own work, and to that of later neo-Marxists, one could claim that their theories, and the criticism they produced, are in fact homologous to the malaise of intellectuals in post-Sartrian France: a group with prestige but with no real power.

Mauron's approach may be viewed as an antithetical response to the same malaise. Instead of drawing attention to the role of social problems, Mauron ties literature to the individual psyche, escaping from historical concerns to the realm of the unconscious, which is both private and universal. Society enters his scheme only to the extent that, by a Freudian logic, complexes and phantasms are generated by real occurrences in family life, including social circumstances that affect it. In the case of Racine, orphaned at the age of three, Mauron assigns the function of the mother to the Jansenist Port-Royal, a women's abbey where the child was brought up, while the king who received the poet at court holds the role of the father. The resulting reconstruction of Racine's unconscious psyche cannot be substantiated. Mauron presents it only as a plausible hypothesis that could account for the presence of obsessive structures in Racine's theater. His psychoanalysis of a dead writer is problematic; but his analysis of the writer's texts still stands today as an exemplary demonstration of Freudian structuralism and a most impressive reading of Racine's tragedies.

Projecting Racine's phantasms onto his heroes leads Mauron to show quite rigorously that most Racinian tragedies are in fact variations of a single obsessive structure, and that the order in which they were written corresponds to a dramatic evolution of that structure. The central character is always a problematic son, possessed by the demons of the Oedipal triangle, object of their power play. In the first plays, the absence of the father minimizes the impact of guilt: early Racinian heroes, pursued by powerful mother figures, still pursue in their turn powerless figures of younger mates, though with a diminishing faith in success. With *Mithridate* (1673; *Mithridates*), the father returns, and guilt destroys the incestuous son. The later phantasms are increasingly grim. The entire scheme is repeated in *Phèdre,* where Racine/Hippolyte projects onto the mother his own incestuous desire, and the returning Thésée deals the expected punishment and dashes all hopes of easing guilt. Throughout Racine's work, Mauron thus weaves a very intricate network of projections and parallel structures that, especially in his interpretation of *Phèdre,* allows for subtle psychological nuances. His brand of Freudian criticism, trivialized by a host of less able successors, has now been superseded in France by Lacanian approaches; but there is no Racine by Lacan.

In some way, neither is there a Racine by Barthes. In the most brilliant of all essays on Racine's theater, Barthes rarely mentions the poet: he deals with the "Racinian man," a Racinian anthropology, Racinian plays. In short, the text becomes everything, and literature the only ground for readings. Not that Barthes reads in a vacuum: he, too, plays with Marxism and psychoanalysis, structuralism and semiotics, eros and *logos;* but everything bears on the autonomous universe of Racine's theater, nothing on its personal or social genesis. Writing after Goldmann and Mauron, and more sensitive than they to the growing intellectual malaise, Barthes manifests the most radical reaction, withdrawing from an alienating society to the free land of literature. Severing Racinian theater from its author and times enables him to reshape its landscape in the mold of his own visions, appropriating textual evidence when it suits him, twisting it to the breaking point when it resists. Thus altered, or *Barthesformed,* Racine's tragedies become an exotic archipelago, where feminoid men and viriloid women practice strange rituals of lust, power, and words.

They obey the order of the Primitive Horde: a dominant father (Agrippine as well as Agamemnon) controlling the life of his sons (Athalie as well as Néron), who both fear and seek to kill him; coveted women; antagonistic brothers. In the softness of shadows, some dream of fraternal love; but tragic passion bursts into flame when eyes meet under a blazing sun. Desire haunts everywhere—or rather, repeated images of desire, for it is not satisfied. Power over the object of love meets rejection, invites violence, brings death. And the law of the tribe is never questioned: victims of power prefer to believe in their guilt rather than in an abusive authority, father or god. There is no escape from the enclosure of tragedy, no issue from its space. But tragedy can be postponed, or prolonged, as long as words ward off events, as long as events remain words. Tragic heroes must withhold as long as possible the secret sign, thought, or action that triggers the fatal end, conceal fatality with words directed at each other and at the audience. Strategies vary from play to play, some more inventive than others. But finally the secret is out; tragedy catches up with the actors, and ends for the spectators.

No one could nor did imitate Barthes, not even Barthes himself on Racine. But the theatrical dimension that, among the New Critics, he alone suggested for Racine tragedies, as well as his explorations of other sources of theatricality, did influence later theories of theater. Although most recent Racine scholarship bypasses Barthes, a series of controversial stagings of Racine's plays in the 1970s seems to have been inspired by his spirit of provocative transformation. From the area of critical debates, Racine's revival has moved overwhelmingly to the stage.

See also 1664, 1687, 1827 (February), 1968 (May).

Bibliography: Roland Barthes, *On Racine,* trans. Richard Howard (New York: Hill and Wang, 1964). Serge Doubrovsky, *The New Criticism in France,* trans. Derek Coltman (Chicago: University of Chicago Press, 1973). Lucien Goldmann, *The Hidden God: A Study of Tragic Vision in the Pensées of Pascal and in the Tragedies of Racine,* trans. Philip Thody (New York: Humanities Press, 1964). Charles Mauron, *L'inconscient dans l'oeuvre et la vie de Racine* (1957; reprint, Geneva: Slatkine, 1986). Raymond Picard, *New Criticism or New Fraud?* trans. Frank Towne (Pullman: Washington State University Press, 1969).

Jean Alter

 1700

At the Close of the Century, Charles Perrault Presents a Roster of Modern French Celebrated Men in the Two Volumes of *Les hommes illustres qui ont paru en France pendant ce siècle*

Classics in the Making

Before the 17th century, the only authors considered classics were Greek and Latin. Literary history as we know it today did not exist. Commentary on authors and works rarely ventured beyond the confines of the ancient world. In the 16th century, critics finally began to recognize the existence of a French literary tradition. Antoine Foclin's *La rhétorique française* (1555; *French Rhetoric*), for instance, included examples of each rhetorical figure from both classical and contemporary poets. In the following century this process of self-examination was rapidly accelerated so that, before the death of Louis XIV, the monarch who presided over most of the 17th century, a radical transformation in the perception of literary classics was under way.

A history of French (modern) authors truly began with the creation of the first notion of periodization, when the term *le siècle de Louis XIV* was accepted as a concept defining the literary production of the 17th century as indissociable from the Sun King's reign. Voltaire's indispensable history of the era, *Le siècle de Louis XIV* (1751; *The Century of Louis XIV*), is the first comprehensive overview written with the benefit of hindsight. His title was but a slight modification of that chosen by Charles Perrault for his poetic manifesto of modernism, "Le siècle de Louis le Grand" ("The Age of Louis the Great"), whose reading during a session of the Académie Française in 1687 ignited the conflict between supporters of ancient and of modern authors because Perrault pronounced authors of his day superior to those of antiquity. Perrault's title was perhaps his most astute invention: with it, he delimited a field of investigation premised on the unity of inspiration behind the political, artistic, and scientific accomplishments of his age, a field of investigation constituted by the will of a single individual, the Sun King.

The promotion thus launched, commentators scrambled to find ways of presenting their contemporaries' achievements as proof that France was indeed experiencing a new golden age. The best-known efforts were variations on Plutarch's reliable formula of a collection of biographies of famous men, in particular Perrault's two-volume *Les hommes illustres qui ont paru en France pendant ce siècle* (1696–1700; *Illustrious Men Who Appeared in France during This Century*) (fig. 1). Perrault inaugurated the practice (followed by Voltaire) of beginning "the century of Louis XIV" before the monarch's birth, with the establishment of the Académie Française by Louis XIII's minister Richelieu. This was a reasonable chronological marker, since the first commentators on the French tradition pointed to political sponsorship as the foundation of the period's literary greatness. Perrault, however, departed from established practice by including famous men from all professions but from only one century. As in both *Le siècle* and his most important polemic in behalf of the modernists, *Parallèle des anciens et des modernes en ce qui regarde les arts et les sciences* (1688–1692; *Parallel between the Ancients and the Moderns concerning the Arts and Sciences*), Perrault portrayed as "illustrious men" not only men of letters but also scientists, military men, and political figures, as long as they had died since the beginning of the 17th century. Thus he praised Richelieu alongside the century's most celebrated military genius, Louis II de Bourbon, prince de Condé, and men of letters such as Corneille and Molière. The compilations were kept up-to-date so that, as soon as famous men died, their entry into the ranks of the illustrious was recorded. Thus in the second volume of his *Hommes illustres* Perrault made a place for

1. "Le ciel en sa faveur forma tant de grands hommes," frontispiece, plate designed by Bonet, engraved by Gérard Edelinck, in Charles Perrault, *Les hommes illustres qui ont paru en France pendant ce siècle, avec leurs portraits au naturel* (Paris: Antoine Dezallier, 1696). (Courtesy of the Beinecke Rare Book and Manuscript Library, Yale University.)

Racine, dead just a year before Perrault's celebration of his literary career was published in May 1700, at the century's chronological end. Perrault's panorama provided the model for subsequent "Moderns," who always based their claim that French authors had become the new classics on the first truly interdisciplinary presentation of literature, literature viewed in its relation to the other fields in which their age had achieved greatness.

But Perrault's was by no means the only system devised to propose 17th-century authors for admission to classical status. Indeed, the last twenty-five years of Louis XIV's reign (1690–1715) witnessed the most impressive jockeying for power in French literary history. To a degree verging on the obsessional, literary debate seems to have looked to the future: Who would be considered the great writers of the age? Who would make this selection, and on what grounds? Numerous anecdotes from the period testify to the prevailing anxiety about literary hierarchies. One of the most revealing gives us the Sun King and Nicolas Boileau in conversation. To the monarch's curiosity about posterity's judgment—"Who was the greatest writer of my reign?"—the literary arbiter replied, as though the answer were self-evident: "Molière." But the king had the last word: "Really, I'd never have guessed it." Their exchange suggests that those who accepted the classification set forth by Boileau in *L'art poétique* (1674;

The Art of Poetry) had no difficulty discerning literary greatness. It also suggests that Boileau's standards were not yet universally accepted, that while the century of Louis XIV was still unfolding, it was not clear to everyone just which authors would be revered by posterity as the classics of the age.

In the decades that followed the outbreak of the Quarrel of the Ancients and the Moderns, both the definition of literary criticism and the identification of the public for whom it was destined were in flux. During this period of transition an impressive number of proposals were drawn up, in the form of either literary histories or suggested reading lists, that were in reality protocanons of the literary production of the age and therefore rivals of Boileau's *L'art poétique*. Before 1660, most of 17th-century literary commentary was destined for erudite readers. Most often—as in the case of the Académie Française's response (1637) to *Le Cid*, criticizing Corneille for his infidelity to Aristotle's rules—it seemed directed almost exclusively at authors themselves, in accordance with the definition of the word *critiqueur* in Randall Cotgrave's 1611 *Dictionarie of the French and English Tongues:* "Controller or corrector of other men's works." Toward the middle of the century, in conjunction with the growing influence of the salons as private academies, a different type of literary commentary began to develop, sometimes referred to as worldly criticism because of its practitioners' ties to aristocratic society. This criticism was composed for readers rather than writers, for a public who frequented the salons, where literature was a primary subject of discussion. It was most often descriptive rather than prescriptive: worldly criticism tried to keep its adult readers informed about the literary production of the day, rather than to dictate what they should read or to influence the future development of literature, as Boileau hoped to do.

The worldly critics provide a valuable sense of the variety of literature prized at the end of the century of Louis XIV. In their work, we find the beginnings of literary history in France. Desiring above all to demonstrate the existence of a French literary tradition, they edited numerous compilations, ranging from simple lists of authors to anthologies that included biographies and selections from their works, devoted exclusively to French (modern) literary figures. The most impressive representative of this genre, attributed by some to Bernard Le Bovier de Fontenelle, by others to Marie-Catherine d'Aulnoy, is the *Recueil des plus belles pièces des poètes français depuis Villon jusqu'à M. de Benserade* (1692; *Collection of the Most Beautiful Works by French Poets from Villon to M. de Benserade*). The anthology provides a history of French poetry in all its stylistic variety, rather than limiting its judgment of great poetry to that promoted by Boileau, the neoclassical style of the generation of 1660–1680. From the mid-17th century all through the 18th, worldly criticism kept the educated public informed about the literary scene by taking over where childhood education had left off. It can thus be seen as a program for continuing education: it shows us what informed adults were reading during the Quarrel of the Ancients and the Moderns. When we compare the lists of authors most often singled out for praise in worldly compilations with Boileau's hierarchy, the results are often surprising. Most impressive perhaps is the realization that, as long as the canon was still in flux, the early tradition of women's writing was widely recognized and prized as one of the glories of French literature in an unbroken series of compilations, from Marguerite Buffet's *Eloge des illustres savantes* (1668; *Eulogy of Illustrious Learned Women*) to Louise Keralio's fourteen-volume *Collection des meilleurs ouvrages composés par des femmes* (1786–1789; *Collection of the Best Works Composed by Women*).

Although pedagogues relied almost exclusively on literary texts to teach all subjects until the end of the 18th century, before the end of the age of Louis XIV modern authors were very rarely part of any curriculum for children's education. In the twilight years of the Sun King's reign, those drawing up curricula for children became increasingly aware that modern authors should no longer be reserved for adults but should be given a major role in the education of French children. This evolution was reinforced by the movement, which had come into its own by the 1750s, for the creation of a standardized national educational system: educators recognized the potential of the French literary tradition to help instill in the youth of France a sense of national identity. From this conjunction of circumstances a new type of literary commentary was born, one whose primary goal was to put an end to the multiplicity of literary classifications still available and thereby to determine which authors would be considered modern classics.

This new critical tradition—ranging from treatises such as Louis Le Blanc's *L'étude des belles-lettres* (1712; *The Study of Belles Lettres*) to comprehensive historical anthologies such as the abbé Claude-Pierre Goujet's eighteen-volume *Histoire de la littérature française* (1740; *History of French Literature*)—is closer than worldly criticism to what we today consider literary history. It was first directed at the same public addressed by worldly anthologies. This time, however, adult education was also conceived as reeducation: the new works aimed to convince adults that they should reject the eclecticism of the worldly literary programs both for themselves and for their children. They also aimed to prove that the curriculum should be centered on those modern authors who could best serve the state's interests as illustrations of the proper values and conduct of the model citizen. Many of these literary commentaries were addressed to the pedagogues who would actually be responsible for implementing a revised curriculum.

Nowhere is this shift in the public for literary criticism away from a general audience and back to a specialized one clearer than in Abbé Charles Batteux's companion volumes *Les beaux-arts réduits à un seul principe* (1746; *The Fine Arts Reduced to a Single Rule*) and *Cours de belles-lettres* (1747; *Course in Belles Lettres*). Batteux's comprehensive program illustrates the process by which, once modern authors became the foundation of the French educational system, the number presented as worthy of the attention of literary commentators, and therefore of pedagogues and their pupils old and young, was severely limited. Worldly criticism had been descriptive. The new pedagogical critics were above all prescriptive: they sought to eliminate from the annals of literary history any work or genre that could not be proposed as a model of civic virtue, and they were prepared to redefine civic virtue in ways that would allow them to exclude authors not considered appropriate models for the schoolboys of their day.

Once the developing discipline of literary history made French authors "classic" in the only sense of the term admitted in 17th-century French dictionaries (Furetière, *Dictionnaire universel,* 1690: "author who is taught in classes"), French literary history turned away from the receptiveness to innovation and variety that had been the rule of the Moderns, who had initially promoted French authors, to espouse a position on literary value close to that of early Ancients such as Boileau. Just after the Revolution, as a result of this complicated process, a new definition of "classic" was in place, the one most familiar to students of French literature today as formulated in the *Grand Robert* dictionary: "that which pertains to the great authors of the 17th century and their period, considered as expressing an ideal." In the general acceptance surrounding this usage, it has too seldom been considered that, since the mid-18th century, only those 17th-century authors have been classified as "great" who promote an "ideal" to which the national, and nationalistic, French educational system has felt schoolchildren should be exposed.

In recent years the canon of 17th-century French literature, the ensemble of works and authors taught in the classroom, has been radically expanded, though more so outside France than within. For the first time since 17th-century authors officially achieved classic status, students thus are often now exposed to writing that was last the object of pedagogical scrutiny during the reign of worldly criticism. Female writers in particular have been given expanded coverage on the new pedagogical horizon, as have all early practitioners of the genre whose rise Boileau and his followers most strenuously opposed—the novel—in addition to philosophical writers and to baroque poets. The early 19th-century definition of "classic," which validates an ideal embodied in the works of the great generation of 1660–1680, no longer seems widely appropriate. We have returned to the earlier, more liberal attribution of classic status.

See also 1634, 1637, 1661, 1687.

Bibliography: Georges Ascoli, *La critique littéraire au dix-septième siècle* (Paris: Centre de Documentation Universitaire, 1934). Roger Fayolle, *La critique littéraire* (Paris: Armand Colin, 1966). Alain Viala, *Naissance de l'écrivain* (Paris: Minuit, 1985).

Joan DeJean

 1704

Antoine Galland Publishes the First Four Volumes of *Les mille et une nuits,* Translated from the Arabic

Sunset Years

The decadence of the last years of Louis XIV's reign, with its wars, famines, empty treasury, persecutions of religious dissent, and a court whose tired rituals often evoked cynicism and boredom, seems to have blighted prose fiction as well. Marie-Madeleine de La Fayette's *La princesse de Clèves* (1678), apogee of the classical novel, is also the end of an era, and one follows the course of fiction in the next two decades for the same reasons one studies the political and social history of the time: in order to see taking shape the forces that would impose themselves in the century to come.

Among the seldom-read productions of this period one finds, first, historical novels whose plots were usually situated in the recent past and which mixed fiction and fact with a disconcerting lack of discrimination. Narrated in the first person singular, they encouraged a trend toward the subjective strategies of the 18th century, when, from Abbé Prévost's *Manon Lescaut* (1731) to Pierre Choderlos de Laclos's *Les liaisons dangereuses* (1782), all the important narrators said "je." A second prolific genre was the novel of gallantry (*roman galant* or *nouvelle galante*), involving passion and seduction among the highly born, with hopelessly stereotyped characters, plots, and style. A third popular genre was formed by a cross breeding of the first two, producing the historical novel of gallantry. Usually laid in the recent past, it turned real historical personages into pretexts for stories of passion and romance.

Almost without exception, the truly talented authors of this period went abroad for their inspiration. A superb example is Marie-Catherine d'Aulnoy's *Relation d'un voyage d'Espagne* (1696; *Account of a Spanish Voyage*). The work is hardly a novel, since parts are taken up by purely historical material, and most of the rest is a real account of her trip from France to Madrid and other cities of Spain. But her power of description, her whole visual sense, is extraordinary in a period that placed such a premium on stylistic abstraction: wintry landscapes (she was one of the first before Rousseau to feel their power); filthy kitchens in country inns; haunting, almost Goyaesque portraits of women's faces. She writes endlessly of women's cloistering, women shut away in convents or locked into their houses for the benefit of husbands who make it a matter of honor not to be faithful in return. Their confinement creates, inevitably, an infinite yearning to slip out of their bondage and to experience the amorous pleasures most forbidden to them. The same furtive gesture is repeated in the author's narrative strategy: from time to time the real world, with all its oppressive harshness, melts away into fiction, and the reader is caught up in some tempestuous tale of passion, heading toward tragedy, bliss, or even comedy.

In 1713, contrary to all expectation, the novel of gallantry produced a minor masterpiece, a work so wittily ironic it can be read with enjoyment in our own cynical time. The action of Anthony Hamilton's *Mémoires de la vie du comte de Gramont* (1713) also takes place abroad, mainly at the English court of Charles II. The society it depicts is exclusively traditional nobility. This is a man's world, and the sole preoccupation of the male characters is in laying siege to some citadel, whether it be a military garrison or another man's wife (an ambiguity the author enjoys playing upon). The games of intrigue are often cruel: slips are not pardoned, nor is physical deformity, and the gallantries are inevitably complicated, since the lady in view may have, in addition to a susceptible husband, frustrated lovers from the past and female rivals as well. It was easy to get caught.

This is England seen through the eyes of a nobleman schooled in France. The people whom he describes and whom the hero meets on a basis of perfect equality did indeed exist, and they have far more historical individuality than the background personages of *La princesse de Clèves*. Hamilton was less of a painter than d'Aulnoy, yet there is an easy elegance in his portraits: the king's slightly infantile mistress and his noble but unloved Portuguese wife; the charming yet slightly sinister figure of the Duke of Buckingham; Milord Arlington with his scars and plaster. There are scenes of great balls and outings in Hyde Park and on the Thames, and of course more private scenes of jealous husbands, jealous mistresses, and jealous wives.

This easygoing, loosely evolving novel is not centered on one event, nor does a series of major scenes form the central structure, as they had in *La princesse de Clèves*. Even the final espousal of the ever-active, if colorless, hero to the lady he has pursued is tossed off with an ironic flip at the end: the one certainty about it is that the hero does not intend to remain faithful after the wedding. Perhaps the novel's most essential quality is unconstraint (*désinvolture*). It shows a truly hedonistic society bent solely on pleasure for its own sake (there are no serious issues beyond that) and determined not to be tied down by rules. In a sense it is the last of the chivalric romances, dedicated entirely to military prowess and the pursuit of passion, a final flaunting of all the moral values and social responsibilities that would be the fighting issues of the future.

Published the same year was Robert Chasles's (or Challes's) collection of seven stories, *Les illustres Françaises* (1713; *The Illustrious Frenchwomen*). Its mysterious author, who is just now emerging from the shadowy anonymity he preferred during his lifetime, was also a practicing lawyer in the Parlement of Paris. Whereas *Mémoires de la vie du comte de Gramont* embodies the most fanciful ideals of the traditional nobility, *Les illustres Françaises* reflects the rulebound mentality of the legal class.

The locus of the stories is France, mainly the Paris region; in fact the collection opens with a brilliant description of a noisy Paris traffic jam. The principal theme of each tale is the one issue Hamilton's novel determinedly never takes seriously: marriage, an event that is perceived not merely as a final curtain or as the end of romance, as in the novel of gallantry, but as a rather solemn rite of passage giving expression to the social and moral values that codify the will of society. In the history of the French novel Chasles comes as a distinct advance in realism. His characters have three dimensions, and the emotion his heroes and heroines feel toward each other can be described as love rather than as mere passion: they relate to each other as whole beings and not simply as sex objects. The author has a poignant sense of how seldom the pieces of the lives he details fit together as they should. Since marriage is seen as a legal matter, the woman becomes less an object of attack or seduction than a potential partner who is being persuaded to enter into a settlement, the basis of which may even sound like equality.

398

Yet the principal ingredient that creates the drama in all the tales is *virtue* (that is, chastity or fidelity), which is always pointedly demanded of the woman, never of the man. In the second and sixth tales, the heroine's virtue has been unjustly impugned, and the plot turns rather ponderously upon her exoneration. The process resembles not only a trial but, in the elaborateness of the ceremonial, a holy rite, a sacrament. With this tearful emphasis on the vindication of virtue in the face of the infinite perils of vice, Chasles helped to create a new breed of heroine whose traits would reappear in novels, plays, and comic operas from Samuel Richardson to Voltaire and Rousseau, and on to Sade. Most of Chasles's heroines are making their way in an aristocratic milieu (either the traditional nobility or the legal caste). The later 18th century found an even more fitting place for such heroines, in dramas of the middle class.

The one-sided nature of the vindication, with the requirement of virtue placed exclusively on the female, casts the woman, confronted with a male-oriented law, in the role of either a potential or an actual victim. This bias becomes clearly visible in *Les illustres Françaises* and reaches its climax in the fifth and sixth tales, in which the heroines eventually pay with their lives because their virtue cannot be vindicated. The consistent onesidedness of the demands upon the female in the first six tales leaves the reader quite unprepared for the last, in which the ethics of virtue, so elaborately put in place and, until now, so emotionally sustained, break down with a suddenness resembling an explosion. The *Françaises* of these anecdotes are anything but *illustres,* and virtue is the last thing required of them by the cynical narrator, who lewdly sets them up as his prey. Eventually the author tips his hand in a dialogue between a worldly-wise widow and her conventional sister. The beautiful widow denounces the unfairness of a system that ties women to philandering husbands in the name of an attribute—virtue—which is contrary to the law of nature, and which women would never practice were they not coerced to do so by the overbearing male. Like Diderot, the beautiful widow comprehends the signal importance of sexual pleasure, and again like Diderot, her philosophy assumes the utility of conforming to outward appearances: she and the narrator will have their passionate affair and produce their illegitimate offspring in secret.

Although Chasles does understand the far-reaching consequences of his widow's insights and, by imagining his narrator's blissful affair with her, even seems to dally for a time with the possibility of accepting them, ultimately he rules them out. In the final episode the hero—for reasons he refuses to specify—breaks off his secret love affair and contracts a conventional marriage of traditional morality. Thus at the end of the collection the reader seems to be returned to the original outlook, though perhaps less convinced now that the tangle of carriage wheels of the opening scene has in fact been straightened out, or that the rules of marital ethics represent anything but oppression in disguise.

The most famous novel—the only international hit—of this period was Alain-René Lesage's *Histoire de Gil Blas de Santillane,* the first half of which was published in 1715. *Gil Blas* was set in Spain and drew liberally on novels of the Spanish golden age. In this picaresque tale, Lesage's hero is everything that *roman galant* heroes are not. Gil Blas is neither well-born nor especially bright. In the first six books he spends most of his time employed, or seeking employment, as a social nonentity, a valet. But the most striking contrast is in the role of money: among highly born heroes and heroines, wealth was of course assumed, and never spoken of except in general terms. In *Gil Blas* money is the central preoccupation of everyone's life. As the author states in so many words at the beginning, in this society people have coins for souls.

In most instances the transfer of money amounts to stealing, and one of Gil Blas' earliest adventures involves a sojourn, really a baptism, in a den of thieves. Whereas in Molière's world the squandering or hoarding of money provokes merely laughter or ridicule, in Lesage's it produces irony: the cash deal invariably shows people up for what they truly are. The grave doctor, the alguazil (marshall), the virtue-protecting duenna, despite their respectable appearances, are all taking or giving money on the sly. In Lesage's earlier *Le diable boiteux* (1707; *The Devil upon Two Sticks*), the devil raises the rooftops of the houses of Madrid to reveal the usually sordid realities hidden within. Money here serves the same purpose.

Paradoxically, however, these cynically described adventures are framed by rather stern moral expectations. For ultimately the author's ethical touchstones turn out to be almost puritanical: hard work, speaking the truth, and honest dealing. Perhaps the end of the sixth book is predictable in this regard: the hero eventually breaks away from the band of thieves with whom he has been consorting and opts for respectability as an intendant (the bailiff of an estate)— thus setting the pattern for Beaumarchais's Figaro.

Yet Lesage is a master at having his cake and eating it too. In most instances Gil Blas behaves no better than the corrupt people the novel exposes and condemns. Of course the author never allows the reader to feel detached enough from his hero to dismiss or pass final judgment on him. At the author's invitation we are pleased to assume that the day will come when Gil Blas will repent his dishonesty and greedy impulses. Meanwhile, the author adroitly insinuates, his character, commonness, and vulnerability to the vicissitudes of fortune belong to us all. With this novel, and with Chasles, realism—rendered almost extinct by the novel of gallantry—returned in all its vitality, to remain a mainstay of the French novel until the end of the old order.

In the last decades of the Sun King's reign another kind of prose fiction surged suddenly into prominence: the literary fairy tale. D'Aulnoy led the way in 1690 with a retelling of the folktale, *L'île de la félicité* (*The Isle of Felicity*). Charles Perrault made his debut in 1696 with *La belle au bois dormant* (*Sleeping Beauty*), in a genre that quickly came into its own: twenty-nine new tales in 1697 and in 1698 (*Histoires ou contes du temps passé, avec des moralités; Stories or Tales of Time Past, with Morals*). Then, just as suddenly, the vogue subsided, and another sort of literary magic, the oriental tale, immediately filled the gap. Inaugurating this movement in 1704 was Antoine Galland's translation of *Les mille et une nuits* (*The Thousand and One Nights*). The chronology dovetails perfectly: the first four volumes (204 nights) in 1704; and two more volumes each in 1705, 1706, 1709, 1712, and 1717. The oriental tale was launched.

Galland's translation is a literary masterpiece in its own right. Its publication brought a whole group of new tales—including *Ali Baba and the Forty Thieves, Aladdin and the Magic Lamp,* and *Sindbad the Sailor*—to join Perrault's *Cendrillon* (1697; *Cinderella*) and *Le petit chaperon rouge* (1695; *Little Red Riding Hood*), d'Aulnoy's *L'oiseau bleu* (*The Blue Bird*), and all the other fairy tales that were already making their way into Western literary consciousness. Of course *Les mille et une nuits* formed only one element—though the crucial one—in a larger movement. The vogue of the oriental tale had numerous other contributory sources, ranging from authentic travel accounts to all manner of fictions, including Giovanni Paolo Marana's famous *Lettres d'un espion turc* (1684; *Letters Writ by a Turkish Spy*). Galland's translation itself inspired sequels, imitations, and parodies, some of which, as in the case of *Les mille et un jours* (*The Thousand and One Days*), in which Lesage had a hand, became almost as popular and influential as the original. Perhaps the supreme importance of these oriental tales for the 18th century lay in their establishing an alternative, nonclassical mythology that seemed to free, or at least loosen, authors from their literary past. Like a magic lamp or a secret cave, these tales opened up a whole range of literary possibilities: new forms, metaphors, characters, moralities; they promised to fulfill any author's or reader's desire. One could find anything in them one wished: stern cautionary tales preaching honesty and thrift, tales of thievery and the delights of pilfering, pure adventure, pure magic, licentious tales, high romance, and all of them—because they came at night from the voluptuous Scheherazade, whose life depended on their effect—seductively infused with eroticism and danger.

Georges May has called *Les mille et une nuits* an "invisible masterpiece." Just so; and perhaps invisibility is the apt word too for the vagaries of its influence, which, like some mysterious perfume, makes its presence felt everywhere but can seldom be quantified. Specialists have determined that Ali Baba's cave recurs in Proust's *A la recherche du temps perdu* (1913–1927; *Remembrance of Things Past*) more frequently than any other image. It is not difficult, given Proust's persuasions concerning language and art, to imagine why this should be so. In 1704, on the other hand, no one concerned with the writing of prose fiction chose to reflect very much upon the significance of these oriental tales for that era. Might one not surmise that their main appeal, in that barren landscape brightened only by fairy tales, was simply *enchantment?*

Bibliography: Robert Chasles, *Les illustres Françoises,* ed. Frédéric Deloffre, 2 vols. (Paris: Belles Lettres, 1967). Antoine Galland, *Les mille et une nuits,* ed. Gaston Picard, 2 vols. (Paris: Garnier-Flammarion, 1967). Anthony Hamilton, *Mémoires de la vie du comte de Gramont,* in *Romanciers du XVIIIème siècle,* ed. René Etiemble (Paris: Gallimard, 1960). Alain-René Lesage, *Le diable boiteux,* in ibid. Lesage, *Histoire de Gil Blas de Santillane,* in ibid.; translated by Tobias Smollett as *The Adventures of Gil Blas of Santillane* (London and New York: H. Frowde, 1907). Jean Lombart, *Courtilz de Sandras et la crise du roman à la fin du grand siècle* (Paris: Presses Universitaires de France, 1980). Georges May, *Les mille et une nuits d'Antoine Galland* (Paris: Presses Universitaires de France, 1986). Raymonde Robert, *Le conte de fées littéraire en France de la fin du XVIIème à la fin du XVIIIème siècle* (Nancy: Presses Universitaires, 1982).

Walter E. Rex

✐ *1707?*

Antoine Watteau Paints His First Theatrical Subject,
Le départ des comédiens-italiens en 1697

Fêtes Galantes

The imagery of the theater is pervasive in the painting of Antoine Watteau (1684–1721), and his interweaving of visual and dramatic representation has figured centrally in almost every commentary on his art. The precise character of the links between canvas and stage has nevertheless remained elusive. Representative in this regard is Edmond and Jules de Goncourt's essay on the artist in their *L'art du dix-huitième siècle* (1873–74; *French Eighteenth-Century Painters*). From the time of its first appearance, this text has remained one of the best known and most influential accounts of Watteau's art, and its treatment of his theatrical motifs celebrates this elusiveness. Although the Goncourts recognize that Watteau began and ended his career depicting the actual scenes and performers of the Parisian comic playhouses, they insist that the figures found in his *fêtes galantes,* his scenes of pastoral pleasure, are only nominally related to the contemporary stage:

> By the introduction of these airy, insubstantial jesters, these graceful mimics, the elegant, musical incarnations of delicate comedy and subtle laughter, of the men and women of such vague corporeity, whose physical presence grows faint beneath the influences of myth and symbol, the painter's conceptions no longer appear to derive from the world of actuality. In the *fêtes galantes,* we may suppose the turf to be trodden by allegorical beings bereft by the spirituality and lightness of Watteau's touch of all resemblance with the actors who may have served as models.   (*Painters,* p. 38)

This retreat from the referent is consistent with the mythology that has surrounded the artist since the time of his early death—the image of the withdrawn, compulsive dreamer who paints a world of pleasure that he cannot enter. Nor has it been contested in more recent scholarship; Watteau's connection with the world of contemporary theater is acknowledged, but discussion of that relationship has tended to trail off in the direction of inconclusive metaphor and reiteration of the artist's "poetic" distance from the material life around him.

One of Watteau's earliest-known theatrical pictures, however, already opens the way to a historical understanding of the ambiguity that characterizes the

1. Engraving by Louis Jacob after Antoine Watteau, *Le départ des comédiens-italiens en 1697* (1707?). (Courtesy of the Bibliothèque Nationale, Paris.)

figures in his paintings. Painted around 1707 (and now known only from a print), *Le départ des comédiens-italiens en 1697* (*Departure of the Italian Comedians in 1697*) (fig. 1) shows Harlequin, Mezzetin, Colombine, and the rest of the commedia dell'arte troupe reacting with histrionic gesture and expression to a public notice announcing their banishment from France. Watteau was making, a decade or so after the fact, a comedic scene out of an actual event. The actors in question were the very polished company of players that held a royal monopoly over their genre and acted before the king at Versailles. Their success had long inspired jealous hostility on the part of the Comédie-Française. One final provocation, a satirical play that seemed to attack the king's morganatic wife, Françoise de Maintenon, induced the state to order the company's suppression.

Though officially banned from the country, the actors found refuge close by in the acrobatic troupes that operated, in Paris, at the fairgrounds of Saint-Germain and Saint-Laurent. With these new recruits, the fair companies began providing a dramatic product that was both exciting and illegal—illegal because it violated the official monopoly held by the Comédie-Française on the presentation of spoken drama of all kinds. When they were not brazenly defying the law, the fair theaters resorted to a series of inventive and hugely entertaining expedients to avoid the letter of the prohibition: dialogue printed on placards suspended above the stage for the audience to recite in unison; plays staged with only one actor on the stage at a time; familiar tragedies presented *en jargon,* that is, in perfect meter but with nonsense syllables in place of the original text. In the process, they evolved a mode of theater unique to themselves, one distinguished by an improbable mixing of genres and crossing of codes. A single performance might include the classics in straight and burlesqued forms, old-style commedia dell'arte, the farce and physical comedy of the festive popular tradition, along with the athletic spectacle of the acrobats. They were so popular among all classes that the financial well-being of the official theater and opera was threatened.

Watteau's mature work does not, however, depict the outlaw comedians in an unambiguous way (his portraits of the Italians date from the years following their official reinstatement). His figures appear in an assortment of theatrical costumes, but the rude and bumptious atmosphere of the fair stages is replaced by one of a markedly different character—the dreamy, vaguely melancholic mood for which his art is most celebrated. He evokes a life of studied idleness in spacious parks dotted with classical statuary, one that resembles more than anything else the pastoral rituals characteristic of the 17th-century high nobility. But in Watteau's lifetime the vernacular culture of the fair comedy and the leisure activities of the high nobility had already begun to overlap. This took the form of a widespread aristocratic enthusiasm for amateur performances imitating those of the fairs. These took place in town but more often in the country, and imitated the crudest and simplest element of fair entertainment: the *parade,* that is, the brief bits of slapstick played on platforms above the theater entrances to entice paying customers. And this overt theatricalization of leisure could spill over beyond the boundaries of the play's schematic structure. One performer might remain in his peasant garb through a whole day's outing, maintaining his crude accent and deceiving new arrivals into taking him as the genuine article; only at the end of the day would he be gleefully unmasked.

This openness to popular culture on the part of the French high nobility was not in fact inconsistent with the larger evolution of its cultural attitudes over the course of the 17th century. Its mode of life had never been identical with the court culture under Louis XIV; still less could it be represented in the high classicism of tragic drama or academic history painting in the grand manner. Increasingly excluded from the practical conduct of power, the great feudal families withdrew from the royal court into a life of conspicuous indifference to the functional demands of rule. In enclaves remote from the king's presence, an ideal form of courtly life was evolved that resisted the legibility and semantic transparency of classical forms. (The high nobility were in general hostile to literary erudition, which for them carried a fatal association with bourgeois pedantry.) The older term of *honnête homme* (cultivated man or gentleman) underwent a shift of meaning in the later 17th century, coming to designate this ideal type of supremely disinterested aristocrat. For such men (and women), the power of words in themselves was devalued in favor of elaborate codes of indirection, nuance, and displacement of meaning in a ritualized and intensely

2. Antoine Watteau, *Les bergers* (ca. 1716), oil on canvas, 56 × 81 cm (Schloss Charlottenburg, Berlin). (Photo courtesy of Jörg P. Anders Photoatelier, Berlin.)

visual theater of everyday life. The essence of *honnêteté* (courtliness or gallantry) lay in the maintenance of artifice and the secret penetration of the artifice of others, the decoding of hidden messages and undeclared desires, the displacement of language into puzzles and enigmas.

The early 18th century saw an even greater shift away from the overt exercise of power into the crafting of leisure, and the amateur *parade* was the medium that joined elite pleasure to the subculture of the fair. The resistance of the fair players to the monopolies of official classical culture, their free mixing of established artistic modes and subversion of established hierarchical boundaries, was incorporated into the work of aristocratic self-definition. A few props, a random collection of fancy dress, or just some flour for whiteface was all that one required; the very openness and formal carelessness of the model were precisely what appealed to its elite imitators. Thus, in a way that has not been much remarked upon, the two distinct zones of cultural practice most evidently linked to the dominant themes in Watteau's painting had already come to overlay one another before his invention of the *fête galante*.

The painter, of course, thanks to the protection extended to him by Pierre Crozat, was no stranger to the life of the wealthiest aristocrats in France. Crozat belonged to the richest family in the country outside of the royal house; he cultivated members of the old nobility and maintained an elaborate pleasure park at Montmorency modeled on earlier aristocratic gardens. In this light, one might then be tempted to see a painting like *Les bergers* (ca. 1716; *The Shepherds*) (fig. 2), with its apparently improbable conjunction of pipe-playing rustic with

405

3. Claude III Audran, design for a ceiling, pen and ink. (Courtesy of the National-museum, Stockholm.)

carefree aristocrats, as an illustration or record of the life around him. To take this as the primary motive behind the new genre, however, would be to misrepresent its origins and limit our understanding of its appeal to a patron such as Crozat and the legion of elite enthusiasts who came after. The *fête galante* was in fact an extension of a distinctly artificial and conventionalized mode of painterly practice—the arabesque—that paralleled, both structurally and thematically, the stylized forms of aristocratic leisure that Watteau later encountered face-to-face. The status of the arabesque as the most fashionable form of painted interior decoration had been established by one of Watteau's teachers, Claude III Audran. Within the light, pliant armature provided by its organic frame, this format allowed the free and loose interpolation of elements from a whole range of otherwise distinct genres: folk symbolism and the moralizing allegorical symbols common in Dutch and Flemish painting were mixed with motifs from classical myth—the latter almost always drawn from the lighter, eroticized segment of that repertoire and including the sort of burlesque on the classics regularly provided by the fair players. Audran allowed his patrons freedom to choose their own motifs for inclusion in the allegorical game, and often the actual performers of the fair theaters were portrayed (fig. 3). The arabesque was an intermediate mode of art, contiguous but not identical with that of the Royal Academy of Painting and the high tradition, that allowed a playful exploitation and subversion of the academy's elevated moral and intellectual posture. In this, it was a zone of practice parallel to that of the theatrical *parade* in both its professional and amateur forms, and all three were indeed involved in a continuous process of exchange with one another.

An arabesque such as Watteau's *L'escarpolette* (ca. 1713; *The Swing*) (fig. 4) produces a deliberate confusion between pictorial unity and free decorative fantasy. The various emblematic elements embedded in the frame—such as the bagpipes that function as a rustic symbol of male sexuality—hover just beyond the reach of the illusionistic space at the center, but closely enough so that their mixed symbolism spills over into our reading of the enclosed drama. At its most subtle, the arabesque format allowed playful and intriguingly layered allegories of desire that could refer to contemporary experience without being merely imitative of it.

Around 1714 it was Watteau's great and original move to project the disjunctive strategies of the arabesque into an apparently unified moment in space and time. The organic, rectangular frame, which had stood for the borders of a metaphoric "garden of love," now appears in the form of an illusionistic garden setting, but whether it is actual, theatrical, or entirely fictional is a moot question: some *fêtes galantes* favor one interpretation more than others, but no conclusive determination is possible. The kinds of players who had occupied the arabesque's central vignette now stand in that fully pictorial space, while the various allegorical symbols from the frame insert themselves into the scene as accessories, instruments, and props. *Les bergers* joins another swinging couple

4. Engraving after Antoine Watteau, *L'escarpolette* (ca. 1713). (Courtesy of the Bibliothèque Nationale, Paris.)

5. Antoine Watteau, *Les fêtes vénitiennes* (ca. 1718), oil on canvas, 56 × 46 cm. (Courtesy of the National Gallery of Scotland, Edinburgh.)

with an actual player of bagpipes in shepherd's costume, the discrete frame of trees around the swing still preserving the effect of a vignette. Likewise in the consummate example of the form, the painting that has come to be called—somewhat inscrutably—*Les fêtes vénitiennes* (ca. 1717; *Venetian Festivities*) (fig. 5), each element from the constellation of symbols that surrounds the lovers in *L'escarpolette* finds a place in the scene. The statue, present in many of his pictures, works as another kind of emblem. Reclining voluptuously, as in *Les fêtes vénitiennes,* or stirring into rude, carnal wakefulness, it serves as a living embodiment of the desire elsewhere hidden beneath stylized costume and restrained gesture.

In Watteau's art, related and artificial systems of representation are maneuvered into productive contact. His genre is a frankly conventional one, however much accuracy of description it might contain. Its allegorical character guarantees the status of his pictures as fiction, as works of and for the imagination; they cannot be read as faithful (and inevitably inferior) reproductions of a pre-existing reality. Watteau's treatment of the human actors reinforces that refusal. His blocking of narrative and emotional unity produces more than enigmas. One of its effects is to prevent the nonhuman elements of the symbolic interplay from becoming mere accessories, that is, from forming a clearly secondary register of commentary at one remove from a self-sufficient human drama. Merely dressing the pleasure seekers in theatrical costume contributes significantly to this end, since Watteau never shows an actual amateur performance. Divorced from any obvious scenario, these might be understood as moments before or after a play, but it would be truer to their fundamental removal from the here-

and-now to say that they posit theatrical disguise as a condition of leisure and therefore of noble life.

Watteau's vision was especially attractive to wealthy financiers such as Crozat who had no deep noble ancestry and only recent acquaintance with its intricate codes. For them the ideal of *honneteté* was more easily available as representation, in the arabesque and *fête galante,* than in participatory performance. But what such individuals lacked in one kind of knowledge, they made up for in another, namely, the cultivation of expertise in art collecting and art history. In fact the *fête galante* as a genre reached its greatest popularity later in the century for patrons who had become ever more distant from the bygone modes of life it memorialized but ever more accomplished as *amateurs* of art. Crozat's great collection had provided the school in which Watteau learned to fit the multiple overlay of codes embodied in elite leisure and its decor to the higher demands for formal coherence, density, and integration embodied in the Italianate high-art tradition. This last matching of code to code constitutes Watteau's greatest achievement, and in this inspired synthesis we can see the practices of painter and patron as locked in a crucial series of exchanges with both the lowest and the highest territories within French society and culture.

See also 1680, 1759 (August–September).

Bibliography: Norman Bryson, *Word and Image: French Painting of the Ancien Regime* (Cambridge: Cambridge University Press, 1982). Thomas Crow, *Painters and Public Life in Eighteenth-Century Paris* (New Haven: Yale University Press, 1985). Edmond and Jules de Goncourt, *L'art du dix-huitième siècle,* 2 vols. (Paris: Rapilly, 1873–74); translated by Robin Ironside as *French Eighteenth-Century Painters* (Ithaca: Cornell University Press, 1981). Margaret Morgan Grasselli and Pierre Rosenberg, *Watteau: 1684–1721* (Washington, D.C.: National Gallery of Art, 1984).

Thomas Crow

✑ 1721

Montesquieu Publishes His *Lettres persanes*

Others

The year 1721 does not mark a beginning of France's curiosity for other cultures or for any—empirical or general—form of "otherness." French readers had already been interested by the works of explorers and commentators for more than a century. A few fictional narratives purporting to recount visits to and from exotic places already existed as well. Much of the preceding travel literature, however, tended to undermine the difference of other cultures either by disputing it (they are just like us despite appearances to the contrary) or by rendering their difference so absolute as to deny any common ground (they are not even Christian/human, have no souls, and so on). The *Lettres persanes* (*Persian Letters*) and the works that it inspired signal a more transformative awareness of the other one, in which France no longer served as a privileged culture of reference against which all others were to be measured.

Differences among cultures are a central concern for Montesquieu. His commentary on the diversity of societies increasingly sought less to measure them against an ethnocentric standard passing for universal, than to understand what caused their real differences. "After examination," he wrote in *De l'esprit des lois* (1748; *On the Spirit of Laws*), "I felt that in this infinite diversity of laws and customs, man was not guided solely by his fantasies" (*Oeuvres complètes*, 2:229). Montesquieu showed that what may seem bizarre in other cultures results in fact from the same processes that produce one's own culture. Cultural differences can be retraced along a logical chain to the diversity of fundamental factors such as geography, climate, history, and demography.

Probably Montesquieu could adopt such a position because he believed that one could perceive all cultures from a totalizing perspective that would give them cogent meaning. Michel Foucault has shown that such a belief is characteristic of the 18th century. And yet, once a global, causal logic was posited, its effects were no less real for being enabled by a passing epistemology. An important if paradoxical consequence of such attention to the causes of cultural difference is that it gives one's own culture some of the very qualities of strangeness that previously were recognized only in exotic societies. Indeed, Roger Caillois introduces the *Lettres persanes* as a "sociological revolution," which he characterizes as "the mental procedure that consists in pretending to be foreign to the society in which one lives, in looking at it from the outside as if one were seeing it for the first time" (1:v).

The *Lettres persanes* is composed of 161 letters, primarily those between the sultan Usbek and his friend Rica, and correspondents back in Persia, during their lengthy visit to France. The epistolary format allows Montesquieu to insert a wide variety of critical and satirical commentary on French mores from a foreigner's point of view. Topics include differences in social behavior, religion, politics, and economics. It is sexual tension and intrigue, however, that provide the novel with a cogent plot, and it is in the sexual sphere that we find the preeminent focus on otherness. The insincerity, frivolity, and licentiousness of the French in sexual matters are shown in stark contrast to the sober, monogamous order that supposedly exists in the Persian harem.

The novel also includes letters to the Persian travelers from home. Usbek's wives and the eunuchs who are supposed to guard them write concerning the rapid deterioration of male-supremacist law in his absence. The injustices of the harem system become increasingly obvious even as Usbek refers to its closed and rigid order as the ideal standard against which to measure the decadence of the French. The novel ends with a suicide letter from Roxane, Usbek's favorite, who reveals that she has had a lover all along even as she feigned devotion to the sultan and obedience to his rules. "I reformed your laws according to the laws of nature," she writes (letter 161). Critical awareness of both cultures is thereby introduced in a manner that refuses to allow either to serve as a privileged reference or standard.

The notion of otherness in the *Lettres persanes* is no longer restricted to exotic lands. It also surfaces at home, even if in a repressed or marginalized form. First, Usbek's commentary repeatedly shows that the "natural" and familiar customs of the French are really quite bizarre; and then Roxane's shattering final letter reveals an alien element in the heart of Usbek's purely Persian universe as well. Roxane's desire for others (here: other than Usbek) is what the sultan has particularly criticized as an alien, French vice, only to discover that it also existed in his own harem. Montesquieu's presentation of Roxane's desire makes it clear that her "reform" of putatively natural (read: Persian, male) law itself occurs in the name of nature. Whichever way we turn, then, the designation "natural" is clearly up for grabs, the focus of a discursive confrontation rather than the self-evident marker of easy truths.

A challenge to notions of a universal, natural law is also discernible in Montesquieu's treatment of the eunuchs whom Usbek left at home as guarantors of the harem system. A familiar rhetoric rehearses the stereotype of eunuchs as "unnaturally" severed from their being, as separated from themselves, with a status derived solely from their role as representatives of the absent sultan. But when the eunuch Cosrou wants Usbek's permission to enter into a marriage of his own, another rhetoric and a new logic again emerge to "reform" these supposed laws of nature. We learn "that eunuchs experience a kind of eroticism with women that is unknown to us; that nature pays itself back for its losses; that it has resources that repair the disadvantage of the eunuch's condition; that one can cease to be a man, but not to have feelings; and that such a state is like being in a third sense in which, so to speak, all one does is change pleasures" (letter 53). This switch in sexual pleasure is a natural process. In this text it therefore falls within the semantic field of "normal," "acceptable," and even "virtuous," echoing Roxane's "reform" of Usbek's laws according to an equally revolutionary understanding of "nature." But Montesquieu's thinking on this prototypical issue has in fact taken him a significant step beyond this modest measure of cross-cultural, cross-gender understanding of otherness.

Among many other sources, Montesquieu has read Jean Chardin's *Voyages en Perse* (1686), elaborating the place and function of eunuchs in the Orient. He is not ignorant. And yet the eunuchs' pleasure is—and remains—as "unknown" as women's pleasure will remain for Sigmund Freud. Although we have no categories for understanding the eunuchs' otherness, their pleasure can still be affirmed as natural. In this way Montesquieu handles otherness, not only as a site of our temporary ignorance on its way to be colonized, but also as something that has its place within "the way things are" even though it remains unknown. In an age that liked to admire itself for its production of *lumières* (the flattering light of total insight), the "darkness" of otherness was beginning to find space for itself within a reformed and reformable construction of knowledge. A healthy blank space was opening, and with it, the possibility that a different voice and a different subjectivity might one day be able to construct itself there.

Twenty-six years later, in her *Lettres d'une Péruvienne* (1747; *Letters of a Peru-*

vian Princess), Françoise de Graffigny echoed Montesquieu when she marveled that the French "seem unable to perceive the shocking contradictions that foreigners notice in them at first glance" (letter 33). Thanks in part to the phenomenal success of the *Lettres persanes* (with some ten reprintings), this viewpoint, this "glance" of the other, became more important in French writings about themselves. Numerous works articulated fictionalized critiques of society from foreign perspectives. In addition to Graffigny's *Lettres d'une Péruvienne*, works such as Voltaire's *L'ingénu* (1767; *The Huron*) and Abbé Prévost's *Histoire d'une Grecque moderne* (1741; *The History of a Fair Greek*) stand out from among paler, often "orientalist" imitations that owe much to Montesquieu's novel.

Not all these texts are marked by the degree of openness to the other that one finds in Montesquieu's novel, however. Voltaire, for example, most often invokes cultural otherness merely as an ironic device to ridicule the blindness of his chosen target. Thus *L'ingénu*, substituting an American Huron for Montesquieu's Persian, uses the foreign visitor as a mere foil for demonstrating the blind parochialism of the French. The Huron is little more than a blank whose principal function in the text is to represent an unproblematic "natural man." "For, having learned nothing in his childhood, he learned no prejudices. His understanding, not having been bent by error, had remained in all its rectitude. He saw things as they are, whereas ideas we are given in childhood cause us our whole life long to see them as they are not" (*L'ingénu*, p. 148).

Montesquieu had used the same phrase, asking us to recall the differences between our perceptions and things "as they are." For Voltaire, however, to see things "as they are" is to penetrate cultural particularity in order to reach the rational norm that defines the way things should be. In Montesquieu's novel the difference between culturally determined perceptions does less to reveal rational norms than to demonstrate cultural relativity itself. In *L'ingénu*, rationality simply is. In the *Lettres persanes*, culture, made visible in the encounter with others, can produce no absolute rationality to legitimate our attitudes or beliefs. Otherness inhabits all culture and can be understood, if at all, only through a shift in outlook of the kind provoked by an outsider.

There were texts that were more successful than Voltaire's in dealing with others, perhaps because they were more attuned to the *Lettres persanes*. In the draft of a revision, Montesquieu explicitly recognizes Graffigny's novel as a descendant of his own. Deserving more attention from modern readers, her *Lettres d'une Péruvienne* is another important work in which cultural and sexual otherness overlap.

The novel begins with the kidnapping of an Inca princess, Zilia, on the day she was to marry Aza, her brother. She winds up in Paris, where she is protected by Déterville, a nobleman who wants to marry her. In her letters to Aza written in captivity, Zilia relates her discovery of French culture. Like Montesquieu's Persians, Graffigny's Inca is able to perceive her surroundings otherwise. Here too, the point is less to present either culture as superior than to reveal the relativity of what appears natural to both.

The Incas are shown to live in a social system in which the sun is god. The overriding ethical imperative is not to break the ties that bind the solar deity to his incarnations on earth. Thus Prince Aza, as the "organ of the sun," was obliged to marry Zilia precisely because she was his closest blood relative. In direct contrast to the French, Graffigny presents the Incas as a culture that resists differentiation.

In Paris, Zilia discovers that she has fallen into a culture in which incest is a transgression because the law demands marriage into a different family. From an Incan perspective, such a law seems to result in a generalized difference from oneself: "With the majority of the French, vices are artificial, as are virtues, and the frivolity of their character allows them to be only imperfectly what they are" (letter 32). The total integrity and self-possession promised her by Incan culture is impossible. This theme is amplified in many subtle ways: French society forces one to use words that differ from the true feelings they are supposed to express; furniture that she thought was made of gold is only wood covered over by a thin veneer of gold leaf; similarly, politeness and piety on the surface are thin disguises for base feelings within. Unlike the Incas, the French treat virtue (and all its cognates) as merely ideal; reality is always different.

As in the *Lettres persanes,* however, the yardstick that allows Zilia to measure French shortcomings in this manner will self-destruct. Aza, "organ of the sun," the incarnation of everything sacred, will convert to Catholicism while in Spanish captivity. In a parallel with Roxane and the eunuchs, Zilia is cut off from her putatively "natural" being as an undifferentiated extension of the male "sun." Like Roxane, she now has to reform the rules.

Graffigny, like Montesquieu, allows a different voice to emerge from this position of otherness with respect to the norms of culture. The once-passive Zilia, a stranger in a strange land, takes charge of an ambiguous situation. She issues a ringing call for an altered relation between herself and her suitor Déterville in which romantic passion would have no part: "Come and learn how to economize the soul's resources and the blessings of nature. Give up tumultuous sentiments, the imperceptible destroyers of our being; come and learn to know innocent and durable pleasures, come and indulge in them with me [*en jouir avec moi*], you will find in my heart, in my friendship, in my sentiments everything that can compensate you for love" (letter 41).

The last phrase, "compensate you for love," resonates with the eunuchs' love, in which "nature compensates itself for its losses." Zilia is speaking in the voice of the "other," unknown to the dominant ideology and yet good. Renouncing the romantic, sexual love that is one of the West's most cherished cultural constructions, she voices an unmistakable affirmation of something else that comes to reform it. Zilia is indeed rare among 18th-century heroines: she emerges alive from this story of altered ideals. She has wealth, property, and a faithful male "friend." She remains an Inca. She will not marry. She will not become a mother. And, most significantly, she is allowed to be. Otherness does not have to be retrieved for ideology by the heroine's death.

In a similar vein, Abbé Prévost's *Histoire d'une Grecque moderne* also allows alterity a place that cannot be entirely subsumed within dominant ideology.

Prévost's heroine is Théophé, a Greek orphan who had been formed in childhood for her present career in a Turkish harem. Like Roxane in the *Lettres persanes,* Théophé starts out being constrained to serve as a mirror of male fantasies, but winds up giving voice to another order.

The novel's narrator, a French diplomat, is much taken with her beauty. Upon meeting her in her harem setting he speaks to her of the totally different life she would enjoy if she were French. Her response is everything that a cultural imperialist could desire. As she will later reveal in her narration of the experience, "The words 'virtue,' 'honor,' and 'decorum,' which I understood without any further explanation, entered my mind and took over in a moment, as if they had always been familiar to me" (p. 53). In *Histoire d'une Grecque moderne,* the very enunciation of the talismanic words of 18th-century French ideology precipitate a total conversion within Théophé. In this tale, however, French culture overwhelms its exotic other with a thoroughly ironic result.

Now that she has in effect become a perfect incarnation of Frenchness, Théophé resists sleeping with her benefactor. To do otherwise would be to reposition herself as a concubine, exchanging sex for protection in violation of her newfound virtue. The narrator is driven to distraction by the unimpeachable logic of a refusal based on the very principles to which he has converted her. Her tenacity in asserting her new, French virtue thus serves to reveal that French culture allows its men in effect to make concubines of its women. What at first was posited as exotic and different returns as the repressed in indigenous French culture. Théophé's refusal reveals the duplicity at the very core of the French system that requires women to be virtuous in order to elicit men's desire to become their masters and rob them of their virtue. Théophé began as an exotic concubine in a Turkish harem, a continent away from France. In the end, however, like Zilia, she reveals the contradiction within French culture even as it attempts to absorb her and neutralize her difference.

The narrator becomes pathologically jealous of Théophé and writes the memoir that is *Histoire d'une Grecque moderne* in an attempt to clarify what he never could ascertain directly: was she in fact chaste in her new role, or was she merely able to manipulate appearances for her own gain? Nothing in the text answers this question empirically. Even so, several important critics (Jean Sgard, for example) have presumed to answer that Théophé either was or was not virtuous—most often not—thereby revealing the pure ideology underlying such unwarranted conclusions. Théophé in this way remains irreducibly other even today. Whereas Montesquieu, Graffigny, and Prévost allow her and her analogues their incomprehensible difference, cultural fundamentalists unwittingly provide the familiar answers that would reduce them to what the West has always "known" about women, "Orientals," "Indians," eunuchs, and all others. No culture can absorb them and what they represent without at the same time revealing something about the mystification behind its most fervent attitudes and values.

See also 1578, 1704, 1847, 1922.

Bibliography: Michel Foucault, *The Order of Things: An Archeology of the Human Sciences* (New York: Random House/Vintage, 1973). Françoise de Graffigny, *Lettres d'une Péruvienne,* ed. Bernard Bray and Isabelle Landy-Houillon (Paris: Garnier-Flammarion, 1983). Alain Grosrichard, *Structure du sérail* (Paris: Seuil, 1979). Charles-Louis de Secondat, baron de Montesquieu, *Lettres persanes,* in *Oeuvres complètes,* ed. Roger Caillois, vol. 1. (Paris: Gallimard, 1951). Montesquieu, *De l'esprit des lois,* in ibid., vol. 2. Abbé Prévost, *Histoire d'une Grecque moderne,* in *Oeuvres complètes,* vol. 9 (Geneva: Slatkine, 1969). Suzanne Pucci, "Orientalism and Representation of Exteriority in Montesquieu's *Lettres persanes,*" *The Eighteenth Century: Theory and Interpretation,* 23 (Fall 1985), 263–279. Jean Sgard, *Prévost romancier* (Paris: José Corti, 1968). Jean Starobinski, *Montesquieu par lui-même* (Paris: Seuil, 1963). Voltaire, *L'ingénu,* ed. William R. Jones (Geneva: Droz, 1957).

James Creech

ᕤ 1725

Twenty-nine Years after the Death of the Marquise de Sévigné, the First Collection of Her Letters Is Published

The Politics of Epistolary Art

The correspondence of Marie de Rabutin-Chantal, marquise de Sévigné, spanning the period 1648–1696, stands at the summit of the epistolary genre. As both stylist and chronicler, Sévigné is described in literary histories as a monument to 17th-century French culture, to a society that cultivated letter writing as one of its most important arts. Yet, whereas the correspondence of other well-known 17th-century epistolary artists was published during their lifetimes or shortly after their deaths (Jean-Louis Guez de Balzac, 1624; François de Malherbe, 1630; Vincent Voiture, 1650; Roger de Bussy-Rabutin, 1697), Sévigné's letters were not published until 1725, almost thirty years after her death. Moreover, recent scholarship has shown—contrary to a widely accepted myth—that Sévigné's letters did not circulate in salon society; they were relatively unknown before 1725.

There is mounting evidence that the earliest admirers of Sévigné's letters, beyond her family circle, were not her literary contemporaries but writers who would shape the critical thought and taste of the early Enlightenment—Pierre Bayle and Voltaire, among others. There is also significant evidence that once Sévigné's letters were published (in four increasingly voluminous editions between 1725 and 1754), she displaced all previous epistolarians as the exemplar cited in private correspondences as well as in letter-writing manuals. Thus, unlike her contemporaries, Sévigné did not come into her own as a woman of letters until the Enlightenment.

Sévigné's appropriation by the republic of letters formed *after,* rather than during, the life of Louis XIV challenges the common assumption that her writing is a logical development of the epistolary art practiced by Balzac, Malherbe, Voiture, and Bussy. Sévigné's significance emerges in a different light when we go beyond the confines of the 17th century to consider the fuller history of letter publication under the ancien régime. Under the ancien régime publication of letters typically consecrated the epistolarian as an exemplary writer, a cultural model to be imitated: between 1539 and 1789 hundreds of real correspondences and letter-writing manuals were published in France, each purporting in some way to offer a model for writing. During this period two major shifts occurred in the type of writing promoted as a cultural ideal. In the 1620s "familiar," "personal," egalitarian, and potentially dissident forms of letter writing—inspired in large part by Erasmus' theories in his influential *De Conscribendis Epistolis* (1522; *On the Writing of Letters*)—were repressed in favor of "courtly" models supporting a hierarchical view of society and an absolute monarchy. Then, between 1725 and 1761—following the impact of Sévigné's unconventional, uncourtly, personal writing—the Erasmian model of "epistolary liberty" (what Erasmus called "illam libertatem epistolarem") returned to preeminence after a century of repression, and the 18th century began to promote independent style and "originality" rather than "imitation" in letter writing as well as in critical thinking.

It is therefore possible to speak of three periods—Renaissance, classical, and postclassical—each with a distinct epistolary ideal. In each instance the *poetics* of letter writing (in both theory and practice) depended upon a *politics:* letter writing under the ancien régime was conducted under the watchful eye of the nation-state and was a particularly important means for forming civic identity. The evolution of epistolary art was thus closely tied to shifts in the political and cultural organization of French society as a whole.

During the Renaissance the publication of missive letters coincided with the rise of national consciousness. Like the poets of the Pléiade, and similarly inspired by the Italian example, a number of prose writers promoted the development of a national literature in the vernacular. Crucial to their purpose was the effort to get educated writers to communicate through letters composed in French instead of in Latin, letters that could nonetheless rival Cicero's in eloquence. Both Etienne du Tronchet in his *Lettres missives et familières* (1569; *Missive and Familiar Letters*) and Etienne Pasquier in his *Lettres* (1586) claimed to be taking the first steps in this direction by publishing their own correspondences. They exhorted others to follow their example by writing letters, as Pasquier put it, in the language that had nourished them "since the mother's breast" (bk. 1, letter 1).

Both Pasquier and du Tronchet helped legitimate the art of letter writing in French. Beyond this shared purpose, however, these two Renaissance epistolarians differed significantly. Du Tronchet's main concern was to provide a set of letters to illustrate what he called "legitimate" court usage, and his letters divide stylistically according to a hierarchy of social relations at the French court. Du Tronchet had served as secretary to Catherine de Médicis; he was thus well placed to provide model letters for the numerous secretaries being hired by an increasingly communicative aristocracy. To make his letters more useful as models, du Tronchet eliminated many historical and personal references from his original missives before publishing them. His letters were reprinted often between 1569 and 1623; after 1623 du Tronchet's collection was rendered stylistically obsolete by a manual that cornered the market in both France and England, Jean Puget de La Serre's *Le secrétaire de la cour* (1625; *The Secretary of Fashion,* 1640), which conveyed court norms established under Louis XIII.

A quite different purpose informed Etienne Pasquier's letter collection. Pasquier gathered and presented his *Lettres* at age fifty-seven as a form of personal writing not unlike the *Essais* (1580, 1588) that his friend Montaigne chose to publish at a similar point in his life and during the same decade of cultural conflict. Written to close friends of diverse persuasions between 1552 and 1586, Pasquier's letters expose his developing thoughts on a number of issues—educational, political, literary, and philosophical. As a practicing historian and lawyer, Pasquier writes attentively about his own life and the life of his nation: childbirth, the marriage of a son, and various incidents in the Wars of Religion (1562–1598) appeal equally to his artistic talents. Pasquier compares the resulting collection to the "mixed merchandise" of a "hardware store," attributing the book's pluralism to the fact that his letters are a "general tableau of all of my ages in life . . . molded by the ages that have diversely determined my opinions" (bk. 1, letter 1). Pasquier refuses to weed out "folly" from "wisdom" or to engage in any pruning of the "tree" composed by his letters. Anticipating that some readers will object to this "mixed merchandise," Pasquier celebrates the right of those readers to differ from him, since "the opinions of men are too diverse to conform in everything and everywhere with mine" (bk. 10, letter 12).

In his regard for cultural diversity and his encouragement of others to develop strong personal voices by writing familiar letters, Pasquier followed the practice of two Renaissance epistolarians who published familiar letters in the vernacular before him—Hélisenne de Crenne and Gaspar de Saillans. *Les épîtres familières et invectives* (*Familiar and Invective Letters*), published in 1539 by the classics scholar and writer Hélisenne de Crenne, constitute the earliest-known volume of missive letters published in French. Hélisenne's familiar letters are highly personal, addressed largely to friends in distress. In the invective letters, she argues against several adversaries who maintain that women are capable only of spinning and should not engage in literary activity. Hélisenne cites a series of predecessors who combined eloquence with wisdom, from the classical Aspasia and Cornelia to her contemporary Margaret of Navarre; Hélisenne is publishing her own letters to remind readers that women are coequals of men in the republic of letters. Like Erasmus before her and Pasquier after her, Hélisenne appeals in her preface to readers who value "variety" in human character.

In 1569 a merchant named Gaspar de Saillans collected the letters that he and his wife, Louise, had exchanged before and after their marriage; he published them under the title *Premier livre de Gaspar de Saillans . . .* (*Gaspar de Saillans's First Book*), for no other reason than "to create a place where my name might survive my body" (p. 30). Intended as a gift for a newborn son, this handsomely adorned letter book offers a fairly detailed image of daily domestic life and conjugal communication in a milieu threatened by plague and religious wars. Although Gaspar and Louise did not write for a larger literary public, they shared a literary credo with Renaissance epistolarians such as Erasmus, Hélisenne, and Pasquier. Indeed, Gaspar used the same metaphor of the unpruned tree—allowed to display the marks of its "savory" individuality—to insist on the value of the book written in one's personal idiom as the record of an individual life.

Publishing practices in Renaissance France encouraged the public representation of a writer's personal life, philosophy, and political ideas. This freedom of personal expression virtually disappeared in correspondences published as exemplary writing between 1624 and 1723, when conventions for respectability in letter writing became quite rigidly codified. The conventions that governed letter writing throughout the classical period were established largely through anthologies of model letters selected from France's "best authors" and "most beautiful minds." These anthologies typically defined a limited number of epistolary situations and offered model letters for each situation. The standard collection—from François de Rosset (1612), Jean Puget de La Serre (1625), and Nicolas Faret (1627) at the beginning of the century to Pierre Richelet (1689), Antoine Furetière (1690), and Pierre d'Ortigue de Vaumorière (1690) at the end—included letters of compliment, gratitude, consolation, recommendation, offers of service, and exercises in gallantry, reflecting the social rituals of court and salon life. The editors of these anthologies were the theoreticians of the aristocratic code of *honnêteté* (Faret), members of the Académie Française (Faret, Richelet, Furetière), or vulgarizers anxious to teach courtly manners to the wider public (Puget de La Serre). As editors they were concerned primarily with codifying grammar and spelling as well as with codes of behavior. Epistolography became an important channel for inculcating courtly conduct.

During this period even collections of letters by a single author conformed to the codes established by the anthologies. When Malherbe's editors prepared his letters for publication early in the century, they eliminated many historical and personal matters in order to reduce each letter to its principal object: consolation, recommendation, or the like. The 1630 edition grouped his letters according to the social rank of the addressees, defined in terms of courtly hierarchies: (1) royal family, (2) Richelieu and bishops, and (3) mistresses. Letters to the poet's son, wife, and his close friend Nicolas Peiresc were not included; although Malherbe had written lively, familiar letters on topics that were considered appropriate by Renaissance publishers (political, religious, and domestic topics as well as journalistic accounts of events), these were no longer considered publishable as art.

Jacques de La Motte–Aigron's preface to the 1624 edition of Guez de Balzac's letters makes it clear that two kinds of topics should henceforth be banished from published letters: "domestic" affairs (which only the "Germans" would be barbaric enough to mention) and criticism of the government ("we no longer live in a period when people are accustomed to accuse publicly the State government"). Like many writers who hailed Richelieu as the architect of national unity after the civil wars, Balzac's 1624 commentator deemed such restrictions salutary. And so the injunction persisted throughout the century: most epistolarians heeded the advice of Puget de La Serre's popular letter manual—to avoid writing anything "about aristocratic leaders and government affairs" that could get the letter writer into trouble (*Le secrétaire à la mode*, p. 5).

Publishing epistolarians did more than heed this advice. They refrained from commenting on political institutions, and they cultivated primarily the art of eulogizing courtly figures. Many of them dedicated their letter collections to rulers who were engaged in repressing strongholds of power outside the king's court. Faret dedicated his 1627 anthology to Richelieu—who was efficaciously breaking Huguenot power between 1621 and 1628—and Balzac asked that the posthumous edition of his letters (1656) be dedicated to the marquis de Montausier, to praise him for putting down the Fronde rebels. Pinchêne's first edition of Voiture's letters (1650) presented the book as the "offering" of a "humble servant's fealty" to the prince de Condé and the whole court, claiming that Voiture's letters were a monument to courtly patriotism. Over a century later Voiture's letters were still being promoted primarily for their "fine and delicate art of praising rulers," as the title page of the 1779 edition announced.

Letter manuals in the Bibliothèque Bleue series (inexpensive paperbacks intended for the working class) taught peasants and workers the proper language for breaking with a mistress or congratulating someone on his success at court; unlike British manuals from the same period, they contained no letters tied to the daily occupations of people outside the court. After the revocation of the Edict of Nantes imposed a single state religion (1685), letter anthologies illustrated the "letter of persuasion" by a letter persuading a Protestant to become a Catholic. Epistolary art in the 17th century was thus an important tool for eliminating cultural difference from the public arena. Letters published as art under classicism typically positioned the writer as a loyal (male) servant of an aristocratic order revolving around an absolute monarch, serving that order through public speech acts that constituted a universally imitable model of courtesy.

Although the period's theoreticians claimed that women surpassed men as letter writers, women writers were strikingly absent from the anthologies of epistolary art published in the 17th century, except in the category of letters from mistresses. It was male epistolarians whose names guaranteed the literary value of letters published in the "best authors" anthologies. Instead, women were published anonymously in Jacques du Boscq's special anthology, *Nouveau recueil de lettres des dames de ce temps avec leurs réponses* (1635; *The Secretary of Ladies*). Du Boscq's anthology of letters by nameless female writers was first published the year that the Académie Française was founded: for the next 345 years authors whom the state recognized as "immortal" would be male.

In marked contrast to the Renaissance, when women published their own letters and entered the world of publication on equal footing with men, only

2 percent of the individual correspondences published in the 17th century were by women, and most of these were published anonymously or against their will. Women's letters were marketed as emanating from a space that was separate from that of men and even more narrowly confined—essentially that of the convent, boudoir, and bedside. The few published correspondences signed by women included *Les épîtres spirituelles* (1644; *Spiritual Letters*) of Jeanne Françoise de Chantal (Sévigné's grandmother), who founded a religious order, and the *Lettres et billets galants* (1668; *Gallant Letters*) of the playwright and novelist Marie Catherine Desjardins (who wrote under the pseudonym of Mme. de Villedieu); the latter were published without the author's permission, when her lover sold them to a publisher, Claude Barbin, who was developing the market for women's epistolary passion. The spaces confining women writers would dominate epistolary novels during the 17th and 18th centuries.

These conditions do much to explain the relatively late publication of Sévigné's letters. Although Sévigné was certainly the product of 17th-century culture, and even the Sun King admired her letters to Nicolas Fouquet when he confiscated Fouquet's papers in 1661, Sévigné's letters did not conform to the norms of epistolary art promulgated through publication under Louis XIV. Sévigné did not illustrate the courtly genres of letter writing, and she did not embody a writer's subordination to superiors within the monarchical order. She wrote in egalitarian terms and primarily to her daughter, addressing her as "ma bonne" in a century that excluded family correspondences and "domesticity" from the field of public representation. In so doing, Sévigné profoundly renewed an earlier tradition of personal writing that went underground after 1623—that of the thoroughly familiar and familial letter—which addressed family and close friends (rather than patrons or gallant lovers), mixed styles and tones, constituted a record of personal experience, and ranged freely over diverse topics, from local events to the interior life of the epistolarian.

For the first edition of Sévigné's correspondence (1725 in France, 1727 in England), the editor selected letters to reflect the life of Louis XIV's court. Editors soon discovered, however, that the interest of Sévigné's letters lay elsewhere, in the style that Sévigné cultivated in her most personal letters, which were published in subsequent editions. Although Sévigné's style and her expressions of maternal affection initially shocked some readers, literary critics quickly began to praise her "singularity" as a literary quality and to propose her as France's outstanding epistolarian. Above all, Enlightenment critics repeatedly referred to Sévigné's "freedom" of speech as the source of her originality.

In 1723 Pasquier's correspondence was reprinted for the first time in a century; it was advertised for the "particularities" of Pasquier's observations on the civil wars. In subsequent decades, the Enlightenment's major epistolarians—Voltaire, Françoise de Graffigny, Rousseau, Diderot—exercised Sévigné's and Pasquier's epistolary freedom; their letters open onto private and dissident spaces, and they are readable as personal autobiography in the same way that Renaissance letter books often were. The publication of the Sévigné correspondence thus constitutes part of a major shift in literary and political focus in the early Enlightenment—away from the life of the court and toward the experience and ideas of the private citizen, away from universally replicable ritual and toward the particularities of historical and cultural difference.

See also 1761 (February), 1782 (March).

Bibliography: Janet Gurkin Altman, *Epistolarity: Approaches to a Form* (Columbus: Ohio State University Press, 1982). Jean-Louis Guez de Balzac, *Lettres du sieur de Balzac,* with preface by Jacques de La Motte—Aigron (Paris: T. du Bray, 1624). Hélisenne de Crenne, *A Renaissance Woman: Helisenne's Personal and Invective Letters,* ed. and trans. Marianna M. Mustacchi and Paul J. Archambault (Syracuse: Syracuse University Press, 1986). Roger Duchêne, *Ecrire au temps de Mme. de Sévigné: Lettres et texte littéraire* (Paris: Vrin, 1982). Desiderius Erasmus, *On the Writing of Letters,* trans. Charles Fantazzi, in *Collected Works of Erasmus,* vol. 25 (Toronto: University of Toronto Press, 1985), 10–254. Jean Puget de La Serre, *Le secrétaire à la mode* (Paris, 1651; first published as *Le secrétaire de la cour,* 1625). Etienne Pasquier, *Lettres* (Paris: L'Angelier, 1586). Gaspar [and Louise] de Saillans, *Premier livre de Gaspar de Saillans gentilhomme citoyen de Valence en Dauphiné . . .* (Lyons: Jacques de la Planche, 1569). Charles A. Porter, ed., *Men/ Women of Letters,* special issue, *Yale French Studies,* 71 (1986). Marie de Rabutin-Chantal, marquise de Sévigné, *Lettres choisies de Madame la Marquise de Sévigné à Madame de Grignan sa fille. Qui contiennent beaucoup de particularités de l'histoire de Louis XIV* ([Troyes], 1725).

Janet Gurkin Altman

 1727

In the Seven Issues of *L'indigent philosophe* Pierre Carlet de Marivaux Suggests What It Is Like to Be a Philosopher

Portrait of the Philosopher as a Tramp

Neither Pierre Carlet de Marivaux (1688–1763) nor other authors of the early 18th century realized that they had stepped across the boundary separating the Age of Ideas (as the 17th century has been called) from the Age of Philosophers. Neither he nor, for that matter, those who came after him thought of themselves as monumental thinkers or writers. The most celebrated of them (Montesquieu, Voltaire, Diderot, and Rousseau) did not produce—and indeed often made fun of—those ponderous, abstruse, and pedantically organized tomes that might have earned them a place in the later, Germanic, and now institutionalized version of the history of philosophy. They remained devoted, for the most part, to an audience that had already defined itself in the time of Louis XIV— an aristocratic and bourgeois audience of casually curious souls, whose weekly salons came to suggest the level, the tone, and the discursive forms of their work. It was an audience concerned above all with the duties, pleasures, and practicalities of the here and now, with truth only as it impinged on their lives, and with life as it was elegantly, though not unspiritually, lived in the world.

What, then, did it mean to "philosophize" in the early 18th century, and with these readers in mind? Was it possible, with the knowledge of all the venerated and contradictory "philosophies" that had preceded, to find a reliably functional wisdom and stability? How, especially, was it possible to abide by an intricate code of social proprieties and at the same time to play the role of the gadfly—to take part in the essentially dissident project of philosophy and yet to preserve those values that knit society into its contemporary manner and form? Was there a speech that was at once accessible and not already completely shot through with complacency? Was it possible to shake the structure of people's beliefs or expose their hypocrisies without calling into question the social ideologies that had spawned and supported them? To all these questions, Marivaux's *L'indigent philosophe* (1727; *The Indigent Philosopher*) brilliantly provides the most telling, if chilling, response of the first half of the century.

Marivaux's *Journaux* (1717–1733: *Journals*), periodical sequences of essays in the manner of *The Tatler* and *The Spectator*—of which *L'indigent philosophe* is but one small sequence—are not yet canonical reading, even though they may be the finest essays in French since Montaigne. They are easily the equal of Marivaux's more famous plays and novels, whose themes they inevitably share. Like so many of the narrators or characters of Marivaux's novels—Pharsamon in *Pharsamon, ou les nouvelles folies romanesques* (1712–13; *Pharsamon, or the Latest Fiction-Inspired Insanities*), Marianne in *La vie de Marianne* (1731–1741; *The Life of Marianne*), or Jacob in *Le paysan parvenu* (1734–35; *The Nouveau Riche Peasant*)—the pauper philosopher does not merely speak and tell stories; he seems deliberately to primp and compose himself in every utterance, to take his unsteady, equivocal bearing and identity from circumstantial and imaginative projections, from illusion itself—or from allusions to other texts. Like these characters, he finds no place of grace, no true, independent existence, except perhaps in the parodic rehearsal of what has found favor in the eyes of his readers, and this includes an aristocratic disdain for wealth and property. Like them, he seductively mimics or flirts with a way of being and speaking, an order of prejudice and received ideas that he cannot fully condone or evade. Every assault upon established precincts turns out, paradoxically, to be an assault upon himself; and parody comes to define itself as an ambiguous instrument of attack, self-defense, and self-recrimination, a device that draws its energies from an unappeased longing for illusory glories or values.

Not surprisingly then, our philosopher quite literally admires himself in a mirror. He cannot get over how wonderful he looks in his "picturesque" rags, symbols not only of a borrowed, remaindered life but of the accumulated debris of practical philosophy—the flotsam and jetsam of Aristotelian, Epicurean, Cynic, and Stoic ideals as they were then vulgarized, promoted, or decried. As he speaks or, rather, attitudinizes, he jauntily mixes all these creeds, indeed ironically pretends to be living by their blessed wisdom while—like Quixote symbolically and portentously struggling with a Knight of the Mirrors—he catches the dancing, faceted reflections of his own self-conscious performance. What is the truest substance of this hero? Where can it be found? In the intertextual and imaginative mirror before him? Or somewhere else, invisibly and inscrutably perhaps, in a merely supposititious self that either has no name and cannot appear or that exists only as an impulse to create appearances? Suddenly, as the philosopher leaps for joy before his mirror, it sends back not his own image but the image of someone else—a more radical variation of the existence that he, as narrator, produces for himself. He sees his drunken comrade, his exaggerated double, who jumps into view by bouncing reflexively out of the mirror, that is, out of the philosopher's literary imagination. Or have the writer and his surrogate narrator, in search of more scandalous embodiments and quotations, deliberately bounced into it? The parodic images of writers, philosophers, and drunkards coalesce and echo one another, the way Marivaux's characters in general and the events of their lives duplicate themselves and spin out an ironic, repetitive drama of analogies and similitudes. If the existences of the philosopher and his comrade resemble nothing so much as those of *pícaros* or scroungers, and if both men seem at times, in their speech and behavior, to incorporate a classical, well-bred "negligence" and "naturalness" or a Rabelaisian drunkenness, it is because Marivaux stitches into their portraits other literary and social allusions—including allusions to his own ideals and manner—that strike him as consonant with the philosophical attitudes he wants to portray.

What all of these attitudes have in common is a mistrust of social norms or a scorn for that single value sponsored by the church, the state, and the enlightened public: society itself. It is therefore not surprising that the 1718 edition of the dictionary of the Académie Française and, in 1732, the *Dictionnaire de Trévoux* describe the "philosopher" in such a way that any opinion or conduct regarded as independently "natural," shocking, irreligious, or self-concerned could be maliciously described as "philosophic." And any man who was "surly, dirty, uncivil, unconcerned with the duties and proprieties of social life" could be labeled a "philosopher." Attacks on the figure of the philosopher as narcissistic lout and heedless naturalist continued through the 1740s in the theater, the *Mercure de France,* the *Journal de Trévoux,* and the works of René de Bonneval, Jean Jacques Lefranc de Pompignan, and Pierre François Guyot Desfontaines. The line between philosophy and libertinage had, it appears, at least in the mind of a certain worldly public, grown so tenuous that someone "above all prejudice and beneath contempt," the viperous Mme. de Senanges of Claude Prosper Jolyot de Crébillon's novel *Les égarements du coeur et de l'esprit* (1736–1738; *The Wayward Head and Heart*), could be described as "one of those women philosophers for whom the Public means nothing" (p. 94).

The image of the philosopher was not to be rehabilitated, at least in print, until more than a decade after Marivaux's *L'indigent philosophe,* in a short but luminously witty manifesto by César Chesneau Dumarsais called "Le philosophe." The fact that it appeared in a volume titled *Nouvelles libertés de penser* (1743; *New Freedoms of Thought*), a book published without official permission and surreptitiously distributed just two years after the number of royal censors had been increased to seventy-nine, provides some sense of the growing difficulties involved in the entire project of philosophical dissent. As thinkers champed more violently at the bit or as their thought itself became more radical toward midcentury, a slandered nobility and church redoubled their persecutions. Dumarsais's new version of the philosopher, which served as the basis for the definition supplied in Diderot's *Encyclopédie* (1751–1772), was bound therefore to make a mildly conservative and conciliatory debut: although he sets himself up as the prophet of a revitalized and critical rationality that abhors the blindness of religious doctrine, he conscientiously separates himself from the old specter of disruptive, yahoo philosophers and happily inclines before the notion of social order and agreeable social exchange. In time, however, this proved to be a difficult position to maintain. Those who followed in the wake of this new philosopher, men like Diderot, but especially women like Marie-Jeanne Riccoboni and Isabelle de Charrière—I deliberately omit thoroughly revolutionary writers such as Gabriel Bonnot de Mably, Jean-Paul Marat, and Louis de Saint-Just—would come to face the inevitable dilemma that pits civility and, if not social order, then social conformity against the possibility of revision and free expression. This tumbled them into irritable misgivings not simply about their role and place in the society of their day, but about their own moral complexion. Rousseau, who, mortifying friends and enemies alike, seriously challenged the very premises of a cherished sociability and of civilized society in general, could not himself escape the guilt and the quandary.

It goes without saying that in the highly ritualized and restricted society of the early 18th century, a society that dared to call itself "the world," it was perilous to avoid good form and no less perilous to one's soul to understand that good form concealed and perpetuated corruption. The early century simply disseminated a view that the classical moralists had elaborated, one that transformed every gesture and expression into an act at once moral and aesthetic—a pragmatic compromise allowing vice and the consciousness of vice to go their separate ways. It is not at all true, as libertine characters often and for their own purposes maintained, that vice was fashionable. It was, as usual, rampant, and the problem was how to manage tendencies as endemic and repetitious as original sin. Seventeenth-century thinkers had, at first, kept themselves triumphantly afloat on Reason; they were only later to discover its existential uselessness and to draw resignedly, as Montaigne had, upon the ancient prudence of Epicurean and Skeptic naturalism. Pious Christians enjoined their readers to study the world—a world given over to concupiscence, illusion, and the arrogance of human convention—in order to reconfirm, in their own minds and existences, the enduring difference between the City of God and the fallen, cyclical City of Man. They summoned their brethren both to test their Christian charity or humility (Antoine de Courtin) and to avoid the "danger of conversation" (Pierre Nicole) while submissively inclining to a secular order whose only virtue was the maintenance of a temporary but necessary tranquillity. Novelists, poets, playwrights, and moralists unveiled the instabilities or miseries beneath social appearances and proprieties while treating these appearances and proprieties as the necessary foundation of all human intercourse. Even while society, orchestrated by Louis XIV and his heir, reluctantly formed itself into a

424

spectacular, hierarchical machine, it was clearly generating its own political, social, and personal discontents.

Marivaux's pauper philosopher steps onto the heaving stretch of this wide, historic landscape, among these ambiguities and paradoxes. Although he is 500 kilometers from Paris—a metaphor for his psychic distance and transcendence—he writes as if he had never stepped beyond its civilized space. And this is true not only because he writes for a Parisian audience, but because he actually plays out and apes its anxieties and hopes in his ironic, comically frenetic, masquerade. His frivolity, his refusal to be a laborious and professional author, even, paradoxically, his espousal of the "natural" and the spontaneous, the desire "to write to the moment" and "without ceremony" or "order," correspond to moral and aesthetic ideals increasingly popular in circles where "natural virtue" seemed more plausible than Reason "spiritual and sublime." These were in fact circles in which any heroic gesture—political, social, or literary—had long been regarded with an aristocratic mixture of defeat, nostalgia, and contempt. The "pleasure of being mad," of delinquencies that eased the burden of rigid social codes, stood against the "pain of pretending to be wise" (*L'indigent philosophe*, in *Journaux*, p. 280). Dissidence had, in other words, become obscurely normalized, rationalized, and moralized. Even more remarkably, it provided deviant modes of being, of acting and of speaking, that allowed "madness"—a combination of repressed anger and hysterical release— to surface in forms that predict the pauper philosopher and, allowance made for changes in belief, milieu, and emphasis, his closest kin, Diderot's *Le neveu de Rameau* (wr. 1761–1774, pub. 1805; *Rameau's Nephew*).

This not uncommon, subterranean permissiveness was accompanied by an obsessive vocabulary of catchwords pinpointing outrageously "philosophic" but still, within good society, tolerable patterns of behavior—gestures, attitudes, performances, an entire semiological field of eccentric manners and expressions that could easily pass for what Diderot would eventually call "moral idioms." They were the smilingly deplored but very intelligible colloquialisms of a more general social grammar. Though marginal, they expressed an undercurrent of malaise that eventuated in some of the most profound stylistic and philosophical upheavals of the century. *Négligence* and *paresse* (carelessness and indolence), *extravagance* and *étourderie* (foolishness and thoughtlessness), *singularité, indifférence,* and *distraction* (peculiarity, indifference, and absent-mindedness)— these are some of the merely lexical traces of what was a need, a disposition to advertise personal deflections from a normative center, an escape from standards of social diligence and wakefulness; and all of them, while suggesting the natural and the casual, could be cleverly, enviously contrived, seductively used to replicate and even to parody what was obviously in short supply. They were thought to be the attributes of unsettled and carefree youth, of unattachably epicene *petit-maîtres* (fops), of slippery libertines, but especially of women, the embodiment of unregularized or natural desire, the very models of a pleasure-loving, restless, disordered temperament. In their presence, in their salons, where, as moralists like Montesquieu and Diderot warned, conversation had lost its starched sequentiality, and men, subject to their influence, had become "feminized," thought fluttered, flew into fragments, or digressed. Oppressed but imitated for those compensatory, liberating qualities that men easily found within themselves, women conveniently bore the blame for a vast and insidious change of rhetoric that, from Bernard Le Bovier de Fontenelle to Nicolas Chamfort, came to mark the entire century: a predilection for brief, informal, or discontinuous genres (dialogues, letters, dictionaries, epistolary novels, short stories), a taste for variety, wit, and swift change, for entertaining, flirtatious vulgarizations. In matters of style and sensibility, everyone had, as Montesquieu noticed privately in his notebooks (*Mes pensées,* 1716–1755; *My Thoughts*), become a woman: "We are all women in spirit" (p. 1234). Protest had imploded, transformed itself into a manner more than an overt or particular content. And the womanly, the undomesticated, the incompletely engaged, the improvised and organic—in short, all that could be called waywardly "philosophical"—was already and fashionably in every knowing wink or voice.

The mounting distaste for rococo art and literature that grew most explicit at midcentury in the work of Diderot, Johann Winckelmann, Rousseau, and the critics of the Louis Petit de Bachaumont and Louis Doublet circle undoubtedly concealed not only a contempt and fear for those shifting, unsettled social, economic, and political realities that women's destabilizing banter and inconstancy came, by association, to symbolize; it also announced a new "sentimental" and, eventually, neoclassical model of what women must become: sequestered, long-suffering mothers and sisters, grave and static guarantors of narrowly defined, republican virtues. Buttressed by an odd mixture of English and ancient examples, it was an appeal for a new kind of masculine and domestic sublimity—fiercely ordered, immutable, wordless, and thrilling in its paroxysmic effects. But the easy, unorthodox forms and the liberated imagination supposedly unleashed by women or their myth had already insinuated themselves into the mainstream of 18th-century rhetoric and shaped the quality and content of its thought. Even Rousseau, who later maintained, more than any other philosopher, the full-blown, defiantly male rhetoric of the schoolrooms he never attended, and whose *Lettre à M. d'Alembert sur les spectacles* (1758; *Letter to M. d'Alembert on the Theater*) may be the most vituperative indictment of women in French literature—even he imbibed and incorporated their careless ways in what he acknowledged to be the fitful, discontinuous structure of his works. In his *Confessions* (1782–1789) and throughout *Les rêveries du promeneur solitaire* (1782; *The Reveries of the Solitary Walker*) he actually, though no doubt unconsciously, dared draw their childlike disengagement and distraction into a positive philosophy of existence.

Typically, then, the indigent philosopher lives as he admittedly writes: from moment to moment, from sentence (occasionally incomplete) to sentence. He thumbs his nose at the reader and deliberately adopts a structure and tone that reflect not only the "beautiful disorder" of his thoughts but also the "natural" and "bizarre" admixture of human clay and animal, vegetative, and spiritual soul. A good Christian repeatedly decrying all forms of vanity—including the pride of authorship—he nonetheless joins the sinful race each time he insists, too defensively, on his invulnerability to criticism and on his desire to be not merely read but cited as well. He is trapped, even in his fictional rags, between attitude and authenticity, disinterestedness and boastfulness, self-mockery and self-love; he compels us to call into question the very possibility of moral and discursive oppositions. Where is nature as distinct from art or society; where is a self untainted by otherness; and where is a language that does not wear man's smudge and share man's smell? He moves within a Pascalian world overwhelmingly saturated with habit, artifice, convention, and literary quotation—not a natural, essential world but a "second nature," a fabricated world, blindly but self-importantly hoisted over the abyss. His impertinence, part of Marivaux's translucent and playful mask, part of that same worldly artifice and convention, glories in its freedom but produces in the reader a sense of paralysis, of being caught between indignation and bemused yet cynical acceptance. Our philosopher does not approve of masks, but he appreciates those who self-consciously lift them and say: "There; charming, isn't it?" (*Journaux,* p. 315). The mask wants to be shocking, sufficiently "unique" to score a moral difference; but our individuality, the shadow of a betrayed desire to be our natural selves, lies only in our comment, in the feeble, offensive-defensive parody of a borrowed phrase: "charming, isn't it?" Since we must all be "ridiculous," this awareness of our folly, the ironic consciousness of the roles we play and the recycled language we speak, presents itself not as a solution to the comedy we must continue to enact, but as a stalled, purely reflexive reaction that keeps us rushing between the stage, the wings, and the pit. Marivaux announces here as well as in his plays and novels an exacerbated form of self-consciousness that hovers between self-creation and self-estrangement, between performance and moral vigilance—a desperate, manipulative lucidity that will overtake authors, but especially their authorial counterparts: Marivaux's own Marianne and Jacob; Crébillon's Meilcour; Diderot's Suzanne, Rameau's nephew, and Mme. de la Pommeraye; Choderlos de Laclos's Mme. de Merteuil.

In the final installment of his periodical *Le spectateur français* (1724), Marivaux, having lost his father and still more recently his wife, describes a young man who, almost penniless, his parents dead, his beloved sister shut in a convent, takes to the road, heading for Paris: "I was no longer to have anyone but myself, and what was this self?" (*Journaux,* p. 261). Pushing into his forties, Marivaux is haunted by the idea of divestment and solitude, by a vision of insular landscapes and abandoned souls. He writes a comedy about an island of slaves and also begins *La vie de Marianne;* he abruptly leaves off writing *L'indigent philosophe* to concentrate on another comedy, *L'île de la raison* (1727; *The Isle of Reason*), in which Blaise, a peasant and drunkard, grows taller than all the other European inhabitants because, without pretense or illusion, he is frank about his vices: "Humility, what a wonderful secret it is for being tall [*grand*]!" (*Théâtre,* p. 216). The ambiguity of the adjective, which might mean "great," ironically suggests that his "secret," surfacing to consciousness, language, and our scrutiny, has already become a boast. And it is in this vein that

427

the deepest variations on the interrelated themes of self-estrangement and social conformity appear in a fittingly recessed narration within *L'indigent philosophe,* boxed in the philosopher's narrative frame. The drunken comrade—son of a drunken musician, whose liquor draws him, as it does his son, to the sources of creation and social forgetfulness, to a music that cannot be transcribed—falls in and out of delinquent service to the army and the church only to end up among a troupe of actors—"good folk" but social reprobates. Living the "natural," uncivil life, an unregulated, "obscure," but varied life of laziness and chance, he falls from grace by becoming a successful actor exposed to public desire, coveted for his body, his face, his style—for everything that he *is not.* If he didn't drink, he would weep.

Wine becomes "a rich parenthesis," a respite in the manipulative and spec- ular engagements of life, which are also, in this comrade's century, the favored engagements of authors with their readers, of speakers with their listeners. Wine violently summons a corporeal present as immediate and "natural" as lips and stomach; it erases all reflection and discourse; it keeps otherness at bay. "Madmen think, wise men act; and I, I drink: to which category do I belong?" He longs for pure being, the death of consciousness, of language, and of any time other than the here and now ("anyone is alive who is not dead"), a reab- sorption into innocent, entirely spiritual, origins and energies. Yet he remem- bers, speaks, and jests, so that being eludes him forever, and in its place stands the parodic figure of a "character," a "philosopher," whose story he tells not only with relish but also (having read Ovid) with an awareness of how poorly he has "arranged [his] narrative" (*Journaux,* pp. 292–298).

The impossible tension between wine and discourse, being and appearance, seeing and being seen, causes reflection and irony, the reflection of reflection, to gather a useless strength—one that circles dizzyingly in its own orbit and sways from the illusion of freedom to a sense of entrapment. Clearly Marivaux's ironists, the philosopher and his comrade, are fools in this world, poetically engendering themselves, parodic ironists for whom this production, the "philo- sophical" flouting of social proprieties, serves merely to confirm the moral ambiguity of their own "natural" existence and ideals of the natural. The intui- tion, the natural certainty that, as the philosopher says, we have a "feeling of our excellence," "intimations of an exalted destiny" cannot entirely override the baleful truth that "there is no expression for it, and the mind perceives what it cannot say" (*Journaux,* pp. 305–306). If every efflorescence of being and truth, every word and presence, becomes the degradation, the destruction, of being and truth, of what La Rochefoucauld called "pure love," a spiritual current hidden not only from others but from ourselves, then all visible existence defines itself as negativity and contradiction. In the philosopher's words, which rather disappointingly signal solutions beyond the text and certainly beyond the world, "Sauve qui peut"—find your salvation where you can!

See also 1761 (December).

Bibliography: Claude Prosper Jolyot de Crébillon, *Les égarements du cœur et de l'esprit,* ed. René Etiemble (Paris: Armand Colin, 1961). César Chesneau Dumarsais, *Le philosophe:*

Texts and Interpretation, ed. Herbert Dieckmann (Saint Louis: Washington University Studies, 1948). Michel Gilot, *Les journaux de Marivaux: Itinéraire moral et accomplissement esthétique,* 2 vols. (Paris: Champion, 1975). W. Pierre Jacoebée, *La persuasion de la charité: Thèmes, formes et structures dans les Journaux et oeuvres diverses de Marivaux* (Amsterdam: Rodopi, 1976). Pierre Carlet de Marivaux, *L'indigent philosophe* and *Le spectateur français,* in *Journaux et oeuvres diverses,* ed. Frédéric Deloffre and Michel Gilot (Paris: Garnier, 1969). Marivaux, *Théâtre complet,* ed. Bernard Dort (Paris: Seuil, 1964). Charles de Secondat de Montesquieu, *Oeuvres complètes,* ed. Roger Caillois, vol. 2 (Paris: Gallimard, 1951).

Jack Undank

✐ 1734

Three Editions of Voltaire's *Lettres philosophiques* Are Published and Banned

Intricacies of Literary Production

Voltaire's *Lettres philosophiques* (1734; *Philosophical Letters*) has passed into tradition as "the first bomb launched against the ancien régime" (Fellows and Torrey, *The Age of Enlightenment,* p. 364). Originally called *English Letters,* the work is composed of letters written home by an imaginary French visitor to England. The narrator alternates between perceptive didacticism and expressions of naïve astonishment, made funny by Voltaire's irony and aphorisms, but the book met with instant popular success as much for its shocking ideas as for its amusing tone. Voltaire's England is first of all a land of religious tolerance; Catholics, Protestants, Jews, Muslims, and others thrive by ignoring differences of doctrine: "If there were only one religion in England, there would be fear of despotism; if there were but two, the people would cut one another's throats; but there are thirty, and they all live happy, and in peace" (letter 6, "On the Presbyterians," in *Candide and Other Writings,* p. 327).

In the opening letters, the Gallic visitor appears rude and intemperate, opposing dogmatic quibbles and blasphemous oaths to his Quaker interlocutor's simple and humane faith. Voltaire holds that, instead of religious debates, the English focus on useful matters: business, commerce, parliamentary government, the arts and sciences. Soon the traveler turns his attention to these subjects and depicts England as a model of progress and prosperity. He discusses English literature, notably Shakespeare, and expounds the ideas of Locke and Newton. *Lettres philosophiques* stands out among early Enlightenment works largely because of its role in spreading English thought in France, especially Locke's sensualism and Newton's physics.

Historians now question the traditional belief that Enlightenment philosophers caused the French Revolution, even indirectly; and in any case, Voltaire was not the first. By the time *Lettres philosophiques* appeared in 1734, there were already many significant books in the same current of thought, including Pierre Bayle's *Dictionnaire historique et critique* (1697; *Historical and Critical Dictionary*) and *Pensées diverses sur la comète* (1682; *Miscellaneous Thoughts on the Comet*), Bernard Le Bovier de Fontenelle's *Entretiens sur la pluralité des mondes* (1686; *Conversations on the Plurality of Worlds*), and Montesquieu's *Lettres persanes* (1721; *Persian Letters*). They share a trust in human reason rather than in divine revelation, ancient authority, or political tradition; a method arising from that trust, dependent upon skepticism and scientific or scholarly analysis; and a style appealing to the public's common sense, not to the expertise of theologians and academicians. They also regularly compare cultures, decentering the perspective of the French reader and viewing French civilization as if it were foreign, at a moment when the French, just emerging from the glorious Century of Louis XIV, liked to consider themselves the most powerful and most advanced nation in the world. For all its brilliance and originality, *Lettres philosophiques* does not mark the start of a philosopher's war on the state so much as a turning point in Voltaire's career.

Even before 1734, Voltaire had acquired some reputation as a troublemaker; indeed, *Lettres philosophiques* was based on an enforced stay in England from 1726 to 1728 because of a quarrel with a French nobleman, the chevalier de Rohan-Chabot. Rohan apparently insulted Voltaire's ancestry, and Voltaire allegedly replied, "I am immortalizing my name, while you are dishonoring yours" (Pomeau, *D'Arouet à Voltaire,* p. 204). Rohan in turn had his lackeys thrash Voltaire, a way of underscoring the difference between the privileges of the nobleman and the obligations of the commoner. Voltaire wanted to seek revenge in a duel and instead was put into the Bastille, from which he was released on condition that he leave France for London.

It is tempting to suppose that, burning with resentment over this injustice, Voltaire became a philosophe in England. It is true at least that he encountered many new ideas and found some of the seeds of his later thought there. He returned from England, however, feeling much resentment toward the English, and with only fourteen of the twenty-four *Lettres philosophiques* written in a first draft. Voltaire actually wrote these fourteen in English, intending to publish them with the title "Letters concerning the English Nation"; they did not include the most original material, the letters on Locke and Newton. For two years after his return, Voltaire abandoned the project, and then took it up again in late 1731, completing it over the next year.

A friend in London supervised the printing of two editions during 1733, one in English, and one in French claiming on the title page to have been printed in Basel. Meanwhile Voltaire arranged with a printer in Rouen named Claude-François Jore to bring out a French edition, with the title *Lettres philosophiques* and a title page giving Amsterdam as the place of publication. While the printing was going on in Rouen, Voltaire was in Paris trying to secure official tolerance for the publication. He showed the manuscript to various well-placed friends, and even to Cardinal Fleury, the prime minister, but concluded that the censor would not approve it. Thus he would not have a royal privilege (comparable to a copyright), but he hoped to obtain a tacit permission, a systematic procedure for winking at evasions of the official regulations, under which the police agreed in advance not to prosecute a work. Or, failing that, he might have a de facto tolerance, meaning that without any formal agreement the police would ignore the book.

Both the London printer and Jore had an edition ready for sale by the summer of 1733. Meanwhile Voltaire allowed another printer, the Parisian François Josse, to see the proofs, knowing that he would pirate a copy. Because negotiations with the police were not going well, Voltaire tried to keep the work from being sold. Despite his efforts, in August 1733 the English-language version was released to the public, and reviews began appearing in periodicals. Later in the year Jore, worried about the sales of his own stock of books, let a few out to see what would happen; he was summoned by the chief of police and threatened, so he kept his copies in storage, in a rented stable in Passy. In March 1734 the "Basel" edition found its way from London to France, and Josse began selling his pirated edition. Jore could afford to wait no longer; in April he put his own copies on the market.

The authorities reacted quickly. Jore was sent to the Bastille for two weeks and lost his license as a printer. By court order the book was burned on 10 June, although according to legend the executioner substituted an innocuous work and took *Lettres philosophiques* for his own library. Voltaire escaped prison only because he was out of Paris for a wedding in Autun. Warned of his impending arrest, he fled to his mistress's château at Cirey, on the border between France and the independent duchy of Lorraine, and remained there most of the time until 1740, studying and carrying out scientific investigations, receiving visitors from all over Europe, and sustaining a prodigious correspondence. The publication of *Lettres philosophiques* thus marks the moment when he ceased to think of himself primarily as a poet and dramatist (although he never gave up writing either poetry or plays) and began to campaign against church and state in favor of certain ideas, what we generally term the philosophy of the Enlightenment.

The story of the publication of *Lettres philosophiques* may seem complex, but it is fairly typical of the 18th-century works read most today. The institutions by which an author's manuscript reached a reading public were chaotic. They reflected conflicting impulses within the government, on the one hand to foster French culture and commerce, on the other hand to control the circulation of ideas and to suppress unorthodox opinions. They also reflected conflicts between individual officials, some of whom worked actively to stifle unorthodoxy, while others openly sympathized with the Enlightenment. Moreover, these institutions had important effects on the works. A complete account of how books were produced, from the raw materials to the distribution of French books abroad, would fill a large volume. It is important at least to recognize that the books we read today do not represent the standard output of typical 18th-century publishers, who turned out huge quantities of pious literature, almanacs, how-to manuals, folktales, and the like. Such items might eventually sell hundreds of thousands of copies in a variety of editions over many years. By contrast, *Lettres philosophiques* probably had a total sale of about 20,000 copies in all its 18th-century editions. Most of what was printed passed through the system without obstacle, but mainly because it was, on the whole, conventional and orthodox; and for those same reasons it is less likely to be read today.

Voltaire by himself could illustrate most of the varied aspects of literary production. His first major triumph was *Oedipe* (*Oedipus*), a verse tragedy, performed at the Comédie-Française in 1718. Like most literary institutions, the Comédie-Française had been established under Louis XIV; it held a royal charter and enjoyed certain monopoly rights. It also suffered some onerous obligations. For most of the century it competed with other theaters, the opera, the Comédie-Italienne, and the theaters of the fairs; but the rivalry was strictly regulated—for example, the opera was supposed to avoid the spoken, and the actors were generally forbidden to use music and dance.

By its nature, a theater is easy to regulate. To stage a play requires a group of people, who must gather repeatedly in a single location and advertise their performances to the public. There is no theatrical equivalent to storing volumes in a stable, making contraband copies, or smuggling them in from abroad. By the same token, a play can more easily reap the financial benefits of a monopoly. For a beginning author, book publication was seldom lucrative; a manuscript could be sold only once, after which the author usually had no more financial interest in it. The author of a play at the Comédie-Française, by contrast, received one-ninth of the receipts during the first run. Thus Françoise de Graffigny had to sell the manuscript of her popular novel *Lettres d'une Péruvienne* (*Letters from a Peruvian Princess*) for 300 livres in 1747; three years later, her play *Cénie* brought in about 2,500 livres in performance royalties and another 1,000 for the publication, which, unlike the novel, benefited from official permission and privilege.

Clearly, the Comédie-Française offered important financial advantages over book publication. The disadvantages lay in the difficulties of having a play accepted. The actors selected their own plays; their capriciousness was legendary. Even when the troupe accepted a play, members might quarrel over the casting and demand revisions in their roles. Shepherding a play through production was stressful and required constant personal attention; these factors alone probably suffice to explain the rarity of women playwrights.

The prestige of the theater in the 18th century of course owed a great deal to the masterpieces of the preceding century. Unlike the great works of Corneille, Molière, and Racine, however, the plays that most pleased the 18th-century public—prior to Pierre Caron de Beaumarchais's *Le barbier de Séville* (*The Barber of Seville*) in 1775—have all disappeared from the boards. The dead weight of tradition was not just in the writers' minds and the public's taste, however; the laws and regulations of the ancien régime ensured the preeminence of the Comédie-Française. It continued to attract Voltaire, whose plays were well received, and Diderot and Rousseau, whose plays were not; but none of them did their best work for the stage. It was a suitable medium for an ambitious and mediocre talent such as Jean-François Marmontel's; he took to heart Voltaire's advice to write for the theater, where one could win fame and fortune all at once, and won a seat in the Académie Française on the strength of his flops, as a contemporary wit put it. The best dramatist of the age, Pierre Carlet de Marivaux, did his best work for the Italians; but because it was not in the great French tradition, it was automatically deemed inferior.

Voltaire was still in his early twenties when he won fame and fortune with *Oedipe*. Unlike most of his fellow authors, he became a rich man, though more from the patronage of wealthy friends than from his writing. For much of his career, he could afford to give away his manuscripts; he was more concerned with the diffusion of his ideas than with the small income he might obtain. With *Lettres philosophiques* he pursued that objective by arranging for several different editions; if the police seized one, another would be available. His novels appeared unsigned or pseudonymously; his coy denials of authorship became a clever form of advertising. He made it a practice to give manuscripts to young writers who asked for help; in exchange for accepting the attribution, they pocketed the profits, and the ideas got into circulation. To polemical works, he sometimes even signed an adversary's name. In such ways Voltaire and others coopted the elaborate machinery of regulation and censorship for their own ends, and illicit literature of all kinds, including pornography, flourished.

Although such tactics were suitable for controversial philosophical writings by a wealthy and established writer, they were inappropriate for works aimed at currying favor with the king and gaining admission to the Académie. Having scored a triumph in the theater, the young Voltaire dreamed of providing France with its national epic poem. This was to be a monument, not a clandestine pamphlet. It had to have high-quality printing and engravings. Given the ease with which works could be pirated, normal publication methods would have proved ruinous, so Voltaire resorted to a subscription. Rich and noble friends and patrons of the arts and literature were solicited, and paid in advance for a deluxe edition of *La Henriade* (1728). As was often the case with Voltaire, in his egotistical enthusiasm he miscalculated; being in England at the time, he dedicated the work to the queen of England and filled the patrons' list with Protestants. Moreover, the work celebrated Henri IV, whose tolerance toward Protestants was no longer French policy. The French court rebuffed Voltaire's overtures, and *La Henriade* did little to win its author advancement on the pension lists or membership in the Académie Française.

The century's most important example of subscription publication was Denis Diderot's *Encyclopédie* (1751–1772). *La Henriade* was simply a deluxe edition of a single work; the *Encyclopédie* was a multivolume project requiring the collaboration of dozens of France's leading writers and thinkers for two decades. An enterprise of such dimensions could not risk the free-for-all of the open market. Despite the efforts of the consortium of publishers to maintain respectability and legality, the *Encyclopédie* was continually beset by threats from conservative enemies on one side, who twice succeeded in stopping publication temporarily; by rival publishers on the other, who did their best to pirate the materials; and by internal quarrels, defections, and betrayals, for in the end Diderot's own publishers secretly censored his work. The full story of the "Battle of the *Ency-clopédie*" reads like a Balzacian melodrama.

Although the *Encyclopédie* crowned Diderot's achievement in the eyes of his contemporaries, and today still seems a remarkable victory of unorthodox ideas over the forces of a conservative and absolutist régime, the works for which he is most admired now could not even be published during his lifetime. Some—*Le neveu de Rameau* (wr. 1761–1774, pub. 1805; *Rameau's Nephew*), *Paradoxe sur le comédien* (wr. 1773–1776? pub. 1830; *Paradox on the Actor*), and the *Supplément au Voyage de Bougainville* (wr. 1772, pub. 1796; *Supplement to the Voyage of Bougainville*)—existed only in manuscript copies given to close friends. Others—*La religieuse* (wr. 1760, circulated 1780, pub. 1796; *The Nun*), *Jacques le fataliste et son maître* (wr. ca. 1773, cir. before 1780, pub. 1796; *Jacques the Fatalist and His Master*), *Le rêve de d'Alembert* (wr. 1769, cir. 1782, pub. 1831; *D'Alembert's Dream*), and the *Salons* (wr. and cir. 1759–1781, pub. 1795–1857)—were circulated in Friedrich Melchior Grimm and Jacques-Henri Meister's hand-copied *Correspondance littéraire* (1753–1790; *Literary Correspondence*). This was, needless to say, an expensive process, technologically obsolete since the 15th century; the subscribers, who never numbered more than fifteen, were crowned heads of central and eastern Europe. Thanks to Grimm's contacts in the diplomatic world and his friendship with Diderot, the *Correspondance litté-raire* is the most important, but by no means the only, instance of manuscript "publication." A number of other Parisian literati, such as Abbé Jean-Bernard Le Blanc and Louis Petit de Bachaumont, kept up literary correspondences. Others, such as Abbé Antoine François Prévost and Charles de Fieux de Mouhy, produced *gazettes à la main,* handwritten periodicals. In the first half of the 18th century, numerous works attacking Christianity were too dangerous to risk printing, so they circulated in manuscript.

Perhaps no genre better reveals the effects of material and political considerations on literary production than does the novel. The novel was a popular genre, without models in classical antiquity, but it had acquired enough stature to attract serious writers. Georges May has shown how the evolution of the novel was affected by the novelists' efforts to respond to moralistic critics, armed with the threat of censorship. The formulaic plots, ending in a tear-jerking dispensation of poetic justice, seem to have been supported by political pressure. Until Chrétien de Malesherbes replaced Henri François d'Aguesseau as chancellor at midcentury, novels seldom got permissions or privileges, without which the author and the printer were at the mercy of pirates. The printers had to recoup their expenses on the first printing, so even the most honest could not afford to pay the author much; to survive, therefore, a writer had to be prolific. Novelists, including Prévost and Marivaux, countered with installment novels; if the first volume succeeded, its successors could command higher prices, since the printer could be more certain of good sales.

Installment fiction requires episodic and open-ended plots. The previous century had provided illustrious examples by Honoré d'Urfé, Georges and Madeleine de Scudéry, and Gautier de Costes de La Calprenède, among others.

Moreover, a rambling tale well suited the 18th century's increasingly prevalent faith in a providential universe, in which good ultimately triumphs. Economic and political factors were therefore not the sole determinants of fictional forms; but, as with the theater, the official institutions of the state reflected or reinforced aesthetic and philosophical tendencies. Alain-René Lesage's *Histoire de Gil Blas de Santillane* came out in three sections over two decades (1715, 1724, 1735); Marivaux and Claude Prosper Jolyot de Crébillon (Crébillon *fils*) left novels unfinished. Later, Jean-François Marmontel, Baculard d'Arnaud, and Nicolas Edme Restif de La Bretonne also wrote frequently in installment form, either collections of stories and sketches, or novels with sequels. Much 18th-century French fiction was episodic and open-ended, even when it was published in one short volume. The popular epistolary form, as practiced by Graffigny and Isabelle de Charrière, seemed inherently open in structure. Prévost's *Manon Lescaut* was conceived as the seventh volume of the rambling *Mémoires et aventures d'un homme de qualité* (1729–1731; *Memoirs and Adventures of a Man of Quality*); and, despite the death and burial of the heroine, Prévost had clearly left open the possibility of resuscitating her for a sequel, which someone else actually wrote.

In short, the influence of political and economic factors on literature was direct and powerful. The French monarchy's effort to control literary production generated a large output of publications, most of it forgotten now because creative authors and perceptive readers could not accept the controls. Other forces in the government, the growth of international trade, and the development of the publishing industry counteracted the effects of censorship and regulation. These marginal and alternative avenues of publication contained their own limitations, but the writers we care about today are those who found creative ways of using and transcending the limits, like Marivaux turning to the Italian theater, Diderot exploiting the freedom of circulation in handwritten form, Prévost keeping open the option of a sequel, or Voltaire pitting censors and greedy publishers against each other from *Lettres philosophiques* to the end of his career.

See also 1680.

Bibliography: Roger Chartier, Henri-Jean Martin, and Jean-Pierre Vivet, eds., *Le livre triomphant 1660–1830*, vol. 2 of *Histoire de l'édition française* (Paris: Promodis, 1984). Robert Darnton, *The Business of Enlightenment: A Publishing History of the Encyclopédie, 1775–1800* (Cambridge, Mass.: The Belknap Press of Harvard University Press, 1979). Darnton, *The Literary Underground of the Old Regime* (Cambridge, Mass.: Harvard University Press, 1982). Otis E. Fellows and Norman L. Torrey, eds., *The Age of Enlightenment* (New York: Appleton-Century-Crofts, 1942). Georges May, *Le dilemme du roman au XVIIIe siècle* (New Haven: Yale University Press, 1963). René Pomeau, *D'Arouet à Voltaire 1694–1734*, vol. 1 of *Voltaire en son temps* (Oxford: Voltaire Foundation, 1985). Voltaire, *Candide and Other Writings*, ed. Haskell M. Block (New York: Modern Library, 1956).

English Showalter, Jr.

The *Mémoires du comte de Comminge* Are Published
Anonymously in The Hague

The Gender of the Memoir-Novel

The *Mémoires du comte de Comminge* (*Memoirs of the Count of Comminge*) were published anonymously in The Hague in 1735. Although neither anonymous publication nor publication in Holland was unusual in the period (as a result of censorship and the system of *privilèges* in France), the fact that Claudine Guérin, the marquise de Tencin, who presided over a powerful Parisian salon, chose, like Marie-Madeleine de La Fayette before her, to publish her novels anonymously nevertheless raises critical questions about the contemporary status of French female writers and their place in the canons of literary history. Thus the *Petit Larousse illustré* (1986) lists Tencin under a description of her brother, Pierre Guérin, cardinal de Tencin, archbishop of Lyons and minister of state: "His sister, Claudine Alexandrine Guérin, born at Grenoble (1682–1749), the marquise de Tencin, maintained a famous salon and was the mother of d'Alembert." There is no mention of her writing. The structuring categories of the entry—sister to the cardinal, mother of the philosophe, *salonnière* to (male) writers and thinkers—body forth in the late 20th century the stereotypes of what was called the "reign of women" in 18th-century France.

Tencin in fact wrote five novels. Three were published anonymously in her lifetime: *Comminge, Le siège de Calais* (1739; *The Siege of Calais*), and *Les malheurs de l'amour* (1747; *The Misfortunes of Love*). The unfinished *Anecdotes de la cour et du règne d'Edouard II, roi d'Angleterre* (1766; *Anecdotes of the Court and Reign of Edward II, King of England*) and *Histoire d'une religieuse écrite par elle-même* (1786; *The Story of a Nun, Written by Herself*) were published posthumously with her signature. For thirty years after the publication of *Comminges,* the secret of its author's name was kept, although Tencin's friends Montesquieu and Pierre Carlet de Marivaux (who left a famous portrait of her as Mme. Dorsin in his own memoir-novel *La vie de Marianne,* 1731; *The Virtuous Orphan*) seem to have been in the know. According to a note added by an intimate to a collection of Montesquieu's published letters, Montesquieu, on the day of Tencin's death, acknowledged her authorship of novels thought by many to have been written by her nephew. Not until 1786, however, did her signature appear on the novel.

If much is known about Tencin's social and political life—she is typically described as an *intrigante* (a plotter, though this is not meant to refer to her novelistic technique)—how and why she came to writing remains a mystery. It appears that at about age fifty, having done as much as she could to advance the career of her famous brother, she invested her energies in a secret literary career and changed the population of her salon from priests to writers.

The social commentator and literary critic Jean-François de Laharpe was one of many to describe *Comminge* as the "equal" of La Fayette's *La princesse de Clèves*

(1678). Indeed, in 1804 the widely read and appreciated *Comminge* was published in an edition combining Tencin's novels with those of La Fayette and Marie-Louise de Fontaines. *Comminge* was republished at least a dozen times until 1835, after which it remained out of print until 1969. Its publication history is emblematic of the fate of 18th-century women's writing and of many 17th-century women's texts as well.

Standard literary history has placed Tencin along with Françoise de Graffigny and Marie-Jeanne Riccoboni under the rubric of the *roman sentimental*, characterizing their novels as poignant fictions of thwarted love that created both the audience for and the posterity of Jean-Jacques Rousseau's masterpiece *Julie, ou la nouvelle Héloïse* (1761; *Julie, or the New Héloïse*). Recent feminist criticism has recast that genealogy, replacing the female writers of the 18th century in a strong literary tradition characterized by a recognizable narrative poetics that begins with La Fayette and continues through Germaine de Staël.

But identifying Tencin's place in this tradition, notably in relation to a powerful line of 17th-century precursors, is only a first step. Replacing women's writing in literary history requires a double revision: women's writing must be seen both in relation to a diachronic female tradition and in synchronic relation to the contemporaneous mix of male (and female) works. This second critical strategy involves more specifically a "reading in pairs": reading women's writing in the weave of men's, and, perhaps more radically, the other way around.

From this double perspective, we might wonder why, for her first novel, Tencin chose the model of a memoir in the masculine. The memoir-novel was, of course, an extremely popular and creative novelistic form from 1690 to 1750. The 1730s, which are generally seen as a decisive moment in the evolution of the French novel, also represent the high point of the form; its best-known examples are Antoine François Prévost's *Manon Lescaut* (1731), Marivaux's *La vie de Marianne* (1731–1741; *The Life of Marianne*), and Claude Prosper Jolyot de Crébillon's *Les égarements du coeur et de l'esprit* (1736–1738; *The Wayward Head and Heart*). The memoir-novel seems to have developed in reaction to complex social and political pressures from critics and commentators both to create texts of greater narrative plausibility and to confront the competing demands of morality and realism. In contrast to the historically framed narrative modes favored in the 17th century, these fictional first-person retrospectives fashioned new spaces within which to represent the relations between gendered subjects and their changing social realities.

Typically the memoir-novel restages the narrator's experience of the world: from entrance into social life at adolescence, through a series of experiences in the apprenticeship of social relations—notably sexual encounters—to a detached view of that experience, generally to a disillusionment with worldly values. Although 17th-century female writers had authored successful and popular pseudomemoirs with female protagonists, by the 1730s the gender of recollection tended to be male.

Few female writers in the 18th century wrote memoir-novels. In the corpus of forty-six memoir-novels studied by Philip Stewart, for example, only three are by women (although some of the still-anonymous memoirs may have been female authored). Female writers were associated instead with the first-person feminine voices of the epistolary novel, which increasingly became the dominant form in the second part of the century; the first-person feminine retrospective was left largely to the male imagination—Marivaux's socially mobile Marianne and Diderot's ambiguous nun Suzanne are the most famous examples of the genre.

The fact that few female writers chose the memoir form in 18th-century France reflects in part the decline in social and political power enjoyed by dominant women in the 17th century. To produce a plausible retrospective fiction of worldliness required a certain indifference to the scandal of being a writing woman, and by the 1730s the protocol regulating the codes of public and private behavior for men and women had significantly curtailed the spheres of women's social autonomy and political intervention. But perhaps 18th-century fiction itself offers the sharpest reading of the consequences for women of going public with a female perspective on the apprenticeship of worldly life. Early in Pierre Choderlos de Laclos's *Les liaisons dangereuses* (1782), for instance, a novel that casts a backward glance at the social and sexual intersections of the pre-Revolutionary elite, the Marquise de Merteuil, a woman of the world not entirely unlike Tencin in her remarkable mastery of social plots, imagines a *rouerie,* a sexual exploit, for the Vicomte de Valmont to include in *his* memoirs, memoirs that *she* would write and have published for him. Later in the novel, however, writing privately to Valmont, she supplies for his edification a condensed memoir of her own; this is the story of her duplicitous self-formation in the world. When the dangerous relations are unmasked at the end of the novel, the public—in the novel—is particularly shocked by the account of a woman's deliberate manipulation of social convention. Merteuil's punishment—social exile and hideous disfiguration—points very specifically to the price women pay for committing to writing the memoir of a female self whose social performance violates the prevailing social codes of masculine and feminine behavior.

Writing in 1735, Tencin had a variety of models to use for her first novel: memoirs of women by male writers *writing as women* (novels of female impersonation); memoirs of men by male authors (generally libertine novels); and third-person "historical" novels of aristocratic manners by women, in particular the works of La Fayette and Mme. de Villedieu (pen name of Marie-Catherine Desjardins). Tencin also had access to the first-person feminine memoirs of Henriette de Castelnau Murat and Desjardins and, closer in time, the explicitly feminist memoir-novels of Mme. Méheust, *Histoire d'Emilie* (1732; *The Story of Emily*) and *Les mémoires du chevalier de . . .* (1734; *The Memoirs of a Chevalier*). By choosing anonymity but taking a man's name in the title of her memoir, Tencin produced an oblique fiction of dissent: a feminist critique of masculine privilege. Tencin's novel of male destiny interrogates the place of woman in patriarchal plots; it exposes the tradition that uses her as a pretext for male narrative, such as that of the exquisite cadaver of Prévost's *Manon Lescaut.*

The full title of Prévost's novel, *Histoire du chevalier des Grieux et de Manon Lescaut* (1731; *Story of the Chevalier des Grieux and of Manon Lescaut*), is rarely used; even less that of the seven-volume *Mémoires et aventures d'un homme de qualité qui s'est retiré du monde* (1728–1731; *Memoirs and Adventures of a Man of Quality Who Has Retired from the World*), to which *Manon Lescaut* was appended. But the wording of the original titles points to both the general narrative project of the memoir-novel and Prévost's role in shaping it. *Manon Lescaut* is the story of the Chevalier des Grieux as told to "the man of quality," the Marquis de Renoncour. In the "Notice" that frames the novel, the marquis presents des Grieux's story as one enough like his own for him to have considered inserting it into his own memoirs, but different enough to deserve narrative space of its own. Thus the older and wiser man of the world frames the account of the younger and authorizes the interest of that experience: "Each deed that is here reported is a degree of enlightenment, an instruction that substitutes for experience; each adventure is a model on which to form oneself; all it needs is to be adjusted to the circumstances one is in. The entire work is a treatise on morality shown entertainingly in practice" (p. 19). The model for formation proposed to the reader, like the relation that connects the two men's stories to each other, assumes a complicity of well-born masculine subjectivities.

Once the framing narrator has introduced the young man and provided him with the occasion to tell the story of his life, he withdraws, and the "I" who speaks tells of his undying passion for a woman, now dead, whose name in the history of the novel has displaced his. Thus although the novel appears to belong to the 18th-century tradition of constructing fictional texts around a heroine's name and fate, in its narrative and in its ideology it is structured by the apprenticeship of masculine identity.

Des Grieux's story begins with a young man's entrance into the world: "I was seventeen and I was finishing my philosophy course at Amiens, where my parents, who belong to one of the best families in P——, had sent me" (p. 27). Destined to join the Order of Malta, des Grieux, a younger son, takes a long detour from his rightful place in the social order by falling in love with a beautiful young woman "of common birth" (p. 31). The disparities of class and circumstance—the faithful (though fallen-from-grace) seminarian and the fickle (though loving) courtesan—combine to create the pathos of opera (which Giacomo Puccini and Jules Massenet capitalized upon in the 19th century). The story follows the familiar sequences of illicit love punished: seduction, fleeting happiness, threat, betrayal, retribution. Despite the love that binds them, each time des Grieux and Manon set up a ménage, their domestic idyll is undermined by Manon's need for money. Des Grieux becomes a gambler, a thief, and a murderer in his efforts to fulfill Manon's desires. Finally, captured by the police and driven from the Old World by the rage of the fathers—his own and the man the young couple has tried to dupe—the couple attempts to find happiness in America. But legitimate and tranquil union is not to be the lot of the ill-fated lovers, prisoners of the state and of their desire: Manon dies of cold and exhaustion in the New World. In perhaps the most famous scene of the novel, des Grieux, after having "remained more than twenty-four hours with my lips pressed to the face and hands of my dear Manon" (p. 188), breaks his sword to dig a grave for the idol of his heart, whom he has wrapped in all

1. Death of Manon Lescaut, plate designed by Pasquier, engraved by Monziès, in Abbé Prévost, *Les aventures du chevalier des Grieux et de Manon Lescaut, par Monsieur ∗∗∗* (Amsterdam: Aux dépens de la compagnie, 1733), facing p. 470. (Courtesy of the Beinecke Rare Book and Manuscript Library, Yale University.)

his clothes (fig. 1). Although he wishes for death, he survives and returns home with his friend, the faithful Tiberge, who has come from France to bring him help. The woman must die in order for the men to reestablish their bonds with each other.

Prévost revised the novel in 1753, and it is this edition that is most commonly preferred. The revisions include a change in the description of Manon's origins from modest to common—generally understood as an attempt to make her ambiguous behavior more palatable to bourgeois readers; a shortening of the time des Grieux spends attached to Manon's dead body, from two days and two nights to twenty-four hours; and an expanded penultimate sentence that shifts the emphasis from the dead father—the words upon which the novel originally ended—to the son's return.

Just before des Grieux reaches his account of Manon's death, he interrupts himself to address the marquis: "Forgive me if I finish in a few words a story that kills me. I am telling you of a misfortune without precedent. My whole life is devoted to weeping over it" (p. 187). It is exactly this posture of the male mourner that Tencin adopts in opening the memoirs of her unhappy hero: "I have no other goal in writing the memoirs of my life than to recall the smallest circumstances of my misfortunes and to engrave them still more deeply, if that is possible, in my memory" (*Comminge,* p. 21). In both cases, a man's love for a dead woman engenders the memorialization of a life.

The plot of Tencin's novel is set in motion by a quarrel between two brothers as a result of a grandfather's will. Two young people whose fathers are mortal enemies meet and fall in love. Comminge decides to hide his true identity from Adélaïde de Lussan, the beautiful young woman whose name (an anagram of "ideal"?) he did not know when he fell in love with her at first sight; then, once she learns the truth from him, he insists upon his right to marry her despite the paternal interdiction. His father imprisons him on the family estates, and Adélaïde sublimely decides to marry the most disagreeable man she can find in order to save Comminge's honor as a son and to free him for happiness. After the marriage, Comminge tries to see Adélaïde, who lives like a prisoner on her husband's estate, and comes to almost fatal blows with the jealous husband. But in the face of Adélaïde's resolve to endure her miserable destiny alone—"If I have not been mistress of my feelings, I have at least been of my conduct, and I have done nothing the most rigorous duty could condemn" (p. 195)—he abandons all hope and withdraws to a Trappist monastery, where toward the novel's end Adélaïde, freed by her husband's death, ultimately finds him. Disguised as a man, she lives among the monks until her early death.

The most famous scene in the novel is the last. Lying on the ashes, on the point of death, Adélaïde, still dressed as a monk, speaks in her woman's voice: she explains that wandering through the countryside after her liberation, she was lured into the monastery by the sound of her lover's voice singing; she followed him around secretly as he performed his spiritual exercises (in particular, digging his own grave), but did not reveal herself to him because she did not want to threaten his salvation. As she expires, Comminge cries out in belated recognition and throws himself on her dead body. The monks forcibly tear him away from their final embrace but allow him to spend the rest of his days waiting for death in a hermitage, where presumably he writes the memoir of his unhappy life. Prévost, in his periodical *Le pour et le contre,* condemned the scene of the deathbed confession as an offense to plausibility, and in general the ending was criticized for not showing enough repentance and respect for religion. From 1764, when François de Baculard d'Arnaud adapted Tencin's novel into a successful play, *Les amants malheureux* (*The Unfortunate Lovers*), until well into the 19th century, the scene was greatly admired for its pathos and moral dimensions. By granting the lovers a moment of recognition—she realizes that he still loves her; he learns that she has always loved him—but no earthly reunion, Tencin, like Prévost, reproduces the narrative logic of much 18th-century fiction.

In *Manon Lescaut,* as in many other male-authored 18th-century novels, passion comes to challenge the class assumptions of the social order, the prejudices that bind property to propriety under patriarchal law. What, then, is the role

441

of passion in a novel based on class identity? Like the 17th-century fictional model of aristocratic relations, passion in the *Mémoires du comte de Comminge* displaces difference from the oppositions of class to focus uniquely on those of gender. What difference does sexual difference make? If in feminist writing passion's ideal form is sublimation, then the difference within that difference is that women are superior to men; they love better.

Tencin's novel ends with her hero miserably rehearsing his second loss of the perfect woman. As Adélaïde explains in the confessional narrative of her own abbreviated memoir, her cherished Comminge, in love with her absence, failed to perceive her presence; fascinated by the fetishistic remains of their thwarted union (her farewell letter to him and her portrait, which he studies in tearful solitude), the man overlooks the woman whose sublimity he reveres.

In its conclusion, the novel sharpens the critique of patriarchy by showing the ways in which the sons *as men* prove to be as blind as the fathers to the fatal embodiment of human relations. More pessimistic and more skeptical about the old realities of patriarchal authority than Prévost—whose novel finally returns the son to the land of his fathers and to his proper place, and perhaps bitter about the limits placed on the life of an exceptional woman forced to operate *through* men in it—Tencin's fiction represents the end of the line.

See also 1678, 1704, 1787, 1788.

Bibliography: Prosper Jolyot de Crébillon, *The Wayward Head and Heart,* trans. Barbara Bray (London: Oxford University Press, 1963). René Demoris, *Le roman à la première personne* (Paris: Armand Colin, 1975). Antoine François abbé Prévost, *Manon Lescaut,* trans. Donald Frame (New York: New American Library, 1961). Naomi Segal, *The Unintended Reader: Feminism and Manon Lescaut* (Cambridge: Cambridge University Press, 1987). Jean Sgard, *Prévost romancier* (Paris: José Corti, 1968). Philip Stewart, *Imitation and Illusion in the Memoir-Novel, 1700–1750: The Art of Make-Believe* (New Haven: Yale University Press, 1969). Claudine Alexandrine Guérin, marquise de Tencin, *Mémoires du comte de Comminge de Madame de Tencin,* ed. Jean Decottignies (Lille: René Giad, 1969).

Nancy K. Miller

✒ 1750

Alexander Baumgarten's *Aesthetica* Inaugurates the Study of the Beautiful as an Independent Discipline

Beauty in Context

In 1750 Alexander Gottlieb Baumgarten, a fairly obscure German philosopher, coined the term *aesthetics* in his treatise *Aesthetica*. By this term he designated the science of knowledge, based upon sensory perceptions, whose aim is beauty and the psychological responses to it, in contrast to logic, whose aim is truth. He also assigned it an independent and equal status as the branch of philosophy concerned with the nature of art, its creative sources, its forms and effects, and the criteria of artistic judgment and taste. Thus to Baumgarten belongs the credit not only of creating the term *aesthetics* but also of promoting the "philosophy of the beautiful" to a rank on a par with the traditional branches of philosophy. Beyond these contributions, however, he had very little impact on the subsequent development of aesthetics, mainly because his views remained rooted in transcendental, abstract, and scholastic metaphysics, whereas French and especially English thinkers generally preferred dealing with the new interest in beauty and aesthetic pleasure through an intuitive, empirical approach.

Enlightenment aesthetics frequently stressed the social usefulness of art. The philosophes, unlike the 17th-century *moralistes,* wanted to improve social and political conditions, and the belief that the artist should not be content merely to create pleasing and decorative works was a tenet shared by 18th-century thinkers as diverse as Jean-Jacques Rousseau and Denis Diderot. This new conception made the Enlightenment to the 18th century what classicism had been to the 17th and what Romanticism would be to the 19th. Although it does not represent the whole spectrum of 18th-century aesthetics, it was nevertheless a central force and its most radical departure.

One of Rousseau's major goals was to formulate a new relation between culture and society. His writings on literature, art, and music make clear that his aesthetics were inseparable from his ethical and political ideas. Both the *Discours sur les sciences et les arts* (1750; *Discourse on the Sciences and the Arts*) and the *Discours sur l'origine et les fondements de l'inégalité parmi les hommes* (1755; *Discourse on the Origin and Foundations of Inequality among Men*) reflect his ideological disapproval of the role of the poet and artist in society. Although music, fiction, poetry, and the theater are intimately intertwined in almost all his works, for Rousseau the development of the arts, the progressive refinement in manners, mores, and standards of beauty and taste, and the impressive advances and achievements in architecture, theater, opera, literature, and painting had not been matched by political and ethical progress and only testified to an everwidening rift between nature and culture as well as to the increasing degeneration of social and moral values and of the human condition in general.

Rousseau's 1758 *Lettre à M. d'Alembert sur les spectacles* (*Letter to M. d'Alembert on the Theater*) occupies a central place in his oeuvre. Rousseau was acutely aware that theatricality plays a necessary role at all levels of personal, social, and political interaction. In the *Lettre* he seeks to transform the very notion of theatricality in order to bring it into greater conformity with his idea of a new society. His attack on the contemporary theater constitutes a passionate plea for one that would involve not just professional actors and actresses, but all citizens united in great patriotic spectacles.

Rousseau's basic thesis, using Molière's *Le misanthrope* (1666) as a paradigmatic case, is that even the greatest playwrights tend to legitimate the status quo, because they depend on pleasing the public for their very survival. And it is precisely because of his admiration for Molière's genius that he launches a fierce attack on his representation of the sincere Alceste as a ridiculous character

443

and of Philinte, Alceste's cynical and accommodating friend, as a spokesman of wisdom. One could of course argue that Rousseau's choice of *Le misanthrope* is unfair to Molière. He could not have made the same case for *Tartuffe* (1664–1669)—a satirical portrait of a religious hypocrite and the dramatist's most controversial play, which caused Molière endless difficulties with the censors. But Rousseau never mentions it in the *Lettre,* even though it would have in fact reinforced his argument: theater is not the place for truth.

Unlike Rousseau, Diderot looked upon the role of art in society, even a corrupt one, as a positive force liberating the most creative human energies and impulses. From the outset, Diderot approached the artist's creative process and procedures and the interrelation between art and society with keen interest and a personal sense of sympathetic, enthusiastic involvement. Whereas Rousseau viewed the arts with suspicion if not outright hostility, Diderot found in them an unending source of delight and spiritual enrichment. Whereas Rousseau perceived a profound cleavage between art and moral values, Diderot sought to reconcile the respective exigencies of the aesthetically pleasing and the socially useful.

All his life Diderot remained concerned with aesthetic questions of a theoretical nature, as well as with art and its function in society. Before Gotthold Lessing, whose influential treatise *Laokoon* appeared in 1766, he had become aware that the notion of the sisterhood of the arts, inherited from the Renaissance, required qualification, for each medium depends on a different set of conventions and symbols. Diderot was especially concerned with the possibilities and limitations of the language of the poet, as distinct from that of the prose writer. Vigorously rejecting the descriptive role generally assigned to poetry in the 18th century, Diderot emphasized its suggestive, symbolic function and its reliance on a subtle intermingling of "hieroglyphs" that surpass the explicit meaning of words and represent the most complex manipulation of language and its associative potentialities.

In 1751 Diderot's article "Beau" ("Beautiful") appeared in the second volume of the *Encyclopédie.* It was widely admired, and as early as 1759 Immanuel Kant recommended it to his friends and disciples. The article offered a survey of major aesthetic doctrines of the time as well as a theoretical definition of beauty that avoided metaphysical abstractions and rejected the notion of an internal, God-given sense of beauty. Diderot opted instead for the Lockean idea that the human capacity for perception of relationships is at the core of our sense of the beautiful. Such an apparently vague and general definition is entirely in keeping with Diderot's experiential relativism and profound distrust of any kind of authoritarian absolutism, aesthetic, ethical, or political.

Although "Beau" represents one of Diderot's earliest statements on art, it firmly links his aesthetics to his materialistic, empirical philosophy and at the same time avoids the excesses of either idealism or sensationalism. Diderot acknowledges diversity in individual aesthetic judgments but at the same time proclaims the existence of an objective, universal law enabling us to perceive beauty in a harmonious relationship of the parts to the whole: the unity within multiplicity. Recognizing cultural and individual vagaries in our ideas of beauty, he emphasizes the universal nature of aesthetic sensibility, which derives from a basic human need for harmony and order.

Before long, Diderot turned from theoretical to more practical and specific considerations. In his biennial *Salons* and his 1766 *Essais sur la peinture* (*Essays on Painting*), he increasingly sought in art qualities that do not necessarily please, but that move, astonish, and shock us out of our complacency. Beauty was no longer the criterion, but rather those awesome, even terrifying aesthetic features associated with the sublime. Diderot's ideal was an art at once grandiose, high-minded, forceful, and morally uplifting, as well as intimate, spontaneous, and immediate in its depiction of human situations, conflicts, and emotions.

The last decades of the 18th century witnessed the emergence of such aesthetic categories as the sublime, the picturesque, the gothic, and the fantastic, exemplifying new modes of perception and symbolization superseding the rational and beautiful; and stressing the overpowering, nostalgic, and melancholy rather than pleasing emotions and experiences. The sublime, in particular, which had been a rhetorical concept in France since the 17th century, acquired a new importance through a growing awareness of the aesthetic potentialities of vast and enthralling scenes in nature.

That sublimity could be a more significant aesthetic category than beauty was demonstrated in Edmund Burke's influential *Philosophical Enquiry into the Origin of Our Ideas of the Sublime and Beautiful* (1757). Basing his analysis on Locke's pleasure-pain principle and linking it to the human passions related to self-preservation, Burke defines qualities of beauty as merely pleasing ones, and those of the sublime as related to such intense emotions as terror and astonishment. Natural scenes connoting overwhelming power, vastness, mystery, and dread—such as towering, snow-clad mountains, steep gorges and dizzying precipices, roaring torrents, violent storms, beclouded and darkened skies, or heavy, turbulent seas—are likely to induce sublimity.

An early work on aesthetics by Kant, *Beobachtungen über das Gefühl des Schönen und Erhabenen* (1764; *Observations on the Feeling of the Beautiful and Sublime*), carried on the debate on the sublime and beautiful. It shares with Enlightenment empiricism a concern for human feelings and psychological motivations. Kant's distinctions between the sublime and the beautiful essentially follow Burke's model: the sublime arouses feelings of astonishment, terror, and awe, whereas the beautiful elicits enjoyment and pleasure. The sublime is therefore more powerful and more intense than the beautiful. At this stage in his philosophical evolution, Kant still remained within Enlightenment thought in defining the aesthetic sense as an immediate, intuitive response to sensory experience and in relating it to ethics.

The appearance of new aesthetic categories stressing strong emotions and effects rather than pleasing ones by no means spelled the demise of neoclassicism. Indeed, the last decades of the 18th century were marked by a revival of the Greco-Roman ideal, closely related to a renewed ethical preoccupation with civic and patriotic virtues. Johann Winckelmann's widely read and admired *Geschichte der Kunst des Altertum* (1764; *History of Ancient Art*) extolled a simple, dignified, virile aesthetic ideal. In painting, the coloristic exuberance and slyly erotic themes of such rococo artists as Jean-Honoré Fragonard and François Boucher were challenged not only by the didactic and melodramatic family scenes of Jean-Baptiste Greuze but also by the sleekly classicizing pictures of Joseph-Marie Vien, the mentor of Jacques Louis David, whose grandly heroic and patriotic compositions were to inflame the Revolutionary generation. At the same time, however, the gothic, nostalgic, and fantastic found expression in the romantically charged ruin landscapes of Hubert Robert, in the visionary paintings of John Henry Fuseli, and in the nightmarish *Caprichos* of Francisco de Goya.

The 18th century did not look upon the arts as above or separate from the difficult business of living in a modern, complex society, and it fostered a creative, at times explosive, confrontation between the old and the new that paved the way for the Romantic revolution. From the outset the century acknowledged the essential roles of passion and enthusiasm in the creative process and of subjective sensibility in aesthetic appreciation and pleasure. At the same time, Enlightenment writers and thinkers insisted that artistic creativity and aesthetic appreciation cannot be separated from their social and moral context. That 18th-century aesthetics demanded and fully expected this relation of art to life, morality, and politics is its most distinctive feature and its greatest legacy to us.

See also 1759 (August–September), 1761 (December).

Bibliography: Alexander Gottlieb Baumgarten, *Aesthetica* (Hildesheim: Olms, 1961). Edmund Burke, *Philosophical Enquiry into the Origin of Our Ideas of the Sublime and Beautiful,* ed. J. T. Boulton (New York: Columbia University Press, 1958). Jacques Chouillet, *L'esthétique des Lumières* (Paris: Presses Universitaires de France, 1974). Denis Diderot, *Essais sur la peinture,* ed. Gita May (Paris: Hermann, 1984). Diderot, *Letter on the Blind and Letter on the Deaf and Dumb,* in *Early Philosophical Works,* trans. Margaret Jourdain (Chicago and London: Open Court, 1916). Diderot, "On the Origin and Nature of the Beautiful," in *Diderot's Selected Writings,* ed. Lester G. Crocker, trans. Derek Coltman (New York: Macmillan, 1966). Immanuel Kant, *Observations on the Feeling of the Beautiful and Sublime,* trans. John T. Goldthwait (Berkeley: University of California Press, 1960). Gotthold Ephraim Lessing, *Laocoon: An Essay upon the Limits of Painting and Poetry,* trans. Ellen Frothingham (New York: Noonday, 1957). Gita May, "Diderot and Burke: A Study in Aesthetic Affinity," *Publications of the Modern Language Association of America,* 25 (1960), 527–539. Philip E. Robinson, *Jean-Jacques Rousseau's Doctrine of the Arts* (New York: Peter Lang, 1984). Jean-Jacques Rousseau, *The First and Second Discourses,* trans. Roger D. and Judith R. Masters (New York: St. Martin's, 1964). Rousseau, *Politics and the Arts: Letter to M. d'Alembert on the Theater,* trans. Allan Bloom (Ithaca: Cornell University Press, 1977). Johann Winckelmann, *History of Ancient Art,* trans. G. Henry Lodge (1872–73; reprint, New York: F. Ungar, 1968).

Gita May

✑ 1751

Denis Diderot and Jean Le Rond d'Alembert Publish
the First Volume of the *Encyclopédie*

Ordering Knowledge

As conceived in 1745 by a group of enterprising Parisian publishers, the *Encyclopédie* began as a business venture limited to bringing out a French encyclopedia modeled on Ephraim Chambers' two-volume *Cyclopaedia* (1728). But by the time the first volume of articles appeared, in 1751, the project, under the editorship of Denis Diderot and the mathematician Jean Le Rond d'Alembert, had already outstripped all original plans. When completed a quarter-century later, in 1772, this monumental work comprised seventeen folio volumes containing 71,818 articles and eleven folio volumes of 2,885 plates. Judged in terms of its innovative conception, the financial and technical means marshaled, the size of its readership (some 4,500 subscribers), and the number of its eventual collaborators (over 150 identified), the *Encyclopédie* stands as one of the greatest projects in the history of French culture and capitalism. Testifying to the Enlightenment belief in the progressive and beneficial results of rational inquiry into all sectors of human activity, the *Encyclopédie* helped crystallize the Enlightenment as an intellectual and reformist movement. Providing great impetus to the technological development of French industry, the *Encyclopédie* contributed as much to the change of ideas during the last decades of the ancien régime as to the exchange of capital. Five subsequent editions, either reprints or revisions, were printed in Switzerland and Italy before 1789; roughly half of these 25,000 copies went to readers in France.

In many respects this massive text of some 20 million words resembles the Tower of Babel that Voltaire called it. Author of only one rather conservative, elitist article, "Gens de lettres" ("Persons of Letters"), Voltaire perhaps sensed that the *Encyclopédie* project radically expanded the definition of the intellectual and thereby promoted areas of investigation and activity with which the philosophe, for personal as well as political reasons, had little affinity. New orders of knowledge take shape in the *Encyclopédie* through the reordering of old ones, whether they involve philosophical and religious questions, economic and political theory, or scientific and technological knowledge. Yet this work was not the product of a revolutionary Third Estate or a homogeneous bourgeois class. In terms of social origins and financial means, the encyclopedists constituted a fairly heterogeneous group. Most were firmly integrated in a feudal and monarchical sociopolitical system. At the same time they were sufficiently independent from it, economically and intellectually, to imagine and promote other orders of knowledge, whether philosophical, sociopolitical, economic, or scientific.

For Diderot, the *Encyclopédie*'s goal was to encourage its readers to think freely, which for him meant resisting any authority, whether divine or human.

447

In the area of religion the encyclopedists tirelessly denounce fanaticism in the name of religious tolerance; attack Christian doctrine, the Catholic church, and its institutions; and present other beliefs favorably. At times this assault on organized religion relies on an artful use of critical irony rivaling Voltaire's. An article presenting a harmlessly orthodox statement of Christian dogma, for instance, may end with cross-references to a virulently atheistic denunciation of theology from the pen of Baron Paul Henri Thiry d'Holbach, and to a deistic apology for religious tolerance. Forcing the reader to rethink accepted ideas, the duplicitousness and irony that infiltrate the system of cross-references are emblematic of the way in which the *Encyclopédie* incites its reader to engage in interpretation and to understand it as a conflictual process. Articles on philosophy extend the conflict, presenting the argument for a deterministic materialism that Diderot relies on to treat the question of ethics. In his additions to articles on the soul and in others written entirely by himself, such as "Nature," "Périr" ("Perish"), "Volonté" ("Free Will"), "Délicieux" ("Delightful"), "Jouissance" ("Pleasure"), and "Chasteté" ("Chastity"), Diderot rehabilitates the passions, according the body a determinate, even autocratic, role in shaping human conduct. Yet although his individual ethics are resolutely amoral, his social ethics rest on the supreme value of virtue, which he presents as the highest form of sociability. The individual may not be free to act, but the conduct of the individual can be freely modified socially and politically. In the area of political theory, Diderot's ethics correspond to a contractual absolutism typical of 18th-century liberal thinkers. In his major entries on political authority and natural law ("Autorité politique" and "Droit naturel"), he argues that individuals assign authority to a sovereign body, not to an individual person, and in return the sovereign's function is to ensure the free play of natural laws, based above all on the notion of private property, which it is the sovereign's principal duty to protect. Reflecting the growing dissatisfaction with absolutism, as well as the parlements' struggle during the 1750s and 1760s to win greater autonomy and power from the crown, the political theory of contractual monarchism expressed in the *Encyclopédie,* though by no means insurrectionalist, represents the political corollary of the encyclopedists' economic liberalism. Thus Louis de Jaucourt's critique of despotism in the name of natural political laws meshes with Anne-Robert-Jacques Turgot's defense of laissez-faire capitalism in the name of equally natural economic laws. Contributors of articles on economy, notably François Quesnay, call for specific reforms in accordance with such laws, including limitation of the power of guilds and monopolies, tax reforms, and increased recognition of the importance of agriculture, trade, and the merchant class.

In addition to the specific positions and programs it contains, the *Encyclopédie* establishes a particular approach to knowledge in general. Its full title, *Encyclopédie, ou dictionnaire raisonné des sciences, des arts et des métiers (Encyclopedia, or a Descriptive Dictionary of the Sciences, Arts, and Trades)*, indicates its double objective. As an analytic or descriptive dictionary, it would contain the general principles and essential details pertaining to all branches of 18th-century science as well as to the mechanical and liberal arts. As an encyclopedia, it would display the order and interrelation of all forms of human knowledge. The encyclopedists sought not only to compile and transmit all existing knowledge but also to order it rationally, according to their understanding of how the human mind works. The *Encyclopédie* thus represents far more than a vast reference work or documentational enterprise, albeit the most massive Europe had ever produced. It also reflects the most powerful tenet of European Enlightenment, the belief in human reason as an individual and innate critical faculty, capable not simply of understanding the world but, more important, of actively organizing all forms of knowledge, thereby representing the world as understandable, that is, able to be grasped, ordered, and ultimately mastered by the rational mind.

In their venture of compiling knowledge, the encyclopedists had several predecessors, including the Académie Française's *Dictionnaire* (begun in 1638), Louis Moreri's *Grand dictionnaire historique* (1674; *Great Historical Dictionary*), and Pierre Bayle's *Dictionnaire historique et critique* (1697; *Historical and Critical Dictionary*). The Jesuits saw in the *Encyclopédie* a dangerous and secular rival to their *Dictionnaire de Trévoux* (1704–1771). Following Francis Bacon in his defense of "mechanical arts," the encyclopedists made free use of the several more technologically oriented reference works that had appeared following the *Description et perfection des arts et métiers* (1761; *Description and Perfection of the Arts and Trades*) that Jean-Baptiste Colbert, minister of Louis XIV, had called upon the Royal Academy of Sciences to produce after its foundation in 1666. Among these are Antoine Furetière's *Dictionnaire universel des arts et des sciences* (1690; *Universal Dictionary of the Arts and Sciences*), Thomas Corneille's *Dictionnaire des termes d'arts et de sciences* (1732), and Jacques Savary-Desbrulon's *Dictionnaire universel de commerce* (1723; *Universal Dictionary of Commerce*). Like its predecessors, the *Encyclopédie* of course remained inaccessible to the French working class, who could hardly have afforded a subscription to it, assuming they could read. But for the better-off educated person the encyclopedic text and illustrations presented a remarkably complete and up-to-date account of the 18th-century French "mechanical arts," now called technology, integrating them within a larger economic, historical, cultural, social, and philosophical context, in a style aimed at a relatively broad readership.

Unlike its predecessors, the *Encyclopédie* has won longevity (as the recent Pergamon complete reprint testifies), and not only as a reference work for ancien régime specialists. One of the most massive attempts of the Enlightenment to present knowledge as a product of human reason and to link the question of knowledge with that of value, the *Encyclopédie* remains a founding document and event of modern Western culture. It played a tremendous role in shaping the 18th-century educated person's way of thinking about knowledge by focusing attention on the values employed to determine how knowledge should be represented. In this way it contributed greatly to consolidating the value system called Enlightenment, which from a contemporary standpoint may well seem to be one of the most natural and essential features of modern thinking. Displaying nothing less than the rational mind at work organizing things and

449

persons into objects of knowledge, the *Encyclopédie* promoted above all the value of instrumental reason, the capacity of the human mind to think dynamically and to bring about organized change according to specific values and criteria, change that since the Enlightenment we call progress. The *Encyclopédie* played a major role in consolidating what was to become the legacy of the Enlightenment: a belief in the progress that would result from reason's power to present a critique of existing orders of knowledge by revealing their arbitrary and motivated basis, and at the same time to promote other orders of knowledge, founded on equally arbitrary yet arguably more productive values. The extent to which we wish to continue to be heirs to the Enlightenment's legacy, which may well have already been a myth in the 18th century, will determine how we read the *Encyclopédie* today. Perhaps we can no longer take pride in finding here a liberating, enlightened, rational critique and must consider as well its enabling conditions, the structures of power on which it is founded and with which it is linked. For in a very modern fashion the questions of knowledge and power merge in the pages of the *Encyclopédie,* not always perhaps as the encyclopedists may have intended, but certainly in a way that requires us to rethink the entire encyclopedic program of ordering knowledge.

Both d'Alembert in the "Discours préliminaire" ("Preliminary Discourse") and Diderot in his article "Encyclopédie" make explicit the ordering process at work in the *Encyclopédie,* the epistemology or theory of knowledge from which it derives, and the critique of institutions of order—especially theological institutions, but social and political ones as well—that the encyclopedic text contains and promotes. Rejecting the idealism of any theory of knowledge that locates the origin of ideas in some divine cause, d'Alembert and Diderot advance the sensationalist argument, taken from John Locke and developed by Etienne Bonnot de Condillac. According to this more empirical, materialist epistemology, knowledge derives not from innate ideas, as René Descartes and the proponents of Cartesianism maintained, unwilling to break the causal link between theology and epistemology, but rather from the senses. Understanding (*entendement*), claim Diderot and d'Alembert, comprises three faculties: memory, imagination, and, chief among them, reason. Reason's function being to combine sense data, it works with its sister faculties to produce all the various categories of human knowledge. These the encyclopedists portray schematically in the form of a "genealogical tree of knowledge," which depicts not only mental order, but encyclopedic and textual order as well. The epistemological model that describes the generation of ideas thus serves as a textual model, explaining the interrelation between every article in the *Encyclopédie.*

In their attempt to interpret their world according to the rule of reason, to represent the most valuable and useful forms of knowledge as grounded in sensory experience and mental operations, not metaphysical, idealist assumptions, the encyclopedists clearly had to take on the question of God, to say nothing of the church. Their "tree of knowledge" illustrates the approach they would take. Here the concept of the divine falls under the rubric of "la science de Dieu," a term that could mean the knowledge possessed by God, but that for the encyclopedists refers only to knowledge about God. This area of knowledge they figure as a subcategory of "general metaphysics," itself a subcategory of philosophy. Needless to say, all these areas are subcategories located under the general heading "reason." Farthest away from reason, both on the tree of knowledge and for the encyclopedists, is the category of religion, labeled "religion, hence, abusively, superstition." In the rational mind as the encyclopedists depict it, theology belongs next to black magic. The encyclopedists thus reorganize the cognitive universe, rejecting the authority of all systems and institutions that claim to deliver up any absolute order of knowledge, and setting in their place more secular, empirical, and arbitrary ones.

This rejection was immediately countered by a hostile campaign launched against the *Encyclopédie* project, notably by the Jesuits and the antiphilosophes movement. The *Encyclopédie* was placed on the church's Index of Forbidden Books, and on two occasions the crown revoked the *privilège,* or royal authorization to publish. In both cases the *privilège* was soon restored, matters of religious orthodoxy playing a smaller role in the crown's decision to provide tacit approval for the project than the question of economic benefit and national prestige for France, especially after the rumor circulated that Catherine II of Russia had offered to support the project if its editors would publish the *Encyclopédie* in Russia.

As in Voltaire's *Dictionnaire philosophique* (1764; *Philosophical Dictionary*), the church and its claims to doctrinaire authority were favorite targets in the pages of the *Encyclopédie.* To be sure, not all contributors professed the staunch atheism to be found in the articles by d'Holbach, or even the probing yet less rigid materialism of a Diderot. In fact numerous articles express Christian belief and dogma in the most orthodox terms. The real issue dividing the encyclopedists and the church involves the relation between power and the encyclopedic representation of knowledge. Diderot and d'Alembert make no claim to present absolute knowledge in the pages of the *Encyclopédie,* for such knowledge they willingly leave to God. Instead they argue that all other systems of knowledge must by necessity be arbitrary, as arbitrary in fact as the alphabetical order of articles. Given the arbitrariness of any ordering principle, the encyclopedists claim themselves justified in adopting the one they have chosen for their text. "Why should we not present man in our work," Diderot asks, "as he is situated in the universe? . . . Man is the sole term from which all must be derived and to which all must be reduced" (*Encyclopédie,* 5:641). Whether in the area of science and technology or that of philosophy and literature, in descriptions of either machines or ideas, all knowledge must be presented as an exclusively human product. More important, it must be judged in terms of its usefulness to humanity. "Man," a term that refers at times to the universal human individual and at others to the educated European male, thus serves as the supreme ordering principle for the encyclopedic representation of knowledge. By claiming not to answer questions pertaining to the ultimate nature of reality, the encyclopedists seek a more limited working knowledge of human experience, partial and provisional as they admit, but in the end more useful. The encyclopedic text sets up a relation between individual and world, thinking subject and object of knowledge, that is underlaid moreover with a particularly utilitarian epistemology.

The real utilitarianism at work in the pages of the *Encyclopédie* lies in the way this text empowers its readers by proposing a particular way in which to view and interpret the world and their place and function in it. The encyclopedic plates are emblematic in this regard. Reflecting a remarkably complete view of mid-18th-century French technology, the plates work to promote a techno-logical understanding of the world. The cross-section drawing, a fairly new form of representation in 1751, not only shows how to construct a machine—the most celebrated example being the stocking-weaving machine and Diderot's article concerning it, "Métier à bas" (fig. 1). It also suggests a way of repre-senting, viewing, and understanding objects that disassembles them, slices through them like the surgeon's scalpel and the viewer's gaze in the anatomy plates, and reassembles them, not as they look, but rather according to an understanding of how they function and produce. The articles also present a similar means for knowing the world; in other words, for constructing a world that can be controlled and made to work. Although the encyclopedists were quick to criticize the reductiveness of Cartesian systematization, their text amounts to an attempt to realize Descartes's dream of a philosophical system that would guarantee technical mastery over and possession of the world. With the *Encyclopédie,* the world of the Cartesian *cogito,* a world of being, explodes into a world of having, filled with objects that must be ordered and put in place. And the order of things in the *Encyclopédie* is determined above all by the status accorded them as belongings, by their usefulness to an ordering subject. Things in the encyclopedic text are not just "out there"; they are meant to be used, and the products of their use are of value, which is one reason for the countless tools, machines, and processes of production depicted in the plates. Nor is it by chance that Diderot invariably employs the metaphor of the voyage to describe reading the *Encyclopédie,* and that of the map to figure how it struc-tures knowledge. Like other maps used to chart the great European voyages of discovery to Africa, the Americas, and the Orient, the *Encyclopédie,* too, holds out the tantalizing promise of power to be achieved and wealth to be had. The encyclopedists' desire to transmit intact to future generations the wealth of knowledge contained in the encyclopedic storehouse begins to resemble uncan-nily the cartoon in which the captain of industry announces with pride to his heir: "Someday all this will be yours."

Only later in the history of rationalism would the consequences of the Enlightenment's self-destructive potential be more acutely felt, as Enlighten-ment transformed itself into mythology, and a philosophy of reason into an ideology designed to rationalize power structures. For the more militant 18th-century encyclopedists, however, theirs were heady times, which they willingly characterized as revolutionary. Post-Revolutionary conservative historians and intellectuals would continue for a century to denounce the *Encyclopédie* for having helped bring down an old order. But such judgments are misconceived,

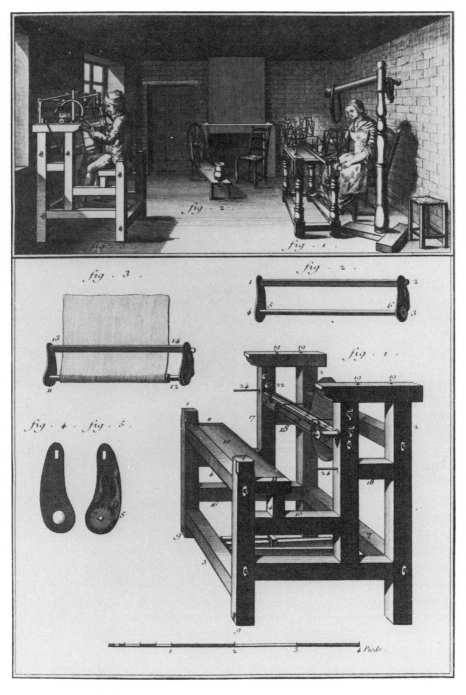

1. "Métier à faire des bas," plate designed by Goussier, engraved by A.-J. de Fehrt, in *Recueil de planches, sur les sciences, les arts libéraux, et les arts mécaniques, avec leur explication,* bk. 1, pt. 1 (Paris: Briasson, David, Le Breton, Durand, 1763), plate 5. (Courtesy of the Beinecke Rare Book and Manuscript Library, Yale University.)

453

the nostalgia they convey masking a fear all too easily transformed into repression. What is revolutionary about the encyclopedic text, or, better yet, most powerful, is the way it works, as Diderot puts it, "to undeceive people." It prompts its reader to seek out unreason in this work, in others, and indeed in all sectors of human activity. Presenting the critical practice of Enlightenment as a way of finally dispelling the shadows, the *Encyclopédie* displays the Enlighteners' awareness of the impossibility of challenging knowledge, however incorrect, irrational, or corrupt, with anything other than knowledge. The only way to dispel the shadows is to show that tenebrous knowledge does not know enough, or does not know strongly enough. The encyclopedists' text makes clear that the discourse of reason can oppose power only by being more powerful than what it sets itself against. Hence the *Encyclopédie* presents a powerful way of coming to knowledge, showing its readers how to "undeceive" themselves by leading them to interpret a world of their own construction, one of their own representation. We must confront the risk contained in such a way of coming to knowledge: the risk of redeception and a knowledge of things, not as they are, but as we desire and will them to be. Pointing out such a risk turns the encyclopedic critique of authority upon itself, in order to question the authority of any such critique. But this apparently more modern, post-Enlightenment view may be no more than Enlightenment's blind spot, already present in the encyclopedic project. The success of later editions of the *Encyclopédie,* especially those whose more cautious and canny editors sought to avoid the confrontation between knowledge and power by concentrating on the natural sciences instead of philosophy and by criticizing Protestantism in the place of Catholicism, bears witness to the ways in which the ordering of knowledge could be shaped to fit the political, social, and ideological exigencies of monarchy, revolution, and empire. Many of the encyclopedists' values and views concerning science and technology, religion and politics, today seem totally natural. The *Encyclopédie* contributed greatly to naturalizing them, that is, to representing such value systems as if they belonged to a natural order of things. We should not forget, however, reading the *Encyclopédie* today mindful of its most critically powerful dimension, that the encyclopedists' work reveals all orders of knowledge—including their own—to be arbitrary and motivated, mediated through and through by the power deployed and channeled by discourses of order. With this realization we may reach the limits of the Enlightenment understanding of knowledge as a kind of light that dispels the shadows of ignorance. Perhaps we must attempt to understand knowledge differently in order to come to terms with a power-knowledge that sometimes produces the well-being and pleasures of technological societies, and sometimes their terror and violence.

See also 1694, 1697, 1727, 1754.

Bibliography: Robert Darnton, *The Business of Enlightenment: A Publishing History of the Encyclopédie, 1775–1800* (Cambridge, Mass.: The Belknap Press of Harvard University Press, 1979). Denis Diderot and Jean Le Rond d'Alembert, eds., *Encyclopédie, ou dictionnaire raisonné des sciences, des arts et des métiers,* 18 vols. (1751–1772; reprint, 5 vols.,

Paris: Pergamon, 1969). John Lough, *The "Encyclopédie"* (New York: D. McKay, 1971). Arthur Wilson, *Diderot* (New York: Oxford University Press, 1972).

Daniel Brewer

◁◊ 1754?

Rousseau Writes His *Essai sur l'origine des langues*

Origins

"Speech distinguishes man among animals; language distinguishes nations from each other." These two assertions open Jean-Jacques Rousseau's *Essai sur l'origine des langues* (*Essay on the Origin of Languages*). As a starting point for such a treatise, the double distinction conferred by language seems obvious enough, conforming as it does to a certain rational order: first speech and then language, first the general faculty of man and then the differentiation within that faculty among men and nations. This order must apply wherever it is a question of *the* origin of something. Before the proliferation of differences that distinguish any one national language from all others, there would have been an origin, the origin; that is, there would have been a single, unified, and self-identical point from which later differences arose and in which they originated.

In fact, however, this double starting point of the *Essai* initiates a pattern whereby differences or distinctions will be marked in two ways: as differences from each other (no two national languages are alike) but also as differences from the origin, as departures from the original manifestation of speech as such. In the latter sense, difference can be measured as a distance or a deviation, a progression or a degeneration from an initial point. What is being measured in that case is not just the distance between two different points, one called the origin and the other its derivative. When languages are conceived of as departing from an origin, the difference in question is that between an undifferentiated point in space and time (the origin) and some force of effraction that breaks with and breaks up unified space. And that is why stories about origins so frequently end up being fables about lost wholeness.

Rousseau told this story once again after a number of his predecessors and contemporaries had already approached the question of the origin of languages in systematic treatises: John Locke in 1690 (*An Essay concerning Human Understanding*), Etienne Bonnot de Condillac in 1746 (*Essai sur l'origine des connaissances humaines; Essay on the Origin of Human Knowledge*), Julien Offroy de La Mettrie in 1747 (*L'homme machine; Man the Machine*), Pierre Louis de Maupertuis in 1749 (*Réflexions philosophiques sur l'origine des langues; Philosophical Reflections on the Origin of Languages*), Anne-Robert-Jacques Turgot in 1751 (*Réflexions sur les langues; Reflections on Languages*). All these thinkers were, to some degree, turning around the void that had begun to open up within the biblical account of how there came to be speech and language: "Whatsoever Adam called every

455

living creature, that was the name thereof" (Genesis 2:19). Although few openly dismissed faith in God's revelation of language to Adam (if only because it was dangerous to do so in a theocratic monarchy), they all sought to give a parallel account of the same phenomenon that relied principally on reason rather than on divine intervention. Like Condillac, whose account is situated after the Flood and traces the invention of language to two children, one of each sex, who had been lost in the desert before learning to speak, Rousseau adopts a procedure for wiping clean the slate of human nature without insulting faith in a divine creator. "Adam spoke, Noah spoke; but it is known that Adam was taught by God himself. In scattering, the children of Noah abandoned agriculture, and the first common tongue perished with the first society" (*Essay on the Origin,* p. 36). It is reason alone that is then taken as a guide in retracing the "progress" of that most fundamental of human institutions, the one without which no other institution is imaginable: language. And reason tells us to seek to know the origin of something if we would understand it in all its manifestations. Yet, by trying to think of language as other than divinely inspired, the philosophes had, paradoxically, let go the only hold on a thoroughly *reasonable* account deriving and developing from an identifiable point of origin. Their accounts, and especially Rousseau's, uncover a ground that reason cannot master because it must yield to the very "object" it purports to describe. Beginning with its own doubled point(s) of departure, the *Essai* performs language as the spacing out of differentiation in a process that can have no single, undifferentiated origin. Rather than reason's circumscribing language, this performance shows language to be always at work before and within reason, deferring at every point the reasonable distinctions that reason would establish in order to know its object.

This would not have been Rousseau's intention, of course. It is only unintentionally, inadvertently or unconsciously, that the *Essai* ends up assigning no origin to languages, deriving them instead from difference at the origin, difference without origin. At one point it is called passion as distinct from need; at another, it is called need as distinct from passion. Language is born as pure voice or vowel; language is born from the articulation of consonants. These different and seemingly contradictory assertions are distributed throughout the text, and even a casual reader of the *Essai* may come away from it dismayed by a dimly recognized pattern in which the oppositions put in place by argument are repeatedly overturned. This is because language has to some extent taken over the controls and is telling the story, but according to its "logic" of articulation among differences that is precisely not the logic of mutually exclusive contraries with which Rousseau, on some level, wants to account for them.

One can only speculate on why Rousseau never resolved to publish his *Essai.* Its first, posthumous publication, in 1781, was in a volume titled *Traités sur la musique* (*Treatises on Music*). (The *Essai*'s full title mentions melody and musical imitation, and eight of its twenty chapters treat of music.) Had he proceeded with the plan to publish it that he entertained in 1761 and again in 1763, then he might also have described more fully the circumstances of the work's composition and forestalled many of the questions that have been raised about when it was begun. According to the draft of a preface to his text, the *Essai* began as a fragment of his *Discours sur l'origine et les fondements de l'inégalité parmi les hommes* (1755; *Discourse on the Origin and Foundations of Inequality among Men*). Rousseau explains that he cut it from the *Discours* because it was too long and out of place, and then returned to it on different occasions over the next years. Although these details are somewhat sketchy, they still provide a plausible account of the *Essai's* composition. Why, then, have some literary historians and scholars nonetheless questioned their accuracy?

The first to do so at some length was Gustave Lanson in 1912. Lanson had been highly influential in revising literary study in France, moving it away from the strictly classical curriculum and remodeling it within the boundaries of a national tradition. In his article "L'unité de la pensée de J.-J. Rousseau" ("The Unity of J.-J. Rousseau's Thought"), Lanson disputed the date 1754, which Rousseau gave to the first version of the *Essai* and which other scholars had supported with reasoned argument. Lanson reasoned that the *"Essai sur l'origine des langues* is most assuredly in contradiction with the *Discours sur l'inégalité,"* whereas the latter work remains of a piece with Rousseau's later, comparable speculations in *Emile* (1762). From this he concluded (being concerned foremost with the *unity* of Rousseau's thought) that the *Essai* should be dated no later than 1750, that is, "from the period in which Rousseau's systematic views had not yet been formed" (p. 5). The *Essai,* in other words, does not fit the view of a unified system of thought which the mature Rousseau would have put in place with the *Discours sur l'inégalité* and from which he then never wavered. Dating the *Essai* before 1754 was necessary to save the unity of Rousseau's oeuvre. At the same time, Lanson's rewriting of this episode served to reinforce the notion of a progressive development of French literary history that could be systematically, rationally studied, one in which a chronological succession of dates would provide a reliable guide to national tradition. The place of Rousseau within such a history was crucial: more perhaps than that of any other pre-Revolutionary writer, Rousseau's thought had come to be identified (for good and for ill) with the course of a nation's history. It cannot be forgotten that some of the earliest and most fiercely systematic readers of *Du contrat social* (1762; *On the Social Contract*) were leaders of the Revolutionary National Convention: Robespierre, Saint-Just, Marat. The question of the internal coherence of that thought has therefore always been an issue for more than just a few literary historians.

Indeed, in 1912, the same year that Lanson published his article, the French government sponsored a celebration of the bicentenary of Rousseau's birth. The Action Française (a vehemently royalist, nationalist, anti-Semitic, right-wing party) seized upon this event as an occasion to attack the French Third Republic and to garner the sort of publicity it needed to attract adherents. Inspired by the Action Française, protests were heard in the Chamber of Deputies against the official glorification of this anarchist, decadent Romantic, while in their literary journal, *La revue critique,* Action Française adherents vilified the "cult" of

Rousseau. The ideologues of this growing political faction applied themselves, in journal articles and in more comprehensive literary histories (such as Pierre Lasserre's *Le romantisme français,* 1907), to demolishing Rousseau's reputation as a serious thinker. Charles Maurras, the undisputed leader of the movement, who devised its intellectual program, wrote, in an article titled "Un ennemi de la France": "Reasoning comes easily to [Rousseau]; however, as he was born a sensitive and versatile soul, completely unable to embrace the truth with the force of conviction, his different reasonings are never in agreement with each other and, to put it bluntly, he is mad . . . He was the very type of the false prophet" (p. 451). This biblical allusion gives a hint of the anti-Semitic rhetoric with which Maurras assailed the writer. Rousseau was, after all, a plebeian; a non-Catholic, and a foreigner.

Vituperations of this sort against Rousseau were not new. They distinctly echo the attacks of some of his contemporaries—Voltaire, for example— although several new and ominous notes were sounded on the protofascist instruments of nationalism and racism. According to Maurras and his followers, Rousseau betrayed and incited others to betray the reasoned ordering of thought, which was the only sound basis of an ordered society and the very core of French national tradition.

In such an atmosphere, Lanson's revised dating of the *Essai* takes on a different appearance. Even though the *Essai* was no doubt little read outside scholarly circles, Lanson would have attempted, in effect, to remove it from the list of Rousseau's "systematic" writings so as to reinforce the argument of their coherent design and to counter the image of a madman's ravings that was fueling the political polemic. What is more, insofar as the *Essai* attempted to define and account for specific characteristics of different languages, it was explicitly concerned with the "national tradition" at issue in this polemic. Whatever its motives, however, the political significance of Lanson's gesture retains an uneasy ambiguity because, as a defense of Rousseau's thought in the face of an ideological onslaught from the reactionary right, it nonetheless ratifies the key terms chosen by the opponent. In one and the other camp, the privilege is given to reason, to system, which is to say, finally, to ordered development from a self-identical origin. From the ideology of such an order to the realization of nationalist and racist states is not, as history was about to demonstrate, a very big leap.

For the more than two centuries that they have been read, Rousseau's texts have provoked many such ambiguous confrontations between seemingly opposed interpretations. It is as if such reading engaged a program operating beyond the reach of oppositional categories and calculating their periodic reversal. The *Essai sur l'origine des langues,* although it has never been regarded as one of the major texts (it remains, for example, as yet unedited in the authoritative collection of the complete works begun by the Pléiade in 1959), has nevertheless played a curiously symptomatic role in this history of reversals. To illustrate: Although Lanson's hypothesis was soon refuted by another Rousseau scholar (Pierre-Maurice Masson, writing in 1913), in 1964 the debate about the *Essai's* chronological place was reopened in an article by Jean Starobinski, author of the highly regarded *Jean-Jacques Rousseau: La transparence et l'obstacle* (1957; *Jean-Jacques Rousseau: Transparency and Obstruction*). Starobinski in effect returned to Lanson's argument that certain of the *Essai*'s key concepts are incompatible with the conceptual design of the *Discours sur l'inégalité* and *Emile*. The interpretation of the *Essai* had come full circle in fifty years, leaving the enigma of its contradictory assertions about the origin of languages fully intact.

This was the situation when, in the mid-1960s, the French philosopher Jacques Derrida began to consider the *Essai* within the long tradition of Western thought about language. His *De la grammatologie* (1967; *Of Grammatology*), after addressing directly the issues of the text's internal contradictions and its inconsistency with other works, proceeded to lead the way out of the alternating explanations of this incoherence and to account for their ambiguous reversibility. The *Essai*, recalls Derrida, belongs to a tradition of thought based on what may be called units of presence, that is, terms considered to be always fully present to themselves, without any difference within them that could cause their meaning or function to deviate. To account for difference, this logic of presence must resort to various versions of accidental intervention from some point external to the unit of presence. Within such a tradition, the position of the origin is always granted the privilege of absolute self-presence—a presupposition that, when dealing with language, leads invariably to placing spoken language closer to the origin than written language: writing is undeniably a mode of "absent presence" (of the writer and the writer's intention) and requires the intervention of elements external to meaning itself (such as the material support of writing), whereas the spoken word seems to remain uncontaminated by this potential difference from itself. Rousseau follows this pattern more or less to the letter. By restoring its outline in the *Essai*, however, Derrida is able to isolate that which exceeds the pattern and falls outside the bounds traced by the logic of presence. He can distinguish, that is, between what Rousseau *meant* to say and what he actually *did* say, or rather, *write*. Rousseau meant to identify an origin of speech, a moment and a space of self-presence; he meant to maintain a clear exteriority of speech to writing, the latter coming to represent the former and, by leading ever further from the origin, to supplant it. Yet this logic of representation of and substitution for an original presence cannot close itself off; it must be supplemented by another logic, which is that, precisely, of the supplement. Rousseau's description of language as a movement of substitution requires that he use the verb *suppléer* in its two, nonsynonymous senses in French: "to supplant" and "to supplement." In the terms *suppléer* and *supplément*, in other words, an *internal difference* forces the logic of presence to have recourse to another logic. According to this other logic, which the *Essai* performs over and against what Rousseau would have meant to say or to describe, there is a lack of presence already at the origin that must be supplied or supplemented by some external, or different, term. In this way, the *Essai* inscribes the origin in a general movement of supplementarity that is itself without identifiable origin. If, then, the origin of languages can tend to become lost or get supplanted, it is because language could never have originated in a single point or term, but only in a supplemental relation among differences.

This, then, is how the *Essai* would have performed the story of language in writing: not as a derivation from an origin that had conferred on each language its separate and unique identity, but rather as a translation across different tongues necessary before there could be anything called an original, national language. This is also why one can neither place Rousseau within the tradition of French literature nor exclude him from it without doing great violence to the language in which he wrote.

Bibliography: Georges Benrekassa, *Fables de la personne: Pour une histoire de la subjectivité* (Paris: Presses Universitaires de France, 1985). Jacques Derrida, *De la grammatologie* (Paris: Minuit, 1967); translated by Gayatri Chakravorty Spivak as *Of Grammatology* (Baltimore: Johns Hopkins University Press, 1974). Guy Harnois, *Les théories du langage en France de 1660 à 1821* (Paris: Mercure de France, 1929). Gustave Lanson, "L'unité de la pensée de J.-J. Rousseau," *Annales de la Société Jean-Jacques Rousseau,* 8 (1912). Pierre-Maurice Masson, *La religion de J.-J. Rousseau,* 3 vols. (Paris: Hachette, 1913). Charles Maurras, "Un ennemi de la France," in *Oeuvres capitales,* vol. 1 (Paris: Flammarion, 1958). Jean-Jacques Rousseau, *Essai sur l'origine des langues où il est parlé de la mélodie et de l'imitation musicale,* ed. Charles Porset (Paris: Nizet, 1969); translated by John H. Moran as *Essay on the Origin of Languages Which Treats of Melody and Musical Imitation,* in *On the Origin of Language: Two Essays,* ed. John H. Moran and Alexander Gode (Chicago: University of Chicago Press, 1966). Jean Starobinski, *Jean-Jacques Rousseau: Transparency and Obstruction,* trans. Arthur Goldhammer (Chicago: University of Chicago Press, 1988).

Peggy Kamuf

ᴇᴥ❧ 1754

Etienne Bonnot de Condillac Publishes His *Traité des sensations*

From Natural Philosophy to Scientific Discourse

How to speak about the material world became a central concern during the French Enlightenment. A major motivation of the Enlightenment philosophers was to develop an authoritative voice able to counter that of the church and the divinely ordained monarchy and to justify working changes in the social and political order. Extending a tradition begun by Montaigne and Descartes that flowered into the Port-Royal *Grammaire* (1660) and *Logique* (1662), they complemented it with Newton and Locke. Essentially, their enterprise involved presenting language as one component in a triadic interactive system: the structure of the world, mirrored in the structure of thought, is expressed in the structure of language. A language perfectly adequate to the world should therefore result in statements whose truth value is self-evident and automatically eliminate issues of competing opinion—for who can argue with nature? The answer to this question was simple and ironic: God. When he created the material world, God both provided its dynamism and set its laws. The philosophers' efforts to build up an authority able to challenge the church's was thus stymied unless the natural world could be recast in terms that dispensed with the necessity of having recourse to God as lawgiver.

This issue became central with the split of natural history, a formerly indistinct mode of speaking about the material world, into two diverging disciplines. With Denis Diderot's *De l'interprétation de la nature* (1753–54; *On the Interpretation of Nature*), which continued the reflections on sight and touch begun in his *Lettre sur les aveugles* (1749; *Letter on the Blind*) and which ended in *Le rêve de d'Alembert* (wr. 1769, pub. 1831; *D'Alembert's Dream*), natural history diverged from positivist science into an explicitly literary program. The second and, to modern readers, less familiar tradition runs from Etienne Bonnot de Condillac to Antoine Laurent Lavoisier's chemical nomenclature, to Pierre-Simon de Laplace, and to the positivist natural sciences of the 19th century.

In 1754 Condillac published the *Traité des sensations* (*Treatise on Sensations*)—the centerpiece of a group of works that included the *Traité des systèmes* (1749; *Treatise on Systems*) and culminated in the *Logique* (1780), his most renowned work. Whereas the *Traité des sensations* intends to give a basis to scientific work by providing a detailed description of the way the body's senses interact with the material world to produce knowledge, the *Logique* describes the structure of thought processes and thus of arguments that are predetermined by such a body. The intersection of these two works shows how Condillac hoped to derive an unshakable authority for all reasoned argument.

Condillac's *Logique* is exemplary of the way the Enlightenment promoted vision into the paradigmatic position for explaining both the structure of the material world and the natural, logical procedures for observing it.

> Now what is this order? . . . it is the order in which nature presents the objects to us. There are some objects which attract our gaze more particularly . . . and all the other objects seem to be arranged around them and for the sake of them . . . Thus we begin with the principal objects: we observe them successively and compare them in order to judge the relations in which they stand. When, by this means, we have grasped their respective locations, we successively observe all those objects which fill the intervals, comparing each one with the nearest principal object and determining its position. At this point we distinguish all the objects whose form and location we have grasped, and we encompass them all in a single gaze. The order which exists among them in our mind is thus no longer successive; it is simultaneous. It is the same as the order in which the objects exist. (*Logic,* bk. 1, chap. 2, pp. 67–69)

The observer then proceeds to tag each object with a word, whence the importance eventually given to tabular scientific nomenclatures, whose structures mimic the relations existing between the objects.

The *Traité des sensations* provides the origin of this sensory construal of observation and knowledge. In it, rather than showing how we can understand our methods of observation, Condillac tries to show how they might have come

461

about. He introduces his famous conceit of the living statue—really a body without a past—that acquires one sense at a time and whose consequent reactions to the material world Condillac analyzes to prove that no knowledge need be innate. (If it were innate, it would thereby imply an ordering providence, which is precisely the function that has to be negated.) The *Traité* differs from the later *Logique* in that the most basic notions, such as identity and difference, past and present, inside and outside, are not explained by analogy with vision, but are derived from touch. Condillac holds that vision becomes in the end the most powerful tool and the sense through which the others are understood, but only after touch has turned *seeing* into *observing*.

For every sense except touch, sensations are perceived by the statue as being only modifications of itself. But all these perceptions are passive; it has as yet no understanding of the notion of self. The statue perceives itself as the perfume of the rose it smells or the color of the tree it sees. "It has no knowledge of its body at the time it experiences such sensations. To discover it, it must be able to analyze, that is to say it must successively observe its *self,* in all the parts in which it appears to be found. Now it is certain that it could not make this analysis without help. It is, then, nature which enables it to do it" (*Treatise on Sensations,* bk. 2, chap. 4, p. 3). By nature, Condillac here means capacities that the statue has as a result of its organization. The one sense that works differently from the others is touch, for it is the only one to produce a doubled sensation: the sensation felt by the statue's touching hand is mirrored by its body's corresponding sensation of being touched until, in its motion across surfaces, it passes to a foreign object. At that point the statue conceptualizes "otherness" and "boundary" and, by opposition, "self." Once it can conceive of otherness, the involuntary movements provoked by pleasure and pain are perceived as motion toward or away from external sources of sensation. It thus learns that it does move and can then will to move, which allows it to explore its own motions. Only touch, therefore, can go from passive perception to willed action.

Motion, then, is always required for discrimination, hence for objectification. The statue conceives of the space around it, then of a succession of objects, and finally the notion of succession (*Treatise,* bk. 2, chap. 3, p. 8). When it understands succession, it not only can will; it also can compare and judge. "It thus analyzes naturally, and this confirms what I have demonstrated in my logic, that nature of itself teaches us to analyze . . . Thus we see why our statue, being without reflexion in the other senses, commences to reflect with touch" (bk. 2, chap. 8, pp. 12, 14). Once it can judge through touch, the statue's passive perception (seeing) is changed into active vision (observing). For then it observes that color, which it had taken to be only a quality of the surface of its eyes, is the index of either a boundary or a volume that it has already felt. Thus vision becomes an extension of touch. Touch has been generalized to become a method, the analytic method of continual, willed comparison and differentiation, as is clear in Condillac's choice of images to describe analytic vision. "We do not have ideas as soon as we see; we only get ideas when we observe with order and method. In a word, our eyes must analyze, for they will not grasp the whole of the simplest shape if they have not observed all its parts separately one after the other and in their natural order" (bk. 2, chap. 3, p. 6). Memory, ordered by the notion of succession, allows the statue to synthesize, and the eyes take over. But the eyes are so powerful that once touch has trained them, they induce weakness in the other senses. The statue forgets that touch was the mother of and remains the pattern for observation; it thinks from then on through the paradigm of analytic vision presented in the *Logique.*

Now the argument followed by Condillac in the *Traité des sensations* has the same structure as the analytic procedure followed by the senses themselves. One tiny step at a time, like the statue, we follow quietly, simply, through a chain of linked observations derived from the relentless operation of reflection on sensations. We move from a state of conceptual insensibility to the synthesized picture of a thinking, judging person furnished with moral principles. The work is dry. Nonetheless, it is rhetorically effective. It soon becomes obvious, however, that this is not merely an astute because effective choice, but that Condillac has chosen to speak this way because he is arguing that it is the only rhetoric that maintains authority. This is a self-justifying rhetoric. (The same neutral tone and analytic structure characterize, perhaps to an even greater extent, the *Logique,* which also functions in a self-authorizing rhetorical mode.)

How does this rhetoric work? The structure of Condillac's analysis requires that language be in its essence denotative. In other words, each sensation must directly yield or eventually reduce to a single idea, represented by one word. Even for categories there is a single form that all elements in the category's set of objects imply. A language that works in accordance with this constraint will always properly, cleanly, designate the world. But, conversely, if a word must always denote one and only one analytic element, it follows that no metaphors, allusions, or suggestions can be used, for they all rely on at least a double referent for an utterance—in other words, on the shift from a denotative to a connotative field. Because poetic or literary uses of language depend on connotative suggestion and figurative multiplications of meaning, literary language for Condillac can lead only into a primordial confusion of referent. The philosopher who writes literarily can neither recall reliably to himself nor indicate clearly to his reader the cause of sensation. He therefore loses his clear analytic grasp of the network of cause-and-effect relationships structuring his world. He can no longer speak truly. He can no longer speak or even think with authority. Metaphor is, for Condillac, at the origin of superstition and religion.

> The statue feels at every moment its dependence on its environment . . . convinced that it does nothing unintentionally, it seems to see design in all the actions it discerns. It only judges them by what it notices in itself . . . It thinks, then, that what pleases it has the intention of pleasing it, and . . . it now wishes the objects to have the intention of loading it with benefits and of warding off evil. It wishes in fact everything to be propitious, and its wish is a sort of prayer . . . In a word it will worship all things upon which it depends. (*Treatise,* bk. 4, chap. 4, pp. 1–2)

The statue's metaphorical extrapolation of its own experience of having intention, of willing, into the external sources of its pain and pleasure is an important mistake in analytic thinking. Desire provokes figurative, poetic thinking. The true Fall, then, is not from faith into pride born of reason, but from reason into religion born by metaphor out of desire. Once the objects of religious faith—the gods as causal agents—are shown to be illusions derived from error, they can hardly be held up as creators of natural law. By showing how such error both could have been avoided and can be conclusively demonstrated after the fact, the analytic method—a "naturally" derived method, both for observation and for exposition—achieves final authority. It is then unassailable with respect not only to its own logical coherence but also to its demonstration of the logical faults supporting its major opponent, religion.

For its authority to be maintained, however, the method' must first be adhered to. Natural history had been a consciously figurative form of persuasion in which knowledge itself and the author's way of presenting it were assumed to be clearly distinct both in reality and to the reader. After Condillac, however, nature had to speak denotatively through the scientist. Any authorial posturing would disturb the denotative functioning. As a result, the materialist scientific reader would assess the truth of an argument partly by looking for neutrality of tone and for the avoidance of literary mechanisms. Condillac's oeuvre is the best model of the new style and rhetoric of scientific writing, a style recognizable to any reader of modern scientific texts. The literature of science was no longer a subset of literature, but was placed in direct opposition to it. Analysis dismissed poetry, and nature superseded the author as the voice in the scientific text.

The hard sciences in France adopted Condillac's authoritative antirhetoric wholeheartedly, as demonstrated most notably by Lavoisier's extensive quotations from the *Logique* in his 1787 reform of chemical nomenclature and his *Traité élémentaire de chimie* (1789; *Elementary Treatise of Chemistry*). Condillac's work taught the scientists a way to reach and transmit scientific truth; the issue of generating authority became subsidiary to that of assessing truth. For two other groups, however, less well known as descendants of Condillac but just as closely tied to his project, the issue of truth was still subsidiary to the issue of authority. Both the Revolutionary polemicists and the Ideologues drew on his work in order to guarantee the efficacy of their own programs not for transmitting knowledge but, like the early Enlightenment philosophers, for bringing about social change. The Revolutionaries, especially Robespierre, wished to purify natural language of the resonances of the ancien régime and to build a powerful political rhetoric. But the Ideologues went much further. They planned to eliminate even the possibility of such inflammatory revolutionary rhetoric by setting up a complex and sophisticated centralized national school system. Its courses would all be taught in the depersonalized language; their content would be the neutral analytic knowledge. Rather than undermining the established modes of authority as the Revolutionaries had wished, the Ideologues' new curriculum was intended to produce obedient, productive, and dedicated citizens for the new post-Revolutionary state.

See also 1751, 1769, 1791 (13 January), 1799, 1808.

Bibliography: Sylvain Auroux, *La sémiotique des encyclopédistes* (Paris: Payot, 1979). Etienne Bonnot de Condillac, *Logic,* trans. W. R. Albury (New York: Abaris, 1980). Condillac, *Treatise on Sensations,* trans. Geraldine Carr (Los Angeles: University of Southern California, 1930). Michel Foucault, *Les mots et les choses* (Paris: Gallimard, 1966); translated (no translator named) as *The Order of Things: An Archeology of the Human Sciences* (New York: Pantheon, 1972). Mary Slaughter, *Universal Languages and Scientific Taxonomy in the Seventeenth Century* (Cambridge: Cambridge University Press, 1982).

Wilda Anderson

✐ *1759, January*

Voltaire Publishes in Geneva His Philosophical Tale *Candide, ou l'optimisme, traduit de l'Allemand de Mr. le docteur Ralph*

On Cultivating One's Garden

Voltaire's *Candide,* published anonymously in 1759 and disseminated illegally as part of the subversive literature that flourished during the ancien régime, is the undisputed masterpiece of its genre, the *conte philosophique,* or philosophical tale. Candide, a young German who has been indoctrinated by Dr. Pangloss, a comical advocate of Gottfried Wilhelm von Leibniz's philosophy, in the belief that "all is for the best in the best of possible worlds," approaches every situation in the naïve hope that it will bear out his optimism. But after being ejected from the "earthly paradise" of a tranquil Westphalian fiefdom, he undergoes repeated misfortunes and failures that teach a common lesson. The adventures of Candide and the little band of friends he acquires bring to light a whole catalogue of injustices and abuses, perversities of fate, irrationalities of custom, and individual vices or follies that, taken together, frustrate on a global scale the natural human pursuit of happiness. The hero's education begins when he finds himself an unwilling soldier in the midst of a "glorious butchery" that violates the most elementary norms of civilized behavior, all "in accordance with law" (p. 92). Deserting to Holland, he suffers the effects of religious bigotry and observes the symptoms of syphilis, a gift from "love, the consoler of mankind," which has meanwhile ravaged Pangloss (p. 96). While journeying to Lisbon, Candide is shipwrecked within sight of port. He survives only to be injured in the terrible earthquake that devastated the city in 1755. He narrowly escapes death at the hands of the Inquisition, which is convinced that roasting a few heretics "over a slow fire" is "an infallible recipe for preventing the ground from shaking" (p. 104). An old woman tells Candide her life story, an unrelieved sequence of horrors that works like a preview for the whole tale. By chance he kills the Grand Inquisitor and must flee to America. In Buenos Aires he is bullied by a dictatorial Spanish governor. Candide then visits the Jesuit colony of Paraguay, where *"los padres* have everything and the people nothing; the government is a model of reason and justice" (p. 135). During another escapade, he learns that the virtue of the noble savage in the state of nature includes a penchant for bestiality and cannibalism. In Surinam he meets a Negro slave who has been disciplined by having his leg and a hand cut off, and who says: "This is the price of eating sugar in Europe" (p. 160). Candide is robbed of a vast fortune in gold and precious stones that he had brought out of Eldorado, a utopian country unknown to outsiders. On returning to Europe, he is duped by swindlers in Paris. While briefly in England, he is shocked to see an admiral of the fleet executed so that "the others might be encouraged" to do battle more vigorously. In Venice he witnesses a different kind of adversity: the deadly boredom of those who have everything they desire. He also discovers, while dining with several deposed kings, that even royal birth confers no sure advantage. Finally, Candide and his followers settle down in the humble "paradise regained" of a farm near Constantinople. Their communal routine of work preserves them from three great ills: want, idleness, and vice. Although Pangloss continues to profess his metaphysics of optimism, the closing remark is Candide's: "That is all well and good, but it is necessary to cultivate our garden."

The dénouement is thus an allegory of social meliorism, but it represents such a small triumph in comparison with the magnitude of evil and pain in the world that a sense of letdown, even of banality, is hard to avoid. There is, moreover, something distinctly selfish and (in Enlightenment terms) unphilosophical about the rescue of a few lucky souls from the desperate human condition that has been depicted. Voltaire ends *Candide* in such a low key not because he thinks his garden apologue is a satisfactory solution to the prevalence in life of so many wrongs and afflictions, but because this particular ending suits best his group of characters and the kind of experiences he has imagined for them. What else could a simpleton like Candide, who requires an avalanche of rebuttals to see at last through the optimistic nonsense of Pangloss, have been expected to do about all the predicaments he encountered? The conclusion is artistically right. But whether it is philosophically right is another matter. Candide should not be mistaken for his creator, Voltaire, who has meanwhile given his own answer to the problem of evil.

Candide came into being from Voltaire's belief that, in the great majority of people, the organ of moral consciousness needed to be revitalized. The human race, for the sake of its peace of mind, had developed over time elaborate defenses against the reality of evil, which was variously minimized, ignored, justified, rationalized, tolerated, romanticized, or denied. The evasions that provoked Voltaire the most were the optimist's claim that manifest evil is hidden good; the Christian's faith in a beneficent providence, the value of suffering, and eternal rewards in heaven; the egotist's unconcern about misfortunes that befall others; the cynic's dismissal of evil by stressing its pervasiveness; and, of course, everyone's wish to forget what is unpleasant. The ideological purpose of *Candide* is to do away with all these escapisms because, instead of lessening the sum of evil, they augment and perpetuate it. The first step in alleviating or curing any human ill is to identify it lucidly and unflinch-ingly—to see and denounce it for what it is: war, religious intolerance, class privilege, poverty, disease, slavery, natural catastrophes, political oppression, superstition, and ignorance.

The philosophical teaching of the tale is, therefore, a redefinition of evil in essentially humanitarian terms. It is shown to consist not in breaking the rules of religion or society, nor even in contravening natural law and the urgings of conscience, which were otherwise so important to Voltaire's deism. God and transcendent symbols or concepts are noticeably absent from *Candide*. Evil is equated, from the sole standpoint of the sensitive human subject, with the immanent experience of loss and misery, which is why no distinction is made between mishaps such as syphilis or earthquakes and those owing to personal acts. Nor is Voltaire interested in explaining why and how evil can exist at all. Knowing intuitively what is bad in human affairs, he wastes no effort on inquiring into its general causation or ontological status (these being issues treated with scorn via Panglossian metaphysics). He operates, instead, on the hope that it can be remedied, if not eliminated completely. The basic message of *Candide,* expressed more by example than by precept, is not retirement to the calm and safety of a garden, but the dangerous duty to oppose *in the world,* as best we can, all practical evils, wherever and in whatever guise, or rather disguise, they may occur. This interpretation has in its favor that it construes *Candide* as the essence of its author's life, personality, and writings.

Voltaire saw his reader as at heart a decent sort but morally stupefied by a brew of religion, metaphysics, political dogma, social convention, and class prejudice. The aim of *Candide* was to bring such a reader, through verbal shock therapy, to an awareness of the cruelty, injustice, and suffering everywhere around him, and at the same time to excite in him, with his consent, an appro-priate reaction of outrage. That Voltaire judged his potential audience with keen foresight is attested by the continued relevance of his masterpiece. Even so, some may protest that this is not philosophy, but merely literature with a gigantic ax to grind. Yet if Leibniz, whose credentials as a philosopher are not in doubt, could write a lengthy book—*Essais de théodicée* (1710; *Essays on The-odicy*)—to argue that evil has no objective validity in the cosmic scheme of things and is therefore nothing to complain about, why should it be unphilo-sophical for Voltaire to reply that evil is objectively real in the *human* scheme of things and a scandal not to be borne? If this was not philosophy as it had come to be known over the centuries, it certainly was philosophy as understood and propagated by the philosophes of the French Enlightenment.

But the success of *Candide* depends ultimately on the skill with which its literary form, style, and tone are adapted to its content. For instance, the rhe-torical figure most often and most brilliantly used is that of irony, which is also

467

the main source of the work's unceasing and mordant satire. The choice of optimistic philosophy as the immediate target in a much wider spectrum of delusion and foolishness was itself a strategic masterstroke, from which everything else follows naturally, for one can hardly think of a motif more vulnerable to ridicule than the Panglossian credo. Optimism serves as a background against which the hideousness of existence can be etched with optimal sharpness. It is beside the point whether or not Voltaire refutes the proposition that "all is for the best in the best of possible worlds." In any event, there could be no question of disproving it, because metaphysical constructs have a built-in immunity to falsification. Thus Pangloss, despite all empirical evidence to the contrary, mouths his opinion to the end, and Candide, who by then knows better, has no means of negating it. He simply ignores it, and behind his attitude of disdain we surmise Voltaire's rejection not only of metaphysical optimism but also of metaphysics in general. As for the mockery heaped on "the best of possible worlds," it works by exploiting an ambiguity in that formula. Although the "best possible" of anything could be "bad" as well as "good," since in logic the notion of possibility implies no judgment of value, the reader cannot but assume that the "best possible" will be something good rather than bad. Having reduced Leibniz's optimism to a convenient quid pro quo, Voltaire plays on it to highlight the contradiction between what the reader imagines optimism to be and what, in a metaphysical sense, it actually is. The resulting incongruity never ceases to be comical and absurd, as we find over and over again that all is for the *worst* in the best of possible worlds.

Although the nature of irony in *Candide* may not be different from that in Voltaire's other works, it manages to be exceptionally corrosive because of the far-ranging thematic structure that sustains and reinforces it. Moreover, ironic discourse, as the art of saying something but meaning the opposite, was well suited to philosophical propaganda under a government that censored and suppressed ideas it considered subversive. At the same time, it created a special bond of complicity between the text and its readers, who were made privy to the hidden sense of a coded message. The irony in *Candide* served also as a veiled imperative to bring about change in the established sociopolitical system. When Voltaire shows how appallingly at odds the world is with Pangloss's belief that "all is well," he does not make a neutral statement of fact. The ironic tension between theory and actuality arouses a feeling that things *ought to be* other than they are. The satire on metaphysical optimism is, consequently, a means by which Voltaire affirms his own nonmetaphysical optimism, that of a practical reformer who wants all to be as well as possible in the human condition.

This philosophical aim of the tale is supported by its rococo manner: light, quippish, playful, amusing, frivolous. Such traits might seem, at first, to be contrary to the moral earnestness, indeed grimness, of its underlying subject. Yet it is no small part of Voltaire's artistry that he turns the rococo aesthetic to his advantage. The jarring contrast between the awful events that are recounted and the apparently smug, even joking, detachment of the author as spectator—for example, in the scene in which the Lisbon ladies sip cool drinks while watching, as if it were a sport, the burning alive of heretics—brings home to the reader, more forcefully than righteous condemnation, the full atrocity of an auto-da-fé. This is so because, instead of being told how to react, we are made to take upon ourselves the responsibility for the indignation we cannot help but feel. In *Candide,* Voltaire treads with dexterity a fine line between smiling aloofness and intense involvement. But there is perhaps an inherent risk in the rococo method of being dead-serious. What if the reader comes away with the impression that the work is meant as a supreme lesson in how to laugh despite, or even at, human misfortune? Although some might understand it that way, one would have to be singularly obtuse, or entirely lacking in empathy, to see *Candide* as nothing but an entertainment.

The Voltairian *conte philosophique* is a sui generis hybrid of fiction and philosophy. The fusion of these two elements yields, as in a chemical compound, a product that differs from either taken separately. The philosophical component, in being fictionalized, is freed from the necessity for analytic examination and logical proof of what it asserts, as well as from the necessity of weighing objections and avoiding inconsistencies. It is content to argue its case and disarm criticism by essentially rhetorical strategies, such as illustration, fabulation, wordplay, wit, irony, and satire. Conversely, the fictional component, by being philosophized, also loses some of its usual qualities. One decisive result is the abandonment of verisimilitude. The literary development of an idea or theme through generalization and a testing of its limits causes the narrative in *Candide* to be not only unrealistic but at times fantastic. The intent behind Voltaire's exaggeration of reverses, injustice, and absurdity is not, of course, to misrepresent the facts, but to emphasize their abnormality, while also preparing the ground for all sorts of comic and satiric side effects. There is an art of exaggeration, as of everything else. It is a measure of Voltaire's mastery that the grotesque and improbable features of the tale soon acquire a plausibility of their own, as realism ceases to be the sole criterion of reality. Besides, by expressing prohibited opinions through a fiction without claims to realistic reference, the author was freer to say what he wanted in a climate of intellectual repression.

Another result of mixing fiction and philosophy is the type of characterization peculiar to *Candide*. Its dramatis personae, instead of resembling flesh-and-blood individuals, are in large part allegorizations of some trait or condition. The hero, as his name connotes, is the soul of candor, guilelessness, and inexperience. Cunégonde, as woman incarnate, is the grand panacea of love that Candide pursues in vain throughout the *conte*. Her brother, the Baron, personifies aristocratic bias and arrogance. Pangloss is the oracle of metaphysical futility. The Old Woman sums up in her desolate person all the indignities and insults to which humanity is heir. Cacambo is the embodiment of friendship and loyalty. Martin, as the foil to Pangloss, speaks for pessimism. The lesser characters may similarly be assigned various labels. Everyone, tending toward metonymy and caricature, substitutes more or less for an abstract idea in the narrative argument. Not only are Voltaire's "marionettes" suitably passive victims of circumstance, but he can manipulate them at will, shaping the story with maximum ease to make whatever point he wishes, since psychological density, being absent, offers no resistance to philosophizing. Despite his pose of affective distance, he is thus ubiquitous in the work, communicating at every turn the views and values he holds as a thinker.

The open-ended episodic structure of *Candide,* resembling that of a pica-resque novel, makes it possible to amass a great quantity of evidence and to keep up a relentless satire on the human condition in rebuttal of the optimistic thesis. When combined with the travel motif, this narrative plan universalizes the problem of evil, implying that the tale concerns humanity, not just a few members of a given society. There is, for the sake of propaganda, much the-matic insistence and repetition in Voltaire's storytelling, but luckily this is redeemed by the swiftness of his tempo. More happens in a dozen pages of *Candide* than in the whole of many full-length novels. Swept along by the restless energy of its prose and by its continually changing peripeteia, the reader is disinclined to complain that each of the episodes amounts to the same dis-illusioning commentary on optimism. The only constraint on the author, in the highly flexible form he has chosen, is the aesthetic one of not boring us. Nor are we disheartened by the exhaustive inventory of human woes. The tale's curiously sanguine tone derives mainly from the liveliness of Voltaire's style and temperament, which counteracts the starkness of his subject. It is owing also to the fact that his little band of characters are "survivors" who, in their con-frontation with the worst, come through with their vitality intact. Their his-tory of defeats and anguish reassures us that stamina and solidarity can win out in the end over both human malice and inhuman fate.

The relative lack of fixed form or rules that typified narrative prose fiction, as compared to poetry and drama, in 18th-century France facilitated Voltaire's encapsulation in *Candide* of a lifetime of experience and reflection. He had something new and difficult to express, for which the existing fictional modes were inadequate; so he invented and perfected one that answered his purpose. *Candide* is also, to some extent, a self-parody that pokes fun at the contempo-rary novel, for nothing in it was meant to appear solemn. True to this casual approach, the work unfolds with the spontaneity of an improvisation. Yet it is probably correct to say that Voltaire's voluminous production as a philosophe and writer is now known to most people only through this one quintessential text. Its popularity from 1759 to the present lies in his unrivaled ability to render an ideology of huge practical importance not merely accessible but fas-cinating to a broad public.

The *conte philosophique* first rose to prominence in France during the 18th century under the stimulus of the Enlightenment. The *conte* as such was widely known and appreciated at the time in a variety of subgenres: the tale of love; oriental tales reminiscent of *The Thousand and One Nights;* the didactic *conte moral;* fairy tales; erotic stories in the tradition of Boccaccio; folkloric *contes* related to the fabliaux; and still others. All these kinds of tale could, and often did, contain material that mirrored the "philosophical" tendencies of the age.

But in Voltaire's hands the *conte philosophique,* while drawing on various features of a rich literary background, achieved a form that was unique. If *Candide* is taken as its most typical and best-realized example, the philosophical tale may be defined as an episodic narrative, more imaginary than realistic, structured by frequent changes of scene resulting from travel, and controlled by a central theme—optimism, destiny, providence, progress, relativism, natural law— that involves the problem of evil. The unfolding of the plot confirms, undermines, or otherwise qualifies the idea under consideration by testing it against a series of concrete experiences and observations in the world at large. Voltaire's other *contes philosophiques*—such as *Zadig ou la destinée* (1747; *Zadig, or Destiny*), *L'ingénu* (1767; *The Huron*), *Micromégas* (1752), *Le monde comme il va* (1748; *The World as It Goes*), *Les voyages de Scarmentado* (1756), *Histoire de Jenni* (1775)—conform in varying degrees to the paradigm. Still other of his tales— *La princesse de Babylone* (1768), *Le taureau blanc* (1773; *The White Bull*), *Jeannot et Colin* (1764), *Cosi-Sancta* (1784)—bear some resemblance to those works but can more accurately be called parables; for, though they deal with some point of moral truth or common wisdom, they do not pose any recognizable problem of philosophy. On the other hand, *Candide* has been likened, as a philosophical fiction, to Samuel Johnson's *Rasselas* (1759) and Denis Diderot's *Jacques le fataliste et son maître* (wr. 1771–1780? pub. 1796; *Jacques the Fatalist and His Master*). What, ultimately, distinguishes the Voltairian *conte philosophique* is its total design, both form and content, in furtherance of the overall aim of the Enlightenment, which was to criticize and correct social and political inequities and the collective mentality behind them.

Bibliography: William F. Bottiglia, *Voltaire's "Candide": Analysis of a Classic* (Geneva: Institut et Musée Voltaire, 1964). Jean Sareil, *Essai sur Candide* (Geneva: Droz, 1967). Voltaire, *Candide, ou l'optimisme,* ed. René Pomeau (Paris: Nizet, 1966). Ira O. Wade, *Voltaire and "Candide"* (Princeton: Princeton University Press, 1959).

Aram Vartanian

ᔈᕫ 1759, 23 April

The Duc de Lauragais Pays the Théâtre-Français an Indemnity of 12,000 Livres to Remove Spectators from the Stage

Clearing the Stage

Voltaire's tragedy *Sémiramis* (1748) was written in an attempt to outdo a play of the same name by Prosper Jolyot de Crébillon, who had since become the royal censor. Its plot wavers between a tragic resolution (in which the prince avenges his father the king's murder by killing his mother) and a sentimental avoidance of tragedy (in which the son forgives his repentant and loving mother, the queen). At the end of act 4, Queen Semiramis reminds her son Arzace of the orders given him (in an echo of *Hamlet*) by the late king's ghost: "Ninus has commanded you to reign in my place; / Fear his vengeful spirits." But Arzace hopes that "they will be moved / By a mother's remorse and a son's tears" (act 4, scene 4). Voltaire finally tries to resolve the conflict by having Arzace kill his mother involuntarily, making the son's hand a "blind instrument" (act 5, scene 5) of the gods' will. At the first performance of *Sémiramis,* there were so many spectators onstage that the actor playing King Ninus' ghost stumbled and nearly fell, completely spoiling the Shakespearean effect. Voltaire is then said to have interrupted the ensuing peals of laughter by bellowing, "Place à l'ombre!" ("Make way for the ghost!").

These onstage seats were one of the more curious aspects of theatrical arrangements during the ancien régime. The most original and significant feature of these narrow, rectangular theaters was the *parterre,* an inclined floor occupying the space of today's orchestra seats, where much of the audience stood for periods of up to four hours. The rest of the audience sat, in various sections of the ground floor, in the loges, or onstage. Not only did these onstage seats hamper the actors' freedom of movement; they also enabled the occupants to become unofficial participants in the spectacle. This practice came to an end on 23 April 1759, thanks to the duc de Lauragais, who paid the actors of the Théâtre-Français an indemnity of 12,000 livres. This complete separation of the actors from the audience is symptomatic of other, more far-reaching changes in serious (noncomic) 18th-century French theater and society. The 18th century is the century of *embourgeoisement,* that is, when bourgeois values and structures permeated and reorganized society. In theater, this process affected not only the kind of plays that were written and produced, but also their performance, staging, and reception—indeed, the very conception of theatrical illusion and space.

The problems encountered at the première of *Sémiramis* by the corpulent actor (Legrand) playing the king's ghost illustrate the nature of these changes. To the extent that our contemporary understanding of these transformations is affected by our own *embourgeoisement,* we can measure the distance that separated Voltaire's audience from Racine's in the previous century. In the bourgeois world, serious occasions require one's undivided attention and quiet respect: at the theater, for example, one is not supposed to make noise or even smoke, let alone interrupt the actors, laugh at them, or flirt with the person across the way. Yet Parisian audiences of the 17th and early 18th centuries were notorious for this kind of behavior, which would today be more appropriate at a baseball game. During tragedies, they chatted continually with each other and with the actors, blew whistles, and yawned as loudly as possible when they got bored. Paradoxically, these same audiences took the story fatally unfolding on stage with perfect, tragic seriousness. For them the story was real, because they thought it not only had really happened in the past but also was taking place again before their eyes (just as Catholics believed that the sacrifice of Christ was actually repeated in the eucharist); and yet they chatted, flirted, or (even in Racine's day) cried. Racine's audiences did not find levity incompatible with religious behavior, nor were they troubled by the presence of actors and spectators on the same stage. Indeed, lack of "seriousness" and onstage seats were part of the same, ritualized conception of theater. As Jean-Marie Apostolidès has argued, French classical tragedy symbolically replayed the king's ritual sacrifice in battle. Yet by Voltaire's time the sacrificed king had turned into a ridiculous ghost, and the presence of actors and spectators on the same stage had become intolerable. It had become impossible to give credence to the reality of tragic action; instead, it was necessary to redefine tragedy as an illusion that one knows is untrue but believes nonetheless: as a *fiction.* Likewise, spectators had to be removed from the stage to the shadows and installed in the respectful silence of bourgeois representation.

When Voltaire shouted "Place à l'ombre!" he was speaking like a man of the French classical age, clinging to the ideology and conventions of classical tragedy (interest of state, the three unities, alexandrines, subjects derived from antiquity) even though he had read Shakespeare (and translated him into the elegant French of regency salons). He demanded the abolition of onstage seats so that nothing might distract the audience from viewing the king's entry with suitable reverence. In his view, the terrifying events of great tragedy should instill a religious awe in the spectator. Yet the most popular new tragedies of the 18th century (such as Antoine Houdar de La Motte's *Inès de Castro,* 1723) testify to the *embourgeoisement* of this aristocratic genre. Fewer tragedies were produced during this period than in the previous century, but audiences continued to attend new tragedies in large numbers and to call for revivals of both Thomas and Pierre Corneille, as well as of Racine. On the other hand, they did not relate to these plays in quite the same way as previously. What the theatergoing public of Voltaire's time found most attractive in the tragedies of the previous century was no longer the spectacle of heroism and violence, but love. The most popular tragic actresses (Adrienne Lecouvreur, Mlle. Gaussin) carried off their greatest triumphs in the role of the tender victim (Ariadne, Racine's Bérénice, Voltaire's Zaïre) whose sufferings moved the audience to tears. Racine's audiences were already sensitive to the sentimental aspects of tragedy, but their 18th-century counterparts no longer believed that human beings were impotent before a fate decided by transcendent powers, or that human conflicts were essentially insoluble. The sense of tragedy, if not the genre itself, had been lost.

When Voltaire cried out "Place à l'ombre!" at the première of *Sémiramis,* he was enjoining the audience (composed largely of royal subjects) to show respect for a representation of the king's ghost. Yet his words take on a very different meaning in the work of Denis Diderot, where the pivotal figure (and ideal spectator) is no longer the king, but the bourgeois father. When the long-lost father makes his first appearance at the end of Diderot's first play, *Le fils naturel* (1757; *The Natural Son*), one recognizes that he has been the absent center of the whole play. The play reenacts events that are supposedly real, and Diderot fantasized a first performance in which the participants would recreate them, for their own benefit, with no audience or actors but themselves. But Lysimond, the natural son's father, having died before he could play his own part, had to

473

be replaced by a friend. The *place à l'ombre* here is that absent, offstage role, without which the performance cannot take place: a place in the shadows occupied first by Lysimond, then by his friend and by Diderot's alter ego (the character called Myself), who waits in the wings during the entire performance. Diderot imagines the ideal spectator in much the same way, as a father-author who feels for his children. With *Le fils naturel* and *Entretiens sur Le fils naturel* (1757; *Commentaries on "The Natural Son"*), followed by *Le père de famille* (*The Father*) and *Discours sur la poésie dramatique* (1758; *Discourse on Dramatic Poetry*), Diderot sought to found the poetics and practice of a new, "serious" genre.

Classical poetics in France precluded the possibility of taking the Third Estate seriously: since they are not noble, Molière's peasants or his M. Jourdain can only be ridiculous. Only the nobility and the interests of state affected by their actions are worthy of tragic representation. Hence the desire to see a new kind of play, in which the bourgeoisie might appear in a different light. This new genre is bourgeois, first, because it portrays strictly private concerns, which have no direct consequences for the state; whereas in a classical tragedy such as Racine's *Phèdre* (1677; *Phaedra*) the welfare of an entire kingdom had depended upon a conflict between father and son. Moreover, regardless of the new hero's social class, he lives a bourgeois life in the intimacy of the nuclear family. Likewise, his feelings and inner life enable him to sympathize with the human family as a whole. He (Diderot's theater is quite patriarchal) understands that beneath the trappings of royal power, Queen Clytemnestra is a mother. Relying upon this appeal to universal human nature, Diderot also calls for a number of related reforms in theatrical composition and performance: prose instead of verse; subdivision of the stage to allow representation of simultaneous actions; elimination of onstage seats and creation of a "fourth wall"; and, in various forms, a new emphasis upon visual rather than verbal elements. The combined effect of these reforms was to make theater more realistic or "natural," unlike the highly stylized, abstract reality of the classical stage.

Diderot's proposals also have a political, critical edge to them. He declares his opposition to those sudden reversals of fortune, which classical theater had labeled coups de théâtre (a convention that belongs to the public world and shifting alliances of the court), and calls instead for a new device, which he names the tableau. The latter portrays a moment when the action has stopped or (as in the opening scene of *Le père de famille*) not yet begun. This pause allows the beholder to take stock of the family drama onstage, to define himself in relation to it, and to react appropriately (that is, sentimentally). Given what he believes is the universally moving quality of a tableau, Diderot expects that every member of the audience will feel a bond of humanity with the character, and will therefore understand that virtue is "a form of self-sacrifice" (*Eloge de Richardson* [1762; *Eulogy for Richardson*], p. 31). When he fully appreciates what it means to be, for example, a father, the beholder ought to be moved to tears. Just as tragedy produced a catharsis of pity and fear, the new *drame* is meant to induce "the sweet pleasure of being moved and shedding tears" (*Discours sur la poésie dramatique*, p. 189). What these tears convey, among other things, is a longing for a better world, in which the people onstage might finally be happy. Theater now provides its audience with the utopian vision of an enlightened social order, just as it moves the audience to tears by portraying the sacrifices that will be necessary for that vision to come true.

The emergence of the *drame,* like that of the novel, implied not only changing class relationships but also a reorganization of sexual markers within the society as a whole. Like the novel, Diderot's *drame* at once reemphasized the "feminine" pleasure of identifying with others and sought to subordinate that pleasure to the "masculine" pleasure of maintaining a critical detachment. Sensing himself unjustly subservient to the cold and "virile" nobleman, the bourgeois found in the *drame* and the novel a means of asserting the ethical superiority of his identification with private experience; simultaneously, he could label that identification as only imaginary, as fiction. By demonstrating a capacity for both tears and critical thinking, the bourgeois could contrast the warmth of ideal family life with the heartlessness of the public, economic world and could designate that very capacity (for sensitivity and detachment) as the virtue that enabled "man" to rule over both the private and the public spheres.

In *Paradoxe sur le comédien* (wr. 1773–1776?, pub. 1830; *Paradox on the Actor*), Diderot makes what is arguably his most radical claim about theater. Great actors, he claims, are totally insensitive beings, capable of producing the symptoms of emotion at will, yet without ever feeling anything themselves. Rather than identifying with a character, the great actor coolly imitates his or her behavior. The actor's paradox is this: what is proper to the great actor is that nothing is properly his. However, Diderot advocates this cool, intellectual acting style for the same reason that he wants to have the onstage seats removed: not (like Voltaire) for the sake of decorum, but better to assure the beholder's passionate identification with the spectacle.

Knowing from his own experience how easily one can be seduced into taking theater for reality, Rousseau agreed with Diderot's analysis of the great actor's skills. Yet his connoisseur's understanding of the workings of theater led him to condemn its moral and political consequences. Whereas Voltaire, the admirer of royalty, attempted to renew the serious aristocratic genre, and the liberal Diderot founded a new, bourgeois genre, Rousseau the Protestant republican viewed theater itself with suspicion. In his public response to the *Encyclopédie* article (instigated by Voltaire) on Geneva, the *Lettre à M. d'Alembert sur les spectacles* (1758; *Letter to M. d'Alembert on the Theater*), Rousseau rejects the notion of establishing a theater in that city and uses the occasion to raise the discussion of theater to a level unparalleled in 18th-century France. What, he asks, are the moral, political, and philosophical conditions and effects of *theater as such?*

Theater, he argues, necessarily isolates the members of its audience from each other, appeals to their vices, and asks them to take illusion for reality. Rousseau believes that by shedding tears over fictional sorrows, we save ourselves the trouble of dealing with real suffering. Although these ill effects may be tolerated (and even desirable) in certain other places, they cannot be allowed in the republic of Geneva. In particular, he claims that classical French theater has the effect of blinding its audience to social reality ("Blind men that we are, amidst so much enlightenment!") and aggravates existing inequalities by making the audience pay for admission. It reinforces the exclusion of the many by the few, and then turns even the few into willing accomplices in their own oppression: "Let us not adopt these exclusive entertainments which close up a small number of people in melancholy fashion in a gloomy cavern, which give them only prisons, lances, soldiers, and afflicting images of servitude and inequality to see" (*Letter*, p. 125).

Whereas in a society of equals, Rousseau implies, everyone would stand confidently together in the light of day. In that society, it would no longer be necessary even to schedule theatrical performances, since festivals (not "theater") would spontaneously flow from the rhythms of daily life. In an egalitarian society, the distinction between audience and performers would collapse: "Let the spectators become an entertainment to themselves; make them actors themselves; do it so that each sees and loves himself in the others so that all will be better united" (*Letter*, p. 126). No one in this society would remain apart, hidden in the shadows of a *place à l'ombre*. No one would remain offstage, and there would therefore be no one, nothing, to show onstage: "What will be shown in them? Nothing, if you please. With liberty, wherever abundance reigns, well-being also reigns" (ibid.). At the very moment when Voltaire and Diderot call for the elimination of onstage seats, Rousseau imagines the elimination of the audience itself, thereby clearing the stage for a theatrical Revolution.

Bibliography: Jean-Marie Apostolidès, *Le prince sacrifié* (Paris: Minuit, 1985). Denis Diderot, *Oeuvres complètes*, ed. Herbert Dieckmann et al., vols. 10, 13, and 20 (Paris: Hermann, 1980). Diderot, *Oeuvres esthétiques*, ed. Paul Vernière (Paris: Garnier, 1968). Arnold Hauser, *The Social History of Art*, trans. Arnold Hauser and Stanley Goodman, vol. 3 (New York: Vintage, 1957). Henri Lagrave, *Le théâtre et son public de 1717 à 1750* (Paris: Klincksieck, 1972). Jean-Jacques Rousseau, *Politics and the Arts: Letter to M. d'Alembert on the Theater*, ed. and trans. Allan Bloom (Ithaca: Cornell University Press, 1960). Peter Szondi, "Tableau and Coup de Théâtre: On the Social Psychology of Diderot's Bourgeois Tragedy," in *On Textual Understanding and Other Essays*, trans. Harvey Mendelsohn (Minneapolis: University of Minnesota Press, 1986). Voltaire, *Le théâtre de Voltaire*, 2 vols. (Geneva: Institut et Musée Voltaire, 1967).

Jay L. Caplan

✑ 1759, August–September
Denis Diderot Writes His First Review of the Exhibitions
Held in the Louvre

Salons

Around the middle of the 18th century in Paris the (mostly biennial) official exhibitions of paintings, sculptures, drawings, and engravings by members of the Royal Academy of Painting and Sculpture began to be the focus of printed critiques, usually in journals but also, with increasing frequency, in independent brochures. Because the exhibitions were then held in the Salon Carré in the Louvre, the critiques themselves came to be known as *salons,* a name that persisted long after the exhibitions were moved to other venues. By far the greatest of the early *salonniers* was the leading philosophe Denis Diderot, who critically reviewed the exhibitions of 1759, 1761, 1763, 1765, 1767, 1769, 1771, 1775, and 1781 for Friedrich Melchior Grimm's *Correspondance littéraire* (1753–1790; *Literary Correspondence*), a miscellany that circulated regularly in manuscript form to a small number of royal and noble subscribers outside France. Like so many of his most significant writings, the bulk of which also first appeared in the *Correspondance,* Diderot's *Salons* were published only after his death, and even then not all at once. As a result, he had no public reputation as an art critic in his lifetime. Publication of his *Salons* during the 19th century, however, made Diderot an important influence on the art criticism of the period and may well have contributed to the popularity of the genre as a vehicle for ambitious writers such as Stendhal, Charles Baudelaire, and Emile Zola.

The traditional view of Diderot's art criticism has been sharply divided. For example, he has been widely castigated for his enthusiasm for the art of Jean-Baptiste Greuze, whose paintings of sentimental genre subjects have been characterized pejoratively as "literary." From such a perspective, Diderot's liking for Greuze has appeared emblematic of his own literary interests and practice as well as of the grossly sentimental tastes of his epoch. At the same time, Diderot's praise of the still-life paintings of Jean-Baptiste Siméon Chardin has been taken as evidence of an admirable sensitivity to the values of "pure" painting, values that, it is claimed, later became dominant in Impressionism and Cézanne. The "bad" Diderot is thus regarded as a child of his times while the "good" Diderot is considered a forerunner of modernity. This ahistorical view posits an absolute and fundamental distinction between "pure" and "literary" painting that is an ideological construct of the later 19th century and defies rigorous application to previous art (if Greuze is "literary," why aren't Nicolas Poussin and Raphael?). An alternative strategy is to try to grasp Diderot's thought as nearly as possible in its own terms. This approach reveals that his writings on painting, for all their copiousness, digressiveness, and apparent spontaneity, propound a single, richly developed conception of the pictorial enterprise, a conception, moreover, that is at work in much of the most interesting and important painting of his age.

At the heart of Diderot's conception is a paradoxical ideal of the relation between painting and beholder. The first writings in which Diderot fully articulates that ideal, *Entretiens sur Le fils naturel* (1757; *Commentaries on "The Natural Son"*) and *Discours sur la poésie dramatique* (1758; *Discourse on Dramatic Poetry*), are principally concerned not with painting but with the theater. In both Diderot repudiates the outworn conventions of the French classical theater according to which actors and actresses appeared in elaborate costumes that lacked all verisimilitude; delivered, while facing the audience, long tirades

477

during which the action of the play was halted; and in general performed in a manner that at every moment addressed the audience as if seeking its approval. Instead he advocates a dramaturgy that would appear to deny the audience's very existence. "In a dramatic representation," he writes in the *Entretiens,* "the beholder is no more to be taken into account than if he did not exist. Is something addressed to him? The author has departed from his subject, the actor has been led away from his part. They both step down from the stage. I see them in the orchestra, and as long as the speech lasts, the action is suspended for me, and the stage remains empty" (*Oeuvres esthétiques,* p. 102). In the *Discours sur la poésie dramatique* he develops these ideas at greater length: "Whether you compose or act, think no more of the beholder than if he did not exist. Imagine, at the edge of the stage, a high wall that separates you from the orchestra. Act as if the curtain never rose" (*Oeuvres esthétiques,* p. 231). The paradox, of course, is that only by seeming to ignore the beholder in this way can the author and actors rivet an audience's attention and indeed move it to tears.

The principal instrument for achieving this double effect is the tableau, which Diderot defines in opposition to the coup de théâtre of the classical theater. "An unexpected incident that happens in the course of the action and that suddenly changes the situation of the characters is a *coup de théâtre,*" he explains in the *Entretiens.* "An arrangement of those characters on the stage, so natural and true to life that, faithfully arranged by a painter, it would please me on canvas, is a *tableau*" (p. 88). A coup de théâtre takes place within the action and marks a sudden change in the consciousness of the characters involved; whereas the grouping of figures and stage properties that constitutes a tableau stands as it were outside the action, with the result that the characters appear unaware of its existence and hence of its effect on the audience. "He who acts and he who beholds are two very different beings" (p. 81). The concept of the tableau at once hypostatizes that difference and defines it as above all one of point of view. A tableau is visible, it can be said to exist, only from the beholder's point of view. But precisely because that is so, it helps persuade the beholder that the characters on the stage are unconscious of his presence.

The same principle is fundamental to Diderot's vision of painting, although its articulation in the *Salons* is less systematic than in his early writings on the theater. A crucial expression of that principle, however, is Diderot's admiration for paintings that persuasively represent figures either deeply absorbed in states of mind or feeling or wholly engaged in certain activities, figures who seem oblivious to everything but the objects of their engrossed attention. Most important, such figures appear oblivious to the beholder standing before the canvas—in this sense they deny his presence—as Diderot all but makes explicit in a striking short passage in his *Essais sur la peinture* (1766; *Essays on Painting*), composed in close conjunction with the *Salon de 1765.* "If you lose your feeling for the difference between the man who presents himself in society and the man engaged in an action," Diderot remarks to a prospective painter, "between the man who is alone and the man who is looked at, throw your brushes into the fire. You will academicize all your figures, you will make them stiff and unnatural" (*Oeuvres esthétiques*, p. 702). In that event the painting will no longer be "a street, a public place, a temple"—that is, the setting it was meant to represent; it will become "a theater," by which Diderot means an artificial construction in which persuasiveness is sacrificed and dramatic illusion vitiated in the attempt to impress the beholder and solicit his applause.

Diderot's use of the word *théâtre* in this connection reveals the depth of his revulsion against the prevailing stage conventions; but it also suggests that superseding those conventions by the new principles Diderot advocated would mean simultaneously the death of theater as he knew it and the birth of something else—call it true drama. And in fact Diderot's conception of painting is profoundly dramatic, in accordance with a new definition of drama that aims above all for the illusion of the character's complete absorption in the represented action and hence for the ontological illusion, the overriding fiction, that the beholder does not exist. "The canvas encloses all the space, and there is no one beyond it," he writes in the *Pensées détachées sur la peinture* (wr. 1776–1781; *Detached Thoughts on Painting*). Paradoxically, however, it is only that illusion or fiction that can transfix the beholder before the canvas and hold him there in the perfect trance of imaginary involvement that Diderot and his contemporaries regarded as the experiential proof of a completely successful painting.

One qualification must be added. Starting in 1763 Diderot's *Salons* present a second, alternative conception of painting which might be called pastoral and which implies a seemingly antithetical but essentially equivalent relation to the beholder. In Diderot's accounts of certain pictures that are unsuited to dramatic rendering because of their subject matter, he takes up the fiction that he is literally inside the painting, in one famous instance—an account of Joseph Vernet's contributions to the Salon of 1767—withholding until near the end of his commentary the information that the peopled landscapes he is describing with great enthusiasm are not real but painted. This approach suggests that for Diderot the function of such works is not to exclude the beholder, as the dramatic conception requires, but rather to absorb him into the representation, a feat that would equally deny his presence before the painting and of course would equally transfix him precisely there. Diderot's account of Greuze's *La piété filiale* (1763; *Filial Piety*) in his *Salon de 1763* leaves no doubt that it exactly fits his dramatic conception of painting, just as his remarks in his *Salon de 1767* on Chardin's still-lifes imply that he sees them in terms approximating those of his pastoral conception. In any case, there is nothing inconsistent about his admiration for both.

Certainly Diderot's beholder-centered aesthetic bears a close relation to much French painting of his time, and the issue of theatricality remains vital to a major current in French painting at least until the advent of Impressionism. But two other points are perhaps of more immediate interest.

First, the issue of beholding is often given a particular inflection in Diderot's writings by considerations of gender. For example, his admiration for Greuze's *Une jeune fille qui pleure son oiseau mort* (1765; *Girl Mourning Her Dead Bird*)

1. Jean-Baptiste Greuze, *Jeune fille
pleurant son oiseau mort* (1765) (Musée
du Louvre, RF 1523). (Photo courtesy of Documentation Photographique de la Réunion des Musées
Nationaux.)

(fig. 1) is correlated with his inability (until near the end of a long passage) to
distract the girl from her sorrow over the loss of her bird, understood as a
metaphor for her loss of virginity. The worldly male critic thus simultaneously
dramatizes the girl's obliviousness to his presence and develops the motif's
sexual implications in ways that leave no doubt that they too are part of the
picture's appeal. By the same token, the biblical subject of Susannah and the
elders is acknowledged by Diderot to present special difficulties to the painter,
precisely because the innocent Susannah must be displayed naked before the
eyes of the beholder and yet appear unaware of the elders spying on her as she
bathes in her garden. In this case the beholder's implicit maleness is part of
the problem: if he is not made to feel excluded from the painting, he is likely
to identify with the elders, which would mean that the subject was no longer a
virtuous but a lascivious one.

Second, questions of theatricality are tacitly or explicitly present in other
18th-century French writing. Thus in Rousseau's *Lettre à M. d'Alembert sur les
spectacles* (1758; *Letter to M. d'Alembert on the Theater*), an argument against
establishing a theater in Rousseau's native Geneva is presented in terms that
indict the very conditions of beholding and being beheld. But the ineluctability
of these conditions also means that theatricality as such is inevitable, and in
fact Rousseau's description toward the end of the *Lettre* of the balls that he
recommends as winter entertainment for unmarried men and women involves
the imposition of strict controls on all spectators and, in that sense, the exploitation of theatricality in the interests of the state. The novels of Pierre Carlet
de Marivaux and of Diderot himself further exemplify the new and disturbing
apprehension of beholding as inherently theatricalizing even as their reliance on
absorptive tableaux bears further witness to the crucial role accorded visual
experience in French 18th-century culture.

See also 1707, 1727, 1759 (23 April), 1771.

Bibliography: Norman Bryson, *Word and Image: French Painting of the Ancien Régime* (Cambridge: Cambridge University Press, 1981). Thomas Crow, *Painters and Public Life in Eighteenth-Century Paris* (New Haven: Yale University Press, 1985). Denis Diderot, *Oeuvres esthétiques,* ed. Paul Vernière (Paris: Garnier, 1959). Diderot, *Salons,* ed. Jean Seznec, 4 vols. (Oxford: Clarendon Press, 1957–1967). Michael Fried, *Absorption and Theatricality: Painting and Beholder in the Age of Diderot* (Berkeley: University of California Press, 1980). David Marshall, *The Surprising Effects of Sympathy: Du Bos, Marivaux, Rousseau, Diderot, and Mary Shelley* (Chicago: University of Chicago Press, 1987).

Michael Fried

ᔐᕋ 1761, *February*
Jean-Jacques Rousseau Publishes *Julie, ou la nouvelle Héloïse*

The Novel and Gender Difference

The appearance in Paris in early 1761 of *Julie, ou la nouvelle Héloïse: Lettres de deux amants, habitants d'une petite ville au pied des Alpes. Recueillies et publiées par J. J. Rousseau (Julie, or the New Héloïse: Letters of Two Lovers, Inhabitants of a Small Town at the Foot of the Alps*) was one of the most important events in the history of French literature. This is sometimes difficult for literate readers or even scholars of French fiction to understand, for the work is lengthy, stylistically self-indulgent, and frequently boring. It is read today mostly by literary historians and academic critics, yet its publication evoked an overwhelming response from an 18th-century public whose definition and numbers were just being understood by novelists, themselves working within a genre not yet considered to be "respectable" literature. Establishment critics were tepid about *Julie* (Voltaire sarcastically remarked that he would rather kill himself than finish it), but the reading public demanded it so ardently that dozens of editions were issued in quick succession. Hundreds of letters, many of them addressed to Rousseau, were exchanged throughout Europe for several years after *Julie's* appearance, reflecting a very emotional reaction to this tale of two young lovers.

What were the reasons for the work's immense popularity? Rousseau had succeeded in deftly combining precise descriptions of recognizable daily life with more general "moral" or "sentimental" themes, thereby giving *Julie* a plausibility—the sense of a verifiable reality—that would capture firmly the attention of its readers, even those who professed never to read fiction. The care with which he organized the chronology of his tale, the attention he gave to the description of the daily lives of his characters, the particularity of his geographic references, and the thorough knowledge he showed of the variety of social codes that determined daily existence in 18th-century France and Switzerland, all united in *Julie* to make it a plausible fiction. In this way Rousseau hoped to enhance markedly the novel's place in the hierarchy of French literature, for he saw narrative fiction as a conduit for inculcating a new value system in an increasingly secularized public.

Rousseau worked on *Julie* for about five years. We know this from the extensive references to the novel's development in his correspondence and in the *Confessions* (1782–1789; especially bks. 9–11), as well as in the two prefaces that accompanied the novel. Both the task and the text preoccupied him, at times to the point of obsession. He even evaluated his relationships with others according to how they responded to his public readings of *Julie* or to the manuscripts he sent to friends. In fact it was Denis Diderot's tepid response to *Julie*—Rousseau had early sent him parts of the manuscript that Diderot had criticized—that contributed to the dissolution of his close relationship with Rousseau. By the time the novel appeared, the friendship was disintegrating.

What sort of novel was this collection of letters, written by a man known for his aversion to "fiction" in all its guises? It is very long, composed of 172 letters (including 9 *billets* or notes) unequally dispersed among six parts; about half of the letters are exchanged between Julie d'Etange (the "new" Héloïse) and a young man with the name of Saint-Preux (recalling the Middle Ages, for *preux* is Old French for "brave"). The other correspondents are Claire (cousin and friend of Julie, later Mme. d'Orbe), Milord Edouard Bomston (friend of Saint-Preux), M. de Wolmar (Julie's eventual husband), and a few minor characters. At the beginning of the novel, Julie is about seventeen and Saint-Preux about nineteen; by the end, they are around thirty and thirty-two. The probable dates of the novel's action fall between 1732 and 1745.

The narrative's plot is uncomplicated. A young man is hired to tutor a young girl. They fall in love, have a brief sexual liaison, but cannot marry because of social differences held to be insuperable by Julie's powerful father, the baron d'Etange. Three years after their first exchange of letters, and soon after their sexual initiation, Saint-Preux is chased from the d'Etange home and goes to live in Paris. Julie marries M. de Wolmar, an older landowner, under pressure from her father and friends. A forsaken Saint-Preux leaves for a trip around the world and is absent for four years, during which time there is no correspondence among the parties. When he returns to Clarens, the home of Julie de Wolmar (now the mother of two boys) and her husband, they invite him to live there. Saint-Preux befriends M. de Wolmar and spends his time writing about the little community of Clarens. He then leaves for Italy with Edouard, and, before his return, Julie, ill from having dived into a lake to save her younger son, dies. The last three letters include one from M. de Wolmar describing Julie's lengthy death, a final one from her to Saint-Preux, and one from Claire d'Orbe asking Saint-Preux to return to Clarens to join Julie's extended family.

As the novel's subtitle affirms, Rousseau intended his readers to recall one of Europe's great legends: the 12th-century story of Héloïse's love affair with her tutor Abélard, a cleric. Abélard had seduced the young girl and was castrated in revenge by thugs hired by her uncle. Both lovers become members of religious communities. Later they exchange four letters, the two from Héloïse being among literature's most touching love letters, especially poignant given the lovers' years of separation and Abélard's sexual incapacity. All the great themes of passionate love are adumbrated in these four epistles: its inevitability, illicitness, repression, and incompatibility with self-sufficiency; its sublimation through the act of writing; and its role in cultural—especially gender—definition.

Why is Julie d'Etange a *new* Héloïse? The "new" in the novel's title implies both a modern rewriting of the medieval story and the "modernity" of the passion of Julie and Saint-Preux (in fact Rousseau at first called his novel "La moderne Héloïse"). In Julie's last letter to Saint-Preux (pt. 6, letter 12), composed on her deathbed and transmitted to him by her husband, she writes: "When you see this letter, the worms will be preying upon your lover's features and upon her heart, where your image will exist no more. But could my soul exist without you? Without you, what happiness could I enjoy? No, I do not leave you; I go to wait for you" (p. 407). By insisting that he accept her death—her ultimate separation from him—Julie demands, as did Abélard, that a new definition be given to love, that it be forever, and forever unconsummated. This time, however, a man, not a woman, must make the decision and withstand the sacrifice of separation and loneliness.

Julie d'Etange *is* a desiring woman; Rousseau presents her "modern" desire as superior to the passions of the men who, for social reasons, order her life. Although she is caught up in relationships with men who, including her father, persist in seeing her as a sexual object, her own desire is more subtle and transcends sexuality. Julie's last letter, from her deathbed, is testimony to the transcendent value of a desire that she recognizes as encumbered, but not defined, by her "crime" in having succumbed to Saint-Preux's sexual attractiveness. Yet, because this desire is different, society must suppress it; Rousseau's novel describes how difficult it is for a desiring *woman* to influence the social codes of a society defined by male values.

Gender and desire: around these poles, Rousseau struggled to make of narrative fiction a genre where questions of epistemology—of how one thinks and organizes thoughts and perceptions—could be discussed without boring his readers. Gender implies difference, and it is the problematization of difference in social discourse that marks 18th-century fiction. The issue of literary genre was gender-specific as well, for one of the most persistent myths of the 18th century—and since—was that the novel was written primarily for and (until Rousseau's too obvious success) by women, not for and by men. Although novel-writing did offer women a rare entrée into the literary world, allowing them to attain increasing prominence as writers, it was regularly criticized as an activity unworthy of serious *men* of letters. Such popular and accomplished writers as Claudine Guérin de Tencin, Françoise de Graffigny, and Marie-Jeanne Riccoboni all had written novels before Richardson and Rousseau astutely recognized that narrative fiction was not only a genre with immense potential for popularity, but also one that could permit the most liberal discussions of what that audience wanted: how emotional relationships operate in a domestic context. The struggle to control and define this relatively new genre is a good place to begin inquiries into the questions of canon formation and the role of women in the history of literature.

The epistolary format played a central role in the working out of the questions of gender, genre, and desire. The female-male correspondence, around the subject of sexual passion, had made the novel truly popular. An exchange of letters allowed, in principle, for an unaffected, transparently sincere form of (nonsexual) intercourse between men and women. Paradoxically, such letters could also be read as a sign of sinfulness, for, by giving verbal proof of a desire for affective relations with another, they could inculpate the writer. The epistolary novel was compelling to those who were trying to understand the psychosocial functions of sexuality, for infatuation with the act of writing can mean the displacement of an original (sexual) desire, the deferral of sexual fulfillment. This is another reason for the public's fascination with *Julie:* the permanent sexual union the two young protagonists cannot have, for reasons external to their mutual affection, becomes less compelling as the union they *do* have, through their letters and communication with friends, subtly replaces it.

Social relations between sexes was the subject of much French fiction, and the epistolary genre problematized the subject further. A letter was a private communication, and epistolary novels reinforced the idea that *sensibilité* gave primacy to the senses as cognitively valid devices; adroit management of verbal styles stressed the role language plays in our definition of self and other. Works such as Marivaux's *La vie de Marianne* (1731–1741; *The Life of Marianne*) and Graffigny's *Lettres d'une Péruvienne* (1747; *Letters from a Peruvian Princess*) had depicted women who were attempting to create and control their own discourse so as to express their difference from masculinity and male society. This "novel" discourse was defined by a fascination with solipsism, by a tendency (or unacknowledged desire) to remove the other from all consideration while focusing on the writing subject (who was frequently also the object), by a manipulation of the past (history) to control the present and the future, and by a general decentering of the male subject, primarily through the exquisite autopsy of power relationships. As a consequence, a genre sensitive to feminism was briefly dominant in 18th-century France; there was the breath of a possibility that subjects for women and written by women could have a position of some prestige in the arts. One of the reasons was the publication and success of Rousseau's *Julie,* which "canonized" what had preceded in this genre, including the translation into French of Samuel Richardson's great epistolary works.

Richardson had died in July 1761, only six months after the publication of *Julie.* His *Pamela, or Virtue Rewarded* (1740–41) was available in French soon after its appearance in England; and *Clarissa, or the History of a Young Lady* (1747–48) had been translated—though bowdlerized—in 1751 by none other than Abbé Prévost, author himself of several lengthy novels, including *Manon Lescaut* (1731). In late 1761, while *Julie* was being welcomed enthusiastically throughout Europe, Denis Diderot composed a valuable treatise on narrative fiction, the *Eloge de Richardson* (1762; *Eulogy for Richardson*). He seconded Prévost's evaluation, arguing that the English novelist had accurately reflected in his novels the ethical universe that should be the subject of contemporary fiction. Discreetly judgmental of Rousseau, Diderot's *Eloge* can be read as one of the earliest substantive critiques of *Julie*. Similar to the two prefaces that Rousseau insisted must accompany *Julie*, the *Eloge de Richardson* sought to define an "ethics" of reading, arguing that reading is never innocent. It is in the definition of the ideal reader that the theories of Rousseau and Diderot intersect. They both felt reading to be an activity that demanded the acuity of truly intelligent and sensitive beings, regardless of gender; but they differed substantially on the "dangers" that the uninitiated, especially young women, ran when they opened a novel.

Eighteenth-century iconography is replete with depictions of the activity of reading, and the *danger* of reading caught the fancy of both male and female novelists. Reading alone was more likely dangerous for young ladies; commentary on and illustrations of reading during the period often reflected on the advantages of communal readings for inhibiting unbridled fantasy. Rousseau felt so strongly about the negative influence of reading fiction that in his preface he compared opening a novel to the first step one took toward a sexual liaison: "No chaste girl has ever read novels, and I gave a title to this one definitive enough that anyone would know what it was about before opening it. She who, despite this title, dares read but one page is a fallen girl; but she should not blame the book; the evil was done [when she opened it]. Since she has already begun it, she should finish it; she has nothing left to lose" (*La nouvelle Héloïse,* in *Oeuvres,* p. 6).

Although many more men than women corresponded with Rousseau after the publication of *Julie,* and lengthily and warmly so, about the sentimental effect the work had had on them, women remained the passive "bodies" on which he and his male contemporaries transcribed the modern novel. The great heroines—Prévost's Manon and Richardson's Clarissa, Diderot's nun Suzanne and Rousseau's Julie—all die at the end; their stories (written, collated, edited by men) come into existence as a result of this ultimate absence. Convinced that it was for women that the genre was created, by and about women that it was primarily written, by women that it was read, male writers—and the public—contradictorily believed that it was from women that it must be kept. Women were warned not to read novels, whose most common subject was female desire. But where else were young women to learn about society and its power relationships, to understand sexuality and the male codes of society? In their struggle to appropriate fiction to their purposes, male writers failed to answer such questions; indeed, this deficiency influenced the development of the novel in the 18th century, as it sought its audience and its place in the literary hierarchy.

Rousseau sought to represent a world of anticipated union in which physical—sexual—possession had only a marginal place. In a utopia, desire's eternal anticipation would equal possession; human sexuality and death would be transcended. The author of *Julie* was concerned that a utopian novel might be seen as boring and thus go unread before his readers could understand his motives. So, Julie and Saint-Preux do make love, early in the novel (between letters 54 and 55 of pt. 1), but only once. Rousseau in effect wanted to change the emotional locus of a type of popular, romantic fiction, fascinated as it was with the titillation of sexual relations, that had prevailed since the 17th century. This is why friendship, a nonerotic relationship, plays such an important role in the novel, for it attenuates sexuality as the sole marker of gender difference. As even a superficial reading of *Julie* will sustain, *amitié*—nonsexual desire—can be ineffably superior to *amour*. Friendship can serve as an attractive "escape" from the erotic imperatives of sexual difference. Julie's creator would have nothing less than a transformation of sexual love into *amitié*, or, more subtly, into the never-to-be-attained yet energizing presence of nongenital desire in human existence.

Rousseau intended to do what Diderot praised Richardson for having done, namely, lead his readers to discover excitement and fulfillment in the emotional and intellectual intensity brought on by nonsexual desire *in conflict with* sexuality, rather than in the libertine exaggeration of passion common to earlier and most other contemporary fiction. To do this, Rousseau relied on the intimacy of first-person narration, which meant that he had to write at times *as a woman;* this truism may help to explain why the direction of French fiction changed after *Julie.*

When there are multiple narrators—whether invented by male or female writers—there is at least the implication of difference. The authority of knowledge is thereby attenuated, for the first-person voice implies the value of multiple perspectives. But after the Revolution, which was truly a watershed in the history of French culture, first-person narration in fiction lost ground, and the so-called omniscient third-person voice dominated. Relativism and the attenuation of (male) domination and authority became of secondary, even tertiary, importance to novelists. The general move away from first-person narration and toward the more "neutral" third-person narrative voice in the early 19th century—facilitated by the high irony of Pierre Choderlos de Laclos's *Les liaisons dangereuses* (1782)—not only was "natural" but also must have been a psychic relief to male writers who had been forced to "write as women."

The success of *Julie* may have hastened this development. An extraordinarily influential and popular piece of fiction, written by one of French literature's half-dozen most original thinkers, *Julie* would literally disappear from the canon of *read* works by the middle of the 19th century, as did most other epistolary and memoir novels. It remains on reading lists in the academy, and major French publishing houses still bring out editions regularly, but the book has become a literary curiosity (untranslated completely into English since the 19th century) rather than a source of ethical and aesthetic inspiration. It may be "canonical," but its unique messages have been repressed by a public that has impatiently substituted for it the authority of more plausible, more accessible, and less unsettling texts about gender difference, sexuality, and desire.

See also 1725, 1735, 1782 (March), 1782 (May).

Bibliography: Nancy K. Miller, "The Misfortunes of Virtue: II. *La nouvelle Héloïse,*" in *The Heroine's Text: Readings in the French and English Novel, 1722–1782* (New York: Columbia University Press, 1980). Jean-Jacques Rousseau, *Julie, ou la nouvelle Héloïse,* in *Oeuvres complètes de Jean-Jacques Rousseau*, ed. Bernard Gagnebin and Marcel Raymond, vol. 2 (Paris: Gallimard, 1964); translated by Judith H. McDowell as *La nouvelle Héloïse. Julie, or the New Eloise,* abridged (University Park: Pennsylvania University Press, 1987). Jean Starobinski, *Jean-Jacques Rousseau: Transparency and Obstruction,* trans. Arthur Goldhammer (Chicago: University of Chicago Press, 1988). Tony Tanner, "Rousseau's *La nouvelle Héloïse,*" in *Adultery in the Novel: Contract and Transgression* (Baltimore: Johns Hopkins University Press, 1979).

Ronald C. Rosbottom

✒ 1761, December

Frederick II the Great of Prussia Writes "Le conte du violon"
in Celebration of the Instruments of Art

What Was Enlightenment?

In a work of history it is certainly reasonable to rephrase Immanuel Kant's well-known "What Is Enlightenment?" in the past tense. Yet this temporal shift may be worth thinking about. Does the Enlightenment now belong to history? Have its values and objectives become unusable as a result of our modern insight into their historical limitations? The Enlightenment thought of itself as universal, but we now know that it was in large measure an ideological instrument of the bourgeoisie in its struggle for political power.

Curiously enough, it is in Germany, where Enlightenment was always fragile and contested, because of its compromising association with absolutism and foreign-influenced courts, rather than in France, where many of its tenets were incorporated into the official ideology of the Republic, that Enlightenment remains to this day a live moral and intellectual force, an armory of weapons against right-wing reaction and obscurantism, and a precious heritage to be defended. Many modern French intellectuals, in contrast, seem intent on breaking up what they apparently regard as an embarrassing or oppressive bourgeois inheritance. They appear to have forgotten that in the last decades of the 19th century and the early decades of the 20th, efforts to discredit the Enlightenment values of rationalism, liberalism, modernization, and political emancipation by exposing them as instruments of exploitation and domination by capitalists and Jews were characteristic not of the left but of the radical right. The question that remains to be answered is whether an authentic and effective critique of economic exploitation or social and political oppression can be based on any principles other than those of the Enlightenment itself.

It is apt that a fable written in French by a German should serve as the occasion of a brief reconsideration of the Enlightenment as a whole. For the Enlightenment was even more universalist in its ideals than the Christianity it aimed to supplant, or at least to transform. It recognized no local values or truths. Whatever was not universal was ipso facto erroneous, a limited, partial vision that had to be transcended by a larger, universal one. Before the bar of universal reason all local truths and local institutions (such as historically based

487

religions or traditional moral codes and legal systems) were judged and usually found wanting. There is no simpler or more grandiose expression of the universalism of the Enlightenment than Kant's famous definition of the categorical imperative: "Act so that the principle of your action can become a universal law." The French language itself, the language not only of Voltaire, Montesquieu, and Rousseau but also of Leibniz, the Royal Prussian Academy, and educated people from Potsdam to Parma and St. Petersburg, was the language of Enlightenment partly no doubt because of French power and prestige, but also because it was considered the least local, the most universal, the most "philosophical" and modern of languages, the language best adapted to rational and analytic thinking, least ambiguous, and least likely to lead to confusion or misunderstanding. (Frederick the Great's *De la littérature allemande* [1780; *On German Literature*] and Antoine Rivarol's *De l'universalité de la langue française* [1784; *On the Universality of the French Language*] are classic statements of this view.)

Enlightenment involved a double movement: the exposure and elimination of error and the discovery and establishment of truth; criticism and invention. The operation of removing the scales from people's eyes, symbolized by Denis Diderot at the beginning of his *Lettre sur les aveugles* (1749; translated in 1750 as *An Essay on Blindness*), in the celebrated cataract operation performed under the auspices of René Antoine de Réaumur, was fundamental. Everything that had been taken for granted was to be subjected to a kind of radical positivist (analytic and empirical) critique. Through the device of the candid and "unprejudiced" onlooker (such as the heroes of Voltaire's tales, the Harlequins in Pierre Carlet de Marivaux's comedies, Diderot's blind men and deaf mutes) or the visitor with a different set of presuppositions (Montesquieu's Persians), common modes of behavior and habits of thought were defamiliarized—broken down into their empirical and observable components. Things familiar and seemingly "natural" suddenly fell apart and were perceived as strange, incoherent, and comical; it was no longer possible to believe in them. Words and phrases whose meaning had been obvious became problematical, even nonsensical. Imposing categories of moral and political control were exposed as "paper tigers," as in act 2, scene 2, of Marivaux's *La seconde surprise de l'amour* (1727; *Love's Second Surprise*), where the heroine reflects on the emptiness of the expression *a woman's reputation* and makes it clear that by accepting it she is acknowledging only the fact of male social dominance, not its rationality or legitimacy. Most important, the beliefs and rituals associated with throne and altar, the pillars of social authority, were defamiliarized and made to seem absurd. The very prose of Enlightenment appeared to shun all but the simplest connectives. The complex hierarchies and the dramatic counterpoint of baroque sentence structure gave way to a limpid, linear prose marked by parataxis and the surface polish characteristic of contemporary rococo painting and decoration. If the conjunctions "and," "but," and "then" in Voltaire's writing signal problematical connections, "because" and "so that" only cover these over with mystified and mystifying pseudoexplanations. The "depth" these conjunctions imply is exposed as a tiresome trompe l'oeil.

Conflict between the Enlightenment and the church was inevitable. The former aimed to liberate from false belief, exactly as the latter had once done. But the dogmas of the Christian churches now headed the list of false beliefs from which liberation was to be achieved. The reader—and the Enlightenment was very much a literary movement aimed at the conversion of readers—was to be emancipated from all "prejudices." If the reader was often represented as a woman, that was not only because many readers were in fact women, but also because for the writers of the Enlightenment, especially those of the first half of the 18th century, woman—socially mobile and a facilitator of movement among men from different social classes—stood close not only to the bourgeois of historical reality but also to the new ideal, derived from the bourgeois, of the emancipated, detached, enlightened individual, the abstract, universal citizen who was no longer defined and restricted by a fixed social role.

Along with Christian beliefs, the great metaphysical systems of the previous century, usually associated with the names of Descartes and Spinoza, were among the chief victims of the new critical, analytical, and empirical outlook, usually associated with the names of Locke and Newton. To most Enlighteners, the metaphysical ambition of accounting for everything and deducing the universe from a few first principles was not only a crazy, if in some respects admirable, pipe dream; it was also presumptuous and potentially repressive, since in all metaphysical systems the whole was favored over the part, the idea over experience, a necessarily transcendent totality over the actual and the here and now, and so, by implication, a divine or cosmic plan over the interests of humankind, the state or the prince over the individual citizen.

At the same time, no age worked harder than the age of Montesquieu, Thomas Malthus, Pierre de Maupertuis, Adam Smith, and Pierre de Laplace to discover the order of the universe, the general *laws* governing all particular phenomena both in the natural world and in the world of human behavior: the laws of physics, of living things, of political societies, of demography, of trade and economics. No age was more committed to the ideal of scientific knowledge or expected more from it. The pursuit of the true, universal laws of the workings of humankind and nature was the complement to the Enlightenment's negative and critical thrust, its attack on error. But the universality to which it aspired was not a transcendent universality. It was grounded in and bounded by human experience. At first there was speculation that, since humans depend for all their ideas on the data of their senses, beings endowed with different, or more, or fewer sense organs would have quite different conceptions both of the world and of what constitutes acceptable human behavior. Locke, Hume, and Diderot all wrestled with this question. By demonstrating that time, space, and causality are the conditions under which any human mind apprehends the world and acquires knowledge of it, Kant restored confidence in universal order and lawfulness; yet these remained a strictly human affair. Although the Enlightenment always sought to subsume the particular under the general, the local under the universal, its idea of the general and the universal was located in the sublunar human world.

It was not by reaching up to a point beyond themselves—to God or Absolute

489

Reality or Truth—that individual human beings rose above local prejudice and personal experience to the universal, but by a negative process of abstraction: everything that failed the test of critical scrutiny had to be sloughed off; what remained would be universal, common to all humanity. At the same time, it was not by discounting the world of experience and deducing the universe from the most fundamental intuitions of reason that the order of the phenomenal world would be apprehended, but on the contrary by seeking the laws of phenomena in the phenomena themselves. Scientific laws, in other words, were not external or anterior to the phenomena they governed; they were not metaphysical but were discovered in and through the encounter between the human mind and the phenomena presented to it. In short, reason was less a transcendent source of true knowledge, which the divine creator had deigned to share with his creature, and through which the latter participated in his truth, than a human instrument of criticism and invention, a means both of subjecting existing hypotheses (and no explanation, however well established, was to be regarded as anything more than a hypothesis) to criticism and of proposing new and more plausible hypotheses to account for phenomena. No idea was immune to criticism. Dogma was rejected as unscientific. Even if the Enlightenment neglected to examine some of its own assumptions, notably the very assumptions underlying the processes of identifying error and discovering truth, by establishing the *principle* that all assumptions are subject to rational scrutiny it acknowledged, at least in principle, that the notion of rational scrutiny was itself open to scrutiny. The very instruments provided by the Enlightenment enable us to identify and try to resolve its own prejudices.

The Enlightenment thus differed from the rationalist philosophical systems of the baroque age as well as from their critics (Pascal). It recognized in principle that the truth it sought was subject to review, and that that was the only kind of truth compatible with freedom. It did not expect or desire absolute truth, only what people could know by their own unaided efforts. The Enlightenment idea of knowledge thus left no place for divine intervention in the human world in the form of revelation or miracles or a special providence. On the contrary, whereas 17th-century philosophy had agonized over what it experienced as man's exile from God and tried to restore the lost connection, the Enlightenment exiled God from the world and appropriated the world for man. As Voltaire put it in *Candide* (1759), God is a captain who does not concern himself with the rats traveling in the hold of his ship; for their part, it is implied, the rats are quite happy to be left alone. Conversely, the rats have no cause to concern themselves with the plans of the captain or with anything else about him, including the question whether he exists or not. As human beings must fend for themselves, devise their own morality and social arrangements, make their own rules and forms of knowledge, and generally assume responsibility for themselves, the proper object of their investigations is nature and themselves, the laws of the physical world in which they live and of which they are part, and the laws of the social world with which they must also come to terms. Our business, as Candide put it, is to cultivate our garden. One of the most curious signs of the autonomy implied by Candide's famous dictum was a proliferation of essays and reflections on suicide (by Pierre Bayle, Diderot, Paul Henri Thiry d'Holbach, Jean-Bernard Merian, Montesquieu, Rousseau, above all Hume). If theological considerations were no longer pertinent to the issue of suicide, if human beings were responsible only to themselves or to each other, it became necessary to reconsider to what extent and in what conditions suicide might be justified. The Enlightenment was thus a major step in the process of secularization that is the hallmark of our modernity.

It is true that most Enlighteners believed or wanted to believe (they were sometimes beset by doubt) that the categories of human understanding, as well as the basic principles of morality and reason, were universal and timeless, common to all human beings in all places and at all times, once they had scraped away their local prejudices. Thanks to this belief, they did not think of their enterprise as purely negative and destructive. A new morality, a new legal and political order, a new philosophy, they were convinced, would be progressively constructed on these universal foundations. Advances in the natural sciences would promote greater control of nature, while the development of the sciences of man and society would enable people to refine their moral and political judgments and create a happier world. In the light both of modern notions of science and morality and of recent historical experience, that confidence may well appear optimistic or naïve.

Yet it is just as plausible to emphasize the continuity between our modern notions and those of the Enlightenment as to underscore the contrasts. The Enlightenment worked hard to avoid falling into the characteristically baroque polarities of reality and appearance, truth and illusion, whole and part, God and man, the effect of which was to devalue the "merely" human. In the baroque scheme, only the divine spark in the human—itself a divine favor—saved the human from absolute nothingness, and human knowledge was valid only insofar as it approximated to the divine and the absolute. By placing the divine beyond the pale and resolutely refusing the transcendent, the Enlightenment made humanity itself responsible for the very criteria according to which one idea or explanation was to be judged "better" than another. Among the major figures of the Enlightenment, Montesquieu and Diderot came very close to a modern view of both science and morality as evolving social practices. Similarly, although the Enlightenment's faith in the positive results that were expected to ensue from increasing rational understanding of man and nature—a faith already challenged in the 18th century by the marquis de Sade—has been rudely shaken by the experience of modern times, it is not clear that it is less rationality rather than more that is needed to solve our problems. Perhaps what is necessary is to find a way of subordinating instrumental reason to practical reason, the world of administration and technology to the rational decisions of moral individuals and communities.

The Enlightenment's practice of a critical positivism, its repudiation of every transcendence, its ideal of a universal, "philosophical" language that would ensure faultless communication and eliminate error and misunderstanding, were not, it is widely believed, favorable to literature and especially to poetry. If literature is defined in terms of the classical genres, such as epic narrative and tragedy, then it is true that there is not much significant 18th-century literature. But if we are willing to recognize literature in the deliberately modest or new genres the Enlighteners deemed appropriate to a modern secularized civilization—essays and parodies, private and public letters, real and fictional travel accounts, novels and short stories—then there is no shortage of wit, talent, or imagination in the Age of Enlightenment. Similarly, if poetry is defined in terms of the Romantics or the baroque, if it is expected to have a mantic or metaphysical mission, then there is indeed no 18th-century poetry in France worth talking about.

The poets of the 18th century themselves encouraged the skepticism with which their efforts are now regarded. Most of them appear to have partly believed that they were impotent epigones of the giants who had preceded them (it should not be forgotten that the so-called *grand siècle* was largely an invention of Voltaire and the Enlightenment) and that "great" poetry was incompatible with the critical positivism, the prosaic worldview they had espoused. Voltaire almost always referred deprecatingly to his poetry, especially his lighter society poems, as "bagatelles." But that is also how he referred to his celebrated tales. And although the classical idea of "Literature" that survived in him led him to this negative judgment, he belied it by carefully preserving all his "bagatelles" and supervising their publication, even while characteristically repudiating his own role in their publication. If it was impossible to take the "bagatelles" seriously—that is, to treat them with the awe traditionally reserved for "Literature"—it was equally impossible for an enlightened writer, a Modern, to take the classical view of literature seriously, as Marivaux had made clear in the early decades of the century in his essays. Some of Voltaire's best verse—the "Epître des vous et des tu" ("Epistle on 'Vous' and 'Tu'"), "Si vous voulez que j'aime encore" ("If You Want Me to Love Again") (nine gossamer verses said to have been written for Emilie du Châtelet), "Ce qui plaît aux dames" ("What Pleases the Ladies")—turns on the contrast of youth and age, illusion and enlightenment, naïve passion and resigned realism:

> O l'heureux temps que celui des fables
> Des bons démons, des esprits familiers
>
> . . .
>
> On a banni les démons et les fées;
> Sous la raison les grâces étouffées
> Livrent nos coeurs à l'insipidité;
> Le raisonner tristement s'accrédite;
> On court, hélas! après la vérité:
> Ah! croyez-moi, l'erreur a son mérite.
>
> Happy the age! Thrice blessed mankind,
> When tales like these belief could find,

Of spirits hovering in the air,
Of demons who make men their care!
. . .

   We of the marvelous are rifled,
By reason's weight, the graces stifled,
Have to the insipid men consigned.
The soul by reasoning is confined;
Still hunting after truth we go;
From error too some good may flow.
("Ce qui plaît aux dames," 1738)

Ainsi je déplorais la perte
Des erreurs de mes premiers ans;
Et mon âme, aux désirs ouverte,
Regrettait ses égarements.

Du ciel alors daignant descendre,
L'Amitié vint à mon secours;
Elle était peut-être aussi tendre,
Mais moins vive que les Amours.

Touché de sa beauté nouvelle,
Et de sa lumière éclairé,
Je la suivis; mais je pleurai
De ne pouvoir plus suivre qu'elle.

'Twas thus those pleasures I lamented,
Which I so oft in youth repented;
My soul replete with soft desire,
Vainly regretted youthful fire.

But friendship then, celestial maid,
From heaven descended to my aid;
Less lively than the amorous flame,
Although her tenderness the same.

The charms of friendship I admired,
My soul was with new beauty fired;
I then made one in friendship's train,
But destitute of love, complain.
    ("Stances à Mme. du Châtelet," 1745;
    "From Love to Friendship")

The "regret" for an earlier time of innocence and imagination never gets out of hand. Irony undercuts both the supposed innocence that has been lost and the wisdom that has been acquired, reducing the distance between them. If the poetical is exposed as ordinary, the ordinary is discovered to have an unsuspected poetical quality. There is never any danger of a revival of baroque tensions. In the end, the irony that prohibits the reader from taking the theme

493

seriously has the effect of throwing its conventionality into relief and focusing attention on the art with which it has been transformed into a poem. A similar effect results from another favorite poetic practice of the age: the working over of a well-known model—as in some verses to Mme. Lullin, a Genevan lady ("Je veux, dans mes derniers adieux," 1773; "Let Me, in My Last Farewell"), which are a variation on the first poem in book 1 of Tibullus' elegies. As this popular piece had been given a French version earlier in the century by the poet Charles-Auguste de La Fare, Voltaire's composition inevitably invited comparison with both that of Tibullus and that of La Fare.

Viewed as a "bagatelle"—like the embroidered silks and the silverware of the rococo craftsmen that Voltaire liked to honor in his verse—the characteristic 18th-century poem is to be admired as their products are: for the wit of the invention and the skill of the execution, the celebrated *difficulté vaincue* (difficulty overcome). By the art of these modest craftsmen, Voltaire points out, banal items of everyday use—vases, earrings, sideboards—are transformed into objects of delight, works of beauty commensurate with a scaled-down but at the same time more intensely human view of our existence. The point at which this Enlightenment aesthetic transcends the baroque forms still present in reduced and humanized guise in the rococo and achieves what Jack Undank calls the "domestic sublime" is no doubt the painting of Jean-Baptiste Chardin and the intimate descriptive prose of Rousseau. For all the writers of the Enlightenment, however, poetry, art, and music are not and should not aspire to be divine or superhuman. In an enlightened age, they can be authentic only by representing a world from which the baroque contrasts of the divine and the human, the spiritual and the material, have been eliminated. Within the traditions of classical versification, the 18th-century poets show the same inexhaustible ingenuity and humor as its silversmiths and cabinetmakers. Of all their predecessors, it is surely with La Fontaine that they show most affinity. If we approach their work in the unprejudiced spirit we bring to other 18th-century artifacts, we will begin to understand what near-contemporaries like Goethe and Pushkin admired in them; why the epigrams and epitaphs of Alexis Piron, for instance, are masterpieces.

Frederick's "Le conte du violon" is not quite up to the standard of Piron. Its author did not owe his sobriquet "the Great" to his poetic achievements. But it is clever enough. Frederick was an accomplished versifier in French. "Le conte" tells wittily of a virtuoso violonist, aptly named Vacarmini (Uproarlet), who receives a request from a member of the audience, after a particularly successful concert, to perform using only three strings, then two, then one—at which point all the art of Vacarmini produces only "a common tune"—and finally no strings at all, with the predictable result. The moral of the little tale?

> Par ce conte, s'il peut vous plaire,
> Apprenez, chers concitoyens,
> Que, malgré tout le savoir faire,
> L'art reste court sans les moyens.

494

Fellow citizens dear, from this tale
You will, if it please you, conclude
That skill is of little avail;
When the means fail, art remains rude.

"Le conte du violon" is not one of the heavier pieces in the royal arsenal of verse. It was jotted down, hastily no doubt, at Breslau, in the last days of 1761—not the most brilliant year, for Frederick, of the Seven Years' War. But it bears testimony in its own way both to the international character of the French Enlightenment and to the place poetry occupied in the "prosaic" 18th century. Since poetry had been desacralized and secularized along with everything else, it could be regarded as an object of everyday use—topical rather than divine or eternal, and available for a variety of purposes—to turn a compliment, to attack an enemy or praise a friend, to make a witty, pungent comment. There was no contradiction, for Frederick, between practical life and poetry. On the contrary, a talent for verse composition (in French) was among the attributes he considered appropriate to an enlightened statesman, soldier, and citizen of the world.

Frederick's elegant little fable makes a point that the royal pupil's master had often made himself: genius and inspiration can achieve nothing, in any field, except through the arts (a word that in the 18th century still included what we would call science and technology) and the instruments that civilization—the collective and cumulative achievement of humankind—puts at our disposal. Like Diderot's blind geometer Nicolas Saunderson, we humans are extraordinarily resourceful at making up for what we do not have. Civilization itself is our collective attempt to make up for our shortcomings as individuals and as a species, and we would be very badly off indeed without the tools we have painstakingly and collectively acquired and labored to improve. Frederick's fable conveys, in many ways, not least through its own unpretentious and slightly self-mocking form, the gist of the modest yet liberating lesson of the Enlightenment.

See also 1647, 1700, 1762, 1770.

Bibliography: Ernst Cassirer, *The Philosophy of the Enlightenment,* trans. Fritz C. A. Koelln and James P. Pettegrove (Princeton: Princeton University Press, 1951). Frederick the Great, "Le conte du violon," in *Oeuvres de Frédéric le Grand,* ed. J. D. E. Preuss, vol. 10 (Berlin: Rodolphe Decker, 1849). Jean-Paul Sartre, *"What Is Literature?" and Other Essays,* trans. Bernard Frechtman (Cambridge, Mass.: Harvard University Press, 1988). Jean Starobinski, *The Invention of Liberty,* trans. Bernard C. Swift (New York: Rizzoli, 1987). Voltaire, *Oeuvres complètes,* ed. Louis Moland, vol. 7 (Paris: Garnier, 1877). Voltaire, *The Works of M. de Voltaire,* trans. T. Smollett (1761–1765), rev. ed., John Morley, vol. 36 (New York: E. Du Mont, 1901).

Lionel Gossman

✍ *1762*

Jean Calas, a Protestant Merchant, Is Executed in Toulouse, and
Voltaire Denounces the Proceedings That Led to His Condemnation

Writing the Political

Political writing in the French Enlightenment took a wide variety of forms.
Alongside such rigorous treatises as Montesquieu's *De l'esprit des lois* (1748; *On
the Spirit of Laws*) and Rousseau's *Du contrat social* (1762; *On the Social Contract*),
which explored in general terms the nature of legitimate authority and the
meaning of political freedom, a number of polemical works by Voltaire and
others stand out as characteristic of the age. As the marquis de Condorcet put
it in his *Esquisse d'un tableau historique des progrès de l'esprit humain* (1794; *Sketch
for a Historical Picture of the Progress of the Human Mind*), the philosophes used
"all the weapons with which learning, philosophy, wit, and literary talent can
furnish reason . . . every mood from humor to pathos, every literary form from
the vast encyclopedia to the novel or the broadsheet of the day" (pp. 156–157).
These polemics are still read today, in part because their main targets—the
abuse of authority based on sectarian prejudice and intellectual complacency—
are part of our own world, in part because of the stylistic brilliance and ingenuity praised by Condorcet. This attention to rhetoric, which is also to be found
in Rousseau's and Montesquieu's most sophisticated works, reflects more than
the simple desire to express ideas more agreeably. It was rooted in the conditions of the time: books were censored, and writers who subverted religious or
political tradition were subject to persecution. The philosophes needed to
defend their principles, which included the autonomy of individual reason, the
secular origin of political systems, and the need for due process of law, in ways
adapted to prevailing circumstances. But in addition to preserving the author's
personal freedom through the use of irony and other stylistic detours, the philosophes' rhetorical strategies helped create a special relationship between reader
and text. Their provocative style, which, in Condorcet's words, covered truth
with "a veil that spared weaker eyes and excited one to guess what lay beyond
it" (p. 157), helped turn public opinion into an active political force.

The interplay of philosophical investigation and historical circumstance in
the definition of public opinion's new role is evident in two important texts
published in 1762. Their authors came to symbolize the political importance
of the independent intellectual in this process. Voltaire's writings on the
Calas case attack the abuses of a judicial system that condemned an innocent
man to death. Rich and well-connected as he was, Voltaire had no legal
standing to justify his intervention. Nor could he rely on anything but "public
outcry" in his effort to have the royal courts reconsider a decision that had
been reached according to established procedures. Rousseau's *Du contrat social*
inquires "whether there can be a legitimate and reliable rule of administration
in the civil order, taking men as they are and laws as they can be" (*On the Social
Contract*, p. 46). Rousseau himself emphasizes that he does not speak as "a

496

prince or a legislator," but merely as "a citizen of a free State" whose right to vote imposes upon him the "duty" to reflect on these questions. Now, it is true that in the 18th century Rousseau's homeland, Geneva, was a republic whose citizens theoretically participated in government, but in reality the city-state was governed by a patrician oligarchy. Far from wishing to foster political self-consciousness among the people, the ruling elite sought to minimize demands for a more democratic exercise of power. But Rousseau ignores this fact. He is determined to show that critical discussion of political philosophy is not the privilege of those with particular social status or professional training.

These two texts illustrate two principal trends in Enlightenment political thought. Voltaire seeks to defend private individuals against the arbitrary power of the state. Public opinion operates to limit the state's prestige and authority. Rousseau, on the other hand, seeks to maximize the citizen's identification with the political association to which he has freely committed himself. The difficulty of reconciling critical independence and wholehearted participation remains an enduring problem in democratic thought.

Jean Calas was a Protestant merchant of Toulouse, which had expelled its first Protestants in 1562. Two centuries later, the city still commemorated that event with a solemn procession, for although some measure of toleration had been granted, sectarian feeling ran deep. When Calas' son Marc-Antoine was found dead, the father was accused of murdering him in order to prevent his conversion to Catholicism (at that time a necessary precondition for a professional career). The evidence was slim; even though the real culprit has never been identified, modern scholars have confirmed Calas' innocence. The city authorities, however, were not inclined to doubt the father's guilt: according to widespread belief, Protestants were fanatics, who severely punished any betrayal of their faith. Jean Calas was convicted and, after two hours of public torture that failed to elicit the desired last-minute confession, executed on 9 March 1762. After initial hesitation, for he was suspicious of any cause involving religion, Voltaire led a successful three-year effort to reverse the conviction, rehabilitate Calas' memory, and repair the harm done his family.

The first step in Voltaire's campaign was to bring the facts into the open. In his efforts to clarify the circumstances of the case, he discovered that the legal proceedings were being withheld even from the defendant's relatives and that such secrecy was quite legal. Access to the records became Voltaire's key demand, since the only cure for fanaticism, he wrote in a 15 April 1762 letter, was "publicity and proof" of the crime (*Correspondance,* letter no. 10414). The evidence must be available to outside scrutiny and open debate. To create more favorable conditions for public examination of the case, and in the absence of the actual records, Voltaire produced letters and depositions ostensibly composed by Calas' widow and surviving sons. Each account carefully marshaled the facts as each witness knew them. Readers were invited to judge and compare the testimony, then decide what additional evidence might be needed to confirm it—evidence the authorities must be urged to release. Whereas, in the past, secrecy could have been justified by worries about hasty judgment by

497

uninformed people, the creation of a mature, enlightened public made secrecy not only unnecessary but undesirable. Only in 1763, after the success of the initial campaign, did Voltaire publish a more general and explicit *Traité sur la tolérance* (*Treatise on Tolerance*) to drive home the points raised in the personal testimony.

And yet Voltaire's "original documents" were written by himself. As in the tragedies he continued to write throughout this period, Voltaire spoke through each character to convey the pathos of the situation and the travails of reason struggling to be heard. Since they were based on interviews, the Calas papers cannot be considered purely fictional, but their ambiguous, pseudodocumentary nature suggests that Voltaire's notion of "publicity and proof" involves something other than simply replacing hearsay by fact.

In earlier usage, "publicity" meant flagrancy; it was a term used to describe the scandal of an open crime. Conversely, the best evidence was self-evident, disclosing the truth to immediate apprehension. The majesty of a king or the power of a miracle are instances of this immediate authority, which for Voltaire rests on illusion. Voltaire shifts the ground of apprehension from direct, transcendent revelation to the intersubjective communication of independent rational minds. Voltaire's polemics create a space in which a horizontal, introspective identification with another person is balanced by critical, skeptical judgment. Calas was a family man, but the bourgeois family does not conduct its life in the open: it reveals itself to others only on intimate acquaintance. He was also a respectable merchant. His reputation is not based, however, on the qualities that shine forth from the nobleman, but on the soundness of his business. Accusations against him should be examined with the same care as his accounts. As Jürgen Habermas has argued, this new outlook is an essential aspect of Enlightenment thought. In terms of literary history, it will find better expression in the 19th-century realist novel than it could in the classical theater, to which Voltaire was still loyal. But Voltaire's easy assimilation of the Calas writings to his dramatic experiments is understandable. It was the critical discussion of aesthetic (and especially theatrical) questions in the salons of Paris that first allowed public opinion, as an intersubjective network of judgment, to become conscious of itself. Voltaire helped bring the exercise of criticism out of the intimate atmosphere of the salons onto the political stage, where the Revolution would soon demand *la publicité des débats* (openness of proceedings).

Rousseau detested prejudice and arbitrary rule as much as Voltaire did, but he did not seek to neutralize these dangers by making public opinion more pluralistic and politically autonomous. Such a division of sovereignty might be necessary in a country as corrupt as France, but it had no place in a genuine political order. *Du contrat social* portrays an ideal republic in which no parties or pressure groups are allowed. Rousseau is confident that where every citizen has an equal voice in fundamental legislation, where all laws must be formulated in general terms, without reference to particular persons or groups, and where no obstacles prevent the citizen from seeking and expressing the public interest, individual rights will be respected.

By making participation in an indivisible sovereignty the highest political value, Rousseau denies legitimacy to any loyalty that might conflict with the citizen's wholehearted identification with the body politic. Allegiance to the god of a particular religion is one such loyalty. To the extent that Christianity, considered in its pure, authentic form, proclaims the existence of an authority above and apart from that of the state, it is incompatible with social unity: "All institutions that put man in contradiction with himself are worthless" (*On the Social Contract,* p. 128). Instead, to ensure that people will obey the laws even when no one is looking, society needs a "civil religion" whose tenets are defined by the state to foster in each citizen an internal sense of moral obligation. Many readers have read a totalitarian intention into Rousseau's text, but we should remember that, in its own time, *Du contrat social* (which was never allowed to circulate in France) was banned in Protestant Geneva as subversive not only of "the Christian religion" but also of "all governments." Rousseau may call for undivided loyalty, but he does so in such a way as to denounce the governments of his own time, which conflate eternal truths and expedient arrangements.

The discussion of religion in *Du contrat social* is typical of the book's disturbing mixture of single-minded doctrine and double-edged criticism. As he expounds the "principles of political right," Rousseau soberly and with apparently unassailable logic draws a series of inferences from his basic premises. This style contributes to the impression that, however democratic in form, his vision is restrictive in spirit, leaving no room for divergence of opinion either in the republic he portrays or in the reading of his text. But when it is examined in detail, the style of the work proves to be a paradoxical one, turning ideas in on each other and provoking the reader to adopt a more critical, independent attitude. One famous example of paradoxical style is Rousseau's claim that, having once committed himself to the political association, the citizen is "forced to be free." On the one hand, this simply means that those who freely enter into a contract are bound to keep their promise: democratic citizens obey the laws they impose on themselves. But the dark overtones of Rousseau's formulation remind the reader that even the most legitimate obligations involve some form of compulsion, that freedom is never simply the opposite of force. One might say that the checks and balances absent from his constitutional scheme operate at the level of discourse itself, which compels readers to grapple with the conflicting values embedded in semantic paradoxes.

Rousseau's paradoxical politics emerged from his speculations on how social organization came into being in a world initially inhabited by isolated individuals. Rousseau acknowledged the advantages of civilization, but the image of independent, "natural" man was still attractive enough to him that he could never ignore the price exacted by even the best political organization. On the other hand, it was foolish to pretend that the state of nature could be recovered. Rousseau's analysis of social development in the *Discours sur l'origine et les fondements de l'inégalité parmi les hommes* (1755; *Discourse on the Origin and Foundations of Inequality among Men*) shows how the rich and powerful were able to exploit the ambiguity of abstract concepts in establishing the first social contract. This pact created an association that extended "equal" protection to all the people against common enemies, but only in the sense that the rich man's wealth was protected as much as the poor man's poverty. Such deceptions were made possible, even inevitable, by the same cognitive and linguistic processes that enabled individuals of very different appearance and capacities to conclude that they were similar enough to have common interests in the first place. Equality is always in some sense a fiction, with both positive and negative possibilities. Even as Rousseau outlined the conditions for a more just social contract, he remained aware of the difficulty of properly evaluating and applying political concepts. His paradoxical style is designed to bring this problem to the reader's attention by displaying the tensions, such as the one between force and freedom, that all those concerned with politics try to resolve—or, in the search for easy answers, to hide.

Because Rousseau traced to ambivalent human motives not only the workings of government but also the very meaning of political ideas, readers have been tempted to interpret *Du contrat social* as the expression of the author's own troubled personality. In turning to autobiography after the condemnation of his philosophical works, Rousseau himself seemed to recognize that the relation between critical consciousness and idealizing identification, between the desire for autonomy and close communication with others, could, in the late 18th century, more easily and acceptably find expression in the language of the self. As in Voltaire's Calas writings, political understanding could not be divorced from the critical exploration and exercise of subjectivity.

See also 1734, 1761 (December).

Bibliography: Felicity Baker, "La route contraire," in *Reappraisals of Rousseau: Studies in Honour of R. A. Leigh,* ed. Simon Harvey, Marian Hobson, D. J. Kelley, and S. S. B. Taylor (Manchester: Manchester University Press, 1980). Patrick Coleman, *Rousseau's Political Imagination: Rule and Representation in the "Lettre à d'Alembert"* (Geneva: Droz, 1984). Antoine Nicolas de Condorcet, *Esquisse d'un tableau historique des progrès de l'esprit humain,* ed. O. H. Prior (Paris: Vrin, 1970); translated by June Barraclough as *Sketch for a Historical Picture of the Human Mind* (New York: Noonday, 1955). Maurice Cranston, *Philosophers and Pamphleteers: Political Theorists of the Enlightenment* (Oxford: Oxford University Press, 1986). Jürgen Habermas, "The Public Sphere," trans. Sara Lennox and Frank Lennox, *The New German Critique,* 3 (1974), 40–55. Jean-Jacques Rousseau, *Du contrat social,* in *Oeuvres complètes,* ed. Bernard Gagnebin and Marcel Raymond, vol. 3 (Paris: Gallimard, 1964); translated by Judith R. Masters in *On the Social Contract with Geneva Manuscript and Political Economy,* ed. Roger D. Masters (New York: St. Martin's, 1978). Voltaire, *L'affaire Calas,* ed. Jacques van den Heuvel (Paris: Gallimard, 1975). Voltaire, *Correspondence and Related Documents,* vols. 85–135 of *Complete Works,* ed. Theodore Besterman et al. (Geneva: Voltaire Foundation, 1968–1977).

Patrick Coleman

◌⁓ 1769

Denis Diderot Writes *Le rêve de d'Alembert*

Reason

Denis Diderot's *Le rêve de d'Alembert* (wr. 1769, pub. 1830; *D'Alembert's Dream*) is a difficult and quirky text consisting of three dialogues: "Entretien entre d'Alembert and Diderot" ("Conversation between d'Alembert and Diderot"), "Le rêve de d'Alembert" ("D'Alembert's Dream"), and "Suite de l'entretien" ("Sequel to the Conversation"). Though written in 1769, when Diderot's thought was already mature, the dialogues, the most fully elaborated example of his materialist philosophy, remained unpublished during his lifetime. Diderot had been writing underground philosophy since the suppression in 1759 of the *Encyclopédie,* (1751–1772), for which he had served as editor-in-chief. "The condition of the sage is really dangerous," he wrote, adding: "What is one to do? Join the insane? No; but one must be wise in secret; it is safer" ("Pythagorisme," *Encyclopédie*). *Le rêve de d'Alembert* is a work profound in the development of a poetics and a philosophy of science that questioned the rational tradition, and extravagant in the daring sequence of conversations among three well-known contemporaries: the mathematician and Diderot's coeditor for the *Encyclopédie,* Jean Le Rond d'Alembert; the literary hostess and d'Alembert's friend Julie de Lespinasse; and the distinguished physician Théophile de Bordeu. Because of the content of the dialogues and because of the roles assigned to their respective characters, both d'Alembert and Lespinasse demanded the destruction of the manuscript. The assertions attributed to d'Alembert represented a potential social and political threat to his position; Lespinasse was angry with her portrayal as a light-headed coquette by a man who hardly knew her. A copy of the manuscript survived, however, in the personal library that Diderot sold to Catherine II of Russia, and this became the basis of the first published edition in 1830.

Materialism, as a philosophy, finds the explanation for the universe in the sole principle of matter, and for this reason remains close to science. By establishing a form of scientific materialism, Diderot confronts philosophy with the possibility of modeling itself on the biological sciences without falling back into inherited schemas of thought and language.

In the first dialogue, Diderot establishes his materialist philosophy with the startling assertion that "stone must feel." Centering his attention on physiology, he presents (as interlocutor in the dialogue) the most important argument: sentience is the property of all matter, the general principle of organization of the universe. Thought exists in a chain extending from passive to active, from inorganic to organic life: "You can make marble out of flesh and flesh out of marble" (*Dream,* p. 149). The question is: When, along this chain, does one pass from inert matter to consciousness in the human being? If through memory a sentient being "links together the impressions he receives, and constructs from this a story, that of his life, and so acquires consciousness of himself, he can deny, affirm, conclude, think" (pp. 155–156).

To demonstrate that thinking in this sense is not simply a matter of finding causes or drawing conclusions through logical reasoning, Diderot turns to musical images. The philosopher and his "instrument" are not separate (the one spirit, the other matter). Rather, they both are "at one and the same time player and instrument." Thought is the activity of connecting "phenomena, the connection between which is either necessary or contingent. [These phenomena] are necessary in mathematics, physics and other exact sciences, contingent in ethics, politics and other speculative sciences" (*Dream*, p. 162). Asking whether the *connection* between phenomena is any more necessary in one case than in another, d'Alembert addresses the crucial question of analogy and analogical thinking. Diderot taunts d'Alembert and suggests that analogy may play tricks on the philosopher; he warns him that d'Alembert will dream about this talk, and the first dialogue ends with d'Alembert's going to bed.

In the second dialogue, the most substantial of the three, Dr. Bordeu pays a visit to d'Alembert, who has spent a fitful night spouting delirious ideas in the dream that Diderot predicted. The dream in this part provides a format for presenting philosophical topics without an apparent rigorous order; it opens up ways of thinking that prefigure Freudian discoveries about the nature of dream-life. Lespinasse presents the dream, because she transcribed it during the night, and she and Bordeu converse about it. Like Diderot, Bordeu is a materialist; his discussion centers on examples and analogies rather than on generalities and concepts. D'Alembert awakens periodically and interrupts the conversation with musings such as this: "Why am I what I am? Who can tell what a thinking and sentient being on Saturn is like?" (*Dream*, p. 179). The characters talk about the mechanical nature of the body and soul, the explanation of life in physiological terms, and a provisional theory of evolution. By mixing subjects, tones, and styles, Diderot reinvigorates the abstract, conceptual language of philosophy through a literary approach to the questions of the day. The sequence of dialogues establishes associative thinking and digression as the way in which both conversation and the order of the text unfold; these are metaphors for the workings of the mind. The conversation jumps from subject to subject, touching on concrete examples to illustrate conjectures: the swarm of bees, the polyp, and the spiderweb.

In the final dialogue the characters discuss the consequences of crossbreeding and genetic experiments along with the ethical problems they create. Like the other two, this dialogue fuses form and content and performs a critique of rationalism by developing a poetics of philosophy. Philosophy takes on the tone of conversation and the whims of associative thinking. Without pretense to a conclusion, this dialogue stops with the following casual repartee:

> *Mlle. de L.:* Well, good-bye, Doctor. Don't stay away for ages, as you usually do, and remember sometimes that I'm madly in love with you.
> If people only knew all the horrors you have been telling me!
> *Bordeu:* I'm quite sure you will keep them to yourself.

> *Mlle. de L.:* Don't you be too sure. I only listen for the pleasure of passing
> things on. But just one word more, and I'll never bring the sub-
> ject up again as long as I live.
> *Bordeu:* Well?
> *Mlle. de L.:* Where do these abominable tastes come from?
> *Bordeu:* Always from some abnormality of the nervous system in young
> people, softening of the brain in the old, from the attraction of
> beauty in Athens, shortage of women in Rome, fear of the pox in
> Paris. Good-bye, good-bye. (*Dream,* p. 233)

In the article "Philosophie" in the *Encyclopédie,* Diderot had described philosophy as the science of possibilities *as* possibilities. At the same time he
maintained, as his contemporaries did, that without the ideal of totality, philosophy would be impossible. For philosophy to exist, all knowledge had to be
linked, and any break in knowledge stemmed from a failure of thinking. In
keeping with the entire Hellenic-Judeo-Christian tradition, Diderot associated
the concept of totality with rational thinking and the notion of being. The
place of this rational being within philosophy, and philosophy within the
system of the universe—what the 18th century called the Book of Nature—
could be ascertained only by addressing questions of truth and method.

For the 17th century, the proper task of philosophy was the construction of
philosophical "systems" through rigorous deduction. The function of reason
was to reduce what is complex to its simple elements; this analytic method,
based on the Cartesian method, was to lead to understanding. Reason played a
unifying role: it provided knowledge of the world according to a constant and
general rule. The 18th century inherited this conception of reason as a principle
prior to all experience, but it turned away from deduction and system formation
in order to seek a new conception of truth. Reason, in the 18th century, no
longer led from this world beyond in a transcendent movement; it was neither
a sum of ideas revealing the essence of things nor a predetermined content of
knowledge. Reason was an *energy,* a force in this world that could be perceived
through its actions and effects.

In searching for a "new" and "original" form of philosophy, the Enlightenment philosophers saw the "spirit of systems" as a hindrance to reason, although
they never abandoned the "systematic spirit." System refers here to system of
philosophy, a term confused with the tradition of metaphysics; systematic
thought ("rational," "logically deduced") was based on the belief that there was
a correspondence between the systematic form of ideas and empirical phenomena; it involved the ordering of ideas. Observation, reflection, and experience replaced metaphysical certitude, as description—based on the model of
the natural sciences—replaced philosophical definition.

Although Diderot never completely abandoned the systematic form of ideas,
in showing language to be an arbitrary system his critique of rationalism passed
from epistemology (as the understanding of how one acquires knowledge) to
aesthetics (the artistic realm) in order to change the function of reason. In many
of his writings Diderot demonstrates the impact of science and technology on

traditional questions of philosophy through a kind of literary laboratory: mimicked experiments in his *Lettre sur les sourds et muets* (1751; *Letter on the Deaf and Dumb*), anecdotes and exchanges of dialogue in *Jacques le fataliste et son maître* (wr. 1771–1780? pub. 1796; *Jacques the Fatalist and His Master*), and *Le rêve de d'Alembert*, all take on a status equivalent to that of facts in the domain of experimental physics. They are there to be tested in the apparently fortuitous conversations and events of the works.

Because each experiment, anecdote, or scene from these works deals with a singular episode, it eludes the form of traditional philosophical discourse, which depends upon conceptual thinking and universality. What interests the "new" philosopher (Diderot) is what is accidental, accessory, and circumstantial, namely, everything that qualifies the person or thing in its singularity. The philosopher's reasoning cannot be solely deductive; it must also be inductive and associative. In his writing Diderot generalizes that which, by definition, cannot be generalized. Each example is taken in its own terms and yields local, not universal, meanings. In this way art resembles matter: "Not a single molecule resembles any other, not a single molecule remains for a moment just like itself" (*Dream*, p. 174).

The swarm of bees, the polyp, and the spiderweb illustrate the need for unifying images to develop this philosophy of science. The image of the swarm of bees raises the question of continuity of being. D'Alembert proclaims that the world, or general mass of matter, is a great hive, and he muses that if one had never seen a swarm of bees before, a person might "take it for a single creature with five or six hundred heads and a thousand or twelve hundred wings" (*Dream*, p. 169). So the question is: What if you wanted to change the swarm of bees into a unity? "Soften the feet with which they cling to each other, that is to say make them continuous instead of contiguous" (ibid.).

Reversing the passage from contiguity to continuity is the polyp, a creature that lives by dividing and multiplying itself. The polyp, discovered by Abraham Tremblay in 1740, remained the metaphor par excellence for conceptual thinking and the model for examining totality in the rationalist tradition well into the 19th century. It posed the problem of location of the seat of the soul: Is it within each new living fragment or in the larger whole embracing the homogeneous plurality of cuttings? In *Le rêve de d'Alembert*, d'Alembert dreams of human polyps: males resolving into males, females into females in a kind of utopian androgyny. He even imagines an entire society of beings formed from the debris of a single being.

The image of the spiderweb raises the crucial question of unity and consciousness within the sensitive being. The center of being, like the center of the spider's web, exists within a network of relations; it is described as "variations on the sense of touch." In the human as in the spider, "it is the constant, invariable relationship between all impressions and the common center which constitutes . . . individuality" (*Dream*, p. 194). Memory confers consciousness of individual history and unity without which life would be an unintelligible stream of sensations, while the faculty of comparison enables the human being to think and reason. The images of the swarm of bees, the polyp, and the spiderweb all raise without resolving the problems of the unity of being, how it is determined, and whether its will can be free, by showing that the spirit is embedded in matter, in a network.

In his early texts Diderot expressed nostalgia for a metaphysical system from which all arbitrariness would be excluded, because the truth of being could be located in the unity and absoluteness of the soul. But the scientific materialism that he develops in *Le rêve de d'Alembert* promises no certainty beyond the existence of matter. As for an intelligence that might order or direct the universe, interlocutor d'Alembert gives the question and response:

> What is a being? The sum of a certain number of tendencies . . . Can I be anything more than a tendency? . . . No, I am moving towards a certain end . . . And what of species? Species are merely tendencies towards a common end peculiar to them . . . And life? A series of actions and reactions . . . Alive, I act and react as a mass . . . dead, I act and react as separate molecules . . . Don't I die, then? Well, not in that sense, neither I nor anything else . . . To be born, to live and to die is merely to change forms. (*Dream,* p. 182)

Lest one harbor the hope of locating a spiritual world in the passage from inert matter to generalized sensitivity, d'Alembert warns in his dream against "the fallacy of the ephemeral," and this discussion ensues:

> *Bordeu:* [This is the fallacy] of a transient being who believes in the immutability of things.
> *Mlle. de L.:* Like Fontenelle's rose, who declared that no gardener had ever been known to die?
> *Bordeu:* Exactly. That is both graceful and profound.
> *Mlle. de L.:* Why can't these philosophers of yours express themselves as gracefully as Fontenelle? We should understand them then.
> *Bordeu:* Frankly I'm not sure whether such a frivolous tone is suitable for serious subjects.
> *Mlle. de L.:* What do you call a serious subject?
> *Bordeu:* Well, universal sensitivity, the formation of a sentient being, its unity, the origin of animal life, its duration and all the questions these matters raise.
> *Mlle. de L.:* For my part I call these things a lot of nonsense, something that I admit we can dream of when we are asleep, but which a reasonable man will not bother about in his waking hours. (*Dream,* p. 177)

Reproducing the paradox of being, this dialogue questions what the proper tone and subjects of philosophy should be. The "new" philosophy will be concrete, descriptive, and alive, opening up problems without solving them, and often relying on dialogue as its favored form. Because dialogue for Diderot is a hybrid form between philosophy and literature, it allows him to challenge the traditional concept of written language as rational discourse directed at rationality. Diderot shows that resistance to order is at the heart of invention. Language is an acquired, not a given, faculty, whose primary function is to establish the connection between thoughts through an order or system independent from all others. That is, Diderot dismantles systems in order to see how they are constructed. Rejecting facile solutions that might allow his thought to fall back into received patterns, Diderot seeks to change the way in which women and men think. He moves playfully, but always rigorously and cautiously, toward new ideas.

By exploring the limits of epistemology in order to found an aesthetics, Diderot describes poetic being as a unity capable of perceiving simultaneous significations. He translates this into the poetic notion of the hieroglyph, an emblem of the mysterious relations between meaning and image. It becomes the figure for a common internal language in which a plurality of meanings recreates the heterogeneity of poetic thought: the mind understands; the soul is moved; the imagination sees; and the ear hears. The recognition of such a language of the senses depends less upon rational content than upon the force of evocation. Since all art, according to Diderot, is imitation, the intelligibility of the affect depends upon translation that no longer opposes reason to instinct; rather, instinct, like the modern concept of the unconscious, guides the individual in her or his relationship to the world.

In his theory of the correspondences among the arts, Diderot proclaims that the orchestra speaks thought, the poet dictates it, and the musician writes what it should say, in the same way that the painter or pantomime may "think" with paint, steps, and gesture. Far from homogenizing all art forms and unifying all thought, Diderot maintains the tensions between the oppositions and differences within the arts and sciences, making discrete meanings intelligible. Using musical images, he compares the mind to a stringed instrument whose operation is governed by the law of connection; just as resonating strings vibrate, causing other strings to resonate, so one idea evokes another. Bordeu says that "ideas awaken each other, and they do so because they have always been related" (*Dream*, p. 220). What emerges from these associations depends on the type of mind making them. The harpsichord is the model for the brain. The sensitive being is endowed with memory, and men and women are composed of a multitude of keys touched both by nature and by themselves. The poet and philosopher both function according to the same musical model. In the genius, association permits extraordinary leaps in thought—comparable to harmonics produced at sometimes incomprehensible levels—as it does for those able to call upon affect rather than reason.

The analogy to music becomes an extended metaphor for the transformation from the rationalist to a "new" form of philosophy. In the *Lettre sur les sourds et muets*, Diderot shows that between one chord and another there is a common sound that resembles the middle term of the syllogism. In *Le rêve de d'Alembert* he substitutes analogical thinking for the syllogism, as the quintessential form of rationalist thought. Analogy becomes the heuristic means to innovating in the arts and sciences. The subjects, form, and tone of philosophy are not preset: the subjects are there in experimental science, the history of philosophy, and the lives of human beings; the forms are as numerous as their objects; and the tone, considered in its etymological sense of stretched ligament, rope, string, or cable, will now be related to the timbre of the sensitive instrument.

In *Le rêve de d'Alembert,* the relations of thought, language, and gender are jumbled through the dialogue of the dreaming mathematician and the associations of his two friends, so that there appears to be no "difference at all between a doctor awake and a philosopher dreaming" (*Dream,* p. 170). As for Lespinasse, her ostensibly secondary role, as scribe of the dream, becomes crucial to change. Comparisons, as she proclaims, may be the realm of women and poets; but so they are too of the "new" philosophy. Indeed, it is Lespinasse who finds herself gleefully spouting a new form of prose without even knowing it; it is she who inaugurates a rhetoric of science establishing the parameters of the future by at once questioning and maintaining the tradition out of which they come. And it is she who, in a discussion of normality and abnormality in genetics, puts forth the "very silly idea" that "perhaps man is merely a woman with freakish malformations, or woman a freakish man" (p. 192). Lespinasse functions as the literary agent of changing thought, leveling the hierarchies of spirit to matter, of man to woman. She engages her cohorts in a heuristics of philosophy that proposes no fixed system, only possibilities for interpretation, discovery, and action: possibilities that future generations, from the "nephews" and *nieces* of the Enlightenment through the 20th century, inherit as the effects of reason in question.

See also 1761 (December), 1771.

Bibliography: James Creech, *Thresholds of Representation* (Columbus: Ohio State University Press, 1986). Denis Diderot, *Jacques le fataliste,* ed. Simone Lecointre and Jean Le Galliot (Geneva: Droz, 1976); translated by J. Robert Loy as *Jacques the Fatalist and His Master* (New York: Norton, 1959). Diderot, *Lettre sur les sourds et muets,* in *Premières oeuvres,* ed. Norman Rudich and Jean Varloot (Paris: Editions Sociales, 1972). Diderot, *Le rêve de d'Alembert,* in *Oeuvres philosophiques,* ed. Paul Vernière (Paris: Garnier, 1961); translated by Leonard Tancock as *D'Alembert's Dream,* in *Rameau's Nephew; D'Alembert's Dream* (Harmondsworth: Penguin, 1966). Christie McDonald, *The Dialogue of Writing* (Waterloo, Ontario: Wilfrid Laurier Press, 1985). Jack Undank, *Diderot, Inside, Outside, & In-Between* (Madison, Wis.: Coda Press, 1979).

Christie McDonald

℘ 1770

Claude-Joseph Dorat Publishes *Les baisers* with Copperplate Illustrations

Kisses, en Taille Douce

Even in a period unsurpassed for the elegance of its styles, no art form gave rise to more exquisite jewels than did copper engraving. Over time, wooden blocks (from which the surfaces that were *not* to print had to be carved away) were almost entirely replaced by copper plates, on which every scratch could hold enough ink (after the smooth surface was wiped clean) to transfer a fine line to paper. Copper is soft enough to etch neatly with acid or sculpt fluidly with a sharp tool—because of this the process was called *taille douce,* or soft carving— yet hard enough to withstand hundreds of printings under great pressure; and a plate of copper can be as small as a vignette or as large as a double folio.

Because it can also be subtly shaded through a variety of techniques, one of its principal uses was to copy great works of art; this monochrome but aesthetically pleasing medium made possible their dissemination to a universal viewership. In the hierarchy of the Academy of Painting, engraving was thus subordinated to painting, as the imitation of an imitation. History, natural history, and travel literature made extensive use of large copper illustrations, and the eleven folio volumes of plates to Denis Diderot's *Encyclopédie* (1751–1772) are, quite as much as Jean-Baptiste Oudry's folio-size plates for the four-volume edition of La Fontaine's *Fables* (1755–1759), among engraving's greatest monuments.

Besides venerable tomes, sacred and profane, such as Paul Rapin de Thoyras's ten-volume history of England (*Histoire d'Angleterre,* 1724–1727), which would grace any fine collection, many literary works, among them Voltaire's epic *La Henriade* (1728), were illustrated. Because the process was labor-intensive and therefore costly, however, illustrated editions could be produced only for the wealthy, who constituted a considerable but limited segment of the market. New and untested works, less certain to appeal to these potential purchasers, were infrequently illustrated. The favorite literary beneficiaries were therefore the established classics, whether of inspirational or comic appeal (Longus, Boccaccio, Torquato Tasso, Ludovico Ariosto), and, beginning with Racine, Molière, La Fontaine, and Fénelon, works believed to be the foundation of a new classical heritage. The expanding use of original illustration for literature brought into being a great tradition—less honored, perhaps, but increasingly prized—of compact, fine engraving (often duodecimo or even smaller), in contrast to the majestic plates (*estampes*) used for paintings and prestige publications.

This general rule could, however, be completely reversed when private motives not directly related to profit impelled another party to bear the expense. *Les baisers* (1770; *The Kisses*), for example, a lavishly illustrated little book of daintily erotic poems by Claude-Joseph Dorat, published probably at his own expense, is a series of twenty fables mostly clad in the worn but remarkably persistent trappings of pastoral lyric and playing titillatingly on the latent ambiguity of *baiser* (kiss/coitus). Such delights are not to be confused, Dorat insists, with "licentious writings, which shock the senses rather than tickling them" (p. 9). Like so many productions of the rococo period, this kind of poem pretends to justify the representation of officially immoral subjects on the strength of its purely stylistic elegance. Each *baiser* is framed by a pair of vignettes (headpiece and tailpiece) after Charles-Joseph Eisen, which are part and parcel of this style. More celebrated for his drawings than Dorat for his verse, Eisen understood perfectly the nature of this aesthetic compromise, the precise balance of sensuality and decency required to arouse libidinous interest without courting censure. Dorat's exploitation of illustration is doubtless an extreme example, given his obvious dependency upon renowned artists to lend luster to his own rather limited poetic attraction: there was an anecdote about a buyer who promptly removed the plates to keep and discarded the rest.

Before the *baisers* stands a twenty-five-page poem titled "Le mois de mai" ("The Month of May"), which, after unfolding as a grand allegory of spring, veers midway toward quite specific political allusion (*Kisses*, p. 34):

> A solemn treaty from of old prevails
> To reconcile Vienna to Versailles,
> When Love—whose counsel is too seldom sought—
> Fresh Vigour, for a tie that pleased him, wrought:
> —Vainly confined by cunning statesmanship
> What worldly wisdom sows, 'tis his to reap—
> Child-master of the gods! There wait thy care
> Theresa's daughter and the Lily's heir.

Versailles and Vienna are invoked for very precise reasons: the Seven Years' War now over, in which Austria and France were allies, the young dauphin of France (designated by the lily—that is, the fleur-de-lis) is marrying Marie-Antoinette (daughter of Maria-Theresa, the Austrian empress). With his paean to a love that thinly rationalizes the designs of state, Dorat is attempting nothing less ambitious than to attract the favorable attention of the royal family. His perfunctory exploitation of contemporary events does not imply that the poet is supposed to interpret history; he is merely to celebrate it. Thus his final sendoff to the felicitous pair (p. 40):

> O! may time's wing, beloved and sacred pair,
> Your happy-shining future ever spare!
> And may the Fates, upon their spindles old,
> Reel off your lives in lengthened threads of gold.

As historical commentary, this can only appear ludicrous in retrospect (they were to be beheaded in 1793), but it well represents the mood of such public occasions and the kind of response their rituals called for.

Eisen's illustrative plate (fig. 1) partly corresponds to, and is explained by, Dorat's mythical hyperboles (p. 37):

> Rejoice then, Hymen! Is thy temple dressed?
> Aye! with festoons thy lavish hand has blessed:
> I see them, snake-like, round the columns turning,
> I see bright Twins o'er the summit burning,
> An eagle bound by Venus there I see
> Exchange his thunder for the fleur-de-lys.

History here is allegorized in a manner characteristic of such precious verse, and the reader had to know how to recognize the allusions of both poem and illustration. This apostrophe to Hymen, god of marriage, justifies the illustra-

1. Plate designed by Charles-Joseph Eisen, engraved by Joseph de Longueil, for "Le mois de mai," in Charles-Joseph Dorat, *Les baisers, précédés du Mois de mai* (The Hague and Paris: Delalain, 1770), p. 29.

tor's fantasy of an antique temple of love, which with its baroque canopy simultaneously evokes the present setting of the royal nuptial. The cupid in front is most likely meant to represent Hymen, his torch resting on the ground so he can better hold what would appear to be a dove, sign of peace. As Louis and Marie-Antoinette join hands across a classical altar, they are crowned with wreaths by a pair of *putti* repeating those above (the "Twins," which are explicitly Gemini in the original), which are placing crowns on the twin heads of the imperial Austrian eagle. The objects in the foreground provide a symbolic promise of abundance and of the flourishing of the arts and sciences.

Smoke issuing left and right from censers, the garlands everywhere, and the allusion to Venus lend a sensuous atmosphere to this epitomization of vernal fertility in the form of a crowned union. These connotations are reinforced by the poem's headpiece (fig. 2), with its commingling of male (*le* Danube) and female (*la* Seine) rivers representing the two national lineages, and by a tailpiece in which the smiling sun of May shines down on a cornucopia full of flowers and royal babies. Since the very inclusion of the crown prince's marriage in a book such as *Les baisers* is rationalized by a common natural-erotic theme, there is nothing surprising about such allusions to the proliferating benefits of regal sexuality. Reference to the conjugal bed (also explicit in the poem) was a publicly acceptable acknowledgment of the procreative duty of all marriage and of the future king's in particular: Marie-Antoinette, despite her popularity, did not acquit herself satisfactorily until she gave birth to a male heir eleven years later.

Both Dorat's and Eisen's allegorizations are typical in their dependence on ancient motifs, a common fund of referents for a readership whose education was relatively uniform and predominantly literary. But text and image are not perfectly congruent. The poem does not mention the second pair of cherubs; and although the eagle in the illustration is perhaps "bound" by the garlands of Venus, "thunder" (lightning, more exactly) and fleur-de-lis are difficult to detect. More curious still is a zodiacal anomaly. Gemini, of course, stands for May (not 16 May, date of the official wedding at Versailles, but 30 May, the date of its Paris celebration); but within the wheel that traverses the altar like a rainbow, Gemini seems to be framed by Scorpio and Libra on the left and Virgo and Aquarius on the right, whereas correctly it is preceded by Aries and Taurus and followed by Cancer and Leo. It is difficult to make any sense of this progression. Similarly odd is the fact that the abstract third character in the other illustration is not mentioned in the corresponding passage of the poem.

Thus the apparent precision of allegorical allusion seems somewhere to have broken down, giving rise to some unsettling disparities. And although the poem and the engraving have the same subject, one would be hard pressed to decide which came first and which was made to match. More generally, any such comparison can serve to exemplify the irreducible difference between a verbal and a visual representation, allegorical or otherwise. Even when an illustration does not conflict with anything in the text, the two cannot totally coincide and will indeed be subject to interpretations somewhat independent of each other. At the same time, an illustration, precisely because of this difference, highlights particular aspects of a text and indeed constitutes a commentary on

2. Headpiece designed by Charles-Joseph Eisen, engraved by Joseph de Longueil, for "Le mois de mai," in Charles-Joseph Dorat, *Les baisers, précédés du Mois de mai* (The Hague and Paris: Delalain, 1770), p. 29.

or imaginative reading of it. Illustrations tend to use iconic language to roughly the same degree as the corresponding texts. But allegorical tools for reading are not always pertinent, for many illustrations refer ostensibly only to the limited scenes framed by the story being narrated, as in a story never before told.

Voltaire wrote a highly irreverent mock-epic of Joan of Arc, *La Pucelle d'Orléans* (1755; *The Maid of Orléans*), which for decades he dared not avow, so dangerous was it to treat lightly the incarnation of an all-but-sacred patriotic myth. It quickly became a minor classic, and its many editions, mostly pirated and all illegal in France, were frequently accompanied by plates in varying taste. Despite its irreverent fancy, *La Pucelle* reflects Voltaire's attitude toward history, for this travesty of the exploits of the national heroine is both an oblique satire of religious tradition and a lesson in respect for natural and human fact. His comic strategy was based on turning Joan's heroic tale into the epic of her maidenhead, which more than her life is subject to constant threat. In consequence, the episodes were usually risqué or worse, that categorical distinction depending upon the reader's sensitivity. Since even an indecent subject can be illustrated in either circumspect or outrageous ways, however, according to the choice of moment and manner of representation, the illustrations are themselves quite diverse. Some of the best of them tend to hedge, bringing out the potential to shock while avoiding sexual explicitness.

One of the plot's contrivances divests Joan of her armor, thrusting her into the ludicrous position of having to enter combat utterly naked against an English band who have invaded a convent. Whereas elsewhere in the poem this paragon of chastity is made to appear an ambiguous transvestite, here her femininity is advertised in the most flamboyant fashion, so that in the eyes of at least one Englishman she is merely a party to the general orgy going on around her:

> Joan was *en cuerpo,* when a Briton's eyes,
> With look unblushing, greet the wished-for prize;
> He covets her, and thinks some maiden gay
> Has sought the sisters to enjoy the fray;
> Then flies the fair to meet, and forthwith seeks
> To taint her modesty with loathsome freaks . . .
>   (*The Maid of Orleans,* canto 11, 41:44)

He thus becomes her sword's first victim. The others are too busy raping nuns to think of defending themselves as Joan wreaks vengence among them. Only one manages to shift his attention so as to confront the danger, and he turns out to be the very one who is wearing her purloined armor.

The plate after Jean-Michel Moreau (fig. 3), probably the greatest illustrator of the late 18th century, contrasts the gothic setting with a general turbulence of nuns and soldiers. Its parallel diagonals of swords and limbs are a parody of the confusion reigning in a conventional battle scene, while Joan's statuesque pose has all the strident, military assertiveness of an early David. It is nowhere visually explicit about the kind of pseudomilitary activity being alluded to, but casts full light on the heroic pose of a starkly and absurdly naked Joan. The

Il a mon casque; il a ma soubrevelle.

Il était vrai; la Jeanne avait raison.

Pucelle Chant 11

3. Plate designed by Jean-Michel Moreau, engraved by Jean-Baptiste Simonet, for canto 11 of Voltaire's *La Pucelle d'Orléans,* vol. 11 ([Kehl]: Société Littéraire Typographique, 1789), p. 198.

enticing beauty of her flesh is sanctioned by a long artistic tradition idealizing the nude; yet by any ordinary standards it is radically out of place, both narratively and visually. The caption—"'He wears my helm and under vestments too.' / Joan reasoned justly, she had truth to quote"—further highlights her exposure by drawing attention to the fact that her rightful armor is worn by someone else. Only through such an arresting incongruity can a drawing alone well express irony (political cartoons, which first appeared in the 18th century, have always been heavily dependent upon verbal support); the engraving is as witty, in its own medium, as the poem.

Any writer was flattered by the prospect of seeing his works embellished by engravings, and some, including Rousseau, pressed their publishers to engage the finest craftsmen for this purpose. Indeed no author ever reflected longer on, or tried more intensely to control, the process of illustration than did Rousseau for his novel *Julie, ou la nouvelle Héloïse* (1761; *Julie, or the New Héloïse*). He even aspired to commissioning that consummately worldly painter (and sometime engraver) François Boucher, assuring his publisher that the engravings alone would make the book a success; but the cost was prohibitive and he eventually made a private arrangement with Hubert-François Gravelot, who was probably

4. "La confiance des belles âmes," plate designed by Hubert-François Gravelot, engraved by Pierre-Philippe Choffard, for Part 4 of Jean-Jacques Rousseau's *Julie, ou la nouvelle Héloïse* (*Recueil d'estampes pour La nouvelle Héloïse*, Paris: Duchesne, 1761).

at that time the best known of all illustrators. Rousseau had prescribed in great detail twelve "sujets d'estampes," and in his letters harshly criticized some of the proofs. We thus have in this instance a whole series of texts in the light of which to understand the illustrations.

In his instructions for the seventh plate, Rousseau first summarizes the moment in the plot—when Wolmar's confidence in Julie's virtue leads him to receive her former lover at Clarens—and then specifies the depiction in extraordinarily precise detail:

> The young man, dressed for traveling, approaches with an air of respect in which one can sense, in truth, some constraint and uncertainty but neither painful discomfort nor suspect embarrassment. As for Julie, on her face and in her behavior can be seen a character of innocence and candor which reveals at this moment all the purity of her soul. She should look at her husband with a modest assurance reflecting the tenderness and gratefulness that such a great token of esteem, and the sentiment that she is worthy of it, afford her.
>
> The inscription of the seventh plate: "The confidence of beautiful souls." ("Sujets d'estampes," p. 766)

514

As Rousseau had earlier admitted, such instructions cannot be followed to the letter; "they are less what the artist must render than what he must know in order to make his work conform as much as possible" to the intention (letter of December 1757, *Correspondance,* 4:408). In this case (fig. 4) he was rather pleased with the result, especially the figure of Wolmar on the right, although he had objected, upon seeing the proof, to Julie's overly long and insufficiently touching face. Gravelot has in fact been content to render the facial expression with great simplicity (the faces are in truth very tiny), reserving lush elegance for the clothing and trees, and emphasizing the dignity of the occasion over its emotional tension; indeed Rousseau had prescribed the instant *following* Saint-Preux's and Julie's "impetuous" embrace, in which they finally turn more calmly toward Wolmar. Necessarily transformed too, both in visual perspective and in the plate's caption, is the *voice* (Saint-Preux's) of the letter relating the story.

When Moreau began to illustrate the same novel a dozen years later, he felt no obligation to respect Rousseau's subjects and sometimes chose episodes more sublime, such as the storm on the lake in part 4, or domestically dramatic, such as the return of Claire in part 5 (fig. 5). A whole chain reaction is captured

5. The return of Claire, plate designed by Jean-Michel Moreau, engraved by Noël Le Mire, for *Julie, ou la nouvelle Héloïse,* in *Collection complète des oeuvres de J.-J. Rousseau,* vol. 2 (London [Brussels]: [J. L. de Boubers], 1774), p. 349.

6. Frontispiece by Charles-
Nicolas Cochin, engraved by
Joseph de Longueil, for *Julie,
ou la nouvelle Héloïse* (Neuchâtel
and Paris: Duchesne, 1764).

here, yet it is only a small fraction of the compact action in the novel, related
again by Saint-Preux:

> Henriette, seeing her mother, leaped up and ran to meet her, crying "Mama!
> Mama!" with all her might, and ran against her with such force that the poor
> child fell backward. This sudden appearance of Claire, that fall, her joy, her
> agitation—all took hold of Julie to such a point that, having stood as she
> extended her arms, with a very piercing cry she let herself fall back and grew
> faint. Wishing to raise her up, Claire saw her friend turn pale. She hesitated:
> she did not know to whom to run. Finally, seeing me pick up Henriette, she
> rushed to aid the fainting Julie and fell with her in the same condition.
>
> (*La nouvelle Héloïse*, pt. 5, letter 6)

The stately height of the room and the muted portrait on the wall provide the
aristocratic frame, while in contrast the sweeping contours of the characters'
arms tracing grand gestures seem complemented by the multiple arabesques of
chairs and garments.

Nonetheless Rousseau and his novel were, for ideological reasons, often allegorized, and the first fully illustrated edition was also furnished with a frontispiece by Charles Nicolas Cochin (fig. 6) that in no way refers to action in the

story. In fact, rather than standing alone it is glossed by a new kind of text common in works of the time, an *explication des figures,* serving to underscore and extend its allegorical content: "To express the larger-than-life impression that can be given by the characters traced in this novel, we have represented the author of *La nouvelle Héloïse* under the emblem of a Painter inspired by the fire of Genius and of Love, and who, in imitating Nature, paints her much larger and more beautiful than she is." This is rather simple as general allegory of artist and truth, but the citation of the novel's title suggests another degree of allegory relative to it specifically: the "painter" is Rousseau, the image of Nature is Julie, Julie is too perfect to be taken literally. The commentary depends, as in all illustration—though in various admixtures—on a reverberation from text to image and back, or vice versa.

For illustration can never be simply "literal." It can be minimalist and conservative or imaginative and provocative; but because it can in no way simply reproduce language, it is always to be "read" in some degree of tension as well as harmony with the text. Its subtleties, and its aesthetic appeal, will also be of a different kind. No one doubts its evocative power, and every reader's memory of at least some works is permanently marked by the illustrations that accompanied them.

See also 1668, 1707, 1751, 1759 (January), 1761 (February), 1761 (December).

Bibliography: Claude-Joseph Dorat, *The Kisses,* trans. H. G. Keene (London: Vizetelly, [1888]). Alexis François, *Le premier baiser de l'amour, ou Jean-Jacques Rousseau inspirateur d'estampes* (Geneva: Sonor, 1920). Owen E. Holloway, *French Rococo Book Illustration* (New York: Transatlantic Arts, 1969). Roger Chartier and Henri-Jean Martin, eds., *Histoire de l'édition française,* vol. 2: *Le livre triomphant, 1660–1830* (Paris: Promodis, 1984). Gordon N. Ray, *The Art of the French Illustrated Book, 1700 to 1914,* vol. 1 (New York: Pierpont Morgan Library and Cornell University Press, 1982). Jean-Jacques Rousseau, *Correspondance complète,* ed. R. A. Leigh, 45 vols. (Geneva: Institut et Musée Voltaire, 1965–1986). Rousseau, *La nouvelle Héloïse: Julie, or the New Eloise. Letters of Two Lovers, Inhabitants of a Small Town at the Foot of the Alps,* abr. and trans. Judith H. McDowell (University Park: Pennsylvania State University Press, 1968). Rousseau, "Sujets d'estampes," in *Julie, ou la nouvelle Héloïse,* vol. 2 of *Oeuvres complètes* (Paris: Gallimard, 1961), pp. 761–771. Voltaire, *La Pucelle d'Orléans,* in vol. 7 of *Oeuvres complètes de Voltaire* (Geneva: Institut et Musée Voltaire, 1970); translated by W. F. Fleming as *The Maid of Orleans,* vols. 40 and 41 of *The Works of Voltaire* (Akron: Werner, 1905).

Philip Stewart

❧ 1771

Denis Diderot Starts to Write *Jacques le fataliste et son maître*

Diderot at the Crossroads of Speech

To a man like Denis Diderot (1713–1784), who suffered from claustrophobia and who, by principle and temperament, clung to the joys of social life and free intellectual exchange, it must have seemed like the sudden materialization of a recurrent nightmare when in 1749 he was imprisoned for the slanderous and unorthodox ideas contained in his *Lettre sur les aveugles* (1749; *Letter on the Blind*), *Les bijoux indiscrets* (1748; *The Talkative Jewels*), and *Pensées philosophiques* (1746; *Philosophical Thoughts*). The fear of disconnection and immurement, physical or figurative, threads itself throughout his work in fields as diverse as science, philosophy, aesthetics, drama, politics, art criticism, and religion. The persecutions of censorship and the intimidations of what he at times angrily referred to as "public opinion" no doubt heightened his anxieties; but he continually meditated on the difficulties involved in overcoming obstacles to communication—difficulties inherent not only in the beliefs that separate us, but in the very nature of society and of language itself. If the purpose of Enlightenment philosophy was to create a brave new world based on the destruction of prejudice and blindly vested interests; if the written word was to be its sanitary engineer as well as its harbinger, the entire enterprise depended as much on the efficacy of speech as on the freedom to reveal new foundations for truth and judgment.

The conceptual framework Diderot was bound to use as he considered the question of the limits and impasses of language derived from John Locke's vastly influential *Essay concerning Human Understanding* (1690), which, if hastily read, made it hard to imagine how human beings might possibly agree or even understand one another. Locke was, in France, shorn of all nuance, but he had made it clear that we are born with no innate ideas—ideas planted in all human souls by the divinity—and that our thoughts are no more than airy, conventional abstractions based on accidentally associated sense impressions. These thoughts, compounded by the cohesive operations of memory, merely describe and ratify the individual experience of particular beings. How, then, given these premises—liberating in the way they disconnect a transcendent power from the operations of the mind, but disturbing in the burdens they impose on the immanent order of man and matter—was anyone able to convince anyone else? Diderot had already in his earliest works—those mentioned, as well as in his translation of Shaftesbury, the *Essai sur le mérite et la vertu* (1745; *Essay on Merit and Virtue*), *La promenade du sceptique* (1747; *The Skeptic's Walk*), *Lettre sur les sourds et muets* (1751; *Letter on the Deaf and Dumb*), and *De l'interprétation de la nature* (1753–54; *On the Interpretation of Nature*)—imaged the clash of fixed and irreconcilable "systematic philosophers." He had convinced himself that all men were not sensorially endowed by their creator with equal and concordant versions of the universe and that lively testimonies of empirical experience or carefully conducted experiments performed on essentially transient things yielded not so much truth as a ground for speculation and interpretation. He even noticed that in this babel and bedlam of dissonant, self-righteous voices, each sealed in its own sounding-box, no voice (including Diderot's own), no necessarily linear speech, could possibly capture the teeming simultaneity of ideas or impressions as they crashed upon consciousness. He hoped for a language as transparent, immediate, and expressive as gesture, as dense and resonant as poetry. Having struggled with the epistemological problem of radically confined subjectivities, the difficulties involved in maintaining the unity of society itself, its social intelligence and communication, he was becoming either free or ripe enough to fathom his obsessive theme.

It is as if, after his imprisonment, after the repeated "spasms of crisis" that attended the publication of the inaugural volumes of the *Encyclopédie*, (1751– 1772), after his quarrel with Rousseau over the very issue of social solidarity—a quarrel launched by Diderot's first "domestic drama," *Le fils naturel* (1757; *The Natural Son*)—he could ponder not only the ramifications of those psychological and physiological differences that divide us from one another; he could reflect also on the material circumstances that compel us to assume the attitudes that constitute our individual being and specificity. Henceforth, however, the most insidious, the most daring of Diderot's voices (whose faint echoes continued to be heard publicly in his plays and the *Encyclopédie*) would move underground, remaining concealed in manuscripts that were either published after his death or consigned to the pages of Friedrich Melchior Grimm's privately circulated *Correspondance littéraire* (1753–1790; *Literary Correspondence*). In 1760 he was to begin *La religieuse* (1796; *The Nun*), a first-person narrative involving a girl named Suzanne who, illegitimate and without dowry, is swept out of society and into the conventual system, where society replicates itself in grotesque ways. She is compelled to learn, among the gothic horrors of confinement and censorship—even as she blackens the page with her pleading letter to the Marquis de Croismare—the importance of "having one's mouth open to speak" (*La religieuse*, p. 146). But she comes to realize that any speech exacts a dreadful price, that by adopting forms of discourse to "move" the different powers and sexes controlling her fate, she has self-protectively and adaptively destroyed her moral self or else scattered it upon the winds of social circumstance. Diderot is here no longer preoccupied with abstract epistemological issues, with idealist considerations of what normal or handicapped subjectivities may know or express, but with the formative pressures of a tyrannical environment that violently executes the mandates of its own "unnatural" or philosophically ungrounded ideology. If social solidarity was to remain an ideal, its founding and operational principles had to be reformulated to accommodate the natural desires and freedom of particular people. Diderot was to struggle with the problem for the rest of his life.

It was precisely the pervasiveness and complexity of contemporary ideology and the obstacles it placed in the path of mutual understanding, persuasion, and social accord that he chose to expose in the first of his many undisputed masterpieces, *Le neveu de Rameau* (wr. 1761–1774, pub. 1805; *Rameau's Nephew*)—carefully situated not in obviously sequestered and institutionalized precincts, but right in the *apparently* open, indeed in the most "libertine" and permissive, spaces of Paris. Strolling to the Café de la Régence from his bench along the favorite cruising paths of the Palais-Royal garden, pursuing his hottest idea like a man chasing after a whore—his thoughts, he says, are his "whores"—the narrator, who never provides his name but simply calls himself

"I," finally catches his idea, his whore, made flesh: Rameau, the debased, unnamed nephew of the "great" composer. Like "I," he is watching the café habitués play chess. Indeed, the dialogue that passes between them resembles a series of moves in some metaphysical but highly personal chess match—a match performed, moreover, with all the slyness and mutual provocation of sexual foreplay. The eerily insubstantial and spongy tokens they push about, hoping to check and checkmate each other, are words like "posterity," "happiness," "dignity," "truth," "beauty," "goodness," and ultimately the no less wobbly concept of being or identity. The serious disjunction within and between their beliefs is counterpointed by the disconcerting aesthetic (sometimes moral) pleasure they take in the display of their own wit and performance or in the spectacle of each other's. And this delight coordinates rather nicely with the predilection, the "taste" they share ("I" begrudgingly, "He" undisguisedly) for power and energy, for the eccentric, disruptive, fiery, and amoral strength of genius, which might, like Shelley's west wind, blindly sweep away the old dispensation—the old boredom of inherited notions, forms, and constraints—but which also threatens to subvert all axiological arguments and rational premises, indeed all their quibbling, their inconsistencies, their distressingly equivocal appeals to "reason," "the greater good," "beneficence," or "personal pleasure."

It becomes increasingly clear, however, that both "I" and "He," in every phase of that dialogic game in which they jockey for power, are representative voices: not so much the voices of two beings or of one head (Diderot's), as the voices of an ideology that is itself swamped with contradiction—a field of power relationships bristling with rules and pieties but energized by a lust for wealth and "position," for the momentary self-affirmation of takeovers and appropriations, the forbidden thrill of duplicitous or unscrupulous victories. There is room here for all masters and all slaves, for censors and their silenced pawns, for acceptably naïve or public-spirited philosophers, but for unscrupulous and self-congratulatory rogues as well. (Rameau's nephew, who once spoke his mind, or one of his minds, with "taste," "wit," and "reason," was actually forced from society; yet his "friends" and sponsors cherish him as much for his outrageous eruptions as for his abject servility.) And there is room, especially, for a slippery semantics that, at any moment, allows for the inversion of all terms and positions. Every misunderstanding, every discursive gambit or evasion—the dialogue is replete with them—rides along the rails of a complex and permissive social "grammar" whose many "idioms" and solecisms accommodate any number of linguistic but also moral and functional errors or crimes. The capacious system may be attacked or satirized, but it remains, flexibly, intact. It deftly patronizes and neutralizes merely theoretical differences, while in private or public practice—where everyone, whether routinely or self-consciously and regardless of social status, both commands *and* obeys—it annihilates difference altogether. "I," the lamely passionate and high-minded philosopher awkwardly defending virtue, but voyeuristically curious about the back streets of Paris and the raucous, sybaritic salons of upstart financiers and actresses; "He," the parasite, the image of the social outcast and failure, longing for his uncle's success and single-mindedness, but a "genius" nonetheless in his brilliant pantomimes and aesthetic judgments, living his life "to the moment," scrounging for a sou, selling wife and child, body and soul (if he has one), for a handout—these are the twin testicles of the imprisoning, commanding organ of society.

It would be unfair to "I" and to Diderot to think, as Hegel did, of an absolute separation between the antagonists, the one "base" (read noble), the other "noble" (read servile and conformist). Rameau's "self-estrangement," his scornful alienation from society and from himself, which, for Hegel, is the mark of Spirit rising to a pinnacle of self-consciousness, is actually the predicament, the disease, of society itself and of all its members. Rousseau had said as much in his *Discours sur l'origine et les fondements de l'inégalité parmi les hommes* (1755; *Discourse on the Origin and Foundations of Inequality among Men*), and Diderot was to supply the more probing ramifications: if self-awareness promotes the acknowledgment of contrary impulses—allows us to spot the residue of a "natural" beneficence impacted beneath our "civilized," that is, disguised, indifference—our selves are at least as tellingly fractured, as Suzanne's was, by the way they necessarily absorb and recapitulate the muffled tensions and duplicities of social life. Because political, economic, and moral urgencies often skirmish among and within themselves, consciousness speaks dispersedly and in many tongues. It casts about among the voices that it encounters not merely outside itself, in the streets, among friends, in books, and in various institutions; it finds what Mikhail Mikhailovich Bakhtin calls a "heteroglossia," a world of multifarious speech, within itself. It speaks others even as it speaks itself: the tools, the languages that guide or help constitute consciousness—even the modalities of "self-estrangement"—are never entirely its own.

Is this why "I" and "He," in spite of their mutual condescension and the dismay they cause each other, never draw blood or break off their discussion? Is the extraordinary civility they observe only a tacit acknowledgment of the *politesse* and ultimately of the scornful, self-preserving detachment that society requires? Or may it also be that every thought, act, or word, however unpalatable, is always in some startling sense latently and inadmissibly one's own, always a recognizable possibility nesting in the ideological and discursive economy? And yet, precipitating unheard, suppressed, sometimes dangerous voices from an inner or outer plenitude, selectively formulating and situating them in particular characters and among countering or sympathetic listeners, Diderot comes increasingly to understand that the act of "voicing" and writing creates a strenuous drama of questionable appropriations, of preemptive power plays that are in no way different from those he sees around him. Where are the words and voices that can resist tendentious authorial focalizations and manipulations? What narration, what dialogue, does not, as in the case of *Le rêve de d'Alembert* (wr. 1769, pub. 1830; *D'Alembert's Dream*), tilt the board or force its characters to speak as though they were not caught in the thrall of their author's "dream"? Can there be a literature that does not act to nudge us toward its own beliefs (even the hesitancies of beliefs) and their ratification? Finally, who or what deserves our greatest pity, the characters, the plot, the setting, the reader, or discourse itself, as the author irremediably maneuvers them to his satisfaction? But wait, we have not considered the plight of the author caught in the vortices of conventional genres and the expectations of readers, driven to "make it new" but, like everyone else, currying favor, torn between his own wayward desires, the desires of characters, and the internalized strictures of the general public.

Having found the apple of his freedom in the privacy of unpublished manuscripts, Diderot in his late fifties and early sixties sinks his "shaky teeth" into it and contemplates, ever more assiduously, the worm at its core—the core of all representation, assertion, and communication. Words or signs of any kind now seem to him irresistibly to arise from the organic character, the controlling passion, and the material, social condition of their users—as he tried with dark humor to demonstrate in his *Satire première* (1773; *First Satire*). Like nature as he conceived of it in his materialist and atheistic philosophy, language appears blindly to produce merely functional and pragmatic results, a swarm of independently viable discourses that never, alone or together, replicate the once and forever given, but reformulate and so recondition the ever-changing, ever-rescrambled sum of reality. The imitative arts, language, all forms of persuasion, do not so much imitate and reproduce the world as cooperate in its tumultuous, generative functions. They work their imaginative will upon mind and matter. They have, in their perfected expression, the ethically suspect and tyrannous capacity to appropriate consciousness, to enthrall, subjugate, or redirect desire.

Artists, for Diderot at this time, come more and more therefore to resemble Rameau's nephew or the projectionists he finds in Plato's cave (*Salon de 1767*) or the actors of *Paradoxe sur le comédien* (wr. 1773–1776? pub. 1830; *Paradox on the Actor*)—con men, con women, mystifiers, and illusionists constructing imaginative metaphors, myths, and contracts the way lovers make promises, forgetting or masking themselves and the erratic, disintegrating, and renovative processes of nature. These discoveries as well as the composition of several stories and what may be the most far-reaching and multifaceted novel of the century, *Jacques le fataliste et son maître* (wr. 1771–1780? pub. 1796; *Jacques the Fatalist and His Master*), run parallel, in Diderot's life, to the recognition of his own personal betrayals, mystifications, and broken engagements; the sudden, irrational death and birth of love; the violence and yet the necessity of persuasion. His finest and last play, the autobiographical comedy *Est-il bon? Est-il méchant?* (1775–1784; *Is He Good? Is He Bad?*), takes up some of these themes, but it is in *Jacques,* the epitome of reflexive thought and narration, that he demonstrates the need both for open social exchange and for dismantling its pretensions and artifice. He gave up writing an ethical treatise "on the good life" in order, as usual, to puzzle over what life had in fact become for him: a matter of facing the distinctly *moral* conundrums and paradoxes of social interaction and speech, the perplexities involved not only in the discovery of Truth, but also (and perhaps above all) in its dissemination.

"How did they meet? By chance, as we all do. What were their names? What difference does it make? Where were they coming from? From the closest spot. Where were they going? Do we ever know? What were they saying? The Master said nothing; and Jacques said that his captain said that all the good and bad that befalls us down here was written up above." This is how the novel begins—in a voice caught between interior dialogue and direct address to an ideal but exacting reader, the two symptomatically and characteristically fused. And it is only the first of the narrator's self-conscious, teasing duels with the reader, with himself, and with the tyrannical sway of received prejudice and traditions of fiction; the first of the many analogous sparring encounters, physical, erotic, or discursive, to be endured and sometimes relished by all subsequent characters and narrators. *Jacques* is not, to say the least, a conventional novel; it is, as the irascible implied reader once actually interjects, a "rhapsody of things, some real, some imagined . . . distributed without order" (p. 293). There is, to be sure, an overarching narrator, and he sets about telling the story of Jacques and his master. He resurfaces sporadically, but the narration runs away from him. He lets Jacques tell the story of his loves, and that story is constantly interrupted—by squabbles with the master, who has, among other things, his own story to tell; by encounters with other characters who have theirs; by indignant questions from the reader or from the narrator himself; and by dialogues between the characters, dialogues in which they offer their opinions about one another and about the tales they have just heard. Whatever staid literary models they use to shape their stories—allegories, memoir-novels, Byzantine or chivalric romances, folk tales, or picaresque fiction—narration and speech itself come off as exercises in manipulative power. The power to seduce, control, or punish through the energies unleashed by words reveals itself in almost every human relationship in the book—most famously in the episode in which Mme. de la Pommeraye contrives to force her faithless husband to marry a prostitute; but this power also attends the strange bond of verbal dependency that ties Jacques to his master and all the narrators to their readers and listeners.

Above the noisy competition of many voices and classes, above the jarring juxtaposition of the many literary genres whose preposterous confinements Diderot exploits and assails, there hangs the final arbiter of Truth, the Scroll "written up above"—authoritative, or so one imagines, but oppressively, tantalizingly silent. The Scroll, whose message is as pervasive, inscrutable, and circumscribing as any ideology, as (arguably) immanent as destiny working through and about us, exists, in its relationship to the characters, the way the characters exist in their relationship with one another: it seems by its very silence to provoke unanswerable questions, to defy a totalizing knowledge, to inspire relationships of dependency and servitude, and to stir up speech as a futile remedy and weapon. Yet speech, in its assertions or, better still, its creative approximations, is where the agitated interval of life transpires. Jacques, raised in the home of his grandparents, who in their entire lifetimes emitted only the words "hat for sale" and "one sou," had to put a gag over his mouth; he now speaks, thrives, and paradoxically reigns as a servant—rather like

Scheherazade or Diderot himself—only because he can, after that pent-up period of censorship, speak, amuse, instruct, and distract his nameless master.

Silence and Truth, then, on the one side, and on the other, a cacophony of words, torments, and hopes, a ceaseless rage and striving: the search for definition, fidelity, and assurance among the fluctuations and ambiguities of human nature and life "down here"; the recognition of an endless, repetitious round programmed into our minds, bodies, or beliefs; the terrible perception of the inadequacies and miscarriages of discourse, at once eminently performative and effective (as in the case of that consummate artist Mme. de la Pommeraye), but likely to boomerang, to shed more light on the moral complexion of its user than on the object it attempts to describe or trap. And yet the exuberance of the narration, of its several narrators, and of their Shandean digressions struggling for more space (always, admittedly, at the expense of someone else's), the fervor with which the characters pursue, interpret, and debate one another, seems to overwhelm this gloom. Although "one never says anything in this world that is understood exactly as one says it" (*Jacques*, p. 71), talk, open talk, for all the misunderstanding it creates, its epistemological dead ends or, as we might say, its doubtful referentiality, manages, though imperfectly, to stave off the incipient anger and violence. Meanwhile, the talk of Diderot's puzzled narrators and their listeners within the novel deliberately labors to complicate or paralyze the vehemence of interpretation, the self-righteous terrorism of any established "understanding" that tolerates no deviance, no infractions of social, celestial, or literary Law. It is talk, dialogue, that placates masters and servants alike; talk that temporarily erects small islands, if not of Truth, then of emerging truths and paradoxes. Above all, it keeps society afloat—a society not finally enlightened by some blistering revelation of Reason or Nature and therefore always ready to wield its club, but a society that is mercifully, edifyingly, perplexed and wondering.

Diderot's final, most poignant, and cautionary message has nothing to do with positive knowledge or ultimate truth. It does not so much say as demonstrate what a fully reflective and reflexive literature may yet contribute to the processes of social exchange and to the fashioning of a socially committed yet morally open and suspensive speech.

Bibliography: Denis Diderot, *Jacques le fataliste et son maître,* ed. Simone Lecointre and Jean Le Galliot (Geneva: Droz, 1976); translated by J. Robert Loy as *Jacques the Fatalist and His Master* (1959; reprint, New York: Norton, 1978). Diderot, *Le neveu de Rameau,* ed. Jean Fabre (Geneva and Lille: Droz and Giard, 1950); translated by Jacques Barzun and Ralph H. Bowen in *Rameau's Nephew and Other Works* (Harmondsworth: Penguin, 1966). Diderot, *La religieuse,* ed. Georges May and Jean Parrish, vol. 11 of *Oeuvres complètes,* ed. Herbert Dieckmann, Jacques Proust, and Jean Varloot (Paris: Hermann, 1975); translated by Leonard Tancock as *The Nun* (Harmondsworth: Penguin, 1974). Elisabeth de Fontenay, *Diderot: Reason and Resonance,* trans. Jeffrey Mehlman (New York: Braziller, 1982). Robert J. Loy, *Diderot's Determined Fatalist: A Critical Appreciation of Jacques le Fataliste* (New York: King's Crown Press, Columbia University, 1950). John Hope Mason, *The Irresistible Diderot* (London: Quartet Books, 1982). Jack

Undank, *Diderot, Inside, Outside, & In-Between* (Madison, Wis.: Coda Press, 1979).
Arthur Wilson, *Diderot* (New York: Oxford University Press, 1972).

Jack Undank

1772

Louis-Antoine de Bougainville Publishes an Account of His Stay
in Tahiti

Utopias

In 1772 Louis-Antoine de Bougainville published a report on his voyage around
the world, including descriptions of the people of Tahiti. His appealing portrait
of this non-Christian yet pacific society aroused Diderot's interest. Why not add
a supplement to the mariner's impressions of this visit, outdoing his descriptions without troubling oneself with a long voyage? Diderot's *Supplément au
Voyage de Bougainville* (*Supplement to Bougainville's Voyage*), written shortly after
the appearance of Bougainville's report but published only in 1796, after Diderot's death, outlined an ideal society whose principles challenged not only the
Christian aristocratic order of the ancien régime but also its Enlightenment
opposition. The *Supplément* was presented as a factual account, not as an exercise
of literary or philosophical imagination. In Diderot's text, two genres merged
into one: travel reports and utopian dreams blended into a discourse that subverted the moral beliefs on which Diderot, editor of the controversial *Encyclopédie* (1751–1772), had based his life.

In the *Supplément,* the eroticism of the utopian Tahitians tantalizes a visiting
French priest (p. 190):

> The young Tahitian girl blissfully abandoned herself to the embraces of a
> Tahitian youth . . . She was proud of her ability to excite men's desires, to
> attract the amorous looks of strangers, of her own relatives, of her brothers.
> In our presence, without shame, in the center of a throng of innocent Tahi-
> tians who danced and played the flute, she accepted the caresses of the young
> man whom her young heart and the secret promptings of her senses had
> marked out for her.

The "natural" world of the "primitives" appears, in Diderot's utopian discourse,
far superior to the "enlightened" world of France. As in his posthumous *Le
neveu de Rameau* (wr. 1761–1774, pub. 1805; *Rameau's Nephew*), Diderot,
siding with Rousseau against Voltaire, is able to suspend his dedication to the
Enlightenment long enough to consider alternatives, paths to moral perfection
that are achieved not by working for social progress through scientific advance,
but rather by listening to the promptings of the heart, by shaping society on
the model of nature. "How far we have departed from nature and happiness!"
laments Diderot's French observer upon hearing a discourse on the laws of Tahiti
(*Supplément,* p. 223).

Yet the *Supplément* is a complex text. On the one hand, Diderot calls into question the Enlightenment idea of progress through the development of the arts and sciences by presenting primitive Tahiti, without highly developed arts and sciences, as morally superior to Europe. On the other hand, he also challenges primitivism, the celebration of natural simplicity: Tahitian society is troubled by internal difficulties and practices infanticide. In this manuscript that he chose not to publish, Diderot was willing to acknowledge doubts concerning his moral choices that he would not allow in his public statements.

The utopian writings of the Enlightenment fell within a tradition that had its origins in Thomas More's *Utopia* (1516). The word *utopia* connected the Greek *eu*, denoting both good and nonexistent, and *topos*, denoting place, hence no place or ideal place. The society More described was far off, perhaps legendary but very definitely conforming, in its institutions and values, with the general ideals of Renaissance Christian humanism. More's Utopia was a placid, unchanging incarnation of a particular blend of classical wisdom and Christian virtues, a world at once remote from Europe and pointedly critical of its mores and conventions. The reader of *Utopia* cannot be certain if it is to be taken as a literary exercise, striving only for elegance and poise, or as an engaged, bitter political statement.

French utopian writers followed closely in More's footsteps. Distant, often bizarre worlds inhabited by noble savages of great variety were presented in François de La Mothe-Fénelon's *Télémaque* (1699; *Telemachus*), Louis Sébastien Mercier's *L'an 2440* (1771; *The Year 2440*), and countless other texts as if they existed somewhere, far away, enduring from year to year as a standard against which to measure the limitations of monarchs such as the Sun King, but not as potential catalysts of revolutionary change. As in More's model, Fénelon's ideal society was of unchanging perfection, a mixture of harmony, simplicity, sensuality, reason, gentleness, and meditative calm, presented as a desirable ideal but not as a design for the transformation of France.

The utopian writings of Nicolas Edme Restif de La Bretonne (1734–1806) in many ways represent a departure from More's model and prefigure the great 19th-century systems of Charles Fourier (1772–1837), Claude-Henri de Saint-Simon (1760–1825), and Auguste Comte (1798–1857). Utopias for Restif were neither idle dreams nor literary exercises: a moral urgency informs his writing on the ideal society, an urgency that became characteristic of such works after the Revolution of 1789. The political events that followed 1789 made it clear to writers and intellectuals that change was possible, indeed that anything was possible; and if the right plans were devised, a perfect society might be instituted in one's own lifetime. That was certainly the marquis de Condorcet's inference from the political upheavals he witnessed: his *Esquisse d'un tableau historique des progrès de l'esprit humain* (1794; *Sketch for a Historical Picture of the Progress of the Human Mind*) traced human development up to his time but concluded with a final chapter in which for the first time in human history the future was foreseen as one of "indefinite and infinite progress." The optimistic view that change was possible and a sense of urgency in bringing it about became characteristically modern elements in utopian literature.

In Restif's utopian writings, many of which were penned before 1789, the sense of urgency may have derived from personal rather than historical exigencies. For he perceived himself not as others did—the peasant boy who achieved fame as a writer in Paris, the capital of European culture—but as a failure, as a "corrupted peasant," one who had been presented with examples of moral rectitude during his youth but had fallen into urban degeneracy. His multi-volume autobiography, *Monsieur Nicolas* (1794–1797), is an obsessively repetitious morality tale of good intentions overwhelmed by sensual passions. Instead of following the lofty example of his Jansenist father, Restif sank into the degradation of pursuing women's sexual favors. In his writing he attempts to expiate the numerous sins of his flesh by showing that passions are too strong to resist, but also—as in *L'anti-Justine* (1798), an anti-Sadian pornographic novel intended for married couples—that, in their proper place, passions are not harmful but beneficial. Utopia, it follows, is a place where Restif's fate could happen to no one. His ideal societies reflect a metaphysical sense that his soul hung in the bargain.

In the history of utopian thought, Restif deserves attention if for no other reason than the quantity of his writings in this genre. In the travel and voyage mode he wrote *La découverte australe par un homme volant, ou le Dédale français* (1781; *Australia Discovered by a Flying Man, or French Daedalus*). In his most famous novel, *Le paysan perverti* (1776; *The Corrupted Peasant*), he included a sketch for an ideal community, "Statuts du bourg d'Oudun" ("Statutes for the City of Oudun"), a practice he repeated in several other novels. His most ambitious work was the six-volume *Idées singulières* (1770–1797; *Singular Proposals*), an extensive compendium of rules and regulations for the creation of utopia. Each volume was a "project of reform" for a particular aspect of society: prostitution (*Le pornographe,* 1770), the French language (*Le glossographe,* 1797), the theater (*La mimographe,* 1770), and on a major scale, men (*L'andrographe,* 1782), women (*Les gynographes,* 1777), and the law (*Le thesmographe,* 1789).

Restif's work demonstrated that the passions are socially organized, not biologically determined. His experience of an abrupt, drastic change of circumstances left a deep scar. This rude peasant from Sacy, a village in Burgundy near Auxerre, who had moved to Paris and been overwhelmed by its excitement and temptations, surmised that the passions were healthy in the countryside but dangerous in the city. Therefore, something in the social structure of each place accounted for the way individuals experienced and dealt with their feelings. In *L'andrographe* Restif expressed his ambivalent feelings and their utopian resolution as follows (pp. 183–184):

> A young country boy came to the city, was instructed there, was taught politeness there and became a savant. But ambition and exalted passions caused him trouble; he regretted the tranquillity of his first environment. You ask him, would he wish to give up his lights? If he is sincere he will reject this proposition with horror. How many times have I posed this question to myself, in certain very unhappy circumstances: would I like still to be a peasant? At first, at an age when experience had not enlightened me enough,

I believed that I sincerely would desire my early tranquillity. I left for my province . . . I returned to simple men. But I was there for eight days only when I found them unbearable: their deference, my superiority, the solitude . . . I returned to Paris. Upon seeing the great city, where I have suffered so much, my heart leaped with joy. I blessed it; I swore never to leave it again.

Utopia, then, was a world where the passions could have free play but at the same time were regulated to prevent the fate of *le paysan perverti.* Restif dreamed of a balance between gratification and restraint, a mean that combined the safety he remembered in the village with the pleasurable delights of the capital.

Hence his interesting ambivalence concerning the method to follow in order to achieve such a balance. The central principle of his utopian projects was the gratification of love, but he had the greatest difficulty deciding whether this was to be realized by permissiveness or by strict regulation. In *La découverte australe,* unrestricted expression of passion is the general order. The beneficial results are proved by its effects: "The entire nation seemed renewed: old age has disappeared in the two sexes; everyone dressed up, everyone friendly, everyone gay and healthy, they aspired equally after the pleasures that a new choice would promise them" (3:526). In *L'andrographe, Le pornographe,* and *Les gynographes,* however, utopia is achieved through the most spartan regulation of the passions.

The next generation, untroubled by Restif's ambivalence, extended his concern for an emotional utopia far beyond the wildest imagining of the Burgundian peasant. Fourier and Saint-Simon, along with Robert Owen in England, completely eliminated the escapism of Morean utopianism. The French Revolution and its Napoleonic aftermath were proof enough for them that both society and human nature were changeable. All that was needed was a genius of social design on the order of Isaac Newton, one who could decipher history's laws of motion and extrapolate from them a guide to the best possible future. In this era of revolutions, utopia was now attached to the dynamic of temporal change, with much the same urgency that Restif had derived from his personal life. No longer a distant, vaguely located place, utopia was now the culmination of a temporal continuum; it was the future.

And the future was near. A simple letter to Napoleon, outlining utopia, might suffice. Saint-Simon wrote such a letter, fully expecting a reply that would bring with it the solution to all mankind's travail. When it failed to arrive, he appealed to capitalists and speculators. Fourier had a different tactic. He let it be known that he would be available in his apartment every day at noon, so that any person of substance might have an interview with him, marvel at his great projects, then donate the funds required to erect a model community, one that would provide palpable evidence that his ideas were viable. With a single community in operation, Fourier was certain that humanity would see the wisdom in his ideas and take up the cue; in short order the earth would be reorganized into palaces of perfection. Although no one arrived at his door with the necessary financing, Fourierist communities were established from Rumania to Louisiana as a wave of utopianism swept the Western world in the middle and late 19th century. Brook Farm, eight miles from Boston, in West Roxbury, visited and written about by Nathaniel Hawthorne, aspired to Fourierism. Indeed a newspaper (the *Phalanx*) devoted to the exchange of information among Fourierist communities survived for several years on the east coast of the United States. The Saint-Simonians were more successful in France, establishing their practical utopia at Ménilmontant, outside Paris.

The reorganization of love was the central theme of Fourier and Saint-Simon, reacting against Enlightenment rationalism, the bourgeois calculating spirit, and the harshness of life under an emerging urban capitalist society. Whereas Ludwig Feuerbach, the young Hegelian across the Rhine, endeavored to bring forth a new social order based on love out of the airy subtleties of dialectical discourse, the French preferred a more organizational discursive strategy: the utopian plan.

Fourier regarded his observations of society as an embryonic social scientific method, and he couched his writings in pseudo-Newtonian terminology. Passionate attraction, not mere gravity, was the basic law of all beings. The entire cosmos was in motion, pushed and pulled by that force in cycles that spanned millennia. Present-day France was at an unfortunate point in a cycle that would lead upward to a better world, one organized in conformity with the laws of passionate attraction. Just as Newton regarded himself as an instrument of God, revealing to mankind His secret plan of the universe, so Fourier was in touch with unseen vital forces of nature. Utopian discourse was Fourier's way of presenting his special knowledge to his fellow Frenchmen. "Passionate attraction alone, without constraint and without aid other than the charm of voluptuousness, is going to establish universal unity upon the globe, and will cause war, revolution, indigence, and injustice to disappear during the seventy-thousand-year period of social harmony which we will enter" (*Harmonian Man*, p. 90).

For many years a traveling salesman, Fourier made it a point to observe and classify the variety of human personality types as he passed from town to town. He concluded from his investigations that 1,610 distinct personality types existed, half male, half female, corresponding to permutations of twelve basic passions. Social orders could be evaluated on how well they empowered the gamut of the passions. Utopia provided for the maximum interchange between complementary passionate types. It ensured that all passions were afforded release because a repressed (*étouffée*) passion becomes harmful by turning into its opposite and leading to poisoned human relations. Such was the case, in his example, of the notorious Mme. Stroganoff, princess of Moscow, who loved one of her maids but, since lesbianism was forbidden by the prevailing morality, took her pleasure by sticking pins into the maid, thereby causing pain not pleasure.

Fourier dreamed and dreamed, obsessively elaborating his projects down to the least detail. Nothing escaped his concerned eye: bourgeois civilization, he complained in *Théorie des quatre mouvements* (1808; *Theory of the Four Movements*), was organized to increase disease and contention by making it the pecuniary interest of doctors and lawyers to proliferate, not eliminate, these social ills. All work must be pleasurable, he insisted, and this is accomplished by ensuring passionate interest. Since adult males regarded garbage collection as demeaning, utopia would organize young boys, who exult in mud and filth, into "little hordes" charged with the duty of its collection. These groups, in quasi-military orders, would compete with one another for badges and other small rewards. Thus in Fourier's utopia the most socially noxious tasks would become simply another occasion for pleasure. Work in general would be ameliorated by hourly job rotation, since the passions sustain interest only for that length of time. And work brigades would be composed of friends and complementary passionate types. Fourier's utopia provided an employment office that counseled individuals not only on their abilities but also on their affinities, a sort of social psychotherapy.

Most important for this lonely salesman was the gratification of love. Harmony, Fourier's name for the ideal society, was designed to maximize, indeed expand, sensual and affectionate pleasures. Although civilization failed to provide an adequate organization of work, its structuring of love was far more inimical to well-being. Fourier ranted against the treatment of women in contemporary France and proclaimed that civilizations may be evaluated by the degree of freedom accorded to women. The bourgeois family, he complained, scored poorly on this account, stifling the passions in a cage of boredom and repression, oppressing women with a pecuniary relation that was little different from prostitution.

In Harmony, every individual would have his or her own apartment, guaranteeing independence. Affectionate and sexual encounters would vary in nature and degree according to the individual's passionate type. The "butterfly" type, for example, prefers continual variation in partners; others might be more monogamous. If garbage collection is the worst problem for the organization of labor, jealousy is its amorous counterpart. A special cadre of attractive people is organized to enfold a disappointed lover in a cloud of affection, gently lifting him or her from despondency to rapture. With these reforms, Fourier announced, each individual would have greatly expanded capacities for sensing and feeling pleasure. The final test of utopia would come when two communities met and, despite being complete strangers to one another, enacted an orgy of sexual-emotional exchanges. "An orgy may be fortuitous, as in the assemblies of the army and the caravan seraglios, but in the regular sessions of the court of love, orgies are prepared by the minister and the female pontiff who arrange delightful reunions and cumulative sympathies that heighten one another" (*Harmonian Man*, pp. 261–262).

Although examples of utopian literature continued to be written and published in France after 1848, the genre slowly died out. After World War II the future became fantasized rather as *dys*topic. Except for a short flurry of interest in utopia after the events of May 1968, exemplified by Swiss director Alain Tanner's film *Jonas qui aura vingt-cinq ans en l'an* 2000 (1976; *Jonah Who Will*

Be 25 in the Year 2000), the future appears no longer a subject for the utopian imagination, except in the genre of science fiction.

See also 1834.

Bibliography: Denis Diderot, "Supplement to the Voyage of Bougainville," in *Rameau's Nephew and Other Works,* trans. Jacques Barzun and Ralph H. Bowen (Harmondsworth: Penguin, 1966). Charles Fourier, *Harmonian Man: Selected Writings of Charles Fourier,* ed. Mark Poster (New York: Anchor, 1971). Fourier, *Le nouveau monde amoureux* (Paris: Anthropos, 1967). Frank E. Manuel and Fritzie P. Manuel, eds., *French Utopias: Anthology of Ideal Societies* (New York: Free Press, 1966). Mark Poster, *The Utopian Thought of Restif de La Bretonne* (New York: New York University Press, 1971). Nicolas Edme Restif de La Bretonne, *L'andrographe, ou idées d'un honnête-homme sur un projet de règlement, proposé à toutes les nations de l'Europe, pour opérer une réforme générale des moeurs, et par elle, le bonheur du genre humain* (Paris: Duchesne et Belin, 1782). Restif, *La découverte australe par un homme volant, ou le Dédale français,* 4 vols. (Paris: n.p., 1781). Pierre Testud, *Rétif de La Bretonne et la création littéraire* (Lille: Université de Lille III, 1980).

Mark Poster

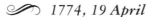 **1774, 19 April**

The Première of Christoph Willibald Gluck's *Iphigénie en Aulide* at the Paris Opera Sets Off Yet Another Storm among Paris Intellectuals

A War at the Opera

On the evening of 19 April 1774, less than a month before the death of Louis XV, Christoph Willibald Gluck's *Iphigénie en Aulide* (*Iphigenia in Aulis*) had its first performance at the Paris Opera before an audience that included Marie-Antoinette. According to the future queen—who, as a member of the Austrian royal family, had been a pupil of the celebrated German composer—the performance of the first "French" opera by Gluck was the occasion of extraordinary public agitation, as intense and divisive as if it had been a matter not of music but of religion (letter of 26 April 1774, in Prod'homme, *Gluck,* p. 197). The feverish literary debate ignited by this operatic event came to be known as the War between the Gluckists and the Piccinists, the latter after Niccolò Piccini, whom Jeanne Bécu, countess Du Barry, Louis XV's influential mistress, brought to France as an Italian rival to Gluck in the composition of operas set to the same libretti. For five years France's literary elite would be splintered into factions, supporters of one or the other artist, as they were already separated over political and religious issues that opposed Jesuits and Jansenists, philosophes and *dévots.*

This "musical war" was in fact only the latest episode in a conflict that had divided cultivated French society for over a century and had transformed it twenty-two years earlier, with the aesthetic debates known as the Quarrel of the Buffoons, into a battlefield of polemical writings on the unlikely subject of French and Italian lyric drama.

For most thinkers of the 17th and 18th centuries, music meant simply lyric music, and it was therefore with special reference to opera that virtually all musical debates during the Enlightenment were conducted. Opera was a hybrid form that embodied an essentially dramatic ideal of total spectacle; through it, the late Renaissance creators of the genre had intended to achieve the perfect union of music and poetic declamation; later, in the baroque imagination, it most nearly achieved the ideal of bringing together all the arts in the richest of aesthetic forms.

Italian opera, introduced to France by Jules Cardinal Mazarin early in the reign of Louis XIV, at first merely whetted the French appetite for an opera in their own tongue. Italian opera emphasized melodic richness and vocal virtuosity, most often at the expense of dramatic tension and theatrical values. With the advent in France in the early 18th century of the less dramatic Italian lyricism, opera seemed to veer inevitably toward becoming an art form in which the pleasures derived from the singing voice, considered since Plato to violate moral limits, would prevail over the verbal, the poetic, the didactic, over whatever elements regulated the questionable delights of melody. Music and text—the eternally conflicting elements of operatic music—were expanded into the thematic polarities that set the French tradition of tragic opera in opposition to the innovative Italian style.

The first musical controversy to divide the early Enlightenment public involved an exchange of essays that either celebrated the freedom of the Italian melodic imagination, unrestrained by rule, or else, in support of the French operatic tradition, called for the rigorous subordination of music to textual meaning. These initial debates, which would later provide significant source material for the more ample midcentury Quarrel of the Buffoons, focused on the music of Jean-Baptiste Lully. Though of Italian origin himself, Lully had become director and guiding spirit of the French national opera. The musical controversy concerning him really constituted an aspect of the larger Quarrel of the Ancients and the Moderns, which split the early Enlightenment between the values of tradition and modernity. French music, by this time, had come to be identified with the ancients, and therefore with the court, with nobility, with royal and aristocratic ceremonial. Inspired by this milieu of tradition and authority, Lully had evolved a style of musical drama that was both elegant and austere and that gave prominence to a vocalization patterned directly upon the style of recitation prevalent in contemporary French classical tragedy.

And so, in the 1730s and 1740s, a new dispute, the battle of the Lullists and the Ramists, structured explicitly around notions of the old and the new, was set in motion. The modernist group identified itself with the music of Jean-Philippe Rameau, who had become the newest divinity of the Parisian musical world. For the generation, Rameau embodied the spirit of the new, youthful, creative freedom identified with the Italian manner. But with the outbreak of the next major episode in the continuing war of operatic styles, the momentous Quarrel of the Buffoons, a radical shift of positions occurred in the musical constellation.

The outbreak of polemics was occasioned by the arrival in France in 1752 of a small company (three performers) of Italian artists known as the Bouffons because their repertoire was drawn entirely from the genre of Italian musical theater known as opera buffa. A revival of Giovanni Battista Pergolesi's comic intermezzo *La serva padrona* (1733; *The Maid as Mistress*), performed without noteworthy reaction six years earlier, precipitated an explosion of inflammatory writings and became, quite simply, an affair of state.

The new controversy divided the intellectual elite into a "king's corner" and a "queen's corner," referring to the vicinity of the respective loges at the Opera occupied by Louis XV and Marie Leszczynska where the partisans of French and Italian music had begun to assemble. For the most part, the encyclopedists, the radicals and Moderns of the age, espousing the Italian cause, aligned themselves with the queen's corner. Among their number were Jean Le Rond d'Alembert, Louis de Cahusac, and the most fanatic supporters, Friedrich Melchior Grimm and Jean-Jacques Rousseau. Those occupying the king's corner, led by Elie Fréron, Jacques Cazotte, and Mathieu de Pidensat, paraded their faithfulness to French music and thereby to patriotic values. Neither group was especially distinguished for its knowledge of music; the polarization of support was manifestly political rather than musical.

The Italian company had arrived at the same time as the launching of the encyclopedist venture, which would constitute the Enlightenment's great testimony to its ideals of intellectual change. And the French opera was, after all, a national and political institution, the creation of Louis XIV and therefore a complex living emblem of the principles of tradition and authority, preserved by a kind of cultural inquisition. In fact, in the third book of his *Confessions* (1782) Rousseau characterized the division within the cultivated Parisian public as comparable to another war of religion. What began as a debate that focused primarily upon musical questions had rapidly come to mirror a discord of greater moment concealed by aesthetic preoccupations.

The opera house had become an extension of the salon, the café, and other intellectual and cultural centers where richly symbolic partisan alignments, pitting king against queen, French against Italian, and even the male against the female principle, reflected a form of political conviction. With their support of Italian opera, the encyclopedists were giving voice to values of free expression and to the hitherto artfully regulated world of feeling. The soaring of Italian melodic genius at the Paris Opera was the musical image of a way of life, an altered dramatic portrait of human desire and possibility. For the enthusiastic camp of the modernist philosophes, Italian music offered cultural evidence for the liberating and fertile notion of progress. And the enemy to progress on the musical battlefield was Rameau, whose name now evoked a stale musical universe of excessively erudite harmonies and superfluous refinement. Meanwhile, for the aristocratic elite and the traditionalists occupying the other "corner," the philosophes were guilty of simply having made common cause with mediocre artists and, perhaps more pertinently, with true buffoons, with contemptible lower-class clowns.

Baron Paul Henri d'Holbach, materialist philosopher and prominent collaborator on the *Encyclopédie* (1751–1772), is credited with having scored the first hit with his charge that French music was "Gothic and barbaric." Grimm's *Le petit prophète de Boehmischbroda* (1753; *The Little Prophet from Boehmischbroda*) intensified the quarrel with a renewed attack. In a style parodying the prophecies of the Old Testament, the pamphlet recounted the dream vision of a young Prague music student in which the decadent state of French operatic theater was revealed and a warning issued by the voice of the spirit of opera to heed the redemptive lesson of Pergolesi and Italian music. Grimm's satire was followed by approximately sixty pamphlets between 1753 and 1754, most of them published anonymously. The level of dispute hardly represented the philosophes' ideal of a free circulation of ideas: the tone was one of intrigue, jealousy, and gossip; the issues of contention were usually petty and without substance; the arguments were repetitive and consisted of little more than a reduction of musical values to stereotyped parallels between two "national" styles.

The richest artistic achievement evoking the debate was surely Diderot's masterpiece, *Le neveu de Rameau* (wr. 1761–1774, pub. 1805; *Rameau's Nephew*), although it was not published until long after the midcentury quarrels had subsided. Diderot's dialogue is virtually a condensation of the musical polemics of his time; his position concerning the appealing "natural" Italian lyricism, passionately endorsed by the nephew of the celebrated composer, is as ambiguous as the entire fictional dialogue.

Yet, until Diderot had earlier entered the fray more directly in 1753, with three brief pamphlets, none of the participants had recognized that the questions dividing the combatants had been poorly posed from the outset. His concern with generic limits, hybrid forms, and the specific imitative capacities of each art permitted Diderot to perceive rapidly that all the arguments being advanced in both camps were nullified by the meaningless comparison of unlike musical forms, French serious lyric tragedy and the lighter pieces in the Italian comic tradition. Establishing these artificial parallels in music criticism was much like comparing Molière and Corneille in order to determine which was the better dramatist.

For the philosophes, political commitment and ideological bias also constituted insurmountable obstacles to the appreciation of Rameau's music and musical theory. Rameau had proposed harmony as the absolute foundation for all music, proclaiming its supremacy over melody and the dependence of melody upon harmony. He saw musical harmony as a reflection of a deeper harmony, of an unchanging natural law that could not be discovered without mathematics. Music possessed an intrinsic rationality that located it beyond the shifting idiosyncrasies of the historical and the national: it was a privileged language that had access to the rational unity of the world.

It is not surprising, then, that Jean-Jacques Rousseau refused to ally himself either with Rameau's identification of the natural with the rational or with his sense of music as mathematical beauty. Rousseau's own opera, *Le devin du village* (*The Village Soothsayer*), which assimilated some Italian flavors into a traditional

French form, had been presented successfully at Fontainebleau in 1752. But his epoch-making *Lettre sur la musique française* (1753; *Letter on French Music*), containing Rousseau's views on French music and language, came to occupy the center of the debate.

In keeping with those of the majority of his contemporaries, Rousseau's preferences resided entirely with vocal music; for Rousseau, instrumental music, being nonreferential and detached from the poetic, was literally without meaning. It was music's natural condition to exist in union with language. In some mythical paradise of the past, man's first language had been song. Nature dictates to our souls not harmonies, but melodies, which alone preserve intact some privileged contact with the conscience, with the voice of "divine instinct." It was language in general and the French language in particular that Rousseau's theory in his *Lettre* was intended to subvert. The French language, he felt, was essentially unfit for musical expression; it was too harsh, and it lacked the sonorous qualities of Italian, its strongly accentuated rhythms, its sweetness. French music was without melody, expressionless; France did not and could never have a genuine music of its own.

Nonetheless, in 1754, after a disruptive visit of less than two years, the Italian artists were expelled from France; the repertoire of French opera had emerged apparently unaltered. The same year, a performance by the actors of the Comédie-Italienne of a play by François Antoine Chevrier satirizing the Bouffons and the queen's corner hailed, in the spirit of the play's title, the return of good taste: *Le retour du goût*. It also marked a tentative conclusion to the controversy over French and Italian musical styles. No triumph could be claimed by either group, and nothing of substance had emerged from the exchange of pamphlets to illuminate the questions of operatic form that had fractured the musical world.

And so, as if propelled by some deeper compulsion fostered by ideological irresolution, two camps were formed once again when Gluck arrived in Paris in 1774 with an opera adapted from Racine and set to a libretto by François du Roullet on the subject of Iphigenia in Aulis. Whereas the Italians had assigned priority to the musical component of opera, Gluck's so-called reform operas would reestablish an equilibrium between the conflicting forces of the operatic medium by inclining heavily toward the poetic and dramatic powers of the lyric art. Despite his famous comment in the dedication of *Alceste* (1769) concerning his goals as composer of opera—"I sought to restrict music to its true function, namely to serve the poetry by means of the expression" (quoted in Weisstein, *Essence of Opera*, p. 106)—Gluck's intention was to create an operatic mode that transcended the prevailing French and Italian styles. Both operatic manners now seemed excessively academic, and Gluck was determined to bring dramatic music closer to its intended ideal, the effective wedding of music to poetic text.

Gluck demonstrated with *Iphigénie en Aulide* that the spirit of Lully, which he had merely preserved and developed, possessed a continuing appeal even for this new public of the late Enlightenment. Despite the dedication of the supporters of the Piccinist-Italian camp, it was Gluck, celebrated by the encyclo-

535

pedists, by the majority of the informed musical public, and even by Rousseau, who emerged as the undisputed master of the French operatic scene. Piccini, who never actively participated in the literary quarrel bearing his name, was a sorry musical rival for Gluck; the outcome of this most recent confrontation of musical styles was ominously prefigured by Piccini's ill-timed arrival in Paris on the day of the première of the French version of Gluck's already-renowned *Orfeo ed Euridice* (31 December 1776; first performed in Vienna, 1762). For approximately five years (1774–1779) an intense controversy, returning again and again to the subjects of the earlier quarrels, hovered around the dominant figure of Gluck. The hostilities ceased with Gluck's permanent departure at the end of 1779 in disappointment at the failure of *Echo et Narcisse*.

The tempest of diatribes and invectives, of acrimonious personal hostilities, produced no musical revolution. Certain values, forceful enough to affect the subsequent evolution of operatic form, did surface in the midst of the tumultuous events surrounding the stylized world of the opera house. The genre of French *opéra comique* had grown out of the combined seeds of other comic and lyrical forms. The extravagance of baroque opera was becoming distasteful to a public whose enthusiasm for musical drama in the regal style was eroding. Opera had emerged as the art that spoke to and from the heart and, perhaps best of all art forms, represented the reality of the irrational. In the next few years, Mozart's genius, assimilating and transforming all the operatic forms, serious and comic, realized the richest possibilities of musical drama. The musical polemics that spanned the century, of dubious value to music history, absorbed the passionate overflow from the fervent debates in politics, morals, and aesthetics that were transforming the image of human nature. Music had come to occupy a place close to the center of a movement of ideas whose cultural force penetrated even the ritual universe of opera.

See also 1680, 1707, 1771.

Bibliography: Denis Diderot, *Ecrits sur la musique* (Paris: Lattès, 1987). Béatrice Didier, *La musique des lumières: Diderot, l'Encyclopédie, Rousseau* (Paris: Presses Universitaires de France, 1985). Catherine Kintzler, *Jean-Philippe Rameau: Splendeur et naufrage de l'esthétique du plaisir à l'âge classique* (Paris: Le Sycomore, 1983). John Neubauer, *The Emancipation of Music from Language: Departure from Mimesis in Eighteenth-Century Aesthetics* (New Haven: Yale University Press, 1986). Alfred Richard Oliver, *The Encyclopedists as Critics of Music* (New York: Columbia University Press, 1947). Jacques-Gabriel Prod'homme, *Christoph-Willibald Gluck* (Paris: Fayard, 1985). Michael F. Robinson, *Opera before Mozart* (London: Hutchinson, 1966). Jean-Jacques Rousseau, *Lettre sur la musique française,* in *Ecrits sur la musique* (Paris: Stock, 1979). Ulrich Weisstein, ed., *The Essence of Opera* (New York: Norton, 1965).

Herbert Josephs

∽ *1782, March*
Pierre Choderlos de Laclos Publishes *Les liaisons dangereuses*

Words and "the Thing"

Published in 1782, seven years before the coming of the Revolution, which would shatter the world that it depicts, *Les liaisons dangereuses* sums up a long tradition of "libertine" literature and gives it a definitive expression. Since the start of the 18th century, as Denis de Rougemont has noted, an aristocracy that no longer could display its potency in military combat had turned to games of erotic conquest. The seducer had become a major literary figure, someone who—in the manner of Molière's *Dom Juan* (1665)—defied the ostensible rules of church, state, and social mores. Seduction as a system of psychological control of others, and thus as social power, had its own game-rules, which had been codified, even theoretized, in dozens of novels that prepared the way for Pierre Choderlos de Laclos's masterpiece. The diplomat Charles Maurice de Talleyrand would exclaim, years later: "Unless you lived before the Revolution, you never really knew *la douceur de vivre.*" The constant quest for pleasure and power in *Les liaisons dangereuses* can give a persuasive image of the sweetness of life lived only for self-gratification. Yet it may also show the critical stresses of such a system: may, in our retrospective view, say something about why the Revolution was at hand.

Les liaisons dangereuses also caps a long tradition in the epistolary novel, reaching back, in France, at least as far as Gabriel de Guilleragues's *Lettres portugaises* (1669; *Letters from a Portuguese Nun*), and best known in the 18th century through Samuel Richardson's *Clarissa* (1747–48) and Jean-Jacques Rousseau's *Julie, ou la nouvelle Héloïse* (1761; *Julie, or the New Héloïse*). In this tradition, novels could be "single-voiced," with all the letters written by one person; dual-voiced, an exchange between two people; or multivoiced, involving the correspondence of a group of people. *Les liaisons dangereuses*— subtitled "Letters Gathered in a Society"—is an example of this last category, and more than any of its predecessors it orchestrates a complex counterpoint of diverse voices. It is, to change the metaphor, so perfect a construction of a drama through letters that no one, in the relatively few examples of epistolary fictions since, has ever been able to rival Laclos's mastery of the genre. It is a perfection that for several reasons may make *Les liaisons dangereuses* a limit-case: the best, the most extreme, and the last of its kind.

Rarely has an epistolary novel so fully and neatly motivated its form: the need to exchange letters is made perfectly clear, and the process of their exchange is an important element, for most of the characters find themselves in situations in which they cannot communicate except by letter, either because they are in separate places or because more direct communication is barred. The Vicomte de Valmont and the Marquise de Merteuil, former lovers and continuing confidants, are each pursuing their separate conquests, Merteuil at home in Paris, Valmont at the country estate of his aunt, Mme. de Rosemonde,

537

where he has discovered the desirable Présidente de Tourvel, the hitherto perfectly chaste wife of a jurist (hence, from the upper bourgeoisie rather than the court aristocracy). Although Valmont is at first mainly interested in the seduction of Tourvel, Merteuil works to persuade him that he should turn his attention to Cécile Volanges, who has just completed her convent schooling and is promised in marriage to the Comte de Gercourt, whom she dislikes and proposes to punish through the deflowering and debauching of his fiancée. Cécile, in turn, becomes infatuated with the young Chevalier de Danceny, whose lack of a fortune makes him an ineligible suitor.

The situation is so arranged that the letter becomes the only possible report on what is happening or, just as often, the only way to make something happen. Danceny, for instance, unable to speak openly of his love for Cécile, must write her a clandestine letter and hide it in her harp. Valmont must postmark a letter from Tourvel's native city of Dijon so that she will open it (thinking it is from her husband). Later, Valmont will use the need to deliver Danceny's letters to Cécile as an excuse for obtaining the key to her room that will allow him to seduce her. He will suborn a servant to retrieve his own letters to Tourvel—and will determine from their condition (all preserved, one tear-stained and pieced together after being torn up in public) the state of her sentiments for him. Merteuil will use a letter to Mme. de Volanges to give a narrative of her adventure with Prévan, knowing that her gossipy correspondent will give its contents such publicity that it will become the "official" version of events. From the very first letter, in which Cécile mentions almost in one breath her boredom and her possession of a writing desk, we are made to see the connection between the games of seduction and writing. And Merteuil sets the rules of the game of the novel when she promises a return to Valmont's bed only after he furnishes proof in writing—in the form of a letter from the "victim"—that he has bedded Tourvel.

Traditionally, the epistolary novel valued the letter as a direct expression of the sentiments. As Richardson noted, letters give a nearly "instantaneous" report of events and the writer's reactions to them: they are preeminently the device of self-expression and of self-analysis. Rousseau capitalized on the letter as the vehicle of pure subjectivity, making the opening chapters of *La nouvelle Héloïse* into a suite of operatic arias in which Julie and Saint-Preux give voice to their intimate feelings. Laclos, who had learned the lessons of these two masters very well, plays on the tradition of the letter as pure subjectivity, but thoroughly complicates it. As the preface of the putative "editor" of the letters warns us, almost all the emotions presented in these examples of a supposedly confessional form are "feigned or dissimulated." Our naïve and natural desire, as readers, to identify with the writer of a letter, to espouse his or her sentiments, is immediately made problematic. And the contrast in tone of the first two letters—the first, childish, saccharine, stupid, from Cécile; the second, worldly, witty, scheming, from Merteuil—puts us on our guard that reading this novel will not involve simple acts of empathy.

Laclos has indeed wrought a major revision of the epistolary tradition. The revision is well summarized in the letter Merteuil writes to a Cécile who has lost her virginity but not her worldly innocence: "When you write to someone, it is for him and not for yourself: thus you should seek to say less what you think than what pleases him more" (letter 105). Letters in this novel are always carefully contrived, written with a view to their reader: they always attempt to anticipate, to control, to incorporate into themselves the reader's response. The masters of the seduction game, Merteuil and Valmont, are masters precisely because they best write into their letters the reader's reading. A notable example of this is letter 48, written by Valmont in bed with the courtesan Emilie—using, he claims, her bare bottom as writing desk—and addressed to Tourvel, but relayed by way of Merteuil so that she can read it first. Whereas for Tourvel the letter is a passionate expression of unrequited love, we, like Merteuil, know the situation of its writing and can decipher in the language the description of his erotic proceedings with Emilie. The letter is a sustained double entendre that demonstrates that "meaning" depends on an act of reading. That meaning can be coherent but contradictory in two different readings is troubling: it destroys any transparency of language and makes the reader look beyond the letter itself, to the system of communication that subtends letters and that, understood and mastered, can give Merteuil and Valmont their nearly mythical power to manipulate others.

Merteuil and Valmont indeed create what André Malraux called a "mythology of intelligence," a potent image of superior minds wholly in control of exterior circumstances through the analytic power to know and to control others. The idea of the game—which also evokes a long tradition, reaching back to 17th-century *moralistes* such as François de La Rochefoucauld and Jean de La Bruyère—is to "penetrate" the hidden motives and desires of others, to understand so perfectly what makes them tick (for they are psychosocial mechanisms) that one can manipulate them while maintaining oneself a kind of protean freedom. The whole "education" of Cécile in debauchery offers a good example of the capacity of the two worldly masters to produce results quite opposite to those willed by the characters in question, and indeed to write the novel of someone else's destiny. Cécile eventually becomes nothing more than a "pleasure machine," a mechanism to be discarded when one has done playing with it; whereas Merteuil, in the joy of her control of other destinies, compares herself to "the Divinity."

Valmont's mastery of others tends to demonstrate itself in the text of his letters through a nearly constant use of parody: of the languages of military conquest, of religious devotion, of sentimental friendship, and of education. He is ever referring to someone else's use of language and showing that he can use it even while undermining its claims to authority by self-consciously overdoing it. In his pursuit of Tourvel, his parodies become ingenious and elaborate, as in his staged scene of benevolence to a destitute family, or in his use of a priest and the simulation of conversion to gain entrance to Tourvel's home. Merteuil uses a related but somewhat different technique, that of citation: her letters are full of terms taken from her correspondent's letters, and italicized (often literally) within her own discourse, in a demonstration that she is capable of incorporating others' speech—and hence their desires, motives, self-conceptions—within her elastic intelligence. Thus she sends back to her correspondents their own words, but changed, unmasked. She will eventually work her victory over Valmont by writing a letter for him: the letter of rupture that he will copy and send on to Tourvel. When the parodist becomes the copyist, he has let himself be entrapped in a plot of citations.

If throughout most of the novel we sense that Merteuil has the edge in her combative collaboration with Valmont, we learn in the celebrated letter on her self-education (letter 81) that this must be so, in that for a woman to play the game at all, she must be smarter than the man. For the rules of the game have been set by the men: all they need do is seduce, and when they choose to give publicity to their seductions, they can add the pleasure of ruining the woman's reputation. The woman, on the other hand, must at the same time gain the public glory of apparent resistance to seduction and the private pleasure of giving in to seduction, while preserving an absolute cover of secrecy. Merteuil has systematized psychology and social behavior to such an extent that she compares herself to a "new Delilah," who wields the scissors that can shear the force of her lovers. She is a self-conceiving and voluntaristic being, who states, in what is perhaps the key expression of her proud declaration of principles, "I can say that I am my own creation" (letter 81). As such, she can write the stories of others.

In a context of such concerted control of self and manipulation of others, the letter always calls our attention to itself as a speech act, as an instrument, even as a weapon, as a linguistic artifact that does not so much reflect reality as create it. In a novel that is ostensibly devoted to the pursuit of erotic pleasure, the sexual act itself is constantly elided, and erotics reinvested in the letter. Merteuil in letter 33 comments that Tourvel is expending her forces in defending herself against the word *love,* and that she will have no strength left to defend herself against *la chose,* the thing itself. This is accurate in that it points out the extent to which Tourvel's letters, in quarreling with Valmont's choice of terms, already accept the communicative network he has set up, and thus, despite her intentions, already prefigure her fall. But one may wonder whether *la chose* has any existence outside *le mot* (the word). Even the seduction of Tourvel has no existence until it becomes a letter.

Writing, and reading, are in this manner highly eroticized. A good example can be found in letter 10, where Merteuil describes to Valmont her six-hour lovemaking with the Chevalier de Belleroche, for which she prepares herself by readings—in the *Contes* of La Fontaine, Claude Prosper Jolyot de Crébillon's novel *Le sopha* (1742; *The Loveseat*), and the sentimental rhetoric of Rousseau's *La nouvelle Héloïse*—in order to be able to strike a range of tones and play a gamut of roles. She becomes an entire "harem" for Belleroche, whose "reiterated *hommages,* though always received by the same woman, were always given to a new mistress." Not only does the letter instance Merteuil's ability to know pleasure without ever allowing herself to be fixed in one role—without ever sacrificing her existential and intellectual freedom; it also demonstrates her capacity to manipulate her *reader*. For ultimately, this linguistic and stylistic harem is deployed for Valmont: letter 10 is designed, first, to make Valmont ashamed of his thus-far sterile pursuit of Tourvel; second, to make him jealous (for he wants Merteuil); and, most of all, to arouse him. We know from Valmont's next letter that she succeeds: her letter has placed him in a voyeuristic role in relation to her lovemaking, made him want to substitute himself for Belleroche: made of his readership an arousing and frustrating business. Our own place as readers is not easy to define, but we may sense that the ideal reading of the novel would be polymorphically perverse: would not be limited to the male or female part, but would find pleasure in the way the scene of writing is itself invested with erotic force.

Les liaisons dangereuses may thus appear a kind of epistolary pleasure dome, where the need to narrate pleasure is at the same time the need to create the conditions of pleasure in writing: where writing is never simply referential, but always performative, intent on creating a reading situation that is itself part of the story, that itself will further the erotic action. The fact that Merteuil and Valmont are separated throughout the novel of course motivates their correspondence—they can communicate only by letters—but it also creates the underlying field of force whose energy charges the novel: Valmont wants to overcome that separation, to become once again the marquise's lover; she wants to maintain the separation, to control his approaches to her. Their erotico-epistolary duel may also suggest the extent to which this paradise of epistolarity is infernal, a place in which desire can never break out of the realm of the letter, of language, to accede to the thing itself.

In letter 5, Merteuil notes that "in the most tender conjugal tête-à-tête, one is still always two people." To this inadequate kind of union, she opposes another ideal: "that entire abandon of oneself, that delirium of voluptuousness in which pleasure is purified by its very excess." We may sense here that beyond the alterity implied by, necessitated by, epistolary exchange, there is an ideal of fusion in which two lovers would become one, the barriers between discrete beings would be broken down, and the burden of self-consciousness and egotism momentarily lifted. It may be the goal of the protagonists to move beyond the necessity for epistolary exchange, beyond letters and beyond language itself, to a capture of bliss in the experience of the thing. One may speculate that Merteuil's jealousy of Valmont's experience with Tourvel—which will lead to the breakdown of communication between the two protagonists, and to their open warfare—may be caused by her sense that Valmont has tasted something of that extralinguistic experience with Tourvel. A reading of letter 125, in which Valmont recounts his bedding of Tourvel, suggests something of the sort, his discovery of a state of being not previously known.

Charles Baudelaire called *Les liaisons dangereuses* a "book of terrible sociability," stressing the way in which its games of pleasure and power depend on the collectivity, on all the *others*, and how this situation creates a desperate alterity and publicity, so that one is always playing to, for, off, and against others. Laclos understands that letters, perhaps more strikingly than any other literary form, take shape in anticipation of their reading: that the "I" of the letter writer is always conscious of the "you" to whom he or she writes, conscious that this "you" in reading the letter will conceive itself as "I." The best letter writers always insinuate themselves into the situation of reading. And if writers in this manner become readers, where, on the one hand, is the literal writer of all letters—the author—and where, on the other hand, are the literal readers of the book? So finely managed an epistolary novel as *Les liaisons dangereuses* makes it impossible to find the author, and impossible for the readers to find a firm normative position from which to evaluate what they have read. This, no doubt, is why *Les liaisons dangereuses* has generated, and continues to generate, so many and such divergent interpretations. There is no narrator, no authoritative narrative voice, no implied authorial attitude: elements that most 19th-century novelists would find necessary. Laclos's "terrible sociability" derives in part from his refusal to step forth from the society of the letters. Whatever bad ends may be meted out to his protagonists, the book offers no alternatives, no worlds elsewhere. When you enter the scene of letter writing and letter reading, you become part of a chain of correspondences; you become perhaps that scene itself. This has its pleasures, and also, if you are looking for certainties, looking to attach words to the thing, its dangers of frustration.

The impression of "terrible sociability" also derives from the historical moment of *Les liaisons dangereuses:* at the tail end of the century famous for its dedication to the pursuit of happiness—very much including erotic happiness—and to the analysis of man in purely secular terms. Some contemporaries suggested that Laclos intentionally created a scandal by unmasking the behavior of high society, and this impression is given increased weight by the role played by Laclos during the Revolution, which began its long course only a few years after the publication of his novel. Laclos early aligned himself with the duke of Orléans, head of the younger branch of the royal family, who became known during the Revolution as Philippe-Egalité and voted for the execution of his cousin, Louis XVI. Laclos's career during the Revolution remains imperfectly known. He seems to have been protected by Danton; he was certainly in prison several times, probably close to execution on the guillotine, during the Reign of Terror; and was saved by the downfall of Robespierre. He was an officer in the Revolutionary armies, fought in Italy under the command of the young General Bonaparte, and experimented with the invention of new hollow artillery shells. Some commentators have decided that his Revolutionary biography reveals most of all the opportunist, intent on being with the winning cause, eager to efface himself in moments of trouble. Be that as it may, one can probably draw at least the inference that Laclos did not display any loyalty to the class and the society that he depicted in *Les liaisons dangereuses.*

More certain is the fact that the Revolution brought an end to the kind of sociability on which the epistolary novel depended. Later examples of the genre tend to be self-consciously nostalgic evocations of the form, or else private correspondences, closer to journals. The sense of a unified and exclusive society that had codified the rules of its public games—as well as the permissible hidden infringements of those rules—no longer existed with such clarity and force after the Revolution. The closure on which Laclos's novel depends was no longer absolute. And the letter would no longer be so indisputably the act through which members of the collectivity created their erotic texts. From after the Revolution until well into the 20th century, *Les liaisons dangereuses* became an underground classic, a book not publicly circulated. Nineteenth-century society wished to maintain a firmer distinction between *le mot* and *la chose* and to classify texts dealing with "the thing" as pornography. Today we have once again become more conscious of the erotics of all writing and can allow ourselves once more to admire the perfect fusion of *eros* and the letter achieved by Laclos.

See also 1725, 1735, 1761 (February), 1788.

Bibliography: Janet G. Altman, *Epistolarity: Approaches to a Form* (Columbus: Ohio State University Press, 1982). Charles Baudelaire, "Notes sur *Les liaisons dangereuses*," in *Oeuvres complètes,* ed. Y. G. Le Dantec and Claude Pichois (Paris: Gallimard, 1961). Peter Brooks, *The Novel of Worldliness* (Princeton: Princeton University Press, 1969). Pierre-Ambroise-François Choderlos de Laclos, *Les liaisons dangereuses,* in *Oeuvres complètes,* ed. Laurent Versini (Paris: Gallimard, 1979); translated by Richard Aldington as *Les Liaisons Dangereuses* (New York: New American Library, 1962). André Malraux, "Laclos," in *Tableau de la littérature française,* vol. 1 (Paris: Gallimard, 1940). Nancy K. Miller, *The Heroine's Text* (New York: Columbia University Press, 1980). Ronald Rosbottom, *Laclos* (Boston: Twayne, 1978). Denis de Rougemont, *Love in the Western World* (1939), trans. Montgomery Belgion (Garden City, N.Y.: Doubleday, 1957).

Peter Brooks

∾ 1782, May
Four Years after Rousseau's Death, the First Part of His *Confessions* Is Published in Geneva

Autobiographical Acts

The *Confessions* of Jean-Jacques Rousseau (1712–1778) has become the model for modern autobiography and illustrates, perhaps more than any other one, the problems inherent in this genre. The first two paragraphs of the *Confessions* raise some of the fundamental questions (p. 17):

> I have resolved on an enterprise which has no precedent, and which, once complete, will have no imitator. My purpose is to display to my kind a portrait in every way true to nature, and the man I shall portray will be myself.
>
> Simply myself. I know my own heart and understand my fellow man. But I am made unlike any one I have ever met; I will even venture to say that I am like no one in the whole world. I may be no better, but at least I am different.

543

What is the relationship of an individual autobiography to the autobiographical tradition? Is it possible to distinguish what is specific to the author's lived experience and what is derived from the constraints of representation? Can any autobiography be "true to nature" and unique?

Claiming to be an inimitable work about a unique individual, the *Confessions* opens with a provocation and a paradox. For despite the assertion that this enterprise "has no precedent," the work's title infallibly recalls at least one well-known literary antecedent, the fourth-century *Confessions* of St. Augustine. Considered in Rousseau's time, as in ours, the first great autobiographical work, Augustine's *Confessions* was copied or alluded to by practically every Western chronicler of a spiritual journey, from Petrarch to St. Theresa. By distancing itself from earlier attempts at autobiography while plainly alluding in its title to the single most influential autobiography of the previous fourteen centuries, Rousseau's autobiography causes us to ponder the epistemological status of the "true" life story we are about to read. Can we be sure of knowing where literature ends and nature takes up? A book that flaunts its literary frame of reference while simultaneously proclaiming itself true to nature must put us perpetually on our guard.

Even if we can get beyond the hubris of the opening paragraphs and accept the premise that the book refers only to the nature of the man himself, we are still left to wonder what constitutes this nature and how one grasps the man. For the adequacy of recollection and the possibility of reconstituting the past are also called into question here: "Here is what I have done, and if by chance I have used some immaterial embellishment it has been only to fill a void due to a defect of memory. I may have taken for fact what was no more than probability, but I have never put down as true what I knew to be false" (p. 17). The existence of "embellishments," the effort to fill "defects of memory," and the allusion, in the title of the work, to an already well-formed tradition of autobiographical narrative warn us that the relation of "portrait" to model(s) is not likely to be simple.

The fact that the *Confessions* is not the only autobiographical work signed "Rousseau" further complicates that relation. Do the four autobiographical *Lettres à Malesherbes* (written to a sympathetic government official in 1762), the *Confessions* (composed in 1767 and 1769), the *Dialogues: Rousseau juge de Jean-Jacques* (*Dialogues: Rousseau Judge of Jean-Jacques,* completed in 1776), and the unfinished *Les rêveries du promeneur solitaire* (*The Reveries of the Solitary Walker,* begun in 1776) tell the *same* life story, in four different ways? Or does the project change, however subtly, with the form? Does each addition to the sequence of stories add to the story of the life, or merely retell or revise it? Do the later autobiographies take the place of the projected third part of the *Confessions,* which Rousseau never wrote, and thus "complete" it? Indeed, is an autobiography ever complete, if it cannot include the whole life up to the end? These questions, raised so insistently by Rousseau's autobiographies, suggest that any life story may be nothing but a construct, the truth of which we may never ascertain.

544

The complexity of autobiography, the difficulty of determining its relationship to an individual's lived experience, has prompted some modern theorists of the genre to search for ways to guarantee the authenticity of the narrative. Defining the author as the source of certain necessary choices that give the work its features—choices of style, subject matter, design—or as the signatory whose name appears on the title page and on the publishing contract, they locate the author at the margins of the text, simultaneously within and outside it. By learning the author's choices or by reading his name, they argue, we can impose a certain stability on the otherwise elusive "I" whose "history" we are asked to judge. But it is possible to understand modern autobiography, and certainly the autobiographies of Rousseau, as turning this idea on its head. Rousseau's *Confessions* may be not the product of an author's extratextual acts, but rather a series of textual or linguistic acts that produce an "author."

In fact Rousseau's *Confessions* renders problematic the related notions of author, authorization, and authority by playing with the Augustinian paradigm. Whereas Augustine's *Confessions* presupposes God's "book"—the history of the world from creation to last judgment—and takes God the "author" as its ultimate reference, Rousseau's story relies on Augustine's (via the shared title and certain commonalities of structure) in order to establish, paradoxically, its difference and to divorce authorship from any transcendental authority. Augustine's story positions the individual life within a universal scheme that gives that life its meaning and the author his force; Rousseau's story claims its identity by rejecting resemblance to any earlier author's work, whether that author be secular or divine.

Yet Rousseau's *Confessions* retains the design of a conversion narrative along the lines of Augustine's: book 8 in both *Confessions* relates the decisive moment of reading when the narrator is changed forever. From this moment forward, Augustine will look back on his former life of sin from the point of view of the exemplary man of God he has become; Rousseau, on the other hand, will find misery, distrust, and exile in his new status as a prizewinning author and will look back on his past with longing. It is at this juncture—in this break with the former self, not at the moment of the narrator's birth—that both autobiographies originate. The life story is made possible by the doubling of the self into a former, narrated "I" and the present "I" of the narrator reflecting on that other self. Each of Rousseau's autobiographies signals such a doubling; but in book 8—and in the second letter to Malesherbes, to which book 8 refers—the turning point is described in terms that distinctly recall Augustine, despite their obvious secularity. Augustine's conversion takes place "under a certain fig tree" in a garden; Rousseau's occurs "under an oak tree" along the road to Vincennes (where he is going to visit his imprisoned friend Diderot). Augustine, taking as divine command an insistent voice he cannot identify, picks up a "volume of the apostle" and reads the first passage he comes across, sure that it is meant for him; Rousseau falls upon an announcement of an academic essay contest in the *Mercure de France,* the newspaper whose name evokes the Roman messenger of the gods, and recognizes his calling as a writer. The events provoke a similar reaction in the two men: a flow of tears and a sudden illumination mark that instant when God converted Augustine to himself and Rousseau "became another man." Rousseau's life story clearly (even humorously) positions itself within a literary tradition.

Augustine's narrative also conforms and overtly refers to previous conversions: when he picks up the apostle's volume, he recalls "how [St.] Anthony had been admonished by a reading from the Gospel at which he chanced to be present, as if the words read were addressed to him . . . and that by such a portent he was immediately converted to you [God]" (p. 202). The allusiveness of the conversion narrative and the association of conversion with reading claim holy authority for Augustine the convert and author. Augustine's life story is exemplary precisely because it replicates the established and authoritative model of Christian typology. In Rousseau's *Confessions,* references to Christian typology are present as a subtle and ironic undercurrent, but the ultimate reference through the Bible to "God's book" is lacking. Rousseau's is a purely secular conversion, in which difference rather than resemblance is the governing principle.

Perhaps the most telling difference between the two *Confessions* is the discourse that is said to result from the conversion moment. Whereas Augustine's first postconversion act is to relate his conversion to his friend Alypius, who is thereby converted in turn, the text Rousseau claims to have composed in his altered state is the portion of the *Discours sur les sciences et les arts* (1750; *Discourse on the Sciences and the Arts,* also known as the *Premier discours,* or *First Discourse*) that he calls "the prosopopoeia of Fabricius." In other words, what remains of the conversion is not a conversion narrative but the beginning of Rousseau's reply to the essay question advertised in the newspaper.

The "prosopopoeia," a brief, highly rhetorical passage, attacks the decadence of imperial Rome by "recalling to life" Fabricius, a hero of Rome's golden age as a republic, in order to have him bear witness to the corruption and degradation to which the city has succumbed:

> O Fabricius! What would your noble soul have thought if, unhappily recalled to life, you had seen the pompous appearance of that Rome saved by your valor and better glorified by your worthy name than by all its conquests? "Gods!" you would have said, "what has become of those thatched roofs and those rustic hearths where moderation and virtue used to dwell? What deadly splendor has succeeded Roman simplicity? What is this foreign language? What are these effeminate mores? What do these statues, these paintings, these buildings mean? Madmen, what have you done? Have you, the masters of nations, made yourselves slaves of the frivolous men you conquered? Are these rhetoricians who govern you? Was it to enrich architects, painters, sculptors and affected actors that you watered Greece and Asia with your blood? The spoils of Carthage are the booty of a flutist? Romans, hasten to tear down these amphitheaters; break these marble statues; burn these paintings; chase away these slaves who subjugate you and whose deadly arts corrupt you. Let other hands glory in vain talents; the only talent worthy of Rome is that of conquering the world and making virtue reign over it. When Cineas

mistook our Senate for an assembly of kings, he was not dazzled by vain pomp or studied elegance. He did not hear there this frivolous eloquence, the object and charm of futile men. What then did Cineas see of such majesty? O Citizens! He saw a spectacle that could never be produced by your wealth or your arts, the most beautiful spectacle which has ever appeared beneath the Heavens, the assembly of two hundred virtuous men, worthy of commanding Rome and governing the Earth. (*First and Second Discourses*, pp. 45–46; translation modified)

Fabricius' (fictive) outburst as he compares the two Romes contains, in miniature, the as-yet-undeveloped argument of the entire *Premier discours:* "the contradictions of the social system . . . the abuses of our institutions . . . that man is naturally good and that it is by these institutions alone that men become wicked" (*Lettres à Malesherbes*, pp. 1135–36). If Rousseau is "born again," it is as a commentator on social institutions who sees the history of the world, like his own history, divided into a "before" and "after" by the catastrophic introduction of the arts and sciences. Rousseau's *Confessions*, written some twenty years after the "prosopopoeia," conforms to and replicates the historical model set out there. His life, we might say, is prefigured by the resuscitated Fabricius and the two ages of Rome. Rousseau's life, like Augustine's, is exemplary of a certain history.

However, unlike Augustine, who views his Christian conversion as a desirable death and longed-for rebirth, Rousseau presents his conversion to authorship negatively, as loss. In the second letter to Malesherbes, the brilliance of the moment is dissipated: "All that I could retain of those throngs of great truths which in a quarter of an hour illumined me under that tree, has been feebly scattered in my three principal writings, which are that first discourse, the one on inequality, and the treatise on education [*Emile*], three works which are inseparable and together form a single whole. *All the rest has been lost,* and all that was written on the spot itself was the prosopopoeia of Fabricius. That is how when I was thinking about it the least I became an author almost in spite of myself" (p. 1136; emphasis added). In the later *Confessions,* it is the possibility of a happy life that falls away: "When I reached Vincennes I was in a state of agitation bordering on delirium. Diderot noticed it; I told him the cause and read him the prosopopoeia of Fabricius, which I had written in pencil under an oak tree. He encouraged me to give my ideas wings and compete for the prize. I did so, and *from that moment I was lost.* All the rest of my life and of my misfortunes followed inevitably as a result of that moment's madness" (p. 328; emphasis added).

The "moment's madness"—the moment of writing—produces a text condemning madness and addressed to madmen, men who have allowed themselves to be corrupted by the "deadly arts" of "foreign" rhetoricians. In other words, the "prosopopoeia" is not just a model for the narrative of Rousseau's life; it is a reflection on the very act of writing, which reveals the turn to authorship as nothing less than alienation and loss of self-control. Whereas Augustine's conversion marks his progress from sin toward redemption, the moment in which Rousseau "became an author almost in spite of [him]self" is doubly negative.

The new self (as "loss") is no compensation for the "death" of the old. Becoming an author—writing—is a kind of death in itself.

In fact the "prosopopoeia" does more than represent writing's nefarious effects; it enacts them. Prosopopoeia, the trope which inaugurates Rousseau's entry into writing, which makes of him an author, is defined in contemporary and classical rhetoric as giving face and voice to an imaginary or absent person—in this case, the legendary, long-dead Fabricius . . . but also Rousseau. Speaking from the place of death or absence, prosopopoeia marks the "outside" of the text as uninhabited. Thus there is no point outside the autobiographies from which the reader or the "author" can control their claims. The mastery of language, the power to overturn rhetoric and govern the world in one's own language, which the Fabricius soliloquy assimilates to an original independence now lost, is shown to be a fiction. Fabricius' speech, replete with direct addresses to an imaginary audience of Madmen, Romans, Citizens, repeatedly reproduces the very trope that generated it. Fabricius is *not* the other of imperial Rome, that which is extrinsic to it and measures its enslavement. He, like the Romans he berates, is *subject to* the power of rhetoric, which is as deadly as it is creative. The "prosopopoeia," the text designated only by the rhetorical figure that constitutes it, exposes the negativity of rhetoric and thereby reflects on its own deadly effects.

The turning point that appeared to divide and double Rousseau (or Fabricius) into a dead and a resurrected self, outside and inside the work, turns out to be, not the act of a transcendental authority, but a figure of speech, a rhetorical turn or trope. The "fallen"—and only—world of Rousseau is a text whose specular structure blurs innocent and corrupt, old and new, past and present in an infinite mirroring. It is from this rhetorical perspective that Rousseau's *Confessions* can be viewed as the "original" work of modern autobiography—the work that unsettles the very concepts of "author" and "origin" on which autobiography is traditionally grounded.

Bibliography: Paul de Man, *Allegories of Reading: Figural Language in Rousseau, Nietzsche, Rilke, and Proust* (New Haven: Yale University Press, 1979). Ann Hartle, *The Modern Self in Rousseau's Confessions: A Reply to St. Augustine* (Notre Dame, Ind.: University Press of Notre Dame, 1983). Thomas M. Kavanagh, *Writing the Truth: Authority and Desire in Rousseau* (Berkeley: University of California Press, 1987). Christopher Kelly, *Rousseau's Exemplary Life: The "Confessions" as Political Philosophy* (Ithaca: Cornell University Press, 1987). Jean-Jacques Rousseau, *Confessions,* trans. John M. Cohen (Harmondsworth: Penguin, 1953). Rousseau, *The First and Second Discourses,* ed. Roger D. Masters, trans. Roger D. Masters and Judith R. Masters (New York: © St. Martin's, 1964; quotation reprinted by permission). Rousseau, *Lettres à Malesherbes,* in *Oeuvres complètes,* vol. 1, ed. Marcel Raymond and Bernard Gagnebin (Paris: Gallimard, 1959). Jean Starobinski, *Jean-Jacques Rousseau: Transparency and Obstruction,* trans. Arthur Goldhammer (Chicago: University of Chicago Press, 1988). St. Augustine, *Confessions,* trans. John K. Ryan (Garden City, N.Y.: Doubleday, 1960).

Virginia E. Swain

✑ 1784, 27 April
Pierre Caron de Beaumarchais's *Le mariage de Figaro*
Triumphs at Last at the Comédie-Française

Pre-Revolution (a Comedy)

The public première of *Le mariage de Figaro* (*The Marriage of Figaro*), by Pierre Caron de Beaumarchais (1732–1799), took place on 27 April 1784, on the stage of the Comédie-Française. In the entire history of French theater, it was awaited for a longer time and more intensely than any other première, and for several reasons.

First of all, Beaumarchais had long been a celebrity, not only because of his few plays, but also because of his financial ventures, his amassing of great wealth, his well-known lawsuits, and his role as a businessman and more or less secret agent in foreign countries in the service of the French monarchy (for example, he furnished a huge shipment of arms to the American insurgents).

Second, after two *drames* and a theoretical essay on that new genre, he had had a triumph with the final version of his joyous comedy *Le barbier de Séville* (*The Barber of Seville*), performed at the Comédie-Française in 1775. In the preface to the published play he alluded to the possibility of adding an act to the adventures of his Sevillan barber, Figaro. Encouraged by his patrons, Beaumarchais wrote not one act, but an entire play, which he seems to have finished in 1778. As was the custom, he read the play in the salons of high society, reworked it, and on 29 September 1781 finally read it to the actors of the Comédie-Française, who accepted it enthusiastically as part of their repertoire. Then began the intricate problems with censorship and with Louis XVI himself. A first censor considered the play performable on condition that a few revisions and cuts be made. But the king, having had the play read to him, forbade the performance. "The Bastille would have to be destroyed," he declared, "in order that the performance of this play not be dangerously irresponsible."

The king's allusion to the Bastille was prophetic only retrospectively. However, in *Le mariage de Figaro* he had to deal with the portrait of a *grand seigneur,* married to a loving wife, who made every effort to sleep with his faithful servant's fiancée; an aristocrat who was to be constantly thwarted and, at the end, humiliated in front of his vassals; and throughout those "follies of a day" (the 1795 English translation of the play's original title, *La folle journée*) Figaro, the servant, took advantage of every occasion to denounce the aristocrats who abused the lowly, the contradictions of justice and the treatment of women, and the unfairness of privileges accorded to birth regardless of worth, in a dazzling display of insolent repartees and incisive one-liners that won the approval of the audience through the laughter they provoked. And the whole was crowned by a long satiric soliloquy cataloguing the absurdities and characteristic arbitrary actions of the ancien régime. Louis XVI thus decided, at the time, not to take any risks. A second censor went along with him and rejected the play.

549

Though denied the play itself, the public was treated to a comic demonstration of the vacillations of the established powers toward the end of the ancien régime. Coincidentally with the king's interdiction, a performance of the play was organized to allow the court to see at last what it was all about, but the performance was forbidden at the very last moment, just as the curtain was about to go up. Shortly afterward a successful private performance took place at Joseph-Hyacinthe de Vaudreuil's, attended by the comte d'Artois, the king's youngest brother. Following that, three new censors approved the play in a very watered-down version, and one of them even praised it. Then suddenly, in March 1784, the king's interdiction was lifted, the performance on 27 April was a great triumph, and the first run spanned sixty-eight performances, a very high figure for the time.

Immediately afterward, however, Beaumarchais was accused of having insulted the powers that be by speaking of "lions and tigers" in a pamphlet in which he defended himself against new charges and explained his struggles to get his play performed. As a result he found himself locked up, not in the Bastille, the royal prison, but in Saint-Lazare, the prison meant for profligates and juvenile delinquents. Outraged public opinion, a polite but strong *Mémoire* addressed by Beaumarchais to the king, and the comte d'Artois's intervention—all resulted in Beaumarchais's release after five days, a gift to him of 800,000 francs, a half-apology from the king, and the staging of *Le barbier de Séville* at the Trianon, in which the comte d'Artois played Figaro, and Marie-Antoinette herself the part of Rosine.

Beaumarchais was not the only writer to endure the alternate waves of favor and persecution, often a reflection of the shifts in the prevailing faction at court; Voltaire and Denis Diderot were other eminent victims of that uncertainty. Not only was the king himself ambivalent; he was surrounded by the "cons"—including Monsieur (the king's brother and the future Louis XVIII), some of his ministers, and the censor Jean-Baptiste Suard—and the "pros," including the queen (guillotined in 1793), the princesse de Lamballe (murdered in 1792), the duchesse de Polignac (who was to emigrate), and the comte d'Artois (who also emigrated and under the Restoration became Charles X, only to be dethroned in 1830 by the July Revolution), as well as the enlightened nobility and royalty of Europe. For example, the impatience of Catherine the Great (Diderot's patron) is a well-known historical fact: as early as 1781 she had her chamberlain write to Beaumarchais, expressing her astonishment at not yet having received a copy of the new and already notorious play—she, who had had *Le barbier de Séville* performed more than fifty times at her court.

Announced and awaited for a long time, an object of controversy in high places, occasionally suppressed but also upheld by influential members of the court, *Le mariage de Figaro* clearly owed its immediate and prolonged success to reasons other than external circumstances.

To begin with, at a time when comedy, weighed down by sentimentality and moralism, was no longer very funny (at least at the Comédie-Française; there was plenty of laughter at the Opéra Comique and in fairground theaters), Beaumarchais's play proved to be a richly integrated repository of devices that had made audiences laugh since before Molière.

Theatrically, *Le mariage de Figaro* is a unique synthesis of an entire past and present. After many comedies fashioned on Molière's and often seasoned with a facile and edifying morality (Philippe Destouches, Louis Gresset), Pierre Carlet de Marivaux (1688–1763) introduced a new and special kind of comedy which did not eliminate types and characters but in which language (most often, that of love) was the driving force of the action. In addition to a few traces of *marivaudage*, Beaumarchais also made use of the *comédie sérieuse*, the serious comedy that was in fashion in the second half of the century. After the success of Pierre Claude Nivelle de La Chaussée and his "tearful comedies" (such as *Le préjugé à la mode* [1735; *The Fashionable Prejudice*], whose heroine is a betrayed wife), Voltaire had already made audiences weep with his *Nanine* (1749). Then came the true "serious" genres, bringing an element of gravity into the portrayal of contemporary domestic life, while the *drame bourgeois* introduced the pathos of tragedy into a contemporary setting. Diderot, Michel-Jean Sedaine, and Beaumarchais himself—with *Eugénie* (1767), about a pregnant girl; and *Les deux amis* (1770; *The Two Friends*), about a bankruptcy—were the masters of that new genre. Thus the end of the 18th century witnessed a blurring of the traditional distinction of genres in classical theater.

In *Le mariage de Figaro*, Beaumarchais used all the available possibilities. Not one of his purely comic devices had not already appeared in farces, *parades*, the Italian comedies, and the works of Molière and his successors. He also used the pathos of the "serious" genre: in the jealous count's violence; in Marcelline's plea for women, accompanied by the indignation of most of the characters; and in the tears of joy in the recognition scenes.

Yet the play is not merely a theatrical exercise. It is in fact a transposition of Beaumarchais's talent for comedy *in real life*—as an intriguer, a literary portrait painter, and an autobiographer—to the place that best suited it, the stage. The autobiographical dimension is one of the original features of the play: Beaumarchais not only expresses some of his ideas through the character of Figaro, but he also introduces a metaphor of his own person and of what he claims is his destiny. Both Beaumarchais and Figaro seek to succeed in the service of an aristocratic establishment (Beaumarchais with the French monarchy, Figaro in Count Almaviva's monarchical microcosm). The character of Figaro offers thus a figure *en abyme*, a miniature image of his creator's life. But the two correspond more than metaphorically. For example, Beaumarchais in effect signs the portrait by endowing his character with the trait that made it possible for him to survive, *gaiety*, which both of them mention often and publicly.

Finally, it is thought today that the play's success with members of all classes must have also been due to the fact that the work contains, simultaneously, an often vengeful satire and a conciliating caution that somehow weakens any truly subversive effect. The basic metaphor (*le droit du seigneur*) diverts attention away from indignation at real and painful abuses and toward amusement at the piquant eroticism of the situations (which Lorenzo da Ponte and Mozart, in 1786, were to transform into the lyricism of love in *Le nozze di Figaro*). Count Almaviva's tyranny consists essentially in trying to sleep with his servants, who, as in the case of Suzanne, are perfectly able to defend themselves. Figaro himself—who clearly far transcends the traditional valets of theater, even the cleverest of them, because of his many professions, his culture, and rich, individualized life—acts and speaks more than he is effectual: his plans are helped along or upset by the charming and supposedly fragile characters—Rosine, Suzanne (whose taking control over the action starting with act 4 is a fine example of protofeminism), and Chérubin—or quite simply by chance, which is all-powerful and ambiguous, and which Figaro complains about when it is used by the nobility to oppress the lowly, but which delights him when it happily resolves delicate situations. As a result, the true action of the play is partly stolen from the protagonist, who, in addition, has no organized plan of reform in his satires and complaints; for neither Beaumarchais nor Figaro is committed to any systematic ideology, and even less to any truly revolutionary activity. Moreover, the count himself, who, according to Beaumarchais's preface, is "humiliated but never degraded," was perhaps considered a reflection—as Jean-Pierre de Beaumarchais, a descendant of the author, remarked—of those members of the nobility who were progressive out of a bad conscience and often prisoners of their liberal impulses, and who contributed to the play's success by getting a good conscience from watching the comic spectacle of their bad conscience. Given a Figaro without any ideology, who, like Beaumarchais, asks only to be happy, free, and secure within the system of his time, and an Almaviva who abuses his power only when urged by his desire for sexual novelty, one could, forgetting the later chapters of history, reduce the play to a fine example of candor in which a courageous author, in the tradition of classical moralists and satirists, grasped the spirit of his time, its contradictions, and its social types and produced this mirror onstage. Confronted with a society whose ideology has become unstable and incoherent, and in which the powers that be are hesitant, the play hesitates, too, and moves between disparate elements that were to be part of an ideology yet to come—and to be taken in hand by the Revolution.

But inevitably, the following chapters of history were written; and during the Revolution the character of Figaro came to acquire mythic status. It is not easy now to detach Figaro from the layers of meaning he has accumulated for over two centuries, from the allegorical iconography that portrays him as the hero striking out at abuses, then the interpretations that transform him into the first *sans-culotte,* all the way to Marxist analyses. Actors, directors, and critics remain divided over what emphasis to give the different levels and elements of the play. *Le mariage de Figaro* is a truly pre-Revolutionary comedy, a comedy between two worlds in which everything ends in song. But is it more than the dazzling dramaturgy of the foibles and follies of a tottering society that, oblivious to impending catastrophe, is merely greedy for a free right to happiness? Or is it the prophetic overture to one of the greatest upheavals in the history of the West?

See also 1759 (23 April), 1791 (13 January).

552

Bibliography: Elizabeth S. Kite, *Beaumarchais and the War of American Independence* (Boston: Richard G. Badher, 1918). Robert Niklaus, *Beaumarchais: Le mariage de Figaro* (London: Grant & Cutler, 1983). A. R. Pugh, *Beaumarchais: Le Mariage de Figaro: An Interpretation* (London: Macmillan, 1968). Joseph Sungolowsky, *Beaumarchais* (Boston: Twayne, 1974).

Jacques Guicharnaud

⁄⁄⁊ 1787

Isabelle de Charrière Publishes *Caliste*

Designing Women

The 18th century—and especially its last few decades—saw the publication of a surprising number of novels by women, most of which have been excluded from the canon. Although students of French literature can usually identify Marie-Madeleine de La Fayette, who wrote in the 17th century, and Germaine de Staël and George Sand, who wrote in the 19th, few have heard of 18th-century writers such as Françoise de Graffigny, Marie-Jeanne Riccoboni, Marie Le Prince de Beaumont, or Anne-Louise Elie de Beaumont. Whereas Staël, by the force of her personality and politics and the sheer volume of her writing, represents the woman writer and intellectual of the early 19th century, the 18th century is characterized instead by scores of women who frequently wrote in obscurity and signed pseudonymously or not at all, and whose works are basic commentaries on the social debates of the era and on woman's place in it. Their experiments with epistolarity, sentimentality, and the figure of the heroine helped shape the emerging novel and establish a public for a genre that was still often disparaged by critics.

Among the period's female writers was Isabelle de Charrière, one of the century's subtlest and most compelling novelists, who has been excluded from the French canon by reason of both her sex and her nationality. Born Isabella van Tuyll van Serooskerken in 1740 to an aristocratic Dutch family (and known as Belle de Zuylen from the name of the family castle), she never belonged to the Parisian intellectual or social milieu. She counted among her lovers Benjamin Constant, and her hand was at one time sought by James Boswell. Her marriage at the age of thirty to Charles-Emmanuel de Charrière, an obscure Swiss citizen, took her from Holland to Switzerland, where she lived until her death in 1805. There she produced in French a voluminous oeuvre that includes novels, essays, verse, plays, and music. Her correspondence reveals her as provocative and sometimes grim, and her novels resemble her personality. She does not conform to the stereotype of the 18th-century female novelist as someone who wrote casually for lack of anything better to do. Like Riccoboni, Graffigny, Isabelle de Montolieu, and countless other women, Charrière worked hard and wrote to sell, and the financial and material arrangements of her publications were of paramount importance to her.

Her best-known novels are written in the epistolary form, which attained its

553

greatest popularity during this period, especially from the pens of women writers such as Graffigny and Riccoboni. With Charrière, the epistolary novel demonstrates its intrinsic suitability to the evocation of woman's life. Where woman's access to the public domain is problematic, the letter form conceals and compensates for her exclusion from history while it gives full play to her lifespace and her private experience of time. It stresses private relations—secrets, confessions, the act of confiding—in short, woman's traditional sphere. Some of Charrière's novels involve an exchange among several correspondents; in others, a single protagonist writes. Unlike many 18th-century novels, Charrière's major works contain no cases of mistaken identity or disfigurement by smallpox; nor a single duel, rape, purloined letter, secret marriage, or lost will. Her writing is a delicate weave of inconspicuous circumstances and almost infinitesimal occurrences whose accumulated weight nonetheless determines the heroines' destinies. For all the careful psychology of its investigation of seduction and betrayal, Riccoboni's *Lettres de Mistriss Fanni Butlerd* (1757; *Letters of Mistress Fanni Butlerd*) appears coarse when compared to the fine texture of Charrière's novels. Charrière, who has been rightly compared to Jane Austen, also dramatizes the domestic, intertwining psychological, aesthetic, and economic concerns and exploring a carefully delimited and vividly depicted interior space where the dropping of a sheet of music, the closing of a door, or a half-muted reproach can resound like thunder. But the situations and destinies the letters narrate gain an exemplary emancipatory strength from this very restrictiveness. By the breadth of her concerns and the finesse of her analyses, Charrière may be considered as epitomizing a group of women who reigned over the novel. But she is simultaneously distinguished by her very foreignness and by the qualities that account for her continuing readability: her economy of means, the psychological distinctness of her work, and the way she uses novelistic conventions such as closure. Coming late in a long tradition of women's epistolary writing, Charrière draws on that tradition while implicitly rejecting the exaggerations often associated with the novel.

Charrière's best work includes *Lettres écrites de Lausanne* (1785; *Letters Written from Lausanne*) and its sequel, *Caliste, ou suite des lettres écrites de Lausanne* (1787; *Caliste, or the Sequel to Letters Written from Lausanne*). The themes of both—woman's marginality, her social and financial vulnerability—eloquently translate the patterns of life into fiction. The first half is the story of seventeen-year-old Cécile, told by her enlightened mother in letters to a friend in France. Without a fortune, Cécile has poor marriage prospects. She has a few viable suitors but loves Edward, a young English lord who is beguiled but insufficiently motivated to propose marriage. When Cécile begins to languish, her mother takes her away for a change of air. And so the story ends—or fails to end.

The sequel, *Caliste*, is an extraordinarily powerful piece and also, like Charrière's other novels, quite short: less than fifty pages. William, Lord Edward's melancholy companion, writes for Cécile's mother his own story and that of the brilliant, artistic Caliste. Caliste is made a child actress by her impoverished mother; then she is more or less bought by an English nobleman who takes her as his mistress but also gives her an impeccable education. After his death, she meets and falls in love with William, bereaved by the death of his twin brother. William never musters the courage either to marry her despite his father's interdiction or to take her as mistress despite her craving for respectability. He finally marries instead a trifling widow of his father's choosing, while Caliste weds a country gentleman. She dies in England in an aura of sainthood (during a performance of Pergolesi's *Stabat Mater*), while back in Lausanne William wallows in self-reproach.

Differences in tone and events do little to undermine similarities between the two stories: *Caliste* is the tragic version of Cécile's story—tragic because William, like Edward, manifests a fatal inertia. Jean Starobinski has noted that William's compulsive abdication of decisive action is accompanied by discreet but insistent suggestions of latent homosexuality. They include, for example, his attachments to a twin brother (during their military service, they spend their free hours studying and making music, while other soldiers "wasted their time on gambling and women") and to a young stepson who resembles the deceased brother. In fact this ten-year-old child accompanies William on a trip (honeymoon?) after William's marriage, while the bride stays at home with her father-in-law. Finally, of course, William attaches himself to Edward. When William falls in love with Caliste, he feels instinctively unfaithful to his brother and, despite his realization of Caliste's passion, shrinks from physical love. He is willing to be treated like a "sister" by Caliste and is indifferent to his own wife's infidelities. Although there is no explicit indication that William feels threatened by Caliste's ardor, this is subtly suggested by his irresolution, his tendency to yield rather than persevere. In most sentimental novels, by contrast, male aggressiveness is a fundamental fact: the men tirelessly strategize to get the women into bed. Here, too, William says he wants to sleep with Caliste, and she says no; but her underlying passion and his passivity, like his virginity and her sexual experience, in effect constitute a reversal of roles. Caliste does not die because she has engaged in illicit sex; instead, she withers away for lack of it. Her death, caused largely by the jealous force of a male bond, is also a commentary on the power of a patriarchal system to exclude a woman who is not "normal."

In their utter social dependence on male initiative, Cécile and Caliste are the victims of a system that makes autonomy almost impossible for women. They are oppressed by habits of mind engraved in a sociological landscape defined by a religion, a culture, and the slow pace of time. While men act, women are obliged to wait and practice female "virtue." In Charrière's work, chastity is motivated by practical considerations. The abstinence that Caliste obsessively practices after the death of her first lover is designed to be rewarded by rehabilitation: because she can aspire to become William's wife only by refusing to become his mistress, she mounts a campaign of intellectual and moral resistance. Although she thereby proves herself "worthy" of William, his own lethargy guarantees that her worth will go unrewarded by sex or marriage, and her obstinate, virtuous victory over desire weakens and ultimately kills her.

Cécile, too, has to resist the physical: her story suggests a new definition of virtuous behavior, which her mother attempts to motivate less with religious arguments than with a more concrete inducement: it helps find a husband. Cécile must therefore artfully conceal the attraction she feels toward the English lord if she is to induce him to marry her. Here virtue functions as imposture—the concealment of what Charrière calls one's *sensibilité*, and what we understand as both sentiment and the sexual urge.

The possibility of domestic happiness is one of Charrière's main concerns. Neither Cécile, nor Caliste, nor most of her other heroines have access to other than domestic satisfactions: their thoughts range restlessly within a cage constructed and reinforced by patriarchal concepts. Yet even the domestic sphere excludes or thwarts them. Conjugal and domestic structures are seen as constituting the principal mode of fulfillment for women, yet such structures are also progressively revealed as the chief obstacle to their happiness. The case of the protagonist of Charrière's *Lettres de Mistress Henley* (1784; *Letters of Mrs. Henley*) is the clearest: her decision (like the author's own) to marry a man of solid and retiring virtue rather than one of ambition and eminence is a choice of the domestic over the worldly. Delimited by the parameters of her spouse's mind and home, Mrs. Henley's fate is wretched, just as Charrière's own life in the village of her stolid Swiss husband was stifling. Is Charrière not suggesting that the male version of happiness for women is a verbal fabrication? Are women not alienated by the complicity of moralizing, rationalizing men with empty words? We are reminded of Louise d'Epinay's remark that "reason" means following the advice you are given.

Just as Edward and William are characterized by an appalling passivity, so Cécile's story is fragmented, its inscription strangely incomplete, except insofar as Caliste's tragic end represents Cécile's. Just as these plots anatomize the critical junctures arising out of the minute incidents of daily life, the ending refuses to transcend the quotidian. This indeterminacy itself mimics the heroines' contingency, their social, economic, or affective estrangement. These very domestic representations of individuality reveal and represent patterns of the literary and the social, especially as they figure in novels by female writers throughout the century. They are dialogues with the late 18th-century European culture in which Charrière lived and worked, a culture in which there seemed to be little salvation for a woman outside of marriage and, as her own experience demonstrated, little hope of personal satisfaction for an exceptional woman within it. In Charrière's world, there exists no recipe for marrying or for marital success, biological and economic imperative though marriage is, and men may lack even the mettle to make love.

Caliste has an unusually rich literary posterity, both in works such as Germaine de Staël's *Corinne* (1807) and Benjamin Constant's *Adolphe* (wr. 1806–07, pub. 1816) and in the real-life connections among their authors. Charrière, who as a young woman had a long (mostly epistolary) relationship with a Swiss officer eighteen years her elder, Baron Auguste Constant d'Hermenches, later counted among her intimates his nephew Benjamin, whom she met when she was in her late forties and he not yet twenty. His tumultuous affair with Germaine de Staël, which began a few years later, embittered Charrière, although she and Benjamin Constant remained in correspondence until her death. Staël, for her part, esteemed her older rival (although she complained about her annoying habit of leaving her novels unfinished) and specifically prized *Caliste:* "How I wish I hadn't read *Caliste* ten times!" she wrote to Charrière during the Terror. "I would have before me the certain prospect of an hour's respite from all my troubles" (31 December 1793, in Charrière, *Oeuvres complètes,* 4:299).

Like William in *Caliste,* Staël's hero (Corinne's lover) irresolutely forsakes the woman who fascinates him to marry the woman of his father's choosing, cementing the paternal bond through the conjugal. *Adolphe* is a male version of the story: here the heroine who dies of despair is rather less genius and more harpy, and the courage that the man lacks is not so much courage to marry as courage to leave. Lovers and (writing) rivals in a triangular relation curiously skewed by their chonological ages and by the historical passage from Revolution to Empire, Charrière, Constant, and Staël each translated a personal drama into a masterpiece of fiction and an essential myth about patriarchy. In each case a novel about female passion and marginality and male impotence is curiously configured by the role of the father/brother for whom the hero feels the profoundest bond, the most inviolable desire.

Caliste glosses the most urgent concerns of the female novel of the late 18th century: love, of course, and marriage, without which vulnerable female protagonists recognize that survival is difficult. The author herself had reason to understand this. The drama of the problematic marriageability of the modestly dowered and too brilliant Belle de Zuylen with her motley band of mostly lukewarm suitors, her dubious decision to accept the hand of the man who promised (and proved) least fit to be her husband—this drama has been amply evoked by her biographers. Her novels also epitomize women's complicated relation to 18th-century sensibility. It was in the wake of Richardson and Rousseau that the notion of *sensibilité* reached its apogee in the French novel and that the novel itself (and especially the epistolary form) became increasingly recognized as an effective means of representing not just morality and sentiment but also complex social realities. Novels by women during this era mediate social conditions and literary conventions: women helped enthrone sensibility, which enthroned women, but they also explored its connections with oppression. Charrière and other women used the novel to write about themselves in a century that saw fewer autobiographies and memoirs than works of fiction. The extent to which sentimentality and apparent morality mask revolt in fiction, and the play between conformism and questioning, help account for the subversions they wrought. By their use of form and by the force of style, Charrière's stories are powerfully seductive. The meaning she invests in morality, domesticity, sensibility, reason, and virtue connects her to a tradition of women's writing. It also suggests the relation of her work to woman's domestic culture and indicates the extent to which a close reading of fictional conventions in the century's female novel may reveal the currents beneath a seemly, seamless surface.

557

Bibliography: Isabelle de Charrière, *Oeuvres complètes,* ed. Jean-Daniel Candaux, C. P. Courtney, Pierre H. Dubois, Simone Dubois-De Bruyn, Patrice Thompson, Jeroom Vercruysse, and Dennis M. Wood, 13 vols. (Amsterdam: G. A. Van Oorschot, 1979–1984). Philippe Godet, *Madame de Charrière et ses amis,* 2 vols. (Geneva: A. Jullien, 1906). Elizabeth J. MacArthur, "Devious Narratives: Refusal of Closure in Two Eighteenth-Century Novels," *Eighteenth-Century Studies,* 21 (1987), 1–20. Geoffrey Scott, *The Portrait of Zélide* (New York: Scribner's, 1927). Jean Starobinski, "Les *Lettres écrites de Lausanne* de Madame de Charrière: Inhibition psychique et interdit social," in *Roman et lumières au XVIIIe siècle* (Paris: Editions Sociales, 1970), pp. 130–151. Joan Hinde Stewart, "The Novelists and Their Fictions," in *French Women and the Age of Enlightenment,* ed. Samia I. Spencer (Bloomington: Indiana University Press, 1984), pp. 197–211.

Joan Hinde Stewart

✐ 1788

The Marquis de Condorcet Publishes *Lettres d'un bourgeois de New-Haven*

Civil Rights and the Wrongs of Women

Marie-Jean Antoine Nicolas de Caritat, marquis de Condorcet, was born in 1743 into a long-established noble family from the south of France that had until the 17th century remained staunchly Protestant. This legacy of stubborn dissent was one that the marquis would not reject.

In Picardy, where the Condorcet family had only recently settled, his mother, from the north, was widowed for the second time when Condorcet was only a month old. She raised him in a frenzy of piety and protectiveness, dressing him in feminine garb until he was eight, ostensibly to spare him from the violence of other boys. What influence this early experience might have exerted on his ability to speak as he did, in 1788 and 1789, for the rights of women can only be imagined.

After a struggle with his family, which had designated a military career for him, Condorcet found his vocation in the study of mathematics and was early accepted into the Academy of Sciences, where Jean Le Rond d'Alembert, the mathematician and collaborator with Denis Diderot on the *Encyclopédie* (1751–1772), became his protector. At twenty-one he had established his scientific eminence with the publication of *Du calcul intégral* (1764; *On Integral Calculus*). Once a member of the academy, Condorcet enjoyed enormous prestige, as the impact of science and technology grew at the century's end. Condorcet took his conception of the "man of science" from d'Alembert: for both, science was an intellectual pursuit that placed its practitioners squarely in the midst of all the great questions of reform that agitated their time. D'Alembert in fact proclaimed that it was the mission of men of science and letters to legislate for the rest of the nation in matters of taste, and Condorcet accepted this assumption, which later generations would come to deem arbitrary and elitist. A second mentor was Anne-Robert-Jacques Turgot, Louis XVI's finance minister from

1773 to 1776, under whom Condorcet served. Turgot was a technocratic advocate of human progress, and Condorcet espoused his views. As early as 1772, the marquis conceived the plan for a great treatise *Esquisse d'un tableau historique des progrès de l'esprit humain* (1794; *Sketch for a Historical Picture of the Progress of the Human Mind*), a work expressing his positive faith in the human capacity to achieve the good, which he was to complete in 1793–94 in hiding, as a proscribed Girondist politician, from the Terror that claimed his life.

Condorcet's belief in the power of human institutions to change entrenched habits and, through education and scientific thinking, to liberate humankind, was one factor in allowing him to think of women in a fresh way. His experience of salon life and his friendship with the "muse" of the *Encyclopédie,* Julie de Lespinasse, and other women of ability played a role in acquainting him with a lively world of mixed gender. Finally, his marriage in 1786 to Sophie de Grouchy may have proved decisive in making him advocate the cause of women. Sophie de Condorcet was a young person of great vivacity and curiosity of mind. With her husband, she founded a political salon where, in the very center of Revolutionary activity, advanced political ideas and projects were passionately discussed. Out of this milieu emerged Condorcet's two remarkable works: a pamphlet, *Lettres d'un bourgeois de New-Haven à un citoyen de Virginie, sur l'inutilité de partager le pouvoir législatif en plusieurs corps* (1788; *Letters of a Resident of New Haven to a Citizen of Virginia on the Uselessness of Dividing the Legislative Power between Various Bodies*)—Condorcet liked to employ the literary convention of commenting on his nation as if he were not a native—and the 1789 essay *Sur l'admission des femmes au droit de cité* (*On the Admission of Women to the Rights of Citizens of a State*). The first text made a philosophical argument for women's rights in a nation-state; the second proposed how such rights might be implemented.

By the 1780s the salon culture of the upper classes had passed its apogee; the preeminence of perspicacious and witty *salonnières* was being effectively contested by the domestic ideal, originally imported from England but enormously inflated by the popularity of the wifely, sanctified heroine of Rousseau's *Julie, ou la nouvelle Héloïse* (1761; *Julie, or the New Héloïse*). Among the poor, women in agricultural settings still lived for the most part within little-altered folk traditions of rustic subordination, while those women who in ever-greater numbers had been forced townward to support themselves by clothmaking or domestic service attempted to keep at bay, or simply succumbed to, a life of prostitution. The continuing rise in illegitimate births and the wholesale abandonment of infants to orphanages and wetnurses—amounting to tacit infanticide—was a painful feature of the pre-Revolutionary era. Perhaps in response, female sexuality became loaded with menace and female chastity an obsession.

The full originality of Condorcet's understanding of women's nature and place becomes clearer when compared with the terms of the late 18th century's intense though not always coherent debate about the nature and role of women. In his 1772 review (never published in his lifetime, but probably circulated by hand) of Abbé Thomas's *Des femmes* (*On Women*), Diderot made it plain that discourse on the female sex was chiefly the preserve of men. "The souls of women are not more honest than ours," he wrote, "but since decency does not allow them to explain themselves with our candor, they have fabricated intricate birdcalls for themselves, and if we use them, we can say anything we like about them, once they have whistled us into their birdcage" (p. 35). Diderot's disgust stemmed from the abbé's conformity to the courtly and figured style of discourse concerning women, a system of surface *politesse* that upper-class women and men had developed in the days of *préciosité* as a means of refining and extending courtship and social mixing of the sexes. But the bourgeois in Diderot restlessly contested what he held to be this namby-pamby aristocratic treatment of women. He sought to rip their protective veils from them: "It is above all in the passions of love, in attacks of jealousy, in their transports of maternal love, in the way they have of spreading emotional epidemics among the people that women astonish us; as beautiful as Klopstock's angels, as terrible as Milton's devils. I have seen love, jealousy, rage, and superstition carried in women to a point that no man will ever know" (p. 38). No less than Freud, Diderot saw women as dominated by their biology and thus as radically—and for him excitingly—different from men in their wild affectivity and unreason. Even as he strove to characterize them more feelingly than had Thomas, he could not resist his zestful manipulation of the angel/devil model of thinking about women.

The place of women in the upper reaches of 18th-century French society was universally regarded by visitors from Europe and the Orient as a marvel. The social skills, elegance, and influence of Frenchwomen were conceded; but all these qualities could be and were construed as negative: as calculation, interference, vanity, and artifice. As Diderot's remarks illustrate, although women's status, talents, and duties were now under wide discussion, they rarely received systematic or serious treatment. The discourse on women by men, even at its most insightful, suffered from the entrenched imperative to verbalize about them in terms of the frivolity and sensuality of "the sex," an approach applied impartially to duchesses and shepherdesses.

Despite their prominence in the salons, the endemic mythology dictated that no woman could be allowed into the most enlightened literary and intellectual ranks on a par with men. Thinking women were well aware of the legal, intellectual, and spiritual limits placed upon them. Louise d'Epinay, mistress to Friedrich Melchior Grimm and friend to Diderot and Rousseau, ruefully commented: "I contend that a woman is not able, by reason of her being a woman, to acquire any knowledge extensive enough to be useful to her kind, and it seems to me that only in such knowledge can one take pride . . . How many things it is forbidden women to approach! All that pertains to the science of administration, of politics, of commerce, is deemed foreign and closed to them: they cannot nor they must not be involved in them, and these are the sole great means by which cultivated men can be truly useful to their fellows, to the state, to their nation" (*Correspondance*, p. 359). The tone of d'Epinay's remark contrasts markedly with that of Diderot's essay. Her language in speaking of women is sober, even somber: it is the language of reason, whereas his revels in fantasy and a deliberate evasion of reasoned discourse about the opposite sex. While the dominant male discourse of this time tends stubbornly to obscure women's human complexity, preferring to concentrate on their "nature" as sexual and reproductive beings, women's discourse does nothing of the sort; they see themselves as social beings, as beings of culture, not as primarily "natural." The great charge against them, lent daunting force by Rousseau, was that women's participation in society was an aberration, and that those who sought to play the game of society with men simply unwomaned themselves.

That unsurpassed novel of seduction, Pierre Choderlos de Laclos's *Les liaisons dangereuses,* toys with the notion of what happens when women's (or one woman's) objectives resemble those of men. This work, the sensation of 1782, contains in its celebrated letter 81, written by Mme. de Merteuil to her collaborator and enemy in the arts of amorous manipulation, a meditation on the hard rock of inequality between the sexes and a proclamation of lucid female will not to be subjected to it. In the context of her triumphant exposure of her control over the hypocrisy society has enjoined upon her, the marquise proclaims herself a general in the war of the sexes, "born to avenge my sex," she tells Valmont, "and to master yours."

The sheer power of release of a painfully repressed female truth in Merteuil's "explanation" testifies to the anxiety aroused in high society by women's more nearly equal place in it. Merteuil's "sin" proves to be that of self-preservation; it is her genius for calculation and mastery of her world that, in the ethos of the novel, unsex her. In contrast to Merteuil, the intended-to-be touchingly chaste Mme. de Tourvel, whom Valmont seduces only to become emotionally obsessed with her, exhibits appropriate feminine vulnerability to love and achieves an ultimate validation by the pathos of her death. But inscribing Merteuil's "revolt," with its bold rejection of victimization, sufficiently heightened Laclos's awareness of the explosiveness of women's situation to impel him to compose a discourse (*De l'éducation des femmes; On Women's Education*) on the question proposed by the Academy of Châlons-sur-Marne in 1783, "What would be the best means of improving women's education?" Laclos replied that, as things then were, there was no way of improving women's education, for in fact they were receiving none; moreover, a woman of good education would be deeply unhappy if she stayed in her place, and dangerous (like Merteuil?) if she sought to depart from it. Urgently summoning women to listen to him, Laclos then uttered a curious statement: "One can break free of slavery only by making a great revolution. Is such a revolution possible? Only you can say, since it depends upon your courage" (*Oeuvres,* p. 391).

If this rhetoric holds women responsible for their own servitude, it at least has the virtue of conceptualizing their rejection of it. Laclos did not pursue this level of plain speaking about women, although he made several more traditional attempts to clarify his thinking about them. Indeed, in his 1782 correspondence with Marie-Jeanne Riccoboni, the respected author of successful novels clearly conceived from the female point of view, we find quite another voice. She wrote to him on 14 April 1782 protesting against the depiction of the malicious marquise: "It is as a woman, monsieur, as a Frenchwoman, as a zealous patriot to the honor of my nation that I felt my heart wounded by the character of Mme. de Merteuil" (*Oeuvres,* p. 759). It is true, as Riccoboni seems to have intuited might be the case, that by virtue of the power of representation Merteuil was to come to appear in historical retrospect to embody all the heartlessness, callousness, and bitterness of human connection under the ancien régime. Laclos retorted that such a woman was of no country, for wherever a woman is born with active senses and a heart incapable of love, some wit and a vile soul, there a Merteuil will be. This prescription clearly, though by indirection, commands women, if they would be "good," to have loving hearts and passive senses. Laclos's correspondence is characterized by that commonplace rhetoric of gallantry that, beneath its apparent grace, attempts almost expressly, by its insistent allusion to women's desirability, to limit the content and style of their expression: "It is to women alone that belongs that precious sensibility, that facile, free-flowing, and smiling imagination that embellishes all it touches and creates objects as they ought to be" (ibid.). We read beneath his flattery: "A woman novelist does not criticize." Laclos is unnerved by Riccoboni's assumption of the role of dissenter. Women may create, provided they do so in all modesty, by analogy with their biological function; but dissent is a failure of the generosity that one has a right to expect from them. *Les liaisons dangereuses* was viewed by a number of women as a work inimical to them, but, as Laclos coyly claimed, this controversy simply bore witness to his preoccupation with them, and "how can one pay attention to them and not love them?" Here the discourse of flirtation effectively blocks dialogue with a female interlocutor.

The silencing of Riccoboni was part of a wider struggle. The longing of women to speak meaningfully or to be heard was expressed fitfully in the midst of the continuing polemic for and against them. In 1772 Canon Edmé Ferlet argued that women's influence upon French culture was no longer positive as it had been: scientists and thinkers were now finding themselves enervated by the need to please women and to make themselves understood by them. Women must never hold, as Ferlet charged they then did, powers of reward and punishment for achievement, nor should they be arbiters of reputation. Ferlet's argument was temperate in comparison with that of the chevalier Feucher d'Artaize. In his *Réflexions d'un jeune homme* (1786; *Reflections of a Young Man*) Feucher treated a theme related to Ferlet's, that of the supposed degradation of man in society and the decadence of taste in the arts and sciences. Both authors fault the same culprit: woman. But Feucher's argument suggests that it had become more and more licit to pit women against society, as foreign to it. He arraigns "our cruel institutions" for drawing women out of the dependency and retreat that is "naturally" theirs, only to set them up in the midst of the whirlwinds of society, where virtue flees in the face of pleasure. Women's sexuality is unmanageable to Feucher, who refers to their desires as "vile," their nature as depraved, corrupt. Feucher's solution? It foreshadows the order of the Revolutionary deputy Jean-Baptiste Amar in 1793 removing women from the public streets, back into the sphere of domesticity. We should, says Feucher, do as Lycurgus made the Spartans do: confine our women and separate them as much as possible from men and from public affairs.

Pre-Revolutionary women were not passive in the face of this attack. Marie-Armande Gacon-Dufour responded to Feucher in 1787 with a *Mémoire* supporting her sex. Admitting (far too readily?) women's "natural" weaknesses, their depths of sensuality and sensibility, she yet holds them innocent of Feucher's charges, claiming that for the past forty years men have striven less to please women: man "finds himself such nowadays that he feels horror for himself" and, to justify himself, "has taken to blaming us" even for women's corruption (*Mémoire*, p. 13). Feucher did not let this rest. In 1788 he answered Gacon-Dufour, insisting that the dissolution of mores had to be ascribed to the sex "hungriest for pleasure." But finally, like Laclos before him, he attempts to withdraw from the bitterness of the chastity/corruption axis by a gallant sally: "I hate women? who am always with them, and never feel at ease except by their side?" (*Lettre*, p. 13).

The 18th century's long and mounting preoccupation with chastity and sensuality—with its implications for the lives of women—came to a kind of apogee in Jacques-Henri Bernardin de Saint-Pierre's novel *Paul et Virginie* (1788). Raised by their mothers in a simple matriarchal exotic idyll on the island of Ile de France (Mauritius), neither Paul nor Virginie has any conception of the evils of French society. It is Virginie who is made to feel the first promptings of sexuality: "For some time Virginie had felt herself stirred by an unknown malady. Her beautiful dark eyes darkened and her complexion became sallow; an irresistible languor came over her body. Serenity left her brow, and smiles departed from her lips . . . The unfortunate girl felt troubled by the caresses of her brother" (p. 266). Virginie's sexual awakening, which finds sensual echoes in the lush tropical perfumes and the rushing waters, must, however, be contained and is in the end repressed; she dies in the stormy seas upon her return from a disastrous voyage to France, calculated to delay her union with Paul. Having refused to remove her clothing to plunge into the waters and be saved, she raises her serene eyes on high "like an angel who takes flight heavenward" (p. 345) (fig. 1). The huge popularity of the angelically self-denying Virginie's gesture confirmed that this solution of the corruption/chastity dualism was about to prevail. But its cost to women was a reaffirmation of an ancient vision of them as foreign to men in their spiritual otherness, their naturalness as opposed to their culturedness—this at a moment when their similarity to men, as Merteuil and Valmont demonstrate, had never been closer.

We can now better comprehend the enormity of Condorcet's daring. In his relentlessly antitraditionalist and rationalist way he inserted in the second of his four *Lettres d'un bourgeois de New-Haven* an extended argument for the right of women to full participation—that is, the right to vote—in a republic.

Condorcet knew exactly how bizarre such a suggestion would seem: "Now I have to raise an objection" (p. 280), he says, marking plainly a hiatus in his

1. "Naufrage de Virginie," plate designed by Pierre-Paul Prudhon, engraved by Barthélémy Roger, in Jacques-Henri Bernardin de Saint-Pierre, *Paul et Virginie* (Paris: Didot, 1806). (Courtesy of the New York Public Library, Spencer Collection.)

text, a turn to momentous dissent and affirmation. He argues, in Rousseauistic fashion, that we call rights natural when they seem to arise from the original nature of man, that state that precedes social institutions. Is it not because men are sentient and sense-making beings, capable of reason and of moral judgment, that we accord them rights? Well then, women must have absolutely identical rights; and yet never, in any so-called free constitution, have women exercised the rights of citizens. Although he is prudent, wishing to limit the franchise to propertied widows and unmarried women, arguing that women are better suited to certain governmental functions than to others, and wondering if they possess powers of inventive genius (but deciding that they may), he nevertheless achieves a remarkable leap out of rigid gender dualism and myth. He notes that citizenship presupposes "the acting out of one's will" (p. 282) (a phrase in which a Merteuil might have delighted) and that civil laws seem to deprive women of such a right. The law ought not to exclude women from any role, says Condorcet, and when in the end it no longer does so, mores and women's education will be so altered that objections to their participation now deemed plausible will seem so no longer.

Condorcet's utopia, then, was not that of the Revolution. Neither was it Rousseau's, and Condorcet expresses a rueful consciousness that in demythologizing women, in speaking of their "rights and not their reign," he might only incur their wrath: "Since Rousseau has earned women's approbation by saying they were made only to take care of us and good only to torment us, I have no hope that they will find themselves approving of me" (*Lettres d'un bourgeois,*

564

p. 287). The presumably independent Germaine de Staël, in her 1788 *Lettres sur le caractère et les écrits de Jean-Jacques Rousseau* (*Letters on the Character and Writings of Jean-Jacques Rousseau*), had fallen into this line: "If Rousseau is outraged against [women] when they want to emulate men, how he adores them arrayed in all the charms, weaknesses, virtues, and faults of their sex! Because he believes in Love, we forgive him all. What does it matter to women if his reason disputes their power, since his heart submits to them?" (p. 8). Condorcet persisted, in the face of women's defection to love, affirming, "It's good to tell the truth, even if it should open us up to ridicule" (*Lettres d'un bourgeois,* p. 287).

Not too long afterward, the Ideologue Georges Cabanis, a former protégé of Condorcet, would expressly hold up as absurd the idea that women's "defects" were the product of education rather than of their biological constitution. As Cabanis described them, these physiologically feeble beings totally subject to their bodily functions could certainly not have handled citizenship nor had a will worthy of enactment.

If a tree fall in the forest, who shall know it? Condorcet's statement was echoed by only a minority among the women and men of the Revolution. Not that women did not notice their exclusion from representation: one of them even wrote, "Perhaps one day we shall see our rights returned to us with interest, when the still useless Assembly of the Estates General changes and, instead of being masculine, will become feminine? This is our secret desire" (*Remontrances,* 1 : 13). Nevertheless, sensing how incongruous such claims would appear to the men who felt women to be alien to government, few women beyond Etta Palm d'Aelders, Olympe de Gouges, and Théroigne de Méricourt would call for the franchise as a means of redress for their "wrongs." And spurning Condorcet, Mary Wollstonecraft dedicated her *Vindication of the Rights of Women* (1792), in a largely political gesture, to that grand political opportunist who was fleetingly influential with the dying monarchy, Charles Maurice de Talleyrand. Yet Condorcet's vision and Wollstonecraft's were one, even though her view was more censorious of women than his. "Let woman share the rights and she will emulate the virtues of man; for she must grow more perfect when emancipated, or justify the authority that chains such a weak being to her duty" (*Vindication,* p. 287). The difficulty was that the joint Condorcet-Wollstonecraft discourse, that of reason and personhood, and the pervasive and tradition-consecrated one of chastity and corruption were incommensurable, irreconcilable. After the conflagration of the Revolution and its deceptions the two discourses would reemerge, only more polarized than before.

See also 1654, 1721, 1782 (March).

Bibliography: Keith Michael Baker, *Condorcet: From Natural Philosophy to Social Mathematics* (Chicago: University of Chicago Press, 1975). Jacques-Henri Bernardin de Saint-Pierre, *Paul et Virginie,* ed. J. van den Heuvel (Paris: Le Livre de Poche, 1974). Barbara Brooks, "The Feminism of Condorcet and Sophie de Grouchy," *Studies on Voltaire and the Eighteenth Century,* 181 (1980), 279–361. Georges Cabanis, *Rapports du physique et du moral de l'homme* (Paris: Crapart, Caille et Ravier, 1802). Antoine Caritat, marquis de Condorcet, *Esquisse d'un tableau historique des progrès de l'esprit humain,* ed. O. H. Prior (Paris: Vrin, 1970). Condorcet, *Lettres d'un bourgeois de New-Haven,* in Filippo Mazzei, *Recherches historiques et politiques sur les Etats-Unis de l'Amérique septentrionale, par un citoyen de Virginie* (Paris: Froullé, 1788). Condorcet, *Sur l'admission des femmes au droit de cité,* in *Oeuvres complètes,* ed. Arthur Condorcet O'Connor and M. F. Arago, vol. 10 (Paris: Firmin Didot, 1847). Denis Diderot, review of Abbé Thomas, *Des femmes,* in *Oeuvres complètes,* ed. Herbert Dieckmann et al., vol. 10 (Paris: Hermann, 1975). Louise de la Live d'Epinay, in Abbé Galliani, *Correspondance,* vol. 1 (Paris: C. Lévy, 1881). Canon Edmé Ferlet, *Le bien et le mal que le commerce des femmes a fait à la littérature* (Nancy: [Lescure], 1772). Feucher d'Artaize, *Lettre à Mme. Gacon-Dufour* (Paris: Chez tous les marchands de nouveauté, 1788). Feucher d'Artaize, *Réflexions d'un jeune homme* (Paris: Royez, 1786). Marie-Armande Gacon-Dufour, *Mémoire pour le sexe féminin contre le sexe masculin* (Paris: Royez, 1787). Madelyn Gutwirth, "Laclos and 'Le sexe': The Rack of Ambivalence," *Studies on Voltaire and the Eighteenth Century,* 189 (1980), 247–296. Pierre Choderlos de Laclos, *Les Liaisons Dangereuses,* trans. Richard Aldington (New York: New American Library, 1962). Laclos, *Oeuvres complètes,* ed. Laurent Versini (Paris: Gallimard, 1979). M.L.P.P.D. St. L., *Remontrances, plaintes et doléances des femmes françaises à l'occasion de l'Assemblée des Etats-Généraux,* in *Les femmes dans la révolution française,* vol. 1 (Paris: EDHIS, 1982). Samia I. Spencer, ed., *French Women and the Age of Enlightenment* (Bloomington: Indiana University Press, 1984). Germaine Necker, baronne de Staël, *Lettres sur le caractère et les écrits de Jean-Jacques Rousseau,* in *Oeuvres,* vol. 1 (Paris: Lefèvre, 1838). Mary Wollstonecraft, *A Vindication of the Rights of Women,* ed. Charles W. Hagelman (New York: Norton, 1967).

Madelyn Gutwirth

✑ 1789

5 May: Meeting of the Estates General; 20 June: the Tennis Court Oath; 14 July: Storming of the Bastille

Seventeen Eighty-nine

The widespread convention of dating the onset of the French Revolution to 1789 is testimony to the importance of a remarkable series of events that occurred from May through October of that year. In May, France assembled the raw material of a representative legislative body when Louis XVI convened the Estates General at Versailles and requested that its delegates address the severe budgetary crisis hobbling his government. In June, the legislative raw material converted itself into a legislature by declaring itself France's National Assembly and claiming sole authority to sanction taxes levied on France's citizens. In July, the people of Paris stormed the Bastille in a shattering demonstration that popular sovereignty was a material force as well as a political principle. In August, the feudal system that had prevailed in France for a thousand years was abolished, and a Declaration of the Rights of Man and Citizen announced that feudal principles were henceforth of interest only to antiquarians. In October, a militant throng of women and men trooped from Paris to Versailles and forced the king and his family to make the return trip with them. The irony is exquisite. In May, the French people sent their representatives to Versailles, seat of royal majesty, at the behest of the king. Less than six months later, the king went to Paris, seat of revolutionary turmoil, at the demand of the French people.

From one perspective, the historic upheavals that began in 1789 and continued through Napoleon's fall in 1815 are less important for literary scholars than for social and political historians. The Revolutionary decades produced few works that have entered the canon of masterpieces, and it has long been commonplace to see the French Revolution as proof that great deeds dull the sensibilities needed for great writings. From another perspective, however, the Revolution is integral to all literary developments in modern France. At no time has the power of language been more blazingly apparent, and much of subsequent French literature has sought to work out that power's implications. The great figures of Romanticism and realism were thoroughly imbued with the Revolution's lessons on human meaning and verbal expression. Victor Hugo saw his poetry as dressing the old dictionary in the costume of a Revolutionary militant. Honoré de Balzac took the Revolution as the setting for the first novel he published under his own name, *Les Chouans* (1829). Stendhal's *Le rouge et le noir* (1830; *The Red and the Black*) inaugurated the great tradition of social fiction by scrupulously describing social fear of the Revolution's return. Nineteenth-century European historiography is a sustained dialogue on the Revolution and its message, and Charles Dickens' *A Tale of Two Cities* (1859) is only the best known of the many works in languages other than French that took France's Revolution as their subject. "The thinkers of this age, the poets, the writers, the historians, the orators, the philosophers, all, all, all derive from the French Revolution. They come from it, and from it alone" (Hugo, *William Shakespeare*, pp. 306–307).

In addition to its influence on texts written after it, the Revolution immediately made itself a presence in the texts written before it. So huge was its impact that 18th-century literature suddenly seemed to demand a new reading as imperiously as France's citizens were demanding a new regime. The writings of Voltaire and Rousseau, claimed as a major inspiration by the most radical activists, had to be reread from beginning to end in the light of the events accomplished in their name. Even texts without major political influence, such as the fiction of Pierre Choderlos de Laclos, conveyed disparate messages before and after the end of the world they represented. When a play based on Laclos's *Les liaisons dangereuses* (1782) opened in New York in 1986, reviewers were almost unanimous in asserting the need to see this fictional drama as a commentary on Revolutionary fact. Such a solid spectator response is a striking reminder of what has long been a dominant reader response to the texts of the 18th century.

The Revolution's effects on the writings that preceded it and its presence in the writings that followed it are strong arguments against any effort to draw neat distinctions between literature and history. In the terms the philosopher

J. L. Austin used to define his concept of speech acts, the French Revolution "did things with words" with such consistency that neither the things nor the words can be understood apart from the other. Verbal meanings became the stake of armed struggles that were themselves often motivated by conflict over the forms of speech able to act on the world. The language of the Revolution was constantly at work in the events of the Revolution, a dynamic interaction of speech and acts with profound implications for literary as well as political history.

No event of the Revolution was more compellingly memorialized in language than the Parisian people's storming of the Bastille. The causes of the assault were a complex mixture of factors such as the king's dismissal of the popular minister Jacques Necker and wide resentment against royal reliance on foreign troops. But the message conveyed by the assault's success was thunderously straightforward. When a symbol of military and judicial oppression that towered over one of the poorest sections of Paris disappeared under the onslaught of the section's inhabitants, the impossible seemed to become real. In the *Manifesto of the Communist Party* (1848), Marx used a striking metaphor, "All that is solid melts into air" (p. 83), to describe the sensation produced in those living in feudal society by the abrupt disappearance of feudal institutions. In the case of the Bastille's destruction, this metaphor is straight description: the most solid of prisons proved the most evanescent of illusions. If the people were strong enough to overcome so massive a physical structure, surely no social or political structure could withstand their will for change.

In Thomas Carlyle's words, "The Fall of the Bastille may be said to have shaken all France to the deepest foundations of its existence" (*The French Revolution,* 1:165). It is with full justification that the date of the Bastille's fall, 14 July, stands as the national holiday of the France created on the new foundations that Revolutionary action was to establish. Nevertheless, the issues animating the Revolutionary struggle are perhaps more vivid in an event that preceded the assault on the Bastille by several weeks, the self-transformation of the Third Estate into the National Assembly on 17 June.

Under the ancien régime, everyone in France was defined as belonging to one of three categories called estates: an estate for praying, an estate for fighting, an estate for working. The first two, clergy and aristocracy, comprised approximately 4 percent of the French population in 1789. The Third Estate consisted of the remaining 96 percent of the people, yet each order was in theory of equal importance to the kingdom's well-being. At times of exceptional crisis, the king could call the nation together in the form of the Estates General, a body of representatives from each of the three estates assembled to advise on matters of government. In 1789 the crisis was a severe and growing budgetary deficit, and Louis XVI accordingly convened the Estates General at Versailles. On the theory that the function of each estate was as vital as that of the others, the Estates General had always before consisted of an equal number of representatives from each order. In 1789, however, strong political pressure by an unprecedentedly powerful and wealthy middle class had secured for the Third Estate a number of delegates equal to those of the other two orders combined.

But the meaning of the Third Estate's double representation was still open to debate when the Estates General convened on 5 May, for the principle of the equal importance of all orders remained officially intact. In the reactionary view, therefore, each order should meet and deliberate separately, and the number of people participating in any one order's deliberations was without practical consequence of any kind. Every matter not unanimously accepted would be decided by a two-to-one vote.

Since the Third Estate had compelling reasons to believe that it would be on the losing side in every such two-to-one decision, its delegates argued aggressively that the Estates General must meet as a single body in which each delegate had a single vote and the bourgeoisie's double representation would effectively double its power. For six weeks after the Estates General convened, the Third Estate dutifully assembled in a hall large enough for all delegates from the three orders and vainly requested that the other delegates join them there. The resulting standoff had a paralyzing effect. Bourgeois representatives were claiming the authority to speak for the French people as a whole; but if they exercised this authority while meeting alone, they would be implicitly accepting the principle that they were the voice not of the whole but only of a part. The Third Estate could take action in isolation only at the risk of destroying all chances to make its actions count.

The dilemma was resolved in a daring move that has come to stand as the first authentically revolutionary act of the French Revolution. After a final, minimally successful effort to convince the other delegates to join them, the representatives of the Third Estate approved a motion by Abbé Emmanuel Joseph Sieyès declaring that they were not after all the representatives of the Third Estate. They were rather the National Assembly of France, a body charged with speaking for the nation in its entirety regardless of whether delegates of certain national constituencies chose not to represent their electorates. At a single stroke, the bourgeoisie converted itself from a group that could do nothing at all into a group responsible for doing everything that mattered in France.

The response of Louis XVI was to reassert royal authority to do what mattered. Three days after the National Assembly declared its existence, the king had its meeting hall closed and forced its members to wander through the rain in search of a place to deliberate. The meeting place they found was a building used for tennis (*jeu de paume*), where the delegates officially convened, repeated that they were indeed the National Assembly, and swore an oath not to disband until they had given France a constitution. This meeting in Versailles, enshrined in French history and legend as the occasion of the Tennis Court Oath, was quickly followed by another opportunity for the National Assembly to assert that it was no longer the Third Estate. On 23 June 1789 the king summoned all three orders together, proclaimed that each must henceforth meet separately, announced that there was no such thing as the National Assembly, and concluded his address with an unequivocal royal command: "I order you, gentlemen, to disperse at once." Clergy and nobility obeyed, but the bourgeoisie remained in place to iterate yet again that it was what it declared and that no declarations other than its own could make it something else.

Considered together, the birth of the National Assembly and the death of the Bastille summarize one of the French Revolution's major object lessons for the world: the interdependence of the concrete actions that establish the conditions of human existence and the abstract forms through which humanity represents its existence to itself. The storming of the Bastille was a real event in the most material sense of what constitutes reality. Violent and bloody, it altered history by altering the arena in which history was produced. Yet it immediately acquired an acute symbolic charge, conveyed and intensified through countless plays, festivals, writings, pictures, and orations. No less than the event itself, the multiple representations of the storming of the Bastille were crucial to the momentum of France's Revolution and the self-understanding of France's Revolutionaries.

As the fall of the Bastille is a reality that became a representation, so the National Assembly is a representation that became a reality. The act originating a political power independent of the king was nothing more than a statement that the power had come to be, and yet that statement was a beginning just as incontrovertibly as the disappearance of the Bastille was an end. The combination of the National Assembly's institution of itself through its words and the king's repeatedly demonstrated inability to dissolve it through his words was a striking display of the mutual impact of linguistic value and sociopolitical force. Given the appropriate connection to collective drives, speech that had been meaningless could make and unmake worlds. In the absence of such connections, speech that had been all-powerful could become an empty phonetic exercise: "I order you, gentlemen, to disperse at once."

As if they sensed the importance for human meaning of what they were doing with words, the delegates of the Third Estate spent a week debating what they would be named after they stopped being the delegates of the Third Estate. Jean-Joseph Mounier proposed the title "Legitimate Assembly of the Representatives of the Larger Part of the French Nation, Acting in the Absence of the Smaller Part," a grotesque horror that at least has the merit of highlighting by contrast what the title "National Assembly" achieved. Mounier's suggestion was to use language for the purpose it was conventionally assumed to have, that of naming things that exist before their name is articulated. The delegates of the Third Estate did in fact represent the larger part of the French nation, and they were in fact acting in the absence of those representing the smaller part. In historic contrast, Sieyès' "National Assembly" situated its validity as a name not on what came before its articulation but on what came after. Without ratification by a militant collectivity, the National Assembly would be neither.

The French Revolution therefore began on a sustained argument that the value of linguistic representation is not a given but a creation and that the forces making representation valid or vain are in continuous conflict with one another. A different alternative to "National Assembly," Honoré Gabriel de Mirabeau's "Representatives of the French People," illustrates the resistance to such an argument even by those who would eventually make it their own. Debate on Mirabeau's proposal centered on the ambiguity of the word *peuple*. Did the title refer to the French people as a whole or only to the class contemptuously referred to as "the people"? To resolve the ambiguity, Latin was invoked, and "people" was alternately identified with the lower-class *plebs* and the gloriously comprehensive *populus*. Before acting out the principle that meaning is a living product of dynamic human struggle, the Third Estate situated meaning in a dead language forever insulated from the changes that struggle brings about.

But the very delegates who sought refuge from a volatile present in a dead past were soon to furnish memorable proof that actions transforming the world must also transform the way the world is spoken. Each month in the summer of 1789 produced a new assault on the former organization of France: 17 June, institution of the National Assembly; 14 July, storming of the Bastille; 4 August, abolition of the feudal system by the new political body formed when the clergy and nobility joined the bourgeoisie's constituent deliberations. After the annihilations of 4 August, the Assembly requested one of its members, Guy Jean-Baptiste Target, to compose a message officially informing the king of what had occurred. When Target read his composition to his colleagues, he was shouted down by an uproar so violent that the windows rattled, for he had chosen to state the arrival of the future in the words of the past. "Sire, the National Assembly has the honor," Target began, and a storm of hoots informed him that there were no more honors in a France that had left feudalism behind; "to place at the feet of your Majesty," he continued, and strident screams of "Down with feet!" made it clear that a standard metaphor had become an obscenity (Campe, *Briefe aus Paris,* p. 224). Between Target's arrival in Versailles and his compositional miseries, the relation of a form of expression to the reality of existence had altered beyond recognition.

The overriding significance of forms of expression as France revolutionized forms of life is stark in the last great event of 1789, the march to Versailles by a Parisian throng led by hungry women resolved to bring the king back with them. From the day of the Bastille's fall, the tricolor cockade of red, white, and blue had been the emblem of all progressive factions in France. The goad for the march to Versailles on 5 October was the news that this cockade had been defiled and trampled at court functions on 1 and 3 October. In response, the people of Paris occupied the château at Versailles, killed members of the royal guard, and forcibly installed Louis XVI, Marie-Antoinette, and the rest of the royal family in Paris, the center of popular agitation against royal privilege. Contemplating the abrupt transition from an insulted piece of cloth to the turbulent overthrow of monarchical principles, Jules Michelet asks: "Who could miss here the omnipotence of the sign?" (*Histoire de la Révolution française,* 1:253). By October of 1789, red, white, and blue had become (Michelet again) "the Revolution itself," and the people of Paris took the Revolution to Versailles in order to defend the meaning they had established for their signs. Constantly recurring displays of the omnipotence of the sign created one of the French Revolution's enduring messages for those concerned with signs' organization into literary texts.

See also 1830, 1848, 1871, 1889.

Bibliography: J. L. Austin, *How to Do Things with Words* (Cambridge, Mass.: Harvard University Press, 1962). Joachim Heinrich Campe, *Briefe aus Paris* (Berlin: Rutter und Loening, 1961). Thomas Carlyle, *The French Revolution,* 2 vols. (London: Everyman's Library, 1931). Victor Hugo, *William Shakespeare,* ed. Pierre Albouy, in *Oeuvres complètes,* ed. Jean Massin, vol. 12 (Paris: Club Français du Livre, 1969). Karl Marx and Friedrich Engels, *The Communist Manifesto* (Baltimore: Penguin, 1967). Jules Michelet, *Histoire de la Révolution française,* 2 vols. (Paris: Gallimard, 1952).

Sandy Petrey

✑ *1791, 13 January*
The National Assembly, Abolishing Royal Censorship,
Establishes the Freedom of the Stage

Language under Revolutionary Pressure

The French Revolution gave high priority to the task of regenerating the art and language of France, so that they might represent the reversal of society and reflect the beginning of a new age. Everything—from shows, spectacles, and festivals to pictures, paintings, and spoken French—was expected to bear witness to and ensure the great political transformation. In the effervescence of events, the jostling of ideas, and the haste of decision making, it sometimes adopted contradictory positions on these issues and often imposed censorship soon after proclaiming freedom. Nonetheless, during the Revolutionary period the modes of representing political power were changed with astonishing speed, as were those of the new political discourse that was developing. A few short-lived linguistic innovations were promoted: "Citizen" became the proper form of address; street and place-names were changed, such as the Ile Saint-Louis, which became the Ile de la Fraternité. More important, a whole new political, administrative, and legal vocabulary was created. Efforts were made to adapt the French language to current events, to democratize its forms, and to ensure its use throughout a nation in which numerous other languages still flourished. Political trials were turned into public spectacles; in the press, eloquence became one of the surest instruments of power; abstract ideas (Liberty, Reason, the Supreme Being) were causes of celebration. Certain men (Jean-Paul Marat, Louis-Michel Lepeletier de Saint-Fargeau, Joseph Bara) were raised to mythic stature, and their image was sold to the public as a commodity by means of artful propaganda. The measurement of space was rethought (the decimal metric system was adopted in 1793), as was that of time (Philippe Fabre d'Eglantine created the Revolutionary calendar in the same year, replacing the seven-day week by a decimal ten-day period called a *décade;* it started retrospectively at the autumn equinox of 1792 and would stay in use until 1 January 1806). The nation was given a new banner, the king's color being framed by those of the city of Paris (blue, white, and red), and a new anthem (the "Marseillaise"); the republic got its motto (*Liberté, Egalité, Fraternité*) and its emblem (the neoclassical statue of the Republic). It was the intent of the Revolution that everything should *signify,* celebrate, and convey the new ideology.

Since before the Revolution, the theater had been extremely sensitized to censorship and to the arbitrary nature of royal power. The problem had arisen in the polemics surrounding Pierre Caron de Beaumarchais's *Le mariage de Figaro* (*The Marriage of Figaro*): after two years of political misadventures, the play finally opened in 1784 and was an unprecedented success. The path was cleared. All during the Revolution, the theater would be an especially significant reflection of political tensions, debates, and stakes. "It is especially in the theater that the people's feelings can be swayed," the actor Abraham-Joseph Bénard, known as Fleury, wrote in his memoirs; "In the theater one must master people's emotions. I am convinced that anyone who wants to renew an epoch should first change the spirit of the theater" (*Mémoires,* 4:184). When Marie-Joseph Chénier's *Charles IX, ou l'école des rois* (*Charles IX, or the School for Kings*), after its 1788 interdiction, was performed at the Comédie-Française in November 1789 (fig. 1), the passions of the moment rose to the surface. In this unflinching portrait of religious fanaticism and princely despotism, Chénier depicts a weak

1. Saint-Prix, *comédien ordinaire du roi,* in the role of the Cardinal de Lorraine blessing the St. Bartholomew's Day assassins, in act 4 of Marie-Joseph Chénier's tragedy *Charles IX, ou l'école des rois* (1789). (Courtesy of the Bibliothèque de l'Arsenal, Paris.)

Charles IX who, as a result of palace intrigue, allows the St. Bartholomew's Day Massacre to take place. The subject matter of the play set up an ideological schism that divided the professional actors into two groups, the "red" and the "black." The young Revolutionaries followed the tragedian François Joseph Talma, who left the Comédie-Française for the theater of the rue de Richelieu. The public was divided as well: on the one hand, the royalists demanded the unconditional withdrawal of the play; and, on the other, partisans of the new ideas reacted violently to the decision to close the play down and demanded its unconditional reopening. The subject of the play and its repression galvanized calls for freedom of expression. The author, with the support of the press, used the play as a symbol, invoking recent memories of the Bastille and of the *lettres de cachet* used arbitrarily by the kings for imprisonment and exile. The play was allowed to reopen in November 1789 and was performed hundreds of times. But the controversy lasted for almost a year.

On 13 January 1791, royal censorship was abolished along with the system of *privilèges,* or permits pertaining to the theater, thereby sanctioning a de facto situation. All citizens were henceforth free to open a theater and to put on the plays of their choice—on condition that the municipality be notified. The written consent of living authors was also required. This situation was modified in 1793, in an attempt to make the theater a more explicitly controlled tool of propaganda. Fleury commented, "The exalted patriots had well surmised which of the arts best stirs up [the passions]; previously Voltaire had advanced the cause of philosophy by putting it into the theater; the patriots thought, and correctly so, that their politics would fly high by the same means" (*Mémoires,* pp. 184–185). In August of the same year, the government of the Convention (1792–1795) ordered the performance three times a week of the tragedies of *Brutus, William Tell,* and other plays "relating the glorious happenings of the Revolution and the virtues of the defenders of liberty." The Convention specified that "any theater at which plays are presented tending to lower public spirit and to reawaken the shameful superstition of royalty will be closed, and the directors arrested and punished to the full extent of the law" (quoted in Carlson, *Theater,* p. 165). The right of censorship was given to the municipalities.

In the ten years separating the beginning of the Revolution and the Consulate (1799–1804), there was a complete upheaval in the formal aspects of the theater: for the audience and the actors, for the architect and the decorator, for the writer and the director (who was henceforth fully responsible for his choices), and for the municipal authorities (who at first were given certain powers of decision, then a real power of censorship). The memoirs of contemporary actors bear witness to the lively nature of the theater in this period. A spectator interrupts the show to demand that some other show be put on, to suggest more "politically committed" lines for the actors, or to climb onto the stage to announce some news "of national importance"; or he leaves to denounce the counterrevolutionary nature of what he has heard. Plays were opened and closed at the request of spectators.

In December 1789, actors were promoted to the status of "citizen" and thus released from their position as outcasts (the church had refused them the sacrament of marriage and burial on consecrated ground); along with Jews and Protestants, actors now had the same rights and the same civil and military obligations as other Frenchmen. As many as forty-five new theaters opened. The comic and lyric Théâtre-Français was inaugurated in 1790, the Théâtre National de Molière in 1791. Interior decorations began to be modified in 1793: the fleur-de-lis was replaced by the emblems of the Republic (the sheaf, the Phrygian cap, the three-colored cockade); the alcoves were filled with statues of the heroes of the moment or with allegories of the Republic; the loges were closed. Between 1789 and 1799 more than 1,500 plays were produced. The classical repertoire remained popular, although it was somewhat restricted as of 1793. Some plays were "adapted" to the needs of the moment (this could mean changing anything from one verse to an entire passage, even adding Revolutionary couplets); the actor François-René Molé was asked to do this with *Tartuffe,* Molière's anticlerical comedy. Numerous contemporary plays were concerned with historical themes. The new heroes were Roman citizens or recent martyrs whom the theater and the plastic arts would immortalize.

In 1790 the Catholic church, linked to royal power through the doctrine of the divine right of kings since Louis XIV, was stripped of its political status as the state religion, and priests were obliged to swear allegiance to the new constitution. The mood of anticlericalism guaranteed the success of the theme of convents and their wretched victims, found in Jacques Marie Boutet's (known as Monvel) *Les victimes cloîtrées* (1791; *The Cloistered Victims*), Pierre Laujon's *Le couvent* (1790; *The Convent*), Joseph Fiévée's *Les rigueurs du cloître* (1790; *The Hardships of the Cloister*), and Olympe de Gouges's *Le couvent, ou les voeux forcés* (1792; *The Convent, or the Vows by Force*). A certain number of plays were considered counterrevolutionary, such as Jean-Louis Laya's *L'ami des lois* (*The Friend of the Laws*)—produced at the time of the king's trial in January 1793—which ran for only a few days (the audience could recognize Robespierre in the character of a self-infatuated demagogue named Nomophage). One of the great successes of 1793, perhaps marking the culmination of the republican spirit, was Sylvain Maréchal's *Le jugement dernier des rois* (*The Last Judgment of the Kings*), in which the monarchs of Europe, along with the pope, are exiled on a volcanic island, where an eruption does away with them once and for all. There were also the so-called Thermidor plays, produced after the fall of Robespierre, which denounced the Reign of Terror and the various power struggles; these included Pierre Ducancel's *L'intérieur des comités révolutionnaires* (1795; *Inside the Revolutionary Committees*) and Jean Charlemagne's *Le souper des Jacobins* (1795; *The Jacobins' Supper*).

The theater of the French Revolutionary period should not be mistaken for a revolution in theater itself. The Revolution was concerned mainly with content, and in this it was closer to Denis Diderot's notion of a *pedagogical* theater than to Rousseau's ideas. The theater of the Revolution was intended to be a *representation of ideas* and was expected to provide civic lessons, to put examples of Revolutionary virtues onstage, to give models to the nation, and to "reread" history and the classics in accordance with the new principles that society was developing. The distinction between comedy and tragedy was carried on in theory, but a good number of productions belong more to the *drame bourgeois;* with their increasing use of dramatic surprise, they anticipate 19th-century melodrama and comedy of manners. The classical alexandrine verse continued to rival free verse, but "natural dialogue," advocated by Diderot, was gaining importance. Successful plays were published and sold, sometimes with financial assistance from the Committee of Public Safety. The committee ordered 6,000 copies of *Le jugement dernier des rois* and overrode restrictions on gunpowder to provide for the explosions in the last act.

Along with the theater, the printing houses were of prime importance in the dissemination of ideas. Speeches, reports, and motions before official tribunes were published on a daily basis; there were also thousands of fliers and pamphlets of all sorts published by private citizens; countless "addresses," "calls," "responses," "letters," and "papers," generally signed with a pseudonym. The counterrevolutionaries published theirs in England.

The press also boomed. The Declaration of the Rights of Man, passed on 16 August 1789, specifically stipulated freedom of the press. Article XI states: "Free communication of thought and opinion is one of man's most precious rights. All citizens may therefore speak, write, and publish freely, except that they may be held accountable for abuse of this freedom in cases determined by law." The freedom was almost absolute through August of 1792. Between that date and July 1794, royalist pamphlets were gradually eliminated; under the Terror, the Girondist and Hébertist newspapers followed the same course. From Thermidor Year II (Robespierre's fall in 1794) to Brumaire Year VIII (Bonaparte's seizing power in 1799), liberalism alternated with moments of repression, notably aimed at Jacobin and royalist pamphlets.

Hundreds of periodicals appeared along the full range of the political spectrum; most of them lasted no longer than two or three years. The counterrevolutionary publications, such as *Les actes des apôtres* (*The Acts of the Apostles*) and *L'ami du roi* (*The Friend of the King*), were quickly eliminated. Among the most famous "patriotic" journals were *Les révolutions de Paris,* edited by the centrist Armand Elisée de Loustalot; *L'ami du peuple,* in which Marat unrelentingly bludgeoned "the enemies of the Republic," exercising his belief in a denunciatory press; *Les révolutions de France et de Brabant,* and then *Le vieux cordelier* (*The Old Friar*), edited by Camille Desmoulins, who, unlike Marat, believed in a conciliatory press; and *Le père Duchesne,* one of the most popular papers of the period, edited by Jacques Hébert.

Along with the theater, the press and the public tribunes continued to spread Revolutionary ideas, and each of these media had to confront a central question: that of language itself. In what kind of language should a revolution be made? The crucial problem was not only to control the meanings of words and to forge a new vocabulary to describe new realities, but also to work toward the "democratization" of the French language: efforts were made to institute French as the real means of communication among all Frenchmen, which had hardly been the case previously.

Revolutionaries and counterrevolutionaries bickered constantly over the meaning of words and never tired of accusing each other of semantic perversion. The royalists complained that the language was being "bastardized" and "trifled with," and these "enemies of the Republic" were themselves accused of using a "feudal" and "mendacious" style. On both sides, suspicion reigned. The predicament is illustrated by Jean-François de Laharpe's *Du fanatisme de la langue révolutionnaire* (1797; *On the Fanaticism of Revolutionary Language*). In this denunciation of anticlerical discourse, Laharpe finds himself trapped in the very "inverted language" he denounces (p. 9) and which he cannot avoid using, since it is made of "common words, but with their meaning turned upside down." Speeches made at the official tribunes, as well as commentaries in the Revolutionary press, betrayed a similar anguish. Again and again, Robespierre constructed his arguments on definitions of words: *virtue, nation, dictatorship.* Until his very last discourse, on 8 Thermidor Year II (1794), he kept deploring the necessity of using the same words as his enemies. And, one day later, the day of their fall, Louis de Saint-Just asked: "What language can I use to speak to you? . . . How can one make palpable an ill that is revealed by language and amended by language?" (*Discours,* p. 202).

On one side were those who challenged the systematic use of words such as *philosophy, tolerance, humanity,* and *liberty* by the National Convention, which would soon be attacked as "bloodthirsty." On the other side were those who sought a new language for new ideas, busily disseminated titles and slogans, propagating the Revolution by creating categories, formulas, and oaths by decree. Louis-Sébastien Mercier, a successful playwright, recorded neologisms and changes of meaning and defended the institutionalization of a new lexicon in his *Néologie, ou vocabulaire de mots anciens à renouveler ou pris dans des acceptions nouvelles* (1801; *Neologism, or Vocabulary of Old Words Revived or Given New Meanings*). Reactionaries scoffed at this and in response published satiric dictionaries such as the *Dictionnaire néologique des hommes et des choses, ou notice alphabétique des Hommes de la Révolution* (1801; *Neological Dictionary of Men and Things, or Alphabetical Directory of the Men of the Revolution*) or the *Extrait d'un dictionnaire inutile* (1790; *Excerpt from a Useless Dictionary*). But the problem was not confined to neologisms. Bertrand Barère stated in his 1794 *Rapport du comité de salut public sur les idiomes:* "We must popularize the language, we must destroy this aristocracy of speech, which seems to establish a civilized nation in the midst of a barbaric nation. We have revolutionized the government, the laws, the customs, the habits, the dress, the commerce, and thought itself; let us therefore revolutionize the language, which is the daily instrument of all these things" (p. 295). It was necessary, for example, to simplify the legislative style: in *Le courrier de Provence* (1790; *The Provençal Courier*) Honoré Gabriel de Mirabeau wrote: "It is time to speak French in French laws, and to bury Gothic style under the rubble of feudalism" (quoted in Brunot, *Histoire,* p. 102). The next

577

task, stated by Antoine Caritat de Condorcet in his 1792 report, would be to build a democratic language through an egalitarian, republican, universal system of public education: "If real equality is to be preserved, the language must stop dividing men of the two classes" (quoted in ibid.).

An important obstacle to the Revolution's efforts to propound and apply its decisions throughout France was the existence of dialects, patois, and foreign languages, spoken by more than half of the population: "One can state without exaggeration that at least 6 million Frenchmen, especially in the countryside, do not know the national language, and that an equal number are unable to carry on a conversation; as a result, there are no more than 3 million who speak French, and still fewer write it correctly," observed Henri Grégoire (known as Abbé Grégoire) in his *Rapport sur la nécessité et les moyens d'anéantir les patois et d'universaliser l'usage de la langue française* (1794 [*Report on the Necessity and the Means of Abolishing Provincial Dialects and of Universalizing the Use of French*], p. 302). For a time, it was decided to *translate* the decrees that emanated from Paris (Decree of 14 January 1790). But this recognition of linguistic pluralism did not last long. The ignorance of French and the linguistic fragmentation of the country, which had for centuries supported royal despotism, now played into the hands of the counterrevolutionaries. According to Barère's *Rapport*, "federalism and superstition speak Low Breton; emigration and hatred of the Republic speak German; the counterrevolution speaks Italian, and fanaticism speaks Basque." It was therefore important for the nation to understand that "knowledge and usage of the national language are important to the preservation of liberty" (p. 295). Barère proposed sending teachers into each village in those départements where a "foreign" idiom persisted (the north, the east, Brittany, Corsica, the Maritime Alps, and the Lower Pyrenees). These teachers "will be required to teach the French language and the Declaration of the Rights of Man to all young citizens of both sexes; every tenth day, they will read to the people and translate aloud the laws of the Republic, giving special attention to those concerning agriculture and the rights of citizens" (p. 298). Abbé Grégoire, assisted by the constitutional bishop of Blois and a member of the Convention, had organized a vast survey on dialects, resulting in his own report, in which he suggested that journalists, songwriters, actors, and writers put their patriotism to work by helping to promote a unified language. He proposed that a new dictionary and a new grammar be prepared in order to fight ambiguities and double meanings, to adjust the lexicon to suit new situations, and to reduce as much as possible syntactic anomalies and exceptions of all sorts. Grégoire's was the only proposal that really took the new linguistic needs of the Republic into consideration, but it got no further than an adoption by vote. The "Revolutionary language policy" met with little success in reaching beyond the level of administrative reports and decrees.

In the years following Bonaparte's rise to power, the situation changed: the theater, subjected to strict censorship, attempted no substantive innovations; except for newspapers that openly supported the régime, the press was held under strict control. The "Revolutionary language policy" was completely abandoned. According to tradition, Napoleon said of his Alsatian soldiers: "Let these people keep their Alsatian dialect—they still kill in French."

See also 1808, 1871.

Bibliography: Renée Balibar and Dominique Laporte, *Le français national: Politique et pratiques de la langue nationale sous la Révolution française* (Paris: Hachette, 1974). Bertrand Barère de Vieuzac, *Rapport du comité de salut public sur les idiomes,* in *Une politique de la langue (la Révolution française et les patois: l'enquête de Grégoire),* ed. Michel de Certeau, Dominique Julia, and Jacques Revel (Paris: Gallimard, 1975), pp. 291–299. Ferdinand Brunot, *Histoire de la langue française des origines à 1900,* vol. 9 (2 books) (Paris: Armand Colin, 1927, 1937). Marvin A. Carlson, *The Theater of the French Revolution* (Ithaca: Cornell University Press, 1966). Fleury (Abraham-Joseph Bénard), *Mémoires,* 6 vols. (La Haye: Vervloet, 1837). Henri Grégoire, *Rapport sur la nécessité et les moyens d'anéantir les patois et d'universaliser l'usage de la langue française,* in de Certeau, Julia, and Revel, *Une politique de la langue,* pp. 300–317. Jean-François de Laharpe, *Du fanatisme de la langue révolutionnaire, ou de la persécution suscitée par les barbares du dix-huitième siècle, contre la religion chrétienne et ses ministres* (Paris, 1797). James A. Leith, *The Idea of Art as Propaganda in France (1750–1799)* (Toronto: University of Toronto Press, 1965). Louis Saint-Just, *Discours et rapports,* ed. Albert Soboul (Paris: Editions Sociales, 1977).

Martine Reid

✒ 1791, *Summer*

The Marquis de Sade, Freed from Prison by the Revolution a Year Before, Publishes His Novel *Justine* Anonymously

Pleasure, Perversion, Danger

After having spent most of his adult life in the prisons of Vincennes and the Bastille, Donatien Alphonse François, marquis de Sade (1740–1814), was freed by the Revolution in 1790. The world that awaited him, born symbolically with the taking of the Bastille, saw itself as being founded in equality and liberty among all citizens. Against the immorality, idleness, and extravagance of the court and aristocracy, Revolutionary France defended the moral values of the family and of work, and thus was violently opposed to Sade's entire heritage: his aristocratic birth, his feudal way of life in his château of La Coste in the south of France, his family, and his friends. But in fact Sade had already suffered so much under the ancien régime—especially as a result of the infamous *lettres de cachet*—that he finally chose the side of the Revolution. The radical disruptions and new ideas based in the Enlightenment, with which he had always been familiar, provoked an intense curiosity in him. In an atmosphere already disrupted by the proliferation of newspapers and pamphlets, in 1791 the fifty-one-year-old Sade published *Justine, ou les malheurs de la vertu (Justine, or the Misfortunes of Virtue)* under the newly established freedom of the press. Because its excessive character and descriptive violence seemed to correspond to contemporary realities, the book had an immediate and great success. This correspondence is all the more remarkable, since *Justine* was the product of many years of solitude in prison. This first published work was an expanded version of "Les infortunes de la vertu" (wr. 1787; "The Misfortunes of Virtue") and was in turn further amplified and rendered even more immoral in *La nouvelle Justine* (1797; *The New Justine*), a progressive elaboration exemplary of Sade's obsessional mode of writing, in which repetitions and variations of a given theme allow digressions only to the extent that they relate to the central issue. This theme—both philosophical and literary—is the omnipotence of crime and evil, and the pleasures derived therefrom.

The vision of evil depicted in *Justine* surpasses any real social tableau: it is without cure, and no Revolution can change it. Quite the contrary: as Sade shows in "Français, encore un effort si vous voulez être républicains" ("Yet Another Effort, Frenchmen, If You Want a Republic," the pamphlet included in *La philosophie dans le boudoir*, 1795; *Philosophy in the Bedroom*), the Revolution must take into account and understand the unleashing of the passions, even though they be negative and perverse. This is not to say that Sade's writing presents a metaphysics. Sade adheres to Enlightenment ideology, but, unlike Denis Diderot and Paul Henri Thiry d'Holbach, for whom materialism means the improvement of human nature, Sade's thought results in an absolute conviction in the permanent existence of evil. What makes him unique among 18th-century philosophers is his rejection of any notion of progress.

Justine centers on the adventures of a young woman, orphaned at the age of twelve and deprived of all means, who has only her innocence and beauty to offer the world. In an exactly symmetrical schema, her sister, Juliette, as dark and nefarious as Justine is blond and gentle, travels the world committing crimes and accumulating happiness (in Sade, both libertine and victim can be of either sex). This world, inhabited exclusively by the worst of libertines, never ceases to victimize Justine. She experiences all the "nuances" of misfortune, described in the greatest detail. The narrative is in the first person. Justine, hands tied, is led away by the police like a criminal. They arrive at an inn where two strangers, to pass the time, ask her to recount the story of her life. Thus the tale has the open picaresque structure in which it is always possible to add another episode. Yet each episode is based upon a single model: Justine, filled with goodwill and religious convictions, seeks moral rectitude and humaneness in every person she encounters. Each interlocutor begins in a virtuous manner and offers Justine aid and an honest job. (Hypocrisy is one of the libertine's pleasures.) Justine, always confident, follows her new protector, seeing in him the end of her misfortunes. But he, excited by the young girl's tales, only dreams of new crimes. The libertine guards his mask of virtue only long enough to gain her confidence (which is not difficult, given her Rousseauistic convictions about the universality of moral consciousness) and to lead her to a "safe" place.

Sade's audacity and irony are inseparable from his treatment of language. He writes with constant attention to formal rules (grammar and *politesse*) while speaking the most scandalous truths and describing the most shocking erotic scenes. Justine is first alerted to the dangers that await her by a sudden change of tone and language. She understands, but too late, that the person she took to be honest is in fact a total pervert. For example, in one episode Justine has saved the life of a young nobleman, Saint-Florent. They traverse the forest at dusk. Justine, somewhat worried, asks her guide if they are in fact on the right road. "'We have arrived, whore,' the villain replied, toppling me with a blow of his cane brought down on my head; I fell unconscious" (*Complete Justine*, p. 502). He then rapes her, steals the little money she has (which she had generously offered to him!), and leaves her half-dead at the foot of a tree.

The sudden change of language—often accompanied by an insulting shift from *vous* to *tu*—has the cruelty of the springing of a trap. This change coincides with nightfall and her arrival at a château, which, because of its remoteness, its fortifications, and the depth of its foundations, could be taken for a prison or a tomb. One need only enter this mortuary architecture to feel oneself entirely isolated, indeed effaced, from the rest of the universe. But Justine endures all tortures, and her faith in virtue is, at the least, equal to the torturers' perversity. She remains a fanatic of the good until the very end, a courageous combatant against her adversaries' immorality.

The character Justine, the quantity of her sufferings, and the setting of her adventures are typical of the gothic novel, or *roman noir* (which was extremely popular in France in the 18th century). Justine evokes Voltaire's hero Candide, as well as the pure and persecuted young woman central to the genre. *Justine* is a particularly admirable example of this dynamic of terror, since the novel's action—conceived as a concatenation of crimes—ceaselessly marks the heroine's very body. In 1933 Maurice Heine noted that Sade, on a manuscript page of his tales *Les crimes de l'amour* (1800; *The Crimes of Love*), had written about his own text: "There is no tale or novel in the entire literature of Europe where the genre *sombre* attains a more terrifying and pathetic level" (quoted in *Le marquis*, p. 211). (Sade noted with the code letter *S* his own such productions.) Heine further claimed that Sade undoubtedly read all the English masters who influenced Ann Radcliffe and Matthew Gregory Lewis a generation later. But, although it is certain that Sade, a voracious reader, knew the English gothic tradition, his primary sources of inspiration were the popular tradition's *histoires tragiques*—collections of violent, bloody, true anecdotes—and the horrifying novels of Jean-Pierre Camus, bishop of Belley (1582–1652), written to restore the reader's virtue through the spectacle of vice. Camus's titles are explicit: *Elise, ou l'innocence coupable, événement tragique de notre temps* (1620; *Elise, or Guilty Innocence, a Tragic Event of Our Time*); *Marianne, ou l'innocente victime, événement tragique arrivé à Paris au Faubourg Saint-Germain* (1629; *Marianne, or the Innocent Victim, a Tragic Event Which Occurred in Paris in the Faubourg Saint-Germain*); *Les spectacles d'horreur* (1630; *The Spectacles of Horror*); *L'amphithéâtre sanglant* (1630; *The Bloody Amphitheater*). A work by Sade's contemporary François de Baculard d'Arnaud (1718–1805), the theatrical horror tale *Les amants malheureux, ou le comte de Comminges* (1764; *The Unfortunate Lovers, or the Count of Comminges*), drew on the same tradition. It was a great success.

In his introduction to *Les crimes de l'amour*, "Idée sur les romans" ("Reflections on the Novel"), Sade grants only secondary importance to "these new novels in which sorcery and phantasmagoria constitute practically the entire merit" ("Reflections," p. 108). Sade has no deep affinity with texts dominated by magic, sustained by the supernatural, and permeated by a diffuse terror essentially bound to a certain place and atmosphere. His writing is opposed to the use of this type of fantastic. However extreme the imagination of torture and the sophistication of crime in his own works, he makes no appeal to the supernatural. Passions in Sade, though undoubtedly excessive and systematically transgressive, are never implausible. They are expressed in the clear, demonstrative language of the encyclopedists. Sade's libertines are animated by the will to say everything, and their exploration of pleasure is always explicit. Justine, embarrassed by the indecency of her own stories, suggests to her auditor, M. de Corville, the desirability of suppressing certain details. He is indignant at the idea, desiring such details in the name of a greater knowledge of mankind:

> You may not fully apprehend how these tableaux help toward the development of the human spirit; our backwardness in this branch of learning may very well be due to the stupid restraint of those who venture to write upon such matters. Inhibited by absurd fears, they only discuss the puerilities with which every fool is familiar, and dare not, by addressing themselves boldly to the investigation of the human heart, offer its gigantic idiosyncrasies to our view. (*Complete Justine,* pp. 670–671)

Sade's great literary models are Samuel Richardson, Henry Fielding, and especially Abbé Prévost (above all, he admires *Manon Lescaut*), all of whom are concerned with "the profound study of man's heart—Nature's veritable labyrinth" ("Reflections," p. 106). Sade takes after those analyses that—from Marie-Madeleine de La Fayette in the 17th century to Claudine Guérin de Tencin in the 18th—attempt to explain the mechanisms of pain and cruelty, not in the form of physical torture, but rather in the more subtle and "decent" form of renunciation and refusal. They analyze in a neutral fashion the impossibility of loving, the torture of the body deprived of caresses and vainly trying to express itself through melancholy, long diseases, repeated fainting.

The corridors, labyrinths, and cellars of the castles do not exist to pique the reader's interest or to create suspenseful anguish in the victim, but rather to protect the libertines' tranquillity. They are purely functional. There is no suspense in Sade. He uses neither allusion nor suggestiveness. Immediately upon imprisonment Justine suffers the caprices dictated by the libertine's lust. After his orgasm, he proclaims his philosophical system. His continual alternation of orgy and discourse causes the victim's ceaseless tears. The abundance of tears and blood shed is equaled by the torrents of sperm ejaculated by the libertine. But these tears are in vain because, instead of creating compassion in the villain, they only excite him further. In fact they provoke no emotion at all and do not blur the extraordinary clarity of the Sadian vision. One must know how to see, and how to keep in sight the necessity of going yet further, even if the scene of pleasure borders on horror. Libertinage is a pitiless exploration of the labyrinths of desire. The libertine confronts an ineluctable truth, that of the absolute egoism of pleasure. Sade's libertine is a sovereign individual. His desire does not proceed from diabolical spells. Nor does it depend upon another person, since it ignores all interpersonal psychology. Justine attends the torture of bleeding that M. de Gernande inflicts upon his wife every three days, and tries to soften the victim's fate. M. de Gernande says: "Do not suppose it is vengeance that prompts me to treat her thus, scorn, or any sentiment of hostility or hatred; it is merely a question of passion. Nothing equals the pleasure I experience upon shedding her blood" (*Complete Justine,* pp. 634–635).

Thanks to this indifference, which is precisely what does not exist in what is commonly termed sadism, a principle of detachment, a lightness, underlies Sade's writing. His characters ignore resentment as well as all guilt and mourning. Justine has no bonds with her persecutors other than the outcomes of pure chance. These crimes are doubly gratuitous: first of all, because Justine is simply one victim among many others. As soon as she arrives in a new seraglio, she is immediately told that she can easily be replaced. Hence the importance of numbers, of quantity, in Sade's novels, whereas in the gothic tale the author wishes to entrance the reader with the heroine's singular destiny; the very manner in which she is both loved and persecuted forces us to see her as totally incomparable. Sade's world is icily libertine and permits no romanticism. Second, this gratuity, from the libertine's point of view, has in the final analysis no justification other than a completely matter-of-fact "It pleases me." Everything is founded on the satisfaction of a passion—but also, anything can become a passion. Sade's discursive monomania parallels the irregularity of his imagination, which invents the most baroque predilections in order to derive from them just as many types of passions.

Justine's misfortunes are truly endless. Injustice pursues her even beyond death. The sole progression of the plot consists in Justine's escaping the torments of one libertine only to become the prey of yet another, with even more painful consequences. And finally, in the last chapter—just as she is ready to live happily with Juliette, who has been converted to the good by Justine's example—she is struck dead by lightning, thus suffering even heaven's outrages. "The lightning entered her right breast, found the heart, and after having consumed her chest and face, burst out through her belly. The miserable thing was hideous to look upon" (*Complete Justine,* p. 742).

This ending recalls that of *Les liaisons dangereuses* (1782), with the marked difference that in Pierre Choderlos de Laclos's novel, the illness that strikes the libertine Merteuil and disfigures her forever has a bearing upon her guilt; her face reveals the depths of her soul. Sade, on the other hand, desires no conclusions based on justice. His dénouements are immoral and offer no reassuring paths, and thus are completely consistent with the internal logic of his system—the logic of the worst.

The absence of any happy ending is also, most certainly, analogous to his personal experience: after having been liberated by the Revolution, he was once again imprisoned during the Terror. Saved from the guillotine by error, he was arrested yet again, this time under the Consulate (1801), as the author of *Juliette* (1797) and both versions of *Justine*. He was then incarcerated in the asylum of Charenton until his death in 1814. The course of Justine's life, from one misfortune to another, parallels the tableau of Sade's own life. Contrary to all received opinion, Sade's name should in fact evoke the image of innocence victimized. Is Justine therefore Sade's double? Certainly not, since she is the figure of blindness itself, and of the obstinate refusal of all pleasure. In "Idée sur les romans" Sade writes that the knowledge most needed in the creation of the work of art is that "of the human heart. Now, every man of intelligence will doubtless second us when we assert that this important knowledge can be acquired only through an intimate acquaintance with *misfortune* and through *travel*" ("Reflections," p. 110).

And yet, although Justine benefits to the maximum from these two conditions of creativity, she can hardly be considered an emblematic figure of the writer. Desperately sincere, eternally in tears, she remains the archetypal victim, without any possible ironic reversal or philosophical liberation.

See also 1837, 1931 (March).

Bibliography: Roland Barthes, *Sade, Fourier, Loyola,* trans. Richard Miller (New York: Farrar, Straus and Giroux, 1976). Jean Fabre, "Sade et le roman noir," in *Le marquis de Sade* (Paris: Armand Colin, 1968). Maurice Heine, "Le marquis de Sade et le roman noir" (1933), in Heine, *Le marquis de Sade,* ed. Gilbert Lély (Paris: Gallimard, 1950). Donatien Alphonse François, marquis de Sade, *The Complete Justine, Philosophy in the Bedroom, and Other Writings,* trans. Richard Seaver and Austin Wainhouse (New York: Grove, 1965). Sade, "Reflections on the Novel," in *The 120 Days of Sodom and Other Writings,* trans. Richard Seaver and Austin Wainhouse (New York: Grove, 1966).

Chantal Thomas

✍ 1794, 8 June
In Order to Establish a Revolutionary Religion, Robespierre
Organizes the Festival of the Supreme Being

Twilight of the Gods

Early summer in the Paris of 1794 was marked by two important events: the splendid celebration of the Festival of the Supreme Being, on 20 Prairial Year II (8 June 1794), and the passage of the famous Law of 22 Prairial, which began, within the Reign of Terror, the months of what historians call the Great Terror. This law expedited the judicial process by doing away with preliminary questioning, depriving the accused of right to counsel, and requiring the court to limit its verdicts to acquittal or death. According to the historian Georges Lefebvre, from the enactment of this law to the fall of Revolutionary leader

Maximilien de Robespierre at the end of July 1794, the Great Terror took the lives of 1,376 people in Paris alone.

The Festival of the Supreme Being was the last and most brilliant of the Revolutionary festivals. The circumstances of its celebration and the commentaries it inspired provide precious indications of the politics of spectacle during the Revolution.

After burning colossal effigies of Egoism, Nothingness, and Atheism, Robespierre led an immense cortège from the Tuileries to the Champ de la Réunion (today's Champ de Mars). The ceremony had been carefully planned by the painter Jacques Louis David. Gathered around a symbolic mountain, the people sang a hymn to the Supreme Being, written by the poet and dramatist Marie-Joseph Chénier. The final stanza proclaimed:

> The slave and the tyrant pay no homage to Thee.
> Thy worship is virtue; Thy law equality;
> In the free and good man, Thy work and Thy deed,
> Thou instillest immortality.   (*Oeuvres*, p. 689)

Soon afterward, on 11 Messidor (29 June), the Commission of Public Instruction denied an author permission to stage a play inspired by the Festival of the Supreme Being. Its decision is a definitive statement on the status of spectacle and religion during the darkest days of the Terror:

> What stage, with its cardboard rocks and trees, its sky in rags and tatters, can rival the magnificence of 20 Prairial or erase its images? . . . Only in memory can we bring back those deep feelings that so moved our hearts: to look elsewhere is to diminish them; to put this sublime spectacle onstage is to make a parody of it.
>
> He who first conceived the idea of staging such festivals has degraded their majesty and damaged their effect . . . The writer who, instead of lessons, offers only needless repetitions, and instead of a grand tableau, offers caricatures, such a man is useless to Letters, to morals, to the State, and Plato would have driven him out of his Republic.   (Quoted in Aulard, *Le culte de la raison*, p. 328)

A few days later the Committee of Public Safety approved the decision in these terms:

> In accordance with these reflections, the Commission of Public Instruction, considering that plays devoted to representing the Festival of the Supreme Being, whatever the talent of their authors, present only a limited framework rather than an immense tableau;
>
> That they are beneath nature and truth;
>
> That they tend to spoil the effect and destroy the interest of the national festivals by breaking their unity into artless copies, lifeless images, by substituting groups for the mass of the people, and by insulting its majesty;
>
> That they hinder the progress of art, stifle talent, and corrupt taste without instructing the nation;

Decrees:

That the Festival of the Supreme Being may not be represented on any stage of the Republic. (*Le moniteur*, 15 July 1794)

This unprecedented decision not only consecrated 20 Prairial as a religious festival, in contrast to a profane theatrical performance, but articulated aesthetic assumptions that defined the nature and function of the Revolutionary spectacle.

All historians of Revolutionary festivals, from F. A. Aulard to Mona Ozouf, have stressed that, although the festival is itself a representation or spectacle, it differs from theater in several ways: it takes place in a large esplanade in the open air instead of in an enclosed, restricted space; nature is directly accessible to experience rather than portrayed by "cardboard trees"; all the "people" are assembled, instead of a small number of viewers. The very structure of theatrical space separates the stage from the audience. The festival, on the other hand, allows for no spectators, only participants. All these distinctions were particularly important to Robespierre, an avid reader of Rousseau. In his *Lettre à M. d'Alembert sur les spectacles* (1758; *Letter to M. d'Alembert on the Theater*), Rousseau had strongly condemned the evil effects of the stage: it encouraged artificial representation of the passions and led the audience to depend on an unhealthy vicarious experience. Rousseau proposed replacing the fictional representation of the theater with open-air festivals to which everyone would be invited, in which literally nothing would be staged or shown, so that the invidious distinction between spectators and performers would be abolished. Representation would be replaced by an aesthetics of "transparency" whereby citizens would mingle in mutual celebration of civic virtues.

The Commission of Public Instruction's decision suggests that theater undermines the sacred character of the festival: it parodies a "sublime spectacle"; it is nothing but "needless repetitions" and "pantomime." The festival's essentially dramatic nature would be degraded on a profane stage. The commission's text also throws light on the complex relationship between the sacred and representation. Unlike the festivals before it, the ceremony of 20 Prairial was organized around something that could not be shown. "When it comes to defining the Supreme Being," wrote Claude-François de Payan, a friend of Robespierre, "we shall have an idea of him that is so *sublime* that we shall not degrade him by giving him a face, or a body similar to ours" (quoted in Aulard, *Le culte*, p. 287). In a deliberate attempt to resist the idolatry of images, the National Convention stressed the idea that the sublime is not representable. The Festival of the Supreme Being therefore tended to fulfill two desires: first, as Mona Ozouf puts it, "the dream of that austere transparency of a festival where . . . there would be nothing to see" (*La fête révolutionnaire*, p. 246); and second, the desire for a religion free of all appeals to the senses. The historian Edgar Quinet later wrote that the day after the Festival of the Supreme Being, Revolutionary France would have converted to Protestantism.

Although the festival of 20 Prairial was organized around a subject sublimely beyond representation, it was nonetheless planned and experienced as a theatrical spectacle. In his speech to the Convention of 18 Floréal (7 May), Robespierre had already affirmed that "the most magnificent of all spectacles is that of a great people assembled." And yet because the festival of 20 Prairial was itself a spectacular representation, it also had the power (emphasized by the Commission of Public Instruction, and intrinsic to all spectacles) of "erasing the image" of the scene that inspired it. Much has been said about Revolutionary theater as an instrument of propaganda, but the commission's decision underlines the equally important notion of Revolutionary spectacle as palimpsest and as a political strategy of erasure.

Indeed the Festival of the Supreme Being had a double goal: to found a religion and to erase the Cult of Reason instituted a few months before during the de-Christianization campaign. Festivals and performances followed one another like so many gestures of simultaneous propaganda and erasure. The Festival of Reason, hurriedly celebrated (10 November 1793), took place at Notre-Dame in order better to emphasize its role as a substitute cult. Until 7 November the plan had included a statue representing Liberty; then, in order to avoid any possible confusion with a statue of the Virgin, it was decided to use living representations of Reason, in the form of women chosen for their "respectable beauty" and the "severity" of their morals. A magistrate's wife incarnated Reason at Saint-Sulpice, and an actress at Notre-Dame. The singing of Marie-Joseph Chénier's "Hymne à la liberté" ("Hymn to Liberty") marked the occasion. As a Revolutionary strategy the Cult of Reason does not seem to have been a complete success. Some of the reasons for its partial failure, at least in terms of general opinion, were summarized in a letter by a certain Picard from Limoges: "What shocks the philosopher's senses and imagination is as much the idea of a woman representing Reason, as the woman's youth. In woman, this purest of faculties is identified with weakness, prejudice, and the very attractions of her enchanting sex" (quoted in Aulard, *Le culte,* pp. 88–89). Payan condemned the Cult of Reason both for its atheistic basis and for its representation by women. In his speech to the Convention on 25 Floréal Year II (14 May 1794), which prepared the way for the Cult of the Supreme Being, he exclaimed: "So did the word *reason* in their mouths take on any and all meanings that could serve their interests. Sometimes it was insurrection against liberty, sometimes a conspirator's wife carried in triumph among the people. One day it was an actress, who on the previous day had played the role of Venus or Juno" (quoted in ibid., p. 284).

At the same time the Committee of Public Safety decreed: "On the facade of buildings formerly devoted to worship, in place of the inscription *Temple of Reason,* these words from the first article of the decree of the National Convention of 18 Floréal will be inscribed: 'The French People recognizes the existence of the Supreme Being and the immortality of the soul' " (quoted in Aulard, *Le culte,* p. 280). The Cult of Reason had been too feminine; the Cult of the

Supreme Being would be resolutely virile. By seeking to erase the Cult of Reason, the Cult of the Supreme Being thus attempted to dismiss both the icon and the feminine role in religion.

Twenty Prairial Year II is also the day when the guillotine was moved from the Place de la Révolution (today's Place de la Concorde) to the Faubourg Saint-Antoine, where it would briefly remain before its removal, further still from the center of Paris, to the Barrière du Trône. Far from signifying a decline in the number of executions, this move preceded the onset of the Terror by a few hours. It also disrupted what had become a familiar spectacle for the Revolutionary crowds. Indeed, the poet André Chénier (who, unlike his brother Marie-Joseph, repeatedly attacked the régime and would be executed three days before Robespierre) decried families who spent their days watching the executions: "[The father] comes home from the show. He goes back with his wife and the children who have been good" (quoted in Scarfe, *André Chénier*, p. 309). According to Jules Michelet's *Histoire de la Révolution française* (1847–1853; *History of the French Revolution*), even the prisoners gave performances inspired by the guillotine: "Grave men, serious women abandoned themselves to frenzied displays, to mockeries of death. Their favorite recreation was the preliminary rehearsal of the supreme drama, to try on their last outfit and the graces of the guillotine. These lugubrious parodies included daring exhibitions of beauty" (*Histoire*, 2:843). Indeed, on 24 Ventôse Year II (14 March 1794) Payan had requested that it be made illegal to bring benches for the audience to the executions. Just as the Festival of the Supreme Being experimented with the possibility of a theater whose very subject would remain beyond representation, the Law of 22 Prairial precipitated a series of deaths that were to be moved away from their usual audience: the sublime and the Terror were thus joined in a gesture that removed them from the spectator's gaze. Sacred and dreadful, "the scaffold would no longer be pressed by the crowd," wrote Michelet: "it was the emancipation of the guillotine. She was to take a deep exterminating breath, outside the civilized world, having nothing more to be ashamed of" (ibid., p. 882).

With the fall of Robespierre began what is conventionally referred to as the Thermidorian Reaction, and with the end of the Terror a profusion of new spectacles. Robespierre's death itself was lived like a festive occasion. Actors performed pantomimes on the prisoners' way, and windows were rented at high prices along the tumbril's route. What Michelet described as a "false tragedy around the real one" inaugurated a change of scene. "After 9 Thermidor," wrote the historian Paul Thureau-Dangin, "everything was diminished, events and men . . . The stage was given over to walk-ons, things fell so low that creatures like Tallien and Barras became characters" (*Royalistes et républicains* [1888; *Royalists and Republicans*], p. 1). Mere theater would prevail over the sublime. The end of 1794 would also witness the transfer of Rousseau's remains to the Panthéon, accompanied by a "Hymne à Rousseau" composed by Marie-Joseph Chénier. But the time of Rousseauistic festivals was past. Already other celebrations were taking place, which parodied the symbols of the Terror and the guillotine.

At the Victims' Ball, dancers exchanged greetings with a nod that imitated the jolt of the prisoner's head when it was forced into the guillotine. At Saint-Sulpice there was dancing on the tombstones, whose inscriptions had been erased.

See also 1794 (25 July), 1802, 1905.

Bibliography: F. A. Aulard, *Le culte de la raison et de l'Etre suprême* (Paris: Alcan, 1892). Marie-Joseph de Chénier, *Oeuvres* (Paris: Ledentu, 1839). E. H. Gombrich, "The Dream of Reason: Symbolism of the French Revolution," *British Journal for Eighteenth Century Studies,* 2 (1979), 187–205. Stanley J. Idzerda, "Iconoclasm during the French Revolution," *American Historical Review,* 60 (1954), 13–26. Jules Michelet, *Histoire de la Révolution française,* ed. Gérard Walter, 2 vols. (Paris: Gallimard, 1962). Mona Ozouf, *Festivals and the French Revolution,* trans. Alan Sheridan (Cambridge, Mass.: Harvard University Press, 1988). Francis Scarfe, *André Chénier, His Life and Work, 1762–1794* (Oxford: Clarendon Press, 1965). Jean Starobinski, *The Invention of Liberty: 1700–1789,* trans. Bernard C. Swift (New York: Rizzoli, 1987). Paul Thureau-Dangin, *Royalistes et républicains* (Paris: Plon, 1888).

Marie-Hélène Huet

✐ 1794, 25 July
André Chénier Is Guillotined

Unfinished Work

In 1794 at the age of thirty-two, André Chénier, accused as an "enemy of the people" by the Revolutionary Tribunal, was guillotined. Before his death, he had published nearly thirty articles on politics and only two poems.

In the context in which Chénier was writing, the Tribunal's decision was doubtless inevitable. Despite his declaration that he owed allegiance to no party, his political articles appeared in journals subsidized by a party suspect for its moderation, the Feuillants. Moreover, Chénier had taken unpopular positions in the troubled times before the Terror, turning his eloquence against the Revolutionary ardor of the people and the policies of the dominant Jacobin party on various issues. He had opposed, for example, the death sentence against Louis XVI. The facts that he had served as secretary to the ambassador in London from 1787 to 1790, and that, upon his return to France, he had maintained a correspondence with several members of the émigré community living in England, also told against him. The government, embattled by insurrection within and war without, had reason to be fearful of foreign interference in its affairs, and England, which had been at war with France since 1793 and where many royalists had taken refuge, was the target of particular suspicion.

It was only upon the publication in 1819 of the first volume of Chénier's works that the public was given any idea of the extent of his poetic production. Before that, only a few poems had appeared, notably "La jeune Tarentine" (1798; "The Young Tarentine") and "La jeune captive" (1795; "The Young

Captive Girl"). Chénier had written numerous poems grouped under titles evoking the Greek models that had inspired him: *Bucoliques, Elégies, Epigrammes, Les amours, Epîtres (Epistles), Hymnes, Odes, Iambes (Iambs)*. He had also tried his hand at the epic in *L'Amérique (America)* and *Hermès (Hermes)* and had written several long pieces on the art of poetry that owe much to the 18th-century didactic or philosophical poem, namely, *L'invention (Invention)* and *La république des lettres (The Republic of Letters)*. Most of these poems are unfinished. Most cannot be dated with any certainty. A number of prose fragments on literature, history, and politics also survive, of which the *Essai sur les causes et les effets de la perfection et de la décadence dans les lettres et les arts* (1914; *Essay on the Causes and Effects of Perfection and Decadence in the Letters and the Arts*) is generally thought to be the most important.

As a result of a combination of anecdotal factors and factors having to do with the texts themselves, Chénier's poetic and political works have been edited and interpreted in a polemical atmosphere. Scholars from left, right, and center have argued over the decision of the Revolutionary Tribunal and over the shape that his fragmented and unfinished work ought to take, with poetic as well as political texts figuring as key evidence in the debate. These quarrels over the shape of various poems have been overtly ideological. According to a recent editor, Gérard Walter, Chénier's first editor in 1819, Hyacinthe de Latouche, made decisive corrections in line with conservative Restoration ideology, often "suppressing passages he considered 'subversive' or indecent" (*Oeuvres complètes*, p. xxxv). In turn, Chénier's literary biographer, Francis Scarfe, has attacked Walter's edition for shaping the poet's oeuvre in line with his own Marxist interests.

The issues involved in the areas of politics and literature are, at first glance, very different. This difference shows up most clearly in the assumptions each makes about language. Politicians and political thinkers address their texts to determinate communities of men, in a language considered to be a fairly reliable tool or vehicle for the communication of messages about the world and its social structures. The messages delivered by political texts may be laws for governing action or promises to undertake future action, but in general we assume that political messages have some direct reference to the context from which they spring. Lyric poetry, on the other hand, is addressed to individual readers; it is less interested in delivering messages about the world outside the poem than in structuring its own world. To that end, it exploits form as much as meaning. In interpreting poems we feel justified in taking into account the appearance of the poem on the page or its various sound patterns (rhyme, alliteration and assonance, meter). No one would dream of trying to understand Hobbes's concept of man's life in the state of nature by referring to the prevailing *sh, s,* and *t* sounds in his definition of it as "nasty, brutish, and short." At most one might say Hobbes was a good stylist and wrote a memorable definition. But in a poem, alliteration can become a central part of the message. Poetry substitutes messages about an imaginary world whose only existence is in language, for messages about the world outside the poem. The medium tends to become the message; in more technical terms, poems are self-referential. From the perspective of these differences, judgments on Chénier's political ideas and editorial decisions on how to make unified poems out of the fragments of his work would seem to be parallel but essentially unrelated activities.

However, Chénier himself occasionally considered the apparently separate domains together. In his first published political work, *Avis au peuple français sur ses véritables ennemis* (1790; *Advice to the French People on Its True Enemies*), he states first of all that writing and politics are inextricably linked: "Everything that has been done in this revolution for good or for evil is owed to writing" (*Oeuvres*, p. 206). He justifies his own entry into the political domain on the basis of his specialized understanding of how writing functions. Moreover, he finds that the best political writing of his time bears some of the characteristics of literary language. The most exemplary feature of the French Revolution— "for which one day the human race will vote its thanks to France" (*De la cause des désordres qui troublent la France et arrêtent l'établissement de la liberté* [1792; *On the Cause of the Disorders that Trouble France and Impede the Establishing of Freedom*], ibid., p. 272)—lies in its having combined a wise political message with a quality of writing that stands up to the severest aesthetic tests. The writings of previous revolutions were marked by rhetorical warmth and political shortsightedness: their writers produced "those atrocious but truly eloquent writings that posterity blames, but loves to reread" (*Réflexions sur l'esprit de parti* [1791; *Reflections on Partisan Spirit*], ibid., p. 242). In contrast, "a remarkable thing in this revolution . . . is . . . that the only good works that we see appearing are also the only wise ones . . . that our malcontents . . . have brought to light only cold exaggerations or insipid scoffing" (ibid.).

Chénier tried to think literature and Revolutionary politics together for several reasons. In the first place, concern with good writing accorded with the conception of revolution as dynamic. He advocated the extension, past any determinate context, of "a just and legitimate insurrection [by which a great nation] restores its rights and upsets the order that has been violating all of them" (*Oeuvres*, p. 199). But the energy of any given revolution is finite. It is impossible to eternalize the moment of revolutionary ardor in a determinate context without sapping the foundations of the revolution and chipping away at the very rights that it reestablishes. A people has already finished its revolution once it has instituted a body to legislate in keeping with the rights it perceives to be fundamental. Once the French Revolution had given legislative power to the National Assembly, for example, it was effectively over; to fan its flames within France could only produce anarchy within the state and would make France into a "sinister scarecrow" (p. 215). It would give to the world the frightening spectacle of a Revolution grown oppressive of the very people in whose name it was undertaken. According to Chénier, understanding of this point was crucial, for on it depended the French Revolution's modeling power for other revolutions, its ability to propagate and disseminate freedom throughout Europe and into future generations (pp. 214–215). The pressing problem to be resolved was: given that any determinate revolution is finite and context-bound, how can one extend its spirit past its "death"? At this point, literature steps into the breach, because literary texts, unlike political ones, are not bound to a determinate time and place. Not only can they travel outside the spatial and temporal contexts in which they appear, not only are they largely autonomous with respect to the determinate ideological battles of their time; but also they reflect upon the vehicle, written language, that allows that transgressive travel. Thus lyric poetry became the unlikely place where Chénier meditated on the extension or dissemination of the Revolution past its demise in France.

Many of Chénier's poems, whether written before or after 1789, have a messianic strain showing that he conceived the mission of poetry, and more especially of the unfinished poem, to be to speak to the broadest and most far-flung audience possible. In the "Epître sur ses ouvrages" ("Epistle on His Works"), a poem that some scholars date to 1787, and others to 1791, Chénier evokes the audience to whom his poetry is addressed. The following passage uses a description of his compositional practices, likened to those of a bell-caster, as the point of departure for a reflection on the poem's missions and its audience (*Oeuvres,* pp. 158–159):

> You have seen under the hand of a caster of bells
> Be formed together, diverse in grandeur,
> Thirty bells of bronze, rivals to the thunder?
> He finishes their mold buried underground;
> Then, by a long canal divided into branches,
> Makes flow in the waves of fiery bronze;
> So that at the same moment, bells, little and big,
> Are ready, and each one awaits and demands only
> To ring some death, and, from high atop a tower
> To awake the parish at daybreak.
> I, I am this bell-caster; of my throng of writings
> I have been preparing for a long time both form and mold,
> Then on all at once I let flow in the bronze:
> Nothing is done today, all will be done tomorrow.

Between the two parts of the parallel drawn between the work of the bell-caster and the creative processes of the poet, there is a vivid vignette of the functions of the bells, or poems. In the first place, it is the poem's function to toll the death of the individual, be it the passing of Chénier, long dead by the time we read the poem, or of any other finite individual. As for John Donne, with his adjuration "Never send to know for whom the bell tolls; it tolls for thee" (*Devotions,* 1629), it is clear to Chénier for whom the message is intended: the bell tolled, tolls, will toll for all individuals. In the second place, the bell's mission is to wake a parish; it peals to a collective body inhabiting a social space organized by buildings (a high tower), by religious institutions (the parish), and by the reach of the bell's sound (all those wakened by the bell belong to the parish). Chénier suggests that poems do not just happen within a social space, they help to define it, to awaken a collectivity to consciousness that it is a collectivity.

But poetry has a third mission as well. The future, *tomorrow,* with which the passage ends is broad enough to include the present day. The last line wavers between the (unfulfilled) promise that the poet will finish his poems soon, and a prediction that they will not be finished in the poet's lifetime, but must await future generations to get a final form. Unlike the bronzed bell that rings from a given tower to the parish in reach of its voice, the unfinished poems do not give forth a sound in any already-defined social space. They are a crowd, a "throng of writings," themselves too fragmented to have elected a single spokesperson or to ring from atop a single tower. The appeal of unfinished poems carries further than a sound could do; it can reach a public broad enough to include even 20th-century English-speaking readers, for example. Chénier is meditating on the mission of his poetic fragments to cast their message further than sound can carry, further than the determinate spatiotemporal context in which they appear and which they help form, to speak to an audience as diverse and as scattered as the printed word can reach. In short, the poem transmits the message of its incompletion to a disseminated audience, which is invited to use its freedom to give the poem the determination and final finish that it lacks.

Chénier couples Revolutionary politics and writing for another reason. The activity of making a poem is analogous to the activity of a revolution, for poetry also subverts conventional forms and points out decays or abuses, albeit in the realm of language. The Revolutionary period was characterized by the recognition that political structures are not natural or God-given structures, but are rather contractual or conventional. It actualized the possibility, attendant on that recognition, that present institutions might have lost their value and become repressive with respect to the original model legitimating them. For Chénier, in keeping with many of the thinkers of the Revolution, the legitimating model was found in Rousseau's *Du contrat social* (1762; *On the Social Contract*). According to Rousseau's hypothesis, the social pact is made by a sovereign people that contracts with itself and delegates its power to a government to rule in the interests of all. The Revolution of 1789, according to Chénier, called into question the absolute authority of the monarchy in the name of an originary social pact underlying all instituted law. The original it called upon was admittedly fictional or utopian, and as such never could be realized in positive law.

Similarly, poetry subverts the tacit convention that language operates as an unproblematic vehicle or medium for the exchange of ideas. By the polish it brings to language's surface characteristics, poetry suggests that our ordinary assumption of linguistic colorlessness might be unwarranted. The telescope through which we think we view the world, language, is a system of forms and structures that may distort or otherwise determine the ideas we gain by its means. It is in the interests of a corrupt political system that the people should believe that signs point transparently to meaning. The monarchy, for example, tried to suggest that the king was the earthly representative or sign of God's order. Poetry can be a powerful subversive weapon because it puts into question the claim that signs express meaning immediately.

The poetic imagination is at work as just such a subversive force in the name of freedom in "La jeune captive," the celebrated ode that Chénier wrote during the four months he waited in the Saint-Lazare prison for a summary trial of almost certain outcome. Throughout much of the ode, a captive girl pleads passionately with absent judges to be allowed to live out her life. In the third stanza, where the girl identifies herself with the emblem of poetic song, the nightingale Philomela, she does not simply ask for freedom, however; she reclaims it as a natural right, her first and most elementary possession by right of her hope, her ability to transcend her current limitations:

> The fecund illusion inhabits my breast.
> Of a prison on me the walls weigh in vain,
>   I have the wings of hope.
> Escaped from the nets of the cruel bird-catcher,
> More lively, more happy, toward the countryside of the sky
>   Philomela sings and soars up.

This stanza states the impotence of outside formal constraints, the prison, to hold the girl. Her freedom depends on her mind, not on the physical walls surrounding her. No institutional walls—be they the walls of Saint-Lazare or of the Conciergerie, where Chénier was incarcerated, or the walls of the Bastille, the prison that symbolized the tyranny of the ancien régime and whose toppling ushered in the Revolution—can stand against her hopeful imagination. But the stanza does not just assert that thought is free. Its language also provides a concrete example of the activity of escaping from a worn-out ideology. The girl takes a tired cliché, the "wings of hope," whose force as metaphor has been all but forgotten and whose terms through long habit have come to mean that hope arises and spreads rapidly. Clichés of this sort do not express an individual's thought about the world, or his desire with respect to it. Rather, they force thought or desire into predetermined patterns. A trite phrase is a language that indeed resembles a prison; instead of expressing a thought, the cliché determines what thoughts are normal in the speakers of the language. In the cliché, thought has all the rigidity and the common currency of an ideology. Chénier takes this cliché and reinvents it in the quoted stanza. He liberates "wings of hope" from their trite meaning by making an extended comparison between the birds' wings, which allow them to escape the snares of bird-catchers, and hope, the "fecund illusion," which lives in the girl's breast and liberates her from her fetters. The parallel between her inner world and the invisible world of nature permits an exchange of properties in a metaphor: hope gets wings that take the girl out of her prison; the birds, in flying upward "toward the countryside of the sky," acquire transcendence. In this reinvented metaphor, wings do not denote speed, but are rather the means for reclaiming the transcendence and autonomy of thought. The stanza persuades us that the girl's mind is as free as she asserts because it contains an example of her having freed the terms of the cliché to express a new idea.

Yet we must be somewhat suspicious about the ability of poetry to persuade us of its truthfulness. Chénier was keenly aware of a potential for reversal that could put the gesture of demystification at the service of new, repressive ideologies. Nothing seems to prohibit, for example, the quotation of the stanza above to justify the reactionary or apolitical view that there is no need to restrict the activity of cruel tyrants, since thought is always free, and indeed seems to demonstrate its freedom best where it is constrained. Conversely, the stanza could be read as advocating a kind of anarchic freedom: all prisons, all restrictions or regulations, all social conventions should be toppled, for all walls are oppressive to the nightingale, and all bird-catchers are cruel. Literature, whose independence from context allows it to call ideologies into question, by virtue of that same independence, can readily be made a tool of any ideology that comes along. For this reason Chénier's poem turns against literature: it is a fiction that denounces the seductions of fiction. The epithet by which the girl's hopeful imagination is characterized—"fecund in illusion"—is the sign given here that Chénier is warning us that the victory celebrated is purely imaginary: the truth is that the girl is a captive languishing in prison, however persuasively she may evoke for us a free Philomela singing and soaring.

A similar concern underlies Chénier's denunciation of the turn the Revolution took during the Terror, when subversive fictions like that of the social contract were transformed into repressive fictions legitimating, for instance, the anarchic power struggle between factions as a struggle over who best represented the people's will. Similarly, the rallying cry of the Revolution—"Liberty, Equality, Fraternity"—degenerated during the Terror into a slogan to be quoted whenever a particularly repressive measure was to be enacted. It even became the site of a pitched battle between various parties, each of which tried to claim that it alone knew how to interpret the slogan. France, Chénier explained in *De la cause des désordres,* is a place where fraternity has become a title limited to members of one's party, "where one oppresses in the name of equality, and where the effigy of Liberty is only a stamp used to seal the wishes of several tyrants" (*Oeuvres,* p. 277). Chénier wrote against a revolution in the Revolution that made it as oppressive as the régime it overthrew.

Chénier's most compelling reason for coupling literature and Revolutionary politics was thus not the celebration of its ability to ring to the ends of the earth any given message of freedom, nor yet its subversive ability to awake a given parish to a consciousness of its oppression. The most profoundly political literature is not enthusiastic about the seductions it produces. Rather, it denounces, in the cold mode of reason, the mystifications it perpetrates. Such a literature must remain as unfinished as the revolution of which Chénier dreams: the revolution will never be over until it has subverted successfully all the ideologies of revolution that it has propagated. Neither will a poem be finished until it has demystified all the illusions its gesture of demystification produces.

See also 1791 (13 January), 1889, 1945 (6 February).

Bibliography: André Chénier, *Oeuvres complètes,* ed. Gérard Walter (Paris: Gallimard, 1958). Paul de Man, "Roland Barthes and the Limits of Structuralism," *Yale French*

Studies 77 (Fall 1989), in press. François Furet, *Interpreting the French Revolution*, trans. Elborg Forster (Cambridge: Cambridge University Press, 1981). Jean-Jacques Rousseau, *The Social Contract*, ed. Charles Sherover (New York: New American Library, 1974). Francis Scarfe, *André Chénier: His Life and Work, 1762–1794* (Oxford: Clarendon Press, 1965). Jean Starobinski, "André Chénier and the Allegory of Poetry," in *Images of Romanticism: Verbal and Visual Affinities*, ed. K. Kroeber and W. Walling (New Haven: Yale University Press, 1978).

E. S. Burt

◈ *1799, 10 October*
On 18 Brumaire, Bonaparte Seizes Power

The Ideologists

Eighteen hundred was not officially the beginning of a new century for the French, who were still under the Revolutionary calendar, in the year VIII or IX; nor was 18 Brumaire (10 October 1799), when young Bonaparte seized power, seen by many at the time as a new beginning; rather, it was just one more of those coups d'état whereby since 9 Thermidor Year II (17 July 1794) the middle-of-the-roaders, the advocates of a bourgeois revolution and an oligarchic government, had managed to crush the royalist right or the Jacobin left. Bonaparte did offer promises of increased stability and efficiency, and both were badly needed, for the Directory, which had governed France from 1795 to 1799, had been beset with problems, and intellectuals such as Pierre Simon Ballanche and Germaine de Staël, who were later to be his bitter enemies, reacted with enthusiasm to his coming to power.

The Directory's problems stemmed basically from a lack of consensus about the Revolution and the appropriate political path for France, and operatively from the fact that the political mechanism offered no way—except by coups d'état—to resolve conflicts between the legislative and the executive. The country was also plagued by inflation, an inadequate system of taxation, and rampant poverty—25 percent of the population was at times on poor relief—while other Balzacian-type sharpers were making—or losing—fortunes. The religious question remained unsolved. The constitutional church was dying a slow death; the government somewhat favored the theophilanthropists, an organization of rational, liberal theists; the Catholics who had remained faithful to the pope were divided between those willing to compromise with the régime and those adamantly opposed, and although their worship was tolerated, there were still no Sundays. And France was a country constantly at war—in Italy and Switzerland against Austria and Russia (with heavy defeats in 1799), in Egypt against England, at home against the royalists (5 August 1799, an insurrection in the southwest). Where there was not division, there was growing political apathy; getting rich and enjoying life became the dominant goals of many.

The Directory should not be judged too harshly, however. In many ways it did a good job in a bad situation, helped stabilize finances, steered a middle path between revolution and reaction. It introduced the metric system and reformed the moribund academies into the intellectually active Institut de France; scholars accompanied Bonaparte to Egypt and founded Egyptology. Indeed, the Directory, especially at the very end of the century, knew great intellectual and creative ferment. The foundations of life may have been shaken, but for some this led not to despair but to a radical revaluation of theories about philosophy, psychology, and aesthetics, including literary form.

Although Germaine de Staël had published before, her career really began with *De la littérature considérée dans ses rapports avec les institutions sociales* (1800; *The Influence of Literature upon Society*), and that career was a novelty. There had been female novelists or poets, women active in politics, women who presided over intellectual salons; Staël was the first woman *mandarin*, a full-fledged intellectual famous as a novelist, as an essayist, and as a political figure. *De la littérature* is primarily a study in literary history and comparative literature, and an archetype in both genres; but it is also about philosophy and quite overtly about politics—fulfilling Baudelaire's later demand that good criticism be "passionate, prejudiced, political." As comparative literary history, it breaks with the Jean-François Marmontel–Jean-François de Laharpe appreciation of works in terms of how well they meet the criteria of classical models. Staël turned rather for inspiration to Montesquieu, suggesting that each culture, each period, produces a certain kind of literature, although she paid less attention to questions of race, of climate. Rather, literature reflects (and influences) the political, social, and religious institutions of a culture as well as its traditions.

The first, revolutionary result of this approach is the elimination of the criteria of absolute beauty; an aesthetic relativism takes their place, and value judgments—she makes them unhesitantly—are based on how sincerely, successfully, even critically the work manifests its culture, and on how that culture should be evaluated; she is closer to Marxist criticism than to Nicolas Boileau. Staël proposed several distinctions that were to be of lasting importance—between the literature of the north and that of the south, for example—and the notion that there are periods of cultural gestation, then of flowering. In the quarrel over taste versus genius, she favored—with measure—genius, praised Shakespeare but with reservations. She was less original in asserting that sentiment, and not just reason, was essential for successful literary creation. Along with Ballanche, and before François-René de Chateaubriand, she acknowledged the considerable contribution of Christianity to culture; in this she aroused much criticism both from those who found her too favorable to Christianity and from those who found her not favorable enough. All these theses are documented with extensive reference to literary works. There, her knowledge is lacunary; she knew the Greeks and Romans fairly well (and generally preferred the latter, strange to us but not uncommon at the time); French literature, as for many of her contemporaries, began with *le grand siècle* plus Montaigne; medieval literature and Renaissance poetry were yet to be discovered. English she could read, and she knew English literature well. She greatly admired their novels; what French fiction was good—except for Rousseau's *Julie, ou la nouvelle*

Héloïse (1761; *Julie, or the New Héloïse*)—was an imitation of Samuel Richardson, Laurence Sterne, Henry Fielding. She could not yet read Italian, and her knowledge of Dante was secondhand; Spanish literature was terra incognita. Nor could she yet read German, but she was familiar with Goethe and Friedrich Klopstock. During the ten years of exile Napoleon imposed on her, she was to become much more versed in foreign literatures and languages, and probably regretted some of the judgments of *De la littérature.*

The book also represents a collaborative endeavor. The picture of Staël saying to the assembled luminaries at her château at Coppet, on the lakeshore near Geneva, "Today we will talk about X," and afterward going to her study to write that chapter, is a picturesque simplification; but she did count among her entourage some noted minds—Benjamin Constant, August Wilhelm von Schlegel, Charles-Victor de Bonstetten, Simonde de Sismondi, and her father, Jacques Necker—and profited from them; she practiced the community of scholarship, and her writing, here as elsewhere, reflects the thought of a group.

That Coppet group steered a middle, liberal path. Faithful in many ways to the Enlightenment, enthusiastic about the bourgeois Revolution of 1789 and horrified by the Terror of 1793, concerned with politics, economics, and history, they hoped for an enlightened oligarchy that would build on the good of the Revolution while eradicating its bad. Today's reader of *De la littérature* is surprised by the importance Staël attaches to eloquence, by her assertion of the perfectibility of literature, and by her concern with literature's moral content; but all three are justified by the political context in which she wrote. In her discussion of eloquence, she is concerned with the political uses and abuses of language and clearly has Revolutionary oratory in mind. She objects to eloquence that is too abstract, devoid of sentiment; words that do not reflect thought; political discourse that is pure propaganda. Eloquence can and should be a major weapon against despotism. When she discusses the moral qualities of literature, the same concern for responsible political freedom is present; words should be used to contribute to improving man and society. Although she was impatient with licentious literature, Staël was no prude; and "morals" (*moeurs, morale*) had a broad sense for her, as it still does in French; she was concerned with the betterment of humankind. That such perfectibility was possible, in literature and society, she was convinced. She was not sure whether the Revolution heralded a new era or had been a terrible interlude; but history for her was the history of progress. The Middle Ages were not a retrogressive moment, but one of intellectual development; even wars often led to scientific discoveries and the spread of civilization. Literature, too, could and must progress; one might admire and appreciate the ancients, but not imitate them; instead, one should forge ahead to create a literature meaningful and valuable for the new age.

De la littérature can be read as the last blast in the Quarrel of the Ancients and the Moderns, a definite valuing of diversity and modernity as opposed to the imitation of old models and uniform standards of excellence, a call for a literature that would be pertinent and hence free in its choice of style and form.

Much caricatured, in part because of her tumultuous private life, in part because she was a pioneering feminist, in part because of her later stalwart opposition to Napoleon, Staël was much admired by the utopian socialist thinker Claude-Henri de Saint-Simon, who appreciated her idea of progress; her sense of the interplay among institutions, customs, traditions; and her conviction of the essential role of the artist in society.

In the same year IX, Ballanche wrote his first book, *Du sentiment considéré dans ses rapports avec la littérature et les arts* (*On Sentiment, Considered in Its Relations with Literature and the Arts*). Its theses are similar to those of Staël, though more extreme, pro-Catholic, and Romantic. My book is organized like an English garden, he proudly proclaims; and he does rather ramble, rejecting the geometric clarity of classicism. Sentiment he defines as a moral power that judges instinctively, without deliberation, lets us know our true being and that of the universe, including the existence of God and of the immortal soul. Sentiment is essential to any appreciation of the arts as well as to the rest of life. (The literature he admires announces the Romantic canon: Shakespeare, Richardson; but he still prefers Racine over Corneille.) Reason without sentiment can produce only vain philosophy, overturn altars and thrones. Ballanche, who was later to accept the Revolution as a meaningful part of history, here terms it the most dreadful political phenomenon in the annals of humanity. But his text offers other germinal ideas. Through sentiment we can perceive that all is harmony in nature, and that "tout est sensible" (the whole chain of being is sentient)—two notions at the core of the poetic creations of Alphonse de Lamartine and Gérard de Nerval. He revivifies the Neoplatonic tradition in French letters. He also justifies the presence of melancholy, sorrow, even ugliness, in life and literature. Unhappiness is necessary for man, tempers his soul, increases his sensitivity—provided it is integrated into the Christian system of sacrifice and expiation. Later he would develop this conviction in conjunction with his progressive theory of history, in which he justified the Revolution—out of evil, good will come—and which was to influence strongly thinkers such as Joseph de Maistre, Félicité de Lamennais, and certain socialists. Ballanche combines a sense of the essentially tragic nature of life with a belief in the harmony and meaning of creation and history, prefiguring the way in which the richest of French Romantic thinkers would manage to entertain both pessimism and optimism with full awareness.

The main intellectual group of the period was the Ideologues, those who continued in the tradition of the encyclopedists, Etienne de Condillac, and the marquis de Condorcet but were also revising that tradition, moving toward a more complex and organic conception of nature, humankind, and society. Among the more famous and exemplary was Philippe Pinel. The tale of Pinel's striking the chains off the mad and that of his facing down the Terrorist Georges Couthon and refusing to let the "royalist" insane in his care be guillotined are probably apocryphal. Pinel was not that kind of dramatic character, and to contrast his "good liberty" with Couthon's "bad liberty" is to oversimplify. But it is also false to suggest, as Michel Foucault does, that Pinel introduced into the world of the insane not science, but simply a new personage, the medical doctor who becomes the father-judge. He also threw out a good deal of the "old" science for treating the insane, including chaining them up and showing them off like monkeys for the amusement of the mob; and he proposed the bases for a new science in his *Traité médico-physique sur l'aliénation mentale* (year IX; *A Treatise on Insanity*). Most of what he suggests seems simply good common sense: decent food (with tales about how hard it was to provide during the difficult winters of the Revolution), cleanliness, manual labor—especially gardening—separating the various kinds of insane, distinguishing them from the epileptics. He rejects not only chains but also indiscriminate bleedings, emetics, or hellebore. Other proposals are more typical of the Ideologues. Records and statistics must be kept, observations made about the efficacy of various treatments, about which kinds of insanity can be cured, which cannot, about the relations between physiology and mental disease. Pinel holds that the prime need is to establish an effective typology of insanity, and he complains about the inadequacy of both Greek and French labels; nosology requires neologisms. His categories (melancholy, mania with or without delirium, dementia, idiocy, and so on) may not be ours but were based on observation and aimed at serving a therapeutic end, and he did demonstrate that cranial deformation and the like had little to do with madness.

L'aliénation mentale is a very readable book, which in its organization is similar to that of a later work inspired by the Ideologues, Stendhal's *De l'amour* (1822; *On Love*). Pinel starts with logical categories but constantly strays off into anecdotes and case histories, some quite developed, suggesting a character or plot for Balzac or Maupassant. Pinel believes that traumatic experiences, in love, in fortune, often trigger attacks of insanity; and the book is rich in descriptions of how the turmoil of the Revolution unbalanced many, providing a sad portrait of its effects on the lives of ordinary citizens. *L'aliénation mentale* combines the logic and mathematical bent of the Ideologues with Romantic sensitivity for the individual and the particular.

Joseph Marie de Gérando was a friend of Germaine de Staël; she read the manuscript of his four-volume *Des signes et de l'art de penser considérés dans leurs rapports mutuels* (year VIII; *On the Mutual Relations between Signs and the Art of Thinking*), which represents a shift from the sensualist Ideologue approach toward a more spiritual conception of humanity. Gérando presented an independent, interior soul as a means of knowing, in addition to the perception of sense data. He thus prepared the way for Maine de Biran and the whole Romantic, spiritualist school of philosophy. Gérando later became a comparative historian of philosophy, just as Staël launched in France the comparative history of literature. His broader conception of the mind led to a renewed interest in Platonism and in German idealism, and he was the father, intellectually, of Victor Cousin and his eclectic school. Another aspect of *Des signes et de l'art de penser* is surprisingly modern: Gérando also maintained that thought can be communicated and known only through signs—not just language, but all signs—which makes him an ancestor of semiotics. Among signs he includes cooking customs, dances, and primitive rituals, to be classed and interpreted as much as words. This anthropological focus also dominated his *Considérations sur les diverses méthodes à suivre dans l'observation des peuples sauvages* (year IX; *Considerations on the Methodology to Employ in Observing Primitive Peoples*). His theory that language originated in onomatopoeia and then evolved through metaphor toward a gradual development of abstraction was commonplace in the period; but he was impatient with various Enlightenment proposals to create an ideal, universal language, completely logical, all denotation and no connotation; one might invent such a language for international travelers or scholars, but it would never replace the organic language systems, and any traveler really interested in a foreign culture would want to learn its language. The study of signs, and hence of language, is the only means of understanding other cultures, ages, people. Gérando was no irrationalist; he greatly admired Locke and Condillac and shared Pinel's notion that new scientific observations should and would continually produce a new, more adequate language. But he was convinced that a purely mathematical analysis of empirical reality was necessarily incomplete; man and reality were more complex than that.

Among the many works of other Ideologues at the turn of the century, Xavier Bichat's *Recherches physiologiques sur la vie et sur la mort* (1800; *Physiological Researches on Life and Death*) merits particular attention. Read with admiration by Maine de Biran and also Schopenhauer, *Recherches* attributes great importance to the notion of force as an interior resistance in each organism that struggles against exterior pressures and constitutes the essential characteristic of organic life. It also distinguishes between organic and animate functions, the brain being the center of the animate function. Thus Bichat introduced the idea of a vital force, which was to be so important for the Romantics, and also developed a relativist conception of personality: the view of a beautiful countryside may produce pleasure for the city dweller, but not for the peasant who tills the fields. Finally, Bichat discussed how social environment and education affect various personality types, and distinguished three basic sorts: those concerned with the satisfaction of the senses, those whose occupations are essentially cerebral, and those who utilize the locomotive muscles. Considerably revised, this triple distinction was to form the basis of Saint-Simon's proposed reconstruction of society. All too often Romantic thought has been read as a break with or reaction against the Enlightenment; in a great many ways, it is rather a revision and complicating, a nuancing, of the Enlightenment heritage, and much of that revision was done by the Ideologues and the Coppet group during the Directory.

In 1799 Sophie Cottin published *Claire d'Albe*, a short, very readable novel that is a precursor of Staël's *Delphine* (1802) and *Corinne* (1807), Juliane von Krüdener's *Valérie* (1803), and her own less successful *Malvina* (1801). The heroine is always beautiful, intelligent, sensitive, most virtuous, and yet deeply involved in a passion to which society seems to oppose insuperable obstacles. Claire is married to an older man, a good, kindhearted father figure, but falls deeply in love with young Frédéric, her husband's protégé. It all ends badly:

they are separated; she is told Frédéric has grown indifferent, he the same about her; the misunderstanding is ultimately resolved, but too late; he rejoins her at her father's tomb, they make love once more, and she then dies of remorse and of her impossible love. The novel provides what is perhaps the first description by a woman novelist of a female orgasm: "that lightning flash of delight, delicious and unique joy; her soul floats in a torrent of voluptuousness" (p. 267). *Malvina* is much longer, more complex, with a cast of character types who foreshadow Jane Austen; but tears, fainting spells, fires, mortal fevers make it very characteristic of the excesses of pre-Romantic sensibility. Yet Sophie Cottin reformulated the function of the woman novelist as portrayer of the plight of women; she moved Marie-Madeleine de La Fayette's heroines into a new psychological and social context, which Staël and George Sand would delineate with increasing feminist fervor and a growing awareness of the social obstacles facing and repressing women.

Thus this turn of the century—which was and was not one—rejected or revised previous categories of thought, and some previous convictions, as oversimplistic. The *homme machine* and simple linear progress were no longer intellectually acceptable; writers moved from a mechanistic, absolutist, and mathematical conception of man, history, literature, life, philosophy, and science to an organic, dynamic, relativist, and empirical one—the difference (as A. J. Lovejoy described it) between classicism and Romanticism. The Napoleonic era, with its censorship, its wars, its cult of national glory, dampened this enrichment of thought begun under the Directory, but the ideas—and some of the actors, especially Staël—would carry the torch until the Restoration (1814–1830), when an even worse political regime would produce an even richer intellectual ferment.

Bibliography: Annie Becq, *Genèse de l'esthétique française moderne, 1680–1814* (Pisa: Pacini, 1984). George Boas, *French Philosophers of the Romantic Period* (1925; reprint, Baltimore: Johns Hopkins Press, 1964). Sophie Cottin, *Claire d'Albe* (Paris: Maradan, 1799). J. Christopher Herold, *Mistress to an Age: A Life of Mme. de Staël* (New York: Bobbs-Merrill, 1958). Martin Lyons, *France under the Directory* (Cambridge: Cambridge University Press, 1975).

Frank Paul Bowman

✑ 1800

Guilbert de Pixerécourt Produces *Coelina, ou l'enfant du mystère*

The Melodramatic Imagination

On the evening of 2 September 1800 the usual queue, composed of petits bourgeois, artisans, and some day laborers, intermingled with a number of more elegantly turned-out members of the upper bourgeoisie, formed before the entrance of the Théâtre de l'Ambigu-Comique for the première of a new play, *Coelina, ou l'enfant du mystère* (*Coelina, or the Child of the Mystery*), by René

Charles Guilbert de Pixerécourt. The play was an immediate hit; it would run for 387 nights in Paris and for 1,089 nights throughout the rest of France, reappearing in revivals over the next thirty years. It came to be considered the first full-fledged representative of a new genre, the *mélodrame,* that was the most successful and perhaps also the most significant new development in French literature between the period of the Revolution and the advent of Romantic poetry and drama in the 1820s.

Traditional histories of French literature present this period as something of a wasteland, redeemed only by a few isolated figures such as François-René de Chateaubriand, Germaine de Staël, and Etienne de Senancour. During the Revolutionary period (1789–1799), much of the cultivated elite of France had left the country, seeking political asylum in Germany or England (or, like Chateaubriand, undertaking exotic voyages, to America or elsewhere). Those who in the ancien régime had set the standards of literary taste were no longer in power. And in any event, the upheavals of the Revolution seemed to require a literature for those without traditional literary culture, something simple, direct, arousing, appealing. Melodrama came to be the most popular and durable embodiment of this new aesthetics. Born during the Revolution, the genre incarnated—in the words of Charles Nodier, an important figure in the early formation of Romantic doctrine—"the morality of the Revolution" (introduction to Pixerécourt, *Théâtre choisi*). What Nodier had in mind was no doubt the democratic character of melodrama. The genre is democratic in at least three senses. First, it is written for a popular audience ("I write for those who don't know how to read," Pixerécourt is reported to have said). Second, its message is essentially democratic, since it regularly shows the humble of the earth standing up to wicked tyrants and voicing their rights to respect and happiness. Third, the presentation of the message comes in a democratic form through signs—verbal, visual, musical—that aim to make unambiguously clear the moral stakes of the drama. These elements did not, however, make the genre subversive of the established order. Although melodrama was later used to urge various social positions—including explicitly socialist doctrines—early in the century its social and ethical content tended to be somewhat conservative, an affirmation of enduring moral verities. As Nodier also said of Pixerécourt's plays, "I have seen them, in the absence of religious worship, take the place of the silent pulpit" (ibid.). At a time when the traditional church, battered by the Revolution, had lost much of its hold on the urban masses, melodrama preached a secular message of virtue.

Melodrama indeed is centrally about virtue: about virtue as innocence that will undergo false accusations of crime and a period of persecution at the hands of the villain (traditionally known in French as *le traître,* but also, significantly, as *le tyran*) during which it wanders in exile from its home, unable to make good its claims to respect, until, finally, the dénouement brings the exposure of the villain and the rehabilitation of persecuted virtue. *Coelina* has most of these elements. In act 1 the modest, virtuous family gathered around Dufour—including his son, Stéphany, and his supposed niece Coelina, who love each other—is troubled by the arrival of Truguelin (a real uncle of Coelina), who wants Coelina to be his son's bride, and a poor old mutilated mute, Francisque, who takes refuge with the family but at once runs afoul of Truguelin, who attempts to drive him out. Act 1 ends with the banishment of Truguelin from the domestic hearth, but not without the menace of his future return. "Tremblez"—tremble, all of you—he says to the Dufour family as he exits. Act 2 takes place in a garden, prepared for the wedding feast of Stéphany and Coelina. The enclosed garden is a topos of melodrama, the space in which the virtuous and innocent celebrate their pleasures and, especially, articulate and celebrate their nature as innocence and virtue. But evil inevitably intrudes into this space: in *Coelina,* it takes the form of a letter delivered by Truguelin's servant, declaring that Coelina is not what she appears, but the adulterine daughter of Truguelin's sister and the wretched Francisque. After reading the letter, Dufour cries out: "No. She's not my niece. She is the child of crime and adultery!" His credulity (typical of the virtuous father-figures of melodrama, who are easily gulled by the villain) is given some substance by Coelina's birth certificate, which Truguelin has enclosed with his letter—the document, true or false but essentially creating a deceptive appearance, is another melodramatic constant, apparent "proof" that will have to be confuted by other, more veracious signs. Upon the reading of the birth certificate, Coelina herself does not hesitate; she immediately throws herself into Francisque's arms: "You, my father!" Nothing, in melodrama, speaks louder than the *voix du sang:* the call of family relation, especially of paternal and filial bonds. The act ends with Francisque's expulsion from Dufour's garden, and Coelina's decision to accompany him into exile from the space of virtue.

Act 3 concentrates on the exposure of the villain and the restoration of innocence to its rightful place. For the audience, there is no ambiguity about where rightful valuations lie. Not only do the virtuous publicly enunciate their moral sentiments in aphorisms and epithets; the villain inevitably has a monologue in which he declares his accursed nature, sometimes accompanied by a remorse that rarely leads to conversion. Thus Truguelin, at the start of the third act, soliloquizes in a "savage place" (where many years earlier he had tried to murder Francisque) during a thunderstorm:

> It seems to me that everything in nature unites to accuse me. These terrible words reverberate ceaselessly in my ears: no rest for the murderer! Vengeance! Vengeance! . . . (*The words are repeated by the echo. Truguelin turns round in fright.*) Heaven! What do I see? This bridge, those rocks, this torrent, here, here it is that my criminal hand shed the blood of an unfortunate. O Lord! thou that I have so long neglected, see my remorse, my sincere repentance. Stop, wretch, cease to outrage Heaven! . . . Ah! if everyone knew what it costs to cease being virtuous, we would see few villains on earth.

Truguelin is discovered by Francisque, and his identity revealed to the virtuous miller Michaud by way of the scar on his hand—result of his past combat with Francisque—in a typically melodramatic proof. There follows an exciting combat that uses the spectacular stage set (with a bridge high above the mountain torrent) and ends in Truguelin's wounding and public exposure—but not his conversion: melodramatic villains are driven out of society, not converted—and in a presentation of a written statement by Francisque that clears up past mysteries, explains the motives of Truguelin's villainy, and assures Coelina's legitimacy. The society of the innocent and virtuous reforms around Dufour, who opens his arms to Francisque and blesses the union of Stéphany and Coelina. An improvised dance ends the play.

The typical structure of melodrama, then, displays the misprision and ultimate recognition of the sign of virtue. By the time the curtain falls, virtue is rewarded—by marriage, riches, and quite often by formal judgment in a trial scene that publicly establishes culpability and innocence. But the reward of virtue really is secondary to its recognition: clearing enigmas that have obscured its sign, making evident to everyone onstage—and in the audience—where correct valuations lie. Hence the importance of the notorious melodramatic token of identity, which came to be known as *la croix de ma mère*, "my mother's cross," from the number of plays in which an apparent orphan or young person of otherwise misattributed parentage is recognized in the last act by a token preserved since birth. In *Coelina,* the scar on Truguelin's hand is such a token; other melodramas provide birthmarks, initials embroidered in baby garments, and the like. These all suggest how melodrama enacts a version of the *anagnorisis,* or recognition, that Aristotle held to be a key structural element in tragedy—but enacts it on the surface, in overt ways. The moral drama of melodrama almost always has to do with making manifest those signs that will allow the virtuous and unprejudiced to judge where good and evil reside, and eventually to make the correct choice in the Manichaean struggle between them.

All the rhetoric of melodrama is predicated on this opposition of simple, primary signs. Epithets frequently give a summary judgment of character. Thus in act 1 of *Coelina* the heroine's confidante says of Truguelin and his nephew: "I believe them to be envious, false, and wicked," while Coelina notes that Francisque "has an honest appearance." People are called "virtuous," "respectable," "interesting" (that is, appealing to one's moral sympathies) or else "vile," "cruel," "tyrannical." Not only do characters thus designate one another; they also speak their own moral natures. The villain almost always soliloquizes, naming himself as essentially evil, and the virtuous hero or heroine, while cast out and under a cloud, usually has an opportunity to affirm the essential rightness of his or her soul, beliefs, and actions. The great moments of dramatic confrontation in melodrama often come from the clash of namings of good and evil: the villain announces: "Tremble, all of you, for I am the man who will destroy you," whereas the representative of virtue claims: "God is my witness that I am innocent." We are in an unrepressed mode, a mode of excess, where everything must be articulated in the starkest possible terms.

The action of melodrama works toward confrontations, showdowns. Early in the play, such a confrontation will put evil in charge, so that it will seem to dictate the action for most of the rest of the play, deluding those who should know better, setting the apparent moral coordinates of society. But there has to be another showdown by the end, in which there will be a reversal. Often the showdown—particularly that of the last act—involves spectacular action: combats that fill the stage, explosions, fires, floods, volcanic eruptions. It is vital that the melodramatic sign be fully legible, that it impose its evidence. And melodrama enlisted a new generation of ingenious stage designers (including Louis Daguerre, who would go on to be a pioneer in photography) who used scenery, gaslight, transparencies, and trapdoors in a newly spectacular way that broke entirely with the classical tradition of French theater.

Styles of acting, too, broke radically with the classical tradition, which restricted gesture to a minimum and observed the formalities of verse, rhyme, and a decorous vocabulary. Melodramatic acting was expressionistic, full of grimaces, grandiose gestures, and an emphatic style of speech. Everything was heightened, slightly superreal, overstated rather than understood. There were frequent asides to the audience, as when the villain announced his assumption of a false face with the sacramental "Dissimulons" ("Let's dissimulate"). An important element of acting was the tableau, the moment when, at a point of crisis, the characters would freeze in a plastic representation of the emotional freight of the situation, each expressing through posture, gesture, and facial expression his or her particular place in the spectrum of reactions. The repeated use of tableaux reflects melodrama's primordial effort to make its signs forceful and intelligible.

The use of tableaux is, to be sure, only a particularly striking instance of a general recourse to silent action, pantomime, highly characteristic of melodrama (and, again, a repudiation of the classical French theater, which was essentially verbal). Historically, melodrama originated in pantomime and a bastard form called *pantomime dialoguée,* which came into existence late in the 18th century in popular theaters because the official theaters—principally the Comédie-Française—had a monopoly not only of the classical repertoire but literally also of the word: the minor theaters were not allowed to mount real plays but only (according to their category) acrobatic acts, animal shows, pantomimes, vaudevilles. The liberation of the theaters in 1791 changed all that, although Napoleon later tried to reinstitute a hierarchy of theaters and designated only a certain number that were allowed to play melodrama. In any event, the new genre kept faith with its pantomimic origins, no doubt because pantomime once again serves to make visible the stakes of the action.

The mute Francisque of *Coelina* is by no means an isolated case: mutes show up with astonishing regularity in melodrama, and their potential pathos is especially marked in dramas (such as Pixerécourt's *Le chien de Montargis,* 1814; *The Dog of Montargis*) in which the mute character is put on trial and must demonstrate his innocence and virtue wholly through gesture and facial expression. It was a virtuoso role. The stage directions of melodramas often become extremely elaborate as the dramatists attempt to describe the gestures to be used, and the effects to be sought, in the mute role. Conversely, we must not forget that melodrama, as its name implies, brought to the stage a new use of music, not only in frequent interludes of song and dance, but also to underscore moments of emotional intensity: the villain's entry onstage, the heroine's falsely secure idyll, the combat of the last act. Music—in melodrama as in the form that would eventually relay it, the cinema—conveys an additional register of legibility.

Pixerécourt, the author of some 120 plays—the majority of them melodramas—came to be dubbed the "Corneille of the Boulevards." The Boulevards were the wide avenues laid out where the walls of Paris had once stood, and which during the 18th century became the locale of fairs and popular theaters, especially the Boulevard du Temple, also known as "le Boulevard du crime" from the number of stage murders, abductions, and other heinous acts produced there. The analogy between Pixerécourt and Corneille is not as trivial as it might appear: as contemporary observers noted, there is something of Corneille's grandeur in Pixerécourt's dramatic style, his reaching toward effects of astonishment that produce in the audience a sense of admiration, a kind of popular sublime. His contemporary Louis-Charles Caigniez was in turn designated the "Racine of the Boulevards," for his dark and passionate melodramas. Along with Victor Ducange, they were the recognized masters of the genre—but there were dozens of other competent practitioners—during roughly the first third of the century, to be succeeded by such dramatists as Auguste Anicet-Bourgeois, Joseph Bouchardy, Adolphe Dennery, Louis Desnoyers, and Félix Pyat, all of whom tended to produce more complex plots (Bouchardy's regularly require a prologue, set some twenty years before the main action, which establishes the preliminaries of birth, orphanage, and so on, necessary to an understanding of the rest) and who often oriented the drama toward social problems: poverty, the criminal population of Paris, illegitimacy, class exploitation.

But the inheritance of melodrama was not confined to melodrama. In many ways the *drame romantique* of Victor Hugo, Alexandre Dumas (both father and son), and others can be seen simply as an "ennobled" version of melodrama, employing more exalted personages and historical situations—often historical personages—and more lyrical language, whether in verse or prose. There was a class difference between *mélodrame* and *drame romantique,* particularly evident when Victor Hugo stormed the citadel of the Comédie-Française with his play *Hernani* (1830). But the Romantics' capture of the Comédie-Française proved to be short-lived, in part because it was difficult to make classically trained actors and actresses adapt to the new acting styles required of them. The famous interpreters of Romantic drama came to be actors and actresses trained on the Boulevards: Bocage, Marie Dorval, and the incomparable Frédérick Lemaître, who with his gestures alone could elicit gasps of horror from the audience.

It was not only the Romantic drama that found a source of imaginative renewal in melodrama: scores of novelists also turned to melodramatic conceptions and modes of dramatization in their own work. The most popular novel of the century, Eugène Sue's *Les mystères de Paris* (*The Mysteries of Paris*), published serially in the daily newspaper in 1842 and 1843, is a compendium of melodramatic devices—and it almost immediately returned to the stage, in

607

numerous theatrical adaptations. It was not only "hack writers" like Sue who found inspiration in the melodramatic mode. The work of Balzac, for instance, is intimately and essentially melodramatic, founded on an expressionist aesthetic which regularly uses grandiose gestures, postures, and articulations of strong and opposed moral and psychological positions, and which plots its fictions toward moments of overt, dramatized confrontation, thunderous showdowns that give us memorable tableaux. Melodrama is a natural vehicle for novelists concerned to represent the conflict of good and evil in a world where old religious valuations no longer seem to have real imaginative force. And the line of melodramatic writers runs from the early 19th century to our own time, including Charles Dickens, Fyodor Dostoevski, D. H. Lawrence, Henry James, Marcel Proust, William Faulkner, and Norman Mailer—in contradistinction to a line of cool tragic ironists and absurdists who owe their allegiance to Gustave Flaubert, including Franz Kafka and Samuel Beckett. And melodrama on the stage has likewise continued well into the 20th century, relayed by the cinema—especially in the early silent film, as in the work of D. W. Griffith—and the television serial. The melodramatic mode, broadly understood, is a central fact of the Romantic and modern sensibility.

The traditional literary history that registers only the line of acknowledged masterpieces, and thus asserts that not much happened in French letters from the time of the Revolution until some years into the Restoration, neglects the effervescent aesthetics of popular literature. In literature aimed at the masses— in particular the urban masses, who were taking on a greatly increased importance in a period in which the population of Paris doubled over thirty years—new modes of representation were being forged. Crude as they often were, they corresponded to the needs of the times and expressed a prevailing imaginative mode. Poet, novelist, and theater critic Théophile Gautier, looking back nostalgically at the heroic period of melodrama he knew during his youth, wrote: "A splendid ray of poetry illuminated the densest minds, a rich sap flowed into the smallest twigs, never has one seen such a flowering of the spirit. We found nothing strong enough, bold enough, passionate enough. Everyone pushed to the limits of his own nature . . . The excessive seemed natural and unbridled lyricism the style of conversation . . . A furious life animates these strange creations and the authors have a rare quality . . . a deep seriousness, an implicit faith in their work" (*Le moniteur universel,* 30 May 1864).

Melodrama assures us that life—at least in our fictional representations of it—can satisfy the most excessive demands placed on it by the imagination.

See also 1791 (13 January), 1827 (December).

Bibliography: Peter Brooks, *The Melodramatic Imagination: Balzac, Henry James, Melodrama, and the Mode of Excess* (1976; reprint, New York: Columbia University Press, 1985). Robert B. Heilman, *Tragedy and Melodrama: Versions of Experience* (Seattle: University of Washington Press, 1968). Guilbert de Pixerécourt, *Théâtre choisi,* 4 vols. (Nancy: privately printed, 1841). Julia Przybós, *L'entreprise mélodramatique* (Paris: José Corti, 1987). J. L. Smith, *Melodrama* (London: Methuen, 1973).

Peter Brooks

〜 *1802, 14 April*

François-René de Chateaubriand Publishes His *Génie du Christianisme;*
Four Days Later the Easter *Te Deum* at Notre-Dame Celebrates the
Concordat between Napoleon and Pope Pius VII

Gothic Revival

The publication of François-René de Chateaubriand's *Génie du Christianisme*
(*Genius of Christianity*) on 14 April 1802, four days before the solemn implementation of the newly signed concordat between Napoleon and Pope Pius VII
in Notre-Dame by an Easter *Te Deum,* undoubtedly promoted the literary
work's immediate success. The relationship between the *Génie,* which set out to
reestablish Christianity by examining its history, practices, monuments, and
artistic influence, and the politics of reconciliation with a church disestablished
by the Revolution seemed to critics and enthusiasts alike to be entirely calculated. Charles Augustin Sainte-Beuve was to remark that despite the fact that
the book "was neither a great book nor a true monument," contrary to the
claim by Chateaubriand's friend and mentor Joseph Fontanes, it was inseparable
from "this ensemble of social circumstances," this "sudden theatrical gesture"
("Etude sur Chateaubriand" ["Introduction to Chateaubriand"], *Oeuvres complètes,* 1:68–69). To the Second Empire critic, the book remained a "decoration
of the *Te Deum,*" a fitting embellishment to the revival of popular spirituality,
a properly spectacular and colorful support to an already theatrical spectacle
stage-managed by a self-proclaimed skeptic.

The work quickly became a canonical reference for religious sentimentality
in 19th- and 20th-century France—anthologized, quoted in sermons, and set
as required reading for generations of schoolchildren, its hyperbolic tone surrounded by a suffocating aura of quasi-lay religiosity. But its anecdotal approach
to history was dismissed by Romantic historians, from François Guizot to Jules
Michelet; its profeudal and monarchical tone distanced it further from the intellectual mainstream during the successive revolutions of 1830, 1848, and 1871.
Thus the *Génie* ceased to be read as literature or history. Unlike the extracts
from it published by Chateaubriand himself, *Atala* (1801) and *René* (1802), it
is read today more as a historical curiosity, as evidence of Chateaubriand's own
ambiguous religious sincerity, than for its literary qualities.

Certainly the *Génie* is hard to classify. Self-consciously combining all the
traditional genres, it is neither novel nor history, polemic nor reverie, philosophy nor ideology, aesthetics nor doctrine. Part collage, part pastiche, part
chain of associations, its sprawling sections deal in turn with religious dogmas
and doctrine, the "poetics" of Christianity, fine arts and literature, and forms
of worship. Its books and chapters seem to be so many discrete fragments
bundled untidily. Yet it is precisely the readily disassembled form of this rambling collection of vignettes that contributed to its popularity. Because it could
be read selectively it appealed to both clerics and laypeople, royalists and republicans, antiquarians and historians. Chapters dealing with ruins, their picturesque effects, and the religious feelings they evoked; with tombs, from

Egyptian times to the present, including excursuses on the moods inspired by country churchyards; with the liturgy and its panoply of props, from bells to vestments—all emphasized the dramatic aspects of Christianity, tinged with the melancholic sublimity of nostalgia for an already irretrievable past and given force by the recent spectacle of the Revolution's vandalism. The *Génie* has traditionally been assigned a founding role in the emergence of medievalism, the sensibility for the Gothic, and the shift in taste that prepared for not only the Gothic revival in France but also the movement for the preservation of historical monuments. Thus Paul Frankl, in his study of the history of attitudes toward the Gothic, demonstrated how Chateaubriand's glorification of the Catholic faith gave special force to his chapter on Gothic churches (*The Gothic*, pp. 481–483). Beginning with the premise that everything in culture has its proper place—the Egyptian temple having none in Athens, the Greek temple none in Memphis or Paris—Chateaubriand gave the Gothic cathedral a place in his aesthetics that it had been denied in the classical tradition: "One may build very elegant, well-lighted Greek temples for the purpose of assembling the *good people* of St. Louis and causing them to worship a *metaphysical god,* but they will always long for these Notre-Dames of Reims and of Paris, these basilicas all covered with moss" (*Génie,* in *Oeuvres complètes,* 2:292). Of all descriptions of the Gothic, Frankl concluded, this was the most poetic, evoking associations rather than describing scenes, providing pictures of subjective consciousness. It was also clearly nationalistic, along the lines of Goethe's and Friedrich Schlegel's defense of "German" architecture at Strasbourg and Cologne cathedrals. For Chateaubriand, French forests transformed into *forêts des Gaules* take the place of German forests as the original model of Gothic vaults. Certainly the impassioned evocation of Christian values embodied in medieval artifacts, the elision of spiritual and aesthetic qualities, strongly increased the appreciation of the nonclassical past. Whereas previous scholarly studies—such as those of Montesquieu or La Curne de Sainte-Palaye—had concerned themselves with the legal, institutional, and moral structures of chivalry, hunting, heraldry, and the like, Chateaubriand focused on objects that were accessible and ubiquitous. Collectors, antiquarians, local historians, and, above all, travelers were now presented with a way to experience the Frenchness of French monuments.

Paradoxically, Chateaubriand himself was wedded to a classical taste; he by no means applauded the Gothic or its revival unreservedly. His real appreciation, even in the *Génie,* is reserved for the 17th century, the "religious century," and the buildings of Jules Hardouin-Mansart, especially the Invalides. Saint Peter's, Santa Sophia, and Saint Paul's are the masterpieces that prove Christianity's beneficent effects on religious architecture, and Chateaubriand reaffirms his point by comparing Mansart's Invalides Church of 1680–1691 and Jacques-Ange Gabriel's Ecole Militaire of 1751–1788: "The former has raised its vaults to the heavens in the voice of the religious century; the latter grovels close to the earth, in the speech of the atheistic century" (*Oeuvres,* 2:290). The Gothic, by contrast, and in accordance with the view common since the Renaissance, has "barbarous proportions"; the cathedrals owe their attraction to something other than the rules of beauty.

Like many followers of Edmund Burke, Chateaubriand preferred to respond to aspects of medieval monuments, the "sublime" as evoking sensations more akin to nature than to art: "One cannot enter a Gothic cathedral without feeling a kind of shiver of awe [*frissonnement*] and a vague sentiment of the Divinity" (*Oeuvres,* 2:293). Burke had associated fear, awe, vagueness, and obscurity with the terrifying sublime and with the forest clearings where the Druids had first worshiped and the dark interiors of Gothic cathedrals. Chateaubriand united these examples in a single image of an architecture that imitated not just the forests or simply the patterns of liturgy, but the very "murmurs" of original worship in nature: "The forests of the Gauls have passed in their turn into the temples of our ancestors, and the woods of our oaks have thus maintained their sacred origin. These vaults carved in foliage, these buttresses supporting the walls and terminating abruptly like broken tree trunks, the coolness of the vaults, the shadows of the sanctuary, the dark aisles, the secret passages, the low doorways: everything in the Gothic church retraces the labyrinths of the forest and excites feelings of religious horror, the mysteries and the Divinity" (ibid.).

Chateaubriand's sentimental rather than aesthetic attachment to the Gothic was illustrated in his attitude toward the emerging cult of the museum. Siding with the neoclassicist critic Antoine Quatremère de Quincy and the sculptor Louis-Pierre Deseine against the creation of what Quatremère called "these cemeteries of the arts," Chateaubriand attacked the deracinating effects of cultural centralization, the piling up of the spoils of Bonaparte's Italian and Egyptian campaigns in the Louvre, and especially the assemblage of medieval and Renaissance fragments in the newly established Musée des Monuments Français (Museum of French Monuments), constructed by the painter and antiquarian Alexandre Lenoir in the former convent of the Petits-Augustins. This institution, gradually formed out of the debris of vandalized tombs and buildings saved by Lenoir from Revolutionary destruction, had, since its official opening in 1795, presented a kind of dramatic tableau to Parisians interested in their national history. Displayed in chronological order, in a sequence of rooms designed in the styles of the centuries, tombs, sculptures, and architectural motifs from the legendary age of Clovis to the present provided a historical equivalent to the popular panoramas. In his *Mémoires d'outre-tombe* (1849–50; *Memoirs from beyond the Grave*), Chateaubriand compared this "collection of ruins and tombs of every century, piled up pell-mell in the cloisters of the Petits-Augustins," to the heterogeneity of Parisian society in the 1790s (*Mémoires,* p. 232).

But despite Lenoir's evident good intentions in saving endangered monuments, Chateaubriand was strongly critical of the museum's cultural program. Advocating a sense of rootedness and place, a religion founded on the true emotions that stem from monuments seen in context, Chateaubriand found himself unmoved by Lenoir's displaced fragments: "One owes much to the artist who has amassed together the debris of our old sepulchers; but . . . the effects of these monuments . . . are destroyed. Confined in a small space, divided up into centuries, deprived of their harmonies with the antiquity of temples and

Christian worship, not having kept even their dust, they no longer say anything to the imagination or the heart" (*Oeuvres,* 2:406). For the young Romantic archaeological enthusiast and religious sentimentalist, ruins were truly effective only in place, living emblems of the *poétique des morts* (poetics of the dead) to be experienced in solitary reflection and contemplation.

Thus, although Michelet was to credit Lenoir rather than Chateaubriand with having contributed to his sense of the medieval past—walking as a child through the sequence of rooms, he had experienced his first intuition of "the true order of the ages" and a revelation of the laws of historical change—it was Chateaubriand who set the terms of the debate between advocates of preservation and enthusiasts of restoration in the 1830s: between Victor Hugo, whose travels convinced him that restoration might kill a building as surely as demolition, and Eugène Emmanuel Viollet-le-Duc, whose fanciful attempts at "complete" restoration satisfied the Second Empire taste for artificial history. It was Chateaubriand too who served the emerging sense of a national patrimony, a geography marked by monumental traces and a still-living historical landscape; his reverie on a wayside cross and soliloquy on the sight of ruins in the landscape provided an easily assimilable version of picturesque aesthetics, more attractive to local historians than the antiquarian disputes of Parisian curators.

In his "war" against the barbarism of the "demolishers," opened in 1825 and made explicit in the polemical article "Guerre aux démolisseurs" in 1832, Hugo was perhaps less indebted to Chateaubriand than to the rhetoric of the republican churchman Henri Grégoire, inventor of the word *vandalism* and leader in the fight to save French monuments from mutilation during the Revolution; but it was Chateaubriand's sensibility for the Gothic sublime that infused Hugo's evocations of eastern architecture in *Les orientales* (1829) and pervaded his grotesque vision of Notre-Dame in *Notre-Dame de Paris* (1831).

Chateaubriand's work was no doubt too religiously and politically biased to appeal to the young Romantics in the first Comité des Monuments (Committee on Monuments), established by François Guizot in 1834. His outdated theories of the origins of Gothic architecture in the imitation of forests, the commonplaces of 18th-century historians, owed more to poetic license, even in 1802, than to archaeological accuracy. Moreover, the spate of heavily illustrated travel books, starting in the late 1780s and increasing through the Restoration, probably had as much to do as Chateaubriand with engendering the "touristic" appreciation of the remains of historical France. Yet Chateaubriand's reputation as a founder of medievalism was, in another sense, well deserved: his descriptions, like those of Johann Joachim Winckelmann on classical statuary a generation before, were paradigmatic; they supplied the proper vocabulary for guidebooks and the proper feelings for tourists in an age when the sensibility for the terrifying sublime was gradually being replaced by the comforting commonplaces of the *Guides Joanne.*

See also 1674, 1791 (13 January), 1836, 1905.

Bibliography: François-René de Chateaubriand, *Mémoires d'outre-tombe,* ed. Maurice Levaillant, vol. 1 (Paris: Flammarion, 1949). Chateaubriand, *Oeuvres complètes,* with an introduction by Charles Augustin Sainte-Beuve, 12 vols. (Paris: Garnier, 1858–1861). Paul Frankl, *The Gothic: Literary Sources and Interpretations through Eight Centuries* (Princeton: Princeton University Press, 1960).

Anthony Vidler

✍ 1808, 17 *March*
Napoleon Establishes a System of National Education

Discipline and Melancholy

On 1 January 1809, at the peak of the Empire, the whole system of education in France came under the governance of the Imperial University, instituted by the Decree of 17 March 1808. Any school that was not authorized by the *grand-maître*—the president of the university—would be suppressed. The Imperial University was legally endowed with an educational monopoly even superior to that which, under the ancien régime, the church had unofficially enjoyed. Nothing would escape the control of the state. As Hippolyte Taine remarked in his study of the French schools and universities (*Le régime moderne,* 1894; *The Modern Régime*), Napoleon had a very specific aim in establishing such a homogeneous system: as he had said in a speech to the State Council on 11 March 1806, he wanted "to secure the means for directing political and moral opinions" (quoted in Taine, *Le régime,* pt. 3, p. 196). The university was centralized in Paris and supervised all public institutions in the *départements* (the Revolution had divided French territory into eighty-three such subdivisions); it administered what had been called since 1807 lycées (high schools), while private schools were forced to pay enormous taxes, or closed, or reduced to simple boarding schools. In the academic year of 1809, the triumphal year of Wagram, the lycées opened under the university regime with a new curriculum. The students were between nine and eighteen years old; the normal curriculum lasted six years: two years of grammar, two of humanities, one of rhetoric, and one of mathematics or philosophy. Literary studies were oriented more toward Latin than toward French; geography was not taught, nor was history, deemed a dangerous discipline that could encourage critical thinking. Napoleon wanted to direct and determine how the new generations thought: the state would never build up a nation with a stable political identity if the young people were not told to be republican or monarchist, irreligious or Catholic. If the state did not monopolize public education, it would constantly confront disorder and change.

Napoleon's schools were organized according to a military discipline. The emperor announced: "I want a corporation, not of Jesuits whose sovereign is in Rome, but of Jesuits who have no ambition but to be useful and no interest but the interest of the state" (Taine, *Le régime,* p. 212). The professors and administrators of the lycées and the university should form a coherent and well-organized civil militia, copying the hierarchy of military ranks, following a similar pattern of promotion. The Decree of 17 March 1808 explicitly stated that no one would reach a superior rank without having passed through the inferior. Like young soldiers, the teachers could dream of glorious careers. "The feet of this great body will be on the college benches and its head in the Senate," Napoleon said (p. 213). The head, the *grand-maître,* became one of the most important civil servants of the Empire, with more independence than the ministers themselves. Professors and administrators of all degrees would feel part of the same association, respect their chief, and enjoy the consideration accorded him: they would form an elite, develop solidarity, and every teacher would become attached to the university, like a soldier to his regiment or a monk to his order. The members of the educational corps would be engaged for three, six, or nine years and could not resign "without giving notice a certain number of years beforehand" (p. 214).

Napoleon admired Catholicism not for its spiritual values, but for its organization. To make the analogy with a religious or a military group even more manifest, he decided that joining the university would involve "taking the cowl," with "some solemnity attached to this act." The civil engagement would be similar to a religious one, "with the difference that the marriage will not be as sacred, as indissoluble" (Taine, *Le régime,* p. 214). Marriage, a family, or any type of private life would weaken a system requiring complete dedication to duty. The 1808 decree established a rule of celibacy in the first years of the teaching career. Napoleon planned to apply it not only to the schoolmasters but also to the principals, censors, and headmasters. So that celibacy and life in common would not be threatened, no women would be admitted into the lycées (state high schools) and collèges (municipal high schools).

Discipline, obedience, hierarchy: in the schools as in the army Napoleon's troops were held together by incentives of emulation, ambition, and pride. The military structure of the lycée, in terms of both its formal organization and the moral values it promoted, reflected the general military atmosphere in France at the time. As Alfred de Vigny recalled in his *Servitude et grandeur militaires* (1835; *The Military Condition*), "I belong to the generation that was born with the century, that was nurtured on the Emperor's communiqués, that had ever before its eyes a naked sword" (p. 5). Vigny's vivid portrayal of the pupils' life in the lycée shows how persistently they were diverted from any intellectual commitment: "In the closing years of the Empire I was a boy at school, but my mind was elsewhere. The war was constantly in our midst; the roll of drums drowned the voices of my teachers, and the arcane language of our books had a frigid, pedantic ring to our ears. Logarithms and figures of speech we regarded as so many steps leading up to the star of the Legion of Honour, heaven's brightest star to children's eyes." No serious reflection could take place; the pupils' minds were "awhirl with the thunder of cannon-fire" (p. 10). Similarly the liberal historian Charles de Rémusat recalled in *Mémoires de ma vie* (wr. 1858–1870, pub. 1958; *Recollections from My Life*) all the horrors of the authoritarian system in the collèges: obedience was only external; everybody lied; a constant state of war existed between masters and students, depriving their relationship of esteem and affection.

Convinced that "without discipline and without obedience, no university could exist" (Taine, *Le régime*, p. 218), Napoleon discouraged political discussion and independent thought. It was not enough to repress the old generation; a younger generation of lycée teachers must replace it, carefully selected and expressly shaped in a special institution. On 30 March 1810 Napoleon set forth new rules for the administration of the Ecole Normale Supérieure. Students would enter at the age of seventeen and be bound to work for the university for ten years. A superintendent would control every movement: they could not spend time alone in their rooms or enter the hall of another division without the superintendent's permission. Only outings in uniform and in groups were allowed, always under the direction of superintendent masters. Napoleon took a particular interest in this normalizing institution: Abel Villemain recalled in his *Souvenirs contemporains* (1855; *Contemporary Recollections*) a visit from the emperor in 1812, when the Ecole Normale was still very small, located in the upper floors of the lycée Louis-le-Grand, and consisted of only forty pupils and four masters. Napoleon disapproved of reading Tacitus, Marcus Aurelius, and Montesquieu and recommended instead Caesar, Corneille, and Bossuet, because they strengthened the established order of things in their times.

Classicism was the official culture of the Empire: Napoleon wanted to restore the admiration for the century of Louis XIV and judged that Louis de Fontanes, a classical poet, an admirer of Virgil and Cicero, of Corneille, Racine, and Bossuet, would be the ideal *grand-maître* of the Imperial University. But the emperor's imposition of classicism provoked a reaction against it: those who were intensively indoctrinated with the classical culture in the lycées became the Romantic generation of 1830. The *mal du siècle* (Romantic spleen) simmered in the militaristic atmosphere of the beginning of the century. Napoleonic censorship, however harsh, did not succeed in converting the official values of discipline and classical order into the dominant mentality. Despotism could not strangle opposition. Absolute power could not suppress contradictions and rebellions. Ten thousand copies of Germaine de Staël's *De l'Allemagne* (1810; *On Germany*) were destroyed by the police; François-René de Chateaubriand was not allowed to republish his *Essai sur les révolutions* (1797; *Essay on Revolutions*); Prosper de Barante was forced to soften the tone of his *Littérature du XVIIIe siècle* (1809; *Literature of the 18th Century*), which explored the relationship between literature and society in the light of Staël's *De la littérature considérée dans ses rapports avec les institutions sociales* (1800; *The Influence of Literature upon Society*). In his official report to the State Council on 27 February 1808 on the condition of French literature since 1789, Marie-Joseph Chénier, the prominent ideologue of neoclassicism, did not even mention *De la littérature;* and of all Chateaubriand's work he alluded only to *Atala* (1801), and that in order to criticize the deterioration of the language and style of classicism.

But nothing could prevent the triumph of Staël's and Chateaubriand's ideas, which promoted a new literature born in the dark skies of the north. Emancipated from the models of the ancients, it substituted Christian and medieval evocations for Greek and Latin mythology and stressed the role of human passions and poetic inspiration. Thus the historian François Guizot recalled in his *Mémoires* (1858) that upon his arrival in Paris in 1807, German philosophy and literature were his favorite studies. He read Kant, Herder, and Schiller more than Voltaire and Condillac. Staël, an enthusiastic reader of Rousseau—her first work was a volume of *Lettres sur le caractère et les écrits de Jean-Jacques Rousseau* (1788; *Letters on the Character and Writings of Jean-Jacques Rousseau*)—had opened the way to an almost religious devotion to German Romantic poetry. She contrasted their poetry, infused with Christian and chivalric values, to the French classics. Meanwhile Chateaubriand, another admirer of Rousseau, created a new type that became an enduring figure in French literature: the melancholic hero. The exalted and dreaming title character of *René* (1802) leaves France and civilized society to be intoxicated by the spectacle of nature in Louisiana. Had not Napoleon himself been enthralled by Rousseau's ideas? In his *Mémoires d'outre-tombe* (1849–50; *Memoirs from beyond the Grave*) Chateaubriand cited these words written by the young Napoleon when he was at the Brienne military school: "Always alone among people, I escape human company to dream within myself and give myself to the fullness of my melancholy" (1:683).

The despot could persecute and immobilize, but he could not obliterate a cultural movement. Benjamin Constant de Rebecque, an important figure in Staël's circle, quoted Rousseau in *De l'esprit de conquête et de l'usurpation* (1814; *On the Spirit of Conquest and Usurpation*): "The laws of liberty are a thousand times harder than the oppression of tyrants" (*Oeuvres*, p. 1052). In the midst of the imperial festivities and ceremonies mimicking the splendor of *le grand siècle*, the imagination of those who, like Constant, defended the principles of individual liberty grew splenetic. Shy, solitary, and scornful, seized by incurable boredom and tormented by vague emotions, such is the hero of Constant's novel *Adolphe* (1816), composed between Coppet and Geneva in 1806–07, while the writer was following Staël in her exile.

In January 1809 Constant published an adaptation of Friedrich von Schiller's tragedy *Wallstein,* with an important preface. Although no theater would produce the play, the first edition of the book was sold out within two months. The setting of *Wallstein* is the Thirty Years' War. In his preface Constant described this war as one of the most remarkable periods in modern history, when the people fought to obtain religious liberty and the princes to keep their political independence against the authority of the Empire. But, in Constant's view, military spirit, since the time of warriors such as Wallstein, had become more and more foreign to the spirit of the people, and now the military condition is under the control of political authority, individual courage being replaced by discipline and obedience. Presenting Schiller's tragedy to the French public was a political as well as a literary act: Constant implied that people would always fight for liberty and emphasized the originality of German drama, like Staël in her condemned *De l'Allemagne*. Less radical in his Romanticism than Staël, Constant altered the character of Thecla, the daughter of Wallstein. Although he did not give her "the regular color of the Greek and Roman heroines" and remained faithful to her melancholy and sensitivity, he did modify her German mystical nature to please the classical and rational expectations of the French public. Constant later regretted this compromise: "I should have foreseen that a political revolution would produce a literary revolution, and that a nation that had only momentarily renounced freedom for the hazards of war would not be satisfied with weak and incomplete emotions" ("De la guerre de Trente Ans" ["On the Thirty Years' War"], *Oeuvres*, p. 881).

Chateaubriand, inspired, after the success of his *Génie du Christianisme* (1802; *Genius of Christianity*), by the religious persecutions under Diocletian, wrote *Les martyrs* (1809), another compromise between classicism and Romanticism, in which he juxtaposed the pagan and the Christian world to the advantage of the latter: Christianity encouraged the development of characters and passions in the epic. Chateaubriand noted in his preface to the 1826 edition: "This work caused my persecutions under Bonaparte to be redoubled: the allusions in the portrait of Galerius and . . . the Court of Diocletian were so striking that they could not escape the imperial police" (*The Martyrs*, p. xviii). The young Guizot wrote an impassioned defense of *Les martyrs* in *Le publiciste*, one of the few political papers that Napoleon did not suppress. And Fontanes, though the champion of classicism, had no doubts about the quality of this work so violently attacked by contemporary critics: "They will come back to it," Chateaubriand recalled his saying (p. xvii). Presented in what Chateaubriand himself acknowledged to be a classical style, the Romantic profile of the Christian hero Eudorus, magnified, like René, by sadness and tears, gained the approval of the *grand-maître* Napoleon had appointed as the head of his university. Chateaubriand was not officially received at the Académie Française, to which he had been elected in 1811, because his speech did not please the emperor, but René's melancholy was about to triumph over the century.

See also 1802, 1814, 1827 (February).

Bibliography: François-René de Chateaubriand, *The Martyrs*, trans. O. W. Wight (1859; reprint, New York: Howard Fertig, 1976). Chateaubriand, *Mémoires d'outre-tombe*, ed. Maurice Levaillant, 2 vols. (Paris: Garnier, 1964). Benjamin Constant de Rebecque, *Oeuvres*, ed. Alfred Roulin (Paris: Gallimard, 1957). Georges Pariset, *Le Consulat et l'Empire*, vol. 3 of *Histoire de la France contemporaine*, ed. Ernest Lavisse (Paris: Hachette, 1921). Antoine Prost, *L'enseignement en France* (Paris: Armand Colin, 1968). Hippolyte Taine, *Le régime moderne* (part 3), vol. 9 of *Les origines de la France contemporaine* (Paris: Hachette, 1912); translated by John Durand as *The Origins of Contemporary France (Selected Chapters)*, ed. Edward T. Gargan (1876; reprint, Chicago: University of Chicago Press, 1974). Alfred de Vigny, *The Military Condition*, trans. Marguerite Barnett (London: Oxford University Press, 1964).

Patrizia Lombardo

✍ 1814, 4 June

In the Constitutional Charter, Louis XVIII Grants Freedom of the Press to the French People

Freedom and Repression during the Restoration

The Restoration deserves better than its name implies. Rather than a return to the ancien régime, this period (1814–1830) witnessed the creation of a public domain in which people and ideas circulated more freely than ever before. During the Restoration the French people took the first timid steps in their apprenticeship in democracy. Inevitably these steps involved conflicts in the views expressed on the question of freedom, and more specifically on freedom of written expression.

The position of the governing powers on this subject was recorded in article 8 of the Constitutional Charter granted to the French people by Louis XVIII on 4 June 1814 (rather than *accepted* by him, as the liberals had hoped): "The French people have the right to make public and to print their opinions, while conforming to the laws that must repress abuses of this freedom." This formulation satisfied the liberals but displeased the "ultras" (as the ultraconservatives were called): it did not provide for prepublication censorship of books and of the press, but instead subjected them to the general regulations for the repression of criminal offenses. From 1814 to 1830 the two extreme poles of Parlement waged an incessant battle: at times the ultras attacked the overly liberal position of the government, and thus the charter itself; occasionally, having successfully influenced royal policy, they managed to establish a system of censorship: in response the liberals, the extreme left wing of the time (there were no longer any Jacobins in the public arena), would counterattack by referring to the letter of the Charter. Louis de Bonald (1754–1840) and Benjamin Constant de Rebecque (1767–1830), the ideologues and respective spokesmen of these two groups, tirelessly published discourses, newspaper articles, and pamphlets on the question of censorship and freedom of the press. Only Bonald's retirement and Constant's death interrupted this exchange, which resembled a duel more than a dialogue. Their writings circumscribe the ideological space of this period, within which other authors followed their serpentine courses (Chateaubriand, for example, managed to align himself with Bonald in 1814 and with Constant in 1827).

Bonald was first and foremost a social theoretician. During the Revolution, while in exile, he published his three-volume *Théorie du pouvoir politique et religieux* (1796; *Theory of Political and Religious Power*); later he amplified and refined his doctrine by applying it, in many other publications, to questions as varied as divorce, the origin of language, and literary theory. Constant was a multifaceted author: in 1806 he wrote a treatise titled *Principes de politique* (*Principles of Politics*), which was not published in its entirety until 1980 but on which he drew for diverse pamphlets, discourses, and articles published during his lifetime; a historian and philosopher of religion, he wrote the monumental three-volume *De la religion* (1824, 1825, 1827; *On Religion*); an attentive observer of his inner life, he wrote a journal, letters, and reminiscences of his childhood (*Le cahier rouge*, 1907; *The Red Notebook*); finally—and this is his principal claim to glory for the modern reader—he was the author of two short novels, one of which appeared during his lifetime (*Adolphe*, wr. 1806–07, pub. 1816) and the other long after his death (*Cécile*, wr. 1810, pub. 1950). These two works inaugurated the modern "psychological novel."

In 1814, after the fall of the Empire and with the return to monarchy, it was

Bonald who led the attack against freedom of expression. His reasoning was as follows. First, the problem itself had to be reformulated: it was not a question of limiting freedom of thought—which in any case could not be done, since thought could use the human mind as an inviolate refuge (Bonald had not conceived of totalitarian brainwashing)—nor even of attenuating freedom of expression in speech or writing, when confined to the private domain. What Bonald wanted to regulate was the freedom to publish, to act on others in the public domain. Starting with this premise, his reasoning took the form of a rigorous syllogism. The major premise was that public speech and writing were actions: to speak was to act; one does things with words. The minor premise was that no government, no society, could accord its subjects unlimited freedom of action; otherwise it would regress to the savage state of war of all against all. The conclusion: it was inconceivable for a reasonable government to make verbal actions, which were the most important in a civilized nation, an exception to the law that it applied to all public actions; consider, for example, the effects of books such as the gospels, Rousseau's *Du contrat social* (1762; *On the Social Contract*), or, later, the *Manifesto of the Communist Party* (1848) and *Mein Kampf* (1925). Prohibition and regulation were therefore necessary.

Bonald contended that the liberals' avowed desire to defend freedom of thought was a matter of playing with words: it was publishing and not thinking freely that the liberals demanded. Furthermore, this was not a question of freedom but of power, the power to control and to judge (a "fourth power," as we would call it today, that of the press). Unlike the other powers (legislative, executive, judiciary), this one was uncontrolled: journalists were not elected and were revocable by neither nation nor king. In order to publish, they simply needed access to the material means or the personal sympathy of those who possessed the means. What could be more unjust, whatever yardstick of justice was used, monarchist or republican? The governments of modern France have remained sensitive to this problem: every change of parliamentary majority entails a change in the personnel of the principal television stations.

To this argument Bonald added another. Recognition of everyone's right freely to express his opinion meant one of two things. Either the opinion in question concerned a subject immaterial to the common good, in which case its publication, being injurious to no one, was in no way alarming. But how could anyone maintain that political, moral, and religious questions had nothing to do with the interests of society when in fact they aroused it most? Or else—if one rejected this view—one had to acknowledge that these were indeed serious questions; but then how could one dare affirm that all answers should be indifferently allowed? Was the better not preferable to the worse? For Bonald, Christian values were superior to all others. Were there not ideologies whose universally acknowledged and confirmed harmfulness made it at the very least imprudent to encourage their circulation? Equal freedom for all opinions implied that all were of equal merit, and thus a renunciation of any hierarchy of values. It was absurd to ignore willingly that some things were better for a society than others. Laws informed people of what was permitted and what was forbidden, and knowledge preferred the true to the false. By what miracle could ideology alone escape the judgment meted out everywhere else?

As for the manner of regulating publications, Bonald preferred censorship to justice; he desired prevention instead of repression, and he attempted to demonstrate that this was the very spirit of the charter. His arguments here were varied. First, one could reason by analogy: was it not better to avert an illness than to cure it? to prevent a crime rather than to punish it? and were the police not a necessary complement of justice? It was true that for other actions the law was satisfied with repression, but in specifying the nature of the offense, it served to dissuade: everyone knew that it was wrong to steal. But it was impossible to write laws for the press in a precise manner: it was impossible to foresee all the forms that an author's heresy could take. Therefore the censor should interpret the law in advance by obligingly informing authors whether the publication of their ideas would or would not constitute a criminal offense. Moreover, censorship would prevent authors from incurring large publishing expenses; and, if it was done discreetly, it would not compromise their good reputation. This procedure would avoid trials that would publicize a work that was to be withdrawn from the attention of readers. "Censorship, severe censorship, universal censorship is necessary for all periodical and other writings" (*De l'opposition dans le gouvernement et de la liberté de la presse* [1827; *On Opposition in Matters of Government and on Freedom of the Press*], p. 149). Thus Bonald acted in accordance with his deepest convictions when he accepted the presidency of the Censorship Committee in 1827.

Bonald's arguments did not lack weight, and his recommendations have been implemented in every country where tyranny reigns; some of them are also to be found even in liberal democracies. Constant's counterarguments were not as radical as some of his formulas, useful for their oratorical efficacy, would lead us to believe. Constant often started from the same observations as Bonald, but he arrived at different results. He showed that the ineluctable character of Bonald's conclusions was illusory, even though his original premises were often correct. Thus he admitted that speech and writing could constitute actions; as such, they should not be above the law. In other words, Constant tacitly accepted Bonald's initial syllogism. Their differences came afterward.

Constant also acknowledged that freedom of the press was a power, but he rejoiced in this fact rather than deploring it. In the republics of antiquity, which were the size of a city, citizens had only to go to the agora to inform their fellow citizens of all that they should know. In this way they were able to participate in the affairs of state. In Constant's time, this participatory "freedom of the ancients" had become impracticable, if only because of the size of states. It had been replaced by the "freedom of the moderns," freedom as autonomy— that is, the establishment of a private domain over which neither the state nor society had any rights. Books and the press offered a way to compensate for the loss of participatory freedom; they informed those who governed of the thoughts of their subjects and at the same time provided citizens with a recourse against the arbitrariness of power: "Publicity," Constant wrote, "is the resource of the oppressed against the oppressor" ("Sur la censure des journaux" [1821; "On Censorship against Newspapers"], *Oeuvres,* p. 1296). Publishing, as the word implies, assured access to the public domain. The printing press was the indispensable tool of modern democracy; but if this tool was to be available to all, the press had to be pluralist, and thus publications uncontrolled in advance: hence each individual had a good chance to find a channel for expression.

Constant, like Bonald, subscribed to a hierarchy of values. When he discussed nihilism, it was to ascertain its progress and not to glorify it. Also like Bonald, he believed in the necessary harmony between means and ends. Bonald acknowledged the revealed truth of the gospels as the ultimate value and accordingly wanted people to accept it and submit to it, not to discuss it freely. But the truth and the values to which Constant aspired had to be the product of reason. It followed that the appropriate way to attain them was not by an injunction addressed by a superior to an inferior, but by free examination and debate with others, which in turn implied freedom of the press. Otherwise, Constant claimed, "the means are not homogeneous" (*Principes,* p. 362). Not only did the use of inappropriate means risk compromising the end (the moment that something worthy was promoted by the police, it became unpopular), but free discussion also had virtues of its own: it led to calm, for it forced the interlocutors to admit that they had one thing in common, namely, the context of discussion itself; good "social exchanges" led to "the rectification of all ideas" (p. 131). Free discussion was profitable both to the state and to individuals: blind acceptance of the truth (the truth of authority) dulled the mind; active searching for truth fortified it.

This reasoning led Constant to the conclusion, not that there should be unlimited freedom of the press, but that the press should be subject to supervision by the courts (with juries) rather than by censors. Constant was no anarchist, and he never failed to state that he found certain verbal actions (certain publications) reprehensible. In *Cours de politique constitutionnelle* (1818; *Lessons on Constitutional Politics*) he enumerated them at length: aspersions on the dignity of a person or collectivity (defamation); inciting to violence in order to resolve individual or social conflicts (the call to murder or to civil war); "invitations to the enemy abroad" (*Cours,* 1:126). But such offenses, like all others, were simply questions of justice and thus did not require the creation of a special agency. Contrary to what Bonald suggested, publishing was not in itself a "dangerous means," even if it could become one; its use could not be proscribed because of its potential for abuse. "To silence citizens for fear that they might commit these crimes is to forbid them to go out lest they trouble the tranquillity of the streets and of the open roads; and it is to forbid them to speak lest their words be injurious" (*Recueil d'articles,* 1:78).

The existence of censorship, on the other hand, had its own particular disadvantages. In order to control everything that was written in a country, it would be necessary to have spies everywhere—that is, to create a police state, whose disadvantages far outweighed its advantages and led unnecessarily to the most extreme of solutions. "In the matter of the freedom of the press," wrote

Constant, "we must either be tolerant or execute" (*Cours,* 1:445); because it was impossible to execute everyone, it was better to be tolerant. Moreover, it would be necessary to close all frontiers; otherwise forbidden writings would be imported from abroad (totalitarian states are not innovative in this regard either). Another disadvantage lay in the fact that the government, in overseeing everything, would find itself led to assume responsibility for everything published; yet there were opinions that, though not constituting criminal offenses, were unacceptable expressions of the government's will. In addition, if every public proclamation was assured by the government, and if the government thus became the sole source of public expression, it would lose all credibility from never being subject to the test of contradiction (in totalitarian states the people do not believe even weather forecasts). Under a system of censorship, power would be still more concentrated in the government; if it was in the hands of judges, the distribution of power, and thus mutual control, was assured. Finally, freedom of expression was also a safety valve: revolutions erupted in places where there was no other way to influence society. In countries that prohibited participation in public life by means of publishing, citizens had the choice of becoming revolutionaries or finding refuge in pure material satisfaction. These solutions were as degrading as they were harmful to the well-being of the country.

The July Monarchy, which succeeded the Restoration in 1830, seemed to support Constant's ideas against Bonald's on a number of issues, but the relative merits of censorship and freedom of the press continued to be debated for many years. Today the Fifth Republic has clearly chosen for Constant's principles in preference to Bonald's. But the best commentary on this controversy is perhaps an anecdote concerning Bonald himself. An article that he published in 1806, "Réflexions philosophiques sur la tolérance des opinions" ("Philosophical Reflections on the Toleration of Opinions"), drew the ire of Napoleon's minister of police, the notorious Joseph Fouché, who sent the following edict to the prefect of Bonald's region: "Assure M. de Bonald that His Majesty the Emperor esteems and rewards only useful talents and positive knowledge, that he welcomes writings that shed light, and that he severely punishes discussions that might create discord in his Empire." It is not enough to prefer the useful, the positive, and the enlightening; it is necessary also to be on the side of those who will give a content to these conveniently vague notions; and the risk of every censor is to find himself one day censored. He who renounces equality must imagine himself not only on the side of the masters but also on the side of the slaves.

See also 1648, 1791 (13 January), 1816, 1830, 1851.

Bibliography: Paul Bénichou, *Le sacre de l'écrivain* (Paris: José Corti, 1973). Bénichou, *Le temps des prophètes* (Paris: Gallimard, 1977). Louis de Bonald, *De l'opposition dans le gouvernement et de la liberté de la presse* (Paris: Dupont, 1827). Bonald, *Oeuvres complètes,* 3 vols. (Paris: Le Clère, 1859–1864). Benjamin Constant de Rebecque, *Adolphe,* in *Oeuvres,* ed. Alfred Roulin (Paris: Gallimard, 1957). Constant, *Cours de politique constitutionnelle,* vol. 1 (Paris: Guillaumin, 1861). Constant, *Principes de politique* (Geneva:

Droz, 1980). Constant, *Recueil d'articles, le Mercure, la Minerve, et la Renommée*, vol. 1 (Geneva: Droz, 1972).

Tzvetan Todorov

✍ 1816, 8 May

The 1792 Law Making Divorce Legal Is Rescinded by the Restoration

Women's Voices in Literature and Art

On 20 September 1792 the Revolutionary Legislative Assembly made divorce legal for the first time in France; this unprecedented and extremely liberal divorce law remained the object of bitter controversy until its rescinding on 8 May 1816. To Revolutionary liberals, the law represented a dramatic assertion of the inalienability of individual liberty, followed as it was on the very next day by the founding of the (first) French republic. Conservatives tended to view divorce as a perverse extension to the family of the spirit of Revolutionary anarchy: the divorce law was ratified, they claimed, in the shadow of the grisly prison slaughters known as the September Massacres and had helped, somehow, to usher in the Reign of Terror.

One principle on which republicans, Bonapartists, and royalists concurred from the 1790s on, however, was that women should not be given a voice in the political arena. The Jacobin dictatorship of the Year II (1793–94) closed down women's political clubs and sent to their deaths female political activists such as Jeanne-Marie Roland, Olympe de Gouges, and Théroigne de Méricourt. In the Revolutionary and post-Revolutionary decades, ambitious women fared much worse than in the days when *salonnières* and royal mistresses could sway the politics of court and town. By outlawing court politics, which had traditionally granted prominent women varying degrees of formal or informal influence, the Revolutionaries redefined the political sphere as an exclusively male preserve.

The moderate and conservative régimes that followed the fall of Robespierre immediately began to revise and restrict the divorce law, and the antifemale bias of the Revolutionary era culminated in the Napoleonic code. Articles 213 and 214 of the code dictate the complete legal submission of a woman to her husband, making the latter's authorization necessary for any judicial act or legal transaction, even of the wife's own property. Although divorce was retained— the emperor himself was, after all, about to change wives—the issue remained controversial, especially in conservative circles.

One of the most articulate voices raised against divorce in the early years of the century was that of the ultraroyalist Louis de Bonald. In his widely read *Du divorce considéré au XIXe siècle* (1801; *On Divorce Considered in the 19th Century*), Bonald argued that the public and private spheres naturally espouse a trinitarian order. In both, a power or will (sovereign or father) and an end or object (subject or child) are linked by a mediator or means (minister or wife/mother). Women

623

or ministers thus serve as mediating forces, "passive to conceive, active to produce," between the active power of the sovereign/father and the passive receptivity of the subject/child. The very ordering of natural language, Bonald continued, proves the pervasiveness of this model: are not sentences made up of active subjects and passive objects joined by a verb or "copule"? Thus divorce settlement between man and wife not only thwarts the rights of the weakest third party, the child born or yet unborn; it also grants an unnatural degree of initiative to the wife, who should remain consigned to her subordinate function as mediator. Women, in Bonald's scheme, do not utter their own (substantive) words; they are the ministers, priestesses, or verbs through whom the father's word is transmitted to the son.

The ideological climate that spawned this pamphlet did not favor female intellectual ambitions. Yet it has been estimated that as many as 150 women novelists were active in France in the first two decades of the 19th century, and the authors of successful novels were more often female than male. Early 19th-century literary successes included Sophie Cottin's *Claire d'Albe* (1799), Juliane von Krüdener's *Valérie* (1803), the last novels of Isabelle de Charrière, and, in the 1820s, the works of Claire de Duras; none of these, however, came close to attaining the popularity of Germaine de Staël's *Delphine* (1802) and *Corinne* (1807). The feminization of certain sectors of the literary world, begun in the 18th century, was accelerated by the historical conditions of the early 1800s: given the thoroughness of imperial censorship and the new channels for social promotion opened up by the Revolution, young men in search of fame and power probably looked to the administration or the army rather than to the world of letters and ideas.

Not that women writing in this period were isolated from the cultural and political realities of the wider world. Many were of foreign birth or had resided for long periods abroad: Staël's parents were Swiss; Charrière, née Van Tuyll, came from Holland; and Krüdener was born in Riga, on the Baltic. Most of them had experienced personal tragedies in the political turmoil of the 1790s. The Revolution had claimed the lives of Duras's Girondist father and Cottin's husband; it had ruined the political career of Staël's father, Louis XVI's liberal minister Jacques Necker, whose dismissal had touched off the Parisian riots of July 1789. Finally, female writers in their thirties and forties under the Empire had come of age in the closing years of the ancien régime, in a cultural environment that afforded talented women a much greater degree of social and intellectual freedom. All of this no doubt accounts for the sense of bitter frustration that so often pervades their writings. Duras may have beautifully fulfilled her role as a mediator by bringing together in her Restoration salon the brightest liberal minds of the day with the conservative allies of her legitimist husband; yet the novels she penned at the end of her life are tales of social exile and personal defeat: *Ourika* (1823) recounts the life of a Senegalese girl raised to gentility in France, whose growing awareness of the barriers of race turns into self-hatred and self-destruction; *Edouard* (1825) chronicles a love stymied by social barriers; and *Olivier* (1824) depicts a passion doomed by sexual impotence.

Duras's contemporary, the critic Charles Augustin Sainte-Beuve, wrote that she became an author "almost by accident"; of others such as Adèle de Souza or Charrière, he remarked that they wrote "as an intimate pastime." Sainte-Beuve was not so much expressing contempt for these women's achievements as reflecting the conventional view that for a society woman, the production of sentimental novels, if practiced quietly and in private, was a perfectly acceptable business. But things were much different where the visual arts were concerned. Since painting and sculpting were much more public endeavors, the efforts of women in those areas usually met with open disapproval or hostility. The early decades of the 19th century witnessed a marked deterioration of the status of women in the visual arts.

To be sure, a few outstanding female painters of the ancien régime, such as Elisabeth Vigée-Lebrun and Adélaïde Labille-Guyard, continued to thrive during the Empire (although Vigée-Lebrun, the most famous female artist of her day, worked mostly abroad and received only one commission from the imperial government). But whereas the Royal Academy of Painting had admitted four female members in the 1780s, the Revolutionary and imperial academies excluded them outright.

Though permitted to exhibit in the Salons, women had never been allowed to take art training in academy schools, nor therefore to compete for the Prix de Rome, and in the heyday of neoclassicism the production of large-scale historical and classical paintings by female artists was greeted with skepticism. The works in that style by Angélique Mongez, a pupil of Jacques Louis David, and by Constance Mayer, who had trained with Pierre-Paul Prud'hon, received mixed reviews: women, explained one critic, were not supposed to attempt such "strong, pathetic, and often terrible conceptions," and social decorum increasingly forbade all but a few from copying human figures from life. Female artists were thus denied even the basic technical skills that would have given them access to a "public" artistic language. Until the second half of the 19th century, most were consigned to the minor realms of domestic genre painting, still life, and, increasingly, the decorative arts.

The work of literature that most enduringly captures the intellectual and artistic frustrations of women in this age of social and political reaction is Germaine de Staël's *Corinne, ou l'Italie*. The full title of the novel points to its most obvious organizing principle, the analogy between gender and national culture. The fate of Italy, overrun by French imperial troops, Staël suggests, is that of creative womanhood, admired for its artistic genius, plundered, and forced into political submission. Napoleon himself, who had exiled Staël from Paris on account of her political meddling, fully recognized, and was angered by, the political overtones of a novel that systematically portrayed French characters as shallow and urbane hypocrites.

Unlike France, Italy allowed for the public, official recognition of female genius. The beautiful poet Corinne first appears to the reader—and to the brooding English nobleman Oswald Nelvil—as a stately, iconic figure, crowned upon the Roman Capitol before throngs of admirers. "Behold her, the image of our fair Italy," an onlooker remarks to Nelvil; "we would be men as

she is woman if men could, like women, create a world within their own hearts"
(p. 50). The opening chapters of *Corinne* simultaneously absorb and reject contemporary political culture (of the male republican and imperial variety) by
portraying the heroine both as a neoclassical allegory of national spirit and as a
real woman of intellect and emotion.

The tensions at work in the novel are familial as well as political. Corinne
initially has no patronymic: her given name is her only identity, for she has
broken off ties to her family in order to fashion an independent life for herself.
But as she and Oswald fall in love, the revelation of the linkage between their
families intrudes upon, and ultimately dooms, their passion. The poet turns
out to be the child of an Anglo-Italian marriage. Oswald's recently deceased
father, who had known Corinne as a young girl in Northumberland, had once
considered her as a possible bride for his son; alarmed by her unusual artistic
gifts and distressingly foreign ways, the older Nelvil had rejected her in favor
of her gentle, submissive, and thoroughly English half-sister, Lucile.

Oswald is tormented by filial guilt, a previous (and sordid) love affair having
kept him away from his father's deathbed; Corinne is culturally and emotionally
rent apart by the tension between the expressive and self-fulfilling longings of
her "Italian" self and her "English" awareness of the virtues of duty and conformity. Together, the lovers give novelistic expression to Staël's anguish over the
recent death of her adored father, with English culture standing in for the stern
moral outlook of her Swiss Protestant parents. Jacques Necker, the most important man in Germaine's life, had admired his daughter's social skills but disapproved of her literary ambitions. (Fanny Burney has left vivid descriptions of
Staël writing her major works before Necker's death "on the fly," leaning against
a mantelpiece.) In the novel, Oswald eventually marries Lucile and returns with
her to Italy, only to witness the death of the heartbroken and half-crazed
Corinne. Corinne is destroyed, as Germaine was undermined, by the posthumous workings of paternal law.

Political, social, and familial pressures thus combine, in the novel, to silence
the voice of female genius. Yet even Staël's glowing portrayal of her heroine's
achievements is fraught with ambiguities. Corinne is happiest, in her Italian
glory days, engaging in minor and ephemeral social arts as a dancer, as an
amateur actress, and, above all, as a brilliant conversationalist. When she gives
free rein to her artistic genius, at the Capitol and then again on Cape Miseno,
it is in the equally ephemeral form of poetic improvisation: her words are never,
apparently—except for the purposes of the novel—consigned to paper for posterity. Corinne's artistic achievements, whether as *salonnière* or as tormented
artistic genius, have a self-limiting quality built into them. Indeed, the specters
of self-doubt and self-censorship haunt the entire novel, most poignantly in the
chapters depicting Corinne's bleak adolescent years in provincial England: "It
is therefore not true that one can simply hold in contempt the words of
mediocre people; they make their way in spite of yourself into the recesses of
your mind, there to lie in wait for those times when superior talents have
brought you suffering" (p. 92).

626

The image that most frequently recurs in Staël's descriptions of Corinne as artist is that of the sibyl or illuminated priestess, according to Madelyn Gutwirth "one of the few licit images of female genius." On the Roman Capitol Corinne is seized by "enthusiasm," an "inspired priestess"; at Miseno she herself proclaims, foreseeing her own doom, that "the priestess through whom the god spoke was shaken by a cruel power" (p. 76). Ironically, Bonald had used exactly the same image in his conservative tract against divorce: one of the proper roles of women, he wrote, was that of conveyors of the word of God the Father: "Hence the priestesses of pagan religion, and the customary disposition of ancient peoples to attribute superhuman traits to women, in particular a fore-knowledge of the future" (*Du divorce,* p. 87). In the repressive climate of the Empire, Staël's tormented self-doubt and Bonald's complacent conservatism came together in a common portrayal of woman as one who does not speak, but is spoken through.

Bonald and Staël emerged in the early months of the Restoration as respective leaders of the ultraroyalist and liberal factions, facing each other across a widening ideological chasm. It was Bonald, however, whose political star was on the rise: elected deputy in August 1815, with the repeal of the divorce law as his main platform, he became one of the leading lights of the short-lived but stridently royalist *chambre introuvable* (undiscoverable chamber). Having satisfied their political vindictiveness through a series of decrees known as the "legal white terror," Bonald and his fellow deputies voted in the spring of 1816 to put an end to "domestic democracy" by making marriage once again indissoluble. Until the end of the century and despite a succession of different political régimes, the private sphere in France remained shaped by the embattled royalism of 1816.

See also 1787, 1788, 1814, 1949.

Bibliography: Louis de Bonald, *Du divorce considéré au XIXe siècle relativement à l'état domestique et à l'état public de la société* (Paris: Le Clère, 1839). Madelyn Gutwirth, *Madame de Staël, Novelist: The Emergence of the Artist as Woman* (Urbana: University of Illinois Press, 1978). Germaine de Staël, *Corinne, or Italy,* trans. Avriel H. Goldberger (New Brunswick, N.J.: Rutgers University Press, 1987). James Traer, *Marriage and the Family in Eighteenth-Century France* (Ithaca: Cornell University Press, 1980). Charlotte Yedham, *Women Artists in 19th-Century France and England,* 2 vols. (New York: Garland, 1984).

Sarah Maza

 1820

Alphonse de Lamartine Publishes *Méditations poétiques*

The Lady in the Lake

The slim volume of elegies published in 1819 by an actress named Marceline Desbordes-Valmore could well be considered the starting point of a new style of French lyric poetry. With its personal and emotional tones and its renewal of the elegiac tradition, *Elégies, Marie et romances* presents many of the characteristics that have come to be associated with Romanticism. But traditional wisdom has it that French Romantic poetry was born a year later to a minor aristocrat named Alphonse de Lamartine. The thirty-year-old Lamartine's anonymously published volume, *Méditations poétiques,* was hailed as a major poetic event. Eighteen-year-old Victor Hugo, for instance, exclaimed in an article published in *Le conservateur littéraire:* "Take heart, young man! you are one of those whom Plato would have showered with honors and banned from his republic! . . . Here at last are poems by a poet, poetry that *is* poetry!" (*Oeuvres complètes,* 1:61).

Despite the early fanfare, however, literary history has not been kind to Lamartine. Rimbaud, in an oft-cited letter, describes him as "strangled by outworn forms." Even the editor of the Pléiade edition of Lamartine's works calls him "terribly dated," a poet "everyone knows but no one likes" (*Oeuvres poétiques,* p. ix). The paradox of a poetics perceived as both inaugural and dated is in fact summed up in Lamartine's own 1849 prefatory self-description: "I am the first to have brought poetry down from Parnassus and to have given to what we used to call the Muse, in place of a lyre with seven conventional strings, the very fibers of man's heart, touched and moved by the numberless vibrations of soul and nature" (*Méditations,* 2:357). These vibrating fibers are of course no less conventional than the lyre's seven strings.

Lamartine's survival is essentially based on one poem, "Le lac" ("The Lake"). Yet that one poem has left an indelible mark on French culture. As a recent French literary manual puts it: "Lamartine's 'Le lac' quickly became a symbol, a key reference in France's cultural patrimony" (Biet, Brighelli, and Rispail, *XIXe siècle,* p. 39). The manual lists quotations in which characters as different as Flaubert's Emma Bovary and *Tintin*'s Captain Haddock recite lines from "Le lac." To be French is apparently to be able to raise one's eyes heavenward and intone: "O Temps! suspends ton vol . . ."

What is it about this poem that has lodged it so firmly in the canon? What kind of cultural work does it perform?

The anecdote on which the poem is based is very much a part of its celebrity. In 1816 Lamartine went to Aix-les-Bains, where he met and fell in love with Julie Charles. The lovers spent three weeks together on the shores of the Lac du Bourget. A year later they arranged to meet again at Aix, but Julie was too sick to make the trip. "Le lac" commemorates this failed rendezvous. It is a lament uttered by the lover who, finding himself alone at the appointed place, recalls the earlier presence of his beloved. Several months later, Julie Charles died.

Nothing in the poem indicates that the beloved woman is not in fact already dead. Lamartine anticipates Julie's death in order to resurrect her voice as one that exists only in memory. Through a complex system of apostrophes, the poem seems to attempt to reanimate the dead by animating the inanimate (the poet addresses the lake, the remembered voice of the woman addresses time, and, finally, the poet enjoins all of nature to speak the words "They have loved"). The desire to exchange attributes between the animate and the inanimate is perfectly natural in an elegy that wishes to bring the dead back to life. But there is something curious about the fact that, by anticipating Julie's death, Lamartine is in fact making the exchange go the other way. It is as though the poem were written not out of a desire to restore the woman to life but rather out of a desire to write her into death. The poetic name "Elvire" by which Julie has come to be known actually predates, in Lamartine's writing, his acquaintance with her, as does his desire to publish a volume of elegies. It is as though his pen were just waiting for a real death to mourn. Could it be that the death of a woman represents not the thwarting but rather the fulfillment of a desire? And could that satisfaction have something to do with the hold "Le lac" has on us?

Romantic poetry seems indeed to give a newly revitalized expressiveness to the equivalence always implicit in lyric poetry between the beloved and the dead, between beauty and death. Wallace Stevens calls death "the mother of beauty"; Mallarmé's Hérodiade says, "A kiss would kill me if beauty were not already death" (*Oeuvres,* p. 44). Petrarch's Laura dies at some point in the course of the sonnet sequence addressed to her, but in a sense, as Nancy Vickers has noted, she has been dead—that is, reduced to a projection—from the beginning. Indeed, dead women seem repeatedly to be inseparable from moments of poetic renewal (Ronsard is another example that comes to mind). But in Romantic poets such as Lamartine, Wordsworth, Gérard de Nerval, and Poe, the revitalization of poetry seems even more explicitly dependent upon the death of a woman. Wordsworth imagines himself anticipating Lucy's death; and Poe goes so far as to assert that "the death of a beautiful woman is, unquestionably, the most poetical topic in the world" ("The Philosophy of Composition," p. 1084).

This apparent necrophilia can be read as a form of poetic self-reflexiveness: woman equals beauty equals the poem itself, which is killed into art. This reading, however, neutralizes the underlying misogyny of such a topos. Another way of understanding the satisfaction inherent in the death of a woman is to see it as a sign of a lover's ambivalence toward the beloved's reality. Thomas Bergin expresses such ambivalence in the introduction to his selection of Petrarch's works: "This Laura, who is, on the poet's solemn assurance, a real woman, may have been Laurette de Noves, married to Hugues de Sade. Some readers may find the embodiment of Petrarch's tender ideal in a matron of the minor nobility, and one given to frequent pregnancies (Laurette de Sade had eleven children), not entirely appealing; fortunately, we are not obliged to accept her candidacy as proven beyond doubt" (Petrarch, *Selected Sonnets,* p. xii). Better dead and idealized than real and pregnant.

The desire for the woman's death may be a response not only to excessive embodiment but also to excessive will. An unkilled woman is always capable of escaping man's control. A main precursor to "Le lac," Rousseau's *Julie, ou la nouvelle Héloïse* (1761; *Julie, or the New Héloïse*) provides a complex illustration of the question of control and ambivalence. In one of the most famous scenes of that novel, Julie, now virtuously married, goes for a boat ride on a lake with her former lover, Saint-Preux, and struggles with the memory of their former passion. Saint-Preux, who recounts the episode in one of his letters, writes that he would find it easier to tolerate her death than her unpossessable proximity. The episode as a whole is a paroxysm of frustration. Not only is Saint-Preux a frustrated lover who cannot even mourn, but also the reader, who would have preferred a romantic ending to Rousseau's concluding dissertation on virtue, is left with an indelible memory of the unsatisfied desire for a love story by a lake. Lamartine, perhaps aided by the coincidence of names (Julie Charles's name, though never revealed in the poems, was known by many readers), acts out a piece of unfinished literary business and provides both delayed satisfaction and revenge for the frustration produced by Rousseau's treatment.

Rousseau's Julie escapes control by taking charge of her own domestic virtue, but ambivalence toward a woman's escape from a lover's control can be expressed even in contexts in which the woman has no power over her fate. In the first piece in his 1822 volume *Poèmes,* Alfred de Vigny, another Romantic poet, narrates the death of Helena, a Greek woman raped and murdered by the Turks. Her Greek lover laments her death until he learns of her rape, at which he recoils in horror. "Why can't I just savor her death?" he cries. "It would be nothing compared to *this* pain. Why didn't I lose her when she was a virgin?" (lines 921–922). Interestingly, Vigny withdrew this poem from later editions of his poems after it was harshly criticized on many points by his mother. About the lover's lament, Vigny's mother wrote, "All these thoughts demonstrate a thoroughly masculine injustice and egoism" (*Oeuvres poétiques,* p. 281).

The idea that for every dead woman there might be a strong living woman lurking in the background is not without foundation. Behind Rousseau's New Eloise is of course the original Eloise. Behind the Lady in the lake there is perhaps The Lady of the Lake, the ambiguous figure who stole the legendary Lancelot as a child and later delivered him to King Arthur's court. Even Lamartine's Julie was not a "mere" love object. She was married to the inventor of the hydrogen balloon and was the hostess of a distinguished literary and political salon. During the four months she and Lamartine were both in Paris between the two lake episodes, she introduced Lamartine to many prominent figures who would later prove useful to him. The salon had indeed long been a locus of female power in French society. The beloved woman was thus also an influence broker, although no trace of this role has accompanied her romantic legend.

That a certain ambivalence toward female power should express itself in a haste toward mourning should come as no surprise. It is even possible that readers in 1820 turned to Lamartine as a way of marginalizing Marceline Desbordes-Valmore. Desbordes-Valmore herself, however, is no less ambivalent toward the female voice. In many poems she depicts herself more as an object marked by love for death than as a desiring subject in her own right. Her voice is a voice that struggles to write its way out of the silences assigned to it by poetic tradition.

French poetry's rebirth was closely tied not only to the death of a woman but also to the political context in which it occurred. Lamartine's debut in both poetry and politics was very much a function of the return to power of the ancien régime. Lamartine, Vigny, and Hugo were indeed initially all devout proponents of aristocracy, monarchy, and Catholicism. Hugo, in the 1824 preface to his *Nouvelles odes* (*New Odes*), is at pains to correct the grounds on which his detractors have criticized the new poetry: "It is precisely, they say, because this *literary revolution* is the result of our *political revolution* that we deplore its triumph and condemn its works.—This consequence is not correct. Present-day literature can be in part the *result* of the revolution without being its *expression*. Society, as shaped by the revolution, did have its literature, which shared its hideousness and ineptitude. That literature and that society have died together and will not be reborn. Order is everywhere returning to our institutions; it is being reborn in letters as well" (*Oeuvres complètes*, 2:472). It is thus paradoxically with political restoration rather than with political revolution that the revolution in poetic language was associated.

If Romantic poetry was a poetry of restoration, what did it restore? One answer, suggested by Laurence Porter, is that it restored classical genres: the elegy, the ode, and the *poème*. Romantic philhellenism was intensified by the Greek War of Independence (1821–1832), which enabled poets such as Vigny to perform a subtle gesture of cultural synthesis: in writing about the liberation of Greece from the Turks, Vigny used the rhetoric of the Revolution (*patrie, liberté*) in the service of a restoration (of the classical Greek past).

As for Lamartine, one of the things he restored was the classical elegy. Again paradoxically, the poetics of restoration here was a poetics of loss. Elegy itself is an attempt to combine loss with restoration, to erect a monument in the place of a lack. If in man's eyes woman somehow herself represents lack ("castration"), then her death becomes the lack of a lack, or another, convoluted, kind of restoration. There may also be a certain overdetermination in an association that goes from the English Lake poets to Lamartine's lake, through the words *lake—lack—lac—lacune* (lacuna)—*lac* + *une* (lake + one). The relation between lakes and lacks continues in French poetry through Baudelaire's swan, who lacks his "lac natal," and Mallarmé's swan, who seems to be stuck in a frozen lake, haunted by "vols qui n'ont pas fui" (*vols* that have not escaped). The word *vol*, which means both "flight" and "theft," already figures prominently in Lamartine's line "O Temps! suspends ton vol . . ." (O Time! suspend thy flight/theft). From this it becomes clear that much of subsequent French poetry constitutes a theft—or a flight—from Lamartine. In some strange way, Lamartine's association with lacks, lakes, and laments had ended up feminizing *him*, so that literary history's ambivalence toward Lamartine may very well itself be an expression of ambivalence toward femininity.

See also 1735, 1835, 1859 (23 July).

Bibliography: Christian Biet, Jean-Paul Brighelli, and Jean-Luc Rispail, *XIXe siècle* (Paris: Magnard, 1985). Elizabeth Bronfen, "Die schöne Leiche," in *Tod und Weiblichkeit in der Literatur und Kunst*, ed. Renate Berger and Inge Stephan (Cologne: Böhlan

Verlag, 1987). Bronfen, "Dialog with the Dead," *New Comparison,* 6 (Autumn 1988), 101–118. William Fortescue, *Alphonse de Lamartine: A Political Biography* (New York: St. Martin's, 1983). Victor Hugo, *Oeuvres complètes,* ed. Jean Massin, vols. 1 and 2 (Paris: Club Français du Livre, 1969). Alphonse de Lamartine, *Méditations poétiques,* ed. Gustave Lanson, 2 vols. (Paris: Hachette, 1915). Lamartine, *Oeuvres poétiques complètes,* ed. Marius-François Guyard (Paris: Gallimard, 1963). Stéphane Mallarmé, "Hérodiade," in *Oeuvres complètes,* ed. Henri Mondor and Georges Jean-Aubry (Paris: Gallimard, 1945). Petrarch, *Selected Sonnets, Odes and Letters,* ed. Thomas Bergin (Arlington Heights, Ill.: AHM Publishing, 1966). Edgar Allan Poe, "The Philosophy of Composition," in *Edgar Allan Poe: Works,* vol. 14, ed. James A. Sarrison (New York: AMF Press, 1965). Laurence M. Porter, *The Renaissance of the Lyric in French Romanticism* (Lexington, Ky.: French Forum, 1978). Nancy J. Vickers, "Diana Described: Scattered Woman and Scattered Rhyme," in *Writing and Sexual Difference,* ed. Elizabeth Abel (Chicago: University of Chicago Press, 1980). Alfred de Vigny, *Oeuvres poétiques,* ed. Jacques-Philippe Saint-Gérand (Paris: Garnier-Flammarion, 1978).

Barbara Johnson

 1823

Stendhal Publishes *Racine et Shakespeare,* His Romantic Manifesto, in the *Paris Monthly Review of British and Continental Literature*

Romantic Historiography

Stendhal (Marie Henri Beyle, 1783–1842) returned to Paris in 1821 after a seven-year sojourn in Italy, where he had imbibed the Italian Romantic movement, met Byron, and collaborated with Alessandro Manzoni. He immediately hurled himself into the political and literary struggles brought on by the conservative reaction of 1820. The government, dominated by the Constitutionnels, fearful of growing liberal strength, and moved to action by the assassination of the duc de Berry, had suppressed civil rights and freedom of the press. Stendhal contemplated starting a new magazine to oppose the religious and monarchist poets of Charles Nodier's *La muse française* and the ultraconservative members of the nascent Société des Bonnes Lettres (Society of Polite Letters), devoted to the cause of legitimacy in both art and politics. This project failed, but in 1822 he found an occasion to set forth a notion of Romanticism quite at odds with those of both François-René de Chateaubriand and his younger successors Victor Hugo, Alfred de Vigny, and Alphonse de Lamartine.

Stendhal's *Racine et Shakespeare,* published as an essay in the *Paris Monthly Review* in 1823 and expanded in a second, pamphlet-form version in 1825, started as a defense of an English company of Shakespearean actors who had been attacked by a chauvinistic Parisian audience. Here he identified Romanticism with whatever was modern in any age and defined the Romanticism of his own time as whatever, in art or life, might give to living peoples "in the existing state of their habits and beliefs, the greatest possible pleasure."

To Stendhal, Shakespeare's Romanticism was manifested in his comedic sense, his willingness to violate the classical unities, and the realism of his characterizations. As for Racine, he had been, by virtue of his formalistic innovations in the theater, a romantic for his own age; but precisely because Racine's practices had become hardened into dogmas that inhibited the innovative experiments of contemporary writers, he had now become irredeemably "classical." Consequently, Racinian theater had to be transcended in a new, freer art that would present tragedies in prose, overturn the rule of the three unities in the interests of verisimilitude, deal with "national" themes, and address the concerns of moderns rather than simply imitate the ancients.

Stendhal's Romanticism thus stood opposed, not only to the classicism of the ultraconservative reaction of the early 1820s, but also to the Christian and chivalric Romanticism of Chateaubriand, on the one hand, and Benjamin Constant de Rebecque's secularist and liberal but generally world-weary Romanticism, on the other. First, it presupposed, against the model of German culture popularized by Germaine de Staël, the positive value of French culture, especially the culture of the recent, Revolutionary and Napoleonic, past. Second, it was resolutely modernist, vesting the problem of meaning in the needs and desires of living generations rather than in models handed down from the past. Third, it was aggressively liberal, even libertarian, in both its political and its aesthetic orientation. And, fourth, it was historicist in its presupposition that the present, no less than the past, must be viewed as belonging to a universal process of social change that necessitates the continual revision of culture.

These four aspects of Stendhal's notion of Romanticism foreshadow a new attitude toward time, social change, historical process, and historiography that would take shape in France during the third decade of the 19th century. The new attitude combined Romantic aesthetic principles and a generally liberal political ideology. Its effects are discernible in the work of the three major professional historians of the 1820s: Auguste Mignet (1796–1884), Adolphe Thiers (1797–1877), and François Guizot (1787–1874). Its principal exponents, however, were two amateur historians: Prosper de Barante (1782–1866) and Augustin Thierry (1795–1856). Their work marked the transition between the conservative Romantic historicism of Chateaubriand and the more radical, even revolutionary Romantic historicism of Jules Michelet. The influence of their work on literary theory and criticism is evident in Hugo's preface to his play *Cromwell* (1827), which, except for its identification of the "grotesque" with the modern sublime, reads today like a synthesis of the ideas of Chateaubriand, Stendhal, and Thierry.

In the first two decades of the 19th century, French academic historiography was moribund. It displayed little of the speculative boldness of the philosophes and even less of the conceptual rigor of its German counterpart. It had remained servile to the demands of the prevailing political régime, first Napoleonic, then Bourbonist. With the exception of Guizot and the literary historian Abel François Villemain (1790–1870), the academic historians of this period remained hopelessly mired in antiquarian concerns and banal notions of objectivity. In their practices they anticipated the directive of the reactionary Commission of

Public Instruction, which in 1820 defined as the aim of historical studies "to engrave on the memory [of students] the principal facts of history" and instructed that commentary on the facts must be limited to classical accounts provided by such stalwarts of the ancien régime as Louis-Pierre Anquetil, Gabriel Bonnot de Mably, Gabriel Daniel, and François de Mézeray.

Outside the academy, however, French historical speculation was stimulated by the progressivist, utopian-socialist visions of Claude-Henri de Saint-Simon and Charles Fourier, Chateaubriand's mystico-aesthetic retrieval of the medieval past, and Constant's agonized reflections on the destructibility of time. These conflicting ideologies of temporality inspired a deep interest among French intellectuals of the 1820s in the new discipline called "philosophy of history." During this decade, Michelet popularized the philosophy of history of the Italian philosopher Giambattista Vico, Victor Cousin that of Georg Wilhelm Hegel, and Edgar Quinet that of Johann Gottfried Herder. These philosophers of history all stressed the functions of human will and imagination in the making of human history, and they had directly confronted the problem of the relation between violence and conflict, on the one side, and historical progress, on the other, in ways less doctrinaire and abstract than had the French philosophes. They also insisted on the primacy of cultural and social, rather than political, institutions for the understanding of historical processes. They thus provided, as it were, a theoretical justification for the similar insight informing Sir Walter Scott's historical novels, which enjoyed a phenomenal success among both French intellectuals and the general reading public throughout the 1820s.

All of these influences informed the new historiography envisaged by Thierry as a necessary basis for a liberal political criticism at once more aggressive than that of his hero Constant and less doctrinaire than that of Guizot.

Thierry, a former secretary to and collaborator with Saint-Simon, turned to reflection on the problem of history in July 1820, in a series of "Lettres sur l'histoire de France" for the liberal journal *Le censeur européen* (later merged with *Le courrier français*). Here he wrote that "the nature [*essence*] of historical studies was yet to be decided." Modern historiography, he argued, required a new subject matter, a new methodology, and a new manner of representation if it was to serve the needs of modern society and its progressive—by which he meant bourgeois—public. The old historiography, written for the edification of political elites, had been content to tell the story of kings and noblemen; the new, which would be written for the political instruction of the people, would tell the story of citizens, subjects, and the masses. The old historiography, whether of the ancient narrative kind or of the more recent philosophical sort cultivated by the philosophes, had dealt in types and abstractions; the new would depict the rich textures of everyday life, the passions of living men and women, and the customs and atmospheres of specific periods of cultural life. Here the model was the novelist Scott, whom Thierry regarded as both the supreme exponent of the "imaginative" method of historical reconstruction and the practitioner of a distinctively modern mode of narrative representation.

Thierry's "Lettres" (collected in *25 lettres sur l'histoire de France,* 1827) proposed both a conception and a scholarly study of historical reality significantly different from those then taking shape in Germany under the leadership of Leopold von Ranke. In the early 1820s, German historians and philosophers were laying the groundwork for historiography's transformation from a branch of rhetoric into a putatively scientific discipline. The political function of their new historiography was to provide a genealogy, and therewith an argument for the legitimacy, of the centralized nation-states arising on the ruins of the Napoleonic empire. Its cultural function was to provide an objective, factual basis for the criticism of the various ideologies, reactionary as well as revolutionary, spawned by the Revolution and its aftermath.

In France, by contrast, interest in a new historiography was inspired by the need of the first post-Revolutionary generation to come to terms with the political and social significance of the Revolution. Unlike the other nations of Europe, France had to confront the Revolution as a domestic problem: the Revolution had originated in France, and the French had experienced its effects in ways both different from and more radical than the other peoples of Europe. The Restoration and its acompanying Reaction had sought virtually to expunge every memory of the Revolution from the public consciousness, to turn back the clock, and to deny what the liberals continued to regard as France's most heroic, if most violent, period. Liberal interest in the history of the Revolution, then, represented an interest in the present as much as a fascination with the past.

In response to this need to come to terms with the present through reconsideration of the immediate past, Thiers and Mignet each began a new, comprehensive history of the Revolution, the first volumes of which appeared in 1823 and 1824, respectively. The Romanticist aspect of Thiers's work lay in his purported effort to write a history that would "unite the poem with philosophy" while continuing to do justice to the "picturesque" and the "factual" (quoted in Johnson, "Historians," p. 294). Mignet stressed the necessity of studying "society" as a whole rather than politics exclusively and, more strikingly, insisted on the historical inevitability of the Revolution. Neither historian broke new methodological or theoretical ground. They wrote straightforward, narrative accounts of the principal political events, actors, and parties of the Revolutionary era. The success of both attested, however, to the general interest in retrieving the immediate past from the obloquy to which the conservatives had tried to consign it. Their popularity also reflected the bourgeois reading public's general desire for a historiography that might be as entertaining as Scott's historical novels.

This desire was satisfied to a large extent by the publication of what are generally recognized today as the two classics of French Romantic historiography produced during the 1820s: Barante's *Histoire des ducs de Bourgogne de la maison de Valois* (1824–1826; *History of the Dukes of Burgundy of the House of Valois*) and Thierry's *Histoire de la conquête de l'Angleterre par les Normands, de ses causes, et de ses suites jusqu'à nos jours, en Angleterre, en Ecosse, en Irlande et sur le Continent* (1825; *History of the Conquest of England by the Normans, Its Causes, and*

635

Its Effects Down to the Present Day, in England, Scotland, Ireland, and on the Continent). These two works are commonly represented as prime examples of the "narrative school" of historiography, a designation more than justified in the case of Barante and Thierry. Their use of novelistic techniques of representation was a result of a conscious and theoretically defended choice of storytelling over explicit commentary and formal argument as the best means of bringing the past to life and even of explaining what had really happened in history.

Barante strove for a perfectly neutral style, for the absolute suppression of the historian's own voice, in order to allow the medieval chroniclers to speak for themselves and to represent the spectacle of the chivalric past, in all its vivacity and variety, as they had witnessed it. He insisted that historians should study the past with an attitude of "love and esteem" for the events, characters, institutions, and conflicts retailed in the chronicles of times past. He took as his own motto Quintilian's instruction "to narrate rather than to demonstrate," allowing the meaning of events to emerge naturally from the narrative. "When it is *sincere*," he wrote in the preface to his *Histoire des ducs de Bourgogne*, "history imparts its lessons loudly and clearly." The historian was to serve as a conduit or medium by which the past would be able to represent itself to the present in a succession of tableaux not unlike the brilliant stained-glass windows of a Gothic cathedral, a Flemish tapestry, a Rubens canvas—or, it might be added, the kind of historical dioramas that Louis Daguerre had begun to produce the year before Barante's masterpiece appeared in print.

Moreover, Barante presented in his concept of local color a theoretical defense of his technique for representing the past. He had borrowed the notion of "local color" from the vocabulary of art criticism and used it in his drama criticism for *Le publiciste* as early as 1806. It had to do with the discernment of the telling "detail" of a scene, personality, or event in which its unique character or inner essence was manifested in a concentrated manner. Chateaubriand had picked up the term and the notion in 1811, hailing it as the very condition of historical truth and accurate representation. In his historical writings, Barante used the term to indicate those "authentic turns of phrase" by which the reader would be forced to "envisage a historical milieu rather than a contemporary one." The right detail would, he thought, transport the reader into an immediate, virtually visual contact with past reality. So intensely did he strive for authenticity that his work often became little more than a pastiche of passages quoted from the medieval chroniclers.

Barante was later criticized for his failure to work in the manuscript sources, to evaluate the printed documents he had used, and to provide a scholarly apparatus. But Barante felt that cumbersome notes and appendixes would detract from the flow of the narrative and distract the reader's attention from the unity of the successive tableaux, of which the various events, scenes, persons, and practices related in his story were all integral parts. His aim was not to dissect Burgundian culture and society or even to explain it, but to bring it to life, to resurrect it; and in this aim he provided a model for the young Michelet, who in the 1830s would try to do the same thing for the whole past of France.

Thierry's *Histoire de la conquête de l'Angleterre* was at once just as Romanticist as Barante's work, but also more scholarly, more openly political in purpose, and theoretically more controversial. The Romantic aspect consisted in Thierry's conviction that the imagination, rather than reason, provided the only certain access to an understanding of the past: "For the imagination," he wrote, "there is no past . . . and the future is of the present." His explicit political aim was to expose the "lies" of every official history, every history written from the standpoint or in the interest of monarchs, the upper classes, the conquerors of history. He enjoyed the advantage, he said, of having been born a commoner and of having experienced the events of an age of revolution. Later on, in his *Considérations sur l'histoire de France* (1840; *Reflections on the History of France*), he argued that political passion and experience in political affairs provided insights into history that neither a "disinterested scholarship" nor "a pure zealous love of truth" could ever yield. In his *Histoire de la conquête de l'Angleterre,* he told the story of the Saxon resistance to the Norman invaders and celebrated the "outlaws" of society and the "rebels" against foreign oppressors, in order to provide models of domestic (as opposed to imperialistic) heroism for the oppressed peoples of his own time.

Thierry's first choice for his proposed new historiography reflected the current general fascination of French intellectuals with the history of England. In his handling of the topic, however, he was concerned to explode the myths of the unity of English history and of the continuity of English constitutional development. He told how the original, "natural" unities of the Saxon and Celtic peoples had been disrupted by the Norman invasion and the populace severed into contending linguistic, political, social, and cultural factions, indenturing the British Isles to centuries of bloody conflict, rebellions, revolutions, civil wars, and unstable settlements. Instead of providing an alternative model to contentious and rebellious France, the vaunted English model of government by negotiation and compromise was shown to have been a product of conflicts as violent as anything produced by the French Revolution. Indeed, Thierry treated the history of England as a synecdoche of the history of Europe. Every nation of Europe had experienced the same struggle by an autochthonous "race" to preserve its "natural" unity against the incursions of foreign invaders. The typical institutions of these nations, therefore, had to be viewed as products of resistance to oppression from without and of more or less just compromises between social classes originally comprising different racial, linguistic, and cultural entities. It was this assimilation of racial to social class differences and the subordination of political to social considerations for the understanding of history that led Marx to hail Thierry as "the father of the doctrine of the class struggle in French historiography" (quoted in Gossman, "Augustin Thierry," p. 25).

But Thierry made no claim to be writing scientific history. Like Barante, he worked only with published sources, did not examine archival materials, and wagered everything on the effect of verisimilitude deriving from the use of Scott's narrative techniques. Also like Barante, he strove for the effect of local color, even to the extent of insisting on the restoration of the archaic spelling of Saxon, Celtic, and Old French proper names. It was not only anachronistic but untruthful, he held, to confuse "the Franks" with "the French."

The real protagonist of every national history, Thierry maintained, was not heroic individuals, great men, or political institutions, but "the people" in its entirety. The oppression, conflict, and violence that marked the history of every nation was a result of a fall of some given "people" out of its original unity into a condition of social schism. Progress in the history of any nation was, therefore, to be measured by the extent to which it succeeded in reunifying itself.

After the Revolution of 1830, of which Thierry was a devoted publicist, he came to view the Third Estate as the principal force and beneficiary of historical progress. In his *Essai sur l'histoire de la formation et des progrès du Tiers Etat* (1853; *Essay on the History of the Formation and Progress of the Third Estate*), he defined the middle class as the very incarnation of "reason" and "the spirit of industry" (in contrast to "the spirit of conquest") in human history. It alone could lead the way to an enlightened, humane, and peaceful future.

Thierry's work was eminently successful among the middle-class reading public, and during the July Monarchy (1830–1848) his kind of historiography provided a dominant model for French historical consciousness, even earning the praise of the aged Ranke some sixty years later. It was soon eclipsed, however, by the work of Michelet, Louis Blanc, and Lamartine, all of whom published in 1848 histories of the French Revolution that surpassed Thierry not only in the depth of their scholarship but also in the fervidness of their political commitment and the brilliance of their narrative techniques. With the appearance of these works and the shock to French society and culture effected by the revolution of 1848–1851, French Romanticism, liberalism, and historiography alike entered a new period in their development.

See also 1677, 1942.

Bibliography: Stephen Bann, *The Clothing of Clio: A Study of the Representation of History in Nineteenth-Century Britain and France* (Cambridge: Cambridge University Press, 1984). Lionel Gossman, "Augustin Thierry and Liberal Historiography," *History and Theory: Studies in the Philosophy of History,* 15 (1976). Douglas Johnson, "Historians," in *The French Romantics,* ed. D. G. Charlton (Cambridge: Cambridge University Press, 1984), pp. 274–307. Stendhal, *Racine et Shakespeare,* ed. Henri Martineau (Paris: Le Divan, 1928).

Hayden White

✍ 1827, February

Charles Augustin Sainte-Beuve Misses the Deadline for the Submission of His Essay on 16th-Century French Literature to the Académie Française

The Invention of the Renaissance

"The time of imitations is over: we must create or translate," Emile Deschamps proclaimed in the preface to his poetic collection, *Etudes françaises et étrangères*

(1828; *French and Foreign Studies,* p. 48), one of the many Romantic manifestos to appear in the years 1827–1829. Rather than being defined by a specific doctrine, Romanticism might in fact be defined by its refusal of canons: imitation is forbidden. René Girard rightly sees the cult of spontaneity and originality, and the fear of imitation, as the heart of what he calls Romantic. Oddly, the Romantics linked this canonless aesthetic to promotion of the Pléiade, the school that made poetic emulation, mimetic rivalry with the classical canon, the very center of its inspiration. Strange patronage: one of Joachim du Bellay's watchwords in *La défense et illustration de la langue française* (1549; *The Defense and Enrichment of the French Language*) had been the exact inverse of Deschamps's: Don't translate from Latin or Greek; imitate in French.

But the 19th-century infatuation with the Pléiade resulted not from theoretical but from historical interest. The Romantic rejection of the classical canon accompanied a revision of literary history. Following the example of Germaine de Staël in *De la littérature considérée dans ses rapports avec les institutions sociales* (1800; *The Influence of Literature upon Society*), it replaced the dogmatic view of a timeless beauty with a sociohistorical approach that contextualized art. The French classics were not so much rejected as reframed, seen as the expression not of a universally valid aesthetic doctrine but of their century, the century of Louis XIV. If no other century equaled it in perfection, it was because no other chose perfection as its ideal. The reign of autocratic uniformity in art is over. Under this pluralist banner, the interesting supplants the beautiful. "Beauty has only one type; ugliness has thousands," Hugo declared in his *Préface de Cromwell* (1827 [*Preface to Cromwell*], p. 55).

The young writers who opposed classicism turned, then, to what classicism had itself opposed. A kind of ancient literary testament suddenly reemerged, under the sign of "not-yet": François de Malherbe (1555–1628) had not yet codified prosody. This version of the 16th century had extremely flexible boundaries: in his *Tableau historique et critique de la littérature française et du théâtre français au XVIe siècle* (1828; *A Historical and Critical Panorama of French Literature and Theater during the 16th Century*), Charles Augustin Sainte-Beuve extended it all the way to Honoré d'Urfé's *L'Astrée* (1607–1627), to Malherbe, and even to the quarrel of *Le Cid* (1637). And Théophile Gautier, in *Les grotesques* (1844; *Grotesque Masters*), after quoting a 1622 poem by Théophile de Viau, sighed: "Admirable 16th century!" explaining: "Théophile and the society around belong to the 16th rather than to the 17th" (p. 131). For the Romantics, the 16th century extended up to the point where Malherbe and Nicolas Boileau had not yet condemned it, and the Renaissance emerged as the primal scene that the censorship of Louis XIV's century had repressed. Castration is often evoked: Charles Nodier, for example, in his 1831 essay on Cyrano de Bergerac, compares Boileau to a eunuch; and Hugo, in the 1826 preface to *Odes et ballades,* describes the gardens at Versailles as the triumph of the shearer, submitted to the same treatment as the trees of Verrières at the beginning of Stendhal's *Le rouge et le noir* (1830; *The Red and the Black*).

But this revival, tied to the Romantic fashionableness of historiography and of Walter Scott, fed more on the turbulence of that age than on its literary productions. The Romantics' Renaissance is the century of the Wars of Religion (1562–1598), of the League (1589–1591), and of the Fronde (1648–1652), a period in which the proud anarchism of the nobility had not yet been totally curbed by monarchical centralization. Alfred de Vigny borrowed from the chronicles of the time the subject matter of his novel *Cinq-Mars, ou une conjuration sous Louis XIII* (1826; *Cinq-Mars, or a Conspiracy under Louis XIII*), which recounts an episode from the nobility's resistance to Richelieu. Its heroes, two young noblemen, Cinq-Mars and de Thou, were executed by order of the cardinal against whom they had plotted. In their punishment Vigny sees the death sentence of the monarchy, which, in suppressing the nobility, had itself prepared the revolutionary turmoil that would carry it away two centuries later, in 1789. Prosper Mérimée, in *1572, Chronique du règne de Charles IX* (1829; *1572, A Chronicle from the Reign of Charles IX*), does not profess as outspoken a philosophy of history, but, at a time when liberals worried about the growing influence of religious orders under the Restoration (1815–1830), the year of the St. Bartholomew's Day Massacre had an almost symbolic value. This fashion for the 16th century was not limited to novels. In 1829 the first Romantic drama, Alexandre Dumas's *Henri III et sa cour* (*Henri III and His Court*), also borrowed its subject matter from the period. And the events of almost all the plays written by Hugo during the riotous years of Romanticism stem from the same preclassical source: in addition to *Cromwell* (1827), which was not staged, *Marion de Lorme* (1829) is set in 1638 under Louis XIII, *Hernani* (1830) in 1519, *Le roi s'amuse* (1832; *The King's Diversion*) in the 1520s, *Lucrèce Borgia* (1833) "in 15 . . ," *Marie Tudor* (1833) in 1553. And Alfred de Musset's *Lorenzaccio* (1834) is set in Florence, under the Medicis.

This fashion also echoes in Balzac's novel *Illusions perdues* (1843; *Lost Illusions*), in which Lucien de Rubempré is writing a novel in the manner of Walter Scott, "L'archer de Charles IX" (The archer of Charles IX). But Balzac, a legitimist, viewed the 16th century differently from the increasingly liberal Romantics. In "Les deux rêves" (1830; "The Two Dreams"), the earliest of the stories collected in *Sur Catherine de Médicis* (1842), he admiringly shows Catherine accepting—aside from all religious conviction, and by the coldest of political realisms—the responsibility for the St. Bartholomew's Day Massacre. She understands that power cannot be shared. For the sake of the unity of the realm she did everything "to lower the high and mighty" (p. 131). Balzac did not think much of *Cinq-Mars*.

But for no Romantic author was the myth of the Renaissance more central than for Stendhal. Mathilde de La Mole, the heroine of *Le rouge et le noir*, hates the vulgarity of her own time. But she partakes of her period through her very flight from it into chronicles of the civil wars of the past by Théodore Agrippa d'Aubigné, Pierre de Brantôme, Pierre de l'Etoile. "The Wars of the League are the heroic age of France," she says. "I love that period" (p. 381). And she wears mourning at her parents' ball, because it is the anniversary of the death of her ancestor Boniface de La Mole, a precursor of Cinq-Mars, beheaded 250 years earlier by order of Catherine de Médicis for having conspired against Charles IX.

Of all the variants of the Romantic aesthetic, Stendhal's correspond most closely to Girard's definition. His passionate cult of spontaneity and originality and the ensuing condemnation of any kind of mediation can be encapsulated in the form of a double-bind: one must not be "as one must be" (*il faut ne pas être "comme il faut"*). This imperative provides the logical basis for the decanonization of the classics in *Racine et Shakespeare* (1823, 1825): for Stendhal, Racine was the exemplar of the artist *comme il faut,* the courtier who incarnated an epoch in which, under the name of restraint, conformity was sanctified. But Stendhal had not waited for the welling up of Romanticism to take Racine to task. In *Rome, Naples et Florence en 1817* (1817), he had already dismissed him in passing as "a soul lit up by the stale monarchy" (*Voyages,* p. 51); and in his autobiography, *Vie de Henry Brulard* (wr. 1835–36, pub. 1890; *The Life of Henry Brulard*), he recalls that as a child he considered him a "stale hypocrite," dead of despair because Louis XIV did not look at him (*Oeuvres intimes,* 2:780). The Renaissance predated the gospel of cant; imitation was neither an aesthetic imperative nor a social duty. Passions then were kept in check neither through fear of ridicule nor through respect for decorum nor through material self-interest. In 1835 Stendhal acquired manuscripts of chronicles from the Italian Renaissance. *La chartreuse de Parme* (1839; *The Charterhouse of Parma*) transposed one of them to modern Italy. The others (including "Vittoria Accoramboni," 1837; "Les Cenci," 1838; "La duchesse de Palliano," 1838; "L'abbesse de Castro," 1839) made up the posthumous collection *Chroniques italiennes* (1855; *Italian Chronicles*). Each of these bloody tales has a brief quasi-anthropological introductory warning that prepares the reader for this lost paradise of violence. Obviously it was not their literary quality but their documentary force that interested Stendhal in the naïve brutality of these stories.

The Romantic revival of 16th-century authors focused on poets. In August 1826 the Académie Française had proposed for its 1828 prize for eloquence the subject "the progress of French language and literature from the beginning of the 16th century to 1610." Charles Augustin Sainte-Beuve, the young critic of *Le globe,* still a medical student, decided to compete for the award. But in February 1827, immersed in the discovery of the authors of the period, he was invited by Hugo to the latter's reading of the *Préface de Cromwell* at the house of Emile Deschamps. One outcome was that he missed the deadline for the Academic competition. Another was that his *Tableau* acquired a range that it had not had at the outset. Literary history became manifesto. Sainte-Beuve, who discovered Pierre de Ronsard at the same time he did Hugo, chose du Bellay's position: the *Tableau* became the *Défense et illustration* of the Cénacle (Inner Circle), the group of Romantic writers assaulting the classical canon. In his own poems (*Vie, poésies et pensées de Joseph Delorme,* 1829; *Life, Poetry, and Thoughts of Joseph Delorme*), Sainte-Beuve, leaving to Hugo the sonorous Ronsardian ode, resuscitated the sonnet, the more personal form through which du Bellay, the Pléiade's theoretician, had achieved poetic fame. In the *Tableau,* scholarly research and nostalgia for works of the past are often a pretext for promotion of the modern school: "I have lost no opportunity of connecting these studies of the 16th century to the literary and poetic questions stirring in our own" (p. 3). Revisionism in literary history begins here: in claiming 16th-century ancestry, Romanticism, instead of defining itself in the negative terms of rejecting the canon, restored a historical continuity that had been disrupted by the negativity of classicism. This new periodization made *le grand siècle* appear as a simple episode, a sort of intermission, or a parenthesis opened within the national tradition. "This royal festival of Louis XIV, celebrated at Versailles between the League and the revolution of 1789, looks to us," Sainte-Beuve declared, "like those short and capricious intermezzos that can scarcely be connected to the action of the play" (p. 281).

The Romantics, however, did not simply take things up at the point where they had been left when classicism intervened. In an 1829 article on Hugo, Sainte-Beuve contrasted his and Ronsard's uses of the ode: Hugo, he wrote, "is the one who truly created it in France. Ronsard, with this form, has only made studies that, though worthy of esteem, are unsuccessful" (*Oeuvres*, 1:297). The objective was not to return to Ronsard but to carry out promises he had not kept. The same year, Hugo wrote in the preface to *Les orientales* (*The Orientals*): "Other nations say: Homer, Dante, Shakespeare. We say: Boileau" (*Oeuvres complètes*, 3:496). Indeed, their rehabilitation of the Pléiade never went as far as canonizing Ronsard. Sainte-Beuve's *Tableau* is not a *Racine* (or *Boileau*) *et Ronsard* comparable to Stendhal's *Racine et Shakespeare*. The Romantics rummaged through the 16th century in vain; they never found a French Shakespeare. Nothing to imitate, only to translate. The other national "Renaissances," Sainte-Beuve said, had their Dante, their Shakespeare, their Cervantes. "In France, unfortunately, there is nothing parallel to this . . . the more I think about it the more convinced I am that a man of genius appearing at the time of Ronsard would have changed the whole picture" (*Tableau*, p. 280). Genius, Valéry would say, is nothing but a long patience. France had the genius to wait. And the Shakespeare France had lacked finally appeared. Hugo said: Boileau. Sainte-Beuve corrects him: "The poetry of the 16th century was a kind of impetuous, avant-garde skirmishing . . . The honor of recommencing and pursuing this knowing work of construction was reserved for Victor Hugo" (pp. 165, 283).

Relations between Hugo and Sainte-Beuve deteriorated. So did Sainte-Beuve's image of 16th-century poetry. In 1842 he reedited his *Tableau*, presenting what, in 1828, was an introduction to Romantic poetry as "an introduction to the history of our classical poetry." The Pléiade was no longer an early Romanticism but "our first, aborted, classical poetry" (p. 1). But Romanticism too was downgraded: instead of achieving what the 16th century had promised, it had merely repeated a century that was full of nothing but promises; it rehearsed the nonachievement of the Renaissance. "In this sense, French poetry of the nineteenth century and that of the sixteenth have one more thing in common as their fate," Sainte-Beuve wrote in the new preface. "Hope dominates it; there are more buds there than harvests" (p. 2). Literary history reconnected with an evolutionary linearity. There was no longer a parenthetical break nor a resurgence: the 16th century contained the origins, the "rough draft," of the 17th.

The same change of heart occurred in Théophile Gautier. Having read Boileau's *L'art poétique* (1674; *The Art of Poetry*) in 1834–35 merely to collect the names of the outlawed, he had in a series of vivid portraits rediscovered the victims of the "envious and unproductive" school of those "grammatical versifiers" Malherbe and Boileau (*Les grotesques*, p. 145): François Villon, Théophile de Viau, Antoine de Saint-Amant, Cyrano de Bergerac, Paul Scarron. Ten years later he collected these in *Les grotesques*. But no longer with the same enthusiasm. "We are in no way proposing the poor victims of Boileau as models" (p. 453).

"There are literary centuries more perfect than the sixteenth; but there are none more energetic and powerful," wrote Jean-Jacques Ampère, the Romantic historian of literature, in his lectures on the Renaissance. "A prodigious time when all the powers of human nature coexisted pell-mell in a fecund chaos: a time of enthusiasm and of irony, of poetry and of science, of art and of politics, of religious fanaticism and of philosophical élan!" (*Mélanges*, 1:389). Gautier speaks of it in the same terms: "Fecund century, over-rich, luxuriant, where life and motion ran over . . . theological battles, riots, duels, kidnappings, dangerous adventures, uninhibited gorging in taverns . . . what an incredible mélange, what inconceivable chaos" (*Grotesques*, pp. 131–132). And Sainte-Beuve describes its "audacious and feckless stylistic comportment, without rules or scruples, marching off randomly according to vagaries of its thought" (*Tableau*, p. 283). Whereas classicism had constituted an aesthetic of restraint, the Renaissance was a century of no reserve—a century of cornucopia, of unregulated productivity, a century before censorship. And it was a century without reserve in another sense as well: it left nothing exemplary, nothing to imitate, no Shakespeare. Unlike other national literatures, "We lack, we French, these immense sacred lakes as reservoirs for the days of regeneration" (ibid.). But this century without a colossus was itself colossal. In a certain way it was emblematized by the chaotic polymorphism of Hugo's figure of Cromwell, "the protean man," at one and the same time soldier, statesman, theologian, scholar, bad poet, visionary, buffoon, father, and husband (*Préface*, p. 78). The unity of the subject is precisely the multiplicity of the man. The Renaissance is a Romantic drama.

See also 1512, 1550, 1627, 1674, 1799, 1823, 1827 (December).

Bibliography: Jean-Jacques Ampère, *Mélanges d'histoire littéraire et de littérature*, vol. 1 (1867; reprint, New York: Johnson, 1970). Honoré de Balzac, *Sur Catherine de Médicis*, ed. Nicole Cazauran, vol. 11 of *La comédie humaine*, ed. Pierre-Georges Castex (Paris: Gallimard, 1980). Emile Deschamps, *Préface des Etudes françaises et étrangères*, ed. Henri Girard (Paris: Presses Françaises, 1923). Théophile Gautier, *Les grotesques*, ed. Cecilia Rizza (Paris: Nizet, 1985). René Girard, *Mensonge romantique et vérité romanesque* (Paris:

Grasset, 1961); translated by Yvonne Freccero as *Deceit, Desire, and the Novel* (Baltimore: Johns Hopkins Press, 1965). Victor Hugo, *Les orientales,* ed. Jean Meschonnic, in *Oeuvres complètes,* ed. Jean Massin, vol. 3 (Paris: Club Français du Livre, 1967). Hugo, *Préface de Cromwell,* ed. Claude Duchet, ibid. François Rigolot, "Sainte-Beuve et le mythe du XVIe siècle," *L'esprit créateur,* 14 (1974), 35–43. Charles Augustin Sainte-Beuve, *Oeuvres,* ed. Maxime Leroy, vol. 1 (Paris: Gallimard, 1956). Sainte-Beuve, *Tableau historique et critique de la poésie française et du théâtre français au XVIe siècle* (Paris: Charpentier, 1869). Stendhal, *The Red and the Black,* trans. C. K. Scott Moncrieff (New York: Modern Library, 1953). Stendhal, *Rome, Naples et Florence en 1817,* in *Voyages en Italie,* ed. Victor del Litto (Paris: Gallimard, 1973). Stendhal, *Vie de Henry Brulard,* in *Oeuvres intimes,* ed. Victor del Litto, vol. 2 (Paris: Gallimard, 1982).

François Rigolot

 **1827, December**

In the Preface to His Unperformable *Cromwell,* Victor Hugo Delivers the Aesthetic Charter of Romanticism

Drama

The extraordinary amount of space in the press devoted to literary or artistic quarrels during the reign of Charles X (1824–1830) stems from their conflation with the settling of political accounts, the defense of established positions, and conflicts between generations. Genuine aesthetic problems were obscured by delusive alliances between political conservatives and young Romantics. At the same time institutions, whether left over from the Empire (1804–1815) or born with the Restoration in 1815, systematically condemned anything that swerved, however little, from the neoclassical tradition.

Ever since the quarrel of *Le Cid* in 1637, the theater in France had been a particularly sensitive arena for conflicts of ideas. An incomplete reading of Aristotle's *Poetics* had led to the formulation of rigid and virtually unchanging doctrine. The supremacy of the theater, particularly of tragedy, and the fixed nature of the rules governing it explain both why young writers staked their fortunes on it and why they encountered severe resistance. When the theater prospers, as it did under the Restoration, a great deal of money can be made from it. Accordingly, in some cases it is difficult to assess what part of the most fiercely conservative reaction reflected true aesthetic conviction, and what can be explained by the desire to preserve established privileges.

Theatergoing was very popular among Parisians. Each dramatic genre had its designated producers, its own theaters, and its preferred actors. Melodramas, vaudevilles, and classical comedies and tragedies were interspersed with hybrid tragedies inspired by the new doctrine of Romanticism that to modern readers seem scarcely distinguishable from the traditional productions. In 1820 theatergoers at the Comédie-Française were introduced to Friedrich Schiller's *Maria Stuart* in a timid adaptation by Pierre-Antoine Lebrun. They saw productions of Shakespeare in English in 1822 and 1827. So young writers, thanks also to new and more reliable translations, had the opportunity to reflect on more flexible dramatic forms that could end the stagnation of the theatrical repertoire. If the translation, in 1827, of Goethe's *Faust* (by a young poet who would become a great one, Gérard de Nerval) did not play a role in the movement toward emancipation, the main reason lies in a strong current of xenophobia that helped the theory of genres maintain its grip and limit innovations, especially when they came from abroad. Those nostalgic for the Empire—liberals and Bonapartists, who together viewed the treaties of 1815 as an unbearable humiliation for France—as well as royalists compelled to align themselves with an exaggerated nationalism, systematically opposed everything that might be considered foreign to the national genius. Only with Alexandre Dumas's *Henri III et sa cour* (1829; *Henri III and His Court*) would a French Romantic drama finally be produced at the Comédie-Française itself.

Victor Hugo's play *Cromwell* has never been staged. But starting in 1827, the year it was published, it was commented on and criticized in important periodicals such as *Le journal des débats, Le globe,* and *La gazette de France.* The play as well as the preface were the target of vigorous reactions.

The *Préface de Cromwell* is a powerful manifesto. To avoid talking in terms of aesthetic norms, which would have misrepresented his purpose, Hugo presents his point of view as a simple observation, based upon an analysis that boldly divides all of human history into three large periods. Like the two earlier periods, the epoch he calls modern has a characteristic literary form: drama. In this Germanizing overview, the term *modern* means the entire Christian era, which permits Hugo to melt in the same crucible medieval art and the Renaissance, Dante and Shakespeare, the cathedrals and Michelangelo. Such a classification allows him to marginalize the century of Louis XIV, too strongly oriented to the classical values of the pre-Christian world—characterized by the epic—so that its theories of the beautiful, and the rules they entail, become insignificant. Hugo needs only to show that the dictatorship of the beautiful as conceived by the neoclassical school is merely an epiphenomenon, and that the modern aesthetic implies an artistic duality that conforms to basic Christian dualism. Drama, according to his definition, is the form capable of rendering this opposition between spirit and matter, between the beautiful and the ugly. The modern writer, who seeks to encompass the totality of the real, must first of all refuse to set up a hierarchy of subjects as a function of a priori aesthetic criteria; this premise leads Hugo to legitimate everything that the classical era has excluded. In particular the monstrous, which coexists with the sublime in reality, is granted the right to literary and artistic existence that classical rules previously denied it. The shadowy double that the irrational element, evil, discovers deep within divine creation now has a name: the grotesque. Opposed to ideal beauty, the *grotesque* yet provides that beauty—through the working of a law of complementarity—with a greater radiance and a new purity. It should therefore be put at the heart of drama, since drama is at the heart of modernity.

Whereas Stendhal in the 1825 *Racine et Shakespeare* preached the use of prose in the modern drama in order to free it from the ponderous conventions of the alexandrine, Hugo remains committed to using verse in theater. Realism as he conceives it is a poetic one—a concentration rather than a mirror of the real. One cannot, in his view, escape from the "routine" by giving the theater over to the common. Verse must be preferred to prose for its plasticity and its power to amplify the entire spectrum of emotions. The historical overview that allowed Hugo to reject normative aesthetics now gives way to highly technical reflections on the alexandrine. Hugo wants to replace the constraints of metrics—filled as they are with paralyzing prescriptions but even more with unjustified prohibitions that have kept verse on a middle path equally distant from the simplicity and freshness of daily experience and from the lyricism of high poetry—with a flexible form capable of covering the entire expressive field. Dramatic verse should be able to communicate both life's trivialities, as in Molière, and its sublimity, as in Corneille.

Hugo himself presents *Cromwell* as unperformable. "That is why the author, despairing of its ever being staged, freely and obediently abandoned himself to compositional fantasies . . . which, even while they distanced his drama from the stage, at least permitted it to be nearly exact from a historical point of view" (*Oeuvres,* 3:81). The fact that its length made it unplayable allowed equally foes to justify their criticisms and its supporters to forgive its weaknesses. Critics focused generally on the license taken with versification or on the reprehensible alliance of the noble alexandrine with the vulgarity of prosaic moments. The tone was set by *Le journal des débats,* part of a politically moderate literary rear guard. But Hugo and his avant-garde friends agreed to debate on these terms: Charles Augustin Sainte-Beuve, for example, stressed in a January 1829 article that Hugo had provided in *Cromwell* the paradigm for the "genuine style and genuine verse of modern drama" (*Oeuvres,* 1:301).

Hugo also invented a transparent dramaturgy, perhaps because his theater sought a much greater public than that of classical tragedy. Hugo's semiotics of costume and color, his use of simple dramatic procedures (asides, a group of madmen very much like a chorus or narrator) or more complex ones (the breaking up of what would be one secondary character in the classical theater into a multiplicity of anonymous voices, the reduction of anti-Cromwell Puritan conspirators to a set of colorful names)—all helped to make the play a landmark in French theatrical history. The second volume of Alfred de Musset's *Théâtre dans un fauteuil, Lorenzaccio* (1834), which until the end of the 19th century remained, in conformity with its title, unperformed "armchair drama," and Paul Claudel's admirable *Le soulier de satin* (1924; *The Satin Slipper*), which waited until 1987 for a complete production, are from many points of view the legacies of this tradition in which the grotesque reigns.

Hugo's emphasis on the specificity of the modern era, his understanding of realism as refraction and condensation (instead of mere reflection), his claims for the poet's right to poetic liberty, and his theory of equality between words and things in the creator's eyes (a theory with a promising future)—all of these elements had specific consequences for poetics in its most general sense. It would soon be clear that the very word *drama* no longer applied to the stage proper but suggested a tonality and a dynamism that could as easily be novel-istic and even lyric. If drama was the form specific to the modern era, it was because the situation of *homo Christianus,* opposed to the pastoral or epic sim-plicity of the primitive epochs, is that of a dramatic duality.

The first phase of Romanticism in France had focused essentially on the-matics. The poetry of ruins, the lyricism of intimacy and cruelty, and the return to "national antiquities," especially to the literature and architecture of the Middle Ages, had expanded the domain of literature beyond that provided by the classical tradition. The emphasis had also shifted from the universal to the particular. The discovery of the self in its singularity, of the other in its differ-ence, the poetic exploration of space and time, all came to be taken for granted. To this thematic renewal and this emphasis on forms of subjectivity, Hugo himself, in his first collections of poetry, *Odes et poésies diverses* (1822; *Odes and Various Poems*)—augmented as *Nouvelles odes* (1824; *New Odes*) and *Odes et ballades* (1826)—had contributed the motif of the poet-magus preaching in the desert, a motif he would later link to a cosmic visionary poetry of which he became the uncontested master. He makes the same type of move when, in the *Préface de Cromwell,* he associates modern subjectivity and melancholy. But, progressively, it became clear that Romanticism involved more than a mere question of con-tent. Even the timid ideologues of *Le globe* came to understand that the oppo-sition between classic and modern involved more than a consideration of subject matter; they began to discuss "rêverie" or "imagination" and the rediscovery of melancholia. But even this was not enough. Hugo and, after him, Sainte-Beuve understood that modern poetry involved a transformation of "poetic diction."

Paradoxically, Pierre Leroux, the most philosophical and doctrinaire of con-temporary critics and at the time director of *Le globe,* best understood what was at stake in the Romantic revolution. In his article "Littérature: Du style poé-tique" (8 April 1829; "Literature: On Poetic Style"), devoted mainly to Hugo's newly published verse collection *Les orientales,* Leroux, completely at odds with most of his colleagues, came to Hugo's defense, explaining that he had trans-formed all of poetry by inventing the "symbolic style." Thanks to this revolu-tion, French, which up to then had been too precise, could now *evoke* what previously it had only been able to *say.* The systematic recourse to the symbol (which Leroux took to mean all metaphorical tropes) leads to the spiritualization of materiality, to the fusion of moral idea and physical image, and to an inter-nalization of the exterior world. As Hugo had already proclaimed in his preface to *Odes et poésies diverses,* "Poetry is everything that is intimate in everything that is."

French poetry would not have become what it did if Hugo had not, one fine day in 1828, invented a bold visual metaphor that quickly became a cliché: "tout ruisselants de pierreries" ("all streaming with precious stones") ("Laz-zara," line 30, in *Les orientales*). Symbolism's connection with the visual was fraught with consequences. Sainte-Beuve, though he himself had reproached Hugo for an imagination "caught by the eyes" (*Oeuvres,* 1:203), came to defend in his own *Vie, poésies et pensées de Joseph Delorme* (1829; *Life, Poetry, and Thoughts of Joseph Delorme*) the picturesque and the use of the right concrete word, both of which had been dazzlingly mastered in *Les orientales*. Hugo's pursuit of local color enriched the lexicon and limited the periphrastic excesses of the neoclassical poets. *Les orientales* profoundly influenced the youngest and most daring poets of the time, and throughout the century all those seeking to promote "art for art's sake" referred to it.

Symbolism's emphasis on the visual had a spiritual corollary. Sainte-Beuve had discussed it at length in October 1825 in relation to the English Lake poets: "All that is visible . . . offers no longer obscure symbols or fantastic emblems, but rather true revelations" (*Oeuvres*, 1 : 135). He had also mined this spiritual lode in his *Joseph Delorme*, which quickly became the "intimist" antidote to the visual orgies of *Les orientales*. In an 1861 article praising as "prophetic" Hugo's "La pente de la rêverie" ("The Inclination to Rêverie") in *Les feuilles d'automne* (1831; *Autumn Leaves*), Charles Baudelaire described Hugo as "the man who is the most gifted, the most manifestly chosen, to express what I would call *the mystery of life*" ("Victor Hugo," *Oeuvres*, p. 704) and laid out in detail the doctrine of universal analogy or correspondences, which Baudelaire elaborated in one of the most celebrated sonnets in *Les fleurs du mal* (1857; *The Flowers of Evil*). "Everything," he wrote in this article, "form, movement, number, color, perfume, in the *spiritual* as in the *natural*, is meaningful, reciprocal, converse, *corresponding*" (p. 705). Both Hugo's *Les contemplations* (1856; *Contemplations*) and Baudelaire's *Les fleurs du mal*, twin but divergent masterpieces, essentially flow out of this prophetic aesthetic outlined by Leroux.

As Hugo practiced it, the symbolic style was not limited to the use of metaphor. The preface to *Odes et ballades* expresses its real ambition: to base a genuine poetic naturalism on an appropriate rhetoric. There Hugo opposes the artifice of a French garden, which he disparages for its "regularity," to the real, profound "order" of the tropical forest. But he was not satisfied with reinventing extreme versions of what may simply be the eternal baroque; he also created, through the rhythms of his sentences and his use of cumulative enumeration, a rhetoric of excess. This fundamentally anti-Aristotelian rhetoric, which can accommodate all possible accidents of thought, attempted to achieve a perfect equation between form and content. This versatility is no doubt the most enduring and personal mark of the style that, above and beyond the peripeties of Romanticism, made of Hugo an artist beyond any norm.

Hugo has been reproached from many political perspectives for describing *Les orientales* as "a useless book of pure poetry." What Théophile Gautier, the spokesman of *l'art pour l'art* (art for art's sake), found enchanting in its uselessness naturally annoys those who seek signs of political commitment in literature. Again it was an editor of *Le globe*, Charles de Rémusat, who in his review of *Cromwell* (26 January and 2 February 1828) explained that for Hugo political awareness resulted from the process of writing itself. The writing of *Cromwell*, the drama of the English Puritan revolution, is what produced in Hugo a shift toward the causes espoused by those then called liberals. Soon (in the preface to his play *Hernani*, 1830) Hugo himself would affirm, rightly, what the confusion of the *Cromwell* debate had obscured: Romanticism is nothing else, all considered, than *"liberalism* in literature" (*Hernani*, in *Oeuvres*, 3:922). We are on the eve of the Revolution of 1830.

See also 1827 (February), 1830, 1834, 1835, 1885 (June).

Bibliography: Charles Baudelaire, *Oeuvres complètes*, ed. Y. G. Le Dantec and Claude Pichois (Paris: Gallimard, 1961). Jean Gaudon, *Victor Hugo et le théâtre. Stratégie et dramaturgie* (Paris: Suger, 1985). Victor Hugo, *Cromwell*, ed. Claude Duchet, in *Oeuvres complètes*, ed. Jean Massin, vol. 3 (Paris: Club Français du Livre, 1967). Hugo, *Hernani*, ed. Jean Massin, in ibid. Hugo, *Les orientales*, ed. Henri Meschonnic, in ibid. Charles Augustin Sainte-Beuve, *Oeuvres*, ed. Maxime Leroy, vol. 1 (Paris: Gallimard, 1958).

Jean Gaudon

✑ *1830, 27–29 July*
The July Revolution Terminates the Bourbon Monarchy and Gives the Throne to Louis-Philippe, the "Citizen King"

An Oedipal Crisis

In just three days—later called *les trois glorieuses* (the glorious three)—the revolution of July 1830 brought an end to the Bourbon monarchy restored after the fall of Napoleon and released the pent-up force of a younger generation that throughout the Restoration had felt itself repressed and alienated from the sources of power. Journalists, significantly, were in the vanguard of the uprising. Although the causes of the revolution were legion and complex, related both to a crisis of political legitimacy (whether the ministers governing France were responsible to the elected deputies, or merely to the king) and to deep social and economic problems, attempts by the government to impose tighter censorship laws were among the immediate catalysts of the insurrection. Journalists, refusing to submit to *la censure préalable*—censorship that could kill articles before they appeared—marched to occupy the printing presses and defend them against government forces. The July Revolution did not accomplish what many had hoped it would: it brought about a "bourgeois monarchy" instead of creating a republic, and Louis-Philippe, scion of the Orléans branch of the royal family (which had long been in conflict with the Bourbon branch) assumed the title "King of the French," instituting what its supporters perceived to be a constitutional monarchy on the English model. The true showdown was put off for another eighteen years, to erupt in more radical (and bloody) form in 1848. But in the symbolic order of literature, 1830 is the year of emblematic showdowns between partisans of liberty and those of order, between the aspiration of a younger generation and the resistance of the old.

The Restoration was a gerontocracy. The kings themselves—first Louis XVIII, then Charles X, both brothers of Louis XVI, who had been guillotined in 1793—were aged men, and so were most of their ministers. The Restoration marked a concerted effort to turn back the clock of history, to regain ancien régime standard time. Prominent both socially and governmentally were émigré nobles who had sought refuge outside France during the Revolutionary struggles, and who returned to their imposing houses in the Faubourg Saint-Germain without a true understanding of the forces unleashed by the Revolution. As Balzac retrospectively summed it up, the Restoration was "cold, petty, and without poetry" (*La duchesse de Langeais* [1834], in *La comédie humaine,* 5 : 332). Balzac, a monarchist who had no use for democracy, was astute in his analysis of the failure of the Restoration to recreate a viable monarchical system: those who held power were afflicted by a profound egotism, they mistook narrow interests of caste for the national interest, and in particular they failed to make contact with the young intellectuals who should have been regarded as the glory of the nation. A monarchy that wanted to put down secure roots should have sought out those men of talent, in the arts, in journalism, in commerce—whatever their class origin—and taken them to its bosom, thus coopting those who would become leaders of the revolutionary bourgeoisie in 1830. Instead, they were condemned to what Balzac called a moral "helotism"; they became "viveurs" (rakes) dissipating their talents in debauchery and irresponsible opposition, best represented, in Balzac's eyes, by a journalism that he saw as increasingly satiric, opportunistic, motivated by a desire to please the public rather than by statesmanlike views (*Illusions perdues,* 1843; *Lost Illusions*).

Balzac's diagnosis of the condition of intellectual and artistic youth during the Restoration finds confirmation from many sources. One of the most famous, Alfred de Musset's *La confession d'un enfant du siècle* (1836; *Confession of a Child of the Century*), portrays his generation in post-Napoleonic France as a careworn youth seated among ruins. When they spoke of glory, of ambition, of hope, love, power, the response they heard was always the same: "Make yourselves priests!" Religion was promoted during the Restoration as a force of social order, and the youthful hero of Stendhal's *Le rouge et le noir* (1830; *The Red and the Black*) understood that this was one of the few careers open to him. Even for those who did not take this advice, black—the black of the modern frock coat, which replaced the more varied garb of the ancien régime—became a symbol of an epoch without hope. When asked in what it believed, youth could answer only, "In nothing." This was worse than disenchantment; it was a state of hopelessness.

It is curious that the forces of artistic renewal that would gain a well-publicized triumph in 1830—shortly before the political revolution broke out—were originally identified with a conservative, Catholic, monarchist politics and with a revival of "medievalism" in art and literature. Most typical is the case of Victor Hugo, who as a very young man founded, along with his brothers, the review *Le conservateur littéraire,* then became an animating force of *La muse française,* a journal that united conservative politics and Romantic doctrine. Political liberals, on the other hand, tended to reach back to the 18th-century philosophes for their literary models: the skepticism and mordant wit of Voltaire offered the proper stance of opposition to a régime that wanted to suppress this very kind of thinking and writing, which had led to the Revolution it was trying to efface. The alliance between liberalism in politics and Romanticism in arts and letters was worked out only gradually, and with many misunderstandings, during the 1820s. Stendhal, who had learned his Romanticism from English and Italian sources, was a key figure in declaring the solidarity of the new in both politics and art, and his *Racine et Shakespeare* (1823, 1825) argued that literary tastes were evolutionary, not fixed for all time. How, he asked, can you expect a public to be interested in the neoclassical tragedies of Racine, and in their tightly controlled versification, when this public has lived, in the Revolution and the Napoleonic wars, the breathtaking changes of modern history? Give us something new, stripped of the old rule of the "three unities," written in prose, and addressed to subjects of real interest. The cause of liberal Romanticism would find expression in a new periodical, *Le globe*. Victor Hugo himself evolved to the point where he declared, in the preface to his play *Hernani* (1830), that Romanticism was simply "*liberalism* in literature" (*Oeuvres*, 3:922).

The première of *Hernani*, on 25 February 1830, marked the public triumph of Romantic doctrine: it planted the Romantic banner in the bastion of institutional artistic conservatism, the Comédie-Française. So great was the prestige of the theater, as a public, sociable genre and institution, one that had been a center of life for good society for two centuries, that a victory in its most illustrious house carried great symbolic value. And *Hernani* was carefully prepared as a symbol. Contemporary memoirs give us a lively picture of Hugo's difficulties in convincing actors and actresses trained in the classical repertoire to speak the new rhythms of his verse and to utter a vocabulary that often broke with the decorum of high tragedy. As for the première itself, all the Romantic youth of Paris was there, notoriously emblematized by Théophile Gautier in his flaming red waistcoat—as were, of course, many of those opposed for both artistic and political reasons to the Romantic movement and its leaders. From the opening curtain, individual lines were both applauded and hissed. Innovations that today seem to us extremely modest—an alexandrine that, instead of being end-stopped, runs on into the following line, a king who casually asks "What time is it?"—threw the house into turmoil. And the turmoil went on night after night, as the audience played out its own psychodrama. The "Battle of *Hernani*," as it came to be known, was won by the Romantics in the sense that their play held on, continued to attract an audience, and gained extraordinary publicity. But in another sense the triumph was short-lived, since Hugo and other Romantic dramatists (notably Alexandre Dumas) increasingly produced their plays in various Boulevard theaters, where they found actors trained in popular melodrama who were more sympathetic to the grandiose rhetoric and action of Romantic drama.

In its action and theme, especially in what might be described as its latent drama, *Hernani* is a curious play to represent the triumph of the younger generation. In fact it appears to represent just the opposite. Hernani's struggle to achieve union with his beloved Doña Sol comes close to success only at the price

651

of abandoning his pledge to avenge his father, who was executed by the father of Don Carlos, king of Spain. The latter is elected Holy Roman Emperor Charles V in act 4. By the end of that act, Don Carlos has given up his claim to Doña Sol's hand in order to assume the lonely eminence of empire, has pardoned Hernani, and has authorized his marriage. But the generation of the fathers has not finished haunting Hernani. Following the wedding feast, in act 5, as he prepares to take Doña Sol to their nuptial chamber, the far-off sound of a hunting horn is closely followed by the entrance of Don Ruy Gomez, the elderly protector of Doña Sol, who also is in love with her. Back in act 3, Don Ruy Gomez saved Hernani's life, hiding him in a secret cell behind the portrait of one of his illustrious ancestors, in his hereditary castle, when Don Carlos was in hot pursuit of the outlawed Hernani. In return for this supreme act of hospitality, Hernani has promised his life to Don Ruy—to be delivered whenever Don Ruy chooses to summon him with the hunting horn. And it is just on the threshold of Hernani's happiness, the resolution of his conflicts in the love of Doña Sol and the restoration of his title as Don Juan d'Aragon, that Don Ruy chooses to exact payment of Hernani's pledge. He brings with him a vial of poison, which he insists that Hernani drink. And such are the laws of Castilian honor (the play is in fact subtitled *L'honneur castillan*) that Hernani must obey. Doña Sol does not disagree. She indeed snatches the vial of poison, drinks half herself, then gives Hernani the other half for his suicide. Their union comes only in the embrace of death, in a final operatic duet.

Summarized in this bald fashion, the play sounds silly enough. It is, like so many of Hugo's plays, well on the way toward becoming grand opera—and Giuseppe Verdi (1813–1901) would in fact use it as the source of his opera *Ernani* (1846), as he would more famously use Hugo's *Le roi s'amuse* (1832; *The King's Diversion*) as the source of *Rigoletto* (1851). What makes *Hernani* a compelling drama despite its contrived plot and grandiose posturings is its youthful poetic spirit; its spectacular use of settings, costumes, light, and symbolic confrontations; and especially its soaring, generous verse, which brought to the French stage a new lyricism and a new lyric definition of character. And the darker, latent side of the plot has a certain sinister force. When Don Ruy returns to claim Hernani's life, he is characterized as "the old man who laughs in the shadows." He appears to be a representative of the paternal law that Hernani has violated in accepting reconciliation with Don Carlos, and in accepting his bride from his father's enemy's hand. The return of Don Ruy figures a return of the repressed, as Hernani appears to recognize by his hysterical reaction to the reappearance of this shadowy representative of a past he thought was behind him. In accepting the validity of his old promise to Don Ruy, in accepting the renunciation of love, happiness, and life in order to make good on his pledge to the old man, Hernani seems symbolically to recognize an unsatisfied guilt toward the generation of the fathers. One is tempted to read Hernani's need to immolate himself to the law of the fathers as an obscure acknowledgment by Hugo that his play is itself an oedipal transgression that calls for atonement. While on the one hand he has overthrown the patriarchs, all those who for years attempted to block the younger generation's attainment of maturity and power, on the other hand he has symbolically enacted the victory of the patriarchs, their continuing power to exact mortal punishment for transgression of the paternal law. *Hernani* is a kind of psychic compromise-formation.

It is in fact striking how many of the literary works of this historical moment record a bitter conflict of generations and the eventual denial of gratification to the sons by the ultimate victory of the fathers. Consider Balzac's *La peau de chagrin* (1831; *The Fatal Skin*), his first great popular success as a serious novelist. Its hero, Raphaël de Valentin, is on the verge of suicide, having gambled away his last sou, when he discovers, in an antiques shop, a magic skin that will grant one's every wish—but at the price of shrinking the skin, thus shortening one's life. The magic skin represents the union of *vouloir* and *pouvoir*, desire and power: the dream of youth. Raphaël's life under his pact with the magic skin is at first an orgy of pleasures, a domination of the world in a frenzy of desire. But as the skin contracts—as in the postorgasmal state—he is forced more and more to live beyond desire, as a prematurely old man, a conservative in the deepest sense since all his attention is concentrated on maintaining life, which necessitates renouncing all desire. Opposed to the union of desire and power in the magic skin is the domain of *savoir*, knowledge, represented by the antiques dealer himself, who has lived to the age of 102 by renouncing all desire, living chastely, finding his pleasures only in the observation of others. Toward the end of the novel Raphaël attempts to join the world of knowledge, to find a rural retreat cut off from the world where he can live under "the conservative law of nature," to become something like a lichen on a rock, living as little as possible just so long as he is living. But it is too late, and the reappearance of his mistress leads to a final paroxysm of impotent desire in which he dies. As is the case with a great many of Balzac's young heroes, youth consumes itself in a flamboyant expenditure of desire. To prolong life means to renounce desiring, to refuse the expenditure of self that desiring entails—the underlying metaphor is explicitly sexual: orgasm is seen as loss—while the renunciation of desire merely brings a kind of death-in-life, best represented in Balzac's work by the ubiquitous usurer Gobseck, who is described as being of "the neuter gender" and who lives to a ripe age through the vicarious experience gained by lending money for others to spend.

No doubt the fullest and most significant representation of the forces in conflict in 1830 can be found in Stendhal's novel *Le rouge et le noir*, originally subtitled "Chronique de 1830." It is a curious chronicle of that year, in that the July Revolution is never directly represented, although everything the novel is about appears to look toward and call for that revolution. Stendhal had in fact conceived the novel and written at least half of it before the *trois glorieuses*—he describes watching the insurrection from the windows of his apartment while correcting proof for book 1 of the novel. He completed the novel without alluding to the change of régime. His silence regarding this major historical event creates some incoherence in the representation of time in the

653

novel: when, in its last chapters, Mme. de Rênal thinks of going to Charles X to beg pardon for Julien Sorel, by the novel's own implied chronology Charles X had been in exile for months. In a curious manner, Julien Sorel's death on the guillotine at the end of the novel figures the Revolution that is never represented. For Julien—like his hero Napoleon—is a "usurper," someone who has claimed a place not rightfully his, not his by inheritance. As he describes himself at the trial that will condemn him to death, he is "a peasant who has revolted against the lowness of his condition" (*Le rouge et le noir,* p. 476), and his execution, while explicitly retribution for his shooting of Mme. de Rênal, stands symbolically as the defensive reaction of the threatened ruling classes to the success of an energetic parvenu. (We might note in passing that Stendhal always reproached the victors of 1830 for *not* using the guillotine: he thought the ministers of Charles X should have been executed.) One can in fact read in Julien's execution the class reaction of the new masters of France—the commercial bourgeoisie—to the proletarian fringe that wanted to take the revolution further, to establish a republic and an egalitarian society. The figure of Julien Sorel looks beyond 1830 to 1848, when, in the uprising known as the June Days, the proletariat would be pitted against the bourgeoisie and crushed by it. In the context of 1830, it is interesting that Julien's career of successful usurpation brings—in the manner of Hernani's success—the revenge of the parental generation. It is explicitly and literally Julien's father, whom he has always detested, who inherits from his son.

Monsieur de Rênal, mayor of the town of Verrières who hires Julien as tutor to his children, reflecting on the fact that these children seem to prefer Julien to their real father, explains at one point: "Everything in this century tends to throw opprobrium on *legitimate* authority. Poor France!" (*Le rouge et le noir,* p. 164). The comment explicitly links political issues of legitimacy and authority with paternity, itself inextricably bound up with the political problem of legitimacy and authority. The entire plot and structure of the novel turn on the key political questions, to whom does France belong, and who shall inherit it? Julien, abandoning his early dream of a career in the army because he understands that the Napoleonic military epic is now a specter to be exorcised, chooses an ecclesiastical career. This becomes an exercise in hypocrisy, dissimulation, role-playing, talents that Julien studies to master. Napoleonic conquest leaves the battlefield to return to its classic ancien régime context, the bedroom: Julien seduces first the wife of his master, Mme. de Rênal, and then, when he has moved on to Paris, the daughter of his new master, Mathilde de la Mole. And in the course of his social ascent he not only repudiates his father, Sorel the carpenter, but also gives his allegiance to a series of father-figures—Abbé Chélan of Verrières, the severe Jansenist director of the seminary Abbé Pirard, and the supremely aristocratic Marquis de la Mole. Each figure represents some ideal of paternity. But as the series implies, Julien never finds stable allegiance to any one father; he always slips out from under the authority of each. The novel in fact sets up a movement of slippage on the issue of paternity and authority that gradually assumes the paradoxical form of Julien's legitimation by illegitimacy.

The hypothesis that he might be the illegitimate son of an aristocrat (a hypothesis that the novel suggests but never validates) is called upon to legitimate his transgressions, to authenticate the place that he has gained for himself in society. As the bastard son of an aristocrat, Julien would no longer be a dangerous and unclassifiable "monster"—a term that he applies to himself—but rather like a foundling from an 18th-century comic novel who by the end of the story discovers his true parents and finds that his instinctual love of grandeur is in fact motivated, and authorized, by his bloodline. But such is not to be Julien's story. At the moment of apparent total success—when he has even received a commission of lieutenant in a regiment of hussars, allowing him to cast off his clerical black for his original dream of the army—the whole of Julien's carefully plotted career comes crashing down, in actions that never seem to be adequately motivated.

Critics have failed to find convincing reasons for Julien's excessive and self-destructive acts—the shooting of Mme. de Rênal, his self-identification as a peasant in revolt at his trial—and no doubt one should recognize that the ending of *Le rouge et le noir* constitutes something of a scandal that can never be, and should not be, covered up by recourse to ingenious psychological explanations. Even the paternalistic authority of the narrator, it appears, is put into question. Although the legacy of Julien Sorel is ironically resolved on the most literal level—when the father becomes inheritor of the son—the larger political question, "Who shall inherit France?" remains unresolved. In the violent death of Julien Sorel, one reads the determination of the masters of France to put down and keep in their place the transgressive, monstrous careers of ambitious plebeians. But the force of Julien's "energy"—a favorite word of Stendhal's—cannot be contained by mere execution. Revolution is sooner or later inevitable.

There are many other examples of generational conflict in the literature of 1830 and its immediate aftermath: novels by Balzac and Stendhal, plays by Alexandre Dumas and Alfred de Vigny—whose *Chatterton* (1835), the tragic drama of a young poet driven to death by an uncomprehending society, provided a powerful emblem of the creative forces of youth in doomed struggle with a utilitarian and middle-aged society—all signal a moment of cultural and political crisis. The Romantic generation won its battle, gained its place in the sun, and changed French literature forever. But the works in which it claimed and recorded this victory seem to suggest that a high price has been exacted—that revolutionary victories do not last, and that the deep forces of social normalization and utilitarianism will always reassert their dominance. King Louis-Philippe's minister, François Guizot, would utter the watchword of the new bourgeois monarchy: "Enrichissez-vous," he said to the French: "Get rich." The heyday of the commercial and industrial bourgeoisie was at hand. The generous heroic idealism of the Romantics of the generation of 1830 could never overcome that kind of imperative.

Bibliography: Honoré de Balzac, *La comédie humaine,* ed. Pierre-Georges Castex, 12 vols. (Paris: Gallimard, 1976–1981). Victor Brombert, *Stendhal: Fiction and the Themes of Freedom* (New York: Random House, 1969). Peter Brooks, "Balzac: Representation and

Signification," in *The Melodramatic Imagination* (1976; reprint, New York: Columbia University Press, 1985). Brooks, "The Novel and the Guillotine, or Fathers and Sons in *Le rouge et le noir*," in *Reading for the Plot* (1984; reprint, New York: Vintage, 1985). Jean Gaudon, *Victor Hugo dramaturge* (Paris: L'Arche, 1955). Victor Hugo, *Hernani*, vol. 3 of *Oeuvres complètes*, ed. Jean Massin (Paris: Club Français du Livre, 1967). Stendhal, *Le rouge et le noir* (Paris: Garnier-Flammarion, 1964).

Peter Brooks

✐ 1833

George Sand Publishes *Lélia;* Charles Augustin Sainte-Beuve Describes Its Lack of Realism as an Aesthetic Monstrosity

The Scandal of Realism

On 29 September 1833, Charles Augustin Sainte-Beuve, the most astute and influential French critic of the century, published in *Le national* a review of George Sand's *Lélia*, which had appeared earlier that year. In his opening paragraph Sainte-Beuve situates Sand's novel, not in the expected contexts of the dominant literary movements of romanticism and realism, but in the unfamiliar context of a "singular moral and literary movement," the rise of women's writing in France (*Portraits contemporains*, 1 : 494). As Sainte-Beuve is quick to note, women, especially a privileged minority in the educated upper class, had always written in a variety of genres; but not until the end of the Restoration, with its "good form" and "moral veneer," and the advent of Saint-Simonism, with its utopian ideals of social harmony and sexual equality, did women begin writing en masse. Indeed, the July Monarchy (1830–1848) produced as many women writers as the entire 18th century, and for the first time in France their numbers included members of the working classes (Elisa Mercoeur, Louise Crombach) as well as of the bourgeoisie (Marceline Desbordes-Valmore, Louise Colet) and the upper classes (Delphine de Girardin, who wrote as Vicomte Charles de Launay; Marie d'Agoult, who wrote as Daniel Stern). Sainte-Beuve rightly sees the emergence of a significant movement of women's writing as participating in and informed by a broader movement of liberation and democratization sweeping France in the early 1830s: "Today, then, everywhere, women are writing: each has her secret, her painful novel in support of the plea for emancipation, and each one betrays it" (*Portraits*, p. 96). Just as authorship is no longer limited to aristocratic women, the constraints of decorum no longer prohibit women from voicing their deepest aspirations to greater freedom and social justice. Thus, according to Sainte-Beuve, women's writing in post-Restoration France was distinguished by its explicit thematization of what we may call feminist concerns; it was not merely writing *by* women, but also writing *about* women's estate. For all its striking originality, viewed in this context, Sand's *Lélia* appears as the most remarkable product of a large-scale literary movement in which Sand inscribed herself from the outset of her independent writing career. *Lélia* can thus be read as the third volume in Sand's feminist triptych, following *Indiana* (1832) and *Valentine* (1832).

Yet Sand's feminism can no longer be taken for granted. In recent years feminist critics and historians have pointed out both her complicities with the régime that recognized her exceptional status and her failure to convert her individual revolt against the inequities of patriarchy into a collective movement of mass political action. She dissociated herself from the Saint-Simonians; in 1848 she refused to stand for parlement as a representative woman, and throughout her life, as a true daughter of Rousseau, she affirmed the difference between the sexes (see in particular *Lettres à Marcie,* 1837; *Letters to Marcie*). Even if we grant that linguistic acts are as political as acts in the public arena, the question remains: in what sense can Sand's fiction, and notably her early fiction, be classified as feminist?

Indiana, Valentine, and *Lélia* focus on the institution of marriage as the keystone in the system of exchange of women between men that organizes patriarchal societies. *Indiana,* the first novel Sand signed with her male pseudonym and the one that brought her instant fame, is about a beautiful young woman from the West Indies who is married to a brutal older man. Though passionately drawn to the egotistical seducer Raymon de la Ramière, the pure, indeed virginal, Indiana—the unconsummated marriage (*mariage blanc*) is a recurrent theme in the antimarriage literature of the period—does not commit adultery. Following her husband's death, in a famously implausible ending, Indiana survives a suicide pact with her devoted cousin, Ralph. Bound together in a chaste companionate relationship, Indiana and Ralph abandon culture for the natural wilderness of Ile Bourbon, where they lead a life dedicated to helping other victims of the social order.

Class differences complicate the scenario of marital misery in *Valentine*. Valentine, an aristocratic young heiress, is married off to a debt-ridden diplomat who, having secured his rights over Valentine's property, goes off to Russia, leaving his intact bride to struggle against her fascination with the plebeian but byronically attractive Benedict. The death of both partners follows almost immediately upon the long-deferred consummation of their passion.

Although—or rather, because—it breaks with many of the novelistic conventions that determine the female protagonist's fate in *Indiana* and *Valentine,* *Lélia* brings to its logical conclusion the critique of marriage set forth in the two preceding novels. Echoing an earlier portrayal of woman as artistic genius in Germaine de Staël's *Corinne* (1807), Lélia is an accomplished and admired woman of independent means whose destiny is not strictly ruled by the constraining narrative syntax of bourgeois realism. To the extent that this bleak howl of despair has a plot, *Lélia* recounts the heroine's final and failed relationship with the idealistic young poet, Stenio. Driven to debauchery by Lélia's refusal to consummate their relationship, Stenio commits suicide. Strangled by the mad priest, Magnus, Lélia is buried on the other side of the lake from Stenio.

Not surprisingly, given Sand's highly charged erotic thematics, the scandal raised by *Lélia* was first and foremost of a sexual nature. As Lélia confesses to her courtesan sister, Pulchérie, in the central section of the novel, she suffers from a disabling sexual dysfunction: frigidity. Readers found this confession scandalous because they tended to assume that all women's writing was highly autobiographical. Their reaction thus obscured the radical criticism of patriarchy in which this confession is embedded. Indeed, as Sand makes clear in the most overtly political of the three prefaces she wrote to *Indiana* (that of 1842), what is at stake in her feminist fiction is an interlocking system of laws that govern women's existence under patriarchy: "I wrote *Indiana* with a feeling, not deliberately reasoned out, but a deep and genuine feeling that the laws which still govern women's existence in wedlock, in the family and in society are barbarous." Lélia's inability to experience that supreme form of sexual bliss known as *jouissance* is not accountable merely to individual pathology or romantic *mal du siècle* (Romantic spleen)—impotence is a prominent symptom of the discontents of Romantic civilization, as in the case of Octave, the suicidal protagonist of Stendhal's *Armance* (1827). Rather, it testifies to the effect of manmade laws on female desire.

Because male subjectivity and its representations in the 19th century (and beyond) are so deeply grounded in the denial of woman as subject of desire, despite her feminism Sand is, as Leslie Rabine has shown, unable to represent a fully desiring female subject: hence the proliferation of female doubles in Sand's fiction. Just as Indiana's purity is purchased at the cost of her milk sister Noun's doomed sensuality—Noun, seduced, impregnated, and abandoned by Raymon, drowns herself—Lélia's frigidity is offset by Pulchérie's orgasmic pleasure: "We did not resemble each other," says Lélia to Pulchérie. "Wiser and happier than I, you lived only to enjoy. More ambitious and less submissive to God, I lived only to desire" (p. 101). But, at the same time that Lélia's insatiable metaphysical desire symptomatizes the devasting dualism of patriarchal discourse, her frigidity functions, as Eileen Boyd Sivert has argued, as the site of resistance to male hegemony. For what Lélia's conversation with Pulchérie makes clear is that under patriarchy the options available to women are exceedingly limited. "Become a nun," says Pulchérie. When Lélia demurs, Pulchérie responds: "Very well, since you cannot become a nun, become a courtesan" (p. 135).

Sand's feminist trilogy, and notably *Lélia,* attests to a profound crisis in the gender-power relations in post-Restoration France. The law that binds Sand's female protagonist is not some great, universal law of human desire; it is the Napoleonic code (proclaimed in 1804), which deprived women of their rights and fixed them in their (inferior) sexual roles, according them the same legal status as minors and madmen. In 19th-century France one did not have to be a feminist, or even a woman, to grasp the full horror of the condition of women under bourgeois patriarchy. And Balzac was neither: in contrast to Stendhal, his feminist contemporary, Balzac espoused a dismal, traditionally Christian view of woman as the long-suffering embodiment of devotion and resignation. Yet because, as Marxist critics have long known, Balzac's exposure of the ideological fault lines of his society constantly belies his explicit conservative politics, *Eugénie Grandet* (1833) is in its own way as scathing a condemnation of the institution of marriage and the symbolic system it serves to perpetuate as is *Lélia*. Like Indiana and Valentine, Eugénie is not free to marry the man she loves; she must submit to the laws of exchange enforced by her capitalistic father. When, toward the end of the novel, her father dies, leaving her an immensely wealthy heiress, and when she learns that her long-lost love is to marry someone else, Eugénie has a conversation with her local priest that uncannily echoes Lélia's dialogue with Pulchérie: "If," says the priest to Eugénie, "you wish to work out your salvation, there are only two courses open to you to follow, either you must leave the world or you must live in it and obey its laws, you must follow either your earthly destiny or your heavenly vocation" (p. 237). The binary opposition between world and convent, courtesan and nun, commands woman's destiny under the Napoleonic régime, forcing both Lélia and Eugénie to devise complex strategies to escape. Both, in fact, choose not to choose: Lélia oscillates between ascetic retreat and immersion in the world; Eugénie opts for the world while refusing to submit to its laws. Thus she agrees to marry her faithful suitor, Bonfons, but only on condition that their marriage remain unconsummated. "Such is the story of this woman, who is in the world, but not of the world," concludes the narrator of *Eugénie Grandet* (p. 248).

The laying bare of the workings of the symbolic order, the indictment of the oppression of women through marriage, is a major theme of 19th-century French realist fiction. It is explicit, for example, in two such diversely paradigmatic works as Gustave Flaubert's *Madame Bovary* (1857) and Edmond Duranty's *Le malheur d'Henriette Gérard* (1860; *The Misfortune of Henriette Gérard*). But there is a crucial difference. Realism was a representational mode wedded to the marriage plot and the binding of female energy. And whereas the male-authored texts never call into question either the system within which marriage functions or realism, Sand's feminist analysis of patriarchy in *Lélia* rejects realism, the patriarchal mode par excellence (at least in France; George Eliot is a notable if problematic exception to this rule). Sand's fundamental aesthetic choice to reject realism signified her refusal to reproduce and hence legitimate a social order inimical to the disfranchised—chief among them, women.

What makes Sand's analysis feminist is that it is not confined to the institution of marriage; it comprehends the imbrication of power and desire. Sexual desire in Sand's early novels does not deploy itself in a timeless universe, according to eternal laws. History and its contingencies shape desire. Sand demonstrates both in the *Lélia* of 1833 and even more in her overtly feminist rewritten version of 1839 that the war between the sexes is culturally constructed. As long as woman is to man as slave is to master, there can be no sexual relations between them: "What relationship, other than that of power, can henceforth exist between him who has the right to exact and him who has no right to refuse? . . . There is no true association in the love between the sexes, because the woman's role is that of the child and the hour of emancipation never rings for her" (*Lélia,* 1839, pp. 385–386). Marriage is targeted in Sand's early fiction because it ratifies the unequal division of power. Viewed in this perspective, as long as men hold all power, until women achieve emancipation, there is no relationship between the sexes that is not on some level a form of prostitution. Not surprisingly, given this analysis, the Lélia of 1839 becomes the abbess of the convent of the Calmadules.

In *Indiana* and *Valentine* the feminine inflections of the marriage plot are restricted to violations of plausibility and explorations of interstices in the grid of patriarchal law: the wild valley of Bernica (*Indiana*), the utopian space of the pavilion (*Valentine*). In *Lélia,* however, Sand appropriates the currently popular genre of fictionalized metaphysics (exemplified in Honoré de Balzac, Etienne Pivert de Senancour, and Charles Nodier) to break entirely with the restrictive conventions of realism. Thus, revealingly for Sainte-Beuve, the scandal of *Lélia* lies not in its feminist thematics but in its aesthetic choices: "Since the initial given of *Lélia* is totally real and has its analogues in the society in which we live, I could not help regretting, despite the prestigious brilliance of this new form, that the author did not confine himself within the limits of the realistic (*vraisemblable*) novel" (p. 501). Sainte-Beuve faults Sand for not having respected the law requiring that a realistic content be matched by a realistic form. The result of this violation is an aesthetic monstrosity, with characters frozen somewhere between verisimilitude and symbolism: "In entering into the state of ideal representation or symbol, the characters or the scenes, whose initial given was, so to speak, grounded, could not avoid in the indeterminate moment of their metamorphosis taking on a mixed and fantastic character that does not satisfy" (p. 502). In her preface to the *Lélia* of 1839, Sand readily acknowledges the novel's hybrid nature: "*Lélia* was and remains in my mind a poetic essay, a fantastical novel where the characters are neither completely real . . . nor completely allegorical" (p. 350).

Sand's deliberate failure in *Lélia* to respect the boundaries that separate allegory from realism, boundaries that cannot accommodate the radical novelty of *Lélia,* resulted in an unclassifiable text that called into question the very taxonomic categories on which literary history depends. The price of Sand's subversion of the canonical hierarchy has been high: whereas *Eugénie Grandet,* written within the dominant tradition, the *roman intime,* was from the outset recognized as a masterpiece of psychological realism and incorporated into the canon, *Lélia*'s status has remained marginal. Allowed to go out of print for long periods, rarely required reading within the precincts of the academy, *Lélia,* undoubtedly one of the major works of women's writing in France, continues to be a scandal repressed by the largely male critical establishment, which Sainte-Beuve, the father of French literary criticism, inaugurated almost single-handedly. *Lélia* will continue to scandalize and hence to be repressed until the aesthetic values so ably naturalized by Sainte-Beuve begin to be questioned and dismantled.

Bibliography: Honoré de Balzac, *Eugénie Grandet,* trans. Marion Ayton Crawford (Harmondsworth: Penguin, 1955). Nancy K. Miller, "Writing from the Pavilion: George

Sand and the Novel of Female Pastoral," in *Subject to Change: Reading Feminist Writing* (New York: Columbia University Press, 1988), pp. 204–228. Leslie Rabine, "George Sand and the Myth of Femininity," *Women and Literature*, 4 (Fall 1976), 2–17. Charles Augustin Sainte-Beuve, *Portraits contemporains*, vol. 1 (Paris: Michel Lévy, 1870). George Sand, *Indiana*, trans. George Burnham (Chicago: Cassandra, 1978). Sand, *Lélia*, trans. Maria Espinosa (Bloomington: Indiana University Press, 1978). Naomi Schor, "*Eugénie Grandet:* Mirrors and Melancholia," in *Breaking the Chain: Women, Theory, and French Realist Fiction* (New York: Columbia University Press, 1985). Eileen Boyd Sivert, "*Lélia* and Feminism," *Yale French Studies*, 62 (1981), 45–66.

Naomi Schor

✐ 1834
Victor Hugo Publishes *Claude Gueux*

Romanticism and Social Vision

In July 1830 a three-day rebellion by the people of Paris toppled the Bourbon régime that had ruled France since the fall of Napoleon I fifteen years before. The July Revolution was crucial to a major reorientation of Romantic sensibility during the first half of the 1830s, a time when some of the most influential French Romantics began to consider social action no less urgent a task for the artist than individual expression. Victor Hugo's evolution during this period both exemplified and furthered a broad effort to make effective political action a central part of the Romantic project.

Like many of his fellows, Hugo began his struggle for far-reaching changes in French aesthetic standards with the conviction that French political organization should be immune to change of any kind. The legitimate Bourbon monarchy was to remain serenely in place while the classical literary forms once associated with the monarchy were ignominiously discarded. But by 1830 Hugo was convinced that liberation from the past was desirable in all areas. Moreover, he had come to understand that the correct name for liberation was a word hateful to all legitimists, *revolution*. Soon after the July uprising, Hugo wrote to the other principal Romantic leader, Alphonse de Lamartine: "Ours too is a question of freedom, it too is a revolution; it will stand intact to walk side by side with its political sister. Like wolves, revolutions don't eat one another" (7 September 1830, *Oeuvres*, 4:1004). At least since 1820, one of the preferred exercises of French authors had been to try to define just what Romanticism was. The approach of the events of 1830 allowed Hugo to give what he considered the definitive explanation. "Romanticism, so often badly defined, is, taken all in all, and this is its real definition, nothing more than *liberalism* in literature . . . Freedom in art, freedom in society, there is the double goal" (*Oeuvres*, 3:1085).

Hugo's ideological development was typical of French Romantics' reactions to the events of 1830. Those previously celebrating individual sensations became acutely sensitive to collective dynamics, a development best symbolized by the editorial policies of *Le globe*. From 1824 to 1830 this self-styled "philosophical and literary journal" published some of the most important French defenses of Romantic theory and practice. After the July Revolution, *Le globe* was bought by the followers of Claude-Henri de Saint-Simon (1760–1825), an important precursor of socialist theory whose major concern was how society as a whole could be organized most productively. The publication that had called itself "philosophical and literary" adopted Saint-Simon's motto: "To each according to his capacities, to each capacity according to its works." From a forum for describing and encouraging Romantic expression in literature, *Le globe* became a platform for planning and exhorting massive transformation in society.

Hugo's progress was less dramatic. His first major work after the July Revolution was *Notre-Dame de Paris* (1831), a stunning novelistic representation of late-medieval Paris and its central point, the great cathedral of Notre-Dame. Although many of the novel's characters are poor and hungry, Hugo concentrates as much on their grotesque and picturesque traits as on their economic problems. *Notre-Dame de Paris* firmly rejects the idealization of the Middle Ages frequent among Romantic apologists for the ancien régime, but this narrative of a hunchback, a gypsy, and a variety of other 15th-century exotics by no means evoked the realities faced by the July Monarchy. Hugo's novel was a hugely influential revelation of the descriptive intensity of Romantic prose, but it did not suggest that literary and political revolution had learned to walk side by side.

In 1832 Hugo brought out a new edition of a work originally published in 1829, *Le dernier jour d'un condamné* (*The Last Day of a Condemned Man*). Purportedly the journal kept by a prisoner awaiting execution, this text is a moving argument against the death penalty that takes its force from detailed notation of the physical and emotional sensations experienced during the final hours and minutes in the life of a prisoner whose head is going to be chopped off. In the 1832 edition, Hugo gave his general plea against the death penalty a specific social content by adding a lengthy preface that sharply contrasted the judicial treatment of rich and poor. The new French legislature, indifferent to the fate of all lower-class prisoners condemned to die, was in distress over the possible execution of four guilty ministers from the previous régime. In Hugo's representation of the thought of France's leaders, killing the poor is fine, but not "killing four men like you and me, four *men of the world*. There's not even a mahogany guillotine!" (*Oeuvres*, 4:483). Justice, always a cardinal virtue for Hugo, had in its application become only another way to distinguish upper-class privilege from lower-class squalor.

The interaction of justice and class is memorable in *Claude Gueux* (1834), the story of a convict who kills to punish the unjust administration of his prison. Claude is in prison because he stole for the sake of his wife and child, and the narrator of his story assertively announces that this theft did not originate in the moral laxity of an individual but in the unjust organization of a society. "I don't know what he stole. I don't know where he stole. What I know is that stealing brought three days of bread and warmth to the woman and child and five years of prison to the man" (*Oeuvres*, 5:235).

Among the multiple torments convicts must endure, the one most painful to Claude is constant hunger. One day another prisoner, Albin, begins to share his food with Claude, and the two become committed comrades. The warden, already jealous of Claude's moral authority over his fellow inmates ("to contain the prisoners, ten words from Claude were worth ten guards"; p. 239), resents the new relationship bitterly. He therefore separates the pair and ignores Claude's frequently repeated pleas for reunion with his comrade. Finally Claude decides that so unjustified a separation demands punishment. He explains his reasoning to the other inmates, who unanimously approve and silently watch as Claude kills the warden with an ax and unsuccessfully tries to kill himself with a pair of scissors. After recovering from his wounds, Claude is tried and condemned to death because he is unable to focus the trial on the real problem. "I stole and I killed. But why did I steal? Why did I kill? Ask those questions beside the others, gentlemen of the jury" (p. 249). Claude dies on the guillotine, and the narrator comments that each paragraph in his story could furnish a chapter heading for the book that will solve "the great problem of the people in the 19th century" (p. 250).

Claude Gueux concludes on a simplistic solution to the problem of the people: educate them so they can prosper if they are able; give them Christian resignation so they will accept their hard lot on earth if they are not. The interest of Hugo's text is less in the solution it proposes than in its representation of the problem as the perversion of social relations. Claude Gueux has a "well made brain" and a "well made heart," but a "badly made society" converts him into a thief and a killer (p. 251). In a challenge to the ideology of the individual central both to the rising bourgeois order and to the founding principles of Romantic expression, *Claude Gueux* comes close to assigning responsibility for human development to the collectivity in which it occurs.

Such emphasis on collective dynamics was widespread in the first part of the 1830s. In *Littérature et philosophie mêlées* (1834; *Literature and Philosophy Together*), Hugo sought to work out the literary implications of the historical changes transforming France and its citizens. He saw the age as characterized by "the great substitution of social questions for political questions" (letter to Jules Lechevalier, 1 June 1834, *Oeuvres,* 5 : 1046), and *Claude Gueux* expressed those social questions with special intensity. Alone among Hugo's works, this story suggests that social conditions can be so atrocious as to invalidate moral principles that persuasively lay claim to being absolute.

For it must not be forgotten that Claude, the victim of the death penalty, also inflicts the death penalty. Hugo's opposition to capital punishment was always explicitly comprehensive. Yet Claude judges, condemns, and executes without textual reprimand. Moreover, whereas Hugo's works are full of characters who, like Claude, responsibly examine their consciences and resolve on an act that will lead to condemnation, Claude is the only character to submit the results of self-examination for group approval. Hugo's other works make it radically unthinkable for a character to sneak up behind a man, smash an ax into his head three times and his face once, and retain narrative sympathy. Claude Gueux not only does these things; he also asks for and receives his fellow prisoners' approval that he do so. Representation of acute internal conflict was among Hugo's most impressive novelistic talents. In *Claude Gueux*, internal conflict remains unrepresented, and the arena of debate shifts from an individual soul to a collective condition. The vast scope of "social questions" in 1834 led Hugo to a narrative structure in which murder is forgivable when its motive is one that a suffering social unit accepts as a legitimate response to oppression.

It was during the period of *Claude Gueux* and the second edition of *Le dernier jour d'un condamné* that Hugo first began to think about the monumental work he would publish thirty years later as *Les misérables* (1862). The problems of society and its organization were critical to him in the early 1830s, and even his reactionary proposal that religion be made a more efficacious opiate of the people has strong connections to the social debates of the age. The Restoration and July Monarchy understood the etymology of *religion* to be *religare*, "to bind together," a derivation that was also taken as an imperative statement of purpose. For conservative thinkers, society could be kept whole only if the religion inherited from the past was preserved intact. For progressive thinkers, creating the society of the future required conceiving programs for change as themselves imbued with profound religious content. Saint-Simon called his last major work *Le nouveau christianisme* (1825; *The New Christianity*), and his followers explicitly adopted some of the monastic and hierarchical customs of the Catholic church. Social problems demanded social solutions, and religion was the model of choice for uniting people in an effective totality.

In the work of Félicité de Lamennais (1782–1854), the old and new concepts of religion came together. The year of *Claude Gueux* was also the year of Lamennais's *Paroles d'un croyant* (*Words of a Believer*), which combined Romantic lyricism and Christian sermonizing with intense appeals for justice in this life. Lamennais's hugely successful and influential work prompted conservative forces to widespread condemnation of Romantic literature as a whole. *Paroles d'un croyant* powerfully displayed the incendiary potential of Romantic expression, and the orthodox Catholic response was not only to excommunicate Lamennais but also to place Hugo and Lamartine on the Roman church's Index of Forbidden Books.

The plans for a better world developed by the social thinker Charles Fourier (1772–1837) also demonstrate the interaction between individual feeling and collective responsibility typical of French Romanticism in the 1830s. Fourier's projects were based on allowing members of a group to act according to their personal desires in a setting that gave those desires the greatest possible opportunity to benefit the group in its entirety. For Fourier, the world of the future would give full collective value to the individual passions Romantic literature had best described: "To be a devotee of Romanticism is to be enamored of passionate attraction and the magnificence it is about to create on this globe" (quoted in Evans, *Social Romanticism in France*, p. 46). Like the Saint-Simonians, Fourier and his followers were acutely sensitive to the fact that sexual relations and gender traits were socially determined and thus demanded collective attention. In the France of the 1830s, social dynamics were understood to be crucial to all aspects of human existence, even those that, like the eternal feminine, had been considered immune to historical influence.

Fourier's and Saint-Simon's thought had an extensive and profound influence on contemporary literature. The Saint-Simonians saw the artist as duty-bound to work for political progress through artistic creation, and their appeals for literary engagement found a ready audience. Théophile Gautier used the preface of *Mademoiselle de Maupin* (1835) to argue for art's freedom from political responsibility in part because so many of his talented contemporaries saw political responsibility as central to their art. George Sand reacted strongly to several of the age's social theories, and Honoré de Balzac gave his own version of rational social organization in *Le médecin de campagne* (1833; *The Country Doctor*). The slight plot of this substantial novel furnishes a pretext for describing the conversion of a poverty-stricken mountain region into a prosperous center of entrepreneurship through the benevolent offices of a physician who operates on society as effectively as on his patients. As with *Claude Gueux*, the details of Balzac's proposals are less provocative than the vision of the world they address. For Balzac's protagonist, Dr. Benassis, "the future is social man" (p. 430), and all concepts of collective existence as a simple accumulation of individual existences must be relentlessly challenged. Balzac's fictional defense of a paternalistic dictatorship relies on the same concept of a social whole that informed more liberal contemporaries' attacks on just such dictatorships.

In the same year that *Le médecin de campagne* appeared, Jules Michelet published the first volumes of his enormous history of France. Michelet's history, a major expression of respect for the people as a mass rather than as a collection of individuals, developed directly from its author's meditations on the lessons Romanticism drew from the 1830 Revolution: "This was the first model of a revolution without heroes, without proper names. Society did everything . . . After the victory, they looked for a hero, they found a whole people" ("Introduction à l'histoire universelle" ["Introduction to the Universal History"], in *Oeuvres*, 2:254–255). The age's orientation toward the social determined its representation of history as well as its construction of fiction.

The concern with social problems typical of French Romanticism in the 1830s received a name destined to have its own impact on history, *socialisme*. The term entered the French language in an 1833 article by Pierre Leroux (1797–1871), the major figure in the conversion of *Le globe* from Romantic to Saint-Simonian programmatics. Leroux contrasted socialism with individualism, itself a term undergoing intense scrutiny by the social Romantics and their contemporaries. That socialism so quickly acquired the sense it has today—militant opposition to the bourgeois order and committed determination to overturn it—powerfully manifests the importance of the shift in Romantic ideas that began with the July Revolution. A different way of looking at the world almost immediately became a militant program for a different way of organizing the world.

Hugo characterized the early 1830s as the time of a great substitution of social questions for political questions. In 1831, 1832, and 1834, this substitution was embodied in the contrast between social revolts by Lyons weavers and political revolts by Paris militants. Karl Marx assigned special importance to the Lyons uprisings in formulating his ideas about the actions necessary for achieving authentic social justice. For Marx, Lyons was the site of a new working-class intervention in history that made all classical political thought obsolete, and we continue to live with the consequences of Marx's insight. The historical circumstances in which French Romantics embraced a social vision were part of a decisive transformation of sensibility that helped make the modern world itself.

See also 1772, 1830, 1840, 1851, 1889.

Bibliography: Honoré de Balzac, *Le médecin de campagne,* ed. Rose Fortassier, vol. 9 of *La comédie humaine,* ed. Pierre-Georges Castex (Paris: Gallimard, 1978). Victor Brombert, *Victor Hugo and the Visionary Novel* (Cambridge, Mass.: Harvard University Press, 1984). David O. Evans, *Social Romanticism in France: 1830–1848* (New York: Octagon, 1969). Victor Hugo, *Oeuvres complètes,* ed. Jean Massin, vols. 3, 4, and 5 (Paris: Club Français du Livre, 1967). H. J. Hunt, *Le socialisme et le romantisme en France* (Oxford: Clarendon Press, 1935). Jules Michelet, "Introduction à l'histoire universelle," in *Oeuvres complètes,* ed. Paul Viallaneix, vol. 2 (Paris: Flammarion, 1972).

Sandy Petrey

✐ 1835

Alfred de Musset Writes "La nuit de mai" and "La nuit de décembre"

Dialogues with the Muse

The lyric sentimentality and poetic forms of Alfred de Musset's verse, exemplified by two of his most famous poems, "La nuit de mai" (June 1835; "May Night") and "La nuit de décembre" (December 1835; "December Night"), represent so completely certain excesses of French Romantic poetry that it is impossible today to read such poetry without a certain ironic distance. Contemporaries, however, admired their author as the very figure of Romantic young genius, representative of the lyric genre itself. In 1835 Musset, only twenty-five, was a celebrated figure in Parisian literary circles; his plays, including *Les caprices de Marianne* (1833; *The Follies of Marianne*), *Andrea del Sarto* (1833), *Lorenzaccio* (1834), *Fantasio* (1834), and *On ne badine pas avec l'amour* (1834; *No Trifling with Love*), had been published; his essays had appeared in major literary reviews; and his long poem, *Rolla* (1833), the lyric evocation of a "child of the times," was celebrated as a landmark of Romantic sensibility. Musset had quickly gained the recognition and admiration of influential advocates of the new literary modernism such as Prosper Mérimée, Charles Augustin Sainte-Beuve, Alfred de Vigny, and, of course, George Sand, with whom he had a stormy public liaison that ended in March 1835. The role of the poet he cultivated was that of the brilliant and extravagant dandy whose public persona is as much an aesthetic production as his texts; sentiment and art were consubstantial. It would take thirty years for the dissociation of the Romantic conflation of person and persona in the lyric to occur. Only with Charles Baudelaire's *Les fleurs du mal* (1857; *The Flowers of Evil*) did the lyric poet lose his claim to represent the poet per se and cease to personify a genre.

Musset's "Nuit de mai" and "Nuit de décembre" typify the Romantic poet's relationship to art and to objects of desire, either human subjects or an aspect of the inanimate world to which the lyric is addressed. "La nuit de mai" is a dialogue: the poet talks and listens to the muse, a divine voice that he can assume as his own. "La nuit de décembre" is a retrospective narrative of encounters with the core of the poet's most intimate subjectivity, allegorically personified as Solitude. Both are lyric confessions recounting how the personal pain inflicted by life and love distracts the poet from his art. Ultimately, however, he embraces this suffering, which authenticates his voice. Romantic morality and aesthetics are never separate for a writer such as Musset: the suffering is the sign of divinely designated greatness, "a holy wound" that provides the poet with an exemplary subjective experience. The muse admonishes him to communicate it through verse. A sense of loss and estrangement in an alien world is thus transformed into an imperative to speak. Solitude, the sign of his alienation from others, becomes, more importantly, the sign of his superiority.

In "La nuit de mai," thinly veiled autobiographical allusions reveal that the "painful martyrdom" upon which these lofty claims are staked is a disappointment in love. The second one, less noble and allegorical, is directly anecdotal: the narrator recounts disengaging himself from a "weak" and "prideful" woman who has abandoned him out of jealousy. He in turn rejects her, saying (lines 172–173):

> Go! go! great Nature did not shower
>   All her good gifts upon your mind.

Despite the rather comic disparity between the triviality of the events recounted and the exemplary value accorded the consequent suffering, both poems make far-reaching claims about the poet and his art. They also share with most Romantic lyric specific assumptions about communication and about the power said to inhere in poetry.

For poets such as Alfred de Vigny, Alphonse de Lamartine, and Victor Hugo, scrutiny of the poet's identity, in solitude as well as in relation to others, and meditations on poetic language always assume that a dialogue is possible. The "thou" addressed in the lyric, whether it be a lover, an absent or dead companion, or, as for Hugo, the soul of a tree, is always presumed capable of response, even if that response is deferred and withheld, not recounted in the poem. Language and the material world are a vast and common repository of figurative forms, which Baudelaire, among others, referred to as the "universal analogy." Most of the pieces collected in Hugo's *Les contemplations* (1856; *Contemplations*) still typify, twenty years after Musset's "Nuits," this metaphysical rhetoric. "Aux arbres" ("To the Trees") is exemplary of such poems in which

667

the lyric narrator addresses the inanimate by means of tropes that transform it into a potentially responsive subject, revealing the underlying assumption that all poetic communication implies an animistic God-centered view of the universe: everything that falls beneath the poet's gaze is a potential interlocutor (lines 1, 9–11, 15–16):

> Trees of the forest, you know my soul!
>
> . . .
>
> You have seen me a hundred times, in the dark valley,
> With these words that the spirit speaks to nature,
> Question softly your throbbing boughs,
>
> . . .
>
> Attentive to your sounds which each speaks a bit,
> Trees, you have seen me flee man and seek God.

For the Romantic, even if the desired response is silenced or withheld, the form of the address, a vocative or apostrophe, presupposes the possibility of a response. The object to which the poet speaks can itself become a subject that enters into colloquy with the poet, as in "Paroles sur la dune" ("Words upon the Dune"), also from *Les contemplations* (lines 33–36):

> Has everything fled? I am alone, I am weary.
>   I call and nothing answers;
> Oh winds! oh waves! Am I also nothing but a breath, alas?
>   Am I also nothing but a wave?

Romantic theories of language and Romantic metaphysics assumed that grand syntheses among mind, matter, and discourse are attainable. A common quest for universal communication should allow subject and object to join. But their relationship, never simple or unmediated, is seldom entirely positive. The subjective presence of the mind, apprehended through language, always rests upon poetic figures. The essence of the subject can be reached only through discourse: the lyric poet is often acutely, even painfully, aware that his quest for presence, unity, and authenticity may be hindered by the artifices of language upon which it depends. Even the most sweeping assertions about the power of poetic language to communicate with the world and to convey truth and presence are tempered by a sustained meditation upon the fragility of the fictions through which these assertions are made. And the most euphoric moments, when poetic truth and affective fulfillment are said to coincide, are answered by more somber ones in which the narrator struggles with the negative implications of his engagement with language.

In Musset's lyric dialogues, apostrophe and use of the vocative narrow the distance between subject and object. The other (the Muse or Solitude) is here, addressed directly, not *as though* capable of animate activity and speech. Furthermore, it is not a potentially elusive, reticent, or enigmatic object of desire, but one readily accessible to the poet. Yet a profound uneasiness inhabits many other Romantic lyrics, for those poets are aware that, if poetry can transform inanimate objects into subjects, death can in turn transform subjects into life-less objects: the poet is always menaced by a return to the inanimate. In Hugo's "Aux arbres" this intuition gives way to a longing for absolute oblivion (lines 35–36, 38–40):

> And so, sacred groves, where God himself appears,
> Religious trees
>
> . . .
>
> It is beneath your august and lonely branches
> That I wish to shelter my own grave
> And that I wish to sleep when sleep overtakes me.

In Musset's texts, on the other hand, the poet himself, or a double of the poet, is the mysterious other to whom the lyric communication is addressed, and art must come to know and accommodate him. In "La nuit de mai" the muse seeks out the silent poet, invites him to a night of love, implores him to yield to his own inspiration (lines 1–6):

> Come, take thy lute and kiss me, poet mine.
> The breezes' breath grows warmer, and to-night
> Is born the Spring and buds the eglantine;
> Among the tender blossoms perching light,
> The birds are waiting for the dawn to shine.
> Come, take thy lute and kiss me, poet mine.

With a coy rhetoric of seduction, the muse cajoles the poet to take up again their amours of the past, and the poet, wounded in love, quite unabashedly withholds his favors. Here he is the one who plays the role of the elusive and enigmatic object of desire. Appropriately, the act of love is represented as the joining of voices, an invitation to sing together. The muse entreats the poet to join her in assuming the various poetic figures and styles that are available to traditional art. The passage reads much like a catalogue of Romantic stereotypes (lines 73–75, 86–88):

> We are alone, the world is at our feet—
> Green Caledon and sunburnt Italy;
> My mother, Greece, where honey is so sweet;
>
> . . .
>
> Come, shall we sing of hope, or joy, or woe?
> The mailed legions shall we bathe in gore?
> Or tell how silken ladders lovers bore?

This artfully ironic effusion elicits a nobly serious response, in which the poet assumes his true attitude to art (lines 134–138):

> But of hope I cannot sing,
> Nor of happiness nor glory,
> Nor, alas! of suffering:
> Dumb the lips are, listening
> To the heart's unuttered story.

669

This answer establishes the context for the central allegory of the poem, elaborated over some thirty-nine lines, in which the muse tells of the pelican who returns to his hungry young after lofty flights. Having searched the sea in vain for food, he can offer only the blood from his open breast, from his own heart, as an expression of sublime love, an allegory for the fate of the great poets (lines 189–191):

> Their worldly passion is a flashing sword
> That traces dazzling circles in the air,
> And yet a drop of blood is ever clinging there.

The poet's last reply, however, lays claim to an even greater suffering, heretofore unknown; a suffering so great that, if he were to take up his lyre, it would "break like a reed."

In "La nuit de décembre," the structure of the lyric address is different: the poet addresses a silent other who accompanies him throughout life, and as the vision speaks in the last three stanzas, he learns that his companion is Solitude. This vision personifies a more perfect form of the poet himself (lines 208–210, 220–225):

> My friend, one father have we both;
> No guardian angel I, in truth,
> Nor yet the evil fate of men.
>
> . . .
>
> Heaven has entrusted me your heart,
> When you have trouble to impart
> Seek me without disquietude.
> I'll follow you along your way;
> But touch your hand I never may.
> My friend—my name is Solitude.

The poem has recounted the stages of the narrator's life—childhood, adolescence, early youth—when he engaged in the distractions of society and, most painful of all, was rejected in love; he is always accompanied, however, by a "friendly shadow": Solitude.

Whereas in "La nuit de mai" the subject experiences his alienation in and from language, the incapacity of language to fit and express a consciousness said to be radically new, "La nuit de décembre" is about a more direct estrangement, a social one, with no special emphasis on the relationship between self and language. Both poems, however, quite unreflectively suggest a way to resolve the difficulties they describe, since both transform estrangement from the world into a purer and fuller form of presence, projecting a quite comfortable conjunction and subjectivity. As for "La nuit de mai," it purports to relate allegorically the incapacity of verse to contain the poet's unique suffering, traditional language being inadequate to the Romantic subject. And that very story of personal loss and the ensuing pain is just what the poem does recount. In doing so, however, it does not invent a radically new poetic language, such as the one it claims to be lacking, but rather repeats the most conventional figures of poetic diction, allegory and irony. In "La nuit de décembre," Solitude, the personification of the poet's difference from other men, paradoxically represents that difference as sameness: what separates the poet from society ultimately unites him with a vision of a self that returns the poet's own image.

Musset's "Nuits" are remarkably explicit in representing the narcissistic relation to the world and to communication that underlies Romantic writing in general. Most Romantic writers pursued and meditated upon a coalescence of the writing subject and the material universe, leading to a transcendent, infinite, yet usually only partially comprehensible subjectivity. But Musset's dialogues lead inward to a self-sustaining and reassuring image of the poet's persona. They are devoid of metaphysical anguish and show no concern that poetry may mediate only in the most fragile or even inadequate way between self and world. To us such poems relay the image of an ultimately rather vain literary persona, decorated in a craftsmanly manner with the tropes and figures of traditional verse. Assembling a set of Romantic procedures, they perform a morally inspired meditation upon the lyric first person, the essence of subjectivity conveyed through the themes of alienation and solitude. These concerns are occasionally intermixed with considerations about the limits of expressive language. But such considerations never exceed the dimensions of formalized anecdotes that can be accommodated by neoclassical rhetoric, shaped to fit a lyric stereotype.

What is it, then, that provokes our resistance in this apparently docile engagement among the poet, language, and alienation? Perhaps it is the presence, behind the self-confident and grandiloquent lyricism, of questions that still haunt us about the relation of subjectivity—our relation—to language and to the symbolic order in general. Psychoanalytic theory, particularly with Freud and Jacques Lacan, has shown that the utterance of the pronoun "I" never guarantees the presence of a unified expressive subject at its source. Mallarmé called the similar dispersal of the lyric subject an "elocutionary disappearance." The disappearance of the Romantic lyric subject, however, leaves traces that nonetheless can be recognized as linguistic signs of subjectivity. What appear today, in Musset's lyricism, as rather glib considerations about desire and the self may serve as reminders of the intrinsic fragility of our own understandings of questions about the self and language that ultimately elude resolution.

See also 1820, 1827 (December), 1859 (7 December).

Bibliography: Victor Hugo, *Les contemplations,* in *Oeuvres poétiques,* ed. Pierre Albouy, vol. 2 (Paris: Gallimard, 1967). Alfred de Musset, *The Complete Works of Alfred de Musset,* trans. George Santayana, Emily Shaw Forman, and Marie Agathe Clarke (New York: E.C. Hill, 1905). Musset, *Poésies complètes,* ed. Maurice Allem (Paris: Gallimard, 1957). Maurice Toesca, *Alfred de Musset, ou l'amour de la mort* (Paris: Hachette, 1970). Philippe Van Tieghem, *Musset* (Paris: Hatier, 1944).

Nathaniel Wing

✒ 1836, 25 October

The Obelisk Given to France by Mehemet Ali, the Pasha of Egypt,
Is Erected in the Place de la Concorde

Egypt in Paris

In 1753 a square was laid out, between the Tuileries and the Champs-Elysées, to glorify Louis XV, then still called the Beloved. It was there that the Revolutionaries first set up the guillotine, there that, in 1793, Louis XVI was beheaded. Witness to the reversals of Revolution, Empire, Restoration, the square bore in rapid succession the names given it by each side (at times Place Louis XV, Place Louis XVI, and Place de la Charte; at times Place de la Révolution), and finally, in a synthesis, Place de la Concorde.

It "could not retain any one name," Victor Hugo commented in *Choses vues* (1887; *Things Seen*):

> It could retain, no less, any one monument. There was the statue of Louis XV, which disappeared; a fountain of expiation was planned, one which would wash the bloodied center of the square and for which the first stone had not even been laid; a monument to the Charter had been sketched; we saw nothing but the base of this monument. Just when a figure in bronze representing the Charter of 1814 was about to be erected, the July Revolution occurred with the Charter of 1830. The pedestal of Louis XVIII disappeared in the same way that the pedestal of Louis XV crumbled. Now in this same place we have put the obelisk of Sesostris. It took the great desert thirty centuries to half bury it; how many years will the Place de la Révolution need to bury it completely? (*Oeuvres complètes,* 1 : 1)

In 1828 Mehemet Ali, the pasha of Egypt, had given France an obelisk that, at the time of its delivery in 1833, it had no idea how to use or to dispose of. After three years of public controversy, the July Monarchy (1830–1848) settled its destination. It was set up in the center of the square on 25 October 1836 in the presence of the royal family and 200,000 spectators. The operation lasted from 11:30 A.M. to 3:00 P.M. (fig. 1). This exploit of French technology was like the second coronation of a régime committed to forgetting the past. Reflecting the prevailing mentality, embodied in the injunction of Louis-Philippe's minister François Guizot, "Get rich," the square had hosted in 1834 a lavish exposition of the products of industry. It was for this occasion that Théophile Gautier, in the antiutilitarian manifesto that was his preface to *Mademoiselle de Maupin* (1835), invented the adjective *luxorien* (both "Luxorian" and "luxurious"). And in 1833, the year of his *Champavert,* Pétrus Borel published a pamphlet, *L'obélisque de Louqsor* (*The Luxor Obelisk*), in which he promised that neither Ramses nor Sesostris would cause Louis XVI to be forgotten. In 1842 Balzac, in *Sur Catherine de Médicis,* made this "huge Egyptian pebble" the emblem of the July Monarchy and "the system of materialist politics that governs us" (*Catherine de' Medici,* p. 6).

1. Ignace-François Bonhommé, "Erection de l'obélisque de Louqsor sur la place de la Concorde à Paris, 25 octobre 1836, à midi," lithograph by Thierry Frères (Musée Carnavalet, Paris). (Photo © Musées de la Ville de Paris by SPADEM 1988.)

This solemn obliteration of memories that four decades of conflicting projects had tried in vain to account for indeed marked the triumph of philistinism. Monuments have commemoration as their function. This one was meant to induce forgetting. In order to soothe a still-livid scar, Louis-Philippe decided to erect, in the center of Paris, the memorial of someone no one had heard of. Against the antiquity of the neoclassics, the Romantics had revived the national past. Decontextualized, transplanted absurdly to the Parisian setting, the obelisk, with its dead language, was the exact opposite of the "living stones" celebrated by Hugo in *Notre-Dame de Paris* (1831).

Jules Michelet was filled with the same indignation against this silent stone whose unreadable presence inhibited the recall of a past through which a much-needed national communion would find its ground. In 1878 his widow published the unfinished *Les soldats de la Révolution* (*The Soldiers of the Revolution*), an 1848 project inspired by the revolution that had just toppled Louis-Philippe's monarchy. In the preface the Romantic historian imagined a monument that would be suitable to the square. But "to start with, let us get rid of, let us ship off to the museum, to a little corner of the courtyard of the Louvre or of the Bibliothèque, this Egyptian obelisk, curious old oddment, good for academic exercises, but ridiculous and out of place at a site at which the Nation alone has the right to be represented" (*Soldats*, p. 8).

Even though a monarchist, François-René de Chateaubriand had, during the Empire and the Restoration, incessantly reproached the survivors of the ancien régime for thinking and acting as if the Revolution had never occurred. In turn, he would reproach the July Monarchy for acting as if regicide had never happened. That the past is past is no reason to let it be forgotten. Ambassador and secretary of state during the Restoration, Chateaubriand resigned upon Louis-Philippe's accession to power in 1830 and redevoted himself to writing his autobiography, *Mémoires d'outre-tombe* (1849–50). The eleventh and last book of

these "memoirs from beyond the grave," published after his death, is given over
to the reign of someone called Philippe, lest the royal name Louis be sullied.
Its dark and biting energy pours a scathing haughtiness, the splenetic violence
of a sixty-year-old Captain Fracasse who has nothing any longer to lose, over an
entire epoch. These pages were written in 1838. After a gallery of portraits—grandiose in their grotesquerie—that ends with the funeral dirge of the
last true king of France, Charles X, Chateaubriand dreams of civil peace, of a
posthumous concord between the parties that have been tearing each other apart
for more than forty years. But this dream is fleeting, suddenly broken by the
newly erected obelisk, the silhouette of which wells up in the last sentence of
the book: "And yet the stone carved by order of Sesostris henceforward buries
the scaffold of Louis XVI under the weight of the ages. The hour will come
when the obelisk of the desert shall find again, on the place of the murders, the
silence and solitude of Luxor" (*Memoirs*, 6:180). Chateaubriand speaks of recollection, but forgetting is what had been instituted. And the memorialist goes
one step further by prophesying that one day there will be nobody left to forget
what the July Monarchy did not want the French to remember.

Whereas the events of July 1830 provided Chateaubriand with an occasion
to establish his loyalty to an irreversibly terminated régime, it afforded Victor
Hugo the opportunity irrevocably to renounce the monarchy. "Dicté après
juillet 1830" ("Dictated after July 1830"), the first poem of *Les chants du crépuscule* (1835; *Sunset Songs*), is filled with the hope generated by the July Revolution. In it Hugo demands of the new régime: "Erase nothing." He, too,
wishes for the reconciliation of antithetical pasts (IV, lines 44–46):

> That no memory weigh on us:
> Let us give back his tomb to Louis Seize,
> His column to Napoleon.

In a note accompanying the first publication of this poem in 1830, Hugo
disapproves of "the change of purpose that seems to be intended for the pedestal
of the Place de la Révolution." The death of a king, he adds, is among the
episodes "that one does not erase from the history of empires" (*Oeuvres poétiques*,
1:1428). Lambs and wolves coexist in the Ark. Memory is a temple where
conflicts are overcome. Hugo dreams of a place where the totality of what has
happened will be offered up to recollection. Those who were separated by what
they thought of the past would be united through the very fact of thinking
of it.

From *Le dernier jour d'un condamné* (1829; *The Last Day of a Condemned Man*)
to *Quatre vingt-treize* (1874; *Ninety-three*), Hugo's work is haunted by images of
the Terror and the scaffold. Just as Hamlet muses in the graveyard over the
skull of Yorick, Hugo mused, in April 1839, in the midst of a public celebration, on the death of the king. "En passant dans la Place Louis XV un jour de
fête publique" ("Passing through Louis XV Square on a Public Holiday"), in
Les rayons et les ombres (1840; *Lights and Shadows*), orchestrates a typically
Hugolian system of antitheses. The initial, synchronic one opposes the rejoicing

of the people to the somber reflections of the poet. The second is diachronic; the populace rejoices on the site where it had executed the king. A third contrast then recalls an earlier celebration: there the people had even earlier feasted the marriage of the future Louis XVI, then dauphin, and Marie-Antoinette. The poet thereby casts the shadow of the scaffold over two festivities, the one that occasions the poem, the other that celebrated a marriage within which he alone sees the seed of death. In "This square where our troubled age / Placed a stone in order to hide an idea" (lines 6–7), under the spell of the obelisk, the populace dances, a forgetful Oedipus, on the stage of its crime. The memory of the Terror burgeons here with the terror of oblivion. The poet denounces, in the forgetting of violence, the figural violence of forgetting.

See also 1770, 1794 (25 July), 1889.

Bibliography: Honoré de Balzac, *Catherine de' Medici,* trans. Katharine Prescott Wormeley (Boston: Little, Brown, 1900). François-René de Chateaubriand, *The Memoirs of François-René, Vicomte de Chateaubriand, Sometime Ambassador to England,* trans. A. Teixeira de Mattos, vol. 6 (London: Freemantle, 1902). Solange Granet, *La Place de la Concorde,* special issue, *Revue géographique et industrielle de la France,* 26 (1963). Victor Hugo, *Choses vues,* vol. 1 of *Oeuvres complètes* (Paris: Ollendorf, 1913). Hugo, *Les chants du crépuscule* and *Les rayons et les ombres,* in *Oeuvres poétiques,* ed. Pierre Albouy, vol. 1 (Paris: Gallimard, 1964). Jules Michelet, *Les soldats de la Révolution* (Paris: Calmann-Lévy, 1878). Musée Carnavalet, *De la Place Louis XV à la Place de la Concorde* (Paris, 1982).

Denis Hollier

ᓚᓚ 1837

Prosper Mérimée Publishes *La Vénus d'Ille*

Fantastic Tales

Modern literary critics' increasing emphasis on narratology, theories of signs and meaning, the rhetorical nature of the literary text and its readiness to produce multiple and incompatible meanings, and especially the reader's contribution to the formation of these meanings has largely influenced the revival of the fantastic. Recent definitions of the genre elaborate on the links between the fantastic and fantasy (*fantasme*), the fantastic and dreams, or the fantastic and death; and they invariably stress the central importance of language in effecting shifts from one element to another. Indeed, the relative freedom of the fantastic from the constraints of verisimilitude has pushed "the suspension of disbelief" advocated by Coleridge to new extremes, thus allowing the fantastic story to encompass elements previously seen as disparate, heterogeneous, or even contradictory.

In 1829 Jean-Jacques Ampère introduced the genre in France with his translation of E. T. A. Hoffmann's *Phantasiestücke in Callot's Manier* (1814; *Fantasy*

Pieces in the Manner of Callot), for which he coined the word *fantastique*. Ampère also wrote an essay sketching the parameters of Hoffmann's fantastic. This early attempt at a definition was rather vague: it promoted antirationalism and fantasy, focused on the actual narrative content of the stories, but did not examine the focus of later definitions, the reading processes such content determines. Ampère's translation had an immediate success in Paris; the term *fantastique* became almost obligatory in the titles of short stories published in newspapers and journals in the early 1830s (although by today's standards some of them would not be called fantastic stories). In 1830 Charles Nodier and Gérard de Nerval published essays in praise of the fantastic. Again, these essays did not so much define a genre as group and defend the various writers who mixed realistic elements with fantasy, dreams, and supernatural elements (ghosts, fairies, vampires, demons, spells, and so on). In addition to Hoffmann, they claimed among their predecessors the English gothic novelists Ann Radcliffe, Matthew G. Lewis, and, to a lesser extent, Walter Scott.

In their search for a native exemplar to legitimate the new trend, French writers of fantastic stories settled upon Jacques Cazotte's *Le diable amoureux* (1772; *The Devil in Love*). Indeed, even Hoffmann had cited Cazotte as a precursor, and traces of *Le diable amoureux* are discernible in Lewis' novels. Ampère, Nerval, Nodier, Théophile Gautier, and Balzac all acknowledged their debt to Cazotte. At first glance, *Le diable amoureux* is a rather simple and conventional story about the seduction of a human by a devilish temptress. The narrative, however, focuses not on the actual process of seduction but on the persistent and tormented doubts of the hero, Alvare, who sees no harm in falling in love (or being seduced), but who suspects that his beloved Biondetta is in fact one of the many shapes of the devil, whom he himself had conjured up in the form of a camel head. Eventually Alvare succumbs to Biondetta's charm only to find out that his fear was well founded and that she is indeed Beelzebub. But the story does not stop here: after this revelation, when the dismayed Alvare visits his mother, he realizes in speaking with her that he must have dreamed most of his marvelous adventures. Most of the characters who he thought took part in the adventures leading to his "surrender" to Biondetta have alibis corroborated by his mother; most, but not all. Because the camel head appeared to Alvare after an intimate moment with Biondetta, there are no witnesses to corroborate or invalidate this particular recollection. At the end of the story, despite the interpretation of events offered by the wise Don Quebracuernos, invited by Alvare's mother to resolve the puzzle, neither the hero nor the reader knows for certain whether the climax of the story—the love scene with Biondetta—belongs to the realm of reality or of dreams, and whether or not Alvare has in fact fallen prey to the devil. These uncertainties wreak havoc with any attempt to encapsulate the story as the prototypical "seduction of a weak man by a beautiful and sinful temptress," "man's fantasies of being ravished by a beautiful woman," or any other generality.

This lack of closure is what distinguishes *Le diable amoureux* from other fairy or fantasy stories. The fantastic is not simply a genre in which the supernatural plays an important role: as far back as literary memory can go, fairy tales, myths, and folk stories have relied on supernatural interferences to the delight of generations of readers. The novelty of the fantastic lies not in the content or message of the story, but in the attitude toward storytelling that it forces on the reader: it does not ask "What happened?" but exploits the very need inherent in reading to know what "really" happened. Reading no longer consists in extracting the meaning that was hidden in the story by the writer for all time, but in being helplessly suspended between possible meanings, between equally plausible albeit mutually exclusive stories that double each other without ever merging into one coherent narrative (for example, was Alvare dreaming or did he really surrender to the devil?). The focus is not on the story itself, but on the reader, or, more precisely, on the inconclusive and slippery hermeneutics of reading. What is being put into question is neither Alvare's moral strength nor an evil woman's power of seduction (although each is an important component), but the reader's need to distinguish between what happened and what might have happened.

This question in itself was not a novelty in the 19th century. Denis Diderot, Laurence Sterne, and Henry Fielding, for example, had already exposed the various paths a story might take and the crucial part played by the caprice of the writer in selecting one story line over another. The novelty of the fantastic thus lies not so much in the discovery and denunciation of the arbitrariness of fiction writing as in the apparent simplicity with which it incorporates the structural open-endedness of all stories (which the writer's authority normally remedies) into the storytelling process itself. Contrary to Aristotelian tradition, which has accustomed Western readers to expect a definite conflict followed by an appropriate dénouement, the fantastic simultaneously weaves at least two contradictory conflicts and dénouements, thus implying that there may be at least two discrete stories in one narrative. The plurality of story lines and dénouements commands hesitations (either the character's or the reader's) that in turn come to constitute the woof and warp of the fantastic story. This practice, an essentially paradoxical one, ends up creating a narrative out of what traditionally undermines the very possibility of narratives: confusion. Reading a fantastic story is therefore not a trip along a road, as the traditional metaphor for reading would have it, but a standstill at an intersection from which one can glimpse various roads and vistas.

The early fantastic (that of Nodier, Gautier, Nerval, and Mérimée) is neither a style nor a genre: like *Le diable amoureux,* it is an attitude toward storytelling (and story-reading) forced upon the reader by the hesitations of the text. Balzac is a borderline case, since his use of the supernatural does not require an additional interpretative effort. In *La peau de chagrin* (1831; *The Fatal Skin*), for example, the shrinking skin is perfectly integrated in a coherent narrative; similarly, *Melmoth réconcilié* (1835; *Melmoth Reconciled*) and *L'élixir de longue vie* (1830; *The Elixir of Long Life*) include supernatural elements in their narrative building blocks, but without the doubling of characters and semantic excess associated today with the fantastic. Such is the case even with the apparent doubling of *Séraphîta*'s (1835) androgynous Séraphîtüs/Séraphîta since Balzac explains in a long quasi-Swedenborgian excursus that double sexuality is not a confusion between the sexes but a higher form of love.

The fantastic exploits the incompatibility between common-sense reality and the supernatural. It establishes a framework in which the supernatural found in fairy tales is no longer acceptable, yet cannot be refuted with certainty: faced with odd events, the characters propose tentative interpretations based on science, mysticism, irony, madness, or dreams to explain phenomena that would otherwise seem supernatural. Yet these explanations fail to abate the doubts of either the reader or the character. At various moments the narrative offers what appear to be (at least) two simultaneous "stories": the supernatural and the other one or ones. The reader (and often the character) is called upon to furnish an explanation, to prolong the story beyond its textual boundaries—in short, to mirror and rival the author. Mirroring effects are therefore not limited to the obvious doubles commonly found in fantasy stories. They surreptitiously encompass semiotic and narrative functions: embedded mini-stories partially mirror each other, thus highlighting otherwise inconspicuous aspects of the main plot; writers (or storytellers) and readers (or listeners) become interchangeable; and signs lose their intrinsic meanings, referring instead to other textual signs.

Gautier, for example, often uses dreams to achieve this effect: in his stories the supernatural would vanish if the character (and the reader) could believe that his adventure was only a dream. But although the reader is invited to adopt the dream explanation, some textual detail points irreducibly to the supernatural. In *La cafetière* (1831; *The Coffee Pot*), when the narrator, finally convinced that he dreamed the lovely woman with whom he fell in love, nostalgically draws her portrait, his host recognizes his sister, dead for two years; in *Le pied de momie* (1840; *The Mummy's Foot*) the narrator finds the next morning on his bureau the amulet his "dream" princess gave him in exchange for her foot. Sometimes Gautier's solution is drugs, as in "La pipe d'opium" (1838; "The Opium Pipe") and "Le club des hachichins" (1846; "The Club of Hashish Smokers").

Nodier, the closest to Hoffmann and the most Romantic, does not oppose to reality dream or madness alone, but a fusion of reality and fantasy. His *Smarra* (1821), for example, can be read as a hallucinatory commentary on the power of nightmare, while "La fée aux miettes" (1832; "The Crumb Fairy") suggests that what we so unimaginatively call madness is in fact an ultimate simplicity of heart and harmony between one's inner life and the surrounding world. Unlike Gautier or Mérimée, Nodier does not attribute hesitations, suspicions, or misgivings to either the main character or the narrator; the fantastic experience befalls "others," unimaginative witnesses of the events who totally lack the charm and appeal of the primary characters. The reader, naturally identifying with the apparently hallucinating, dreaming, or mad characters rather than with the pedestrian and unattractive ones, is spared the impossible semantic hesitations the fantastic normally imposes, while enjoying all the doubling and mirroring effects programmed by the text.

The masterpiece of the early fantastic is undoubtedly Mérimée's *La Vénus d'Ille* (1837; *The Venus of Ille*). A young man playfully puts the wedding band destined for his bride on the finger of a statue of Venus recently discovered by his archaeologically inclined father. Despite his efforts to retrieve his ring, it remains stuck, as if the statue had bent its finger to hold onto it. On his wedding night he is found dead in bed, where, according to his terrified young wife, a huge body had joined them. The police disqualify her testimony on the grounds that the horror of that night has left her insane. The ensuing criminal investigation uncovers a rivalry between the bridegroom and another man, who thus becomes a likely suspect with a motive, but the man's footprints do not match those left in the garden by the killer. Was the young man murdered by a resentful rival? Did the statue come to claim her groom? The first hypothesis is dismissed for lack of conclusive evidence; no one explicitly advances the second. Even the narrator, a blasé archaeologist from Paris, does not offer any comments, despite the irony and marked condescension he expresses toward the villagers. The death of the young man remains unsolved, notwithstanding the strong indications that the statue must be the culprit.

The inconclusiveness of the narrative stems mostly from the narrator's blindness to the supernatural explanation that the story obviously invites. The reader's dilemma is that, to interpret the "facts" in order to solve the mystery of Alphonse's death, it is necessary to rely on the account of the narrator, whose perception is clearly inadequate: the reader may never know the "real" facts. Mérimée makes extensive and masterly use of such problematic narrators— knowledgeable witnesses (a professor, a minister, an archaeologist, a worldly traveler) who remain surprisingly blind to the oddity of the events they relate. Their very blindness to the inescapable implications of their accounts calls attention to them as narrators: it highlights their crucial role in the story as interpreters and thus implicates both them and the storytelling process in the odd events that they relate.

Mérimée's clever use of citations further emphasizes the doubling effect and muddling of boundaries. Inevitably, a citation summons the text from which it is taken and superimposes it on the main story, creating multiple narrative planes. Studded with such citations, *La Vénus d'Ille* is a matrix of literary texts parasitizing one another. All address the problem of doubling and its effect on language and narrative. One comes from Molière's *Amphitryon* (1668), in which an ever-amorous Jupiter adopts Amphitryon's appearance, while Mercury, his companion, chooses the appearance of Sosie, Amphitryon's servant. The result is twofold: on the one hand, Amphitryon's loving and unsuspecting wife mistakes Jupiter for her husband, and on the other, language no longer functions properly because of the proliferation of referents. Another citation, from Virgil's *Aeneid,* refers to the precise moment when Dido's love for Aeneas outweighs her moral obligation to her deceased husband: she decides to remarry. A third one evokes Racine's *Phèdre* (1677; *Phaedra*), in which a married woman faces the consequence of confessing her adulterous love for her stepson. The last literary citation comes from Lucian's *The Lover of Lies, or the Doubter,* in which, to illustrate what a lie is, the narrator tells the story of an animated statue who took revenge on the man who had wronged her. All these texts evoke the dire consequences of doubling of either meaning or spouses and thus contribute further to the scrambling of the narrative and sexual doubling sketched by the main plot.

The late writers of the fantastic, among them Auguste de Villiers de l'Isle-Adam (1838–1889) and especially Guy de Maupassant (1850–1893), were markedly influenced by Edgar Allan Poe, whose stories Baudelaire translated between 1852 and 1867. In Maupassant's writings the supernatural is internalized: it becomes the mysteries of the human mind. In "Lui?" (1884; "Him?"), "Un fou" (1884; "A Madman"), "Qui sait?" (1890; "Who Knows?"), and mostly in "Le Horla" (1887; "The Horla"), hypnotism, magnetism, and insanity replace ghosts, demons, and spells. "Le Horla" is the diary of a man recording how he is first baffled and then terrified as he comes to believe that a creature that he names the Horla is living in his house and imposing its will on him. The story does not focus on the exploits of the mysterious creature, but on the narrator's growing terror and his attempts both to understand and to escape its grasp. Finally, convinced that his house is possessed by an alien creature determined to destroy and succeed the human race, he sets the house on fire. Only then does it occur to him that the creature may have escaped the fire by possessing him; the story ends with the narrator weighing suicide in order to destroy the Horla. The narrative itself is in the thrall of various digressions or subplots pulling the story in contradictory directions: some lead us to believe that the narrator is insane; others hint at a science fiction horror story in which aliens intend to take over the human race; still others suggest hypnotism. The narrator, the reader, and the narrative confront the same perplexing and unanswered questions. (In an earlier, 1886 version, the narrator, a patient in a mental institution, is convinced of the existence of the alien Horla; the final version undermines this conviction and offers a text and a narrator beset with contradictions and perplexity.)

Today the boundaries between fantastic and realist literature have collapsed. Readers have been trained (in part by the writers of fantastic stories) to accept the ambiguities and doubling effects that once distinguished the fantastic. Perhaps more important, Freud's decisive essay "Das Unheimliche" (1919; "The Uncanny"), in which the distinction between *heimliche* (familiar) and its opposite collapses while giving rise to doubling and mirroring effects, has furnished a strikingly cogent framework suitable for the elaboration of theories of the fantastic. Following Freud's example, literary critics have collapsed boundaries while highlighting doubling and repetitions. Among the most productive are the collapse of the distinction between writing and reading and the mirroring effects between reader and writer. The tenets of the fantastic have thus been generalized and extended to all literary texts. It no longer comes as a surprise to modern readers that their reactions are in fact programmed by the literary text and therefore are textual rather than simply subjective and private.

See also 1704, 1791 (Summer), 1830, 1886.

Bibliography: Jean Bellemin-Noël, "Note sur le fantastique (textes de Théophile Gautier)," *Littérature,* 8 (1972) 3–23. Pierre-Georges Castex, *Le conte fantastique en France: De Nodier à Maupassant* (Paris: José Corti, 1951). Tzvetan Todorov, *The Fantastic: A Structural Approach to a Literary Genre,* trans. Richard Howard (Ithaca: Cornell University Press, 1975).

Ora Avni

1839

Stendhal Publishes *La chartreuse de Parme*

Body Bildung and Textual Liberation

Nothing succeeds like success: in the story of Rastignac's triumphant initiation into the rules, signs, and codes of a pointedly "modern" society, Balzac's *Le père Goriot* (1835) provided European fiction with its master narrative—not to mention its master narratology—for at least the rest of the century. Of all the approaches to this success story (Balzac's no less than Rastignac's), the most forceful today is one that the story has most interest in cutting off to traffic: taking a good look at Rastignac's good looks.

For characters, narrator, and reader alike, Rastignac's *beauté,* cited throughout Balzac's novel, situates a desire whose somewhat scandalous connotations could only precipitate—well beyond the cross-gendered couple—in a frankly polymorphous range of erotic sites, practices, and pleasures. Such a desire finds its nearest narrative acting-out one melodramatic night at the Pension Vauquer, when Vautrin's opiated wine delivers the hero's appealingly insensible body ("Looks very handsome when he's asleep, doesn't he?" p. 180) over to an impromptu touch-group that eagerly forms around it. Vautrin's own kiss follows up on Goriot's embrace only a short while earlier. "Lay your head on his shoulder," Mme. Vauquer advises Mme. Couture, no doubt with her usual prurience, but Rastignac falls instead on top of Victorine, who not only "drops a kiss on his brow," but who also could, "without sin, feel the young man's heart beating against her own" (p. 181). The scene explicitly lays Rastignac's dormant body open to numerous pleasures and dangers, of which Vautrin's homoerotic admiration (said to make Rastignac tremble "in every member") presents the most anxiogenic instance.

The would-be representative Rastignac thus fails momentarily to be identified with the male body elsewhere so immodestly covered up in 19th-century representation, the body whose power and prestige depend on its vanishing into a gaze that cannot effectively be returned. In large measure, *Le père Goriot* is the story of how this identification comes to be achieved. What the text calls

Rastignac's famous "aplomb" (his perpendicularity, his straightness) requires submitting his body to correction, to its most profitable sociosexual appropriation and disposition. For example, Rastignac needs to dress for the success that he seeks, as the text aptly notes, "à corps perdu" (to the point of losing his body, himself), for along with his illusions, it is precisely his body—as a host of pleasures—that he must sacrifice, whether that loss be connoted in the mutilating work of the tailor through whose help he cuts, at last, only a figure; in the bondage of a tie that, even before anyone shows him the ropes, he knows to wear high on the throat; or in the imperforate ideal reflected in the highly polished surface of his boots. Even standing in front of a mirror, Rastignac is less the narcissist spellbound in pleasure at the sight of his own body than the semiotic manager alert to ensure that his body is bearing the signs proper to its social integration.

The heterosexual terms of the vocation to which Rastignac's body is ultimately called cannot therefore be reduced to the issue of a drama of "sexual preference." For what is arrested along with Vautrin is not just the explicit homoeroticism that circulates, in and as the narrative, around Rastignac's body, but also, more important, the pleasurable visibility of the male body as such. That visibility spells capture as directly as Vautrin's arrest follows on the denuding of his muscular torso, on the revelation of those "fatal letters" of identification that—*Le père Goriot* is still being written even in our own American day—have been branded on his broad shoulders. In contrast, by the time of Rastignac's final appearance in the novel, he is visible only as vision itself: hidden in the failing light, he surveys from the heights of Père Lachaise the good things of a world that he wants to "pump" and "penetrate." "And as the first move in the challenge he was flinging at society, he went to dine with Madame de Nucingen" (p. 275). As a metonymy for the decisive heterosexual coupling, however, dinner with Delphine manifests how little this coupling has to do with sexuality. In the role of his mistress, Delphine will network Rastignac into the society of young lions he enviously glimpsed at the opera; in the part of Nucingen's wife, she will offer access to the banker whose tenebrous financial affairs will help make Rastignac's fortune. Moreover, although the screwing never gets beyond so purely exploitative a turn, Delphine is implied to deserve nothing better: she is being justly "punished" for her part in parricide, the murder by exploitation and neglect of her father, Goriot; and the punishment will receive a Dantesque refinement when, many years later, Rastignac abandons her to marry her own daughter. Dining with Mme. de Nucingen serves a worldly ambition; it serves a patriarchal morality that justifies the practices of this ambition; but (partly for these reasons) it does not noticeably advance the cause of the pleasure it appears to be euphemizing. As though making *her* were just another part of the arduous self-discipline involved in making *it,* pleasure disappears into the homosocial ceremonies that, by holding a figurative place for pleasure, have become its literal replacement.

The mortification of Rastignac's body is a primary condition and effect of his social success. As such, it represents his correct understanding and incorporation of the novel's theme of "the death of the father." Naïvely, old father Goriot thinks that when he dies, the society that "turns on fatherhood" will go with him; on the contrary, the working of Balzac's patriarchy exacts the death or disembodiment of him who would bear the name of father. For its symbolic capacity to structure the flow of meaning and power, this name depends on *not* being identified with the all-too-vulnerable or desirable bodies of actual men, who must instead learn to identify with the impersonal role of facilitating the circulation, whether of women, workers, or other "goods," between them. The lesson is as antipathetic to Goriot, who would jealously keep his daughters to himself ("No more marrying!" p. 262), as it is to the novel's other failed father figure, Vautrin, whose unrealized dream of becoming a slaveowner in the American South betrays the same inaptly ancien régime understanding of paternity as a hoarding of bodies by a sovereign who thinks he may remain fully embodied himself.

The abstraction of the male body thus assists in the capitalist construction of a male subject of exchange, who at his most efficient tends to the lack of particularity, the mobility, and the infinitely removed finality of money. Just as Rastignac's body disappears into its symbolic function, so too does his psychology gradually (in subsequent appearances in *La comédie humaine* [1842–1850; *The Human Comedy*]) get flattened to the series of social roles the last of which, epitomizing the development it also crowns, is minister of the interior. The price of success under Balzac's patriarchal capitalism is a rigorous ascesis—an ascesis that consists not in the renunciation of desire but, less traditionally, in the renunciation of anything that might interfere with desire in motivating an endless exchange of commodities.

Balzac's text bears the marks of having instructed itself in the same lesson it teaches its hero. It adheres to the mimetic project that accumulates an abundance of details about the world but only as part of a deeper commitment to the semiotic project that unceasingly encodes this abundance into signs, types, socially usable meanings. Even its garrulity—its recurrent need to demonstrate its competence in the codes that it also has a recurrent need to invent—serves the fantasy of a terse economy of design in which every part is recovered in the eventual legibility it procures. The sheer telling of this success story dramatizes in its own compulsive self-mutilation the same conversion of flesh into word, "reality" into "semiology," that is the condition for success within the story. The flattening of the hero's psychology is perfected only in the narrator—if that term does not already falsify a narration that characteristically refuses to assume the person of its utterance. This narration circumvents even the more obliquely personal affirmation of an imaginary identification with a character by shifting such identification so systematically that its ultimate identification becomes one with the process of shifting itself. Similarly, as he undoes the ending of one novel by resuming the story or reintroducing its characters, often from a different angle, in another, Balzac elides the satisfactions of narrative closure, as though, no less than its hero, the text must be always maintained in a state of desire. From the legendarily abusive accompaniments of

Balzac's composition—the masturbation calculated to stop just short of climax, the consumption of coffee only to intensify the desire to consume it—down to the workaholic prose that never stops to smell, much less to scent, its own floridity of language, and is thus prevented from giving off the dilatant redolence of *style*—everything proceeds as though nothing might more jeopardize this world, this text, this author, than the irrecoverable waste of pleasure. To Balzac goes the credit of inventing for modern French literature the text without pleasure—or rather, the text with no pleasure that it can afford to know.

Balzac himself grasped the affinity of *La chartreuse de Parme* (1839; *The Charterhouse of Parma*) to his own achievement. Or at least, likening the novel in a review to Machiavelli's *The Prince,* he implicitly underlined the perception at the basis of such affinity—that the power at stake in worldly mastery (and in the strictly rationalized plot of such mastery) depends on the elaboration of a knowledge that, in its need to establish and stabilize the links between certain signs and certain meanings, is specifically semiological in kind. Even the configuration of roles in *La chartreuse* picks up that in *Le père Goriot:* the good-looking Rastignac becomes Fabrice, "one of the best looking men in Italy" (p. 130); Vautrin, with his contraband bank and his private agents, goes straight in Mosca, Parmesan minister of finance and police; and the relation between the younger and older man (uneasily varying from mentorship to rivalry) is articulated in terms of a choice between a woman who knows (Delphine, Gina) and a woman who does not know (Victorine, Clélia) how to make the most of her own homosocial instrumentalization. The peripety everywhere implied in Balzac's success story—that the semiology to which worldly desire entrusted its profitable operation was itself a kind of confinement (of the world no less than of the self)—is in Stendhal as explicit as the literal prisonhouses in which his landscape abounds. Yet if Stendhal's novel postulates a Balzacian world, it does so as the condition of what can then be seen, not least in the erotic sense, as its resistance to such a world. This resistance is figured, most obviously, in Fabrice's inability to cathect the plot of worldly ambition that Gina and Mosca seek to promote for him. Whereas Mosca has successfully transformed himself from an officer in the republican army into a minister at the reactionary court of Parma, his example is altogether lost on Fabrice, who seems temperamentally unable to hold the stage in the black Restoration comedy that develops in the wake of Waterloo. Unable, even, to perform: for his indifferent compliance with Mosca's schemes in his behalf is of a piece with the erotic frigidity that returns even his pursuit of love to the boredom it was meant to relieve. Only during his imprisonment in the Farnese tower, at the very moment when such schemes of advancement have most evidently failed, does Fabrice make the abrupt and overwhelming discovery of the erotic passion he doubted he would ever feel. "By a paradox to which he gave no thought, a secret joy reigned in the depths of his soul" (p. 301).

Although joy reigns in the novel's value system as well, this does not mean that the narrator identifies with Fabrice, who after all gives no thought to the paradox the narrator compels us to consider. Insofar as Fabrice is the textual focus for a point of view that puts (erotic) value outside narrative and ultimately outside language itself, then in his own terms, Fabrice would have no terms at all. By contrast, if only by virtue of his status, the narrator is committed to elaborating a plot that, although Fabrice may have no use for it, is indispensable to giving the latter the opportunity for self-affirmation. In occasional remarks, the narration may well appear to take Fabrice's side in the oppositions it constructs; nonetheless, as a construction, it cannot help being on the side of the oppositions themselves. The novel is thus characterized by an irresolvably split identification with, on the one hand, the "divine happiness" that cannot be told and, on the other, the "endless details" of the narrative that can never tell it; with self, spontaneity, and youth, and also with society, mediation, and middle age; with the Charterhouse, the last venue of Fabrice's many seclusions, and with Parma, where only the quintessential courtier Mosca survives—to tell the tale, as it were, of the *amour fou* (mad love) that proves literally killing to the others. The interplay of these oppositions issues in a somewhat different value scheme from that implied by the romantic, Fabrician priority of passion to plot or of self to world. No doubt, the sheer existence of such oppositions implies a political refusal of the tendency to uniformity in the Balzacian success story, where self and society cynically prove more than adequate to each other. Yet because the oppositions regularly provide the conditions for a pleasure that emerges (as in Roland Barthes) on the border or fault-line of an antithesis, this refusal seems itself the prerequisite of a more fundamental attempt to alter the erotic state of the text: Stendhal's narratology is therefore best grasped as an *ars erotica*, a body of techniques for bringing about—in a world and in a textual régime of unrelaxed desiring—the disparate conjunctions hospitable to pleasure. Since the rigors of desire are epitomized in the functionalism of Balzac's plots, the pleasure of Stendhal's resistance to this functionalism erupts most remarkably in torsions and distortions of the narrative line. In itself, plot is not erotic in Stendhal. It becomes so through characters such as Fabrice, for whom it falters, or Gina and Mosca, for whom the possibility of abandoning it at any moment continually qualifies its elaboration. But neither then does eros lie in the simple absence of plot: Fabrice's vague inwardness (whether transcendent or merely spaced-out is impossible to say) participates in his general frigidity until, in the Farnese tower, it suddenly becomes *intriguing*, quickened into the articulations of code and contrivance by the sight of Clélia. In relation to the story it seems to want to tell, Stendhal's plot never stops wavering between overelaboration and outright ellipsis—as though pleasure could only be more and less by turns than the desire it thus perverts.

A "sexual liberation" of the text? Only if we fail to grasp the melancholy that, no longer traditionally restricted to the mournful aftermath of gratification, saturates the pleasure of Stendhal's novel even as it may be thought to occur. With the character of Mosca, the text figures the counterfinality of a pleasure that takes flight from the relentless rationality of business in the world only to be rationalized as this very flight. Pleasure comes to acquire the function of mitigating functionalism, to which it gets assimilated in the process. In no way disrupting the mastery of self and world, such pleasure merely applies to mastery's good conscience the balm of a *savoir-vivre*. The game of cards or dice to which Mosca and Gina continually compare the social world recognizes the constrained nature of participation therein (Gina to Fabrice: "Would you raise any objection to the rules of whist?" p. 121) at the same time that it seems to make such participation optional, less than totally absorbing (Mosca to Gina: "As at the game of tric-trac, *let us get out,*" p. 401). The seam thus implied between the game and its sidelines, between the person of the player and his structurally prescribed position, gives an edge to what may then be taken as a pleasure in the game itself. Although Mosca frequently dreams of abandoning the court, he never comes close to doing so; and in any case he casts his dream in such worldly terms—Gina's teas in Naples would attract the best company, and so on—that it looks less like retirement than like going part-time. It is as though the fantasy of getting out were finally nothing more than a yoga for staying in, and Mosca imagined a self in excess of its professionalization the more thoroughly to identify with the consummate courtier that Gina will sooner die than forgive him for being.

On the other hand, against the pleasure that does no more than make bearable the worldly practices that easily assimilate it, the text sets another kind of pleasure that, because it is less tractable, is also less sturdy, discernible mainly in its own wake. Clélia's death sentence—"she had the joy of dying in the arms of her lover" (p. 482)—is exemplary in directly linking this pleasure to the tableau of its unviability in a world whose business is to elide pleasure. In the premature mortality that claims Sandrino, then Clélia, then Fabrice, then Gina (is something going around?), pleasure is registered only as the exorbitance of the price paid for it—a price so far exceeding the high toll taken by renunciation that someone like Mosca who survives the debacle of the others may be said to be "immensely rich." Should the social order not succeed in making pleasure merely pleasant, the results get thus tragic: whatever liberations cannot be domesticated in the trivial pursuit of a protoyuppie culture are exiled in the catastrophe of a venereal morbidity, staged for effects of wonder and set somewhere beyond recognition. Such lack of recognition makes pleasure, in Stendhal, characteristically insistent and—what comes to the same thing—dubious, in danger of being confused with its opposite, the mere *desire for* pleasure. We feel the pressure of the doubt on the curious acceleration of the narrative toward the end of *La chartreuse* where, by way of ever-more-elaborate but ever-more-perfunctory sequences, the novel multiplies its characteristic "pleasure effects" to the point of paroxysm, as though in a panic to prove what therefore becomes improbable—that haste makes rush.

On the last page of the novel, we are told that Gina did not long survive Fabrice, "whom she adored"—and, a sentence later, that the insipid young prince Ernesto V was "adored by his subjects." With a facility that only adds to the pathos, the code word of bliss dissolves into a formula of public relations. "Divine happiness" has passed away with Clélia and Fabrice; even "every appearance of happiness" has gone with Gina; in such a context, the famous dedication ("To the happy few") that Stendhal puts at the end of the novel is an elegy or even a malediction, hardly the smug invitation to "living well" dear to Stendhal's cult. For by the end of the novel, the few who have been happy are either dead or, like Mosca, happy no longer. The dedication rather bespeaks Stendhal's perversely heroic allegiance to a value that is always on the verge of becoming—may already have become—impossible to practice.

It is no surprise that 19th-century French culture "selected" the text of male desire rather than the text of "unmanning" pleasure: the former model better served (as rationale, as mythology) the various repressions and injunctions on which its social organization depended, and these in turn anchored the representation in a kind of verisimilitude. It is even in keeping with the logic of this model that it should have generated so large a progeny, since reproduction of the species is what passes, when compared to pleasure, as utility. But neither is it inappropriate to the drift of Stendhal's text—all but unrecognized throughout the century—that this text had to await the modern construction of the category and the subject we call "homosexual" before, first with André Gide and later with Roland Barthes, it could be actively revived as a writing practice. Perhaps the only social formation in which the minor, minoritizing value of pleasure has managed to strike root is that composed of those "without progeny": fitted by the chances of a certain minority of their own to understand not just the precariousness but also the necessity of resurrecting Rastignac's body.

See also 1830, 1911.

Bibliography: Honoré de Balzac, *Père Goriot,* trans. Henry Reed (New York: New American Library, 1962). Roland Barthes, "One Always Fails in Speaking of What One Loves," in *The Rustle of Language,* trans. Richard Howard (New York: Hill and Wang, 1986). Leo Bersani, *Balzac to Beckett: Center and Circumference in French Fiction* (New York: Oxford University Press, 1970). D. A. Miller, "Balzac's Illusions Lost and Found," *Yale French Studies,* 67 (1984), 164–181. Stendhal, *The Charterhouse of Parma,* trans. C. K. Scott Moncrieff (New York: New American Library, 1981).

D. A. Miller

 1840

The Académie des Sciences Morales et Politiques Advertises a Competition for the Best Essay on the Topic "What Constitutes Misery?"

Discourses on Misery

In June 1840 the Academy of Moral and Political Sciences awarded 2,500 francs to a journalist named Eugène Buret for his essay on the topic "What constitutes misery? By what signs does it manifest itself in different nations? What are its causes?" Buret died of tuberculosis at the age of thirty-one, leaving a sick widow, an infant daughter, and a fleeting reputation as a student of what was called "political economy." He is unread and forgotten today. The tale, not the teller, warrants our initial attention.

France under the July Monarchy (1830–1848) was awash in alarm and concern over urban poverty, especially with crime and suffering in the streets of Paris. Readers were captivated by the presence of a mysterious and fatal other: *les misérables*. This term, which consigned the destitute to a separate social category, continues to defy translation. There is a historical explanation for this problem: the "meaning" of *les misérables* was encoded from the start. Buret's treatise on "the great social fact of our time," as he called it, is a key to understanding the ambiguous, evasive, and contradictory discourses of misery as they existed around 1840. The first step is to identify common elements among the competing voices.

The subject of misery in 1840 was charged with the memory of barricades (revolution in 1830, rioting in 1832 and 1834, a failed radical uprising in 1839) and haunted by the specter of the cholera epidemic that struck the capital in 1832. The population of Paris was rapidly approaching a million. The precise number offered by the authorities (928,071) is deceptive; there were so many crumbling warrens, shacks on the outskirts, and homeless people that the size of what was called "the floating population" was only estimated. Tension increased that summer as the cost of a loaf of bread rose from seventeen to forty sous, and a wave of spontaneous strikes sent thousands into the streets to protest wage cuts and working conditions in the city. The French economy was beginning a spurt of industrial expansion. A child labor law was passed to regulate textile factories in 1841, and the Railway Act of 1842 stimulated the production of iron. The boom would end by 1848, however, and the July Monarchy collapsed during an economic depression.

Both the cabinet and Parlement made pronouncements on misery in 1840. In February, Minister of the Interior Charles de Rémusat launched a policy review of private and public charity in the face of growing demand for relief. He knew the workhouses in England distinguished between the poor "who can work" and "those who will work." ("It is only by keeping these things separated . . . and by making relief in all cases less agreeable than wages, that any . . . improvement can be hoped for," noted the English Poor Law Commission of 1834.) Should France make the same distinction? In June, Alexis de Tocqueville addressed the Chamber of Deputies on the question of prison reform. Since 1830, he reported, there had been a 36 percent increase in convictions, and the rate of recidivism among convicts was 40 percent. Did incarceration reform individuals or create hardened criminals? Rémusat, for his part, saw the threat of prison as "the unique moral sanction, the last guarantee of the social order." In accordance with a long tradition of official discourse he linked "the institutions of charity and repression" as solutions (quoted in Moreau-Christophe, *Du problème de la misère*, 1 : 457).

Literary portrayals of misery shared this duality. In March 1840 Honoré de Balzac's play *Vautrin* opened in the popular entertainment district known as the "Boulevard du crime." The sinister title character appears in several of Balzac's novels. In *Splendeurs et misères des courtisanes* (1838–1847; *A Harlot High and*

Low), Vautrin's confinement in the Conciergerie prison provides the opportunity for an extended description of a separate criminal underworld. "Prostitution and theft are . . . living protests, male and female, of THE STATE OF NATURE against society," he stated. To "the CONTRARIES in civilization," Paris is "what the virgin forest is for savage beasts" (p. 31). Although Balzac did acknowledge "the vice and crime that result from the circumstances of the unfortunate poor" (p. 293) in *La cousine Bette* (1847), in *Splendeurs* he gibed: "Modern reformers produce . . . nebulous theories, or philanthropic novels; but the thief acts!" (p. 31). One of the writers he undoubtedly had in mind was George Sand, whose novel *Le compagnon du tour de France* (*The Journeyman on the Tour of France*) also appeared in 1840.

Sand's hero, a worker named Pierre Huguenin, was inspired by an actual person (the carpenter Agricol Perdiguier, who later wrote an autobiography). The story, however, is a romance in which the fate of this humble artisan is entwined with that of a count. Poverty was regularly depicted through such melodramatic codes. Félix Pyat moved theater audiences with the plight of society's outcasts in *Les deux serruriers* (1841; *The Two Locksmiths*) and *Le chiffonnier de Paris* (1847; *The Ragpicker of Paris*), but used tricks with identity to save the situation: on his deathbed poor Sam reveals his children's secret inheritance, while foul-smelling Jacques unmasks the villainous baron. Feuilleton (serial) writers also conformed to deadlines, space limitations, and the tastes of newspaper readers. Eugène Sue's novel *Les mystères de Paris* (1842–43; *The Mysteries of Paris*), originally published in *Le journal des débats*, revealed the secret life of misery through a sequence of dramatic installments. Sue, who had a keen interest in money and frequented the snobbish Jockey Club, was delighted when this potboiler became a literary sensation, arguably the first French bestseller. Victor Hugo began his epic tale of a saintly convict (then called *Jean Tréjean, ou les misères*) in 1845, but *Les misérables* was not completed until 1862.

Eighteen-forty was a bounty year for the "nebulous theories" that so irritated Balzac. Louis Blanc's *L'organisation du travail* (*The Organization of Labor*), which demanded a right to work, "social workshops," and the elimination of private production, sold out its first edition in a single month. Flora Tristan's *Promenades dans Londres* (*Strolls in London*) proclaimed: "England resounds on every side with cries of revolt and destruction" (p. v). Pierre Joseph Proudhon's *Qu'est-ce que la propriété?* (*What Is Property?*) condemned private ownership as "theft," an unjust source of inequality. Etienne Cabet's *Le voyage en Icarie* (*The Voyage in Icaria*) portrayed a utopian community that he called a "communist society." Pierre Leroux, a follower of Claude-Henri de Saint-Simon, wrote *De l'humanité, de son principe et de son avenir* (*On Humanity, Its Principle and Future*) and encouraged George Sand with her worker novel *Le compagnon du tour de France*. And *L'atelier*, a monthly newspaper written by and for workers, began to circulate Pierre Buchez's ideas of Christian socialism. The simultaneous appearance of this cluster of works makes clear why, when Karl Marx arrived in Paris in 1843, his fellow German Arnold Runge called it "the new laboratory where world history is formed" (quoted in Pinkney, *Decisive Years*, p. 98).

Misery was also being scrutinized by a fledgling social science. A phalanx of researchers was visiting slum neighborhoods, combing records, and assembling surveys on prostitution, illegitimacy, suicide, and murder. H.-A. Frégier's *Des classes dangereuses de la population dans les grandes villes* (*The Dangerous Classes in the Population of Large Cities*) and L.-R. Villermé's *Tableau de l'état physique et moral des ouvriers* (*Portrait of the Physical and Moral Condition of Workers*), both published in 1840, exemplify a shared attitude among these moral statisticians. Frégier, a bureaucrat, was alarmed by the behavior of "the vicious and poor classes that swarm in the city of Paris." Of "the ragpicker and the nomad," he wrote: "When the proletarian . . . aspires to quaff the cup of pleasure reserved for the wealthy . . . instead of mitigating his poverty by sobriety and thrift . . . his degradation is the deeper for his desire to rise above himself" (quoted in Chevalier, *Laboring Classes,* p. 458). Villermé, a physician, studied the textile industry and reported: "The workers of the manufactures lack sobriety, economy, savings, proper manners, and very often it is their own fault that they are miserable." In general, he concluded, "their condition is better than it has ever been" (*Tableau,* 2:351 and 346). Dangerous class or working class, the solution to the problem of *les misérables* lay in improving their character.

Villermé belonged to the Academy of Moral and Political Sciences, and it was he who announced Eugène Buret's award. This august branch of the Institut de France was composed of economists, legislators, and other social experts distinguished for their political moderation and their allegiance to an unfettered economy. The academy regularly sponsored essays on contemporary questions, and its "glorious suffrage," as one member termed it, could launch the career of an aspiring intellectual. Buret was disappointed by the results, however. The competition was for 5,000 francs, but the committee failed to agree on a laureate and decided to divide the prize; it also announced the next contest: What was "the most useful application" of "the principle of private and voluntary association" to the alleviation of misery? Disgusted by such "questions and answers on to eternity," Buret used the academy's money to witness English poverty for himself, added a 100-page introduction to his manuscript, and published it in two volumes under the title *De la misère des classes laborieuses en Angleterre et en France* (*On the Misery of the Laboring Classes in England and France*). The appearance of this text at the end of 1840 added a fresh meaning to the term *les misérables*.

Buret was born in October 1810 in Troyes, a town long known for its hat-making and knitting industries. His father, a shopkeeper, invested his savings in "the education of a son" (as Buret *père* stated in a letter), but nothing is known about his youth or when he arrived in the Latin Quarter; he translated a German volume on geography in 1835 and contributed to *Le courrier français* the next year. Around this time he read *Nouveaux principes d'économie politique* (1819, rev. 1827; *New Principles of Political Economy*), by Simonde de Sismondi, a Genevan who was among the first to grasp the importance of a passage in *The Wealth of Nations* (1776) where Adam Smith laments that "the progress of the division of labour" induces a corrupted "state into which the labouring poor . . . must necessarily fall, unless government takes some pain to prevent it"

(*Wealth,* pp. 734–735). Whether it was Sismondi's influence or the fact that knitting machines and hat factories had appeared in Troyes, or both, Buret decided to make his mark as a man of letters by entering the academy's competition. After his death he was praised for "the independence of his spirit" by Adolphe Blanqui, a political economist and academician, who thought him the best theorist of his generation.

Buret shared his contemporaries' conviction that urban poverty had become severe and appeared to be worsening. Part of his originality lay in a bold dismissal of received wisdom. Not only did he consider it "beyond the power of private or public charity to decrease misery"; he also disagreed with "those distinguished writers who blame the vices of the poor for the suffering and privation they endure" (*Misère,* 1:391). Instead, he transmuted "the social mystery we are trying to solve" from an objective into a subjective reality. "Misery," Buret stated, "is poverty felt morally . . . a phenomenon of civilization; it presupposes . . . the higher development of the human consciousness . . . Certain classes of mankind suffer the most extreme poverty, but not misery in our sense. The Picardy peasant . . . is as poor as a man can be, but he . . . is not *misérable*" (p. 118).

While Alexis de Tocqueville looked across the Atlantic to discern the habits of a democratic society (the second volume of *De la démocratie en Amérique* [*Democracy in America*] appeared in 1840), Buret described the moral landscape of an industrialized world in England. What was truly controversial about his analysis was his insistence that "the picture of the wealth of nations must be confronted with the picture of the misery of nations" (1:13). Few at the time were prepared to accept his implication that *les misérables* were the creatures of progress.

"Walking in the streets of London and other large cities . . . will teach you more . . . than the most learned statistics," Buret wrote. "In the very heart of the busiest centers of industry and trade you see thousands of human beings reduced to a state of barbarism . . . outside society, outside the law" (2:327). "Under the present industrial system," he reported, "no kind of moral bond exists between master and worker . . . In the mind of the owner, workers are not men but units of energy . . . rebellious instruments, and less economical than tools of iron and fire" (2:269–270). Machines "divide the population engaged in production into two distinct classes, opposed in their interests: the class of capitalists, owners of the instruments of work, and the class of wage workers" (2:146). Since "the industrial army offers no advancement," he noted, "a silent hostility exists between workers and employers, which breaks out on the least occasion and each time with a redoubled violence" (2:142). His term for this incipient conflict was "social warfare."

"Must we conclude that liberty is everything?" Buret asked; "should not the first duty of social authority . . . be to ensure that liberty for some does not become the servitude of others? Absolute *laisser-faire* is not better in industrial than in political affairs; its true name is anarchy" (1:17). "The poor," he warned, "have already inspired their theoreticians, who maintain that political institutions are the cause of the people's suffering. Let governments beware!" (1:74). *De la misère des classes laborieuses* was an undeniable herald of the *Manifesto of the Communist Party* (1848): it anticipated Friedrich Engels' *The Condition of the Working Class in England* (1844), and Marx's journal of 1845 contains passages copied from it. That is not how Buret was heard in 1840, however. His treatise was taken as an accusation that the July Monarchy was creating "masses of *misérables*" by its economic policy.

A final piece of evidence to add to the discourses of misery is the end of Buret's own life. The sources are slight—an obituary in the *Journal des économistes* and a dusty file in the Archives Nationales—but the story they tell is like a missing chapter from Henry Murger's account of the poor intelligentsia of the 1840s, *Scènes de la vie de bohème* (1851; *Scenes of Bohemian Life*).

Eugène Buret lived for less than two years after the publication of his treatise on misery. Late in 1840 he married the twenty-year-old daughter of a poor tax clerk; a daughter was born in July 1841. By that time Buret's illness was serious enough for him to seek the Algerian sun. The need to support his family would not let him rest, however. He returned to Paris and wrote three articles and a book favoring French colonization in North Africa before he died in August 1842, within a few days of Sismondi, allegedly while annotating a volume by Adam Smith. His wife struggled to survive on 600 francs from the minister of public instruction. "Two years of pain and suffering," she explained, "have exhausted our few resources. I find myself with a child of fourteen months and my health greatly compromised" (Archives Nationales F17 312B: 10 September 1842). Auguste Blanqui, who had arranged the modest pension, informed the minister that she would soon "follow her husband to the tomb" (ibid., 4 September 1842). After Buret's widow died in March 1843, their orphaned daughter was sent to reside with Buret *père,* who described himself as living "in near indigence" (ibid., n.d.). The old man sent a petition to Paris asking to receive his son's pension; he also got the mayor of Troyes to vouch for his character. There is no record of his response when the request was denied.

Bibliography: Honoré de Balzac, *La cousine Bette,* ed. Anne-Marie Meininger, vol. 7 of *La comédie humaine,* ed. Pierre-Georges Castex (Paris: Gallimard, 1977). Balzac, *Splendeurs et misères des courtisanes,* ed. Pierre Citron, vol. 6, ibid. Eugène Buret, *De la misère des classes laborieuses en Angleterre et en France,* 2 vols. (Paris: Paulin, 1840). Louis Chevalier, *Laboring Classes and Dangerous Classes,* trans. Frank Jellinek (New York: Howard Fertig, 1973). L. M. Moreau-Christophe, *Du problème de la misère et de sa solution chez les peuples anciens et modernes,* 3 vols. (Paris: Guillaumin, 1851). David H. Pinkney, *Decisive Years in France, 1840–1847* (Princeton: Princeton University Press, 1986). Hilde Rigaudia-Weiss, *Les enquêtes ouvrières en France entre 1830 et 1848* (1936; reprint, New York: Arno, 1975). Adam Smith, *An Inquiry into the Nature and Causes of the Wealth of Nations,* ed. Edwin Cannan (New York: Modern Library, 1937). L.-R. Villermé, *Tableau de l'état physique et moral des ouvriers,* 2 vols. (Paris: Renouard, 1840).

Robert Bezucha

◯◯ *1843, 9 June*

The Last Part of Honoré de Balzac's *Illusions perdues*
Begins to Appear in Serial Form

Publishing Novels

In May and June 1843, Honoré de Balzac, closeted in his printer's shop, was feverishly writing the third and last part of *Illusions perdues* (*Lost Illusions*), "Les souffrances de l'inventeur" ("Eve and David"), which, following "Les deux poètes" (1837; "Two Poets") and "Un grand homme de province à Paris" (1839; "A Distinguished Provincial at Paris"), brought to completion, in his words, this "capital work within the work" (quoted in Chollet, "Introduction," p. 3). On 9 June, though still unfinished, this last part began to appear in serial form. It then joined the eighth volume of *La comédie humaine* (1842–1850; *The Human Comedy*), the Dantesque title under which, after 1842, Balzac regrouped the near totality of his fiction, past and future. This fragmented mode of publication was typical of Balzac's practice and of the conditions of production during the July Monarchy (1830–1848). The previous year Balzac had written the famous "Avant-propos" ("Foreword"), outlining the extraordinary scope of his project in *La comédie humaine*. Drawing a parallel between humanity and animality, it propounds Balzac's conception of social species, together with his unitary theory of energy and "thought" (all affective and intellectual processes): society both improves and corrupts, and thought is both a social and a destructive force. The writer, who studies the reason behind social effects and the *spirit* of forgotten laws, is equal or superior to the statesman.

A *Bildungsroman* of epic proportions and encyclopedic content, *Illusions perdues* also thematizes its own creation and takes the whole institution of literature as its object. It reflects on political, economic, and social power and, implicitly, on the crises of power. Although its action is set in 1821–22, the novel is written with the hindsight of the July Monarchy; and although it describes the rise of the Romantic movement, it is written during its ebb. The theme of disillusion develops around the opposition between Paris and the provinces (represented by Angoulême, a city known for its paper factories) and soon focuses on the contemporary transformation of literature into a material and intellectual commodity. Only in Paris can Lucien Chardon, one of Balzac's distinctive type of talented, ambitious young men, become rich and famous, that is, find a publisher for his novel and volume of poetry, and obtain the king's ordinance that will allow him to repudiate Chardon, his father's name, and grant him the name of his noble maternal ancestors, de Rubempré. Although the first goal is more salient, both determine Lucien's actions in Paris. And his failure will be the direct result of his weakness and vanity. The mechanisms of the literary market even become part of Balzac's usual depiction of monomania—understood as a concentration of energy on a single passion—for the demon of invention that possesses and temporarily ruins Lucien's devoted friend, David

Séchard, drives him to experiment tirelessly with the formula for a cheaper kind of paper. "In a volume which," in Balzac's words, "owes its existence in book form to the paper industry no less than to the printing-press" (*Works,* 8 : 107), David's passion serves as an introduction to the long historical and technical digression of the first part on the making of paper. "Les souffrances de l'inventeur" narrates the capitalist exploitation of David's "discovery" of vegetal paper by his powerful competitors, who steal his secret, in one of those minute private conspiracies and intricate legal schemes that Balzac was a master at devising.

The very first line of *Illusions perdues* singles out the Stanhope press as a major innovation in printing. This and other technical improvements contributed to the overproduction of books, and the picture presented in "Un grand homme de province à Paris" (the second part of the novel) probably owes something to the commercial crisis of 1827–28, which had been fatal to Balzac's own printing shop, as well as to the stagnation of 1836. When Lucien arrives in Paris after eloping with Anaïs de Bargeton (who, realizing her poet's insignificance, soon forsakes him), he finds it impossible to get his novel published. The various stages of his ordeal illuminate the incredible mismanagement of the book trade. From 1810 until the Revolution of 1848, printers and booksellers, subjected to surveillance, obtained their licenses on the basis of their moral and political character. The printer-publishers, themselves exploited by the booksellers, in turn exploited the authors, and the price of books was beyond the reach of most people: Lucien reads at the Bibliothèque Sainte-Geneviève or, for a small fee, in a *cabinet de lecture* (commercial reading room). Authors could legally *sell* their books to publishers, and often thus renounced their ownership—for a very low price if they were unknown. Even after becoming a journalist and literary critic to be reckoned with, Lucien falls victim to this situation. Dauriat, a successful publisher-bookseller, buys his poems to pacify him but never publishes them, because of overproduction in poetry. And the lesser publisher who buys Lucien's novel goes bankrupt, a frequent occurrence. The novel appears, but is sold in bulk and peddled out on the bridges and banks of the Seine. The text also alludes to the competition of Belgian piracy, whose heyday was actually between 1830 and 1840: the Belgians would reprint a three-volume novel, selling at 7.50 francs per volume, in a single-volume large-size edition at 3.50 francs. In 1838 Gervais Charpentier became the first French publisher to launch similar cheap editions on the French market.

Balzac's picture leaves out exceptional success stories on the model of Victor Hugo's, but Lucien's adventures amply show that, with the disappearance of patronage, most writers, in order to survive, had to turn to *petit journalisme* (the small literary sheets written at least in part by hack journalists). Too frequently corrupt—and, according to Balzac's preface of 1839, even more so in 1839 than in 1821—*petit journalisme* is the object of a forceful and systematic satire. Once they become journalists, the former victims of the book trade turn into its exploiters: the intricate plot brings out the *petit journal*'s disastrous action. In order to sell, publisher-booksellers have to advertise. The high price of advertisements supports the newspaper but ruins the bookseller (hence the stretching of novels over two or three volumes in order to recoup the expense of advertising), and the *réclame,* a form of publicity somewhere between the advertisement and the book review, substitutes venality for free judgment. Charles Augustin Sainte-Beuve also denounced this circular effect a few months after the publication of "Un grand homme" in his article "De la littérature industrielle" (1839; "On Industrial Literature"). Lucien soon becomes adept at turnabouts and betrayals, the bartering of favors, the reselling of free books and theater tickets, and the little game of veiled threats and false stories (although he stops short of blackmail). Some episodes demonstrate how the mostly liberal literary papers, though not allowed to treat political matters, nevertheless contributed to the fall of Charles X by means of insidious, ad hominem attacks.

Repeatedly faced with choices between the authentic values of high literature, represented by the (future) great novelist d'Arthez, and the shallow values of journalism, Lucien invariably opts for the second, but, in the words of one journalist, "all ideas, Janus-like, are binary" (9:225). The neat oppositions that denounce the quantification of quality and the prostitution of ideas are contradicted by the high value set on work—an important condition of quality, and yet a bourgeois value that partially depends on quantity. One of the greatest scenes in *La comédie humaine,* toward the end of *Illusions perdues,* further compounds the scrambling of values. After liberals and royalists have joined forces to ruin him, a repentant Lucien returns home to Angoulême, where, once more duped by flattery, he becomes the unknowing instrument of David's arrest for debt and departs, leaving a suicide note behind. On his way to death he meets a Spanish Jesuit, Carlos Herrera, who derides laws and moral principles and outlines the ruthless code of ambition. He praises virile affections and promises to realize all of Lucien's frustrated hopes in exchange for Lucien's compliance. Some readers understand Herrera's somber satire as an invitation to revolt, although his professed, cynical intention is to exploit a corrupt social state to his own advantage. Seduced by the sight of gold, by Herrera's brilliant rhetoric and seeming political leverage, and by the prospect of unqualified support and love, Lucien instantly accepts the Faustian pact. *Splendeurs et misères des courtisanes* (1838–1847; *A Harlot High and Low*) recounts his resurrection in Paris, his ascent into aristocratic society, and his downfall and final suicide in prison.

The dialogue and narrative often designate Lucien as "the poet." At first associated with an idealist, Romantic, and all-embracing conception, the term is used ironically after Lucien's encounter with the realities of the literary market, until finally he is described as "a continuous novel." And indeed, through the self-reflective and metafictional dimension of *Illusions perdues,* it is the novelist who emerges as the true poet. Of the three contradictory reviews that Lucien has to write about the novel of another character, Nathan, the first two constitute significant samples of literary criticism (the third one is barely touched upon). The first review introduces Balzac's familiar opposition between a literature of ideas, in Voltaire's dry narrative manner, and a literature of images, the new novel of Romanticism, with passion and drama, ample dia-

695

logues and descriptions. The second review expounds Balzac's own ambition, "to give expression to ideas through images, [thus achieving] the highest form of art" (9:227). More attuned to the dramas of the past thirty years, this new novelistic form supersedes comedy as the major genre. Combining all other genres, it is "the greatest creation of modern days" (9:227).

Thus *Illusions perdues* both theorizes and exemplifies Balzac's own archaeological, encyclopedic, and poetic project. Among many unity- (and "realism"-) producing devices, the most salient is probably Balzac's invention of reappearing characters. In *Splendeurs et misères*, Carlos Herrera turns out to be none other than Jacques Collin, alias Vautrin, a former convict, from *Le père Goriot* (1835): he will end as head of the Paris police. As for the first part of what was to become *Splendeurs et misères*, though published (under the title *La Torpille*) one year before "Un grand homme de province," it already contains the sequel to the not-yet-published Lucien's adventures in Paris. And the successful, mature d'Arthez of *Les secrets de la princesse de Cadignan* (1839; *A Princess's Secrets*) appeared the same year as the unknown, destitute d'Arthez of *Illusions perdues*. Balzac pulls the strings of nearly 2,000 characters through ninety-six novels and short stories. To plunge into this parallel universe and find one's way in its space and temporality is a unique experience.

Illusions perdues does not describe the development of the main newspapers, but it bears its mark in several ways. Lucien professes an aristocratic indifference to the matter of the signature, but in 1829, in the newly founded *Revue de Paris,* the insertion of the author's name under each piece testified to a new sense of literary ownership, related to the end of patronage. This concern, which Sainte-Beuve deplored in regressive, elitist terms, led to the foundation of the Société des Gens de Lettres (Society of Authors) in 1838, in which Balzac was instrumental. And on 1 July 1836 a decisive event for the novel occurred: the launching of two dailies, *La presse* and *Le siècle,* by Emile de Girardin and Armand Dutacq, respectively. They reduced the price of yearly subscriptions by half (there were hardly any sales by issue), developed advertising on a large scale, and introduced the serial publication of novels, which easily doubled or tripled circulation. Within a year most new and old dailies had to follow suit. Balzac's *La vieille fille* (23 October 1836; *The Old Maid*) was the first French novel in France to be published originally in installments in a daily. By 1839–40 this form of lucrative prepublication prevailed, and the serial novel—whose masters were not Balzac, but Paul Féval, Alexandre Dumas, Frédéric Soulié, and Eugène Sue—had developed specific techniques. Fiction became directly dependent on the financial and political interests that controlled the press, not the least influential of which was the buying public. And serial publication temporarily decreased book sales while, together with the spread of literacy, it enlarged the readership. (Between 1820 and 1834, except for bestsellers, novels were published in editions of about 1,000 and often less. By 1841 the size of editions had risen to 1,500, although the actual number of titles had somewhat decreased.)

The advent of serials affected the novelistic genre in two ways. First, while trying to accommodate the tastes of less sophisticated readers, it also modified the reading expectations and possibly the tastes of the traditional, educated audience. It highlighted the suspense and drama, historical background, or sentimental and gothic variations of Romantic fiction but discarded its metaphysical questioning and poetic innovations, avoided lengthy descriptions, was heavy on dialogue and action, and subjected the plot, if not always to the happy ending of the popular formula, at least to a reassuring conclusion in an orderly world. Plebeian and criminal characters, previously confined to melodrama, began to appear as protagonists and in their own setting. Social Romanticism, which expanded after 1836, is characteristic of this new trend in fiction.

Second, publication in installments sometimes directly influenced the progress of the story while it was still being written. An outstanding example is *Les mystères de Paris* (19 June 1842 – 15 October 1843; *The Mysteries of Paris*), by Eugène Sue. Even before the advent of daily serials in 1836, Sue had advocated the episodic novel in the preface to his novel *Atar-Gull* (1831), and he had no idea of where he was going when he wrote the first chapters of *Les mystères de Paris,* whose instant, fabulous success forced him to pick up the thread. The plot is governed by the themes of paternity, crime, and redemption. Prince Rodolphe, the protagonist, had raised his hand against his father and thus will be punished in his paternity. His daughter was kidnapped as a child, and he finds her again many years later on the street in Paris, a beautiful flower still pure in spirit. She is redeemed but will die of remorse and, in Marxist terms, of religious alienation. First a Christlike figure, Rodolphe is above all God the Father, the providence of the poor and good, the scourge of the wicked, and his actions become more and more identified with the charismatic Word of Sue the novelist. In the early episodes it was clearly an aristocratic reader whom Sue took slumming in the social depths of Paris, and it was the fears of the upper classes, faced with the massive urban expansion of the 1840s and the increase in crimes and in general mortality, that his picture reflected. But the cultural disparity between the novelist and his eventual actual readership led to a disruption of aesthetic and referential norms: the outside "real" irrupted into the novelistic universe. As letters kept pouring in, Sue assumed the role of social reformer that most readers ascribed to him, and, in his words, abandoned "art" in favor of a social mission. Adopting a pedagogical form similar to Balzac's, but more obviously contrived, he conducts a systematic review of strategic social points, with alternation of disquisitions and episodes explicitly destined to provide the evidence. From a naïve advocate of private charity, the narrator turns into a spokesman for doctrinal and utopian socialism, proposing a system of government rewards for deserving workers, loan banks for the unemployed, and a reform of the legal, penal, and medical systems. His strong statements on the exploitation of women as commodities in and out of marriage point toward a restructuring of gender relations. Some isolated letters from working-class readers proposed radical rather than specific reforms. Sue himself did not voice the need for a general restructuring of society, but this need could easily be inferred from his massive investigation, notwithstanding the indictment of

Les mystères de Paris in Marx and Engels' *Die heilige Familie* (1845; *The Holy Family*). Such at least was the view of Sue's contemporaries. Sue's tremendous impact on all social layers was believed to have contributed to the Revolution of 1848, and in 1850 a new press law, taxing the publication of novels in installments, tolled the end of the first golden age of the serial novel.

See also 1734, 1839.

Bibliography: James Smith Allen, *Popular French Romanticism: Authors, Readers, and Books in the Nineteenth Century* (Syracuse: Syracuse University Press, 1981). Honoré de Balzac, *Lost Illusions,* trans. Ellen Marriage, Clara Bell, and R. S. Scott, vols. 8–10 of *The Works of Honoré de Balzac* (1901; reprint, Freeport, N.Y.: Books for Libraries Press, 1971). Jean-Louis Bory, *Eugène Sue, le roi du roman populaire* (Paris: Hachette, 1962). Roland Chollet, "Introduction, Notes and Variants to *Illusions perdues,*" in Balzac, *La comédie humaine,* ed. Pierre-Georges Castex, vol. 5 (Paris: Gallimard, 1976). Umberto Eco, "Rhetoric and Ideology in Sue's *Les mystères de Paris,*" International Social Science Journal, 19 (1967), 551–569. René Guise, "Balzac et le roman feuilleton," *L'année balzacienne 1964,* pp. 283–338. Charles Augustin Sainte-Beuve, "De la littérature industrielle," in *Portraits contemporains,* vol. 2 (Paris: Michel Lévy, 1870). Anne-Marie Thiesse, "L'éducation sociale d'un romancier: Le cas d'Eugène Sue," *Actes de la recherche en sciences sociales,* 32–33 (April–June 1980), 51–63.

Lucienne Frappier-Mazur

1847, 23 December
The Algerian Resistance Leader 'Abd-al-Qadir Surrenders to the French

Orientalism, Colonialism

The capitulation in Sidi-Brahim of the Algerian leader 'Abd-al-Qadir on 23 December 1847, after prolonged resistance, was seen by French authorities as their rightful, if hard-won, conquest of an ancient but "half-civilized" society. The pretext for the subjection of Algeria to the French *mission civilisatrice* (civilizing mission) had been provided when Hussein Pasha, the dey of Algiers, struck the French consul-general in the face with a peacock-feather fly swatter in the spring of 1827. The French blockaded the port; by July 1830 their flag was flying over the Casbah, and 7,000 kilograms of gold were under French "protection." These events, foreshadowing the imperial expansion that would soon put most of the globe under European control, stand in a disconcerting relation to contemporary intellectual and artistic movements. One of the most important of these is the preoccupation of 19th-century Europe with "the Orient."

Orientalism must be seen from a dual perspective. For participants in the movement, the Orient was an intellectual adventure based on realistic acts of *description;* from a late 20th-century point of view, "orientalism" is a political mythology passing itself off as objective truth. The initial view is defined by the *Larousse du XIXe siècle* (1866–1879), in which orientalism is not merely the "new science" of the "Orient" (a term Larousse admits is excessively vague), but also a belief in the primacy of the East. Five years before 'Abd-al-Qadir's surrender, an idealistic young historian named Edgar Quinet had proclaimed an "Oriental Renaissance," in which Europe and Asia, twin "echoes of the same Word," would find their common ground again and form an "alliance." This second renaissance would reform Western thought as the 16th-century one had, but under the powerful influence of Indian, Persian, and Islamic traditions. What relation can there be between the bloody victory of 1847 and the peaceful project of scholarly inquiry described by Quinet in 1842? Answers to such questions are provided by retrospective studies, which have revealed the manipulative nature of orientalist thought. The French scholar Raymond Schwab, in his exhaustive study *La renaissance orientale* (1950; *The Oriental Renaissance*), asserted that orientalism "undermined the wall" between East and West, but that "the dismantling was done in the West's self-interest" (p. 1). Edward Said's influential *Orientalism* (1978) goes deeper into political questions and defines orientalism as "a Western style for dominating, restructuring, and having authority over the Orient" (p. 3).

It was in fact clear from the beginning that orientalism was a question of power. In *Le génie des religions* (1842; *The Nature of Religions*), Quinet shows that distinctions between artistic expressions and political movements were negligible: the "sovereign *poet* who, better than any other, cemented the union between Europe and Asia . . . writing the poem of alliance in lines of blood," was Napoleon (p. 61). Bonaparte's Egyptian expedition (1798–1801) was indeed an intellectual as well as a military enterprise; it led to the founding of the Institut d'Egypte in Cairo, which would eventually produce the twenty-three-volume *Description de l'Egypte* (1809–1828; *Description of Egypt*). The occupation also expanded French power and paved the way for future interventions. The Rosetta Stone, discovered by Bonaparte's troops in 1799, symbolized the mystery of the Orient, as Jean-François Champollion's deciphering of its hieroglyphics in 1821 symbolized the power of orientalism. Mastery of the territory permitted mastery of its secrets. Napoleon, a fellow and vice-president of the Institut, set the tone for French orientalism, with its peculiar blend of raw power and intellectual curiosity. The close alliance between these two faces of orientalist discourse is ambiguous and troubling: when the administration of the Collège de France considered whether to discontinue the chair of archaeology in 1837, the decision not to do so was based on the importance that had accrued to the field (as an administrator put it) "through the works of oriental scholars, through the conquests of Champollion, and *thanks to our armies in Egypt, Greece, and Asia,* through the discovery of so many monuments" (Schwab, *Oriental Renaissance*, p. 389; emphasis added). Scholars and soldiers were engaged in parallel enterprises.

The Orient before the 19th century was largely a conventional image, used for exoticism, invented to suit the agenda of, for example, Montesquieu's *Lettres persanes* (1721; *Persian Letters*). In the late 18th century, philologists and linguists began to explore languages previously unknown to Westerners, and a new Orient began to emerge. Silvestre de Sacy, author of *Chrestomathie arabe* (1826; *The Arab Chrestomathy*) and numerous other anthologies and compilations, invented the new orientalism almost by himself; he became the authoritative source for all who would enter the field in the 19th century. Along with Edward Lane in England, Sacy was read and studied by scientific and literary orientalists throughout the 19th century. The literary ones who did not travel (like Hugo) found their Orient in books by European scholars; those who did travel (such as Gérard de Nerval, Théophile Gautier, and Flaubert) perceived the Orient through the perspective their readings had given them. Nerval copied passages from Sacy and Lane into his own writings; plagiarism was widespread among travel accounts.

Raymond Schwab suggests that Romanticism in its entirety may be understood as a reflection of orientalism; the Oriental Renaissance is synonymous with Romanticism as affirmation, as assent to all things in a united world "where one did not have to choose between yes and no" (*Oriental Renaissance*, p. 485). It is certain that Romanticism and orientalism coincided historically and shared common themes, and that the intellectual genealogy of both passes through Germany. It was Friedrich Schlegel who at the turn of the 19th century stated: "We must seek the supreme Romanticism in the Orient" (quoted in ibid., p. 13). Victor Hugo echoes this call in his preface to *Les orientales* (1829) and obeys it in the poems that follow.

Les orientales is the first major manifestation of orientalist Romantic literature. The preface implies that a new poetic force is to emerge here, one that the poet can channel but not completely control: "The Orient, as an image or as a thought, has become for the intellect and for the imagination a sort of general preoccupation that the author of this book has obeyed, perhaps unwittingly. Oriental colors, as if by themselves, came to be imprinted on all his thoughts, all his reveries; and his reveries and thoughts each turned out to be, and without wanting it to be so, Hebraic, Turkish, Greek, Persian, Arab, even Spanish" (*Orientales*, p. 580).

Hugo's description of his oriental thoughts as semiautonomous entities beyond his creative control is not merely a conventional disclaimer. Seen from a late 20th-century perspective, the important point is not the oriental colors themselves but rather the power of such a "preoccupation" to control the thoughts of a generation. Orientalism was a *discourse*, a body of linguistic and extralinguistic expressions capable of shaping the perception of reality. *Les orientales* was a revolutionary work in many ways, with fantastic catalogues of images, elaborate footnotes on Arabic and Persian literature (on which Hugo was coached by the novelist and translator Ernest Fouinet), and innovations in verse form (for which he was accused of writing "verses in prose"). All these features seem to increase the sheer power of the work. But the power belongs more to Hugo than to the Orient: it is the power to assert, to designate, to marshal "a hundred idols," "monsters born of hideous couplings," bridges, mountains, and somber avenues, and then to make them disappear. It is also the erotic power to see "Sara la baigneuse" ("Sara Bathing") through her veil and robe, to know her inner thoughts, or rather to create them for her. As an exercise in power *Les orientales* was never equaled in other French orientalist poetry. And it is clear that the revolutionary Romanticism of these poems derives its strength mainly from a manipulation of the Orient as a figure.

Many of the most important writers of the day sought inspiration from the Orient not only through reading, as Hugo did, but also through direct contact. Their travel accounts are the richest documents available to us. For these writers, *le voyage* was both a physical movement and a literary genre that allowed new freedoms. From François-René de Chateaubriand, through Baudelaire, to Pierre Loti and Maurice Barrès, the *voyage en Orient* was not merely an escape from the ennui of Europe but also a pilgrimage designed to enrich one's artistic production. Chateaubriand stated in 1811, "I set off to seek images, that is all" (*Itinéraire de Paris à Jérusalem* [*Journey from Paris to Jerusalem*], p. 169). Eugène Delacroix, part of an official mission to Morocco in 1832, came back with thousands of drawings, which he used as a dictionary of images for the rest of his career. Théophile Gautier called his own trip a "pious pilgrimage to the places on earth where beauty makes God more visible" (*Oeuvres complètes*, 2:6). And Flaubert saw the Orient as a source of "color, poetry, things sonorous, hot, beautiful" (Bruneau, *Le "conte oriental" de Flaubert*, p. 70).

The voyages of the Romantics are rather ambiguous in their intent and their effect. Writers asserted the primacy of oriental civilization in order to place themselves at odds with their own bourgeois culture; they used the Orient to pry themselves away from classicism. Yet once exposed to the actual people and places of the East, they often reverted to the ethnocentric values of Western civilization.

Chateaubriand's *Itinéraire de Paris à Jérusalem* established a route that many would follow: clockwise around the Mediterranean, to Greece, Turkey, Lebanon, Jerusalem, Egypt, Tunis, and home through Spain. "My *Itinéraire* was no sooner published than it became a guide for whole crowds of travelers," states the author in a preface (*Itinéraire*, p. 695). Chateaubriand makes no claim to have familiarized himself with the peoples he visited, but this does not prevent him from judging their level of civilization. His goal, to compare the sites of the Orient with their descriptions in the Bible and in the writings of the ancients, is frustrated by oriental actuality: the old civilization is dead, and in its place there is only Islam, with "neither a civilizing principle nor a precept capable of improving the character" (p. 908). The European traveler must therefore pick over the ruins: "An obscure traveler, passing over the erased path of vessels that bore the great men of Greece and Italy, I had set off to look for the muses in their homeland; but I am not Virgil, and the gods no longer live on Olympus." The mission was nonetheless a success in that Chateaubriand found the "exact images" he was looking for and could now "correct" and "give local color" to his tableaux of these famous places (p. 892).

Alphonse de Lamartine traveled, from 1832 to 1833, as a *grand seigneur*, surrounded by servants and retainers, for whom he had to rent numerous houses and buy numerous horses. The French Byron could not overcome the barriers between himself and the Orient. Lamartine presents his *Souvenirs, impressions, pensées et paysages pendant un voyage en Orient* (1835; *Remembrances, Impressions, Thoughts, and Landscapes during a Journey in the Orient*) "regretfully," as "fleeting and superficial impressions" written for himself alone, "without science, history, geography, or customs" (*Oeuvres*, 9:6–7). Critics have agreed, finding Lamartine the least reliable of commentators. Charles Augustin Sainte-Beuve reproached him for claiming to resolve all questions concerning a people after a visit of a few weeks. At the end of the four volumes, Lamartine unveils an expansionist political agenda, the manifest destiny of European hegemony over the Orient. By "the right of humanity and civilization," European powers must divide among themselves the "magnificent debris" of the Ottoman Empire, "so that the human race will multiply and grow there, and civilization will be expanded" (12:321). Of course preexisting tribal rights and nationalities will be respected, so long as the population is obedient: "This is merely an *armed* and *civilizing tutelage* that each power will exercise over its protectorate" (p. 323). An overcrowded Europe would thus be able to relieve itself in an Asia that Lamartine sees as empty, "reduced to nothing" (p. 309).

Gérard de Nerval followed the itinerary of Chateaubriand and Lamartine, but his attitude is less explicitly that of a lord and master. His *Voyage en Orient* (wr. 1844–1850, pub. 1851; *Journey to the Orient*), published eight years after his journey, is perhaps the culmination of the genre. Although it does not necessarily depict accurately the countries he visited, it is an openly personal work that makes no claim to total control over the world in its reflections. But the more poetic quality of Nerval's reflections does not leave him unconstrained by the power of orientalist discourse. Nerval's chapter "Le masque et le voile" ("The Mask and the Veil") reveals the narrator's erotic desire to "lift the veil" between himself and the women of Cairo: "Let us stay and try to raise a corner of that austere veil which the goddess of Saïs wears . . . In actual fact, they [the women of Cairo] enjoy more liberty than European women . . . There is certainly the veil, but possibly it is not such a ferocious obstacle as might be imagined . . . From behind that rampart, ardent eyes await you, with all the seductions they can borrow from art" (*The Women of Cairo*, pp. 2–3).

The city is likened to its women; to unveil the women of Cairo, Nerval disguises himself as an Egyptian, touring the city incognito, knowing only one word: *tayeb*, "very good." Following the advice of the neighborhood sheikh, that it is imprudent to live without a "wife," Nerval, struggling against his "European conscience," complies by buying a Javanese slave girl. He teaches her to say "Ze souis one bétit sovaze" (*Voyage*, p. 375), "Eh em a leedle sovidge" (*Women*, p. 151). From her he learns the complement to *tayeb: mafisch*, which "includes all possible negations" (p. 130). Nerval seeks oneness and harmony, the assent of an embracing *tayeb*. But the desire for fusion with the Orient, a world that he sees as a "perfect antithesis of ours," works in strange ways. He concludes that the women of Egypt are freer behind their veils than European women, and that the beliefs of Muslims make them almost "a sort of Christian sect" (*Voyage*, p. 794). The moment of synthesis is a moment of appropriation that obliterates the other, the "oriental," who is not by accident a woman. The project of understanding dead-ends in the politics of power. Choices between yes and no, between *tayeb* and *mafisch,* seemed inescapable, and in that Romanticism failed to find a world of pure affirmation.

Nerval's unremitting desire to lift the veil is symbolic of orientalism as a whole; the Westerner's fantasy of penetrating the harem or the bath is a commonplace theme. In Jean-Auguste-Dominique Ingres's *Grande odalisque* and *Le bain turc* (*The Turkish Bath*), Delacroix's *Femmes d'Alger* (*Women of Algiers*), and countless other paintings, women are observed as if through a peephole, in an intimate privacy that the artist has violated. Not only for Delacroix but also for writers, the Orient was an important source of color: whether metaphorical or visual, "color" was what the Orient could provide.

In Flaubert and Baudelaire the orientalist tradition begins to self-destruct. In Flaubert's life and writings, the Orient is a recurrent, quirky figure; fragments of his personal Orient are scattered throughout his works, both before and after his travels there. Flaubert's voyage, with Maxime Du Camp, covered the usual route and lasted from November 1849 to June 1851. The fact that Flaubert's travel notes and letters were not intended for publication may explain to some extent their special value in the history of orientalist writing: in contrast to Nerval's decorous if persistent striptease of the women of Cairo, Flaubert's comments are openly leering. The Orient for Emma Bovary is a dreamworld of heightened sensuality; Flaubert is ironic about Emma's Orient, yet he sought and experienced something similar while he was actually there. Flaubert's sensual experiences were a good deal earthier than Emma's fantasies: the Orient satisfied the author's taste for the bizarre, the perverse, and the grotesque. In a letter to his mother, Flaubert says that the Orient is equal to and even greater than what he expected: "It is often as though I were suddenly coming upon old forgotten dreams" (quoted in Steegmuller, *Flaubert in Egypt,* p. 75). But to friends he reveals the nature of those dreams: much talk of sodomy, some observations of bestiality, and, most important, the author's adventures with an Egyptian dancer and courtesan named Kuchuk Hanem. "Kuchuk's bedbugs . . . were for me the most enchanting touch of all" (p. 220). Yet the "Oriental woman is no more than a machine" for him, sensual but sterile: not unlike himself. Although Flaubert persistently uses the Orient in his works, most notably in *Salammbô* (1862) and *Hérodias* (1877), he produced no *Conte oriental* and published no travel account. The latter Flaubert considered to be beneath him as an artist. The oriental tale was a project that Flaubert worked on both before and after the voyage, finally abandoning it in 1854. It was supposed to be "antehistorical" but concerned with oriental *humanity,* a challenge to research and to understanding that may have proved too much. We do not know why Flaubert abandoned the project, but his having done so is perhaps an acknowledgment of the limits of Western knowledge, symbolic of the wane of the "Oriental Renaissance." The Orient in Flaubert's works is largely a backdrop: meticulously constructed but portending none of the intellectual fusion with the East that Quinet had announced.

Baudelaire's orientalism sums up and undercuts the Romantic tradition. His parents sent him on a voyage to India in hopes that his poetry would thereafter derive from "better sources than the sewers of Paris." Baudelaire turned back before reaching India, but not before seeing enough to alter his conception of beauty. As defined in his review of the 1855 Paris Exposition, "the beautiful is always bizarre," exotic, unexpected; a European who has visited the tropical, colonial world is in a privileged position to produce beauty. In poems from *Les fleurs du mal* (1857; *The Flowers of Evil*) such as "A une dame créole" ("To a Creole Lady"), "La chevelure" ("The Head of Hair"), and "L'invitation au voyage" ("Invitation to the Voyage"), a fragile but clear economic dependence is described, in which the object of beauty is processed and enhanced by poetic discourse. But although Baudelaire formulates a late orientalist aesthetic, his discourse lacks the sheer confidence and power of *Les orientales*. In "Sed Non Satiata" ("But Unsatisfied")—one of Baudelaire's most scandalous poems—the white male speaker is reduced to impotence by a black female "demon without pity"; power is reversed, playfully. In "Le cygne" ("The Swan"), the discontinuity between worlds that is at the heart of orientalism is expressed as an allegory of pandemic exile and nostalgia, in which no one has a home. All of a sudden the world seems decentered.

Although literary orientalists rarely again displayed the confidence of Hugo and Lamartine, politicians of the late 19th century took up Lamartine's dream of colonization and came close to fulfilling it. Stéphane Mallarmé, in his preface to William Beckford's *Vathek* (1865), describes orientalism as a "veil . . . over political or moral abstractions." As that veil is lifted, the political agenda of colonialism will be articulated as a *mission civilisatrice*. By the end of the 19th century, most of the globe was subjected to what Edward Said calls "manifest orientalism," myth turned into government policy and imposed on colonized peoples. It was mainly in black Africa (the other Orient) and in Algeria that France would most actively play out its orientalist dreams. The word *orientalism* is now seen as synonymous with the power of discourse to create and destroy worlds, to inquire and ignore at once.

See also 1578, 1721, 1933 (February).

Bibliography: Jean Bruneau, *Le "Conte oriental" de Flaubert* (Paris: Denoël, 1973). François-René de Chateaubriand, *Itinéraire de Paris à Jérusalem*, in *Oeuvres romanesques et voyages*, ed. Maurice Regard, vol. 2 (Paris: Gallimard, 1969). Théophile Gautier, *Oeuvres complètes*, vol. 2 (Geneva: Slatkine, 1978). Victor Hugo, *Les orientales*, in *Oeuvres poétiques*, ed. Pierre Albouy, vol. 1 (Paris: Gallimard, 1964). Alphonse-Marie-Louis de Lamartine, *Souvenirs, impressions, pensées et paysages pendant un voyage en Orient*, in *Oeuvres de Lamartine*, vols. 9–12 (Brussels: Méline, 1849). Christopher L. Miller, *Blank Darkness: Africanist Discourse in French* (Chicago: University of Chicago Press, 1985). Gérard de Nerval, *Voyage en Orient*, in *Oeuvres*, ed. Claude Pichois and Jean Guillaume, vol. 2 (Paris: Gallimard, 1960–61); partially translated by Conrad Elphinstone as *The Women of Cairo* (London: George Routledge, 1929). Edgar Quinet, *Le génie des religions*, in *Oeuvres complètes*, vol. 1. (Paris: Pagnerre, 1857). Edward Said, *Orientalism* (New York: Vintage, 1978). Raymond Schwab, *The Oriental Renaissance*, trans. Gene Patterson-

Black and Victor Reinking (New York: Columbia University Press, 1984). Francis Steegmuller, ed., *Flaubert in Egypt: A Sensibility on Tour* (London: Bodley Head, 1972).

Christopher L. Miller

✐ 1848

25 February: Proclamation of the Second French Republic;
23–27 June: Repression of Workers' Uprising

Class Struggles in France

Eighteen-forty-eight: *another* revolution. That "otherness" defines our vision of 1848. From the beginning, the insurrection that occurred in that year has appeared to exist alongside itself, in the image of something else. Its representation has been dominated by the representations of France's earlier uprisings. Those who fought in 1848 suffered from the uncanny impression that they were living not so much an action as an imitation. As they thought about the peculiar alienation of their own experience, the generation of 1848 became conscious of the process and problem of representation itself—of how in modern societies things come to be conceived and perceived.

Authoritative claims have been made that 1848 was France's most significant 19th-century revolution: more fundamental in the contradictions it brought to light than the July Revolution of 1830, more complex and consequential even than the Commune of 1871. Yet those who lived and recalled 1848 as the turning point of the century's political, social, and personal life nonetheless hesitated to credit the revolution with the authenticity of an event truly unprecedented, truly decisive. They seemed to agree that 1848 had made them into what they had become; but they hardly seemed to understand how. And had it really made *history?* Was it *real*—or simply a play of images? The generation of 1848 lacked inner conviction of their revolution's genuineness. In representing the revolution they seem to have been preoccupied with establishing their own reality in the face of a subversive but somehow ineradicable suspicion that there was something absent or defective in them and in their experience.

This failure of authenticity was perceived immediately. In *Der achtzehnte Brumaire des Louis-Napoléons* (1852; *The Eighteenth Brumaire of Louis Bonaparte*) Karl Marx devastatingly characterized the 1848 revolution as an involuntary parody of 1789: "the first time tragedy, the second time farce" (p. 10). But Marx was not alone in detecting this theatrical troping of the French Revolution by its mid-19th-century offspring. Alexis de Tocqueville, who was active in the government in the early stages of the revolution, wrote a remarkable memoir of the period, *Souvenirs* (1850; *Recollections*). For Tocqueville the minds of his revolutionary colleagues were so full of images of 1789 that they "performed the French Revolution rather than continuing it . . . We sought without success to warm ourselves at our fathers' passions; we imitated their gestures and their

705

poses as we had seen them in the theater . . . It all seemed a vile tragedy staged by a provincial troupe" (*Recollections,* p. 53). The convergence of views between the liberal nobleman Tocqueville and the revolutionary socialist Marx is remarkable. But they also shared an even more significant perception: that beneath the ludicrous exterior of 1848, something epochal was occurring. As Tocqueville put it, "the imitation was so visible that the terrible originality of the facts remained hidden" (ibid.).

What happened in 1848? What was the originality that the generation who lived the revolution believed had constituted them, and yet simultaneously felt they could never quite be sure about?

Like those of 1789 and 1830, the events of 1848 overthrew a monarchy and a dynasty. The 1848 revolution proclaimed a republic and enacted a liberal constitution. But the Second Republic lasted only until late in 1851, when Louis-Napoleon, Napoleon I's nephew, who had been elected president of the new republic, overthrew it and built his way toward assuming his uncle's title of emperor. Thus strictly political history gives a strikingly thin image of 1848, as no more than a republican interlude between the authoritarian forms of government of Louis-Philippe's July Monarchy (1830–1848) and Napoleon III's Second Empire (1852–1870).

Social and economic analysis reveals more fully the particularity of the events we know as 1848, for it presupposes precisely the lessons concerning representation that the generation of 1848 was so stressfully in the process of discovering. Unlike political history, which in chronicling a succession of rulers and régimes recounts events that are imagined to bear their meanings openly on their faces, social analysis assumes that its object is veiled or mystified and must be brought to light through the demystifying midwifery of what we have come to call social science. In 1848 these nascent sciences underwent a crucial test.

Again Tocqueville and Marx concur about what was really happening beneath the theatrical posturing of the politicians. Tocqueville conceived the revolution as acting out the drama of "society cut in two: those who had nothing united in a common envy; those who had anything, in a common anguish." The stakes of the revolution were not "the form of government, but . . . the order of society. It was not . . . a political battle, but a battle of classes" (*Recollections,* pp. 98, 136). As for Marx, 1848 was "the first great battle . . . between the two great classes which divide modern society. It was a fight for the preservation or destruction of the bourgeois order" (*Class Struggles in France, 1848–1850* [1895], pp. 58–59).

Before examining the cultural and literary resonances of the battle that emerged into consciousness in the 1848 revolution, let us rapidly outline the stages of the battle itself. For its very chronology had an interpretative significance that was not lost upon those who fought or witnessed it. The years preceding 1848 in France had been ones of severe agricultural and economic crisis: wages dropped 30 percent; food prices more than doubled; unemployment soared. When this led to demonstrations in February 1848 and brutal repression by the government, middle-class revulsion and workers' outrage produced such a powerful reaction that within a few days Louis-Philippe was compelled to abdicate and flee. The multiclass coalition founded a provisional government. But its efforts to accommodate the divergent aspirations of the groups that had overthrown the monarchy collapsed in June in a civil war that pitted the forces of the bourgeoisie against those of the working class. Thousands died, and the workers were brutally repressed. A resolutely middle-class constitution was proclaimed, elections were held, and Louis Bonaparte became president of the Second Republic in December 1848.

The interclass conflict of June 1848 transformed the fraternal allies of the previous February into mortal enemies. And from the violence of the bourgeoisie's repression of the poor, the generation of the 1848 revolution discovered a truth about their own society that they had hardly suspected before. The values of "fraternity" and "equality" inherited from 1789 had never been forgotten—particularly by middle-class idealists, intellectuals, and artists. But now the universalizing ideals that up to 1848 had undergirded *all* the French revolutions seemed to have been liquidated along with the working-class protesters. The revolution of 1848 revealed that these values were *themselves* representations—subject to manipulation, to slippage, to all the effects of power directly or indirectly exercised. The republic governed in their name; yet its fraud seemed patent. The novelist George Sand put this disillusionment poignantly: "I can no longer believe in a republic that starts out by killing its workers" (quoted in Duchet, *Manuel d'histoire littéraire,* p. 19).

The dissonance between the intense idealism that surfaced in the revolution's early stages and the brutality that unmasked itself later is at the source of the perception held by the generation of 1848 that their time was out of joint, their period and their experience somehow counterfeit. This dissonance had broad and profound cultural effects.

After 1848 the separation between elite and popular culture rigidified. Once the dream of fraternity between the classes was shattered by the brutality of June 1848, it was as if what Marx named "classes" and "class struggle" suddenly became primary and incontrovertible perceptual structures. Divisions deepened. The literary canon itself directly reflects the efforts of the increasingly centralized educational bureaucracy after 1848 to define what would be taught (and what excluded) in France's schools. Clearly, in this conscious marshaling of representations by the ruling bourgeoisie, such formative choices were political.

Literary scholars in France and elsewhere have devoted relatively little study to the culture of those who lost the revolution of 1848. The art historian T. J. Clark puts it cuttingly: "Not many . . . writers or politicians or painters . . . gave faces to the People in the nineteenth century. They were the mass, the invisible class; they all looked alike" (*The Absolute Bourgeois,* p. 29). There were inevitably exceptions, such as Honoré Daumier's, Jean-François Millet's, and Gustave Courbet's images of peasants and workers. Eugène Sue's *Les mystères de Paris* (1842–43; *The Mysteries of Paris*), one of the first serial best-sellers, sketched an image of the urban poor that reflected the working class's own self-consciousness in 1848. Later, Victor Hugo in *Les misérables* (1862), Emile Zola in *L'assommoir* (1877), and Jules Vallès in the Jacques Vingtras trilogy (*L'enfant* [1879; *The Child*], *Le bachelier* [1881; *The Bachelor*], *L'insurgé* [1886; *The Insurgent*]) sought, among others, to represent both the voices and the perspectives of the exploited, the poor, and the dispossessed.

But our image of this period is inevitably the image of bourgeois culture. And the contradictions that preoccupied the middle class are the substance of the literature of the mid-19th century. After 1848, such contradictions could hardly be repressed. They were inherent in the social situation of the bourgeoisie—and of the intellectuals and artists who, born within it and nurtured according to its values, nonetheless felt increasingly alienated from it. Essentially such contradictions arose in the tension between the sincere humanist ideals of their own class self-conception, on the one hand, and, on the other, powerful tendencies toward an unrestrained and corrosive individualism and toward the instrumentalization of others (particularly the members of subordinate groups, including women, workers, and the poor). The violence of June 1848 seemed a supreme unmasking of these negative dynamics within what would henceforth be a social formation overtly dominated by the bourgeoisie and by its conflicted values.

Moreover, this vision of 1848 has persisted to our own time. From the Hungarian Marxist Georg Lukács to the French semiotician Roland Barthes, the June revolution marks the moment beyond which the harmonization of bourgeois values and the integration of bourgeois consciousness simply became impossible. This image of 1848 as the moment when middle-class self-consciousness became irretrievably divided has its roots in the representations of their culture by the generation of 1848 itself. Both Baudelaire and Flaubert, for example, centered important later texts upon the experience of the revolution.

Although Baudelaire fought alongside the insurgents in June 1848, by fifteen or so years later his view of the revolution had changed diametrically: "1848 was charming only because of the very excess of its ridiculousness" ("Mon coeur mis à nu" [1887; "My Heart Laid Bare"], in *Oeuvres complètes*, p. 1274). But in one of his most striking prose poems, "Assommons les pauvres!" ("Let's Smash Poor People!" from *Petits poèmes en prose*, 1869; *Little Poems in Prose*), he depicts the tensions that underlay the revolution much more directly. In this staging of the antagonism between middle class and lower class, the social dialectic appears quite naked. The text manages to devaluate the positions of *both* classes through corrosive satire. A comically befuddled intellectual conceives the theory that one could induce consciousness of their degradation in the poor by mugging them randomly in the street. So he goes out and beats up a beggar. But in a second moment the power of the underclass rebounds, and the beggar lays the bourgeois flat. We are left with two battered Frenchmen and the sense that neither has understood a thing as the result of his drubbing. There is, of course, a third consciousness in the poem: that of the poet, who may be saying that the transformation of social conflict into poetry—

its aestheticization—is the only means by which such degraded and intractable material could or should be handled, at least for the middle class after 1848.

Flaubert places 1848 at the center of his historically most significant novel, *L'éducation sentimentale* (1869; *Sentimental Education*). But it is an uncannily decentered center. In 1848 Flaubert had been in the National Guard (one of the arms of bourgeois power in the June Days). But during the insurgency he had only observed, never fought. The novel reproduces this sense that the action of the revolution happens *alongside* the concerns of its characters, but never engages them directly. This peculiar link between the historical and the fictional—not so much an integration as a kind of uncomfortable cotenancy of the same novelistic space—today seems to many critics brilliantly to symbolize the uneasy relation between art and social life that was represented at about the same time in the slogan of "art for art's sake." History is profoundly *in* Flaubert's novel, to be sure. Flaubert worked through the chronology of the events of the revolution with meticulous care. In a crucial scene at the center of the novel, Frédéric Moreau, the hero, has finally succeeded in obtaining an assignation with Mme. Arnoux, the woman with whom he has been in love since adolescence. He waits for her outside an apartment he has rented for the purpose of seducing her. Meanwhile, street demonstrations are going on in several parts of the city: it is 22 February 1848, the beginning of the insurrection. Frédéric, waiting for Mme. Arnoux on a street corner by coincidence adjacent to the site of the Reform Banquet at which the insurrection started, witnesses the revolution's opening events. But he refuses his friends' appeal to join them in the demonstrations. When he sees some of them being arrested, he hides.

Mme. Arnoux never arrives. However, her decision not to come turns out to have had nothing to do with the revolution at all. These most consequential historical events, in other words, are without consequence for the hero of this most characteristic of midcentury novels. The "outside" world of social existence is there—*outside*. But it seems to have nothing to do with the inner drama of "feeling" (*sentiment*) that is played out in what Flaubert himself termed the "sentimental history of the men of my generation" (letter to Mlle. Leroyer de Chantepie, 6 October 1864). History and feeling seem to have become as disjunct as the classes whose initial alliance and later conflict determined the physiognomy of 1848. Paradoxically, then, *L'éducation sentimentale* is a "novel of education" in which nothing is learned about the world at all. The characters start out with plans to conquer whatever confronts them; they end up caring about scarcely anything at all. When, in one of the final scenes, Mme. Arnoux finally offers herself to Frédéric, in a confused mixture of disinclination and embarrassment he turns away and rolls a cigarette. Yet the controlling voice of the novel's narrator and the careful orchestration of its simultaneous (if disconnected) episodes, indeed the very form of the novel, urge us to conceive the power of the determinations that, in Flaubert's generation, had produced a view of human beings according to which determination was simply not *seen* as operative.

It would be reassuring to be able to claim that some edifying lesson was learned from 1848, to see some form of transcendence to compensate for a whole generation's sense of counterfeit, incompleteness, and frustration. Of course the revolution did move history forward—if that was the direction of more or less unrestrained capitalist development, with its equivocal but undeniable achievements. Working-class movements, of course, found in the June Days of 1848 a moment of indispensable clarification. A vision of their own interests arose out of their bloody repression by the middle class.

But for the intellectual bourgeoisie whose cultural objects still tend most to preoccupy readers, scholars, and critics, the revolution was a profoundly consequential and ineradicable fiasco. Flaubert sardonically characterized it thus in *L'éducation sentimentale:* "It turned intelligent people into imbeciles for the remainder of their lives" (p. 338). These words ring with the sorry authenticity of the truth about 1848 for the middle class and, in its image, for an entire tradition in the West.

Bibliography: Charles Baudelaire, *Oeuvres complètes,* ed. Y.-G. Le Dantec and Claude Pichois (Paris: Gallimard, 1961). T. J. Clark, *The Absolute Bourgeois: Artists and Politics in France, 1848–1851* (Princeton: Princeton University Press, 1973). Claude Duchet, ed., *Manuel d'histoire littéraire de la France, 1848–1917* (Paris: Editions Sociales, 1977). Gustave Flaubert, *L'éducation sentimentale,* ed. Edouard Maynial (Paris: Garnier, 1964). Georg Lukács, *Studies in European Realism,* trans. Edith Bone (New York: Grosset and Dunlap, 1964). Karl Marx, *Class Struggles in France, 1848–1850,* in *Surveys from Exile,* ed. David Fernbach (Harmondsworth: Penguin-Pelican Marx Library, 1973). Marx, *The Eighteenth Brumaire of Louis Bonaparte* (Moscow: Progress, 1954). Richard Terdiman, *Discourse/Counter-Discourse: The Theory and Practice of Symbolic Resistance in Nineteenth-Century France* (Ithaca: Cornell University Press, 1985). Alexis de Tocqueville, *Recollections,* trans. George Lawrence (Garden City, N.Y.: Doubleday, 1970).

Richard Terdiman

✑ 1851, 2 December

The Eighteenth Brumaire of Louis Bonaparte

Literature Deterritorialized

Unlike, say, 1830 or 1857, 1851 was not an especially notable year for literature. But it forms a watershed in literary history because of the significance of a political event. Louis-Napoleon's successful coup d'état of 2 December, soon followed by a plebiscite, confirmed the authoritarian trend that had marked the evolution of the Second Republic since the bloody repression of working-class revolt in June 1848, and made him emperor of the French. Disabused by the failure of the 1848 revolution and now subject to strict political and moral surveillance, writers retreated from their intense and enthusiastic involvement in the making of history. As Baudelaire put it, with angry emphasis, in a letter of 5 March 1852: "The 2nd December has *physically depoliticized me* [m'a *physiquement dépolitiqué*]" (*Selected Letters,* p. 45). His statement can stand as a motto for the literature of the midcentury and after, which found itself—to borrow a metaphor from Gilles Deleuze and Félix Guattari—"deterritorialized." Only Victor Hugo, from his exile, was free to pursue the practice of art as a direct intervention in political life (most notably in *Les châtiments*, 1853; *The Chastisements*).

Deterritorialized art entered a period of confused self-interrogation concerning the referential value of artistic signs: what was art to be "about"? A formalist movement proclaimed the separatist doctrine of "art for art's sake," which had tempted Théophile Gautier since his preface to *Mademoiselle de Maupin* (1835), itself a response to the July Monarchy's authoritarian turn. It was to flourish in the Parnassian movement (Charles Leconte de Lisle, Théodore de Banville, José Maria de Heredia), which dominated French poetry in the latter half of the century, influencing Rimbaud and Mallarmé before the emergence of symbolism. But symbolism also had roots in the midcentury, and its idea—an ancient one—that artistic signs could be a medium for expressing the mysteries of ideal, superreal, or spiritual reality gained impetus from a wave of "spiritualist" thinking and a craze for tablerapping that reached France from New England in the 1850s. The work of Edgar Allan Poe, combining spiritualist beliefs with a formalist aesthetic, was to be a major influence on French art until well into the 20th century. The translation and presentation of Poe became a major preoccupation for Baudelaire in the early 1850s.

But although Baudelaire's enthusiasm for Poe (and for Gautier) made him a major proponent of the new formalism and idealism, his work, like Flaubert's novel *Madame Bovary*, was judged in 1857 by a court of law in terms of an aesthetic of "realism," that is, as the imitation of material life (especially in its sordid aspects). Realism's notable theorists in the 1850s were Philippe Duranty and Champfleury (Jules Fleury-Husson); their essay *Le réalisme* appeared in the same year as *Les fleurs du mal* (*The Flowers of Evil*) and *Madame Bovary*. Indeed the "realist debate," sparked in part by the showing of Gustave Courbet's revolutionary painting *L'enterrement à Ornans* (*The Burial at Ornans*) and nourished by the new technology of photography, was the most prominent aesthetic issue of the early 1850s. After 1870, the "naturalism" of Emile Zola would be the most important descendant of 1850s realism.

But it is striking that, whereas *Les fleurs du mal* and *Madame Bovary* were put on trial, from within a realistic referential perspective, for "outrage to good morals," a self-proclaimed realist novel of the period such as Ernest Feydeau's *Fanny* (1858)—which has clear thematic resemblances to *Madame Bovary*— never drew unfavorable attention from the authorities. This fact has led commentators to think that it was not the subject but the writing in *Les fleurs du mal* and *Madame Bovary* that was troublesome to contemporary readers; and it is indeed clear to us that these works are the first masterpieces of literary modernism. Their writing has an elusive quality that resists interpretative closure and makes it difficult, perhaps impossible, to locate a subject in which an "intended meaning" would have originated. As a result, reading modern works becomes a literally interminable procedure, and in both the text and its interpretation the insistence of unconscious forces—that is, of desire—becomes impossible to ignore. At the same time, it is easy to understand this recourse to deterritorialization, to forms of textuality that produce constant instability (instability about the text's referent, about how and what it "means," instability of the reader caught up in the dynamics of a text that always means more than it says, or says more than it seems to mean), as a response, with its own political force, to the imposition of order and control that characterized the dominant social discourses and practices of the Second Empire (1852–1870).

In this period, then, the referential value of artistic signs hovered between positions as diametrically opposed as those of realism and spiritualism, and literary production between concepts that allowed simultaneous allegiance to a formalist ideal (that of the beautiful object, not unrelated to the importance of the artisanal *objet de luxe* in Second Empire craftsmanship) and to a "depersonalized" writing in which desire circulates freely, with no subjective anchorage. Baudelaire's work, self-proclaimed as formalist, supernaturalist, or both, but read by his contemporaries as scandalously realist and by us as interestingly modernist, stands at the center of this confused and confusing midcentury crisis of the deterritorialized artistic sign. So it is symptomatic that much of Baudelaire's critical writing of the 1850s and 1860s was devoted to a retrospective evaluation of Romanticism, then clearly perceived to be over.

Unlike the new literature of the 1850s, Romanticism had been an intensely political moment. Not that a collective political will was discernible in the movement, apart from a broad swing away from monarchism to republicanism, a swing resulting in part from disenchantment with the July Monarchy (1830–1848). But Romantic writing was typically involved in immediate political questions and was conscious of its own part in the making of contemporary history. Honoré de Balzac's reactionary politics made him, after 1830, the ideal observer of the values and ideology of a country now devoted to capitalist expansion, while Stendhal's novels—especially *Le rouge et le noir* (1830; *The Red and the Black*), *Lucien Leuwen* (abandoned as unpublishable in 1835), and *La chartreuse de Parme* (1839; *The Charterhouse of Parma*)—explored the pettiness and duplicity involved in the struggle for power in post-Napoleonic Europe. In the 1840s Eugène Sue's immense, socially conscious, serial novel *Les mystères de Paris* (1842–43; *The Mysteries of Paris*) had extraordinary impact. And an important theme of the period, discernible in Alfred de Musset's *Lorenzaccio* (1834), in Gérard de Nerval's *Léo Burckart* (1838), and in *La chartreuse,* was the consequences of intellectuals' involvement in the exercise of power—a role illustrated by the real-life careers of François-René de Chateaubriand, Alphonse de Lamartine, and Hugo, each of whom participated in different ways in government.

When the exiled Karl Marx took refuge in Paris (1843–1845), he found the city's intelligentsia engaged in a ferment of political and social speculation, mainly humanitarian, "harmonian," and utopian. Auguste Blanqui, the most intransigently revolutionary figure of the time, was in prison from 1839 to 1844 but would be active again until his reincarceration in May 1848. Saint-

Simonian and Fourierist journalism and monographic writing flourished; there was an active feminist movement, with its own journal, *La tribune des femmes* (*Women's Rostrum*); and in 1840 Pierre Leroux published *De l'humanité, de son principe et de son avenir* (*On Humanity, Its Principle, and Its Future*), and Pierre Joseph Proudhon *Qu'est-ce que la propriété?* (*What Is Property?*), proclaiming that "Property is theft." Louis Blanc's *L'organisation du travail* (*The Organization of Labor*) had appeared the previous year; Etienne Cabet's *Le voyage en Icarie* (1840; *The Voyage in Icaria*) was soon to inspire disastrous social experiments in Ohio and Texas; and the earlier enthusiasm aroused by Félicité de Lamennais's democratic-Christian *Paroles d'un croyant* (1834; *Words of a Believer*) was far from forgotten. George Sand gave novelistic resonance to much of this humanitarianism (learned especially from Leroux and Lamennais). It is against this excited babble of "socialist" voices that the political *silence* of the 1850s needs to be measured.

But the silencing of humanitarian socialism was not exclusively the result of the Second Empire's authoritarianism. After the unanimous insurrection of February, the bourgeois June 1848 repression had made clear the facts—largely occulted in the preceding era—of class and of class conflict: the bourgeois basis of the universalist dream was revealed, as were the group interests it had both concealed and subserved. There seemed little point in pursuing it. It is symptomatic that the last manifestation of directly political writing in the Romantic tradition was the post-1848 phenomenon of worker poetry, represented most prominently by Pierre Dupont's *Chants et chansons* (*Cantos and Songs*), for which Baudelaire wrote a warm preface in 1851. And 1851 also witnessed the publication of the last bourgeois writing in which the spirit of the 1840s was still clearly discernible, Nerval's *Voyage en Orient* (wr. 1844–1850; *Journey to the Orient*). The work is infused with initiatory mysticism, social idealism, and the harmonian ideal of tolerance combined with an oppositional aesthetic. In the tradition of Romantic political involvement, it also demonstrates a desire to have its "say," particularly with respect to what was already the "Middle Eastern question."

But by 1851 Nerval had turned in a new direction. The early signs of what was to be the literature of the 1850s are also apparent in the work of Baudelaire, who published in journals or sent to friends early versions of poems that would appear in *Les fleurs du mal,* and in the career of Flaubert, who returned from his own trip to Egypt and the Levant to begin *Madame Bovary.* The key transitional figure, however, is certainly Nerval. In his work of 1850–1852, profound nostalgia for the sense of community that pervaded the 1840s combined with experimentation in realism to produce writing that was already clearly modernist. In the fall of 1850, in direct response to the repressive Riancey Amendment, one of a series of measures that increasingly limited press freedom, Nerval produced an exemplary model of deterritorialized writing in "Les faux saulniers" ("The Smugglers"), a feuilleton piece that ran intermittently in *Le national* from 24 October to 22 December and from which "Angélique" was later extracted for *Les filles du feu* (1854; *The Daughters of Fire*). The new law, aimed at restricting the success of the popular—and often populist—*roman feuilleton*, often loaded with political undertones, created a penalty for newspapers publishing fictional writing. The plot centers on the narrator's search for a book about one Abbé de Bucquoy that would allow his text to be registered as historical writing and enable *Le national* to keep publishing it without facing the enormous fine.

The new legal requirements of nonfictional representation and personally signed writing (clear manifestations of an ideology requiring linguistic referentiality associated with an autonomous, *responsible* subject) are creatively eluded and mocked through the diffraction of the narrative voice, pluralized by means of quotations to the point of merging and disappearing into a collective harmony. This disappearing act foreshadows Mallarmé's "elocutionary disappearance of the poet" ("Crise de vers," 1896; "Crisis of Verse") but gives it political point. Simultaneously, in "Les faux saulniers," the requirement of referentiality is trivialized—everything that is related is the case, but nothing particularly matters—and subverted through the motif of the elusive book that would enable history to be written, but is itself only a book, that is, a representation.

"Les faux saulniers" launched a witty modernist polemic against an official and repressive doctrine of realism. In another feuilleton, "Les nuits d'octobre" ("October Nights"), which ran in *L'illustration* in October and November 1852, Nerval's target was an *aesthetic* doctrine. "Realism" being once more imposed as the rule of the game, the text asks what reality it should represent. The realism that represents the rational world of material reality is clearly associated with the constraints of a bourgeois worldview, the judgmental moralism of a strictly policed society—in short, a politics of control. Against this, the text presents a realism of the repressed, including Parisian low-life in its nocturnal haunts and the fancies, dreams, and nightmares of the "imagination"—figures of a plural and divided subject enacted in "endless digression," the permanent parabasis recommended by the German Romantic theory of writing. Here too, a fruitless quest allegorizes the "subjectlessness" of the writing, "subject" here referring both to the speaking self and to the subject matter.

Nerval's modernism is a subversive variant of official realism: it is realism taken to its logical consequences and thus helping us understand how Flaubert's and Baudelaire's later modernism was "mistaken" for realism. But in 1850 the ambiguities of realism had been demonstrated in a different way by Courbet's controversial *L'enterrement à Ornans* (fig. 1), which combined the huge dimensions previously associated with the Romantic genre of history painting with subject matter drawn, as in genre painting (but without its compositional and painterly prettiness), from the vulgarity of everyday life. Courbet's straggling representation of a top-hatted funeral procession, with its flat composition, its dark colors, and its suspected allegorical intentions (the burial of the property-owning class?), was interpreted as an open attack on the bourgeoisie. To us it looks more like a realization of the art Baudelaire had called for in the *Salon de 1846*, a *celebration* of the black-suited (male) middle class and of the "heroism

1. Gustave Courbet, *L'enterrement à Ornans* (Musée d'Orsay). (Photo courtesy of Documentation Photographique de la Réunion des Musées Nationaux.)

of modern life." But such seems to have been the uncanny appropriateness of realism to the confused aspirations and ambivalent social situation of midcentury art: rooted in bourgeois ideology, it simultaneously had the power to embarrass official culture by what it made visible.

After the death of Romanticism, the label "realism" applied to a range of newly visible cultural realities, from the "heroism of modern life" to the "disappearance of the subject." As early as 1847, Baudelaire's short story, "La Fanfarlo," identified the relation of realism to nonrealist (modernist) modes as the central aesthetic question of modernity, and tellingly defined the dynamics of that relation as one of mutual entailment. It is no exaggeration to say of "La Fanfarlo" what Baudelaire himself said of E. T. A. Hoffmann's "Prinzessin Brambilla" (1820; "Princess Brambilla"), that it is a "catechism of the higher aesthetics": it identifies the options and sets the agenda for the whole of the coming half-century.

"La Fanfarlo" opposes two spheres of life and art: on the one hand, a world of domestic (bourgeois) decorum and comfort, associated morally with virtue and "naturalness," and aesthetically with the referentiality of signs, or realism, of which Balzac's descriptions stand for the novelistic illustration; and, on the other hand, an "artistic" or bohemian universe, associated with seduction and erotic stimulation and, aesthetically, with nonreferentiality, that is, with the formal autonomy and "artificiality" of signs, and with a form of supernaturalism embodied in the theatrical genre of pantomime. It is the story of a poet recruited by a bourgeoise to seduce an actress the lady's husband has fallen for, so that she can get him back. The ensuing action weaves complicated connections between the two spheres, establishing that each supposedly distinct domain—the bourgeois and the bohemian, the natural and the artificial, the referential and the superreal—depends on repression of the other. The bourgeois world condemns the artistic as artificial (but still needs it), whereas the supernaturalism of artistic signs "forgets"—as the poet-hero forgets his court-ship of Mme. de Cosmelly in the arms of the *danseuse*—the "naturalness" of bourgeois reality and the materialism of the world. But each world's repressed returns to haunt it: the natural and virtuous Mme. de Cosmelly becomes a seductress to get her husband back, while the actress—all artifice and provo-cation—settles down to produce babies.

This interrelatedness of two mutually exclusive worlds and their artistic equivalents entails an infinitely greater complexity and trickiness than either sphere acknowledges, especially in the status of the sign, which cannot be defined in terms of referentiality (whether supernatural or natural), but only by the cleavage of which it is a trace, the exclusion it manifests or the absence of which it is the site. It thus suggests a paradoxical link between these two apparent opposites, modernism and realism: the referentiality of realism entails the writerliness of modernism as what it represses; but, inversely, modernism functions as the repression or "forgetting" of realist representation. Baudelaire's short story stages a similar subversion of Balzac's realist narration: whereas Henri de Marsay, the seducer in the latter's *La fille aux yeux d'or* (1834; *The Girl with the Golden Eyes*), inhabits an ultimately rational universe in which desire has an object and in which "mystery" is violently eliminated, Baudelaire's hero, Samuel Cramer, lives with La Fanfarlo in a state of permanent sexual excitement (but forgets Mme. de Cosmelly).

The literature of the later 19th century, with its kaleidoscope of aesthetic configurations and its jumble of isms, was to act out the implications of Bau-delaire's sense of the sign as the site of repression. Art itself is the repressed other of the bourgeois world; but within its deterritorialized space two mutually exclusive régimes of the sign coexist: a sign subjected to naturalistic referen-tiality—something like the inheritance of Balzac (who died in 1850)—and a sign made available for the nonrealistic compositions of desire. And this is so whether those constructions are described in terms of the art-for-art's-sake cult of "pure Beauty," or in terms of some supernatural—or indeed psychic—"other world," or, finally, as Baudelaire gets close to hinting in "La Fanfarlo" (where the dancer is described as "poetry equipped with arms and legs"), in terms of a certain *materialism* of the writerly sign—a materialism that, to us, has a sur-prisingly modern ring.

See also 1848, 1866.

Bibliography: Charles Baudelaire, *La Fanfarlo,* trans. Greg Boyd, ed. Kendall E. Lappin (Berkeley: D.S. Ellis/Creative Books, 1986). Baudelaire, *Les Fleurs du Mal,* trans. Richard Howard (Boston: Godine, 1982). Baudelaire, *Selected Letters of Charles Baude-laire,* trans. Rosemary Lloyd (London: Weidenfeld and Nicolson, 1986). Gérard de Nerval, "Les faux saulniers," in *Oeuvres complètes,* ed. Jean Guillaume et Claude Pichois, vol. 2 (Paris: Gallimard, 1984). Nerval, *Journey to the Orient,* abr. and trans. Norman Glass (London: Haag, 1984). Nerval, *Selected Writings,* trans. Geoffrey Wagner (New York: Grove, 1957).

Ross Chambers

✐ *1852, 2 December*

Louis-Napoleon Bonaparte, President of the Second Republic,
Becomes Emperor Napoleon III of the Second Empire

Bonapartism

The year 1852 in France was framed by two shocks to the continuity and the
legitimacy of the state: the overthrow of the Second Republic, which had
emerged from the 1848 revolution; and the establishment of Napoleon III's
Second Empire. These events affected political and cultural life for several
decades.

The 1848 revolution had brought France a new republican régime. When
elections were held in December 1848, Louis-Napoleon Bonaparte, nephew of
Napoleon I and heir to his legend, was overwhelmingly elected president.
Despite intense conflict with the new National Assembly, he governed France
for nearly the full three years provided for by law. But on 2 December 1851, as
his term in office was about to end, he abruptly overthrew the republic; and on
the anniversary of that date in 1852 he declared himself emperor.

Bonaparte's 1851 coup d'état had long been foreshadowed; he had tried to
seize power twice before, in 1836 and again in 1840. But these forewarnings
by no means forearmed the politicians, military officers, journalists, and other
dignitaries who were efficiently arrested on the night of the coup, many of them
in their beds. Although there was some bloodshed, in general the change of
régime was nowhere effectively contested. The coup, by all accounts, was brilliantly and meticulously planned. It has become a model for modern seizures of
power.

After the coup Louis-Napoleon dissolved the National Assembly and declared
himself president of a new republic. He increased the presidential term from
three years to ten and reduced the powers of the legislature. Behind these
changes lay a political theory or tendency, Bonapartism, that Louis-Napoleon
and his supporters had been shaping since the period of the July Monarchy
(1830–1848). For its inspiration, it reached back to the French Revolution and
the Empire (1789–1815).

Bonapartism's power resided largely in the strength of the Napoleonic
legend—what E. J. Hobsbawm has termed the world's "first secular myth"
(*The Age of Revolution, 1789–1848*, p. 98). In France, as a series of revolutions
had shown, the body politic was profoundly fragmented. This fragmentation
reflected the existence of multiple and seemingly irreconcilable constituencies,
and the competition of apparently incompatible theories of government. Most
recently, after a protracted series of other upheavals, these divisions had generated the bloody conflicts of the 1848 revolution.

In this situation, allegiance could be focused upon the fabled figure of Napoleon I as upon no other in the political spectrum—the more so because at the
time his nephew engineered his coup in 1851, the idea of Napoleon and of the
glorious period through which he had led France had acquired the patina of

nearly four decades of concerted mythologizing. Thus after 1848 Bonapartism seemed to promise an end to a long series of conflicts, to offer the possibility of unification of a deeply divided state.

The Napoleonic myth personalized Bonapartist power and conceived the structure of government as a paradoxically authoritarian democracy, based on a mystically unmediated relationship between ruler and people—what Bonapartists called "confidence from below, authority from above." After the coup, in a practical application of this principle, Louis-Napoleon restored universal male suffrage in order to hold a plebiscite concerning the coup. Seven million Frenchmen (against a mere 600,000 dissenters) confirmed and in effect retroactively legitimated the régime that he had installed at the price of more than 20,000 arrests and deportations.

But in the new Bonapartist republic even a weakened Assembly still exerted a significant countervailing power. Accordingly, a year later Louis-Napoleon organized a second plebiscite, on the question of establishing an imperial form of government. This time more than 8 million voters supported him. On 2 December 1852 he swept the republic away and declared himself Emperor Napoleon III.

The new régime, called the Second Empire, lasted until France's disastrous defeat by the Prussians at Sedan in 1870. The changes it wrought and the developments it encouraged may have been the most significant in 19th-century France. It instituted the most intense and most sustained economic growth that France had ever known. And the writers and artists whose careers began or flourished during the Second Empire—Gérard de Nerval, Victor Hugo, Théophile Gautier, Gustave Flaubert, Charles Baudelaire, Edmond and Jules de Goncourt, Charles Leconte de Lisle, the Comte de Lautréamont (Isidore Ducasse), Paul Verlaine, Stéphane Mallarmé, Jules Verne, Emile Zola, Gustave Courbet, Jean-Auguste-Dominique Ingres, Edgar Degas, Edouard Manet, Paul Cézanne, Claude Monet, Camille Pissaro, Pierre-Auguste Renoir, Auguste Rodin—form an extraordinary group of innovators whose prestige has remained high to our own period. Yet from the beginning the Second Empire has had a notoriously bad press.

In 1852, in a brilliant trope in *The Eighteenth Brumaire of Louis Bonaparte,* Karl Marx derisively measured Louis-Napoleon's coup d'état against Napoleon I's armed overthrow of the Revolutionary Directory on 9 November 1799 (in the Revolutionary calendar, 18 Brumaire). Marx satirized the nephew's coup d'état as a base, derivative forgery of the uncle's epochal seizure of power. This theme of an ignoble imitation of a prestigious original dominates numerous accounts of the event and of the régime it inaugurated. It defined the attitudes of many intellectuals toward the Second Empire.

Yet the reality of Napoleon III was considerably more complex, and contemporary readings of him and his régime were in fact extraordinarily diverse. Such divergence suggests the degree to which 19th-century politics were increasingly played out in the volatile realm of the imagination. Not that Louis-Napoleon was characterless; rather, his character and his political identity were oddly contradictory, a fact that makes him extraordinarily difficult to assess. Cogent evidence can be adduced for each of the seemingly irreconcilable opinions concerning him and his politics. This uncanny plasticity allowed for adherence to Bonaparte and Bonapartism by French citizens holding very diverse political views. The difficulty of defining an authentic Bonapartist "reality" may help account for the exasperation that Louis-Napoleon elicited in a number of contemporaries.

Napoleon III has most frequently been portrayed as a reactionary, as in Marx's account referred to earlier, or in Hugo's contemporaneous *Napoléon le Petit* (1852; *Napoleon the Small*). Though different on almost any other scale, both Hugo and Marx were committed to some form of republicanism in France. Independently, both organized their attack along the lines of a contemptuous comparison between uncle and nephew. Yet the fact that their target was the first popularly elected ruler in French history made these denunciations in the name of democracy somewhat paradoxical. From a radically contrary position, the reactionary François Guizot lamented the coup of 2 December 1851 as a triumph of socialism (Marx, *Eighteenth Brumaire,* p. 103). And indeed there was some basis for such a claim, for in 1844 Louis-Napoleon had written a pamphlet, *Extinction du paupérisme* (1844; *The Suppression of Poverty*), that incorporated the theories of several socialists (particularly Claude-Henri de Saint-Simon, with whose ideas Bonaparte always had had considerable affinity) and claimed considerable sympathy with the problems of working people. These sorts of contradictions in his political identity made it possible for one critic to call Napoleon III a simpleton while another condemned him as a consummate Machiavellian (Campbell, *The Second Empire Revisited,* p. 1), or, on another scale, for commentators to embrace—or condemn—him from nearly any position in the political spectrum. Napoleon III and the régime he led were not so much neutral as radically multifaceted.

The emperor thus exhibited a bizarre ideological capaciousness, in which objective oppositions and conflicts were somehow muted or diverted into other modes of expression. Bonapartism became a kind of indefinable third entity standing not so much between the alternatives of republicanism and monarchism, which framed so many battles in the 19th century, but somewhere off to the side of the fissure dividing these traditional antagonists. It was through something like this sort of mechanism that, at least at the beginning of the Second Empire, Bonaparte became the first chief of government available for symbolic investment by nearly all the diverse elements of a modern social formation.

Whatever its origin in Napoleon III's own personal uncertainties or his tendencies to opportunism, this quality—what might be termed a constitutive heterogeneity—produced a new configuration not only in the conduct of politics but also in the political resonance of culture. For around the time of the Second Empire, it was to cultural production, and in particular to literature, that the task largely fell of sorting out the more diffuse and elusive meanings that functioned within an increasingly complex and diverse society, engaged in an extremely rapid, inevitably disorienting industrialization and urbanization. Indeed in the face of such changes it was the stabilization of these meanings that permitted such a society's functioning. In effect the mysterious underdetermination of Napoleon III's régime itself might be said to have determined the production of a new hermeneutics—an unprecedented science of meaning whose field of investigation was no longer simply the assignment of political valence based on a stable structure of parties and interests, but the teasing out of significance in all the increasingly variegated and mystified realms of social space.

Evidence of this tendency is perceptible in the period's two masterpieces, Flaubert's *Madame Bovary* and Baudelaire's *Les fleurs du mal* (*The Flowers of Evil*). Both were already in early stages of composition in 1852, and both appeared just five years later. Moreover, upon publication both met with the judicial scrutiny that the Second Empire's stringent censorship reserved for writing upsetting to its homogenizing and pacifying norms.

Neither of these books explicitly intended to evoke politics at all. On the contrary, each in its own ways resolutely aestheticized the art work, apparently removing it from the political realm altogether—a tendency that was becoming prevalent among the intellectual avant-garde. Yet by interrogating the complex and contradictory character of social existence and attempting to trace back to their mysterious imaginative and interpersonal origins the sources of a profound dissatisfaction characteristic of the contemporary world, both works testify to a new and baffling obscurity in what used to be termed the political domain, or what we could call the public sphere. Flaubert and Baudelaire reflect a new perception of reality, in which the very causes of human experience appear to have left this public sphere, and seem disconnected from social institutions and from political interests. They thus appeared uncoupled from the preoccupations over which, since 1789, so many revolutions had been fought. They seemed to have migrated into some other place, which it became the task of literature to frame and explicate.

If they can be said to have themes at all, both *Madame Bovary* and *Les fleurs du mal* manifest a preoccupation with the means by which desire is engendered in society. In their own ways both Flaubert and Baudelaire clearly perceived the paradox that the very society that creates desire—by an increasingly dense circulation of images of social mobility and economic success, by an increasing identification of the erotic and the commercial—at the same time stringently restricts the means by which desire can be satisfied. The satisfactions that are permitted turn out to be ambiguous and somehow unfulfilling. This effort to understand how social existence is fashioned *outside* the realm of the explicitly political brings into focus a characteristically modern form of malaise.

Not that politics stopped being an issue, particularly for writers. The Second Empire censorship prohibited publication of political attacks on the emperor or the form of government he had instituted. Yet within the limits established by such repression, it seems clear that the emperor intended to attract the widest possible allegiance to the régime. To this end he consciously manipulated public opinion in all its aspects. Newspapers, pamphlets, even novels and plays were created or enlisted in this effort.

But as these genres suggest, the tools for manipulating public opinion lay almost wholly within the realms of writing and publishing. So by a structural necessity of the new régime, writers found themselves solicited to play a new role in the political process. And they discovered that the best way to discharge this role was to seem not to be playing it at all. Just as newspapers in the period were discovering the means by which they could forge a mass audience and thereby achieve mass circulation (notably by banishing the explicit political partisanship of the older forms of journalism in France), by analogous means political discourse and rhetoric were made to serve what the emperor sought to conceive as an authentic mass politics.

Of course, the belief that one could unify a polity as divided as 19th-century France was transparently utopian. Despite the Bonapartist ideology of harmonizing differences, conflict did not end. In important ways Napoleon's régime remained a classic theater of oppositions. Liberals and monarchists were allowed to express themselves as long as they did not attack Napoleon by name. But the threat of censorship, leading to fines that might put a publication out of business, frequently succeeded in moderating their antagonism. On the other hand, Napoleon believed the republicans could not be reconciled to the régime, and they were more or less systematically silenced. Many of them abandoned active politics and devoted themselves to other pursuits. A prestigious few chose—or were forced to choose—exile. Thus Edgar Quinet remained in Switzerland, writing a study of the failure of the 1848 revolution. Louis Blanc, one of the major figures in that conflict, finished his *Histoire de la Révolution française* (1870; *History of the French Revolution*) in London. The most celebrated, Victor Hugo, also chose exile.

Hugo was surely as much of a paradox as Napoleon III. But whereas Louis-Napoleon seemed indefinable, Hugo's stability and constancy, in this century characterized by disruptive change, made him seem almost impervious to the mutability of history itself. Hugo's career was so long and so illustrious (no other literary figure in 19th-century France even came close to the reverence and the celebrity he enjoyed in the later part of his life) that his lack of evolution comes as something of a shock. In his early years—at the time of *Hernani* (1830), for example—he figured among the Romantic enfants terribles; but later, when the literary originality that he had once so powerfully exemplified had become a norm within the culture, he seemed satisfied to reproduce the forms and themes he had been employing for decades. Thus during the Second Empire, at a time of great cultural effervescence, Hugo began to look something like an old master. But such an appearance, with the impression of authority that attached to it, was perhaps optimally suited to the political and moral role that Hugo elected to play after Bonaparte's coup.

At a time when disenchantment with politics pervaded artistic and literary aestheticism—for example, in the movement known as "art for art's sake"—Hugo threw himself into active *political* opposition against Napoleon III.

But he battled through his books. This struggle began directly after the 2 December coup.

Hugo went first to Brussels, where he wrote two works denouncing the overthrow of the republic: an account of the coup titled *Histoire d'un crime* (1852; *History of a Crime*) and the previously mentioned satire *Napoléon le petit*. He then left Brussels and took refuge in the Channel Islands, eventually settling on Guernsey, within sight of the French coast. In 1853 he published an entire volume of poetry directed against the "Usurper" who had seized the state, *Les châtiments,* a title translatable not only as "punishment" but also as "retaliation." In this collection Hugo defines the republican ideal subverted by Bonaparte's power. He mercilessly chastizes the parodic emperor and the degraded period over which he presides: "Times like ours are History's sewer" ("L'Histoire a pour égout des temps comme les nôtres," *Châtiments,* bk. 3, 13). In "Ultima Verba" ("Last Words"), the most celebrated line of the collection, and one of the most famous Hugo ever wrote, declares his intransigent opposition to the new régime. He hopes for popular support, but he will continue to fight no matter what others do: "And if there's only one [opponent] left, I'll be that one" ("Et s'il n'en reste qu'un, je serai celui-là").

Napoleon tried to coopt this stirring—and disruptive—politics of opposition by offering Hugo amnesty in 1859. Hugo disdainfully refused. As he had put it in *Les châtiments* to those tempted to collaborate with the régime, "Go ahead and eat well; I prefer the black bread of freedom" ("Chanson").

Hugo's opposition to the emperor and the régime never abated. He returned to France only after Napoleon III abdicated in 1870. This moral and verbal battle established an enduring paradigm for relations between the artist and the state. Napoleon III was devising a new form of power, rooted in intangibles such as "public opinion" and sustained by more or less subtly "guided" media. Writers after midcentury were devising a new aesthetic, defensively closed in and intent upon itself. Hugo's refusal to adopt either of these patterns put both into revealing perspective. In this confrontation, something like a new power— the power of language; the power of those producing culture—was itself affirmed, by an artist unexpectedly engaged in politics, and by the modern state itself.

See also 1848, 1851, 1871.

Bibliography: Rondo Cameron, *France and the Economic Development of Europe, 1800–1914,* 2d ed. (Chicago: Rand McNally, 1961). Stuart L. Campbell, *The Second Empire Revisited* (New Brunswick, N.J.: Rutgers University Press, 1978). E. J. Hobsbawm, *The Age of Revolution, 1789–1848* (New York: Mentor, 1962). Victor Hugo, *Les châtiments,* in *Oeuvres poétiques,* ed. Pierre Albouy, vol. 2 (Paris: Gallimard, 1967). Natalie Isser, *The Second Empire and the Press* (The Hague: Martinus Nijhoff, 1974). Dominick LaCapra, *Madame Bovary on Trial* (Ithaca: Cornell University Press, 1982). Karl Marx, *The Eighteenth Brumaire of Louis Bonaparte* (Moscow: Progress, 1954). Richard Terdiman, *Discourse/Counter-Discourse: The Theory and Practice of Symbolic Resistance in Nineteenth-Century France* (Ithaca: Cornell University Press, 1985).

Richard Terdiman

1853

L'artiste Publishes "Le corbeau," Charles Baudelaire's Translation
of Edgar Allan Poe's "The Raven"

French Poe

The 20th-century French poet Paul Valéry thought Edgar Allan Poe the only
truly "impeccable" writer (*Correspondance*, p. 163). Harold Bloom, on the other
hand, has echoed most of Poe's English-speaking readership with his claim that
"no reader who cares deeply for the best poetry written in English can care
greatly for Poe's verse" ("Inescapable Poe," p. 23). Critics such as Bloom have
found the French esteem for Poe as incomprehensible and perverse as similar
accolades of the disgraced American president Richard Nixon and the derided
comedian Jerry Lewis: in France it is not unusual to hear them also called
geniuses. French literary culture has memorialized Poe as one of the greatest
writers of the 19th century, whereas in his own language, his work is commonly
regarded as minor and more than slightly, and entirely unintentionally, silly.
Poe's striking absence from American lists of great American writers and his
prominence in the French tradition moved Simone de Beauvoir to remark,
during her tour of the United States, that Americans must consider Poe French
(*America Day by Day*, p. 55).

Since his translation by Baudelaire and Mallarmé, Poe has been regarded
alongside these two French symbolists and Gérard de Nerval, the Comte de
Lautréamont, and Rimbaud as one of the great *poètes maudits*, or damned
poets—those who, in one way or another, in myth or reality, followed Rimbaud's dicta that the poet must "degrade himself" as much as possible, that
poetic vision can be produced only by a willful "disorganization of *all the senses*"
(*Oeuvres*, p. 344). In the 20th century, Poe became one of the "saints" of surrealism. The surrealist Antonin Artaud wrote to Henri Parisot in 1945: "Everything that is not a tetanus of the soul or does not proceed from a tetanus of the
soul, like the poems of Baudelaire and Poe, is not true and cannot be accepted
as poetry" (*Selected Writings*, p. 448). That Baudelaire should be so conjoined
with Poe in Artaud's statement is a felicitous coincidence, for in fact French
Poe—the French understanding of Poe, in French—is the result of a collaboration involving first Baudelaire and then Mallarmé, in which Poe himself was
an entirely passive partner. In the eyes and through the language of these two
French writers, Poe became, as Mallarmé put it, "this exception, in effect, and
the absolute literary case" (*Oeuvres complètes*, p. 531).

It is not only through surrealism, however, that French Poe survives, indeed
flourishes, to the present day. Valéry praised him for "opening up a way,
teaching a very strict and deeply alluring doctrine, in which a kind of mathematics and a kind of mysticism became one" (*Leonardo, Poe, Mallarmé*, p. 207).
This statement confirms the assertion by Poe's recent biographer, Julian
Symons, that the writer was torn between two contradictory imperatives, which
Symons describes as the "Visionary Poe," who was fascinated by the mysterious
and occult, and the "Logical Poe," who insisted that every aspect of literary

composition be precisely executed according to a logical plan. What Symons regards as a serious flaw in Poe's literary makeup seems to Valéry a positive virtue. It may well be that the French affinity for Poe's scientific mysticism is related to the general tendency among French literati such as Valéry to believe in the possibility of a quasi-scientific purity and rigor in literary study and practice—a belief usually dismissed by English-speaking counterparts as just one more amusing instance of Gallic pedantry. Thus in French, and to the French, this aspect of Poe's work, which appears ludicrous in English, is considered not only praiseworthy but even the mark of genius.

Still, it is probably Poe as seen by Artaud, as filtered through surrealism, who most embodies French Poe today. Artaud's Poe is mystical: there were, wrote Artaud, "collective magic spells in connection with Baudelaire, Poe, Gérard de Nerval, Nietzsche, Kierkegaard, Hölderlin, Coleridge, and also in connection with van Gogh" (*Selected Writings,* p. 486). Artaud insists that these artists are "correct" in their representations of the human psyche, more so than mere empirical science would allow. But the association of Poe's "genius" with "collective magic" is especially apt, if by collective magic Artaud may be understood to mean a *collective misreading,* a misconstrual occurring across and through translation, which appears to have improved the original even as it vitiated it, got it "wrong."

An important space in Baudelaire's works is occupied by his translations of Poe, the first one published in 1848, the last one in 1865. They constitute five of the volumes he published during his lifetime: *Histoires extraordinaires* (1856; *Extraordinary Tales*), *Nouvelles histoires extraordinaires* (1857; *New Extraordinary Tales*), *Aventures d'Arthur Gordon Pym* (1858), *Euréka* (1863), *Histoires grotesques et sérieuses* (1865; *Grotesque and Serious Tales*). Out of the introductions Baudelaire wrote for them, a fascinating misreading, comes the strange figure of French Poe. Baudelaire's idolatrous misrepresentation of the life of Poe is well known, thanks to the work of W. T. Bandy and others. Poe first became an object of French literary mythology, following Baudelaire's presentation, as the very type of the well-born though decadent southern aristocrat, the very incarnation of one of his own characters—for example, Roderick Usher in *The Fall of the House of Usher* (in *Tales of the Grotesque and Arabesque,* 1840)—and a perfect transatlantic counterpart to the hyperbole of male stylishness and affectation so promoted by Baudelaire as *dandysme* (dandyism). Baudelaire knew Poe's life largely through a southern partisan, John M. Daniel, who was at pains to depict Poe as just such an archetype, a *dandy* of the American South—brilliant, well-born, cultivated yet drawn irresistibly to every sort of dissipation, an aristocrat in a democracy, spurned by his countrymen because he was superior to them. Following Daniel, Baudelaire wrote that "Edgar Poe was thus raised in a noble affluence, and received a complete education" ("Edgar Allan Poe, sa vie et ses ouvrages" [1852; "Edgar Allan Poe, His Life and His Works"], in *Oeuvres posthumes,* 1:251). Anticipating Beauvoir, he went on to say: "His countrymen find him scarcely American, and yet he is not English" (ibid.). What set Poe apart was his negativity. "If you talk with an American, and if you speak to him about Mr. Poe, he will admit his genius; willingly, even, perhaps he will be proud of it, but will finish by saying, in a superior tone: 'But myself, I am a positive man'" (p. 248).

Thus there is a paradox implicit in such statements as: "All of Edgar Allan Poe's stories are, so to speak, biographical. One finds the man in the work" (*Oeuvres posthumes*, 1:251). The man, as Baudelaire conceived him, was as much a fictional, literary phenomenon as the work—all the more so for not being acknowledged or recognized as such. A second version of his essay on Poe does not substantially alter the initial misrepresentation. It speaks of Poe's "quasi-miraculous intelligence" and of his family as "one of the most respectable of Baltimore" (p. 250), which could hardly have been more mistaken: Poe's grandfather, a spinning-wheel maker, had come from Ireland, himself the grandson of a tenant farmer. Baudelaire refers to him as "General" Poe, held in esteem by Lafayette, whereas in fact David Poe was a major in the American Revolution. John Allan, who adopted Poe, was not a "wealthy merchant," but plainly, if comfortably, middle class. Admittedly, the source of much of the misinformation was Poe himself. He was as assiduous in the cultivation of his own myth as in the composition of any poem or story; had Baudelaire known this, he probably would have praised Poe for it as well because it coincided so perfectly with the French poet's theories of art and style, which extolled artifice above all else. Poe did not receive the education and upbringing of a wealthy aristocrat any more than he ever went to Greece or Russia, although both versions of Baudelaire's essay repeat popular myths that he did.

But even with Poe's own collaboration in the manufacture of false biography, it is unlikely that the modern myth would be anywhere near the same without the efforts of Baudelaire and Mallarmé to "translate," to transpose Poe into the alien but eagerly hospitable medium of French. Clearly, they were anxious to import the American writer because the peculiar mixture of fact and fiction subsumed by the name of Poe fitted so well with their own attitudes toward and theories of art and life. In Poe they found "this delicate monster," "my likeness—my brother," evoked by Baudelaire at the opening of *Les fleurs du mal* (1857; *The Flowers of Evil*), a reflection that would allow them to shape their own literary identities.

There is no question that, in translating such works as "The Raven" (*The Raven and Other Poems*, 1845), which is often mocked by English critics for its clanky rhymishness and luridly melodramatic tone, Baudelaire and Mallarmé left out most of what appears offensive or silly in the English and added touches of their own or—quite by accident—elements inherent in the French language that gave Poe's poems and tales a gloss and subtlety they badly needed. Baudelaire's translation of "The Raven," like Mallarmé's later translation of Poe's poems (1863, pub. 1888; *Les poèmes d'Edgar Poe*), is in prose, denuded of the trappings of verse, and thus, for Poe, of its entire generic, structural integrity. One cannot blame Baudelaire for this, although the logical Poe probably would have: Baudelaire admitted in his preface that "in the casting of prose applied to poetry, there is inevitably a certain imperfection; but the harm would be even greater in a rhymed mimicry" (*Oeuvres posthumes*, 1:356). Yet what seems grotesque in English often comes out in French as sublimely allusive and metaphorical, and what seemed to sound a wholly discordant note in American letters made a perfect harmony with the emerging French schools of symbolism and decadence. So it is through the misunderstandings of Baudelaire and his literary heirs, and because of properties inherent in French, that Poe was improved upon by becoming French Poe. And today, of course, French Poe has so colored our concept of Poe generally, in English, that it would be exceedingly difficult to say exactly where French Poe ends and English Poe begins. What can be said unequivocally, however, is that Poe holds a far more important place in the history of French literature than in that of American letters, and that his positive influence on modern American writers has occurred mostly through their reading of French writers such as Baudelaire, Mallarmé, and others influenced by them and, through them, by Poe.

Bibliography: Antonin Artaud, *Selected Writings*, ed. Susan Sontag, trans. Helen Weaver (New York: Grove, 1976). W. T. Bandy, Introduction to Charles Baudelaire, *Edgar Allan Poe, sa vie et ses ouvrages* (Toronto: University of Toronto Press, 1973). Charles Baudelaire, *Oeuvres posthumes*, ed. Jacques Crépet, vol. 1 (Paris: Conard, 1939). Simone de Beauvoir, *America Day by Day*, trans. Patrick Dudley (New York: Grove, 1953). Harold Bloom, "Inescapable Poe," *New York Review of Books*, October 11, 1984, pp. 23–37. Shoshana Felman, "On Reading Poetry: Reflections on the Limits and Possibilities of Psychoanalytic Approaches," in *The Literary Freud: Mechanisms of Defense and the Poetic Will*, ed. Joseph M. Smith (New Haven: Yale University Press, 1980). *French-American Literary Relationships*, special issue, *Yale French Studies*, 10 (1952). Jefferson Humphries, *Metamorphoses of the Raven: Literary Overdeterminedness in France and the South since Poe* (Baton Rouge: Louisiana State University Press, 1985). Patrick F. Quinn, *The French Face of Edgar Poe* (Carbondale: Southern Illinois University Press, 1957). Arthur Rimbaud, *Oeuvres*, ed. Suzanne Bernard (Paris: Garnier, 1960). Julian Symons, *The Tell-Tale Heart* (New York: Harper & Row, 1978). Paul Valéry, *Correspondance d'André Gide et de Paul Valéry 1890–1942*, ed. Robert Mallet (Paris: Gallimard, 1955). Valéry, *Leonardo, Poe, Mallarmé*, trans. Malcolm Cowley and James R. Lawler, vol. 8 of *Collected Works*, ed. Jackson Mathews (Princeton: Princeton University Press, 1972).

Jefferson Humphries

ᕗ 1857

In January Gustave Flaubert Is Prosecuted for *Madame Bovary;*
in August Charles Baudelaire Is Condemned for *Les fleurs du mal*

Two Trials

In January and August of 1857 Gustave Flaubert and Charles Baudelaire, respectively, were indicted for "offense to public and religious morality and to good morals." Flaubert went on trial for *Madame Bovary,* and Baudelaire for *Les fleurs du mal* (*The Flowers of Evil*). Flaubert was acquitted with a severe reprimand and not awarded costs for the trial. Baudelaire's trial was a miniaturized replay of Flaubert's; even the prosecuting attorney, Ernest Pinard, was the same. This time the state won, and six poems of *Les fleurs du mal* remained censored until 1949, when an attorney named Falco convinced a court of appeals to overturn the condemnation. Falco obviously believed that the issues in the two trials were similar, and that is why he invoked the case of Flaubert while pleading for Baudelaire. He even intimated that Adolphe Billaut, minister of the interior in 1857, may have wanted to bring Baudelaire to trial to avenge the court's earlier acquittal of Flaubert.

Flaubert and Baudelaire were brought to trial under legislation originally passed on 17 May 1819 and supplemented by a decree of 17 February 1852. During the Second Empire, those accused no longer had the right to a jury trial but went before a magistrate presiding over a *tribunal correctionnel,* where common criminals such as pimps and prostitutes were the customary delinquents. Literary prosecutions were not exceptional under this régime of censorship. But the fact that works of more manifestly "prurient" interest and of markedly low aesthetic quality escaped prosecution makes these two trials significant. In 1857 the *Revue de Paris,* where *Madame Bovary* was first published in serial form, was already an object of government suspicion. Its editor, Maxime Du Camp, felt that the prosecution of Flaubert was a pretext to repress the periodical, and Flaubert agreed with him. But the Flaubert and Baudelaire trials involved much more than local political repression: exceedingly complex literary and sociocultural interests were at stake.

Baudelaire lost his case in part because his defense lawyer, Chaix d'Est-Ange, was rhetorically less effective than Flaubert's lawyer, Marie-Antoine-Jules Sénard. Oddly, although the prosecutor Pinard won the Baudelaire case, he himself seemed decidedly less invested in the trial—and the text—of Baudelaire than he had been in that of Flaubert. Because *Les fleurs du mal* retained, to his mind, more vestiges of Christian faith than *Madame Bovary*—and Pinard was a man who believed Christianity to be the very foundation of Western civilization—he even convinced the court to drop the charge of outrage to religious morality and to consider Baudelaire's text only as an offense to public morals.

Pinard's subsequent account of the two trials in his *Journal* of 1892 is remarkable for its inaccuracies:

> The novel *Madame Bovary* reveals a true talent; but the description of certain scenes goes beyond all bounds [*toute mesure*]; if we close our eyes, Flaubert will have many imitators, who will go even further in the same direction. In addition, the *chambre correctionnelle* had just condemned Baudelaire's *Les fleurs du mal;* it inflicted a fine upon the author and ordered the suppression of certain passages. If we abstain, people will say that we are easy on the strong and the heads of schools and that we are accommodating toward our own but inflexible for opponents. Baudelaire had many friends in the camp of the republicans while Flaubert was an assiduous, feted guest in the salons of Princess Mathilde. (Quoted in Pasquet, *Ernest Pinard,* p. 10)

Even André Pasquet, who attempted to retrieve Pinard's reputation, admitted in discussing this entry that "Ernest Pinard's memory betrayed him in an extreme way. It is difficult to accumulate more errors in a few lines" (*Ernest Pinard,* p. 11). Yet an account of the facts indicates a degree of evasion and repression that goes well beyond loss of memory or simple mistakes.

First of all, the condemnation of Baudelaire could not have influenced Pinard's decision, because *Les fleurs du mal,* which appeared on 25 June 1857, was condemned on 20 August of that year, six months after Flaubert's trial. In addition, Flaubert's relations with Princess Mathilde began only in 1860, three years after the trial. As for Flaubert's renown, he was, at the time of the trial, hardly a powerful *chef d'école.* He had published nothing. He became a figure-head for "realists" and "naturalists," much to his dismay, only after the trial. Furthermore, as Flaubert surmised in his own letters, those who had brought him to trial probably were not aware of his family's social importance, although his lawyer made much of it during the trial. Baudelaire's stepfather, General Aupick, was a figure of national prominence, whereas Flaubert's physician father enjoyed only regional fame. And Pinard's strict separation of the writers on the basis of their sociopolitical circles obscures the fact that Baudelaire and Flaubert themselves immediately recognized the commonality of their aesthetic views. Pinard's "tricks" of memory must have indicated a powerful ambivalence toward *Madame Bovary.* Feeling the temptations the novel conveyed, he was unable to articulate them fully; he therefore opposed the book all the more strongly.

The defense lawyer, Sénard, made *Madame Bovary* out to be altogether conventional and harmless. It was nothing more, he claimed, than an extended moral lesson to demonstrate that a farmer's daughter should not be educated to have desires and ambitions beyond her station in life. And he found it less risqué than acknowledged classics in the literary canon: he delighted in comparing the famous fiacre scene in *Madame Bovary* to a scene in Prosper Mérimée's *La double méprise* (1833; *The Double Mistake*), where Mérimée had been so bold as to reveal what went on inside a closed cab. Pinard, in contrast, seemed particularly susceptible to the allure of Emma Bovary, whose existence might be imaginary but whose effects certainly were not. Pinard's comments during the trial indicate that he felt poisoned or contaminated by the novel's portrayal of passion and, when faced with his own temptation, set out in a kind of quest for self-preservation to find a legal antidote to Flaubert's writing. He suggests, for example, that even men may be "feminized" by literature, and then evokes in almost Platonic fashion an image of the law as guardian of public morality and religion:

> Who will read the novel of Monsieur Flaubert? Will it be men who busy themselves with political or social economy? No! The light pages of *Madame Bovary* will fall into even lighter hands—into the hands of young women, sometimes of married women. Well, when the imagination has been seduced, when seduction has descended into the heart, when the heart has spoken to the senses, do you believe that a very cold reasoning will be very strong

against this seduction of the senses and of sentiment? In addition, even men must not drape themselves too much in their force and virtue; men, too, harbor instincts from below and ideas from above, and, with everyone alike, virtue is the consequence of effort, very often painful effort. Lascivious paintings generally have more influence than cold reasonings.   (Quoted in Flaubert, *Oeuvres,* 1:631–632)

It is striking how many unspoken assumptions and expectations were shared by prosecution, defense, and judges at both the Flaubert and Baudelaire trials. They conceived the nature of true art in a similar manner, and they all believed that the larger sociocultural and political context of the trials and the texts was basically legitimate. They could not explicitly recognize that the texts of Baudelaire and Flaubert placed in question the context and the norms on which the court relied to render judgment. The trial proceedings could go no further than to pit ordinary conformity against ordinary deviance or crime, a simple binary opposition. Neither defense nor prosecution could admit that the texts in question involved an ideological offense, an extraordinary transgression rather than a mere crime. Indeed it was the defense at both trials who insisted the most on normalizing or domesticating the texts, thereby reducing them to a conventional level. Only Pinard came close to disclosing facets of the text that went beyond simple or standardized deviance. Twice he pointed out the scandalous nature of the following phrase from *Madame Bovary:* "the defilements of marriage and the disillusions of adultery" ("les souillures du mariage et les désillusions de l'adultère"). The second time, he tried to explain why he found the phrase disturbing: "Often when one is married, instead of the unclouded happiness one expected, one encounters sacrifices and bitterness. The word disillusion might be justified; that of defilement could never be" (quoted in Flaubert, *Oeuvres,* 1:625). He obviously was upset by Flaubert's radical reversal of cliché and struggled to restore the standard formula—marriage can disappoint, but only adultery can sully.

Madame Bovary itself neither praises adultery in order to condemn marriage nor attacks adultery in order to defend marriage. It creates instead a drastically unstable social and ethical universe in which as fundamental an opposition as that between adultery and marriage threatens to become a distinction without a difference. Emma's real tragedy is that little of substance differentiates her husband from her lovers, her ordinary reality from her imagined one. Seeming opposites become deadly repetitions of one another, and the despised husband seems in the end to be the only one who loves her. Not only does he keep an adoring vigil at her coffin while others sleep or are absent; he ends his life imitating hers as he establishes Emma as an undefiled romantic idol despite all evidence to the contrary.

Madame Bovary's unsettling treatment of marriage and the family is matched by an often outrageous and satirical critique of religion. The binary opposition between the sacred and the profane proves to be as untenable as that between marriage and adultery. There is, for example, little to distinguish the priest Bournisien from his ridiculous secular counterpart Homais. Appropriately, these two finally "recognize" each other as they eat and sleep together over Emma's coffin.

Most subtly unsettling is Flaubert's style of narration. His famous *style indirect libre* (free indirect style) makes it impossible for the reader to tell if it is the narrator or the character who is thinking or speaking. Voice and perspective are thus modulated in such a way as to keep all expectations off center. Figures of speech or thought that deviate from the norm combine with this narrative device to unsettle the self-sufficient bourgeois individual, the subject who in the normal confines of storytelling is considered to be the fount of judgment and interpretation. Pinard sensed this problem when he exclaimed to the court that there was no vantage point within the novel from which Emma Bovary could be forthrightly condemned.

Foremost among the legal charges levied against both Flaubert and Baudelaire was their adoption of the aesthetic doctrine of "realism"—realism understood as an alluring representation of the ugly and the evil, marked by lascivious coloration and lack of a legitimate sense of *mesure,* of limits. As Pinard put it in Flaubert's trial, "art without rules is no longer art; it is like a woman who takes off all her clothes" (quoted in Flaubert, *Oeuvres,* 1:635). Or, as the court put it in its judgment, realism as practiced by Flaubert was "the negation of the beautiful and the good" (p. 683).

Madame Bovary and *Les fleurs du mal* do to some extent invite conventional or symptomatic interpretations on realist grounds. Both texts operate between traditional expectations and experimentation; both swerve between a hyperbolic realism and rhetorical strategies that seem to escape realism. *Les fleurs du mal* combines traditional poetic harmonies with the disconcerting attempt to extract "beauty" from the ugly and the evil—an attempt that involves an ambivalent fascination with transgression. Baudelaire enacted in his poems the double or ironic consciousness that for him defined the condition of the artist: "two simultaneous postulations, one toward God, the other toward Satan" ("Mon coeur mis à nu" [1887; "My Heart Laid Bare"], in *Oeuvres,* p. 632). In *Madame Bovary,* Flaubert employed an elaborate strategy of double inscription involving, in addition to the *style indirect libre,* the re-citation and recycling of cliché, which is simultaneously a linguistic definition of social reality and a manifestation of stupidity.

Along with this ironic undermining of realism, Baudelaire and Flaubert seemed to share other aesthetic ideals, and they came to recognize and to enunciate an elective affinity: each sought a pure art that would transcend any content or theme it might convey. (See especially Baudelaire, "Gustave Flaubert, *Madame Bovary,*" in *Oeuvres,* pp. 449–453.) In Baudelaire a "religion of art" sanctified the attempt in a pure poetry ("poésie pure") to transubstantiate the ugly into the beautiful, even into the sublime. In Flaubert it induced an image of the artist as the Christ of art. Flaubert also dreamed of a "livre sur rien"—a book about nothing. A "book about nothing" might conceivably be made up entirely of recycled clichés. Liberated from their practical functions and transformed into ritualistic but secular blazons, these clichés could be used in complete independence from their referents.

When, in 1949, attorney Falco asked the court to overturn the 1857 verdict against Baudelaire, he stressed the need for a more enlightened understanding of civil liberties in relation to art. He urged the court to understand more "symbolically"—a word the court took to mean "spiritually"—the same Baudelaire poems that the 1857 judges had read and condemned in "realistic" terms. The crux of his appeal was a rather embarrassing anomaly: six poems by Baudelaire, then as now one of the most widely disseminated classic authors of French literature, were still condemned by law. The judgment in Baudelaire's favor was therefore pragmatic. And yet the theoretical understanding of true art on which the 1949 court relied resembled that of the 1857 court. The judiciary's aesthetic was idealistic. It demanded that a work of art provide purely symbolic and "spiritual" resolution of the problems it disclosed and explored. What changed in 1949 was the judgment: certain portions of *Les fleurs du mal,* once deemed offensive, were found to be uplifting. And this change of view was facilitated by the process of canonization, which the court's revised decision itself sanctioned.

Read in narrowly formalistic ways, the texts of Baudelaire and Flaubert would seem to exemplify the ideology of "pure art" that these writers themselves at times professed. The texts would attain—or at least approximate—a self-referential, self-sufficient, or "autotelic" status. Yet the trials of these writers suggest that formal experimentation itself may in certain historical contexts have broader sociopolitical and cultural effects. One issue for readers today is whether a different, "noncanonical" reading of the canon, which resists symbolic resolutions as well as narrowly formalistic interpretations, may be one force in reopening texts to the broader sociopolitical effects that were operative, however uncritically, in the trials of Flaubert and Baudelaire.

Bibliography: Charles Baudelaire, *Les fleurs du mal précédé du Dossier des Fleurs du mal,* ed. Claude Bonnefoy (Paris: Pierre Belfond, 1965). Baudelaire, *Oeuvres complètes.* ed. Marcel A. Ruff (Paris: Seuil, 1968). Gustave Flaubert, *Oeuvres,* ed. Albert Thibaudet and René Dumesnil, vol. 1 (Paris: Gallimard, 1951). F. W. J. Hemmings, *Culture and Society in France 1848–1898* (London: B.T. Batsford, 1971). Barbara Johnson, *Défigurations du langage poétique: La seconde révolution baudelairienne* (Paris: Flammarion, 1979). Dominick LaCapra, *"Madame Bovary" on Trial* (Ithaca: Cornell University Press, 1982). André Pasquet, *Ernest Pinard et le procès de Madame Bovary* (Paris: Savoir Vouloir Pouvoir, 1949).

Dominick LaCapra

✑ *1859, 23 July*
Death of Marceline Desbordes-Valmore

Poète Maudite

Marceline Desbordes-Valmore (1786–1859), the only woman to join—in the second edition—Paul Verlaine's famous study of 19th-century poets, *Les poètes maudits* (1888; *The Damned Poets*), was France's best female poet since Louise Labé (1526–1566).

The youngest surviving child of a family impoverished and separated by the economic and social upheavals of the Revolution, Marceline Desbordes was put to work as an actress at age eleven to help her mother make ends meet. Never financially secure, she learned to eke out her own living from then on. An unmarried mother at twenty-four, she raised her son alone until his death in 1816. So strong was her sense of independence and privacy that scholars still cannot agree whether or not the writer Henri de Latouche was the child's father and her lifelong lover. In 1817 she married Prosper Valmore, an actor seven years her junior, and bore four more children, three of whom survived past infancy.

Because her husband was frequently on the road when not unemployed, Desbordes-Valmore raised the children alone for long periods and contended with securing their subsistence. She worked in the theater until 1823 and then lived hand to mouth as a free-lance writer, selling children's and other stories—*Contes en vers* (*Tales in Verse*), *Contes en prose* (*Tales in Prose*), *Livre des mères et des enfants* (*The Book of Mothers and Children*), all in 1840; *Huit femmes* (1845; *Eight Women*), *Anges de la famille* (1849; *Angels of the Family*), and *Jeunes têtes et jeunes coeurs* (1855; *Young Heads and Young Hearts*)—lyrics for musical romances; and an autobiographical novel, *L'atelier d'un peintre* (1833; *A Painter's Studio*). From 1813 on, she also sold her poems by the piece. Her collections of poetry include *Poésies* (1830), *Les pleurs* (1833; *Tears*), *Pauvres fleurs* (1839; *Poor Flowers*), and *Bouquets et prières* (1843; *Bouquets and Prayers*). A lingering battle with cancer left her housebound and unable to write anything new for the last two years of her life, but at the time of her death, she was editing what is generally agreed to be her finest collection, the posthumous *Poésies inédites* (1860; *Unpublished Poems*), which includes "Les cloches et les larmes" ("Bells and Tears"), "Allez en paix" ("Go in Peace"), "Les roses de Saadi" ("The Roses of Saadi"), "La couronne effeuillée" ("The Barren Crown"), and "Une nuit de mon âme" ("A Night of My Soul").

The historical and cultural disadvantages against female poets highlight the scope and quality of Desbordes-Valmore's poetic achievement. Few women then received schooling of any kind beyond the primary grades, and Desbordes-Valmore was no exception. Higher learning was reserved for males of privilege. Moreover, although Romanticism exalted emotion and nature over learning and artifice, literary genres were still systematically defined according to paradigms based on gender—and poetry was for and by men. Most major poets described the reading and writing of poetry in metaphorical terms referring to male genital activity, such as virility, potency, and insemination. The animal imagery widely used by Romantic writers contributed further to this association. In "La mort du loup" (1843; "The Death of the Wolf"), for instance, Alfred de Vigny created a lasting symbol of the ideal poet, embodied in the male of the species and the stereotypical ideal of the pater familias. Alphonse de Lamartine, in his poem "A Mme. Desbordes-Valmore" (1831; "To

Mme. Desbordes-Valmore"), follows the same gender pattern in distinguishing between two kinds of poetry, identified with two types of boats: the great ocean-going vessel of virile poetry, with exclusively male passengers, ejaculates a frothy seminal liquid in its wake; the frail houseboat represents poetry by and for "others." The gender-based hierarchy is replicated in the titles of the publications in which Desbordes-Valmore's work appeared: *Hommage aux dames* (*Homage to the Ladies*), *Hommage aux demoiselles* (*Homage to the Maidens*), *Guirlande des dames* (*The Ladies' Garland*), *Les femmes poètes* (*Women Poets*), *Almanach des dames, Almanach des demoiselles, Chansonnier des dames* (*The Ladies' Songbook*), *Chansonnier des grâces* (*The Graces' Songbook*), *Chansonnier des belles* (*The Beauties' Songbook*), and *Conseiller des femmes* (*The Ladies' Counsellor*). Female poets were regarded as minor, second-rate, or subordinate, writing for other women; first-rate poetry was by and for men. Indeed, among the most striking and moving aspects of Desbordes-Valmore's poems are the references to being silenced—at the sound of a lover's approaching footsteps or in awe of God the Father—a silencing fundamentally different from the metaphysical kind of writer's block that haunted Mallarmé and his followers.

This view of female poets as second-rate did not cease with Romanticism. Shortly after Desbordes-Valmore's death, Baudelaire, the spokesman of modernist aesthetics, wrote in 1861 a commemorative essay praising her as "natural" and "feminine." The very sign of her femininity *is* her naturalness: her simple, direct, spontaneous style, coming from the heart. Baudelaire concludes by likening her work to a romantic garden. For Baudelaire, however, the vegetal, organic, and irregular were antithetical to true art or poetry; he scorned the profuse, wild, and uncultivated earthiness exalted by Romanticism. Thus the terms he uses to praise Desbordes-Valmore in fact devalue her poetry. Hence his difficulties in accounting for Desbordes-Valmore's subversion of Romantic themes, images, and stylistic features to her own very different account.

Although several of her poems satirize the educational system as the center and source of misogynistic forms of culture, for the most part Desbordes-Valmore turned the disadvantages of her gender to creative advantage. In the first place, she speaks of and to her muse as a kindred spirit, with none of the sexual tensions—the defensiveness, hostility, and embarrassment—that frequently characterize male lyric apostrophes. Able to speak woman to woman (as in "A Madame A. Tastu"), she finds in these sororal bonds a source of strength rather than emotional bondage, and attributes her own verbal creativity, candor, and courage to this feeling of sisterhood with the muse.

Second, her lack of formal education left her free to bypass a stultifying rhetorical tradition. In an 1839 letter to her husband (*Lettres*, 1:151), she explicitly rejects the traditional sonnet (which Baudelaire was going to revitalize in *Les fleurs du mal*)—her more than 600 poems include only 3—calling it nothing but a brilliant straitjacket created by men. Instead, by experimenting constantly with verse forms, original metrical and rhythmic patterns, and diction, she achieves a musicality based on actual spoken language: a series of short interjections or imperatives, common verbs, rapid-fire questions followed by staccato answers, frequent repetitions, strings of subjects and verbs without subordinate clauses, and formulaic, colloquial, and prosaic expressions from contemporary speech. Her lexicon includes nonpoetic words such as *raser* (shave or skim), *ciment* (cement), and *forceps* (forceps), all of which become powerful images, because they were then uncommon in literary writing. The conversational rhythms harmonize with her frequent use of irregular or free verse instead of the classical alexandrine, which favors intricate rhetorical effects and a periodic sentence structure.

Many of Desbordes-Valmore's poems take the form of dialogues—between two mothers, two trees, two dogs, two pigeons, and so on—perhaps as a result of her theatrical background. The dialogue structure frequently heightens her unique orality and highlights the theme of intersubjectivity. Neither the speakers represented in the poem nor the poet's own lyric voice is disembodied: instead of using universal paradigms, such as the essence of humanity or poetic genius, which are traditionally masculinized, she makes the feminine both visible and audible, through her choice of nouns, pronouns, and adjectives.

Desbordes-Valmore's landscapes are settings for extremely vivid, intense, and complicated emotions—anxiety, trepidation, defloration, regret, sorrow, pain and guilt, the bitterness of paternal reprimands and the loneliness that results—but also, and perhaps primarily, for positive feelings—joy, warmth, and sometimes freedom, including sexual freedom. With their hidden recesses in thickets and undergrowth or undulating, dark, and moist knolls, their odors, flowers, and valleys, they are as strikingly erotic as the images of the 20th-century painters Georgia O'Keeffe and Léonor Fini. Whispered desires and caresses are exchanged in shadowy enclosed gardens bursting with fruit. The same gardens at other times are inundated with rays of sun that either gush or pierce. Or they have cracks and crevices that quiver quietly by themselves. In these landscapes, flowers become concrete figures of female genitals and sexual activity. Minutely described in terms of friction, swelling, and respiration, flowers embody various forms of sensory arousal, compliant bending, and emotional gestures such as the willing acceptance of vulnerability. "L'augure" (1839; "The Omen") presents the earth as a woman opening her belted robe to the sun's rays, her smiling lips exuding a sweet odor in the context of penetration: her "invisible smile fills nature with incense / And her hymn to the sun will rise from the flowers." Such imagery provides an important document of the way 19th-century women described their own bodies and their sexuality.

The sensory calm of lush undergrowth frequently prompts memories of pleasure shared with others. Images of fertilization, fructification, and insemination abound, but phallic brutality is absent. Gratification is oral, olfactory, mutual. In the following verses from "Une ruelle de Flandre" (1860; "A Small Street in Flanders"), the surface meaning seems innocent enough, for the ostensible subject is a neighbor's garden, which the poet recalls from her girlhood. But in their atmosphere of slightly vibrating leafiness and dilation, the reminiscences can be read on a deeper level not only as images of specifically female physical experience, but also as expressions of palpable erotic delight in genital sexuality.

734

She recalls a narrow, dark, breathless, and suffocating street, which an invisible good fairy dilates (*dilatait*) with a tingling breath of fresh air:

> Wandering among perfumes from all these green trees,
> Plunging our foreheads boldly under their half-opened bodies,
> We flirted with the embalmed roses
> Which returned the favor, happy to be loved!

Desbordes-Valmore celebrates female friendship in terms interchangeable with those used for heterosexual relationships. In fact "Les deux peupliers" (1829; "The Two Poplars") has been (mis)read as a conventional love poem, although her letters show that in writing it she had in mind one or two female friends. In it she addresses two poplar trees: below the ground, "the vital juices that join you return inward to your hearts," while above ground "your quivering limbs and foliage murmur in unison; / married in the earth, through beloved knots, / you live for each other." Similarly, in "Les roseaux" (1839; "The Reeds"), dedicated to her sister, two reeds

> . . . intertwined their days
> and nights
>
> . . .
>
> made themselves one in order to stay together forever as two
>
> . . .
>
> And from this fresh wedding came forth a harmony
> Which spoke! Which sang! sad, intimate, infinite.

The harmony of this "hymen" is destroyed by an intruding male. The poem's images and themes apply as well to special female bonds as to love or marriage. Heterosexual love no longer functions as the ultimate reference, according to which all other relationships receive meaning and value; it is only an indicator of relationships and values more heartfelt. When images of marriage are used thus to refer to friendship, and images of sorority evoke marriage, male and female cease to be objects of desire and become instead interchangeable subjects. Because Desbordes-Valmore's "love" poems are not focused exclusively on amorous and erotic gratification with or for men, they disrupt the entrenched habit of "immasculation," of interpreting strong emotional expressions normatively in relation to men, their self-conceptions, and their definition of heterosexuality.

Desbordes-Valmore's vision of creativity also distinguishes her from her contemporaries. Unlike most Romantics, she does not depict poetry as a special power or destiny acquired at birth. Nor does she make the poet heir to a tradition or subject to divine inspiration. Such images, she was well aware, linked the definition and self-image of the poet to the ideology of patrimony, primogeniture, and biological birthrights that signaled in yet another way the masculinization of the genre. She also excludes the Old Testament notion of genesis ex nihilo by God the Father. Instead, she describes the making of poetry in terms of transformation or metamorphosis within existing life forms—a caterpillar in its cocoon becoming a butterfly, a fruit becoming the flower or vice versa, a girl becoming a bird, a mother merging into the flesh of her child.

Desbordes-Valmore explores the permeable boundaries that exist between the self and nature—childbirth, poetic creativity, and death—and treats them all as transformative rather than destructive events. She expresses none of the fear, commonly voiced in Romantic male lyric, that nature will overwhelm the poet and deprive him of his uniquely human capacity for inspiration. Her themes, imagery, and style set her apart from what, in Joyce Carol Oates's view, characterized masculine Romanticism, the feeling and loneliness of having "lost the cosmos." Rather, Desbordes-Valmore empathizes with that which is other than, but not inferior to, herself, transforming a sororal or maternal mystery into a source of knowledge and joy. In his recent introduction to her poems, Yves Bonnefoy notes that Desbordes-Valmore's nature poetry captures the authenticity and intensity of being finite. Nature is neither a barren wasteland nor the mirror or lamp with which to illuminate her own ego. Her landscapes are female and teem with interwoven, transitional forms of life—insects, birds, the bodies of the children and parents she has buried, her own future corpse—whose affinity with human forms need only be recognized to be loved and enjoyed.

Desbordes-Valmore could hardly have been read in this way by her contemporaries. Even 20th-century perspectives have not diverged from Baudelaire's paradigm assessing women's poetry in terms that subordinate it to men's. Critics have praised her ability to write like Hugo, Racine, Théophile Gautier, and even Baudelaire. They have largely ignored her part in enriching French poetry with oral folk material, themes, and rhythms, and in integrating music into poetry. Yet Verlaine's, Guillaume Apollinaire's, and Bonnefoy's intense musicality owes much to her previous "musicalization" of poetry.

Desbordes-Valmore's style suggests only one of the ways in which the history of French literature should be rewritten to take into account the contributions of female poets. Desbordes-Valmore deserves a place in literary history precisely as the voice of difference. For contemporary readers, her poetry gives renewed access to the world of the female imagination, where eroticism is not controlled by men. Her flowers, as metaphors of an active, autonomous sensory life, constitute an alternative to Baudelaire's *flowers of evil*. Her images of female sexuality are the flowers of otherness.

See also 1555 (July), 1820, 1837.

Bibliography: Francis Ambrière, *Le siècle des Valmore* (Paris: Seuil, 1987). Charles Baudelaire, "Marceline Desbordes-Valmore," in *Oeuvres complètes,* ed. Y.-G. Le Dantec and Claude Pichois (Paris: Gallimard, 1961). Yves Bonnefoy, Preface to Desbordes-Valmore, *Poésies* (Paris: Gallimard, 1983). Boyer d'Agens, ed., *Lettres de Marceline Desbordes à Prosper Valmore,* 2 vols. (Paris: Sirène, 1924). Marceline Desbordes-Valmore, *Les oeuvres poétiques de Marceline Desbordes-Valmore,* ed. Marc Bertrand (Grenoble: Presses Universitaires de Grenoble, 1973). Eliane Jasenas, *Marceline Desbordes-Valmore devant la critique* (Geneva: Droz, 1962). Jasenas, *Le poétique: Desbordes-Valmore et Nerval* (Paris: Delarge, 1975). Alphonse de Lamartine, *Oeuvres poétiques complètes,* ed. Marius-François

Guyard (Paris: Gallimard, 1963). Charles Augustin Sainte-Beuve, *Memoirs of Madame Desbordes-Valmore with a Selection from Her Poems*, trans. Harriet W. Preston (Boston: Robert Bros., 1873). Paul Verlaine, *Les poètes maudits*, in *Oeuvres en prose complètes*, ed. Jacques Borel (Paris: Gallimard, 1972).

Michael Danahy

ᥱᥬᕤᕥ 1859, 7 December

Charles Baudelaire, Preparing the Second Edition of *Les fleurs du mal*,
Encloses "Le cygne" in a Letter to Victor Hugo

Exile from Within, Exile from Without

The edition of Charles Baudelaire's *Les fleurs du mal* (*The Flowers of Evil*) that we read today is not the one originally published in 1857, but the second, 1861 edition, reorganized and enlarged by the addition of thirty-five new poems. Shortly after the appearance of the first edition, Baudelaire was brought to trial for "offenses to public morality"—obscenity. Six of the poems were condemned, and the poet was ordered to pay a fine. The judgments of the court address moral and aesthetic transgressions against sexual and religious decorum, yet they remain blind to more profoundly threatening aspects of the poems. Though never explicitly political, these frequently undermine prevailing systems of representation in which the subject assumes a place not only in the lyric itself, but also in the wider symbolic systems of social discourse.

Les fleurs du mal first appeared just a few months after the publication of Victor Hugo's great collection of Romantic poems, *Les contemplations* (1856; *Contemplations*). In 1861, in the second edition, three poems of the new section, "Tableaux parisiens" ("Parisian Scenes"), were dedicated to Hugo: "Le cygne" ("The Swan"), "Les sept vieillards" ("The Seven Old Men"), and "Les petites vieilles" ("The Little Old Women"). In the same year Baudelaire published an essay on the Romantic poet: "Réflexions sur quelques-uns de mes contemporains: Victor Hugo" ("Observations on a Few of My Contemporaries: Victor Hugo"). This reading of Hugo, as well as the poems dedicated to him, exemplifies the radically different relations between history and poetic language in the work of the two writers.

From his exile in the Channel Islands, Hugo overtly opposed Louis-Napoleon; a maguslike figure, he spoke both as poet and as polemicist. Baudelaire, on the other hand, disdained politics yet wrote from within the city about a different kind of exile, the alienation of contemporary life. His political opposition, a complex and even perverse one, did not result in the *poet's* becoming a directly political figure, but was performed instead by the *poem's* symbolic operations, by the figures of the texts themselves. The themes of poetic communication, the rhetorical strategies, and the relations to memory and history assumed in Hugo's *Contemplations* and in *Les fleurs du mal* are radically different. Why, then, did Baudelaire dedicate to Hugo these three poems in the new

737

"Tableaux," including one of his most important ones, "Le cygne"? In what ways did Baudelaire adhere to or diverge from the lyric tradition that reached its apogee with Hugo?

In "Réflexions sur mes contemporains" Baudelaire compares Hugo to a biblical prophet whom God has ordered to eat a book. The poet consumes the French lexicon, and it emerges from his mouth as "a world, a colored, melodious, and moving universe" (*Oeuvres complètes*, p. 705). This is a somewhat monstrous version of the important topos of Romantic poetry describing the world as a book and the poet as a privileged reader whose verse deciphers the mysteries of the universe. Here Baudelaire pays homage to Hugo's astonishing verbal genius and prodigious output and acknowledges him as the major lyric poet of mid-19th-century France. But Baudelaire's other writings show that he considered Hugo's poetics revisionary, amplifying the practices of an earlier Romanticism rather than radically revitalizing language; expressive lyricism is no longer viable, even in the case of its most powerful exemplar. In his notebooks Baudelaire ironically observes that Hugo thinks a "fiat of Providence" has transformed "Jersey into Saint Helena" ("Mon coeur mis à nu" [1887; "My Heart Laid Bare"], in *Oeuvres complètes*, p. 1262): exiled in 1852 after his campaign against the establishment of the Second Empire, Hugo has become an unwittingly ironic figure of the first Napoleon. For Baudelaire the heroic stance is an anachronistic reminder that contemporary French artists, now mired in increasingly reactionary politics, have failed to transform the nation's history. Exiled from daily events in France, Hugo speaks with authority the truths of his personal life, as if they were also those of an ethical, contemporary history, adjusted by the visionary's view of the universal. He is, in Baudelaire's words, "a genius without frontiers" (p. 707). Baudelaire, on the other hand, writes of the subject's alienation in modern Paris . . . exiled from within.

Hugo's preface to *Les contemplations* states that the book should be read as the memoirs of a dead man; death is the fulfillment of a personal narrative of suffering and expiation. For Hugo, all poetic discourse is an expression of presence and communication, not of alienated subjectivity—of what Baudelaire calls, in "L'irrémédiable" ("The Irremediable"), the "heart's exchange / with its own dark mirror" (*Les Fleurs du Mal*, p. 81). The lyric "I" and "thou," subject and object, are interchangeable in Hugo and enter into a dialogue taking on cosmic proportions, with the divine as its origin and ultimate subject.

In *Les contemplations* both the many poems addressed to a beloved and the lyric complaint assume the possibility of a response from a figure that either intercedes between the poet and the ideal or in some other way represents a desired understanding or emotion. In those texts in which the poet speaks to nature, exploring the integration of life, the human has a place within a vast, obscure, though comprehensible, creation. The poet is a dreamer ("La vie aux champs" ["Life in the Fields"], "Aux arbres" ["To the Trees"], "Paroles sur la dune" ["Words upon the Dune"]) whose walks engage him in a dialogue between the animate and the inanimate. Baudelaire notes: "He converses with the waves and the wind" ("Réflexions," p. 702). The very act of seeking dialogue, even when frustrated, affirms the possibility of communication. He who contemplates, observes Baudelaire, derives a "morality of things" that respects the obscurities of the "universal analogy." Thought, dream, and quest coincide. Every object functions as a subject, capable of language and of expressing presence and meaning. The poems are written within a schema of address in which the "I"/"thou" relationship can always be reversed and the narrating "I" become the receiver of a message ultimately deriving from a divine spirit: "Oui, je suis le rêveur" (["Yes, I am the dreamer"], *Les contemplations,* bk. 1, xxvii).

The many poems in which the narrator meditates upon personal, social, and cosmic history reiterate the discovery of a comprehensive order. Dialogues between the poet and his past ("A Villequier"; "At Villequier"), with contemporaries ("Ecrit en 1846"; "Written in 1846"), or with the infinite ("Ibo" ["I Will Go"], "Ce que dit la bouche d'ombre" ["What the Mouth of Shadows Said"]) are all immense affirmations of the possibility of progress. The poet joins the destiny of those who, like him, seek and suffer ("Les malheureux"; "The Unfortunate Ones"), who comprehend the permanent unity of things ("Les mages"; "The Magi"). On the personal and social levels, the obstacles to this quest are the death of the innocent (*Les contemplations,* bk. 4), the silence it imposes, doubt, and persistent social injustices ("Melancholia"). On the universal scale, there are the unknowable enigmas of the "sinister spiral" of "Immensity" and "Eternity" ("Magnitudo Parvi"; "Greatness of the Small"), and the "obscure barrier of creation," which separates man from God. The poems thus rely on an unshaken confidence in language and in narrative. If everything is available to interpretation, implicated in comprehensive analogical relations, and difference and otherness always the province of the poet, then even the most purely metaphorical texts are charged with relating a narrative of universal interpretability. This confidence reaches its apogee with Hugo; with Baudelaire it can no longer hold.

Baudelaire's verse preface to *Les fleurs du mal,* "Au lecteur" ("To the Reader"), establishes a very different relation between poet, text, and reader from that advanced by Hugo. It is a "prosy" text, its declamatory, moralizing tone quite inconsistent with most of Baudelaire's poems. The first stanza enumerates the moral failings, sins, and foolishness occupying our minds and working upon our bodies and accuses reader and poet alike of complicity with these evils; we feed our "affable remorse" "the way a beggar nourishes his vermin." The great moral categories, even if they survive in the notion of sin, have broken down and commingle with the trivial, the foolish. The poem is peopled with personifications of evil—Satan Trismegistus, the Devil, Demons, and Death—yet destiny is figured as a "banal buckram" that our souls lack the vigor to embellish. Among the monsters in the menagerie of our vices, the ugliest, meanest, and filthiest is Ennui, who would "swallow all creation in a yawn," his eye filled with an involuntary tear. The poet and the reader are debilitated figures, having outlived the moral canon of the past, capable of nothing grand. Mind and body are constantly divided from within, inhabited by forces not our own; the subject is fragmented and corrupt. The last two lines lash out:

> Reader, you know this squeamish monster well,
> —hypocrite reader,—my alias,—my twin!   (*Les Fleurs du Mal*, p. 6)

The hypocrite is an actor, one who assumes a role, who dissembles. Communication between the poet and the reader, the material world, or a transcendent subject, implicit in the traditional lyric, as in *Les contemplations,* is an impossibility that can be considered only ironically. The traditional rhetoric of the text (apostrophe, personification, periodic syntax) suggests in its very exaggeration that poetic language itself has become problematic, an obstacle rather than a shared communication.

Baudelaire often insisted that *Les fleurs du mal* was not just a collection of verse, but that it was structured coherently, with a beginning and an end. Its "secret architecture" was to create an overall thematic and narrative unity recounting a descent into the abyss, after the failure of love and ideals, and various forms of self-destructive vice. This moral narrative, though in many ways similar to that of Hugo's *Contemplations,* is fundamentally different, and not simply because of its pessimism. Baudelaire had no faith in progress based upon either a concept or an experience of history as a continuum. Furthermore, in *Les fleurs* there is no implicit narrative of the universal interpretability of life. These observations are borne out by the final poem, "Le voyage," which repeats and radically modifies the topos of life as a journey. Here the poet addresses Death as an "old captain" whom he entreats to set sail, and

> we can plunge
> to Hell or Heaven—an abyss will do—
> deep in the Unknown to find the *new!*   (*Les Fleurs du Mal*, p. 157)

There is no ultimate enlightenment here at the end of life's journey, just the desperate hope that death will bring something different.

To interpret the collection as a drama with a dénouement, following Baudelaire's admonitions, is to impose a moral teleology on a collection deriving much of its force from its disruption of grand narrative schemes. Baudelaire's relation to these issues is characteristically ambivalent; he alternately seeks meaningful completeness and questions its possibility. The second poem of "Tableaux parisiens" is emblematic in this respect. In "Le soleil" ("The Sun") the narrator wanders through the modern city:

> sinking into slums
>
> . . .
>
> I venture out alone to drill myself
> in what must seem an eerie fencing-match,
> duelling in dark corners for a rhyme
> and stumbling over words like cobblestones
> where now and then realities collide
> with lines I dreamed of writing long ago.   (*Les Fleurs du Mal*, p. 88)

Poetic "inspiration" is not a discovery of a transcendent natural order, as in the Romantic lyric, but something of an accident, a shock, an only partially conscious activity. The narrator assembles fragments, bits and pieces of meaningfulness, already partially "there" within consciousness, but disjoined and jolted forth by the very unsystematic collision with the "real." Meaning is a partial affair, a struggle with the distinct, contingent, and mutually resistant components of consciousness, language, and "reality."

"Le soleil" condenses forms of meaning and attitudes toward poetry encountered throughout Baudelaire's verse, sometimes distinct and separate, sometimes in tension. Many of the texts develop and refine the Romantic aesthetic of universal analogies in which the world is a metaphor or a hieroglyph; in others, self and world are fragmented, irrevocably different and discontinuous.

The famous sonnet "Correspondances," like several others in the first section of *Les fleurs,* celebrates the symbolic unity of the universe, the interrelatedness of the affective, the material, and the ontological. The poem develops the Romantic simile of the natural forest as a temple, from which emerge "confused words"; man proceeds through "forests of symbols," which look at him "with accustomed eyes." Physical senses, sounds, the visual, and the olfactory "answer one another," like echoes. The poem does not personify these "correspondences" in a narrative of revealed truth, as so often occurs in Hugo; the emphasis is upon possible combinations of senses, between mutually implicating levels of metaphoricity, "the senses' raptures and the mind's" (*Les Fleurs du Mal,* p. 15).

The many love poems of the collection—"La chevelure" ("The Head of Hair"), "Le serpent qui danse" ("The Dancing Serpent"), "Le balcon" ("The Balcony"), "Ciel brouillé" ("Overcast"), "L'invitation au voyage" ("Invitation to the Voyage"), "Chant d'automne" ("Autumn Song")—develop analogies between the object of desire and components of a world represented in the text: a distant country, the sky, a cityscape. Their particular force derives in part from their paradoxical and ironic renewal of the lyric "I"/"thou" connection; by representing the desired other as available only through its difference from the poet, the most intimate moments are those in which the reverie is most distant from its immediate object. Quite traditionally, the beloved is often called upon to mirror the poet's desire, returned as the same, but repeated in the forms of difference making it accessible. The poems represent not simply fulfilled desire but also the mobility of desire and meaning.

Negative versions of correspondences marking the dispersal and destruction of the self occur most powerfully in the series of "spleen" poems, which evoke an insistent melancholy: "La cloche fêlée" ("The Cracked Bell"), four pieces titled "Spleen," and others at the end of the first section. In one "spleen" poem, "Quand le ciel bas et lourd . . ." ("When skies are low and heavy . . ."), the physical universe and its affective analogues contract; the earth is transformed into a damp prison cell. The progressive restriction of symbolic space and the dissolution of the material world deplete energy and dissipate being. This is not just a blocked relation with the infinite, a negative version of the Romantic topos, but the figuration of the dissolution of emotion and being.

In recent years much critical attention has been given to "Tableaux parisiens," in part because it is thematically the most explicitly "modern" section of the collection; most of its poems are set in the recognizably contemporary décor of mid-19th-century Paris. Many of them are "modern," however, in still another sense: they often bring into conflict motifs and forms of the traditional lyric with a radically different poetic language, transforming both the forms of the lyric and the subjectivity it relates. In dedicating three of these texts to Hugo, Baudelaire produces complex ambiguities that dramatically underscore the collision between the dominant poetic tradition, represented by Hugo, and the "new shock" ("le frisson nouveau") produced by *Les fleurs*. The poems' protagonists are figures of the dispossessed, the debris of modern civilization; thus Baudelaire, as he acknowledged in his correspondence, is in one sense daring to rival Hugo on his own ground. But the outcast, including the poet himself, assumes very different relations to the immediate experience of the modern world, to memory, and to the future from those in Hugo's poetry. In dedicating "Le cygne" to Hugo, Baudelaire is addressing poetry itself, as the title, a pun on its French homonym *signe* (sign), indirectly confirms. The poem is an allegory of exile and alienation set in modern Paris, in a park being reconstructed as part of Baron Georges Haussmann's renovations; it represents man's displacement from modern urban space. In this construction site the poet finds debris from a former zoo and disparate objects, "a confused bric-a-brac" (line 12). Object relations that might constitute the poet as subject, as in traditional lyric, are in disarray. The allegory seems to offer a narrative of exile, placing the alienated self in its "wrongful" place as the unwanted other. The poem begins with an apostrophe to Andromache, widow of Hector and prisoner of Pyrrhus in an exile emblematic, as the second section says, of all exiles. The narrator also recounts having seen a swan escaped from its cage, "drenching its enormous wings in the filth" (line 21). The second section of the poem likens the two figures to all exiles, both ridiculous and sublime, eaten away by endless desire. Several other figures are evoked that expand the narrative (lines 41–44):

> some black woman
>
> . . .
>
> peering through a wall of fog for those
> missing palms of splendid Africa,

and, in the following stanza, "those who lose whatever can be found" (line 46), until the final line: "and so many more" (line 52). Here signs, swans, lovers, and poets are dislodged from any stable and meaningful place in the modern world; their place is to be ever out of place. Similarly, this gap between subject and world is repeated by a gap between poetic diction and poetic experience. Allegories and apostrophes continue to have meaning, but they are no longer felt to be commensurate with experience; they symbolize less meaning apprehended and communicated than the possibilities of language to add new, ultimately endless symbols of humans' displacement from both world and language.

Contrasting attitudes toward lyricism, narrative, and history separate Hugo and Baudelaire. Baudelaire's revisions of *Les fleurs du mal*, his writings on Hugo, and the complex engagement with the poet represented throughout the collection and most specifically in "Tableaux parisiens" mark their profound differences. Hugo, dislodged from contemporary France, considered himself secure in History. Baudelaire, distanced from the myths making poetry possible, an alienated citizen of modern Paris, was constantly displaced from the immediate present and rejected any progressive vision of the future. From exile in Guernsey, Hugo communicated with an extensive audience; Baudelaire, who wrote for a few, for whom lyric eloquence had become suspect, is now the most widely read of French poets.

See also 1834, 1835, 1851, 1857.

Bibliography: Charles Baudelaire, *Les Fleurs du Mal,* trans. Richard Howard (Boston: David R. Godine, 1982). Baudelaire, *Oeuvres complètes,* ed. Y.-G. Le Dantec and Claude Pichois (Paris: Gallimard, 1961). Walter Benjamin, *Charles Baudelaire: A Lyric Poet in the Era of Capitalism,* trans. Harry Zohn (London: Verso, 1983). Ross Chambers, "Mémoire et mélancolie," in *Mélancolie et opposition* (Paris: José Corti, 1987). Jonathan Culler, "Apostrophe," in *The Pursuit of Signs* (Ithaca: Cornell University Press, 1981). Victor Hugo, *Les contemplations,* ed. Jean Gaudon, vol. 9 of *Oeuvres complètes,* ed. Jean Massin (Paris: Club Français du Livre, 1967). Suzanne Nash, *"Les Contemplations" of Victor Hugo: An Allegory of the Creative Process* (Princeton: Princeton University Press, 1976). Nathaniel Wing, "The Danaïdes Vessel: On Reading Baudelaire's Allegories," in *The Limits of Narrative: Essays on Baudelaire, Flaubert, Rimbaud and Mallarmé* (Cambridge: Cambridge University Press, 1986).

Nathaniel Wing

✐ 1866

The First Volume of *Le Parnasse contemporain* Appears

The Dream of Stone

In 1849, introducing the new edition of his *Méditations poétiques* (1820; *Poetic Meditations*), Alphonse de Lamartine boasted that he had brought poetry down from Parnassus and replaced the lyre with the very fibers of the human heart. However, there soon arose a movement to transplant poetry back to the mountain of the classical muses, le Parnasse.

Le Parnasse contemporain (Contemporary Parnassus) was the somewhat self-contradictory title chosen by a group of young poets for what began as a little poetry magazine, launched through the combined efforts of Catulle Mendès and Louis-Xavier de Ricard, and ended as a series of three collective volumes, soon published by Alphonse Lemerre, above whose bookstore the young poets held rowdy poetry readings. *Le Parnasse contemporain* became a major forum for the poetry of its day. It stands as a monument to the complex interaction between Romanticism and symbolism.

The first and best-known volume, published in 1866, contained poems by thirty-seven poets, ranging from the well established (Théodore de Banville, Charles Baudelaire, Théophile Gautier, Charles Leconte de Lisle) to the soon to be famous (Stéphane Mallarmé, Paul Verlaine) to those destined to remain obscure. Two successive volumes, one dated 1869 (but not actually published until 1871 because of the Franco-Prussian War), the other dated 1876, brought the total number of contributors to ninety-nine. The spectrum could in fact have been even broader: Victor Hugo, for example, was asked to contribute but declined; and fifteen-year-old Arthur Rimbaud sent Banville a poem that was not published. But within the full range of styles represented in the three volumes, "Parnassian" poetry, characterized by impassivity, impersonality, and the "cult of form," has been considered the most important.

For the Parnassians, form was the essence of art. According to Banville, in his *Petit traité de poésie française* (1872; *Short Treatise on French Poetry*), all of poetry could be summed up by the notion of rhyme. If poetry were simply equated with the overflow of emotions, with the search for truth, or with moral or political vision, it would lose its specificity. As Baudelaire put it, "the poetic principle is strictly and simply the human aspiration toward superior Beauty . . . independent of passion, which is the intoxication of the heart, and of truth, which is the nourishment of reason. Passion is a *natural* thing, too natural even, not to introduce a discordant, wounding tone into the domain of pure Beauty" (*Oeuvres complètes*, 2:114). Echoing Kant's definition of beauty as a form of purposiveness without purpose, Baudelaire went on to define poetry as an end in itself: "Poetry cannot, on pain of death or decay, be assimilated into science or morality. Truth is not its object; its only object is itself" (p. 113).

Gautier, to whom Baudelaire had dedicated *Les fleurs du mal* (1857; *The Flowers of Evil*), was the acknowledged progenitor and leading poet of the first *Parnasse contemporain*. Although he had once worn the Romantic *gilet rouge* in the 1830 battle of *Hernani* at the Comédie-Française, he had become increasingly critical of the strain of Romanticism that aimed to enlist poetry in the service of social utopianism, embodied in the writings of Claude-Henri de Saint-Simon and Charles Fourier. He bemoaned utilitarian notions of art, whether socialist or bourgeois: the function of art was to be beautiful—and useless. As he wrote in the preface to his novel *Mademoiselle de Maupin* (1835): "Nothing is really beautiful unless it is useless; everything useful is ugly, for it expresses a need, and the needs of man are ignoble and disgusting, like his poor weak nature. The most useful place in a house is the latrine. For myself . . . I am among those to whom the superfluous is necessary . . . I prefer to a certain useful pot a Chinese pot which is sprinkled with mandarins and dragons" (p. 39).

Thirty years later, the young Mallarmé showed himself to be a faithful disciple of Gautier. In his poems in *Le Parnasse contemporain*, Mallarmé depicts himself giving money to a beggar on condition that he *not* spend it on bread ("A un pauvre"; "To a Poor Man"), turning his back on "life" ("Les fenêtres"; "The Windows"), and attempting to leave behind "voracious art" in order to paint fine designs on a Chinese cup ("Epilogue," later titled "Las de l'amer repos . . ."; "Weary of bitter rest . . .").

Thus Parnassianism can be seen as a critique of the dominance of the concept of need. As social theory, such a critique seems to have little to recommend it. But when viewed in psychoanalytic terms, Parnassianism appears as an attempt to reserve a space for the intractability of human desire. Jacques Lacan's definition of desire makes clear the inadequacy of equating it with need: "Thus desire is neither the appetite for satisfaction, nor the demand for love, but the difference that results from the subtraction of the first from the second" ("The Signification of the Phallus," in *Ecrits,* p. 287). In other words, desire is what is left of absolute demand when all possible satisfaction of real needs has been subtracted from it. It is by definition both indestructible and unsatisfiable. As Gautier's hero boasts (and laments) in *Mademoiselle de Maupin,* "the impossible has always pleased me" (p. 142).

The equation between desire and impossible satisfaction is often represented by the Parnassians as the love of a statue. Whereas Lamartine's poetry focuses on a dead woman, the Parnassians yearn for a woman of stone. Gautier again provided the rationale in *Mademoiselle de Maupin:* "[If] there is something noble and fine about loving a statue, it is that your love is quite disinterested, that you need not fear the satiety or weariness of victory, and that you cannot reasonably hope for a second wonder like the history of Pygmalion" (p. 142).

The Parnassian passion for sculpture arises out of several sources. Sculpture stands as a serene and objective figure for pure form: it is visible, durable, unchangeable, and impassive. Parnassian poetry is often sculptural in its stanzaic patterns. Although many complex forms were used, the place of honor went to the sonnet, with its blocklike solidity and slight asymmetry. Indeed, the 1866 volume of *Le Parnasse contemporain* ended with a series of sonnets by diverse hands.

The poet's craft is often compared to that of a sculptor. In an exchange of poems in the journal *L'artiste* (May 1856 and September 1857), Banville and Gautier agree that the poet must be a "stone cutter" who wrests a shape out of rebellious matter. The last stanza of "L'art," Gautier's contribution, which he later included in the second edition (1858) of *Emaux et camées* (1852; *Enamels and Cameos*), urges the poet to

> Sculpt, file, chisel;
> Let your floating dream
> > Be sealed
> In the resistant block!   (*Poésies complètes,* 3:130)

This aesthetic of desirable difficulty requires a muse who wears narrow shoes or chains (like Keats's "sandals more interwoven and complete") so that the rhythm scanned by the (metrical) feet will not be overly facile. The force of resistance of the material (or of the muse) must be discernible.

Another factor in the choice of marble sculpture as a poetic subject may have to do with marble's whiteness. The whiteness of the beloved woman has always been celebrated in French literature, but the Parnassians seem more than usually obsessed with whiteness. Gautier's "Symphonie en blanc majeur" ("Symphony in White Major"), also in *Emaux et camées,* is a monochromatic tour de force in which a woman's body is compared to snow, satin, marble, frost, silver, opal, ivory, ermine, alabaster, dove down, swans, hawthorn flowers, and other white substances. Yet in this celebration of whiteness *resistance* remains the ultimate desideratum:

> Beneath the ice where calmly it resides
> Oh! who can ever melt this heart!
> Oh! who might induce a blush
> On this implacable whiteness!   (*Poésies complètes*, 3:24)

Whiteness is loved as a refusal to submit, but the ultimate goal is the blush.

Joseph-Arthur de Gobineau's *Essai sur l'inégalité des races humaines* (1853–1855; *Essay on the Inequality of the Human Races*) is proof that this obsession about whiteness was present on other levels of 19th-century French discourse. It is difficult, in fact, not to link it, even in the Parnassians' poetry, with something that has to do with race. Such a subtext is at least suggested by the fact that among the poems to marble and alabaster women in *Le Parnasse contemporain* there is one written to a black woman, Baudelaire's "A une Malabaraise" ("To a Malabar Woman"), which begins:

> Your feet are as delicate as your hands, and your full hips
> Would be the envy of the most beautiful white woman;
> To the pensive artist your body is sweet and precious;
> Your velvet eyes are blacker than your flesh.

The most obvious source of the Parnassians' interest in sculpture was the growth in European studies of ancient Greece. The image of Greek purity, harmony, and serenity (whose appeal was not unrelated to the political and racial turbulence of the 19th century) was celebrated through a vast increase in historical and linguistic research. The lyrics of Leconte de Lisle and Louis Ménard in particular owe more to philology than to psychology.

Orientalist and classicist references combined to produce a large number of Parnassian poems about sphinxes and Venuses. In Leconte de Lisle's 1846 poem "Vénus de Milo" (in *Poèmes antiques,* 1852; *Ancient Poems*), the Greek sculpture, recently installed in the Louvre, stood as "the admirable symbol of impassive happiness." Banville, too, in an 1842 poem, addressed her as a "great poem of stone" and imagined her regaining her arms, dropping her tunic, and giving herself to him as he himself turns into a stone lover. But not all lovers of statues are so lucky. Baudelaire's sphinx, in "La Beauté" ("Beauty"), is made both to attract and to wound:

> My beauty, mortals, is a dream of stone;
> My breast, where each in turn comes to be wounded,
> Is made to fill the poet with a love
> Eternal and mute, like matter itself.   (*Oeuvres complètes*, 1:21)

A breast of this "matter" (or of this *mater?*) wounds rather than nourishes. In a similar poem by Gautier, "Le sphinx," the sphinx is actually called a bad mother:

746

Thus it is with all our chimeras:
Their charming face hides ugliness beneath.
We take their breast, but these bad mothers
Don't give our lips a single drop of milk. (*Poésies complètes*, 2:123)

One begins to suspect all these cold, statuesque muses of being figures for the bad mother. Yet despite the pain and frustration they cause, these figures inspire admiration in those they reject. Is there something desirable about having a stone mother? Yes, if one wishes to be a stone child.

As a reaction against the excesses of Romantic vulnerability, the Parnassian celebration of impassivity is in part a desire to attain a state of needlessness. The fantasy of needlessness can on the one hand be understood as a reaction to the mother's failure to satisfy needs. But it may also arise from another source, equally fundamental to the formation of a human subject. According to Jacques Lacan, a decisive step in human development is taken when a baby first recognizes his or her own image in a mirror. The image with which the baby identifies looks fixed, stable, and complete. Lacan calls this version of the self "the statue in which man projects himself" ("The Mirror Stage," in *Ecrits*, p. 2). Thus the image that the baby assumes as his or her "I" is a fiction, a vision of wholeness that disregards the functioning of need. The fantasy of needlessness is built into the very formation of the self. To deny need is, however, to deny life. This was the error of Narcissus, who stopped eating and drinking when he fell in love with himself as pure form. Indeed, Ovid describes Narcissus' body as being "like a statue carved from Parian marble" (*Metamorphoses*, bk. 3, p. 155). Narcissism may very well be the desire to love, or to become, a statue.

Baudelaire, for his part, was not only an enthusiast but also a lucid demystifier of the cult of form. In "Le fou et la Vénus" (1862; "The Fool and the Venus"), a late prose poem, he describes a costumed fool crumpled at the feet of a statue of Venus, imploring her to take pity on him for his love of beauty. As an inanimate object, she can only look blankly off into space with her marble eyes. And in his essay "L'école païenne" (1852; "The Pagan School"), Baudelaire writes: "The immoderate taste for form leads to monstrous and unforeseen disorders . . . Any literature that refuses to march fraternally between science and philosophy is both homicidal and suicidal" (*Oeuvres complètes*, 2:49).

Baudelaire once claimed that the rights of man should include the right to contradict oneself. And certainly this fraternal notion of art contradicts his pronouncements elsewhere about art for art's sake. But perhaps this contradiction within the cult of form lies at the very heart of Parnassianism. The statue can be loved only *as* resistance. The claim that the concept of need does not suffice cannot be turned into the claim that need does not exist. That would be both homicidal and suicidal. But then, Baudelaire also promoted the right to commit suicide. What the Parnassians celebrated was the irreducibility of a dimension of art—or even of human experience—that is precisely not equivalent to "life."

See also 1820, 1885 (June), 1940–1944.

Bibliography: Théodore de Banville, *Petit traité de poésie française* (Paris: Charpentier, 1872). Charles Baudelaire, *Oeuvres complètes,* 2 vols., ed. Claude Pichois (Paris: Gallimard, 1976). Robert Denommé, *The French Parnassian Poets* (Carbondale: Southern Illinois University Press, 1972). Théophile Gautier, *Mademoiselle de Maupin,* trans. Joanna Richardson (Harmondsworth: Penguin, 1981). Gautier, *Poésies complètes* (Paris: Nizet, 1970). Jacques Lacan, "The Mirror Stage" and "The Signification of the Phallus," in *Ecrits: A Selection,* trans. Alan Sheridan (New York: Norton, 1977). Charles Leconte de Lisle, *Oeuvres,* ed. Edgard Pich, 4 vols. (Paris: Belles Lettres, 1977). Christopher L. Miller, *Blank Darkness: Africanist Discourse in France* (Chicago: University of Chicago Press, 1985). Monica Nurnberg, "Animated Sculpture: A Paradox of the *transposition d'art* from Chénier to Hérédia," *Parnasse,* 1 (May 1983), 41–49. Ovid, *Metamorphoses,* trans. Frank Justus Miller (Cambridge, Mass.: Harvard University Press, 1971). *Le Parnasse contemporain: Recueil de vers nouveaux* (1866; reprint, Geneva: Slatkine, 1971).

Barbara Johnson

✐ 1869

Les chants de Maldoror par le Comte de Lautréamont Is Printed in Belgium

Tics

When Isidore Ducasse was found dead in his apartment on 24 November 1870, during the siege of Paris, he was twenty-four years old. The cause of his death is unknown—as are most aspects of his life. Born in Montevideo and raised by his father, at age fourteen Ducasse was sent to France, where he attended the lycée at Tarbes from 1859 to 1862 and at Pau from 1863 to 1865. We lose sight of him for the next three years. His last two years he spent in Paris as an aspiring poet, publishing two collections of prose poetry and maxims at his own expense.

His posthumous fame rests on the pseudonymous volume *Les chants de Maldoror par le Comte de Lautréamont* (*Lautréamont's Maldoror*), banned in France, printed in Belgium in 1869 but not distributed until 1874 (the first canto of *Les chants de Maldoror* was published separately in France in 1868); and *Poésies* (1870), to which he signed his name. Only in 1890 was *Maldoror* reedited and published in France. Aside from a few indignant reviews, these works went virtually unnoticed until André Breton and the surrealists enthusiastically adopted Lautréamont as their champion half a century after his death. Since then, Lautréamont has been generally acclaimed by all schools of literary criticism as a symbol of modernity.

Les chants de Maldoror is composed of six cantos, each consisting of from five to sixteen stanzas. Each stanza is a separate "prose poem"; that is, it offers the density and richness normally associated with poetry, without exhibiting any of poetry's formal markers. In the first three cantos, each stanza forms a discrete narrative, complete with recognizable "stories" and recurrent themes. The fourth and the fifth cantos consist of apparently senseless rambling, studded with truncated subnarratives or pseudoscientific digressions and poetic notations. The sixth and last opens with an explicit break with the previous five, promising a new series of short novels "of about thirty pages." It then proceeds with the story of the seduction of an adolescent boy by an evil character, in the manner made fashionable in France by the *romans feuilletons* (literary serials published in the newspaper) and especially by Eugène Sue (in fact Ducasse's pseudonym, Lautréamont, comes from the name of one of Sue's characters, Latréaumont). Soon, however, the narrative breaks down again and gives way to apparently incoherent digressions; when it picks up anew, its pace accelerates and it reads like a sketch for a story. At the conclusion, Maldoror's last victim, the young Mervyn, is holding a wreath of flowers and dangling from the dome of the Panthéon, the burial place for France's most illustrious figures. In this last ironic twist Lautréamont immortalizes Mervyn, his creation, among France's literary masters.

Yet some elements remain constant throughout the six cantos. One is Maldoror, the odd hero with whom the narrative voice often identifies, a sinister character, waging war on God and man, engaged in a series of gory encounters with God or his messengers. His cruelty seems limitless, matched perhaps only by that of the Creator (whom he catches, for example, gorging on human bodies). Odd fights between hybrid creatures alternate with equally odd matings (Maldoror and a female shark, a bulldog and a little girl). Metamorphoses of characters into animals or even monsters punctuate the narrative.

A more important unifying element is the cantos' persistent preoccupation with their own literary status. *Maldoror* constitutes a meditation on literary history and traditional rhetoric. The introductory stanza sets the tone:

> May it please Heaven that the reader, emboldened, and become momentarily as fierce as what he reads, find without loss of bearing a wild and sudden way across the desolate swamps of these sombre, poison-filled pages. For unless he brings to his reading a rigorous logic and mental application at least tough enough to balance his distrust, the deadly issues of the book will lap up his soul as water does sugar.

By opening with a classical poetic topos (the evocation of heaven), the canto identifies itself as "a poem," as if pulling its reader's sleeve to say, "Look, I am poetry too!" The rest of the stanza also works· on two planes: it *constitutes* the "story" or the "poem" while *commenting* on stories and poetry—particularly on contemporary poetic practices. For example, the introductory evocation *is* already the poem. At the same time, it informs its reader of its poetic nature (it is "fierce," "sombre," "poison-filled," uncharted—in brief, dangerous), establishes a list of the qualities required of its reader ("emboldened," "become momentarily as fierce as what he reads," capable of "rigorous logic and mental application," distrustful), and eliminates from the ranks of its readers the "timid souls," incapable of detours and transgressions ("it would not be good for everyone to read the pages which follow"; p. 1). Furthermore, it sets up a program defining what reading is: engaging in reading is akin to finding one's way across a desolate and perilous terrain. A long simile, comparing the "timid reader" to migrating cranes that, upon sensing an approaching storm, deviate from their original itinerary and adopt "another—safer and more philosophical—course" (p. 2), confirms the topographical importance of detours and maneuvers as an integral part of the relation between the text and its reader. By actually *reading* the warning about the dangerous nature of reading (rather than shunning the ominous text the way the cranes shun the storm), one tacitly identifies oneself as the opposite of a "timid soul" (who is a nonreader), that is, as a *reader*. In progressing from one line to the next, the reader is necessarily "emboldened and become momentarily as fierce as what he reads"—not so much because such qualities are idiosyncratic as because "reading" is construed as a relationship with a text that generates boldness and fierceness rather than a passive surrender to the dissolving power of the poem ("unless . . . the deadly issues of this book will lap up his soul as water does sugar"; p. 1).

The introductory stanza mentions only "the text" and "the reader": the poet himself, the lyric "I," is conspicuously absent. In *Maldoror,* poetic communication bypasses the "author": it proceeds from a peculiar encounter between the text (the poem) and an act of reading become so fierce and emboldened that it usurps the power traditionally attributed to the poet. Whereas the Romantic tradition invites the reader of poetry to track an inspired "I," Lautréamont undermines the priority and mastery of the poetic "I." This attitude is particularly explicit in *Poésies,* in which Ducasse proclaims that "the poetic moans of this century are only sophisms" (p. 33), that "personal poetry has had its day of relative juggling tricks and contingent contortions" (p. 51), and engages in virulent diatribes against

> the Great-Soft-Heads of our epoch . . . the old ninnies, Chateaubriand, the Melancholy-Mohican; Sénancourt [*sic*], the Man-in-Petticoat; Jean-Jacques Rousseau, the Socialist-Grouser; Anne [*sic*] Radcliffe, the Crazy-Spectre; Edgar Poe, the Mameluke-of-Alcohol-Dreams; Mathurin [*sic*], the Accomplice-of-Darkness; George Sand, the Circumcised-Hermaphrodite; Théophile Gautier, the Incomparable-Grocer; Leconte, the Devil's-Captive; Goethe, the Suicide-through-Weeping; Sainte-Beuve, the Suicide-through-Laughter; Lamartine, the Maudlin-Stork; Lermontoff, the Tiger-Who-Howls; Victor Hugo, the Funereal-Green-Spindelshanks; Misçkiéwicz, the Imitator-of-Satan; Musset, the Shirtless-Intellectual-Dandy; and Byron, the Hippopotamus-of-the-Infernal-Jungles. (Pp. 51–53; translation modified)

In short, he blasts the *Who's Who* of Romanticism.

Furthermore, whereas Romanticism, breaking with classicism, glorified the personal inspiration of the poet, and hence originality, *Maldoror* shamelessly borrows themes, situations, and styles commonly identified with canonical writers. Baudelaire, Byron, Dante, Goethe, Hugo, Lamartine, Sade, Scott, Shakespeare, and Sue provide the most obvious subtexts. Lautréamont's vision of intertextuality extends beyond literature proper, however. He lifts verbatim whole paragraphs from scientific texts (in particular, from Jean Charles Chenu's *L'encyclopédie d'histoire naturelle,* 1850–1861; *The Encyclopedia of Natural His-*

tory). For example, in a passage acknowledged as one of the tours de force of modern literature, he opens the fifth canto with a long "borrowed" description of starlings, whose complex flight constitutes a remarkably astute rendering of the composition of *Maldoror*, while undermining the individuality and authority of the poetic voice:

> Flights of starlings have a way of flying which is theirs alone and seems as governed by uniform and regular tactics as a disciplined regiment would be, obeying a single leader's voice with precision. The starlings obey the voice of instinct, and their instinct leads them to bunch into the centre of the squad, while the speed of their flight bears them constantly beyond it; so that this multitude of birds thus united by a common tendency towards the same magnetic point, increasingly coming and going, circulating and crisscrossing in all directions, forms a sort of highly agitated whirlpool whose whole mass, without following a fixed course seems to have a general wheeling movement round itself resulting from the particular circulatory motions appropriate to each of its parts, and whose centre, perpetually tending to expand but continually compressed, pushed back by the contrary stress of the surrounding lines bearing upon it, is constantly denser than any of these lines, which are themselves the denser the nearer they are to the centre. (*Lautréamont's Maldoror*, p. 141)

Poetry is therefore not the creation of a poet mysteriously inspired by the muses, but a collective effort that results in the creation of *sens* (both "meaning" and "direction"); one in which each poet is rewriting and rereading his predecessors, and in which each reading, each interpretation, constitutes a rewriting of the text. Apart from this never-ending process, intimates Lautréamont's work, the "poem" has no existence. "Poetry should be made by all. Not by one. Poor Hugo! Poor Coppée! Poor Corneille! Poor Boileau! Poor Scarron! Tics, tics, and tics" (*Poésies*, p. 77).

Bibliography: Ora Avni, *Tics, tics et tics: Figures, syllogismes, récit dans "Les chants de Maldoror"* (Lexington, Ky.: French Forum, 1984). Maurice Blanchot, *Lautréamont et Sade* (Paris: Minuit, 1949). Isidore Ducasse, *Lautréamont's Maldoror*, trans. Alexis Lykiard (New York: Crowell, 1972). Ducasse, *Poésies and Complete Miscellanea by Isidore Ducasse also Known as Lautréamont*, ed. and trans. Alexis Lykiard (London: Allison & Bushy, 1978). Marcelin Pleynet, *Lautréamont par lui-même* (Paris: Seuil, 1967).

Ora Avni

✐ *1871, 15 May*

From Charleville, Arthur Rimbaud Sends Paul Demeny an Important Letter That Begins with a Poem, "Chant de guerre parisien"

Commune Culture

When Adolphe Thiers and the other dubious bourgeois republicans who had claimed power on 4 September 1870 capitulated to the Prussians, they announced a "peace" to Napoleon III's disastrous war for which the working people of Paris would be made to pay. Class antagonism, which had smoldered under the authoritarian social measures of the Second Empire, intensified; and on 18 March 1871 workers, many of them women who had borne the brunt of the hardships of the long Prussian siege of Paris the winter before, revolted. For seventy-three days a largely leaderless revolutionary government declared Paris an autonomous Commune and set about the free organization of its social life—free, that is, except for the constant threat of military reprisal from Thiers's army at Versailles, which became a reality, with unprecedented carnage, in the final week of May. More people died during that week than in any of the battles during the Franco-Prussian War or in any of the previous massacres in French history. Some 25,000 Parisians, most of them workers, died in the streets at the hands of the Versaillais; many of the 40,000 Communards arrested were deported to New Caledonia, where those who withstood the atrocious conditions waited nine years for the amnesty that allowed them to return to France.

The Commune was not just a political uprising; it was perhaps even more a revolt against deeply entrenched forms of social regimentation. The Commune was both the rallying cry and the event, the sign and the lived experience. This pervasive meshing of text and act contributed to the effervescence of the Communards' improvisational experiments in extending the principles of association and cooperation to the workings of everyday life. Impassable divisions established under the rigid censorship of the Second Empire (1852–1870) and the constraints of the bourgeois market—between genres, between cultural and political discourse, between artistic and artisanal work, between high art and reportage—were addressed as issues in extravagant verbal and visual form by artists, poets, artisans, journalists, cartoonists, and songwriters in a whirlwind of contradictory efforts for and against the Commune.

Catulle Mendès' memoirs, *Les 73 journées de la Commune* (1871; *The 73 Days of the Commune*), exemplify a genre prevalent immediately after the demise of the Commune: the hurriedly written eyewitness account or journal documenting everyday life during the insurrection. Mendès' journal recounts the furtive and fearful existence of an anti-Communard who agonizes daily about why he stayed in Paris rather than fleeing to Versailles with the other *amis de l'ordre* (friends of order). The publication and distribution of such texts in the early summer of 1871 coincided with and helped justify the violent repression of the Commune—a violence with which the novelist and art collector Edmond de Goncourt, in his *Journal* (1887), heartily concurs: "The bloodletting is a bleeding white; such a purge, by killing off the combative part of the population, defers the next revolution by a whole generation" (31 May 1871; *Paris under Siege*, p. 312). *Pro*-Commune memoirs such as those by Elie Reclus, whose anarchist brother Elisée was to found social geography in France, or by the songwriter Jean-Baptiste Clément, composer of one of the better-known Commune songs, "Le temps des cerises" (1866; "The Cherries' Brief Season"), tended to be published outside France in the early 1870s, or in France only after the 1880 amnesty.

In *Les 73 journées* Mendès, a poet and cofounder in 1866 of the journal *Le Parnasse contemporain,* recounts imaginary late-night conversations between himself and Gustave Courbet. Fifty-one years old in 1871, Courbet, whose status and reputation as a painter was already well established, was serving as president of the Fédération des Artistes under the Commune. The Artistic Federation was responsible for the organization of various concerts and cultural events; it was primarily concerned with education and organization rather than with artistic questions. Mendès finds Courbet's position ridiculous. Doing a little bit of everything, even politics, is excusable and comprehensible if you are good for nothing else, but not if you paint as well as M. Courbet. If any poet or artist ever tried to get him to "federate," Mendès announces, he would reply, "Leave me in peace, *Monsieur de la Fédération! Je suis un rêveur, un travailleur* [I am a dreamer, a worker]" (*Les 73 journées,* p. 167).

A dreamer, a worker. In order best to reaffirm the privileges of art for art's sake, Mendès here appropriates the term *travailleur* and, to describe his own position as a poet, inflects it with the full logic of the *métier* (craft, trade): the professional specialization that alone defines one's being. For workers or artisans, of course, such a specialization, dating back to the justification of the division of labor in Plato's *Republic,* is simply the prohibition against doing something else. In a well-constituted state, each person has a proper task that no other can do in his or her place. A shoemaker is first of all someone who cannot also be a warrior; by the same logic a poet is someone who should not participate in politics. Politics, like poetry, is a particularized, specialized set of activities, occasions, and institutions; the proper task of the poet is to keep such boundaries and specializations carefully delineated.

Travailleur, one of the most frequently used terms in the political discourse of the period, had, by the end of the Second Empire, taken on thick revolutionary connotations that it would lose in the following decades when a specifically Marxist vocabulary (*classe ouvrière*) began to prevail. Its equally widespread usage in economic, political, and social discourse pointed to an interdependence of the three structures that in 1869 some were not willing to admit. In exile in 1866 Victor Hugo titled his novel about fishermen *Les travailleurs de la mer* (*The Toilers of the Sea*); in June 1871 the Communard Eugène Pottier, composing "L'Internationale," included the verse "Ouvriers, paysans, nous sommes / Le grand parti des travailleurs" ("Workers, peasants, we are / The great party of those who work")—*travailleurs* in this case overcoming the Versaillais promotion of ideological differences between Communard Paris and the provinces. In a letter from Charleville written at the same moment as Mendès' imaginary conversations with Courbet, Arthur Rimbaud announces his own, quite different identification with the term *travailleur:* "I will be a worker [*travailleur*]. That's what holds me back when a wild fury drives me toward the battle in Paris, where so many workers [*travailleurs*] are still dying while I am writing to you! Work, now? Never, never. I'm on strike" (13 May 1871, *Complete Works,* p. 100). I *will be* a worker. Rimbaud's phrase is both affirmative and negative. At some future moment, when new social relations have been achieved—when the structure of work, as we know it, has come to an end—Rimbaud will be a worker. Now, however, he identifies with a group whose joint, combative subjectivity lies in abandoning the identity of "good worker" as constituted under the present social division of labor.

"I have a horror of all *métiers*," writes Rimbaud in *Une saison en enfer* (1873; *A Season in Hell*, in *Complete works*, p. 194); and "It seemed to me that everyone should have had several *other* lives as well" (p. 208). Rimbaud resists the *idiotisme*—both the idiocy and the idiom—of the *métier*, of viewing the world only according to the limitations of one's trade, whether one's role be that of boss or of worker: "Bosses and workers, all of them peasants, and common" (p. 194). He rejects the social division of labor that in the late 19th century was beginning to be pushed to the limits of overspecialization. The unprecedented events of the Commune caused Marx, too, to focus more strongly on the division of labor. Marx saw in the Commune a completely new democratic governing structure and the abolition of a separate political sphere whose very existence represented an alienation of human social powers. The greatest social achievement of the Commune was not its laws or reforms but rather "its own working existence" (Marx, *The Civil War in France* [1871], p. 65). The Commune, in other words, was nothing more than a sustained attack on the divisions of labor that render the workings of government "mysteries, transcendent functions only to be trusted to the hands of a trained caste" (*Civil War*, p. 59). Both Edmond de Goncourt, mourning the recent death of his brother during the siege of Paris, and Courbet, functioning as a member of the Commune, a delegate to the municipal administration (*mairie*), a member of the Commission on Education, and president of the Artistic Federation—in his own words, "up to my neck in political affairs"—would have agreed. "In short," wrote Goncourt on 20 March, "for the moment France and Paris are under the control of working men who have given us a government composed solely of their men. The unbelievable rules" (*Paris under Siege*, pp. 231–232). And Courbet: "I get up, I eat breakfast, I sit down and preside twelve hours a day. My head begins to feel like a cooked apple. Despite all this torment of the head and of my understanding, which I'm not used to, I'm in a state of enchantment. Paris is a true Paradise" (quoted in Dommanget, *L'enseignement, l'enfance et la culture sous la Commune*, p. 19).

Mendès, for his purposes, adopted a myth of the *travailleur* that coincides in part with Pierre Joseph Proudhon's image of the artisan and of labor as redemptive agency; Rimbaud chose another—expansive and forward looking. Such volatility of the sign, whereby the overdetermination of a given ideological symbol can be shaken like a loose tooth, is revealed most fully during times of social crisis or revolutionary change. Signs, terminology, and political images become disputed and debated, appropriated and *intended* for different uses. During the Commune the proliferation of songs and slogans, posters, small revolutionary periodicals, caricatures and cartoons did not serve as décor for the "real" social conflict taking place—it served to *articulate* that conflict. Caricatures that appeared in popular newspapers such as *La charge*, which published Rimbaud's "Trois baisers" (1870; "Three Kisses"), and *Le hanneton*, whose editor, Eugène Vermersch, played an important role in Commune culture and politics, were often printed on separate sheets. Colored by hand, sold by street vendors, they were stuck up on walls and fences. Their sheer accumulation in the streets, along with the many publications of Commune proceedings, could not be ignored. "During this time the walls burst out laughing. *Paris-gavroche* [guttersnipe-Paris], *Paris-voyou* [punk-Paris], *Paris-catin* [slut-Paris] are convulsed in front of the caricatures that ingenious merchants hang with pins on their front doors . . . Who is drawing these strange images, devilishly colored, vulgar, rarely pleasant, often obscene?" (Mendès, *Les 73 journées*, pp. 159–160).

In a letter written 17 April 1871, Rimbaud celebrates this cacophony of verbal and visual images in the streets as the focus of his experience of Paris: "Let's talk Paris . . . We stopped in front of engravings by A[drien] Marie, *Les vengeurs* [*The Avengers*], *Les faucheurs de la mort* [*Death's Reapers*]; and especially caricatures by [Jules] Draner and Faustin [Betheder] . . . The items of the day were *Le mot d'ordre* [Henri Rochefort's Commune newspaper] and the admirable fantasies by [Jules] Vallès and [Eugène] Vermersch in *Le cri du peuple*" (*Oeuvres complètes*, p. 266). "Such was literature," he concludes, "from 25 February to 10 March." Rimbaud expands the boundaries of literature to include propaganda, political "fantasies," engravings, and caricatures: ephemeral, satirical genres afloat in a complex set of social discourses and representations. Literature's function, it appears, is to point directly to an entirely revolutionary situation; its affiliation is with the slogan, the call to action (the *mot d'ordre*). More than any other 19th-century French poetry, Rimbaud's work, like a forgotten synecdoche of the Commune, has been transmitted to 20th-century readers mainly in the form of a series of slogans: "Changer la vie" (Change life); "L'amour est à réinventer" (Love must be reinvented); "Il faut être absolument moderne" (We must be absolutely modern).

Partial liberalization of the press laws had occurred in 1868, but the progressive collapse of censorship from September 1870 to June 1871 brought unparalleled experimentation in political imagery. Some seventy new periodicals and journals sprang up during the Commune's brief existence. His immersion in this material led Rimbaud, who composed a "communist constitution" (now lost) based on the organization of the Commune, away from early Parnassian influences. In Paris in March 1871 he made the acquaintance of the Communard engraver André Gill and sought out the address of the freemason and poet Vermersch, whose political "fantasies" he admired—and in whose London apartment the following year he would take refuge, along with Prosper Olivier Lissagaray, author of the most widely esteemed history of the Commune, Paul Verlaine, Jules Andrieu, and other exiled Communard *lettrés*. In his letters of 13 and 15 May—what have come to be called the "Letters of the Visionary," his artistic manifestos—Rimbaud includes not poetry but a "fantasy" ("Le coeur supplicié"; "The Heart on the Rack") and what was probably his most successful attempt to overcome the barrier between high art and reportage, his "contemporary psalm," the "Chant de guerre parisien" ("Parisian War Song").

LES TROIS GRACES (Musée de Versailles.)

Ernestine ———— La grosse Lolotte ———— Julie.

1. "Les trois Grâces (Musée
de Versailles): Ernestine—La
grosse Lolotte—Julie," lithograph (from Susan Lambert,
ed., *The Franco-Prussian War
and the Commune in Caricature*
[1870–71], London: Victoria
and Albert Museum, 1971,
no. 92).

The poem, which features Thiers; his minister of the interior, Ernest Picard;
and his minister of foreign affairs, Jules Favre, in its cast of characters, assumes
that its readers are familiar with popular caricatures of Favre weeping crocodile
tears after negotiating the capitulation to Prussia and with the anonymous caricature "Les trois Grâces" ("The Three Graces"; fig. 1), which depicted these
three leaders of the Versailles government as nude political prostitutes cavorting
for the favor of royalist régimes. "They are all great friends [*familiers*] of the
Grand Turk," writes Rimbaud; in the working-class slang of the period, "the
Grand Turk" had come to signify the king of Prussia.

The culture of the Commune cannot be abstracted from the working-class
movement and cultural forms that preceded it. Nor can it be isolated from its
own interaction and debates with the bourgeois culture surrounding it. Still,
certain aspects of the verbal and visual forms of the Commune are both striking
and particular: the uninhibited use of erotic imagery and the stylistic perfection
of the art of invective. Deeply affective vocabulary and insult were by no means
a specialized discourse; they were widely integrated in the political and social
language of all classes, and they were manipulated by both left and right. Anti-
Communard invective sought to establish a *racial* connection between "savages"
and workers. Thus the novelist Alphonse Daudet referred to the Commune in
a letter as "Paris au pouvoir des nègres" (Paris in the hands of the blacks), and
Goncourt pondered in his journal, "Is it possible that in the great law underlying changes here on earth, the workers [*travailleurs*] are for modern societies
what the barbarians are for ancient societies, convulsive agents of dissolution

and destruction?" (10 March 1871, *Paris under Siege*, pp. 236–237). When Communard Vermersch in *Le cri du peuple* proclaimed, "We belong to the *canaille* [rabble]!" or when popular singer Rosalie Martin, called la Bordas," intoned the refrain "J'en suis" ("I'm one of them") of Joseph Darcier's 1865 song "La canaille" to a crowd of thousands in the Tuileries in April, they were embracing the most prevalent of the derogatory bourgeois designations for the Communards. When Rimbaud in the "Mauvais sang" ("Bad Blood") section of *Une saison en enfer* "becomes" a barbarian or an African, he adopts much the same procedure of reappropriating and refashioning to his own ends the anti-Communard rhetoric that aimed at establishing a massive, racially constituted category encompassing animals, workers (especially working-class women), barbarians, blacks, savages, and thieves. In "Mauvais sang" Rimbaud affirms the *political* connection that indeed existed between workers in European capitals and the colonial oppressed at the historical moment when even the most exotic lands were being opened to European mercantile interests. Mendès appropriated *travailleur;* Rimbaud adopted *barbare, assassin, nègre.* Much of Rimbaud's poetry from 1871 and beyond—*Une saison en enfer,* "Solde" ("Sale"), "Le bateau ivre" ("The Drunken Boat"), "Démocratie," "Métropolitain" ("Metropolitan"), and others—as well as his written collaboration in the proto-Dadaist group, the Zutistes (from *zut!,* "Shucks!"), can be read in the light of its manipulation of political stereotypes and affective forms. In this enterprise he was joined not only by Vermersch, Louise Michel, Pottier, and other Commune poets, but also by a poet who died at the age of twenty-four a few months before the insurrection of 18 March, Isidore Ducasse, the Comte de Lautréamont. Like Rimbaud, Ducasse called for a new "objective" poetry and a transformation of the poet's role as citizen. His *Poésies* (1870) anticipate in important ways the forms of Commune culture, and *Les chants de Maldoror* (1869; *Lautréamont's Maldoror*) still awaits the materialist and historical interpretation called for by Aimé Césaire that would reveal in that "mad epic an aspect ignored by many: that of an implacable denunciation of a very precise form of society, such as it could appear only to one of its sharpest observers around the year 1865" (*Discours sur le colonialisme,* p. 45).

See also 1848, 1869, 1873.

Bibliography: Aimé Césaire, *Discours sur le colonialisme* (Paris: Présence Africaine, 1955). Maurice Dommanget, *L'enseignement, l'enfance et la culture sous la Commune* (Paris: Editions-Libraire de l'Etoile, 1964). Jean Dubois, *Le vocabulaire politique et social en France de 1869 à 1872* (Paris: Larousse, 1962). Edmond de Goncourt, *Paris under Siege, 1870–1871: From the Goncourt Journal,* ed. and trans. George Becker (Ithaca: Cornell University Press, 1969). Prosper Olivier Lissagaray, *L'histoire de la Commune de 1871* (1876; reprint, Paris: Maspéro, 1967). Karl Marx, *The Civil War in France,* and V. I. Lenin, *The Paris Commune* (New York: International Publishers, 1940). Catulle Mendès, *Les 73 journées de la Commune* (Paris: E. Lachaud, 1871). Adrian Rifkin, "Cultural Movement and the Paris Commune," *Art History,* 2 (June 1979), 201–220. Rifkin, "Well-Formed Phrases: Some Limits of Meaning in Political Print at the End of the Second Empire," *Oxford Art Journal,* 8 (1985), 20–28. Arthur Rimbaud, *Oeuvres complètes,* ed.

René Rolland de Renéville and Jules Mouquet (Paris: Gallimard, 1963); translated by Paul Schmidt as *Complete Works* (New York: Harper & Row, 1976). Kristin Ross, *The Emergence of Social Space: Rimbaud and the Paris Commune* (Minneapolis: University of Minnesota Press, 1989).

Kristin Ross

✍ 1873
Arthur Rimbaud Leaves *Une saison en enfer* at the Printer's Shop

Exit and Save

Arthur Rimbaud (1854–1891) is known as the poet who stopped writing. Indeed, he stopped writing before many poets start; his entire oeuvre was written before his twentieth birthday. *Une saison en enfer* (1873; *A Season in Hell*), a collection of nine prose poems, is the only volume he took the initiative to publish. Other works (*Illuminations*, 1886; *Poésies complètes*, 1895) appeared under the auspices of others. Rimbaud's ambivalence toward his own work became so legendary that rumors circulated that he had made a bonfire of the whole edition of *Une saison*. But in 1901 a Belgian bibliophile chanced upon all 500 copies of it at the publisher's shop. Rimbaud had never paid the printer.

Nothing, however, became Rimbaud's literary career like the leaving of it. It is hard not to be seduced by the image of a meteoric adolescent poet burning himself out in rage against the constraints of Western culture, ceasing all literary activity, sailing off to become an arms dealer in Africa, and returning to France, having lost a leg, to die at age thirty-seven. The combination of Rimbaud's precociousness, his abandonment of literature, the dearth of facts about his life (did he participate in the Commune? what was he doing in England, Germany, Italy, Crete, Scandinavia, and Indonesia before settling in East Africa?), and the difficulty and intensity of his texts has given rise to a body of contradictory myths, summarized by René Etiemble: Rimbaud the symbolist, the vagrant, the surrealist, the Bolshevik, the bourgeois, the crook, the pervert, the prophet, the superman, the Christian, and more. But the most paradoxically attractive aspect of the myth for literary history remains the fact that, as Stéphane Mallarmé put it, "he amputated himself, alive, from poetry" (*Oeuvres complètes*, p. 516).

In reality, the chronology of Rimbaud's departure from literature is unclear. Scholars long considered *Une saison en enfer* to be his last work because it ends with a poem entitled "Adieu" ("Farewell"). This literary farewell to literature made a good story, but there now exists considerable evidence to suggest that some of the texts collected in *Illuminations* (edited by Paul Verlaine in 1886) were written after *Une saison*. And indeed, a close reading of Rimbaud's work indicates that it consists all along of various attempts to escape "literature," along with rueful admissions that "no one leaves" (*Complete Works*, p. 195). In a sense, Rimbaud never stopped writing. His Ethiopian correspondence makes up the bulk of the recent (1972) Pléiade edition of his complete writing. The challenge to the reader, then, is to learn how to read Rimbaud's escape from literary boundaries *within* his poems and not just *after* them.

From the first, Rimbaud's aim was to escape the constraints and comforts of existing literature. In a series of letters he wrote at age sixteen, he outlined a poetics of monstrosity:

> The first task of the man who wants to be a poet is to study his own awareness of himself, in its entirety; he seeks out his soul, he inspects it, he tests it, he learns it. As soon as he knows it, he must cultivate it! That seems simple . . . But the problem is to make the soul into a monster . . . Think of a man grafting warts onto his face and growing them there.
>
> I say you have to be a visionary, make yourself a visionary.
>
> A Poet makes himself a visionary through a long, boundless, and systematized *disorganization* of *all the senses.*   (*Complete Works*, p. 102)

Rimbaud here takes the Romantic image of the poet as visionary and radicalizes it. Through the paradox of a "systematized disorganization" (*raisonné dérèglement*), he seeks to bring the forces of reason and the forces of madness together in such an explosive way that "all the senses"—physical, semantic, and geographical—will be shattered and renewed. "So what if he is destroyed in his ecstatic flight through things unheard of, unnameable; other horrible workers will come; they will begin at the horizons where the first one has fallen!" (*Complete Works*, pp. 102–103).

Through this cultivation of monstrosity, Rimbaud blurs the distinction between perception and language, life and literature, enormity and norm, self and other. In one of his most celebrated formulas, he goes so far as to assert that "*I* is an *other*. If brass wakes as a bugle, it is not its fault at all. That is quite clear to me: I am a spectator at the flowering of my thought: I watch it, I listen to it: I draw a bow across a string: a symphony stirs in the depths, or surges onto the stage" (*Complete Works*, p. 102).

Rimbaud here offers a poetics not of intentionality but of instrumentality. The poet does not express a knowledge he already possesses; he is, rather, the instrument and the spectator of his own thought.

In these letters of May 1871 known as the "Lettres du voyant" ("Letters of the Visionary"), Rimbaud thus sets forth a poetic program. In *Une saison en enfer* (April–August 1873), he evaluates it. Two of the prose poems in particular take stock of the visionary's impasses. In "Délires I" ("First Delirium"), Rimbaud literalizes his dictum that "I is an other" by recounting his stormy affair with Verlaine from Verlaine's point of view, casting Verlaine as the Foolish Virgin masochistically attached to an Infernal Bridegroom. In his "Délires II: Alchimie du verbe" ("Second Delirium: The Alchemy of the Word") he quotes a number of his earlier poems, accompanying them with commentaries that express both scorn and mourning for his former poetic hopes. The text ends enigmatically by closing a door and yet refusing to show what is beyond it: "All that is over. Today, I know how to celebrate beauty" (*Complete Works*, p. 209).

Problematic boundaries can indeed be seen as Rimbaud's trademark. In "Le bateau ivre" ("The Drunken Boat"), the poem through which he introduced himself to Verlaine, Rimbaud describes the chaotic voyage of an unmoored boat torn between the desire to dissolve and the desire to return. And the last paragraphs of the poem "Adieu," which ends *Une saison,* are as unclear as they are emphatic about the nature of the conversion experience they depict:

> One must be absolutely modern.
>
> Never mind hymns of thanksgiving: hold onto a step once taken. A hard night! Dried blood smokes on my face, and nothing lies behind me but that repulsive little tree! The battle for the soul is as brutal as the battles of men; but the sight of justice is the pleasure of God alone.
>
> Yet this is the watch by night. Let us all accept new strength, and real tenderness. And at dawn, armed with glowing patience, we will enter the cities of glory.
>
> Why did I talk about a friendly hand! My greatest advantage is that I can laugh at old love affairs full of falsehood, and stamp with shame such deceitful couples—I went through women's Hell over there—and I will be able now *to possess the truth within one body and one soul.* (*Complete Works,* p. 213)

It is fitting that scholars remain unable to determine whether this is indeed Rimbaud's last text, or whether, as seems probable, some of the prose poems published as *Illuminations* were written subsequently. The thematics of transgressed boundaries are amply illustrated not only *by* the poems in *Illuminations* (by the fact that they come after Rimbaud's "Adieu"), but also *within* them. Some of the manuscripts of those poems are not in Rimbaud's handwriting, and it is sometimes not entirely clear where one poem ends and another begins. But more strikingly, many of the poems are characterized by a transgression of boundaries—between appearance and reality, or between the expectations created in the reader throughout most of a poem and a final, shocking, violation. Several poems set up a picture or story, only to destroy it at the last moment. In "Les ponts" ("Bridges"), Rimbaud describes a city scene and ends with the sentence "A white light falling from the heights of heaven obliterates this scene" (*Complete Works,* p. 228). "Nocturne vulgaire" ("Ordinary Nocturne") ends: "One breath dispels the limits of the hearth" (p. 164). And "Enfance" ("Childhood") concludes: "I am Master of Silence. But why should the appearance of an aperture gleam white in the corner of the vault?" (p. 157). Many poems end with a withholding of knowledge, as in "Après le Déluge" ("After the Flood"): "And the Queen, the Witch who lights her fire in an earthen pot, will never tell us what she knows, and we do not" (p. 220); or in "Parade": "Only *I* have the key to this savage parade" (p. 159).

By thus questioning the boundaries of literature, Rimbaud became canonized within literature. He stands as a Januslike figure whose poetry constantly attempts to capture the nonliterary on the point of becoming literary. It is a sign both of the success and of the failure of his enterprise that even his radical rejection of poetry has been appropriated by literary history as his most enduringly poetic act.

See also 1871, 1924.

Bibliography: Robert Greer Cohn, *The Poetry of Rimbaud* (Princeton: Princeton University Press, 1973). René Etiemble, *Le mythe de Rimbaud,* 3 vols. (Paris: Gallimard, 1952–1961). *Littérature,* special issue on Rimbaud, 11 (October 1973). Stéphane Mallarmé, *Oeuvres complètes,* ed. Henri Mondor and Georges Jean-Aubry (Paris: Gallimard, 1945). Georges Poulet, *Exploding Poetry,* trans. Françoise Meltzer (Chicago: University of Chicago Press, 1984). Arthur Rimbaud, *Complete Works,* trans. Paul Schmidt (New York: Harper & Row, 1976). Rimbaud, *Oeuvres complètes,* ed. Antoine Adam (Paris: Gallimard, 1972).

Norbert Bonenkamp

✍️ 1874

Stéphane Mallarmé Writes, Edits, and Publishes the Ladies' Magazine
La dernière mode: Gazette du monde et de la famille

Haute Couture and Haute Culture

In August 1874 Stéphane Mallarmé, the intense, elusive poet and weary lycée English teacher, paused yet again from the literary masterwork that was his life's ambition to undertake the bimonthy publication of a fashionable ladies' magazine, *La dernière mode: Gazette du monde et de la famille* (*The Latest Fashion: A Gazette of Society and the Family*).

Eight issues of *La dernière mode,* dated 6 September through 20 December 1874, appeared under the editorship—as the decorative cover announced—of a certain "Marasquin" (fig. 1). Marasquin, however, was just one of many noms de plume that Mallarmé donned for this project. Between the covers of the magazine he became Marguerite de Ponty, authoritative columnist on "La mode"; Ix, the man-about-town reporting on books, theater, and art for the "Chronique de Paris" ("Paris Chronicle"); Miss Satin, cosmopolitan commentator on *le high-life* for the "Gazette de la Fashion"; and the nameless "Chef de bouche de chez Brabant" who provided elaborate menus for faultlessly elegant meals. For the "Carnet d'or" ("The Golden Notebook"), which offered household hints for stylish living, Mallarmé might wear the hat of the interior decorator Marliani, or of Zizi, the mulatto maid with a recipe for coconut jam. Only on the last page of each issue did the name Stéphane Mallarmé appear plainly in print, as the correspondent to whom all information regarding books, theater, travel, society, and the fine arts was to be addressed.

In fact, except for the poems and short stories contributed for the literary segment of the magazine by his friends—Théodore de Banville, François Coppée, Alphonse Daudet, Armand Sully Prudhomme, Léon Valade, and others—Mallarmé wrote all the articles from cover to cover of *La dernière mode.*

The association of Mallarmé, the serious, exacting poet of unusual difficulty and delicacy, with a frivolous fashion magazine has always struck readers as an odd detour in an already unusual literary career—odder by far than, for instance, his excursions into English philology or classical mythology several years later. And yet, when Paul Verlaine requested a few biographical details

1. Front page of *La dernière mode*, no. 2 (20 September 1874).

from Mallarmé to include in the popular series *Les hommes d'aujourd'hui* (1886; *The Men of Today*), Mallarmé wrote back on 16 November 1885:

> In moments of financial difficulty or in order to buy expensive little rowboats [for the children], I had to take on some regular work and nothing more (Ancient gods [*Les dieux antiques,* 1880], English words [*Les mots anglais,* 1877]), about which the less said the better; but aside from that, the concessions to necessities—as to delights—were not frequent. At one point, nevertheless, despairing of the despotic book that I had let loose from myself, I tried, after hawking some articles from here and there, to edit all by myself—dresses, jewelry, furniture, and even theater and dinner menus—a magazine, *La dernière mode,* the eight or ten published issues of which inspire me still, when I groom them of their dust, to dream on at length.   ("Autobiographie," in *Oeuvres complètes,* p. 663)

However peripheral to Mallarmé's poetic corpus *La dernière mode* may appear, it remained for him a source of reverie and apparent pride long after the magazine had folded. Nor is it difficult to read traces of the original pleasure and reverie that informed Mallarmé's poetic spree with fashion. For indeed, the splendid, fashionable world that Mallarmé conjured forth in issue after issue of *La dernière mode* is a world of tantalizing surfaces, where words share in the dazzle of jewels, the delicacy of lace, the soft transparency of feathers, the flutter of fans, and the bewitching insignificance of bibelots—the very images, that is, that haunt Mallarmé's poems.

Although most features in *La dernière mode* concentrated on the latest fashions in women's dress—each issue contained five or six fashion illustrations, with commentary, and one full dress pattern—the magazine also presented the latest offerings in theater and literature. Many of the important literary works published in 1874 were introduced as part of a bimonthly list of fashionable "things to do"; these included Gustave Flaubert's *La tentation de saint Antoine* (*The Temptation of Saint Anthony*) and Jules Barbey d'Aurevilly's *Les diaboliques* (*Diabolical Women*), as well as major collections of tales and verse for that period by Banville, Coppée, Daudet, Zola, and others.

The standards for judging literature were outlined in the first issue of *La dernière mode* by the intriguing gentleman "Ix." ("Ix" represents the French pronunciation of *X*, the impersonal signature par excellence.) Readers more knowing than the general subscriber no doubt recognized Mallarmé's playfulness behind the suggestive anonymity of the pseudonym, for by 1874 he had already baffled many friends and admirers with an obscure, untitled, poetic tour de force that was known even then as his "Sonnet in -ix,"—a sonnet famous for the opening of the second stanza (*Oeuvres*, p. 68):

> Sur les crédences, au salon vide: nul ptyx
> Aboli bibelot d'inanité sonore
>
> On the sideboards, in the empty room: no ptyx
> Obliterated bibelot of vacuous sonority

Rather than obscure his relation to the dapper chronicler of Paris, Mallarmé thus insinuated a meaningful analogy between his own dense, hermetic poetry and the beautiful but "meaningless" bibelots that filled the space of the fashionable world—and fashionable magazine—in which his chatty personae circulated. The language of Ix's declaration further heightened that association ("Chronique de Paris," 6 September 1874):

> To speak, of course, of the works of the mind, but always according to the taste of the day . . . Let such a volume [of verse] linger for eight days, half-opened, like a bottle of scent, on silk cushions embroidered with fantasies [*chimères*]; and let that other volume [of tales] pass from this testing ground onto the lacquered surface of a heavy cabinet—jewel-boxes near at hand, locked shut until the next party: this is our simple way of judging.

In the rarefied spheres of "the latest fashion," the literary work assumes its place in the insubstantial world of a lady's boudoir amid perfumes, silks, and jewels. Not surprisingly, Mallarmé's descriptions of that enclosed world of subtle nuances often reflect the syntax and metaphors of his most famous poems. His accounts of new variations in dress suggest an almost physical pleasure derived from reciting the exact, exotic terms for the latest brooches, fans, hairdos, and hats: the "thousand charming nothings, indispensable finish for a daytime toilette" ("La mode," 4 October 1874). Like the words of his poems, each detail of dress, and each detail of the description of that dress, is designed to suggest less the materiality of a present object than a magical, fleeting, overall effect: "Peindre, non la chose, mais l'effet qu'elle produit" ("To paint not the thing, but the effect it produces"; letter to Henri Cazalis, October 1864, *Correspondance*, p. 137).

Perhaps, then, what has most unsettled readers of the poet is less the strangeness of Mallarmé's writing in *La dernière mode* than its closeness to aspects of his more "serious" corpus. And yet, just as the poet's evocation of ball gowns—"to render light, ethereal and airy, for that superior manner of movement that is called dancing, the divinity who appears in their cloud" ("La mode," 15 November 1874)—fulfills a certain logic in what Jean-Pierre Richard called the "imaginary universe of Mallarmé," so too the poet's resolute attention to the fact of fashion and to the idea of fashionability in his own time fulfills a certain logic within the history of 19th-century French literature.

A general preoccupation with fashion informs much of the period's literature. In Balzac's novels (published individually since 1830 but collected in *The Human Comedy* between 1842 and his death in 1850), detailed descriptions of dress encode relations of wealth and power in a changing bourgeois society. As early as 1830, Balzac had reflected on the significance of fashionability in modern French culture in a series of amusing, provocative essays: "Des mots à la mode" ("On Fashionable Words"), "Physiologie de la toilette" ("The Physiology of Dress"), and the "Traité de la vie élégante" ("Treatise on Elegant Life"). Mallarmé's immediate predecessors, Théophile Gautier and Charles Baudelaire, furnish further telling examples of the emergent 19th-century poetics of fashion.

Gautier was a symbolic godfather to two generations of French poets. When he died in 1872, few writers in France were unaffected by the loss. Mallarmé joined with friends and disciples of the poet in paying homage to Gautier by composing a haunting poem in his memory, "Toast funèbre" (1873; "Toast in Memory"). It was in fact the last poem that Mallarmé published before the appearance of *La dernière mode*. Despite the apparent irreverence of this sequence, no greater tribute could have been paid Gautier than Mallarmé's passage from a funeral toast to fashion forecasts. For few authors had so utterly identified the world of "high" art with the world of fashion as Gautier.

It was, in some sense, Gautier who legitimated the theme of fashionability by redefining the status of dandyism in the culture of his time. His urbane, ironic tales—such as *Fortunio* (1837)—transformed the dandy from a shallow anglophile fop into something of an aesthetic rebel and intellectual hero. Gautier represented the dandy as a new aristocrat of taste who defied the utilitarian values of bourgeois society through his utter devotion to beautiful detail. As Barbey d'Aurevilly theorized in his essay "Du dandysme et de George Brummell" (1844; "On Dandyism and George Brummell"), the dandy's bold commitment to fashion represented no less than a quest for new standards of creative achievement in a world of staid manners and conventional beliefs.

In a pamphlet published in 1858, *De la mode* (*On Fashion*), Gautier defined fashion as an index for the changing standards of beauty in the modern world. Addressing his essay to those painters who refused to represent their models in contemporary dress because modern fashion fell so short of the "classical" ideal, Gautier eloquently defended not only the general standards of contemporary dress but even that most extravagant aberration of Second Empire fashion, the oversized crinoline (pp. 26–28):

> A young woman, in a low décolleté, arms bared, hair coiffed as we have described, with billowing trains of antique moiré, satin, and taffeta behind her, with her double skirts and multiple flounces, seems as beautiful and as finely costumed as can be; we do not very well see what Art could possibly have to reproach her with. Unfortunately, there are no contemporary painters; those who seem to be living in our time belong to an older era, long past . . . They possess a preconceived form of beauty, and the modern ideal is unknown to them.

For Gautier, therefore, the ideals of modern art were to be patterned on an appreciation of modern fashions. To be sure, in addition to being the first major author to introduce the word *crinoline* into French literature, Gautier is credited with the important 19th-century neologism *la modernité* (modernity), a term that is firmly rooted in fashion: *la mode*.

The poet who most clearly expressed the intimate association between fashion and the art of modernity, however, was not Gautier, but his most famous disciple, and Mallarmé's most famous mentor, Charles Baudelaire. In "Le peintre de la vie moderne" (1863; "The Painter of Modern Life"), Baudelaire developed Gautier's intuitions on fashion and ideal beauty into an aesthetic program for modern art, characterizing the exemplary painter as a dandy and a man of the crowd whose "business" it is to extract from fashion, especially from the ever-changing display of women's fashion, glimpses of an ideal beauty that weds eternal and ephemeral truths:

> If a fashion or the cut of a garment has been slightly modified, if bows and curls have been supplanted by cockades, if *bavolets* have been enlarged and *chignons* have dropped a fraction toward the nape of the neck, if waists have been raised and skirts become fuller, be very sure that his eagle eye will have already spotted it from however great a distance . . . It is much easier to decide outright that everything about the garb of an age is absolutely ugly than to devote oneself to the task of distilling from it the mysterious element of beauty that it may contain.   (*The Painter . . . and Other Essays*, p. 11)

Fashion, Baudelaire declares, should be considered as the permanent and repeated attempt to improve upon crude Nature; it should thus be considered as "a symptom of the taste for the ideal" (p. 32). By his own analogy, therefore, fashion and art share a common purpose—to transcend the impermanence and imperfection of nature with beautiful illusions; but at the same time both must partake of the "transitory," "fugitive," "modern" spirit of the day. Otherwise, Baudelaire warns the artist, "you cannot fail to tumble into the abyss of an abstract and indeterminate beauty" (p. 13).

765

It is striking that Gautier's and Baudelaire's reflections on fashion and its relation to modern art should both be framed by discourses on painting. In the case of Mallarmé, too, the excursion into fashion coincided with a discovery of the painting of his day. For it was especially in the area of painting that the issues of what a "modern ideal" of beauty might be, and how (or whether) to represent contemporary social reality, produced the fiercest debates in the second half of the 19th century. And 1874, the year of *La dernière mode,* marked a turning point in the history of these debates on fashion, modernity, and art.

On 15 April, two weeks before the official opening of the state-sponsored Salon of 1874, there opened at the Paris studios of the photographer Nadar (Félix Tournachon) an independent show of paintings that came to be known as the First Impressionist Exhibition. Among the exhibiting artists were a number of young painters—Edgar Degas, Claude Monet, Berthe Morisot, Camille Pissarro, Pierre-Auguste Renoir, and Alfred Sisley—all of whom had been influenced by the acknowledged leader of the modern movement in painting, Edouard Manet. These painters, one critic wrote, were to be characterized by the new term *impressionnistes,* for they sought in their work to render not the landscape, but "the sensation produced by the landscape" (Castagnary, "L'exposition"). Although many of the works exhibited by the newly named Impressionists did in fact represent scenes and sensations of landscape, some, like Degas's exquisite *Aux courses en province* (*At the Races in the Country*), with its representation of a handsome family in their carriage, also sought to convey sure impressions of modern elegance. Subject matter aside, the earliest experiments of Impressionist art clearly sought to enact a visual equivalent of Mallarmé's poetic ambition: "to paint not the thing, but the effect it produces."

In 1874 Mallarmé was not yet familiar with the Impressionist painters, but he had recently met and befriended Manet, their respected mentor. To the dismay of his followers, Manet did not participate in the independent exhibition of 1874 but chose rather to affirm his artistic legitimacy by submitting his paintings to the official, though aesthetically reactionary, Salon.

Manet's paintings of the early 1870s often translated impressions of the modern, changing social landscape about him. Indeed, since the early 1860s, when he was closely associated with Baudelaire, Manet had acquired notoriety as a radical and controversial "painter of modern life." It did not come as a total surprise, therefore, when only one of the three paintings he submitted to the Salon of 1874, *Le chemin de fer* (1872–73; *The Railroad*), was accepted by the conservative jury. Ironically, it is this painting, which boldly sets off a fashionable young woman and beautifully dressed girl against a sketchy backdrop of modern smoke and steel, that has since become emphatically identified with the techniques and iconography of Impressionism.

Mallarmé, upon learning that the Salon had rejected two of Manet's paintings, quickly drafted an indignant article in defense of the artist's work, "Le jury de peinture pour 1874 et M. Manet" ("The Jury on Painting for 1874 and M. Manet," in *Oeuvres complètes*). In that article, written only months before *La dernière mode,* Mallarmé passionately protested the exclusion of Manet's painting

Le bal de l'Opéra (1873–74; *Masked Ball at the Opera*), an extraordinary scene of "high life" that crowds together Parisian swells and flirtatious costumed women. The poet defended the subject of the painting, "a showcase for the display of a modern crowd," and extolled Manet's technique for capturing this stunning vision of contemporary festivity. Once again, the spirit of modernity had been caught by the hand of an artist with an eye for fashion.

But fashion and fashionability were by no means the exclusive artistic property of the avant-garde. While Impressionist artists and their critics were being drawn to fashion for fleeting images of their rapidly changing environment, academic theorists were looking to fashion otherwise, for a reassertion of the constant principles of art. Charles Blanc, directeur des beaux-arts (state minister for fine arts) from 1848 to 1852 and from 1870 to 1873 and founding editor of the *Gazette des beaux-arts* (1859), became famous for his influential manual on art, *Grammaire des arts du dessin* (1867; *The Grammar of Painting and Engraving*). Soon regarded as the most important work on practical aesthetics published in France, it became one of the best-known books on theory among late 19th-century artists. Less well known, however, is the fact that in 1874 Blanc published a sequel to this manual, devoted entirely to the laws of fashion: *L'art dans la parure et dans le vêtement* (*Art in Ornament and Dress*).

Blanc's dissertation on fashion first appeared in the *Gazette des beaux-arts* in four installments, from 1 February to 1 July 1874. As he had for painting and engraving, Blanc assumed for fashion a set of unchanging principles that could be defined and domesticated. Some chapter titles serve as an indication of his scope and method: "De l'assortiment des couleurs dans la parure" ("The Harmony of Colors in Dress"), "A l'harmonie de la toilette concourent les parties secondaires ou accessoires telles que les souliers, les gants, l'éventail . . . les dentelles" ("On the Accessories of the Toilet—Shoes, Gloves, the Fan . . . Laces"), "L'ordre, étant une condition essentielle dans la composition d'un bijou, les modes qu'il faut y employer . . ." ("On Design in the Composition of a Jewel").

Blanc thus provided something of a scholarly encyclopedia for all those magical and elusive effects of personal adornment that Mallarmé sought to evoke in *La dernière mode*. Yet two more different approaches to fashion would be hard to imagine: whereas Mallarmé reveled in the indefinable pleasures and charms of fashion, Blanc sought to reduce them to useful, universal laws. Despite such manifest dissimilarities, however, *L'art dans la parure* and *La dernière mode* presupposed and promoted one same overriding premise: that fashion is an art. That message had been transmitted obliquely in French literature throughout the 19th century. It was, however, more than literature, sweeping changes in the material production of womens' clothing during the Second Empire that had transformed the former "craft" of fashion into a new and significant art form.

Many technological innovations affected the production and distribution of "the latest fashion" in the latter half of the 19th century: improvements in the sewing machine, for instance, radically increased the number of gowns a single dressmaker could produce in a week, and an ever-expanding railroad system allowed for the dispersion of the latest Parisian gowns across the Continent. But it took the imagination, the skill, and the ambition of one man to consolidate the potential of these technical changes; in the process, he fundamentally redefined the structure and status of fashion in the modern world.

Charles Worth, an aspiring young Englishman with an intimate knowledge of fine fabrics and a keen appreciation of tailoring techniques, arrived in France in the late 1840s to work as a sales assistant for the leading fabric merchant of Paris. By the 1860s, his name and the name of the "house" that he founded had become synonymous with the highest standards of fashion in Europe and the New World. In *La dernière mode,* Mallarmé repeatedly defers to him as "the Great Worth," "the master of ceremonies for the sublime, daily pageants of Paris, Vienna, London, and Petersburg," "the great magician." Just what did Worth's magic consist of?

At the time of Worth's arrival in Paris, the production of fashion was still very much a local and haphazard collaboration between mercers, seamstresses, and the aristocratic ladies who paid them: a lady would select a fabric at her mercer's, have it delivered to her dressmaker, and inform her of the design she wanted. The dressmaker had little control over the textures, colors, or pattern of the gown she sewed; the end result, however uneven, was meant to reflect the tastes of the patron. Worth revolutionized this procedure. Recognizing that the form and fabric of a well-made garment were truly inseparable, he began to create rather simple, elegant dresses whose design was based on the properties of materials that he personally chose. The formula proved a huge success: Worth was awarded a first-class medal for his gowns at the Universal Exhibition in Paris in 1855, he opened his own dressmaking establishment on the rue de la Paix in 1858, and by 1863 he was the official dressmaker to the imperial court. In a bold and unprecedented gesture—doubly unprecedented for a man— Worth consolidated all the peripheral activities of fashion under one roof and assumed total control over the wardrobes of his distinguished clientele. He became, in his words, an "artist" who "composed toilettes." Even the empress Eugénie had to submit to Worth's taste: he would dictate the color, the fabric, the design, and the accessories for her gowns right down to the last detail. The House of Worth thus achieved its own distinctive style. Its standard for excellence would persist long after the government of his patrons had collapsed. When the Third Republic came to power, Worth's own empire was stronger than ever; from his seat in Paris, he dictated the frivolities of high fashion from New York to St. Petersburg.

The fashions that intrigued Gautier in 1858, fascinated Baudelaire in 1860, and preoccupied Mallarmé in 1874 were thus all by-products of the House of Worth. More than any individual poet or painter, Charles Worth succeeded in creating an aura around fashion and promoting it as a new art for modern times. As "Miss Satin" wistfully remarked in her "Gazette de la fashion": "We have all dreamt of this gown, without knowing it. Monsieur Worth, alone, knew how to create a *toilette* as elusive as our thoughts" (1 November 1874). It was therefore not entirely a matter of chance that poets strolling in the streets of Paris in the late 19th century saw in the display of contemporary fashion a model for the "painting of modern life." It is, however, to their visionary credit that these poets recognized what few before them could have even imagined: that in the era that ushered in the fortunes of mass production, the quintessential art of modernity would also be an industry.

Bibliography: Charles Baudelaire, "The Painter of Modern Life," in *The Painter of Modern Life and Other Essays,* trans. and ed. Jonathan Mayne (London: Phaidon, 1964), pp. 1–40. Charles Blanc, *Art in Ornament and Dress* (London: Chapman and Hall, 1877). Jules Antoine Castagnary, "L'exposition du boulevard des Capucines: Les impressionnistes," *Le siècle,* 29 April 1874; reprinted in Hélène Adhémar and Sylvie Gache, "L'exposition de 1874 chez Nadar," in the exhibition catalogue *Centenaire de l'impressionnisme* (Paris: Grand Palais, 1974). Théophile Gautier, *De la mode* (Paris: Poulet-Malassis, 1858). Sima Godfrey, "The Dandy as Ironic Figure," *SubStance,* 36 (1982), 21–33. Stéphane Mallarmé, *Correspondance, 1862–1871,* ed. Henri Mondor and Jean-Pierre Richard (Paris: Gallimard, 1959). Mallarmé, *La dernière mode: Gazette du monde et de la famille,* facsimile ed. (Paris: Ramsay, 1987). Mallarmé, *Oeuvres complètes,* ed. Henri Mondor and Georges Jean-Aubry (Paris: Gallimard, 1945). Diana de Marly, *The History of Haute Couture, 1850–1950* (New York: Holmes and Meier, 1980), esp. chaps. 1–2. Georg Simmel, "Fashion (1904)," in *On Individuality and Social Forms,* ed. Donald N. Levine (Chicago: University of Chicago Press, 1971), pp. 294–323.

Sima Godfrey

✐ 1876

George Sand Dies While Gustave Flaubert Is Writing
Un coeur simple for Her

Idealism

At George Sand's funeral on 10 June 1876, Gustave Flaubert, whom Sand addressed fondly in their correspondence as her "old troubadour," wept "like a calf." His deep grief over the loss of his beloved "old master" was made all the more poignant by its timing, in the midst of his work on a tale he claimed to have written "exclusively" for Sand, "solely to please her" (*The Letters of Gustave Flaubert,* p. 239). During the dark year 1875–76, when Flaubert struggled against the depression brought on by his diminished financial and literary prospects, Sand had given him a crucial piece of advice: "Write something more down to earth that everybody can enjoy" (*Letters,* p. 222). That something was to be *Un coeur simple* (1876; *A Simple Heart*), the tale of an ignorant woman called Félicité, who spends her entire adult life in devoted servitude to a single mistress, Mme. Aubain. Much of the critical debate over this most enduringly popular of all Flaubert's writings has focused on the problematic status of irony in a tale that constantly strains toward pathos. In keeping with its intended receiver, Flaubert defended his text against the ironical reading. "This is not at all ironical as you may suppose," Flaubert wrote to Edma Roger des Genettes, "but on the contrary very serious and very sad. I want to move tender hearts to pity and tears, for I am tenderhearted myself" (quoted in *Three Tales,* p. 15). Nevertheless, despite Flaubert, the ironical reading has with some rare exceptions prevailed, simultaneously obscuring the tale's pathos and Flaubert's debt to Sand.

Unquestionably, as many have noted, Sand and Flaubert form the oddest of literary couples: on the one hand, a writer celebrated for her prolixity; on the other, a legendary perfectionist; on the one hand, the good lady of Nohant, author of classics of children's literature; on the other, the hermit of Croisset, the precursor of modernism. And yet, as their remarkable thirteen-year correspondence demonstrates, their differences enabled and enlivened their dialogue rather than impeding it. The intertextual relationship between Sand and Flaubert is not limited to *Un coeur simple;* it spans forty years of French literary history. The young Flaubert, like all his contemporaries, read Sand; and the case could be made that Sand's fictionalized feminist critiques of the institution of marriage provided part of the cultural context for *Madame Bovary* (1857). Sand, in turn, took on the theme of adultery in *Le dernier amour* (1865; *The Last Love*), a late, now-forgotten novel dedicated to Flaubert in which she set out to depict adultery free from the immorality that characterized Flaubert's work. It was precisely on the issue of morality and its place in literature that Sand and Flaubert disagreed most interestingly during the final years of their correspondence.

The shared conviction of Flaubert and his fellow realists was, as the young Henry James sarcastically observed, "that art and morality are two perfectly different things, and that the former has no more to do with the latter than it has to do with astronomy or embryology" (*Letters,* p. 225). For Sand—and this perhaps explains why in the 19th century her literary fortunes exceeded Flaubert's among both Russian- and English-speaking readers—art and morality were, on the contrary, intimately linked. Hence Sand totally rejected Flaubert's vaunted doctrine of impartiality, his belief, as he famously expressed it to her in 1875, that the writer must appear "in his work no more than God in nature" (p. 227). The writer, far from being absent from his work like a *deus absconditus,* must, according to Sand, intervene, judge his characters, and above all provide his readers with a moral compass. To "make a mystery of the moral and beneficent meaning of his book" (p. 229), as did Flaubert in *L'éducation sentimentale* (1869; *Sentimental Education*), is to court the reader's indifference, even rejection. But what Flaubert termed the "essential difference" between himself and Sand lies elsewhere, for in the final analysis what Sand objected to in Flaubert's writing was less its failure to take a moral stance than its refusal to provide moral examples: "Don't hold virtue to be a cliché in literature," Sand pleaded with Flaubert. "Give it its representatives; portray the honest man and the strong, along with the maniacs and dolts you so love to ridicule" (p. 230).

Unambiguously virtuous characters are indeed in short supply in Flaubert's fictional universe, peopled as it is with a depressing conglomeration of deluded, self-centered, or cynical characters entirely lacking in any redeeming virtue. Representatives of goodness can be counted on one hand: Catherine Leroux, the exploited domestic servant who is awarded a medal at the agricultural fair in *Madame Bovary;* Dussardier, the altruistic worker who dies on the barricades in *L'éducation sentimentale;* and, of course, Félicité, the big-hearted servant in *Un coeur simple,* who ends up conflating a stuffed parrot with the Holy Spirit. In each instance, goodness is alloyed with stupidity (*bêtise*) or, at the very least, with naïveté. The situation could not be more different in Sand's seventy-odd novels. The long list of her virtuous characters includes such luminous figures as Edmée Mauprat, Fadette, the Marquis de Villemer, and the Meunier d'Angibault (the miller from Angibault). What is more, in Sand's fiction, virtue is always rewarded, unequivocally endorsed by the author. The essential difference between Sand and Flaubert involves ethics and its place in fiction, and it is this difference that divides Sand not only from Flaubert but also from Balzac—in short, from the major representatives of realism in France.

Sand's debate with Flaubert echoes at a distance of nearly half a century the very terms of her debate with Balzac, the friend and model of her youth. "You," Flaubert wrote to Sand, "always in whatever you do, begin with a great leap toward heaven, and then you return to earth. You start from the *a priori,* from theory, from the ideal . . . I, poor wretch, remain glued to the earth, as though the soles of my shoes were made of lead; everything moves me, everything lacerates and ravages me, and I make every effort to soar" (*Letters,* p. 230). Similarly, as Sand recounts in *Histoire de ma vie* (1855; *Story of My Life*), sometime around 1830 Balzac had said to her: "You seek man as he should be; I take him as he is" (*My Life,* p. 218). The opposition between the idealistic and idealizing woman writer and the hard-nosed, earthbound virile writer who bravely confronts reality head-on is a perennial cliché of (male-authored) literary history and criticism. Thus, when Balzac goes on to say, "Idealize only toward the lovely and the beautiful: that is woman's work," he is speaking with the authority and nonchalance of the purveyor of popular wisdom.

In Sand's case, however, there was a perfect fit between received ideas about gender and genre and her own aesthetic theory and practice. For, in contrast to the dominant male aesthetic of realism that linked the masters of 19th-century French fiction, Balzac, Flaubert, and Zola (their differences notwithstanding), Sand affirmed a competing aesthetic, idealism.

In the 19th century, following Immanuel Kant's fundamental formulation of the centrality of the ideal in aesthetics (1794; *Critique of Judgment*), realism was yoked to idealism. As idealism's binary opposite, realism signified only in relation to idealism—so much so that to consider one term in complete isolation from the other is to deplete, even distort, its significance. And yet so massive, so crushing has been the triumph of realism that at least in literature—in painting, where the opposition first arose, the story is quite different—idealism has all but vanished from our critical consciousness, taking with it the literary reputation of its most eminent French representative, George Sand. It is not because Sand was a woman, but because she is associated with a discredited representational mode (itself associated with the feminine), that she, unlike her great friends Balzac and Flaubert, is no longer ranked among the canonical authors.

The notorious terminological slipperiness that affects realism—is realism a "perennial mode" or the name of a specific historical movement? do realist works mirror reality or shape the real in the service of class interests?—also affects idealism. The immensely popular and influential lectures on aesthetics, *Philosophie de l'art* (1880; *Philosophy of Art*), by the philosopher Hippolyte Taine, who was one of Sand's most eloquent admirers, provide the best key to understanding Sand's practice of idealism. In the section "De l'idéal dans l'art" Taine argues that the ideal in art can take two forms: to heighten the essential or to promote the higher good. Taine's double definition of aesthetic idealism makes clear the necessary slippage between the formal and the ethical dimensions of idealism. Thus, whereas Balzac could be said to be an idealist in the first sense, because, as both he and Taine agreed, he idealized characters "in reverse, in their ugliness or folly," only Sand in the 19th century can be described as an idealist in the full, double sense of the word. Her conflation of hyperbolizing and meliorative idealization is what makes Sand in Taine's eyes the paradigmatic idealist novelist, whereas Balzac, for all his larger-than-life character types, remains stuck in the lower ethical spheres of realism. The hierarchical reversal brought about by Taine is stunning: viewed from the unfamiliar vantage point his aesthetics provide, realism appears as a lesser, even a failed, idealism; it is Sand and not Balzac who is the major French novelist of 19th-century France.

Sand's form of idealism—not to be confused with the more traditional Germanic and misogynistic strain of idealism illustrated by fin-de-siècle authors such as Auguste de Villiers de l'Isle-Adam—found its consummate expression in the pastoral or "rustic" fictions of her middle period: *La mare au diable* (1846; *The Devil's Pool*); *François le Champi* (1847); *La petite Fadette* (1848; *Fanchon the Cricket*); and *Les maîtres sonneurs* (1853; *The Bagpipers*). But idealism in Sand is transgeneric and informs her most melodramatic love stories as well as her most preachy *roman à thèse*. The poetics of idealism always entails a double process: first, the erasure of the very contingent details that are according to Sand herself constitutive of realism; second, the heightening in importance of a protagonist who embodies the "chief feeling or idea of the book" (*My Life*, p. 218), almost always love in its most sublime or sublimated form. It is no accident that Sand repeatedly invokes the archetypal Western model of an ethical eros, the courtly love rituals sung by medieval troubadours. Frédéric Moreau's obsessive quest for the unattainable lady of his fantasies, the ideal figure of Mme. Arnoux in Flaubert's *L'éducation sentimentale,* gestures toward the same model but at the distance of parody: hopelessly mired in the degraded, desublimated universe of Flaubert's realism, neither the narcissistic Frédéric nor the bourgeois Mme. Arnoux achieves the transcendental union toward which each aspires. In Sand's fictional universe, where women are never represented as fully desiring subjects and where men are capable of almost indefinite deferral of their instincts for carnal possession, the courtly love model is appropriated to feminist ends, and an alternative erotic grammar is elaborated. What distinguishes Sand's love stories from those of Flaubert (while calling to mind those of Hugo and Balzac) is that in her novels, the quest for the love ideal is inseparable from an aspiration toward a better world. For all her reading of what George Eliot called "silly women's novels," when Indiana fantasizes, it is not as Emma Bovary will, about the beautiful people and Paris, but rather about freedom for herself and all her fellow slaves. And when in the epilogue of *Indiana* (1832)—so roundly condemned by contemporary male critics such as Charles Augustin Sainte-Beuve for its implausibility—Indiana and her faithful cousin Sir Ralph retire to the wilds of Bernica, they devote themselves to freeing the old and infirm black slaves. Similarly, when, at the end of *La petite Fadette,* Fanchon and Landry marry and live happily ever after, Fanchon founds and presides over a school for the needy children of the commune. Altruism is a central component of Sand's eros. And altruism is, of course, the virtue symbolized by the long-suffering Félicité, who, in Flaubert's words, "loves one after the other a man, her mistress's children, a nephew of hers, an old man whom she nurses, and her parrot" (quoted in *Three Tales,* p. 15). Hers is, like the ignorant Indiana's, the "intellect of the heart." Félicité's serial love objects, unlike those of Flaubert's other protagonists, are none of them narcissistic. Love under the régime of idealism is anaclitic. Whatever else one can say about Félicité's heterogeneous choices, they all testify to her unique capacity to love the Other. After all, what is the parrot if not the absolute Other, first as animal, then as inert matter, and finally as transcendental signifier? For all the text's duplicities, for all its manipulations of irony, there is little doubt that in *Un coeur simple* Flaubert does give virtue its due, does reconcile the poetics of realism with the aesthetics of idealism.

Idealism and realism, the two dominant representational modes of 19th-century French fiction, are not irreconcilable opposites: just as in *Un coeur simple* Flaubert combines realistic effects grounded in superfluous details with the idealization of the protagonist, Sand in her own writings is always careful to surround her idealized protagonist with realistic secondary characters whose function is to ensure verisimilitude, hence the text's legitimacy. It is perhaps in the fiction of the other George, George Eliot, who owed so much to Sand, that the meeting of opposites is most strikingly bodied forth. In *Adam Bede* (1859), where Eliot famously devotes a chapter to stating her repudiation of the prevailing idealism in favor of a revolutionary prosaic realism, her protagonist is, for all his human flaws, a highly idealized figure, a paragon of lower-class virtue patterned on Sand's Meunier d'Angibault. Nevertheless, despite its tendency to collapse, as all oppositions do, the opposition between idealism and realism must be revived and revised if the hegemony of patriarchal realism is to be challenged and Sand recanonized.

Bibliography: Victor Brombert, *The Novels of Flaubert* (Princeton: Princeton University Press, 1973). Ross Chambers, "An Invitation to Love: Simplicity of Heart and Textual Duplicity in 'Un Coeur Simple,'" in *Story and Situation: Narrative Seduction and the Power of Fiction* (Minneapolis: University of Minnesota Press, 1984). Jonathan Culler, *Flau-*

bert: The Uses of Uncertainty (Ithaca: Cornell University Press, 1974). Gustave Flaubert, *The Letters of Gustave Flaubert*, vol. 2, trans. Francis Steegmuller (Cambridge, Mass.: Harvard University Press, 1982). Flaubert, *Three Tales*, trans. Robert Baldwick (Harmondsworth: Penguin, 1961). George Sand, *My Life*, trans. Dan Hofstadter (New York: Harper & Row, 1979). Naomi Schor, "Idealism in the Novel: Recanonizing Sand," *Yale French Studies*, 75 (1988), 56–73. Hippolyte Taine, *Philosophie de l'art* (Geneva: Slatkine, 1980).

Naomi Schor

✍ 1877
Emile Zola Publishes His First Working-Class Novel, *L'assommoir*

Nature, Society, and the Discourse of Class

When Emile Zola published *L'assommoir* in book form in 1877, he added a preface in reaction to the monumental controversy provoked by the novel's appearance as a newspaper serial the year before. The preface defined *L'assommoir* as "a work of truth, the first novel about the common people which does not tell lies but has the authentic smell of the people" (p. 21). This statement raises three issues to be considered here: the ideology of how the people smell, the problem of how fiction avoids lying, and Zola's need to qualify the claim that no novel before his had taken the common people as its subject.

In fact an illustrious series of novels before *L'assommoir* had incorporated characters from among those whom Zola's contemporaries across the English Channel were calling the Great Unwashed. Peasants had been prominent in French fiction since the 18th century, and such major figures as Honoré de Balzac and George Sand were among the peasantry's 19th-century chroniclers. As for the urban poor who were the subject of *L'assommoir* (the novel's heroine, Gervaise Macquart, is a Parisian laundress), both Eugène Sue's *Les mystères de Paris* (1842–43; *The Mysteries of Paris*) and Victor Hugo's *Les misérables* (1862) had already acquired immense audiences in many countries by representing the down and out in Paris.

In 1864 Edmond and Jules de Goncourt published *Germinie Lacerteux,* a novel about a domestic servant. Its preface has several points in common with the essay Zola wrote to introduce and defend *L'assommoir* more than a decade later. The Goncourts, too, wanted their fiction to be read as truth: "The public likes false novels; this novel is a true novel." They, too, saw themselves as the first to represent what life was like among society's forgotten majority. "Living in the nineteenth century, at a time of universal suffrage, democracy, liberalism, we wondered whether those called 'the inferior classes' did not have a right to the Novel" (*Germinie Lacerteux,* p. 1). Since Zola was an outspoken supporter of the Goncourts in general and of *Germinie Lacerteux* in particular, his claim that *L'assommoir* opened new territory for the French novel obviously cannot stand solely on its introduction of working-class characters.

Zola was far from alone in thinking that something different had come into

774

being with *L'assommoir,* however. His outraged readers agreed, and their response to that difference inaugurated the high-pitched personal and aesthetic invective that was to greet many of Zola's novels for the remaining twenty-five years of his life. Henri Mitterand quoted two examples in his invaluable commentary to the Pléiade edition of *Les Rougon-Macquart,* the cycle of twenty novels among which *L'assommoir* is the seventh: "This is not realism, it's filth; this is no longer crudeness, it's pornography"; "*L'assommoir* belongs less to literature than to pathology" (*Les Rougon-Macquart* [1871–1893], 2:1558, 1561). Although assessments of its value diverged widely, author and readers of *L'assommoir* were in full accord that this novel brought something new to the fictional universe.

One component of the newness was certainly that Zola's narrative depended for its interest on urban workers alone. *L'assommoir* neither develops a dramatic plot that would grip regardless of its characters' class nor defines workers by juxtaposing them with their social superiors. Zola's original title for his novel was "La simple vie de Gervaise Macquart" ("The Simple Life of Gervaise Macquart"), and his constant compositional rule was to resist the temptation to attenuate the simplicity of working-class life either by filling it with action or by contrasting it to its bourgeois counterpart.

The explanation for the stupefying violence with which readers excoriated *L'assommoir* may therefore lie in the prevailing bourgeois ideology of literary propriety. The novel is in many ways a bourgeois genre: it not only developed in tandem with the bourgeoisie's material and political progress but also depended on bourgeois existence for its readers and its plots. The workers of *L'assommoir* were therefore interlopers in a restricted area, profaners of a sacred space, and they performed their transgression at a time when the bourgeoisie's worries about its claims on government gave special urgency to its claims on plot. Hugo, Sue, and the Goncourts represented the Parisian lower classes before the Paris Commune of 1871, the great revolt that Karl Marx called "the political form at last discovered under which to work out the economic emancipation of labor" (*The Civil War in France,* p. 60). *L'assommoir* appeared after the Commune, and its use of workers to motivate innovations in literary form resonated strongly with workers' own innovations in political form five years earlier.

Zola rejected bourgeois decorum with as much determination as he rejected bourgeois narrative; his discourse gives his characters' physical being a force unprecedented in legally published French fiction. It was the insistent description of bodily functions in *L'assommoir* that stimulated the greatest stridency among the novel's early readers, whose shocked indignation had strong political overtones. Jean Borie has argued that Zola's novels elicited so furious a reaction because they contested the two major operations of a single psychosocial defense mechanism. The 19th-century middle class cultivated a complex system of repression that kept both the body and the workers below the level of consciousness. In the spatial metaphorics of the age, being truly human required willing oneself to rise above both physical demands and economic indigence. By placing bodies and workers at the center of the novel, an imaginative enterprise with imposing credentials for expressing the truly human, Zola collapsed an opposition essential to an age's basic sense of identity.

Borie contends that the much-debated ideological thrust of Zola's novels was fully specified long ago. Any body of fiction that drove conservatives to such tantrums must have struck at the foundations of conservative principles. Persuasive though such reasoning is, it skirts the fact that Zola's combined display of a repressed body and a repressed class could also have the effect of justifying each repression by the other. If to be human was to move away from animals and toward angels, and if workers entered the novel while following the opposite trajectory, then to keep workers in their place was to keep humanity on its course. Such a message may explain both why some socialist critics were also appalled by *L'assommoir* and why the bourgeois reading public ignored the diatribes of bourgeois critics, buying up ninety-one editions of the novel in the five years following its publication.

Among many other functions, ideology has the task of naturalizing the social, of representing as eternal and hence as beyond human control what is actually a historical human creation. By correlating the natural fact of the body's existence with the social fact of class division, by always insisting that the correlation was not a product of his fiction but the simple truth of a writing that would not lie, Zola made ideology's tasks his own. Like the smell of the people, the place of the people became a natural given rather than a social artifact.

To define society as natural is therefore to condemn visions of social change as the purest fantasy, a reactionary position that seems to be implicit in the name Zola chose to denote his novelistic practice: naturalism. The etymological suggestion of immobility is magnified by Zola's many theoretical definitions of naturalism as the transposition into literature of methods developed by the natural sciences. Although the contradictions between Zola's theory and practice have become a dominant theme in criticism of his work, the novels themselves do incorporate aspects of a vision in which human and natural events are subject to the same laws. Moreover, the immobilizing concept of society implicit in a natural model is also apparent in the discourse of naturalism as Zola practiced it. In *L'assommoir,* as in almost all his other works, Zola saw an absolute good in the transparency of language that does nothing more than name. Naturalism's stylistic exaltation of the material universe, roundly condemned by the Marxist philosopher Georg Lukács in several celebrated essays, combines effortlessly with a vision of the world for which class is the same unchangeable given as material reality. That vision produced a plot with few suggestions of workers' ability to take control of their destiny. Gervaise Macquart, abandoned by her lover, marries a construction worker and opens a successful laundry. After her husband is injured in a fall and becomes alcoholic, Gervaise herself takes to drink and loses both her laundry and her virtue when she resumes her affair with the lover who had abandoned her. Widowed and again abandoned, Gervaise dies in filth to be buried in a pauper's grave, a seeming victim of her own lack of character. The progressive implications of Zola's introduction of workers into the novel are countered by the reactionary effect of a narrative representing workers as dissolute and irresponsible.

Ideology determines how we think more than it determines what we think about. Applied to a novel, that principle directs attention to the manner rather than the object of composition; much of Zola's manner strives to naturalize the writing process and thus reinforce bourgeois certainties. As the scholars associated with the French critical movement called sociocriticism have argued, the descriptions Zola defined as purely objective are in actuality no such thing. Far from being neutral notation, the naturalist style accepts prevailing norms and must consequently refuse all methods of description other than those that articulate the world's inertia.

Sociocritics have also argued, however, that *L'assommoir* does problematize the writing process in at least one extraordinary way. The novel that brought workers' lives into fictional plots also brought workers' speech into fictional style. The lexicon and syntax of the streets both invade the novel's narrative voice and characterize its spoken dialogue, a stylistic experiment Zola considered a sufficient explanation for all the antagonism his work encountered. The preface defining *L'assommoir* as a novel that does not lie also said that its truth was unpalatable solely because of the language expressing it. "Only its form has upset people. They have taken exception to words. My crime is that I have had the literary curiosity to collect the language of the people and pour it into a very carefully wrought mould. Form! Form is the great crime" (p. 21). The "carefully wrought mould" is of course the novel form, the "great crime" to have shown that bourgeois discourse and bourgeois existence are equally irrelevant to the bourgeois genre. People took exception to words because those words alienated their property.

In a perceptive combination of statistical and thematic analysis, Jacques Dubois has shown that the presence of workers' language in the narrative sections of *L'assommoir* repeats and expands the semantic uncertainties of free indirect discourse as practiced by Gustave Flaubert. When form commits the great crime of erasing the barrier between reliable and unreliable utterances, the very category of reliability—of language that does not lie—becomes problematic. But whereas Flaubert exploited primarily the psychological effects of a representation of the world that might or might not be true, Zola used free indirection to convey a social message. The signs that the author has yielded the floor in *L'assommoir* may not reveal who has taken his place, but they always announce that the new speaker is not from the middle class. *L'assommoir* uses socially marked language to establish a precise identity that, in the ultimate violation of the carefully wrought form, is not individual but collective.

The effect of the socialized language prominent in *L'assommoir* is to introduce polyphony into the canonically single-voiced structure of naturalist description. And to use Mikhail Bakhtin's term *polyphony* is to invoke Bakhtin's principle that no voice in dialogic interaction with another can be assumed to have the power to call the dialogue to a halt. Applied to *L'assommoir,* this means that

1. Four paperback translations of Zola's *L'assommoir: The Dram Shop* (London, 1913); *The Gin Palace* (New York, 1952); *Drunkard* (London, 1958); *L'assommoir* (London, 1970) (from Graham King, *Garden of Zola*, New York: © Harper & Row Publishers, Inc., 1978).

the purely objective, truth-speaking language of authorial narration is redefined as well as interrupted by the free indirect discourse of anonymous workers. When two forms of language are in conflict and one is insistently defined through the class of its speakers, the other cannot pretend to come from a world in which class is inoperative. In his preface, Zola said that the aim of *L'assommoir* "was to do a purely philological study which is, I think, of very great historical and social interest" (p. 21). That project was paradoxical, for pure philology is a fantasy if the interest of language is its historical and social construction. The pages following Zola's statement of purpose continuously highlight the paradox by setting all pure assertions of truth among repeated demonstrations that any assertion is a combatant in social and historical conflicts.

The ideological implications of naturalist description in *L'assommoir* must consequently be evaluated in the context of a work that delineates those implications for us. The language claiming to be transparent, neutral, and true accepts juxtaposition with language that is insistently opaque and unmistakably socialized.

In Zola's original title, "La simple vie de Gervaise Macquart," a proper noun and proper meanings coalesce in a cogent demonstration that language is as simple as a worker's life. In the final title, the untranslatable *L'assommoir* (fig. 1), proper meanings vacillate irremediably. The word *assommoir* comes from the standard French *assommer,* meaning to knock cold. But the noun form was strongly marked as popular speech, and the novel applies the term to so many different things that it loses any capacity for what should theoretically be objective naturalist notation. Jacques Dubois has analyzed how the multiple senses of *assommoir* establish a purely connotative term that relentlessly subverts the denotative foundation of the naturalist fiction for which this pure connotation furnishes the name. Analogous conflicts between absolute and socialized meanings recur until the vagaries of the word *assommoir* stand as a figure for all of the novel *L'assommoir.* Every stylistic display that language does not lie is permeated with the smell of the class that claims the exclusive right to distinguish between lies and reality.

Eight years after *L'assommoir,* Zola published *Germinal* (1885), the narrative of a miners' strike that fails. This second novel about workers has also been subject to perversely dissonant ideological interpretations, for it too simultaneously practices and denounces descriptive techniques that immobilize society and its constituents. And it, too, begins denunciation with the word that inaugurates the textual universe, the title. The month of Germinal was a component of the calendar created during the French Revolution to signal for the world that time as previously endured had become history as currently produced. Because it both recalls that the bourgeois world began in violent struggle and suggests that it can end the same way, the title page of *Germinal* undermines every suggestion of immobility in the 500 pages that follow.

In *L'assommoir,* the unimpeachable authority of an omniscient naturalist voice is dispersed by clear class identification of the voices that objective narration overcomes. In *Germinal* this dispersal is explicitly political. The miners' vision of economic change challenges all the claims to an origin above change inherent in naturalist discourse, and the novel's title continuously recalls that challenges from the dispossessed can make every discourse obsolete. Although Zola's narratives of working-class struggle are superb validations of middle-class stylistics, they are also telling commentaries on the ways in which class and stylistics reinforce each other. Each novel contains innumerable instances of language claiming to say what is, without fear or favor. Yet each novel also gives such language a setting that makes its fears and favors unmistakable. The memorable critical controversies on the ideological impact of Zola's working-class texts are the effect of the unresolved conflicts that each of those texts has with itself.

See also 1848, 1871.

Bibliography: Erich Auerbach, "Germinie Lacerteux," in *Mimesis,* trans. Willard Trask (Princeton: Princeton University Press, 1953). Jean Borie, *Zola et les mythes* (Paris: Seuil, 1971). Jacques Dubois, *"L'assommoir" de Zola: Société, discours, idéologie* (Paris: Larousse, 1973). Edmond de Goncourt and Jules de Goncourt, *Germinie Lacerteux* (Naples: Edizioni Scientifiche Italiane, 1968). Georg Lukács, *Studies in European Realism,* trans. Edith Bone (New York: Grosset and Dunlap, 1964). Karl Marx, *The Civil War in France* (New York: International Publishers, 1962). Emile Zola, *L'assommoir,* trans. Leonard Tancock (Harmondsworth: Penguin, 1971). Zola, *Les Rougon-Macquart*, ed. Henri Mitterand, 5 vols. (Paris: Gallimard, 1961–1967).

Sandy Petrey

✑ 1880

Forty-five Thousand Copies of Emile Zola's *Nana* Are Sold on Its Publication Day

Prostitution in the Novel

The prostitute is one of the primary vehicles in 19th-century artistic practice for male fantasies about female sexuality. She serves to focus male ambivalence about desire, money, class, and the body. Novelists such as Honoré de Balzac, Gustave Flaubert, Emile Zola, and Joris-Karl Huysmans evoke the fascinating allure of the prostitute's sexual availability only the better to justify a fear of desire and the urge to close, repress, even obliterate the female erotic body. This ambivalence has important consequences for narrative structure. The prostitute's deviance, her transgressive existence on the margins of society, makes her an attractive source of narrative energy. Moreover, her function as a vehicle of erotic release for members of widely varying social strata enables her to operate across class lines as an integrating narrative principle. But the risk of this unifying operation is a potential breakdown of culture. The prostitute's erotic appeal threatens to reduce men to their libidinal drives, mediated only by monetary exchange, and challenges women to adopt the same impersonal mediation in their own pursuit of wealth and pleasure. The result is a vision of cultural ruin in which individuals become easily replaceable substitutes for one another, and the encroachment of a universal mediocrity threatens all differential structures of meaning. The various strategies devised by 19th-century novelists to police the prostitute's narrative destiny are in large part defensive responses to the vision of disaster they associated with her public sexuality.

Many of the components of this vision are already present in the work of the public health official Alexandre Parent-Duchâtelet, who wrote the first modern study of prostitution, *De la prostitution dans la ville de Paris* (1836; *Prostitution in the City of Paris*). Though a meticulous pragmatist and early practitioner of statistical methods, Parent-Duchâtelet was also obsessed by his objects of analysis, most of which involved animal flesh and excrement in various stages of rot and decomposition. There was a logical continuity, in his mind, between his study of sewers and his study of *putains* (the French word for whore that derives from "putrid"): both channels for the disposal of waste were necessary for the well-being of the city and should be properly supervised and regularly sanitized. Therefore, he supported the administrative system that regulated Parisian prostitutes throughout the 19th century, whereby they were deprived of many civil rights, were forced to register with the police, were enclosed, to the extent possible, in officially sanctioned brothels called *maisons de tolérance*, and were required to undergo regular medical inspections for venereal disease.

What worried Parent-Duchâtelet most was the possibility that prostitutes might transgress the established social boundaries and infiltrate the bourgeoisie and upper class. The strategies he recommended to control this potential contamination from below by germs of disease and desire are analogous to the strategies of plot and style devised by 19th-century novelists to control their fantasies of woman's threatening sexuality. The Romantic figure of the prostitute with a heart of gold, popular in the first half of the century, perfectly satisfies the repressive demands of patriarchal ideology. Her glorious destiny is to sacrifice the successful commercial exploitation of her body and wit—she is usually a popular courtesan—for the love of one man. An essential aspect of this myth of the whore redeemed through love is the strict limitation of her aspirations: she may teach an elevating moral lesson, but she must also condemn herself as irredeemably marked by her sexually deviant past. Thus the prostitute's golden heart typically urges her to renounce a golden future: Hugo's Marion de Lorme, in his 1831 play by that name, never even dreams of marriage to her adored Didier; Eugène Sue's Fleur de Marie, the heroine of his immensely popular serial novel *Les mystères de Paris* (1842–43; *The Mysteries of Paris*), though finally recognized as à princess and loved by a prince, has so successfully internalized the patriarchal moral code that she wastes away in guilty expiation for her erstwhile sexual sin; and Alexandre Dumas *fils'* consumptive Marguerite in *La dame aux camélias* (novel 1848, play 1852) sensibly allows herself to be persuaded to renounce her one true love.

Marguerite was one of the last of her kind, largely, it seems, because the public no longer found the self-sacrificing courtesan an even marginally credible type. The courtesan under the Second Empire was a well-known public personality, whose flamboyant doings were chronicled daily in the press. She was a figure of conspicuous consumption, a gaudy emblem of the bourgeoisie's appetite for pleasure. Ostentatiously displaying herself on Baron Haussmann's wide new boulevards, the courtesan of the 1860s was a brilliantly artificial construction. Her spectacular theatricality appealed to the misogynous artists at mid-century because it obscured the libidinal animal they imagined to lurk under her synthetic surface. Thus Baudelaire, declaring in "Mon coeur mis à nu" (1887; "My Heart Laid Bare") that "woman is *natural,* that is to say abominable" (in *Intimate Journals,* p. 65), extolled makeup, jewelry, and costume as means to transform woman into what Flaubert claimed she should be, "a product of man . . . a factitious work" (letter to Louise Colet, 27 March 1853, *Correspondance,* p. 284).

As a prime representative of Woman in male fantasy, the prostitute comes to play a double role. She is associated both with the primitively instinctual and biological and with the disguise of this base naturalism behind the masks of male artistic invention. These denaturalizing masks are often correlated with literary procedures of fragmentation, heterogeneity, and reflexivity that disrupt traditional unities and continuities of character portrayal and plot development and signal the birth of modernism in the arts.

In this as in many other respects, Balzac marks the transition from the old to the new. His melodramatic novel *Splendeurs et misères des courtisanes* (1845–

1847; *A Harlot High and Low*) tells at first the trials of the courtesan Esther Gobseck, whose reformed sexuality the archvillain Vautrin wants to return to the marketplace in the interest of her ambitious lover, Lucien. She commits suicide rather than compromise her ideal love, exiting from the novel less than halfway through. But the idea of prostitution survives her as the motor force of the plot, now operating in the (latent?) homosexual relation between Vautrin and Lucien. Lucien is much more suitable than Esther to perform in Vautrin's play of venal substitutions and exchanges because he is essentially superficial and malleable, whereas Esther, like any woman in Vautrin's chauvinist opinion, "is too much governed by her organs" (*Harlot*, p. 518). As directed by Vautrin, Balzac's alter ego, the plot of Lucien's prostitution, full of disguises, subterfuges, and forgeries, takes on some of the qualities of arbitrariness and discontinuity we associate with the modernist sensibility.

Flaubert's novels, which embody that sensibility, offer radical examples of the association of prostitution with the male denial of female sexuality. In the epilogue to *L'éducation sentimentale* (1869; *Sentimental Education*), the two childhood friends Frédéric and Deslauriers agree that their lives have been failures and that the best time they ever had was their visit as adolescents to the local brothel. What makes this definition of cherished happiness peculiarly Flaubertian, and modern, is that the visit failed to accomplish its goal of sexual initiation: Frédéric fled in panic at the sight of so many available women, forcing Deslauriers, who had no money, to follow. So prostitution here signifies the avoidance of woman's sexual body, and the two friends' telling each other the story of this happy avoidance identifies it as the motive for the narrative act itself.

There is also a historical dimension to Flaubert's portrayal of prostitution. Examples of literal and figurative whoredom are so pervasive in *L'éducation sentimentale* that the entire period covered in the novel, from 1840 to 1868, seems to breathe the atmosphere of venal exchange. The prostitutional motif links those at the highest echelon of society with those at the lowest: whether man or woman, all are willing to sell out to the highest bidder. Women circulate like fetishized commodities to be traded speculatively on the marketplace. Not even the virtuous mother figure, Mme. Arnoux, remains outside the commercialized system of values that debases every human relationship in the novel. The defeat of France in the 1870 war with Prussia would, Flaubert felt, have provided his book with a perfect conclusion.

This is precisely the closure chosen by Flaubert's admirer Zola for his great novel of prostitution, *Nana* (1880). Zola tears away all veils, masks, and disguises from that figure so terrifying to 19th-century male fantasy, the natural woman. The novel's opening scene dramatizes this stripping away of all cultural shields as Nana appears with progressively less clothing on the stage of a theater that its director insists is a brothel. When she finally appears naked, the power of her sexuality, the intensity of her female odor, is such that she reduces her audience to a single mass of lusting, panting flesh. "The book has to be the poem of the cunt," Zola wrote in his preparatory sketch, "and the moral will lie in the cunt turning everything sour" (*Nana*, p. 13). This crude physical reference is important because it suggests the degree to which Nana's personality is independent of her biology. She is, Zola maintains, "good-natured above all else, never doing harm for harm's sake" (p. 12). Her "good nature" is as much the victim of her sexual nature as are the men who destroy themselves to possess her. The mythic dimension of Zola's vision identifies female sexual desirability with biological decomposition and organic decay. Parent-Duchâtelet's obsessional concerns return in Zola magnified into an almost hallucinatory picture of cultural collapse.

In *Le roman expérimental* (*The Experimental Novel*), published the same year as *Nana,* Zola observes: "In society as in the human body, a solidarity exists linking the different members, the different organs, so that, if an organ putrefies, many others are affected, and a very complex illness breaks out" (p. 78). This theory identifying society and the body accounts for the catastrophic contagions that so often infect and destroy Zola's fictional worlds. For the origin of these worlds is a break in the body's health, a deviation from the social order: Nana's blood is tainted by her inheritance of poverty and alcoholism, and her sexual organ is "nervously deranged" (*Nana,* p. 221). This organic derangement is only partly a function of Nana's working-class origins. Zola sets up a parallel between the poisonous crack in Nana's physiology and a similar crack, marking "the birth of an appetite for enjoyment" (*Nana,* p. 84), that fissures the proper aristocratic surface of the Countess Sabine, ultimately driving her to rampant promiscuity. Sexual desire, the generative force of life, is conceived by Zola as potentially the most destructive of deviations from life's wholesome balance. He implies that, once perverted by desire, any woman, whatever her class background, will embrace prostitution as her natural mode and spread the virus of her degenerate infection.

The idea of degeneration was one of the most powerful myths of the fin de siècle. Bénédict Auguste Morel argued in his *Traité des dégénérescences physiques, intellectuelles et morales de l'espèce humaine* (1857; *Treatise on Physical, Intellectual, and Moral Degenerative Diseases in the Human Species*) that a hereditary predisposition to pathology becomes increasingly destructive as it mutates to more malevolent forms in subsequent generations, reducing the organism's capacity for physical resistance to disease and for moral resistance to instinctual impulses. Zola shared this model of evolutionary decline with numerous social scientists of his day, who treated such matters of public concern as crime, madness, alcoholism, prostitution, the defeat of 1870, and the declining birthrate as evidence of progressive degeneracy in both the individual and the nation. For example, the influential Italian criminologist Cesare Lombroso argued in 1893 that all women were prostitutes in primitive times and are easily subject to atavistic regression to this original state. From this perspective, the prostitute is simply woman as she is fundamentally—precociously vicious, childish, perverse, without logical or moral capacity.

In the closely related literary and medical imaginations of the fin de siècle, the prostitute is also the carrier of the venereal prototype of all degenerative pathology, hereditary syphilis. The image of this dread disease, which remains latent for decades, even generations, only to surface with renewed virulence in the blood of an innocent descendant, haunted the anxious bourgeoisie as the undoing of its genetic and economic destiny. Nana's horrifying death from smallpox (*la petite vérole*), contracted from her neglected child, is evidently meant to suggest venereal disease, the pox (*la grande vérole*). Nana's sexual contagion infects men and women alike, decomposing them, making them like her, eroding their differences, until all are absorbed into her putrefying corpse, symbol of the disintegration of an entire age and of its fantasmatic obsession. (Guy de Maupassant, himself syphilitic—like his confrères Baudelaire, Jules de Goncourt, Flaubert, and Alphonse Daudet—reverses this symbolic paradigm in his 1884 story "Le lit 29" ["Bed 29"], in which a syphilitic prostitute, instead of curing herself, deliberately sleeps with as many Prussian soldiers as possible, using her disease as a patriotic weapon.)

Though declaring his disenchantment with Zola's naturalism, Huysmans, in the crucial novel of the so-called decadent movement, *A rebours* (1884; *Against Nature*), does not so much break with his master's morbid biological vision as revitalize its sources in the unconscious. Huysmans elaborates a horrifying set of fantasmatic equations: female sexuality = prostitution = castration = syphilis = the organic world. Huysmans' vivid dream narratives are full of the repellent imagery of castration, but woman's imagined mutilation never signifies a loss of power: on the contrary, castration in Huysmans' nightmare visions is a diseased hemorrhage that infects and decomposes all biological organisms. The decadent program, which originated with Baudelaire, of creating artificial imitations and representations of natural substances had its psychological basis in a desperate need to avoid the imagined female degeneracy of all organic life. "Everything is syphilis," observes the sickly hero of *A rebours*. "And he had a sudden vision of the unceasing torments inflicted on humanity by the virus of ages past" (p. 101). Huysmans' vision encounters death at both its extremes, through syphilitic corruption on the one hand, through sterile artifice on the other. His literary solution to this dilemma once again demonstrates the origins of modernist literary techniques in a fantasized denial of the female sexual body: he invents a highly ornamental style, an encrusted verbal surface, that obscures the imagined underlying corruption, and he subverts the organic model of narrative development by juxtaposing largely self-contained units of plot.

The syphilitic prostitute is the prototype of the numerous versions of the femme fatale that proliferate in the art of the fin de siècle: the vampire, the Sphinx, Salome, Judith. These figures are often represented in the flowing, curvaceous, vegetal forms of art nouveau, their luxuriant hair a typical feature, in images that express male fascination with the dissolving, potentially strangulating qualities of female beauty. The biological panic reflected in these images dissipates after the discovery in 1909 of an arsenic-based treatment for syphilis and the great cataclysm of the First World War. The last two decades of the 19th century do, however, bear an uncanny resemblance to the period we are living in now: AIDS has taken the place of syphilis both in the reality of personal suffering and in the fantasies of a frightened population that feels itself justified in associating deviant sexuality with deadly contamination and imminent cultural disaster.

See also 1840, 1884, 1892.

Bibliography: Honoré de Balzac, *A Harlot High and Low,* trans. Rayner Heppenstall (Harmondsworth: Penguin, 1970). Charles Baudelaire, *Intimate Journals,* trans. Christopher Isherwood (Hollywood: Marcel Rod, 1947). Charles Bernheimer, *Figures of Ill Repute* (Cambridge, Mass.: Harvard University Press, 1989). Jean Borie, *Zola et les mythes* (Paris: Seuil, 1971). Victor Brombert, *The Novels of Flaubert* (Princeton: Princeton University Press, 1973). Alain Corbin, *Les filles de noce* (Paris: Albin Michel, 1978) (translation forthcoming at Harvard University Press). Gustave Flaubert, *Correspondance,* ed. Jean Bruneau, vol. 2 (Paris: Gallimard, 1980). Joris-Karl Huysmans, *Against Nature,* trans. Robert Baldick (Harmondsworth: Penguin, 1959). Alexandre Parent-Duchâtelet, *De la prostitution dans la ville de Paris* (1836); abridged as *La prostitution à Paris au XIXe siècle,* ed. Alain Corbin (Paris: Seuil, 1981). Emile Zola, *Nana,* trans. George Holden (Harmondsworth: Penguin, 1972). Zola, *Le roman expérimental* (Paris: Garnier-Flammarion, 1971).

Charles Bernheimer

⤜ 1884

Joris-Karl Huysmans Publishes His Novel *A rebours*

Decadence

Joris-Karl Huysmans first became known as a disciple of Emile Zola, and thus as an adherent of naturalism—the school founded on the premise that literature could, and should, precisely imitate the scientific and cyclic patterns of nature. In practice naturalism required a rather journalistic, laboriously detailed prose narrative that omitted nothing in the name of good taste (hence contemporary descriptions of Zola's work as "pornography," although by today's standards it seems quite politely discreet). In 1877 Huysmans published *Emile Zola et L'assommoir,* in which he proclaimed his allegiance to Zola and naturalism. The publication of *A rebours* (1884; *Against Nature*) is usually thought to represent a break with the realistic practice of naturalism, and with Zola. It certainly did coincide with a rift between the two writers, as Huysmans himself admitted in his preface to the 1902 edition of the novel, but how and to what extent *A rebours* broke with realism and with the literary past is a more difficult question.

It certainly is true that *A rebours* became, almost instantly, the manifesto of a new literary school with which novelists such as Auguste de Villiers de l'Isle-Adam and poets such as Jules Laforgue, Tristan Corbière, and even, to some extent, Stéphane Mallarmé would become associated. A year before *A rebours,* Paul Bourget had used "théorie de la décadence" as a subtitle in the section devoted to Baudelaire in his *Essais de psychologie contemporaine* (1883; *Essays on Contemporary Psychology*), and in fact *A rebours* coincided with Huysmans' return to the darker, more explicitly Baudelairian side of himself apparent in his earliest published work. In appropriating the term to describe the protagonist of *A rebours,* des Esseintes, Huysmans changed the history of French letters. Des Esseintes became a sort of fictional cult hero for a whole generation of young would-be literati and was memorialized by Mallarmé in the well-known poem "Prose pour des Esseintes" (1885).

But *A rebours* might also be considered a manifesto of realism, of a *return* to realism as understood by Flaubert before Zola. The novel is in fact as much a logical development of the "realistic," laconically descriptive style thought by many to have reached its zenith in Flaubert, as it is a renunciation of Zola's naturalism. Decadence has long been assumed to reflect a "decline in values," if not in literary quality, a turning away from the realist/naturalist project of reflecting, even duplicating empirical phenomena in the realm of language, toward symbolization and a preoccupation with the grotesque and phantasmagorical. As surely as the word comes from the Latin *de-cadere,* "to fall from," a fall is implied, but one that in fact began with Flaubert. The object of Flaubert's realism is not the same as Zola's. The 'real' for Flaubert is rather our perception of the real than anything that may exist apart from or prior to our perception. This concept of reality echoes that of the German philosopher Arthur Schopenhauer, whose pessimism has long been known to have influenced Huysmans profoundly in his formulation of decadence. Only when Huysmans' debt to Flaubert's realism is understood can the extent of his innovation in *A rebours* be properly addressed.

A rebours and its hero, des Esseintes, pursue with relentless rigor the logic of realism as literary practice—fiction as *truquage,* literary special effects, the manipulation of the reader's senses and desire through language in an effort to elicit the momentary hallucination that there is no difference between the text and the real, no difference between the fiction being recounted, or imagination, and actual events. Des Esseintes withdraws from the world and seals himself off from it in an effort to attain perfect control over his reality and to reduce to nothing, within the walls of his house, the difference between imagination and reality, artifice and nature. He attempts in effect to create the illusion of various realities in order to modulate his own sensations.

The same effort in Flaubert's practice of realism is nowhere more clearly elaborated than in *Trois contes* (1877; *Three Tales*), the collection of his three short stories: *Un coeur simple (A Simple Heart), La légende de saint Julien l'hospitalier (The Legend of St. Julian the Hospitaler),* and *Hérodias.* The unity of *Trois contes,* so often overlooked or misunderstood by critics of Flaubert's work, is grounded in the representation of three kinds of religious experience. In the naïveté of the first story's main character, Félicité, there is no difference between the text of the Bible and reality, between a map and the terrain that it represents, between a parrot and God—the real and its representation are one in her ecstatic, hallucinatory simplemindedness. In the second story, another animal—the stag, which speaks a prophecy to Julien—becomes the same sort of figure as the parrot—representing the way in which the mute, brute, objectively real depends on language, on representation, on human perception, to embody and to become what we understand as "real." His encounter with the stag causes Julien to suffer a kind of madness of uncertainty. He is no longer sure of the difference between the real and the text (of the real), between blood-lust (material desire) and another, spiritual, *script*-ural desire. This discrepancy is collapsed in his final hallucinatory experience of God. Similarly, in *Hérodias,* Herod's erotic, material desire is contrasted with the scriptural, religious desire of John the Baptist. Salome, the object of Herod's physical desire, is mute movement; the Baptist is nothing but a voice crying in the wilderness, housed, like the stag's and the parrot's voices, in a "brutish" body. The reality, the desirability, of both Salome and the Baptist is a matter of the way they are perceived. The contrast at the end between the Baptist's head as, on the one hand, just an item among the detritus of the night's festivities, and, on the other, a religious talisman, is one more representation of this paradox.

Des Esseintes must be read as an individual who has determined to live his life by the same precepts and logic that govern Flaubert's fiction. Des Esseintes means to control and willfully to manipulate his own sensations with such care and precision as to create a "real fiction" so enveloping that it leaves no room for contamination by any exterior, alien, and uncontrolled reality. He has a preference for Latin authors because their language is "dead," no longer spoken and subject to the modifications of use; he carefully and artificially duplicates the smells and décor of travel so that he need not leave his house to have all the sensations of being in London; he has a "mouth organ" (*orgue à bouche*), a collection of liquors of various tastes correlated to approximate an analogue of music: "Each liqueur corresponded, according to him, to the sound of an instrument. Dry curaçao, for instance, to the clarinet" (*A rebours,* p. 99). Sometimes he transposed or "duplicated," by taste, an already existing musical composition, and sometimes he "composed melodies himself" (p. 100). In a word, "artifice seemed to des Esseintes the distinctive mark of human genius" (p. 80). He believes it possible "to satisfy desires reputed to be the most difficult to please in everyday life by a light subterfuge, by an approximative sophistication of [surrogate for] the object pursued by those very desires" (p. 79). He lives by the rule and practice of *adroit mensonge,* adroit lying.

He keeps a pet cricket rather than a parrot, which, however, plays the same role as Félicité's Loulou in *Un coeur simple:* just as the bird serves to manipulate Félicité's experience of the real, subsuming all sorts of meanings, such as her nephew's whereabouts, the Holy Spirit, and the New World, des Esseintes's cricket serves to manipulate his perceptions, memories, emotions, sensations. The difference is that des Esseintes knows very well that he is being manipulated, is in fact manipulating himself. He is as sophisticated and subtle a "reader" as one could wish for, unlike the naïve Félicité. This, indeed, is the governing principle behind his careful orchestration of all the physical sensations to which he is subject, all of his surroundings. The manipulation of the reader (des Esseintes) by the author (des Esseintes) or the author's words, which occurs here within the text (in des Esseintes's effort to create a "real fiction"), perfectly duplicates Flaubert's project as a realist: to create a literary reality more credible, more immediate, than phenomenal reality, to manipulate the reader's imagination so adroitly as to collapse the gap between the text and the real. Des Esseintes is a realist even more zealous than Flaubert: he practices, in his life, the very stylistic principles that caused Flaubert to try to allude to at least three of the senses in his descriptive passages. Des Esseintes's pet cricket is the figure of a logic implicit in the parrot Loulou, in the stag that prophesies to Julien, in the head of John the Baptist and the dance of Salome, but the cricket is more explicitly a figure for Flaubert's *self-conscious* realistic style, the manipulation of imaginary sensation. Although he "hallucinates" in the cricket's voice all sorts of meanings that are not there, precisely as Félicité does with the parrot, he knows perfectly well what he is doing (pp. 69–70):

> Thus, out of hatred, out of scorn for his childhood, he had hung from the ceiling of this room a little cage of silver wire in which an imprisoned cricket sang, as they had [in his childhood] in the ashes of the fireplaces of the castle of Lourps; when he would hear this sound, heard so many times before, all the constrained and mute evenings at his mother's, all the abdication of a suffering and repressed youth rose up before him, and then, in the thrashings of the woman whom he was caressing mechanically and whose words or whose laugh broke his vision and brought him brusquely back to reality, in the bedroom, on the ground, a tumult would rise up in his soul, a need of vengeance for the sorrows endured, a raging desire to soil by turpitude these familial memories, a furious desire to pant on cushions of flesh, to exhaust to their last drops the most vehement and the most bitter carnal excesses.

Both Huysmans, in *A rebours,* and Flaubert are ultimately phenomenal rather than empirical realists like Zola. They believe, unlike Zola, that the real does not exist apart from our perception of it. If we can manipulate our own perceptions, we can manipulate our reality. Huysmans goes one step further in showing how the principles of realistic style, and the implications of Flaubert's realism, apply not just to literature but to life, to our real perception of the real. Decadence, then, must be a *return* to Flaubert's (and Schopenhauer's) view of reality, and a departure from Zola's pseudo scientific literary empiricism.

Bibliography: Roland Barthes, "The Reality Effect," in *The Rustle of Language,* trans. Richard Howard (New York: Hill and Wang, 1986). Ross Chambers, "An Invitation to Love: Simplicity of Heart and Textual Duplicity in 'Un Coeur Simple,'" in *Story and Situation: Narrative Seduction and the Power of Fiction* (Minneapolis: University of Minnesota Press, 1984). Jonathan Culler, *Flaubert: The Uses of Uncertainty* (Ithaca: Cornell University Press, 1974). Gustave Flaubert, *Oeuvres,* vol. 2, ed. Albert Thibaudet and René Dumesnil (Paris: Gallimard, 1952). Richard Gilman, *Decadence: The Strange Life of an Epithet* (New York: Farrar, Straus and Giroux, 1979). Jefferson Humphries, "*Bouvard et Pécuchet* and the Fable of Stable Irony," in *Losing the Text: Readings in Literary Desire* (Athens: University of Georgia Press, 1986). Joris-Karl Huysmans, *A rebours* (Paris: Garnier-Flammarion, 1978). Suzanne Nalbantian, *Seeds of Decadence in the Late-Nineteenth-Century Novel* (New York: St. Martin's, 1983). Mario Praz, *The Romantic Agony,* trans. Angus Davidson (New York: Oxford University Press, 1970).

Jefferson Humphries

1885, *February*

Symbolist Poets Publish *La revue wagnérienne*

The Music of the Future

Richard Wagner once told two of his earliest French disciples, Judith Gautier and Catulle Mendès, that no one had better understood his work than the French. Indeed, from the 1860s on, French *wagnérisme* (the term preceded the German *Wagnerismus* and the English *Wagnerism*) acquired both the intellectual cachet and the semblance of a coherent avant-garde "movement" that made it eminently marketable to the rest of Europe—not unlike those other Parisian export labels *réalisme, impressionnisme,* and *symbolisme,* with which it was often confused. Significantly, however, the history of Wagnerism in France had less to do with Wagner's actual music than with the aesthetic and political discourses his work enabled. Gérard de Nerval is an early case in point. Long considered to have been one of the pioneer French Wagnerites, Nerval apparently never heard a single note of the composer's work. Delayed en route to Weimar in 1850, the French translator of *Faust* missed the première of *Lohengrin*—and then went on to publish a ground-breaking essay on the opera in *La presse,* ghost-written, as it now turns out, by Franz Liszt's personal secretary.

Although Wagner began achieving a certain notoriety in France in the 1850s, few had yet heard what newspapers referred to as his "music of the future." Journalists spoke of him as the "Courbet of music," but it was primarily because the catchword *realism* so easily attached itself to the perceived socialist message of his work (Wagner had been expelled from Dresden for his participation in the May 1849 insurrection). In the eyes of his conservative critics, Wagner had done the unpardonable: he had explicitly injected ideology into music by transposing the militant tone and tactics of the failed 1848 revolution to his work. Much of the subsequent history of Wagnerism is an attempt to work out the ambiguous implications of this displacement of the utopian avant-garde political discourse to avant-garde art.

When Wagner arrived in Paris in 1859, the scene was therefore set for the political and ideological controversies that culminated in the theater riots surrounding the 1861 performance of *Tannhäuser* at the Opéra. While in Paris, Wagner acquired the influential backing of Comtesse Marie d'Agoult, converted to Wagnerism by her lover Franz Liszt (their illegitimate child, Cosima, eventually became Wagner's second wife) and the socialite figurehead of the republican opposition to Napoleon III. But it is a measure of Wagner's political opportunism that while eliciting support from left-wing artists, students, and bohemians, he was also courting powerful members of the political and intellectual establishment who were drawn to Wagnerism's aura of radical chic. In any event, it was at the personal request of the wife of the Austrian ambassador that Napoleon III, anxious to assuage the Hapsburgs and to mollify the opponents of his régime, finally issued an imperial decree authorizing the performance of *Tannhäuser* in March 1861. The former firebrand of the Dresden revolution had become the official darling of the French court.

The irony was not lost on the emperor's adversaries. The aristocratic members of the Jockey Club seized on the opportunity to create mayhem during the first three (and only) performances of *Tannhäuser,* drowning out the entire event with choruses of catcalls and dogwhistles. Ostensibly a protest against Wagner's refusal to insert the traditional grand ballet in the second act of his opera (which allowed latecomers to admire their favorite dancers), the demonstration by the legitimist rowdies of the Jockey Club clearly signaled a humiliating defeat for Napoleon III. Wagner left Paris in disgust, but at least he had finally managed to make his mark on the capital: a dress called *le manteau Tannhäuser* enjoyed a brief vogue; caricatures of the German musician by Cham (Comte Amédée de Noé) and André Gill were widely circulated; and Champfleury (Jules Fleury-Husson) published a trendy portrait gallery of *Grandes figures d'hier et d'aujourd'hui* (1861; *Celebrities of Yesterday and Today*) in which Wagner was ranged with Balzac, Nerval, and Gustave Courbet. But the most influential voice to emerge from the Wagner controversies of 1860–61 was that of Charles Baudelaire. His essay *Richard Wagner et Tannhäuser à Paris* (*Richard Wagner and Tannhäuser in Paris*), published as a pamphlet in the spring of 1861, set the agenda for literary Wagnerism in France over the following three decades.

Baudelaire's essay was primarily inspired by Wagner's 1860 Parisian concerts of the overtures to *The Flying Dutchman, Tannhäuser, Tristan,* and *Lohengrin*—the pandemonium at the later full-scale production of *Tannhäuser* was such that nobody really heard the opera. Like much of his late criticism, Baudelaire's essay is essentially an extended meditation on translation. He begins by comparing three independent "translations" of the *Tannhäuser* overture—Wagner's concert program notes, Liszt's published study of the opera, and Baudelaire's own subjective (and overwhelmingly erotic) impressions. To Baudelaire's surprise, he discovers that all three translations are virtually identical: all three involve the same imagery (intense luminosity, immense expanses of space), and all three register the same moods (solitude, lucidity, sensuality). Baudelaire accordingly concludes that "true music evokes analogous ideas in different brains" (*Richard Wagner and Tannhäuser,* p. 116). His intimation that behind the varieties of individual experience there lie certain shared, universal "ideas" harks back to Neoplatonic tradition while prefiguring the "thematic" approach practiced by such 20th-century phenomenological critics as Gaston Bachelard, Georges Poulet, and Jean-Pierre Richard.

Pursuing this notion of translatability, Baudelaire goes on to quote his sonnet "Correspondances," from *Les fleurs du mal* (1857; *The Flowers of Evil*), to illustrate his claim that "things have always found their expression through a system of reciprocal analogy—as when sounds suggest sights, or colors suggest smells, etc." (*Wagner,* p. 116). Better known as synesthesia, Baudelaire's theory of the intertranslatability of different senses and media would exercise a profound impact on symbolist poetics. Arthur Rimbaud parodies it in his 1871 sonnet "Voyelles" ("Vowels"), in which each vowel stands for a specific color; des Esseintes, the decadent hero of Joris-Karl Huysmans' novel *A rebours* (1884; *Against Nature*), invents a special synesthetic "mouth organ," each note of which releases a liquor whose flavor he associates with the sound of a specific instrument; René Ghil's *Traité du verbe* (1886; *Treatise on the Word*) develops an intricate semiotic system in which the letters of the alphabet are correlated with different musical instruments. If the symbolists thought such experiments were Wagnerian in inspiration, the fault probably lay with Baudelaire's influential confusion of synesthesia with Wagner's concept of the *Gesamtkunstwerk* (total work of art). Wagner envisaged the alliance of all the arts in a single object or event; poetry and music were to be combined in order to express what neither of them could articulate in isolation; but nowhere does he suggest, as Baudelaire does, that the two are substitutable for or translatable into each other.

Baudelaire notes that Wagner's music is so evocative of images, ideas, and moods because "there is always a lacuna which is filled in by the listener's imagination" (*Wagner,* p. 114). The act of listening (or reading or viewing) is therefore, according to Baudelaire, always an act of auxiliary imagining or supplemental translation, an act whose recreative impulse parallels that of the artist himself (who is in turn also a species of translator). Baudelaire's supple notion of translation, in short, allows him to blur the boundaries between creation and interpretation, between the original invention of the artist and the secondary elaboration of the critic or theorist. For Baudelaire, Wagner's modernity, like Edgar Allan Poe's, lies precisely in the fact that he managed to do *both* simultaneously. This portrait of the artist as the self-conscious theorist of his own creative practice exercised a considerable attraction for later symbolists and postsymbolists such as Stéphane Mallarmé, Paul Valéry, Marcel Proust, and T. S. Eliot, convinced as they were that modern writing was henceforth inseparable from its reflections upon itself.

The most important portion of Baudelaire's essay on Wagner is its discussion of the role of myth in modern art and its relationship to primitive thought and to dreams. Although these Wagnerian views were already commonplaces of German Romanticism, and although such earlier French poets as Alfred de Vigny, Gérard de Nerval, and Victor Hugo had extensively resorted to myth and legend in their writings, Wagner's oeuvre played a key role in stimulating the symbolist fascination with nordic and oriental mythology and with occult wisdom—as is borne out by the work of Auguste de Villiers de l'Isle-Adam, Jules Laforgue, or, for that matter, by Eliot's *The Waste Land* (1922). Baudelaire observes that it is precisely Wagner's use of myth that makes his operas so suggestive, so translatable: the situations and images he presents are "universally intelligible" because they are rooted in the "universal heart of man" (*Wagner,* p. 123). Baudelaire here comes close to suggesting a pre-Jungian theory of unconscious archetypes, but he also prefigures the structural anthropology of Claude Lévi-Strauss (himself an ardent Wagnerite) when he describes myth as something innate to the fundamental workings of the human mind, as a phenomenon that bespeaks "the absolute principle and the common origin of all beings" and whose functioning has very much to do with the binary oppositions generated by psychic duality (p. 131). The mythic substratum of *Tannhäuser,* for example, involves "the struggle between the two principles that·have chosen the human heart for their chief battlefield" (p. 126)—heaven and hell, Satan and God, sensuality and spirituality. Although Baudelaire's interpretation of the opera converts it into a baroque Christian allegory, his grounding of Wagnerian myth in psychomachia nonetheless points forward to Lévi-Strauss's definition of myth as an attempt to surmount or mediate irresoluble contradictions by acting them out. According to Lévi-Strauss, it is through this purely structural play on oppositions that myth most resembles music.

The history of French Wagnerism over the next three decades is largely a working out of the intellectual and artistic implications of Baudelaire's 1861 pamphlet. During the 1860s, the number of *wagnéristes* continued to grow. *La revue fantaisiste,* under the direction of Catulle Mendès, attracted younger writers such as Villiers de l'Isle-Adam into the Wagnerian orbit. Mendès' wife (and later Wagner's lover), Judith Gautier, published a number of important articles on the composer in *La presse.* A Wagnerite journal, *L'esprit nouveau,* was founded to promote the radically populist and pacifist message of the master's work. Many of the painters who in the 1870s would come to be known as Impressionists were also drawn to Wagner's music: Pierre-Auguste Renoir and Edouard Manet attended the increasing number of concerts of his works, and both Henri Fantin-Latour and Paul Cézanne painted canvases inspired by *Tannhäuser.* The Franco-Prussian War (1870), however, aroused considerable nationalist revulsion against Wagner's work. He had not helped matters by publishing his truculently chauvinistic *Deutsche Kunst und deutsche Politik* (1868; *German Art and German Politics*), but when he gratuitously crowed over the humiliating French defeat in his satirical pamphlet *Eine Kapitulation* (1873; *A Capitulation*), he lost much of the public support that had been building over the previous decade. Concerts featuring Wagner met with demonstrations, a pattern that persisted through the 1880s as French revanchism against Germany gathered momentum. In 1882, the year the Ligue des Patriotes was founded by Paul Déroulède, a scheduled production of *Lohengrin* at the Opéra was withdrawn for fear of nationalist riots. In 1887, at the height of a grave diplomatic crisis with Germany over Alsace-Lorraine and fueled by public fervor for General Georges Boulanger, the same opera was canceled after one performance. Even as late as 1891, angry demonstrations in front of the Opéra marred the final entry of *Lohengrin* into the official repertoire.

Wagner's operas were clearly a casualty of the broader anti-German sentiment that developed in France after 1870. No longer the idealized motherland of poets, musicians, dreamers, and philosophers that had exerted so powerful a seduction on the French imagination ever since Germaine de Staël's *De l'Allemagne* (1810; *On Germany*), the unified Germany of Bismarck had now come to be perceived as a military monster, enemy and corruptor of traditional French values. French caricaturists easily assimilated Wagner into the new stereotype of the barbaric *boche*—the composer as Hun, spike-helmet and all. French Wagnerites of the 1870s and 1880s accordingly attempted to save the day by dissociating the master's artistic message from his Aryan supremacist politics (significantly, Wagner had imported the term *Aryan* from France, where it had been coined by Joseph-Arthur de Gobineau). Inspired by the world-weary pessimism of Arthur Schopenhauer, French Wagnerism after the Franco-Prussian War and the 1871 Commune increasingly retreated into the ahistorical mists of Teutonic myth or into the exquisite solipsism of decadent aestheticism.

With Wagner's operas effectively banned from the French stage, Parisian audiences of the 1870s and 1880s had to content themselves with orchestral excerpts presented at regular concert programs by Edouard Colonne and Charles Lamoureux. His more devoted disciples made the pilgrimage to Bayreuth, which had opened in 1876 with the première of *The Ring of the Nibelungen*. By the time the master died in 1883, a new generation of Wagnerites, many of them also acolytes at Mallarmé's Tuesday gatherings, had established itself in Paris: the fashionable amalgam of Wagnerism, decadence, and what would soon come to be called symbolism is well captured by Huysmans' *A rebours*. Perhaps breathing a collective sigh of relief at the passing away of Victor Hugo in May 1885, the Parisian literary avant-garde launched an extraordinary number of manifestos and interfactional skirmishes both in the popular press (Jean Moréas' 1886 symbolist manifesto appeared in *Le Figaro*) and in such little magazines as *Lutèce, Le chat noir, Le décadent, La vogue,* and *La revue indépendante*. First published in early 1885, *La revue wagnérienne* added its own *wagnérisme* to this chorus of *décadisme, idéalisme,* and *symbolisme*. Its young founder, Edouard Dujardin, a disciple of Mallarmé and a dandy given to wearing Lohengrin's swan as an insignia on his vests, shared editorial duties with the Polish-born pianist Teodor de Wyzewa and the British germanophile Houston Stewart Chamberlain.

Devoted above all to promulgating Wagner's theoretical writings, *La revue wagnérienne* also functioned as a monthly bulletin covering the various performances of Wagner's work at Bayreuth and throughout Europe. Its pages included book reviews, press clippings, musicological analyses, occasional lithographs by Fantin-Latour and Odilon Redon, and translations of Wagner's essays and libretti. For the most part the magazine avoided politics, although its April 1886 number included an essay by the editor of the *Bayreuther Blätter,* Baron Hans von Wolzogen, that envisaged a Europe under the Gallo-Nordic hegemony of Germany and France, triumphantly united to "free Christianity from the chains of Semitism"—coincidentally or not, Edouard Drumont's anti-Semitic *La France juive (Jewish France)* was published the same year. But the affinity between French Wagnerism and anti-Semitism would not fully surface for another decade: Wyzewa became a vocal anti-Dreyfusard; Chamberlain published his racist *Die Grundlagen des neunzehnten Jahrhunderts (Foundations of the Nineteenth Century)* in 1899, a work that subsequently served as a breviary for the young Adolf Hitler and Joseph Goebbels; and later still, an aged Dujardin, author of a collaborationist encomium to dictators, sentimentally made his pilgrimage to nazified Bayreuth in 1943.

The major impact of *La revue wagnérienne* during its three-year existence from 1885 to 1888 proved, however, to be primarily literary. Dujardin certainly exaggerated in his memoirs when he claimed that Wagner's philosophy and aesthetics were the wellspring of symbolism, but the magazine undoubtedly did a great deal to encourage public perception of the new poetry as a "movement." There was a considerable overlap between Wagnerite and symbolist milieus; in fact, while editing *La revue wagnérienne* Dujardin was simultaneously running the symbolist *Revue indépendante* from the same office, often drawing on the same contributors for both magazines. For example, *La revue wagnérienne's* special tribute to Wagner in January 1886 included poems by Mallarmé, Paul Verlaine, René Ghil, Stuart Merrill, and Charles Morice. An indication of the journal's eclecticism is Wyzewa's June 1886 essay, "Littérature wagnérienne" ("Wagnerian Literature"), which lumps together such diverse writers as Zola, Huysmans, Paul Bourget, Laforgue, Verlaine, Villiers de l'Isle-Adam, and Mallarmé, all of whom seem to share little more than a vague Schopenhaueran pessimism and a Hegelian longing for spiritual redemption through art. Much of the criticism featured in *La revue wagnérienne* reads today like modish mush: heavily laced with Germanic majuscules, the essays of Dujardin, Wyzewa, and Chamberlain gesture toward metaphysical concepts only to lose themselves in a purple fog of *Götterdämmerung* prose. In the process, however, they generated something akin to "theory," that is, a metalanguage that enabled contemporary poetry to reflect upon itself philosophically and thus to constitute itself into a self-consciously avant-garde program for the transformation of all the arts.

Mallarmé's "Richard Wagner, rêverie d'un poète français" ("Richard Wagner: A French Poet's Reverie"), published in the August 1885 issue of the magazine, remains the most significant encounter between Wagnerism and symbolism. Mallarmé's essay, which he described in a letter as "half article, half prose poem," is a typically sibylline performance. Except for attending one of Lamoureux's concerts with Dujardin, he had heard little of Wagner's music and seen none of his operas—in short, it was more the *idea* of Wagner that inspired his reverie rather than any specific work. Having himself experimented with dramatic form in such works as "Hérodiade" (1864), "Igitur" (1869), and *L'après-midi d'un faune* (1876; *The Afternoon of a Faun*), Mallarmé was obviously fascinated by the Wagnerian dream of a total spectacle fusing music, dance, and poetry. Wagner's musical dramas, Mallarmé observes, represent a decisive break with the "authoritarian and naïve concept" of realism or verisimilitude in theater. Rather than imposing the "gross fiction" of plot and character on the spectator, Wagner's theater of suggestion instead encouraged the viewer to create the events on stage by his own projective imagination. By conjoining drama and music, Wagner had managed, in Mallarmé's terms, to "empty" the stage, to "abstract" it, to render it a "strictly allegorical" space in which the mind could mirror itself at play. He had thereby returned theater to its most archaic beginnings in ritual and myth: by distancing and depersonalizing its characters into mental deities "clothed in the invisible folds of a tissue of chords," he conveyed the hieratic acting out of the cosmic "secret of origins" (*Oeuvres complètes,* p. 544).

Intrigued though he was by Wagner's deployment of myth and legend, Mallarmé nonetheless criticized him for being at once too anachronistic and too nationalistic in his use of this material. The French, Mallarmé notes, being "more strictly imaginative and abstract" than Wagner's German audiences, are little inclined to indulge in "enormous and crude anecdotes" concerning their collective past. If theater is indeed to be "the rite of the acts of Civilization," it must also be able to find its myths in modernity—Mallarmé puckishly wonders in a footnote whether it would be possible to imagine Brunhild at a Universal Exposition or how Siegfried would go about handling contemporary transfers of political power. Noting that the 19th century had dissolved myths in order to reforge them philosophically, Mallarmé argues that the theater now demands not familiar or fixed myths, but rather a poetico-philosophic fable or symbol that would be "virgin of everything," devoid of "any known place, time or person," a supreme fiction "inscribed on the page of the heavens." Its hero, at once contemporary and eternal, would lack even the medieval specificity of Wagner's supermen; he would be "a type with no prior denomination," a "spiritual fact," a "saint of saints, but mental"—a kind of Hamletic knight of the absolute whom Mallarmé calls "La Figure que Nul n'est" (*Oeuvres,* p. 545)—the Figure of Nothing (or Nobody) that is.

Mallarmé never achieved the ideal drama envisaged in his reverie on Wagner, although elements of it are at work in his late *Un coup de dés* (1897; *A Dice-Throw*) and in his fragmentary notes toward the utopian Book ("Le Livre") that he hoped would at last provide "the Orphic explication of the world." Wagner's *Gesamtkunstwerk* had pointed the way to the Oeuvre of the future, but had failed to pursue its aesthetic and philosophical implications to their very limit. As such, it provided only a temporary way station, a comforting shelter against "the menacing summit of the absolute" whose blankness no musician could ever scale. Poets perhaps had a better chance at achieving this ultimate opera of silence, or at least so Mallarmé was almost convinced. Wagner had wedded music to poetry but had done so only by juxtaposition, by superadding one to the other in a "harmonious compromise" that did not totally transform either. True poetry, by contrast, needed no musical accompaniment because music already inhered in it as its essence—hence Mallarmé's celebrated (and perhaps apocryphal) retort to Claude Debussy when the latter asked him permission to set *L'après-midi d'un faune* to music: "But I thought I had already done that!" Despite the musical metaphors that Mallarmé so subtly deployed throughout his poetry and criticism, the music he was after had finally very little to do with what he took to be its clangorous Wagnerian embodiment. It was instead to be discovered in the silent, sacred music of St. Cecilia, a music purely of and for the mind, an act of mute symphony such as occurs when eye and inner ear perform their solitary apperceptions within the concert of the written page.

Mallarmé's highly intellectualized conception of music reaches back to the Pythagorean doctrine of music as a mathematical microcosm of macrocosmic order—music as pure grammar. But he equally reverts to the Platonic tradition of viewing music primarily in terms of its emotional or physiological effect on the listener—music as a branch of rhetoric. Much of the symbolist discourse about poetry as music wavers between these two poles. Ghil's doctrine of "verbal instrumentation" provides perhaps the most extreme example of the rhetorical orientation toward musical effect—phonemes conceived as analogous in timbre to musical instruments, each instrument in turn provoking a specific state of mind or mood. Verlaine's celebrated injunction to poets in his 1884 "Art poétique" (in *Jadis et naguère; Once and Yesterday*)—"De la musique avant toute chose" ("Music before all else")—advocates the same elaborate use of assonance, alliteration, rich rhymes, and paronomasia found in much French symbolist poetry of the 1880s and 1890s. This sustained attention to the purely acoustic dimensions of the signifier distinguishes symbolism, *grosso modo,* from French Romantic or Parnassian poetry, both of which tended to be more oriented to the visual or plastic arts. In its recourse to lush and often contrived musical effects, symbolism was nonetheless attempting to reclaim poetry's oral origins in spells, incantations, riddles, and charms—all techniques of placing the reader/listener in a trancelike condition of heightened suggestibility, not unlike the experiments in hypnosis that Jean-Martin Charcot was undertaking at the Salpêtrière hospital during these same years.

The Symbolist concept of music as pure grammar in turn found its most persuasive formulation in the writings of Schopenhauer, prominently featured in the pages of *La revue wagnérienne.* According to Schopenhauer, music was not, like all the other arts, merely the mimetic reflection of appearances, but rather the direct expression of the Will (or Idea), which is objectified in these appearances; whereas the other arts merely convey the shadows of phenomenal reality, music reveals the noumenal essence of the real. If, as Walter Pater claimed, all arts aspired to the condition of music, it was because music exemplified a purely abstract, nonfigurative, nonrepresentational art, an autotelic event whose very form *was* its content. This, at any rate, was how Mallarmé took music; indeed, he reproached Wagner for not being musical *enough,* for being still too intent on conveying a programmatic "content" or "message." Mallarmé's final opus, *Un coup de dés,* comes closest to realizing this dream of absolute music. Its fleeting words and phrases typographically arranged on the page like a musical score punctuated by blanks and rests, the poem functions both spatially and temporally, vertically and horizontally. Read (or heard) sequentially, the text conveys something of the evanescence of a melodic line by Debussy as it follows the prismatic intermittences of a train of thought. Seized visually, the page in turn functions as a single chord or constellation, imploding into the unison of its own stillness.

Music and letters, Mallarmé insisted, were the alternate faces of the same coin of the Idea: both served as metaphors and translations for each other. Starting with Dujardin and Wyzewa, however, a number of literary historians have attempted to draw more precise causal connections between certain features of Wagner's music and the development of certain modern literary forms and genres. Dujardin, for example, links Wagner's free, open-ended handling of the musical phrase to the emergence of *vers libre* (free verse) during the 1880s (*Mallarmé par un des siens* [*Mallarmé, by One of His*], p. 173). The analogy between Wagner's "endless melody" and the dissolution of conventional metrical measure is suggestive, but it is enough to look at the internal history of the French alexandrine over the course of the 19th century (or, for that matter, at Rimbaud's earlier experiments in free verse or at Laforgue's 1886 translations of Whitman) to see how little this phenomenon ultimately owes to Wagner's music. The same holds true for Dujardin's claims concerning the Wagnerian influence on the development of the French prose poem. Although *La revue wagnérienne* certainly featured a great deal of writing that might be termed prose poetry (notably Huysmans' sadomasochistic reverie on Wagnerian heroines), the genre can hardly be said to have arisen out of the Wagnerian *Gesamtkunstwerk,* dating back as it does to early French Romanticism. Dujardin is on slightly firmer ground when correlating Wagner's use of the leitmotif to the introduction of interior monologue into narrative prose. Dujardin's own novel, *Les lauriers sont coupés* (1888; *We'll to the Woods No More*), is a Wagnerian experiment in rendering the obsessional recurrence of certain motifs within the free associations of a wandering consciousness. James Joyce read *Les lauriers sont coupés* as a young man and later handsomely honored Dujardin as the discoverer of the stream of consciousness technique that would find its finest development in *Ulysses* (1922).

More than the novel or poetry, however, it was the French fin-de-siècle theater that felt the impact of Wagner's music dramas. The festivals at Bayreuth, visited by so many French pilgrims, contributed to a profound transformation of the audience's relation to the stage. Unlike the French theaters, which traditionally kept the houselights on during the entire performance (thus effectively maintaining the audience itself as part of the spectacle), Bayreuth plunged its public into a community of shared darkness. With all attention reverently directed at the illuminated stage, the entire aesthetic experience of drama thus took on the mystical quality of a religious event—the theater as temple, the audience as anonymous officiants at a redemptive rite. This Wagnerian sacralization of the stage exercised a considerable influence on the non-naturalistic experimental theater of the 1880s and 1890s, particularly on the work of the director Aurélien-Marie Lugné-Poe, who founded the Théâtre de l'Oeuvre in 1893. Lugné-Poe's 1893 productions of Maurice Maeterlinck's *Pelléas et Mélisande* (1892) and of the works of Henrik Ibsen and August Strindberg introduced a new minimalist aesthetic to the French stage—decor stripped down to its bare essentials, emphasis on cryptic lighting effects, actors transformed into mere shadows (or symbols) dispersed across dreamscapes. Lugné-Poe's mise-en-scène of Alfred Jarry's *Ubu roi* (1896; *Ubu Rex*) is at once the consummation and liquidation of this symbolist theater, a parodic rite of passage from the legacy of Wagnerism to modernism. Upon attending its première in Paris, William Butler Yeats remarked, "After us the Savage God."

See also 1827 (December), 1853, 1885 (June), 1886, 1889, 1898, 1913.

Bibliography: Charles Baudelaire, *Richard Wagner and Tannhäuser in Paris,* in *The Painter of Modern Life and Other Essays,* ed. and trans. Jonathan Mayne (London: Phaidon, 1966). Elaine Brody, *Paris: The Musical Kaleidoscope, 1870–1925* (New York: Braziller,

1987). Peter Burbridge and Richard Sutton, eds., *The Wagner Companion* (New York: Cambridge University Press, 1979). Edouard Dujardin, "La revue wagnérienne," in *Mallarmé par un des siens* (Paris: Albert Messein, 1936). Raymond Furness, *Wagner and Literature* (New York: St. Martin's, 1982). Léon Guichard, *La musique et les lettres en France au temps du wagnérisme* (Paris: Presses Universitaires de France, 1963). Martine Kahane and Nicole Wild, eds., *Wagner et la France* (Paris: Herscher, 1983). David Large and William Weber, *Wagnerism in European Culture and Politics* (Ithaca: Cornell University Press, 1984). Stéphane Mallarmé, "Richard Wagner, rêverie d'un poète français," in *Oeuvres complètes*, ed. Henri Mondor and Georges Jean-Aubry (Paris: Gallimard, 1945).

Richard Sieburth

1885, *June*

Victor Hugo Is Buried; Stéphane Mallarmé Writes "Crise de vers"

The Liberation of Verse

On 1 June 1885, after a wild nightlong vigil, France bade farewell to Victor Hugo. It was, writes Roger Shattuck, "a wake and a funeral such as Paris had never staged even for royalty . . . The endless procession across Paris . . . included several brass bands, every political and literary figure of the day, speeches, numerous deaths in the press of the crowd, and final entombment in the Panthéon. The church had to be especially unconsecrated for the occasion. By this orgiastic ceremony France unburdened itself of a man, a literary movement, and a century" (*Banquet Years*, pp. 4–5).

In response to the hyperbolic passing of France's most hyperbolic author, Stéphane Mallarmé described his own sense of unburdenment in a short but quietly revolutionary essay titled "Crise de vers" ("Crisis of Verse"), first published in 1886 as an "Avant-dire" ("Preface") to René Ghil's *Traité du verbe* (*Treatise on the Word*). Literature, Mallarmé asserts, is undergoing a crisis; even the daily newspapers are talking about it. So this century will end, like the last one, with an upheaval, but this time it is occurring far from the public square.

> A French reader, his habits interrupted by the death of Victor Hugo, can only feel disconcerted. Hugo, in his mysterious task, boiled all of prose, philosophy, eloquence, history down to verse, and, since he *was* verse, personally, he confiscated from anyone who thinks, discourses, or narrates almost the right to speak. A monument in the desert, far away with silence; thus, in a crypt lay the divinity of a majestic unconscious idea: that the form called verse is simply literature itself; that there is verse as soon as there is style. Verse, I think, had been respectfully waiting for the giant who had identified it with his firm, tenacious blacksmith's hand to depart, in order to, itself, sunder.
> (*Oeuvres complètes*, pp. 360–361)

One of the things Mallarmé is talking about in these lines is evidently his own prose style: after the death of Hugo, Mallarmé developed an unprecedented genre of complexly sundered and soldered prose that he called the "critical poem." But Mallarmé is also talking about a subject that was hot enough to interest the press: the invention of "free verse." Why was the "liberation" of verse a sign of literary crisis?

French prosody, strictly and painstakingly codified by François de Malherbe in the early 17th century, had changed little from the classical period until the Romantics. The basic unit of verse was the alexandrine, a twelve-syllable line divided into two halves (the hemistiches) by a pause (the caesura). In the most classical alexandrine, the hemistiches are further subdivided, so that the line breaks down into four rhythmic sections. This quadripartite line is called a tetrameter. Victor Hugo was considered revolutionary in his day for using a three-part alexandrine (the trimeter). Indeed, the whole battle of *Hernani,* his 1830 drama, could be said to have been fought over the placement of the caesura.

Against the background of innovations no more radical than the displacement of a pause from its normal place, the notion that a poem could be written in irregular lines of differing lengths was quite a disruption of the French reader's habits. Indeed, when asked in 1894 to lecture at Oxford and Cambridge on the state of French literature, Mallarmé returned to the newsworthiness of free verse with undiminished aplomb:

> I do indeed bring news. The most surprising news. Such a case has never been seen.
>
> Verse has been tampered with [*On a touché au vers*].
>
> Governments change: prosody always remains intact: whether because during revolutions no one notices it or because the coup does not impose itself with the opinion that such a dogma can change.
>
> It is fitting to speak about it, like an invited traveler who breathlessly testifies to an accident known and in pursuit: for the reason that verse is everything; once one writes. Style, versification, once there is cadence, and that is why any prose by a sumptuous writer, ornamental rather than functionally haphazard, counts as a sundered verse, playing with its timbres and its dissimulated rhymes: according to a more complex thyrsus. The very flowering of what was once called the *prose poem.*   (*Oeuvres,* pp. 643–644)

French poetry had thus moved a long way not only from classical prosody but even from the Parnassian poetics codified as recently as 1872 by Théodore de Banville in his *Petit traité de poésie française* (*Short Treatise on French Poetry*). In fact Banville had written: "Can there be poems in prose? No, there cannot, despite Fénelon's *Télémaque* [1699; *Telemachus*], Baudelaire's admirable *Petits poèmes en prose* [1869; *Little Poems in Prose*], and Aloysius Bertrand's *Gaspard de la nuit* [1842; *Gaspard of the Night*]; for it is impossible to imagine a prose, however perfect, to which one could not, with a superhuman effort, add or subtract anything. It is thus always in process, and never the finished product, the ποίημα (*Petit traité,* pp. 6–7). Yet Mallarmé was able both to imagine such a prose and to institute a revolutionary practice not only of writing but also of reading. For in Mallarmé, the finished product *is* an interminable process. Banville asserted that there was no such thing as the prose poem; Mallarmé went so far as to assert that "there is no such thing as prose" (*Oeuvres*, p. 867).

Mallarmé's critical theory brings to Western letters a productive hypersensitivity to the functioning of language as such rather than as a mere equivalent for an extralinguistic meaning. In his elaboration of a critique both of the emotional outpourings of the Romantics (poetry as the expression of a self) and of the documentary novels of the naturalists (writing as the scientific representation of social reality), Mallarmé stressed the autonomy and materiality of writing itself: "Literature exists in exception to everything" (*Oeuvres*, p. 646). It is not that language does not refer ("suggest," or "allude," as he puts it), but that there is something about language that makes it more like a prism than like a window. As soon as one writes, one disappears behind the initiatives that words themselves begin to take.

While referring to the free verse experiments of poets such as Gustave Kahn and Jules Laforgue, Mallarmé himself continued to write regular (though extremely difficult) sonnets mostly in classical alexandrines. The formal radicality of his writing lies in its syntax, whether in verse or prose, not in the number of syllables in a line. It is just that the discovery of free verse revealed something fundamental about linguistic materiality, something about language as a workable material with sonorous, semantic, syntactic, and spatial properties that transcend the one-to-one correspondence with a meaning, something to which poetry, in fact, had always pointed. Mallarmé's one monumental experiment in something like free verse goes so far beyond the irregular meters of other poets that it inaugurates a whole new genre. *Un coup de dés* (1897; *A Dice-Throw*) is a typographic symphony in which the titular sentence is spread out over several pages in huge letters, while intricate subordinate clauses in various styles of smaller type cluster in spatially significant groups around it. With this use of space—of page and print as design elements—Mallarmé initiated a whole tradition of concrete poetry in France. But it is in his use of "blanks" that Mallarmé was most innovative and radical.

Already in his contributions to the 1866 *Le Parnasse contemporain*, Mallarmé had begun to write about the writing process in material terms. While other Parnassian poets celebrated the statuesque whiteness of women's bodies, Mallarmé spoke of the whiteness of the yet-unwritten page. Playing on the dual meaning of *blanc*—both "white" and "blank"—Mallarmé created a scintillation between presence and absence, between paper as material whiteness and paper as mere spacing. In Mallarmé's writing, the blank spaces are just as significant as the words. Interestingly, despite this process of radical depersonalization and abstraction, the traditional gender roles remain unchanged in his work. The poet is still male, the text female. Cutting the pages of a new book is described as rape; writing covers the white page like the veils of a dancer. It is just that instead of an ultimate nudity Mallarmé's textual unveiling reveals "the ultimate veil that always remains" (*Oeuvres*, p. 307), the veil of writing itself.

The experience of reading a Mallarmé text can be disconcerting for a reader trained to seek a message "behind" or "beneath" the text. Mallarmé does not present a meaning but institutes a process. Rather than figure out what the poet meant, the reader must figure out what the language is doing. In other words, the reader learns to see the *search* for meaning as illuminating and meaningful in itself. Just as Mallarmé transformed the nontransparency of writing into the very subject of his writing, his texts can teach their readers to consider the struggle with ambiguity and obscurity not as an *obstacle* to understanding but as the very *experience* of understanding—of understanding as interminable process.

See also 1627, 1866.

Bibliography: Théodore de Banville, *Petit traité de poésie française* (Paris: Charpentier, 1872). Jacques Derrida, "The Double Session," in *Dissemination,* trans. Barbara Johnson (Chicago: University of Chicago Press, 1981). Barbara Johnson, *Défigurations du langage poétique* (Paris: Flammarion, 1979). Johnson, "Les Fleurs du Mal Armé: Some Reflections on Intertextuality," in *A World of Difference* (Baltimore: Johns Hopkins University Press, 1987). Julia Kristeva, *La révolution du langage poétique* (Paris: Seuil, 1974). Stéphane Mallarmé, *Oeuvres complètes,* ed. Henri Mondor and Georges Jean-Aubry (Paris: Gallimard, 1945). Roger Shattuck, *The Banquet Years* (New York: Vintage, 1955).

Barbara Johnson

✑ 1886

Auguste de Villiers de l'Isle-Adam Publishes His Last Novel, *L'Eve future*

The Phantom's Voice

Many 19th-century authors were preoccupied with explaining or dramatizing the enigmatic workings of the mind. Numerous novels and tales dealing with spiritualism, ghostly apparitions, hallucinations, and other altered states of awareness demonstrate this concern with the unconscious and its manifestations. Literary scholars have frequently sought to analyze such occurrences through reference to the writings of Sigmund Freud. The works of the French psychoanalysts Nicolas Abraham and Maria Torok, however, offer a new perspective from which to consider and interpret them.

According to Freud, certain strange, seemingly nonsensical utterances and acts can be attributed to the "return of the repressed," to the reappearance, in disguised form, of an event or fantasy an individual has unknowingly removed from consciousness because of its disturbing nature. The analytic process consists in recounting one's past experiences and thoughts so that the disturbing event or fantasy can be brought from hiding and consciously confronted. Its power to disrupt the psyche can thereby be dissolved. When numbers of their patients did not respond to this therapeutic process, Abraham and Torok developed the theory of the phantom to explain instances of enigmatic utterances and behavior beyond the reach of the Freudian model of repression. Hypothesizing that their patients' symptoms were not caused by what they themselves had repressed, but must be related to something that someone else had concealed, the analysts concluded that an individual can keep secret a disturbing, shameful event or fantasy and then silently transmit it, through cryptic language or behavior, to someone else. The speech and behavior of the individual who is unknowingly hosting this "phantom" will appear incongruous, inexplicable, or hallucinatory because these phenomena have in fact originated with another person. The patient becomes a kind of ventriloquist's dummy, an unwitting medium through whom someone else's disembodied voice "speaks."

Abraham and Torok use this image of the disembodied voice in a metaphorical sense to underscore the linguistic nature of the symptoms produced by a phantom. Whether they are verbal tics or lexical patterns, physical illnesses, obsessive behavior, or phobias, these symptoms can be "translated" and read as words or lexical entities that tacitly "voice" a secret belonging to someone else. Frequently the voice belongs to someone in the same family; the phantom can in fact infiltrate entire family lines and be passed down through successive generations. For this reason it can open to new interpretation such mainstays of gothic and fantastic literature as the notions of demonic possession and the haunted house.

Auguste de Villiers de l'Isle-Adam (1838–1889) was one of the principal contributors to the French symbolist movement during the second half of the 19th century. An admirer of Charles Baudelaire and a close friend of Stéphane Mallarmé, Villiers's works include poems, plays, short stories, and two novels. Most of these works link the themes of voice reproduction and transmission with haunting, motifs of possession, the return of the dead, and disembodied spirits. Thus Villiers's oeuvre may be viewed as a systematic and versatile exploration of the various aspects and incarnations of the phantom. *L'intersigne* (1867; *Intersignum*), the earliest and most accomplished of the *Contes cruels* (1883; *Sardonic Tales*), contains the fullest exposition of a phantom to be found in his short stories. It addresses not only the manner in which a phantom's haunting presence is given voice, but also where the phantom originates and how it may be transmitted.

The phantom structure in *L'intersigne* is elaborated within a mystical, spiritualist framework. At a gathering of friends one evening, the baron Xavier de la V***, a young man prone to attacks of anxiety for which he has sought solace through spiritualist séances, tells of his visit to an old family friend, the priest Maucombe, now dead. This account, for which Xavier offers no commentary, in fact originates with Maucombe. During Xavier's visit, Maucombe cryptically transmitted to him a secret too shameful to utter, undoubtedly the cause of Xavier's mental anguish: he, Maucombe, is Xavier's real father. This secret becomes apparent to the reader from the events and conversations Xavier recounts, such as Maucombe's emphasis on the special "kinship" the two men share, his and his house's "diseased" and "decayed" state, his wish to cure Xavier, and his insistence that the young man wear his (Maucombe's) cloak on the journey home.

Xavier remains unaware both of his true kinship with Maucombe and of Maucombe's desire that Xavier take as his own the disease shrouding the priest's "house," or family. When the priest dies shortly after Xavier's departure, the possibility of explicit communication is permanently foreclosed, and Xavier's fate is determined. He will henceforth be the unwitting bearer of Maucombe's secret, the medium of his father's unspeakable message, and thus voice the words of someone else, all the while deaf to their content and unable to comment upon them. Although Xavier's attendance at spiritualist séances evokes the idea of communication with the beyond, the beyond in his case is not some supernatural, otherworldly sphere, but something beyond Xavier's comprehension.

The series of tales written after *L'intersigne* testifies to Villiers's continuing preoccupation with the disembodied voice and the haunting effects of the phantom. His focus shifts, however, from an overall elaboration of the phantom structure to an examination of its various incarnations and properties. *Véra* (1874), for example, demonstrates that the voice can be used to convoke and then exorcise a phantom. After locking in the family mausoleum the remains of his deceased wife, Véra, Count d'Athol returns home, where memories of his beloved gradually overwhelm him. Sensing that Véra is nearby, he begins to read aloud from his wife's favorite book. As he reads, Véra's presence grows more tangible until Athol finally hears her speak his name and realizes at that moment that "they were in reality *but one single being*" (*Sardonic Tales*, p. 21). Athol's voice is thus both the instrument that convokes a disembodied utterance and the medium through which this utterance is voiced. It is also the tool that puts the phantom permanently to rest; for, moments after hearing Véra's voice, Athol emerges from his stupor and exclaims, "You, you are dead!" With these words, the specter vanishes. In the framework of an apparently mystical, fantastic tale, Villiers demonstrates the curative power of speech to conjure a haunting presence and to bury it forever. Ten years before the publication of Freud's first major essay, Villiers's mystical allegory anticipates what the psychoanalyst would later call a "talking cure."

Finding a cure for those haunted by others' voices is the theme of one of Villiers's most ironic stories, *Le traitement du docteur Tristan* (1877; *Doctor Tristan's Treatment*). The doctor has invented a treatment for patients troubled by various noises in the ear, including disembodied voices such as those suffered by Joan of Arc. His cure consists in rupturing the eardrum by repeating words such as *humanity, generosity,* and *faith* and then passing an electric current through the ear canal. A scathing criticism of the excesses of modern science and a frightening premonition of electroshock therapy, the tale is also a corollary to *Véra.* However perverse the doctor's treatment, it effectively shifts the phenomenon of hearing voices and troubling sounds from the mystical to the psychotherapeutic arena. Hearing disembodied voices is a sign of "troubles in the head," of some mental disorder susceptible to cure.

In *L'inconnue* (1876; *The Unknown* [*Woman*]) Villiers pursues the link between hearing voices, hiding secrets, and mental affliction, this time in relation to deafness. Count Félicien falls in love with a mysterious woman at the farewell performance of a famous soprano. The unknown woman refuses Félicien's offer of marriage, explaining that she is deaf. Félicien, she says, will ultimately grow impatient with this condition, which gives her the ability to escape the intellectual deafness so common to others and to "hear" the hidden meaning in people's words by reading their faces and attitudes. Tormented by the idea of hearing the painful thoughts Félicien will inevitably feel toward her but will dare not utter, she bids him adieu and vanishes. By reversing the traditional ideas of hearing and deafness, Villiers dramatizes the particularity of the phantom structure in which an unspeakable message is transmitted and "heard" without being pronounced. He also firmly links a state of mental anguish with the transmission and reception of something unutterable. The story's setting, a performance of Bellini's opera *Norma,* provides an artful objectification of the phantom configuration while linking its origin to the concealment of a secret; for in singing the role of Norma, the soprano gives voice to the words of someone else whose drama involves keeping secret an illicit love affair.

One of Villiers's most amusing tales, *Le secret de l'ancienne musique* (1878; *The Secret of the Old Music*), dramatizes the idea that a phantom can be transmitted through successive generations. The orchestra of the National Academy of Music needs an antique military instrument to play an exceptionally challenging piece. A retired professor of the Old Music, who alone possesses the secret of this instrument, undertakes to play the part that consists of a "vast *crescendo* of silences" (*Sardonic Tales,* p. 124). The professor's mute performance, to which the orchestra "listens" admiringly, suggests that secret knowledge can indeed be transmitted silently. The possibility that such a secret can pass from generation to generation is illustrated at the story's end when the professor, protesting the difficulty of the piece, falls into the monstrous bowels of the bass drum and vanishes "like an apparition" (p. 125), carrying with him the secret of the Old Music. Entombed in the beating heart of this corps of young musicians, the professor and his secret become the perfect image of a phantom lodged in another's body. We are left to wonder what kind of haunting performances the presence of this unspoken secret will henceforth inspire in the orchestra.

To be haunted is precisely what the main character of *Le désir d'être un homme* (1882; *The Desire to Be a Man*) seeks. An actor, tired of speaking others' words and feigning their emotions, starts setting fires in the hope that his victims' ghosts will haunt him and bring him true feelings of remorse. Frustrated at still not feeling true emotion, he begs for just one ghost to appear, "not realizing that he was himself what he sought" (p. 155; translation modified). The story's last sentence makes clear that the actor (suggestively named Esprit, "Spirit") is already possessed, inhabited by someone else's spirit. Villiers's insight here is to portray an actor, who by definition consciously incarnates other characters and gives voice to their words, as the unwitting recipient of a phantom.

Villiers's most complex exploration of the phantom and the disembodied voice is found in *L'Eve future* (*Tomorrow's Eve*), his novel about the creation of a robot that speaks. Inspired by the technological innovations emerging in Europe and America in the late 19th century, this pioneering contribution to the nascent genre of science fiction was begun in 1877, the year after Alexander Graham Bell's invention of the telephone, and was published in 1886, three years before Villiers's death. The novel takes place in the Menlo Park, New Jersey, laboratory of Thomas Alva Edison, inventor of the phonograph, the incandescent light bulb, and the hearing aid. An old acquaintance, Lord Ewald, comes to bid Edison farewell before committing suicide. Ewald is in love with a beautiful singer, Alicia Clary, but is repulsed by the disparity between her exquisite body and her vulgar, infantile intellect. Her personality, Ewald explains in dismay, is "absolutely FOREIGN" to her body. She is a "living hybrid" (*Tomorrow's Eve,* p. 36), a "child subject to influence from every direction," whose "words seem out of place in her mouth" (pp. 30, 31). Her singing, moreover, is that of a mere "performer," entirely "mechanical" in nature and reminiscent of the utterances of "monkeys" and "puppets" (pp. 43, 41). It is hard not to hear in these and numerous similar comments the description of a woman haunted by a phantom, inhabited by the disembodied voice of someone else speaking through her like a ventriloquist. Villiers uses the theme of the body/soul duality, a major preoccupation of the Romantics and of authors of gothic and fantastic literature (such as Mary Shelley's 1818 *Frankenstein*) to elaborate this psychic configuration. At the same time, he expands upon the possibility, implied at the end of *Le secret de l'ancienne musique,* that a phantom may be transmitted to others. For it is not Alicia but Ewald who speaks of "poisoned existence," of feeling "possessed," and of being unable to free himself from Alicia except by suicide. And it is Ewald, not Alicia, whom Edison proposes to "cure."

Edison invites Ewald into his underground laboratory and unveils the cure he has in mind: Hadaly, a mechanical woman animated by electric currents passing through a complex of interlaced wires resembling nervous and circulatory systems. Edison proposes to transfer Alicia Clary's physical image onto Hadaly's exterior while providing the robot with an intellect to match Clary's magnificent body. The source of this intellect will reside in two golden phonographs, forming Hadaly's lungs, containing recorded words of the greatest poets, metaphysicians, and novelists of the century.

The formidable intellect Edison intends to give Hadaly thus consists of others' disembodied words, which will be voiced through her as a puppeteer's words are mouthed by a puppet. Edison's creation is an objectification of Alicia Clary's psychic structure. Using the phonograph, which separates voice from body, Edison duplicates in tangible form the phantom that haunts and speaks like a ventriloquist through Alicia Clary. In making Alicia's phantom concrete, the robot will bring its presence into the open and thereby dissolve its haunting influence over Ewald.

L'Eve future brings together and amplifies the different aspects of the phantom dramatized in Villiers's short stories. It explores more fully the idea that a disembodied voice may speak through someone else (*L'intersigne*). It also elaborates on the possibilities of exorcising a phantom (*Véra*), of linking disembodied voices with mental disorder (*Le traitement du docteur Tristan*), of receiving or "hearing" an unspoken message (*L'inconnue*), of passing such a message through several generations (*Le secret de l'ancienne musique*), and of physically incarnating someone else and giving voice to his or her words (*Le désir d'être un homme*). Villiers's innovation in *L'Eve future* is to combine the mystical, gothic, and symbolist motifs of his short stories in a scientific setting to reflect upon the domain of the psyche. Uncannily anticipating some of the theories and techniques of the soon-to-be invented science of psychoanalysis, Villiers's texts ask in various ways: what mental or psychic conditions might lead someone's voice to speak through someone else? and what would it mean to "cure" someone inhabited or possessed by such a disembodied voice? In addressing these questions, Villiers's works expand upon the traditional definitions of gothic, fantastic, symbolist, and science fiction literature and suggest a new perspective from which to analyze the works of E. T. A. Hoffmann, Théophile Gautier, Edgar Allan Poe, Nathaniel Hawthorne, and Jules Verne.

See also 1837, 1885 (February), 1889.

Bibliography: Nicolas Abraham and Maria Torok, "Notes on the Phantom: A Complement to Freud's Metapsychology," trans. Nicholas Rand, *Critical Inquiry,* 13 (Winter 1987), 287–292. Abraham and Torok, "A Poetics of Psychoanalysis: The Lost Object-Me," trans. Nicholas Rand, *SubStance,* 43 (1984), 3–18. William T. Conroy, Jr., *Villiers de l'Isle-Adam* (Boston: Twayne, 1978). Philippe Auguste Mathias de Villiers de L'Isle-Adam, *Contes cruels* and *L'Eve future,* in *Oeuvres complètes,* ed. Alan Raitt, P.-G. Castex, and J. M. Bellefroid, vol. 1 (Paris: Gallimard, 1986). Villiers, *Sardonic Tales,* trans. Hamish Miles (New York: Knopf, 1927; quotations reprinted and modified with permission from Alfred A. Knopf, Inc.). Villiers, *Tomorrow's Eve,* trans. Robert Martin Adams (Urbana: University of Illinois Press, 1982).

Esther Rashkin

ॐ **1889**

The Third Republic Celebrates the Centenary of the French Revolution

Commemoration and the Themes of Revolution

Eighteen eighty-nine: the year of Auguste de Villiers de l'Isle-Adam's death was ironically the year when France loudly celebrated the centenary of the French Revolution. Not everyone appreciated Villiers's sarcasm or shared his love-hate for science and his distaste for what the Revolution had brought about. In 1889 the apotheosis of Victor Hugo—high priest of republican virtues, whose remains an entire population solemnly accompanied to the Panthéon—was still a fresh memory. Hugo's life (1802–1885) and work almost literally filled the century, and it was the century he had come to embody that was now being celebrated.

The festive commemoration of the fall of the Bastille was indeed meant to glorify the 19th century—a century that began under the shadow of the Revolution and had repeatedly reactivated revolutionary dreams and fervor, although it had also been a century of historical discontinuities, counterrevolution, and repression. But in 1889 the régime in power could claim that it was the heir to the principles of 1789.

The Universal Exposition and the Eiffel Tower, 1889's answer to the razed Bastille, monumentalized the centenary. There was a pervasive sense of the enormous: allegorical ceremonies, huge exhibits, stupendous illuminations, solemn inaugurations (for instance, the great amphitheater of the Sorbonne), massive parades. On 18 August there was a parade of 15,200 mayors of metropolitan France and overseas territories. The centenary also consecrated the preeminence of Paris, heart and capital of the nation.

Neither France nor Paris, however, was univocal, as is attested by the great variety of books published in and around 1889: Henri Bergson's *Essai sur les données immédiates de la conscience* (1888; *Time and Free Will*), Maurice Barrès' *Un homme libre* (1889; *A Free Man*), Paul Bourget's *Le disciple* (1889), Jules Lemaître's *Révoltée* (1889; *Rebellious*), Ernest Renan's *L'avenir de la science* (1890; *The Future of Science*), Paul Verlaine's *Parallèlement* (1890). It was the period of André Antoine's Théâtre Libre, of Victorien Sardou's facile plays, of Zola's mounting glory. Stéphane Mallarmé's *mardis* (Tuesdays) were already legendary. The intellectual scene was surely heterogeneous. In the same year the French state voted to publish a national edition of Jules Michelet's *Histoire de la Révolution française* (1847–1853). Michelet, by then dead for some fifteen years, was clearly considered, along with Hugo, one of the patriarchs of the Third Republic.

During the last three decades of the 19th century the ideology of the Third Republic, which lasted until the French defeat of 1940, stood on the pillars of anticlericalism, combative optimism, financial opportunism, parliamentary factionalizing, and patriotic poses often inspired by the *revanchard* spirit that had become endemic after the defeat of 1870. The lay schoolmaster, *l'instituteur,* was its unsung hero, and the "intellectual" (the word came into its own at the time) its political consciousness and model leader. Albert Thibaudet in fact later defined it as "la république des professeurs."

This dominant ideology did not, however, go unchallenged. Bourget's *Le disciple,* a frontal attack on positivism, scientism, and the nefarious prestige of professors, coincided with the euphoric celebrations of the centenary. Such attacks, of course, were not new. As early as the 1840s, various pamphlets and books, largely encouraged by the Catholic press, had denounced the pernicious influence of professors on France's youth. The last two decades of the 19th century witnessed a major offensive against the intellectual establishment. Bourget's *Le disciple* proposed the thesis that teachers are directly responsible for the moral and ideological effects of their philosophy on their students and should be held to account. Many of the anti-intellectual pronouncements of the late 1880s and 1890s were reactions to thinkers such as Renan, who in *Dia-*

logues et fragments philosophiques (1876; *Dialogues and Philosophical Fragments*) and *L'avenir de la science* (published in 1890, but written in 1848–49) had implicitly and explicitly called for new spiritual guides. It was possibly Renan whom Bourget had in mind when, in the preface to his novel, he alluded to the eloquent master whose paradoxes had fascinated and corrupted the impressionable younger generation.

The real target, beyond the intellectuals who supposedly sapped France's finest traditions, was of course the democratic mystique, and beyond that, the Revolution, which was held responsible for all contemporary social and moral ills. The spiritual uprootedness and loss of traditional values for which the Revolution and professors were being blamed were soon denounced in Barrès' *Les déracinés* (1897; *The Uprooted*). But negative assessments of the consequences of the Revolution could also be found in the very writings of the suspect intellectual masters. Hippolyte Taine's *Les origines de la France contemporaine* (1875–1894; *The Origins of Contemporary France*) was hostile to the Revolution. Even Renan, though he asserted that the Revolution had been the French epic par excellence and considered the event of the Revolution "sublime," in the final analysis judged it a failure ("expérience manquée") and referred to it as "odious and horrible" (*Oeuvres complètes*, 1:12–13; 2:1081).

The commemorative festivities of 1889 were hardly necessary to focus attention on the French Revolution. Many undoubtedly preferred to occult its more violent aspects, but the Revolution could not possibly be forgotten. Nor could it be considered a closed chapter. Its mission, after all, had never been fulfilled. The history of the 19th century had been marked by a series of caesuras, discontinuities, relapses. On the other hand, repeated revolutionary moments had kept the Revolution's momentum (and the fear of that momentum) alive: 1830, which introduced the constitutional monarchy; 1848, which led to the coup d'état of Louis Bonaparte; the Commune of 1871, which brought about the fiercest of repressions.

Thus it is not surprising that literary works from Balzac to Zola, even when they do not deal directly with the events of the Revolution, are filled with allusions, echoes, and thematic references. Old Goriot is not merely a doting and profaned father, a latter-day degraded Lear or a pathetic "Christ of paternity"; he had been chairman of a Revolutionary section and a profiteer during the great famine when he sold wheat to the "coupeurs de têtes" (head choppers) of the Committee of Public Safety, and thus had earned the retrospective appellation "vieux Quatre-vingt-treize" (Old Ninety-three). Danton and Robespierre are repeatedly referred to with awe, fear, and respect in Stendhal's *Le rouge et le noir* (1830; *The Red and the Black*), whose first epigraph is a stark statement of bitter truth attributed to Danton. As for Zola's title *Germinal* (1885), the name of the month marking the threshold of spring in the Revolutionary calendar instituted in 1793 by the Convention, it is evidently a reference to the most violent period of the Revolution; yet it also signals the novel's hope-filled theme of a political awakening of the still ignorant *peuple* and seems to point to the struggle that lies ahead.

The perspective remains characteristically bidirectional. The 19th century seems determined (or condemned) to think forward by looking backward. Past and future are brought into ironic tension, and this not merely because there are repeated attempts to set back the clock and to treat the period 1789–1815 as though it had been a scandalous and irrelevant parenthesis, but also because progress-oriented ideologies, and in particular revolutionary thought and action, are at every level compelled to look back to an already anachronistic model, thus conceiving history as both linear and repetitive, and promoting ironic and parodistic structures. Commenting on a remark made by Hegel, Karl Marx observed, after the events of 1848–1851, that historical facts and personages tend to occur twice, "the first time as tragedy, the second as farce" (*The Eighteenth Brumaire of Louis Bonaparte* [1852], p. 13). The same principle is illustrated by Flaubert in the chapter on the political clubs in *L'éducation sentimentale* (1869; *Sentimental Education*), where everyone seeks to model himself on a past public figure, "one copying Saint-Just, another Danton, and yet another Marat," while Frédéric Moreau tries to resemble Blanqui, "who in his turn imitated Robespierre" (*Sentimental Education*, p. 301).

Flaubert was evidently hostile to political activism and basically afraid of popular uprisings. His escape into aestheticism was in fact an escape from the sound and fury of history in the making. Many others, however, though they may also have felt anxiety as they witnessed the acceleration of history, espoused ideas of becoming and change and tried to justify the deeper meaning of revolutions. Alphonse de Lamartine, who was to play an important political role in 1848, is a case in point. In the second episode of *Jocelyn* (1836), significantly set not in 1789 but in 1793, he deplores the crimes and horrible reprisals associated with the Revolution, calling it a "bloody abyss" that brought only horror and misery to those who participated in it. But he also sees the Revolution as part of a divine scenario. God wanted it and lent it his creative hand; for revolutions illustrate the basic creative principle that brings birth out of death and suffering. In his ode "Les révolutions" (1831), Lamartine views political violence in the service of progress as the will of a God who knows no rest, whose message is "Forward!" and whose work is forever unfinished. God as revolutionary. Lamartine's poem anticipates some of Hugo's vatic pronouncements on God's immanent participation in history's mysterious processes. Lamartine even comes within one letter of sacralizing revolution as he speaks of "saintes évolutions" (line 96).

The messianic view of art and literature in the service of a larger epic that not only relates the spiritual adventure of mankind but also helps bring it about, characterizes many of the great Romantics. To a large extent such a view defined the sense of the epic as the 19th century understood it. The works of Pierre Simon Ballanche, Félicité de Lamennais, Edgar Quinet, and Michelet—not to mention Hugo's *Les misérables* (1862) and *La légende des siècles* (1859–1883; *The Legend of the Centuries*)—illustrate this notion that a greater spiritual force animates history and the evolution of humanity toward its highest destiny.

Even though for a while there was a reluctance to confront directly some extreme features of the Revolution—as happens after periods of great turmoil—an impressive number of important histories of the Revolution were written during the 19th century. Among the *Histoires de la Révolution française,* those by Adolphe Thiers (1823–1827), Auguste Mignet (1824), Louis Blanc (1847–1862), Lamartine (*Histoire des Girondins,* 1847; *History of the Girondists*), Alexis de Tocqueville (*L'ancien régime et la Révolution,* 1856; *The Old Régime and the Revolution*), and Quinet (*La Révolution,* 1865) are the better known. But the most compelling, in large part because of its mythopoeic qualities, is Michelet's *Histoire de la Révolution française,* written during one of the most turbulent periods of popular uprisings and violent changes of régimes, and consecrated by a national edition in the celebratory year 1889.

It would seem that the commemorative spirit was built into the French Revolution, for it was from the start exceedingly date-conscious: 14 July, 6 October (the march on Versailles), 20 June (the oath of the representatives in the Tennis Court), 10 August (the storming of the Tuileries)—not to mention 21 September, 31 May, Germinal, Thermidor—quickly became household references. Retrospectively, however, the entire Revolutionary period seems politically and thematically polarized around two symbolic dates: 1789 and 1793, the year of the Bastille and the year of the Terror.

Seventeen eighty-nine, or the myth of the Bastille: the stormed fortress was already legendary in stories, images, memoirs. A symbolic, at times even mythical, vocabulary and iconography overdetermined it as an archetype of oppression and political monstrosity. Tracts, pamphlets, dramatic dialogues, tales, and poems had fed this legend. The popular uprising and the assault on 14 July 1789 were thus quickly perceived as both a closing and an inaugural moment of the highest import. In the words of Michelet, the taking of the Bastille was an "act of faith"; Pétrus Borel called it a "holy rebellion." For Michelet, the event had an apocalyptic meaning; it was a "jugement dernier," the last judgment of the past. In the preface to the 1868 edition he evokes the unforgettable days when all of Europe was delirious with joy at the news of the Bastille's fall. But Michelet knew that even as he was writing about the epic liberating events, other Bastilles existed in a world that was still far from free. The Bastille remained archetypally alive. "The world is covered with prisons from the Spielberg to Siberia, from Spandau to the Mont-Saint-Michel" (*Oeuvres complètes,* 1 : 122).

Historically and symbolically, 1789 remained associated with the image of a collective euphoria. It is a joyful date, as attested by the dancing that has become traditional every year in the streets of all French towns. For Michelet, it is the key date. Although he is fascinated by the figure of Robespierre, and although he praises the "sublime" patriotic élan of 1792, he remains emotionally committed to the day the Bastille fell: "Let this great day remain one of the eternal celebrations of mankind" (*Oeuvres complètes,* 1 : 239).

Michelet focuses on more significant features of the Revolutionary events, above all on the profoundly peaceful spirit of the "holy Revolution." He points out that the Revolution left no dead monuments, only living spiritual values.

He stresses the guiding role of Paris and the supreme importance of "le Peuple," the chief protagonist of the saga, whose spontaneity and unanimous action gave the true impulse to what he defines as a "period of unanimity." Characteristically, however, Michelet, in glorifying the notion of the sovereign People, representative of ideal unity, refuses to entertain the concept of class struggle. On this point he is in major disagreement with Louis Blanc, whose views on the Revolution are colored by socialist doctrine. Moreover, Michelet considers the People as essentially silent and in need of a voice—that of the philosopher-historian.

Such views bring Michelet very close to Hugo, who was also unwilling to see the class war and refused to challenge the prevailing social and economic order. But Hugo's myth of "le Peuple," also associated with Paris—specifically through the metaphor of the child Gavroche—is problematized by deep uneasiness and even fear of popular violence. In his works the term *peuple* easily degenerates lexically into crowd, mob, rabble, *fex urbis* (city scum). And possibly Hugo's patriotic fiber, his sense of *gloire,* was complicated by the fact that his father had been a general in Napoleon's army (which had its roots in the Revolution), whereas his mother, born in Vendée, was a royalist attached to ancien régime values and fiercely hostile to Napoleon.

This family rift—the parents had in fact angrily separated—may explain in part Hugo's obsession with civil strife (the Vendée royalist uprising became a symbol) and with revolution as violence and hatred. Whatever the causes, Hugo's lasting fascination, unlike Michelet's dithyrambic attachment to 1789, has to do with the somber year 1793. In his last novel, *Quatre vingt-treize* (1874; *Ninety-three*), written after the events of the Commune, he describes 1793 as an "ulcer," a "hemorrhage," a theater of cruelty in which inflexible doctrinaires and demagogues, serving the reign of the guillotine, lead France to an apocalypse. Yet it is this catastrophic nature that also endows the year of the Terror with an epic dimension. Hugo describes the "epic heap of antagonisms" and resorts repeatedly to oceanic metaphors of storms, foam, reefs, shipwrecks, and the inevitable abyss.

This Hugolian abyss is indeed indicative of forces at work, forces that are greater than either the political leaders who think they control events or the popular masses that storm fortresses and sack royal residences. Like Lamartine, Hugo believes that the text of history is a divine scenario, except that for Hugo, God's immanence in history reveals a disturbing alliance with darkness and evil. He is the "enormous and sinister author."

Hugo's most troubled meditations on the Revolution were repressed for a long time. The 1857 poem "La Révolution" (justifying revolutionary violence) and its immediate disclaimer-sequel "Le verso de la page" (1857–58; "The Other Side of the Page") were not published until many years later, and then only after having been dismembered or inserted in a totally different context. "La Révolution" describes the nocturnal encounter of the stone or bronze statues of the great kings of France with the full horror of the guillotine. At the precise point of their assignation with history, there is a vision of horror in an apocalyptic setting: a geometric silhouette marks the threshold of nothingness tragically inscribed for all time in the fateful number 93, while oozing blood seems to be smearing across the paving stones the ironic word *Justice.*

The poem is nonetheless a justification of the Revolution. All the tyrannical deeds of the past, all the prisons and torture chambers, all the sobs of the downtrodden, call for retribution and expiation. Revolution is a "divine monster." But the executioner must not have the last word. That is the message of "Le verso de la page," which goes so far as to show compassion for the king, to speak of his "martyrdom," and to suggest that we are all murderers so long as the scaffold exists. For Hugo could not forget that even though regicide (a form of collective parricide) was to be understood as a never-to-be-repeated salvational event, this unique expiatory act was also a justification of capital punishment, against which Hugo had all his life fought with genuine vehemence.

Hugo's suppression of the two poems is strikingly paralleled by a collective desire to forget, accompanied by the inability to do so. The erection in 1836 of the obelisk in the very square where Louis XVI had been beheaded (now symbolically called the Place de la Concorde) was symptomatic of a desire to erase the past. The 19th century is the century of commemorations but also of forgetfulness.

What France tried to forget or repress, but could not efface from its collective memory, was the bloody episode of 21 January 1793, which was quickly perceived as far more than the beheading of a king. For this beheading, implicitly or explicitly understood as a parricide, was even more disquieting than the symbolic murder of the father. It signified the breakdown of political structures and societal hierarchies, and the ultimate questioning of the very notion of authority.

The psychopolitical link between father and king was also quickly fictionalized. Stendhal, writing at the same time that Louis-Philippe was trying to create a myth of unity and oblivion, relives in *Vie de Henry Brulard* (wr. 1835–36, pub. 1890; *The Life of Henry Brulard*) that determining moment, in 1793, when the young Henri Beyle is seated in front of his father, in his father's study, as the news of the king's death arrives, and the little boy, watching his father's grief, experiences "one of the keenest raptures of joy" he was ever to experience (p. 634).

The 19th century was evidently haunted, though not always overtly, by the writings of Joseph de Maistre (Hugo's bête noire)—the archreactionary political theorist who had glorified the figure of the public executioner as the mysterious agent of divine justice and the indispensable foundation of the social order. But this exaltation of punishment, expiation, and violence in the service of order was double-edged and could be exploited by conflicting ideologies. Strife is indeed of the essence, even behind the apparently festive façade of the commemorative year 1889. The 19th century, in this self-congratulatory year— torn between belief in progress and nostalgia for a lost "order," at times placing God and his plans in the service of melioristic philosophies, but also challenging the notion of forward-looking linear history by deeper allegiances to mythical structures and cyclical notions of time—could see itself (as Hugo proposed in *William Shakespeare,* 1864) as the child of the Revolution, as a climactic epoch in which true civilization was to be born, but also as a torn and problematic century, and an immensely fertile one because it remained in splendid contradiction with itself.

See also 1789, 1794 (8 June), 1799, 1830, 1836, 1871.

Bibliography: Gustave Flaubert, *Sentimental Education,* trans. Robert Baldick (Baltimore: Penguin, 1969). Victor Hugo, "La Révolution" and "Le verso de la page," in *Oeuvres complètes,* ed. Jean Massin, vol. 10 (Paris: Club Français du Livre, 1967). Alphonse de Lamartine, "Les révolutions," in *Oeuvres poétiques complètes,* ed. Marius-François Guyard (Paris: Gallimard, 1963). Karl Marx, *The Eighteenth Brumaire of Louis Bonaparte,* trans. C. P. Dutt (New York: International Publishers, [1935]). Jules Michelet, *Histoire de la Révolution française,* vol. 1 of *Oeuvres complètes* (Paris: Flammarion, 1893). Ernest Renan, *Oeuvres complètes,* 10 vols. (Paris: Calmann-Lévy, 1947–1961). Stendhal, *Vie de Henry Brulard,* in *Oeuvres intimes,* ed. Victor del Litto, vol. 2 (Paris: Gallimard, 1982). Hippolyte Taine, *The Origins of Contemporary France* (Chicago: University of Chicago Press, 1974). Albert Thibaudet, *La république des professeurs* (Paris: Grasset, 1927).

Victor Brombert

 1892

Oscar Wilde Tries to Have His *Salomé* Performed in London with Sarah Bernhardt in the Title Role

Writing and the Dance

In the latter part of the 19th century, the figure of woman as femme fatale was a prevalent one in literature and the arts, especially in such mythological types as Medusa, the Sphinx, Medea, female vampires, and the Sirens. This misogynous vision of woman as a dangerous beauty, devouring and above all destructive in her sexuality, competed with an equally strong notion of woman as the angel of the home, the embodiment of the Victorian ideal of the good (and therefore sexless) mother.

Salome, the princess whose lascivious dance caused the death of John the Baptist, was a dominant figure from the Middle Ages onward. Her popularity reached its apogee, however, in this later period. One reason for her sudden importance may lie in the fact that she embodies *both* extreme views of woman. On the one hand, of course, her sexuality is deadly. Moreover, Salome is the daughter of another femme fatale: Herodias, who married the tetrarch Herod Antipas without bothering to divorce her first husband, and as a result had been branded a harlot by John the Baptist. So even before her fatal dance, Salome is already tarnished by her lineage. On the other hand, Salome retains a certain possibility of innocence: both Matthew and Mark, the New Testament sources of her story, suggest her extreme youth. Both also make clear that Salome dances at the insistence of her stepfather, Herod, and that when, in return, he offers her anything she wants, she asks her mother what she should demand of him. It is Herodias who tells her to ask for the head of John the Baptist. Salome is a figure of fascination because her deadly sensuality is evident, but her guilt and evil are not. Her relationship to Herodias is equally ambiguous: is Salome the victim of a lecherous stepfather and a vengeful mother, or is she the willing extension of both, eagerly anticipating the death of John? This intriguing complexity, together with the popularity of what was called orientalism at the end of the last century, combined to render the dancing Semitic princess all the more mysterious and attractive.

Gustave Flaubert, Joris-Karl Huysmans, Oscar Wilde, and Stéphane Mallarmé contributed in cumulative and, in some cases, interactive ways to her elaboration. For Mallarmé, the Salome story takes on an added, important dimension: the poet ties the notion of the dance, and of decapitation, to the act of writing itself. It is because of Mallarmé's final vision that the Salome story takes on an added importance in the French literary tradition.

The "modern" Salome begins with Flaubert's *Salammbô* (1862), a historical novel about the wars between Rome and Carthage (3rd century B.C.). Salammbô is the beautiful daughter of the greatest general in Carthage and a devotee of Tanit, the Semitic goddess of the heavens. In addition to the obvious orientalist context, Salammbô is reminiscent of Salome because she causes a man (who is in love with her) to be captured, tortured, and, finally, killed before her eyes. The novel was a favorite of the painter Gustave Moreau, who had already been interested in the fate of John the Baptist. But Flaubert's painstaking portrayal of the beautiful, exotic Salammbô, and in particular his precise description of her ornate dress, shifted the painter's attention onto Salome: more than half of Moreau's 120 sketches foreground the princess. Two of Moreau's completed renditions of the story were displayed in the 1876 Salon exposition: the oil painting *Salomé* and the watercolor *L'apparition* (*The Apparition*), which shows Salome standing in horror before the bloody, floating head of John. In both of these works, as in most of Moreau's other portrayals of Salome, the princess is dressed nearly identically to Flaubert's Salammbô. The painter had found his Salome in the high headdress, flowing gowns, and jewels of Flaubert's Carthaginian priestess.

The debt was reciprocated. Flaubert, overwhelmed by Moreau's vision of Salome, began his own version of the story in the same year of the Salon show. Although, like Moreau, his initial interest was the story of John the Baptist, Flaubert became fascinated with the relationship between Herod and Herodias (whom he elsewhere describes as "ferocious") and especially with Herodias' jealousy of her beautiful young daughter: she has kept Salome hidden from Herod, fearing that he would find her too seductive. When he finally does meet Salome, he is promptly enchanted: looks just like Herodias in her youth, he thinks.

Not only has Herodias withheld her daughter; Flaubert withholds her textually as well: Salome does not appear until the end of the tale. All mention of the dance, too, is delayed until the last few pages, adding to the suspense. She dances with her feet in the air (as she does in the tympanum of the Rouen cathedral, which Flaubert knew well)—a touch of the perverse, perhaps, or of what was perceived as "exotic." When she has finished her dance, she lispingly asks, "like a child," for the head of the Baptist, her childishness clashing with her heavy makeup and revealing costume. The story ends, in an understated fashion, with two disciples of John taking turns carrying the saint's head "because it was very heavy." With *Hérodias,* the third of his *Trois contes* (1877; *Three Tales*), Flaubert returned to the style and scenery that characterize the longer, more epic *Salammbô.*

The same two Moreau paintings, *Salomé* and *L'apparition,* that had so moved Flaubert are described in detail in Huysmans' novel *A rebours* (1884; *Against Nature*). The protagonist, des Esseintes, is a wealthy decadent who hides from the world in his opulent home, surrounding himself with rare books and a collection of art objects that includes the two Moreau paintings. In des Esseintes's lengthy reveries, Salome figures as the incarnation of evil (he is completely uninterested in Herodias). In the oil *Salomé,* he is fascinated by the depiction of the dance about which the Bible is silent. But he most admires the watercolor *L'apparition,* since in his misogynous view Salome is here the intriguing "harlot" who is "obedient to her passionate and cruel female temperament," the murderess who, mesmerized by the floating head of her victim, has "the charms of a great venereal flower, grown in a bed of sacrilege" (*Against Nature,* p. 68). Des Esseintes sees Moreau's Salome as a vampire woman who "saps the morale and breaks the will" even as she reignites the old tetrarch (p. 65).

In *A rebours,* Huysmans also ties Salome to the notion of writing. On the one hand, des Esseintes admires the Moreau paintings because they depict what is not written in the gospels. But his trancelike, lengthy verbal meditations on the painted works also attempt to fill another lack of sorts: if Moreau is able to paint the dance that the gospels omit, the novel (through des Esseintes's descriptions) gives words to what the paintings also hold in silence. *A rebours* renders the relationship between writing and painting both symbiotic and problematic; each professes to compensate for the other's inadequacies.

These concepts of painting and writing come directly to the fore with Mallarmé's treatment of the Salome story. As early as 1864, Mallarmé was corresponding with his friend Henri Cazalis about an idea for a poem to be called "Hérodiade." The ending *-iade* here suggests that this is the tale of the family of Herods (just as, for example, the *Aeneid* is the story of Aeneas). But the title also purposely blurs the distinction between Salome and Herodias, even in name, for Hérodiade is mother and daughter combined: evil, youth, and the cynicism of experience coupled with the "horror" (as Hérodiade puts it) of virginity.

From the outset, Mallarmé saw this work both as being *about* poetry and as a demonstration of a new kind of verse. In October 1864 he wrote to Cazalis: "I have finally begun my 'Hérodiade.' I am terrified, because I am inventing a new language that must necessarily spring from a very new poetics, which I can define in this way: *one must paint, not the thing itself, but the effect it produces.*

In such a poetry, a line of verse is fashioned with intentions, not with words" (*Correspondance*, p. 137). Painting is here a metaphor for writing; a metaphor that continues more subtly the interaction between the two activities. The idea of painting the effect rather than the thing itself, one of the hallmarks of symbolist verse, was inspired by the story of Salome and resulted in Mallarmé's new poetics—one that concentrated on effect rather than on representation.

"Hérodiade" contains three parts: "Ouverture," "Scène," and "Cantique de saint Jean" ("Saint John's Song"). In "Ouverture," Hérodiade's childhood nurse pronounces an incantation that includes her forebodings for the events of the dawning day. "Scène," a dialogue between the nurse and Hérodiade, is filled with cold images of sterility and despair—"Yes, it is for myself alone," says Hérodiade, "that I bloom, desertlike"—and ends with Hérodiade's statement that she awaits "something unknown." There has been no mention of the dance, of Herod, of a mother and daughter. Mallarmé has indeed painted the effect, and not the thing. His Hérodiade, with her glacial torrent of hair and her sterile virginal beauty, becomes a symbol, not of the femme fatale, but of the pure poetry Mallarmé was striving to attain.

The idea of pure poetry is reinforced in the short "Cantique de saint Jean." Here the saint, at the moment of decapitation, turns his martyrdom into a metaphysical meditation on what he terms "the ancient disharmonies" between the head and the body. The notion of baptism becomes a baptism of the poet: the principle, says John, "that elected me" (line 27). Hérodiade is the muse who cuts the head from its body; who insists upon a baptism of ideal thought in electing the poet; whose sensuality is one of mind, not of body. Once decapitated, John becomes like the sun—a center of incandescent radiance, worthy of "grace" (not unlike the floating head that radiates an eerie light in Moreau's *L'apparition;* fig. 1). John is the symbol of the Mallarmean poet: both destroyed and rendered "elect," true poet (pure thought), by his dangerous muse.

"Hérodiade," though never completed, was published in various versions throughout Mallarmé's lifetime (without, however, the "Cantique de saint Jean," which appeared for the first time in 1913, fifteen years after the poet's death) and was well known by his followers. The unfinished state of the poem may have prompted Oscar Wilde, who had met Mallarmé in 1891, to write his own version of the story, and to write it in French. In his ambitious enthusiasm, he no doubt wanted to compete with the master. But Wilde had already been drawn to the story by the texts of Huysmans and Flaubert. "I want [Salome] to dance on her hands," he writes, "as in Flaubert's story" (quoted in Ellmann, *Oscar Wilde*, p. 343). Wilde also saw Salome from the misogynous perspective of des Esseintes: "Her lust must needs be infinite," he muses, "and her perversity without limits. Her pearls must expire on her flesh" (p. 342). Another reason for Wilde's choice of French was that his *Salomé* was to be a play, and he wanted the great French actress Sarah Bernhardt to play the title role. Wilde began rehearsal for his *Salomé* in London in 1892, a full year before it was officially published in its original French version. Bernhardt had accepted the role (although she was displeased that the play's main character was Herod, and

1. Gustave Moreau, *L'apparition,* watercolor (Musée du Louvre, Cabinet des Dessins). (Photo courtesy of Documentation Photographique de la Réunion des Musées Nationaux.)

not Salome) and had granted the rehearsals her blessing and participation. But British censors banned the play, and Wilde had to give up his dream of seeing his Salome's words spoken in French before the English public by the most famous actress of the age.

Wilde's Salome is in love with the saint, who rejects her and her advances. He has to be dead, Salome decides, for her to be able to kiss him. She is the one and the only one who insists, driven by her own desire, upon John's death. Wilde's Salome is in many ways like des Esseintes's "venereal flower" come to life. Indeed, she partakes of the French literary canon not only because the play was written in French, but also because she is so much the descendant of her earlier French versions: "My Salome is a mystic," Wilde remarked, "a sister of Salammbô." Even his Herod "is like the Herod of Gustave Moreau, wrapped in his jewels and sorrows" (quoted in Ellmann, *Oscar Wilde,* p. 376).

Meantime, Mallarmé was still writing about the problem of writing, and about a poetry whose subject is itself. In 1886 he published notes on the theater, mimes, and the dance. One of these, "Ballets," returns to the problem of the dance and its specific relation to writing an "effect" instead of "the thing itself." Although Salome is never mentioned by name, it is clear, given the issues the story had elicited in the poet in 1864, that she is present—but now as a metaphor:

> Let it be known that the ballerina is *not a woman dancing,* that, within these juxtaposed motifs, *she is not a woman,* but a metaphor summarizing one of the elemental aspects of our form, sword, goblet, flower, etc., and that *she is not dancing,* suggesting, by the wonder of ellipses or leaps, with a corporeal writing, that which would take entire paragraphs of dialogued as well as descriptive prose to express in written composition: a poem detached from all instruments of the scribe. (*Oeuvres complètes,* p. 304)

This difficult passage becomes comprehensible in the light of what Mallarmé said the story of Salome had taught him: that the modern poet should evoke ("paint") an effect, and not try to represent or describe a thing. Here, in "Ballets," Mallarmé seems to suggest that the dancer can achieve this type of pure, mental "poetry" or writing by her dance alone. Her dance is a "writing" that, for Mallarmé, suggests (and thus evokes) far more than could "entire paragraphs" of prose. Because it is a dancer's task precisely to evoke an effect and not a "thing," Mallarmé sees her as the truest poet of all—a poet who produces immediately a writing freed from "all instruments of the scribe"—no need of paper or pen. It is in this sense that we should understand Mallarmé's statement that the ballerina "is not a woman dancing" nor indeed a woman. She is above all the perfect metaphor of the kind of pure poetry he spent his life trying to achieve: a poetry removed from things and their concrete representation; a poetry that represents itself being written.

In "Ballets" Mallarmé has found the image of his poetic project. It is a Salome who is important, not because of the consequences of her dance, but because through her dance she becomes the writing of pure thought. And this writing is "corporeal," achieved through the body. Thus the dance overcomes the ancient "disharmonies" between the mind and the body of which John had spoken in "Hérodiade." The dancer is triumphant for Mallarmé because, like the poetry he imagined but knew was impossible to attain, she represents only the story of writing itself, and so "paints not the thing itself, but the effect it produces."

See also 1874, 1884.

Bibliography: Christine Buci-Glucksmann, *La raison baroque de Baudelaire à Benjamin* (Paris: Galilée, 1985). Richard Ellmann, *Oscar Wilde* (New York: Knopf, 1988). Gustave Flaubert, *Salammbô* (Paris: Garnier, 1961). Flaubert, *Trois contes* (Paris: Garnier-Flammarion, 1965). René Girard, "Scandal and the Dance: Salome in the Gospel of Mark," *New Literary History,* 15 (1984), 311–324. Joris-Karl Huysmans, *Against Nature,* trans. Robert Baldick (Harmondsworth: Penguin, 1959). Stéphane Mallarmé, *Correspondance, 1862–1871,* ed. Henri Mondor and Jean-Pierre Richard (Paris: Gallimard, 1959). Mallarmé, *Oeuvres complètes,* ed. Henri Mondor and Georges Jean-Aubry (Paris: Gallimard, 1945). Françoise Meltzer, *Salome and the Dance of Writing: Portraits of Mimesis in Literature* (Chicago: University of Chicago Press, 1987). Linda Seidel, "Salome and the Canons," *Women's Studies,* 2 (1984), 29–66. Oscar Wilde, *Salomé* (Paris: Librairie de l'Art Indépendant, 1893); translated by the author as *Salomé* (New York: Dutton, 1927).

Françoise Meltzer

ᗡ 1895

Gustave Lanson Publishes His *Histoire de la littérature française*

Literature in the Classroom

Two rival traditions, broadly termed philology and rhetoric, have existed in French literary studies at least since the 16th century. The viewpoint of the philological tradition is the particular or the singular: this author and this work. It is historical and erudite, in that it researches contingent facts. The rhetorical tradition, on the other hand, conceives of literature in terms of general categories or universals: genres, narrative techniques, and stylistic figures. The opposition of particularists and generalists is based on differing conceptions of the text as *given* or as *possible.* The particularists are interested in it because it exists, because it is the work of an individual under specific conditions; the generalists are interested in the same text because it exemplifies a system or embodies a structure that might have led to other unrealized texts; through this text they aim at the structure, that is, at literature in its most comprehensive as well as its essential sense (the totality of possible texts and the nature of the literary).

The two traditions began to be perceived as rivals when the Benedictines espoused particularism and the Jesuits generalism. After the Revolution, when the Benedictine abbeys and the Jesuit colleges were dispersed, particularism took refuge in the Academy of Inscriptions and Letters, while rhetoric flourished in the Napoleonic universities established in 1803. The situation changed after the defeat of 1870, which many observers saw as the defeat of France's educational system. According to Ernest Renan, for example, it was the German system of higher education, founded in reaction to Napoleon's victory at Jena in 1806, that triumphed at Sedan. By then the French universities were practically nonexistent, having no other function than to award diplomas and to constitute juries for the baccalaureate examination. After the defeat of 1870, rhetoric, discredited, was to be replaced by literary history in lycées and universities. In the twenty years after 1877, under the leadership of Jules Ferry, the French universities became professional schools as well as research centers.

The reformers of the French educational system were essentially a few historians, "a well-organized gang," as Charles Péguy called them in his famous pamphlet against the Sorbonne, *L'argent suite* (1913; *Money Follow-up*). Historians propagated the discipline of the positivist method for establishing facts, as opposed to the faith in philosophies of history that had prevailed until Hippolyte Taine. History, based on this cult of facts, became the science that would prepare the nation for revenge on Germany. And their bête noire was literature, which was irretrievably associated with rhetoric. The reaction of Romain Rolland, then a student at the Ecole Normale Supérieure, was typical when in 1887 he hesitated between philosophy and history: "As to pure literature," he wrote, "I will not even speak of it. It is meager nourishment. I need more substantial food" (*Le cloître de la rue d'Ulm* [1952; *The Cloister at the Rue d'Ulm*], p. 124). Literature seemed to be doomed by the rise of the historians and their positivistic clique.

Notions of literary history were specifically introduced into the programs of secondary education beginning in 1880. But the literary faculty, who were rhetoricians, did not know how to teach them, and in 1890 the task was reassigned to historians. The demise of rhetorical instruction left the literary faculty powerless, without a pulpit. Until then, the professors of rhetoric had had the upper hand in the lycées: they initiated students into the highest discipline, the art of discourse. But schools founded on rhetoric were now reproached for being oriented to and perpetuating the specific class of those who produced discourse: lawyers, writers, and journalists. Rhetoric was a holdover from the ancien régime in the Third Republic. As rhetoric was aristocratic, history would be democratic.

In 1890 literary studies thus seemed condemned to decline and eventual extinction. But a savior appeared, to whom, it is no exaggeration to say, literary studies in France owe their survival. Gustave Lanson (1857–1934) became the champion of literary history against Ferdinand Brunetière (1849–1906), the last eloquent rhetorician, who had been his mentor. One of Lanson's claims to glory—to the point that French literary history still identifies itself with him under the name *Lansonism*—was to have published in 1895 a *Histoire de la littérature française* (*History of French Literature*). The notorious "Lanson," as his textbook was soon called, made it possible for professors of rhetoric to retrain themselves into the historical method, a generation after the historians had done so.

Brunetière, the leader of the literary faction, was a self-made man. He did not belong to the university, but edited the fashionable *Revue des deux mondes*. He fought the rear-guard struggle against the invasion of literary studies by German erudition. Convinced that criticism had to become a science if it wanted to avoid falling prey to positivist history, he unfortunately chose the wrong model and made a fool of himself with his theory of the evolution of the genres, based on borrowings from Darwinism. Finally he converted. He was an anti-Dreyfusard while the historians in power were secularists and Dreyfusards, and the university faculty despised him.

Lanson came at just the right moment. He never pretended to have invented anything but simply to have opened a new field to erudition, which until then had been applied only to ancient and medieval literature, whereas literature from the Renaissance on had been the object of taste and sympathy. He insisted that the techniques of philology would give scientific legitimacy to literary studies; he split literary history from criticism, literary studies from literature. He eliminated from literary studies "impressionistic imagination" and "systematic dogmatism" (dogmatism being simply a subjectivity that does not know itself). He linked the teaching of literature through history to the ultimate goals of the education system of the Third Republic. And Lanson himself, who was still just a professor of rhetoric in a lycée in 1895, became the pope of literature after the Dreyfus Affair: a professor at the Sorbonne and the director of the Ecole Normale Supérieure following World War I. In the lycées, the professors trained in Lansonism based their teachings on the two new key pedagogical exercises: the *dissertation,* or essay, and the *explication de textes,* or textual analysis. The first took the place of the discourse, with which rhetoric was identified; the second, based on inductive reasoning, which was deemed more democratic than deductive thought, replaced the lessons on the rules of good writing.

Thus did literary history justify itself by the democratization of society. When sympathy with the French classics, the texts of the Great Century, was no longer passed on in families and when new social classes arrived at the lycées, *explication de textes* had to be invented as a means of teaching a literature that had become every bit as foreign to the mass of students as Greek or Latin literature. Similarly, literary history took over in the university as a reaction to the decline of bourgeois culture: the new spirit was defensive. Yet it was also on the offense, identifying itself with the official ideology of the Third Republic, "solidarity." In contradistinction to rhetoric, literary history gave work to all, just as the analytic exercise of *explication de textes* addressed itself to all. It was a collective labor requiring teamwork: for some the small investigations, for others the grand syntheses.

And Lanson himself did not relax. His great contribution to literary history, at the base of the entire edifice, was the monumental five-volume *Manuel bibliographique de la littérature française moderne* (1909–1914; *Bibliographical Handbook of Modern French Literature*), which brought together 23,000 references and 200 supplementary pages for the use of students and researchers. It was accompanied by two critical editions that served as models to several generations of researchers: that of Voltaire's *Lettres philosophiques* (1909; *Philosophical Letters*) and that of Lamartine's *Méditations* (1915). These editions inaugurated source criticism, with which literary history soon identified itself. "The idea would be," Lanson wrote in his preface to *Lettres philosophiques,* "to discover for each sentence the fact, the text, or the connection that had set the intelligence or the imagination of Voltaire going" (pp. l–li).

Unlike his disciples, however, such as Daniel Mornet and Gustave Rudler, who quickly reduced the goal of literary history to source and influence studies,

Lanson also attempted a synthesis between the positivist history of Charles-Victor Langlois and Charles Seignobos and the sociology of Emile Durkheim. He refused to enclose literary history in minor erudition and never renounced his global ambitions. Citing Germaine de Staël and Abel-François Villemain, who were the first, along with Louis de Bonald, to examine the relations between literature and society, he sought to determine the social conditions for the production of literary works. As might be expected, his enterprise was welcomed by Marxists, particularly in an article by Georgi Plekhanov in 1897. Literary history begins with the establishment of texts and the editing of unpublished materials, followed by the writing of biographies and the compilation of bibliographies, through the study of sources and influences. But Lanson also defined the next step, most significantly in his "Programme d'études sur l'histoire provinciale de la vie littéraire en France" (1903; "Program of Studies on the Local History of Literary Life in France"), to which Lucien Febvre, the founder of the *Annales* school of history, would respond enthusiastically. Here Lanson substituted the notion of the "literary life" for that of "literature," with the intention of working on a "literary history of France" alongside a "history of French literature." No longer would there simply be a catalogue, a canon, a collection of monographs on the great writers, focusing on their lives and their works. Rather, he had in mind the "portrait of the literary life of the nation, the history of culture and of the activity of the faceless crowd of readers as well of the famous elite of writers" (*Essais de méthode,* p. 87). Unfortunately, this excellent program was not realized until the *Annales* historians systematically undertook it during the 1960s.

On the other hand, Lanson continually warned against treating literary works only as archival documents; for literary works remain alive: this is their paradox and their genius. Earlier criticism had indeed regarded all literature as contemporary, that is, as timeless or eternal, instead of situating works in history. But the recognition of historical relativity did not rule out an emotional reaction to beauty. The object of method is not to dismiss the impression, but "to reduce the part of personal sentiment in our knowledge to an indispensable and legitimate minimum, while still granting it all its value" ("La méthode de l'histoire littéraire" [1910; "The Method in Literary History"], in *Essais de méthode,* p. 35). Sacrificing itself to history, literary studies would not cut itself off from sociology or aesthetics, and all seemed for the best. But the precautions with which Lanson surrounded himself remained dead letters, and literary history, renouncing the self and the world, the reader and society, shriveled up around the text. Was it the fault of the disciples of Lanson, the *sourciers,* or source-hunters, as they came to be known? Or was the destiny of French literary history set from the time of the founder, even though Lanson, an old fox of rhetoric, continued to write popularizing articles and to address a cultivated public until his death?

The technique of literary history is well known: it is essentially the application of philology to modern literature. Its ideology is also obvious: it is that of the Third Republic, with solidarity its principle, and democracy, pedagogy, and the division of labor its motto. But what was its theory? Was the reconciliation of history and sociology in the literary text possible? The work is historical, but it is also living; it is social, but it is also individual, Lanson said. A prisoner of these paradoxes, he refused to choose, to settle once and for all, and literary history proved in effect unshakable, more institutionally resistant than the history of Seignobos and the sociology of Durkheim. Once Lanson declined to define the literary object in positive terms, the study of literature was quickly reduced to a search for sources. This superficially reconciled the concern for individuality and the desire for causality while seeming to resolve individual facts into a social sequence. Literary history claimed to withstand criticism from Charles Augustin Sainte-Beuve to Taine and Brunetière, to withstand a process that attempted to bind the literary work ever more tightly to determinants—to Sainte-Beuve's man; to Taine's race, milieu, and moment; to Brunetière's genre—and failed to recognize genius. All our analyses, Lanson frequently repeated, are "approaches to genius." But genius was never grasped otherwise than as the residue of historical, sociological, and generic determinisms. As a result, Lanson's attack upon Taine was futile, for the true theory of literary history would remain a conception of man that Taine best expressed in *De l'intelligence* (1870; *On Intelligence*). The intellectualist notion of the human spirit and of literary creation that Lansonism perpetuated had its origins in associationist psychology: "The materials of a work of genius are not genius itself," Lanson still wrote in 1920. "But in making an inventory of these materials, one comes through analysis to isolate an irreducible element that the novelty and the personality of the author will consist of" (*Essais de méthode*, p. 425). The Lansonian mania for sources and influences was thus contained in the essential conformity of literary history to 19th-century positivism.

Lansonism quickly became an object of ridicule to the cultivated public. The polemics that the reactionary circles of the Action Française launched around 1905 against the techniques of erudition and in defense of the humanities proved to be the swan song of rhetoric. However, it was not the end of the quarrel between the particularists and the generalists. The two traditions reappeared intact in the 1960s, during the dispute between the old Lansonian Sorbonne and the *nouvelle critique* (New Criticism), which claimed to take its inspiration from Ferdinand de Saussure's linguistics, Freudian psychoanalysis, Marxist sociology, and so on—that is, from the new social sciences. The dispute between Raymond Picard and Roland Barthes is exemplary. Author of *La carrière de Jean Racine* (1956; *The Career of Jean Racine*), Picard was typical of a Sorbonne committed to the biography of authors, whereas Barthes based *Sur Racine* (1963; *On Racine*) in psychoanalytic anthropology to challenge the myth of the "sensitive Racine." But Lanson's mark on French education was so profound that it is doubtful whether New Criticism, despite its popularity with the cultivated public, did much to shake the institutional domination of literary history. Today, with New Criticism somewhat out of fashion, France—at least literary France—may be politely returning to Lansonism, unless the ancient opposition between the generalists and the particularists, the Jesuits and the Benedictines, finally lapses.

See also 1808.

Bibliography: Antoine Compagnon, *La Troisième République des lettres, de Flaubert à Proust* (Paris: Seuil, 1983). Gustave Lanson, *Essais de méthode, de critique et d'histoire littéraire,* ed. Henri Peyre (Paris: Hachette, 1965). Lanson, *Histoire de la littérature française* (Paris: Hachette, 1895). Romain Rolland, *Le cloître de la rue d'Ulm: Journal de Romain Rolland à l'Ecole Normale, 1886–1889* (Paris: Albin Michel, 1952). Gustave Rudler, *Techniques de la critique et de l'histoire littéraires* (1923; reprint, Geneva: Slatkine, 1979). Voltaire, *Lettres philosophiques,* ed. Gustave Lanson (Paris: Cornély, 1909).

Antoine Compagnon

1898

Emile Zola Publishes "J'accuse," an Open Letter to the President of the Republic in Which He Denounces the Irregularities Leading to Dreyfus' Condemnation

The Dreyfus Affair

In October 1894 the French army, hard pressed to identify the author of an anonymous letter offering military secrets to the German military attaché in Paris, arrested Captain Alfred Dreyfus, an Alsatian Jew for whom the high command had no particular affection. It subsequently exploited the secrecy of a court-martial to misrepresent the evidence in a trial that led Dreyfus to be convicted of treason and sentenced to lifelong detention on Devil's Island. By the time a series of coincidences had revealed first to Lt.-Colonel Georges Picquart, then to Dreyfus' brother, Mathieu, that the author of the letter was the flamboyant Commandant Walsin Esterházy, any demonstration of Esterházy's guilt would have implicitly demonstrated the irregularity of the original proceedings. Whereupon the army general staff closed ranks to exonerate (and conspire with) the actual traitor, did its best to discount the revelation that a crucial incriminating document against Dreyfus had been forged (by Colonel Hubert Joseph Henry), and proceeded to reaffirm Dreyfus' guilt—albeit with "attenuating circumstances"—in a second, limply prosecuted show trial at Rennes in 1899. On the morrow of the Rennes verdict, Dreyfus was pardoned by the president of the republic, but the toll he had paid in suffering endured and time wasted had already proved devastating.

Such was the bureaucratic drama at the focus of the conflict that unleashed widespread anti-Semitic violence throughout France in 1898 and divided French opinion throughout the closing years of the century. That division, particularly marked within France's intelligentsia, was reflected by literature in rather ironic ways.

Véritards was one neologism coined (by the Socialist Jules Guesde) to refer to the partisans of Dreyfus' innocence, and a mystique of Truth—on or off the march—was so much part of the Dreyfusard cause that it may be wondered whether the interests of fiction (or literature) were not above all served, however unwittingly, by the adversary camp. Consider the two great—chance—discoveries of the Dreyfusard campaign: the identification of Esterházy, in 1896, as the author of the treasonous letter; and the revelation, in 1898, that a second incriminating document had in fact been forged by Henry. Those two bits of empirical reality, once ascertained, were milestones in the establishment of truth, the pursuit of justice. But in retrospect the challenge—or shock—to contemporary imagination lay ultimately less in the dissemination of those demystifying truths than in their remystified inscription as fragments of a larger fiction, instruments of the anti-Dreyfusard cause. That Esterházy, precisely to the extent that his handwriting was identified as that of the letter, should have been widely viewed as a surrogate paid by the Jewish "syndicate" (that is, further evidence of Dreyfus' guilt) and that Henry's forgery and subsequent suicide should have been judged acts of military valor are ultimately more imaginatively stunning responses to events than the dogged, almost positivist hunting after evidence that characterized the Dreyfusard effort. (Indeed the sudden transformation of the disgraced Henry into a national hero, effected by Charles Maurras in an article in the *Gazette de France* on 5 September 1898, was the initial source of fame of the future royalist leader of Action Française.) Between the twin impulses to Truth and Literature, the slow progress toward rehabilitation of an innocent and the relentless pressure toward invention that it elicited from his adversaries, there are grounds for positing a primordial discordance.

At the time of the affair, the young Marcel Proust, self-styled "first of the Dreyfusards," was at work on the long and ultimately aborted manuscript of *Jean Santeuil* (published posthumously in 1952), an autobiographical novel so preoccupied with the vindication of persecuted innocence that it has been viewed by some as a Dreyfus Affair in miniature. *Jean Santeuil* relates the protagonist's feverish attendance at the Zola trials, inflates a rather grandiose figure of Chief of Staff General Raoul de Boisdeffre (which it punctures before allowing him to testify), but is most interesting on the figure of the Dreyfusard hero Lt.-Colonel Picquart. He is described at length as a "philosopher" and friend of Jean's philosophy teacher, Monsieur Beulier; his devotion to truth is such that the narrator rhapsodically evokes Socrates. Now at the conclusion of the novel's section on the affair ("La vérité sur l'affaire Dreyfus"), in a series of quick and quintessentially Proustian reversals, it is suggested that Esterházy—as well as Dreyfus—was innocent, that the "philosopher" Picquart had in fact forged the notorious document establishing his guilt but that, in the envenomed and mendacious atmosphere of the affair, he had done so in an effort to produce a counterlie that would alone validate his own "philosophical" intuition of the truth. Picquart remained no less the philosopher-hero, but his commitment to truth was underwritten by a strategic fiction (entirely of Proust's invention). In fact, though, the motif of heroic forgery was less Proust's invention than an application of the anti-Dreyfusard exaltation of Henry to the case of the Dreyfusard Picquart. To the extent that the posthumous editing of *Jean Santeuil* is coherent, it may be concluded that the Dreyfusard Proust was inclined to clinch his novelistic point by borrowing a ploy from the anti-Dreyfusard camp.

That development is not entirely surprising. A division between the life and art of the writer would eventually become part of the ideological baggage of the author of *A la recherche du temps perdu* (1913–1927; *Remembrance of Things Past*)—a work in which the metaphor of the twin "curses" of "Jewishness" and homosexuality came to dominate the sense of life's shortcomings. A Jew and a Dreyfusard, Proust would later write of both the ethical malaise and the aesthetic delight he derived from having chosen the "cruelly" anti-Semitic *L'action française,* edited by Léon Daudet, as his daily newspaper. And already in *Jean Santeuil,* his narrator expresses gratitude to the "science" of the Dreyfusard handwriting experts who strengthened the commitment of those Jews all too ready to "understand anti-Semitism," those partisans of Dreyfus masochistically inclined (or imaginatively disposed) to "understand" the jury that condemned Zola. Plainly, Proust was referring to Jews and Dreyfusards such as himself.

Proust's reference to the "science" of handwriting analysis points to the fact that the Dreyfus Affair was from the outset obsessed with issues of writing. The most influential expert at Dreyfus' first trial (1894) was the chief prosecution witness, Alphonse Bertillon, whose testimony was regarded as so extravagant that it eventually became an embarrassment to the anti-Dreyfusards, almost a source of solace to their adversaries. Yet Bertillon, chief of the Paris police's Service of Juridical Identity, founder of the fledgling science of anthropometrics, perhaps because of that very extravagance, has earned a place in literary and intellectual history. His efforts have recently been linked in a nontrivial way with the Freud who, in "The Moses of Michelangelo" (1914), discussed the profound affinities between psychoanalysis and the art-historical method of Giovanni Morelli. In all *three* cases, human (or artistic) identity is tied to a formally determinable coefficient of *unintendedness* invested in (the inscription/depiction of) a bodily fragment. For the connoisseur Morelli, in his attributions, the idiosyncratic configuration of ear, hand, or fingernail was the touchstone of inimitable authenticity. For Freud, the "component or partial object," in its articulation with the "unconscious," was the analogous instance. For Bertillon, at the time of the Dreyfus Affair, the index of identity oscillated between the multilinear patterns at and upon one's fingertips—that is, between handwriting analysis and fingerprint detection.

Writing analysis was for Bertillon a vanguard "structuralist" struggle against those "graphologists" intent on interpreting handwriting as the *expression* of human identity. Against them, in 1897, he posited that identity to be construable in no other terms than *as* the idiosyncrasies of script. What makes his case of particular interest to literary history—and links it more provocatively to that of Freud—is that his endeavors turned into a laboratory for perfecting techniques of textual superimposition. (The future of Freudian literary criticism in France would be crucially linked to Charles Mauron's subsequent insight that

"textual superimposition"—a model borrowed from the photographic technique of Bertillon's rival, Francis Galton—would alone allow one to compensate
for the lack of "free associations," without which psychoanalysis is an impossibility.) Given two writing samples whose common attribution was to be
decided, Bertillon would photograph and enlarge them, cut the enlargements
into individual words, glue the word-representations to differentially colored
(red or blue) pieces of paper, shuffle the two color series into a single deck, and
redistribute the combined deck according to such criteria as alphabetical order,
inverse alphabetical order, and rhyme. In each case adjacent blues and reds were
superimposed: the greater the degree of coincidence, the surer the attribution,
with the exception of total coincidence, interpreted as an index of forgery (that
is, tracing).

In the Dreyfus case, Bertillon concluded that Dreyfus, as a precaution, had
forged his own handwriting (in order to be able to invoke the excuse of
"forgery" were he caught). The text offered what Stéphane Mallarmé might
have called a "fallacious appearance of presentness," generated through what
Bertillon's superimpositions concluded to be tracings from a template consisting
of two minimally discrete chains of the word *intérêt* repeated over and over.
There was thus a doubly inscribed protowriting generating the illusion of a
"naturally" written message, a protowriting that the Dreyfusards, in their
conviction that the letter had been a "spontaneous" communication from Esterházy, could but seek to repress. Bertillon's system of superimpositions constituted an elaborate (if delirious) machine from which nonetheless a talented
bricoleur (tinkerer) might well be able to reconstruct many of the motifs of what
a recent generation has come to regard as "literary theory" at its most forceful.

Whereas Bertillon was the most extravagant of the anti-Dreyfusards, Maurice
Barrès, among writers, was the most prominent. Indeed Léon Blum later wrote
of his shock at realizing that the artist who served as *the* guide to his generation
had not enlisted in the Dreyfusard camp. Yet it is clear in retrospect that Barrès,
long before his engagement as an anti-Dreyfusard (and already during his years
as a left-wing Boulangist), was on his way to being a central figure among the
French elaborators of what would later be called fascism.

Having advanced his aesthetic beyond its earlier investment in the cultivation of the self, Barrès, largely under the influence of Jules Soury, professor of
"physiological psychology" at the Ecole des Hautes Etudes, had arrived at a
political aesthetic of the "unconscious." That unconscious was deemed to be
fundamentally collective, the transtemporal reality of the national community
in its fundamental intolerance of the pretensions of the individual ego, the
intelligence, and specifically those self-styled "aristocrats of thought," who at
the time of the Dreyfus Affair had begun to be called "intellectuals." Thus in
Les déracinés (1897; *The Uprooted*), a novel deploring the effects of democratic—Parisian—centralism on a generation lured away from its local (provincial) roots by universalist ("Kantian") metaphysics: "What a paltry thing, at
the very surface of ourselves, intelligence is. Certain Germans don't say 'I
think,' but 'it thinks in me'" (p. 318).

With his cult of "the Land and its Dead," Barrès came to see in anti-Semi-

tism the popular formula par excellence. He was an admirer of Edouard Drumont, whose lengthy *La France juive* (1886; *Jewish France*), an attempt to found
anti-Semitism as *the* political philosophy of modern times, was one of the two
best-selling books in France during the latter half of the 19th century. The
extraordinary mobilizing effect of anti-Semitism at the time of the Dreyfus
Affair continues to strain the imagination. In *La révolution dreyfusienne* (1910),
Georges Sorel, a former Dreyfusard, self-consciously adduces Karl Marx's *The
Eighteenth Brumaire of Louis Bonaparte* (1852) as a subtext in order to underscore
the cynicism whereby a pro-Dreyfusard government, *against the will of the French
public,* manipulated the judiciary to effect the rehabilitation of Dreyfus and
consolidated its abusive power in the process. The coup against democracy, that
is, came with the wholesale contempt for the popular—and left-wing (Charles
Fourier, Alphonse Toussenel, Pierre Joseph Proudhon, Drumont)—tradition of
anti-Semitism.

   The relative unpopularity of the Dreyfusard—or "intellectual"—cause in
France is one aspect of a situation that has led Régis Debray to see the exemplary Dreyfusard not at all as the writer but—despite Zola and Anatole
France—as the teacher or professor (electively, of philosophy). (In this, moreover, the Dreyfusard Proust of *Jean Santeuil* and the anti-Dreyfusard Barrès, who
regarded his *Les déracinés* as a premonition of the affair, concur.) The Dreyfu-
sard/anti-Dreyfusard split in the intelligentsia would be less between unestab-
lished and established writers than between teachers (with their inevitably
limited audiences) and writers (promoted by the mass-circulation press). On the
one hand, the Sorbonne (Charles Andler, Lucien Herr, Gabriel Monod); on the
other, the Académie Française (Barrès, Jules Lemaître, François Coppée). Similarly, in an affair whose principal arena was less parlement than the press, one
might oppose the circulation of such anti-Dreyfusard newspapers as Drumont's
La libre parole (500,000) and *Le petit journal* (1,500,000), on the one hand, and
that of *L'aurore* (100,000, doubled for the publication of "J'accuse"), on the
other. And whereas the Dreyfusard Ligue des Droits de l'Homme (League of
the Rights of Man), founded in February 1898, never had more than 8,000
adherents, the anti-Dreyfusard Ligue de la Patrie Française (League of the
French Fatherland), founded in December of that year, was able to collect
100,000 signatures at its inauguration. Moreover, Debray's reading of the
Dreyfus Affair as a victory of teachers over writers, of a lower intelligentsia over
an upper one (sustained in its pretensions by the press), reinforces our initial
suspicion that the interests of literature—or writing—may indeed have been
nurtured above all in the anti-Dreyfusard camp.

   What then of the major Dreyfusard figures of Anatole France and Emile
Zola? The two indeed form such an odd literary couple that it was enough for
Sorel to quote the young France's denunciations of Zola ("among those wretches
of which it may be said that it would have been preferable for them never to be
born"; quoted in *La révolution dreyfusienne,* p. 29) for him to be able to launch
his reading of the "Dreyfus revolution" as farce. The skeptic France's enlistment
in the Dreyfusard cause was in fact as perplexing to his disciple Barrès as Barrès'

own enlistment in the adversary camp was to Blum: France was interested in establishing less Dreyfus' innocence, he speculated, than the general guilt . . . The suggestion, concerning France's initial interest in Dreyfus, is not without merit. In a fragment of *L'anneau d'améthyste* (*The Amethyst Ring*), first serialized in April 1898, Monsieur Bergeret, France's fictional surrogate throughout the affair, speculates ironically on the opportunity to rehabilitate Macbeth. Elsewhere, France would attempt as much for Blue-Beard. Might not the initial interest in Dreyfus' rehabilitation have been of the same perversely paradoxical and virtuoso sort? In any event that interest soon changed, a transformation that may be traced through the decreasing irony (or growing fervor) of Monsieur Bergeret in *Monsieur Bergeret à Paris* (1901). These are the years of France's conversion (through Dreyfusism) to socialism; they resulted in what is by no means the most successful of his numerous versions of the Affair. Ironically, even more than the brilliant satire of Dreyfusards and anti-Dreyfusards in *L'île des pingouins* (1908; *Penguin Island*), France's masterwork on the affair is perhaps the short story "Crainquebille" (originally published as "L'affaire Crainquebille" in Charles Péguy's *Cahiers de la quinzaine,* 1902; *Biweekly Notebooks*). This story, in many ways that of a Dreyfus who would never have been rehabilitated, suggests that when France's imagination is free to shape him, Dreyfus need fail, for the sake of art, the sake of the tale. Again: the interests of literature and the anti-Dreyfusard cause perversely intertwined.

And Zola, whose legendary "J'accuse" (1898; "I Accuse"), published in *L'aurore* after Esterházy's acquittal, remains the most celebrated document of the affair? Zola, who had been defeated numerous times in his quest for election to the Académie Française, was (like Dreyfusism itself) a cultural product consumed with far greater enthusiasm abroad than in France—for which reason Barrès could write him off as a foreigner, a "deracinated Venetian." But even within his own considerable oeuvre, the occasionally megalomaniacal tone of *La vérité en marche* (1901; *Truth on the March:* "I end the century, I begin the next century," p. 134) seems to partake of the humanitarian sentimentalism marring Zola's fictional transposition of the affair in *Vérité* (1903; *Truth*). In retrospect, Zola during the affair—even to the detail of his exile—appears to have been the last man of the 19th century (or the first of the 20th) to have taken himself for Victor Hugo. In the apotheosis of *Vérité,* the horizon of Zola's vision lay in a "universal embrace": no more religious wars; no more Catholics, and thus "no more Jews" (p. 1444). To have drawn that lesson from the affair is in many ways to have reversed the lesson learned by the man whom Zola supplanted as the "literary" hero of the affair, a figure promoted to "sainthood" by Péguy, Bernard Lazare. Lazare, author of *Une erreur judiciaire: La vérité sur l'affaire Dreyfus* (1896; *A Judicial Error: The Truth about the Dreyfus Affair*), moved from the symbolist milieu of Mallarmé's salon (where he was much resented by the anti-Dreyfusard Paul Valéry and the tepidly Dreyfusard André Gide) to a proto-Zionist struggle, against the dream of assimilation, for Jewish identity. A symbolist experience of the affair deeper than (Zola's) naturalist one? To claim as much is to overlook the fact that the engagement in the Dreyfusard cause was for Lazare in effect a farewell to symbolism—and to French literature as well.

See also 1905, 1945 (6 February).

Bibliography: Maurice Barrès, *Les déracinés* (Paris: Charpentier, 1897). Christophe Charle, "Champ littéraire et champ du pouvoir," *Annales,* 2 (March–April 1977), 240–261. Régis Debray, *Teachers, Writers, Celebrities: The Intellectuals of Modern France,* trans. David Macey (London: NLB, 1981). Cécile Delhorbe, *L'affaire Dreyfus et les écrivains français* (Paris: Aittinger, 1932). Bernard Lazare, *Une erreur judiciaire: La vérité sur l'affaire Dreyfus* (Brussels: Monnom, 1896). Geraldi Leroy, ed., *Les écrivains et l'affaire Dreyfus* (Orléans: Presses Universitaires de France, 1983). Georges Sorel, *La révolution dreyfusienne* (Paris: Rivière, 1910). Emile Zola, *Vérité,* in *Oeuvres complètes,* ed. Henri Mitterand, vol. 8 (Paris: Cercle du Livre Précieux, 1968). Zola, *La vérité en marche* (Paris: Fasquelle, 1901).

Jeffrey Mehlman

✎ 1905, 9 December

The Legislative Assembly Passes the Law concerning the Separation of Church and State, Ending the Concordat of 1801

On Schools, Churches, and Museums

Throughout the Dreyfus Affair, the church rushed to defend the honor of the army. The widespread collusion between the two leading orders of the ancien régime, between saber and aspergillum, discredited the church's recent politics of support for the Third Republic and provoked a strong resurgence of the anticlericalism that had been latent throughout the 19th century. Thus, in the defeat of the anti-Dreyfus camp, pro-Dreyfus intellectuals saw confirmation that the time was ripe for a secular ministry. The time had come for the fulfillment of Claude Frollo's prophecy in Victor Hugo's *Notre-Dame de Paris* (1831): "This will kill that"—the book will kill the church.

The campaign for the separation of church and state that followed the Dreyfus Affair featured the same cast of characters: Emile Zola and Anatole France, partisans of the separation as they had been of the retrial; and Maurice Barrès, opposed to both. But there were also realignments: Charles Péguy, former Dreyfusard, denounced the betrayal of Dreyfusism by the intellectual party; and Proust, recovered from his fervor for justice, set himself to wondering about the fate of art in a secularized society.

At the opening of the new century France still operated under the Concordat, a protocol fixing the relationship between the Catholic church and the French state, signed in 1801 by Bonaparte (at the time still First Consul of the French Republic) and Pope Pius VII. Although the Concordat had avoided any mention of the former divine right of kings, in it the republican government had recognized Catholicism as "the religion of the great majority of Frenchmen." Under it, bishops were appointed by the government as state employees would be (with the pope only confirming the appointment afterward) and were placed along with priests on the state's payroll. Rome, in committing itself to respect the autonomy of the internal affairs of the state, thereby gained a kind of religious national monopoly: all threat of schism was avoided. The Concordat stated: "There will be but one liturgy and one catechism for all the Catholic churches of France." It was this arrangement that the law passed on 9 December 1905 brought to an end, declaring that "the Republic neither recognizes, nor funds, either through salary or subvention, any cult whatever."

The campaign for secularization began in connection with school politics, in the thick of the Dreyfus Affair. Zola's novels reflect this development. There is not a single teacher in the family tree of *Les Rougon-Macquart* (1871–1893), the twenty-volume novelistic series to which Zola devoted the first half of his career. Only in his trilogy *Les évangiles* (1899–1903; *The Gospels*) does school appear in his work. In fact the plot of *Vérité* (1903; *Truth*), the third gospel, combines the recent Dreyfus Affair, with its struggle for justice, and the current campaign for the separation and the secularization of schools. It moves from Paris to a provincial town, Maillebois. Dreyfus becomes Simon. He is no longer an officer but a schoolteacher. And, because he is Jewish, a cabal of zealots accuses him of a crime—in this instance a sexual one—that he has not committed. But the innocent one, soon condemned to transportation to the colonies, leaves the stage to the real hero of the novel, Marc, also a schoolteacher, who, following Zola's steps, as it were, enters the lists against all comers in order to see that justice is done. And it will be done, with its final victory reverberating even at the national level. At the end of the novel, the triumphal return of the innocent martyr coincides with a legislative coup de théâtre: "A terrible blow had just been dealt to the Church; the last Chamber had finally voted the total separation of Church and State" (*Vérité*, p. 1431). When it had assimilated to the civil service a clergy otherwise deprived of service by the coming of an industrial society, the Concordat had enabled the churches to survive the disaffection of the public. Zola was scandalized by such an infraction of social Darwinism: "When a function disappears from social life, the monument and the man, necessary before but henceforth useless, disappear" (p. 1432). The Separation put a full stop to what he saw as an anachronistic state funding of parasitism. Zola exulted, "The churches became, like the theaters, places of public spectacle, enterprises of simple commercialism, supported by paying spectators" (p. 1431).

Vérité is a posthumous work. Zola died accidentally in 1902, just after the electoral victory of the coalition of left-wing parties that, three years later, with Emile Combes as prime minister, would effect passage of the Law of Separation. In fact his funeral rites were one of the opening events of the campaign that achieved the triumph described in the most committed of his novels. The Third Republic, in effect, buried its writers with the pomp that the ancien régime had reserved for its generals. Anatole France gave the eulogy. This ironic and skeptical Academician, a dilettantish and misanthropic humanist, had ear-

831

lier disapproved of the humid naturalism of the deceased. But solidarity in combat overrides aesthetic incompatibility. Besides, France's anticlericalism was not new. Advocate of a natural morality, he never missed a chance to use his Voltairian sarcasms against the sublimity of revelation. In his four-volume *Histoire contemporaine* (1897–1901), especially the ecclesiastical chronicles of *L'orme du mail* (1897; *The Elm-Tree on the Mall*), he had already satirized the political intrigues that absorbed the provincial clergy. And whereas Zola had predicted that the Separation must transform churches into theaters, for France this metamorphosis was already an accomplished fact. The modern world had no place for the sacred. "The church is an establishment more civil than religious, which takes after the city hall and the concert chamber. Women show off their clothes there" (*L'église et la république* [1904; *The Church and the Republic*], in *Trente ans de vie sociale*, 2:80).

France would become, for the Separation, what Zola had been for the Dreyfus Affair. In 1904 he published two diatribes, *Le parti noir* (*The Black Party*) and *L'église et la république,* and wrote the preface for *Une campagne laïque* (1902–03) (*A Campaign for Secularization*), a collection of Combes's speeches. But it was not the Separation per se that he defended; he saw it as the prelude to the extinction of the separated church. "A priest who ceases being a civil servant," he jested, "is constrained to become a holy man, and that's a drastic extreme" ("La Séparation devant le Sénat" [1905; "The Separation before the Senate"], in *Trente ans,* 2:134). Could one imagine a head desiring its own decapitation? Therefore, what we are witnessing, he implied, are the final days of the condemned. "It is always from temporal Powers that Religions have drawn sustenance. Separated, they languish and die" (ibid.). France defended the Separation because he believed no more in a separated church than in a disincarnated soul.

Both Zola and France saw the Separation as the logical consequence of the Dreyfus Affair. Péguy, on the other hand, saw the Separation as its betrayal: as he put it, a mystical experience had degenerated into a political one. Writer, printer, publisher, and bookseller, Péguy had started *Les cahiers de la quinzaine* (*Biweekly Notebooks*) in 1900, published from his shop in the rue de la Sorbonne. A craftsman of the book, he was also an angry metaphysician, a fiercely independent polemicist.

The debate soon moved from pedagogical concerns to artistic ones. In his "Réponse brève à Jaurès" ("Short Reply to Jean Jaurès") of 1900 (the socialist leader was still his ally and friend), Péguy remembered his first visit to the Louvre. He had just arrived from Orléans. "I wonder if during our lifetime we ever felt a comparable religious emotion" (*Oeuvres,* p. 567). But it was precisely the memory of such intense religiosity that made him, in 1900, condemn the museum. "Réponse brève" describes the passage from the religious to the artistic, the birth of aesthetic freethinking, a personal relation to individual works supplanting the religious and collective relation to the artistic institution. Jaurès anticipated the collective ownership of works of art as one of the benefits of socialism. But Péguy was not inspired by the idea of art for all. His anarchist view of socialism opposed the depoliticization of art to its collectivization.

At the time, he was not a believer. The campaign to reopen the Dreyfus case had been a campaign for freethinking, and he blamed religion for always arguing from the grounds of its own authority. The Dreyfusard mystique, in this sense, already entailed for Péguy a certain form of separation, the separation of reason and politics, analogous to those of art and the museum, of the infinite and the finite. Certain substances do not mix. There is the state, there is reason; but there will never be state reason. There must not be a state metaphysics (nor a philosophy, an aesthetic, a religion). Thus, in the separation of church from state, Péguy did not see anything like the severance of head from trunk that Zola and France anticipated, but the respectful recognition of the distinction between spiritual and material substances. It was not for him a matter of replacing, but of separating. The state will not become an up-to-date version of the church. Some realities are not susceptible to modernization. A childhood is irreplaceable. And although one may leave Orléans to become a man in Paris, Paris can kill neither Orléans nor Chartres.

In this way Péguy came to distance himself from most of his former Dreyfusard allies, who, under the Separation, were urging a transfer to the state of the church's former pedagogical authority. Ever irreligious, Péguy required that the place of the absent God remain empty. As early as 1901, in "De la raison" ("On Reason"), he condemned the substitution of a secular catechism for a Catholic one. He denounced those who wished to install "a clergy of reason," "to start again in secular form the abuses of the Church" (*Oeuvres*, p. 840). Committed to the separation of reason and authority, he saw in the separation of church and state a mere conflict between authorities. Péguy returned increasingly to the Catholicism of his childhood: the unbeliever, who wished to establish an absolute difference between clericalism and reason, came gradually to accept a religion from which the Law of Separation had stripped much of its authority.

Barrès tells in his journal, *Mes cahiers* (1929–1957; *My Notebooks*), of having planned, with his nationalist friends, a demonstration to disrupt the funeral rites for Zola. They found no one to follow them. It was the hour of the radical triumph. Barrès himself had just been defeated in the elections of 1902. He sought consolation for his defeat in Venice. "La mort de Venise" ("The Death of Venice") opens his *Amori et Dolori Sacrum* (1902). Barrès did not like museums any more than Péguy did. Let the experts of restoration refrain from making Venice into one! Let us fear irreparable repair. "I pity Venice," he says, "but I would not want my pity to rebuild it" (*Amori*, p. 23). Why return life to something that death enhances?

Meanwhile, in Paris, Combes and his radical deputies worked toward the Separation. Barrès would finally be elected in 1906. By then, the Separation had been voted through, but the new deputy would make its implementation the occasion of debates in the course of which his Venetian aesthetic underwent a significant change. His speeches before the Assembly were collected in 1914 in *La grande pitié des églises de France* (*The Great Pity of France's Churches*). "Let us not speak of beauty that dies," the former author of "La mort de Venise" now says (*La grande pitié,* p. 393). He who had insisted on letting expire that which is inclined toward death, became more restrictive: "It was a matter of Venice and of the pleasure of aesthetes" (p. 404).

His rejection of museums relied on grounds opposite to Péguy's. Whereas Péguy opposed aesthetic free thought to the religiosity of museums, Barrès saw artistic connoisseurship as the symptom of free thought most dangerous to the religious. In his speeches before the Assembly, he continually denounced the artistic reconversion of the sacred, the supplanting of the faithful by tourists, art historians, and collectors. "I do not come to speak out for beautiful churches" (*La grande pitié,* p. 82), Barrès claimed. Yet the aesthete in him insisted on resurfacing: "But no church is ugly for a man of taste" (p. 144). It is not because they are beautiful that it is necessary to save the churches, but it is beautiful that churches are not art objects and that people go there, not because they have good taste and these edifices are worth the trip, but because they believe. Mass is more beautiful than the church. "For it to exist, its content, its cult must exist, because a deconsecrated church, without the faithful, without prayers, without the Eucharist, dies and will soon be nothing but an expensive burden" (p. 395). Barrès, himself an unbeliever, opposed the prospect of art's taking over religion, but he did so for reasons that, in the last analysis, were more artistic than religious: the desacralization of churches now transformed into works of art will result in a loss that is primarily aesthetic.

Proust, an early Dreyfusard, opposed the Separation. In a long letter to his friend Georges de Lauris, with whom he had just been discussing the pending law, he summed up with a single question the arguments he had used against secularization: "Will there be an anticlerical art?" (29 July 1903, *Correspondance,* p. 385). Although Catholicism could be credited for the most brilliant centuries of European artistic production, one could not expect anticlerical passions to become a similar source of inspiration. One year later, in "La mort des cathédrales" ("The Death of the Cathedrals"), published on 16 August by *Le Figaro,* Proust's position had not changed. But his reasoning had: it was no longer art whose survival he doubted, but the difference between art and religion. "It is better to tear down a church than to deconsecrate it," he replied to those who proposed the conversion of churches into museums (in *Contre Sainte-Beuve,* p. 774). Proust's motives, indeed, shifted significantly: having first rejected anticlericalism for its artistic sterility, he then refused to defend Catholicism on artistic grounds. Proust wanted to prevent art from becoming the religion of those who do not believe.

"La mort des cathédrales," contemporary with Barrès' "La mort de Venise," begins in a science-fiction mode. Proust imagines that Catholicism is dead, forgotten. Archaeologists have finally managed to reconstitute the details of its rituals. And the government decides to fund their reenactment. The job is entrusted to artists who are inspired, conscientious, irreproachable; yet, whatever their professional qualification, they are still artists, acting the part of men who do not act, but who believe. Nothing happens for real. Proust then returns to the situation that the Separation will put an end to: everything is real in a church. "Gesture, psalmody, and chanting are not entrusted here to artists. These are the very ministers of the cult who officiate, in a sentiment not of aesthetics but of faith, and all the more aesthetically" (*Contre Sainte-Beuve*, p. 143). All the more beautiful that it is not a question of art: here religion has, as with Barrès, the beauty of things that do not pretend to beauty. But, also as with Barrès, this beauty offers itself up to the contemplation of someone who does not believe. Does one go to a church to verify that it is not a theater? The faithful might not be spectators themselves, but what about those who watch the faithful, those who do not take part but simply witness the participation of others? "The actors," as Proust calls those who are not acting, "could not be wished more lifelike, more sincere, because it is the people themselves who, without taking note of it, undertake to act for us" (ibid.). Proust and Barrès wanted to maintain the distinction between temple and museum, between priest and actor.

At the end of André Malraux's novel *La condition humaine* (1933; *Man's Fate*), the sage Gisors dreams of the future. "The factory, which is still only a kind of church of the catacombs, must become what the cathedral was" (*Man's Fate*, p. 330). The same vision inspires *L'espoir* (1937; *Man's Hope*), where, thanks to the civil war, the Spanish cathedrals are endowed with a present, living content: they have been converted into military depots by the Republican forces. From Pierre Drieu la Rochelle to the members of the Collège de Sociologie, from Louis Aragon to Sartre, the list of authors who, in the 20th century, have wanted to reinvent a place for the sacred that will fit the modern world, to refind a religion beyond the Separation, is endless. For Malraux, the myth of revolution had been the first response to this dream; the museum would be the second. "This entire century obsessed by cathedrals will leave only one of them behind: the museum," he wrote in *Le musée imaginaire* ([1947; *The Museum without Walls*], p. 69). The museum gives life back to the dead gods whom it recycles. What had begun, with Zola and France, as cultural desacralization, with Malraux transformed itself into the sacralization of culture—not a secular art but a religion of art. Against this, Péguy's views or those of Proust in "La mort des cathédrales" hint at a modernism that would find its inspiration in the resistance of art to all religious posturing, in the will to maintain, especially in a world that has ceased to be religious, the distinction between art and faith.

See also 1808, 1898, 1959 (9 January).

Bibliography: Maurice Barrès, *Amori et Dolori Sacrum* (Paris: Félix Juven, 1902). Barrès, *La grande pitié des églises de France* (Paris: Emile-Paul, 1914). Barrès, *Mes cahiers*, vol. 3 (Paris: Plon, 1931). Anatole France, *L'église et la république* and "La Séparation devant le Sénat," in *Trente ans de vie sociale,* ed. Claude Aveline, vol. 2 (= vol. 27 of *Oeuvres complètes*) (Paris: Cercle du Bibliophile, 1970). France, *The Elm-Tree on the Mall,* trans. M. P. Willcocks, vol. 8 of *The Works of Anatole France,* ed. Frederic Chapman (London: J. Lane, 1910). Maurice Larkin, *Church and State after the Dreyfus Affair: The Sepa-*

ration Issue in France (London: Macmillan, 1974). André Malraux, *Man's Fate,* trans. Haakon M. Chevalier (New York: Random House, 1961). Malraux, *Le musée imaginaire* (Paris: Gallimard, 1965). Charles Péguy, *Oeuvres en prose complètes,* ed. Robert Burac, vol. 1 (Paris: Gallimard, 1987). Marcel Proust, *Correspondance,* ed. Philip Kolb, vol. 3 (Paris: Plon, 1976). Proust, "La mort des cathédrales," in *Contre Sainte-Beuve précédé de Pastiches et mélanges,* ed. Pierre Clarac (Paris: Gallimard, 1971). Michael Sutton, *Nationalism, Positivism and Catholicism: The Politics of Charles Maurras and French Catholics* (Cambridge: Cambridge University Press, 1982). Emile Zola, *Vérité,* in *Oeuvres complètes,* ed. Henri Mitterand, vol. 8 (Paris: Cercle du Livre Précieux, 1968).

Denis Hollier

✑ 1911

Under the Title *C.R.D.N.* Anonymous Dialogues on Homosexuality Are Printed in Belgium in a Twelve-Copy Private Edition

From Exoticism to Homosexuality

Written over a seven-year period (1896–1903), the four little texts that constitute *Amyntas* (1904) range from an initial Loti-like incantation to the disenchanted scrutiny we recognize today in the "travel writing" of a Graham Greene or a V. S. Naipaul. The little book, largely overlooked in the canon, is a sort of hinge in André Gide's career, for it marks—under a name borrowed from Theocritus and later assigned by Virgil to a shepherd of enterprising but melancholy eros—an articulation of consciousness: far from being a merely decorative opuscule whose rhapsodies have hitherto evaded translation and even commentary because of their apparent submersion in local and exotic color, *Amyntas* accounts for how the author of *Les nourritures terrestres* (1897; *The Fruits of the Earth*), that Nietzschean apostrophe to hedonist liberation, became the author of *Corydon* (1911), those insistently subversive dialogues on the nature of human sexuality and on the place of the homosexual in society. Gide began writing *Corydon* as soon as *Amyntas* was published, and hoped for a preface to this "second shepherd's play" from Freud himself.

Amyntas, then, is a work of disintoxication, in which Gide attempts to separate himself—ruefully, gingerly—from the North African prospects and panoramas that had hitherto formed his entire erotic spectrum. Of course he was working in a great French convention—Flaubert and Eugène Fromentin, Eugène Delacroix and Pierre Loti had shown him the way; yet only Gide achieved the right tonality of eros in his ecstatic dedication to certain landscapes, certain desolations of weather and light. Perhaps Gide's commitment, his ardor, was so tenacious precisely because the desert is the one place where a man's thirst cannot be quenched.

Years later, when considering the possibility of a reprint with illustrations, Gide was to murmur reproaches in his *Journal* (to others? to himself?) about the reception of *Amyntas:* "Few realize I have never written anything more perfect than *Amyntas*. People look for descriptions, for the picturesque, for information about the country and its customs. Yet there is virtually nothing in the book I could not just as well have written elsewhere—in France, any-where. To whom could the secret value of the book speak? Only to the select few. Others were disappointed" (December 1910).

In *Amyntas* the stupefying rhetoric of exoticism collapses; the identification with a certain "primitive" languor falters. The book is the secret narrative of one more impoverishment, a destitution that will lead the author to his authentic riches, his characteristic fictions: *Les caves du Vatican* (1914; *Lafcadio's Adventures*), *Les faux-monnayeurs* (1925; *The Counterfeiters*). Exorcism is perhaps the one constant in Gide's metamorphic career, an anthology of returns—from symbolism, from exoticism, from homosexuality, from communism. And of course, in order to return, one must make a departure. From his very first work, *Les cahiers d'André Walter* (1891; *The Notebooks of André Walter*), published before he was twenty, Gide was concerned with wrenching himself from his comforts, chronicling his consequent lacerations, and accepting no easy solace. André Walter, like Rainer Maria Rilke's Malte Laurids Brigge (fragments of whose diaries Gide was to translate in 1911), would commit suicide; Gide, like Rilke, would survive into a new realism, a new reality. By tracing the decline of the substitutive persona, Gide managed to save himself, to become, as he put it early on, the most irreplaceable of beings.

It was not easy. The disappointments of the insistently returning lover—the connoisseur of landscape, of *Stimmung*—are bitter, sometimes comical in the chronicling. But these are undergone in *Amyntas* for the sake of grander claims, intimations—to be made clear in *L'immoraliste* (1902; *The Immoralist*)—of a more active eros: adulthood! Indeed, the value of *Les nourritures terrestres* is only in the subsequent transcending of its message. The modest *Amyntas* is an enact-ment of just such manumission; it ends in the Normandy autumn, Gide's per-sona racked by his longing for that discarded polymorphous perversity he had once discovered for himself in "De Biskra à Touggourt" ("From Biskra to Toug-gourt," the first piece in *Amyntas*). The opposite of a neurosis, Freud was to say, is a perversion. So Gide was to discover, and *Amyntas* represents the lyrical working out of that maturation which I should call *barbarism and its discontents* if I had not already called it *Gide's Way*.

L'immoraliste was finished in 1901, a year after Freud's *The Interpretation of Dreams*, and published—"so far behind me," Gide wrote in his *Journal*, "that I cannot bear to correct the proofs" (2 March 1902)—in an edition of 300 copies in 1902, a year before Nietzsche's posthumous *The Will to Power*. Whereas *Amyntas* is dedicated to Gide's wife, *L'immoraliste* is dedicated to de-stroying her. Freud and Nietzsche are the landmarks by which to locate this narrative, this voice raised almost to the tension of the lyre as it fills the night on the terrace of Sidi b. M. If there is anything immoral about Michel it is his style—languorous, sometimes complacent, yet with all the terrible energy of a man who has made it his duty to be happy. In it we recognize Gide's very charged sense that only excess may be recompensed, that only *too much* thirst is to be slaked. This recital might as well be called "Civilization and Its Discon-tents" as "Toward a Genealogy of Morals."

Certainly skepticism is what resonates at the end of the trajectory beginning with *Les nourritures terrestres* and ending with *Corydon*. Who was this last, so hemmed and hawed over? Certainly he was a shepherd in Virgil's second Eclogue, in the first line of which we learn that he burned for fair Alexis (another shepherd). To the classically educated Frenchman, the name alone would be, even now, an indication of sexual status, although in the Anglo-Saxon pastoral tradition—in Spenser, for example—Corydon is merely a shepherd and quite as susceptible of being matched with a shepherdess.

Gide was fond of the names that strew the Theocritean canon. One of the most important is that of Ménalque (Menalchas), who first appears in 1895 in a prose fragment of that name, later incorporated into *Les nourritures terrestres*. Apparently *L'immoraliste* was to have been a life of Ménalque before it became Michel's interior drama; the rather "nineties" tempter and catalyst, evidently drawn from Gide's entranced observations of Oscar Wilde, is yet endowed with a resonance we recognize in another connection:

> Lately an absurd, a shameful lawsuit with scandalous repercussions had given the newspapers a convenient occasion to besmirch his name; those whom his scorn and superiority offended seized this opportunity for their revenge; and what irritated them most was that he seemed quite unaffected. "You have to let other people be right," was his answer to their insults. "It consoles them for not being anything else." But Society was outraged, and those who, as the saying goes, "respect themselves" felt obliged to cut him, thereby requiting his contempt. (*L'immoraliste*, p. 425)

Obviously this is the same man who, "I had been told, made no objection to certain unnatural tendencies attributed to him" (*Corydon*, p. 3). Gide has managed to accommodate much of what remains outside his fictions in the figure of Ménalque, and not only the "I" of *Corydon*—a frequently boorish, utterly un-Gidian bigot—but also Corydon himself are the book's real success (as we so often feel that Plato's real success is the figure of Socrates and the décor of the polis, the attribution to philosophy of a site and a voice). Some of the best comic touches occur at the very beginning of Gide's little subversion, already adumbrated so subtly in *Corydon* (p. 4):

> On entering his apartment, I admit I received none of the unfortunate impressions I had feared. Nor did Corydon afford any such impression by the way he dressed, which was quite conventional, even a touch austere perhaps. I glanced around the room in vain for signs of that effeminacy which experts manage to discover in everything connected with inverts and by which they claim they are never deceived. However I did notice, over his mahogany desk, a huge photographic reproduction of Michelangelo's *Creation of Man*, showing Adam naked on the primeval slime, reaching up to the diving Hand and turning toward God a dazzled look of gratitude. Corydon's vaunted love of art would have accounted for any surprise I might have shown at the choice of this particular subject. On the desk, the portrait of an old man with a long white beard whom I immediately recognized as the American poet Walt Whitman.

In *Lolita* (1955) Vladimir Nabokov provides a parody of this scene. Humbert Humbert is delighted to discover some comfort in the analogous sufferer and pederast Gaston Godin, who "always wore black, even his tie was black; he seldom bathed . . . Upstairs, he had a studio—he painted a little, the old fraud. He had decorated its sloping wall with large photographs of pensive André Gide, Tchaikovsky, Norman Douglas, two other well-known English writers, Nijinsky (all thighs and fig leaves) and Marcel Proust. All these poor people seemed about to fall on you from their inclined plane" (p. 166).

By the time Gide had reached *Corydon,* the century had turned and the pervert's lair was no longer represented as the incense-blued den of decadence (pages of illustrations); Corydon's asceticisms are just as clear props and signs. Only the narrator is taken in.

To be taken in—to be deceived, especially self-deceived—was for Gide an abomination. It was what he knew to be wrong with his culture (even with symbolism, which he declared to Valéry left too much out). And this was the realm of lies and fraudulence, which alone could rouse Gide from his own lair by any number of youthful solicitations. As the years have gone by, his steadfast refusal to lie has glowed steadily like a declarative beacon played on a much-vexed darkness. The pursuit of truth and its essential Gidian corollary, the refusal to lie, make *Corydon* worth reading. For despite his painstaking recourse to an appallingly rigged and anthropomorphized zoology, despite his other recourse—the two are always found together in the period's apologies for the homosexual in society—to the literary and historical vestiges of Greek culture, Gide was on to something; indeed, the very indecisiveness of his vocabulary affords a clue that his translators have often chosen to overlook. Precisely when we are discovering that there is no such massive and unitary object of discourse (or experience) as homosexuality, Gide's fluctuations in nomenclature must be rendered as an index of a mind reluctant to dignify confusion by calling it uniformity. The terms he uses in *Corydon* may seem to us merely quaint—*uranism, pederasty, inversion, degeneracy,* not to mention *urnings* and *the third sex*—but at least they question, they even jeopardize, conventions of classification that impose a false unity of conceptualization. Like the Freud he had not read and the D. H. Lawrence who never read him, Gide suggests, in the very variety (instability) of his nomenclature as well as in his liberalizing proposals to a relentlessly repressive and therefore libertine society, that the language of desire is not "about" a continuous unitary sexual experience. Rather, as we learn from *Amyntas,* that language produces and constitutes such experience. What we say structures "instinct" and generates the scripts in which experience and sensation, in themselves, are registered and understood. Or at least received.

Begun in 1907, *Corydon* gestated for thirteen years. It was first published in 1911 in an unsigned private edition of twelve copies with the title *C.R.D.N.* and consisted of only the first two dialogues and a bit of the third; in 1920 another unsigned private edition of twenty-one copies contained all four dialogues and a preface; finally, in 1925, it was published, titled *Corydon,* in a signed, commercial edition, much reprinted subsequently. In 1921, deter-

mined upon its general publication (partly as a result of the wrenching alienation from his wife, who had burned all his letters to her upon realizing that
Gide had accompanied young Marc Allégret to England), Gide made a great
discovery. He began to read Freud, the Freud who seemed to echo his own
thoughts when he had written: "Psychoanalysis resists entirely the attempt to
regard homosexuals as a specially formed group and to separate them from other
men . . . It finds that all men are capable of a homosexual object choice and
that they have in fact performed it unconsciously . . . The exclusive sexual
interest of a man for a woman is equally in need of explanation and cannot be
taken for granted as an underlying chemical attraction" (*Three Essays*, pp. 11–
12). So delighted was Gide to learn that Freud regarded a man who experienced
no homosexual desires rather than one who did as the oddity, that he asked his
translator, Dorothy Bussy, to consider whether her brother, James Strachey,
Freud's English translator, might not intercede for him: would not Freud be the
ideal authority to supply a preface to *Corydon,* thereby sheltering it from many
of the misconceptions and antagonisms it was bound to provoke? Apparently
communication broke down somewhere between Bussy, Strachey, and Vienna,
but it is noteworthy that Gide began psychoanalysis (five sessions) at about this
time, and that he went so far as to speculate: "Perhaps I might present *Corydon*
as 'translated from the German' . . . a preface by Freud might emphasize the
book's usefulness and timeliness" (*Journal,* April 1921). The perceived con-
gruity of purpose between Freud and Gide echoes a larger historical structure:
the apprehension of unity within apparently opposed or agonistic energies,
whether sexual or psychic. *Corydon* remains one of the books crucial to an understanding of the development of the Western mind in the first quarter of the
20th century.

   Corydon participates in the intuition of ecstatic wholeness that appears to be
the ruling metaphysical pathos of its period. From *L'immoraliste* and *Les nourritures terrestres* to *Si le grain ne meurt* (1921; *If It Die*), Gide's first autobiography,
Gide's apprehension of discursively determined rhapsodic experience remains
unequaled in French literature for the scope and frankness of its scrutiny. Gide's
secret, as Camus once remarked, is that he never lost, among all his doubts,
the pride of being human. His is not a great mind, wrote E. M. Forster in
1951, in his obituary of Gide, but a free one—"and free minds are as rare
as great, and even more valuable at the present moment" ("Gide's Death,"
p. 232).

   Like other works of the period, *Corydon* explores not the nature of human
sexuality but the history of its repression; it peers, sometimes gracefully, sometimes grotesquely, beneath what Gide called the veil of lies, convention, and
hypocrisy that still stifles an important and not contemptible part of humanity.

   The same year that Hitler published *Mein Kampf,* Gide published *Si le grain
ne meurt,* the program of another battle, another subversion. Indeed, the
strategy had been laid four years before, when Gide first spoke of these memoirs
to Marcel Proust: "Spent an hour of yesterday evening with Proust . . . I take
him *Corydon* of which he promises not to speak to anyone; and when I say a

word or two about my memoirs: 'You can tell everything' he exclaims, 'but on condition you never say: *I.*' Which does not suit me" (*Journal,* May 1921). During the years in which Gide enabled the discussion of homosexuality with *Amyntas, Les nourritures terrestres, L'immoraliste, Corydon,* and *Si le grain ne meurt,* Jean Cocteau, Marcel Jouhandeau, and Jean Genet devised and perfected their own idiolects of heterodoxy. The argument implied by Proust's comment to Gide has in fact little significance in comparison to the enormous freedom that the Marcel of *A la recherche* acknowledges and enjoys in speaking of sexual subjects. Thenceforth the dialogue among Gide, Proust, and these writers was just that, a dialogue, in contrast to the previous series of sensational (and sometimes preposterous) soliloquies. Frequently the tone was snappish: Gide portrayed Cocteau in *Les faux-monnayeurs* as Count Robert de Passavant; Genet dismissed Gide with "I do not like judges who bend amorously over their victims"; Jouhandeau bandwagoned, "How amused I was, reading *Les faux-monnayeurs,* to see that we have dealt with the same scene, you know, the 'child suicide,' and perhaps at the same moment. It is an episode in my tale that Kahnweiler is to publish next autumn, and which has as its epigraph: Everyone wakes with a minor preoccupation: that of murdering God" (*Correspondance,* p. 62). But these were intramural sports. Much later, as a result of their struggles, the subject of homosexuality acquired the status of legitimate literature.

In the last twenty-five years, largely as a result of Gide's work, there has been a change in both the status and the language of the homosexual writer in France. The homosexual writer in France today is born simultaneously with his text: or rather, his text brings him into being. He does not exist as a glorious or scandalous progenitor; he is not supplied with a being that precedes or transcends his writing. If there is a certain invisibility about him, it is because he no longer needs to present himself as a *monstre sacré.* When the homosexual is no longer the subject of which his book is the predicate, then he eludes the scandal and parade of *before* and *after:* there is the time of writing, which is also the time of our reading, and the problem (is this not what Gide was trying to tell us?) becomes the solution. Of course solutions raise other problems, but that is no more than the dialectics of life itself; in our oedipal tradition of parricide and piety, as Cocteau has shown, one stages a symbolic murder of one's father (as classical literature is received and devoured as the ancestor of French literature), but the other great inheritance, the other great theme of descent, is then realized: the theme of the Possession of the Mothers.

See also 1847, 1922, 1925 (November), 1933 (February), 1962.

Bibliography: E. M. Forster, "Gide's Death," in *Two Cheers for Democracy* (New York: Harcourt and Brace, 1951). Sigmund Freud, *Three Essays on the Theory of Sexuality,* trans. James Strachey (New York: Basic Books, 1962). André Gide, *Amyntas,* trans. Richard Howard (New York: Ecco Press, 1988). Gide, *Corydon,* trans. Richard Howard (New York: Farrar and Straus, 1983). Gide, *L'immoraliste,* in *Romans, récits et soties: Oeuvres lyriques* (Paris: Gallimard, 1958). Gide, *Journal* (1889–1939) (Paris: Gallimard,

1951). Gide, *Oscar Wilde: In Memoriam (Reminiscences), De Profundis,* trans. Bernard Frechtman (New York: Philosophical Library, 1949). Marcel Jouhandeau, *Correspondance avec André Gide (octobre 1922–septembre 1946)* (Paris: Marcel Sautier, 1958). Vladimir Nabokov, *Lolita* (New York: Berkley, 1973).

Richard Howard

∝ *1913*

Guillaume Apollinaire Publishes His First Collection of Poems, *Alcools*

Lyrical Ideograms

Literary historians have called 1913 the annus mirabilis of the 20th century. Proust had published *Du côté de chez Swann* (*Swann's Way*); Gide was polishing *Les caves du Vatican* (1914; *Lafcadio's Adventures*); Valéry took up poetry after a decade of silence and began drafting *La jeune Parque* (1917; *The Young Fate*). At the same time Guillaume Apollinaire saw *Alcools* go to press. Writers who had lived through the Promethean 19th-century visions of literature were now yielding ground to new generations of painter-poets. Influenced by optical revolutions in the path of Paul Cézanne, these experimenters explored retinal aspects of writing, painting, and motion. They used rapid travel in cars and trains to glimpse the fleeting relations between language and sensation. Max Jacob's *Le cornet à dés* (1917; *The Dice Cup*) cast its prose poems by chance and haphazard placement. A voyager who lived in transit for the sake of poetry, Blaise Cendrars wrote verbal photographs called *Kodak* (1924) and transcribed pell-mell impressions of railway travel across Russia in *Prose du Transsibérien* (1913; *Prose from the Transsiberian*). His epic of rhymed sensations, "Les Pâques à New York" (1912; "Easter in New York"), was about to inspire the vision of Apollinaire's "Zone."

In 20th-century literature Apollinaire's two major collections, *Alcools* (1913) and *Calligrammes* (1918), mark a decisive shift from musical to visual poetry. In 1912 the poet championed the cubist painters in articles that were gathered in *Les peintres cubistes: Méditations esthétiques* (*Cubist Painters: Aesthetic Meditations*) the following year. From Georges Braque and Picasso, Apollinaire learned how words, letters, and images could be incorporated into verbal collages. He explained how the new painters were dismantling the "subject" of painting in favor of concrete meditations on the origins and limits of visibility. He noticed that ciphers on limited palettes of gray, beige, white, and tan fields were depriving painting of depth and confusing the acts of reading and seeing. With the advent of collage in the immediate prewar years, spectators' eyes were forced up against the tactile qualities of newsprint, wrappers, and debris glued to the canvas; this new genre showed Apollinaire how the printed page could also become a field of experiment that could strip poetry of its musical, narrative, and emotive registers.

How, since the impact of the cubists, he implied, could writers *not* cast doubt upon the field of illusion that had been the stuff of literary language?

842

Their experiments in mixed media required readers to behold language in its concrete, graphic shapes. It could not be read or merely followed along linear axes. Thanks to the cubists, poetry could become utterly visual; it could also take leave of the transcriptive and dialectical elements that the symbolists had championed. Music, Stéphane Mallarmé had arcanely affirmed in *La musique et les lettres* (1895; *Music and Letters*), was "prestige located at this point of breath and of almost abstract vision, becoming meaning" (*Oeuvres*, p. 649). Music and letters "were alternative means extended toward the shadows" (ibid.) cast down from great spiritual realms. Apollinaire rejected this kind of aura. Following the critical work initiated in *Les peintres cubistes*, he conceived of the page as a canvas that blocks symbolic language—of sensation, pathos, lyrical vision—from moving from object to essence. The page becomes a support that stages experiments with relations between figure and ground, between centers and circumferences, between crosshatched shapes and vectors broken off and begun again. Apollinaire could have recast Mallarmé's legendary remark to Degas, "It is not with ideas, but with words, that poetry is written," to read, "It is not with words, but with shapes, that lyrics are painted."

Cubism and poetry converged in about 1912. *Alcools* assembled most of the verse Apollinaire had written since 1902. Except for "Zone," written just before the collection was published, most is musical and melancholic. The earlier lyrics evoke the figure of an amorous subject, displaced from his northern origins, who gains a sentimental education through travel and failed romance. "La chanson du mal aimé" ("The Song of the Ill-Loved") sings an epic of love betrayed in tones of German lieder. "Rhénane d'automne" ("Autumn Rhine-Song") hits notes reminiscent of the errant poets Jules Laforgue and Rimbaud. Melancholy "between love and disdain" prevails in "Clotilde" and "Les colchiques" ("Autumn Crocuses"). "Le pont Mirabeau" ("The Mirabeau Bridge") sings of love lost over the waves of time.

Not so with "Zone," where a visual lyric abounds. The title designates the outer limits of a modern city, not suburbs or residential quarters, but an industrial landscape—of migrant workers' quarters, gutted buildings, railroad depots—comprising a peripheral but seemingly infinite extension at the end of the modern city. "Zone" tells of the poet's travels to and from Paris; to places and names taken from the map of central Europe and Greek mythology; to cathedrals offering sanctuary in the midst of literary tourism; to Rome, Japan, the Orient; finally, to the world of Oceanic figurines that adorn the apartment in which the poem is written. Cast in free verse, the poem disorients the eye and ear accustomed to the strict measure of the French alexandrine. It sustains a rhythm that veers toward assonance all the while its couplets build a visibly graphic measure. Punctuation marks are absent. The poem displays a cinematic aspect of extended "lap dissolve," or what the film director Sergei Eisenstein would soon theorize as movements established by tensions among space, line, letters, and forms in passage.

Several technical innovations detach it from the vocal tenor of symbolist poetry. First, exclusive use of the present tense casts the wandering poet into the here and now of an absolute present. Flashbacks punctuate the voyages, but they are no less immediate than the impression of the present instant. Like a collage, the verbal texture pulls the shadows of a past tense or repressed dimension of experience onto a single verbal plane. Depth of field, the element that painters and cineasts use to produce illusion (or even psychology and ideation), has an analogue in poetry in the play of past and present tenses. Apollinaire radically flattens narrative depth by pushing the future *down* and pulling the past *up* into the play of graphics before our eyes.

Second, in its narratives classical verse weaves a complex relation of pronouns. When the traditional poet spoke in the third person of the historian, the first person or implied reader was held in the shadows of description. From the play of pronouns a poet could fabricate an illusion and gain omniscience. The second person went unnamed in the verbal field, since the effacement of the spectator or the reader (the "we" or "us") had to be assumed in order for the picture of the narrative to achieve its illusion. In "Zone" *je* (I) and *tu* (the familiar "you") are unified, disallowing articulation of human space and volume. *We* wander together as subjects seeing the very figures that the "I" is scripting or affixing to the page. The shifters produce an air of intimacy that differs radically from the other poems of *Alcools*. Impressions pass in review but are shared between speaker and viewer only in the evanescence of their montage. Wherever affective tones are stated—"Tu as souffert de l'amour" ("You have suffered from love"; line 117)—surrounding parades of sensations scatter all sentimentality (lines 11–12):

> Tu lis les prospectus les catalogues les affiches qui chantent tout haut
> Voilà la poésie ce matin et pour la prose il y a les journaux

> You read the ads the catalogues the posters that sing on the highest line
> That's poetry this morning for prose the newspaper is fine

The imagery ascends, but the writing brings rapture back to earth. The lyrics will themselves seek to defy gravity, to break all records—of flight, sport, and poetry—but are anchored in objects readily made or found. A healthy *obviousness* is captured in the collage of things common—newspapers, posters, and signboards—that jolt the subject out of his pathos (lines 21–22):

> Les inscriptions des enseignes et des murailles
> Les plaques les avis à la façon des perroquets criaillent

> Inscriptions of signboards and on every wall
> Posters plaques like parrots peck and call

The "je" and "tu" ambulate along avenues whose walls turn the city into a mass of newsprint. Intimacy that would be gained in the familiar address is undone by the shrill tones of street life, in whose continual passage the subject and reader are drawn through a field of recognizable and highly legible shapes.

"Zone" aspires to be a modern hieroglyph. Its immediately "sacred" language owes much to imitation of Christian scripture. A number of visible markers produce analogical cohesion, such as the recurrent letter Z that traces the poet's itinerant zigzag through the city or surfaces in the name of René Dalize (line 27); the O of the rose window and of God's eye (line 32); the X at the axis of the miniature calligram, "Pupille Christ de l'oeil" ("Pupil Christ of the Eye"; line 41). Clearly, the dominant figure is the chiasm that combines a standard Christian symbol with icons of modernity. The X, an unknown quantity, an enigma, is a playfully primal "mark" that codes the poet's path through the modern city. It is first suggested by the Eiffel Tower, then denoted by the latent calligram of Christianity, in the vocative "Seul en Europe tu n'es pas antique ô Christianisme" ("Only in Europe you are not old, O Christianity"; line 7) that implies the cipher ✕ , which alludes to a pedestrian's sight of the Eiffel Tower from beneath its four legs. The letter recurs through reference to "L'Européen le plus moderne c'est vous Pape Pie X" (line 9—the "most modern" Pope Pius having decorated the aviator Louis Blériot, who crossed the English Channel in 1909), but the meaning jumps from the prelate's Roman numeral to the shape of the airplane formed by the crossing of wing and fuselage. In the Mediterranean movement (lines 88–91), the poet and reader descend into the sea to behold, in marvel, "octopuses of the deep" and, floating in seaweed, "fish images of the Savior." The octopus recurs as a sort of X with eight arms that reach out to the four corners of the page. The most resonant chiasm, in which painting and writing crisscross, sallies from a couplet defining the poem as a whole and the rapport that "Zone" keeps with the French lyric tradition it relegates to shadows (lines 79–80):

> C'est un tableau pendu dans un sombre musée
> Et quelquefois tu vas la regarder de près

> It's a painting in a somber gallery
> Sometimes you'll look at it pretty carefully

Because the picture *hangs* in a museum, the lines suggest that wires are fastened to the stretchers on the backside of the frame. The poem is the very picture whose support is the crossing, the X, that holds the pictural and verbal representation in suspension together.

Apollinaire writes "Zone" to revive the Quarrel of the Ancients and the Moderns. He implies that his graphic wizardry is anything but "new" and that, in the early 20th century, the painter-poet must be Christian. Modernity owes its renewal of force, its youth, its daring, and its graceful style to the dominant church of France. Far from launching an ideology, Apollinaire indicates that future literature should be invested with Christian values. The modern, he foresees, cannot fail to reach back to a sacred iconography and history of forms. Hence "Zone" disinters a tradition of Christian poetry inspired by visual form. The *versus intexti* (woven verse) of the age of Constantine, with its combination of narrative abstraction (*lex*) caught by figures spelling its messages (*hex*), counts among the origins. Advertising and poster art, the opening lines suggest, go back to Rabanus Maurus (776?–856), who combined pictures and orthography

845

LA CRAVATE ET LA MONTRE

LA CRAVATE
DOU
LOU
REUSE
QUE TU
PORTES
ET QUI T'
ORNE O CI
VILISÉ
OTE- TU VEUX
LA BIEN
SI RESPI
RER

COMME L'ON
S' A M U S E
B I E N
E N

les   la
heures

            beau

et le   Mon

vers   cœur   té

dantesque

luisant et

cadavérique   de

               la

le bel   les

inconnu   Il   yeux   vie

      est   Et

       —   tout   pas

      5   se

les Muses   en   ra   se

aux portes de   fin   fi

ton corps   ni   l'enfant   la

               dou

l'infini   leur

redressé   Agla

par un fou   de

de philosophe

            mou

           rir

semaine   la main

Tircis

1. Guillaume Apollinaire, "La cravate et la montre," in *Calligrammes* (Paris: © Editions Gallimard, 1930), p. 59. (Courtesy of the Beinecke Rare Book and Manuscript Library, Yale University.)

in the *De Laudibus Sanctae Crucis* (*Of the Glory of the Holy Cross,* circulated in manuscripts but first printed in 1503). Visual poetry ranks among the innovations of the *grands rhétoriqueurs* of the later Middle Ages, especially Jean Molinet (1435–1507), a clerical historiographer who composed poems that could be read in all directions on the basis of an artful confusion of letters and ciphers. François Villon, a devoutly Christian criminal, had incised names and numbers in his ballads. A century later Pierre de Ronsard, a tonsured bard, occasionally practiced the same arcana (deaf though he was, he wrote extensive praise of music). Apollinaire unearths the tradition with uncanny fidelity to its past.

What Apollinaire discovers in "Zone" acquires pronounced ideographic force in his second major collection, *Calligrammes: Poèmes de la paix et de la guerre* (1918; *Calligrams: Poems of Peace and War*), written in 1913–1916. The work is a diary recording the poet's last prewar days, the mobilization of 1914, and the lyrical tenor of strife in the trenches. Some of the verse is scratched on postcards, printed, and sent to friends behind the lines. He called it a "book of war" intended to innovate poetry in free verse, but with greater graphic experiment and precision. There is a residue of the lyrical strain of the years before "Zone," but in general the verse, like gunfire in the sky of northern France, explodes and scatters. Calligrams record gratuitous impressions that further extend language as a function of chance and pictorial tension. Pathos, longing, combat, and boredom are arranged through juxtaposed letters, manuscript, and stamped or printed matter on postcards. In a 1918 letter to André Billy, Apollinaire called his lyrical ideograms "an idealization of free-verse poetry and a typographical precision at a time when typography is brilliantly ending its career, at the dawn of the new modes of reproduction that are the phonograph and the cinema" (*Oeuvres,* 4:778). He soon remarked in his famous 1917 lecture, "L'esprit nouveau et les poètes" ("The New Spirit and the Poets"), that "typographic artifices have the advantage of giving birth to a visual lyricism almost unknown before our epoch" (*Oeuvres,* 3:901). *Calligrammes* bears literal proof of his version of graphic and cinematic movement that had begun just before the war.

One of the most celebrated prewar calligrams, "La cravate et la montre" ("The Necktie and the Watch," *Oeuvres,* 3:183) (fig.1), traces the poet's discovery of the lyrical ideogram. According to Serge Férat, the two calligrams took shape in a café while the editors of *Les soirées de Paris* (in which the poem was destined to appear) were conversing around a table: Apollinaire loosened his tie and placed it on the table, and Férat drew his timepiece from his vest to signal that midday and lunch were beckoning. That moment is framed in a piece of visual time.

The poem must be read and seen simultaneously. The reader effectively removes the tie as the eye descends from the incipit at the neck to "respi / rer" (to breathe) at the poem's first pendant flourish. Yet a baroque visual effect is at work: the watch is magnified while the necktie, reduced in size through the effect of a depth of field, hovers in the background. The lefthand side of the watch has larger, darker blocks of words than the right, yielding an anamorphic view of the object. On the right perimeter, "La beauté de la vie passe la douleur

847

de mourir" ("Life's beauty exceeds the pain of death"), followed along its arc clockwise, like a hatched line of shade, elides the verbal beginning—a proverb-like cliché about the triumph of life and time over death—with the circle and leads toward its closure at the bewitching hour of twelve o'clock.

Then hours, words, and ciphers combine. "La," the article, signals the first person singular, the *one* (1), adjacent to "mon coeur," the one heart, at the first station. "Les yeux" (2), two eyes, are placed at two o'clock. Three o'clock (3) is the hour of "l'enfant," the child, the third, unwelcome party who disturbs the lyrics of love but who also instigates "primal scenes" of visibility. "Agla," the youngest of the Graces, a name of four digits, set at four (4), has a promising future: she glides with three as "l'enfant Agla." "La main," the hand (5), is the five-fingered form at five o'clock. The number rhymes centripetally with the − 5 (*moins cinq,* "five to [noon]") at the axis of the calligram, just when the poet and his editor get ready to leave their table and cocktails ("Et tout sera fini"—everything will be over) to have lunch. "Tircis" (6) is Virgil's shepherd (in the seventh Eclogue) who sings with Corydon, but now sits at six as if by fate, simply because the name draws—and fires—its lot at six, as in *Tir-6.* The visual pun suggests that when the needle is aimed at six o'clock they will have "killed" some time. "Une demi-heure de tirée," a half-hour of time has been drawn—and drunk—from the bottom of the barrel. Now seeds are sown on the seventh hour and seventh day: "semaine" (7) verbalizes the number 7. At eight, Eros is on the rise with the needle moving up to "l'infini redressé par un fou de philosophe" (8) (infinity fixed up by some crazy philosopher), in other words, infinity awakened, a figure turned on its side to make 8 a supine figure that becomes a matter of standpoint and perspective, as in ∞. The ninth hour (9) is transcribed as "les Muses aux portes de ton corps" (the Muses at your body's doors). The act of love, anticipated by the opening of the body's nine portals, gives way to "le bel inconnu" (10), the lovely unknown, in the algebra of Roman numbers: X. The ten or *dix* does not quite utter (*dit*) the erotic homonym (*un con nu,* "a bare cunt") that would be why the minute hand has risen so acutely to the eleventh hour. There (11), the number and the hour of the devil (in iconography but especially in the diabolic doubling of the same digit that spells the cardinal sin of representation), are anglicized in "*et le vers dantesque luisant et cadavérique*" (and the glowing and cadaverous Dantesque line). Finally, the poem "rhymes" as the line turns like the glowworm of its homonym, *vers,* in the dark of night.

Love and death are captured in the hour of the worm. The verse comes full circle at twelve o'clock high, where the alexandrine, the heroic line of the French poetic tradition, would otherwise reign supreme. The line buckling the circle (12), "comme l'on s'amuse bien" (how much fun we are having), turns the ratchet into the picture of an eye perched on the watch. Or else, like a corkscrew, the crowning figure is placed on a trajectory spiraling down to Tircis. At the axis, however, is located the only integer in the poem. It resembles the montage of *cou coupé* (neck cut off) at the end of "Zone," in "− / 5 / en / fin / fi / ni" (5 / to / fi / nal / ly / fi / nished), by which 5 refers to the *fünf* of scripture, the five, but also *fin,* which is not an end, but merely the act of division that splits voice and image within writing. The splayed shape of the two "hands" of the clock repeats and inverts the bifurcated writing at the bottom of "La cravate," assuring a graphic tension binding the two accoutrements of everyday life.

Suspended on the page, the two units can be read multifariously. Their meanings can be found anywhere and everywhere, but especially between the visual layers of Apollinaire's prosody. Language concretizes what it would otherwise convey in the illusion of metaphor. As the poem follows its career, the ponderously banal themes of time and life announced on the outer arc—the carpe diem, the memento mori, the eye of Saturn, the serpent eating its tail, allegories of growth and decrepitude—are cast aside in favor of a poem celebrating twelve stations of an extended rebus.

The righthand margin pulls the eye along the poem and draws its first arc, which reads: "The beau ty of life pas ses o ver the sor rows of dy ing." The line of 1914 is almost prophetic in its summation of *Calligrammes,* which all but dispels the context of World War I. The painting-poems embody what, upon his return from the trenches, wounded and trepanned, Apollinaire would theorize in "L'esprit nouveau et les poètes." His lecture, delivered at Jacques Copeau's Théâtre du Vieux-Colombier, foresaw the coming of new genres, especially the "birth of a visual lyricism" spurning at once the dialectical vision of Wagner in French drama, "colossal Germanic Romanticism," and, finally, the "rustic tatters" of a tradition of intensity and truth associated with Rousseau. No doubt he rejected everything associated with *presence* or the sublime understood as coherence, musical harmony, self-containment, or logocentrism. "Zone" and *Calligrammes* were the artillery of a new aesthetic.

Apollinaire's poetics held true to the work begun in his studies of cubism. The play of chance, the rendering of an entirely mute but supremely visible poetry, and the automatic translation of words and letters into figures revived a repressed tradition of pictorial writing, catalyzed surrealism, and embraced the new technologies of aviation, cinema, and recorded sound. From "Zone" to *Calligrammes* is traced an itinerary leading to silence. Voice dies, but pictures live. Today's readers hear howitzer fire through the verse, as World War I seems both to inspire and to extirpate Apollinaire's later life and work. *Calligrammes* marks a unique moment in the history of visual poetry, whose brevity is especially unsettling in view of Picasso's evolution, after 1915, away from abstraction and back to illusion and a calmer palette of human forms. The great experiments leading from 1910 into the war years were virtually annihilated. Few of Apollinaire's friends ventured into the battlefields, but those who did—and who managed to survive—were indelibly marked by the bloodshed of modernity. The *esprit nouveau* faced collective murder and disappeared under the revulsion of patriotic gore. A dazzling moment of creation ends, and a grisly chapter of French literary history begins.

Bibliography: Guillaume Apollinaire, *Oeuvres complètes,* ed. Michel Décaudin, 4 vols. (Paris: Balland, 1965–66). Apollinaire, *Apollinaire on Art: Essays and Reviews 1902–1918,* ed. Leroy C. Breunig, trans. Susan Suleiman (New York: Viking, 1972). Stéphane Mallarmé, *Oeuvres complètes*, ed. Henri Mondor and Georges Jean-Aubry (Paris: Gallimard, 1945). Massin, *Letter and Image*, trans. Caroline Hillier and Vivienne Menker (New York: Van Nostrand Reinhold, 1970). Roger Shattuck, *The Banquet Years* (New York: Vintage, 1968).

Tom Conley

∿ 1914–1918
World War I

Visions of Death and Dissolution

The general mobilization of 1 August 1914 marked the beginning of a European conflict that would soon become known as the Great War. After an initial German advance, the war quickly bogged down into opposing lines of trenches that stretched across northern France, where the fighting caused widespread devastation. The use of newly developed weapons such as the machine gun radically changed the nature of combat, producing enormous casualties and leading to the creation of mass conscript armies. Although the Allies emerged victorious, the four years of trench warfare left over a million and a half Frenchmen dead.

Like all other segments of French society, writers were immediately touched by the war. An anthology published in the 1920s by a veterans' association included the work of 525 writers killed in the war, among them such eminent figures as Charles Péguy and Alain-Fournier, the novelist of *Le grand Meaulnes* (1913; *The Lost Domain*), as well as many younger men. For those who survived, the war inaugurated what Paul Valéry soon saw to be a major intellectual crisis, calling into question the assumptions on which European civilization had long been based. Not surprisingly, the literature that emerged from the trenches expressed a new perspective on war and provided the basis for a literary challenge of the society in which it had its roots.

Barely fictionalized accounts of combat experience began to appear even before 1918, bringing the novel abruptly back into contact with the contemporary social reality it had abandoned with naturalism. Henri Barbusse's *Le feu* (1916; *Under Fire*) and Roland Dorgelès' *Les croix de bois* (1919; *Wooden Crosses*) were prototypes of a genre that remained important for the next few decades. Both Barbusse and Dorgelès had seen frontline combat, and the primary inspiration for their works was the simple imperative of communication: the need to explain the reality of life in the trenches to a civilian population whose view of war had been shaped by 19th-century mythologies and more recent wartime propaganda. Many combat novels contain scenes in which disillusioned veterans are struck dumb by confrontations with civilians who mouth patriotic clichés. In *Le feu* Barbusse gives a sarcastic account of a visit to the front by a group of top-hatted journalists, who regard the muddy infantrymen as exotic curiosities. But when the reporters question them, the soldiers find it impossible to articulate their experience. It was to give these men a voice that the war novel came into existence, as its authors were eager to state.

The World War I novel typically adopts the limited point of view that, at least since Flaubert, had become a characteristic of modern fiction. But here the perspective is that of the helpless common soldier, who has no more understanding of the larger picture than did Stendhal's Fabrice del Dongo at the Battle of Waterloo. Such a perspective was appropriate for a war in which modern technology soon moved beyond human control, and it continued to dominate literary representations of 20th-century human experience. The protagonist of the war novels was not an elite individual, as in the work of André Gide and Marcel Proust, but a collectivity, a heterogeneous group of soldiers from all walks of life. Dorgelès begins *Les croix de bois* by using the pronoun *nous* (we), and Barbusse subtitles his novel, "Journal of a Squad." The perspective of the platoon, which has become a commonplace of war fiction and film right through the war in Vietnam, reflects the reality of a war fought, for the first time, by conscripts rather than by the elite 19th-century cavalrymen who make a farewell appearance in Jean Renoir's 1937 film, *La grande illusion* (*The Grand Illusion*). Twentieth-century technology had created a war that could be fought only by large masses of infantrymen, rendering the heroic individual obsolete. This technology was also responsible for reducing combat to stagnation in the trenches, a situation in which it was hardly possible to speak of individual battles and still less of victories. For the characters of *Le feu* and *Les croix de bois,* victory consists in simply staying alive—and few characters do survive.

Les croix de bois closes with the author's apology for any possible falsification he may have imposed by writing about the experience of his now-dead comrades. In its concern for remaining true to the reality it depicts, the war novel resists inflation of either language or exploit. Narrative passages are simple, and the dialogue employs regional accents and the rich, often obscene slang of the trenches. Philosophical abstractions, such as courage and patriotism, are absent from the soldiers' experience, and situations are built on the concrete activities of eating, finding shelter, coping with mud and lice, and surviving under fire. Jean Paulhan's short combat novel, *Le guerrier appliqué* (1917; *The Conscientious Warrior*), is a particularly striking attempt to convey an experience stripped of the meanings imposed by conventional literary language. Many novels abound with images of dismembered bodies, devastated landscapes, and muddy trenches filled with human excrement—a vision of war summed up in the final scene of *Le feu,* where the opposing lines of trenches are dissolved into a sea of mud filled with bloated corpses.

Concerned primarily with the experience of the front lines, the early war fiction reflects the slow rhythm of life in the trenches, alternating between combat and repose. Episodic in nature, the novels often portray small acts of personal bravery, but these are shown to be without influence on the progress of events. Like the war itself, the plots reveal neither a logical progression toward a climactic event nor an explanatory dénouement. Their end is determined by the inevitable dissolution of the combat unit, as more and more of its individual members succumb to enemy fire.

Even an accurate and nonpolemical description of life in the trenches, such as *Les croix de bois,* constituted an indictment of the official war rhetoric. And Barbusse, always polemical, had already begun to relate the suffering of the war to the fundamental injustice of the society that had produced it; it is no accident that *Le feu* stands behind the powerful indictments of French society that emerged in the 1930s. Throughout the intervening years, the stream of wartime memoirs or novels of *témoignage* (testimony) continued to flow, but the dominant trend of the 1920s, in literature as in politics, was to deny the changes wrought by the war and to seek distraction in material pleasure or exotic adventure. Even the rebellion of disillusioned young radicals such as the surrealists expressed itself in playful gestures rather than in direct political confrontation. At the end of the decade, however, as the menace of European fascism was sharpened by worldwide economic depression, the movement of revolt so long repressed by the men in the trenches finally burst forth.

In the hands of World War I veteran Louis-Ferdinand Céline, the war novel suddenly enlarged its scope to express a ferocious indictment of the whole modern world—European colonialism, American capitalism, and, ultimately, the structure of French society itself, even universal human nature. As Céline's vision of society, like that of many of his contemporaries, had been formed by his experiences in the Great War, so the form of the combat novel lies at the heart of his creative achievement in *Voyage au bout de la nuit* (1932; *Journey to the End of Night*). *Voyage* begins as a war novel, one heavily influenced by *Le feu.* The hapless protagonist, Bardamu, participates uncomprehendingly in supply details and combat, is wounded, and is evacuated to the rear. His wartime adventures constitute less than a quarter of the novel; yet they provide its language and governing images and establish the perspective from which Bardamu will view his subsequent experience.

Céline's characteristic language would hardly have been possible without the precedent set by the combat novels, which opened respectable fiction to colloquial speech and even vulgar slang. The use of obscenity is even more extensive in *Voyage au bout de la nuit,* where it moves beyond the dialogue to pervade the narrative itself. Appropriate to the struggle for physical survival in the mud and *merde* of the war, Céline's extended use of slang becomes a powerful expression of hatred and revolt.

The constant replacement of a polite term by a vulgar one (eating, for example, as *bouffer* rather than *manger*) tends to deflate rhetorical pretension and to rob human activity of a dignity seen as inherently false, an effect reinforced by the narration of the episodes themselves. In the opening sequence, a terrified Bardamu watches in horror as an officer is reduced by wartime shelling to a shapeless mass of marmalade, later likened to a mass of rotting meat. Céline's description of the effect of war on the human body is not unlike that of earlier combat novels, but the process of dissolution begun in the war continues to haunt his peacetime vision. In the African colonies the colonizers and their families melt away under the onslaught of tropical diseases while their constructions are eaten by insects. Back in France, the Paris suburb of La Garenne-Rancy is described as a muddy latrine, and its polluted air corrodes the laboriously accumulated possessions of the petite bourgeoisie. Under Bardamu's gaze the world seems constantly to dissolve into meaninglessness. The viscous blood of the decapitated officer later reappears in the scene of a Parisian abortion, and Bardamu finds that death and violence are as prevalent in the African colonies, the Detroit auto factories, and the Parisian streets as they were in the war. This truth is revealed by Bardamu's visit to a carnival shooting gallery, which he sees as summing up his experience in the war and in civilian society as well. In Céline's view, all of human life can be understood, as he says of the African colonies, as a "guerre en douce," a thinly veiled struggle between egoistic and rapacious human beings. This almost unrelievedly negative vision of human nature is related to a critique of society, which he sees as divided into two opposing groups: oppressors and oppressed. This vision, too, arises from the war, with its division of the world into victimized conscripts and exploitative civilians.

Perhaps the most negative image of the novel is that expressed in its title. The journey to the end of night is that which Bardamu originally undertakes in the nighttime supply duties and scouting missions of the war, and it is later repeated in the image of civilians wandering blindly through a night like that of the trenches in *Le feu*. The outcome of the voyage is suggested by the fate of Bardamu's wartime companion Kersuzon, who is finally shot in the course of his nocturnal wandering. And Bardamu's vocation as a writer who will record a blackened vision of reality is suggested by Kersuzon's repeated attempt to describe the world he perceives: "It's as black as an asshole" (*Journey*, p. 21).

Céline's novel opens under enemy fire, but it quickly moves away from combat to focus on civilian society and its unmistakable contiguity with the war. In this, it is typical of the war fiction of the 1930s, which generally takes place far from the front lines. Its aim is no longer the description of combat but the analysis of its meaning, an analysis that frequently comports a bitter judgment. Jean Giono's 1931 novel *Le grand troupeau* (*To the Slaughterhouse*) sets scenes already familiar from the combat novel into a narrative of peasant life. Giono's lyrical elevation of the natural life of the countryside serves as counterpoint to and condemnation of the mechanized slaughter of the trenches, and the novel's dominant image, the unending flock of sheep relentlessly driven to their own destruction, sums up his vision of the fate of men in war. In *La comédie de Charleroi* (1934; *The Comedy of Charleroi*) Pierre Drieu la Rochelle places his combat experiences in the context of the postwar world. As his narrator visits the Charleroi battlefield with his dead comrade's mother, he comes to see her as embodying the decadence of contemporary society, and he looks back nostalgically to the almost mystical experience of leading a charge on the battlefield, an experience that would determine Drieu's own evolution toward fascism. Renoir in *La grande illusion* refracts events of the war through the limited world of French prisoners of war, and Louis Guilloux in *Le sang noir*

(1935; *Bitter Victory*) does the same with a small provincial city, where the slaughter in the trenches merely serves to intensify the effects of an oppressive and life-denying social order. Like that of Drieu la Rochelle, Guilloux's fictional universe is divided along generational lines, and his novel is dominated by the revolt of the young, who reject both the war and its grounding in contemporary intellectual values.

The war fiction of the 1930s is distant from the trenches not only in space but also in time. Although Jules Romains devotes two volumes to the battle of Verdun, much of his twenty-seven-volume cycle, *Les hommes de bonne volonté* (1932–1946; *Men of Good Will*), concerns the prelude to war. Louis Aragon's novelistic series—*Les cloches de Bâle* (1934; *The Bells of Basel*), *Les beaux quartiers* (1936; *The Elegant Districts*), and *Les voyageurs de l'impériale* (1942; *Passengers of Destiny*)—ends with the outbreak of hostilities, as does the long penultimate volume of Roger Martin du Gard's Thibault saga, *L'été 1914* (1936; *Summer 1914*). More interested in tracking down the causes of war than in describing the war itself, these writers were oppressively conscious of the parallels between the historical background of the Great War and their own turbulent era, which indeed would soon be known as *l'entre-deux-guerres*.

As war again loomed on the horizon, war fiction became increasingly obsessed with the image of asphyxiation. The "black blood" of the French title of Guilloux's novel was the oxygen-deprived blood of those who have been stifled by an inhuman social structure. As the decade moved to a close, this suffocation was more specifically related to the experience of war and the inexorable historical process that seemed to be leading there again. Renoir's prisoners of war found their oxygen running out as they tried to tunnel their way to freedom, mirroring the doomed efforts of Renoir's own contemporaries to escape the forces of history. The equation was made apparent in Martin du Gard's novel *Epilogue* (published after the outbreak of hostilities in 1940), in which Antoine Thibault observes his own slow death from the effects of poison gas as he speculates on the postwar era. By the time Martin du Gard wrote this final volume of *Les Thibault,* the hopes for world peace he had expressed in his 1937 Nobel Prize acceptance speech had all but disappeared, and the slow process of his character's demise had become emblematic of the postwar experience.

The poison gas that slowly destroys Antoine Thibault's lungs was indeed a horrible weapon of World War I, but it made its appearance in fiction only with the approach of World War II, when it came to epitomize the experience of war itself. A detailed account of a poison-gas attack occurs in André Malraux's last novel, *Les noyers de l'Altenburg* (1943; *The Walnut Trees of the Altenburg*), where this single image of World War I is framed by scenes of the 1940 invasion of France. In this retrospective vision of the Great War, Malraux combines the motif of asphyxiation with the images of dissolution that had already become central to the literary portrayal of war: the wave of poison gas not only destroys the soldiers' lungs but also reduces the entire natural landscape to a blackened, viscous mass, from whose clinging tentacles the men must shake themselves free as they struggle for air. In the discussion that inevitably accompanies action

in Malraux's fictional universe, the characters suggest a reason for the pervasiveness of poison gas in the fiction of this era: it is a weapon against which human
courage is of no avail. For Malraux, a leader in the fight against fascism
throughout the 1930s, it surely reflected the inexorable movement of historical
forces, which seemed to reduce human projects to meaninglessness. In the language of this era, poison gas comes to represent the absurd.

In Malraux's hands, however, these images of war give birth to new meaning.
For Barbusse and Céline, the violence of the war had reduced men to the level
of animals, stripping them of human dignity. Malraux's soldiers, in contrast,
are shocked by the effects of their own weapon, and they abandon their attack
in order to aid their victims. In *Les noyers de l'Altenburg* the experience of horror
and meaninglessness becomes an occasion for the reaffirmation of a fundamental
humanity. Malraux was writing not long after the fall of France, at a moment
when his own values as well as those that had constituted French culture as a
whole seemed to have been destroyed. In responding to the collapse of 1940,
he found himself forced to confront once again the images of death and dissolution that had haunted the French consciousness since the Great War. In this
confrontation Malraux found the will to resist, the human meaning that is born,
as Jean-Paul Sartre would later say, "on the far side of despair."

See also 1913, 1934, 1945 (6 February).

Bibliography: Henri Barbusse, *Under Fire,* trans. Fitzwater W. Ray (New York: Dutton,
1918). Louis-Ferdinand Céline, *Journey to the End of Night,* trans. Ralph Manheim (New
York: New Directions, 1983). Pierre Drieu la Rochelle, *The Comedy of Charleroi and
Other Stories,* trans. Douglas Gallagher (Cambridge, Mass.: Rivers Press, 1973). Frank
Field, *Three French Writers and the Great War* (Cambridge: Cambridge University Press,
1975). Jean Giono, *To the Slaughterhouse,* trans. Norman Glass (London: Owen, 1969).
M. J. Green, *Fiction in the Historical Present: French Writers and the Thirties* (Hanover,
N. H.: University Press of New England, 1986). Holger Klein, ed., *The First World
War in Fiction* (London: Macmillan, 1976). Robert Wohl, *The Generation of 1914*
(Cambridge, Mass.: Harvard University Press, 1979).

Mary Jean Green

❧ 1920

Jeanne d'Arc Is Canonized

Bourgeois Sin

Was Jeanne d'Arc (known to English speakers as Joan of Arc) a sinner? Declared
a heretic, she was burned at the stake in Rouen on 30 May 1431 at age nineteen. Rehabilitated in 1456, she was beatified in 1909 and canonized in 1920,
just at the time when Catholic writers in France were producing a cluster of
aesthetic masterpieces distinguished by their quality from works produced by
earlier or later generations. The great sin of the modern world is that it no

longer believes in sin. The Catholic writers of the interwar years, François Mauriac, Georges Bernanos, and Paul Claudel, took up the challenge to concretize sin and expose it beneath the surface of modern materialism and skepticism.

From the interwar years through the German Occupation, Joan of Arc was an emblem of this recurring sense of sin. The Vichy régime, seeking a symbol to concretize France's guilt and shame for its abysmal defeat in 1940, attempted to substitute her feast day (11 May) for 14 July and 11 November as the official holiday. Joan's self-sacrifice for the welfare of the collectivity was presented as a necessary corrective to what was officially held to be France's prewar decadence exemplified in an exaggerated importance accorded to the individual over the group. The fact that Joan was burned on French soil under English occupation played into the hands of those who saw in Albion the most perfidious of false friends.

François Mauriac (1885–1970), a novelist, essayist, and journalist, was the foremost Catholic writer of the interwar years. Thanks to the publication of an early collection of poems, *Les mains jointes* (1909; *With Joined Hands*), which was hailed by Maurice Barrès as the work of an emerging talent, Mauriac was lucky at the outset of his career. He had left Bordeaux for Paris in 1906 to take a degree as an archivist at the Ecole des Chartes, France's library school, but his real ambition, like that of so many provincial novelists before him, was to make his name in Paris as a writer. His fame rests primarily on a group of novels published within a decade: *Le baiser au lépreux* (1922; *A Kiss to the Leper*), *Genitrix* (1923), *Le désert de l'amour* (1925; *The Desert of Love*), *Thérèse Desqueyroux* (1927), and *Le noeud de vipères* (1932; *Vipers' Tangle*). Only one later fictional effort, *La pharisienne* (1941; *The Woman of the Pharisees*), can be ranked with them.

Mauriac faced persistent criticism from conservative Catholics, who blamed his novels for depicting lives from which God seems to be terribly absent. But Mauriac, who had been nourished by Jansenism both at home and in school, saw sin almost everywhere. Like the two great Jansenist writers of the 17th century, Pascal and Racine (both of whom subscribed to the basic Jansenist conviction that grace is not given freely by God, but must be earned by each individual, and that sins associated with human sexuality are especially heinous because they flow from the basic impurity of the human body), Mauriac sought to give artistic expression to the human tensions engendered in him by his religious beliefs. His *Vie de Jean Racine* (1927; *The Life of Jean Racine*) and *Blaise Pascal et sa soeur Jacqueline* (1931; *Blaise Pascal and His Sister*) are emblematic of this inspiration.

In *Le baiser au lépreux,* most of the major components of Mauriac's fiction are already in place. The novel, like virtually all of Mauriac's, is set in the Bordeaux region. Almost all its main protagonists belong to the well-connected landowning class and, obsessed with their money, wall themselves up in their mansions. Suspicious of outsiders, they remain close to home, where a strictly observed system of class distinctions, in which the external trappings of Catholicism are a major ingredient, reinforces their ascendancy. The physical setting is also a major motif: the pine forests of the Landes and the wine-growing sections of the Bordelais, but also the excruciating heat and blinding light of summer (redolent of divine grace), elemental forces against which his characters instinctively protect themselves.

Jean Péloueyre is the "leper" of the novel's title. From his reading of Nietzsche, this homely, introverted man concludes that he is a slave and not a master. His widowed father arranges for him a marriage with a healthy but somewhat dumpy peasant girl whose parents support the idea wholeheartedly for financial motives. Jean feels revulsion for his own body, and Noémi is unable to articulate her feelings. Because she does not share his sexual longings, Jean suppresses them in the most traditional Catholic manner by physically distancing himself from his wife. At the prompting of his parish priest, he goes off to Paris to work on a research project. Not long after his return, he dies of tuberculosis. Upon his death, Noémi dutifully plays the role of bereaved spouse, especially since it has been made clear that she and her family will forfeit their inheritance if she should marry again. An epilogue offers a glimpse of Noémi several years later; she has gained a bit of weight, but is still dressed in black in memory of her deceased husband. To outsiders, she might appear to be a saint, but this is precisely Mauriac's point: the form and substance of Catholicism and those of sainthood are two different matters. Although the townspeople imagine her as having given to Jean "the kisses that in other times the lips of saints would give to lepers," the reader knows that this is not the case.

Thérèse Desqueyroux and *Le noeud de vipères* are also novels of failed communication between spouses. In *Thérèse,* which is based on a real murder case that Mauriac, like many 19th-century novelists, had followed in newspaper accounts, the protagonist attempts to murder her husband, Bernard. After the whole affair has been hushed up, Bernard decides that the best solution is for Thérèse to leave her daughter behind and move to Paris, where she will be out of sight. In the final scene, some type of reconciliation seems to be possible, but Bernard is unable to get her to tell why she has tried to kill him. Like Racine's Phèdre, Thérèse seems condemned to do evil, but she is at a loss to explain why, and her motives can be understood only through a Jansenist reading of human nature. *Le noeud de vipères,* written in the first person, takes the form of a letter—to be opened after his death—from the protagonist, Louis, to his wife, Isa. A lifetime of hatred for his family followed the confidence that his wife had made to him, shortly after their honeymoon, about a brief childhood romance. Now, as his adult children (who take their father to be insane) await his death and the inheritance it will bring, he seeks to even the score. But as he writes the letter, he softens, affected by the stirrings of grace within his soul. His wife unexpectedly dies before him. After his own death, in the epilogue, his son Hubert finds the letter, reads it, and reacts negatively; but Louis's granddaughter, Janine, sees it for what it is: the man who had spent his life in a family likened to a "knot of vipers" has been redeemed. In Mauriac's Jansenistic universe, the gift of grace has transformed the inner reality of Louis's life even though the external trappings have remained unchanged.

Georges Bernanos (1888–1948), a father of six children for whom he could never adequately provide, somehow survived four years in the trenches during World War I. Married to a direct descendant of Joan of Arc's brother, he subscribed all his life to a medieval view of chivalry, which dictated the obligation to live in service to others. This view is forcefully expressed in his devotional biography of the saint, *Jeanne, relapse et sainte* (1934; *Sanctity Will Out: An Essay on St. Joan*). His novels also reflect an aspect of Catholicism that is largely absent from Mauriac's work: a view of the devil as an active, personal agent of evil in the spiritual life of all mankind.

Whereas there is no fully developed portrait of a priest in all of Mauriac's oeuvre, the devil's preferred battleground in Bernanos' novels is the soul of the priest. A living contradiction in a materialistic and hedonistic society, the priest lives on the frontier between good and evil. Bernanos' first novel, written in railroad coaches as he traveled across the French countryside as an employee of an insurance company, sets the tone for the later works. *Sous le soleil de Satan* (1927; *The Star of Satan*) presents an encounter between a country priest, the abbé Donissan (modeled on Jean-Marie Vianney, curé of Ars, canonized in 1925), and evil as incarnated in a horse trader. On a dark night, Donissan, who is becoming lost in the middle of the countryside, suddenly realizes that the man he has met is in fact Satan. When later Donissan grabs hold of him to stare into his face to get a better understanding of the nature of evil, he sees his own face staring back. In this scene—as in all his work—Bernanos challenges the modern belief that evil is a purely psychological phenomenon and not a metaphysical reality. His effort to show that evil exists outside the mere realm of subjectivity is perhaps overstated, but the effect is nonetheless powerful.

Subsequent novels, such as *La joie* (1927; *Joy*) and *Un crime* (1935; *The Crime*), continue in this vein. *Journal d'un curé de campagne* (1936; *Diary of a Country Priest*), however, ranks among the half-dozen most powerful French novels of the 20th century. The young unnamed priest of the title, only recently ordained and referred to simply as "le curé d'Ambricourt," a small village in French Flanders, finds that his parish is consumed by ennui. His parishioners do not believe in anything as much as in money, power, or pleasure. Their lack of faith eats away at their lives just as stomach cancer, of which the young priest is not yet aware, eats away at his own.

Sprung from a socially and culturally impoverished background, he tries to express in his diary the frustrations caused by his many failures as a priest. His greatest problems arise in his contacts with the local nobility: the count and countess, their daughter, Chantal, and the latter's governess, Mlle. Louise. The countess hates both her husband and God because of the death of her infant son. Chantal is estranged from her father because she has learned of his affair with Mlle. Louise. The curé, like the abbé Donissan of *Sous le soleil de Satan*, is able to see into the very souls of certain people. In a pivotal scene he confronts the countess and gets her to accept God's will. But when she dies suddenly the next day of a heart attack, he holds himself guilty for having caused so much stress in her life. As his health deteriorates, he seeks medical care in the nearest city, Lille. There he dies in the company of his friend, ex-priest and former seminary classmate, Dufréty. It is the latter who finds the diary and who, in a brief letter appended to the novel describing the curé's final hours, offers it to the reader. The diary form gives *Journal* an internal coherence and unity that are often lacking in Bernanos' other novels. Again and again, the curé tells of his disappointments in not having succeeded in doing what he takes to be God's work. But Bernanos makes clear that what the curé takes to be his failures are in fact, in the eyes of God, so many successes. This powerful theme, which resonates throughout Bernanos' oeuvre, is expressed in the last words that Dufréty attributes to his dying friend: "Tout est grâce" (Everything is grace).

Like Mauriac, Bernanos early on voiced his opposition to fascism, especially in Spain. For this, both earned many enemies among conservative Catholics. Whereas Mauriac wrote principally as a journalist in the 1930s and 1940s, Bernanos took the route of the traditional French polemicist. *Les grands cimetières sous la lune* (1938; *A Diary of My Times*), a diatribe filled with indignation against Franco and his Catholic supporters, is the most powerfully strident of all his political essays.

Paul Claudel (1868–1955) had an established reputation, principally as a poet, before World War I. As a disciple of Mallarmé, whose Tuesday-evening gatherings he had attended as a young man, and an admirer of Rimbaud, in whose work he discovered a thirst for knowledge of the ultimate mysteries of life, Claudel was by temperament a symbolist, drawn to write about life in the abstract and the universal rather than in specifically social or political terms. Having abandoned the Catholicism of his childhood, he subsequently experienced a mystical conversion at Notre-Dame on Christmas 1886. This revelation colored everything he did for the remainder of his long life. Thus his early works, including the poetic masterpiece *Cinq grandes odes* (1910; *Five Great Odes*) and his early plays, are symbolist in technique and Catholic in subject matter and worldview. Most of Claudel's plays—notably *Partage de midi* (1906; *Break at Noon*) and *L'annonce faite à Marie* (1912; *The Tidings Brought to Mary*)— are so long and involved that they could not be produced as written. Neither of these works reached a wide theater audience until after World War II.

Le soulier de satin (1924; *The Satin Slipper*) is undoubtedly Claudel's greatest theatrical achievement. Composed between 1919 and 1924, and three times longer than any of his other plays, it represents his personal summa, a reflection of his intellectual debt to Thomas Aquinas. The play combines key themes and techniques from his earlier plays with a baroque variety of dramaturgic techniques, including the use of puppets and elements borrowed from the Japanese Kabuki theater. At the heart of the work is the great theme earlier adumbrated in *Partage de midi:* certain pairs of individuals are destined to interact mysteriously on earth, and their words and deeds are symbolic of a deeper, hidden spiritual and mystical reality. The action takes place in a Hispanic setting in 1600, at the dawn of the modern era, when the Old World and the New are just beginning to give meaning to each other. Spain's naval and military power allows her to spread the Christian message throughout the known world. Central to the play is the adulterous (but ultimately chaste) love between Don

859

Rodrigue and Doña Prouhèze. Though separated physically throughout most of the play, they are nonetheless united through their love. Claudel powerfully compresses time and space in order to communicate the ultimate message that despite sin and shortcomings, whether of individuals or of the church, God ultimately makes things right. The power and reality of the invisible and spiritual in human life are best summed up in the Portuguese proverb quoted in the preface to the play: "God writes straight, but with crooked lines." The intoxicating effect of this symbolist drama—which was not staged until 1943, when Jean-Louis Barrault produced a drastically shortened version of it at the Comédie-Française—is inseparable from Claudel's elongated line, the *verset claudélien*, with its stylized, incantatory rhythms that are unique in 20th-century French literature.

Another masterpiece is *L'annonce faite à Marie,* which Claudel rewrote several times between 1892 and 1911. The mystical couple at the heart of the play are the peasant girl Violaine and the church builder Pierre de Craon. A year before the action opens, one day after having tried to rape her, he discovered that he had contracted leprosy. When he sets out for Reims, where he has been commissioned to build a church in honor of St. Justice, Violaine, already engaged to Jacques, offers him a chaste farewell kiss as a sign of forgiveness. Now she too is a leper. Once her malady becomes evident, she will have to live apart and forsake her friends and family. This is the price that one pays for going beyond justice to love. Likewise, her father, a prosperous farmer, sets out on a pilgrimage to the Holy Land in search of a higher good, voluntarily renouncing the happiness that in all justice he could have enjoyed by remaining at home. In the third act of this neomedieval mystery, set during a Christmas night, Violaine, the leper, brings her sister Mara's daughter back to life while, amid the sounds of trumpets and church bells, Joan of Arc, bringing the future Charles VII to be crowned at Reims, passes by offstage. At the end of the play the father returns, carrying the body of Violaine, killed by her jealous sister. But France now has one king and the world one pope (unlike the case at the beginning of the play); unity and harmony have been restored thanks to the freely accepted sacrifices of people such as Violaine and her father. Claudel tacitly implies that, with the end of the Middle Ages and the advent of the modern world, such meaningful correspondences between the visible and the invisible worlds would become impossible. But in his work Joan of Arc is more than a backdrop figure for *L'annonce.* Claudel also wrote the libretto for an oratorio, *Jeanne au bûcher* (1935; *Joan at the Stake*), with music by Arthur Honegger, which was produced in Orléans in 1939.

See also 1664, 1905.

Bibliography: Georges Bernanos, *Diary of a Country Priest,* trans. Pamela Morris (London: Boriswood, 1937). Bernanos, *The Star of Satan,* trans. Pamela Morris (New York: Macmillan, 1940). Gerda Blumenthal, *The Poetic Imagination of Georges Bernanos* (Baltimore: Johns Hopkins Press, 1965). Paul Claudel, *The Satin Slipper,* trans. John O'Connor (New York: Sheed and Ward, 1945). Claudel, *The Tidings Brought to Mary,* trans. Wallace Fowlie (Chicago: Regnery, 1960). Joy N. Humes, *Two against Time: A Study of the Very Present Worlds of Paul Claudel and Charles Péguy* (Chapel Hill: University of North Carolina Press, 1978). François Mauriac, *A Kiss for the Leper,* trans. Gerard Hopkins (London: Eyre and Spottiswoode, 1950). Mauriac, *Thérèse,* trans. Gerard Hopkins (London: Eyre and Spottiswoode, 1947). Mauriac, *Vipers' Tangle,* trans. Warre B. Wells (New York: Sheed and Ward, 1953). Robert Speaight, *François Mauriac: A Study of the Writer and the Man* (London: Chatto and Windus, 1976).

David O'Connell

✐ *1922, 18 November*

Death of Marcel Proust

Death and Literary Authority

How do we "enter" art? Proust's massive work can be thought of as an attempt both to refine the terms of that question and to provide an answer. The Proustian narrator's literary education culminates in the discovery—a discovery recorded in *Le temps retrouvé* (1927; *Time Regained*), the final and posthumous volume of *A la recherche du temps perdu* (1913–1927; *Remembrance of Things Past*)—that the only life worth living is life "réalisée dans un livre" (realized in a book) (*Remembrance,* 3:1088). Outside a book, that life is both worthless and a source of suffering: hence the narrator's astonishing and relentless condemnation of his meticulously recorded experience. If he continually reproaches himself for having friendships, for going into society, even for falling in love, it is, he suggests, because he should have been at home trying to get to the bottom of his impressions of friendship, of society, and of love. In the work of art, representation will operate both as an escape from the objects it represents and as a justification (retroactive, we might even say posthumous) for having had any experiences at all. In Proust, art simultaneously erases, repeats, and redeems life. Literary repetition is an annihilating salvation.

"The function and the task of a writer," the narrator concludes in *Le temps retrouvé,* "are those of a translator" (*Remembrance,* 3:926). Art is "our true life . . . reality as we have felt it to be" ("notre vraie vie, la réalité telle que nous l'avons sentie") (p. 915). But how are we to understand a translation more real than its original? The superiority of the former depends, above all else, on the suppression of the latter. After reading in the Goncourt brothers' *Journal* a description of Mme. Verdurin's salon (this masterful Proustian pastiche occurs early in *Le temps retrouvé*), the narrator feels a peculiar curiosity about Mme. Verdurin's home and her guests—peculiar because he has himself often been her guest. But, he adds, unlike the Goncourts, he has never been able to listen to people or to look at them: "If I went to a dinner-party I did not see the guests: when I thought I was looking at them, I was in fact examining them with x-rays" (p. 738). That is, there is a kind of seeing that depends on not seeing, or on our preventing the objects of our vision from interfering with our view of them.

861

This condition can perhaps best be satisfied in memory, where the images of others are no longer sullied by their presence. The shock that the narrator suffers at the final Guermantes *matinée* suggests the extent to which he has always been remembering people, even before they have become part of his past: his surprise at discovering that his friends have grown old can at least in part be explained by the success with which, until now, he has managed to suppress the signs of their living in time—that is, the signs of their living—in his x-ray "knowledge" of them. The "remembrance of things past" in *A la recherche* begins even before the narrator's introduction to others, and reminiscing in Proust is therefore a curiously intransitive phenomenon, one that works best when the world has been cleared of its inhabitants.

Another way of putting this would be to say that, for Proust, literature depends on death. The superiority of literature's translation of the real is a function of "lost time"—not, as the Proustian title appears to indicate, of time recovered and saved from loss, but rather of time, of the past, permanently disposed of, buried. We know—as the narrator knows—that he is close to realizing his vocation when he manages to see the living already in their graves—even better, to see only their tombstones from which time has obliterated names. "A book is a huge cemetery in which, on the majority of the tombs, the names are effaced and can no longer be read" (*Remembrance,* 3:940). In literature, individuals disappear into their truth. The Proustian narrator even goes so far as to suggest that people willingly sacrifice themselves to the writer so that, in death, the reality of their lives may finally be manifested. "All those men and women who had revealed some truth to me and who were now no more, appeared again before me, and it seemed as though they had lived a life which had profited only myself, as though they had died for me" (p. 939).

It is thus particularly fitting, in a history of French literature, to place Proust in the year of his death. For he is perhaps the greatest modern representative—and the glorious culmination—of what might be called a mortuary aesthetic in our culture, of a view of art's redemptive power as dependent on the annihilating imitation of its models. In Proust the devaluation of experience, hidden in the tradition of mimesis, becomes explicit. Traditional notions of the masterpiece—of the moral and epistemological monumentality of the great work of art—are perhaps inseparable from this dismissal of life; the monument is a tomb. More exactly, the putting to death permits the resurrection of others as redemptive truths. *A la recherche du temps perdu* reflects upon this process; the subject of Proust's novel is the relation between truth and existence, and, in an unprecedented fashion, the work is continually problematizing the position that phenomena will occupy in an essentializing version of them.

To a certain extent, the particular is viewed as an inferior mode of reality in *A la recherche.* "It is superfluous to make a study of social mores," the narrator notes, "since we can deduce them from psychological laws" (*A l'ombre des jeunes filles en fleurs* [1918; *Within a Budding Grove*], in *Remembrance,* 1:552). The fictions that the Proustian writer-hero invents for his work have a wholly different ontological status from those he invented in his past: they are no longer illusions doomed to be shattered by reality, but are rather heuristic lies. They are, we might say, what art adds to philosophy: the perhaps always necessary degradation of laws into vivid exemplary illustrations of laws. The Proustian novel would, then, seem to realize a certain dream in Western thought of literature as *serving* philosophy, as providing an addendum of examples to a purer (but perhaps inherently unreadable) discourse of truth.

Is it possible to go even further, to free the novel itself from its exemplifying function—that is, to eliminate from it the impurities of novelizing? Ideally, art would be truth liberated from phenomena, and the stretching of the Proustian novel toward this extreme (and inaccessible) limit gives to the later volumes—where the general laws are predominant—their austere beauty, the beauty of a novel that has nearly abstracted itself from its own fables . . . And yet, in the most curious way, the novelistic nourishment that *A la recherche* brings to its philosophical projects poisons the discourse of truth. What might be called the descent to a referent—whether that referent be the narrator's "real" life or a life he has invented on the basis of the general laws deduced from his actual experience—shatters the epistemological monument, as if *any* transitivizing of the discourse of truth dismantled the very opposition of fiction and truth on which such discourses depend.

In a move perhaps designed to discredit self-identification, with all its existential impurities, the autobiographical "I" of *A la recherche* is not named until we are more than two thousand pages into the novel. Even then, we get only a first name, which may not be his "real" name, since the narrator suggests that he is momentarily borrowing the author's first name: Marcel . . . And yet Proust's work becomes a novel only to the extent that the transcendence of the particular—and of the autobiographical—is *not* accomplished, that is, to the extent that such a move is at once motivated and resisted by the painful experience of the autobiographical self as shattered, or impenetrable, or perhaps simply empty. Those very attributes meant to discredit the psychological subject make its transcendence gravely improbable. As the last of the great French realists, Proust both makes explicit the annihilating imitation of the models associated with the tradition of mimesis and raises the infinitely subversive possibility that there is nothing to be annihilated. If *A la recherche*—like all great art as the Proustian narrator defines it—expresses an individuality more general than that traced by the particular history of an individual subject, its own generality consists in a massive—massively reiterated and illustrated— anxiety about an unidentifiable, perhaps unfindable particularity. In Proust, the particularity of a human subject fails to constitute itself as a self that art might redemptively translate into an essence or a region of Being. Consequently, the *individuel* that the novel elaborates, far from expressing a plenitude of being, is nothing more substantial than a movement of ontological aspiration.

The narrator insistently asks: how can *I* be? The question is generated by "Marcel's" shattering discovery—or at least suspicion—that *others are*. Anxious subjectivity is not an original or first state in Proust; it is constituted by someone else's move away from the subject. *A la recherche du temps perdu*—and in this it is unique in the history of literature—traces the inescapable repetitions (at, we might say, various levels of sublimation: in our relation to nature, to society, to the people we sexually desire, to art) of the child's shattering discovery that the mother's body can move without him. Both self-pursuit and intersubjective relations—but they are in fact the same—are initiated by the trauma of separation. And the most potent metaphor for the envy and pursuit of being is sexual jealousy (the mechanisms of which are repeated in Proust's elaborate portrait of social snobbery). In anxiously seeking to find out, after her death, if Albertine made love with other women, he was not, the narrator asserts, asking "secondary, insignificant questions, questions of detail," but rather "essential questions: In her heart of hearts what was she? What were her thoughts? What were her loves?" (*La fugitive* [1925; *The Fugitive*], in *Remembrance*, 3:526–527). And a letter that describes what may have been some of Albertine's lesbian adventures reaches "in Albertine and in myself . . . the quintessential depths" (p. 527). "In Albertine and in myself": is there no difference? In Proust, it is precisely at the moment when the loved one turns away from her lover—becomes most mysterious, most inaccessible—that she (or he) is rediscovered within the lover—as if that essential secret being pursued by the lover were the lover's own secret, his own otherness. As long as Marcel's desire is, so to speak, carried for him by his mother, he needs to ask no questions about either her or himself. But once the loved one abandons Marcel's desiring, the most turbulent displacements occur: she is catapulted out of herself and into Marcel in order to torture him with the remoteness of *his* desires, the mystery of *his* subjectivity.

Proust astonishingly, and profoundly, suggests that the consequence of not being desired is an incapacity to identify one's own desires—perhaps most catastrophically, an incapacity to desire at all. The desiring of others is the model of the subject's own desires. It is as if desire were a learned activity, or an already fallen state from the narcissistic plenitude of oneness with the mother. We might even think of desire as an evolutionary conquest, as the mechanism by which we experience the lack or absence of a desired object as a lack of being (a failure to possess is read as a failure to be), and which therefore invests living in the world with endless promises of pleasure. We are, so to speak, seduced into relations by our misinterpretation of otherness as lost sources of narcissistic ecstasy.

There is what might be called a Proustian failure to evolve. Consider Marcel's suspension between this adaptive, independent desiring and a prolonged dependence on the other's desiring in order to keep the mechanism functioning. When that model is withdrawn, the Proustian subject must frantically reconstruct the other's desires in order to save himself from the always renewable sense of being possessed by the alien images of his own desires. This means that the most painful—and the most central—relation in the novel can only be that created by a heterosexual's jealousy of homosexuality in the other sex. Albertine suddenly transplanted inside Marcel as a consequence of her suspected lesbianism is the anguishing otherness of Marcel's own interiority. Albertine's love for other women is a relation of sameness that Marcel, as a man who desires women, is condemned to see as an irreducibly unknowable otherness. His jealousy of a lesbian Albertine therefore dramatizes (and novelizes) a nearly inconceivable and inescapable identity of sameness and otherness in Marcel's relation to his own desires. Marcel Proust the homosexual had to submit to the torture of being heterosexual for the sake of his art. Gide, who was shocked by what he saw as the complacent bad faith with which Proust transformed the men he loved in his life into the women of his fiction, failed to see this—failed, that is, to realize that the tragedies of love are always heterosexual, that is, tragedies of *inconceivable* desire.

These anguishing dramas of desire are, however, somewhat deceptive in Proust. The move to art in *A la recherche* is not only an annihilating and redemptive replication of experience; nor does it simply document the narrator's failed effort to constitute the "I" that the *individuel* of art might fix and transcend. Writing in Proust also makes possible a kind of posthumous responsiveness to surfaces, a redefining reenactment of Marcel's interest in the world. From this perspective, art would be our "real life" not in the sense of an essentializing version of experience, but rather as a first or original (but originally missed) contact with phenomena. The perspective of death is the condition not only of a redemptive transcendence of life, but also of a restoring to the world of those differences that had promoted anxious desire in the first place. In his work, and especially in the early volumes, the narrator recreates the exhilaration (and not only the panic) of discovering his absence from the world. Thus Albertine is not only embedded in Marcel's consciousness as a kind of painful allegory of alienated and alienating desire; she is also the girl Marcel saw at Balbec *before* he loved her, when, in a kind of metonymic intoxication, he simultaneously reduced and enriched Albertine and her friends through those extrahuman associations by which, for example, they are metamorphosed into stems of roses profiled against the sea. Perhaps the most somber *and* invigorating lesson of *A la recherche* is that pleasure always precedes desire and is probably never its consequence.

This is, however, a lesson that depends on the narrator's *not* writing the book that he seems ready to write at the end of *Le temps retrouvé*, a lesson that can be given only in *this* book, that is, in a book whose existence we really cannot imagine. *A la recherche du temps perdu* is constantly raising doubts about its own status as a vehicle of those essences that, according to Proust, become visible in great art. On the other hand, it is by no means clear, within the fictional logic of Proust's work, why—or indeed when—his narrator, having discovered his vocation, would have written three thousand pages not to realize that vocation but to trace the steps of a long, often misdirected and confused apprenticeship. But the superiority of *A la recherche du temps perdu* to its own premises and conclusions depends on, precisely, its own improbable status. Proust's novel defeats its redemptive project—the petrifying translation of life into truth—only by failing to provide us with any reasons for its own existence; its greatness, in short, is inseparable from the impossibility of its ever having been written.

Bibliography: Samuel Beckett, *Proust* (New York: Grove, 1931). Leo Bersani, "Proust and the Art of Incompletion," in *From Balzac to Beckett* (New York: Oxford University Press, 1970). Gilles Deleuze, *Proust and Signs,* trans. Richard Howard (New York: Braziller, 1972). Gérard Genette, *Narrative Discourse: An Essay in Method,* trans. Jane E. Lewin (Ithaca: Cornell University Press, 1980). Gaëtan Picon, *Lecture de Proust* (Paris: Mercure de France, 1963). Marcel Proust, *A la recherche du temps perdu,* ed. Pierre Clarac, 3 vols. (Paris: Gallimard, 1954). Proust, *Remembrance of Things Past,* trans. C. K. Scott Moncrieff and Terence Kilmartin, rev. Andreas Mayor, 3 vols. (New York: Random House, 1981).

Leo Bersani

✎⌀ 1924

André Breton Publishes the *Manifeste du surréalisme* and Launches, with His Friends, *La révolution surréaliste*

From Text to Performance

André Breton's *Manifeste du surréalisme* (1924; *Surrealist Manifesto*) did not appear out of the blue. By 1924, Breton and several of his friends, particularly Louis Aragon, Philippe Soupault, Paul Eluard, and Robert Desnos, were recognized writers and conspicuous personalities. Their notoriety resulted from their part in the provocative agitation staged by the Dadaists after World War I, an agitation that had entertained a small avant-garde audience and scandalized the general public.

Breton and his group also enjoyed the modicum of power that accrues in literary circles to those who edit reviews. From 1919 to 1924 they ran *Littérature.* During the heyday of dadaism and the early phase of surrealism, this ironically entitled periodical was the most radical of avant-garde publications. Yet, as early as 1920, Jacques Rivière, the editor of the established *La nouvelle revue française,* had published the extremely perceptive "Reconnaissance à Dada," an essay praising the talent and seriousness of Breton's group: their bold, paradoxical poetics was taking them beyond the confines of Western literature and art. Moreover, Paul Valéry's endorsement of *Littérature* and his mentorship of André Breton symbolically conferred upon the group a claim to Stéphane Mallarmé's legacy, which enjoined a haughty dismissal of literature as it is generally understood.

As a result of this broad recognition, Breton and his friends found themselves in a theoretical and moral bind: most of them had published a body of poetic works, a brilliant career was open to them, and this literary success was incompatible with their being surrealists. Aragon (who secretly kept writing novels) and Breton were also eloquent essayists; their theoretical articles and chronicles of surrealist activities had in fact become indispensable components of the surrealist enterprise, since they revealed to the public verbal and nonverbal activities that otherwise would have remained unknown and therefore unlikely to foster the cultural revolution they were meant to bring about. In short, it was impossible to forgo literature, since literature played a necessary role in announcing the good news that literature had been superseded by something else, namely, surrealism.

As a result, several evangelical essays besides the *Manifeste* were published in 1924. Aragon's "Une vague de rêves" ("A Dreamwave"), reporting on surrealist séances, echoed Breton's 1922 article "Entrée des médiums" ("Enter the Psychics"), which was reissued in *Les pas perdus* (1924; *Not So Wasted Steps*); Aragon's *Le paysan de Paris* (1924–1926; *Nightwalker*) chronicled the surrealist quest for urban wonders and sketched a theory of the "modern myth" as a mediation between consciousness and the unconscious. These were admirable texts *about* surrealism, but inherent in them was the danger of a fictionalization of surrealist practice. Inasmuch as their eloquence and their mimetic power recreated the excitement of uncanny encounters in the Paris streets or the verbal wonders of a hypnotic séance, these texts turned into illusionistic representations of the event. Yet they were not, properly speaking, surrealism itself, nor were they "surrealist texts"; this designation was reserved for the nonliterary products of *écriture automatique* (automatic writing). The enduring fame of these chronicles (and a few later ones, such as Breton's *Nadja,* 1928) testifies to the literary talent of their authors; it also reveals the hegemonic power of narrative and the extent of its ascendancy over surrealism, even at its most revolutionary. By 1924 the furious phase of surrealism was over; the narrative and programmatic texts published in the mid-1920s were already fraught with a certain nostalgia. They were witness to a past that, though recent, would not be recaptured: it could only be chronicled and monumentalized for history. Surrealism, as a successful tapping of the unconscious and a substitution of irrational impulses for consciousness in the conduct of everyday life, had become, in the main, a myth of origin, a poignant memory, to some a bore or even a fraud.

Weakened by doubts and the centrifugal pull of individual ambitions but reinvigorated by newcomers such as Antonin Artaud, Breton's group decided to forge ahead with peremptory pronouncements and public gestures: it started a new review, *La révolution surréaliste,* and a Bureau de Recherches Surréalistes (Bureau of Surrealist Research), under Artaud's direction, which endeavored to devise new surrealist experiments. This flurry of activity masked the waning of a radical challenge to Western poetics. From then on, Breton's surrealism would become a neoromanticism pervaded by occultism and Marxist revolutionary ideology. This syncretism was formalized in Breton's *Second manifeste du surréalisme* (1930; *Second Surrealist Manifesto*). The radical poetics of the early phase had given way to politics and to a quasi-religious quest.

Breton's challenge to Western poetics in the period immediately following World War I, a dissidence that was initially called *automatisme* and later *surréalisme* (before the 1924 *Manifeste* the two terms were interchangeable), was hardly compatible with a Marxist social praxis. In contrast to Dada's public derision of bourgeois culture, automatism was a very private affair, sometimes termed a "new vice." Inspired by Breton's wartime initiation into psychiatry and the theories of Jean-Martin Charcot, Sigmund Freud, and Pierre Janet, who in the late 19th century had studied the splitting of the neurotic psyche between manifest deficits and nonconscious constraints, automatism purported to explore the subconscious mind. However, rejecting the views held by the discoverers of the unconscious, Breton claimed that the workings of the nonconscious mind were freer, far more interesting than consciousness, and quite easily accessible. Hence the definition included in the *Manifeste:* "SURREAL-ISM, *n.* Psychic automatism in its pure state, by which one proposes to express—verbally, by means of the written word, or in any other manner—the actual functioning of thought. Dictated by thought, in the absence of any control exercised by reason, exempt from any aesthetic or moral concern" (*Manifestoes,* p. 26).

In another part of the *Manifeste,* Breton explained how the subconscious train of thought could be revealed by means of a simple mental strategy that might be carried out in the banal context of a Parisian café, where paper and pens were put at the disposal of the customers (p. 30):

> After you have settled yourself in a place as favorable as possible to the concentration of your mind upon yourself, have writing materials brought to you. Put yourself in as passive, or receptive, a state of mind as you can. Forget about your genius, your talents, and the talents of everyone else. Keep reminding yourself that literature is one of the saddest roads that leads to everything. Write quickly, without any preconceived subject, fast enough so that you will not remember what you're writing and be tempted to reread what you have written. The first sentence will come spontaneously, so compelling is the truth that with every passing second there is a sentence unknown to our consciousness which is only crying out to be heard.

Such sentences presented a wealth of *images* that the conscious mind, controlled by a purposive orientation toward the pragmatic context and constrained by both moral imperatives and cultural commonplaces, could not begin to match with hard work and deliberate poetic invention. Unlike the ordinary composition of poems, automatic tapping of the subconscious did not constitute a preliminary phase in a complex act of textual communication. Automatism, in and by itself, was an intransitive speech/writing act whose primary purpose was the removal of such obstacles as block the release of a repressed, underlying discourse. This act, of course, was predicated on the belief that the subconscious mind, like the Romantic imagination, was an ever-prolific matrix freely producing new and arresting verbal combinations. Though interesting and mysterious, the dreamlike verbal strings released by surrealist strategies were not properly the goal or end product of surrealism: the automatic event itself, regardless of its yield, was the focus of the early experiments. Hypnotic trances and automatic utterances borrowed from the turn-of-the-century discoverers of the psychological unconscious who had in turn diverted them from spiritism (in the context of which they enabled psychics to speak and write for the dead) became, at the hands of the surrealists, the main elements of a new poetics. Under the guise of releasing a flux of subconscious discourse (supposedly arising from an "inner sea" that washed away individual differences), these devices shifted the emphasis of poetics from the textual aftermath of inspiration to the performance itself in the course of which a psychic otherness swept aside the ever purposive ego of the Western poet or maker.

Surrealist games and automatic practices were not meant to produce enduring artistic monuments. Instead, they generated aleatory happenings, contingent performances, which squandered images for the sole benefit of a group of friends gathered in a familiar setting. The surrealist event was context dependent: it demanded of the participants faith in its outcome and the sort of enthusiasm that usually characterizes religious sects and psychic séances. This climate explains the addictiveness of automatism during the period in which Robert Desnos spoke surrealist at will in his hypnotic "sleep" and the onset of pathological reactions, suspicion, and boredom soon thereafter.

Equivocation beset surrealist practice from the beginning, because the participants were also poets and writers in the ordinary sense of those words. The conspicuous waste of images occurring in the automatic verbal strings was of interest to them primarily insofar as it could be construed as a *hyperpoetry* of which only the works of the Comte de Lautréamont and Arthur Rimbaud had given an inkling in the past. Thus, in "Entrée des médiums," Breton praised automatic utterance for teeming with "first-rate poetic elements" (*Les pas perdus,* p. 124), an ambiguous judgment since, while extolling the automatic performance as a whole, it also assesses the poetic value of discrete verbal elements that, under the standard poetic dispensation, might be stockpiled and then spliced into a denser poetic text. Inevitably, given the importance of a shift from text production to automatic performance, there was some ideological backsliding, as well as an unresolved hesitancy between taking the automatic performance for an end in itself and exploiting its poetic yield as raw material for future poems. Theoretically, the surrealist discovery of automatic performances as a means of passing at will from consciousness to a mental state resembling dreaming, from reason to imagination, and from a "prosaic" to a "poetic" verbal mode, had put an end to the *making of poetry*. Surrealism introduced, at least within the confines of Western print culture, a new poetic economy, whereby unreserved psychic and libidinal expenditure was substituted for the cumulative parsimony and crafty forethought that, in our textual economy, is the price to be paid for the communicability and durability of the "work of art." In principle, then, the surrealists were anxious to squander instantly the images lavished on them by automatic ecstasy. But they also wished to make some sort of sense (and some sort of profit) out of the oracular traces they preserved as the by-products of enthusiasm: by preserving these traces, they inevitably textualized them. Though theoretically not *poems* in the ordinary sense, the "surrealist texts," such as Breton's and Soupault's *Les champs magné-*

869

tiques (1920; *Magnetic Fields*) or Breton's *Poisson soluble* (*Soluble Fish*), to which the 1924 *Manifeste* served as an overgrown preface, have de facto become *prose poems:* at any rate, they were received as such, and their very publication, which cast them into the textual economy, fully justified this unavoidable categorical mistake.

Although he emphasized the nonlogical, nonconscious compulsiveness of the imagination at work in surrealism, Breton had a marked preference for *arbitrary images,* which, according to him, pulled together logically unrelated "realities." Such a violent rapprochement was in the nature of an enigma, a message from a supralogical zone that could be rationalized as the unconscious or as the occult order of the world itself. According to this conception, an image appears to be the puzzling local manifestation of another coherence, or an allegory pointing to an alien web of sense that could not readily be translated into "practical language." This explains why Aragon and Breton likened surrealism to a narcotic or to a hallucinogenic drug, which, while multiplying contextual irrelevancies and paranoid coincidences, also intimates the existence of a compelling order beyond the reach of reason. If surrealism was in all respects an experimental allegoresis, it reserved interpretation, deferring it sine die, in order not to impede the flow released by the various automatic practices between sense and nonsense, or between what an anthropologist might call the profane and the sacred. This deliberate confusion, analogous to the spilling at will of the dream state into waking life, and of madness into sanity, served as a rationale for the surrealist way of life, which was chronicled in Aragon's *Le paysan de Paris* and in Breton's *Nadja* and *Les vases communicants* (1932; *Communicating Vessels*). The surrealist poetics, then, was the language-oriented part of a larger attempt to revolutionize the rationality that confers meaning upon all aspects of life. To put it perhaps too simply, the surrealists endeavored to live a poetic life rather than to produce poetic (and artistic) works. Their relative failure should not obscure the boldness and the magnitude of their undertaking: it amounts to an anthropological mutation. According to ethnology, the pursuit of which eventually attracted Michel Leiris as a makeshift approximation of surrealism, many traditional societies retain cultural traits akin to those the surrealists tried to implement against the grain of Western culture. They attempted to translate a primitive otherness, which the Romantic myth attributes to the poet, into the working features of a frail microculture wherein "possession," dreamways, and the beckonings of alien powers would provide a protection, and perhaps an offensive weapon, against the dominant economy of a culture that had perpetrated World War I and the spiritual numbness that angered the surrealists.

It is true that, in keeping with 1920s ideology, the surrealists believed they were primarily interested in the release of subconscious mental activities, which they claimed to be more genuine, interesting, and subversive of the cultural order than had been the traditional practice of literary and artistic invention, perhaps because the Freudian vulgate insisted on the sexual nature of the unconscious libido. As members of a textual culture, as inveterate writers (in the ordinary sense), as assiduous readers and reorderers of the textual canon, the surrealists were bound to underplay the most radical transgression inherent in their practice of automatism, namely, the leap from textualization to performance. A surrealist utterance cannot be confused with the ravings of an insane person, nor indeed with poetry (even when automatism mimics madness, poetry, or any literary genre), so long as one is aware of the precise context of its performance.

Performance, and especially the type of performance called automatism, entailed a dissociation from literature in general, including any avant-garde signifying practices meant to produce durable texts. Thus Artaud, who joined the surrealist group in 1924 and left it soon thereafter to become the theoretician of a textless theater of psychic aggression, came closer to understanding the cultural stakes of the surrealist revolution than did those surrealists who were still deeply enthralled by the textual economy, and who therefore elaborated or adopted ideologies that allowed them to keep on producing texts. In its later phases surrealism reverted to the textually centered system of Western poetics, which it attempted to motivate afresh by reinscribing those occultist beliefs according to which the text, down to the letter, is an analogue of the hidden order of the world, as well as a means of effecting changes in its manifestations.

It may well be that surrealism in its first phase, which ended in 1924, came too early in the century to realize the implications of its shift from textual production to automatic performance. The legitimate desire to preserve traces of extraordinary verbal events, and to make them known to the public, inevitably led to textualization, including ex post facto elaboration and equivocation about the nature of the texts themselves. It also led to the production of brilliant narratives and clever theoretical texts intended to be both monuments to surrealist happenings and self-serving contributions to the textual economy. In the absence of recording equipment and video cameras, this was the only alternative to oblivion and ineffectualness.

Now that performance is a notion commonly available to anthropologists and to art critics, it has become almost too easy to assess the prophetic significance of the cultural shift pioneered by the surrealists. In its automatic phase, surrealism moved beyond textual monumentalizations by focusing, as the electronic media later would, on the event, the performer, the fleeting speech act, the gesture, writing on water.

See also 1935.

Bibliography: Louis Aragon, "Une vague de rêves," *Commerce,* 2 (Summer 1924), 89–122. Richard Bauman, *Verbal Art as Performance* (Prospect Heights, Ill.: Waveland Press, 1984). Marguerite Bonnet, *André Breton: Naissance de l'aventure surréaliste* (Paris: José Corti, 1975). André Breton, *Manifestoes of Surrealism,* trans. Richard Seaver and Helen R. Lane (Ann Arbor: University of Michigan Press, 1969). Breton, *Les pas perdus* (Paris: Gallimard, 1969). Mary Ann Caws, ed., *About French Poetry from Dada to "Tel Quel": Text and Theory* (Detroit: Wayne State University Press, 1974). Michel Leiris, *L'Afrique fantôme* (Paris: Gallimard, 1934). Jacques Rivière, "Reconnaissance à Dada," *La nouvelle revue française,* 82 (1920), 216–236.

Michel Beaujour

At Fifty-six, André Gide Publishes *Les faux-monnayeurs,* His First Novel

Mise en Abyme

André Gide was fifty-six years old when *Les faux-monnayeurs* (*The Counterfeiters*) appeared in 1925. It was not his first narrative piece. But Gide called *Paludes* (1895; *Swamps*) and *Les caves du Vatican* (1914; *Lafcadio's Adventures*) *soties* (farces), a term he revived from the repertoire of medieval genres. As for *L'immoraliste* (1902; *The Immoralist*) and *La porte étroite* (1909; *Strait Is the Gate*), they were presented as *récits,* stories. *Les faux-monnayeurs* is thus his first and only novel.

The first lines of André Breton's *Manifeste du surréalisme* (1924; *Surrealist Manifesto*) had just denounced the novel's inherent servitude to realism. After recalling Paul Valéry's impatience with phrases such as "la marquise sortit à cinq heures" (the marquise went out at five), Breton derided the gratuitous details in which description requires the writer to indulge: "Will he be fair-haired? What will his name be?" The point is taken up again in *Les faux-monnayeurs.* At the beginning of the novel, a young man of letters, Dhurmer, complains about a novelist he is reading: "He speaks of a woman and I don't know whether her dress was red or blue" (*Counterfeiters,* p. 5). But a few pages later another character, Edouard (no last name, no hair color), himself a novelist, hence (and as many have speculated) spokesman for the author, expresses the opposite opinion: while reading a letter, he wonders if there is anything in it that would permit a reader to guess the hair color of the woman who wrote it, a pretext for protesting against novelists who provide every detail and, "by a too exact description of their characters, hinder the reader's imagination rather than help it" (p. 73). The contradiction in these two attitudes, the conflict between Dhurmer's realist demands and Edouard's affirmation of the rights of the imagination, gives Gide's novel its general structure. Thus, one year after the *Manifeste, Les faux-monnayeurs* takes up, via Edouard, Breton's accusations against the genre, but now the charges against the novel are made from within one. In a vertiginous palinode this novel is simultaneously an indictment and an illustration of the genre.

This ambivalence begins with the title. On the one hand, it refers, quite realistically, to a 1906 newspaper clipping that gave Gide his first idea for the novel. Young people from good families had got involved in the fabrication of counterfeit money. The clipping joined excerpts from Gide's journal, collected, after the novel, under the title *Journal des Faux-monnayeurs* (1927; *Journal of "The Counterfeiters"*). But the novel itself loads this anecdote with an allegorical dimension, a specular value, and transforms it into a kind of discrete mirror where the novel itself is reflected, places itself *en abyme,* according to the expression that Gide borrowed from heraldic language, giving it the meaning it has today in literary criticism: a detail repeats the whole, part of a work represents the totality that contains it.

Gide's fascination with this self-reflective structure is long-standing, as evidenced by a note from his journal as early as August 1893. After noting that "in a work I rather like to find transposed, on the scale of the characters, the very subject of that work," he then evokes "the device of heraldry that consists in setting in the escutcheon a smaller one *'en abyme.'*" Already the narrator of *Paludes* was writing a book itself entitled *Paludes*. Entire sections of *Les faux-monnayeurs* consist of excerpts from the journal in which the writer, Edouard, notes his (and Gide's) reflections on novelistic art: he is working on a novel to be called *Les faux-monnayeurs*. However, this title does not have for him the referential and anecdotal anchorage that it has for Gide: counterfeit money here has a metaphorical value from the outset. "Edouard had in the first place been thinking of certain of his fellow novelists when he began to think of *The Counterfeiters*" (p. 191).

It is here that the novel turns into a critique of the novel, becoming at once novel, antinovel, and theory of the novel: in counterpoint to the characters' adventures in Gide's *Les faux-monnayeurs*, the "Journal d'Edouard" introduces "a running criticism of my novel—or rather of the novel in general" (p. 189). In the middle part of Gide's novel, Edouard explains to his interlocutors the project of his own *Faux-monnayeurs*.

For Edouard, who is Mallarmé's and Valéry's contemporary, the representative value of language implied in the realist novel is most problematic. His counterfeiters are precisely the novelists whom he accuses of wanting to pass off as real what is at best only a copy of the real. Pure art is one of the aesthetic mottoes of the period. Edouard, who tends naturally toward abstraction, dreams of a "pure" novel, a novel that has eliminated everything exterior to it, a novel purged of any kind of anecdotal subject, devoted entirely to the pure celebration of its own form, an equivalent, he says, to J. S. Bach's *Art of the Fugue*. Already when he complained of intrusive novelists who deny the reader the freedom to imagine the hair color of their characters, he had noted: "I should like to strip the novel of every element that does not specifically belong to the novel . . . Even the description of the characters does not seem to me properly to belong to the *genre*. No; this does not seem to me the business of the *pure* novel (and in art, as in everything else, purity is the only thing I care about)" (*Counterfeiters*, p. 74).

While Edouard develops his antirealist indictment of novelistic counterfeit, one of his listeners pulls out of his pocket the very thing he is talking about. It is the return, in the novel, of the anecdote with which Gide began.

> "But why start from an idea?" interrupted Bernard impatiently. "If you were to start from a fact and make a good exposition of it, the idea would come of its own to inhabit it. If I were writing *The Counterfeiters* I should begin by showing the counterfeit coin—the little ten-franc piece you were speaking of just now."
>
> So saying, he pulled out of his pocket a small coin, which he flung on to the table.

> "Just hear how true it rings. Almost the same sound as the real one. One would swear it was gold. I was taken in by it this morning, just as the grocer who passed it on to me had been taken in himself, he told me. It isn't quite the same weight, I think; but it has the brightness and the sound of a real piece; it is coated with gold, so that, all the same, it is worth a little more than two sous; but it's made of glass. It'll wear transparent." (*Counterfeiters,* p. 192)

The counterfeit coin is summoned, at the center of the novel, as the central image representing novelistic activity. The piece of gold itself symbolizes the credence given novelistic representation, considered as a direct expression of the real. The false piece of gold, on the other hand (which seems to be solid gold but in fact is glass and transparent inside), becomes the image of the antinovel, the one Edouard is thinking of but also in a certain way the one we are reading. In this way Gide denounces the fiction of a linguistic régime that would continue to pass itself off as the homologue of the gold piece. He denounces the belief in a referential language, bonded by the real, illusively maintained after novelistic signs have lost their capacity to evoke, in a naïve and univocal way, a transcendent, stable, and independent reality. They are now only tokens, uncovered checks, whose convertibility no treasury guarantees, and to which no fixed and eternal standard gives the power to measure the world.

A whole (complete, denotative) language, as reliable as the gold standard, assuring immediate access to the truth, would not require the reader to check the linguistic medium. Also, when the overthrow of the status of representation no longer allows us to think of language either as a gold piece or even as a convertible bank note, when the sign becomes a simple check or a forced-rate currency, a loss of confidence disturbs its value: as Strouvilhou, another literary figure in the novel whose declarations in favor of destructive linguistic games make him a caricature of modernist avant-garde experimentations, points out, the sign is nothing more than a game that no referent and no transcendental signified can guarantee.

A single solution remains at the disposal of the novelist conscious of this crisis: to write a counterfeit novel. It would be realist in appearance (with plots, characters, novelistic situations) but in reality abstract, a specular novel, worked from within by an autoreflection on the conditions of its linguistic production, a novel worried by the problematic status of its medium. Two readings of such a novel are possible: one, naïve, accepts the story as ready money, the life of the characters as cold, hard cash (this is the reading of the grocer who, in Bernard's story, had first accepted the coin); the other discovers beneath the gold covering the crystalline transparence of a pure abstract construction (the reading of the connoisseur, aware of the dissimulation and attentive to the stratagem).

Until 1914 gold pieces were still in circulation; but World War I put an end to the gold standard in France. From then on, monetary signs become inconvertible. On 30 July 1919, just after having begun to write *Les faux-monnayeurs,* Gide notes in his journal: "The whole story of the counterfeit gold pieces can occur only before the war, since at present gold pieces are outlawed" (*Journal of "The Counterfeiters,"* p. 413). The struggle, in the novel, between the system of realist representation (linked to the gold coin) and the denial of the representational value of language (linked to the glass coin) reduplicates in some ways the temporal ambiguity resulting from the fact that the action of this novel begun *after* the war takes place *before* the war. The ensuing chronological bifocalization overdetermines the monetary imagery for language that is at work in Gide's novel. At the border between two régimes of exchange, *Les faux-monnayeurs* reflects and cultivates a hesitation between the nostalgic attachment to the circulation of gold and the acceptance of the vertiginous novelty— inconvertibility.

Novelistic writing today is split between realist representation and deconstruction of the representative illusion, this deconstruction itself leading to a purely specular construction, without basis in things. *Les faux-monnayeurs* prefigures a half-century of formal literary research and philosophy of language. In it, Gide gave an early formulation of the problems to be encountered by literature in its transition toward the régime of inconvertible signs. He was able to recognize that from then on the novelist would have to choose between a reflection on the linguistic medium (leading to a writing at once specular and structural) and the affirmation of the radical senselessness of language, in the drift of uncovered tokens.

But the crisis of standards that *Les faux-monnayeurs* reveals goes beyond the limits of the economic and the linguistic. All the central values of the symbolic system are upset. A general demonetization of the value of paternity leads to the theme of the "counterfeit father," which constitutes one of the most insistent melodic lines of Gide's novelistic fugue. The first note of the novel is Bernard's discovery of a letter revealing that Maître Profitendieu is not his true father. Later, before the mortal remains of his own father, the young Gontran de Passavant will be incapable of feeling any sublime emotion, no call toward the hereafter that might evoke the transcendence of the dead father. As for Armand Vedel, he suspects his, a pastor, of lacking faith, of pronouncing empty words covered by no wealth of interior life. Three times the paternal function fails: in the register of real procreation (Profitendieu), of ideal ancestrality (Passavant), and of language's symbolic value (Vedel). Thus *gold, language, the father,* the three axes that permit measurement of value or meaning, have lost their stability, their power to regulate. And, in the absence of any solid standard to rely on, an endless game opens the totality of exchanges to a generalized counterfeiting. The crisis of novelistic representation itself appears as merely one component of a more general crisis, the loss of guarantees and referentials, a rupture in the measuring function of general equivalents of which money, properly speaking, is but one area.

Some critics have noted a "cubist aesthetic" in *Les faux-monnayeurs:* alternating plots cutting at heterogeneous and fragmentary angles, multiple modes of enunciation, a distancing from the characters and the narrative choices of a text that, behind a straightforward novelistic appearance, develops into the novel of the novel being written. It contains a novel of apprenticeship (Bernard's discovery of his illegitimacy), a detective story (the counterfeiting orchestrated by Strouvilhou), a *roman noir* (the suicide of little Boris), several loosely linked sentimental adventures (the tragic passion of Vincent and Lady Griffith, the homosexual attraction of Edouard for his nephew Olivier), not to mention a quantity of sketchy secondary plots, so many narrative threads often dropped and often taken up again, to which must be added the "Journal d'Edouard," with Edouard's reflection in and reflections about *Les faux-monnayeurs*, the novels in which he is a character and of which he is the author. The labyrinthine interweaving of these threads evokes in its own way the same collapse of standards, the absence of a unique point of view whose authority would impose on life the organization of a unicentric perspective.

This effect, indeed, is what Gide intended, eager to turn his back not on reality proper, but on its conventional representation, eager to approach as closely as possible the ambiguities and the complexity of life. Whereas traditional novelists use a unitary dramatic time that they take or wish to be taken for reality itself, Gide denounces the unthought narrative convention that hides itself in this linear arrangement of the plot. "On all sides life offers us many beginnings of drama, but only rarely do these continue and take shape as the novelist is accustomed to spin them out. And this is exactly the idea I want to give in this book, which I shall have Edouard express" (*Journal of "The Counterfeiters,"* p. 447). Life itself always lacks a middle and an end; it is dispersed, unfocused, uncentered. A well-spun narration results from an artificial narrative elaboration; it is never a given of reality. The counterfeiters are perhaps not who we think.

See also 1925 (December), 1953.

Bibliography: Maurice Blanchot, "Gide et la littérature d'expérience," in *La part du feu* (Paris: Gallimard, 1949). Lucien Dällenbach, *Le récit spéculaire: Essai sur la mise en abyme* (Paris: Seuil, 1977). André Gide, *The Counterfeiters,* trans. Dorothy Bussy, and *Journal of "The Counterfeiters,"* trans. Justin O'Brien (New York: Knopf, 1955). Gide, *Journal* (*1889–1939*) (Paris: Gallimard, 1951). Jean-Joseph Goux, *Les monnayeurs du langage* (Paris: Galilée, 1984).

Jean-Joseph Goux

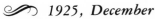 **1925, December**

Paul Valéry Writes a Short Introduction for Ronald Davis' English Translation of *La soirée avec Monsieur Teste*

"I Cannot Abide Stupidity"

Paul Valéry (1871–1945) resists unified, coherent presentation. His life is of little interest. Born into a bourgeois family at Sète, on the Mediterranean, he studied law at Montpellier, then moved to Paris, where from 1900 to 1922 he was employed as secretary to the director of the Havas Press Agency before dedicating himself entirely to his literary work. His best-known texts are extremely abstract and very short: a dozen pages for *La soirée avec Monsieur Teste* (1896; *An Evening with Mr. Teste*), and scarcely more for the celebrated poem *La jeune Parque* (1917; *The Young Fate*). No major one work in his oeuvre provides a focused, more distinct, identity.

Valéry, a man of experimentation and dispersion, refused to consider literature as an end in itself. He thought of his many short texts as traces of an intellectual study rather than as actual works. Writing, for him, had the value of a mental exercise, equivalent to the mathematical speculations that he practiced jointly for many years. From 1897 to 1917, practically without publishing, he continued to write for himself. This long silence gave rise to almost as many speculations among his contemporaries as Arthur Rimbaud's silence had several decades earlier.

Valéry also practiced all literary genres without concentrating on any one. But his poetry, narrative, essays, literary criticism, aphorisms, drama, and dialogues, his linguistic, psychological, and philosophical work reflect a single mental quest, with varied and contradictory aspects. Valéry addressed an identical question in each work: how to account for the power and the potential of the human spirit?

Valéry gave this question a fictional incarnation in Edmond Teste, the "hero" of *La soirée avec Monsieur Teste,* who preoccupied him until the end of his life. Several sequels, some published posthumously, form what we call the "Teste cycle." These brief, half-fictional, half-philosophical fragments deal with the existence of a character who, like Valéry himself, persistently eludes classification.

Who is Teste? Valéry gives the most precise description in his preface to Ronald Davis' 1925 English translation of *La soirée, An Evening with Mr. Teste:* "He is none other than the very demon of possibility. His concern for the whole range of what he can do rules him" (*An Evening,* p. 16). Heir to "cerebral" heroes such as Balzac's Louis Lambert (1832; *Louis Lambert*) or Joris-Karl Huysmans' des Esseintes in *A rebours* (1884; *Against Nature*), distant cousin of Leonardo da Vinci and René Descartes (on whom Valéry wrote several essays), Teste is a man of pure possibility. His sole question is "What can a man do?" (p. 43). Not what does he do. Hence, he is clearly anything but a man of action. To succeed, to carry out something, to be "someone," does not interest him, whatever the possible sphere of action. He nourishes himself exclusively on projects and programs that he never feels any need to execute, and contents himself with the certainty that he could complete them. An insignificant-looking person, he earns his living by performing unimportant transactions on the stock exchange, takes all his meals in the same little restaurant, and lives in sparsely furnished lodgings, where the narrator of *La soirée* is astonished to see neither books, papers, nor pens—nothing to indicate any writing or reading in progress: "I never felt more strongly the impression of *whatever*. It was the whatever lodging, similar to whatever point of a theorem—and perhaps as useful. My host lived in a most common-place home" (p. 44). A subject without attributes, Teste is a depressed ancestor of Robert Musil's man without qualities. He is known for no peculiarity or vice. Just as he lives in "a most common-place home," he has sacrificed all personality and all singularity to an existence based only on general laws that allow him to avoid errors and illusions. His slogan could be the first sentence of *An Evening:* "I cannot abide stupidity." He refuses to be someone in order to exist as the entire world. His existence is theoretical, a fact that makes him a very impractical candidate for representation in a novel.

His name, Teste, is *tête* (head), spelled in the old way. How does one write a novel about a character who, on principle, satisfies himself with thinking? Teste never acts, never falls in love, distrusts words, speaks infrequently, and falls asleep when he invites the narrator to smoke a cigar at his home. He is the main character of an antinovel that disappears as soon as one tries to write it, because he is a character about whom there is nothing to say. More than any other figure, he incarnates not only Valéry's relation to narrative, but also his paradoxical and ambivalent relation to literature in general, if indeed literary practice presupposes the affirmation of an identity or of a singularity.

Valéry's questioning of the possibility or the necessity of an oeuvre (which accords with his silence and his refusal to publish) made him one of the leading literary "terrorists" of the century, to use Jean Paulhan's word. His silence fascinated many avant-garde artists who, sometimes for different reasons, also refused the notion of oeuvre. Among those were André Breton, for a long time a close friend to Valéry, and Marcel Duchamp, a great admirer of his *Introduction à la méthode de Léonard de Vinci* (1895; *Introduction to the Method of Leonardo da Vinci*), which represents the "theoretical" complement to *La soirée:* like Teste, Leonardo da Vinci is evoked by Valéry in order to support the dream of a rigorously objective analysis of the powers of the spirit.

Valéry was properly speaking a poet only during his youth. In the 1890s he attracted attention with some poems clearly influenced by the symbolists, especially by Stéphane Mallarmé. But the desire to learn about his own potential led him to dissociate himself from poetry as a genre and to escape from the influence of Mallarmé, who gave language precedence over the "self" and claimed that the writer should "cede the initiative to words." In 1912, in a letter to Albert Thibaudet, author of the first major study of Mallarmé (*La poésie de Stéphane Mallarmé,* 1912), Valéry said of his elder: "I worshiped that extraordinary man at the very time when I saw in him the one—invaluable—head to cut off in order to decapitate all Rome" (*Leonardo, Poe, Mallarmé,* p. 419). Valéry's attempt to distance himself from Mallarmé was an attempt to distance himself from literature and from language itself. A determination to count, assess, and rely only on his own strengths led him to break more and more radically with the practices and thoughts of others and to be suspicious of language. Language never really belongs to anyone: it is to be distrusted as much as those who shared it with him. "I intended not to let myself be maneuvered by language" he notes in his notebooks (*Cahiers,* pp. 181–182). This statement summarizes Valéry's entire career and accounts for his destiny as a writer with almost no works, who wanted to do without words. When he returned to poetry much later, he had no illusions about the expressive or communicative powers of language. He took up poetry again as a simple exercise.

In 1912 Valéry was approached by his friend André Gide and other editors of the young *Nouvelle revue française* who wished to republish *Teste* and Valéry's early poetry. He finally agreed but wanted to add one or two new pieces of verse. He set to work without believing too much in it; then he got caught up in the game. It took him more than four years to finish his "morsel," and for his longest, most celebrated poem to see the day. *La jeune Parque* has been frequently interpreted, notably by the philosopher Alain (pseudonym of Emile Chartier), as the song of an "I" who awakens to discover herself divided and betrayed by the presence of an unapprehendable other. *La jeune Parque* takes up again, in a form other than *Teste* or *Léonard,* Valéry's dream of a shadowless conscience, transparent to itself. Valéry, however, valued the formal aspect of the poem more than its content. He wanted not so much to express a "meaning" as to present a purely verbal study emphasizing the musicality of words and establishing, as much at the level of words as at the level of images, the effects of resonance, transition, repetition, and variation within a perpetually open structure. In his return to language and to literature, Valéry took certain precautions. He did not seek to communicate something to another, but rather to demonstrate all that can be done with language if one works according to certain rules—in this case, the rules of classical prosody. *La jeune Parque,* written in alexandrines, is an extraordinary stylistic achievement. World War I was raging. "I likened myself to those monks of the early Middle Ages who heard the civilized world collapse around their cloister, who no longer believed in anything except the end of the world; and who nevertheless wrote lengthy poems with great pains, in hard, obscure hexameters, for no one. I confess that French at that time seemed to me to be a dying language. I had schooled myself to consider it *sub specie aeternitatis*" (*Oeuvres,* 1 : 1637−38). In the middle of the war, Valéry thus created a tomb for classical French poetry at a time when literary forms were exploding, as if to preserve a language and a form that had no more currency. And perhaps only the fact that he himself had no more currency, that he was out of step with his age, distanced and without any hold over his period or engagement in its concerns, allowed him to recommence writing.

Valéry's *Cahiers,* the least known but the most monumental part of Valéry's oeuvre, also testify to his desire not to commit himself. Begun in the 1890s and continued until his death, they constitute an enormous, intimate intellectual journal, an "infinite conversation with the self," according to their author. Every morning for more than fifty years, before dawn and the awakening of others, Valéry wrote for himself, searching in some sense for the apparition of his own spirit. "Here I write down ideas that come to me. But I haven't accepted them yet. It is their first state. Still not quite awake" (*Cahiers,* p. 7). A kind of daily mental jogging, at Valéry's death the *Cahiers* contained more than 30,000 pages of thoughts, aphorisms, and barely articulated notes. They stand as one of the most considerable undertakings in the history of private writing, their sheer volume rivaled only by Henri Frédéric Amiel's *Journal* (published in part in 1883−84).

The *Cahiers* are a compendium of reflections on subjects as diverse as literature, art, morality, psychology, dreams, the body, science, mathematics, and politics. Toward the end of his life, Valéry drew on them frequently as he prepared collections of thoughts such as *Tel quel* (1941; *As Is,* translated as *Odds and Ends*), in which he revived a literary tradition with roots in the 17th-century salons, that of the moralists. For their author the *Cahiers* were, above all, an immense *reserve* that enabled him to escape indefinitely from the gaze of the other, which could never seize him in his totality. They allowed' him to maintain a blind spot, a point of illegibility, in his work. "I sense all the things that I write here, these associations, as an attempt to read a text, and this text contains a mass of bright fragments. The ensemble is black" (p. 6). In the *Cahiers,* Valéry escapes more completely than ever from identification. He appears as a plural subject, dispersed, fragmentary, ever changing, who professes only the religion of incredulity. This most modern aspect of his oeuvre was insufficiently appreciated until recently; the publication of a complete edition of the *Cahiers* has only just begun. Made famous by *La soirée avec Monsieur Teste, La jeune Parque,* the early poems collected in *Album de vers anciens 1890–1900* (1920; *Album of Ancient Verses*), and the later ones collected in *Charmes* (1922; *Charms*), Valéry was the last French writer to be honored with a state burial, in 1945, when France interred an author whose work, for the most part, she had still not read.

More than all his other works, the *Cahiers* show how Valéry developed something like paraliterature: a literature which no longer acknowledged itself as such, which refused to remain within traditional genres or to be accepted as fiction; a literature obsessed ·with *lucidity*. Better to do nothing (or, at least, publish nothing) than to risk not knowing what you have done or to be the plaything of your beliefs. Knowledge about literature became the center of literary activity, took precedence over the traditional production of literature. From this perspective, Valéry also was ahead. In many ways his work prefigured the polyvalent intellectuals who dominated French culture after World War II. Without being a "pure" writer, Valéry set what was going to remain the platform of literary activity for at least a generation, in much the same way that Roland Barthes would at the end of the 1960s.

Valéry's concern with a rigorous awareness of the limits of language and of writing inevitably led him to become one of the first literary "theorists"—one of the first to insist, in several published texts and above all in innumerable fragments of the *Cahiers,* on a set of criteria designed both to account for the purely literary uses of language and to capture its literary specificity. The poet was subsumed in the poetics specialist, a kind of physicist of words, who calculated their weight, their relations, their potential, and their effects. In 1937, ten years after his admission to the Académie Française, Valéry was offered the chair of poetics, created for him at the Collège de France. Of course, Valéry's poetics were not systematic: they must be reconstituted through the fragments, hypotheses, and sketches of the *Cahiers*. And it would be another thirty years before these issues assumed a central place in the universities: in the 1960s the structuralists acknowledged their debt to him for giving precedence to the

rational analysis of literary forms over interpretation of meaning. The importance of his poetics lies in the possibility they provided for a new approach to
literature. The development of Valéry's work suggests that behind the theorist's
or specialist's claim to lucidity, there is a mistrust of the inevitable seduction of
literature. This poetics is, perhaps, historically rooted in the development in
France of a literature devoted to endlessly recommencing its own indictment
and demystifying itself.

See also 1885 (June), 1941, 1960.

Bibliography: Alain, *Commentaires de "La jeune Parque"* (Paris: Gallimard, 1936). Jacques
Derrida, "Qual Quelle: Valéry's Sources," in *Margins of Philosophy,* trans. Alan Bass
(Chicago: University of Chicago Press, 1982). Vincent Kaufmann, *Le livre et ses adresses*
(Paris: Méridiens-Klincksieck, 1986). Daniel Oster, *Monsieur Valéry* (Paris: Seuil,
1981). Paul Valéry, *Cahiers,* ed. Judith Robinson-Valéry, vol. 1 (Paris: Gallimard,
1973). Valéry, *An Evening with Mr. Teste,* trans. Ronald Davis (Paris: Ronald Davis,
1925). Valéry, *Leonardo, Poe, Mallarmé,* trans. Malson Cowley and James R. Lawler,
vol. 8 of *Collected Works,* ed. Jackson Mathews (Princeton: Princeton University Press,
1972). Valéry, *Oeuvres,* ed. Jean Hytier, vol. 1 (Paris: Gallimard, 1957).

Vincent Kaufmann

1928, 3 May
Jean Giraudoux's First Play, *Siegfried,* Is Staged by Louis Jouvet at the
Comédie des Champs-Elysées in Paris

Amnesias

Walter Benjamin observed that men came home silent from the battlefields of
World War I: not richer, but poorer in communicable experience. In Jean
Giraudoux's first play, *Siegfried,* the protagonist (who goes by the name Siegfried
von Kleist) returns from the Great War to civilian life utterly speechless,
stripped of his memory. He is a man without a past, bereft of identity—a
living, breathing Unknown Soldier.

Fate lands him in Gotha, where a devoted nurse instructs him so well in
history, geography, and language skills that he becomes a walking textbook.
He assumes a prominent government position and promises to the whole of
Germany—that once-colorful patchwork of decorative kingdoms, each rich
with its own turbulent past and laden with poetry—a modern destiny: administrative efficiency, systematic rationalization. The modern state, a featureless
corporate entity (*société anonyme*), gets the nameless, impersonal executive it
deserves.

But this statesman is miserable. He longs for some distinctive personal traits,
an ingrained habit or two linking him to a family, attaching him to a landscape,
recalling a particular climate. On one afternoon each week he receives the relatives of soldiers missing in action, in the hope that someone will recognize him,
tell him who he really is, restore to him the remembrance of things past.

Siegfried is one of a number of figures in postwar literature to whom history will not attach. The shell-shocked Gaston, in Jean Anouilh's 1936 play, *Voyageur sans bagage* (*Traveler without Luggage*), is discovered by a public-spirited dowager in an asylum where he languidly tends vegetables. She trots him around to the good families of her acquaintance to see which will ring a bell with him and in what respectable social context he might successfully be reintegrated, but he encounters—even in the household that proves to be his own—nothing recognizably proper to him, nothing he is moved to claim, no one he is inclined to settle in with, only strangeness. The rootless, aimless Gonzague, the glamor boy of vaguely foreign origins and indefinite background in Pierre Drieu la Rochelle's short story *La valise vide* (1924; *The Empty Suitcase*), is another such abstracted, disengaged character. He cannot connect with women (except through inconclusive phone calls), or with anyone or anything else.

The past ought to have weight; it ought to form something substantial you can resolutely pick up and carry along with you; and it should make a link between you and the world, between you and other people; but Siegfried's is unhappily, as he says, like a letter he has neglected to write, an obligation that remains to be seen to and that stands between him and everything he would like to undertake: life, love. He is in a state of arrested animation, a sort of limbo. He is a ghost, living and at the same time dead, as one of his acquaintances in Gotha observes. He is like Gaston in this respect, or rather, like Jacques, the extraordinarily disagreeable man whom Gaston turns out to be, the phantom whose clothes Gaston has to don, whose sheets he is obliged to sleep in, and whom he cannot recall at all, who strikes him as an utter stranger, a repellent alien. Sartre's Orestes complains, in *Les mouches* (1943; *The Flies*), that he is the most ghostly of all the ghosts that haunt Argos, for he cannot recollect his native city, he cannot see it as *his,* and his own sister Electra, when he rejoins her there, fails to recognize him. He wonders what city to drift along to next, and to haunt.

These wandering shades of real men, these pale reflections of dense human passions, are themselves haunted. It is their dearth of memories, their general disconnectedness, that gives the past its power to haunt. The American millionaire who, in René Clair's 1936 film *Fantôme à vendre* (*The Ghost Goes West*), can do no better than to *purchase* some background and a little tradition in the form of a Scottish castle, finds himself saddled with the resident phantom. Orestes' guilt-ridden mother, Clytemnestra, defines the horror of a past that will not be laid to rest: she says it defies genuine appropriation. You can never see it as yours. "It is not *I* who did that!" she says. That cannot be *my* deed. It is as though, in the aftermath of the Great War, history had proved unrecognizable. Alien; impossible to *have* as one's own; impossible to collect, recollect, assume—unbearable. It is that strange, eerie history that Sartrian engagement aims to exorcize. Orestes finally commits an act that he can claim; the victims of this crime are *his* dead and the murder itself *his* burden of guilt to shoulder; thus he packs up the troubles of all Argos (the intruding specters of the resentful deceased, all the futile, gnawing remorse) and bears the whole trunk manfully away.

Gaston is just as resolute in Anouilh's play, but not so serious. He simply shrugs off the past, and all the tiresome admonitions as well, addressed to him by pompously responsible people, that he accept himself, acknowledge the bad along with the good, act his age, be a man. Nobody can remain a child forever . . .

But everyone would *like* to: that is the dream of all men, Gaston declares. To be restored to infancy. To begin again from scratch, from a genuine origin, innocent and unencumbered, lightened of the burden of past mistakes and accumulated obligations, lifted up and transported by sheer newness. And since it is my luck to have such an opportunity, why then, he decides, not seize it?

So maybe Siegfried is foolish to feel foolish as an "adult baby." Perhaps he is misled when he attaches such importance to the one small piece of baggage to which he can lay claim—his one vague and meager memory (a single word, an adjective that inexplicably delights him), the only insoluble part of himself, he says. Perhaps he is misled, for elsewhere in Giraudoux we meet *transparent* beings of extraordinary, indeed "angelic," beauty. Like the immortal mermaid in *Ondine* (1939): she leaves no trace of her passage; if she goes away even for an instant, she has never been there at all. Like Jérôme, in *Cantique des cantiques* (1938; *Song of Songs*): ageless, and clear, too, translucent as the water that Ondine comes from. No deposit, no precipitate, no accumulated sedimentation. He has no memories, and the woman he loves loses hers upon meeting him. She has, since becoming his betrothed, the impression of having just been born, wearing *this* dress, *these* stockings, equipped with *this* very toothbrush. He owns but one suitcase—that is plenty to hold his scant personal effects—just as he has "but one word for saying it's raining and that he's in love" (*Théâtre complet*, p. 744).

Maybe Siegfried is foolish to wish he had more than that to say to anyone. Often in Giraudoux love comes as an attack of amnesia. Maybe Siegfried is foolish the way people generally are foolish, and inept at love, in Giraudoux. They want love to be *something:* something dense, opaque, substantial; and it obliges: it comes between them . . .

But maybe it is possible to recollect how to forget. "Let's confront our memories!" Gaston jokes gaily at the very end of *Voyageur sans bagage,* as he abandons the family to which he has been restored ("You're just not for me!"), casts off the past they load upon him (the guilt, the debts, the old quarrels, the misery), and sets out festively for parts unknown, choosing for his sole forebear an orphan child whom, by a great stroke of good fortune, he happens to have just met, and who is both extremely rich and completely ignorant of any parents, grandparents, aunts or uncles, friends, or acquaintances. Siegfried's savior (his forgotten fiancée, Geneviève) is, like Gaston's, an orphan. A last obstacle threatens to arise just as she is about to lead him across the border to the country of love, where, as she assures him, the true past is a happy leap toward the future. The customs official requires that they declare what is in their luggage. "We have none," she explains. "You must have sent it ahead, then," the official responds—"in which case it's not my affair: you'll get it at the baggage claim." Yes, she agrees, "We sent our trunks seven years ahead" (*Théâtre complet*, p. 71).

We do not drag the past along behind us, we do not carry it in our arms or on our shoulders or even in our hearts: we forward it, and travel light.

Giraudoux was a virtuoso stylist: a master of French with an aristocrat's flair for the effortlessly brilliant juxtaposition, the unexpected but telling formula, the delightfully elaborate digression, the elegant syntactical flourish, the enchanting play on words. With *Siegfried,* an adaptation of his novel *Siegfried et le Limousin* (1922; *Siegfried and the Man from Limousin*), he began his long and successful association with the great theater director Louis Jouvet. It is for his fifteen plays that he is best known, although it has sometimes been said that it is better to read them than to buy a ticket to see them. They are too precious, it is said, too rarefied, too "literary" or "metaphysical" to play well on stage; too hard for an audience to follow and comprehend. To this objection Giraudoux replied in *L'impromptu de Paris* (1937; *The Paris Impromptu*) that it is silly to seek "understanding" at the theater; you go there of an evening to let your soul receive the thousand glints and glimmers of style. "I once knew a child who wanted to understand the kaleidoscope. He wrecked all its joys. His friends understood that there were blues and reds, rainbows, mirages, fiery stripes, hell, pleasure, death. But *he* didn't understand anything, and broke his little machine" (*Théâtre complet,* p. 705).

Most of Giraudoux's plays were written between the two world wars, and he was, in more ways than one, a man of interims, interludes, intervals: an in-between man. The boundary between France and Germany was one of the fine lines he trod. He worked for the French Ministry of Foreign Affairs as an official spokesman of French culture—after having been a student of German literature. He was, before World War II, one of the two or three favorite authors of the fascist, germanophile writer Robert Brasillach, and the literary figure most often interviewed by the ultraconservative journal *Je suis partout;* yet, in 1944, at quite the other end of the political spectrum, *Les lettres françaises* devoted an entire issue to Giraudoux after his mysterious death, apparently of food poisoning. Brasillach's famous vindication of his collaborationist activities ("I have slept with Germany and found it sweet") is for all intents and purposes a quotation of a line from *Siegfried*—yet Giraudoux is included in Jean Paulhan's and Dominique Aury's anthology of Resistance literature, *La patrie se fait tous les jours* (1947; *The Fatherland Is a Daily Task*). In 1935, with World War II inexorably approaching, he wrote *La guerre de Troie n'aura pas lieu* (*The Trojan War Will Not Take Place,* or *Tiger at the Gate*). *Ondine,* adapted from a novel by the German Romantic writer Friedrich La Motte–Fouqué the year the war broke out, includes a poem with alternating lines in French and German, and it is said that at the dress rehearsal Giraudoux had to leave the theater to hide his grief at the thought of the clash of arms that would halt such a friendly intermingling of the two languages.

The plight of the amnesiac in *Siegfried* is initially presented as a problem in Franco-German relations. When the play opens, the German patriot, Zelten, has just discovered what, as he says, he has always suspected: that Siegfried von Kleist is not German. That nameless, all but speechless man found ten years ago feebly murmuring "Wasser" on a battlefield in Germany, who was nursed back to health and lovingly taught to speak (German) by a splendid blond paragon of German womanhood, Eva; and who, instructed in the glories of German history, has become a statesman and constitutional authority of national repute, destined, it seems, to save Germany, restoring it to greatness after its humiliating defeat in 1918—this man called Siegfried is in fact no other than the Frenchman Jacques Forestier, Geneviève Prat's fiancé, who disappeared seven years ago soon after his mobilization and has never been heard of since. Zelten secretly plans a coup d'état: he means to oust the Frenchman from German territory, where his innovations are altogether inappropriate, and restore him to his native land. Zelten has sent to France for his old friend Robineau, asking him to bring Geneviève along to Gotha; upon their arrival he asks their help in an undertaking upon which "the fate of Franco-German relations depends" (p. 12).

Typically Giraudoux's plays turn upon a certain choice: Alcmène's, for example, between the love of a man and that of a god, in *Amphytrion 38* (1929); or Isabelle's, in *Intermezzo* (1933), between a ghostly, supernatural, and a down-to-earth, human suitor. Siegfried, inasmuch as he is placed between two women, Eva and Geneviève, each of whom calls to him—one extolling the German nation, the other evoking France—might well be considered to occupy a position analogous to Alcmène's and Isabelle's, especially since the alternative he is faced with (between Frenchness and Germanness) is elaborated, just as in *Amphytrion* and *Intermezzo,* as a choice between two styles: one clear and measured, which keeps rigorously to human proportions; and one stormy, immoderate, imbued with mystery and a passion that exceeds human dimensions. But decisions in Giraudoux are rarely trenchant, and no doubt Siegfried speaks for Giraudoux when, bidding farewell to Germany toward the end of the play and setting out for France, he says, I'll unite in myself the Frenchman and the German; "I'll dig no trenches in myself" (p. 68). But the really typical Giraudoux touch consists in rendering all choices paradoxical. Thus, in *Siegfried,* Frenchness and Germanness weave in and out of each other, and the problem of Franco-German relations becomes an intriguingly knotty problem of translation. Siegfried is recognized by Zelten—who objects to his introduction of reason, clarity, and moderation into the German language and into German culture—as Forestier, the French writer who sought to introduce mystery and passion into French. Siegfried is visibly the German translation of Forestier. Zelten wants Germany to declare herself in the original German, and her would-be savior, the so-called ideal German, to return home across the border, or translate himself back into French. But Zelten himself—even as he exclaims, in an argument with Eva, that Germany's proper destiny is not to be "great" under the leadership of Siegfried, but to be "German" (with *him* at the helm)—may well be speaking German in French. For in Eva's eyes at any rate, he is a "German" such as exist only in the cafés of Montparnasse, where, indeed, Zelten spent his youth, among colorful expatriates and international conspirators, and where he returns (crossing the border just ahead of Siegfried) when his coup d'état fails. If Siegfried is no proper German but just a translation, Zelten, it would seem, is no proper German either, but a traitor, or transfuge; moreover, if the amnesiac Siegfried is a Frenchman lost in translation, there are plenty of Germans, with very long memories, who—like Siegfried's military chief, the fiercely anti-French General Fontgeloy—are Frenchmen *saved* in translation: descendants of Huguenots transplanted in the 17th century to German soil.

So the frontier between France and Germany—the boundary marking off two cultural traditions and two national personalities—spreads like a network of crisscrossings over the whole map of Giraudoux's play. Zelten shows Robineau—by way of proving that Siegfried is none other than Forestier—a text written by Siegfried in German, which he claims is a plagiarism of a French text by Forestier. Robineau is a philologist: that is why Zelten offers him this particular form of evidence. And Robineau remarks that all literatures are plagiarism, except the original, which is unknown. "What German philologists these French philologists are!" moans Zelten (pp. 16–17).

Zelten learns that, just as he has always suspected, Siegfried is not German, is not Siegfried at all. I've discovered something, he tells Siegfried, and "it's not about Siegfried, but about you" (p. 48). Zelten has discovered who somebody is. Who *who* is? Who is it that Zelten, notwithstanding his discovery, continues to call Siegfried? Geneviève, from the first moment she sees him, knows he is Jacques. But when Robineau reminds her, early on, not to neglect to tell him who he is, she asks: "Who is he?" She has instantly recognized someone to be Jacques. But whom?

He never does remember—not, at any rate, in the way one would expect. Nothing whatever comes back to him at the dramatic moment when Geneviève tells him he is her fiancé. "You're French, you're my fiancé, Jacques is you!" she breathlessly informs—whom? He has no idea. Whence the question that haunts him: Who's Jacques? It would seem he would have to know *before* he could begin to find out. The answer toward which the whole play hesitantly moves appears to be prerequisite to the first stirrings of that movement. Indeed, *Siegfried* constantly intimates that it must reach its dénouement in order to get under way at all. Thus the solution to the mystery of origins, the disclosure of the secret of birth—the play itself, even as it transpires—seems deferred. And *Siegfried,* in fact, *is* a delay. It starts in the waiting room of Siegfried's official chambers in Gotha and ends in the waiting room of a train station at the Franco-German border. But this interval allows for some flirtatious dallying—a little play during the play such as must sometimes occur during rehearsals: two strangers, two actors repeating their lines, learning their parts in a romantic drama, must sometimes have time to fall in love. So in the course of Siegfried's (of whose?) discovering Jacques (who's he?)—so in the course of *Siegfried*—does someone fall in love, learning thus who it is who loves to hear Geneviève, a stranger, speak to him of Jacques, and teach him about Jacques. Who it is, in other words, he's discovering to *be* Jacques. Who the unknown is. It's Siegfried! "I've got something to tell you, Jacques," Geneviève confides, just before they board the train (p. 76):

Siegfried: A secret?
Geneviève: It will be a secret when I've told you. Do you hear me, Jacques?
Siegfried: Jacques hears you.
Geneviève: Siegfried! Siegfried, I love you!

"It will be a secret when I've told you . . ." In the course of disclosing the secret of birth (in the course of *Siegfried*), there transpires another play, or another discovery, which is the prerequisite of the first. It is Jacques's discovery—and Geneviève's—during the time they have been spending together (during *Siegfried*), of Siegfried. It is their recognition of the secret: they have come, bit by bit, upon the unknown. So *Siegfried* might well be thought of as a translation of *Siegfried*. A preliminary translation, prerequisite to the original. For during the German's discovery of the Frenchman, the Frenchman has been discovering the German, and while the German has been *solving* the riddle, the Frenchman has been *finding* it. To experience *Siegfried* is to be in attendance at the birth of the secret of birth; to divine a prelude to the play, an overture to the original; and to know that, when the last act finishes, *Siegfried* will come back. The play is sheer promise of the play.

See also 1914–1918, 1945 (6 February).

Bibliography: Jean Anouilh, *The Collected Plays,* trans. Lucienne Hill, vol. 1 (London: Methuen, 1966). Walter Benjamin, "The Storyteller," in *Illuminations,* trans. Harry Zohn (New York: Schocken, 1969). Jacques Body, *Giraudoux et l'Allemagne* (Paris: Didier, 1975). Pierre Drieu la Rochelle, "La valise vide," in *Plainte contre inconnu* (Paris: Gallimard, 1924). Jean Giraudoux, *Théâtre complet,* ed. Jacques Body (Paris: Gallimard, 1982). Charles Mauron, *Le théâtre de Giraudoux* (Paris: José Corti, 1971). Jeffrey Mehlman, "A Future for Andromaque: Aryan and Jew in Giraudoux's France," in *Legacies of Anti-Semitism in France* (Minneapolis: University of Minnesota Press, 1983). Jean-Paul Sartre, *No Exit and Three Other Plays,* trans. Stuart Gilbert (New York: Vintage, 1957). Ann Smock, *Double Dealing* (Lincoln: University of Nebraska Press, 1986).

Ann Smock

1929

Jean Larnac Publishes a *Histoire de la littérature féminine en France*

"Odor di Femina" [*Sic*]

In 1929 Fascism was in place in Italy and National Socialism on the rise in Germany. In the United States the stock market crashed, precipitating a global social and economic crisis; and in the Soviet Union Stalin imposed the massive collectivization of land and the elimination of the kulaks. In France Raymond Poincaré was president, Aristide Briand prime minister, and confrontations between the left and the fascist right were becoming more frequent.

All of these events played a part in exacerbating an intellectual trend that had begun at the end of the 19th century, a trend legitimated by social Darwinism, intensified by nationalism, and sustained by discourses describing the threats posed to the values and fabric of Western civilization by degenerate Jews, inferior races, and hordes of ineptly writing amazons. These features were present in such influential literary criticism of female writers as Jules Barbey d'Aurevilly's *Les bas-bleus* (1878; *The Blue Stockings*), Charles Maurras' "Le romantisme féminin" (1905; "Feminine Romanticism"), and Paul Valéry's "Destin intellectuel de la femme" ("The Intellectual Destiny of Woman"), a public lecture delivered in 1928 and published in 1929.

Jean Larnac's *Histoire de la littérature féminine en France* (1929; *History of Feminine Literature in France*) announced itself as a survey and a defense of the long tradition of female writers in France. Though invaluable as a well-documented compendium of the debate between "féministes" and "antiféministes" (Larnac's vocabulary) known as the *querelle des femmes* and of proper names and titles of works, Larnac's *Histoire* repeated and reaffirmed some of the most pernicious clichés about the inevitable inferiority of women, both as women and as writers.

In his preface Larnac states his intentions: he has come to set the record straight, to study the long history of French female writers without succumbing either to the rhetoric of the "antiféministes," which condemns women as evil, or to the rhetoric of the "féministes," which extols them as paragons. He situates himself in opposition to such early 19th-century writers as Joseph de Maistre, who in a letter to his daughter enumerated the artistic masterpieces of the Western world and emphasized the fact that not one had been produced by a woman. In the last paragraph of the preface Larnac articulates the major questions that inform his study: Have women been unable to create works of art comparable to those created by men because they have not been exposed to the proper social and cultural environments or because, despite social changes, women are inherently incapable of creating such works? Is it true that physiological circumstances determine intellectual differences that neither social nor cultural change can efface? Is it true that women attempt to create works of art because they are unsuccessful in love? Larnac's thesis, enunciated in the preface, reiterated throughout the first part of his study, and defined theoretically in the second part, is that women are fundamentally different from men and that as a result their writing is also different: although women have not created those works of art Joseph de Maistre cited to his daughter, they have created other ones, in conformity with their nature and their genius.

This insistence on women's difference sustains Larnac's discourse in the first and longer part of his study. The nine chapters, following a chronological order, are grouped around major figures: Marie de France, Christine de Pisan, the marquise de Sévigné, and Marie-Madeleine de La Fayette, Germaine de Staël, George Sand, Marceline Desbordes-Valmore, Anna de Noailles, and Colette. Many other women writers are also presented, along with the ironic or flattering rhetoric used about them in earlier histories, critical studies, or journalistic accounts. In his attempt to challenge post-Darwinian notions of women as mediocre, facile, and marginal writers, Larnac exaggerates the binary oppositions that organize his analyses. His categories seem to become more absolute as his text progresses. The masculine is inevitably the sign of intelligence, reason, effort, abstraction, production, muscles, and normality; the feminine is just as inevitably the sign of sensitivity, inspiration, spontaneity, emotion, reproduction, nerves, and abnormality.

The polarity between normality and abnormality, tentatively delineated throughout the first part of the text, becomes central to Larnac's argument at the end of the second part, when his reliance on what he considers *true* scientific theory reinforces the most negative aspects of earlier attacks on female writers as unnatural, as imitators of men, and finally, as abnormal—that is, as no longer women, neither beloved wives nor loving mothers. Larnac's lack of a coherent methodology is partially responsible for his unintended conclusion. Because he has a thesis rather than a method of investigation, his study is not an inquiry from which theory emerges; it is merely a repetitious description of an unchanging condition. In this regard, it is useful to compare Larnac's study with Sigmund Freud's 1932 essay "Femininity." Rather than assuming difference from the beginning, Freud raises the question of the effects produced by sexual difference and then suggests hypotheses that might account for difference, and the consequences of these hypotheses. Freud has a method of investigation, Larnac does not.

In the second part of the *Histoire,* "Les femmes et la littérature" ("Women and Literature"), Larnac cites psychologists, physiologists, doctors, educators, ontogeneticists, and phylogeneticists, all of whom have concluded from their research that there are fundamental differences in intelligence between women and men. The only question that remains unanswered, according to Larnac, is whether these differences are inevitable or whether they may be attributed to a long history of "slavery." Here Larnac clearly relies on Valéry's "Destin intellectuel de la femme," Maurras' "Romantisme féminin," and, perhaps most important, Barbey d'Aurevilly's *Les bas-bleus,* which misquotes a line of Lorenzo Da Ponte's libretto from Mozart's *Don Giovanni,* an error that Larnac repeats.

In act 1, scene 4 of the opera, Don Giovanni tells his servant, Leporello, that he has fallen in love with a beautiful woman. As he is speaking, Donna Elvira appears at the rear of the stage, and Don Giovanni exclaims: "Zitto! mi pare sentir odor di femmina" ("Be quiet! I think I smell the odor of woman"). Woman's presence is revealed by her odor, an odor that Don Giovanni recognizes without any further evidence. In the introduction to *Les bas-bleus,* Barbey d'Aurevilly asserted: "Women can be and have been poets, writers, and artists in all civilizations, but they have been female poets, female writers, female artists. Study their works, open them at random! At the tenth line, and without knowing by whom they are, you are warned; you smell woman! *Odor di femina* [*sic*]. Even when they have the most talent, they lack male faculties as radically as Hercules' organs are lacking to Venus di Milo, and for the critic it is as clear as natural history" (p. xxii).

In *Histoire de la littérature féminine en France,* Larnac quotes this passage, reproduces the misspelling *femina,* and adds this commentary: "And, in effect, feminine literature displays a frenzy of vibration that is opposed to the serene calm of the art that masculine geniuses achieve. Masculine intelligence, feminine

889

sensitivity; we find this opposition even in the style of the two sexes" (p. 271). Earlier, in his preface to *Colette: Sa vie, son oeuvre* (1927; *Colette: Her Life, Her Work*), Larnac had written: "I maintain the hope that I will be able to share the pleasure I have had in breathing in the intoxicating odor of hay that emanates from her work" (p. 9). Here, it is the work rather than the woman that is recognizable by its odor, but the association is still with the feminine, and exclusively with an odor.

Odor di femina is the unconscious of Larnac's text through which his under-lying convictions are acted out: for him difference is ultimately grounded in the physiological and the sexual. His study of women writers thus begins with literature and the differences between the writing of women and men, but ends with their physiological differences, their respective roles in the sexual act, and their psychological differences. Larnac seems unaware of the implications of his thesis. He does not see the connections, as Maurras apparently does, between believing in the physiological differences between the sexes and their mode of writing and believing in physiological differences between Catholics and Jews, between nations, between races. Nor does Larnac see that difference is inevi-tably hierarchical and that, by insisting on difference, he is reiterating a belief in the inferiority of female writers, who contaminate the superior, male culture. Nor is he aware of the discrepancy that exists between his intentions and the unconscious of his text.

The same *odor di femina* that betrays Larnac's attitude toward women as human beings and as producers of culture finds an interesting echo and chal-lenge in Colette's *Sido* (1929). There, as if to consecrate this belief in the iden-tifying power of the feminine odor, Colette describes her mother's returns from occasional trips to Paris in the following terms: "She never knew that, each time she came home, the smell of her gray squirrel pelisse, impregnated with her own blonde scent, chaste and feminine and far removed from all base, bodily seductions, bereft me of speech and almost of sense" (p. 149).

In *Sido* Colette not only emphasizes the odor of her mother but also, like Larnac, insists on the mother as the feminine figure par excellence. In this instance, Larnac, Colette, and the Freud of "Femininity" appear to be in agree-ment. But whereas in Larnac and in Freud there is no other figure to compete with the figure of the mother, in *Sido* there is the figure of the writing daughter, the daughter who writes in the place of the mutilated father, who takes over his project and creates the figure of the mother. There is no *Sido* without Colette.

For Larnac, as later for the psychoanalyst Erik Erikson, a woman is never not a woman. His *Histoire* solidifies, as it attempts to liberalize, an official unprob-lematic discourse on women. During the same period, from 1928 to 1932, other female writers—Djuna Barnes, Natalie Clifford Barney, Gertrude Stein—and two psychoanalysts—Freud and also Jacques Lacan, in the second part of his doctoral dissertation, "Le cas 'Aimée,' ou la paranoïa d'auto-punition" (1932; "The Case of 'Aimée,' or the Paranoia of Self-Punishment")—were beginning to question the notion of a fixed sexual identity and to suggest, albeit in different ways, that masculine and feminine were constructs imposed by social organization and language. But, as Freud points out in the opening pages of "Femininity," the first question of sexual identity—Is it a man or a woman?—is the first difference, the first distinction that we are accustomed to make. Three of the major questions that have preoccupied writers and theorists during the second half of the 20th century began to emerge in 1929: What is a woman? What is literature? And what are the possible connections between them? Unexamined in Larnac's text and in the texts of the predecessors on whom he relies, the first of these questions was formulated by Colette. *Sido* provides not only the writing daughter who picks up, as it were, the father's limp pen and who writes to speak his and her love for Sido, but also the figure of the mother jealous of her daughter's attraction for a woman, Adrienne, who nursed her daughter when she was an infant. Desire circulates between daughter, mother, and wetnurse, defying Larnac's official notion of the normal woman and the permissible forms of love.

Colette's text also calls into question official notions of what constitutes literature. Larnac isolates women writers in what are for him feminine genres: correspondence, poetry, and the novel. But *Sido,* like many of Colette's texts, does not conform to traditional genre boundaries any more than does the name with which, after 1923, she signed her writings. Colette, both her father's last name and a feminine first name, violates both the tradition of Madame de . . . and the tradition of the male pseudonym. It seems reasonable to conclude that in 1929, while Larnac was making order in what he believed to be *the* official tradition of female writers in France, Colette was actively, if unconsciously, disrupting the b(i)ases of that tradition, questioning both the foundations of Larnac's title: "littérature" and "féminine"—and the infallible flair of Don Juan.

See also 1542, 1787, 1816, 1859 (23 July), 1949, 1975.

Bibliography: Jules Barbey d'Aurevilly, *Les bas-bleus* (Paris: Société Générale de Librairie Catholique, Victor Palmé, 1878). Colette, *My Mother's House and Sido,* trans. Una Vicenzo Troubridge and Enid McLeod (New York: Farrar, Straus and Giroux, 1981). Lorenzo Da Ponte, *Don Giovanni* (Milan: Ricordi, 1964). Erica Eisinger and Mari W. McCarty, eds., *Colette: The Woman, the Writer* (University Park: Pennsylvania State University Press, 1981). Sigmund Freud, "Femininity," in *New Introductory Lectures on Psychoanalysis,* ed. and trans. James Strachey (New York: Norton, 1964). Jacques Lacan, "Le cas 'Aimée,' ou la paranoïa d'auto-punition," in *De la psychose paranoïaque dans ses rapports avec la personnalité suivi de Premiers écrits sur la paranoïa* (Paris: Seuil, 1975). Jean Larnac, *Colette: Sa vie, son oeuvre* (Paris: Simon Kra, 1927). Larnac, *Histoire de la littérature féminine en France* (Paris: Simon Kra, 1929). Charles Maurras, "Le romantisme féminin," in *L'avenir de l'intelligence* (Paris: Flammarion, 1927). Michèle Blin Sarde, *Colette: Free and Fettered,* trans. Richard Miller (New York: Morrow, 1980). Béatrice Slama, "De la 'littérature féminine' à 'l'écrire femme': Différence et institution," *Littérature,* 44 (1981), 51–71. Paul Valéry, "Destin intellectuel de la femme," in *Remarques extérieures* (Paris: Cahiers Libres, 1929).

Elaine Marks

༄ *1931, March*

Maurice Heine Publishes the First Volume of the Marquis de Sade's
Long-Lost Novel Les *120 journées de Sodome, ou l'école du libertinage*

Sadology

In 1923 Maurice Heine, a curious figure in the Parisian avant-garde who
devoted his life to collecting and editing the marquis de Sade's manuscripts,
created the Société du Roman Philosophique (Society for the Philosophical
Novel), whose main purpose was to publish (though not to sell) the still mostly
clandestine works of the 18th-century writer. The first reliable edition of *Les
120 journées de Sodome* (*The 120 Days of Sodom*) appeared in three volumes from
1931 to 1935.

Les 120 journées portrays four libertines' exercise of unlimited power over their
kidnapped and carefully selected victims and culminates in gruesome sexual
tortures and mutilations. Sade wrote it in 1785 while incarcerated in the Bastille. He always claimed it was his masterpiece. The scroll on which it was
written, however, was stolen from him a few days before the storming of the
prison in July 1789. It resurfaced only at the end of the century. Iwan Bloch,
a German psychiatrist who specialized in sexual perversions, published it for
the first time in 1904. But he made so many errors in transcribing Sade's handwriting that Heine went to Berlin to buy the manuscript and edited the version
he made available in 1931.

All through the 19th century, Sade's legend had been growing. On the one
hand, medical theory was emphasizing more and more the importance of sexuality in human behavior, especially with regard to its pathology. Thus psychia-
trists came to consider Sade's fictions as exemplary documents on the sexual
perversion that they soon labeled with his name: sadism, or pleasure felt in
inflicting pain, in destroying the object of one's own desire. At the same time,
for Romantic writers, Sade became a fascinating and unspeakable figure, hero
and victim of a Luciferian revolt, the prototype of the *maudit* (damned) figure.
The protagonist of Pétrus Borel's 1839 frenetic novel *Madame Putiphar* shares a
cell with Sade and feels ennobled by the proximity of "one of France's glories,
a martyr."

Guillaume Apollinaire's publication of the first anthology of Sade's works,
L'oeuvre du marquis de Sade (1909; *The Work of the Marquis de Sade*), marks the
first attempt to let Sade out on parole. In the introduction to the volume,
Apollinaire announced: "This man, who seems to have counted for nothing
during the whole 19th century, might become the dominant figure of the 20th"
(*Oeuvres complètes*, p. 231). He was right. Sade's writing was becoming available.
Along with Arthur Rimbaud and the Comte de Lautréamont (Isidore Ducasse),
he was soon to emerge as one of the major figures in the surrealist pantheon, at
once a prophet, a pioneer, and a martyr to modernity. Freud having shown that
sadism was part and parcel of the constitution and development of the human
psyche, Sade could now be praised as an unhypocritical—albeit extreme—

expression of nature, testifying to the variety and complexity of natural impulses rather than to an individual pathological depravity.

Essential to this rehabilitation was the claim that there was nothing realistic about Sade's novels. "Sade is surrealist in sadism," says André Breton in the *Manifeste du surréalisme* (1924; in *Manifestoes of Surrealism*, p. 26), stressing precisely that Sade's excesses are imaginary, unreal or "surreal." Paul Eluard, celebrating St. Justine's Day in the journal *La révolution surréaliste,* summarized this view: "All the figures born from the imagination must become the absolute mistresses of the realities of love," adding that Sade "wanted to liberate the amatory imagination" (December 1926, p. 9). Implicit in these celebrations of Sade's literary sadism is the view that, according to Maurice Blanchot's later formula: "Everything must be said" ("L'inconvenance majeure" [1965; "The Major Misconduct"], p. 20). Censorship is intolerable when language is concerned. But one must not leap from words to the conclusion of facts: no piece of literature can incriminate. In presenting Sade in his *Anthologie de l'humour noir* (1939; *Anthology of Black Humor*), Breton focused on passages from his novels that demonstrate what he called "obvious overstatement": "They allow the reader to relax and to think that the author is no dupe" (*Anthologie,* p. 39). In the surrealist golden age of sexuality, there is place for sadism, a mix of *amour fou* and *humour noir,* mad love and black humor, sex and freedom, blessed with the infinite possibilities opened by imagination.

Maurice Heine, in the preface to his 1930 edition of Sade's *Les infortunes de la vertu* (*The Misfortunes of Virtue*), dedicated to his surrealist friends, gave such a view its strongest expression. Sade's sadistic fantasies are not the cause but the result of his imprisonment. They also work as its denial, allowing the triumph of desire over objective reality. "Physically a prisoner, a small amount of ink and paper will suffice to free his mind" (*Le marquis de Sade,* p. 64). No sooner did Sade start writing than the Bastille turned into "the tower of Liberty." Sadism, here, has nothing to do with real pain inflicted on real bodies, but (reduced to another innocuous surrealist game) strictly with imagination and the pleasure principle.

Georges Bataille was ostracized from the surrealist movement for opposing such views. He saw the transformation of Sade into a literary hero as another form of betrayal. Troppman, the protagonist of his 1935 novel *Le bleu du ciel* (pub. 1957; *Blue of Noon*), denounces the literary cult of Sade. "Listen to me, Xénie," he tells his lover. "You've been involved in literary goings-on. You must have read De Sade. You must have found De Sade fantastic. Just like the others. People who admire De Sade are con artists, do you hear? Con artists!" (*Blue,* p. 68). After the legalistic suppression of the 19th century, the avant-garde "sweetening" of Sade is just another—symmetrical—way to deflect the horrifying, inassimilable core of his experience, linking sexuality not to pleasure but to terror.

Pierre Klossowski developed similar views in a 1939 lecture commemorating the 150th anniversary of the French Revolution at Bataille's Collège de Sociologie, as well as in the essays he collected in *Sade, mon prochain* (1947; *Sade, My*

Neighbor). Such readings mark a shift toward an interpretation that focuses less on Sade's erotics than on the terror they inspired, mirroring the "legalized carnage" that characterized both the Revolutionary Terror of 1793 and contemporary Nazi violence. The surrealists had conceived this "mirror" as a revolutionary doctrine, turning it into a set of prescriptive laws. But like Bataille, Klossowski contended that Sade's work could never be claimed by any ideological or prescriptive system. Far from recognizing the Terrorists as his disciples, Sade, Klossowski contended, "came close to experiencing the legalized carnage of the Terror as a caricature of his own system" (*The College,* p. 221). During the 1930s the surrealists' celebration of Sade began to appear terribly naïve in the face of a political violence that seemed to replicate some of Sade's horrible scenarios.

See also 1791 (Summer), 1924, 1937 (March).

Bibliography: Guillaume Apollinaire, "Les diables amoureux," in *Oeuvres complètes,* ed. Michel Décaudin, vol. 2 (Paris: Balland, 1965). Georges Bataille, *Blue of Noon,* trans. Harry Mathews (New York: Urizen Books, 1978). Bataille, "Dossier de la polémique avec André Breton," in *Oeuvres complètes,* vol. 2 (Paris: Gallimard, 1970). Maurice Blanchot, "L'inconvenance majeure," preface to Sade's *Français, encore un effort si vous voulez être républicains* (Paris: Jean-Jacques Pauvert, 1965). Pétrus Borel, *Madame Putiphar,* 2 vols. (Geneva: Slatkine, 1967). André Breton, *Anthologie de l'humour noir* (Paris: Le Livre de Poche, 1966). Breton, *Manifestoes of Surrealism,* trans. Richard Seaver and Helen R. Lane (Ann Arbor: University of Michigan Press, 1969). Jane Gallop, *Intersections: A Reading of Sade with Bataille, Blanchot, and Klossowski* (Lincoln: University of Nebraska Press, 1981). Maurice Heine, *Le marquis de Sade,* ed. Gilbert Lély (Paris: Gallimard, 1950). Pierre Klossowski, "The Marquis de Sade and the Revolution," in *The College of Sociology, 1937–39,* ed. Denis Hollier, trans. Betsy Wing (Minneapolis: University of Minnesota Press, 1988). Françoise Laugaa-Traut, *Lectures de Sade* (Paris: Armand Colin, 1973). Donatien Alphonse François, marquis de Sade, *The 120 Days of Sodom and Other Writings,* trans. Richard Seaver and Austryn Wainhouse (New York: Grove, 1966).

Carolyn J. Dean

✒ *1931, June*

The Translation of Martin Heidegger's "Was ist Metaphysik?"
Appears in the Final Issue of the Avant-Garde Journal *Bifur*

Plenty of Nothing

"Whereas the philosopher of the past had nothing so much in mind as shielding himself from the vicissitudes of life and searching for security in his own thoughts, the philosopher of the future will no longer avoid the risks that every life implies and will no longer be afraid to face the unknown." It was against just such a development, as Bernard Groethuysen described it in his *Introduction à la philosophie allemande depuis Nietzsche* (1926; *Introduction to German Philosophy since Nietzsche*), that Julien Benda, in *La trahison des clercs* (1927; *The Betrayal of the Intellectuals*), denounced the taste that modern thinkers had developed for life: the defenders of eternal values were becoming less and less disinterested, entering into the service of increasingly temporal passions. Although this outburst made a considerable splash, it did not persuade committed intellectuals to head back to their cloisters. At the close of the Roaring Twenties, a militant younger generation dedicated itself, in the manner of Nietzsche, to "philosophy as a hammer-blow." The domain that had formerly been reserved for patiently wrought dissertations and careful treatises was now invaded by the manifesto and the insult. Emmanuel Berl's *Mort de la pensée bourgeoise* (1929; *Death of Bourgeois Thought*) was followed in the same year by *Mort de la morale bourgeoise* (*Death of Bourgeois Morality*). Above all there was, in 1932, *Les chiens de garde* (*The Watchdogs*), the vitriolic pamphlet that the young Communist writer Paul Nizan flung at the Parisian philosophical establishment. "Today," it declared, "whoever wants to think humanly will think dangerously" (p. 58). Nizan used a letter from the readers of *Iskra,* the Bolshevik newspaper, as the epigraph to his novel *Le cheval de Troie* (1935; *Trojan Horse*): "We have written this letter to *Iskra* so that it may teach us not only 'whence to begin,' but also how to live and to die."

Nizan was a Marxist. But the same hatred for thought's quiescence, the same wish to tie intellectual activity to risk, to danger, to personal commitment, underlay the sudden fashionableness of Martin Heidegger, himself linked to the political convulsions that were shaking Weimar Germany. In 1932 Arnaud Dandieu associated "the philosophy of anxiety" (Heideggerian existentialism) with "the politics of despair" (National Socialism). The success—"both extremely rapid and deep"—of the German philosopher, he commented in *Revue d'Allemagne,* should be accounted for in the "extraphilosophical zones of influence of his thought" ("Philosophie de l'angoisse et politique du désespoir" ["Philosophy of Anxiety and Politics of Despair"], p. 883).

In effect, this philosophy was no longer conceived of as a theory of knowledge or a philosophy of the sciences, but as an analysis of existence; its object was life. In his inaugural lecture of 1929, "Was ist Metaphysik?" ("What Is Metaphysics?"), Heidegger had differentiated logical questions from metaphysical ones: science interests itself in what is, thus overlooking the nothing; but the affective experience of anxiety reveals to consciousness that to which science is blind; "the idea of 'logic' itself disintegrates in the turbulence of a more original questioning" (p. 107). The thinker, thus caught, cannot keep his distance. "The question of the nothing puts us, the questioners, in question. It is a metaphysical question" (p. 111). Dandieu commented: anxiety forbids the philosopher "to claim, in the name of wisdom, the role of observer" ("Philosophie de l'angoisse," p. 885).

For the generation of the 1930s, existentialism answered the urge to destroy the double frontier separating philosophy from both life and literature. Georges Bataille later recalled the impact Heidegger's essay made on him: "What was so seductive from the very first glimpse of this new philosophy was the way it opened directly onto life." But a philosophy that opens directly onto life ceases to differentiate itself from literature. "In this way," he continued, "philosophy was finally reduced to literature" ("L'existentialisme," p. 83).

Shortly after the publication of "Qu'est-ce que la métaphysique?" in *Bifur*, Raymond Queneau, a former surrealist, wrote his first novel, *Le chiendent* (1933; *The Bark Tree*). His first purpose had been to bring to an end a particular form of separation between philosophy and life—namely, their linguistic separation—and to submit philosophy to the test of what the French call the living language —that spoken by concierges and toughs. In order to "kick the ass" of philosophical language, he therefore embarked on "a little attempt at translating Descartes's *Discours de la méthode* [*Discourse on Method*] into spoken French . . . It is with this idea in mind that I applied myself to writing 'a something' that became a novel that would later be called *Le chiendent*" (*Bâtons, chiffres et lettres* [1950; *Strokes, Numerals, and Letters*], p. 17).

Queneau spent the summer of 1932 in Greece, a circumstance that prompted a shift in the philosophical godfather: the *Discours de la méthode* was soon mixed with Plato's *Parmenides*, itself strongly colored with Heideggerian accents. Witness the dialectic of being and nonbeing that Saturnin, the philosopher-concierge of *Le chiendent*, develops in the course of a meditation every bit as metaphysical as that to which his celebrated piece of wax inspired Descartes. In this case its object is a lump of butter: "The lump of butter isn't everything it isn't; it isn't everywhere where it isn't, it stops everything else being where it is, it hasn't always been and won't always be, ekcetera, ekcetera. So that we can say that this lump of butter is up to its eyes in an infinity of nonbeing . . . It's as simple as Hello. What is, is what isn't; but it's what is that isn't. The point is that nonbeing isn't on one side and being on the other. There's nonbeing, and that's all, seeing that being isn't" (*The Bark Tree*, p. 244). Man, according to Heidegger, is "a lieutenant of the nothing"; he is the one who reveals the nothing as belonging to the Being of being. Saturnin fits this definition perfectly; attentive to the strangeness of beings that he experiences as detaching themselves against a ground of what they are not, he maintains existence at the interior of nothingness, contrary to his brethren, who busy themselves with chores whose familiarity hides from them the experience of nonbeing. In the midst of a banquet Saturnin gloomily watches his fellow men finishing off their plates: "They didn't suspect that a full plate conceals an empty plate, as being conceals nothingness" (p. 174). But because the plates had only the time to remain empty that it took the assiduous waiters to refill them, the melancholy Saturnin concludes, "That's how you escape from anxiety." The plot of *Le chiendent* is itself an allegory of this experience. A door, painted blue, unleashes a completely picaresque treasure hunt. Strangely hung on the wall of a junk dealer's hovel, it must hide something. But, like a mask without a face, like a being that covers nothingness, the revelation is that it conceals nothing.

At the core of Queneau's novels there is always a character—an unwitting metaphysician—who thinks about nothing. The hero of *Les derniers jours* (1936; *The Last Days*), Vincent Tuquedenne, having arrived from Le Havre to study philosophy at the Sorbonne, is suddenly seized, in a Parisian garden, by the paucity of the reality of what surrounds him and ends up "about to cry, moved as he was by the nonexistence of things" (*Les derniers jours,* p. 170). In *Le dimanche de la vie* (1953; *The Sunday of Life*), it is not a blow of the hammer but a sweep of the broom that turns Valentin Brû into a philosopher. He handles this annihilatory instrument with metaphysical fire: after having busied himself with the garbage on the sidewalk, he proceeds to sweep the passersby, the houses, the streets, the landscape itself, until he has reached the nonexistence of things (*Dimanche,* p. 174).

Queneau's novels give to metaphysics, in short, the aura of objects picked up at the flea market. As do the poems he wrote. The best of them lead one to imagine what Heidegger's *Sein und Zeit* (1929; *Being and Time*) would be like if the philosopher had set his magnum opus as a song for Marlene Dietrich. But the issue, here, is not a celebration of spoken language. Claude Simonnet has demonstrated that Queneau's rhetoric focuses less on speech proper than on the oddities of its written transcription. Transcribing the language people speak is no less bizarre than translating philosophy into the vernacular. Instead of effacing itself by passing itself off as speech, writing makes manifest, by a tiny gap, the strangeness of speech itself, just as metaphysics makes manifest that of daily life.

It was Nizan, then editor of *Bifur,* who published the French translation of "Was ist Metaphysik?" He introduced the German philosopher to the readers of the journal with this brief note: "Has founded the philosophy of nothingness." In many respects Nizan's communism was to be a reaction against this philosophy. Like those of Queneau, the characters of his novels experience the nonexistence of things. But instead of being moved by this, they rebel against it.

Nizan's first novel, *Antoine Bloyé* (1933), traces the life of a worker whose ambition and success has led him to abandon his class of origin. One spring day, out of the blue ("Antoine was thinking of nothing"), he stumbles over the experience of nothingness. "And suddenly, on the sidewalk of the Rue de Tolbiac, where men and women passed with their accustomed stride, busy with their everyday affairs, Antoine discovered he was going to die. He was suddenly cut off from the passers-by, who continued calmly in their eternal life" (*Antoine Bloyé,* p. 219). He was caught up by "the vast and indifferent whirlwind of nothingness" (translation modified). The chapter is given over to a phenomenology of anxiety that takes up, sometimes word for word, the motifs developed by Heidegger. Nizan concludes it: "It takes a great deal of force and creation to escape from nothingness" (p. 229).

This force that would permit one to resist anxiety and nothingness is at the center of Nizan's next novel, *Le cheval de Troie.* Pierre Bloyé, son of Antoine, becomes a political activist in order to escape the anxiety that haunted his father's last days. In the provincial lycée where he teaches philosophy, one of his colleagues is Lange, a fellow graduate student of the Ecole Normale Supérieure. "The idea of death was in the air of those days," Bloyé remarks (*Trojan Horse,* p. 139). But these two "intellectual heroes" react to it in opposite ways. Bloyé

897

interprets it in political terms: anxiety, the experience of the nothingness of all things, is not inherent in the human condition but only in that of man in a futureless society. In his view, capitalism is condemned to disappear, not because commodity fetishism hides the nothing, but because it masks injustice. Lange opposes his own metaphysical radicalism to such political activism. Heidegger's essay ends with a question: "Why are there beings at all, and why not rather nothing?" ("What Is Metaphysics?" p. 112). This is Lange's question also. When Bloyé speaks of transforming the world, he retorts: "It's difficult to imagine a more disgraceful world than that in which we are unfortunate enough to live now. But any world would be equally disgraceful. The really disgraceful thing is that worlds exist at all . . . I find that Valéry is most naïve in being astonished that things are as they are, instead of being indignant that they exist at all. My anger is more basic than yours" (p. 59). Lange is the novel's lieutenant of the nothing. When, after he has pronounced, "Really there is only metaphysics," and is asked to explain himself, he replies, "Simply that there are no political problems" (p. 118).

In the same issue of *Bifur* that carried the Heidegger translation appeared "La légende de la vérité" ("Truth's Legend"), by Jean-Paul Sartre, a fellow student of Nizan's from the Ecole Normale Supérieure who, when *Le cheval de Troie* was published, recognized himself in the character of Lange. And it was in 1931 that Sartre began the long process of writing his novel *La nausée* (1938; *Nausea*), one of the major literary events of the century.

Whereas, according to André Malraux, Faulkner's *Sanctuary* (1931) marks the intrusion of Greek tragedy into the detective story, *La nausée* marks that of metaphysics into the novel. But Sartre's metaphysical fiction is a philosophical tale without a thesis. Instead of being the medium of a demonstration, it is the site of an experience. Roquentin is a partisan neither, like Lange, of metaphysical nitrogen, nor, like Bloyé, of political oxygen. His experience is metaphysical first of all because he is not a professional philosopher. It takes place in the first person and in the form of a diary.

When Heidegger has to describe what a crisis of anxiety consists of, he does so in a retrospective manner. Once the crisis is over, the subject wonders what had been its cause. "It was 'really'—nothing. Indeed: the nothing itself—as such—was there" ("What Is Metaphysics?" p. 103). Roquentin's estrangement is a function of the same elusive experience. Fredric Jameson observes in *La nausée* "a special sensitivity to events in which 'nothing' happens" (*Sartre*, p. 32). This is the keynote on which the book starts. On the opening page of his diary, after having tried to give an account of the first of his crises, Roquentin notes, "One shouldn't make something strange out of nothing [*mettre de l'étrange là où il n'y a rien*]" (*La nausée*, in *Oeuvres romanesques*, p. 5). This formula contains in germ the whole critique of the narrative, of the way writers generate novels by looking retrospectively at facts that by themselves had nothing novelistic about them. It is impossible to recount without traducing it (without making it strange) the advent of (the) nothing. It is impossible not to make it strange if it is nothing that has happened and that one wants to recount. "For the most banal event to become an adventure, you must (and it is enough) begin to recount it" (*Nausea*, p. 56). Adventure exists only in books.

Roquentin's diary, in this sense, is that of his *unhappenings,* the diary of his disengagements and losses, of his decathexes. "We can get no hold on things," Heidegger says in relation to anguish. The first of Roquentin's experiences is an inability to grasp, to take, to hold: a stone falls from his hands. What follows will be nothing but the generalization of this accident, a sort of ascesis in which it happens to him that nothing happens to him. Roquentin loses his objects one after another; it is the story of a relinquishment and of what Edmund Husserl had termed a bracketing-out.

This is also the meaning of the famous scene in front of the chestnut-tree root in the Bouville public park, during which—like Vincent Tuquedenne in his garden, like Antoine Bloyé on the rue de Tolbiac—Roquentin's Heideggerian experience reaches its climax. Ordinarily hidden behind things and events, existence (like nothingness for Heidegger) suddenly unmasks itself. Things abruptly appear to him in their contingency, manifesting less their presence than the fact that they could just as easily not be. "Existence had suddenly unveiled itself . . . The root, the park gates, the bench, the sparse grass, all that had vanished: the diversity of things, their individuality, were only an appearance, a veneer. This veneer had melted" (*Nausea,* pp. 171–172). This denarrativized novel is also the diary of a kind of metaphysical undoing of events. As the young, then unknown critic Maurice Blanchot commented: "Nausea is the shattering experience that reveals to Roquentin what it is to exist without being, the pathetic illumination that puts him in contact, among existing things, not with the things, but with their existence" (quoted in Sartre, *Oeuvres romanesques,* p. 1708). Emmanuel Levinas, the philosopher who had introduced existentialism into France, described this experience of "existence without existing" as the horror of the *there is.*

This amorphous quality of the existential experience has its equivalent, from the point of view of the subject, in the impersonal mode of its development. In relation to anxiety, "Was ist Metaphysik?" evoked "the impersonal existential ground"; "it is not as though 'you' or 'I' feel ill at ease; rather it is this way for some 'one'" ("What Is Metaphysics?" p. 102). The ultimate degree of this depersonalization is attained at the end of *La nausée* when, Roquentin having relinquished all his projects and having renounced Anny, who has forgotten him, his diary takes on a strangely impersonal grammatical form. Its writer loses the use of his first-person voice. "And suddenly the 'I' pales, pales, and fades out . . . Nobody lives there any more. A little while ago someone said 'me,' said *my* consciousness. Who? Outside there were streets, alive with known smells and colors. Now nothing is left but anonymous walls, anonymous consciousness. This is what there is: walls, and between the walls, a small transparency, alive and impersonal" (*Nausea,* p. 227). From time to time, the thought of Anny returns and causes a pang: "Consciousness of Anny, of Anny, fat old Anny in her hotel room, consciousness of suffering . . . There is consciousness of all that and consciousness of consciousness. But no one is there to suffer and wring his hands and take pity on himself" (p. 229). Roquentin is absent from his own pain. Like existence behind things, consciousness behind subjectivity formulates itself in the modality of the *there is*.

Jean Lacouture, in his biography of Malraux, reports that Manuel Azaña, the president of the Spanish republic, when asked in 1938 about *L'espoir* (1937; *Man's Hope*), replied, "Ah! these Frenchmen! Trust them to get an officer of the *Guardia Civil* to philosophise!" (*André Malraux,* p. 249). The characters of these existentialist novels fill Victor Brombert's category of "intellectual heroes." But they are the green version of it. They speak of death and anxiety, of the meaning of life more often than of the pleasures of love. Ideas do not display a thesis here. They lack the senile wisdom of experience; rather, they explode with adolescent aggressiveness, the teenager's pretentiousness. They try to prove nothing, to draw no moral from history. They are a bit unripe. And raucous. They are less involved in bringing the action to its conclusion than in interrupting it. These are not so much novels by philosophy professors as novels by philosophy students. Stendhal said that in a work of art politics is as cacophonous as a pistol shot at a concert. Metaphysics, in these novels (at the time often associated with the terrorist's revolver), has the same detonating effect. And that gives them their high rhetorical efficacy.

See also 1933 (December), 1941, 1945 (15 October).

Bibliography: Georges Bataille, "L'existentialisme," in *Oeuvres complètes,* vol. 11 (Paris: Gallimard, 1988). Julien Benda, *The Betrayal of the Intellectuals,* trans. Richard Aldington (Boston: Beacon, 1955). Victor Brombert, *The Intellectual Hero: Studies in the French Novel, 1880–1955* (Philadelphia: Lippincott, 1960). Arnaud Dandieu, "Philosophie de l'angoisse et politique du désespoir," *Revue d'Allemagne, et des pays de langue allemande,* 60 (1932), 883–891. Bernard Groethuysen, *Introduction à la pensée philosophique allemande depuis Nietzsche* (Paris: Stock, 1926). Martin Heidegger, "What Is Metaphysics?" in *Basic Writings,* ed. and trans. David Farrell Krell (New York: Harper & Row, 1977). Fredric Jameson, *Sartre: The Origins of a Style* (New York: Columbia University Press, 1984). Jean Lacouture, *André Malraux,* trans. Alan Sheridan (New York: Pantheon, 1975). Emmanuel Levinas, *De l'existence à l'existant* (Paris: Fontaine, 1947). Paul Nizan, *Antoine Bloyé,* trans. Edmund Stevens (New York: Monthly Review Press, 1973). Nizan, *Les chiens de garde* (Paris: Maspéro, 1964). Nizan, *Trojan Horse,* trans. Charles Ashleigh (New York: Fertig, 1975). Raymond Queneau, *The Bark Tree,* trans. Barbara Wright (New York: New Directions, 1968). Queneau, *Bâtons, chiffres et lettres,* 2d ed. (Paris: Gallimard, 1965). Queneau, *Les derniers jours* (Paris: Gallimard, 1936). Queneau, *The Sunday of Life,* trans. Barbara Wright (New York: New Directions, 1977). Jean-Paul Sartre, *La nausée,* in *Oeuvres romanesques,* ed. Michel Contat and Michel Rybalka (Paris: Gallimard, 1982); translated by Lloyd Alexander as *Nausea* (New York: New Directions, 1964). Claude Simonnet, *Queneau déchiffré* (Paris: Julliard, 1962).

Denis Hollier

∽ *1933, February*
After Two Years of Ethnographic Research, the Mission Dakar-Djibouti Returns to Paris

Negrophilia

The Mission Dakar-Djibouti was science on a grand scale. For twenty months a team of ethnologists and linguists led by Marcel Griaule crossed subsaharan Africa from the Atlantic to the Red Sea. Reminiscent of other transcontinental exploits of the period, such as the "Croisière Jaune" and the "Croisière Noire" (across Asia and Africa, with Citroën vehicles), the mission was a resounding success. It added more than 3,000 objects to the collections of the Musée d'Ethnographie du Trocadéro, and it contacted the Dogon, a West African people who would later attain considerable ethnographic renown through the work of Griaule and his colleagues. The mission's results were reported in a special issue of Albert Skira and Etstratios Tériade's lavish art journal, *Minotaure*. It produced scores of scholarly articles and monographs, along with Michel Leiris' *L'Afrique fantôme* (1934; *Phantom Africa*), a unique specimen of surrealist ethnography. The expedition was followed with interest by Parisian socialites as well as by academic scholars at the recently founded Institute of Ethnology. Members of both groups were on hand in evening attire at the Cirque d'Hiver on 15 April 1931 when the black Panamanian boxer and welterweight champion Al Brown staged a benefit.

The Mission Dakar-Djibouti played to the negrophilia that was sweeping avant-garde music, literature, and art. The African sculpture that Pablo Picasso, André Derain, and Guillaume Apollinaire had prized before 1914 emerged after the war as *l'art nègre,* a subject for exhibitions and passionate debates. In the 1920s Paris was flooded with things *nègre,* an expansive category that included North American jazz, syncretic Brazilian rhythms, African, Oceanian, and Alaskan carvings, ritual "poetry" from south of the Sahara and from the Australian outback, the literature of the Harlem Renaissance, and René Maran's *Batouala* (subtitled "véritable roman nègre"), which won the Prix Goncourt in 1921. The writings of the anthropologist-collector Leo Frobenius, recently translated from German, proposed East Africa as the cradle of civilization. And the widely read philosopher Lucien Lévy-Bruhl's *La mentalité primitive* (1922; *How Natives Think*) gave scholarly credence to a common image of black societies as "mystical," "affective," and "prelogical."

"Africa" was by definition primitive, wild, elemental. In the 1920s, however, a series of stereotypes long associated with backwardness and inferiority acquired positive connotations and came to stand for liberation and spontaneity, for a simultaneous recovery of ancient sources and an access to true modernity. This modernist primitivism was perhaps most widespread in the postwar vogue for American jazz, the success of bands such as the Southern Syncopated Orchestra and Lew Leslie's Black Birds, or Josephine Baker and Sidney Bechet's success with La Revue Nègre at the Théâtre des Champs-Elysées. Michel Leiris recalled the scene in *L'âge d'homme* (1939; *Manhood*, p. 109):

> In the period of great license that followed the hostilities, jazz was a sign of allegiance, an orgiastic tribute to the colors of the moment. It functioned magically, and its means of influence can be compared to a kind of possession. It was the element that gave these celebrations their true meaning, with communion by dance, latent or manifest exoticism, and drinks, the most effective means of bridging the gap that separates individuals from each other at any kind of gathering. Swept along by violent bursts of tropical energy, jazz still had enough of a "dying civilization" about it, of humanity blindly submitting to The Machine, to express quite completely the state of mind of at least some of that generation: a more or less conscious demoralization born of the war, a naïve fascination with the comfort and the latest inventions of progress, a predilection for a contemporary setting whose insanity we nonetheless vaguely anticipated, an abandonment to the animal joy of experiencing the influence of a modern rhythm, an underlying aspiration to a new life in which more room would be made for the impassioned frankness we inarticulately longed for. In jazz, too, came the first appearance of *Negroes*, the manifestation and the myth of black Edens which were to lead me to Africa and, beyond Africa, to ethnography.

Leiris was not alone in linking jazz with ethnography. His colleague on the Mission Dakar-Djibouti, the great ethnomusicologist and fieldworker André Schaeffner, had recently written (with André Coeuroy) *Le jazz: La musique moderne* (1926; *Jazz: Modern Music*). Georges-Henri Rivière, an afficionado of black music who organized the Al Brown gala, would become (in collaboration with Paul Rivet) the chief reorganizer of France's ethnographic and folklore museums. Postwar negrophilia permeated and linked the domains of music, art, anthropology, literature, and dance. "La création du monde" ("The Creation of the World") of 1923 was an African cosmogonic "ritual" performed at the Ballet Suédois. Fernand Léger's sets, costumes, and curtain featuring African motifs included actual masks from the Congo and Ivory Coast. Darius Milhaud's music incorporated rhythms of Brazil and New York jazz; the text by Blaise Cendrars was based on West African Baoulé myths.

Two years earlier Cendrars had published his *Anthologie nègre* (1921; *Negro Anthology*), a collection of black poetry culled from diverse sources, questionable works of exoticism with titles such as *Le Sénégal drôlatre* (*Weird Senegal*), as well as the best contemporary ethnographies by Maurice Delafosse, Carl Meinhof, and Arnold van Gennep. By raising African "folklore" to the status of "poetry" Cendrars challenged its common association with mere physicality, rhythm, and savagery. At the same time his emphasis on the themes of fetishism, totemism, and magic reinscribed the prevailing ideology in the register of "literature." Cendrars's own *poèmes nègres*—"Continent noir" (1922; "Black Continent"), "Les grands fétiches" (1922; "The Big Fetishes")—drew on extended contacts with black cultures, sojourns in the *favellas* of Rio, in Harlem, in the jungles of Guyana. Journalist, merchant seaman, foreign legionnaire, compulsive reader, Cendrars had an understanding and enthusiasm for things *nègre* that fell somewhere between cultural translation and romantic exoticism. In his committed, quasi-ethnographic involvement, however, Cendrars went further than most of his contemporaries—for example, Paul Morand, whose travel writing featured sensational exoticism (*Magie noire,* 1928; *Black Magic*) and stylish slumming (*New York,* 1930).

At about the time Cendrars began to bring African motifs and jazzlike compositional patterns into his writing, the Zurich dadaists were organizing their notorious "Soirées" at the Cabaret Voltaire. The program for 14 July 1916 announced "noises, Negro music (trabatgea bonooooooo oo ooooo)." Hugo Ball and Tristan Tzara beat on drums and intoned invented "Negro" chants, simulating a return to wild, purely rhythmic, presyntactic forms of expression presumed to be typical of black cultures. These racist displays—stereotypical savagery recast as scandal and poetic regeneration—were short-lived. But the influence of black culture on Tzara's "poèmes nègres" (most of them unpublished during his lifetime) was more enduring. He was a more critical collector than Cendrars, drawing on the best-documented sources of his time, especially the respected Swiss anthropological journal *Anthropos.* Transcribing African or Australian aboriginal myths and chants, Tzara used scholarly word-for-word translations rather than smoothed-over, "literary" versions. His literalism resulted in obscure, syntactically disjointed "poems" that, like the language experiments of the Italian and Russian futurists, estranged and reassembled basic linguistic components. Whereas for Cendrars black cultures were a source of poetic inspiration, for Tzara the promised renewal presupposed a destruction of civilized literature and proper forms of discourse.

Jean Paulhan had already undertaken a more rigorous experiment in translating non-Western "poetry" during his sojourn in Madagascar from 1908 to 1910 when, in his early twenties, the future editor of *La nouvelle revue française* taught French in Tananarive. An enthusiastic student of ethnology and the Malagasy language, Paulhan became fascinated by popular oral performances called *hain-tenys.* These gnomic, often amorous, poem-proverbs were customarily recited in formal disputations. Moved by their compressed eloquence and poetic force, Paulhan took every occasion (often to the detriment of his teaching) to discuss their meanings with indigenous authorities and to hear them performed in villages of the Merina sections of the island. On his return to Paris he published a selection, *Les hain-tenys* (1913), with a long introduction, Malagasy texts, literary French translations, and explanatory notes. Throughout his career Paulhan cherished the idea of writing an academic thesis on the subject, and he continued to revise his translations. In 1939 Gallimard published an edition of *Les hain-tenys* with a new introduction and no Malagasy texts.

Paulhan had taken a rather scientific tone in 1913, presenting his goal as one of clarifying, contextualizing, and explaining the poems' obscurities. In his 1939 introduction he wrote instead of their irreducible "difficulty." He presented his translations and notes as a means of partial access to an exotic poetry and as a record of his own translation experience, including its "awkwardness and errors." Cultural expressions that in 1913 had seemed accessible to Western ethnographic interpretation and literary translation had, by the eve of World War II, become problematic. Much of the power of the "hain-tenys," Paulhan suggested in 1939, lay in the uncertainty and effort they imposed on their readers.

As writers such as Cendrars, Tzara, Paulhan, and Leiris became seriously engaged in the translation rather than the simple collection of exotic forms, they had to confront African, American, or Melanesian cultures in their specificity. Indeed, alongside the many more or less stereotypical appropriations of 1920s negrophilia one can discern a more complex ethnographic engagement with black cultures. Between 1925 and 1938 a modern, fieldwork-oriented anthropology emerged at the Paris Institute of Ethnology and the renovated Trocadéro museum. A regular exchange of ideas and personnel linked academic and avant-garde milieus. For example, Leiris, Griaule, Schaeffner, and Rivière were active in Georges Bataille's dissident surrealist journal *Documents* (1929–30). They also attended Marcel Mauss's lectures at the Ecole Pratique des Hautes Etudes, finding employment at the Trocadéro and later at its successor, the Musée de l'Homme. The cultures studied by ethnography were sources for an enlarged Western vision of human possibilities. In Mauss's classic analysis of exchange, the *Essai sur le don* (1923; *The Gift*), non-Western examples provided powerful alternative perspectives on European forms of life. This kind of critical, political use of ethnographic knowledge was as integral to the engaged socialism of scholars such as Rivet, Lévy-Bruhl, and Mauss as it was to the cultural criticism of the avant-garde.

Leiris' *L'Afrique fantôme* was perhaps the most striking hybrid to emerge from the interwar encounter of the literary avant-garde and academic anthropology. "Secretary-archivist" of the Mission Dakar-Djibouti, Leiris meticulously kept its scientific records while writing a journal for a more personal history of the expedition. What emerged, anything but a proper history, was a diary recording observations, research problems, encounters with Africans, idle thoughts, moods, speculations, dreams (waking and sleeping), draft prefaces, notes for a novel—"data" relevant to the subjective states of an ethnographer in contact with a problematic, "phantom" reality. The journal, sent in batches to his wife in Paris, was published without emendation in 1934. Leiris' relentless "objectivity," sparing neither himself nor his colleagues, undermined the scientific rhetoric of the expedition. Rather than stressing the number of objects collected, rituals witnessed, photographs taken, articles written, and so forth, *L'Afrique fantôme* dwelt on ethnography's interpersonal frictions, its alternation of feverish work and depression, its implication in both tribal and colonial politics. Leiris revealed that some of the museum pieces collected by the mission had been stolen. He described his own research on initiatory language among the Dogon and on spirit possession in Ethiopia as at best a kind of methodical groping, a constant struggle for authority.

Leiris had been attracted to ethnography as a source of "authentic" contact with radically different cultures. By 1930 he had begun to find the exoticist negrophilia of the preceding decade vicarious and abstract. But after twenty months of fieldwork, social observation seemed equally problematic. Leiris was repelled by its scientific neutrality and lack of real involvement. "I'd rather be possessed myself than study possessed people" he blurted in his journal (*L'Afrique fantôme,* p. 324). And overall he experienced only "an ardent sensation of being at the edge of something whose depths I will never touch, lacking, among other things, an ability to let myself go as necessary, the result of diverse factors very hard to define but among which figure prominently questions of race, of civilization, of language" (p. 359).

Ethnographic work cured Leiris of escapist exoticism. Africa was complex and elusive, providing no release from all-too-familiar intellectual and erotic predilections. Concluding that a really engaged ethnography was possible only at home, he resolved to concentrate on his own society, and particularly on its most mysterious "native"—himself. In the late 1930s, with Georges Bataille and Roger Caillois, Leiris founded the Collège de Sociologie, a short-lived experiment in subversive cultural analysis. For example, the Collège applied techniques from Emile Durkheim's analysis of Australian aborigines to a study of modern "sacred" forms, of sacrifice and transforming ritual in 20th-century France. At about this time, adapting his earlier African research methods, Leiris began to keep "fieldnotes" on himself, methodically recording observations, experiences, dreams, thoughts, and memories. The note cards he accumulated were later classified, "written up"—actually written over and over—to produce the continuous self-investigations that are his most original contribution to 20th-century writing. Beginning with *L'Afrique fantôme* and *L'âge d'homme,* continuing with four volumes of *La règle du jeu* (1948, 1955, 1966, 1976; *The Rule of the Game*) and then *Le ruban au cou d'Olympia* (1981; *The Ribbon on Olympia's Neck*), Leiris wrote about himself from the position of an oddly detached but passionate participant observer. His subjective "culture," like the hybrid Caribbean societies he studied ethnographically after World War II, was open-ended and inventive. Indeed, Leiris' self-ethnography problematized the conventions of both autobiography and anthropology, the former positing a whole, representable, personal experience, the latter describing an objectified cultural domain.

What Leiris saw in 1934 as a frustrating "phantom"—and what he took primarily as an occasion for public introspection—emerged after 1945 as a historical force, *négritude.* During the 1930s Aimé Césaire, Suzanne Césaire, René Ménil, Jules Monnerot, Léopold Sédar Senghor, and other Antillean and African students were living in Paris, writing in the journals *Légitime défense* and *L'étudiant noir.* Aimé Césaire's *Cahier d'un retour au pays natal* (1939; *Notebook of a Return to the Native Land*) was first published there. But only after the war did this seminal poem and a diverse, emergent black poetry have an impact on white negrophilia and anthropology. In the early 1950s the journal *Présence africaine* provided a forum for the collaboration of black writers with anthropologists such as Leiris, Griaule, Schaeffner, Georges Balandier, and Théodore

Monod. The new situation was heralded by Sartre in "Orphée noir" ("Black Orpheus"), his introduction to Senghor's *Anthologie de la nouvelle poésie nègre* (1948). Senghor's anthology was a far cry from Cendrars's primitivist collection, for it presented black voices speaking eloquently, coherently, and without translation on a world stage. "French literature" had become a contested, genuinely international phenomenon. Moreover, the relations of power that had permitted exoticist and social scientific collections of black culture during the 1920s and 1930s were coming into question. Césaire's *Discours sur le colonialisme* (1955; *Discourse on Colonialism*) rejected Western claims to dominate and define colonized peoples. Black cultures were no longer "traditional" sites for appropriation and appreciation by "advanced" artists and scholars. They were powerful discourses, modern in their own terms, resistant to European-centered definitions of evolutionism or history.

In the preface to the 1951 edition of *L'Afrique fantôme,* Leiris registered the dramatic historical changes that now made the book seem "left behind by the times." Leiris had recently returned to West Africa as a member of an official team investigating labor abuses. He had also visited Martinique, where, through his friendship with Aimé Césaire, he came into direct contact with anticolonial protests and locally based cultural dynamism. If Africa once seemed a phantom, he wrote in 1951, this was essentially a symptom of his own "dreamer's subjectivism" and an inability to perceive exploitation except in its most naked forms. He saw much more clearly now that Africa in 1933 was "quite real," caught up in the emerging struggle between colonizers and colonized. A real humanist bridging of cultural and racial boundaries was not to be achieved by romantic gestures of identification or the detachment of ethnographic science, by (symbolically) plunging into a "primitive mentality" or gaining access to a rite or secret. Instead, the new historical situation offered a prospect of "effective solidarity with men who have a clear consciousness of what is unacceptable in their condition and who are mobilizing the most positive means for changing it" (p. 9). In the 1950s the reality of anticolonialism forced Leiris to reject not only the exoticist illusions recorded in *L'Afrique fantôme* but also the book's implicit claim that one could acquit oneself in an unjust world by means of "an escape and a confession."

Four years later Claude Lévi-Strauss published a more famous farewell to prewar travel and ethnography: *Tristes tropiques* (1955; *Tristes Tropiques*), certainly the midcentury's literary and anthropological masterpiece. Ostensibly an account of the author's travels during the 1930s in Brazil, but also touching on his flight from occupied France to New York City and on visits to India and Pakistan, *Tristes tropiques* reinvents the 18th-century philosophical voyage, juxtaposing personal reminiscences; ethnographic vignettes; excursuses on archaeology, history, and epistemology; bravura evocations of cities and sunsets; and metahistorical speculations.

The narrator's various journeys fuse into a single anthropological voyage, Proustian in its divagations and folds of memory. A personal experience of moving between cultures and continents evokes humanity's great journey—

from the origins of cities in the Indus Valley to the invention of literacy and the modern state, along the separate historical paths followed by America and Europe until their contact in the Age of Discovery and current fusion in a global leveling of human differences. Everywhere he goes, Lévi-Strauss feels the impossibility of escape from a relentless development. The sharply different tribal societies he encounters in Amazonia are fast disappearing; his Rousseauistic quest for an example of humanity living in scale with its environment yields only pathetic shreds. Occidental expansion ruins all it touches. "The first thing we see as we travel round the world is our own filth, thrown in the face of mankind" (*Tristes Tropiques,* p. 38).

Lévi-Strauss's goodbye to exoticist travel implicates its alter ego, scientific ethnography. For even if radical human differences could still be found and if the barriers of culture, race, and civilization that had oppressed Leiris could be partially overcome, the resulting "understanding" of other societies would always entail a reduction of their difference. The anthropologist inevitably abolishes otherness, not only by making it less strange but also by participating in a global increase of cultural communication that simultaneously makes people want to know about others while it wears down the significant distinctions among them. All that remains for the anthropologist (whom Lévi-Strauss calls an "entropologist") is a labor of (re)collecting the records of humanity's cultural experiments as precious bases for the comparative study of underlying mental structures. *Tristes tropiques* portrays ethnographic travelers as trapped in an impossible temporal bind. Either they can scramble to rescue a vanishing past or they can attend to the present, confronting all the richness of experience denied them in the past but lacking the hindsight to distinguish what is important. In either case ethnographers work with fragments in search of elusive cultural and historical wholes. Lévi-Strauss's personal response, announced in *Tristes tropiques,* is to leave ethnography to others while cultivating an anthropological "view from afar" (and after), beyond the fray of current culture contact, destruction, resistance, and invention.

Tristes tropiques, like *L'Afrique fantôme,* registers a profound disruption in Western forms of travel and crosscultural understanding. Successes such as the Mission Dakar-Djibouti or enthusiasms such as the prewar negrophilia seem increasingly hollow. Lévi-Strauss takes a long historical view, portraying the violent collapse of differences in an increasingly interconnected world. Leiris, linked to the emergent *négritude* movement, confronts more immediate, alterable, cultural/political relationships. He sees not entropy but colonialism, struggles for power, and the reinvention of identities. Western literary and social-scientific writers still hesitate between these two postcolonial visions, the one global, elegiac, and anthropological, the other local, emergent, and ethnographic.

See also 1937 (March), 1939, 1968 (February).

Bibliography: James Clifford, *The Predicament of Culture: Twentieth-Century Ethnography, Literature, and Art* (Cambridge, Mass.: Harvard University Press, 1988). Clifford, "The

Tropological Realism of Michel Leiris," *Sulfur*, 15 (1986), 4–22. Jean Jamin, "Objets trouvés des paradis perdus: A propos de la Mission Dakar-Djibouti," in *Collections passion*, ed. Jacques Hainard and Roland Kaehr (Neuchâtel: Musée d'Ethnographie, 1982), pp. 69–100. Michel Leiris, *L'Afrique fantôme* (Paris: Gallimard, 1951). Leiris, *Manhood: A Journey from Childhood into the Fierce Order of Virility*, trans. Richard Howard (San Francisco: North Point Press, 1984). Claude Lévi-Strauss, *Tristes Tropiques*, trans. John and Doreen Weightman (New York: Atheneum, 1975).

James Clifford

✒ *1933, November*
William Faulkner's *Sanctuary* Is Translated
with a Preface by André Malraux

Americans in Paris

The publication of William Faulkner's *Sanctuary* (1931) in translation—the first of his novels to appear in France—marked the opening of an "Age of the American Novel," the effects of which would extend well into the postwar period. André Malraux's dramatic preface set the tone: "*Sanctuary* is the intrusion of Greek tragedy into the detective story." Later in the same year came translations of Ernest Hemingway's *The Sun Also Rises* and John Dos Passos' *The 42nd Parallel* (the first volume of *U.S.A.*). These works, followed by translations of Erskine Caldwell's *God's Little Acre* in 1936 and of John Steinbeck's *Of Mice and Men* in 1939, convinced the French public that they were encountering not individual genius but a national phenomenon. Reception was all the warmer in that the French literary establishment was beginning to question the continued vitality of a novelistic tradition of reasoned psychological analysis. The American novel was to the 1930s and 1940s what the Russian novel had been to the 1880s.

It is not surprising that French readers were tempted to ascribe the qualities of these novels to a specifically American experience; the barbarian vitality that Pierre Drieu la Rochelle celebrated in his 1931 preface to *A Farewell to Arms*—and welcomed as an antidote to French decadence—appeared to be the expression of a young, unintellectual civilization not yet "stuffed with words," as Claude-Edmonde Magny put it in *The Age of the American Novel*. What is surprising is the degree to which French critics and writers resisted the temptation and concentrated instead on the techniques used. The American novel was first and foremost "a veritable revolution in the art of telling a story," proclaimed Jean-Paul Sartre in 1946 ("American Novelists in French Eyes," p. 116). The regional character of Yoknapatawpha County that so attracted American critics (especially northerners) went largely undiscussed in France, as did the social critique implicit in Caldwell's novels. What attracted French readers was the phenomenological exoticism of the text rather than the specifics of setting.

By the close of the decade the definition of the American novel had crystallized as a set of distinctive traits: narrative discontinuity, an objective or impersonal style, simultaneity of action, and dialogue (or monologue) that did not so much express thought or sentiment as reveal the uncertainties of all forms of human communication. Such a list of attributes did not necessarily add up to a novel by Faulkner or Hemingway, as French critics themselves recognized, but the existence of the model legitimated the rejection of linear psychological development. In this sense, the influence of the American novel ran concurrently with that of the cinema; indeed, from the early 1930s on their similarity was one of the staples of French criticism. The ellipse, the abrupt shift in angle of approach, the vision "from the outside," were considered common to both. Both furnished techniques adapted to modernity.

By labeling American writers "behaviorist," French critics were also engaging in a form of cultural critique. The absence, in the American novel, of the finely drawn and coherently presented character portraits to which French readers were accustomed suggested that in the United States the inner (spiritual) life was less developed. Fragmentation as a literary technique represented the crisis state of modern man's alienation, the source of which was the capitalist system. By deliberately choosing disorder as a principle of composition, American novelists were seen as expressing their protest on the level of form itself. Their modernity was tinged with subversion.

American novels were grandly introduced to the French public with prefaces by Malraux, Drieu, Valéry Larbaud (*As I Lay Dying,* 1934), Jean Prévost (*The Sun Also Rises,* 1933), André Maurois (*God's Little Acre,* 1936), Raymond Queneau (Faulkner's *Mosquitoes,* 1948), or through stage adaptations such as Jean-Louis Barrault's 1934 version of *As I Lay Dying, Autour d'une mère* (*Around a Mother*), and Albert Camus's 1956 *Requiem for a Nun.* Most were admirably translated, in particular by Maurice Edgar Coindreau, whose influential prefaces and critical articles also sharpened French taste. In the case of Faulkner the chronology of the translations played a role: the French version of *As I Lay Dying* appeared well before that of *The Sound and the Fury* (1938) and thus had far greater impact in France as a revelation of Faulkner's genius. Hemingway's laconic violence led to his being bracketed (by Gide and others) with Dashiell Hammett, who figured prominently in early anthologies of the new American school.

In general French critics discussed the philosophical dimension (Malraux on fate in *Sanctuary,* Sartre on Faulkner's metaphysics of time, Georges Bataille on Hemingway and Hegel), but with the purpose of showing that 'this dimension was inseparable from "rebarbarization," the process by which a literary genre is vitalized through its annexation of popular culture—in this case the detective story and the cinema—and through its appropriation of oral modes of narration. Such an approach, although it gave full weight to what were considered native American idioms, downplayed sociological content. Faulkner's Popeye (*Sanctuary*) was seen less as an impotent derelict of southern society than as the archetypal hard-boiled private eye who would find his way, via gangster movies and translations of James Hadley Chase criminal stories, to the mass-produced Série Noire, a popular collection of detective thrillers launched after World War II by Marcel Duhamel (who himself translated Hemingway's *To Have and Have Not* in 1945). Such associations predisposed the French public to find Faulkner more timely than Americans did; indeed, until 1947 Faulkner sold better in France than in the United States.

Reactions of individual French writers to the American novel varied greatly. Queneau, an early admirer, knew English well enough to read Faulkner in the original. This fact, together with his acquaintance with the Anglo-American literary community already established in Paris—including Gertrude Stein; the legendary Shakespeare and Company, which published Joyce's *Ulysses;* and bilingual reviews such as *Transition*—meant that he read the new American school in a context very different from that of mainstream Paris intellectuals, whose view of America was largely fashioned by Georges Duhamel's *Scènes de la vie future* (1930; *Scenes from Life in the Future*), a classic visitor's guide to American culture that ran through countless editions in the course of the decade. For Queneau, Hemingway's early short stories, first published in English in Paris, were an offshoot of the experimentation of the Anglo-American community in exile. Queneau was early attracted to the formal elements of Faulkner's work. Commenting on *The Sound and the Fury* in his preface to *Mosquitoes* (which he dismisses as a "prenovel"), Queneau describes Faulkner as a mathematician who has set himself a particularly difficult equation to solve. Creativity springs not from personal inspiration (this is in effect the basis of Queneau's criticism of *Mosquitoes*) but from richness of innovation within a set of self-imposed restraints.

Few other French critics, however, shared Queneau's concerns. Most regarded American writing paradoxically as both radically different *and* as a stage toward which the French novel was naturally evolving. In Malraux's formulation, American writers were close to what French writers were seeking—before having read them. To shake off the Proustian legacy, to come to grips with "fundamental man," as Malraux put it, required the abandonment of a centralizing narrative voice through which human experience was filtered—and denied. Whatever the differences between Faulkner and Hemingway (or Hammett), they were seen to share a concern to register human activity in its raw immediacy and a willingness to set readers adrift, to leave them to their own devices in making sense of the whole. The first chapter of Malraux's *L'espoir* (1937; *Man's Hope*) can stand as an illustration of the technique: the novel opens with a series of hurried telephone dialogues in which the Loyalists in Madrid's central railway station interrogate railpoints to the north. Each time, the question is repeated: "Who's speaking?" And the replies ("Worker delegate" or "Falangist") map the division of the country into two opposing camps and set the stage for the Spanish Civil War. Stendhal, in the Battle of Waterloo chapters of *La chartreuse de Parme* (1839; *The Charterhouse of Parma*), had exploited the device of restricting narrative focus to what a given character could take in. But Malraux, unlike Stendhal, does not use an outsider-hero to mediate between narrator and reader. His manner of representing characters as totally absorbed in the activity of the moment functions as an implicit rejection of the reader, whose interests appear to have been ignored. The frequent shifts of focus, not only between the 146 scenic units that make up the novel but also within units and even within paragraphs, impart a nervous rhythm that conveys a basic dissatisfaction with any form of telling. Malraux multiplies fragments of scenes as substitutes for an unrepresentable whole, or rather as a statement of the unrepresentability of the whole. The barely marked transitions work against the reader's natural desire to formulate coherence. Only rarely is there a sustained climax, as when the peasants, in grandiose procession, bring the wounded airmen down the mountainside on their shoulders. For the most part each microunit constitutes a new beginning, and this scattering technique eliminates any impression of cumulative depth. The net effect is to leave intact the mystery of what impels men to heroism.

Action in *L'espoir* is seen exclusively from the Republican side, on which Malraux had fought as leader of an international brigade of combat pilots; but within Republican ranks an ethical question arises: must one sacrifice a sense of humanity in order to wage war effectively? It is tempting to try to resolve the characters' conflicting opinions (and behaviors) in terms of a synthesis that would be that of the narrator, or of Malraux; but to do so compresses *L'espoir* into a novel of moral or political education. Men differ in ethical outlook, just as they differ in their way of hugging the ground under an artillery barrage or inching forward under sniper fire. What counts is the tenuous sense of exhilaration that binds together those who have accepted violence and death in the name of a common cause. It is this theme that the narrative technique expresses by deliberate refusal of any hierarchical ordering of points of view. No one character (much less the narrator) stands as the privileged interpreter of the continuing action; the sharing of the narrative focus among characters equally immersed in the events represents fraternity.

Sartre, a more assiduous reader of American novels than Malraux, judged American writers in terms of their compatibility with his own philosophical views. His 1939 article "La temporalité chez Faulkner" ("Time in the Work of Faulkner") amounts to a condemnation. Not only are Faulkner's characters deprived of a future (and hence of that liberty required by any existential project); they are also denied experience of the here and now; the present exists only in retrospect. It could be argued that Sartre's criticisms (based in large part on flagrant—but revealing—misreading of passages from *The Sound and the Fury*) testify to a greater degree of complicity with Faulkner than he cared to admit; but Sartre was adamant in his disapproval of Faulkner's vision of a present time "full of holes" through which characters freefall into the past. He was equally insistent in his admiration for Dos Passos: "I regard Dos Passos as the greatest writer of our time" (*Literary and Philosophical Essays*, p. 103).

In *Qu'est-ce que la littérature?* (1947; *What Is Literature?*) Sartre described how the writers of his generation met the obligation to integrate history into the novel. Dos Passos provided the model. *L'âge de raison* (1945; *The Age of Reason*), the first volume of *Les chemins de la liberté* (*The Roads to Freedom*), which Sartre began writing in 1938, describes, as if in mockery of the trilogy's title, a series of concentric circles: Mathieu Delarue makes the rounds of the Paris streets in quest of money to pay for his mistress's abortion. The novel multiplies images of envelopment: a stuffy bedroom, a museum, a night club, a taxicab—metaphors for the protective shell within which each character obsessively inventories his states of mind as if they were, by a bourgeois logic of proprietorship, possessions that could define the self. History makes its entrance in the second volume. *Le sursis* (1945; *The Reprieve*) shatters these private concerns by introducing a radical shift of canvas. Individual consciousness is swamped in a tidal wave of events embracing the entire European continent. In effecting this shift Sartre applied the lesson he had drawn in his 1938 article "A propos de John Dos Passos et de *1919*" ("John Dos Passos and *1919*"). As in *U.S.A.*, the narrative jumps from one story line to another. *Le sursis* opens on 23 September 1938 and ends with the signing of the Munich pact on 30 September, a period of mobilization swept by rumors of imminent war. The uncertainties of history serve as an object lesson addressed to the characters, whose fragile private constructs are repeatedly broken up by incidents occurring miles away—in Sudetenland, London, and Berlin. To drive the point home, Sartre—pushing to its logical extreme Dos Passos' concern to reproduce the simultaneity of events—slices the narrative horizontally at an ever increasing pace: Monday, 26 September, 4:30 P.M. in Biarritz, then in London, then in Marseilles . . . a time lapse of one or two hours and then a sampling from other points of the compass. The reader is mercilessly shunted from one setting to another, forced to keep tabs on some fifty individuals, sometimes allowed only a sentence-long glimpse of one context before being immersed in another. For the war, or threat of war, is not simply an issue that confronts each character at a given stage in his or her trajectory (as was the case in *U.S.A.*); it modifies the very grounds on which the self exists.

Dispossessed of an individual destiny, the characters in *Le sursis* are also dispossessed of the very words they use. Commenting on *Sartoris* ("*Sartoris,* par W. Faulkner," 1938), Sartre had remarked that the language of Faulkner's characters does not belong to them as individuals. He was struck, in *U.S.A.*, by the use of ready-made phrases. It is as if, as Sartre put it in his Dos Passos article, there existed somewhere a vast storehouse of set expressions from which each of us picks the one best suited to our situation. Language does not emanate from a (deep) self but is borrowed from a common fund. Language is always a secondhand approximation, a loose fit of hand-me-downs. When individuals account for themselves, they are obliged to choose from the same stock of prefabricated formulas, with the result that the line between private and public experience is eroded.

In *Le sursis* Sartre combines the technique of simultaneous representation and the concept of language as collective by making words into switching points between story lines: a term (often a banal one) that is used by (or applied to) a character in one setting but that could also fit into a (geographically) distant scene occurring at the same moment serves literally to transport the reader from the first setting to the second. Characters are plugged into a language network that exists independently of them. Meaning is constantly deferred (*en sursis,* in a state of reprieve) until all quarters are heard from, just as Europe itself is suspended between peace and war. In the third volume, *La mort dans l'âme* (1949; *Troubled Sleep*), the hero is precipitated into combat.

In *Le sursis* historical forces shatter the individual's closed world. The narrative fragmentation of Camus's *L'étranger* (1942; *The Stranger*) is of another sort. Meursault kills a man under a torrid sun on a beach on the outskirts of Algiers. In the course of the ensuing trial, the prosecuting attorney constructs a sociopsychological portrait of the assassin that convinces the jury to find him guilty of first-degree murder. Yet it is made obvious throughout that this portrait of Meursault, though coherent in itself (Meursault has an unfeeling nature, demonstrated by his lack of reaction to his mother's death; his motive is personal gain, as proved by his association with a notorious local tough), bears no relation to the circumstances of his act. The prosecutor's case can be read as a parody of a reader's insistence on making a connected story out of any succession of events. Summoned to give his own explanation, Meursault can only reply confusedly that it was because of the sun. Whereas society (in the guise of the prosecutor) establishes a chain of events, Meursault, who senses himself an intruder in his own trial, can grasp only an arbitrary disordered succession. Even his "thoughts" do not add up to "thinking," but remain isolated impressions of the moment that he observes from a distance. To produce this effect of estrangement, Camus applies a Hemingway technique: narration is reduced to instant-long notations as if the frames of a movie film had been run through slowly enough for the cuts between frames to appear. Experience and consciousness are dismembered—even the inner life is given behaviorist treatment. To be sure, an ingenious critic can read the text against the grain and explore those lapses that afford glimpses of Meursault as a more fully rounded human being; indeed, Nathalie Sarraute suggested that Camus wrote *L'étranger* to prove the *impossibility* of doing away with psychology. No matter. What we are witness to in *L'étranger* is the appropriation of a technique characteristic of what Sartre called the "neo-realist American" school to serve a specific end (Camus's description of absurd man) that has nothing in common with that school itself: proof that the "American novel" had by then been naturalized and was operating within the French register.

See also 1914–1918, 1933 (December), 1953.

Bibliography: Mary Jean Green, *Fiction in the Historical Present: French Writers and the Thirties* (Hanover, N.H.: University Press of New England, 1986). Denis Hollier, *The Politics of Prose: Essay on Sartre,* trans. Jeffrey Mehlman (Minneapolis: University of Minnesota Press, 1986). Claude-Edmonde Magny, *The Age of the American Novel: The Film Aesthetic of Fiction between the Two Wars,* trans. Eleanor Hochman (New York: Ungar, 1972). André Malraux, "A Preface for Faulkner's *Sanctuary,*" *Yale French Studies,* 10 (1952), 92–94. Nathalie Sarraute, *The Age of Suspicion,* trans. Maria Jolas (New York:

Braziller, 1963). Jean-Paul Sartre, "American Novelists in French Eyes," trans. Evelyn de Solis, *Atlantic Monthly,* August 1946, pp. 114–118. Sartre, *Les chemins de la liberté,* 3 vols. (Paris: Gallimard, 1945–1949); vols. 1 and 2 translated by Eric Sutton as *The Age of Reason* and *The Reprieve,* vol. 3 translated by Gerard Hopkins as *Troubled Sleep* (New York: Knopf, 1947–1950). Sartre, "William Faulkner's *Sartoris,*" "Time in the Work of Faulkner," and "John Dos Passos and *1919,*" in *Literary and Philosophical Essays,* trans. Annette Michelson (New York: Criterion, 1955).

John Atherton

⚖⁀⊃ *1933, December*
André Malraux's Novel *La condition humaine* Wins the Prix Goncourt

"Terrorists Ask No Questions"

"To spit, only to spit, on the condition that one produce a Niagara of spit." Such, argued Pierre Drieu la Rochelle in the preface to *Gilles* (1939, p. 18), was the only imaginable option for the novelist of the 1930s hardy enough to focus steadily upon the spectacle of contemporary France. A writer in this period must be witness to "the winter of the society and history, the winter of a people." "I found myself," wrote André Malraux's friend, "like all the other authors of my time, faced with a crushing fact: the decadence of France. Each in his own way, all my colleagues had to react to this fact" (p. 10). The alternative to convulsive expectoration, Drieu observed, was flight from an exhausted France, such as Malraux had chosen, for whom there was no one at home available to insult, no one even to describe: "Since there were no Frenchmen, he chose to study the Chinese . . . What else could he do?" (p. 17).

The turn to the Orient was to no avail, however; the unraveling China of 1927 described in *La condition humaine* (1933; *Man's Fate*) offered less the saving, contrastive pole suggested by Drieu than the phantasmagoric exaggeration of the collapsing, autonomous, will-suffocating Europe that had to be fled. The novel's decomposing China is traversed by the complex and shifting play of Western expansionism, the interests of rival military régimes, and—the specific focus of the book—the struggles within the revolutionary coalition of Chiang Kai-shek's Nationalist party (Kuomintang) and the Chinese Communist party (CCP), itself split between Marxists loyal to the Comintern and those refractory to the dialectic-chilling strictures of party discipline. In 1923 the CCP had agreed to join the Kuomintang and recognize it as the center of the revolutionary movement. The strategy of the Communists was to accept Chiang's leadership temporarily but eventually to seize control of the entire movement. After the Nationalists had taken Shanghai in 1927, a rift developed between the leftists and the more conservative supporters of Chiang, who had been laying their own plans against their allies. At this moment the central leadership of the CCP agreed to check revolutionary excess and give all support to the Kuomintang leadership, but others in the CCP, notably Mao Tse-tung, felt that the mass revolution should be encouraged to run its course unfettered. Conservative Kuomintang members—business leaders and some army commanders—encouraged Chiang to expel the Communists, which he did in the spring and summer of 1927. After a bloody failed effort to ignite a popular uprising against Chiang, the Communists withdrew to military bases in the mountains and plains of central China, far from the centers of Nationalist power.

Malraux's narrative focuses on the personal and political lives of a cell of students, professors, and foreign advisers with major roles in the ill-fated Shanghai insurrection. Of central importance in the almost all-male cast are three figures—Kyo, son of a Japanese mother and of a French intellectual (the Marxist aesthete, old Gisors); Katow, a Russian militant, the perfect comrade; and Ch'en, the ecstatically suicidal terrorist, the only Chinese of the team. Two other powerful personalities are crucially involved: the cynical banker Ferral, master and victim of the volatility of market forces; and Clappique, the scheming Hoffmannesque extravagant. At the novel's climax, Kyo and Katow have been arrested by Chiang's police and are waiting, with other detainees, to be thrown into the scalding boiler of a locomotive. Both have cyanide pills. Kyo swallows his own and dies, while Katow, seeing two frightened comrades, offers them his pill and goes unflinchingly to an agonizing death.

Instead of reaching deeply into ideological argument and the somber enormity of this particular world-historical situation, Malraux takes as his central concern the description of two irreconcilable types of terrorists, their respective psychologies and roles in the turbulent preparation for a new society.

Malraux was acquainted with *Les réprouvés*, the translation of German novelist Ernst von Salomon's *Die Geächteten* (1930; *The Outlaws*). In it, the adventurer/terrorist asserts: "To march straight ahead did not mean for us a movement toward a specific military goal, toward a specific point on the map . . . Rather, it meant the rupture with all the ties that bound us to a corrupt world, a world in disarray with which the true warrior could have nothing in common" (*Die Geächteten*, p. 89). And further: "What we wanted, we did not know, and what we knew we did not want. The question 'why?' was eliminated in our endless struggle" (p. 89). In another book with which Malraux was familiar, *Mort de la pensée bourgeoise* (1929; *Death of Bourgeois Thought*)—it was dedicated to Garine, the protagonist of Malraux's *Les conquérants* (1928; *The Conquerors*)—Emmanuel Berl wrote in praise of the terrorist: "To go without asking where is the first and only nobility in thought and in life" (*Mort*, p. 9). And Malraux himself, in *La condition humaine*: "[Terrorists] asked no questions" (*Man's Fate*; p. 160). Later, in the essay "Sur Saint-Just" (1955; "On Saint-Just"), he would put it less exclusively and argue that they did not ask a certain question. With anguished accents Robespierre was said to have habitually demanded: "In the name of what?" He always required a knowledge of the specific result that would legitimate a Revolutionary cruelty. This question involved him in what Malraux called "the mythology of ends," an acquisitive, goal-oriented behavior that removed from a disruptive gesture the sublime aura of sovereign anomaly of which it would be possessed if it had been for itself alone. Uninvolved in this mythology was the contrasting Saint-Just: "He seems to have aimed at exemplary acts for their own sake," observes Malraux approvingly ("On Saint-Just," p. 476).

In *Les conquérants* Malraux had already distinguished between Marxists of "the Roman" and of "the conqueror" types; the latter is represented by Garine, whose thoughts are described as entirely occupied with Saint-Just. The Roman can offer no saving example because of his accumulative and abjectly obedient nature, because of his conserving drive to defend the acquisitions of the Revolution, because he is concerned with banking violence, with turning it to account. The conqueror, however, inclines toward a view of revolution as pure and gratuitous expenditure, toward a taste for a self-hoarding violence that declines to place itself in the service of a transcending goal that would obscure a deed's status as a sovereign end in itself. Garine says: "My life is action, and I'm indifferent to everything that isn't action, including the results of action" (*The Conquerors,* p. 154). This violence is not simply unafraid to turn against itself; rather, it *must* do so if it is to drive to the end of its logic of unbridled self-assertion. Revolution in this sense is wastefulness and the incapacity to collect and convene itself, whether in the temporal unity of the duration of its outliving, in the unity of social life, or in the totality of a concept. It thus resembles Hegel's vision of the Terror of the French Revolution, which became familiar to French intellectuals such as Georges Bataille and Maurice Blanchot through the teaching of Alexandre Kojève. According to this reading, the Terror, in its drive to experience absolute freedom and to exhaust all possibilities, necessarily concluded its course by coldly putting itself to death. Without suicide, the gratuitous act is compromised, for it would be merely a *selective* refusal of implication in the world of practical reason and deferred gratification.

Although Malraux's two types of terrorists, "the Roman" and "the conqueror," share a contempt for bourgeois values, they differ in an all-important way. The act of the man who poses the servile question "In the name of what?" remains instrumentalized and trapped in the circuits of desire because it defines itself in terms of a lack it seeks to overcome; whereas the gesture of the Saint-Just figure, precisely to the extent to which it is impotent and delightedly guarantees its own worldly failure, communicates a triumph over desire itself and, rather than bleeding into a future to which it is abjectly subordinated, constitutes by itself the only experience of absolute freedom available in the here and now. For the avatars of Saint-Just the revolution can occur only in miniature, only in the act of irresponsible revolt itself, only when a man is reunited with himself in pointless death—pointless of necessity because an end will always disturb the intimacy of the terrorist's unfiltered relation with his act. Through the insane (because irreducible) act, the utopia of unmediated relation with self is born, fully achieved, and passes out of existence in one and the same moment.

Ch'en meets with the same difficulty that had confronted Garine: each will be excluded by the Roman after he has unwillingly but necessarily used the conqueror. The conquerors must refuse to submit to the authority of the strategically patient and acquisitive Roman, who by his very constitution is unable to grasp the fact that if the revolution will not risk death, it either cannot succeed, or, if it does, the world it will create will not be significantly distinguishable from the one it has been scheduled to replace. Even if the revolution triumphs in the only way that it can, by feeding upon the enterprising energies of a Ch'en, it will fail as far as the conqueror is concerned, for it cannot fold into itself the volitional bravado of the corrosive figure who draws his energies from a personal despair at the pointlessness of human aspiration.

Much to the dismay of the Comintern strategists, the inheritors of the "Asiatic" legacy of Soviet power relations and the representatives of "scientific" Marxism, Ch'en decides to assassinate the leader of the Nationalists when it becomes clear that Chiang is planning to turn violently against the CCP. The bomb-carrying conqueror throws himself in front of the car incorrectly assumed to be carrying Chiang. Although Ch'en's purpose had ostensibly been to heighten tensions between the bourgeois and the Communists, to provide an occasion for the revolution to return to itself as risk of death, Kyo strongly suspects that the gesture was merely a pretext for the vertiginous self-possession that can be achieved only in the gratuitous suicidal act. Although it may (though doubtfully) have served the cause, the gesture simultaneously condemns a revolution unable to absorb the sovereign vitality that was required to bring about the new order, but could not be of that new order itself. It is the act's dual function that gives *La condition humaine* its peculiar sadness.

Although Ch'en's taste for the eccentric gesture makes him an outcast in Malraux's China, it had many analogues in French literature between the two world wars. In André Gide's *Les caves du Vatican* (1914; *Lafcadio's Adventures*), hapless Amédée Fleurissoire is twice exposed to eccentric violence, first in the form of an idea for a novel and subsequently in a real-life version of the act described in the projected text. Shocking the pious sensibilities of his brother-in-law, Amédée, Julius de Baraglioul tells him of a story that would describe a disinterested act of evil, an inexplicable deed performed as a luxury, for the sake of sport, out of a need for pointless expenditure. Such an achievement would surely be "the stamp of a certain aristocracy" (*Lafcadio's Adventures*, p. 171). After hearing of the novelist's plan, Amédée is himself killed, thrown from a train by one Lafcadio Wluicki, who has sought, through this arbitrary murder of an arbitrarily designated victim, to achieve a supreme self-possession and detachment from the world of practical reason. In the *Second manifeste du surréalisme* (1930; *Second Manifesto of Surrealism*) André Breton had written that "the simplest Surrealist act consists of dashing down into the street, pistol in hand, and firing blindly, as fast as you can pull the trigger, into the crowd" (*Manifestoes*, p. 125). Drieu la Rochelle writes of his protagonist in *Le feu follet* (1931; *The Fire Within*): "He became even more attached to his idea of gratuitousness. Naïve dandy that he was, he assumed that everything should be swift, ephemeral, immediate—a brilliant trajectory that disappears into nothingness" (*The Fire Within*, p. 139). In Bataille's *Le bleu du ciel* (wr. 1935, pub.

1957; *Blue of Noon*) the Marxist militant Lazare eccentrically seizes control of a prison rather than the arms depot she is expected to attack. The reason: the prison is useless. This willfully unproductive deed earns the admiration of Troppmann: "She is the only one who understands the revolution" (*Blue*, p. 110). This is the act of the figure whom Bataille in *Sur Nietzsche* (1945; *On Nietzsche*) called "the total man"—"the man for whom life is an 'unmotivated' festival, a festival in every sense of the word, a laughing, a dancing, an orgy that subordinates itself to nothing, a sacrifice that mocks ends, morals, and the accumulation of goods" (*Oeuvres*, p. 22).

A typical case of terrorist reverie appears in Sartre's short story "Erostrate" ("Erostratus"), collected in *Le mur* (1939; *The Wall*). In his description of the fantasies of obscure office rat Paul Hilbert, Sartre appears to lampoon both Breton and Ch'en (p. 93):

> I felt a strange power in my body when I went down into the street. I had my revolver on me, the thing that explodes and makes noise. But I no longer drew my assurance from that, it was from myself: I was a being like a revolver, a torpedo or a bomb. I too, one day at the end of my somber life, would explode and light the world with a flash as short and violent as magnesium. At that time I had the same dream several nights in a row. I was an anarchist. I had put myself in the path of the Tsar and I carried an infernal machine on me. At the appointed hour, the cortège passed, the bomb exploded, and we were thrown into the air, myself, the Tsar, and three gold-bedecked officers, before the eyes of the crowd.

The drive to break out of literature toward the experience of the pure event and to bring to life the other of representation reached its logical extreme in the situationist movement, whose leaders advocated the self-securing spontaneous, irresponsible act of unlived poetry unsubordinated to any goal. Characteristically they also espoused the reintegration of art into life, in the hope that the vessels of aesthetic autonomy would be destroyed and their contents scattered throughout life. As Guy Debord wrote in *La société du spectacle* (1967; *Society of the Spectacle*): "Dadaism wanted to suppress art without realizing it; Surrealism wanted to realize art without suppressing it. The critical position later elaborated by the Situationists has shown that the suppression and the realization of art are inseparable aspects of a single supercession of art" (*Society*, para. 191). Recalling the willed failure of Ch'en, the situationists emphasized the value of the failure of the act, praising, for example, the incompetence of the leaders of the Paris Commune, which resulted in the movement's inability to perpetuate itself.

These various though similarly (un)motivated gestures share an affective structure that involves the exact synchronization of omnipotence and impotence—the trademark of aesthetic modernism. In each case the provocation to desire consumes itself at the very moment its powers of seduction are revealed. The experience of these collapsed contraries permits desire constantly to migrate away from its objects and to flow back to the originating subject. Organized by the system of trap and release, and thus detached from the haven of a final gratification, desire is freed from the authority of this gratification and remains unstabilized by an ultimate meaning. Untransformed by sovereign identifications, unable to be drawn and held to that by which it would not be released, desire is revealed to be without any transcendent sense; desire is revealed to be only desire.

Bibliography: Georges Bataille, *Blue of Noon,* trans. Harry Mathews (New York: Urizen Books, 1978). Bataille, *Sur Nietzsche,* in *Oeuvres complètes,* vol. 4 (Paris: Gallimard, 1973). Emmanuel Berl, *Mort de la pensée bourgeoise* (Paris: Grasset, 1929). André Breton, *Manifestoes of Surrealism,* trans. Richard Seaver and Helen R. Lane (Ann Arbor: University of Michigan Press, 1969). Guy Debord, *Society of the Spectacle* (Detroit: Black and Red, 1977). Pierre Drieu la Rochelle, *The Fire Within,* trans. Richard Howard (New York: Knopf, 1965). Drieu la Rochelle, *Gilles* (Paris: Gallimard, 1939). André Gide, *Lafcadio's Adventures,* trans. Dorothy Bussy (New York: Vintage, 1960). T. Jefferson Kline, *André Malraux and the Metamorphosis of Death* (New York: Columbia University Press, 1975). Jean Lacouture, *André Malraux,* trans. Alan Sheridan (New York: Pantheon, 1975). André Malraux, *The Conquerors,* trans. Stephen Becker (New York: Holt, Rinehart and Winston, 1976). Malraux, *Man's Fate,* trans. Haakon M. Chevalier (New York: Random House, 1961). Malraux, "On Saint-Just," trans. Lionel Abel, *Partisan Review,* 22 (Fall 1955), 465–479. Ernst von Salomon, *Die Geächteten* (Berlin: C. Bertelsmann Gütersloh, 1930). Jean-Paul Sartre, "Erostratus," in *The Wall,* trans. Lloyd Alexander (New York: New Directions, 1948).

Douglas Collins

ᨒ 1934, 6 February

Fascists Riot in the Place de la Concorde (15 Dead; 1,435 Wounded)

Birthrate and Death Wish

On 6 February 1934, veterans' groups of the extreme right marched down the Champs-Elysées and clashed with the police in the Place de la Concorde in front of the Chamber of Deputies, for them the symbol of democratic corruption. This night of antiparliamentary violence exacted a heavy toll: fifteen dead and hundreds of wounded. It was one year after Hitler's election as chancellor of the German Reich. And it would be France's most direct expression of fascist violence with internal origins. The parties of the left responded by organizing the Popular Front for Defense against Fascism, which triumphed in the elections of May 1936.

For forty-year-old Pierre Drieu la Rochelle the crisis of February 1934 provoked a different decision: after many oscillations between left and right, he committed himself irreversibly to fascism. Although his enthusiasm for the cause would fluctuate, until his suicide in 1945 (following the execution of Georges Brasillach, another collaborationist writer), he remained its most brilliant intellectual. In "Ecrit dans la rue" ("Written in the Street"), a section of

Socialisme fasciste (1934; *Fascist Socialism*) inspired by the riots, he expressed his political decision in strange words: "I have given up Asia and children" (p. 110). Drieu's choice for fascism was indeed the ultimate expression of what Pierre Andreu and Frédéric Grover, his biographers, have called Drieu's "refusal of life." It opened up onto an apocalyptic adventure whose mysticism would acquire a suicidal dimension.

Reminding his readers that it was a Frenchman (Achille Guillard) who invented the very term *demography,* Theodore Zeldin devotes an entire chapter of his *France 1848–1945* to the anxiety that had gripped the French since the mid-19th century over the drop in their rate of population growth. "Frenchmen," he writes, "became neurotic about their virility and about their capacity to survive as a great power" (5:184). Anxiety, according to Freudian theory, is an affect that arises from sexual sterility, from an accumulation of stored-up libido that has been shunted away from its reproductive goals. No doubt such an anxiety is responsible for the frequency and variety of reproductive motives in the interwar novels, as well as with their intentionally apocalyptic tone. But the pattern is already in place with André Gide's *L'immoraliste* (1902; *The Immoralist*), whose female protagonist, Marceline, will serve as a prototype for many narrative pregnancies. Hers is a pregnancy doomed from its very start, overlapping as it does with an illness. Instead of promoting promised life, it not only withholds motherhood from her but also signs her death warrant. In contrast to its near contemporary, Zola's *Fécondité* (1899; *Fruitfulness*), Gide's novel does not aim to denounce, through its hero, the suicidal egotism of a civilization that refuses to populate its future. Quite the contrary: Michel's account of his life—his stoic selfishness during and after his wife's fatal miscarriage—is forwarded by his listener, the narrator, to the prime minister as the most convincing of job applications. Such a demonstration of Nietzschean immoralism establishes Michel's readiness for political leadership; the state, the narrator argues, should take advantage of so much strength of mind.

Twenty-five years later the political allegory becomes more explicit in André Malraux's *Les conquérants* (1928; *The Conquerors*). Garine's international revolutionary career begins with a forced exile after he is compromised in an abortion scandal. The role of father is taboo for this revolutionary Oedipus: life must be changed before it can be reproduced.

Marcel Arland's *L'ordre* (1929; *Order*) takes up the motive of sterility but strips it of the revolutionary aura Malraux had given it. The novel ends with the agony of its hero, a grim caricature of a repentant pseudosurrealist adventurer who spreads his own sterility like a disease. His deathbed becomes the site of a hopeless reckoning: "Suddenly he was flooded by the distress of having no child to prolong his being. He dreamed of the one that Renée could have given him, whose existence he had been afraid of before" (p. 510). We are in a time of various kinds of "law and order." In 1929 the Prix Goncourt was awarded to this stale condemnation of an avant-garde whose "immoralism" deprived others of the future it itself held in contempt.

Les cloches de Bâle (1934; *The Bells of Basel*), Louis Aragon's first novel after his turning Communist, sheds on this demographic dead-end the light of the class struggle. This work, in which the bourgeoisie commits suicide while the workers are killed by ruling-class thugs, portrays the failure of childbirth by means of a homology. Judith Romanet, a worldly artist, gets an abortion and then dies from the operation; the worker Jeannette, happily pregnant, has a miscarriage. The moral of the allegory: abortion sums up the suicidal behavior to which a class without a future, the bourgeoisie, is necessarily reduced (Judith Romanet, says one of the characters, "had died because she had not wanted a child"; *Bells*, p. 316), whereas Jeannette's miscarriage illustrates the repression exerted against proletarian fecundity: the bourgeoisie wants to prevent the workers from giving birth to a future it itself will never have.

Marxism's ambivalence toward the issue of abortion is treated with greater subtlety by another Communist novelist, Paul Nizan, in *Le cheval de Troie* (1935; *Trojan Horse*). A worker dies as a result of an abortion that her husband finds difficult to justify, in Marxist terms, as a revolt "against a society which imposes the duty of child-bearing" (p. 100).

No work is more desperately trapped in the doublebinds of demographic anxiety than that of Drieu la Rochelle. *Mesure de la France* (1922; *France within Measure*), the essay that launched the career of the twenty-nine-year-old veteran who had been publishing in the journals of the presurrealist avant-garde, is stamped with these ambiguities. Here Drieu draws the lessons of World War I. Crushed in 1914 by the German horde, France survived only through the intervention of the American one. *Mesure de la France* denounces the French "crime," that is, the genetic "moderation" of oversensitive bourgeois who refuse to multiply. Yet he wants at the same time to save France from German proliferation, and so conclusions are not far from the most elitist of notions: "It is necessary to forswear populousness" (p. 111). In the Europe he dreams of, victorious France, instead of competing with German growth, would impose on Germany its own demographic moderation. "One must not multiply the European like the Oriental. We are not Coolies. One must not produce workers and soldiers indefinitely" (p. 85). *Pullulate* is not an Indo-European verb. Asia and children did not have to wait for 1934 in order to merge in Drieu's fantasies. "These Germans are absurd. Thank God there was someone in Europe to stop that blind proliferation" (pp. 31–32). Thus behind his clamorous denunciation of the French pleasure in withholding, one senses a fascination with the suicidal sterility of the warrior ("The men of France are stingy with their seed, but not yet with their blood"; p. 25).

Drieu's novels, among the most brilliant of the interwar period, abound with Don Juans cursed by childlessness, torn between two mutually exclusive versions of virility: that of the warrior (*La comédie de Charleroi*, 1934) and that of the lover (*L'homme couvert de femmes*, 1925; *A Man Buried in Women*), the virility of the ladies' man versus that of the comrade-in-arms. It oscillates between the anxious heterosexuality of a misogynous off-duty soldier and powerful nostalgia for the front, where the nearness of death excludes women.

Gilles (1939), Drieu's most famous novel, is an autobiographical work.

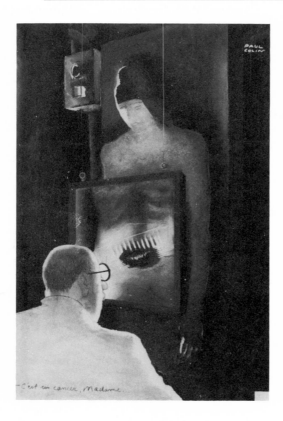

1. "C'est un cancer, madame
. . ." Paul Colin, *Marianne
malade,* exhibited at the Salon
des Humoristes, Paris, 1934.
(Photo © Harlingue-Viollet,
Paris, 1988.)

Beginning with the First World War and ending on the eve of the Second, its plot follows the major political and literary movements of the interwar period. The riots of February 1934 form the nexus of the penultimate section, "L'apocalypse." Gilles, at age forty, has just renounced politics. Western civilization, having reached its final stage of moral and biological decadence, will be reborn only from its own ashes—or from its own blood. But the riots interrupt these apocalyptic reflections, provoking other thoughts entirely. Will France not live thanks to this first slaughter since the war? However, in the ensuing parliamentary compromise the brushfire of February is smothered. No one wishes to honor the promises of a day whose futureless mystique degenerates into politics. France is beyond saving. Gilles leaves to fight and die in Spain amid Franco's batallions.

Running parallel to the insurrectional burst of hope and its betrayal is another crisis, one that shakes Gilles's private world. Several months earlier, his mistress, Pauline, has told him she is pregnant. The allegorical significance of these two series of parallel events needs no underlining. Like a woman with child, the virile blood spilled in the streets stood for the oxymoronic promise of a future. But Pauline's pregnancy will have no more future than February's riots. The fascist uprising is overturned; as for Pauline, scarcely is she pregnant when, in the best tradition of *L'immoraliste,* she is stricken with uterine cancer. In order to operate on her, the surgeon must kill the child, and thus she who should have been the carrier of life bears only the seed of her own extinction. With the cause of her illness tied to a (suddenly introduced) past of prostitution, this punishing, cruel, clinical episode follows the right-wing iconographic stereotypes of the February crisis (fig. 1) in giving an allegorical dimension to Pauline's fate: her cancer duplicates that of a France prostituted by the rampant promiscuity of a multiple-party system. Pauline's agony begins on 6 February. It ends along with the hopes fed by the rioting. "France was dying while Pauline died" (*Gilles,* p. 425). And they both die of the same sterilizing disease, bourgeois capitalism, the cancer of a representational democracy in which signs devour reality. As Pauline's illness advances, its allegorical dimension is made more and more explicit. Drieu describes her as "sterile, marked by death, but above all, become bourgeoise" (p. 408).

A similar episode forms the subject of an earlier short story, "Le journal d'un délicat" ("The Diary of a Fragile Man"), which Drieu began to write in July 1934. But this time, in accordance with the autobiographical experience on which it is based, the woman's fecundity is untainted until the narrator-father refuses the child she is bearing. The abortion he forces upon his mistress renders her sterile. "Life was before me and I refused it" (*Histoires déplaisantes* [*Unpleasant Stories*], p. 75). He who in *Mesure de la France* had still wondered, "I was alone, oh my father. But will I have a son?" (p. 25) has ceased hesitating. Now that he is fascist, he answers in the negative. His strange formula in *Socialisme fasciste* ("I abandoned both Asia and children") bears the date July 1934.

It is clear that the ending of *Gilles* was inspired by the conclusion of Malraux's novel *L'espoir* (1937; *Man's Hope*), where the final note is the victory of the Republican forces at Guadalajara. Likewise, in the final pages of *Gilles* the hero falls before a victorious Republican assault. It is the same relation of forces as in Malraux, but seen from the opposite vantage point. There is, however, another difference. *Gilles* was published two years after *L'espoir.* And if the most optimistic of Malraux's readers could still share, in 1937, a hope in the Republican victory, those of Drieu, in 1939, could have had no doubts. Franco had been master of Madrid since 28 March. *Mesure de la France* had already shown that Drieu's experience of victory was far from euphoric. The conclusion of *Gilles* makes one wonder, against the grain of the events themselves, if his fascism was ever triumphant. How strange to show it dying in 1939. The victory itself is experienced as the expression of the death wish, as the paradoxical form through which a project of self-destruction works itself out.

The triumph of death is part of a somber mysticism that is indissociable from fascist ideology. Sartre, in *Qu'est-ce que la littérature?* (1947; *What Is Literature?*), correctly sums up Drieu's work as "the old Heraclitean myth according to which life is born from death" (p. 163). For this enemy of daily life, only global conflagration could give birth to a radically new future. Following Drieu's doctrine—a sort of catastrophic palingenesis—the only conceivable regeneration would follow a total destruction. Whosoever wants to save life shall lose it: the future does not germinate in the wombs of women but in the blood of men.

See also 1914–1918, 1933 (December), 1937 (March), 1937 (12 July), 1945 (6 February).

Bibliography: Pierre Andreu and Frédéric Grover, *Drieu la Rochelle* (Paris: Hachette, 1979). Louis Aragon, *The Bells of Basel,* trans. Haakon M. Chevalier (New York: Harcourt, Brace, 1936). Marcel Arland, *L'ordre* (Paris: Gallimard, 1929). Pierre Drieu la Rochelle, *Gilles* (Paris: Gallimard, 1939). Drieu la Rochelle, "Journal d'un délicat," in *Histoires déplaisantes* (Paris: Gallimard, 1963). Drieu la Rochelle, *Mesure de la France* (Paris: Grasset, 1922). Drieu la Rochelle, *Socialisme fasciste* (Paris: Gallimard, 1934). Alice Y. Kaplan, *Reproductions of Banality: Fascism, Literature, and French Intellectual Life* (Minneapolis: University of Minnesota Press, 1986). Paul Nizan, *Trojan Horse,* trans. Charles Ashleigh (New York: Fertig, 1975). Jean-Paul Sartre, *"What Is Literature?" and Other Essays,* trans. Bernard Frechtman (Cambridge, Mass.: Harvard University Press, 1988). Zeev Sternhell, *Ni droite ni gauche: L'idéologie fasciste en France* (Paris: Editions Complexe, 1987). Theodore Zeldin, *France 1848–1945,* vol. 5: *Anxiety and Hypocrisy* (Oxford: Oxford University Press, 1979).

Denis Hollier

✍ 1935, 6 May

Antonin Artaud Stages the First of Seventeen Performances of
Les Cenci at the Théâtre des Folies-Wagram

Staging the Plague

Antonin Artaud's directing career was brief. When, in April 1933, the thirty-nine-year-old avant-garde director was invited to give a lecture at the Sorbonne, all that was known about him was that André Breton had bitterly excluded him from the surrealist group in 1929 and that, in a manifesto published in 1932 by the influential *Nouvelle revue française,* he had ominously called for "Le théâtre de la cruauté" ("The Theater of Cruelty"). Two years after the lecture he would leave the theater. No one hearing him talk at the Sorbonne on "Le théâtre et la peste" ("The Theater and the Plague") could have imagined that some thirty years later the whole Western theatrical avant-garde, from Jerzy Grotowski to Peter Brook to the Living Theatre, would claim him as their precursor.

"Le théâtre et la peste" begins with the story of a ship refused entry to the ports of Sardinia in 1720 by a viceroy who had been warned in a dream that the ship was infected with the plague, and which, upon having been diverted to Marseilles, in fact brought a deadly pestilence. Could the plague be, Artaud asks, more than a virulent microbe? Could it be an intelligent force in the service of fate? Describing with clinical precision the irruption of the disease on the bodies of the panicked victims, the buboes discharging their internal putrefaction, the epidemic's invasion of the streets, spreading terror everywhere, leading to institutional anarchy and the collapse of the social order, arousing the most futile behavior, the most delirious beliefs, Artaud goes on to make a startling claim. "And at that moment," he says, "the theater is born. The theater, i.e., an immediate gratuitousness provoking acts without use or profit" (*Theater,* p. 24). The plague exhausts itself in an organic crisis, but the theater maintains contact with the force that inspires it, bringing to light the "depth of latent cruelty" (p. 30) usually masked by morality or convention. In its very excess, Artaud concludes, the theater affects the sensibilities of the spectators with the strength of an epidemic.

But how does one communicate to the public such an apocalyptic view? Anaïs Nin describes Artaud lecturing, his face tortured with anguish: "One could see the perspiration dampening his hair. His eyes dilated, his muscles became cramped, his fingers struggled to retain their flexibility. He made one feel the parched and burning throat, the pains, the fever, the fire in the guts. He was screaming. He was delirious" (*Diary,* p. 192). When Artaud had finished, he was face down on the floor . . . and the room was empty. "They always want to hear *about* something," Artaud said angrily a little later. "And I want to give them the experience itself, so they will be terrified, and awaken." He added somberly: "This is agony I portrayed. Mine, yes, and that of everyone who is alive." Then, Nin recalls, getting up in front of the deserted lecture-hall, "he walked straight up to me and kissed my hand. He asked me to go to the café with him" (ibid.).

This little lecture-hall drama both prefigures the failure of his show *Les Cenci* and exemplifies his teachings about the theater. Artaud felt the upheaval of the contemporary world too powerfully to treat anything metaphorically. On 27 November 1927, while playing an angry and sulfurous Marat in the film *Napoléon,* he wrote to its director, Abel Gance: "I have the plague in the soul of my nerves and I suffer from it" (*Selected Writings,* p. 168). The mental erosion accomplished by a childhood attack of meningitis, which he recounted with paradoxical mastery in his *Correspondance avec Jacques Rivière* (1924; *Correspondence with Jacques Rivière*), forced Artaud to question everything that did not directly affect his senses. For him, the true modern disease was not the black death of the plague, but the "mal blanc," the invisible and insidious "white disease" of a discursive thought that never ceases to dissolve the life it claims to express. It was out of hatred for his own abstraction that Artaud strove to "make the logical, discursive aspect of speech disappear beneath the physical and affective side" (*Theater,* p. 119). Never has a prophet been more estranged from the very matter of his own thought.

"Le théâtre et la peste" was collected in *Le théâtre et son double* (1938; *The Theater and Its Double*), the volume of manifestos and essays that the 1960s almost religiously rediscovered, worshiping Artaud as the greatest theoretician of the theater in this century. But when the book appeared, Artaud had already succumbed to madness. After his release from an asylum, in 1945, he wrote and published the shattering *Van Gogh, le suicidé de la société* (1947; *Van Gogh, the Man Suicided by Society*) and the imprecatory *Pour en finir avec le jugement de Dieu* (1948; *To Have Done with the Judgment of God*), which started a wave of protests when Artaud read it in a radio program. He died in 1948, either from his cancer or from an overdose of laudanum.

During Artaud's lifetime he was never celebrated as a director, a fact for part of which the sorry state of the Parisian theater was to blame: neither the stiffness of the Comédie-Française, with its dusty repertoire, nor the flatness of the Boulevard theaters, dominated by Sacha Guitry, could understand or satisfy a young innovator. But stage direction was only briefly the central activity of Artaud, who, by turns a poet, actor, director, art critic, scriptwriter, painter, and prophet, never stopped hesitating between different callings.

Upon his arrival in Paris from Marseilles in 1920, Artaud enthusiastically joined Charles Dullin's new Théâtre de l'Atelier, where he trained for a year in Russian improvisational techniques and where he first encountered the ritualistic and mystical dimension of oriental theater. Growing impatient with the still-too-realist Atelier, the unemployed actor Artaud shifted to the (still silent) cinema, which provided him with his essential ideas on theatricality. Like silent cinema (and morphine, to which Artaud was addicted), the theater should act, he thought, not on the mind through language but directly on the brain by means of concrete, compact, and convulsive images. In the late 1920s the ultimate triumph of the "talkies"—"that stupidity, that absurdity, and the negation of cinema" (letter to Yvonne Allendy, 26 March 1929, *Oeuvres,* 3 : 144)—sent him back to the stage.

In 1926, along with Roger Vitrac, a dropout from the surrealist group, Artaud launched his first big theatrical venture, the Théâtre Alfred Jarry, where in the following years he staged spectacles that reflected certain of Breton's ideas. The theater, Artaud proclaimed, should rejoin life; it is even more real than life, since it can bring to light the elements usually hidden in the unconscious. What happens onstage is in the nature of magic and dreams, but a dream that, contrarily to Freud's views, does not express only sexual desires but the totality of man, and therefore defies interpretation. The short-lived Théâtre Alfred Jarry having ceased for lack of money, from 1929 to 1935 Artaud devoted most of his writing to theater theory and developed the views on a "théâtre de la cruauté" that, after his death, along with those of Bertolt Brecht, would inspire modern theater.

Artaud's theories called for an absolute break with the humanist, neoclassical tradition inaugurated by the Renaissance. The theatrical event must stop subordinating itself to the written text and to the parasitical authority of canonical "masterpieces." It must give up psycho-logical analysis (character, plot, development, resolution) based on the supremacy of verbal abstraction to become, like painting, "the visual and plastic materialization of speech" (*Theater,* p. 69). The author must give way to the director, who, instead of using words alone, must deploy all the physical means at his disposal: music, dance, pantomime, action, intonation, architecture, lighting, décor. Through this vast register of ideographic and material symbols, the theater would attain the intensity of poetry, arousing a conflagration of feelings and sensations capable of putting the audience in direct contact with the metaphysical questions confronting humanity: the mystery of fate and the need for a transcendent state of life that existing dogmas are no longer able to satisfy. Like the mystery plays of the Middle Ages, the theater must become a total spectacle, both physical and metaphysical, of which cinema, music hall, the circus, and life are still only vague approximations.

In 1931, Balinese dances induced in Artaud the revelation of this metaphysical dimension. This oriental form of traditional theater appeared to him like a pure mirage of signs, the accomplished form of a poetry of gestures so precise and so impersonal that it turned the automatism of the dancers into "a kind of primary Physics from which the Spirit has never been separated" (*Writings*, p. 221). The Balinese theater does not talk about but presents abstraction, the unknown, and mystery physically, mathematically, through symbols in action and corporeal ideograms. This world, manifested ritually with rigor and application, is what Artaud calls *cruauté*.

Cruauté: the term is disquieting, and this is why Artaud continued to use it despite all the misunderstandings that surrounded it. Cruelty is not sadism, although violence necessarily has a place in it; it is the implacable and excessive drive to stimulate conflict in order to conjure up the somber and irrational face—the "double"—of the human spirit.

At the same time that he published "Le théâtre de la cruauté," Artaud became infatuated with an uncanny historical figure and wrote *Héliogabale, ou l'anarchiste couronné* (1934; *Heliogabalus, or the Anarchist Crowned*), which constitutes the best illustration of what he had in mind for the stage. A pagan emperor, the young Heliogabalus, who was also the priest of the Sun, was bent on perversely introducing "the theater and, through theater, poetry to the throne of Rome . . . and poetry, when it is real, is worthy of blood; it justifies the shedding of blood" (*Writings*, p. 318). Like the plague, Heliogabalus implacably liberates, through scandal, murder, and excess, all the fury of the instincts in order to punish "the Latin world for no longer believing in its myths" (p. 319). His radical—but regal—anarchism allows him, by cruel and double-edged gestures, to crystallize even in his ignominious death a metaphysical and superior idea of order.

Artaud put all these ideas to the test in the tragedy *Les Cenci,* presented at the Théâtre des Folies-Wagram in May 1935. This Renaissance story of incest and murder in an aristocratic Roman family, earlier adapted by Stendhal and Shelley, was rewritten by Artaud in the spirit of Elizabethan theater, with its indifference to convention and its metaphysical outbursts. The old Cenci is, like the historical referent of Georges Bataille's *La tragédie de Gilles de Rais* (1959), a "sacred monster," with a limitless appetite for violence. He publicly delights in the murder of his two sons, terrorizes his guests, braves the authority of the pope and the judgment of God. After having raped his own daughter, Béatrice, he pushes her to parricide and dies, gruesomely, from a nail stuck in his head. An innocent murderer, Beatrice in turn is condemned to death. This physical punishment sums up all the injustice of the world.

Using a spare and geometrical set inspired by Balinese theater to discourage any psychological identification, Artaud had his actors gravitate around a few axes, either moving mechanically, like zombies, or swarming onto the stage like a pack of wild dogs. By pushing each scene to the limit, he hoped to attain the point of incandescence where images turn into magic, words into incanta- tion, and effects into cosmic revelations.

Although *Les Cenci* was Artaud's most ambitious attempt to prove that he was not only a theoretician, he was constrained to use hastily trained actors and space ill suited to his needs. His décors, designed by Balthus, his cos- tumes drenched with heavily symbolic color, and sound waves of Incan rhythms surrounding and converging on the audience baffled them. In a letter to Artaud, Eugène Gegenbach described the reaction: "Around me spectators were laughing hysterically, like mad men laughing like hyenas" (*Oeuvres*, 5:55). As Artaud later recognized, the French public was not "ready for this feast of the gods"; and inasmuch as he had hoped to "bring the spectator to submission, to compel him to participate in the action" (5:300), this admission was an acknowledgment of defeat.

For Artaud *Les Cenci* was hardly an opportunity to disprove the critic's claims that the theater of cruelty is per se impossible to realize: he had made a major concession to writing, imposing on his actors a text that restricted them to merely verbal violence. Colette, reviewing the show, remarked that Cenci "keeps announcing something horrible that never materializes" (*La jumelle noire* [1935; *The Dark Binocular*], p. 247). *Les Cenci* was an imperfect realization of Artaud's ambitions, a single-edged spectacle evoking less terror than perplexity.

Artaud's most cherished project for *le théâtre de la cruauté, La conquête du Mexique* (*The Conquest of Mexico*), incorporated all his ideas on theater. It was never produced (it was not published until 1950, two years after his death); but, instead of staging it, Artaud somehow realized it physically by traveling to Mexico alone in 1936 to tap the metaphysical wealth of pre-Columbian religions. But Mexico, still reeling from a political revolution, was more interested in Marxism and European culture than in its aboriginal roots, in the old culture that Artaud had envisioned while writing *Héliogabale*, one in which "theater was not on the stage but in life" (*Oeuvres*, 7:34). The "mad Frenchman," as he was soon called, was just as misunderstood in Mexico City as he had been in Paris.

While in Mexico, suffering severely from withdrawal from drugs, Artaud traveled to an isolated tribe to participate in a curative peyote ritual. *D'un voyage au pays des Tarahumaras* (1937; *From a Voyage to the Land of the Tarahumara*) and related texts written between 1936 and 1948 recount both his vision of a mys- tical land where he saw a secret primary language unfold and the brutal oscil- lations of his existence in France after his return from Mexico. They register in filigree, as if on a seismograph, his collapse in Paris, his extravagant voyage to Ireland armed with St. Patrick's cane, up to his confinement in the Rodez asylum, where he entered for a while, after shock treatments, the "stupid men- tal condition of the *convert*" (*Oeuvres*, 9:38). The *Lettres de Rodez* (1946; *Letters from Rodez*), and especially the hallucinatory continent of the *Carnets de Rodez*

(*Notebooks from Rodez*), reveal the breadth of the mental battle that Artaud waged in the hope of cleansing himself of the seeds of Western culture and the scars of the Catholic religion. The failure of *Les Cenci* threw Artaud into the violence of his own martyrdom. He found there not only the inverse and diabolical image of the world he had previously wanted to subjugate through theater, but also the temptation, never exorcized, to play the propitiatory victim, competing in suffering and humiliation with the Savior whose Passion he often vehemently claimed as his own.

Le théâtre et son double is now considered a classic. Despite the emulation of Artaud during the past two decades, one can only wonder if the theater retains, as Artaud had hoped, the ability to cure a society estranged from "the world of organically civilized men" (*Theater*, p. 11). In this sense, Artaud appears to be, as Susan Sontag describes him, "one of the last great exemplars of the heroic period of literary modernism" (*Writings*, p. xix), a heroism whose failure constitutes the paradoxical but only possible form of accomplishment. Not having been able to save occidental culture, the only thing left for Artaud was to submit himself to his own treatment, his personal suffering becoming in the eyes of the world the spectacle of cruelty he did not succeed in bringing to the stage.

See also 1924, 1954, 1959 (28 October).

Bibliography: Antonin Artaud, *The Cenci*, trans. Simon Watson-Taylor (New York: Grove, 1969). Artaud, *Oeuvres complètes*, ed. Paule Thévenin, 13 vols. (Paris: Gallimard, 1958–1987). Artaud, *Selected Writings*, ed. Susan Sontag, trans. Helen Weaver (New York: Farrar, Straus and Giroux, 1976). Artaud, *The Theater and Its Double*, trans. Mary Caroline Richards (New York: Grove, 1958). Colette, *La jumelle noire*, vol. 2 (Paris: Ferenczi, 1935). Jacques Derrida, "La parole soufflée," in *Writing and Difference*, trans. Alan Bass (Chicago: University of Chicago Press, 1978). Anaïs Nin, *The Diary of Anaïs Nin, 1931–1934*, ed. Gunther Stuhlmann (New York: Harcourt, Brace and World, 1966).

Sylvère Lotringer

⚮ 1937, March
Three Former Surrealists Found the Collège de Sociologie

The Avant-Garde Embraces Science

The Collège de Sociologie (College of Sociology), founded by Georges Bataille, Roger Caillois, and Michel Leiris, had a brief existence, appearing on the Parisian scene in 1937 and disappearing in 1939. The Collège was not an institution of "higher learning" in the American sense, but a set of partners, conspirators, or "friends," in the sense of the Latin *collegium*, "partnership." As such, it existed within a long tradition of Parisian avant-garde groups, which have always been seen as having a political as well as an aesthetic mission (or whose aesthetic mission has inevitably had a political impact): examples include the Romantics of Hugo's day, the various symbolist factions, the surrealists, René Daumal's Le Grand Jeu (The Big Game) group, and even more marginal Marxist groups, of the kind caricatured in Paul Nizan's *La conspiration* (1938; *The Conspiracy*). The Collège met every two weeks in the back room of a bookshop in the rue Gay-Lussac, and the sessions were well attended (around fifty people on a good night). Each one featured a lecture on a given topic, usually related to the individual or social experience of the sacred, followed by discussion. The first year featured mainly Bataille and Caillois. Reflecting the growing timeliness of the Collège's concerns, some lectures in the second year were given by outside speakers, including Pierre Klossowski (who in the late 1930s was intensely committed to a rereading of Sade), Anatole Lewitzky, Hans Mayer, Jean Paulhan, Denis de Rougemont, and Jean Wahl. But Bataille and Caillois were unquestionably the preeminent participants. Caillois, only twenty-four years old in 1937, had been trained as a classicist but was an assiduous student of anthropologists and cultural historians such as Marcel Mauss and Georges Dumézil. Bataille, Caillois's senior by some fifteen years, was a librarian working in the coins and medals collection at the Bibliothèque Nationale. He, too, was widely read in history, sociology, philosophy, Freudian theory (Bataille was perhaps the first French writer to be psychoanalyzed, in 1927), and avant-garde aesthetics. (Bataille's job was singularly conducive to the role he played in the Collège, where he brought together people with widely disparate interests: working in France's largest library, he came into contact with any number of searchers or researchers, including Leiris, the dadaist Théodore Fraenkel, the painter André Masson, and Walter Benjamin.)

Bataille in the late 1920s and early 1930s had been a kind of postsurrealist (although he was never a member of the official surrealist group). Though excoriated by André Breton in the *Second manifeste du surréalisme* (1930; *Second Manifesto of Surrealism*), his work from the outset—including "La vieille taupe" (1930, pub. 1968; "The Old Mole"), "La notion de dépense" (1933; "The Notion of Expenditure"), and "La structure psychologique du fascisme" (1933–34; "The Psychological Structure of Fascism")—attempted to situate the radical experience advocated by the surrealists (dreams, deliria, simulated or real madness) in a different milieu. In other words, he worked to revise surrealism by reinterpreting its ground. In Bataille's view, the violence of the phantasms that surrealism sought to embody and communicate were not necessarily isolated individual expressions in bourgeois art forms such as poetry or painting. Instead, Bataille came to see the "religious" experience, in its broadest sense, as one fundamental to all society, although it had been repressed and nearly forgotten in modern democracies. Thus the radical individual experiences the surrealists stumbled upon were not simply a sign of artistic decadence or impotence; on the contrary, they marked an awareness of the force of the sacred—of the *heterogeneous*—that for Bataille was fundamental to all social life and was the only hope of a culture that had lost its raison d'être. Hence Bataille's interest not only in anthropology in general, but especially in the study of the secret societies that, in many cultures, serve as the guardians and catalysts of the sacred. And "study" for members of the Collège meant more than an academic exercise; the "student" also hoped to be a "sorcerer's apprentice," an acolyte sworn to spark a revival of chance, danger, and ecstasy in a moribund culture. Thus the Collège was itself modeled on a secret society; it too was the embodiment of the human tendency to form social groupings around the experience of delirious and spectacular profligacy. The traditional French literary *cénacle* (coterie) was transformed into a more or less private movement that harbored, that indeed was, the last repository of the heterogeneous. (The secrecy of the marginal organization was even more pronounced in another group founded by Bataille at the same time, which apparently attempted to revive various pagan rituals: Acéphale.) In and through Bataille, the would-be surrealist became the (secret) high priest of a force that would put civilization back in contact with its most fundamental urges.

At the same time, the Collège sought to ground its conclusions in science. Caillois was widely read in anthropology, and Leiris was both a former surrealist and a trained ethnologist who had spent several years doing fieldwork in Africa. Finally, it seemed, the avant-garde was becoming scientific; or rather, it was learning that it had been, even in its wildest ravings, scientific all along. It was coming to realize that the experiences it promoted, however extravagant, were not fundamentally different from the social activities studied in "primitive" cultures by ethnologists; at the same time, the fact that many modernist writers already studied similar experiences *in their own lives* made them, so to speak, anthropologists *avant la lettre* (this in fact is the formula for all of Leiris' autobiographical writings). Caillois's important lecture "La fête" ("Festival," in *The College,* pp. 279–303) revealed that the "revaluation of all values" for which the followers of Nietzsche longed was nothing other than a version of the orgiastic, often murderous celebrations commonly practiced by non-Western peoples to assure personal rebirth and social renewal. Thus the student of "primitive" culture was obliged to implement his conclusions in his own culture: given the fundamental identity of all cultures, "primitive" and modern, "objective" science was an impossibility because scientific truth, like all other cultural phenomena, was dependent on, or posterior to, an excessive experience (of transgression, of "chaos") that went beyond the bounds of all stable knowledge. The members of the Collège were therefore left with a strange science—one that made possible the perception of the "truth" of all cultures but that, at the same time, because of the very nature of that "truth," precluded a pure, detached knowledge; instigated by sociologists who were also enthusiasts, it mandated the implementation of that truth throughout a hitherto stultified, bourgeois society. Like so many other thinkers of the 1930s and 1940s, the members of the Collège, in their own way, were *engagés,* committed.

The Collège attempted to rewrite not only the avant-garde, and especially surrealism, but also French academic sociology and anthropology. Bataille and Caillois based many of their investigations on the anthropological works of Emile Durkheim and Marcel Mauss. Durkheim and Mauss were rationalists of the middle-years period of the Third Republic, former supporters of Dreyfus.

Durkheim, a professor of education at the Sorbonne, was deeply concerned with the secularization of the French school system, a project dear to French republicans since 1789. Secular morality, for Durkheim, was based on his discovery that "primitive" peoples, in their spectacular and excessive rites, were in fact worshiping the energy of society itself. *Mana*, the force that manifested itself through sacred objects, places, and activities, was a kind of reification of the energizing but fundamentally rational power that all people experience in and through social life. The teacher was to be a kind of secular priest, and the "religion" of civic duty taught in the public schools was a morality, based on reason, that would enable citizens to "believe in," and therefore derive strength from, modern society and its highest totem, the person. In a similar way, Durkheim's follower Mauss, in his study of gift-giving among groups such as the Trobriand Islanders and the Indians of the American Northwest, concluded that the spirit of generosity, which these peoples confused in their rituals with mythical beings and the spirits of their ancestors, could, when regrounded in rationality, serve as the basis for revitalizing economic exchange in modern, industrialized economies. Both Durkheim and Mauss, then, recognized the fundamental importance of the sacred for all cultures; they wanted to demystify it, to discover what they took to be the rational, comprehensible basis for its power, and then to implement that power in a secular, egalitarian society.

Bataille, Caillois, and their followers, working in the crisis years of the 1930s, when the democratic center was being shattered in Western Europe, saw only the imminent demise of the society for which Durkheim and Mauss had labored. By this time the dream of a just, capitalist democracy seemed so severely threatened that many people came to envisage a future under either communism or fascism. The Nazi rallies, such as the one that took place yearly at Nuremberg, triggered many questions in the minds of people such as Bataille. What if the force of crowds, of ecstatic masses of people, of the *sacred*, instead of being rational, as Durkheim had argued, was fundamentally irrational? What if the fascists had discovered and exploited a social impulse that neither the democrats nor the communists up to then had had the foresight to recognize? French academic sociologists had never adequately studied the sacred. Bataille considered it a dangerous mistake to leave the monopoly of its political exploitation to the fascists, the only ones so far to have recognized its importance. (Throughout the 1930s Bataille was a Marxist, though never a member of the Communist party.) His view of the sociological importance of the sacred, like Durkheim's and Mauss's, was tied to an emphasis on the secular. But the force behind the sacred, far from being reasonable or even fully comprehensible, was unknowable, radically negative, *impossible*. For this reason Bataille's "secular priest" was no longer a schoolteacher, but a conspirator, a fanatic struggling in a secret society against the dead weight of the very bourgeois culture that Durkheim had championed. Simultaneously, the notion of an autonomous, sacred subjectivity, so important to Durkheim's humanism, was replaced with a virulent absence of self, or a self torn open to the nonhuman through death or ecstasy.

Both Mauss and Alexandre Kojève, the commentator of Hegel's *Phenomenology of Spirit,* had grave reservations about the project of the Collège. Mauss clearly objected to the stress placed on the irrational and on the idea of the "sociologist's" active intervention in society (on the model of the shaman instead of the schoolteacher or the intellectual). Kojève, a Marxist, though he agreed to come and give a lecture, was equally hostile to the principle of a social force identified with "nonknowledge" ("non-savoir"). He also disapproved of Bataille's efforts to revive ritual, saying that Bataille put himself "in the position of a conjurer who wanted his magic tricks to make him believe in magic" ("Les conceptions hégéliennes" ["Hegelian Concepts"], in *The College,* p. 86). Yet Kojève's investigations, like those of Durkheim and Mauss, were of considerable importance to the members of the Collège. Bataille, Caillois, and many others (such as Raymond Queneau, Jacques Lacan, and Jean Hyppolite), were faithful auditors of Kojève's extremely influential lectures on Hegel's *Phenomenology.* These lectures, given at the Ecole Pratique des Hautes Etudes from 1933 until the outbreak of the war, not only renewed French understanding of Hegel but also shaped the existentialism of the 1940s and 1950s.

Kojève's analysis of Hegel was anthropological in that he interpreted negativity not in metaphysical terms, but in a purely social and cultural light: the question of the "Absolute Spirit," so important for the idealist version of Hegel, was as irrelevant for the Marxist's reading as were the conundrums of a rationalist, analytical philosophy. Kojève regarded the master-slave dialectic as the fundamental conflict in Hegel; its resolution was carried out in the realm of applied negativity: the slave won mastery over the master, so to speak, through the application of a kind of creative destruction in the productive process of labor. Negativity in this context meant the inevitable agonistic force of destruction and death that enabled the dialectical process to operate in society, in history, and in philosophy as well.

What fascinated Bataille in this model was the idea that the evolution of society and even of truth (in the dialectical process of philosophy) was a function of a purely destructive force: the dialectic marched onward through succeeding negations, revolutions, and deaths. The violence and madness of the decapitation of the king, and of many other revolutionary crimes and wars, were necessary after all for the productive advance of humanity.

Bataille's response to Kojève's version of Hegel was straightforward: if human history was nearing its end, as Kojève claimed, if the final (Soviet) revolution had occurred and no fundamental (dialectical, historical) change could take place thereafter, then nothing new could happen, and "negativity was out of a job" (letter from Bataille to Kojève, 6 December 1937, in *The College,* p. 90; translation modified). At the end of history, this negativity would not simply disappear, because it is an integral element of social relations. Instead, it would be unemployed, and therefore freed; it would manifest itself in unproductive expenditure, eroticism, sacrifice, and so on. The end of history would allow us finally to recognize the true nature of negativity, which had been there for us to see all along in "primitive" cultures.

This tour de force of argumentation allowed Bataille both to affirm Marxism and to posit a post-Marxist, posthistorical, and even posthumanist era in which negativity would revert to its most basic manifestations. If society itself was a kind of organism, as many French sociologists claimed, then its "cells," individuals joined together to make a larger entity, were united not through a peaceful organizing force (as Durkheim would have argued), but through a violent, negating one that was also a force of repulsion and dissemination. In his Collège lectures of 22 January and 5 February 1938, Bataille stressed the importance of conceiving the "center" around which a society develops (be it a church or any other sacred site) as a locus of the transformation of the sacred: if the sacred is dual, composed of both a repulsive and deadly "lefthand" side (characterized by transgression and transgressive objects, such as rotting bodies, menstrual blood, and aroused sexual organs) and an attractive but repressive "righthand" one (characterized by interdiction, the containment of the spread of death and obscenity, and, consequently, the maintenance of society), it is impossible to state that the social and topological "center" exists solely to contain negativity, to transform the "lefthand" sacred into a "righthand" one (as Durkheim and his followers argued); that center can just as easily be said to exist in order to transform the sacred of the right into that of the left. Thus for Bataille the social "center" was composed as much of a radically unrecoverable negativity (a "center of silence") as it was of a stabilizing, constructive, and positive force. "In fact the central nucleus of primitive agglomerations seems to be no less a space of license than a space of prohibition. Prohibition is obviously the primitive phenomenon that stands there in the way of expending forces, but, if it is at this particular spot that it stands in the way, it is because that is precisely where expenditure can take place" ("Attraction et répulsion" ["Attraction and Repulsion"], in *The College,* p. 123). Conservation is a logical after-effect of transgression and expenditure. Moreover, nothing can guarantee that the unrestrained, negative force can be controlled or that its dynamism, necessary to the constant renewal of society, can be prevented from one day tearing apart the very society that it makes possible.

Bataille's uncompromising commitment to an irrational sacred divided the members of the Collège. Leiris always kept his distance; the one lecture he read at the Collège, "Le sacré dans la vie quotidienne" ("The Sacred in Everyday Life"; *The College,* pp. 24–31, 98–102), was concerned more with an autobiographical, and much less apocalyptic, experience: how the sacred reappeared in the seemingly harmless rituals of his middle-class childhood. Leiris objected also to what he perceived as Bataille's lack of rigor—which was in fact a deliberate straying from the principles of sociological method as laid down by Durkheim and Mauss. Others, such as Jean Paulhan, objected to Bataille's emphasis on the "negative" (lefthand) elements of the sacred. Finally, for Caillois, the sacred implied hierarchy and an elitist model of the secret society, whereas Bataille conceived of a tragic "headless" (acephalic) model of the social group, without a dictator or any other "righthand" principle of organization.

The outbreak of the war in September 1939 put an end to the Collège; Caillois was teaching in Argentina, and other members of the group were dispersed or drafted. In the last years of the war and in the decade that followed it, the "new wave" was existentialism, and Sartre did not look kindly on the Collège; in his 1943 article on Bataille, "Un nouveau mystique" ("A New Mystic"), he argued that attempting to study an unknowable negativity by means of scientific methods was simply contradictory. Whether this criticism is valid or not, Sartre's harsh judgment, which is not far from Leiris', together with the essentially humanist and subjectivist orientation of the existentialists in the 1950s, eclipsed the concerns of the Collège until the 1960s. The 1960s saw a resurgence of interest in the "death of man," madness, collective frenzy, and marginality—especially after May 1968. The *Tel quel* group in the late 1960s and early 1970s owed much to the Collège: like its predecessor of the 1930s, it was a collective effort to link the radicalized social sciences (semiotics, anthropology, history, psychoanalysis) with left-wing politics and avant-garde aesthetic theory. The preoccupations of the Collège are therefore discernible in what has recently come to be known as poststructuralism: Michel Foucault's refusal of rational humanism and his concern with "power"; Gilles Deleuze's obsession with marginality and desire; Jean Baudrillard's critique of production and utility; and Jacques Derrida's interest in the left- and righthand aspects of the *pharmakon* (and of writing) in "La pharmacie de Platon" ("Plato's Pharmacy")—the methodology, and indeed the driving force, of all of these projects can be traced to the more iconoclastic and disruptive efforts of the Collège de Sociologie.

See also 1931 (March), 1933 (February), 1935.

Bibliography: Georges Bataille, *Lettres à Roger Caillois: 4 août 1935–4 février 1959,* ed. J.-P. Le Bouler (Romillé: Editions Folle Avoine, 1987). Bataille, *Visions of Excess: Selected Writings, 1927–1939,* ed. Allan Stoekl, trans. Allan Stoekl, C. R. Lovitt, and D. M. Leslie, Jr. (Minneapolis: University of Minnesota Press, 1985). Roger Caillois, *Man and the Sacred,* trans. Meyer Barash (Westport, Conn.: Greenwood Press, 1980). Jacques Derrida, "Plato's Pharmacy," in *Dissemination,* trans. Barbara Johnson (Chicago: University of Chicago Press, 1981). Denis Hollier, ed., *The College of Sociology, 1937–39,* trans. Betsy Wing (Minneapolis: University of Minnesota Press, 1988). Alexandre Kojève, *Introduction to the Reading of Hegel,* ed. Allan Bloom, trans. J. H. Nichols, Jr. (New York: Basic Books, 1969). Jules Monnerot, *La poésie moderne et le sacré* (Paris: Gallimard, 1945). Jean-Paul Sartre, "Un nouveau mystique," in *Situations, I* (Paris: Gallimard, 1947).

Allan Stoekl

ᏋᏊ 1937, 12 July

Picasso's *Guernica* Is Exhibited in the Spanish Pavilion
at the Paris World's Fair

Committed Painting

When the Spanish pavilion opened its doors at the World Fair in Paris on 12 July 1937, the civil war in Spain had been raging for almost exactly a year. On

18 July 1936 the right-wing military uprising against the recently elected Popular Front government had spread from the coast of Spanish Morocco to the mainland, inaugurating what has been variously called "the last romantic war in Europe" and "the first battle of the Second World War." By August of that year, Spain's greatest modern poet, Federico García Lorca, was dead, murdered by General Francisco Franco's "rebel" troops.

To many artists and intellectuals the world over, the murder of García Lorca confirmed that what was at stake in the Spanish war was not only the survival of a democratically elected government in the face of Fascist aggression (from the beginning, Franco was aided by Hitler and Mussolini, who sent arms, planes, and fighting men), but also the survival of art and culture—indeed, of all humane values in the West. Louis Aragon, who had left the surrealist movement and renounced surrealist poetry in the early 1930s to join the Communist party and write realist novels, expressed a general sentiment among French liberal and left-wing intellectuals when he wrote, in an emotional essay published in December 1936, that "the affair in Spain is the one worth dying for to the shores of the Pacific" ("Ne rêvez plus qu'à l'Espagne" ["Dream No Longer but of Spain"], *Europe,* no. 42).

To be sure, not all French intellectuals were on the side of the Republic. In a country with a long tradition of reactionary thought, where some still looked back to the Dreyfus Affair with vitriolic hatred for "the traitor Dreyfus," there was no lack of champions for General Franco, defender of "le Christ Roi" (Christ the King). Whereas Aragon called for a "crusade of poetry and art" in defense of the Spanish Republic, writers such as Robert Brasillach (who was executed in 1945 for collaboration with the Nazis) and Pierre Drieu la Rochelle (who committed suicide in 1945 to avoid the same fate) called for a crusade against "the Reds," in defense of Christian and aristocratic values. The conservative Catholic Georges Bernanos, on the other hand, denounced the fascist atrocities he had witnessed while living in Majorca during the first months of the war (*Les grands cimetières sous la lune,* 1938; *A Diary of My Times*). Just as in the Dreyfus Affair the writers we now call great were almost all in the Dreyfusard camp, so in the Spanish Civil War those we now think of as the best and the brightest were on the side of the Republic.

Some went to Spain to fight and died on Spanish soil. Others contributed in more indirect ways: raising money, writing, speaking, and generally publicizing the Republican war effort. The number of book-length eyewitness accounts published about the war while it was still going on, by sympathizers on both sides, is astonishing, as Marc Hanrez's *Les écrivains et la guerre d'Espagne* attests. Some, like André Malraux, the most celebrated French writer of the time, both fought and wrote: his novel *L'espoir* (*Man's Hope*), published in December 1937, is based on his experiences as a volunteer aviator during the first eight months of the war, when there was still hope that the Republic would win. *L'espoir,* together with Picasso's *Guernica* (1937) and Ernest Hemingway's *For Whom the Bell Tolls* (1940), remains the most important artistic work to have come out of the Spanish Civil War. And it shares with *Guernica* the fact that it was produced while the war was still going on: far from Wordsworth's famous definition of poetry as "emotion recollected in tranquillity," these two major artistic achievements were the products of emotion and passion lived on the spot. Furthermore, each one could hope to arouse the same passion in its viewer or reader, and thus to exert a direct influence on contemporary history. Rarely is it given to a writer or artist to feel so immediately *useful* in the practice of his or her art.

Picasso, unlike Malraux, did not travel to Spain during the war. In fact the Spanish painter never set foot on Spanish soil after a visit to his native Barcelona in 1934. (He died in 1973, two years before Franco, and thus did not witness *Guernica*'s 1981 installation in "democratic Spain," after forty-two years in New York's Museum of Modern Art, as he had stipulated a few years before his death.) He followed the war in Spain closely, however, and in September 1936 accepted the largely honorary post of director of the Prado Museum as a sign of support for the Republic. A few months later he accepted a commission from the Spanish government to paint a mural especially for the Spanish pavilion at the upcoming Paris World Fair. For an artist who had conspicuously avoided political themes and rarely accepted commissions, let alone commissions with a propagandistic cast, this was a highly significant step. But it was in fact not a first step. In January 1937, just before accepting the commission, Picasso had done a series of etchings violently satirizing Franco, the *Songes et mensonges de Franco* (*Dreams and Lies of Franco*), which were used by the Spanish government as anti-Franco propaganda and were later sold in large numbers for Spanish war relief. These etchings were published in the Spring 1937 issue of the luxury art magazine, *Cahiers d'art*. Clearly, the mood of the moment, even among "difficult" modernists, was for a politically committed art.

The Spanish pavilion was planned from the start as a propaganda effort for the Republic, designed to elicit both material and moral support from the millions of visitors who were expected at the World Fair. Spain, to be sure, was not alone in thinking of the event as a propaganda vehicle: the French Popular Front government headed by Léon Blum planned to make of it a great manifestation of popular support, and arranged for special trains and buses to bring workingmen and women from the provinces to Paris throughout the summer. Nazi Germany and the Soviet Union built the biggest, most monolithically imposing pavilions, facing each other pugnaciously at the center of the grounds, far overshadowing the "Column of Peace" that was supposedly its centerpiece. Not the smallest of the ironies connected with the fair was that by the time it opened, Blum had been toppled as prime minister, and the glorious days of the French Popular Front were over.

Picasso's great mural (actually, a twenty-six-foot-long painting on canvas) occupied an entire wall in the entrance hall of the Spanish pavilion. The title as well as the theme of the painting had been furnished to Picasso, courtesy of General Franco, on 27 April 1937, when three German bombers attacked without warning and almost completely destroyed the historic Basque town of Guernica. Such an attack on a civilian target was unprecedented in military history, and foreshadowed the bombings of European and Asian cities in World War II. The outcry of world opinion was immediate, as was Picasso's own reaction. During the month and a half following the bombing, he drew dozens of preliminary sketches and went through no less than seven stages of the painting-in-progress, all of them photographically documented by his then companion, the surrealist photographer Dora Maar. Paul Eluard, the great surrealist poet and friend of Picasso, watched the progress of the painting and composed his own poetic testimony to the bombing, "La victoire de Guernica" ("The Victory of Guernica," in *Cours naturel*, 1938; *Natural Course*), ending with the brave but unfulfilled prophecy that "victory will be ours" ("Nous en aurons raison").

That *Guernica* is Picasso's masterpiece, perhaps the greatest single painting of the 20th century, is acknowledged by most art historians today. But how useful was this painting in promoting the cause of the Spanish Republic? This was precisely the question that Jean-Paul Sartre asked some years later, in the opening pages of his manifesto of "committed writing," *Qu'est-ce que la littérature?* (1947; *What Is Literature?*): "And that masterpiece, *The Massacre of Guernica*, does anyone think that it won over a single heart to the Spanish cause?" (p. 28). In claiming that it did not, Sartre was not criticizing Picasso's painting but merely confirming his own theory of *engagement*. In his view, painting, like poetry, did not lend itself to the expression of ideas; only the writer of prose should have an instrumental attitude toward language, using it to "persuade, insult, supplicate, insinuate."

But Sartre's postwar views were not necessarily shared by the poets and artists who were caught up in the passions of the 1930s, when Sartre himself was largely apolitical. Eluard wrote several poems about the Spanish war, some of which he included in a volume of "political poems" published in 1948 (*Poèmes politiques*); and Tristan Tzara, who in his Dada days had proclaimed the senselessness of all art, wrote two beautiful poems about Spain in 1936 and 1937. One of them, "Chant de guerre civile" ("Song of Civil War"), first appeared in a slim brochure handset by Nancy Cunard and Pablo Neruda: *Les poètes du monde défendent le peuple espagnol* (1937; *The Poets of the World Defend the Spanish People*). The sad irony of a situation in which it was up to poets to "defend the Spanish people" was not lost on Tzara, who ended his poem with the bitter lines:

> It is I who have written this poem
> in the solitude of my room
> while to those for whom I cry
> death is sweet they stay there.   (*Oeuvres complètes*, p. 317)

The policy of nonintervention observed by the democratic governments of France and Britain, despite the flagrant intervention of the Fascist régimes, was a continuing cause of indignation to intellectuals who supported the Republic and was a recurrent theme in their writing about the war.

As for *Guernica*, Picasso himself said about it in an interview in 1944: "There is no deliberate sense of propaganda in my painting . . . except in *Guernica*. In

that there is a deliberate appeal to people, a deliberate sense of propaganda"
(quoted in Oppler, *Picasso's Guernica*, p. 151). And in a practical sense, at least,
there was no question about *Guernica's* usefulness. After its exhibition at the
World Fair, attended by more than 30 million people, the painting and its
preliminary studies traveled to London, New York, and other American cities,
with all proceeds from those shows benefiting the Spanish war relief. At about
the same time, Malraux was traveling around the United States raising money
for the same cause.

But apart from its immediate usefulness, how effective was *Guernica* as a
political statement? This question, whose implications obviously go beyond
this single painting, was a source of commentary and debate from the start. For
the writers and critics associated with *Cahiers d'art,* which devoted its entire
Summer 1937 issue to Picasso's *Guernica,* there was no doubt that the painting
was both a masterpiece and a clear political statement. "This admirable canvas
tells us the simplest thing with obvious clarity," wrote José Bergamin: "it
means Spain and the wrath of the Spanish people" (quoted in Oppler, *Picasso's
Guernica,* p. 212). Jean Cassou, a writer engaged in left-wing causes (he was a
contributor to the weekly *Vendredi* (Friday), which strongly supported the Popular Front), compared Picasso to Goya as a witness to the horrors of war, while
Michel Leiris, an ex-surrealist who would become one of France's great writers
(his first autobiographical volume, *L'âge d'homme* [*Manhood*], was published in
1939), read *Guernica* as "our own obituary: everything we love is going to die,
and that is why right now it is important that everything we love be summed
up into something unforgettably beautiful" (quoted ibid., pp. 209–210; translation modified).

Not everyone shared *Cahiers d'art's* enthusiasm, however. When plans were
under way for a reopened fair in 1938 (they never materialized), some members
of the Spanish Republican government proposed replacing *Guernica* with a
realist depiction of the war. For them, Picasso's work was not sufficiently clear.
"Instead of an inspiring call to arms for all to hear," comments Ellen C. Oppler,
"the gray-white and black composition held a terrifying jumble of faces and
limbs, massacred animals and human beings, all painted in a difficult modern
style" (*Picasso's Guernica,* p. 72).

In New York in 1941, by which time the Spanish Republic was dead, the
Marxist critic Vernon Clark mounted an all-out attack in the winter issue of
Science and Society: "Is there to be found here a forceful condemnation of Fascist
brutality? Does the treatment as a whole reveal confidence in the justice and
ultimate victory of the cause that the artist has undertaken to support? Or is
this merely the self-pitying wail of a bourgeois Brahmin who sees in the ruin
of Spain a threat to his own cozily introspective life?" (quoted in Oppler, *Picasso's Guernica,* p. 253). As the rhetorical nature of Clark's questions makes clear,
he knew the answers: the painting was far too ambiguous to be anything other
than bourgeois. The bull, symbol of Fascist aggression, is "the only figure in
the mural that has any dignity," while the horse and the warrior, symbols of
the Republic, appear "decrepit and broken down" (ibid.) (see fig. 1).

939

1. *Guernica,* by Pablo Picasso, in the Spanish Pavilion at the 1937 Paris Exposition Internationale (*Cahiers d'art,* July 1937, p. 289). (Photo courtesy of Archives Cahiers d'Art.)

Clearly, *Guernica* did not live up to the socialist realist aesthetic, which demanded positive heroes and an unambiguously positive message. But did that lessen its power as a form of political protest art? Clark argued yes; history, however, has proved him wrong, for Picasso's images—the dying horse, the woman with a dead child, the broken sword with a flower growing next to it—have exerted an extraordinary influence on artists, including politically committed ones, who came after him. The British art critic Herbert Read probably delivered the more just assessment of *Guernica*'s significance when he characterized it, at the time of its exhibition in London in 1938, as a "negative monument." In modern times, Read wrote, the affirmative monumental art of a Michelangelo or a Rubens is no longer possible, for that would require that the artist, and the age, "have a sense of glory." In our time (and Read was writing before Auschwitz), the great artist can "at best make a monument to the vast forces of evil which seek to control our lives: a monument of protestation" (quoted in Oppler, *Picasso's Guernica,* pp. 217–218).

Read's assessment, if correct, may explain *Guernica*'s enduring power to speak to us, who live after Auschwitz and Hiroshima and have heard of torture and massacres on nearly every continent since then. It may also explain why, when we read even as fine a novel about the Spanish Civil War as *L'espoir,* we have the sense that it belongs to a different age. Malraux was no simpleminded celebrator of heroic values; he had a deep sense of the complexity and fragmentation of the modern age. His novel, with its polyphonic and multilayered composition, its cast of hundreds of characters and its division into short, choppy chapters, reflects that sense. At the same time, however, *L'espoir* must be read as an attempt to create a modern epic, with the necessary simplification and "larger-than-life" representation that epic requires.

If there is such a thing as a just war, the Spanish Civil War certainly qualifies, and Malraux was its finest bard. The critic Lucien Goldmann accused him of writing a "Stalinist" work in *L'espoir,* glorifying the idea of the "chief." Such a reading points to the problem a modern writer faces in trying to write a novel that celebrates "men in battle," even just men fighting a just battle. Malraux's Republican heroes, perhaps best represented by the intellectual-turned-army-commander, Garcia, know that violence, force, and submission to a strong military chief are not values in themselves. In this they differ from the "fascist man" celebrated by Brasillach in his novel *Les sept couleurs* (1939; *The Seven Colors*), whose hero becomes a Legionnaire, an admirer of Hitler, and eventually a fighter for Franco, and from the eponymous hero of Pierre Drieu la Rochelle's *Gilles* (1939), who goes to Spain to find "the great white virile God." And yet Malraux's heroes must affirm violence and hierarchy in the short run, as the inevitable, even tragic consequence of their choice to fight for the values they do believe in: justice, fraternity, freedom.

This reasoning (which is thematized in the novel by means of numerous philosophical conversations among the characters) is noble and subtle. Does it work for us today? In one of the early chapters of *L'espoir,* the Spanish painter and sculptor, Lopez, talks about the possibilities of revolutionary art with the American journalist, Shade. What an artist who wants to "talk to the people" needs, Lopez says, is not directives on what to paint or how to paint, but simply a blank wall. Give the artist a wall, and he will find a style. Malraux found the style of a modern epic, the closest approximation to an affirmative monumentality for his age. Picasso, on the other hand, contested the very notion of epic: the vision of war that *Guernica* gives is not of men engaged in noble battle, but of blind animal fury and the destruction of women and children.

Valentine Cunningham has remarked that the Spanish Civil War exists for us today chiefly as "text," or, more exactly, text*s*. We may look with a certain nostalgia at the urgency and passion of the texts inspired by that war. But we should not let the nostalgia for "committed art" blind us to the horror of the events that art converted into words, or images.

See also 1933 (December), 1934, 1940–1944.

Bibliography: Frederick R. Benson, *Writers in Arms: The Literary Impact of the Spanish Civil War* (New York: New York University Press, 1967). Herschel B. Chipp, *Picasso's Guernica: History, Transformations, Meanings* (Berkeley: University of California Press, 1988). Valentine Cunningham, ed., *Spanish Front: Writers on the Civil War* (New York: Oxford University Press, 1986). Pierre Drieu la Rochelle, *Gilles* (Paris: Gallimard,

1939). Lucien Goldmann, *Towards a Sociology of the Novel*, trans. Alan Sheridan (London: Tavistock Press, 1975). Marc Hanrez, ed., *Les écrivains et la guerre d'Espagne* (Paris: Panthéon Press France, [1974]). Ellen C. Oppler, ed., *Picasso's Guernica: Illustrations, Introductory Essay, Documents, Poetry, Criticism, Analysis* (New York: Norton, 1988). Jean-Paul Sartre, *"What Is Literature?" and Other Essays*, trans. Bernard Frechtman (Cambridge, Mass.: Harvard University Press, 1988). Susan Rubin Suleiman, *Authoritarian Fictions: The Ideological Novel as a Literary Genre* (New York: Columbia University Press, 1983). Hugh Thomas, *The Spanish Civil War*, 3d ed. (London: Hamish Hamilton, 1977). Tristan Tzara, "Chant de guerre civile," in *Oeuvres complètes*, ed. Henri Béhar, vol. 3 (Paris: Flammarion, 1979).

Susan Rubin Suleiman

✒ 1939

Before Returning to the French West Indies, Aimé Césaire Publishes
Cahier d'un retour au pays natal in Paris

Surrealism and Négritude in Martinique

From the abolition of slavery in Martinique in 1848 until 1939, the few non-white bourgeois literati on the French island had contented themselves with imitating bloodless French symbolist and Parnassian models. These literary trends, with their aesthetic of emotional distance, were ideally suited to a black intellectual elite who chose to write with their privileged heads in the sand. Their literature not only ignored racial themes and social injustices but also, in its identification with the white colonizer, embodied a style so "bleached" that it never disclosed the race of its authors.

Onto this scene burst the passionate Caribbean poet Aimé Césaire (b. 1913). Upon returning home in 1939 after eight years of study in Paris, he brought with him not only a visionary surrealist style but also inspiration from contacts with blacks from all over the world. Paris in the 1930s yielded up exposure to an African experience undreamed of by the isolated island student. Here Césaire formed lifelong bonds with the poet and future statesman Léopold Sédar Senghor from Senegal and with Léon Gontran Damas from Guyana. These young writers from the French colonies, as students in a Paris indifferent or even hostile to them, struggled with the dawning consciousness of their common blackness and its potential as a unifying force.

The rich literary, cultural, and ethnographic exchanges among black intellectuals in Paris in the 1930s heightened both Césaire's awareness of belonging to a larger community and an ancient heritage, and his realization of the need for cultural renewal. In Paris he discovered America's Harlem Renaissance in the unbleached black writing of Langston Hughes, Countee McCullen, and Claude McKay. In Paris, too, the French translation of the German ethnographer Leo Frobenius' *History of African Civilization* first appeared in 1933. Though later discredited for its lack of scientific rigor, Frobenius' work had a powerful impact on Césaire's imagination and self-esteem. Frobenius' account of the grandeur and high civilization of past African cultures sought to challenge the European prejudice against the "barbarous Negro," and his demonstrations of the unified characteristics of African style nourished the formulation of Césaire's concept of *négritude,* first as consciousness of and pride in the vast ensemble of the African heritage, and then as a springboard for political engagement.

The first black students in Paris to try to reaffirm black cultural values were three Antilleans—Etienne Léro and René Ménil—who published, with Jules Monnerot, the only issue of *Légitime défense (Legitimate Defense)* in 1932. Borrowing this title from the pamphlet in which André Breton, in 1926, had declared surrealism's solidarity with communist revolution, these black editors, all communists and surrealists, attacked the assimilationism of contemporary island poetry, as well as social and economic disparities, while encouraging political revolution. Their journal paved the way for another one, with a less regional constituency: *L'étudiant noir (The Black Student),* published by Césaire, Damas, and Senghor in the mid-1930s. This review served as a sounding board for Césaire's articulation of the political and cultural identity of the black man, which he called *négritude.*

In writing the *Cahier d'un retour au pays natal (Notebook of a Return to the Native Land)* toward the end of his student years at the Ecole Normale Supérieure, Césaire came to understand, through willed remembering, the devastating isolation, alienation, exploitation, and repression of the people of the French Antilles in the 1930s. He recognized that slavery and the ensuing colonial structures had instilled a totally devalued sense of self in the indigenous population, later analyzed in the works of the Martinican psychiatrist Frantz Fanon. Césaire's *Cahier* was published in the Parisian review *Volontés* in 1939, on the eve of his return to Martinique to take a teaching position along with his wife, Suzanne, at the Lycée Schoelcher in Fort-de-France. Although its publication went virtually unnoticed at the time, the *Cahier* was to have a major impact first on Caribbean literature and, soon thereafter, on the writers of all nations struggling with decolonization.

The *Cahier* was both a culmination and a beginning, a taking stock and a prophetic expression of desire for the amelioration of an intolerable reality, both subjective and objective. This lengthy, lyrical, autobiographical poem, alternating between verse and prose, which James Arnold calls the "epic of negritude," represented a radical break with previous Antillean literature and reflected the influence of Césaire's poetic predecessors: the Comte de Lautréamont, Arthur Rimbaud, Charles Baudelaire, and Stéphane Mallarmé, the great *poètes maudits* (damned poets) of the late 19th century. From them Césaire learned the primacy of the image as an instrument to reveal the self by sounding unknown and forbidden zones of the unconscious; the power of trenchant humor and transgressive irony; the arbitrariness of words that had to be respected in their own right if one were to forge a new poetic language. The choice of the word *négritude,* however, was far from arbitrary. Arising from the

943

depths of self-hatred that characterize confessional sections of the poem, Césaire proclaims (pp. 67–69):

> my negritude is neither tower nor cathedral
> it takes root in the red flesh of the soil
> it takes root in the ardent flesh of the sky
> it breaks through the opaque prostration with its upright patience

The poetic subject, that is, the one that by saying "I" constitutes itself in and through discourse, is triumphantly assuming phallic *négritude* and thereby inscribing a unique solution to alienated consciousness, assimilating poetic fathers to ancestral ones. *Négritude* combines the primitive and the poetic, the African and the Ur-French, to forge a new identity. This coinage of a new signifier in the *Cahier* is what allows Césaire to reconcile his intellectual engagement, his poetic ambition, with his visceral engagement, his social ambition. The poetic subject is dramatized as Césaire experiments with the concepts of identification, limitation, definition, freedom. It is constantly being decentered by commenting on and erasing itself in various guises. And from now on the identity of Césaire as autobiographical subject, that is, the man in the world himself, will be linked to his poetic praxis, from the *Cahier* throughout the rest of his poetic career. For writing confers both being and self-knowledge. Incorporating several poetic voices, including imaginary interlocutors, the *Cahier* reads as a relentless series of confrontations between a poetic subject in past, present, and future incarnations and the pitiful reality that surrounds it and that it can no longer deny. The surrealist image, envisioned in Breton's *Manifeste du surréalisme* (1924; *Manifesto of Surrealism*) as an instrument of psychic liberation because it links terms according to intuition rather than according to logic, functions in the *Cahier* to uncover multiple unknown worlds and selves previously repressed by shame. The discovery of such repressed material provokes both moral outrage and the desire for change. Although surrealism, as a critique of rational bourgeois Western society, always had an inherent political dimension, its targets seem abstract and amorphous in comparison with the concrete detail of the harsh reality articulated in the *Cahier* (pp. 37–39):

> the panting of a deficient cowardice, the heave-holess enthusiasm of supernumerary sahibs, the greeds, the hysterias, the perversions, the clownings of poverty, the cripplings, the itchings, the hives, the tepid hammocks of degeneracy. Right here the parade of laughable and scrofulous buboes, the forced feedings of very strange microbes, the poisons without known alexins, the sanies of really ancient sores, the unforeseeable fermentations of putrescible species.

Césaire's painful personal journey in this poem requires acknowledging, in order to overcome, a specific racial image—that of the *nègre*. By stripping reality bare in his identification with his race and island, he reaches a bedrock level from which he can rebuild, through poetry and community, all that has been alienated (p. 77):

> I accept both the determination of my biology . . . and negritude . . .
> measured by the compass of suffering
> and the Negro every day more base, more cowardly, more sterile, less pro-
> found, more spilled out of himself, more separated from himself . . .
>
> I accept, I accept it all.

"It is through the image, through the revolutionary image, the distant image, the image which overturns all laws of thought, that man finally breaks through the barriers," Césaire stated in "Poésie et connaissance" (1944; "Poetry and Cognition," in *Tropiques,* January 1945, p. 166). The *Cahier* can certainly be said to practice this ethos and aesthetic of the image and, as such, to echo the surrealism of Breton's 1924 *Manifeste.* Césaire later claimed that he was writing surrealist poetry at the time the way Monsieur Jourdain, Molière's would-be gentleman, was speaking prose—that is, without realizing it or being consciously committed to it ideologically. But it is less important to pinpoint exact influences than to realize what values were predominant in an intellectual community and to what extent Césaire's emergence as a poet was the result of his experience of an extraordinary historical moment. At the same time, Césaire's text was not just a Martinican extension of surrealism. His unconscious use of the surrealist metaphor, which juxtaposes realities that are as distant from each other as possible, is what puts his writing in touch with his black, African, Martinican specificity, what allows the subject to discover those ancestral rhythms, myths, images, "my deepest internal vibration" ("Lettre à Lilyan Kesteloot," p. 205).

Historical circumstances were such that surrealism and *négritude* coincided and flourished in Martinique. Shortly after the fall of France in June 1940, the French Antilles came under Vichy rule. To the insult of colonialism was added the injury of fascist domination. In response first to the former, then to both, Césaire, his wife, and René Ménil, their colleague from Paris and at the Lycée Schoelcher, founded the journal *Tropiques,* whose first issue appeared in April 1941. Its purpose as a cultural review was to raise native consciousness of and pride in both Martinique's unexplored African heritage and its unique richness as a tropical Caribbean island. Valuing the indigenous was a hitherto unheard-of, indeed revolutionary, project. Although the official régime's censorship policies made it difficult for the authors to give any direct political content to their essays or poems, their position was clear from the outset. Their goal was to root their discourse in the specifics of their Antillean legacy and to use those values creatively to liberate a country of ex-slaves from whatever still bound them intellectually and psychologically. Césaire wrote as the introduction to the first issue: "Wherever we look, darkness is gaining ground . . . But we are among those who say *no* to darkness. We know that the salvation of the world depends on us, too" (p. 6).

The poems Césaire published in *Tropiques,* eventually collected in the volume *Les armes miraculeuses* (1946; *The Miraculous Weapons*), constitute his most overtly surreal texts. The values and techniques of surrealism, to the extent that they

945

coincided with those of the editors and collaborators of *Tropiques,* provided them all with a "miraculous weapon" to accomplish the self-appointed task of psychic liberation of the blacks.

"Objective chance," the surrealist notion that there is an actual but often buried truth to apparent coincidence when desire meets its object, brought surrealism to Martinique. In April 1941 André Breton, fleeing Vichy France, was interned in Martinique before being granted passage to New York, where he would set up a community of surrealists in exile. Upon his release from internment, as he roamed the streets of Fort-de-France, he happened upon the first issue of *Tropiques* in the window of a shop kept by Ménil's sister. Breton described the impression Césaire's poems made on him—at once aesthetic, moral, and social—in "Martinique charmeuse de serpents: Un grand poète noir" ("Martinique Snake Charmer: A Great Black Poet"), published in the May 1944 issue of *Tropiques.* Breton recognized an affirmation of his own values and arranged to meet Ménil and Césaire immediately. Césaire recalled the significance of this meeting in a 1978 interview with Jacqueline Leiner: "Breton brought us courage . . . he shortened our research and our hesitations. I realized that most of the problems I was struggling with had been resolved by Breton and surrealism . . . The meeting with Breton was a confirmation of the truth that I had found on my own" (*Tropiques,* p. vi).

Césaire had already established his own powerful poetic voice in the *Cahier.* It is more in the writings of his fellow collaborators on *Tropiques* and, perhaps more important, in the very structure and organization of the journal that Breton's surrealist ideals and practices had a direct impact. For several issues after the meeting of the two men, the French poet became not only the main character in numerous articles but also the *maître penseur* (mastermind) behind many others. In "André Breton, poète," in the October 1941 issue, Suzanne Césaire quoted from his first and second manifestos and lauded the optimistic side of his surrealist poetic quest. This act of uncritical allegiance was followed by three poems by Breton, two of them reprinted from *Le revolver à cheveux blancs* (1932; *The Revolver with White Hair*) and a new one, dedicated to Suzanne Césaire.

The same issue contained the philosopher René Ménil's "Introduction au merveilleux" ("Introduction to the Marvelous"), whose very title situates it in the surrealist framework. Ménil stressed the vitality of two literary forms, the tale and the poem, reading them as manifestations of mankind's continued aspiration toward the marvelous. Without actually citing Breton, he paraphrased the credo from the *Second manifeste du surréalisme* (1930; *Second Manifesto of Surrealism*) that, in the world of wonder, opposites cease to be perceived as mutually exclusive. The article itself could have been written by Breton. However, a short but telling introductory note, emblematic of the entire group's stance, distinguished it, and all of *Tropiques* for that matter, from its European counterparts, in the exhortation addressed to Caribbean writers to look for their identity by rediscovering their indigenous literature: "Martinican Narcissus, where then will you recognize yourself? Focus your gaze in the mirror of the marvelous: your stories, your legends, your songs" (*Tropiques,* October 1941, p. 7).

To the extent that surrealism sought to put mankind in touch with its deepest, repressed desires, the *négritude* contributors to *Tropiques* enthusiastically espoused its methods and goals. But they also understood that alienation could be overcome only through a revitalization of the autochthonous. The same reasons led to Césaire's 1956 resignation from the French Communist party, which he had come to consider unable adequately to address Martinican specificity. To Maurice Thorez, the party chairman, he wrote: "My concept of the universal is that of a universal rich in all the particular . . . coexistence of all the particulars" (*Les écrits d'Aimé Césaire,* p. 367). And in its juxtaposition of such heterogeneous articles as "Les dénominations génériques des végétaux aux Antilles françaises" ("Generic Plant Names in the French Antilles"), "Réflexions sur quelques phénomènes de mimétisme" ("Reflections on Some Phenomena of Mimicry"), "L'idéologie de Vichy contre la pensée française" ("Vichy Ideology against French Thought"), "Note sur le hasard" ("Note on Chance"), "Que signifie pour nous l'Afrique?" ("What Does Africa Mean to Us?"), "Note sur la pratique de l'hindouisme" ("Note on the Practice of Hinduism"), "Horace, poète bi-millénaire et l'art social" ("Horace, Two-Thousand-Year-Old Poet and Social Art"), "Contes créoles" ("Creole Tales"), plus numerous poems or texts on or by Breton, Césaire, Lautréamont, Mallarmé, Charles Péguy, McKay, and Francis Picabia, *Tropiques* spoke both to the particularity of the Martinican experience and to the universality of the surrealist experience, thereby releasing something new and unknown that surpassed both and gave birth to an authentic and unmystified Antillean cultural consciousness.

Tropiques ceased publication when the war ended in 1945. Political action was now called for. To his surprise, Césaire was immediately catapulted into active political life, simultaneously elected mayor of Fort-de-France and the island's representative to the National Assembly, positions he has held ever since. He cosponsored the bill that in 1946 gave Martinique the dubious status of an overseas département of France. Soon after leaving the Communist party in 1956, he founded Martinique's socialist-leaning Progressive party, with greater responsiveness to local than to global issues.

Césaire has continued to write despite his heavy political commitments: four volumes of poetry: *Soleil cou coupé* (1948; *Solar Throat Slashed*), *Corps perdu* (1950; *Lost Body*), *Ferrements* (1960; *Ferraments*), and *Noria* (1976); an accusatory essay titled *Discours sur le colonialisme* (1955; *Discourse on Colonialism*); a full-length historical study of the Revolutionary Haitian hero, *Toussaint-Louverture* (1962); three plays dealing with decolonization: *La tragédie du roi Christophe* (1963; *King Christophe's Tragedy*), *Une saison au Congo* (1965; *A Season in the Congo*), and *Une tempête* (1969; *A Tempest*); and numerous essays. All of these demonstrate Césaire's unique blend of lofty poetic innovation, passion for social justice, erudition, and black authenticity.

Césaire has worked diligently for an autonomous Martinique since 1939. It is a poignant comment on his original vision in the *Cahier* that he continues to strive for this goal despite the obstacles of bureaucracy, mediocrity, racism, unemployment, fear, poverty, illiteracy, and indifference. Only such a poetic alchemist as Césaire could continue to make the uses of such adversity powerful.

See also 1924, 1933 (February), 1968 (February).

Bibliography: A. James Arnold, *Modernism and Negritude: The Poetry and Poetics of Aimé Césaire* (Cambridge, Mass.: Harvard University Press, 1981). André Breton and André Masson, *Martinique charmeuse de serpents* (Paris: Sagittaire, 1948). Aimé Césaire, *Cahier d'un retour au pays natal* (*Notebook of a Return to the Native Land*), in *The Collected Poetry* (*1939–1976*), trans. Clayton Eshleman and Annette Smith (bilingual edition) (Berkeley: University of California Press, 1983). Césaire, "Lettre à Lilyan Kesteloot," in Lilyan Kesteloot, *Aimé Césaire* (Paris: Seghers, 1962). Césaire, *Lettre à Maurice Thorez*, in *Les écrits d'Aimé Césaire: Bibliographie commentée*, ed. Thomas Hale (Montréal: Presses de l'Université de Montréal, 1978). Césaire, *Oeuvres complètes*, 3 vols. (Fort-de-France, Martinique: Désormeaux, 1976). Aimé Césaire and René Ménil, eds., *Tropiques* (1941–1945), 2 vols. (Paris: Jean-Michel Place, 1978). René Ménil, "Introduction au merveilleux," in Césaire and Ménil, *Tropiques*, no. 3, 1:7–16. Ronnie Scharfman, *Engagement and the Language of the Subject in the Poetry of Aimé Césaire* (Gainesville: University of Florida Press, 1987).

Ronnie Scharfman

✑ 1940–1944

During the German Occupation, the Resistance Finds a Voice in Clandestine Poetry

The Honor of Poets

"Never have we been so free," Sartre wrote rather startlingly in 1944, "as under the German occupation" ("La république du silence" ["The Republic of Silence"], in *Situations, III,* p. 11). It might likewise be said that rarely had the French been such poets. When France was abruptly torn from the grandeur of its past and its apparent security, when time itself seemed wrenched off its hinges, when nothing could be taken for granted except deprivation, humiliation, and the likelihood of imprisonment and death—when, as Sartre recalled, just to utter an honest sentence constituted a resolute exercise of freedom in the face of tyranny, and when to speak such a sentence in French was an expression of national solidarity—poetry experienced a renaissance. "Everyone is a poet today," said the directors of the then clandestine publishing house Les Editions de Minuit, in the introduction to *L'honneur des poètes* (1943; *The Honor of Poets*), a collection of Resistance poetry.

Some writers turned to poetry during the war as a means of getting around the censors. Novelists became poets. Former poets began writing verse again when they realized how eagerly poetry was being received. And a chorus of new poetic voices made itself heard. But the purpose of the numerous poetry journals founded during the war was not so much to launch a new generation of poets equal in importance to the Romantics, the symbolists, or the surrealists as simply to ensure that in this time of emergency certain things be said, against all odds, by students, by underground fighters, by prisoners of war, by those deported. There was ample reason to conceal or disguise the identity of these patriotic authors, but in an important sense their names did not matter. What counted was the defiant affirmation of an ineradicable cultural tradition, rooted in the soil of the nation. Louis Aragon, removed from his former iconoclastic surrealism, returned to forms and rhythms long ingrained in the French language, writing verses reminiscent of Chrétien de Troyes, Charles d'Orléans, Agrippa d'Aubigné, Guillaume Apollinaire, and Paul Verlaine. Among the poems collected after the war in his *La diane française* (1945; *Reveille in France*) is the long and lyrical "Le conscrit des cent villages" (1942; "The Conscript from a Hundred Villages"), fashioned almost entirely out of the "beloved names" of French villages (*Les yeux d'Elsa* [*Elsa's Eyes*], p. 214):

> Adieu Forléans Marimbault
> Vollore-Ville Volmerange
> Avize Avoine Vallerange
> Ainval-Septoutre Mongibaud
>
> Fains-la-Folie Aumur Andance
> Guillaume-Peyrouse Escarmin
> Dancevoir Parmilieu Parmain
> Linthes-Pleurs Caresse Abondance

Robert Desnos, another witty and daring surrealist, wrote in measured alexandrines during his last months at Auschwitz and Terezin. And Paul Eluard, celebrating France's liberation in "Liberté" (1944; "Liberty"), employed the familiar cadences of devotional poetry (*Oeuvres complètes*, 1 : 1105):

> On my schoolboy's books
> On my desk and the trees
> On the sand on the snow
> I write your name
>
> . . .
>
> On all willing flesh
> On the brow of my friends
> On every hand outstretched
> I write your name
>
> . . .
>
> Liberty

Earlier, in answer to the notices plastered on walls all over France by the occupying forces—giving orders, making threats, announcing the names of hostages killed—and in memory of Georges Dudach, a Communist journalist shot by the Germans, Eluard wrote this "Avis" (1942; "Notice," in *Oeuvres complètes*, 1 : 1253):

The night before his death
Was the shortest of his life
The thought he still lived
Boiled the blood in his veins
His flesh was too heavy
His strength made him groan
In the depths of this horror
He started to smile
He had not ONE friend
But millions upon millions
To rise up in vengeance
And day dawned for him.

Poets began to organize immediately after the Vichy armistice, well before there was any Resistance properly speaking. In September 1940 Pierre Seghers inaugurated the monthly journal *Poésie* from Villeneuve-lès-Avignon, in the nonoccupied zone. Traveling to Carcassonne, he met Aragon and Elsa Triolet, who had taken refuge there with other intellectuals. Aragon read Seghers the manuscript of "Les lilas et les roses" (1940; "The Lilacs and the Roses")—a sorrowful commemoration of the spring they had just survived (in *Le crève-coeur* [*The Heartbreaker*], p. 45):

O blossoming month, metamorphosis month
Cloudless May, June knifed
I'll never forget the lilacs or the roses
Or those for whom springtime was a shroud . . .

Aragon agreed to help Seghers with *Poésie;* they thought of it as the medium of a "conspiracy" of writers. Before the end of the year, Seghers had made contact with Eluard and with Pierre Jean Jouve. Pierre Emmanuel and Loÿs Masson gave him their current poetry. Other journals were being born: Max-Pol Fouchet launched *Fontaine* in Algiers, where, a year later, Jean Amrouche inaugurated *L'arche* (*The Ark*); in Lyons, René Tavernier revived *Confluences*. But individual poems also passed from hand to hand in the form of illicit tracts or leaflets. The verses published at the end of the war in *La diane française* or in Eluard's *Au rendez-vous allemand* (1944; *Rendezvous with the Germans*) had been printed numerous times during the preceding years in underground journals, learned by heart all over France by refugees and partisans, recited and sung over Allied radio stations, received abroad by exiles and foreign friends of France.

Just to obtain paper was difficult. Printers stole type from Nazi-controlled newspapers. Poems printed outside France were parachuted along with arms and medicine. Distributors of *Les lettres françaises* (the clandestine journal of the National Committee of Writers) stuffed 1,500 envelopes every month, mailed them from 100 different mailboxes, and gave out over 10,000 additional copies to networks of teachers, students, and doctors to distribute. Soliciting and collecting texts was hard, risky work. Aragon had to keep on the move to elude the authorities and, eventually, like Loÿs Masson, was obliged to live in hiding.

Jean Cassou, writer and art historian, spent eighteen months in jail in Toulouse for anti-Vichy propaganda. Scarcely had the first mimeographed issue of *Les lettres françaises* been distributed than Jacques Decour, one of its founders, was arrested and shot. The commitment of writers persisted undiminished; no other occupied country saw so great a literary output during the war years as did France.

The surrealist poet Benjamin Péret took a dim view of this productivity. In *Le déshonneur des poètes* (1945; *The Dishonor of Poets*), a diatribe written in Mexico, he compared Resistance poetry to ads for pharmaceuticals. Not that Péret was not in complete sympathy with the antifascist struggle. It was the relation between action and poetry (between literature and La France, between writing and the fatherland) that he construed differently from his former surrealist friends Aragon and Eluard. Indeed, even Cassou, who kept himself going during his months of solitary confinement by composing sonnets—in his head, for he was allowed nothing to write with—is reported to have said later that his *Trente-trois sonnets composés au secret* (1944; *Thirty-three Sonnets Written in Confinement*) were of no importance: what mattered was the physical struggle, the acts of sabotage he committed before his arrest. He composed poetry in the Resistance but never considered that it was as a poet that he had been a partisan. René Char felt it *was* as a poet that he fought (he commanded a section of the clandestine armed Resistance in the Basses-Alpes); but he believed he was true to poetry by taking up arms and by *not* producing any poem. A number of poets seem to have felt likewise that the meaning of their poetry after 1940 lay in its interruption. When Seghers invited René Lacôte to contribute to *Poésie*, the latter replied: "I've read your letter and frankly I must answer you that I couldn't be less sympathetic. My literary attitude under the current circumstances can be expressed only by silence" (quoted in Seghers, *La Résistance et ses poètes* [1974; *The Resistance and Its Poets*], p. 384). When human history, wrote Char, undergoes the icy assault of an evil based in the most disreputable aspects of human nature, the poet, at the very eye of this hurricane, will "complete the sense of his message by the refusal of himself, and then he will join the ranks of those who, having removed from suffering its mask of legitimacy, guarantee the eternal return of the obstinate burden-bearer, the ferryman of justice" (*Seuls demeurent* [1945; *They Alone Remain*], in *Fureur et mystère* [1948; *Furor and Mystery*], p. 91). A brushfire, he said, might just as well have been the publisher of the notes he kept while engaged in combat: *Feuillets d'Hypnos* (1946; *Leaves of Hypnos*) could have been no one's or anyone's, he went on; the bloody events they intermittently documented reduced their importance to nothing. But then again, the battlefield that definitely is *not* that of poetry may well—through a paradox characteristic of all Char's art and thought—be the very terrain that poetry transfigures: "In our darkness there is not one place for Beauty. The whole place is for Beauty" (*Feuillets d'Hypnos*, in *Fureur et mystère*, p. 160).

Char refused to publish anything during the occupation. So did Pierre Reverdy. So did the young René Leynaud, a fighter in the Combat network of the Lyons region, who was murdered by the Germans in 1944 and in whose honor Francis Ponge composed "Baptême funèbre" (1945; "Funeral Baptism"): Leynaud was a man so close to perfection, Ponge wrote, that his friends never felt much like talking about him, or about anything at all in his presence, and of his silence now, his definitive absence, his martyrdom, "HOW CAN I SPEAK?" (*Lyres,* p. 26). "I've often wondered," Leynaud wrote to Albert Camus, "if I didn't practice poetry in order to demonstrate to myself that I wasn't a poet . . . Sometimes I feel disgust for poetry, my deep passion" (quoted in Seghers, *La Résistance,* p. 387).

Péret's objections to the poetry of the Resistance bore primarily on its patriotic nationalism and its edifying religiosity. With scorn he quoted Masson: "Christ, grant that my prayer gather strength from deep roots" (*Le déshonneur,* p. 21). And Emmanuel (pp. 22–23):

> O France seamless robe of faith
> Soiled by traitors' feet and by spit
>
> . . .
>
> O robe of hope's purest linen
>
> . . .
>
> You are ever the sole vestment of those
> Who know the price of nakedness before God.

Such pious effusions dishonor poetry, Péret thought; such "relevance" is ludicrous. Poetry is not useful and does not "apply" any more than fantasies are airy distractions. It is upheaval, revolt, and blasphemy through and through. Not a profession of faith or a social program, but a risk, man's disequilibrium. Specific events in history may well call upon poets, as upon everyone else, to fight; but poetry must not confuse its cause with the battles of any nation or of any party. If a poet mixes up the terrain of poetry with that of social action, he will simply cease to be a poet, which is to say a revolutionary. In Péret's view, Guillaume Apollinaire made a sad mistake when he took World War I for a poetic subject, and the "poets" of the Resistance simply perpetuated his error.

Ponge found a really perfect subject for poetry, he thought, in soap—a commodity notoriously hard to come by during the Occupation. So, in the rare free moments his Resistance activities allowed him, he worked at providing himself and others with *Le savon* (*Soap*). By the end of the war he had accumulated quite a thick dossier; he finally finished *Le savon* in 1967 when invited to contribute a text to be read on a German radio station. In 1942 he had written a much briefer poem in praise of "La lessiveuse" ("The Washtub"). Masson, Jouve, Emmanuel, and others wrote about mankind's redemption; the "spiritual purity of man" was a frequent theme in Resistance poetry. Ponge had a related concern, although he also preferred to wash his hands of "purification" and "nakedness before God." He had, he said, a violent yen to get clean. Surely he meant: to eliminate injustice and (he would scarcely make the distinction) sloppy rhetoric, which repelled him at least as much as it did Péret. *Le savon,* however, is nothing if not useful ("la toilette intellectuelle" requires it); *Le savon* applies. And effusiveness—a bubbly, frothy lather—is the rigorously appropriate result. A brisk rinsing process, when *Le savon* has had its extravagantly luxuriant say, leaves all about its readers (its users) a delicately perfumed polish: in the name of what, after all, if not such elegantly agreeable propriety, would a Frenchman—and a revolutionary—Ponge cheerfully inquires, fight, and write?

See also 1937 (12 July), 1966.

Bibliography: Louis Aragon, *Le crève-coeur* (Paris: Gallimard, 1946). Aragon, *Les yeux d'Elsa suivi de La diane française* (Paris: Seghers, 1968; quotation reprinted with permission from Editions Robert Laffont). René Char, *Fureur et mystère* (Paris: Gallimard, 1948), Char, *Leaves of Hypnos,* trans. Cid Corman (New York: Grossman, 1978). Paul Eluard, *Oeuvres complètes,* ed. Lucien Scheler, 2 vols. (Paris: Gallimard, 1968; quotations reprinted with permission from Editions de Minuit). Ian Higgins, ed., *Anthology of Second World War French Poetry* (London: Methuen Educational, 1982). Louis Parrot, *L'intelligence en guerre* (Paris: La Jeune Parque, 1945). Benjamin Péret, *Le déshonneur des poètes* (Mexico City: Poésie et Révolution, 1945). Francis Ponge, *Lyres,* vol. 1 of *Le grand recueil* (Paris: Gallimard, 1961). Ponge, *Soap,* trans. Lane Dunlop (London: Cape, 1969). Jean-Paul Sartre, "La république du silence," in *Situations, III* (Paris: Gallimard, 1949). Pierre Seghers, *La Résistance et ses poètes* (Paris: Seghers, 1974). Allan Stoekl, "Ponge's Photographic Rhetoric," in *Politics, Writing, Mutilation: The Cases of Bataille, Blanchot, Roussel, Leiris, and Ponge* (Minneapolis: University of Minnesota Press, 1985).

Ann Smock

✍ 1941
Maurice Blanchot Reviews Jean Paulhan's Enigmatic *Les fleurs de Tarbes*

How Is Literature Possible?

At the start of World War II, in France, a literary exchange whose importance went relatively unnoticed took place between two writers, Maurice Blanchot and Jean Paulhan. The circumstances of their meeting and the story of their ensuing relationship are fascinating enough from a literary historical point of view. On a purely textual and theoretical level, this encounter produced an important contribution to the debate of the 1940s in France on the status of literature, and it had a profound impact on the subsequent evolution of Blanchot's literary criticism. It came as Paulhan was about to publish what was to become his most celebrated work, *Les fleurs de Tarbes, ou la Terreur dans les lettres* (1941; *The Flowers of Tarbes, or Terror in Literature*), a significant enough occasion in itself to provide Blanchot with an opportunity to publish his first independent literary critical essay, *Comment la littérature est-elle possible?* (1942; *How Is Literature Possible?*), a review of Paulhan's book. The essay originally appeared as a series of three articles in *Le journal des débats* in October, November, and December 1941. In the first article Blanchot makes an explicit claim, edited out of the subsequent version, that Paulhan's book is nothing less than "one of the most important works of contemporary literary criticism."

Paulhan had been promising his book ever since 1925, when he first mentioned its imminent appearance in a letter to Francis Ponge, and he clearly reveled in the suspense generated by its anticipation. A reader expecting to find a work of great profundity and seriousness would, in light of this anticipation, be somewhat disappointed. *Les fleurs de Tarbes* seems to be merely another exposition of a set of obsessive concerns that pervade Paulhan's oeuvre, from his earliest essays on Malagasy proverbs to his late texts of the 1960s—concerns that could briefly be described as a lifelong meditation on the uncertain, paradoxical nature of language. Despite its long incubation, *Les fleurs de Tarbes* in no way represents the culmination of a painstaking theoretical labor. Its construction seems to owe more to collage than to any careful architectural plan; its examples are drawn indiscriminately from literature and ordinary language; and its tone is light and playful. The book, Paulhan admitted, is not even finished, and he was never to produce the promised sequel. Like all Paulhan's works, it is an opuscule rather than an opus, and it seems merely to repeat and to reformulate questions already dealt with in *Jacob Cow le pirate, ou si les mots sont des signes* (1921; *Jacob Cow the Pirate, or If Words Are Signs*) and in *Entretien sur des faits divers* (1910–1945; *Conversation about Miscellaneous News Items*). Small wonder, then, that Jean-Paul Sartre should have seen in Paulhan nothing but "obscurity" and an "irritating veneer" (*Situations, I,* p. 174). So why should Blanchot have been led to make such exaggerated claims about the work?

Paulhan had been chief editor of *La nouvelle revue française* since Jacques Rivière's death in 1925, and he quickly established a reputation as the éminence grise of French literature during the period between the wars. We now know that he rarely limited his role to that of a promoter of new authors, but that he also lent them an unusual amount of intellectual, moral, and even—in the case of Antonin Artaud—financial support. Yet he preferred to confine his own writings to the margins of the main literary and linguistic developments of the period, and we might speculate as to whether or not this self-effacing modesty was a deliberate strategy that permitted a subtly effective theoretical engagement with contemporary writers. In a later, commemorative essay after Paulhan's death in 1968 ("La facilité de mourir," 1969; "The Ease of Dying"), Blanchot reflected on Paulhan's marked tendency to publish his books during wartime and suggested that it was "perhaps to leave them in the margins of time; or perhaps because we all need this vast lack that frees us from everyday literary society, so that even the act of publishing in our own name, in a time outside of time, still leaves us anonymous, or allows us, without too much immodesty, to hope to become so" (*L'amitié* [*Friendship*], p. 172). Indeed, in the years before and during the war Paulhan published a number of crucial theoretical texts besides *Les fleurs de Tarbes,* such as "La rhétorique renaît de ses cendres" (1938; "Rhetoric Is Reborn from Its Ashes") and *Clef de la poésie* (1944; *Poetry's Key*). All focus on the same fundamental, almost Heideggerian question of the essence of literature. Toward the beginning of *Les fleurs de Tarbes* Paulhan poses the question explicitly as "this childish question: 'What is literature?'— childish, but one that we spend our whole life avoiding" (p. 24). The title of Blanchot's essay on the book, "Comment la littérature est-elle possible?" can thus be read quite literally as a return to the "childish" question with which Paulhan's book concerns itself.

In *Les fleurs de Tarbes* Paulhan discusses the two diametrically opposed conceptions of language and literature that he considers to have structured literary history since the French Revolution, which he calls "la Terreur" (Terror) and "la Rhétorique" (Rhetoric). The reference to the period of executions carried out by the Committee of Public Safety in 1793 and 1794 underlines the dramatic shift that Paulhan finds in French literature from pre-Revolutionary classicism, when writers submitted happily to the various rules imposed by traditions of genre and rhetorical composition, to Romanticism, whose "terrorism" consisted in abandoning accepted literary form in search of a more authentic, original expressiveness. In short, Terror is the precedence of thought over language, and Rhetoric the priority of language over thought. For Paulhan, the rift is by no means confined to this one turbulent moment in French history, since the persistence of the antagonism between "terrorists" (writers such as Arthur Rimbaud, Guillaume Apollinaire, and Paul Eluard) and "rhetoricians" (Paulhan's examples include Théophile Gautier, Paul Valéry, and Léon-Paul Fargue) is an indication that the question "What is literature?" transcends its specific historical manifestations.

The most immediate answer to this question is provided by the terrorists (or "misologues"—word-haters—as Paulhan refers to them at one point in *Les fleurs de Tarbes*). According to terrorist writers, an excessive concern with language inhibits the potential of literature to be what it is capable of, in all its innovative creativity. Terror is literature that rejects all literary commonplaces and conventions in an attempt to reach a perfectly authentic expression (as in Rimbaud's rejection of the "poetic oldfashionedness" of his literary predecessors). Paulhan unmasks the futility of this ambition by showing that terrorist writers are victims of an optical illusion, since they are in fact endlessly preoccupied with their language, forever trying to rid it of the impurities of commonplace expressions. Paulhan's fondness for exposing these kinds of perceptual errors is already apparent in *Entretien sur des faits divers,* where he discusses a whole series of similar illusions, such as the illusion of totality (by which one deduces the whole from a part) or the illusion of a "prediction of the past" (by which one establishes the motive, or cause, after the event or effect). The terrorists want their language to be transparent, like a window, but its inevitably refracting, distorting quality shows it to be necessarily rhetorical.

This paradox becomes clearer in the context of the little allegorical narrative that frames *Les fleurs de Tarbes* and gives it its title. A notice at the entrance to the public garden in Tarbes is something of a terrorist slogan: "IT IS FORBIDDEN TO ENTER THE GARDEN CARRYING FLOWERS" (p. 24). As the story goes, the sign was erected by the keeper of the garden (which is the "garden of literature") to prevent people from taking the flowers (the flowers of rhetoric or literary commonplaces) and claiming they had brought them into the garden with them. But some visitors are determined to carry flowers and find several ways around this interdiction, which correspond to the different "alibis" that authors give when confronted with the accusation of theft; for example, they carry ever more exotic flowers (the claim to a perpetual originality), or they say the flowers just fell into their hair from the trees (the denial of authorial responsibility). The keeper's ban fails to solve the problem. As Paulhan explains, it is merely compounded, since the visitors' continuous ingenuity makes it increasingly difficult to determine whether the flowers are their own or are stolen public property. The fundamental paradox of the book, then, is: how can we tell whether the authors intend their words to be read as commonplaces or as original thoughts? Commonplaces thus become for Paulhan symptomatic of a deep-seated tension within language and literature and, far from being common are, as Blanchot rightly points out, monsters of ambiguity.

Paulhan apparently resolves the paradox by turning back—in a reversal typical of the ending of many of his texts—to rhetoric. From the point of view of rhetoric, the author is freed from a constant preoccupation with language precisely by submitting to the authority of commonplaces. In order to have a renewed contact with the "virgin newness of things" (*Les fleurs de Tarbes,* p. 164), authors should mutually agree to recognize clichés *as* clichés, thereby instituting a common, communally agreed upon rhetoric as a means of resolving the perplexing ambiguity that characterizes commonplace expressions. The solution is thus a redoubled or, as Paulhan says, a "reinvented" rhetoric, and in his essay Blanchot likens this reversal at the end to a Copernican revolution, whereby thought, in order to rediscover its authenticity, is made to revolve around and be dependent on the constant gravitational pull of language. Accordingly, the allegory is concluded when the sign at the entrance to the garden is changed to "IT IS FORBIDDEN TO ENTER THE GARDEN WITHOUT CARRYING FLOWERS" (*Les fleurs de Tarbes,* p. 165). The visitors, too burdened with their own flowers, will not even think of stealing the public ones.

The allegory does not, however, close the book, which in fact ends with the enigmatic retraction: "Let's just say I said nothing" (p. 168). These words remove any sense of comfortable completion and force the reader to reconsider the status of Paulhan's text. As Blanchot puts it, a second, "secret" book seems to have written itself despite Paulhan's best intentions, one that starts to work on the reader once the "first" book has been finished. According to Blanchot, "It is only through the uneasiness and anxiety we feel that we are authorized to communicate with the larger questions he poses, and he is prepared to show us these questions only by their absence" (*Comment la littérature,* p. 16). How are we to read the book's ultimate disavowal? Is it to be taken literally, as an authentic expression of the author's feelings? But then how could the book be "nothing," since in that case we could not even read the final sentence? Or is it to be read figuratively as something that is just said, a cliché, a careless, throwaway remark? But then was the whole book composed in an equally negligent fashion? In Paulhan's own terms, it is strictly undecidable. The book is thus a performance of the very radical ambiguity he talks about, an ambiguity that is not simply an equivocation about *what* the book is saying, but that suspends it between saying and doing, stating and performing—between

Terror and Rhetoric. As Blanchot says of the conclusion, Paulhan "factors in this equivocation and does not attempt to dispel it" (p. 25).

In his essay Blanchot is highly attentive to this "nothing" and this radical undecidability. For him, the "nothing" is the reappearance and reaffirmation of the Terror that Paulhan's "first" book so carefully discredited. A reinvented Terror, to be sure, but one that is for Blanchot the very "soul" of literature. It testifies to the persistence of literature's claim to authenticity and originality despite the demonstrated impossibility of this claim (since it is always preempted by rhetoric). Blanchot goes on to make what may seem a surprising comparison between Paulhan and Stéphane Mallarmé: one could hardly imagine two forms of language more different from each other than Paulhan's everyday, vulgar style and Mallarmé's exalted and very difficult poetry. But Mallarmé, too, acknowledged an essential absence at the heart of literature. His poetry attempts to allow this pure negativity to come into play by a simultaneous denial of both language and its referents. Paulhan's reinvented Terror, though expressed in more mundane language, is animated by a similar aspiration toward absolute perfection, and the two authors converge, for Blanchot, in their insistence on literature's radical impossibility as constituting literature's defining characteristic, or even, paradoxically, its condition of possibility.

Once we begin to take into account the evolution of Blanchot's own critical concerns, it becomes clear how powerfully his encounter with the writing of Paulhan affected his own work. Mallarmé is one of the writers to whom Blanchot obsessively returns, and his pairing of Mallarmé and Paulhan makes them equally important sources of an oeuvre that is generally considered to be one of the profoundest meditations of our age on the radical negativity of language. This influence is apparent in Blanchot's most important theoretical statement of the 1940s, "La littérature et le droit à la mort" (1949; "Literature and the Right to Death"), which starts out with the proposition that literature only truly begins with its own radical self-interrogation, then focuses on the period of the Terror in its discussion of literature and revolution, and toward the end states that "literature is language turning into ambiguity" (*The Gaze of Orpheus*, p. 59). What better description could we have of *Les fleurs de Tarbes?*

Paulhan, however, would be the first to deny that his book, as some critics have claimed, is an inauguration of modern literary theory. For the paradoxical originality of *Les fleurs de Tarbes* is to show, in a deceptively naïve manner, that the very distinction between original and commonplace is a radically undecidable one. Many of the commonplaces of contemporary literary theory are already discernible in Paulhan's text: the need to account for the rhetorical dimension of language, the focus on the perplexing ambiguities in literary texts, the problematic nature of citations, and the transfer of linguistic structures to the study of literature, psychology, cultural phenomena, history, and metaphysics. Yet it is all too easy to read these critical commonplaces *as* commonplaces, which, in Paulhan's terms, is no longer to read critically. Paulhan's continual reaffirmation of Terror in literature implicates the reader and the writer equally, and warns us of how relentlessly vigilant an activity reading, as well as writing, has to be.

Blanchot's article on *Les fleurs de Tarbes,* the first of several on Paulhan's texts, is one such exemplary instance of a truly critical reading.

Bibliography: Yvon Belaval, ed., *Cahiers Jean Paulhan 3* (Paris: Gallimard, 1984). Jacques Bersani, ed., *Jean Paulhan le souterrain* (Paris: Union Générale d'Edition, 1976). Maurice Blanchot, *Comment la littérature est-elle possible?* (Paris: José Corti, 1942). Blanchot, "La facilité de mourir," in *L'amitié* (Paris: Gallimard, 1972). Blanchot, "Literature and the Right to Death," in *The Gaze of Orpheus and Other Literary Essays,* ed. P. Adams Sitney, trans. Lydia Davis (Tarrytown, N.Y.: Station Hill Press, 1981). Paul de Man, "Impersonality in the Criticism of Maurice Blanchot," in *Blindness and Insight: Essays in the Rhetoric of Contemporary Criticism,* 2d ed. (Minneapolis: University of Minnesota Press, 1983). Maurice-Jean Lefebve, *Jean Paulhan: Une philosophie et une pratique de l'expression et de la réflexion* (Paris: Gallimard, 1949). Jean Paulhan, *Les fleurs de Tarbes, ou la Terreur dans les lettres* (Paris: Gallimard, 1941). Paulhan, *Oeuvres,* ed. Jean-Claude Zylberstein, 5 vols. (Paris: Cercle du Livre Précieux, 1966–1970). Jean-Paul Sartre, *Situations, I* (Paris: Gallimard, 1947).

Michael Syrotinski

✐ 1942

Lucien Febvre Publishes *Le problème de l'incroyance au seizième siècle: La religion de Rabelais*

The Problem of Belief

In 1929 Lucien Febvre (1878–1956), a professor of history at the University of Strasbourg, founded, with Marc Bloch of the same faculty, the journal *Annales d'histoire sociale et économique* (Annals of social and economic history). During a sea voyage to Brazil some years later, Febvre met a young man, Fernand Braudel (1902–1985), who expressed great enthusiasm about the new history polemically advanced by the *Annales* against the dominant mode of event-filled, politically oriented historiography. The two men were attracted to each other at this first meeting almost as father and son, Braudel later wrote. When Braudel returned to Paris in 1938 he began collaborating with the *Annales,* doing some of the book reviews.

Then came the war. Braudel was mobilized, captured, and imprisoned in Germany. Marc Bloch, a Jew, went to southern France and eventually joined the Resistance. The *Annales,* which had not yet attained academic respectability, began to wither as the war tightened its grip. Febvre, in semiretirement at his home in Franche-Comté from the languishing Collège de France in Paris (occupied by the Germans), returned to an old project: what was the character of the beliefs of the protean Renaissance writer François Rabelais? The result was *Le problème de l'incroyance au seizième siècle: La religion de Rabelais* (1942; *The Problem of Unbelief in the Sixteenth Century: The Religion of Rabelais*).

For Abel Lefranc, dean of the Rabelaisian scholars in the 1930s, Rabelais was an atheist and hence a modern man, a rationalist. Febvre disagreed. Is it surprising that in 1942, amid the carnage of World War II, he decided that one way to demonstrate the error of Lefranc and those who followed him was to discuss Rabelais's ideas of life and death?

To argue that Rabelais was an atheist because he believed that life entirely dissolved at death was to "distort . . . certain words in the language of the sixteenth century," Febvre wrote (*Problem*, p. 197). The verb "to die," for example, did not signify a total extinction of body and soul. The body, it is true, was conceived in the 16th century as "subject to annihilation." In Gargantua's letter to his son Pantagruel, Rabelais defined death as "the bringing to naught of that so stately frame and plasmature, wherein man was first created" (quoted in *Problem*, p. 198). But although "man dies wholly," Febvre suggests, Rabelais does not mean that he dies "irrevocably." Even as he forsakes a precarious life here below, man "knows he will be reborn, if God wishes, to true life, life eternal. It is," concludes Febvre, "a magnificent hope" (pp. 197–199).

According to Febvre, his wartime book was not really about Rabelais, but about "the meaning and spirit of the sixteenth century" (p. 1). It was not difficult to show that Abel Lefranc's atheistic interpretation of Rabelais was anachronistic; Febvre's quarry was larger, nothing less than to demolish all perception of Rabelais's time as an era of secular humanism. The 16th century, which after all was the period of the Reformation and Counter-Reformation, was "a century that wanted to believe" (p. 455); it did so in terms that, if they were not always Christian in a perfectly orthodox sense, never went beyond the parameters of medieval Platonic and Aristotelian extensions of Christianity.

When it first appeared, Febvre's book was scarcely a success. But after the war *Le problème de l'incroyance* acquired growing readership and esteem. Today the book is read not only for its rich evocation of the ambiance of Rabelais's writing but also for its way of thinking about culture. That way, now called the history of mentalities, has become dominant among French cultural historians. It was propagated not only by the book but also by the revivified *Annales*, which after 1946 Febvre continued to edit under the significantly revised name *Annales: Economies, sociétés, civilisations*.

Until after World War II the two dominant—and antagonistic—theories of historical knowledge were historicism and positivism. Febvre, who had little taste for theory but much aptitude for methodology, depended epistemologically upon both theories even while frequently attacking their historiographic effects. Under the rubric of positivism, Febvre assaulted historians' complacent tendency to line up "facts" in chronological order without questioning the conceptual schemes determining their selection and definition. Such had been Lefranc's procedure in passing from the "facts" of Rabelais's unbelief in the body's life after death to modern conclusions about living and dying.

Historicist theory represented culture as the emanation of mind. Some historicists have regarded the mental force that creates culture as collective; thus in Johann Gottfried Herder's concept of "folk spirit," the ideational power exhibited by millions of individuals over many generations creates an organically cohesive uniqueness in each great nation, a unified national culture.

Others have formulated this expressive force in more individual terms; in *Le siècle de Louis XIV* (1751; *The Century of Louis XIV*), for example, Voltaire praised the many individual works of "new and remarkable genius" that together gave Louis XIV's age its uniqueness. In either case the central idea was that minds are stimulated primarily by other minds. One man's ideas, one group's ideas, proceed from others. Collectively they create the spirit of an age, somehow combining their individual uniqueness to form an overall uniqueness particular to time and place.

Positivists have generally explained culture as a phenomenon in which the mind shapes and is shaped by its natural and social environment. Usually materialistic and mechanistic rather than spiritualist and organicist in its basic assumptions, positivism played an important role in the marquis de Condorcet's *Esquisse d'un tableau historique des progrès de l'esprit humain* (1794; *Sketch for a Historical Picture of the Progress of the Human Mind*). Condorcet affirmed, among other things, that as time passes, technologies produced by the interaction between mind and matter become a secondary environment, accelerating historical change and creating ever more positive progress. Auguste Comte's idea of culture enlarged upon Condorcet's, representing a humanity that progresses in its search for truth from religion to philosophy to science. In this science-oriented vision of cultural change, ideas develop in continuity from one age to the next, at once supported and propelled forward by successive revelations of the nature of the material world.

There are of course similarities as well as differences between the two theories. But with respect to Febvre's innovative combination of them to create a new approach to cultural history, the paramount difference is between historicism's view of cultural epochs as individual organisms, emphasizing the spiritual origins of ideas, and positivism's tendency to see culture as a mechanical accumulation, emphasizing the material conditions amid which ideas occur.

When Febvre announces in *Le problème de l'incroyance* that his purpose is to define the "meaning and spirit" of Rabelais's times, he begins with a historicist approach. In the first sections he investigates the personal relationships of Rabelais and his friends and rivals, analyzing their early poetic and critical publications, which were full of extravagant moral denunciations and grandiose praise. Febvre is not concerned here to establish Rabelais's place in the development of a more objective and scientific notion of the world. He is interested in the meaning of words: "atheist," "death," "drunkard," "philosopher." Febvre's aim is to establish the boundaries of 16th-century thought, arguing in classic historicist terms that these boundaries were neither broader nor narrower, neither more nor less progressive than those of other eras, but simply incommensurate with them. This incommensurability afforded Rabelais's contemporaries ways of judging and regarding each other that are now lost:

> What was Rabelais like mentally? Something of a buffoon . . . boozing his fill and in the evening writing obscenities? Or perhaps a learned physician, a humanist scholar who filled his prodigious memory with beautiful passages

from the ancients . . . ? Or better yet, a great philosopher, acclaimed as such by the likes of Theodore Beza [Théodore de Bèze] and Louis Le Caron . . . Our ancestors were more fortunate than we are. They did not choose between two images. They accepted them both at the same time, the respectable one along with the other.   (Pp. 94–95)

Against the complacent notion that great men are the antennae of the human species, uncannily predicting the future, Febvre insists that no one is a precursor. Rabelais had two images: he was both exalted and denounced, not because his ideas, eternally true, were loved by the good and hated by the bad people of his time, but rather because his ideas had such resonance that they stimulated people's thoughts in very mixed ways. But it is a mistake even to say that the ideas were "his." They belonged to a common pool of discourse, uttered or half-uttered, generally felt even if scarcely articulated other than by Rabelais. His works are important, Febvre urges, not because they speak beyond their time but because they offer readers broad insight into that era. They oblige the conscientious scholar to unearth Rabelais's sources, to disinter books by the dozens that would be otherwise forgotten, and thus to reconstruct the richness of competing cultural movements, the perplexing panoply of intellectual choices confronting the writer and his contemporaries. The pluralism of this context is matched by its uniqueness, which separates it from all others. What seemed to Lefranc and other positivist historians of literature and culture to be a straight shining arrow leading from Rabelais's time to ours shows cracks and splinters and on closer inspection proves not to be aimed in our direction at all.

In the last section of *Le problème de l'incroyance* Febvre stops reconstructing the boundaries of thought shaping the actions of Rabelais, his mentors, interlocutors, and contemporary critics. Here he formulates new objects of inquiry by adapting the ideas of mental function developed in contemporary social science. He abandons the historicist approach and makes use of such positivist methods as Emile Durkheim's social functionalism and Isaac Meyerson's collective psychology. For these thinkers the mind is a plasmalike stuff apt to receive any and all kinds of experiences, both those that train it to acquire routines and those that assault it with such diversifying effect that it becomes an assortment of dogmatic and incoherent, rigid and flexible attitudes. Mental activity is full of swerves, veering between the search for order and stability and the desire to accommodate every possible stimulus, a desire that leads to and indeed requires some indefiniteness, some mental disarray.

The first of these two tendencies accounts for the rise of technology. Like Condorcet and Comte, Febvre suggests that the course of Western history shows mentality becoming more precise and exacting. Eventually "true" scientific procedures emerge, the experimental method and the critical method. In the 16th century, however, these methods were so poorly developed that "all opinions [were] of equal value," based on little more than "impressions, prejudices, or vague analogies" (p. 462). In this part of *Le problème de l'incroyance,* the second tendency of mind, its flexibility and inchoateness, its intuitive and inventive properties, is portrayed negatively or as a mere reservoir from which useful mental modes emerge.

The idea of culture that came to be called the history of mentalities designates both these tendencies as objects of research: mental attitudes and mental "tools," proclivities or preferences that are mixtures of emotion and thought, floating and flexible, and routines, habits of analysis, means of conceptualization used to implement the proclivities. Febvre explained the way in which a proclivity or mental preference turned into a tool thus: "An idea that seems to men . . . to be a valid explanation of things—and hence is for them confused with truth—is what accords with the technical means available for modifying and predicting the behaviors of those things. These technical means are acquired from the sciences" (p. 357). Febvre repeatedly juxtaposes the 16th and 20th centuries, appealing to readers' commonplace sense of the superior mental tools available to them today rather than discriminating among particular individuals' verbal usages, as in the first sections of his book. This present-minded orientation of his commentaries, with its unquestioning acceptance of science as the measure of truth, is not fundamentally different from Lefranc's.

But Febvre does more than catalogue the strong and weak points of 16th-century sciences. One of his strategies is to displace attention from concepts and experimental procedures to the words used to describe them. He makes a list of abstract substantives that 16th-century philosophers lacked, to show that this handicapped their ability to think about perceptions and experience. The "perfect disorder" of French syntax, its "incoherence" and "lack of perspective," made it difficult to express clearly what they did think. Scholars before Febvre had turned their attention to historical syntax and style; Leo Spitzer and Ferdinand Brunot had done so precisely with reference to Rabelais. But no one until Febvre had used the study of neologisms over the course of an epoch or the analysis of shifts in substantive-verb-adjective relations to define the mind of an age generally. After indicating the lacunae among scientific terms, Febvre formulates the contours shaping mentality in the absence of science. These contours were not only philosophical and theological but also mythic; Febvre indicates, for example, the influence of doctrines of magic and witchcraft upon Christian ideas of the supernatural.

Febvre daringly coordinated very grand with very particular features of language. He wanted to connect the intricacies of style and grammar with nothing less than ideology on one hand and sensory experience on the other. He suggested that different epochs discriminated among sensory experiences in different ways. Rabelais's, Pierre de Ronsard's, and Joachim du Bellay's references to the senses show that "the 16th century did not see first, it heard and smelled, it sniffed the air and caught sounds" (p. 432). The "structure" of their "intellectual equipment" was not the same as ours (p. 424). In another equally suggestive chapter Febvre surveys the material tools available to would-be scientists in Rabelais's time. Instruments to measure time and space exactly, he concludes, not to mention those involving more highly sophisticated mathematical operations, were almost entirely lacking.

Febvre provides bold and wide-ranging generalizations but few examples of these verbal, sensory, and mathematical tools, and those he does provide are exemplified largely by members of elites, particularly the humanist elite. Such a selection would perhaps be appropriate in the biography of a humanist writer, but not in a study discussing the "meaning and spirit" of the 16th century as a whole. There is a glaring lack of attention in this book to the way different mental tools and emotive-intellectual proclivities are apportioned among different social classes, and how they are (and are not) made available to them. Even so, the concluding chapters of *Le problème de l'incroyance* effect the destruction of traditional cultural history as it had been built up since Rabelais's own era by philological study, connoisseurship, the ideological sovereignty of philosophical thought, and the methodological sovereignty of psychic individuation.

How did Febvre accomplish this? In the first chapters, his object of inquiry is the traditional one of relating text to context by connecting the works of Rabelais and his acquaintances to their sources of inspiration and to social, economic, and other circumstances of writing. In the last chapters, the object of inquiry is something intermediate between persons and their inspirations or surroundings: mentality here is not an imputed substance inside the head or beyond the world, and it is also not something embedded in and explainable by material conditions. Mentality is equivalent to its symbolic modes: languages, numbers, gestures, smells and their classification, foods and their preparation, and so on.

The epistemological status of this new object, mentality, is unclear—and that is its forte. It is almost as if Febvre stumbled across it in the course of writing. He had in fact been led toward it by years of enthusiasm for developments in history's sister disciplines, not only Meyerson's psychology and Durkheim's sociology, but also the anthropology developed in the 1920s and 1930s by Marcel Mauss (Paris), Alfred Kroeber (Berkeley), and Alfred Radcliffe-Brown (Oxford). For them, long before Febvre, culture was no longer a special category of human endeavor but a dimension of all behavior, coordinating and coercing daily life in every respect. Just as these anthropologists used a broadened concept of symbols to break away from the old habit of defining "primitive man" by cataloguing his material possessions on one hand and his religious habits on the other, so Febvre employs notions of mental tools and mental impressions to break down the old ways of approaching culture. He combines quantitative and qualitative, spiritualist and materialist approaches purely with an eye to their operative effectiveness, paying no attention to their ideological or theoretical compatibility. A historically changing mentality could henceforth be discovered wherever changes in people's actions take place, which is to say everywhere.

Such a broadly diversified concept of cultural history cried out for imple-

963

mentation in many different directions. Febvre did just this. When he died in 1956, he left behind him a number of research files, notes, and documents called "An Introduction to the Modern French Intellect," which his student and associate Robert Mandrou used to construct his own *Introduction à la France moderne 1500–1640: Essai de psychologie historique* (1961; *Introduction to Modern France, 1500–1640: An Essay in Historical Psychology*). The book's subsections, which Mandrou says reflect Febvre's "research coordinates," include foods and diet, clothing, housing, diseases, remedies, demography, sensations, passions, spoken versus written language, concepts of space and time, concepts of nature and of the environment, marriage, the family, love, sexuality, country versus town parishes, youth societies, feast days, peasant technologies, artisan technologies, economic thought, sports, dancing, gaming, the concept of artist and of artistic style, humanists, the printed book, encyclopedism, the sciences, freethinkers, moralists, pilgrimages, soldiers, escapism, mysticism, witchcraft, suicide. These categories of investigation are both more particular and more general than those of 1942. Pursuing Febvre's ideas about mentality simultaneously specifies and loosens one's ideas of what is relevant to inquiry. This is its advantage over more methodical programs of research. Febvre's approach leaves not only his historical subjects but himself as a historical writer room to dream.

By 1961 a new generation of historians, stimulated by the postwar development of economic and demographic research, had begun to take Febvre's cultural history in a sharply quantitative direction. In an article in *La nouvelle histoire* (1978; *The New History*), an encyclopedic handbook of the innovations introduced by Febvre, his associates, and his heirs in the so-called Annales school, Philippe Ariès defines the "history of mentalities" thus: "Economic facts (prices . . . taxes, credit . . .) influence the daily life of everyone (. . . penury or prosperity, famines, epidemics, mortality rates)." These facts have been sufficiently recorded that "the regular *series* of their quantified distribution allows for a reading of daily life that is not merely anecdotal." Each economic series has its cultural side: no birth, marriage, or death was without its ritual gestures, its gifts, bequests, or denials of obligation to church, state, and family members. The more historians study the adaptations of population groups to the changing circumstances of their economies, the more aware they become that the adaptations are mediated by "an optical system which modifies the real image: the system of mentalities" (pp. 405–409).

Febvre contributed to one example of such quantified cultural history, *L'apparition du livre* (1958; *The Appearance of the Book*), an examination of the influence of printing on 16th-century life generally, which he wrote in collaboration with Henri-Jean Martin and a team of specialists. In this case analysis of the feedback relations between the consumption of printed materials and their appearance, pricing, distribution, and contents generated a cultural history that was automatically massified. It became the history of ordinary rather than exceptional people such as Rabelais. Such history offers no more total cultural history than the history of great men and their ideas, which Febvre wanted to displace. But it did take a step toward unraveling what Febvre in *Le problème de l'incroyance* called "the most important problem" for the historian, the relation of individuality—here the book's creation by an author—to what is socially, collectively composed. In the two generations since the appearance of *Le problème,* the solid forms of mass culture in early modern Europe have emerged in historical description. This concretization of a hitherto shadowy or ignored realm is a grand achievement. More epochal, however, is what inspired the achievement: a vision of culture as composed of junctures between ideas and emotions, rituals and innovations, instruments and their applications, rather than of either the ineffable insights of some special class of nations or individuals or the automatic inventiveness of materially stimulated masses.

Given the parallel developments in the human sciences briefly mentioned here, it clearly would be wrong to claim that Febvre's idea of mentalities, developed in the devastating early years of World War II, was the sole source of the new vision of cultural or "anthropological" history, as it is now frequently termed. To argue that way would distort the insights of 1942 into the collective nature of mentality. They were insights that were lived as well as written about.

Lucien Febvre was sixty-four years old in 1942, well esteemed but essentially out of work as a result of the German occupation. The problem confronting the author of *Le problème de l'incroyance* was how to live in these difficult, destructive conditions; it was how not "wholly" to "die," in spite of being "subject to annihilation."

Febvre's book is dedicated "to Fernand Braudel, in hope." Braudel, the future leader of the Annales group, who would preserve and extend the research programs of its founders, exemplifying and advertising the usefulness of long-term, quantifiable methods in a manner that made Annaliste methods an international cultural force, was writing a thousand-page book in a German prison camp. He wrote from memory. He sent the pages of his manuscript, little by little, to Febvre in Franche-Comté. During five years of war this went on. At the end of it *La Méditerranée et le monde méditerranéen sous Philippe II (The Mediterranean and the Mediterranean World)* was complete. Amid the still worse pressures of a fugitive life, Marc Bloch also worked on a manuscript, *Le métier d'historien* (1946; *The Historian's Craft*), a handbook of Annaliste methods—and hopes—which, though incomplete, was published by Febvre in memory of his friend after Bloch's death at the hands of the Germans in 1944.

In terms of the professional passion to which they had dedicated themselves, World War II was for Febvre, Bloch, and Braudel a nontime. The very idea of a "new kind of history," as Febvre phrased it, must often have seemed absurd. Their research programs were scarcely imaginable because they depended, no less than on archival probes, on scholarly, intellectual, social-scientific exchanges, on free and fearless travel across physical and mental frontiers of every kind. Febvre, Bloch, and Braudel were in this sense equally prisoners of war, heartened in that state of suspension only by the "mentality" engendered during the years of work together, few indeed in Braudel's case, on the *Annales.*

Le problème de l'incroyance au seizième siècle was begun in order to prove that systematic disbelief was impossible in Rabelais's century. It ended by doing something different, exploring less disbelief than the mentalities predisposing people to believe. Underlying this analysis was another, left unsaid: the *need* of people such as Rabelais to believe during an era of warring faiths . . . as Febvre's was in 1942. How to live is how to believe.

See also 1532, 1534 (Fall).

Bibliography: Lucien Febvre, *The Problem of Unbelief in the Sixteenth Century: The Religion of Rabelais,* trans. Beatrice Gottlieb (Cambridge, Mass.: Harvard University Press, 1982). Jacques Le Goff, Roger Chartier, and Jacques Revel, eds., *La nouvelle histoire* (Paris: Retz, 1978). Robert Mandrou, *Introduction to Modern France, 1500–1640: An Essay in Historical Psychology,* trans. R. E. Hallmark (New York: Holmes and Meier, 1975).

Samuel Kinser

✐ *1945, 6 February*
Condemned to Death for His Activities as a Collaborator,
Robert Brasillach Is Executed by Firing Squad

Literature and Collaboration

The Germans abandoned Paris in August 1944 after four years of military occupation. The literary establishment had tolerated, and in some cases even supported, them. Books pointedly favoring collaboration—Henry de Montherlant's meditative *Le solstice de juin* (1941; *The June Solstice*) and Lucien Rebatet's diagnostic *Les décombres* (1942; *The Ruins*) sold well. When people were not reading essays that explained the events, they wanted escapist novels, the longer the better, as long as the paper supply held out: Jean Giono's translation of *Moby-Dick* was a big success. *La nouvelle revue française,* the literary magazine published by Gallimard and the prewar embodiment of all that was prestigious in French letters, continued to publish in occupied Paris. Its owner, Gaston Gallimard, replaced the magazine's previous editor with Pierre Drieu la Rochelle, an irregular supporter of Jacques Doriot's fascist Parti Populaire Français who had remained a member in good standing of the literary elite. Drieu's 1941 *Nouvelle revue française*—as ambivalent as he—contained collaborationist polemics alongside literary criticism by Paul Valéry and André Gide.

France was not occupied in its entirety until 1943. The southern and inland part of the country had retained its own government and was called "Vichy France," with the spa town of Vichy as its capital. Vichy was governed by World War I hero Philippe Pétain, who had signed an armistice with the Germans in 1940 and would come increasingly under the influence of Hitler; finally his "free zone," too, was occupied in 1943. Pétain's government tried all the while to foster the illusion of an autonomous "conservative revolution" based on family, work, fatherland. On the cultural front, Pétain named as minister of education the writer Abel Bonnard, who, in a 12 July 1940 lecture at the Sorbonne, had called for an end to those "morbid, don juanesque prewar novels." Hard-line fascists found Vichy's conservative nationalism soft and ineffectual and preferred the life in Paris; worldly writers who wanted literary life as usual preferred to be in Paris, too. Many Jews and anti-Nazis who could, hid or went into exile.

A specific literary genre, the anti-Semitic pamphlet, had an audience in both zones of France among those who blamed the Jews for France's defeat; it had a champion, dating back to the prewar years, in Louis-Ferdinand Céline (the pen name of Louis-Ferdinand Destouches). When his *Voyage au bout de la nuit* (*Journey to the End of Night*) appeared in 1932, Céline was a literary outsider, a physician working in the impoverished northern suburb of Clichy. His populist verve and epic narration nearly won him the prestigious Prix Goncourt for this first novel; a bitter fight on the Goncourt jury left him with a second-place Prix Renaudot instead. In 1936, enraged at the relatively poor reception of his second novel, the burlesque autobiographical *Mort à crédit* (*Death on the Installment Plan*), Céline embarked on a new career in writing polemics and produced in quick succession the pamphlets *Mea Culpa* (1936; *My Sins*), *Bagatelles pour un massacre* (1937; *Trifles for a Massacre*); *L'école des cadavres* (1938; *School for Corpses*); *Les beaux draps* (1941; *A Pretty Pickle*)—all, with the exception of *Mea Culpa,* anti-Semitic; all violently antiwar, anticommunist, obscene, occasionally rich in syntax, and sometimes very funny. Vichy banned *Les beaux draps,* while in occupied Paris *Bagatelles pour un massacre* and *L'école des cadavres* were reedited with illustrative photos.

Céline was at best an unreliable collaborator and cannot be easily assigned to either the Parisian or the Vichy group. When invited to the German embassy with elegant peers such as Drieu la Rochelle, Céline, dressed as usual like a bum, either sulked in silence or ranted, mocked the food, maligned Hitler. He did not hesitate to ask collaboration officials for favors—supplies of paper and permission to reedit his books—but he refused offers to visit the Reich or to write officially for the pro-German press. He did write vociferous letters to editors of collaborationist newspapers. His pamphlets, and the persona of the pamphlets, made Céline a symbol of evil for the Resistance and an anticipated object of revenge. By the end of the war he was receiving drawings of tombstones in his daily mail. He needed to get quickly to Denmark, where he had stashed some gold, and he had to cross Germany to get there. He left Paris in 1944, soon after the Allied landing in Normandy.

Céline had good reason to fear for his life. The underground Resistance anticipated the official state trials by summary executions, and among its targets were men of the pen and of the press: the Radio-Paris announcer Philippe Henriot fell in June 1944, the racist anthropologist Georges Montandon in July. Soon after Céline reached Denmark his editor, Robert Denoël, was killed in the Place des Invalides while waiting for his car to be towed. Vichy ministers and Parisian fascists—who hoped they had nothing in common and disliked one another intensely—ended up under German protection at Sigmaringen, a castle in Germany. Céline, en route to Denmark, spent four months with them there.

One collaborationist intellectual, Robert Brasillach, did not flee. Though nowhere nearly as important a writer as Céline, he was made to account for all the writers of the collaboration in a way that makes his story exemplary of a civil war in occupied France, of the intellectual life that came before it, and of the new one that came after. Editor of the fascist weekly *Je suis partout* (I am everywhere), Brasillach was a chronicler, a novelist, and a prolific reviewer of literature, film, and theater. He also wrote scholarly books on Virgil and Corneille, and in the last days of the occupation, while his friends worried about summary execution, Brasillach was in the Bibliothèque Nationale working on an anthology of Greek poetry. In the last days of his life, chained in the prison at Fresnes, he finished a critical study of André Chénier, martyr of the French Revolution. He was a cultural entrepreneur of the grandest sort—Céline made fun of Brasillach, saying he wanted to be minister of culture, minister of cinema; and indeed he is supposed to have been offered the job by Vichy, and refused it.

Brasillach was tried on 19 January 1945 and executed by firing squad at the Montrouge fort on 6 February—eleven years to the day after the riots in the Place de la Concorde that he and the German press had dreamed would be the dawn of fascism for all of France. He was thirty-four. Brasillach, in dying by execution, became the exemplary fascist intellectual and in so doing probably saved the lives of the minor intellectual fascists who went on trial after him. For who, other than Brasillach, was available in that angry first month of 1945 to play the symbolic criminal role? Céline was too low-life, too anti-institutional—and, like Brasillach's colleagues at *Je suis partout,* he had left town; Drieu la Rochelle had been too self-hating, melancholic, and ambivalent in his politics: he died by his own hand on the fourth try just as the purge began. Only the young and talented Brasillach could have represented in quite so pure a form the promise of French letters, and in so sincere a form the great political mistake. Nor was it necessary to bring Brasillach to justice; out of patriotism, he had refused to leave France, and he had turned himself in at police headquarters when he learned that his mother and brother-in-law had been taken to jail.

"No sins allowed intellectuals," Charles de Gaulle is supposed to have said when asked why he let Brasillach die despite a petition in his favor signed by fifty-nine French intellectuals, including Albert Camus, Colette, and Paul Valéry; despite a personal visit to de Gaulle by François Mauriac, who, as columnist for the newspaper *Le Figaro,* had taken upon himself the role of great mediator between the Vichy patriots and the patriot resisters.

Brasillach died in 1945 because of what he had written: praise of a Franco-German alliance, condemnations of an allegedly Communist Popular Front and of what he denounced as Jewish pressure to wage war. It is tempting from an American perspective to look for a drama about freedom of speech in Brasillach's story, but misleading in the French context of 1945. The defense of Brasillach by Jacques Isorni was based neither on Brasillach's right of expression nor even on his innocence of physical wrongdoing. It was based first on his talent and then on the relativity of justice. The letters that Isorni used to argue Brasillach's case were literary analyses: Marcel Aymé claimed for him an unrivaled encyclopedic knowledge of French letters; Mauriac read in him the voice of an entire generation; Valéry cited critical talent and originality; Paul Claudel wrote of a talent that honored France. Brasillach was, after all, a product of the Ecole Normale Supérieure, an institution accessible only through rigorous written and oral competition. He said before his trial that he felt as if he was preparing the oral part of an examination. Clearly, talent was not the best defense: the greater Brasillach's literary talent, the greater his betrayal of literature in its mission as keeper of society's truths and arbiter of values. To allow Brasillach to continue to write would be to devalue literature, to render it a thing of no moment or weight. Such a devaluation was unthinkable in the France of 1945, where literature, bound to the restoration of national identity, needed to matter. Literature was not perceived as a freedom but as an act. It was therefore essential to the dignity of literature and the nation that Brasillach's writing be found guilty.

According to the prosecutor, Marcel Reboul, Brasillach had not editorialized; he had *denounced*—denunciation being the worst crime in a country split by civil war—and his denunciations were all the more vile for their *politesse*. "We must strike [*Il faut frapper*]," he had written in 1941, and "What are we waiting for to shoot [*Qu'attend-on pour fusiller*] the jailed Communist representatives?" but he had used not "we" (*nous*) but "one" (*on*) and "it is necessary" (*il faut*), thus lending an academic impersonality to his damning pronouncements. Because two political targets of *Je suis partout*, Georges Mandel and Jean Zay, did die by assassination at the hands of the collaborationist law-and-order squad known as the Milice, prosecutor Reboul claimed an eye for an eye when he asked the postwar jury to condemn Brasillach to death by the liberation government firing squad. Isorni, Brasillach's attorney, could only counterargue the moral ineptness of a court of justice that months before, during the occupation, had defended collaboration much as Brasillach had defended it: as the lesser of evils. Isorni read to the court a Brasillach poem about the prison at Fresnes, where the poet finds the names of Resistance heroes, "fraternal adversaries," so recently scratched on the wall.

There are two kinds of high tragedy in the French tradition, each linked to a 17th-century playwright. Corneille's is a tragedy of duty and honor competing with passion; Racine's is a tragedy of unalterable fate and of passion's law, informed by a severe branch of French Catholicism called Jansenism. Brasillach lived his own trial as the young Corneille he himself had portrayed eight years earlier in a series of lectures he gave to a group of Parisian fascist intellectuals. Characterized by a submission to personal destiny, by sacrifice, Brasillach on trial was a good Cornelian hero who never forgot he was onstage, never slipped in his own self-esteem. Simone de Beauvoir was one of the courtroom spectators, and in "Oeil pour oeil" (1946; "Eye for Eye"), her February 1946 essay on the event published in *Les temps modernes,* she translated his Cornelian heroism into the heroism of her future, an existential heroism:

> And in his box, alone, cut off from everybody else, was a man whom the circumstances were stimulating to show the very best that was in him. There he was face to face with his death, and consequently with his life too, whose whole burden he had to assume, now that he was about to die. Whatever that life had been, whatever the reasons for his death, the dignity with which he bore himself in his extreme situation enforced our respect. We wanted the death of the editor of *Je suis partout,* not the death of this man who was completely absorbed in dying well. (*Politics,* July–August 1947, p. 140)

Beauvoir, who had refused to sign the petition in Brasillach's defense, now understood why: by dying, Brasillach allowed us to understand that justice is not relative, that we can indeed distinguish good from evil in the use that human beings make of their liberty, and that therefore we can will the good. Prosecutor Reboul, for his part, played the haunted Jansenist Racine to Brasillach's Corneille: "If I hadn't accepted my duty," he claimed, "too many dead voices would have whispered from beyond the grave in my ear that terrible phrase that you prepared for others: What are we waiting for [*Qu'attend-on*]?" (*Le procès de Robert Brasillach* [1946; *The Trial of Robert Brasillach*], p. 170).

Brasillach's death was one of many issues debated throughout 1945 by a National Committee of Writers that included Sartre and Camus but was dominated by communist intellectuals of the Resistance. They argued among themselves the relative guilt of writers versus editors. They made lists of banned writers and debated the lists; they debated the punishments and the death penalty. They sat through endless meetings.

It was Sartre, and not writers who had been far more active in the Resistance (such as Vercors, the pseudonym of Jean Bruller, or René Char), who took the leading role in postwar French letters. Sartre's literary career had come to fruition in occupied Paris, and some postwar intellectuals found it compromising that he had obtained German permission to stage *Les mouches* (*The Flies*) there in 1943. While he lived and published in the occupied capital, Sartre also wrote for the Resistance press, and his essays—"La république du silence" (1944; "The Republic of Silence"), "Paris sous l'Occupation" (1945; "Paris under the Occupation"), "Qu'est-ce qu'un collaborateur?" (1945; "What Is a Collaborator?")—still bristle today with the atmosphere of the occupation, the anticipation of the Liberation. In his postwar writing, Sartre did much more than offer an analysis or a denunciation of collaboration; he offered a future for literature. And this is probably why he came to stand in the public mind for the antifascist cure. In 1945 Sartre founded *Les temps modernes.* The magazine was funded by Gaston Gallimard, anxious to redeem himself from his association with Drieu la Rochelle at *La nouvelle revue française.* In the first issue of *Les temps modernes* Sartre referred to the "temptations of irresponsibility" of bourgeois writers (October 1945, p. 1), and in its fifth issue Beauvoir published her stand on Brasillach's death, a death that served as a sanction for this whole new intellectual universe. It drew a line between the prewar aesthetes—Valéry, Jean Giraudoux, André Gide—and committed intellectuals who conceived their literary and social activities as ethical stands. Their existentialism was in large part a response to the 1944–1947 purge, and as much a part of the postwar recovery as the Marshall Plan.

Diametrically opposed to this existentialist narrative is the recovery story of Louis-Ferdinand Céline. He had been imprisoned by the Danes in 1946 to await extradition, but in 1951, after lengthy maneuvers by lawyers and friends, Céline returned to France. Under his nonliterary name, Destouches, he had benefited from a special amnesty available to World War I veterans wounded in the line of duty. In 1957 Gallimard published Céline's *D'un château l'autre* (*Castle to Castle*). Still the buffoon, Céline presented madcap impressions of the collaborationist milieu at Sigmaringen. The reading public, curious about collaboration—and saturated with legends of the Resistance—was drawn to the novel's setting. So was a school of French intellectuals primarily concerned with Céline's technique: his transposition of reality, his fractured narratives, his assault on syntax—all the aspects of a structuralist poetics. *D'un château l'autre* marks Céline's reinclusion in a postwar literary canon in which the moral hold—and the necessity—of existentialism was beginning to wane. Structuralist poetics, with its formal analyses of texts, provided a new freedom from the ambiguities of accusation, from the righteous triumphs and mistakes of the postwar intellectual purge. So in this movement away from existentialism and toward structuralism—in this commitment to language—we can still see the influence of the trauma of war. How many more years must pass before the wounds of collaboration completely close?

See also 1794 (25 July), 1934, 1945 (15 October).

Bibliography: Pierre Assouline, *Gaston Gallimard: A Half-Century of French Publishing,* trans. Harold J. Salemson (New York: Harcourt Brace Jovanovich, 1987). Simone de Beauvoir, "Eye for Eye," abr. trans. Mary McCarthy, *Politics* (July–August 1947), 134–140. Robert Brasillach, *Oeuvres complètes,* ed. Maurice Bardèche, 12 vols. (Paris: Club de l'Honnête Homme, 1963–64). Louis-Ferdinand Céline, *Castle to Castle,* trans. Ralph Manheim (New York: Delacorte Press, 1968). Henri Godard, *Poétique de Céline* (Paris: Gallimard, 1985). Jacques Isorni, *Le procès de Robert Brasillach* (Paris: Flammarion, 1946). Alice Yaeger Kaplan, *Relevé des sources et citations dans "Bagatelles pour un massacre"* (Tusson, Charente: Editions du Lérot, 1987). Henry de Montherlant, *Le solstice de juin* (Paris: Grasset, 1941). Lucien Rebatet, *Les décombres* (Paris: Denoël, 1942). Jean-Paul Sartre, "Paris sous l'occupation," "Qu'est-ce qu'un collaborateur?" and "La république du silence," in *Situations, III* (Paris: Gallimard, 1949).

Alice Yaeger Kaplan

✍ *1945, 15 October*

The First Issue of Jean-Paul Sartre's Journal, *Les temps modernes,*
Is Published by Gallimard

Rebellion or Revolution?

What defines change in culture? How does it occur? The German occupation of 1940–1944 was a major historical determinant of the existentialist sensibility that pervaded French culture during the decade following World War II. Existentialism extended inquiry into consciousness and subjectivity from philosophy to literature and the arts, where it popularized concepts such as commitment, situation, and the absurd. These, in turn, were increasingly challenged as the euphoria of peacetime faded. The postwar evolution of *littérature engagée* (committed writing) illustrates the nature of cultural change as an interplay of concepts, institutions, and practices.

The history of postwar existentialism in France is chiefly the tale of a monthly review and its founder. Soon after the liberation of Paris in August 1944, Jean-Paul Sartre began to put together the editorial board of *Les temps modernes* (Modern times), a monthly review he was starting with Simone de Beauvoir and Maurice Merleau-Ponty. The venture was, in part, a holdover from Socialisme et Liberté (Socialism and Freedom), a short-lived resistance group he had organized in 1941. Once peace was imminent, the question for Sartre and his colleagues was how best to turn the Resistance into a serious political force. Renovation was a key motive: new forms of literature and journalism held the promise that France's postwar experience would be different from that of the recent past. Sartre and his colleagues would be hunters of meaning; they would tell the truth about the world and about their lives in order to account for the new ("modern") times.

Even before its first issue appeared, *Les temps modernes* was a prime candidate to assume the preeminence of *La nouvelle revue française* ("la NRF"), founded in 1908 under the sponsorship of André Gide. By the time la *NRF*'s publisher, Gallimard, brought out Sartre's *La nausée* (1938; *Nausea*) and *Le mur* (1939; *The Wall*), he was already writing articles for the journal and drawing a salary as a Gallimard consultant. After the publication of *L'être et le néant* (1943; *Being and Nothingness*) and the plays *Les mouches* (1943; *The Flies*) and *Huis clos* (1945; *No Exit*), Sartre emerged from the German occupation as a major writer and philosopher whom Gaston Gallimard was understandably ready to promote.

Another young Gallimard writer had a reputation as novelist and essayist that was enhanced by his role in the wartime underground. Long before the Germans were out of Paris, Albert Camus was using his skills as a journalist to make *Combat* the first of the clandestine newspapers to herald the liberation. The mystique of Resistance hero surrounding Camus was one Sartre could never match; it set the tone for a rivalry that came to affect their relations as friends and colleagues. Despite a certain camaraderie, Camus always kept a safe distance from Sartre's intellectual circle. Like André Malraux, he turned down

Sartre's invitation to join the board of the new monthly. The implications of that refusal resurfaced in the dispute over Camus's *L'homme révolté* (1951; *The Rebel*).

Les temps modernes embodied Sartre's attempt to articulate philosophy, literature, and politics. Under his signature in the first two issues, "Présentation des *Temps modernes*" (1945; "Introducing *Les temps modernes*") and "La nationalisation de la littérature" (1945; "The Nationalization of Literature") announced a program of *littérature engagée* that was revised and expanded in *Qu'est-ce que la littérature?* (1947; *What Is Literature?*). For Sartre in 1945, awareness of history was a prerequisite to action: "The writer is *situated* in his time; every word he utters has reverberations. As does his silence" (*What Is Literature?* p. 252). In *L'être et le néant*, Sartre had defined freedom as the individual's capacity to act on the basis of a free and conscious decision for which he or she was accountable. The concept of situation inscribed that capacity within specific circumstances; it modified free choice into conscious choice and portrayed the individual as a historical subject and agent. In terms of the former, choice was never free from circumstance; in terms of the latter, awareness of this limitation allowed for an understanding leading to the action in and on history that Sartre termed *praxis*.

Littérature engagée consisted of three closely connected elements: *embrigadement* (joining up), *embarquement* (embarking), and *témoignage* (bearing witness). *Embrigadement* was understood in a strict sense as collective action and was thus distinct from doctrine or party line. "Présentation des *Temps modernes*" echoed Marx's call for philosophers to transform rather than merely interpret the world. But immediately after the war, Sartre's relation to the philosophy of Marxism was oblique and his attitude toward the French Communist party guarded. *Témoignage* and *embarquement* were both concerned with thought and action. Ideally, the form of action associated with *témoignage* devolved from active reflection on one's situation beyond the simple awareness of circumstance conveyed by the notion of *embarquement*. In terms of Sartre's own writings, it was as though *littérature engagée* would resolve the impasse of *La nausée*'s narrator, Antoine Roquentin: lucidity would promote rather than inhibit action.

Initial reactions to *Les temps modernes* were mixed. In the Catholic *Esprit*, Emmanuel Mounier called it a "review-event" and noted the similarities of its vision to his own personalism of a decade earlier. Gide, ever the brahmin, was cool and circumspect; in the short-lived weekly *Terre des hommes*, he described the new monthly's first issue as disturbing. Predictably, the Communists attacked *Les temps modernes* as a symptom of bourgeois decadence, ranking Sartre alongside proponents of surrealism ("the Trotskyism of literary cafés") as the party's major ideological enemies. When the Catholic philosopher Gabriel Marcel referred to him as the leader of a new movement, Sartre refused the label, replying with Socratic irony that he did not know what existentialism was.

Outwardly, the monthly thrived as a forum of debate on postwar politics and culture. Literature was very much in evidence; early issues included texts by Antonin Artaud, Samuel Beckett, Jean Genet, Violette Leduc, Francis Ponge, and Nathalie Sarraute. Beauvoir's *Les mandarins* (1954; *The Mandarins*) con-

973

tained a fictionalized account of *L'espoir,* a postwar journal openly modeled on *Les temps modernes.* During the same period Sartre was writing *Les mains sales* (1948; *Dirty Hands*) for the stage while he completed *La mort dans l'âme* (1949; *Troubled Sleep*), the third novel in the series *Les chemins de la liberté* (*Roads to Freedom*). But despite appearances, the journal was riddled by political differences from both outside and within. The June 1946 issue carried Sartre's name alone on the masthead as director after the departures of Raymond Aron and Albert Ollivier, two editorial board members wary of what they saw as the review's proximity to the Communists. Merleau-Ponty agreed to serve as editor-in-chief but refused to be listed as such.

Qu'est-ce que la littérature?—serialized in *Les temps modernes* from February to July 1947—gave full form to *littérature engagée* while affording Sartre the opportunity to reassess his role as director of the monthly. Questions serving as titles of its first three sections—What is writing? Why write? For whom does one write?—provided the basis for the literary program set forth in the concluding "Situation de l'écrivain en 1947" ("Situation of the Writer in 1947"). Sartre began with a definition of writing that opposed prose to a poetic attitude focused on the materiality of language. Whereas the prose writer saw words as tools or as extensions of the body ("a sixth finger, a third leg; in short, a pure function"), the poet considered them primarily as objects ("natural things that sprout upon the earth like grass and trees"). Subsequent chapters portrayed literature as a pact of generosity in which the work of art prompted a mutual recognition of freedom between writer and reader that was set apart from the general experience of conflict between self and other. Whereas *L'être et le néant* had characterized this conflict as a law of human existence, *Qu'est-ce que la littérature?* seemingly offered the promise of alternative relations. Choice—in its revised form as limited and conscious—was still an essential condition; the reader ultimately accepted or rejected the recognition offered by writing. In so doing, he or she completed the process of disclosure leading to the reflective consciousness that Sartre described as the subjectivity of a society in permanent revolution.

The centrality of the work of art in Sartre's program remained problematic, for the experience of recognition it induced was modeled on a phenomenon of disclosure (*dévoilement*) such as that set forth in Martin Heidegger's 1936 essay, "The Origin of the Work of Art." In this sense, *Qu'est-ce que la littérature?* brought out a conflict within *littérature engagée* between a definition of freedom that was ultimately aesthetic and an objective that was markedly political. Hence the paradox that seemingly turned committed writing against itself: the more *engagée* literature became, the less "literary" it was. Disclosure and recognition had intrinsic value for the individual, but the question remained how the progression toward collective action was to occur. As Sartre later recalled this bind in *Questions de méthode* (1960; *Search for a Method*), he was convinced at one and the same time that historical materialism furnished the only valid interpretation of history and that the only concrete approach to reality was existential.

Over the next two years Sartre extended *littérature engagée* beyond writing and journalism. In October 1947 he launched "La tribune des *Temps modernes*," a weekly radio program of commentary and debate that was canceled after less than two months. A more sustained effort was the Rassemblement Démocratique Révolutionnaire (Revolutionary Democratic Group), a movement—a "gathering" rather than a political party—begun in 1948 as an alternative ("third way") to steer France clear of both the Soviets and the Americans. Although group rallies drew thousands to hear Sartre, Camus, André Breton, and Richard Wright call for an "internationalism of spirit," unity remained tentative. Disillusioned by the pro-American posturing of his colleagues, Sartre resigned from the group in October 1949, hardened in both resolve and isolation. By 1950 he had become a staunch opponent of anticommunism whom the French Communist party nonetheless saw as an enemy of the working class.

The notorious 1952 dispute between Sartre and Camus grew out of differences of ideology and temperament going as far back as the occupation. When the two first met in 1943, each had ties to the antifascist left. After the liberation and Hiroshima, the threat of ("hot") nuclear war led to realignments with either the United States or the Soviet Union. This choosing of sides also occurred on a personal level: one was either for the United States (because one supported capitalism against Russia and communism) or for the Soviet Union (because one supported communism against the United States and capitalism). Sartre blasted the anticommunists who claimed to defend the free world while they protected their material interests at the expense of the workers. In 1949 Camus chided *Les temps modernes* for its ambivalence over revelation of the Soviet labor camps. While Sartre moved toward an independent Communist position, Camus asserted the priority of human rights over politics and party doctrine.

Despite his reputation as a proponent of the absurd, Camus saw himself primarily as a moralist whose essays, novels, and plays asserted revolt as an attitude of personal defiance against life's meaninglessness. *Le mythe de Sisyphe* (1942; *The Myth of Sisyphus*) was neither a treatise nor a defense of the absurd; it purported only to describe the alienation resulting from a frustrated desire for meaning and order. Unlike Sartre and Malraux, who used the term *absurd* differently, Camus emphasized its emotional force as so overwhelming that it seemingly made suicide the only serious philosophical issue. Yet suicide, often erroneously identified with Camus's position at the time, was more properly the pretext for an assertion of value and meaning toward which his writings consistently pointed. From the start, Camus set revolt—or, at least, its potential—alongside the absurd. This assertion took on a collective meaning in *La peste* (1947; *The Plague*), Camus's ficitonalized chronicle of an epidemic and its effects on those forced to confront it. Like Sartre's play *Les mouches, La peste* allegorized the occupation. But whereas Sartre's Orestes rebelled against a régime based on murder and guilt, the evil resisted by Camus's characters in the quarantined city of Oran was that of arbitrary suffering. Sartre dramatized resistance against an unjust social order that Camus transposed into a more metaphysical "plague" condition.

In "Remarque sur la révolte" (1945; "Remark on Revolt"), Camus wrote that when political revolution aspired to absolute justice, it opposed the very nature of revolt. Six years later, *L'homme révolté* expanded this point into a critique of the imperative contained in the revolutionary's claim to absolutism. For Camus, the metaphysical rebel was at odds with the violence and injustice ("rational murder") of the literary and historical revolt represented in the writings of the marquis de Sade, Hegel, Marx, Nietzsche, Charles Baudelaire, Arthur Rimbaud, Breton, and Sartre. *L'homme révolté* was a treatise against political revolution—synonymous for Camus with historical revolt—as a degraded form of metaphysical revolt. Even when freedom initiated revolution, its compromise was inevitably the price of belief in historical necessity. As Camus tried to transpose his moral position onto the plane of political philosophy, *L'homme révolté* recast metaphysical revolt into a denial of the Marxist interpretation of history. If the result had only limited success, it was because Camus seemed more concerned with discrediting Marxism than with providing alternatives to it.

When *L'homme révolté* appeared, *Les temps modernes* remained silent while Camus was applauded by the right. Finally, a review by Francis Jeanson took him to task for eliding the historicity of revolution. Camus responded—to Sartre rather than to Jeanson—that he did not deny history but only those who made it into an absolute end in hopes of justifying untenable means. Sartre's reply, published in *Les temps modernes*, "Réponse à Albert Camus" (1952; "Reply to Albert Camus"), was harsh and direct; it accused Camus of judging history from the outside and implied that he lacked the competence in philosophy required to support the position he wanted to take. Even more, it was cast in a tone of disappointed friendship—"You had been for us—you could again be tomorrow—the admirable conjunction of a person, an action, and a work" ("Reply," p. 91)—that was openly insincere. The exchanges resulted in mutual intransigence. Camus regarded Sartre as a communist ideologue whose monthly was a mouthpiece for the Soviet Union while Sartre regarded Camus as a moralist who rejected the historical present in favor of eternal values.

The dispute over *L'homme révolté* exploded a final myth of the Resistance mentality, ending any hopes that solidarity between Communists and noncommunists would outlast the war. Merleau-Ponty resigned in 1953; the editorial board appointed in 1954 contained none of the original members. From 1945 to 1952 *Les temps modernes* marked a specific phase in the evolution of French existentialism. Its program of *littérature engagée* symbolized an end to philosophy in the sense that it extended an imperative to action imposed by wartime into a permanent militancy. Alongside the popular notion of existentialism as a cultural style, the monthly continually redirected inquiry into subjectivity and consciousness toward issues of politics and ideology. As Sartre duly noted in 1945, the occupation forced him to take stock of his responsibility as a writer. But raising awareness was only a preliminary to the collective action prescribed by Sartre's postwar mission to disclose the historical present as a challenge to human freedom. Following the liberation, Sartre's conversion became the model of a militant existentialism engaged increasingly with political issues. Today *Les temps modernes,* after more than forty years and 500 issues, seeks to maintain that militancy.

See also 1931 (June), 1933 (November).

Bibliography: Ronald Aronson, *Jean-Paul Sartre: Philosophy in the World* (London: Verso, 1980). Simone de Beauvoir, *The Mandarins,* trans. Leonard M. Friedman (Cleveland: World, 1956). Anna Boschetti, *The Intellectual Enterprise: Sartre and "Les Temps Modernes,"* trans. Richard C. McCleary (Evanston: Northwestern University Press, 1988). Michel-Antoine Burnier, *Choice of Action: The French Existentialists on the Political Front Line,* trans. Bernard Murchland (New York: Random House, 1968). Albert Camus, *The Rebel: An Essay on Man in Revolt,* trans. Anthony Bower (New York: Vintage, 1956). Annie Cohen-Solal, *Sartre: 1905–1980,* trans. Anna Cancogni (New York: Pantheon, 1987). Dominick LaCapra, *Preface to Sartre* (Ithaca: Cornell University Press, 1978). Mark Poster, *Existential Marxism in Postwar France* (Princeton: Princeton University Press, 1975). Jean-Paul Sartre, "Reply to Albert Camus," in *Situations,* trans. Benita Eisler (New York: Braziller, 1965). Sartre, *Search for a Method,* trans. Hazel E. Barnes (New York: Vintage, 1968). Sartre, *"What Is Literature?" and Other Essays,* trans. Bernard Frechtman (Cambridge, Mass.: Harvard University Press, 1988).

Steven Ungar

✐ 1946, July

"Suite," by Samuel Beckett, Appears in *Les temps modernes*

Samuel Beckett Emerges as a French Writer

Samuel Beckett, an Irishman who would become a leading French writer, was born in 1906 near Dublin to a Protestant middle-class family. After attending local elementary and secondary schools, he studied French and Italian at Dublin's Trinity College. He began an academic career but soon abandoned it to devote himself entirely to writing. Beckett's first works—the novels *More Pricks than Kicks* (1934) and *Murphy* (1938)—were in English, but after settling in Paris in 1937, he composed poetry in French. Beckett returned to his native language for his next novel, *Watt* (1953), which he wrote during the Nazi occupation as he hid in the French countryside because of his Resistance work.

For about a decade following the war, Beckett wrote extensively in French. In July 1946 Jean-Paul Sartre's journal *Les temps modernes* was the first to publish a major work by Beckett in his adopted language: this was "Suite" ("Continuation"), a truncated story that would appear in its entirety as "La fin" ("The End") in *Nouvelles et Textes pour rien* (1958; *Stories and Texts for Nothing*). Other works by Beckett from the same period include the plays *En attendant Godot* (1952; *Waiting for Godot*) and *Fin de partie* (1957; *Endgame*), and the novels *Molloy* (1951), *Malone meurt* (1951; *Malone Dies*), and *L'innommable* (1953; *The Unnamable*). Beckett returned to English with the plays *All That Fall* (1957), *Krapp's Last Tape* (1958), and *Embers* (1959); he then composed the novel *Com-*

ment c'est (1961; *How It Is*) in French. Since that time Beckett has written original texts in both his native and adopted tongues, and he either translates them into the other language, or (far more rarely) collaborates with another translator.

It surprises us that an author would express himself in a language other than his own, although for centuries poetry and philosophy were written in Latin rather than in the vernacular. Other modern writers have also abandoned their mother tongues: Joseph Conrad, a Pole, and Vladimir Nabokov, a Russian, wrote in English; and the Rumanians Eugène Ionesco and E. M. Cioran chose French. But as Martin Esslin has noted, Beckett is unique: others left their own languages to write in tongues more widely spoken, whereas Beckett stopped using English, the lingua franca of the 20th century.

Of course, as an Irishman, Beckett could not have had an easy relationship with his mother tongue. Although English is the sole language of most Irish people, it is still felt to be a foreign tongue imposed on them by the British conqueror: their condition resembles that of Beckett's narrator in *The Unnamable*, "a stranger in [his] own midst, surrounded by invaders" (p. 396). Nonetheless, like James Joyce before him, Beckett has expressed little interest in the Irish nationalist revival of Gaelic. His indifference to the pathos underlying such a cause is figured ironically in *Molloy:* "Tears and laughter, they are so much Gaelic to me" (p. 37). Yet in their own way, Joyce and Beckett distanced themselves from English. In *Finnegans Wake* (1939) Joyce grafted elements of all tongues onto English, and for several years Beckett used French as his principal literary language.

The Irish characters in *All That Fall* give further indication of Beckett's ambivalence toward English (p. 80):

> *Mrs. Rooney:* No, no, I am agog, tell me all, then we shall press on and never pause, never pause, till we come safe to haven.
>   (Pause.)
> *Mr. Rooney:* Never pause . . . safe to haven . . . Do you know, Maddy, sometimes one would think you were struggling with a dead language.
> *Mrs. Rooney.* Yes indeed, Dan, I know full well what you mean, I often have that feeling, it is unspeakably excruciating.
> *Mr. Rooney:* I confess I have it sometimes myself, when I happen to overhear what I am saying.
> *Mrs. Rooney:* Well, you know, it will be dead in time, just like our own poor dear Gaelic, there is that to be said.

The death of English referred to in this dialogue is not to be understood in a simply historical sense—that just as Gaelic was wiped out by the British colonizer, so someday English will give way to the language of a greater empire. Rather, English is dead in the way any language is dead, when we are taken aback by the weightiness, the inadequacy, the otherness of our words.

Even before Beckett had written much in French, he had made language appear strange. In his novel *Watt,* language undergoes a process of disintegration. In one passage, words and sentences are presented backwards; in another, a word is separated from the thing it represents: "Looking at a pot, for example, or thinking of a pot, at one of Mr Knott's pots, of one of Mr Knott's pots, it was in vain that Watt said, Pot, pot . . . For the pot remained a pot, Watt felt sure of that, for everyone but Watt. For Watt alone it was not a pot, any more" (pp. 81–82).

Despite Watt's belief that the pot remains a pot for everyone else, the word *pot* is made unfamiliar for us as well as for Watt through its insistent repetition and rhyme with the names Watt and Knott, which resonate as "what" and "not." We learn that "Watt's need of semantic succor was at times so great that he would set to trying names on things, and on himself, almost as a woman hats" (p. 83). Watt is in a passive position with respect to language: hence the comparison to the stereotypical woman. Recently Beckett suggested that Watt's experience was not far removed from his own, claiming that he left English partly because in *Watt,* "language was running away" with him (personal interview, 23 June 1983).

Thus Beckett exchanged his native language for a foreign one, in which he would have to be more disciplined and self-conscious. The use of French allowed him to "impoverish" and "weaken" himself and to write without "style" or "poetry" (quoted in Cohn, *Back to Beckett,* pp. 58–59). But when critics suggest that French lends itself to sparse expression because it has a smaller vocabulary and a more fixed word order than English, they forget that French is capable of extreme complexity: witness the arcane syntax of the 19th-century poet Stéphane Mallarmé. Thus it is the foreignness of French, rather than any positive characteristic of the language, that attracted Beckett to it.

It becomes less surprising that Beckett should write in French when we consider he is descended from Huguenots who fled France, and that *Beckett* resonates in French as *petit bec,* meaning "little beak." The suggestion that a name alluding to an organ of speech in French might predispose its bearer to write in that tongue implies a certain belief in linguistic determinism. Such arguments are common in French psychoanalysis, whose leading theoretician, Jacques Lacan, extended Freud's assertion that in the unconscious words are treated like things. Positing the "primacy of the signifier," Lacan emphasized that in psychic processes, a word can play a more determinant role than the thing it represents. In Beckett's universe as well, language has great power. He places his creature Watt in a passive position with respect to language, his own explanations for using French imply his assumption of the impotence he felt in the face of language, and the narrator of *The Unnamable* ascribes his very being to words: "I'm in words, made of words . . . I'm all these words" (p. 386).

Sociological factors also influenced Beckett's choice of language. He was attracted to Paris because of the literary life there, and no doubt to the French language because of its literary prestige. Yet eschews the elegant style that is the hallmark of the language in such authors as André Gide or Marcel Proust: he employs an elementary manner, at once conversational and laborious.

Beckett was not the first French author to use colloquial forms, but his work contains neither the bilious rambling of Louis-Ferdinand Céline's *Voyage au bout de la nuit* (1932; *Journey to the End of Night*) nor the ironic populism of certain chapters in Raymond Queneau's *Exercices de style* (1947; *Exercises in Style*). Beckett's halting tempo makes even Albert Camus's simple style in *L'étranger* (1942; *The Stranger*) seem classically literary. Thus in *Molloy*, the words "quelle langue" (literally "what a language," but translated by Beckett as "what rigmarole") suggest exasperation with French:

> Ce dont j'ai besoin c'est des histoires, j'ai mis longtemps à le savoir. D'ailleurs je n'en suis pas sûr. Alors voilà, je suis fixé sur certaines choses, je sais certaines choses sur lui, des choses que j'ignorais, qui me tracassaient, des choses même dont je n'avais pas souffert. Quelle langue.   (P. 16)

> What I need now is stories, it took me a long time to know that, and I'm not sure of it. There I am then, informed as to certain things, knowing certain things about him, things I didn't know, things I had craved to know, things I had never thought of. What rigmarole.   (*Molloy,* trans. Bowles and Beckett, p. 13)

What arrests our attention here is the succession of relative pronouns—*des choses que, qui, dont*—and the rhythm in *"ce dont j'ai besoin c'est des* histoires." In this passage apparently devoid of embellishment, grammar itself takes on rhetorical charge. We become intensely aware of the syntactic pivots of the sentence; it is as though Beckett made art out of the stuff of language textbooks. As Jean-Michel Rey has observed, "Samuel Beckett forces us . . . to learn to read our language all over again . . . He works on the very matter of the French language in memory of English, that is, with the attention to the least particles of the language that can be given by an exterior, foreign view: immense detour at whose end our language is capable of surprising us, of returning to us in an unforeseen form. Beckett's dialect disarms us" ("Sur Samuel Beckett," pp. 63–64).

Beckett's own remarks suggest that he began writing in French as an exercise in humility in the face of language, but it is clear that his French functions as something foreign within French, alienating the French from their own speech. It is as though Beckett transferred to his adopted tongue the ambivalence he felt toward English, thus accomplishing what the narrator of *The Unnamable* set out to do: "I'll fix their gibberish for them . . . I'll fix their jargon for them" (pp. 324–326). The Unnamable is not speaking simply about a foreign tongue. Rather, he experiences his own language as foreign: "I have no language but theirs" (p. 325).

Lacan's view of human development illuminates such ambivalence toward language. For Lacan, a child's accession to the realm of language humanizes his desires, makes his wishes understandable to others, but it also entails an alienation from his wishes, the death of his most individual desires and his assumption of the ghosts of desire dwelling in the words of others. The otherness of language that constitutes the human being as a speaking subject transcends any opposition between native and foreign tongue. Thus the Unnamable says that the words he uses are "others' words . . . I'm all these words, all these strangers" (p. 386); in the French original, the last phrase reads "je suis tous ces mots, tous ces étrangers," which can be rendered as "I'm all these words, all these foreigners" (*L'innommable,* p. 204).

Given the foreignness of his own speech, the Unnamable has no interest in other languages: "All solicit me in the same tongue, the only one they taught me. They told me there were others, I don't regret not knowing them. The moment the silence is broken in this way it can only mean one thing" (pp. 336–337). The equivalence of all language and languages as interruptions of a desired silence is suggested as well in *Nouvelles et Textes pour rien:* "C'est un autre langage, mais qui revient au même" (p. 154); in *Stories and Texts for Nothing,* Beckett translates this remark: "It's another story, but the burden is the same" (p. 102); literally, it means: "It's another *language,* but which comes out to the same." Likewise, in *Endgame* Clov says to Hamm: "I use the words you taught me. If they don't mean anything any more, teach me others. Or let me be silent" (p. 44).

If all language is equivalent, there is no reason to prefer one tongue over another. Although Beckett once said that writing in French was "more exciting" (Cohn, "The Weakening Strength of French," p. 58), by the mid-1950s the charm appears to have been lost. Beckett could then return to his native language: his English writings no longer "run away with him" as *Watt* did, but have the sparseness that characterizes his French texts. Indeed, just as Jean-Michel Rey claims that Beckett taught the French to read their language all over again, we may find that Beckett's latest writings are so bare that they approach an idiom other than English. A good example of Beckett's minimal syntax—or "midget grammar," as he calls it in *How It Is* (p. 76)—would be these sentences from his recent book *Company* (1980), originally written in English: "See hearer clearer. Which of all the ways of lying supine the least likely in the long run to pall?" (p. 56). No doubt Beckett learned to apply the same stringency to his English writings as to his French when he translated his French works into English. The task of translation was a school for discipline, as was the task of writing in a foreign tongue.

Insofar as translation restates a previous text, Beckett's translations of his own works partake as well of a tendency opposed to his stringency: his repetitiousness. It is a critical commonplace that Beckett's writings deal with the repetitiousness inherent in the human endeavor, and the first person to point this out is Beckett's narrator himself. At the end of "L'expulsé" (1945; "The Expelled"), one of Beckett's earliest French works, we read: "I don't know why I told this story. I could just as well have told another. Perhaps some other time I'll be able to tell another. Living souls, you will see how alike they are" (*Stories and Texts,* p. 25). Later, *The Unnamable* notes: "All things here recur sooner or later" (p. 299), and in *How It Is* one hears "always the same song pause SAME SONG" (p. 97). In *Company* the narrator observes: "Another trait its repetitiousness. Repeatedly with only minor variants the same bygone" (p. 16). Other examples of Beckett's repetitiousness: the second act of *Waiting for Godot* presents much of the same action as the first, and the characters affirm time and again that they are "waiting for Godot"; in *Happy Days,* where a woman buried in sand repeats, "This will have been a happy day."

Yet in *Endgame, The Unnamable,* and *Texts for Nothing* the characters insist that silence is better than speech. How can we reconcile the desire for silence with the repetitiousness that characterizes Beckett's work? *The Unnamable* offers a solution to this paradox. The narrator's desire for silence is so strong that its fulfillment must ever and again be put off, so that silence may be all the more enjoyed when it finally comes: "However that may be I think I'll soon go silent for good, in spite of its being prohibited. Then, yes, phut, just like that, just like one of the living, then I'll be dead, I think I'll soon be dead, I hope I find it a change. I should have liked to go silent first, there were moments I thought that would be my reward for having spoken so long and so valiantly, to enter living into silence, so as to be able to enjoy it, no . . ." (p. 396).

Beckett's insistence on translating his own writings participates in the dialectic between the wish for silence and the compulsion to repeat. For translation does not simply repeat an earlier work; since what can be said in one language cannot necessarily be said in another, translating a text entails deciding what of it not to translate. By suppressing as well as repeating, Beckett's translations in their own way realize, and yet delay, the silence longed for in his works.

See also 1959 (28 October).

Bibliography: Samuel Beckett, *All That Fall,* in *Krapp's Last Tape and Other Dramatic Pieces* (New York: Grove, 1957). Beckett, *Company* (New York: Grove, 1980). Beckett, *Endgame,* trans. Samuel Beckett (New York: Grove, 1958). Beckett, *How It Is,* trans. Samuel Beckett (New York: Grove, 1964). Beckett, *Molloy* (Paris: Minuit, 1951); trans. Patrick Bowles and Samuel Beckett, in *Three Novels by Samuel Beckett* (New York: Grove, 1965). Beckett, *Nouvelles et Textes pour rien* (Paris: Minuit, 1958); translated by Samuel Beckett and Richard Seaver as *Stories and Texts for Nothing* (New York: Grove, 1967). Beckett, *The Unnamable,* trans. Samuel Beckett, in *Three Novels by Samuel Beckett* (New York: Grove, 1965). Beckett, *Watt* (New York: Grove, 1959). Ruby Cohn, "The Weakening Strength of French," in *Back to Beckett* (Princeton: Princeton University Press, 1973), pp. 57–60. Martin Esslin, "Samuel Beckett: The Search for the Self," in *The Theater of the Absurd,* rev. ed. (Woodstock, N.Y.: Overlook Press, 1973), pp. 13–65. Jean-Michel Rey, "Sur Samuel Beckett," *Café Librairie,* 1 (1983), 63–66.

Alan Astro

✐〇 1949

Simone de Beauvoir Publishes *Le deuxième sexe*

An Intellectual Woman in Postwar France

Of all her books, Simone de Beauvoir (1908–1986) once remarked, *Le deuxième sexe* (1949; *The Second Sex*) was the one that brought her the most lasting satisfaction. It also brought her continuous harassment from spiteful and lecherous men. As soon as the first excerpts appeared in the May 1948 issue of *Les temps modernes,* Beauvoir became the target of an unprecedented range of vicious and sexist attacks. Right-wingers and Communists alike cast her as a depraved nymphomaniac or, alternatively, as a humiliated, sexually frustrated bluestocking lecherously choosing to inflict her own unfulfilled erotic obsessions on the unsuspecting French public. In addition, the Communists accused her of betraying the socialist revolution, which in and of itself would solve women's problems at a stroke. Camus upbraided her for making the French male look ridiculous. The Catholic bourgeoisie claimed to be shocked by her language (she calls penis a penis), although they used fairly unambiguous terms themselves in their efforts to blacken Beauvoir's name. François Mauriac, that respectable old *bien-pensant,* could not restrain himself from writing to one of Beauvoir's friends that after this Beauvoir's vagina no longer held any secrets for him.

That Beauvoir's book provoked such intense hostility was partly due to the fact that it appeared when the Cold War was escalating. In the United States, Senator Joseph McCarthy and his cronies were launching their infamous witch-hunting campaigns against radical artists and intellectuals. And although the French left was in a much stronger position than its American counterpart, in France too the Cold War produced a deeply divisive intellectual climate in which *all* political and cultural interventions were subjected to the harshest and most summary of black-and-white judgments. In 1949 Beauvoir, like the rest of the group around *Les temps modernes,* belonged to the beleaguered nonaligned French left. This in itself was enough to make her an obvious target for attacks from the right and the Communists alike. Equally important is the fact that *Le deuxième sexe* was published only five years after French women obtained the right to vote, at a time when there was no women's movement to speak of in France. Nor did Beauvoir in any way see herself as a feminist when she wrote the book. (She did not declare herself a feminist until she joined the new women's movement in 1971.) In 1949 the political isolation of *Le deuxième sexe* made the book an exposed and vulnerable target for all kinds of masculinist aggression.

At one level, *Le deuxième sexe* was from the start curiously out of step with its own historical moment, written as it was at a time when Western capitalism was kicking women out of the factories in order to hand their jobs over to the boys back from the war, and published just as the West was about to embark on that most antifeminist of decades, the 1950s, the era of starched petticoats, ponytails, and the big Hollywood bust. But the very scandal surrounding *Le deuxième sexe* at the time of publication (the first volume sold 22,000 copies in its first week) helped make the book available to many women. In the 1950s many middle-class women secretly turned to Beauvoir's book for support in their struggle for the right to want more in life than just home, babies, and bust. For Beauvoir's uncompromising message was clear: motherhood and marriage alone can never make a woman happy; paid work alone secures a woman's independence. In the 1950s, however, her devastating critique of the oppression of women was too radical to be easily accepted by women thoroughly in the grips of patriarchal ideology. In the economic boom and the politically radical and antiauthoritarian climate of the 1960s, on the other hand, *Le deuxième sexe* became liberating and inspiring reading for thousands of young women who went on to create the new women's movement. In 1949 Beauvoir anticipated almost all the issues that became crucial to the feminist struggle in the 1960s and 1970s. There can be no doubt that *Le deuxième sexe* remains the most important feminist book of this century.

Le deuxième sexe is divided into two parts. The introduction to the first volume, "Les faits et les mythes" ("Facts and Myths"), outlines Beauvoir's analysis of women's oppression. Criticizing the sexism of biology, psychoanalysis, and historical materialism, Beauvoir concludes that these discourses cannot really explain *why* women are oppressed. But the fact remains that they are, and accordingly she launches a dauntingly massive discussion of the history of women and women's oppression from the earliest times until 1940 (this section has unfortunately been considerably abridged in the English translation), before finally examining some examples of the representation of femininity in literature written by men. The second volume, "L'expérience vécue" ("Woman's Life Today"), deals with the education of girls, emphasizing the ways in which they are made to conform to dominant notions of femininity, and examines the social and psychological situation of the adult woman, before outlining three major—but ultimately unsuccessful—ways of manifesting female ambition within the strictures of patriarchy: narcissism, romantic love, and mysticism. This volume contains chapters on lesbianism, motherhood, abortion and contraception, prostitution and sexuality. The final chapter, "La femme indépendante" ("The Independent Woman"), offers a quick glance toward liberation.

This marvelously energetic book presents a wealth of information about women's lives and history. More than a generation later, surprisingly (and disappointingly) little of Beauvoir's material is out of date. With her massive accumulation of facts and relentless debunking of patriarchal ideology, Beauvoir almost succeeds in making us forget that even after reading her 1,000-page effort, we still do not really know *why* women are oppressed. In this way, *Le deuxième sexe* leaves us with the image of an oppression without a cause, as the French feminist philosopher Michèle Le Doeuff has shown. It is as if the whole argument of the book is constructed around a central absence. The effect of this void is powerfully dialectical, Le Doeuff argues, producing the impression that patriarchy is desperately trying to fill a never-ending series of gaps and fissures: "Lacking any basis on the side of the involuntary (nature, economy, the unconscious), the phallic order must secure itself against every circumstance with a forest of props—from the upbringing of little girls to the repressive legislation of 'birth control,' and from codes of dress to exclusion from politics" (Le Doeuff, "Simone de Beauvoir and Existentialism," p. 286).

Beauvoir's analysis of women's oppression is based on two simple principles: (1) Woman in patriarchal society is defined as man's *other;* patriarchal ideology defines her as immanence, passivity, negativity, object-being, and man as transcendence, activity, striving, subject-being. (2) There is no such thing as a female nature, no essence of womanhood. All theories of "eternal femininity" (Goethe's "das ewig Weibliche") are patriarchal mystifications. Beauvoir's firm refusal of female essentialism is a logical consequence of her existentialist rejection of any kind of human essentialism. In the case of women, Beauvoir assumes, any form of essentialism will in the end favor the patriarchal project of keeping woman in her "place." But if "woman" has no essence, it follows that neither has she a "place" to which she can be confined. Beauvoir's proverbial dictum "One isn't born a woman; one becomes one" neatly encapsulates this aspect of her analysis.

Given Beauvoir's philosophical starting point, Sartre's *L'être et le néant* (1943; *Being and Nothingness*), it is obvious to her that *every* consciousness is constantly reaching out to define the world in relation to itself. There can be no sense in which women "spontaneously" seek to perceive themselves as other. Their "otherness" is forced upon them by society. If some women come to collude in the patriarchal attempt to cast women as other (that is, as negative, inferior, dependent, and "relative" beings), they are not necessarily guilty of *bad faith* (that is, of presenting man-made myths as inevitable, natural, or God-given realities that cannot meaningfully be opposed), since many women have been effectively deprived of any chance of seeing through the patriarchal game. Women, Beauvoir points out, have traditionally been not only sexually and economically exploited, but also deliberately kept in a state of poverty and ignorance that objectively makes them dependent on men for their very survival. Under such circumstances it does not make sense to talk about women's "bad faith" or collusion in their own oppression, any more than it makes sense to claim that blacks in the United States were responsible for their own enslavement. Having thus surreptitiously tacked a form of materialism onto Sartre's tragic ontology, Beauvoir concludes that women will never achieve their freedom as long as they are not able to earn their own living. But although she sees economic independence as the indispensable foundation of every other form of independence, it does not follow that economically independent women automatically achieve emotional and intellectual freedom as well: patriarchal conditioning is likely to be more recalcitrant than that. Beauvoir's point is simply that economic liberation is the sine qua non of every other form of liberation.

The whole project of *Le deuxième sexe* is based on the assumption that knowledge is both a value in itself and a powerful agent for change. But this knowledge must be expressed in language. Much like her lifelong companion Sartre in *Qu'est-ce que la littérature?* (1947; *What Is Literature?*), Beauvoir holds that the author writes in order to reveal a truth that in its turn will transform the world. For Beauvoir as for Sartre, truth or knowledge is always perceived in visual terms: knowledge is *insight* or *lucidity;* to write is to *expose* the truth, to *throw light on, illuminate,* or *elucidate* the situation. Discovering and representing the truth is the double task of the intellectuals, and it is their specific form of action. Words are not to be handled lightly. As Beauvoir herself puts it: "I am an intellectual, I take words and the truth to be of value" (*Force of Circumstance,* p. 378).

Beauvoir's obsession with knowledge does not surface only in *Le deuxième sexe.* "My desire to know the world is closely linked with my desire to express it," she writes in *La force des choses* (1963; *Force of Circumstance,* p. 287). Even in her first published novel, *L'invitée* (1943; *She Came to Stay*), a powerful and subtle dissection of the philosophical and emotional implications of female jealousy, the heroine, Françoise, is driven by an intense desire to *know* what goes on inside her rival's head. To have knowledge is to master oneself and events; not to have it is to be powerless. Destruction is preferable to ignorance: Françoise ends up by killing the opaque Xavière. The novel gains its impact from the way in which it poses the question of the existence of the other not simply as a philosophical puzzle, but as a concrete, emotional problem, an insoluble dilemma that drives the protagonist to an existential and emotional crisis in which murder suddenly seems to be the only solution. No wonder, then, that Françoise is endowed with a quite exceptional power to "live an idea body and soul" (*She Came to Stay,* p. 302). If Beauvoir is fascinated by ideas, it is not because they are theoretical; on the contrary, Françoise argues: "to me, an idea is not a question of theory. One feels it or . . . it has no value" (p. 302, translation modified). There is little trace here of the traditional patriarchal division between intellect and emotions, mind and body, so frequently criticized by feminists. Beauvoir returns to the problem of the existence of others, this time focusing on our responsibility toward others, in *Le sang des autres* (1945; *The Blood of Others*), one of the first novels about the Resistance to be published after the liberation of France. In her immensely ambitious novel *Les mandarins* (1954; *The Mandarins*), for which she received the prestigious Prix Goncourt, she problematizes the issues of engagement and responsibility as they presented themselves to left-wing intellectuals in France in the first postwar years.

The same drive for knowledge, a knowledge that is never purely intellectual but always also a matter of emotional experience, made Beauvoir undertake the massive task of writing her autobiography. According to many critics, the four volumes of her memoirs—*Mémoires d'une jeune fille rangée* (1958; *Memoirs of a Dutiful Daughter*), *La force de l'âge* (1960; *The Prime of Life*), *La force des choses* (1963; *Force of Circumstance*), *Tout compte fait* (1972; *All Said and Done*)—and her account of her mother's death (*Une mort très douce,* 1964; *A Very Easy Death*) and of Sartre's death (*La cérémonie des adieux,* 1981; *Adieux: A Farewell to Sartre*) together make up her most powerful and moving literary statements. Behind this massive autobiographical enterprise is not only the desire to understand herself and her own choices, but also the conviction that an honest examination of her own life will be of interest to others: "If any individual . . . reveals himself honestly, everyone, more or less, becomes involved. It is impossible for him to shed light on his own life without at some point illuminating the lives of others" (*The Prime of Life,* p. 8). It would seem that she was right: *Mémoires d'une jeune fille rangée* in particular, the evocation of her childhood and youth in a stiflingly conformist bourgeois and Catholic family, and her subsequent break with her background in favor of a life of intellectual and emotional freedom, is considered by many to be her most outstanding book.

Beauvoir's memoirs present a fascinating account of the life of a female intellectual in the mid-20th century, in a country where leading intellectuals are not only unusually influential but also almost exclusively male. Moreover, they show that Beauvoir lived both ideas and politics "body and soul." After the war she declared herself a socialist and began an unending struggle against all forms of oppression and exploitation. Her account of her life in France during the country's ignominious colonial war in Algeria (1954–1962) conveys, together with her rational grounds for opposing the war, her visceral revolt against the nauseating climate of lies, immorality, and silence in which she found herself forced to live. In 1962 with Gisèle Halimi, the lawyer of the victim, she published *Djamila Boupacha,* an account of the French torture of a young Algerian woman.

Beauvoir's voracious appetite for knowledge and experience is reflected in the great scope and variety of her work: autobiography, philosophical essays, theater, literary criticism, novels, short stories, and travel books on the United States and China. Her two massive investigations of women and old age, *Le deuxième sexe* and *La vieillesse* (1970; *Old Age*), defy all generic categorizations. The scope of her essays indicates an intense thirst for *totality,* a desire to encompass the world in her own understanding and to leave her mark on it. Such an ambitious undertaking is singularly lacking in the traditional marks of femininity. There is no modesty, no domesticity, no emphasis on traditional female topics. As an intellectual, Beauvoir saw herself as a human being, not as a woman.

There is something intensely liberating in discovering such limitless confidence and ambition in a woman. Yet many feminists have been made uneasy by Beauvoir's seemingly effortless escape from the female condition. Is she not simply embracing patriarchal values? Should she not have made a greater effort to praise the traditional domain of women? Does her exceptional life (no husband, no children, no permanent home until she was almost fifty) somehow disqualify her from speaking "as a woman"? Or did she rather sin by not being exceptional enough (was she not far too subservient, too traditional, in her relationship with Sartre)? Are not her memoirs also full-fledged attempts to forge a model life for herself? And is Angela Carter not right when she claims that "one of the most interesting projects of the life of Simone de Beauvoir has been her mythologization of the life of Sartre. Her volumes of memoirs are devoted to this project" (quoted in Appignanesi, *Simone de Beauvoir,* pp. 137–138)? Beauvoir's works have proved no less controversial among feminists than among other politically minded readers. Mary Evans, for instance, has provided a searching—some would say ungenerous—critique of Beauvoir's politics from a modern feminist perspective. But such academic and intellectual disputes tend to mask a more important fact: almost from the start of her career

Beauvoir was an immensely *popular* writer. Her novels and essays were often runaway best-sellers; they have been translated into dozens of languages and are constantly in print in both French and English. For a woman who as a teenager used to dream of making herself loved through her books, such lasting popular success must have been the greatest satisfaction of all.

See also 1945 (15 October), 1975.

Bibliography: Lisa Appignanesi, *Simone de Beauvoir* (Harmondsworth: Penguin, 1988). Simone de Beauvoir, *Force of Circumstance,* trans. Richard Howard (Harmondsworth: Penguin, 1987). Beauvoir, *The Prime of Life,* trans. Peter Green (Harmondsworth: Penguin, 1988). Beauvoir, *The Second Sex,* ed. and trans. H. M. Parshley (Harmondsworth: Penguin, 1984). Beauvoir, *She Came to Stay,* trans. Yvonne Moyse and Roger Senhaouse (London: Fontana, 1987). Mary Evans, *Simone de Beauvoir: A Feminist Mandarin* (London: Tavistock, 1985). Michèle Le Doeuff, "Simone de Beauvoir and Existentialism," *Feminist Studies,* 6 (1980), 277–289.

Toril Moi

 1953

Les gommes, Alain Robbe-Grillet's First Novel, Launches a Period of Narrative Experimentation

The Nouveau Roman

In 1953 Les Editions de Minuit, founded during World War II to aid the Resistance, published Alain Robbe-Grillet's *Les gommes* (*The Erasers*). In the years following, the same press published Robbe-Grillet's *Le voyeur* (1955; *The Voyeur*) and *La jalousie* (1957; *Jealousy*); Michel Butor's *Passage de Milan* (1954; *Milan Passage*), *L'emploi du temps* (1956; *Passing Time*), and *La modification* (1957; *A Change of Heart*); Claude Simon's *Le vent* (1957; *The Wind*) and *L'herbe* (1958; *The Grass*); and a new edition of Nathalie Sarraute's 1939 *Tropismes* (1957; *Tropisms*). By the late 1950s it became clear that this corpus constituted a different kind of fiction, one that did away with the methods of the 19th-century novel and its avatars, dismissed the anthropocentrism of the existentialist works that had dominated French literature in the postwar era, seemed utterly insensitive to immediate (sociopolitical) problems, showed unusual interest in its own procedures, promoted experimentation, and stressed the relative.

Some applauded this innovation as a profound examination of fictional language and fictional space, the ways in which we articulate and understand ourselves and the world, the processes through which our views of reality are produced. Many condemned it as excessively formalistic, often unreadable, and thoroughly lacking in humanity. Theoretical and polemical texts by Robbe-Grillet (collected in 1963 in *Pour un nouveau roman; For a New Novel*) and Sarraute (*L'ère du soupçon,* 1956; *The Age of Suspicion*) contributed to the prominence of the so-called New Novel. So did substantial articles by Roland Barthes and others. Other writers, several of whom published their work at the Editions de

Minuit, would be identified as New Novelists: Robert Pinget—*Graal flibuste* (1956; *Filibustering Grail*), *Baga* (1958), *Le fiston* (1959; *Sonny*), *L'inquisitoire* (1962; *The Inquisitory*); Claude Mauriac—*Le dîner en ville* (1959; *The Dinner Party*) and *La marquise sortit à cinq heures* (1961; *The Marquise Went Out at Five*); Claude Ollier—*La mise en scène* (1959; *The Staging*); and, at least for a while, Marguerite Duras—*Le square* (1955; *The Square*) and *Moderato cantabile* (1958). Although the term *nouveau roman* probably did not appear in print until 1957 (as the cover-page title of an article in *Critique* by Maurice Nadeau), the New Novel became the most important French literary phenomenon of the 1950s and early 1960s.

Several reasons can be advanced to account for the *nouveau roman*'s apparent lack of concern for ordinary human interests and ideals, for its self-consciousness, relativism, and emphasis on technical exploration. World War II had dealt a severe blow to universalizing humanistic beliefs. France's postwar capitalist society may have encouraged a focus on things rather than on people. Of course, the New Novelists' individual talents and goals should also be considered. But so should various aspects of the 20th-century French cultural landscape. In philosophy, for example, the influential phenomenological movement spurned explanations resorting to some absolute mind. It underlined instead the reciprocal influence of self and world and maintained that what we call reality does not preexist human consciousness, just as what we call human consciousness does not preexist reality. In science, prestigious new models of the universe discarded beliefs in the possibility of adopting a godlike point of view and abandoned positivistic ambitions to describe the world in itself. Theoretical constructs were viewed as provisional modes of accounting for a set of data rather than as exact representations of the way things are. Uncertainty replaced certainty. Relativity became a byword. Together with the ascendancy of the physical sciences, both the development of the social sciences and the thriving of new artistic and mass media (film, radio, television) suggested that "literary" fiction had to redefine its territory. It could no longer claim preeminence either as a document about the real world or as a narrative of fictional adventures. What it could properly aspire to was examining its own nature and tracing the processes of human consciousness. The very achievements of the great 19th-century realist tradition and its descendants had exhausted a rich vein of fictional possibilities; besides, other novelists (and other artists), in France and elsewhere, had provided examples of an art that was self-exploratory, adopted new modes of organization, and seemed more in harmony with 20th-century conceptions of human experience.

Like the reasons given for the birth of the *nouveau roman,* the exact year of its birth is a matter of contention. Perhaps 1953 has the strongest claim, since it was primarily in terms of Robbe-Grillet's early works that the activity of the New Novelists was interpreted and since both Sarraute's *Martereau* and Duras' *Les petits chevaux de Tarquinia* (*The Little Horses of Tarquinia*) were published the same year as *Les gommes.* However, Pinget's *Mahu, ou le matériau* (*Mahu, or the Material*) came out in 1952, Sarraute's *Tropismes* first appeared in 1939, and in the preface to her 1948 *Portrait d'un inconnu* (*Portrait of a Man Unknown*) Sartre called the novel an *anti-roman*, an antinovel attempting to subvert from the inside accepted novelistic forms and formulas. Furthermore, the new fiction got its "official" name only in 1957, and only in 1957, when *La modification* was awarded the Prix Renaudot, did it reach a wider public.

The very name *nouveau roman* and its appropriateness are likewise contestable. In fact many other designations were proposed, including *école de minuit* (school of midnight), because of the role played by Jérôme Lindon and his Editions de Minuit in the promotion of the New Novel; *école du regard* (school of looking), because of what was felt to be the New Novelists' exaggerated concern with the visual perception and description of inanimate and seemingly trivial objects (the title *Le voyeur* is revealing, and the "protagonist" of *La jalousie*, who is never described but whose looking pervades the novel, is often called the "eye"); *école du refus* (school of refusal), because the relevant works refused the essentialist psychology, the linear chronology, the mechanistic chains of cause and effect, the notion of a perfectly stable, wholly coherent, fundamentally meaningful, and thoroughly decipherable universe that formed the basis of traditional fiction; *nouveau réalisme* (new realism), because for the New Novelists, unlike the 19th-century realists, reality was *constructed*, simultaneously discovered and invented by our perceptions and conceptions; *roman expérimental* (experimental novel), because Robbe-Grillet and Butor, Sarraute and Simon, Mauriac and Pinget underscored in their theory and practice the importance of experimenting; and *anté-roman* (pre-novel), because the New Novelists seemed more interested in discussing the constituents of fiction than in creating it.

Indeed, like any other newness, that of the *nouveau roman* is relative to a context. The novels of Robbe-Grillet, Simon, and Sarraute were new in relation to the 19th-century version of realism, to the postwar existentialist fare of Beauvoir, Camus, and Sartre, and to traditionally constructed works by Antoine Blondin, Jacques Laurent, Roger Nimier, and Françoise Sagan, which were so popular around 1950 that they led Maurice Nadeau to speak of a rebirth of classical fiction. They were much less new in relation to the work of, say, William Faulkner (whose influence on Claude Simon has often been noted) or James Joyce. And earlier in the century in France itself Raymond Roussel and Marcel Proust had abandoned 19th-century assumptions and procedures; Gide had explored some of the boundaries of fiction in *Les faux-monnayeurs* (1925; *The Counterfeiters*); Paul Valéry had wondered how a novelist could write, in all seriousness, such trivial sentences as "The marquise went out at five"; André Breton, in his surrealist manifestos and in *Nadja* (1928), had violently rejected the realist aesthetic; Louis-Ferdinand Céline had refashioned novelistic voice and style with *Voyage au bout de la nuit* (1932; *Journey to the End of Night*) and *Mort à crédit* (1936; *Death on the Installment Plan*); Sartre's *La nausée* (1938; *Nausea*) had underlined the differences between narrative and life and had paved the way for fictions grounded in phenomenology; Camus's *L'étranger* (1942; *The Stranger*) had criticized facile causal explanations and undermined the notion of psychological interiority; in 1951 the Editions de Minuit had published Samuel

Beckett's *Molloy* and *Malone meurt* (*Malone Dies*); and in the 1930s, 1940s, and early 1950s, writers such as Raymond Queneau and Boris Vian, Georges Bataille, Maurice Blanchot, Jean Cayrol, Louis-René des Forêts, Pierre Klossowski, and Jean Paulhan had been discarding conventional plotting and characterization, creating new fictional worlds, and inventing new languages. More generally, it can be argued that the adjective "new" is redundant when used with the noun "novel" (as English more than suggests). What is commonly taken to be the first novel—Cervantes' *Don Quixote* (1605–1615)—is, paradoxically, also the first antinovel; as early as 1633 Charles Sorel called his *Le berger extravagant* (*The Extravagant Shepherd*), in which he ridiculed the commonplaces of pastoral fiction, an *anti-roman;* and the New Novelists themselves took pains to emphasize that good writers are always new in their own time.

Finally, it is not at all clear that the term *nouveau roman* designates a homogeneous production or that the New Novelists were sufficiently similar in their practice to be considered a coherent group. Unlike the surrealists, for example, they did not write joint manifestos or present themselves as members of a school or movement. They even protested being grouped together. Indeed, there were always obvious differences between, say, Robbe-Grillet's interest in the surface of things, Sarraute's preoccupation with psychological depths, the comic verve and linguistic play of Pinget, and the baroque lyricism of Simon.

Still, there are several reasons—beyond pedagogical convenience or blind critical will to order—for placing these writers under the same label. The New Novelists all spurned the techniques of "Balzacian" fiction, the metaphysical assumptions they implied, the intellectual reassurances they provided, the aesthetic stereotypes they encouraged. They stressed relativity, uncertainty, unpredictability. They showed little concern for *vraisemblance,* for modeling worlds on hackneyed views of reality. They rejected or problematized such conventional novelistic props as character and plot. Sarraute, for example, traces the subtlest, most evanescent psychological movements without firmly locating them in well-defined beings; Robbe-Grillet in *La jalousie* and Claude Simon in *La route des Flandres* (1960; *The Flanders Road*) make it difficult or impossible to separate "real" time from personal time, to speak of a beginning, a middle, and an end, to extract a sustained story line. Moreover, the New Novelists invoked the same precursors and admired the same tradition (or antitradition): Flaubert, Roussel, Joyce and Kafka, Faulkner and Woolf. Above all, perhaps, they prized the study and broadening of the territory of fiction. Pinget's *Mahu, ou le matériau,* for instance, examines the elements of which novels are made. Butor's *L'emploi du temps* analyzes and exploits the links between the time of the telling and the time of what is told. His *La modification* explores the dimensions of second-person narrative. In *Les gommes, Le voyeur,* and *La jalousie* Robbe-Grillet transforms the nature and function of description by deanthropomorphizing its language. The New Novelists consistently tried to reinvent the novel, and their writings call for different modes of reading.

This readiness to experiment explains in part the heterogeneity of the New Novelists' production. Going wherever their research may lead them, they not only differ from one another but also from themselves: Robbe-Grillet's *Dans le labyrinthe* (1959; *In the Labyrinth*) does not resemble *Les gommes;* nor does Butor's *Degrés* (1960; *Degrees*) resemble *Passage de Milan.* Moreover, it explains in part why even critics sympathetic to avant-garde endeavors and mindful of their diversity and specificity did not abandon the designation *nouveau roman.* If it is true that the New Novelists had a number of forerunners, it is equally true that their work systematized and elaborated many of those precursors' achievements and contributed significantly to liberating the novel from the schemes and imperatives of traditional fiction. It stressed the realities of representation instead of the representation of realities; or, as Jean Ricardou once argued, it focused on the adventures of writing rather than on the writing of adventures. Although the New Novel did not issue from a school or movement, it did represent a moment in 20th-century French fiction: in the 1950s, several writers published by the Editions de Minuit appeared on the literary scene and many readers perceived, however dimly, the importance of their production and its undeniable—albeit relative—novelty.

In the mid-1960s, the New Novel began to lose its dominant position. It was not so much that its practitioners changed their orientation or lost their talent. Although Robbe-Grillet seemed to show more interest in moviemaking than in writing fiction, and although, after *Degrés,* Butor turned to composing texts that could hardly be called novels and did not aspire to the name—*Mobile* (1962) and *6 810 000 litres d'eau par seconde* (1965; *Niagara*)—there is a remarkable continuity in Sarraute's work from *Tropismes* or *Le planétarium* (1959; *The Planetarium*) to *Entre la vie et la mort* (1972; *Between Life and Death*) and *"Disent les imbéciles"* (1978; *"Fools Say"*); similarly, in *Le libera* (1968; *The Libera*), *Passacaille* (1969; *Passacaglia*), or *L'apocryphe* (1980; *The Apocryphal*), Pinget pursued his exploration of fictional building blocks and of narrative voice; and Claude Simon, who deservedly won the Nobel Prize in 1985, deepened his investigation of the links between history and fiction, memory and desire, reality and representation in such works as *La bataille de Pharsale* (1969; *The Battle of Pharsalus*) and *Les géorgiques* (1981; *The Georgics*). Rather, the very success of the New Novelists had made their production more familiar and therefore, perhaps, less provocative. Besides, a younger generation of avant-garde writers, closely associated with the periodical *Tel quel,* further radicalized many of the already radical practices of the New Novel. Whereas Robbe-Grillet, Simon, and Butor had been interested in the factors governing the writing of fiction and the construction of fictional space, Philippe Sollers, Jean-Pierre Faye, and Jean Thibaudeau concentrated on the factors governing writing, period, and the elaboration of textual space. By the late 1960s the Editions du Seuil, which published their work, had replaced the Editions de Minuit as the most visible purveyor of avant-garde texts, and the *roman Tel quel* or *nouveau nouveau roman,* the New New Novel playfully announced by Robbe-Grillet himself in one of his critical essays, had displaced the *nouveau roman.*

The contributions of the *nouveau roman* were substantial. In barely a dozen years the New Novelists enriched the French literary canon with well over two dozen texts outstanding for their redefinition of the novelistic domain, their illumination of the writer's activity, and their new visions of the world. They encouraged their readers to relearn how to read and allowed them to read afresh earlier writers (including Balzac and the realists). They contributed to the rejuvenation of the theory and criticism of fiction (so much so that they were sometimes viewed as primarily made for critics and professors). Finally, they helped to free their successors from limiting assumptions, rules, and norms and decisively transformed the possibilities of fictional practice.

See also 1925 (November), 1933 (November), 1966.

Bibliography: Roland Barthes, "Littérature objective," *Critique,* 10 (July–August 1954), 581–591; translated by Richard Howard as "Objective Literature," in Barthes, *Critical Essays* (Evanston: Northwestern University Press, 1972). Stephen Heath, *The Nouveau Roman: A Study in the Practice of Writing* (London: Elek, 1972). Vivian Mercier, *The New Novel from Queneau to Pinget* (New York: Farrar, Straus and Giroux, 1971). Maurice Nadeau, "Nouvelles formules pour le roman," *Critique,* 13 (August–September 1957), 707–722. Jean Ricardou, *Pour une théorie du nouveau roman* (Paris: Seuil, 1971).

Gerald Prince

ᕗ 1954, January

Cahiers du cinéma Publishes François Truffaut's
Vitriolic Manifesto against French Cinema

On Certain Tendencies of the French Cinema

In the thirty-first number of *Cahiers du cinéma,* dated January 1954, against the bland uneventfulness of cultural life in the Fourth Republic, there dramatically appeared "Une certaine tendance du cinéma français" ("A Certain Tendency of the French Cinema"), the first major article signed by François Truffaut on his way to wrest power from the old guard. Five years later Truffaut's *Les quatre cents coups (400 Blows)* would initiate the *nouvelle vague* (new wave), a deluge of films whose bold search for self-expression overwhelmed the traditional and heavy *cinéma de qualité* (cinema of quality), forming the most significant movement in film history since Italian neorealism. Truffaut's essay dealt the first blow in this outright struggle for control of French cinema. Its vitriolic tone, even after having been diluted by the magazine's wary editors, André Bazin and Jacques Doniol-Valcroze, provoked immediate screams of pain and anger from the film establishment. From its inception in 1951 *Cahiers* had grown increasingly rancorous toward the cinematographic establishment, but the outright violence of "Une certaine tendance" was unprecedented; it was a bomb designed to maim and injure, not to alter behavior through mere polite criticism.

Paradoxically, *Cahiers* waged its battle for cinematic modernism under the banner of "literature," generally deemed a stronghold of the establishment. Truffaut alleged that the dozen directors and handful of screenwriters dominating the French film industry had betrayed cinema because first of all they

993

had betrayed the literary tradition from which they presumptuously saw themselves evolving. The *cinéma de qualité* of the postwar years thrived on adaptations of novels by Zola, Stendhal, Balzac, Flaubert, Gide, Raymond Radiguet, and Colette. Even productions that purported to be "original" displayed the literary dialogue and carefully sculpted sets, costumes, and acting that the French seemed to associate with the good taste of literary values. But to the editors of *Cahiers du cinéma,* the conception of literature fostered by the "quality approach" was puerile, ingratiating, and debilitating both to the medium and to culture. Truffaut wrote: "I consider an adaptation of value only when written by a *man of the cinema.* [Jean] Aurenche and [Pierre] Bost [two prominent representatives of the quality approach] are essentially literary men, and I reproach them here for being contemptuous of the cinema by underestimating it. They behave, vis-à-vis the scenario, as if they thought to reeducate a delinquent by finding him a job."

It was a simple thing for Truffaut to ridicule the pretensions of a style whose identifying label, "quality," was so obviously part of a national advertising campaign that sought to promote French cars, perfumes, and haute couture as well. It was an even simpler thing for him to prove their so-called adaptations utterly meretricious. Indeed, how could Gide and Stendhal come out looking and sounding like each other as they did in Jean Delannoy's version of *La symphonie pastorale* (1946; *The Pastoral Symphony*) and Claude Autant-Lara's rendition of *Le rouge et le noir* (1954; *The Red and the Black*)? Something stood between these novels and their cinematic representation, something that leveled them into competent but flat movies. Truffaut assumed it was the glibness of the writers (primarily Aurenche and Bost), together with the uninspired attitude of businesslike directors who were satisfied to stage these watered-down scripts in the most commercially efficient way possible.

Today we would put the issue differently. What Truffaut objected to in this "tendency" was a tired but rigid *écriture,* a dull and lifeless cinematic writing that translated literature into merely competent movies. What he called for was a specifically cinematic *écriture.* In short, the institution of the cinema during this era fostered a belief that it descended from the venerable institution of literature, but it did so only by weakening, through institutionalization, the very process and energy of writing. Instead, Truffaut allied himself to directors such as Jacques Becker, Robert Bresson, Jean Cocteau, Jacques Tati, and, above all, Jean Renoir, for whom making movies was a material gesture of writing. Through strong cinematic *écriture* even the maligned enterprise of literary adaptation could come to life. Such was the case, Truffaut believed, with Bresson's version of Georges Bernanos' *Le journal d'un curé de campagne* (1950; *Diary of a Country Priest*)—a film whose stylistic rigor provoked Bazin to claim that it "is faithful to the original because, to begin with, it *is* the novel . . . The resulting work is not, certainly, better but 'more' than the book . . . The aesthetic pleasure we derive from Bresson's film . . . includes all that the novel has to offer plus, in addition, its refraction in the cinema" (*Cahiers,* no. 3, June 1951).

Truffaut was sensitive as well to purely cinematic gestures, such as Mr. Hulot's gait in Tati's comedies, and the wonderful cinematic tricks that take Orpheus into the underworld in Cocteau's *Orphée* (1950; *Orpheus*).

The distinction between writing and literature, implicit in Truffaut, was explored intensively after World War II, not only by Sartre in *Qu'est-ce que la littérature?* (1947; *What Is Literature?*) and by Roland Barthes in *Le degré zéro de l'écriture* (1953; *Writing Degree Zero*), but also by the young filmmaker Alexandre Astruc, a friend of Sartre and a prominent figure in the *ciné-club* movement that preceded *Cahiers du cinéma*. In "La naissance d'une nouvelle avant-garde: La caméra-stylo" (1948; "The Birth of a New Avant-Garde: The Camera-Pen"), Astruc wrote what many consider the first apology for the modern cinema, anticipating Truffaut by admonishing directors against merely mounting preconceived blocks of acting called "scripts." He urged young directors to think instead of the camera as a kind of pen, supple enough to express feelings and ideas of all sorts—supple enough, Truffaut would add, to mimic or respond to many literary styles if it were intent on adaptation. Ten years before the first new wave films Astruc wrote: "This of course implies that the scriptwriter directs his own scripts; or rather, that the scriptwriter ceases to exist, for in this kind of filmmaking the distinction between author and director loses all meaning. Direction is no longer a means of illustrating or presenting a scene, but a true act of writing" ("Birth," p. 22). Literature, then, was a model for the cinema only insofar as it was conceived as process (writing), not as institution (a set of completed masterworks).

In linking his goal for a new avant-garde with a discussion of the literary enterprises of the cinema, Astruc followed a long French tradition. Whereas the cinematic avant-gardes of most countries sought a specific zone explicitly free from the paternalism of literary culture and conventions, Astruc and Truffaut followed Louis Delluc, Jean Epstein, Abel Gance, and the Parisian *ciné-club* movement of the 1920s in measuring the health of the cinema through its relation to literary values. By 1930 cinema had gained widespread respect among the French intelligentsia. The surrealists, for instance, used the cinema in their war against standard conceptions of literature and culture. And René Clair, once a Dada-inspired filmmaker (*Entr'acte,* 1924; *Intermission*), who argued for a "pure cinema" of movement and rhythm, one that owed nothing to verbal language, nevertheless took his place in 1960 alongside the country's literary craftsmen in the Académie Française. Clair's chief antagonist in the first years of sound, Marcel Pagnol, was also elected to the Académie after a distinguished career in both theater and cinema. Pagnol's sensationally successful adaptations of Jean Giono during the 1930s—including *Angèle* (1934), *Regain* (1936; *Harvest*), and *La femme du boulanger* (1938; *The Baker's Wife*)—attest to the broad appeal of a literary cinema in the era of the Popular Front, an appeal that novelists such as André Gide, Roger Martin du Gard, Antoine de Saint-Exupéry, André Malraux, and Colette all actively tried to engage. The Paris publisher Gaston Gallimard went so far as to arrange for an adaptation of

995

Madame Bovary directed by Jean Renoir in 1934, and his publishing firm underwrote a subenterprise known as SYNOPS, which was explicitly concerned with cinematic adaptations of the books of his prestigious authors.

This increasing cultural acceptance had its effect on intellectuals such as Malraux who had at first evinced disdain for the medium. In Barcelona, in 1938, he personally directed the filming of *Sierra de Teruel,* an adaptation of the novel he had just published, *L'espoir* (1937; *Man's Hope*). Two years later he wrote one of the most substantial theoretical monographs on this new art form, *Esquisse d'une psychologie du cinéma* (1946; *Sketch for a Psychology of the Cinéma*). Further, at the time of the liberation Gide was working unofficially on the adaptation of his *La symphonie pastorale,* and Sartre took time out to write film criticism, to help adapt his plays for the screen, and to develop the original scenario for *Les jeux sont faits* (1947; *The Chips Are Down*). This was the prevailing cultural environment when *Cahiers du cinéma* came into being. It is no wonder that the *Cahiers* critics immediately endeavored to replace "quality," a term laced with crass economic connotations and old-fashioned snobbery, with a certain tendency of their own, significantly labeled "the *auteur* policy." The prestige of authorship was an essential element in the culture, and at this time it clearly extended to the cinema.

In literature of course authorship has always been a stable, defining value, yet for its first half-century the cinema struggled to adopt this concept. France adopted it soonest and most passionately, extending copyright (*droits d'auteur*) to the artistic originators of films in 1930. The French courts insisted as early as 1934 that the cinema must be considered an artistic medium with a status similar to that of literature.

By 1954 the notion of authorship had become spiritually bound to that of *authenticité,* a term sacred to the existentialist ethic of postwar Europe. Authenticity, calling to mind notions of originality, is clearly the criterion by which Truffaut judged the filmmakers of his day, before other incidental attributes, such as whether one constructs stories with words or with photographic images. Thus Aurenche and Bost, both of whom enjoyed literary careers outside the cinema, were not considered *auteurs* by Truffaut because they were indifferent to their adaptations' lack of authenticity. Selling the cinema short, they gave up their rights and their heritage.

In the pages of the same journals that launched Truffaut, *Cahiers du cinéma* and *Arts,* the upstart Jean-Luc Godard insisted that cinema take on the responsibility of representing the values of its age, a responsibility that, in his view, contemporary literature had largely abandoned. "The crisis in contemporary literature over the last twenty-five years has caused the cinema to answer for errors which are the responsibility of literature. Our period writes so badly that it is amazed by such polished speeches as those of the American cinema . . . the ease of these transatlantic filmmakers once found its echo in our own amiable and unfortunate 18th century" (*Godard on Godard*, p. 26).

Like Truffaut, Godard maintained that the stodgy architects of the *cinéma de qualité* should have learned from Hollywood; instead they had bartered the relevance and spontaneity of cinema for a trumped-up "intelligence" that they presumed was literary. A voracious reader, Godard elaborated his central intuition that authentic art comes from sincere authors who extend the sacred tradition only when they forget tradition and forge the present with their tools of expression. "Tell me whether the destiny of the modern cinema does not take the same form as it did for the belated partisans of romanticism. Yes, *with new thoughts let us make old verses*" (*Godard on Godard,* p. 28). When he eventually took up a camera, Godard developed his scripts and dialogue himself (often on the spot). He saw himself as an heir to a literary tradition in an era in which filmmaking had replaced literature as the authentic mode of writing and representation. In his first feature, *A bout de souffle* (1960; *Breathless*), he explicitly but casually alluded to William Faulkner, Rainer Maria Rilke, and Dylan Thomas, filmed books in closeup, and whispered passages from Louis Aragon and Guillaume Apollinaire offscreen. Throughout the winding trajectory of his dozens of films, such irreverent homage to the world of books has remained a trademark.

Godard's ambivalence toward tradition and toward literature masks an anxiety over the distinction between the "authentic" and the "specious"—an anxiety that seeps into Truffaut's 1954 essay when he hesitates over the case of France's most celebrated scriptwriter, Jacques Prévert. Prévert had ceased working in cinema before 1950, but it was to the films he wrote for Marcel Carné that the term *qualité* always harked. The "literary" character of Prévert's dialogue was obvious, as was the symbolism of his algebraic plots. Yet Prévert did not adapt novels. He was nothing if not inventive. A former surrealist, his early years had been devoted to spontaneous versification, later to sacrilegious and salacious theatrical improvisation. Truffaut could respect his ability to treat the cinema as the equal of literature, although this stemmed from Prévert's utter disregard of the sanctity of the classics. When, after the failure of the Popular Front, he gave himself over to imagining the poetic realist world that Arletty, Pierre Brasseur, and Jean Gabin would populate in *Quai des brumes* (1937; *Port of Shadows*) and *Les enfants du paradis* (1944; *Children of Paradise*), was he working authentically for the cinema or from facility and disdain? Truffaut could not decide. The criterion of authenticity was far too airy.

Truffaut's qualms about Prévert may be attributed to the latter's anticlerical anarchism. Jean Aurenche, whose career likewise began with surrealism, flaunted his "advanced ideas," as Truffaut called them, in a most presumptuous way, and in a way that turned the cinema into a forum for liberal political views. Truffaut's 1954 essay exposed the *Cahiers* revolution as potentially one of reaction, perhaps even a revolution of the cultural right. So thought rival factions of the time, chiding the *Cahiers* critics for their hagiographic treatment of American directors such as Nicholas Ray in the midst of the Cold War. Later, as filmmakers, the new wave (particularly Claude Chabrol, Eric Rohmer, and Truffaut) would be excoriated for resurrecting a cinema based on personal conscience and private salvation in the midst of a mysterious and incomprehensible world, whereas leftist critics could agree that the *cinéma de qualité* at least had the good sense to analyze the social origins of its dramas and to look for social solutions or cast social blame.

Regardless of the ideology of the *Cahiers* critics and filmmakers, their notions of cinematic art and of the modern world were exactly the ideas that were needed in the mid-1950s. They believed in a new future for the cinema, one they refused to define in advance. They were certainly not out to proclaim a cinema secure in its ideas, for this was precisely what they objected to in the self-satisfied *cinéma de qualité*. Sartre gave to them, as he did to the whole era, a sense of the risk that permeates the creation of culture and must attend every legitimate expression. The *Cahiers* critics and filmmakers understood this risk as an ethics of writing. This is the measure of their modernity; this is why they can be said to have made possible a modern cinema no matter what sorts of films the new wave would ultimately produce.

The strongest vindication of the historical aptness of Truffaut's 1954 essay comes from the concurrent appearance of a parallel group whose conception and practice of cinematic *écriture* would indeed link up with the most advanced tendencies in French culture, right through the 1960s and 1970s. The Rive Gauche (Left Bank) group, made up of Chris Marker, Agnès Varda, and, most important, Alain Resnais, was supported by *Cahiers*, although its members never wrote for that journal or engaged in explicit polemics against the establishment. They worked their way into film culture by means of a series of haunting (and award-winning) documentaries, many of which emphasized commentaries of a literary nature. Resnais addressed the mystique of books in a short subject on the Bibliothèque Nationale (*Toute la mémoire du monde*, 1957; *All the Memory of the World*). He used a poem by Paul Eluard for *Guernica* (1950), and, for *Le chant du styrène* (1957; *The Song of Styrene*), he had Raymond Queneau compose a witty celebration, in alexandrine verse, of the polymerization of plastic resin. In his disturbing masterpiece on the Nazi concentration camps, *Nuit et brouillard* (1956; *Night and Fog*), Resnais interwove his ethereal camera movements with an incantatory narration written by novelist Jean Cayrol to explore a transpersonal, nearly metaphysical, space. When he turned to the fictional mode, Resnais put into play a radical reexamination of the function of character, one that drew on the aesthetic of the *nouveaux romanciers*, Marguerite Duras, Alain Robbe-Grillet, and Nathalie Sarraute, who at just this moment were railing against the wax figure characters of 19th-century fiction. In this way Resnais and the Left Bank group helped the *Cahiers* critics overturn the conventional "psychological" realism of the *cinéma de qualité* directors that, since World War II, had produced nothing but solidly motivated humanoids in stilted dramatic situations.

Because of his close association with the most advanced literature of the day, Resnais ultimately provoked more lasting aesthetic questions than the *Cahiers* critics. His *Hiroshima mon amour* (1959), scripted by Duras, altered the handling of time and space, dialogue, and character far more than the inaugural new wave masterpieces, *Les quatre cents coups* and *A bout de souffle*. Resnais's next film, the enigmatic *L'année dernière à Marienbad* (1961; *Last Year at Marienbad*), was made in collaboration with Robbe-Grillet, then reaching the summit of his influence. Its play with states of consciousness, time, character identity, and the formal properties of the image and of language is unmatched in the history of French cinema.

Whereas the new wave directors, especially Rohmer and Godard, had taken upon themselves the responsibility of scripting their films and had in every case considered themselves *auteurs* of the camera, just as Astruc had predicted, Resnais's projects were more complicated. He insisted on preserving the alien quality of the literary themes and dialogue that Duras and Robbe-Grillet wrote for him so as to make the "literary" interact as an element with the very different elements of the lyrical documentary form he had developed in his short films. Resnais's work became a thriving hybrid, whose specific and calculated effects were different from both the purely literary and the purely cinematic.

The literary impulse in French cinema came full circle in the 1960s when, on the basis of their experience with Resnais, Robbe-Grillet and Duras began directing their own films, confounding writing and filmmaking in what can only be termed an experiment in expanded *écriture*. Robbe-Grillet's *Trans-Europ-Express* (1966) featured the author himself working on a thriller while riding a train. The tale he develops comes to involve his own journey. Here the peculiar intersection of fiction and film is cleverly manipulated for striking, if somewhat traditional, effects. Robbe-Grillet later experimented with serial composition when in *L'Eden et après* (1971; *Eden and After*) he fragmented a dozen independent episodes into core elements arranged according to an abstract sequential algorithm.

Duras' engagement with the cinema has been even more productive and far more influential. After consulting on adaptations of her stories by directors such as Peter Brook and Jules Dassin, Duras got behind the camera herself for *Détruire, dit-elle* (1969; *Destroy, She Said*). After that, many of the situations and characters originating in her prose fiction began to reappear in the cinema. *La femme du Gange* (1974; *Woman of the Ganges*), combining characters from several earlier novels, in turn served as the basis for a play from which another film, her most famous, was made: *India Song* (1975). The mesmerizing soundtrack of *India Song* in turn generated still another film. And so on.

Duras, Robbe-Grillet, and other less renowned authors working directly in the cinema have been supported by the development of a sophisticated critical atmosphere that brought film studies into the universities under the banners of structuralism and semiology. The fact that Duras has become a central figure in French culture allows us to measure the distance traveled since 1954. Cinema, literature, and critical writing are interwoven in this author and in an expanding cultural venture that Truffaut could have neither imagined nor condoned, but that his essay helped initiate. The practice and the field of literature, contaminated throughout this century by the cinematic imagination, has now been recognizably remade so that the term *écriture* must stand beyond authorship and beyond texts in a productive, though anxious, relation to culture and to subjectivity.

Bibliography: Dudley Andrew, *André Bazin* (New York: Oxford University Press, 1978). Alexandre Astruc, "The Birth of a New Avant-Garde: La Caméra-Stylo," in *The New Wave,* ed. Peter Graham (Garden City, N.Y.: Doubleday, 1968), pp. 17–23. André Bazin, *"Diary of a Country Priest* and Robert Bresson's Stylistics," in *What Is Cinema?* trans. Hugh Gray (Berkeley: University of California Press, 1967), pp. 125–143. Jean-Luc Godard, *Godard on Godard,* ed. and trans. Tom Milne (New York: Viking, 1972). Jim Hillier, ed., *Cahiers du Cinéma: The 1950s* (Cambridge, Mass.: Harvard University Press, 1985). François Truffaut, "A Certain Tendency of the French Cinema," in *Movies and Methods,* ed. Bill Nichols (Berkeley: University of California Press, 1976), pp. 224–235.

Dudley Andrew

✐ 1959, 9 January
President Charles de Gaulle Appoints André Malraux
France's Minister of Cultural Affairs

The Ministry of Fate

It was André Malraux's view that his most important legacy as de Gaulle's minister of cultural affairs was the network of cultural centers (*maisons de la culture*) that he had instituted, stretching from Caen to Thonon-les-Bains, Rennes to Firminy, Saint-Etienne to Paris' Ménilmontant, Amiens to Grenoble. "For the cost of twenty-five kilometres of highway," he had argued to the Chamber of Deputies on 27 October 1966, "France may, in the next ten years, become once again, thanks to the cultural centers, the first cultural country in the world" (quoted in Lacouture, *André Malraux,* p. 414).

This notion of forcibly decentralizing French culture, of making it popularly accessible, of "doing for culture what Jules Ferry [the 19th-century legislator of compulsory secular schooling in France] did for education," combined with the cleaning and repointing of the most beautiful buildings of Paris to form the double legacy by which Malraux's ministry is remembered.

Yet this legacy achieved an ironic afterlife when, during the early 1970s, two projects—one initiated by his régime, the other an indirect product of it— were realized that both contravened his efforts as minister and constituted its climax, its logical conclusion. These projects were the destruction of Victor Baltard's great iron-and-glass pavilions of Les Halles and the building of Paris' own massive cultural center, the Centre Georges Pompidou. The contradictory connection that these activities bear to Malraux's cultural policy exemplifies the internal contradictions of that policy itself. For the postwar Malraux was both populist and theocrat. "What matters more than anything to me is art," he had said. "I am in art as one is in religion" (quoted in Lacouture, *Malraux,* p. 363). And again, when on an official visit to the United States, hosted by the Metropolitan Museum, he was asked if he agreed that America's cathedrals were her railroad stations, he answered, "America's cathedrals are her museums" (p. 387).

But if the date of the climax of Malraux's cultural policies is arguably posterior to that of his ministry, the inception of his ideas about culture predates it
by many decades. Malraux signed *Les voix du silence* (1951; *The Voices of Silence*),
the volume that gathers together the various strands of his famous argument
for the *musée imaginaire*, "1935–1951." That sixteen-year period, during which
he returned again and again to the notion of human destiny spoken through the
composite but silent chorus of the world's art, coincides with the span of time
in which international events carried Malraux into a very different sphere of
action. In 1936 and 1937 Malraux led an air squadron for the Republican forces
in the Spanish Civil War. It was therefore not until 1938 that he was able to
take up his project again (originally conceived by him as a "psychology of art"),
publishing a series of short texts from his nascent study in the art magazine
Verve. But the shooting of a film based on *L'espoir* (1937; *Man's Hope*) occupied
him in 1938–39, and it was only after the defeat of France in June 1940 that
Malraux, in the free zone, began once more to write. By the end of 1942
Malraux, having once more taken up arms, this time for the Resistance, nonetheless continued work on his psychology of art. In 1947 *Le musée imaginaire*
(*The Museum without Walls*) was published, followed by the full study, now
retitled *Les voix du silence* (*The Voices of Silence*), in 1951.

The "museum without walls" was the cultural idea that had preoccupied
Malraux for several decades. It was an idea born of the fusion of three sources,
all of them German but given a special Gallic twist by Malraux's mode of syn-
thesizing them. The sources were Heinrich Wölfflin, Daniel-Henry Kahnweiler,
and Walter Benjamin. The first was the art historian who, with his *Kunst-
geschichtliche Grundbegriffe* (1917; *Principles of Art History*), had both fathered that
discipline and formulated an idea of it as a history without heroes or masterpieces, a history of art, as he expressed it, "without proper names." Kahnweiler,
Pablo Picasso's dealer, was the author of *Der Weg zum Kubismus* (1918; *The Rise
of Cubism*), the first text to grasp cubism's inner coherence as a revolutionary
style. The critic and theorist Benjamin was important to Malraux as the author
of "The Work of Art in the Age of Mechanical Reproduction," the first essay to
have explained—beyond the superficial issues of style—the impact of photography on the history of art.

Indeed, it was photography that functioned as the very medium of Malraux's
museum without walls—his museum raised to an entirely new conceptual level
through the power of photographic reproduction. The photographic archive
itself, insofar as it is the locale of a potentially *complete* assemblage of world
artifacts, is a repository of knowledge in a way that no individual museum could
ever be. But beyond its possibility of producing knowledge as the total picture
of something, the photograph is capable of recontextualizing the work of art far
more radically than the museum's merely imperialist gesture of detaching it
from its original site and displacing it to the "neutral" walls of the collection.
Photography's resiting, for Malraux, constituted the recreation of the work of
art, through massive disruptions of original scale (tiny cylinder seals enlarged
to become the same visual size as monumental bas-reliefs), of stunning reinven-

tions by means of camera angle or lighting (with ancient Sumerian terracotta figures thereby emerging as the cousins of 20th-century sculptures by Hans Arp or Joan Miró), and, most important, of cutting or cropping, by which the camera, wresting from a larger work a dramatically framed fragment, surgically intervenes in the aesthetic unity of the original to enable new and startling grafts. "Classical aesthetics proceeded from the part to the whole," Malraux wrote, "ours, often proceeding from the whole to the fragment, finds a precious ally in photographic reproduction" (*The Voices of Silence,* p. 30).

In speaking of photography as the "precious ally" of a modern aesthetic, Malraux was, of course, using only one part of Benjamin's analysis of the reproductive media. The total thrust of Benjamin's argument had been to demonstrate the way art's function is tied to its mode of production, so that mechanical reproduction—by which he meant photography—would necessarily alter the function of art, and thus the very idea of the "aesthetic," beyond recognition. Before photography, Benjamin argued, at least part of art's power was vested in the way it objectified the given touch of its master, or the indelible mark of its period, or the trace of its succession of owners. This was the "aura" of the work of art, and it was a direct function of the uniqueness of the original work—the very meaning of the work's status as an original. The structural change effected by photography's material base is that it is a medium of direct copies, where there exist multiples *without* an original. The photographic reproduction of a work of art not only multiplies the image a thousandfold but, stripping it of the experience of uniqueness, strips it also of its aura. A culture that has entered the age of mechanical reproduction will not only experience the passing of the auratic work of art but will also, Benjamin prophesied, develop a totally new function for art, one that will be a product of the photographic system, most probably documentary in nature.

Malraux's museum without walls, dependent on the way that photography—and specifically the photographic *reproduction*—transforms the original object, did not, however, take Benjamin's final step toward the notion of a post-auratic art. For Malraux, photography simply transferred the experience of aura—or the power exerted by art—from the elitist spaces of the 19th-century museum to the more widely accessible, and preeminently 20th-century, pages of the art book. Thus the imaginary museum was filled with a continued, though transformed, condition of aura. Which is to say that the imaginary museum was filled with "meaning."

One of Malraux's very first texts, a preface to an exhibition catalogue, published in 1922, already presents this notion of art as a vast semiotic system, a multiple chorus of meaning. Indeed, Jean Lacouture writes of this little preface that "here in a few lines is almost everything that the author of *The Voices of Silence* was to develop thirty years later." For there Malraux had written: "We can feel only by comparison. He who knows *Andromaque* or *Phèdre* will gain a better idea of the French genius by reading *A Midsummer Night's Dream* than by reading all the other tragedies by Racine. The Greek genius will be better understood by comparing a Greek statue to an Egyptian or Asiatic one than by acquaintance with a hundred Greek statues" (quoted in Lacouture, *André Malraux,* p. 35).

Malraux, at the age of twenty, did not stumble by himself onto this conception of the aesthetic as comparative and therefore as fundamentally semiotic. Apprenticed to Daniel-Henry Kahnweiler at age eighteen, Malraux was indoctrinated into an experience of the visual arts that was informed by both German art history and cubist aesthetics—which is to say, a way of seeing that had dispensed with the idea of form as beauty in favor of a conception of form as "linguistic." Classical art, as an aesthetic absolute for Western taste, had instituted beauty as the ideal of artistic practice and experience. Wölfflin had relativized this absolute by arguing that classicism can be "read" only within a comparative system through which it can be contrasted to the baroque. Setting up a group of formal vectors through which to make such comparative readings—the tactile versus the optical, the planar versus the recessive, the closed versus the open—Wölfflin transmuted form into the condition of the linguistic sign: oppositive, relative, and negative. Form no longer had value in itself, but only within a system, and in contrast to another set of forms. The aesthetic component was no longer beautiful; it was significant.

Kahnweiler's connection to this early, structuralizing art history in Germany influenced his own understanding of cubism. For Picasso's dealer saw the cubist exploitation of African art, for example, as a breakthrough to the production of forms that would function as signs. "These painters," he wrote, "turned away from imitation because they had discovered that the true character of painting and sculpture is that of a *script.* The products of these arts are signs, emblems, for the external world, not mirrors reflecting the external world in a more or less distorting manner . . . The [African] masks bore testimony to the conception, in all its purity, that art aims at the creation of signs" (*The Sculptures of Picasso,* preface).

Malraux took this dictum, that art aims at the creation of signs, and never forgot it. Art produces signs that can be read comparatively. Comparison decentralizes and dehierarchizes art, for the comparison works on the juxtaposition of systems—*all* systems: east versus west, high versus low, courtly versus popular, north versus south. And photography, by fragmenting and isolating the signifying elements from within a work's complexity, is the ultimate aid to this reading (see fig. 1).

In *Les voix du silence* Malraux attempts to give voice to the "texts"—which he calls "fictions"—that such readings can produce, and to find in them a great, inspiring, master-text. So he speaks of the way the world's vast variety of artistic production—miniatures, frescoes, stained glass, tapestries, Scythian plaques, pictures, Greek vase paintings, "details," and statuary—enters the "museum without walls" (the art book) as "plates." "In the process," he concedes, "they have lost their properties as *objects;* but, by the same token, they have gained something: the utmost significance as to *style* that they can possibly acquire" (*The Voices of Silence,* p. 44). And it is this transformation into a system of meaning that makes up for what reproduction takes away, leaving no room for

1. André Malraux amid the illustrations for *Le musée imaginaire*. (Photo courtesy of Paris-Match/Jarnoux.)

regret that these figures have lost "both their original significance as objects and their function (religious or other); we see them only as works of art and they bring home to us only their makers' talent. We might almost call them not 'works' but 'moments' of art. Yet diverse as they are, all these objects speak for the same endeavor; it is as though an unseen presence, the spirit of art, were urging all on the same quest, from miniature to picture, from fresco to stained-glass window" (p. 46). And it is this "spirit of art" that reproduction liberates to tell its story, no matter how silently: "Thus it is that, thanks to the rather specious unity imposed by photographic reproduction on a multiplicity of objects, ranging from the statue to the bas-relief, from bas-reliefs to seal-impressions, and from these to the plaques of the nomads, a 'Babylonian style' seems to emerge as a real entity, not a mere classification—as something resembling, rather, the life-story of a great creator. Nothing conveys more vividly and compellingly the notion of a destiny shaping human ends than do the great styles, whose evolutions and transformations seem like long scars that Fate has left, in passing, on the face of the earth" (ibid.). For the first time, Malraux exults, this story is becoming, thanks to reproduction, "the common heritage of all mankind."

The need for and urgency of telling this story of a universal artistic culture ring through the concluding passages of Malraux's long study. "The first culture to include the whole world's art," he proclaims, "this culture of ours, which will certainly transform modern art (by which until now it was given its lead), does not stand for an invasion but for one of the crowning victories of the West. Whether we desire it or not, Western man will light his path only by the torch he carries, even if it burns his hands, and what that torch is seeking to throw light on is everything that can enhance the power of Man" (*The Voices of Silence*, p. 640).

There were, of course, readers of Malraux's text who found this hymn to technology's progressive abstraction of the work of art and its transformation simultaneously into "plate" and "sign" objectionable. Georges Duthuit, a former participant in the Collège de Sociologie, greeted *Les voix du silence* with a review that later grew into a three-volume condemnation, *Le musée inimaginable* (1956; roughly, *The Off-the-Wall Museum*). Everywhere, Duthuit said, Malraux merely reinforced the imperialist gesture of the Western collector and museologue, who rips out trophies from foreign cultures to make of them so many abstract "pictures": "The words *conquest, annexation, possession,* ceaselessly resound in *The Voices of Silence* like a rousing clarion call" ("Malraux et son musée," p. 345). Duthuit also impugned Malraux's own participation in the kind of adventurism that was, in his book, being transformed into the disinterested ideal of a new, global aesthetic. Quoting a passage in which Malraux invokes the happy accidents by which "chance" turned Greek sculpture into so many formally revelatory fragments, Duthuit comments, "Chance . . . And Malraux, who sets the example and blasts out several panels from the temple at Angkor with dynamite, stands off to the side laden down with a ton of imaginary stock" (p. 346). (Duthuit refers here to Malraux's expedition to Cambodia in 1923, when, having detached bas-reliefs from the Khmer temple at Banteai-Sre, he was charged with pillaging monuments and sentenced by the French colonial government. Malraux made this the subject of his 1930 novel *La voie royale; The Royal Way.*)

That Malraux, whose postwar political career was committed to the idea of nationalism and the rise of national cultures as the 20th century's response to the crushing internationalist, imperialistic adventures of the 19th, should have embraced an aesthetic that annihilates the particularities of place, of material, of substance, in favor of the abstraction of "text," is indeed a contradiction. And perhaps "Beaubourg"—the Centre Georges Pompidou—is the monument that most vividly embodies the contradictions of Malraux's meditation on art's fate. For Beaubourg, Paris' own cultural center (a constellation of public library, industrial design center, center for experimental music, and the National Museum of Modern Art), became the site of an ambitious cycle of anthologizing exhibitions. These exhibitions, conceived as efforts to embed works of art in their real historical context, combined paintings and sculptures with cases of research documents, with films and video screened on the walls of the galleries, with ranges of documentary photographs, and with exhaustive wall-texts. And from this anthological process there emerged the mutation of "art" into "information" and of the exhibition into the textual event of a book.

Malraux had wanted art to "speak" through the signifying eloquence of its form. This was the possibility he had gleaned from his experience of modernist art. Paris' cultural center acted to engage 20th-century art in the production of speech, and the result—a kind of staccato of information—is seen by many as one of the heralds of postmodernism.

See also 1905, 1937 (12 July).

Bibliography: Georges Duthuit, "Malraux et son musée," *Les lettres nouvelles,* 2 (March 1954), 357–384; expanded into *Le musée inimaginable,* 3 vols. (Paris: José Corti, 1956). Daniel-Henry Kahnweiler, *The Sculptures of Picasso,* trans. A. D. B. Sylvester (London: R. Phillips, 1949). Jean Lacouture, *André Malraux,* trans. Alan Sheridan (London: André Deutsch, 1975). André Malraux, *Museum without Walls,* trans. Stuart Gilbert and Francis Price (Garden City, N.Y.: Doubleday, 1967). Malraux, *The Psychology of Art,* trans. Stuart Gilbert, 3 vols. (New York: Pantheon, 1949, 1950). Malraux, *The Voices of Silence,* trans. Stuart Gilbert (Princeton: Princeton University Press, 1978).

Rosalind Krauss

1959, 28 October

Jean Genet's Play *Les nègres* Is Performed in Paris

The Theater of the Absurd

The première of Jean Genet's *Les nègres* (*The Blacks*) on 28 October 1959 at the tiny Théâtre de Lutèce was both a bombshell and a triumph. Directed by Roger Blin—who had staged Samuel Beckett's *En attendant Godot* (1952; *Waiting for Godot*) in 1953 and *Fin de partie* (1957; *Endgame*) in 1957—and performed by a company of unknown black actors, Genet's fourth play incorporated even more radical concepts of theater than his previous dramatic works, *Les bonnes* (1947; *The Maids*), *Haute-surveillance* (1949; *Deathwatch*), and *Le balcon* (1956; *The Balcony*).

Genet was already notorious as a writer of exquisitely crafted, poetically provocative homoerotic fictions and autobiography as scandalous as the author's criminal past and assertive homosexual practices at a time when these were not yet accepted subject matter for literature. But Genet's plays, which postdate most of his fiction, are not autobiographical, and their appeal is much wider: they are more distanced, less self-indulgent, elevated to a mythic dimension, and based on the enactment of rituals. The shock value of Genet's theater is more deeply rooted; a lyric outburst of stylized hatred by outcasts against oppressors; a radical subversion of traditional dramaturgy; a rare stylistic splendor of dazzling imagery and language, frequently contrasted with jolting vulgarity.

Genet subtitled *Les nègres* "Clownerie" ("Clown Show"). The play starts with a group of blacks who have killed a white woman and, in front of her coffin, enact a ritual of hatred and revenge under the watchful glance of a white court. But nothing is what it seems to be. The blacks, in fact, have *not* killed any white; the catafalque in the middle of the stage that is supposed to contain the dead woman is revealed to be nothing more than two empty chairs with a cloth draped over them; the real killing takes place offstage: another black, a traitor to the cause, is brought to summary justice. The action onstage has been a diversionary tactic for the benefit of the whites. Furthermore, the whites—a Queen and her Valet, a Governor, a Missionary, and a Judge—are not white at all; they are blacks wearing grotesque white masks, their black skin and kinky hair clearly apparent, caricaturing the dominant power structure. The distorting mirror reflects the experience of blacks as outcasts in a white world, their humiliation, their loathing, their revolt. Written by a white dramatist for a white audience (Genet insisted that at least one white spectator, be it a symbolic one, be present at all performances), *Les nègres* portrays what a white playwright thinks that blacks think that whites think that blacks think.

This complex interplay between reality and illusion, both being elements of theater and representation, constitutes what Martin Esslin has called "a hall of mirrors" in which truth becomes indistinguishable from fiction. Indeed, Genet forces to their ultimate limit the paradoxes of the "theater-within-the-theater" technique used by Luigi Pirandello in *Six Characters in Search of an Author* (1921) and *Tonight We Improvise* (1930).

To achieve these resonating circles within circles of a play within a play within a play, Genet uses theatrical references throughout *Les nègres*. "This evening we shall perform for you" (*The Blacks,* p. 12), proclaims Archibald, the master of revels, directly to the audience; to the "white" court he confides: "We are actors and organized an evening's entertainment for you" (p. 99). To his fellow blacks, Archibald explains why they are "performing" for whites: "They tell us that we're grownup children. In that case, what's left for us? The theater! We'll play at being reflected in it" (p. 38); and he chides them when they drift from the spirit of enactment: "This is the theater, not the street. The theater, and drama, and crime" (p. 58). The blacks' gestures are deliberately theatrical, and their frequent, shrill, orchestrated laughter punctuates the artificiality of the process. Words such as *stage, performance, actor, spectator,* and *backstage* recur as constant reminders that the action is a deliberate and distanced nonrealistic representation whose only truth is symbolic. As a further jolt to the fourth-wall convention of the traditional theater, a spectator is brought onstage to hold a prop.

Genet uses strongly antirealistic techniques to undermine all realistic models of the depiction of reality. In the play, blacks and pseudowhites engage in highly structured rituals designed to *enact* (rather than relive) reality. Real life, in Genet's dramas, is always represented via the distortion and the mythologizing associated with rite and ceremony; ritualistic elevation and ceremonial simulacrum disguise form a veil of illusion that cloaks reality. For Genet the interesting feature of real life is its ability to generate the permanent truth of myth. Thus one looks in vain in his plays for a probing political or sociological reflection on their manifest content: blacks in a white world (*Les nègres*); servants subjugated by masters (*Les bonnes*); the sublimation of revolt in the make-believe of the closed world of the brothel (*Le balcon*); North Africans spurned by dominant white European ideology (*Les paravents,* 1966; *The Screens*); criminals versus the "straight" world (*Haute-surveillance*). However fascinating these conflicts may be in themselves, to Genet they are mere pretexts for his relentless examination of the dialectic that separates—and glorifies—the social outcast. Blacks, maids, whores, Algerians, convicts—all have in common their deliberate rejection of the "normal" order of society, whose corruption they despise and denounce. Only in this sense can Genet's theater be deemed autobiographical: the events are not linked to Genet's life as thief and prostitute on a literal level, but rather through the glorification of the pariah based on Genet's contempt for accepted values in a codified, bourgeois society and on his loathing for those right-thinking, self-satisfied citizens whom Sartre called swine (*salauds*).

The pariah-protagonists of Genet's inverted world are forced into their isolation by the society that rejects them, but their particular genius is to assume—even to demand—responsibility for their exclusion. They will assume their fate and glorify it. This is the basis for Sartre's approach to Genet's own life; he calls him a "saint" in his *Saint Genet, comédien et martyr* (1952; *Saint Genet, Actor and Martyr*), less by analogy to the hero of Jean Rotrou's 17th-century play, *Le véritable saint Genest* (1646; *The True Saint Genest*), than in recognition of Genet's proud insistence that his criminality was of his own choosing and not attributable to the excuse that he was an abandoned child, brought up in orphanages, and introduced early to crime. The sainthood claimed by Sartre for Genet and, by extension, for Genet's characters is the exaltation of behavior diametrically opposed to "normal" modes of comportment—the sainthood of evil.

Les nègres introduces us to a topsy-turvy world in which life is turned inside-out, like a glove. Superficially, the blacks conform to white values and to the way whites expect them to act; they carefully dance the white man's minuet to Mozart's music, and they obligingly hurl stereotypical insults at the whites. But Genet allows the characters of *Les nègres* to carry their revolt further than in his earlier plays—not all the way to a successful overthrow (that will never happen in Genet's world), but to a greater awareness and militancy. The blacks of the play have not yet been liberated; they still are prisoners of white stereotypes and are shackled by white language, but their hatred is real and more effective than the impotent and finally self-destructive hatred of the two maids for their Madam in *Les bonnes*. Félicité, one of the blacks, warns the "white"

Queen of things to come: "To you, black was the color of priests and under-takers and orphans. But everything is changing. Whatever is gentle and kind and good and tender will be black. So will the opera to which we shall go, blacks that we are, in black Rolls Royces to hail black kings, to hear brass bands beneath chandeliers of black crystal" (p. 106). As it becomes clear that the blacks are prepared to subvert white values, white language, and the white power structure, the menace to the white world becomes more palpable.

Despite Genet's claim that he was not interested in the social problems of his characters, there is a progressively political undertone in his plays. *Haute-surveillance* and *Les bonnes* shunned political concerns; *Le balcon* is much more in touch with them through a kind of Brechtian distancing; with *Les nègres* and finally *Les paravents* Genet's theater moves closer to real political and social issues. In their reliance on metaphor and nonrealistic dramaturgy, these are not "committed" plays in the Sartrian sense, but they are radical depictions of sen-sitive situations. Indeed, the first production of *Les paravents,* in 1966, at Jean-Louis Barrault's nationalized Odéon–Théâtre de France, scandalized its audience with its mordantly critical view of the French presence in Algeria at a time when the wounds of the Algerian War (1954–1962) had not yet healed.

Les nègres did not have the same subversive political resonance in France where, in 1959, widespread racial discrimination was not yet a burning issue. But in its first New York production, in 1961, at the off-Broadway St. Mark's Playhouse during a period of intense racial tension, *The Blacks* galvanized the public as no other play had done. Presented before the explosion of black theater in the United States, it was the first play to bring a sizable black public to off-Broadway. The author's "hall of mirrors" reflected right into the audience and produced tensions between black and white spectators in the theater and in the lobby. The brilliant New York production boasted a cast of those who were to become the most famous black actors of their generation (and the founders of the Negro Ensemble Company, which established its home at the St. Mark's Playhouse): Maya Angelou, Roscoe Lee Brown, Godfrey Cambridge, Charles Gordone, Louis Gosset, James Earl Jones, Cicely Tyson. *The Blacks* ran for over three years—Genet's biggest hit by far in the United States.

Genet's plays were part of the astonishing avant-garde that shook the theater in Paris around 1950—with aftershocks throughout the Western world ever since. *Les bonnes,* staged in 1947 by the last major director of the interwar years, Louis Jouvet, demonstrated a new dramaturgy, a new sensibility. But the flood-gates opened in 1950, and by the end of the decade the new theater had swept everything else away. The first major event was the production of Eugène Ionesco's *La cantatrice chauve* (1950; *The Bald Soprano*) at the minuscule Théâtre des Noctambules. With its madcap, dislocated language and its nonsensical and non-sequitur humor, *La cantatrice chauve* forced onto the spectator a new perception of the modern world as grotesque and dehumanized, halfway between nightmare and farce, a world populated by interchangeable characters lacking depth and reality. Arthur Adamov, Georges Schehadé, and Boris Vian also produced their first plays in 1950. The new wave continued with Ionesco's

La leçon (*The Lesson*) in 1951, *Les chaises* (*The Chairs*) the following year, and a rapid succession of other works by these and other playwrights. Most memorable was the première of Samuel Beckett's *En attendant Godot* (*Waiting for Godot*) in January 1953; like *La cantatrice chauve*, Beckett's work invented an entirely new theatrical language, palpable and comprehensible images of the absurd, and unforgettable metaphors of the human condition. Didi and Gogo's wait, their pathetic yet marvelous system of trying to fill the emptiness of their abandonment with bits of trivial conversation; Godot, the supposed savior whose only clear definition is that he does *not* come; the tyrant, Pozzo, who is both the tormentor and the victim of his servant, Lucky: these many reflections of the absurdity of existence, which have become part of our general frame of reference, communicate directly, viscerally, without any need to resort to rational analysis.

Starting with a very small public, the new theater caught on quickly throughout the 1950s. By the end of the decade Ionesco and Adamov had presented many more short plays, Beckett had added *Fin de partie* (1957; *Endgame*) and *Krapp's Last Tape* (1958), and Genet *Le balcon* and *Les nègres*. Schehadé and Vian continued to offer occasional new works; other playwrights who were to be more active in the 1960s and thereafter had their first plays performed: Fernando Arrabal, François Billetdoux, Roland Dubillard, Marguerite Duras, Armand Gatti, René de Obaldia, Robert Pinget. The new theater soon inspired dramatists in other countries to write in their respective languages: Edward Albee, Max Frisch, Jack Gelber, Arthur Kopit, Slawomir Mrozek, Harold Pinter.

Critics devised a number of labels to classify these new forms of theater: "antitheater," "metaphysical farce," "theater of derision"; although Esslin's "theater of the absurd" won widest acceptance, none is entirely satisfactory. Perhaps it is best to follow the example of Geneviève Serreau and speak, simply, of "new theater," much in the way one refers to the "new novel." The French avant-garde dramatists did not try to form a school or to work deliberately along similar lines. There are as many differences as similarities among them: Genet's verbal brilliance contrasts sharply with the aridity of Pinget's language, and Beckett's dark pessimism is far removed from Schehadé's gentle optimism. They do all share a deeply felt revolt against realistic conventions and a tendency toward more primitive forms of nonliterary spectacle such as farce, puppet shows, cabaret, ballet, pantomime, ceremonial.

The notion of the absurd, though not omnipresent, understandably predominates in this new theater. Before, during, and right after World War II, playwrights such as Jean Anouilh and Armand Salacrou faced the absurdity of contemporary existence tentatively, in an approximate, humanistic manner; Camus and Sartre tried to demonstrate the absurd dimension of existence by means of rational analysis. Going one step further, what has been termed the theater of the absurd depicts the absurd with absurd *means*. A realistic drama poses a theatrical problem and then moves on to its resolution. In the antirealistic new theater, it is not so much a matter of *what* happens (even if often very unexpected things happen), but rather the possible *meaning* of what is happening. The progression of events is not logical and sequential, but arbitrary and beyond the realm of causality. The author deliberately keeps the audience on the outside, disoriented, incapable of identifying with characters who cannot be placed in a "situation." On discovering that the rational structures they had thought to be operative in life are illusory, the spectators are finally confronted with the irrational element of their own individual existence and of existence in general, of the human condition. As in the *nouveau roman,* reason, plot, social context, and psychology take second place to a "new" realism of interiorized, metaphoric (rather than literal) truth.

By the mid-1960s the theater of the absurd had carried the day. In Paris, where it was born and bred, its authors were no longer limited to pocket-sized playhouses. Beckett, Genet, and Ionesco had become—and remain—household words; some of their plays became part of the permanent repertoire of that repository of French theatrical tradition, the Comédie-Française. Beyond France, the Parisian playwrights of the absurd have become the leading figures in world theater and have influenced dramatists on every continent. In 1967 Jacques Guicharnaud wrote that they had become "the new Establishment"; they have not yet been displaced. It is a remarkable success story for an avant-garde movement.

See also 1935, 1946.

Bibliography: Peter Brooks and Joseph Halpern, eds., *Genet: A Collection of Critical Essays* (Englewood Cliffs, N.J.: Prentice-Hall, 1979). Richard N. Coe, *The Vision of Jean Genet* (New York: Grove, 1968). Martin Esslin, *The Theater of the Absurd* (Harmondsworth: Penguin, 1980). Jean Genet, *The Blacks,* trans. Bernard Frechtman (New York: Grove, 1960). Jacques Guicharnaud, with June Guicharnaud, *Modern French Theater, from Giraudoux to Genet* (New Haven: Yale University Press, 1972). Jean-Paul Sartre, *Saint Genet: Actor and Martyr,* trans. Bernard Frechtman (New York: Braziller, 1963). Geneviève Serreau, *Histoire du "nouveau théâtre"* (Paris: Gallimard, 1966).

Thomas Bishop

✑ 1960

The First Issue of *Tel quel* Is Published

As Is

Tel quel, "as is": to an English-speaking reader, the phrase evokes nothing so much as damaged furniture at a warehouse sale. But to French readers with some claim to literacy, especially if they are over thirty, the phrase has a quite different resonance. It evokes not the furniture mart but the temple of art, or, for the more pragmatic-minded, the cultural and literary marketplace. *Tel quel* was the title given by Paul Valéry (a high priest in the temple) to two volumes of his aphorisms and miscellaneous reflections on literature and life, published in the 1940s; it was also the name under which a group of young writers with more than ordinary ambition (their leader, Philippe Sollers, was at twenty-three already the author of a much-praised novel, which he would soon disavow as an error of youth) launched a new literary journal in Paris in 1960.

The time seemed right for such an enterprise. Sartrian existentialism and its attendant theory of *littérature engagée* (committed writing), which had dominated the French intellectual scene since World War II, was showing signs of age. A new word, *structure,* soon to drown out *existence,* was being murmured after the publication of Claude Lévi-Strauss's *Anthropologie structurale* (1958; *Structural Anthropology*). There was talk of a *nouvelle vague* (new wave) in cinema and a *nouveau roman* (new novel) in literature. Alain Robbe-Grillet, already the best known of the "new novelists," whose first two works had received exceptionally attentive and perceptive commentary by a rising critic named Roland Barthes, was publishing polemical essays against what he called "outdated notions": nature, humanism, tragedy. Albert Camus, perhaps the greatest contemporary representative of those very notions, had been killed in an automobile accident the year before. Meanwhile, the new Fifth Republic, under its new president, General Charles de Gaulle, was trying to extricate itself from a bloody colonial war in Algeria that most intellectuals opposed.

Enter *Tel quel.* With an epigraph from Nietzsche ("I want the world and want it AS IS, want it again, want it eternally"—to be read not as applause for the status quo, but as an affirmation of appetite); a brief opening "Declaration" in favor of "poetry," sufficiently insolent to function as a manifesto even though it had no political or philosophical content (the point was precisely to challenge *littérature engagée* and Sartre's journal, *Les temps modernes*); a lead poem by Francis Ponge, a major poet whose status was not yet fully recognized; a respectable mix of fiction by newcomers and slightly older writers, all of it heavily influenced by the *nouveau roman;* a gesture to precursors in the form of an essay titled "Flaubert et la sensibilité moderne" ("Flaubert and Modern Sensibility") and a translation of Virginia Woolf, as well as the promise of "important unpublished work by Paul Eluard" and a "survey on surrealism" for the second issue, *Tel quel* got off to an auspicious start. Still, nothing in that first issue indicated that this journal would, over more than two decades, come to occupy a central place in French literary and cultural life; nor that its name would eventually, for a time, designate the latest incarnation—some would say the last gasp—of the European avant-garde.

What made *Tel quel* an avant-garde movement, and when did it stop being one? Did it stop being one? And how are these questions related to a present that seems to define itself primarily as an age of "post": postmodern, post-Marxist, post–avant-garde, post-post?

In an interview published in one of the last issues of *Tel quel* (no. 85, 1980; the last issue was no. 94, 1982), Sollers summed up nearly fifteen years of his own and his friends' activity in a few pithy sentences:

> We have relived an old adventure to which we have ourselves doubtless put an end, which is the adventure of all the Western avant-gardes of the twentieth century: the contradiction between art and political engagement . . . In any

case, what has never varied is the concern to maintain the experience of writing, of literature, as rigorously independent . . . And you will see, there will be no reason to regret all the little dramas that *Tel quel* gave rise to, for I would be very surprised if we had ignored or opposed anything really important in our time. I would be extremely surprised if we didn't have a chance to continue asking essential questions. On the contrary. We are less academic today than when we were Maoists. We are more revolutionary today than when we were Maoists. Precisely because we have abandoned that division between political proclamations on the one side and, on the other, the quest for an experience that is opposed to them.

This statement is so packed with allusions to the history of *Tel quel* and with assumptions about the nature and function of writing and of avant-gardes that one hardly knows which way to turn, and how to assess *Tel quel*'s turn. Did *Tel quel* break out of the circle of repetition ("reliving an old adventure") into something new? Or was that breaking-out itself part of a process of repetition, part of the very adventure to which Sollers claims to have put an end?

Part of the answer may be found in the promise on the back cover of the first issue of *Tel quel:* a "survey on surrealism" to appear in the next issue. The survey consisted, Sollers later recalled, of a questionnaire he had sent to André Breton, a founder and chief spokesman of the surrealist movement. By 1960 surrealism was a dream of the past struggling to maintain the illusion that it still had something to offer the present: a revolutionary aesthetic *and* a revolutionary politics, unaffiliated with any party but based on an uncompromising notion of individual and collective liberation. Breton was sixty-four years old, a literary lion presiding over dwindling followers but endowed with enormous personal prestige—and endowed as well with the ambiguous aura of the 1930s. He did not respond to *Tel quel*'s questionnaire in time for the second issue; but in every issue after that, up to his death in the fall of 1966 and even beyond (to no. 29, 1967), his name appeared on the inside back cover among "forthcoming contributors."

Breton never did contribute to *Tel quel; Tel quel,* however, began to devote increasing attention to Breton and surrealism. The more the journal moved away from its original apolitical espousal of "literature concerned with its own rules" toward a conception of writing (*écriture*) as an experimental practice indissociably linked to social and economic revolution, the more it felt the necessity to differentiate itself from surrealism, which had proclaimed the same link throughout the late 1920s and the 1930s. Sollers' declaration in 1970, at the height of *Tel quel*'s political phase, that "one cannot make an economic and social revolution without making at the same time, and on a different level, a symbolic revolution" (no. 43, 1970), resonates uncannily with Breton's often-quoted statement, made in a speech in 1935: "'Transform the world,' said Marx; 'change life,' said Rimbaud: for us, these two watchwords are one" (*Manifestoes of Surrealism,* p. 241).

The *Tel quel* group knew the history of surrealism as well as anyone else. They knew that the surrealists had brought about (in Sollers' words) a "change in 'point of view' on art and literature," based on the conception of a radical break (*rupture*) with tradition; they knew that the surrealists had been the first to insist on both the literary and the ideological importance of "writers of rupture" such as the marquis de Sade and the Comte de Lautréamont (Isidore Ducasse); they knew that they had been among the first promoters of psychoanalysis in France and had attempted systematically to explore, in their works, the relations between waking life and dreams and the unconscious; finally, they knew that the surrealists had had a stormy and complicated relationship with Marxism, the Soviet Union, and the French Communist party, involving several splits within the surrealist group and culminating in Breton and Trotsky's denunciation of Stalinism and the Stalinist doctrine of socialist realism in the name of an "independent revolutionary art" ("Pour un art révolutionnaire indépendant," 1938).

Tel quel, too, based its theory of literature on the notion of *rupture;* it, too, considered Sade and Lautréamont as essential precursors, along with Stéphane Mallarmé and James Joyce; it, too, attributed primary importance to psychoanalysis and the unconscious—and it, too, concurrently with all this, lived through a stormy relationship with Marxism and the French Communist party. Given these coincidences, why did *Tel quel* try so hard to distinguish itself from surrealism? And why did it so relentlessly criticize it?

There is no simple answer to this question. As a start, one could invoke Harold Bloom's notion of the "anxiety of influence" and suggest that precisely because *Tel quel* felt surrealism to be its strongest precursor, it had to "overcome" it. This oedipal paradigm, though in some ways enormously appealing, has only a limited explanatory value, especially if one is trying to take account of ideology and history. (Oedipus, being "eternal," is also ahistorical.) Historically, there are probably two main reasons for *Tel quel*'s desire to establish its difference from the earlier movement. First, the new developments in philosophy, semiotics, and the "human sciences" that exploded on the French intellectual scene in the late 1960s and early 1970s (now loosely called "poststructuralism") appeared to many as an intellectual revolution after which none of the epistemological foundations of Western culture would remain intact. Humanism, the continuity of history, the unity of the self, the stability of the written text—all were called into question by Jacques Derrida's notion of "logocentrism," Jacques Lacan's conception of the "split subject," Michel Foucault's view of history as a series of "epistemic breaks," and Louis Althusser's critique of ideology. In every case, what seemed to be involved was an enterprise of rereading that would change not only our view of the past but also our sense of the future.

Tel quel not only "did not ignore or oppose" these developments, as Sollers stated in his 1980 interview; it promoted them through publication and commentary and significantly contributed to them through the theoretical work of Julia Kristeva. Kristeva, who arrived in Paris as a brilliant young student from Bulgaria in 1965, met Sollers the following year (they were later to marry) and published her first important essay in the Spring 1967 issue of *Tel quel*. In 1969 a volume of essays, *Séméiotikè: Recherches pour une sémanalyse* (*Séméiotikè: Studies toward a Semanalysis*), established her as a major literary theorist. It was partly thanks to Kristeva (as well as to her countryman Tzvetan Todorov) that the Russian formalist critics became widely known in France; she published one of the first essays in the West on the now famous but then barely known Soviet theorist Mikhail Bakhtin. Bakhtin's concept of "dialogism" served as the basis for her own concept of *intertextualité* (intertextuality), a term that has entered the standard critical vocabulary. Above all, it was she who elaborated, in an ambitious synthesis of Derrida's, Lacan's, and Bakhtin's concepts, as well as some others borrowed from contemporary linguistics, the influential theory of the "text as signifying practice," with which *Tel quel* was thereafter identified.

Given the importance attached by *Tel quel* to the epistemological revolution of the 1960s, it is hardly surprising that the journal sought to emphasize its difference from surrealism. The theme that recurs most often, in the articles on the earlier movement published by various members of the group between 1968 and 1971, is that although the surrealists recognized the importance of Marxism, psychoanalysis, revolutionary politics, and the "writers of rupture," they profoundly *misunderstood* all of them: in Marx they saw only Hegel, in psychoanalysis they were closer to Jung than to Freud, in revolutionary politics they ended up with the Trotskyist "deviation," in Lautréamont they saw only the poet, not the hard-headed political thinker. In short, the surrealists were idealists, untheoretical and unscientific; *Tel quel,* on the other hand, as Sollers announced in "La grande méthode" ("The Grand Method"), would use its proper understanding of dialectical materialism and its scientific theory of the text to analyze "the relations between intellectuals and the revolution" (no. 34, 1968).

Idealism thus became the password in *Tel quel*'s critique of surrealism. Ironically, the accusation had already been formulated by critics of surrealism in the 1930s, notably by Georges Bataille. Bataille, who died in 1962, had interested the *Tel quel* group from the start, as had Antonin Artaud, another "dissident" surrealist. *Tel quel* was among the first to reevaluate, and recognize the importance of, the work of both these "writers of rupture." However, the use *Tel quel* made of Bataille's previously unpublished 1929 essay against Breton, "La 'vieille taupe' et le préfixe *sur* dans les mots *surhomme* et *surréaliste*" (no. 34, 1968; "The 'Old Mole' and the Prefix *Sur* in the Words *Surhomme* [Superman] and *Surrealist*"), shows a certain lack of historical perspective. The editors did not take into account the specific circumstances of Bataille's attack—itself a response to Breton's attack on Bataille in the *Second manifeste du surréalisme* (1930; *Second Manifesto of Surrealism*)—which should have alerted them to its possible polemical exaggerations; nor did they consider the fact that Bataille, whom they used to criticize Breton's idealism and "mysticism," displayed more than a small dose of mysticism (albeit of the transgressive kind—Sartre called it Bataille's "black pantheism") in his writings. By promoting Bataille as the counterexample to Breton, *Tel quel* may already have inscribed its individualistic turn of 1980, with its insistence on the "experience of writing"— *L'expérience intérieure* (1943; *The Inner Experience*) is the title of one of Bataille's most important books—into its revolutionary Marxist politics of the late 1960s and early 1970s. On the other hand, by extending Bataille's critique of Breton (he especially blamed Breton for wanting to "abolish contradictions," the surest sign of idealism; Sollers, following this lead, wrote several articles in the 1970s on the necessity of recognizing and maintaining contradictions), *Tel quel* was able to maintain its self-image as an avant-garde movement, revolutionary both politically and aesthetically.

Thus *Tel quel*'s primary reason for attempting to establish its difference from surrealism (more exactly, from "orthodox" surrealism as represented by Breton) was, broadly speaking, theoretical: as Jean-François Fourny has noted, it sought to emphasize the radical innovations in thought of the 1960s and at the same time to revive a strain of 1930s thought (Bataille's) that had been "suppressed" by surrealism. The second reason is more immediately related to the political history of surrealism: in 1935, after trying for several years to place—as the title of their journal had it—"Surrealism in the Service of the Revolution" through a political alliance with the French Communists, Breton and his friends broke with the party; not because they stopped believing in the necessary union between political and aesthetic revolution, but because they felt that the party had compromised its own revolutionary principles by its blind allegiance to the Soviet Union, which under Stalin was sinking into dogmatism. From then on, the drama—or perhaps the tragedy—of surrealism consisted in its effort to maintain its Marxist politics even while proclaiming its ideological and artistic independence. In this attempt, the surrealists failed: more and more isolated politically, surrealism came to be regarded as an "elitist" artistic movement that owed its continued existence to the support of the very bourgeoisie it claimed to detest. Revolutionary in its ideology and aspirations, it ended up as a luxury consumer item on the capitalist market.

This was the fate that *Tel quel* sought to avoid by differentiating itself from surrealism. In an extremely perceptive essay published in 1966 (just before *Tel quel*'s turn toward politics) and prophetically titled "Les problèmes de l'avant-garde" ("The Problems of the Avant-Garde"), Marcelin Pleynet, a member of *Tel quel*'s editorial board, noted with dismay that surrealism had become simply a salon phenomenon: "One can be truly astonished that a revolutionary movement should end up this way, especially when, as in the case of surrealism, it was an organized movement." Pleynet's prognosis for the avant-gardes of the 1960s (coming chiefly from the United States) was pessimistic: "In our time, no more transgression, no more subversion, no more rupture . . . or rather, in my opinion, a parody of transgression, a parody of subversion, a simulacrum, repetition of rupture." Despite his pessimism, Pleynet concluded his essay by suggesting that a possible way out of the impasse of repetition lay in "the new conception of writing made possible by the recent work of Derrida, Lacan, Foucault, Sollers" (no. 25, 1966).

For the next ten years *Tel quel* attempted to blaze the way out of the impasse so lucidly analyzed by Pleynet; and the further it advanced, the more it repeated, with its own variations, the political adventure of surrealism. From

1967 to 1971, the years of revolutionary fervor associated with the events of May 1968, it pursued an alliance with the French Communist party; then, late in 1971, just after publishing its most sustained and virulent critique of surrealist "idealism" (no. 46), *Tel quel* broke with the Communists "from the left," accusing them of "revisionary dogmatism" and proclaiming its own authentically revolutionary avant-garde struggle. Just as the surrealists had repudiated Stalin in favor of the theorist of permanent revolution, Trotsky, *Tel quel* now became a champion of the Cultural Revolution in China and of its leader, Mao Tse-tung. In 1974, when the French Communists and the Socialists established a political alliance that again smacked of "revisionism," *Tel quel* even broke with Jacques Derrida, who supported the alliance.

But in the summer of 1974, after a trip to China that at first elicited great enthusiasm, a new crack began to appear. Kristeva, who was beginning to train as an analyst, published an article in *Tel quel* (no. 58) in which she flatly asserted: "There is no such thing as a Marxist politics for subjects in process." Because the "subject in process" is a central concept in Kristeva's theory (referring, among other things, to the practitioner of avant-garde writing), this statement could be read as an outright condemnation of Marxism, whether Maoist or other. It took another two years, however, before *Tel quel,* in the Winter 1976 issue, formally dissociated itself from Marxism: "The events that are occurring right now in Peking must definitely open the most reluctant eyes to what we must no longer hesitate to call 'the Marxist structure' . . . We must finish with myths, *all* myths." In the next issue Jean-Louis Houdebine, who had been one of surrealism's most relentless critics, published an indignant essay on the adoption of "socialist realism" in the Soviet Union in 1934, with its condemnation of Joyce and other modernist writers; in passing, he praised Breton's steadfast rejection of both Stalinism and socialist realism.

And so *Tel quel* came full circle: "We have relived an old adventure, to which we have ourselves doubtless put an end." Looking back in 1980, Sollers perceived the repetition in *Tel quel* and claimed to have left it behind. The theorist of the 1960s and 1970s who had celebrated contradiction now celebrated the end of a particularly vexing one, which has haunted (and daunted) every Western avant-garde: "the contradiction between art and political engagement."

Was Sollers repeating, fourteen years later, the pessimistic conclusions enunciated by Pleynet just before *Tel quel* embarked on its adventure: "In our time, there can be only a parody of transgression, a simulacrum of rupture"? In the same interview Sollers stated: "I believe that the history of the European avant-garde is over . . . Avant-garde was a term that implied society would follow, evolve, etc.; well, many experiences and experiments {*expériences*} have shown that, not at all, there is a contradiction, and the people of the avant-garde find themselves in assigned places—they are, if you will, the parrots of those in power."

Interestingly, the influential Marxist theorist Peter Bürger has made a similar claim: the notion of the avant-garde must be considered exclusively "historical"—past and done with, over already with surrealism. And yet, as the history of *Tel quel* demonstrates, the appeal of the avant-garde enterprise as the parallel pursuit of two equally compelling imperatives—change life, transform the world—recurs as a possibility for every new generation. *Tel quel* is dead, but the dream it once represented may not be.

See also 1924, 1937 (March), 1953, 1985.

Bibliography: Georges Bataille, *Visions of Excess: Selected Writings, 1927–1939,* ed. and trans. Allan Stoekl (Minneapolis: University of Minnesota Press, 1985). André Breton, *Manifestoes of Surrealism,* trans. Richard Seaver and Helen R. Lane (Ann Arbor: University of Michigan Press, 1969). Breton, "Pour un art révolutionnaire indépendant," in *La clé des champs* (Paris: Sagittaire, 1953), pp. 36–41. Peter Bürger, *Theory of the Avant-Garde,* trans. Michael Shaw (Minneapolis: University of Minnesota Press, 1984). Jean-François Fourny, "La deuxième vague: *Tel quel* et le surréalisme," *French Forum,* 2 (1987), 229–238. Danielle Marx-Scouras, "The Dissident Politics of *Tel quel,*" *L'esprit créateur,* 27 (Summer 1987), 101–107. Maurice Nadeau, *The History of Surrealism,* trans. Richard Howard (Cambridge, Mass.: Harvard University Press, 1989).

Susan Rubin Suleiman

✐ 1962, November
After Eight Years of War, Algeria Becomes Independent

The School of Independence

Throughout the Third Republic (1870–1940), most French people's knowledge of Algeria was comprised of clichés they recalled from Alphonse Daudet's gradeschool classic, *Tartarin de Tarascon* (1892). In the imagination of a decadent elite, the vast expanses of Algerian territory began to function, during the same period, as a preserve where one might experience otherness under the protection of the French flag. Seen as a mixture of sensuality and proud purity, of oasis and desert, Algeria served as a catalyst for writers in search of a break with Parisian culture. André Gide waited until his subsaharan *Voyage au Congo* (1925) to discover (and denounce) colonialism; in Algeria, in 1893, he discovered pleasure: its oases converted him to the taste of earthly fruits.

It was around the time of World War II that, tired of being described, the Algerians entered French literature as subjects rather than as objects; but, even so, they had to use the language of their colonizers: Maghrebian (Algerian, Moroccan, Tunisian) voices made themselves heard in the first person of a foreign language. This distinction seemed, to the Tunisian writer Albert Memmi, a particularly painful aspect of the alienation suffered by the colonized. Analyzing the colonial situation in *Portrait du colonisé précédé du Portrait du colonisateur* (1957; *The Colonizer and the Colonized*), he wrote of the "linguistic conflict" within the colonized individual: "His mother tongue is that which is crushed. He himself sets about discarding this infirm language, hiding it from the sight of strangers" (*The Colonizer,* p. 142). The successful struggle for national liberation would entail the end of this self-mutilation. On the eve of independence, an Algerian literature "written in French" seemed a contradiction in terms: political independence, it was thought, would be quickly followed by cultural and linguistic independence. Yet since 1962 there has been a flowering of works in French by Maghreb writers. Memmi himself recanted thirty years later, in the anthology *Ecrivains francophones du Maghreb* (1985; *Francophone Writers from the Maghreb*): "Without ceasing to believe that the Arabic tongue will ultimately find the place it deserves, I have had to admit that the inertia of custom is more powerful than logical or sentimental expectation" (p. 11).

This outcome reflects the linguistic plurality of Algeria. Besides dialectal and classical Arabic, many other languages were spoken in Algeria, even before the French conquest: Kabyle in the mountains of Kabylie, Tuareg in the desert, Mozabite in the oases. These languages are themselves divided into dialects. Moreover, Algeria's biggest problem has been and remains illiteracy: in 1962, 85 percent of the population not only did not speak French but also neither read nor wrote Arabic. Today the vast majority of Algerians are still illiterate. Algerian writers had to find their literary public in France.

Before independence, most Algerian writers were teachers and thus products of the colonial educational system. The poet Jean Amrouche and the novelist Mouloud Feraoun are notable examples (Feraoun was executed by the extreme right-wing terrorist organization, the OAS, which desperately sought to sabotage de Gaulle's eventual acknowledgment of Algerian independence). The writing of these men is emblematic of the contradiction in which Maghrebian literature is rooted, a contradiction that independence has not resolved. Amrouche translated folksongs into French. In the introduction to *Chants berbères de Kabylie* (1939; *Berber Songs from Kabylie*), he emphasizes the maternal roots of this oral popular poetry: "A man whose life is not separated from the life of the Mother," he writes, "is naturally a poet" (*Chants,* p. 13). But in *Chants berbères,* song becomes literature only as it exiled, into French: transcription and translation, here, are one and the same gesture of estrangement. Amrouche's collection is representative of contemporary Algerian literature: a literature born by breaking with the natural poetry of the mother tongue.

In 1960 Feraoun produced a volume of the same type, a translation of the poetry of Si-Mohand, the most famous 19th-century Kabyle bard (*Les poèmes de Si-Mohand*). But Feraoun was primarily a novelist. His first original work, *Le fils du pauvre* (1950; *The Poor Man's Son*), is autobiographical. Through the colonial educational system a young Kabyle escapes the poverty weighing on his people by becoming a teacher. French is not his native language. Yet, in this tale of apprenticeship, the crossing of the linguistic barrier leaves almost no textual mark. A few Arabic or Kabyle words do appear in the novel, translated at the bottom of the page. But the narrator never focuses on the split between the language he spoke as a child and that in which he teaches and writes as an adult. When the narrator recounts his first days as a student at the French school, no special reaction signals the significance of the linguistic boundary he is crossing. Only years later, after he received his diploma, does he remark: "He was surprised and happy to prove that he knew French" (p. 104). Encouraged by this first success, he attempts the competitive teachers' qualification exam and faces the following composition topic: "Your father, a worker in France, is uneducated. He talks to you of the difficulties encountered there by those who don't know how to read or write, of the regret he feels for not being educated, of the usefulness of learning" (p. 108). The candidate's essay is not reproduced in the novel, but the novel itself somehow makes the student the scribe of his illiterate father. *Le fils du pauvre* inverts the situation addressed in the examination topic: the telling of the poor man's son's story is precisely what differentiates the poor man and his son. On the one hand, his father, who did not know how to write, had to expatriate himself to Paris, becoming a worker in a country where he did not speak the language; on the other hand, by becoming a teacher Feraoun escaped the fate of the immigrant worker but in doing so lost his mother language. During the war, the independence fighters reproached Feraoun for defending the colonial educational system as emancipatory. And he had indeed internalized the pedagogical ideal of the Third Republic: for him, the boundary between two languages (between Kabyle and French, or even between spoken and written language) was less important than that between those who do and those who do not know how to write.

For Mohammed Dib (1920–), another teacher-novelist, the pitfalls of assimilation carried out in the colonialist schoolroom were more apparent than they had been for Feraoun. One of the first scenes in *La grande maison* (1952; *The Big House*) takes place in a "Franco-Arab" school, one of the rare institutions in which a few Arab children have been authorized to receive a French education. It is 1939, the beginning of World War II. The day's lesson is the idea of homeland. The Algerian teacher proposes a definition: "When strangers coming from outside pretend to be the masters, the homeland is in danger" (p. 22). This definition is followed by a coup de théâtre, which Omar, the young protagonist, will need the whole novel to understand fully. "Omar, surprised, heard the master speaking in Arabic. He who forbade them to speak it! Omar knew that the master was a Muslim—since his name was M. Hassan—he knew also where he lived, but Omar could not believe it. He would never even have thought it possible for him to speak in Arabic. But in a low voice pierced by an intriguing violence, the master said in Arabic, 'If you hear someone tell you that France is your homeland, it is just not true'" (p. 23). The novel ends with sirens screaming for an air-raid drill. But Omar has little sympathy for the troubles of the French, those foreign invaders invaded in turn by outsiders claiming to be their masters.

For the French, the end of World War II was a liberation; not so for the Algerians. In May 1945 a general uprising was followed by savage repression in which tens of thousands died. As a high-school student, Kateb Yacine (1929–) took part in these anti-French demonstrations, was imprisoned, and thereafter barred from further education. In his first novel, *Nedjma* (1956), Kateb interweaves memories of school with the insurrection. Lakhdar, a student expelled from high school after the riots, takes the train home. The only traveler in his compartment who can read the names of the stations, written in

French, he discovers that the educational system from which he has just been expelled would have made him betray his linguistic world. "If we had our own trains . . . First of all, the farmers would be comfortable. They wouldn't be fidgeting at each station, afraid of missing their stop. They could read. And in Arabic too! I'd have to reeducate myself in our own language" (p. 84). The French school in this episode ceases to be presented as a catalyst of conciliation, an agent of assimilation; it exposes and explodes the contradictions. Whereas Feraoun's school was a symbol of pacification, Kateb's intensifies a sense of impasse, revealing a loss and a betrayal. The strongest image of insurrection in *Nedjma* is that of the old Si Mokhtar, who in Constantine in May 1945 "walked through the city alone, past the fascinated police officers, with a gag in his mouth showing two slogans of his own invention that crowds of people engraved in their memory: 'Long live France / And Arabs silence!'" (p. 206). This scene embodies Kateb's description of his novel as an Arab work written in French. "Conceived and written in French," he writes in the preface, "*Nedjma* remains a profoundly Arab work" (p. 6).

Linguistic violence also concludes Kateb's second autobiographical novel, *Le polygone étoilé* (1966; *The Starred Polygon*). The narrator, born into a literary family, remembers that from his childhood everyone expected him to become a writer—in Arabic *kateb* means writer—but a writer, precisely, in Arabic, "like his father, like his mother, like his uncles, like his grandparents" (p. 179). Yet his father, a Muslim magistrate, sends him to a French school. This decision leads to the final outburst of jealousy: his mother cannot bear that her son should seek to please the French schoolmistress, who she thinks seduced him in a language that she herself does not speak. Kateb recalls this dramatic moment of betrayal: "Never have I ceased, even on the days of success with the teacher, to feel deep inside me that second rupture of the umbilical cord, that interior exile that reconciled the schoolchild with his mother only in order to tear them, each time a little more, from the murmuring of blood, from the reproachful reverberations of a banished language, secretly, by a common accord broken as quickly as it is concluded . . . Thus I had lost all at once my mother and her language, the only inalienable treasures—and yet alienated!" (p. 181).

Some novelists, such as Rachid Boudjedra (1951–), have tried to resolve this conflict by writing in Arabic and publishing in Algiers. But language is only one piece of a much larger system: the novelistic genre itself is alien to the Maghrebian literary tradition and, like the French language, symptomatic of postcolonial Parisian cultural domination. Thus Kateb's evolution toward popular theater constitutes another effort to recover the oral inspiration of a culture in which, even recently, narration was not tied to print.

"For whom does one write?" The question posed by Sartre in *Qu'est-ce que la littérature?* (1947; *What Is Literature?*) becomes dramatically problematic in a culture that has no literary public. Kateb settled in Algiers with the explicit intention of creating an Algerian public. His choice of public becomes clear in *Mohammed prends ta valise* (1971; *Mohammed Grab Your Suitcase*), the first play he produced in popular Arabic, which enjoyed great success among Algerian audiences in both Algeria and France. The central figure is an immigrant worker, a typical figure in contemporary Algerian life. But around this modern deterritorialized proletarian echoes from traditional nomadic culture multiply, such as popular songs and ancient stories or legends. Unlike the rigidity of the printed language, the flexibility of speech in a theatrical performance can reflect the complexity of everyday language, the plurality of tongues that coexist in Algeria. It permits the avoidance of strict linguistic choices tied to the written and even more to the printed word, and thus of the uniformity and impoverishment that these entail. Kateb's play of languages stirs up the linguistic chaos in which most of today's Algerians live.

Jacqueline Arnaud compares Kateb's return to an oral medium to the collecting of Valois songs so important to Gérard de Nerval. There are in fact several ways to consider this renewal of Si-Mohand's model—of the bard speaking to a people who cannot read. But Kateb's experiments in popular theater cannot be reduced to a simple return to the orality of the mother tongue. Kateb is not, like Amrouche, nostalgic for the lost unity of the mother country, for a culture spared separation and nostalgia. In Kateb's plays, the return to the oral does not constitute the resurrection of an archaic Algerian essence that colonization has destroyed or corrupted, but rather a kind of provisional linguistic morality, friendly to heterogeneity and seeking lively means of communication beyond those long institutionalized by the book-producing industry. This radicalism reminds Arnaud of Antonin Artaud's fight, in the 1930s, against the colonization of theatrical performance by the authority of the written text. Kateb, she says, "questions the very concept of the Maghreb writer of French" (*Recherches,* p. 1009); he chose "to risk his very existence as a writer in French" (p. 1011). Perhaps, she suggests, he even contests the concept of writer.

There is a Maghrebian literature. It denounces a system that, by giving it a voice, made it lose its language. The question it faces is not "Who will have the last word?" but rather "In which language will this word be pronounced?" Does every work written in French belong ipso facto to French literature? Is nationality a category that applies to a literary work as it does to the individual who produces it?

See also 1847, 1911, 1935, 1968 (February).

Bibliography: Jean Amrouche, *Chants berbères de Kabylie* (Paris: Charlot, 1947). Jacqueline Arnaud, *Recherches sur la littérature maghrébine de langue française: Le cas de Kateb Yacine,* 2 vols. (Paris: L'Harmattan, 1982). Réda Bensmaïa, "'Traduire' ou 'blanchir' la langue," *Hors cadre,* 3 (1985), 187–206. Mohammed Dib, *La grande maison* (Paris: Seuil, 1952). Mouloud Feraoun, *Le fils du pauvre* (Paris: Seuil, 1954). Henri Gobard, *L'aliénation linguistique (Analyse tétraglossique)* (Paris: Flammarion, 1976). Kateb Yacine, *Nedjma,* trans. Richard Howard (New York: Braziller, 1961). Yacine, *Le polygone étoilé* (Paris: Seuil, 1966). Abelkébir Khatibi, *Le roman maghrébin* (Paris: Maspéro, 1968). Albert Memmi, *The Colonizer and the Colonized,* trans. Howard Greenfield (New York: Orion Press, 1965). Memmi, *Ecrivains francophones du Maghreb* (Paris: Seghers, 1985).

Réda Bensmaïa

⚲ 1966

The Poetry Journal *L'éphémère* Appears

The Place of Poetry, the Poetry of Place

In France, as everywhere else, the publication of works that are unlikely to have a large readership is at best problematic, and poetry, of all the literary genres, is the most likely to suffer. Indeed, the pragmatic policies of publishers are but one indication that poetry has no guaranteed place, that poetry is always, and everywhere, in search of a place.

In 1988 Michel Deguy discussed this issue. He is a poet familiar with it at first hand and in its most practical aspects, having served for several years on the reading committee of France's most influential publishing house, Gallimard. His book *Comité* (1988; *Committee*) attacks the big publishers' policy of using poets and other writers whom they publish only rarely or not at all, to determine what works will eventually be published, and thus publicly accorded value. The authors who significantly help the large and powerful publishing houses in this task of evaluation are rewarded only by the displacement of their own writing, which is marginalized, relegated to the humbler status afforded by a small or "little" review. What is, then, the place of poetry? The answer seems to be, a small one indeed.

But perhaps the place that is at issue in and for poetry does not really lie between the material covers of a book. In France especially, avant-garde poetry reviews have often been associated with the art world and characterized by an interdisciplinary impulse. The verbal/visual collaboration of, say, Alberto Giacometti and Yves Bonnefoy acquires a resonance beyond the printed page. In 1966 there appeared a journal that was explicitly devoted to the notion not so much of lodging or dwelling as of passage and of passing—or rather, to the paradoxical thought of the ephemeral *as* a dwelling-place. In part for exactly that reason, *L'éphémère* indelibly marked the art and the poetry of the eight years of its existence. It ceased publication in 1973, deliberately enacting its own transitoriness.

Bonnefoy, Jacques Dupin, and André du Bouchet are the poets most closely associated with *L'éphémère*. They brought to their poetry and to their critical and lyric prose deep philosophical preoccupations. Their work links Heraclitus, for whom being is always experienced in passing only (since dwelling in any one moment or in any identical place is humanly impossible), and Friedrich Hölderlin, according to whom poetry alone makes dwelling possible, because only poetry has the ability to call forth or to name both place and moment. "Poetically," Hölderlin said, "man dwells on earth." For Martin Heidegger, who interpreted Hölderlin in the light of his own philosophy, poetic language founds a dwelling-place adequate for human meaning, deep enough to include both the movement of passing and the impulse constantly to abide, thus retaining in this staying the intensity or "amazement" of being newly named. In the lineage of these reflections, the major poets concerned with acknowledging the truth of human passage and, simultaneously, with searching for the ground of dwelling that Hölderlin and Heidegger examined and celebrated, each in different ways, have developed over the last twenty years in France a poetry of place.

A strong sense of the local, mingling with an equally strong sense of the cosmic, characterizes the work of René Char (1907–1988), a former surrealist active in the Resistance during World War II. His poetry, universal in scope, is situated in the countryside of the Vaucluse, in Provence, with its Petrarchan spring (the Sorgue) and mountain (the Ventoux), its memories of Van Gogh, and its ancient stone dwellings. These constructions, formed from dry walls alone, without any mortar added to assure cohesion, are akin to what Char called the "pulverized poem," with its miraculous, fragmentary but eternal holding power. Char builds, in this era of nuclear peril: he starts mankind's poetic enterprise once more, counting upon the strength of dry walls—relying, that is, upon the power of myth. The figures of this newly formed yet ancient structure are familiar to art, to reading, and to the watchers of the millennial sky. In *Aromates chasseurs* (1976; *Hunter's Aromatic Herbs*), Orion the hunter, blinded by Diana, passes like a human meteor, hunting his own being in order to construct in steel now, and "toward us," a correspondence between earth and the heaven he has left, dedicating himself (and, by extension, the poet he represents, and all of us), to human tasks (*Selected Poems*, p. 285):

> Orion
>
> . . .
>
> His countenance darkened by the calcinated iron,
> His foot always ready to avoid the fault,
> Was content in our midst
> And remained.
>
> Whispering among the stars.

This profoundly pagan sense of the universe has also a deep ecological and local dimension: to dwell poetically on earth is to dwell politically in one's time and to find one's true, if embattled, place. Char protested against the pollution of the river Sorgue in the poetic play *Le soleil des eaux* (1951; *The Sun of the Waters*). More recently, joined by Picasso, he protested against the installation of nuclear warheads in silos next to Mont Ventoux, in his pamphlet *La Provence point oméga* (1965). In Char's poetry at its strongest, this very sense of the specific— whether in protest against or in mourning for the desecration of an actual place—speaks clearly, with urgent yearning, for a human truth, a human place that will not succumb to violation but will be, finally, our own. His consciousness of exile is as poignant as his will to rediscovery, so that in *Le nu perdu* (1971; *Nakedness Lost*) the body, wandering lost in a time of terror, bereft of its dwelling-place, signals the soul's displacement: there is for the soul no space that could seem an adequate origin or a source for future nourishment. And yet, the superb title *Retour amont* (1966; *The Return Upland,* or *The Return Upstream*) announces a return against the slope and the current, and the landscape itself (the stream, the slope) suffices to compensate for the bareness of the forlorn human state, for exile and nostalgia.

Yves Bonnefoy (1923–) is the contemporary poet most clearly associated with a poetry of place. One of his recurring themes—"le vrai lieu" (the true place)—links a sense of plenitude with a consciousness of mortality, and this conjunction is infused with memories of artistic and literary traditions, from Shakespeare and the baroque to the Orient. In his firmly poetic architectural sensibility, Bonnefoy resembles Baudelaire. His strongest, most persistent images are those of construction and of limit. They resonate with Heidegger's thoughts of threshold. *Dans le leurre du seuil* (1975; *The Lure of the Threshold*) takes as its epigraph a quotation from *The Winter's Tale:* "They looked as they had heard of a world ransomed, or one destroyed"; it is a poem epic in length and in feeling; its abundant images are heavy with classical reminiscences: a ferryman cries toward a far shore, and, later, an infant is found and saved upon a beach (*Poems,* p. 93):

> Further than the star
> In what is,
> The child who bears the world
> Bathes simply.

Simple things are reestablished, and the sense of the here and now reigns supreme, as in the autobiographically lyrical *L'arrière-pays* (1972; *The Country Behind*). That country is always another place, away from where one is or might be in the world, as if the intense presence of this world, here and now, depended upon the way it seems to beckon to us from afar. The special light of Bonnefoy's poems, often called metaphysical, has a softness and a fullness unique in contemporary poetry; this "douceur" is a dwelling unto itself (*Poems,* p. 169):

> And at its windows the leaves are closer
> In the brighter trees. And the fruit rests
> Under the mirror's arch. And the sun
> Is still high, behind the basket
> Of a few summer flowers here, on the table.

This vision in no sense reflects a frivolous optimism, and not all the days are summer ones. A darker side, the "black spot upon the sun," provides the grave tones of *Ce qui fut sans lumière* (1987; *What Was without Light*). But here too the focus is on stitching the world together once more, on finding the threshold and the presence and promise of words somehow able to contain a universe of human thought and generous vision, where the smells of damp grass, an afternoon thunderstorm, and the simplest flower take on the depth of a modern consciousness.

In his consciousness of passage as the ultimate human truth and in his ways of seeing art and poetry afresh, Jacques Dupin (1927–) resembles Bonnefoy; unlike Bonnefoy, however, he is concerned above all with the actual process of writing. In *L'embrasure* (1969; *The Insetting*), he examines both the constructive methods of setting elements into others within the continuity of the poetic text and the necessarily destructive violence of poetic creation: "Everything is given to us, but in order to be forced, to be broken into, in some sense to be destroyed—and to destroy us" (p. 146).

Henri Michaux (1899–1984), the genially imaginative explorer of poetic and mental space and an experimenter with mind-altering drugs such as mescaline, celebrated not dwelling but voyage in all its various modalities, from trip to trip. He is often associated, in the public mind, with surrealism, if only because of the counterlogical bent of his writing. In 1966, the year that marked the official end of surrealism with André Breton's death, Michaux published *Les grandes épreuves de l'esprit et les innombrables petites* (*The Major Ordeals of the Mind and the Countless Minor Ones*), sketching out the trials of tripping, as well as a book on passage called *Parcours* (*Itinerary*), illustrated by his own etchings, and *L'espace du dedans* (1945; *The Space of Inside*), an expanded edition of his previous works relating to an interior space rather than to that of exterior reality.

Michaux's descriptions of mental processes under the effect of mind-altering drugs reflect his central desire to lift the veil, to reveal the complex mechanisms of the brain and thus to enable the mind to seize at—if not quite completely to grasp—its own attempts to grasp, and the unique nature of thought to which, in Michaux's own estimation, thinking is only rarely and uncomfortably equal. His mental experiments develop Baudelaire's earlier musings on the effects of drugs upon the poetic mind, but they bespeak a modern sensitivity—unsentimental, observational in its essence, and clear-eyed even in its experiments with its own limits. Elsewhere, Michaux the traveler of real and invented space continues the ironic and pseudoepic wanderings undertaken in the 1930s in *Plume* (*Pen*), through a series of newly created myths, of countries and beings, in long narrative poems in which storytelling tenuously controls the disorders of the mind in flight from its interior chaos, that very frightening *interior space*.

But poetry's place is also the literal space of the page, as documented by the "language poets" with their poetry-in-the-making. In *La fabrique du Pré* (1971; *The Making of the Meadow*), Francis Ponge (1899–1988)—a poet whose inheritance was claimed by the review *Tel quel*—describes how words create land and creation itself. In *Le parti pris des choses* (1942; *The Side of Things*), his dry wit and his ability to enable the smallest object to claim its own unique and joyous space of play between his lines aim at converting the reader to perception itself. The "objeu"—the object-game, or the thing manifest from word to work in the text as the play among its multiple aspects—provokes the "objoie," both the object's rejoicing and the reader's share in its joy.

Other poets aligned with this side of things—that is, roughly speaking, the formalist or verbally playful project of poetry-enacted-as-process—include during the 1970s the younger poets of *Tel quel* (Marcelin Pleynet and Denis Roche) and the continuing group of OuLiPo (Ouvroir de Littérature Potentielle, or Workshop of Potential Literature). This group works in an enthusiastically ludic tradition that finds in the constraints imposed by poetic conventions (such as rhyme and meter) or by other arbitrary rules invented for the sheer fun and challenge of them—the possibility of numberless unforeseen and unpredictable effects.

This technical and upbeat enterprise is quite different from the meditative seriousness of Char, Bonnefoy, and the poets of *L'éphémère,* grounded in an ineradicable sense of existential exile. The Egyptian Jew Edmond Jabès, who lives out his own personal exile in Paris, haunted by the question of place and loss of place in relation to writing, is among the most significant thinkers of what we might call poetical alienation. His examinations of word and page, of speech in the form of question and dialogue, are both prose and poetry. He writes on behalf of the people of exile, the people of the book; for him all riches lie in thought and its wandering, homeless, written expression. His *Livre du dialogue* (1987; *Book of Dialogue*) follows on his seven-volume *Livre des questions* (1984; *Book of Questions*) and continues the soul-searching narrative of half-fictive individual lives. The space of the book is seen as the true space, in which exile and promised land somehow, in poetry and in question, meet.

The poetry of place, then, with its bereavement and its persistent hope of finding against all odds a contemporary dwelling-place, is marked, in all its philosophical and formal aspects, by a desire for specific location or by sorrow over its loss. Whether the project be one of endurance or of game, the stakes and the determination are serious. French poetry has only rarely before manifested such a high-spirited, brave sense of its testimonial value, whether that witness be borne to passing, to philosophical meditation, or to play and process. In all its vast stretch of representation and interpretation, the true place of that poetry is now unchallengeable.

See also 1913, 1939, 1940–1944.

Bibliography: Yves Bonnefoy, *Poems, 1959–1975,* trans. Richard Pevear (New York: Random House, 1985). Malcolm Bowie, *Henri Michaux* (Oxford: Clarendon Press, 1973). Mary Ann Caws, *The Presence of René Char* (Princeton: Princeton University Press, 1976). René Char, *Selected Poems of René Char,* trans. and ed. Mary Ann Caws and Jonathan Griffin (Princeton: Princeton University Press, 1976). Michel Deguy, *Given Giving: Selected Poems of Michel Deguy,* trans. Clayton Eshleman (Berkeley: University of California Press, 1984). Jacques Derrida, *Signéponge = Signsponge,* trans. Richard Rand (New York: Columbia University Press, 1984). Jacques Dupin, *L'embrasure* (Paris: Gallimard, 1969). Robert Greene, *Six French Poets of Our Time* (Princeton: Princeton University Press, 1979). Edmond Jabès, *The Book of Dialogue,* trans. Rosmarie Waldrop (Middletown, Conn.: Wesleyan University Press, 1987). Jabès, *The Book of Questions,* 3 vols., trans. Rosmarie Waldrop (Middletown, Conn.: Wesleyan University Press, 1976–77). John Naughton, *The Poetry and Poetics of Yves Bonnefoy* (Chicago: University of Chicago Press, 1984). *Oulipo: A Primer of Potential Literature,* ed. and trans. Warren F. Motte (Lincoln: University of Nebraska Press, 1986).

Mary Ann Caws

✑ *1968, February*

Ahmadou Kourouma Africanizes French in *Les soleils des indépendances*

Francophonie and Independence

As student revolts occurred throughout the industrialized world in 1968, a quiet revolution took place in African literature written in French. Ahmadou Kourouma's *Les soleils des indépendances* (*The Suns of Independence*), published in February of that year, changed the way the French language would be used by citizens of the African states colonized by the French and granted independence in 1960. For the first time, the norms of standard, "universal" French were violated, infused with the expressions and rhythms of the Malinke language of West Africa. A different order is evident from the first lines of the novel, although the distinctiveness is lost in the English translation: "One week had passed since Ibrahima Kone, of the Malinke race, had met his end in the capital city, or to put it in Malinke: he'd been defeated by a mere cold" (*Suns,* p. 3).

Dozens of phrases in *Les soleils des indépendances* are literal translations from Malinke, which the narrator carefully explains: "the era of Independence (the suns of Independence, the Malinke say)" (p. 3); "the doctor had called it a 'hysterical pregnancy' and the Malinke, a 'spirit pregnancy'" (p. 33); "they sat in mourning (they would remain cloistered for forty days)" (p. 88). Using parenthetical and contextual explanations, Kourouma strikes a delicate balance between linguistic revolt and making sense. This is not, after all, a novel written in Malinke. But, if the idea is Africanization, why is *Les soleils des indépendances* written in French?

The colonizers' languages continue to be essential to modern African literature, particularly in the francophone nations, although generally less than one-third of the population knows French. French is the language of literacy. What writing there is—from signboards and street names to poems and novels—is mostly in French: establishing mass African-language literacy, and a literature to nurture it, has only begun. Africans continue to rely on European languages to communicate with each other—across ethnic and national boundaries—and with the rest of the world. Literature, as far as it is identified with written text, was imported and imposed in most of subsaharan Africa by colonialism. In colonial schools African children read French books and learned lessons about "our ancestors the Gauls"; literacy brought with it colonial ideology and European literary genres and standards. Not the least formidable among imported cultural notions was the sanctity of the French language. Ahmadou Kourouma recalled: "Little black children were expected to 'respect a language' that in no way corresponded to their vision of the world" (Badday, "Interview avec Kourouma," p. 7). *Les soleils des indépendances,* according to the author, was "thought in Malinke and written in French." It is significant that this first successful African subversion of French grammar was initially published in Montreal, where there is long-standing experience of French-with-a-difference.

The oppressive culture of colonialism thus proved to be strangely invertible:

the language and literacy of the colonizer (whose role is often symbolized by Shakespeare's Prospero, in *The Tempest*) are seized by the colonized writer (Caliban), who turns the weapon back on his master, curses him, and sets out to forge a new sense of identity. But the history of modern African literature is more complex than this schema, involving a continuing dialectic of dependence and contingent liberation. The history also begins in a peculiar way.

René Maran's *Batouala* (1921; *Batouala: A True Black Novel*) is widely considered to be the first francophone African novel, even though Maran was from the Caribbean island of Martinique and lived in Africa only as a French civil servant. This conflation of things African and Caribbean is typical of the period before independence, when the distinction seemed less important than the common ground of being black and colonized by France. The preface to *Batouala,* however, shows how little Maran identified with Africans: "On moonlit evenings on my porch, stretched out in my chaise longue, I listened to the conversations of these poor people . . . They suffered and laughed at their suffering" (p. 8). At the same time, in impeccably elegant French, Maran also indicts the French "mission to civilize": "You build your kingdom on corpses" (ibid.). Although *Batouala's* treatment of colonialism now seems rather mild, the language of the preface was strong enough to provoke a ban on the novel throughout the French colonies.

Literary works written by Africans began to appear in the 1920s. The earliest novels—such as Ahmadou Diagne's *Les trois volontés de Malic* (1920; *Malic's Three Wishes*), Bakary Diallo's *Force-Bonté* (1926; *Force-Goodness*), and Félix Couchoro's *L'esclave* (1938; *The Slave*)—were often marked by an ideological commitment to French colonialism, or at least an openness to European values. Largely written for a French readership, they belonged to a corpus of "colonial novels," which included the works of white French writers such as Pierre Loti.

The ideology of negritude contrasted sharply with these novels. Created in Paris by black Africans and West Indians, negritude brought together poets from the black diaspora. First articulated in Aimé Césaire's *Cahier d'un retour au pays natal* (1939; *Notebook of a Return to the Native Land*), it was later canonized with the publication of Léopold Sédar Senghor's *Anthologie de la nouvelle poésie nègre et malgache de langue française* (1948; *Anthology of Negro and Malagasy Poetry in French*). Among its more emblematic verses are these by the Haitian poet Léon Laleau, from "Trahison" ("Treason"; p. 108):

> . . . do you feel this suffering
> And this despair that cannot be equaled
> To tame with words from France
> This heart that came to me from Senegal?

Introducing the *Anthologie,* Jean-Paul Sartre's brilliant essay "Orphée noir" ("Black Orpheus") offers the first philosophical elaboration of negritude as an "anti-racist racism" (p. xvii) and as the "being-in-the-world of the negro" (p. x). Over the years, negritude became identified almost exclusively with Senghor, who explicated and codified in dozens of essays and speeches the idea that Césaire evoked poetically in the *Cahier*. But, partly as a result of their national identities, the two men soon diverged on the uses of negritude. Césaire, a political leader in Martinique, rejected any political or biological usage of the term, pointing to its abuses by dictators such as François Duvalier in Haiti; the word dropped out of his poetic vocabulary. Senghor, the first president of independent Senegal (and the first black to be inducted into the Académie Française, in 1984), insisted in *Liberté* (1964; *Liberty*) that negritude meant "assimilating instead of being assimilated" (3:469), that is, embracing "the civilization of the universal" without losing one's identity. Senghor initially defined negritude as "the whole of the cultural values of the black world"; the black and white worlds are separated by an essential difference: "emotion is black [*nègre*], as reason is Hellenic" (1:24). Negritude was known for its romanticized depiction of Africa and for its justifications of African culture.

For critics of a later generation, negritude ideology was too dependent on the eurocentrism it claimed to oppose. It is true that both Senghor and Césaire constructed images of Africa after reading European ethnographers such as Leo Frobenius; Senghor's philosophical references are often to European sources, from Hegel to Pierre Teilhard de Chardin. But such critics often fail to ask how it could have been otherwise, how the discourse of colonialism could have been countered without some echoing of its terms.

The African novel began to come into its own in the 1950s. Camara Laye's *L'enfant noir* (1953; *The African Child*) and *Le regard du roi* (1954; *The Radiance of the King*), Sembène Ousmane's *Les bouts de bois de Dieu* (1960; *God's Bits of Wood*), Mongo Beti's *Le pauvre Christ de Bomba* (1956; *The Poor Christ of Bomba*) and *Mission terminée* (1957; *Mission Accomplished*), and Ferdinand Oyono's *Une vie de boy* (1956; *Houseboy*) are all now considered canonical texts.

L'enfant noir provoked disparate responses in France and Africa. In France, where it was reviewed with adulation and awarded the Prix Charles Veillon, it was and is seen as an evocation of timeless, universal values. Some Africans, however (most notably Mongo Beti), complained that the novel ignored colonialism and presented a falsely idyllic image of Africa. There is indeed no explicit criticism of the colonial system in Camara's autobiographical novel, and there is considerable nostalgia in this story of a Malinke boy's partial initiation into his culture before moving into the space of modern economy and losing touch. *L'enfant noir* seems to make the most sense when it is read not as universal but as a local signifier, tied as much to ancient traditions as to literate modernity. The novel is profoundly caught between worlds, straining to reveal all the secrets of Malinke culture but stopped short by the narrator's ignorance, the result of one fact: "I left my father's house too soon" (*African Child*, p. 12).

Oyono's *Une vie de boy* is more typical of its period. Written as the fictive diary of a servant boy, Toundi, this novel is a brilliantly witty attack on the psychology of colonialism. Toundi is a dutiful worker whose comments are all the more scathing for being delivered deadpan. He perceives all the hypocrisy of his French masters. The narrative develops as a battle of the glance between colonizer and colonized; Toundi, the houseboy, dares to look back because he has discovered that his master the commandant is uncircumcised and therefore, according to African tradition, impotent. Once he has symbolically castrated the master in this way, Toundi says: "His eyes had once struck panic into me. Now I stood unconcerned under their gaze" (*Houseboy,* p. 33). His immunity to white power does not go unnoticed, and it causes his demise: "You see, he can't look us in the eye. His eyes are shifty like a pygmy's. He's dangerous" (p. 91). Arrested, whipped, and brutalized, Toundi escapes to a neighboring Spanish colony, only to die from his wounds.

The 1960s, which brought political independence to almost all of Africa, also brought the realization that African literature would continue to be written in European languages, and that the re-Africanization of discourse about Africa—in law, politics, philosophy, and literature—would not be accomplished overnight. At times the struggle against colonialism seemed to have led only to the discontents of neocolonialism, internal strife, one-party politics, and increasing class conflict. This sense of disillusionment is strong in *Les soleils des indépendances.* Fama Doumbouya, the central character of Kourouma's novel, is a fallen nobleman for whom the new era represents poverty, sterility, and the end of legitimate caste distinctions. "Born to gold, food in plenty, honour and women" (*Suns,* p. 5) but lacking the French colonizers to support his commerce, he becomes a "prince who's practically a beggar" (p. 6), roaming a world "turned upside-down" (p. 70). The last of a dynasty of chiefs, childless, Fama pines for a world remote from modern politics: "Politics has no eyes, no ears, no heart; in politics, true and false wear the same cloth, just and unjust go hand in hand, good and evil are bought and sold at the same price" (p. 109).

Les soleils, then, airs the resentments of a ruling caste that has lost control, and a nostalgia for the precolonial world; but it was ahead of its time in portraying the real situation of African women. The earthy existence of Fama's wife, Salimata, is presented from her point of view. Her mind is dominated by horrific memories of the excision of her clitoris—because, according to tradition, it "represented impurity, confusion, imperfection" (p. 22)—and of her rape by a sorcerer.

Les soleils des indépendances, however, was initially overshadowed by the controversy surrounding another novel, Yambo Ouologuem's *Le devoir de violence* (1968; *Bound to Violence*). The pattern of reception was the same as for *L'enfant noir:* celebrated in France as the first "true" black novel, awarded the prestigious Prix Renaudot, *Le devoir* was criticized in Africa for its political stance. Unlike Camara's work, however, Ouologuem's made the disturbing assertion that Africans, instead of being passive victims of European colonialism, were active participants in the process of exploiting each other.

Africa is depicted as a continent of eternal violence, ruled by dynasties of exploiters who merely allowed the Europeans the illusion of conquest and control: "The Whites devised a system of international colonial law consecrating the principle of spheres of influence and legitimizing the rights of the first occupant. But to Nakem [a fictive West African empire] the colonial powers came too late, for with the help of the local notables a colonial overlord had established himself long since, and that colonial overlord was none other than Saif [the dynastic ruler of Nakem]. All unsuspecting, the European conquerors played into his hands" (*Bound to Violence*, p. 24).

Along with this controversial view of African history came another problem. Four years after the publication of *Le devoir de violence*, scholars discovered that Ouologuem had borrowed heavily from other writers, mostly from André Schwarz-Bart's *Le dernier des justes* (1959; *The Last of the Just*) and Graham Greene's *It's a Battlefield* (1934) but also from the Bible, African Arabic-language chronicles, and Guy de Maupassant. Accusations of plagiarism followed, and the novel was withdrawn from circulation. With a very creative disregard for legalities, Ouologuem, a Malian educated in élite French institutions, had lifted passages from numerous texts, adapting them to his needs, interweaving them in the style of African oral narration to produce a brilliantly complex patchwork. Most critics now agree that *Le devoir de violence* nevertheless remains one of the most significant African novels.

Since the 1970s African literature has turned away from global theories such as negritude and has become increasingly involved in elucidating specific local problems. Political satires account for a large part of the literary production. When they are not subject to the censorship practiced in some form by most African states, these novels mix the intimate, the ordinary, and the fantastic with ethical questions on the state of African affairs. Sembène Ousmane, who in the 1960s turned to film as a medium for closer communication with the masses, returned to the novel with *Le dernier de l'empire* (1981; *The Last of the Empire*). Set in a barely fictive country called "Sunugal," Sembène's narrative explores the politics of power in a period of transition. Léon Migname, "le Vénérable" president of the republic and proprietor of the ideòlogy of "Authe-negraficanitus," is an obvious satire of Senghor and negritude. The plot centers on the political and cultural question of *caste:* what would happen if a politician from the lower caste of traditional society were to rule the nation? This is the kind of local, ethnic, but also ethical concern that contemporary African fiction takes as its object.

Works such as Sony Labou Tansi's *L'état honteux* (1981; *State of Shame*) and *L'anté-peuple* (1983; *The antipeople*), Henri Lopes' *Le pleurer-rire* (1982; *The Laughing Cry*), and Sylvain Bemba's *Léopolis* (1984) deal with similar social concerns but are more fantastic in their realism and more experimental in their narrative form. Thus, one-third of the way through the text, *Le pleurer-rire* contains its own critique, cast in a different typeface: discussing "the satirical and critical memoirs of a slice in the life of a dictator during the last part of our century," a respondent worries, "Now, by the way the manuscript is developing . . . I fear that in yielding too much to intimate memories, you are mixing up genres and losing sight of the objective of all committed writing. And the African book coming from these times, and having any respect for itself, cannot choose but to be committed" (*The Laughing Cry*, p. 95). All three of these writers from the Congo are in fact "committed" to two projects at once: the critique of society and the exploration of new literary styles and forms. Other innovators include M. a M. Ngal (*Giambatista Viko, ou le viol du discours africain,* 1984; *Giambatista Viko, or the Rape of African Discourse*), from Zaire; Jean-Marie Adiaffi (*La carte d'identité,* 1980; *The Identity Card*), from the Ivory Coast; and the Senegalese Ibrahima Sall (*Les routiers de chimères,* 1982; *The Truckers of Chimera*).

In the mid-1970s the emergence of female writers changed the direction of francophone African literature. The reasons for this long delay in women's participation lie deep in Africa's triple heritage of indigenous culture, Islam, and European colonialism. Although in traditional cultures women often actively participated in oral performances, Islam tended to silence them, and colonial schools were open almost exclusively to boys.

Mariama Bâ's *Une si longue lettre* (*So Long a Letter*) and Aminata Sow Fall's *Le revenant* (*The Ghost*), both published in 1976, protest (though in a limited way) the limitations placed on women's lives. Bâ's character Ramatoulaye, married for twenty-five years, mother of twelve children, learns that her husband plans to take as his second wife the friend of one of their daughters. An obedient Muslim, Ramatoulaye remains faithful to him until his death; her period of mourning leads to a new consciousness about the condition of women, articulated in a letter she writes to a friend during her seclusion. The letter is the text of the novel, and within it is a clear statement about the power of literacy, the ability of literature to represent and defend those who have been silenced. Ramatoulaye writes to her friend:

> Books saved you. Having become your refuge, they sustained you.
>
> The power of books, this marvellous invention of astute human intelligence. Various signs associated with sound: different sounds that form the word. Juxtaposition of words from which spring the idea, Thought, History, Science, Life . . . Books knit generations together in the same continuing effort that leads to progress. They enabled you to better yourself. What society refused you, they granted. (*So Long a Letter,* p. 32)

The fact that Ramatoulaye's friend has liberated herself by leaving Africa and moving first to France, then to the United States, seems to support the view, common in Africa, that feminism can only be a Western importation, a form of cultural betrayal. In practice, however, both Bâ (who died in 1981) and Sow Fall have distanced themselves from Western feminism and tried to emphasize the African specificity of their work. Ramatoulaye identifies herself as "of those who can realize themselves fully and bloom only when they form part of a couple . . . I have never conceived of happiness outside marriage" (*So Long a Letter,* p. 56). But this apparent conservatism in regard to family life does not extend to the realm of politics; *Une si longue lettre* voices clear appeals for continuing progress: "Nearly twenty years of independence! When will we have the first female minister involved in the decisions concerning the development of our country?" (p. 61). Advances in politics and in literature remain to be made; against the background of an overwhelmingly male literary tradition, this first generation of francophone female writers has begun to change the canon.

As a direct outgrowth of colonialism, francophone literature in Africa operates between the need for universal communication and the desire for local autonomy. The ideology of *francophonie,* promoted as articulating but also transcending politics, race, and ethnicity, is for the moment tied to the preservation of French interests in Africa, which are considerable. French governments support and promote African literature through their cultural centers and through the state-sponsored literary journal *Notre librairie.* African literature is still largely consumed in the West, and the non-African, nonlocal reader is still accommodated by explanatory footnotes and translations of local terms. Does this mean that there is no independence? Perhaps not total independence, but rather an emerging state of complexity and specificity, including the work of fiercely independent authors such as Sembène. African critics have been debating whether national literatures yet exist—whether there is yet an identifiably Senegalese canon of novels as distinct from a Camerounian or Zairian canon. The fact that this debate has taken place is itself a sign that Africans are looking toward increasingly local horizons.

See also 1847, 1933 (February), 1939, 1962.

Bibliography: Mariama Bâ, *So Long a Letter,* trans. Modupe Bode-Thomas (Ibadan, Nigeria: New Horn Press, 1981). Moncef S. Badday, "Interview avec Ahmadou Kourouma," *Afrique littéraire et artistique,* 10 (1970), 2–8. Frantz Fanon, *Black Skin, White Masks,* trans. Charles Lam Markmann (New York: Grove, 1967). Lilyan Kesteloot, *Black Writers in French: A Literary History of Negritude,* trans. Ellen Conroy Kennedy (Philadelphia: Temple University Press, 1974). Ahmadou Kourouma, *The Suns of Independence,* trans. Adrian Adams (New York: Africana Publishing, 1981). Camara Laye, *The African Child,* trans. James Kirkup (London: Fontana, 1959). Henri Lopes, *The Laughing Cry,* trans. Gerald Moore (London: Readers International, 1987). René Maran, *Batouala: A True Black Novel,* trans. Barbara Beck and Alexandre Mboukou (Washington, D.C.: Black Orpheus, 1972). Yambo Ouologuem, *Bound to Violence,* trans. Ralph Manheim (London: Heinemann, 1971). Ferdinand Oyono, *Houseboy,* trans. John Reed (London: Heinemann, 1966). Jean-Paul Sartre, "Black Orpheus," trans. Arthur Gilette, *Stand,* 5 (1962), 2–12, and 6 (1963), 7–20. Léopold Sédar Senghor, ed., *Anthologie de la nouvelle poésie nègre et malgache de langue française* (Paris: Presses Universitaires de France, 1948). Senghor, *Liberté,* 3 vols. (Paris: Seuil, 1964–1977).

Christopher L. Miller

❧ *1968, May*

Ten Million Workers Strike in France; Students Demonstrate Worldwide

"Actions, No! Words, Yes!"

The years 1966–1970 witnessed the emergence of an international student movement, whose chief centers were Berkeley, Berlin, Milan, Paris, and Tokyo and whose mobilizing theme was the Vietnam war. In France, among the specific factors at the forefront of this movement were the large and rapid expansion of the university sector and various attempts by the government to break up the academic ghetto and integrate it within the social fabric. Paradoxically, this effort at modernization was itself one of the sources of student discontent. One of the leaflets of May 1968 declared: "We refuse to become teachers serving a mechanism of social selection in a school system operating at the expense of working-class children, to become sociologists drumming up slogans for governmental election campaigns, to become psychologists charged with getting 'teams of workers' to 'function' according to the best interests of the bosses, to become scientists whose research will be used according to the exclusive interests of the profit economy" (quoted in Geismar, July, and Morane, *Vers la guerre civile [Toward Civil War]*, p. 411).

The expansion of those sciences of uncertain epistemological status—the so-called human sciences (psychology and sociology)—gave rise to disquiet about the position of the university and of knowledge within society. Earlier criticisms had reproached the university—still not entirely freed from the Napoleonic model—with being maladapted to contemporary society, of serving as a refuge for ridiculous mandarins; but now critics accused it of the reverse—of being an institution of normalization, the place where, in the name of knowledge, those hierarchies that permit political and economic powers to reproduce themselves were being sustained.

Two events assumed emblematic status during this period. The first was the entry of the police into the precincts of the Sorbonne. This unleashed the Latin Quarter riots, with their street fighting, their night of manned barricades, and finally the weeks-long student occupation of the Sorbonne. The myth of the university charters, which made it possible for knowledge to imagine itself independent of power, collapsed: "When the university structures no longer managed to integrate and absorb a confrontation, the shotguns of the riot squads and the grenades of the C.R.S. [security police] took over the shift with perfect smoothness" (*Vers la guerre civile,* p. 59). Parallel with the student uprising, a wave of factory strikes swept France, the largest ever, estimated at 10 million workers. The second exemplary event of May 1968 is linked to these strikes: the students who had occupied the Sorbonne opened it to the workers, in a gesture symbolic of their rejection of professional and social segregation and of the subordination of manual to intellectual labor. Each in its own way, both these events called into question knowledge's claim of extraterritoriality in relation to social struggles.

During this crisis over the status of theory, the notion of the intellectual that had prevailed since the 19th century underwent a transformation. Traditionally, the impartiality of the scholar, theorist, or writer had endowed him or her with moral prestige. The specialist in universal truths was held to be above partisan interests; and this detachment from the practical world was precisely the source of theory's authority in nontheoretical matters. But once the police intervened to maintain order on the campuses, this became an untenable illusion. The production of knowledge now itself appeared to be an arena of activity in which multiple strategies were played out, submitted to competition between diverse interests. There is a politics of science, of truth. Knowledge was fractured into local knowledges, and it became clear that access to information was not free of charge. The intellectual ceased to be the omniscient giver, the paternalistic advocate of others who used to place his universality at the service of those suffering. No longer a representative, he became the example of a revolutionary way of speaking for oneself whose formula was given in one of the most famous graffiti of the time: "Don't liberate me, I'll take care of it."

Another graffito said: "Actions, no! Words, yes!" (Besançon, *Les murs ont la parole* [*It's the Walls' Turn to Speak*], p. 171). This ironic slogan decomposed another form of representation, the one implied by the segregation between signs and things, defining words as representatives of things. Michel de Certeau described the events of May 1968 as a "taking of the floor," a seizing of the right to speak analogous to what the taking of the Bastille had been in July 1789. Language, from an instrument of representation, becomes action as well. It is not limited to representing things; it changes them. The events of May 1968 have been interpreted as the end of structuralism. And this was indeed the period in which, significantly, the interest of linguistics in structures gave way to the analysis of the modalities of language's acting-out: shifters and performatives.

At the beginning of 1968 the linguist Oswald Ducrot, following Emile Benveniste and J. L. Austin, developed a pragmatic view of language that anticipated the scenes of confrontation to unfold later in the year. Language is not limited to the transmission of knowledge, to the communication of information; rather, it places the interlocutor under the obligation to reply, thereby imposing a role, an attitude, a universe of discourse on the receiver. Verbal exchanges are not simply matters of conflicting positions; before any consideration of content, they imply the acceptance or the refusal of the institutional frame of the exchange (what Ducrot called the presuppositions):

> The rejection of presuppositions constitutes a polemical attitude very different from a critique of what is set forth: specifically, it always implies a large dose of aggressiveness that transforms the dialogue into a confrontation of persons. In rejecting the presuppositions of my interlocutor, I disqualify not only the utterance itself, but also the enunciative act from which it proceeds. In presenting certain ideas as presuppositions, one can thus make a kind of bet, tendering an "all or nothing." Either the interlocutor, fearing to aggravate the argument, will accept without discussion the intellectual frame one is holding out to him, or—and here is the risk run by the speaker—he will undertake a refutation that can explicitly put the very legitimacy of the given speech act at stake. (Ducrot, "La description sémantique des énoncés français" ["Semantic Description of Utterances in French"], pp. 51–52)

The frame of an exchange is not anterior to or independent of this exchange. It is instituted by the enunciative act itself, by the presuppositions that one of the speakers succeeds (or does not succeed) in imposing on the other. Thus it is by means of the frame that it imposes, a frame that is not a convention but that all convention presupposes. At the heart of all transmission of information there is a relation of force. All acts of speech, before communicating a message, induce a modification in the addressee's right to speak. Developing these analyses in *Dire et ne pas dire* (1972; *With or without Saying It*), Ducrot would give two examples of situations of this kind: a university examination and a police interrogation.

Without fearing, as Ducrot says, to "aggravate the argument," the actors of May 1968 made manifest the presuppositions of the impartial and authoritative discourses. As the authors of *Vers la guerre civile* stated: "Everyone agrees on ceding the floor. But when someone wants to take it, no one agrees" (p. 185). Unauthorized voices made themselves heard, refusing to accept the turn to speak that they had been offered, taking unbidden a turn that no one had given them, authorizing themselves to contest the authority of the guardians of speech's turn. They broke the contracts, refusing to answer in exams, calling their professors by their first names, and so on. Once the forms were no longer respected, the relations of force became apparent. Refusing the presuppositions of one's adversary forced that adversary to fall back on the institutional presuppositions that guaranteed his or her authority. In this way, through the acts of speech of 1968, many walls became apparent, those on which the authorities leaned for support. Against the backdrop of this off-balance dialogue there would develop reflections—such as Michel Foucault's 1969 lecture "Qu'est-ce qu'un auteur?" ("What Is an Author?")—on the institutional machinery through which a society authorizes a discourse.

One episode in this guerrilla war of speech acts was the taping of an analytic session during which the patient, equipped with a tape recorder, called into question the univocal presupposition of the therapeutic relation. Summoned to speak, the analyst took fright and called the police. Sartre's publication of the transcript of this exchange in *Les temps modernes,* in 1969, expanded this little drama, stirring up throughout the French therapeutic community a disturbed resistance that multiplied the one of the original psychiatrist, demonstrating how deeply a society identifies with its verbal rituals, how essential it is to a society that forms of linguistic exchanges be respected.

Gilles Deleuze, in *Nietzsche et la philosophie* (1962; *Nietzsche and Philosophy*), had already expressed the desire for an active linguistics. In French "to mean" is *vouloir dire,* literally, "to want to say." Behind a meaning, Deleuze says, one must always look for a will: "A word only means something insofar as the speaker *wills* something by saying it" (*Nietzsche and Philosophy,* p. 74). Thus one must treat "speech like a real activity" (ibid.), wondering not what this or that word means but what its user wants. The central element is no longer the content of a message, the sense of a proposition, but the will in which it is rooted: what type of will produces a given type of thought—and in particular, what type of will gives rise to the theorists, the searchers for truth, those who dissociate knowledge from wanting, wisdom from will, those who speak of abstracting themselves from what they think and say, imagining themselves to be looking for truth for its own sake, a truth they assume to be independent of all relation to force, to authority. The question is not: Is it true? but: Who says that it's true? Who wants it to be true? According to Deleuze: "Truth expresses a will: who wills truth? And what does he who says 'I am seeking the truth' will?" (p. 73). Theoretical man is precisely the one who refuses to speak in terms of will, of self-interest. He calls himself detached. But what is the genealogy of this detachment? What is this will that refuses to want? What interest invests itself in this disinterestness? Who has interest—and what (perverted) interest—in claiming to be or in actually being disinterested? It is no longer a matter of researching meanings, of interpreting messages, but of detecting the power plays that underwrite utterances. "We are never referred to the real forces that *form* thought, thought itself is never related to the real forces that it presupposes *as thought*" (p. 104). In a 1972 discussion with Deleuze, Foucault would praise him for having "under the ancient theme of meaning, of the signifier and the signified, etc. . . . developed the question of power, of the inequality of powers and their struggles" ("Intellectuals and Power," p. 213).

In his *Folie et déraison* (1961; *Madness and Civilization*) Foucault embarks on a cognate project: to show the ties between a discourse of scientific pretensions and the interests, possibly obscure ones, of a society. In this genealogy of the medical discourse on madness, psychopathology is related not to its object but to the presupposition of its enunciative act. What is involved is not only a study of the history of science, a discipline that considers the history of discourses whose objects are nonhistorical themselves. The question is not to know if psychopathology speaks truth or falsehood, or—in a progressivist view of the history of science—of determining the date at which it discovered the truth concerning its object, of deciding at what point the discourse on madness acceded to the status of a positive science. Rather, the question is one of determining the decisions, the forces (historical, social, political) that the claim to such a status presupposes: what does a civilization want that labels madness as "mental illness" and relegates it to the subdivision of psychology called psychopathology? Here science does not limit itself to knowing: the epistemological claim hides dark areas of exclusion, fear, condemnation. "Isn't it significant of our culture that unreason was only able to become an object of knowledge for it to the extent that it had previously been the object of excommunication?" (*Folie et déraison*, p. 129). Reason's discourse on madness is not merely descriptive or, as linguists say, constative; it is performative and constitutive. There is nothing neutral or inactive in the way knowledge relates to "madness." Madness is an object only to the extent that psychopathology objectivizes it. A discourse having thus been reconducted to the juridico-political protocol of its enunciative act, "a whole architecture of protection" (p. 555) appears in the place of knowledge, solid structures—some discursive, some not—that make madness into a fact.

Just as Deleuze would develop the implications of his *Nietzsche* in *L'anti-Oedipe* (1972; *Anti-Oedipus*), Foucault would pursue the most radical intuitions of *Folie et déraison* in *Surveiller et punir* (1975; *Discipline and Punish*). This later book uncovers the genealogy of the anthropological disciplines by describing their relations with the positive forms of power (norms, tests, examinations, and the like), whereas *Folie et déraison* had been limited to its negative, repressive forms (confinement, exclusion). The emblem of this modern power is the Panopticon, the ideal prison conceived in 1791 by Jeremy Bentham, an institution that satisfies all the aspirations toward performativity that disciplinary architecture could put in place. The principle of this circular prison is to assure the constant visibility of each cell, imposing on the detainee the uninterrupted consciousness of being, in his solitude, submitted to observation. Given this fact, this "architectural apparatus," as Foucault calls it, does not stop at incarcerating; it also transforms the individuals it shelters: "Architecture . . . would be an operator for the transformation of individuals" (*Discipline and Punish*, p. 174). Of course, the efficacy of this architectural causality is not limited to the formation, the breaking (training), of the individual. While the prisoner behaves as if he were observed, the warder indeed turns him into an object of observation. Once again knowledge and power are tightly linked, as the double sense of the central concept of the book, that of discipline, indicates. The "disciplined" individual is simultaneously subjected to the technology of disciplinary power and exposed as an object to the disciplines of the so-called human sciences. "Any growth of power could give rise in them to possible branches of knowledge; it was this link, proper to the technological systems, that made possible within the disciplinary element the formation of clinical medicine, psychiatry, child psychology, educational psychology, the rationalization of labor. It is a double process, then: an epistemological 'thaw' through a refinement of power relations; a multiplication of the effects of power through the formation and accumulation of new forms of knowledge" (p. 224).

All sorts of walls, of frames, of margins, were made to speak and to provoke speech in the aftermath of May 1968—not only those of museums and of asylums, but also those of political parties and of organized religions. More and more, institutional analyses brought to the fore instances of enunciation, by means of messages taking their context into account, underlining their own circumstances. Such is the case of the first dated text by Jacques Derrida, a lecture written for an international conference of philosophy, hosted by an American university. It is dated 12 May 1968. Derrida reminds his American audience of the Vietnam war and of Martin Luther King's assassination. He also mentions the fact that, while he was typing it, "the universities of Paris were invaded by the forces of order—and for the first time at the demand of a rector" (*Margins of Philosophy*, p. 114). The preamble specifically analyzes its own context from a more pragmatic point of view, thematizing the institutional presuppositions of the philosophical communication, addressing the question of the boundaries of universality, the limits of transparency, which is to say, the decision on the basis of which "a certain group of languages and 'cultures,'" those that Edmund Husserl called European, is linked together through philosophy conceived of as a project that precisely implies the possibility of something like an international colloquium.

In 1980 Derrida, finally a candidate for a Ph.D., introduced the customary thesis defense with a text in which he explained how he came not to write a thesis. The date of 1968—"that event," he says, "which one still does not know how to name other than by its date, 1968" ("The Time of a Thesis," p. 44)—reappeared once again: what happened during that year was essential in the process that led to such a decision. The thesis as such could not survive the shake-up that May 1968 had forced the authorizing institution to face. An institution is able to tolerate any message, including the most subversive ones, so long as they remain messages and do not call its code into question. Therefore, it is the very form of the thesis that needs to be contested. No thesis is going to be subversive as long as the form of the thesis is not being subverted. Nineteen sixty-eight and its consequences made Derrida realize that the stakes of deconstruction were "not primarily a matter of philosophical contents, themes or theses, philosophemes, poems, theologemes or ideologemes, but especially and inseparably meaningful frames, institutional structures, pedagogical or rhetorical norms, the possibility of law, of authority, of evaluation, and of representation in terms of its very market" (p. 45). The theses of deconstruction had to end up in the deconstruction of the thesis.

See also 1789, 1871.

Bibliography: Julien Besançon, *Les murs ont la parole* (Paris: Tchou, 1968). Michel de Certeau, *La prise de parole* (Paris: Desclée de Brouwer, 1968). Gilles Deleuze, *Nietzsche and Philosophy,* trans. Hugh Tomlinson (New York: Columbia University Press, 1983). Jacques Derrida, *Margins of Philosophy,* trans. Alan Bass (Chicago: University of Chicago Press, 1982). Derrida, "The Time of a Thesis: Punctuations," in *Philosophy in France Today,* ed. Alan Montefiore (New York: Columbia University Press, 1983). Oswald Ducrot, "La description sémantique des énoncés français: La notion de présupposition," *L'homme,* 8 (January 1968), 37–53. Ducrot, *Dire et ne pas dire* (Paris: Hermann, 1972). Michel Foucault, *Discipline and Punish: The Birth of the Prison,* trans. Alan Sheridan (New York: Pantheon, 1977). Foucault, *Folie et déraison: Histoire de la folie à l'âge classique* (Paris: Plon, 1961). Foucault, "Intellectuals and Power" and "What Is an Author?" in *Language, Counter-Memory, Practice,* ed. and trans. Donald B. Bouchard (Ithaca: Cornell University Press, 1977). Alain Geismar, Serge July, and Erlyne Morane, *Vers la guerre civile* (Paris: Editions et Publications Premières, 1969). Hervé Hamon and Patrick Rotman, *Génération,* 2 vols. (Paris: Seuil, 1988). Jean-Paul Sartre, "The Man with the Tape-Recorder," in *Between Existentialism and Marxism,* trans. John Matthews (New York: Pantheon, 1974).

Denis Hollier

 1973

The Daily *Libération* Gives the 1968 Generation a Voice in the Press

French Lib

When Jean-Paul Sartre held a press conference on 4 January 1973 to announce the founding of the newspaper *Libération,* no one believed it would last more than a few months. The first issue was launched on 18 April (after five trial runs) despite an administrative, financial, and ideological turmoil that seemed to promise an early demise. But for about fifteen years *Libération* constituted one of the most exhilarating experiences of the French press since the mythical days of the 1944 . . . liberation. With a circulation that skyrocketed in a decade from 10,000 to over 200,000 copies daily, it could hardly have been more successful.

Its impact on French journalism has indeed been considerable. Acknowledging a strong debt to the American press, it was the first Parisian "news journal" (as distinct from a "journal of opinion") to call a spade a spade. No fudging of the facts, and no moralizing: "We'll call a murder an 'accident' only if such is the case," proclaimed the manifesto distributed at the press conference. As a result, although *Libération* is a chronic defendant in numerous lawsuits, its boldness has forced even an established but declining newspaper such as *Le monde* into a more "with-it" stance.

Libé has become an adjective. There are Libé prices (moderate), and there is a Libé style. Applied to a person, *style Libé* first of all indicates a regular reader of the newspaper: high-school student, prisoner, immigrant worker, or—increasingly—yuppy, left-wing but undogmatic, slightly anarchist but not paranoid, interested in alternative issues, open to all kinds of social and cultural experience, "in" without excessive snobbery, and, most important, feeling part of a politicoaffective community as a result of being a reader. Applied to language, *style Libé* indicates a tone that is sometimes abrasive but always humorous, sometimes flaky but always cheeky. This tone is an attempt to create a formula of the spoken/written to intercept the conflicting signals of an accelerating world. In a country whose media have been characterized chiefly by linguistic primness (if one leaves aside the satirical paper *Le canard enchaîné*), *Libération's* combination of dadaist laughter with "just-the-facts-ma'am" inquiries, of passionate lyricism with keen political analyses, of generosity with total disrespect, breathed fresh air into a stuffy environment. More than its ideological content, which is not at all homogeneous, although it has increasingly tended to become so, it is this irreverent tone that engages its readers' complicity.

May 1968 had opened a Pandora's box of language; poetry was in the streets—as the cliché had it. And it is true that people did begin to talk to each other, that political slogans were transformed into surrealist verse ("Under the paving stones, the beach"; "Be realist, ask for the impossible"). But the harsh political restoration that followed, under President Georges Pompidou's "Louis-Philippe" style of administration, dealt a severe blow to the hopes raised by the outburst of May. With its monopoly over radio and television, its control of the national news agency (Agence France-Presse), its alliance with press magnate Robert Hersant (today's French William Randolph Hearst), and the transformation of its police into a paramilitary force, the growing authoritarianism of the state forced the leftist groups that had led the May revolt to organize more or less clandestinely. Mostly doomed to bankruptcy or to outright censorship, many newspapers went underground. Those that lasted the longest were the products of the most coherent sector of the French left (which was otherwise divided to the point of caricature), the Maoists, often called *Mao-spontex* for their insertion of libertarian spontaneity into the teachings of the Chinese Red Sun. Like the many other revolutionaries of the time, they spoke a formulaic, wooden idiom. But they were more clever. To circumvent the recurrent bans, they sought out the protection of Sartre as director. Though as a writer he was rather foreign to their rhetoric, Sartre was fascinated by their desire to break down the capitalist division between manual and intellectual labor (many of them went to work in factories, including Serge July, the current director of *Libération*).

The political arena was not the only one in turmoil. Social groups stressing their *différence* began to organize: the MLF (Mouvement de Libération de la Femme), the French Women's Liberation; the FHAR (Front Homosexuel d'Action Révolutionnaire), the first large gay organization (aligned on Maoist positions!); Michel Foucault's GIP (Groupe Information Prisons), established to collect testimony from jail inmates. In this time of dissent there was a dream of direct democracy: against the authoritarianism of the state, let us save the free speech of May 1968; let the people speak to the people. Foucault's dictum, "No one has the right to speak for anyone else," was a kind of byword.

Cacophony was extreme. Leftists were more divided than ever. Delusive triumphalism alternated with nihilistic depression. But one single event suddenly realigned the various fronts: not only all leftist groups but the whole intelligentsia and the whole journalistic profession united in protest against the official cover-up of an incident of police brutality against a free-lance journalist. A group of Maoist militants called for the creation of a free news agency, on the model of the American Liberation News Service, existing since 1968 in the United States. The Agence de Presse Libération (APL) was founded on 18 June 1971, a date carefully chosen for its Gaullist connotations (on 18 June 1940, the birthdate of the Resistance against the Nazis, de Gaulle broadcast his address from London calling on the French people to refuse Pétain's surrender to Germany). The beginnings were modest, the technological apparatus that of the urban guerrilla. The first texts had all the symptoms of the "infantile illness of leftism," as Lenin would have said. The news proffered by APL's bulletin caused little stir. But another official cover-up, in February 1972, brought the agency to the fore. APL released a series of photographs displaying, step by step, the cold-blooded assassination of a young worker by a member of the private guard of the government-owned company Renault; and overnight, APL became a respected source of information concerning all censored issues. Yet it retained its collective and amateurish character. None of its editors was a trained journalist, and none had a special field of interest. The news was gleaned from the multiple contacts established by the Maoist organization, counterchecked, and anonymously published.

In the fall of 1972, APL drafted its plan for a popular newspaper, to be called *Libération*, again with Sartre as its godfather. Controlled by its readers, devoid of advertising, resistant to the hierarchy of a differential salary scale and the division of labor, it was to—and did—uncover and publish repressed issues, to be in tune with its time, constantly to take the pulse of the "population." The Maoists astutely realized that their only chance of success was to function on a broad political platform. They built an ecumenical team around the motto "The information must come from the people and return to the people." Amid grotesque internal strife, they initiated a promotion campaign with the support of Michel Foucault and a few other intellectuals. Committees were formed all over France. While their primary functions were fundraising and organizing the newspaper's distribution, they were also supposed to institutionalize the reader's control over the editorial board, a role they never fulfilled.

The first issues of *Libération,* published during the presidential campaign of 1973, were far from impressive, the journal being in the grip of unremitting conflict. Again, it was to be saved by events. Protesting against the liquidation of their clockmaking company, the workers of Lip, in Besançon, having confiscated both the products and the means of production, set up a cooperative to manufacture and distribute watches. This move, upsetting all the rules of organized trade unions and all the prescriptions of political analysts, became a social symbol that marked the end of traditional leftism in France. Very much on the scene at Lip, *Libération* was welcomed by a festive working class, conscious of its pioneering role and using a language reminiscent of May 1968 and of the Popular Front of the 1930s. This support rejuvenated the newspaper and overshadowed the ideological battles within the Paris bureau. A page of the newspaper was offered daily to the workers, who used it with a devastating sense of humor. The rigid language of confrontation was definitively abandoned. Through the events of Lip, *Libération* found its tone. Internal political differences remained, but the idea of a "direct contact with reality" prevailed: thinking of this, Sartre later said: "*Libération* is part of my oeuvre."

Having survived many crises, duly reported in its own columns, in 1982 *Libération* finally adopted the customary practices of an institutionalized press—advertising, a hierarchical scale of salaries, a traditional division of labor, the introduction of external capital. Although it was in a way the beginning of its end, *Libé* did not abandon its freedom of language, publicizing on a large scale, especially in its pun-laden headlines, a type of mordant irony indebted to the broadsheets of the 1920s avant-garde. Two anticlerical issues devoted to the pope's trips to France—the one in 1980 printed on incense-scented paper; the second, in 1987, sporting the headline "Pope Show"—provide good samples of this tone. Indeed, it was set from the very first issue, in 1973: speaking about the failed launching of two French satellites, *Libération* splashed, "Castor et Pollux: Plouf [Splash!]." The most memorable example of this peculiar humor remains the first-page obituary of Jacques Lacan (fig. 1), the French psychoanalyst famous for having introduced outrageous puns into the most abstruse matters: "Tout fou Lacan," a pun on *tout fou* (totally mad) and *tout fout le camp* (everything scrams).

Like all other newspapers, *Libération* has a few great writers (Serge July's Machiavellian and epic analyses of French politics are unequaled in France), but

1. *Libération* (11 September 1981, 2 August 1983, 15–16 June 1985). (Photo by Thomas Hollier-Larousse.)

it is its general stenographic wit that distinguishes its pages. Despite the increasing specialization of its collaborators, *Libération* treasured a kind of editorial anarchism until its last major transformation, in 1987. Thus a review of Kafka's letters might be written by a specialist in rock music; or a tennis game might be reported with a passionate commentary by Serge Daney, a veteran of the *Cahiers du cinéma,* whose film columns are the gem of the paper; and sprinkled throughout were the NDLC (*note de la claviste*), by which the typesetters, like so many wry kamikaze pilots, buzzed the columns with strange parenthetical interjections. The wish to be true to one's experience remained pervasive, but it had changed side, moving from the call-to-the-readers of the early years to the later highly subjective idiom of the journalists. Thus the Lebanese conflict leading to the Sabra and Shattila massacres was covered by a native of Beirut whose hymn to his city was greeted as a magisterial piece of lyrical prose. The force of the newspaper lay not in its frequent scoops—the publication of names and addresses of Central Intelligence Agency operatives in France; the uncovering of a document proving that during the 1968 crisis the government had planned to round up political dissidents in a stadium; the conduct of an exclusive interview with Norodom Sihanouk—but in its presentation of firsthand testimony of all aspects of daily life and current experience.

Two features enhanced this aspect of the paper and were innovations in France: a weekly supplement of free personal ads (terminated when it began to resemble Krafft-Ebing's encyclopedia of sexual perversions); and a daily page of letters to the editor, which became both a sociological monument and the catalyst of a new literary genre. Published as a "collective novel" in 1983 under the title *La vie tu parles* (*Life Live* and *Life? No Kidding!*), a chronological and anonymous selection of these letters provides the most polyphonic and dialogic accounts of a decade. Full of anger *à la Céline* or elegiac happiness, of dreary repression or merry exhibitionism, the letters represent a kind of grid of all the events of French social experience as they affect individual lives, and, at the same time, the purest of *Libération* as a literary undertaking, its marginal center, as it were.

Today the newspaper is endangered by its own success and a certain drift away from its principles under the spell of a growing fascination with high-tech modernization and the frenetic hype of fashion. In 1987 *Libération* moved its quarters and adopted the newest computerized printing techniques, and each member of the staff was assigned a special field of interest: it was claiming publicly that it had stopped being the ugly duckling. But at the same time, it lost its peculiar character, and its readership began to decline: puns started to look stale, audacity of tone artificial. In finally taking up the standards of the established press, *Libération* had ceased to define a community of readers: its heyday is obviously over. For more than a decade, however, it remained the only voice able to give a live account of the evolution of what one could call French civilization.

See also 1945 (15 October), 1968 (May).

Bibliography: Patrick Combes, *La littérature et les événements de mai 68: Ecriture, mythes, critique, écrivains 1968–1981* (Paris: Seghers, 1984). Serge Daney, *Ciné-journal*, with preface by Gilles Deleuze (Paris: Cahiers du Cinéma, 1986). Françoise Filliger, Jean-Marie Bartel, and Bruno Montels, eds., *La vie tu parles, roman collectif 1973–1983*, with preface by Serge July (Paris: POL, 1983). Serge July, *Dis maman, c'est quoi l'avant-guerre?* (Paris: Alain Moreau, 1980). François-Marie Samuelson, *Il était une fois Libé . . .* (Paris: Seuil, 1979).

Yve-Alain Bois

∾ *1975*

The Journal *L'arc* Devotes Its Sixty-first Issue to
"Simone de Beauvoir et la lutte des femmes"

"French Feminism"

In the second half of the 1970s, academic literary critics in the United States began to talk about something called "French feminism." In France as throughout the world, the late 1960s and early 1970s witnessed an enormous surge of feminist consciousness and activity. The term *French feminism,* however, referred to only a narrow sector of feminist activity in France, one that was perceived outside France as peculiarly French. "French feminism," then, designates a current of intellectual and literary activity by some women in France, but this current is named and thus *constituted as a movement here* in the United States.

Its central text is a translation by Keith Cohen and Paula Cohen of Hélène

Cixous's "Le rire de la méduse" (1975; "The Laugh of the Medusa"), published first in 1976 in *Signs,* the best-known and most widely read American academic feminist journal, and reprinted in 1980 in Elaine Marks and Isabelle de Courtivron's anthology *New French Feminisms,* which in effect represented and canonized the phenomenon.

In America the movement called "French feminism" is also called *écriture féminine,* a term that generally remains untranslated. More than any other text, "Le rire de la méduse" defines *écriture féminine.* It also asserts that "it is impossible to *define* a feminine practice of writing" (*New French Feminisms,* p. 253)—*define* connoting here both limitation and containment. Cixous's woman writes from her "libidinal economy," an economy of abundance that overflows the tight, patrolled boundaries of masculine thrift. Man's libido is phallocentric; woman's libido has another economy: her various bodily drives are not dominated by any one center. Cixous envisions the revolution in thought and living that will be produced by a writing that carries such prodigious female sexuality: bodily, multiple, and insubordinate. The sort of writing that Cixous imagines as "feminine" has more in common with what has traditionally been called poetry than with prose, either theoretical (subordinating writing to the "thrust" of the argument) or novelistic (subordinating everything to the plot's "climax"). This *écriture féminine* is more an ideal than a description of how women have actually written: Cixous can name only Colette and Marguerite Duras as women who have achieved this truly feminine writing. We may add to this short list Cixous herself, a prolific producer of poetic fictions.

In the mid-1970s a number of French women's texts explored this analogy between female sexuality and writing; examples include Annie Leclerc's *Parole de femme* (1974; *Woman's Word*); Luce Irigaray's *Ce sexe qui n'en est pas un* (1977; *This Sex Which Is Not One*); Cixous, Madeleine Gagnon, and Leclerc's *La venue à l'écriture* (1977; *Coming into Writing*); and various articles in newly formed women's journals such as *Cahiers du grif* and *Sorcières.* But although these texts can be taken together as reflecting a literary movement we might call *écriture féminine,* it never was organized as such. These women were not so much influencing each other as they were all influenced by the concept of *écriture* in French male literary theory at the time. In the late 1960s and early 1970s theorists more or less loosely connected with the journal *Tel quel* (Roland Barthes and Jacques Derrida, among others) were promoting a notion of *écriture* as something insubordinate to "logocentric" discourse, discourse in the service of a governing idea. The politics of *écriture féminine* involved wresting "writing" away from this male avant-garde high culture and claiming it for the common woman. So Irigaray writes: "Her sexuality, always at least double, goes even further: it is *plural.* Is this the way culture is seeking to characterize itself now?" (*This Sex,* p. 28). The great male literary movements of modernity, she claims, are trying to get where women already are: beyond the novel, beyond metaphysics, beyond "phallogocentrism." Rather than banging at the gates of high literary culture, a token woman let in now and then, *écriture féminine* would make women the insiders, construe male high culture as the parvenu.

The French feminism that is best known outside France is largely literary, in part because the international propagation of culture is filtered academically through departments of literature, literature appearing as the least political part of culture and thus being allowed to cross borders without arousing suspicion. *Ecriture féminine,* a specifically literary aspect of feminist activity, would thus seem to belong in a history of literature; but in order to find its place in a history of French literature, it must be returned to its French context. Cixous's "Le rire de la méduse" must be reinserted in the 1975 issue of the intellectual journal *L'arc,* where it was originally published. It is the only literary piece in a collection that includes sociological, biological, and political essays. By returning the piece to its original French context, we reframe it in a broader intellectual history.

In the mid-1970s, in response to the burgeoning of feminist consciousness, a large number of French intellectual journals published special "women's issues": *Partisans* (no. 106, 1972); *Les temps modernes* (April–May 1974); *La quinzaine littéraire* (August 1974); *Dialectiques* (Spring 1975); *Tel quel* (Winter 1977); *Revue des sciences humaines* (October–December 1977). *L'arc* no. 61 was part of this general phenomenon, but a particular problem arose with producing a feminist issue of this journal. Each issue of *L'arc* is devoted to a famous person, a cultural hero, artist or intellectual. Though a journal of ideas, not of personalities, it organizes the presentation of those ideas around or through what the editors of the sixty-first issue, Catherine Clément and Bernard Pingaud, called "figures, names, 'great' names" (p. 1). So its 1975 issue on feminism was attached to a proper name, that of Simone de Beauvoir.

Beauvoir was the first woman to be the subject of an issue of *L'arc.* Yet entering a woman's name in the roster of great men entailed a contradiction, articulated by the issue's editors: "Now never, in the history of the journal, will the choice have been more appropriate [*juste*]; but also never will it have been more questionable in its very principle" (p. 1). It is only "just" finally to include women in history, but this inclusion turns out to challenge the very principles behind this sort of history. The feminist issue of *L'arc* raises two general questions: What does it mean for a woman to become a "name"? And what does it mean to organize the history of ideas around such names?

Clément and Pingaud describe how Beauvoir's contradictory status centers on the question of proper name: "Simone de Beauvoir is a historic name, but today in this issue, her choice . . . is to be . . . a woman among others, nameless [*anonyme*]" (p. 1). Beauvoir is represented in this issue by two texts, both conversations. In the first she "interrogates" Jean-Paul Sartre about feminism. Throughout the interview he is known only as "Sartre," she as "Simone de Beauvoir." In the second conversation she discusses feminism with four women; all four choose to identify themselves by first name only, by what in French is called not a name but a *prénom,* literally a "prename." Beauvoir is the exception; she is identified as "S. de Beauvoir." In contrast to Sartre, she has a *prénom;* in contrast to the women, she has a name. She belongs both with the man who *is* a name (her boyfriend who has already had his issue of *L'arc*) and with the women who choose to remain prename, and not quite with either.

Beauvoir's two interviews appear at the beginning of the journal, separated by one short essay, Clément's "Enclave esclave" ("Enslaved Enclave"). By thus positioning her own writing, the female editor of the issue seems to be placing herself between the two aspects of Beauvoir's dilemma. Clément recounts an experience as a podium speaker: in the audience, passion "circulates anonymously [*anonyme*] from woman to woman. On the podium, one is necessarily in a contrary position: nonymous [*nonyme*], called to the podium because of one's name . . . *'Bravo, sir.'* A woman, among others, sends forth this salutation from the balcony" ("Enslaved," in *New French Feminisms*, pp. 132–135). On the podium, Clément is cut off from what circulates "from woman to woman." From the point of view of a woman "among the others," *anonyme,* the nonymous woman is on the other side, on the side of the men. Clément, like Beauvoir, appears in *L'arc* as the only woman in a list of men; in her case it is the editorial board on the masthead.

L'arc no. 61 begins: "The position taken [*parti pris*] by this journal has been, for a long time, to choose figures, names, 'great' names: those names [*noms, nouns*] that are called proper." "Le rire de la méduse" has something to say about the "proper": "If, by means of laws, lies, blackmail, and marriage . . . her name has been extorted . . . she has been able . . . to see more closely the inanity of the 'proper'" ("Laugh," in *New French Feminisms*, pp. 258–259; translation modified). The word *proper* (*propre*) set off in quotes has a sense of propriety (the sexual insubordination of "Laugh"), a sense of property (the attack on masculine thrift), and, in resonance with patriarchal "extortion" of woman's name, a sense of *nom propre,* the proper noun. If *L'arc* takes its stand on the proper name, within the covers of this 1975 issue "Medusa" is laughing at precisely what the journal takes very seriously, its *parti pris.*

Clément belongs to this journal that writes nonymous history. Cixous seems to belong in the balcony, glorying in namelessness among the women. Yet the research Clément was presenting from the podium was published in 1975 in a book she coauthored with Cixous, *La jeune née* (*The Newly Born Woman*), inaugurating a series—"Féminin Futur" (Feminine Future)—that the two women edited together at Union Générale d'Editions. *La jeune née* is an unsynthesized dialogue between two different positions, as if the nonymous speaker and the anonymous woman in the balcony decided to work together without suppressing the space dividing them.

As name that would be nameless, with the man and with the women, Beauvoir's position in *L'arc* is double. Clément likewise is doubly represented in the issue: as editor with a man in the introduction, and in her own article as one woman among women writing. "The token woman . . . is an ambiguous creature," says Sartre in his interrogation (p. 11). The woman chosen to join the ranks of men disproves the exclusion of women, but she is also there as a token of, a marker for, all the women excluded. In the 1974 women's issue of *Les temps modernes,* Beauvoir recognized that she had "more or less played the role of the token woman." In her issue of *L'arc* she wants to play that role knowingly, assuming her place in male high culture as token, and thus as reminder, of the nameless women.

The token woman shares this ambiguity with the bourgeois wife who, again according to Sartre, has a double relation to her cleaning woman: as women they share confidences and a certain female complicity, but through her relation to her husband the affluent woman has authority over the other woman. Whether through entry into marriage or into the boardroom, into the ruling class or into history, a woman's access to name and power puts her in an ambiguous position unless she denies her connection to other women.

There is a third ambiguous creature in *L'arc* no. 61. According to the editors, the "names, 'great' names: those names that are called proper . . . are most often . . . in an ambiguous position: innovators, but already recognized enough to be the stake of a special issue" (p. 1). What makes a thinker historic seems to be his originality, but it also must be the widespread influence of his thought. If the thought were literally "proper" to him, belonging to him alone, it would have no effect. If he is a historic thinker, then his work must be widely shared. The great names in the history of ideas are also tokens, markers of all the nameless who shared their ideas, both those influenced by and those influencing the "name."

If Beauvoir is a "historic name," it is because *Le deuxième sexe* (1949; *The Second Sex*) nourished the international feminist movement of the second half of the 20th century. It had this broad effect because masses of women reading that book recognized their own knowledge there. Had her knowledge been truly singular, Beauvoir would not have become a "name."

The first woman chosen to be a "name" by *L'arc,* she makes a difference. But the nonymous woman insists on keeping her connection to the nameless women who have entitled her. Chosen in keeping with the journal's format, Beauvoir ends up calling that format into question. Breaking with its usual practice of the lone name, the sixty-first issue of *L'arc* has in fact a double title—"Simone de Beauvoir et la lutte des femmes" ("Simone de Beauvoir and the Women's Struggle").

See also 1929, 1949.

Bibliography: Hélène Cixous and Catherine Clément, *The Newly Born Woman,* trans. Betsy Wing (Minneapolis: University of Minnesota Press, 1986). Hélène Cixous, Madeleine Gagnon, and Annie Leclerc, *La venue à l'écriture* (Paris: Union Générale d'Editions, 1977). Verena Andermatt Conley, *Hélène Cixous* (Lincoln: University of Nebraska Press, 1984). Luce Irigaray, *This Sex Which Is Not One,* trans. Catherine Porter (Ithaca: Cornell University Press, 1985). Annie Leclerc, *Parole de femme* (Paris: Grasset, 1974). Elaine Marks, "Review Essay: Women and Literature in France," *Signs,* 3 (1978), 832–842. Elaine Marks and Isabelle de Courtivron, eds., *New French Feminisms: An Anthology* (Amherst: University of Massachusetts Press, 1980).

Jane Gallop

✑ 1976, 15 November

The Separatist Parti Québécois, Having Captured the Majority of Seats in the Provincial National Assembly, Comes to Power in Quebec

Hubert Aquin and Quebec Literature

When the Parti Québécois (PQ), dedicated to leading Quebec out of the Canadian confederation, won the provincial elections on 15 November 1976, the novelist Hubert Aquin (1929–1977) was jubilant. Like many other writers of his generation in Quebec, Aquin believed political independence to be an essential step toward cultural autonomy. "Now that we have named the unnameable," he wrote, as if the electoral victory were part of a therapeutic process, "the collective unconscious has been freed and can discharge all the energy dammed up until that moment" ("Après le 15 novembre 1976" [1980; "After 15 November 1976"], p. 24). Although literary activity had in fact begun to accelerate two decades earlier, Aquin had historical reasons for speaking of politics in linguistic terms. Since the British conquest of Canada in 1763, survival of the beleaguered French community had always been closely linked to that of its language, threatened as it was by the predominance of English across North America. Overcoming the repressed, colonial mentality induced by its minority status could thus be likened to the breaking of a taboo, the undoing of a repression. Aquin's "unnameable" was in fact only partly political; it involved self-definition in the most literal sense. Thus the PQ's first act was to establish French as the language of work and public life, since the use of French was the most basic element of the Québécois' self-definition. In doing so, ironically, it blunted the appeal of separatism, since much of the psychological pressure behind the movement had been relieved. Still, sheer weight of numbers (6 million francophones in a continent of 250 million) and ease of assimilation meant that cultural survival would always depend in some way on political will.

The Québécois' neighbors in English-speaking Canada (including those within Quebec) and in the United States, many of whose families had originally not spoken English but had become assimilated into the linguistic mainstream, were often puzzled, if not offended, by so insistent a commitment to French. Language to them was merely a means of expression, a tool for getting ahead. The preeminence of English encouraged a view of other languages as a "heritage" devoid of practical significance. But the Québécois rejected any folklorization of their native tongue, established in the St. Lawrence Valley since the beginning of European settlement. French had been accorded official recognition in 1774 by a British government anxious to secure the loyalty of its new subjects at a time when the American colonies were about to revolt. Its survival had also been aided by the long association of language with religion, for French Canadians were Catholics in a country where, until the mid-19th century, an English speaker was usually a Protestant. The church saw the French language as a bulwark of the faith well into the 20th century. French was so much a part of the symbolic structure of Quebec life that even after religion became less important as a means of self-identification, the Québécois remained convinced that to abandon their language would be to make the human landscape unrecognizable. Speaking French, in this context, becomes in itself an act of self-expression, the conscious reaffirmation of a self-image whose content, whatever else it may include, is the means used to portray it.

The tendency to link self-expression so closely to a specific means of expression had its dangers, however. It could introduce a regressive element into political debate and another kind of folklorization into Quebec culture itself, celebrating local customs and traditions simply because they existed as proof of the "French fact." But the more acute intellectuals, notably those grouped around *Liberté,* a vital literary-political review founded in 1959, recognized the limitations of such a perspective and strove to fashion a specifically French identity while rejecting fetishistic cultural ideals. The real challenge was not to identify with a language; it was to give that language new creative energy. As the essayist André Belleau (1930–1986), who with Aquin helped the poet Jean-Guy Pilon found *Liberté,* put it in 1986: "We do not need to speak French, we need French in order to speak" (*Surprendre les voix* [*Overhearing the Voices*], p. 119).

In the past, the need to survive in a harsh climate made this a difficult task for the small French community, cut off from any real contact with the mother country, first by the British conquest, then by the church's rejection of secular, post-Revolutionary France. The first Quebec novel and collection of poems did not appear until the 1830s, for writers were slow to emerge in such circumstances. In the century that followed, these artists were torn between the desire to "write well," according to French literary conventions far removed from local usage, and the need, frustrated by religious restrictions and by the absence of a broad-based literate public, to reflect their own reality. Not until World War II did industrialization (especially in the Montreal area) and advances in communications make it possible to get beyond the false alternatives of regionalism and cosmopolitanism.

The poets of the 1950s were the first to embody the free self-assertion evoked by Aquin in his postelection statement. Marked by surrealism and the wide-ranging verse forms of Henri Michaux and Pierre Jean Jouve, writers such as Paul-Marie Lapointe (1929–) and Gaston Miron (1928–) celebrated the power of language to name feelings hitherto inchoate as well as the specific features of the "territory" (poetic as well as political) they surveyed. The lyric mode they favored allowed form and content to be fused by the power of incantatory speech. But the poets also created the institutional structures without which a native literature could not flourish. In addition to new journals and publishing houses, broadcast media helped writers find an audience, for public radio and television have played a key role in Quebec's cultural development.

Yet the process of emancipation was a difficult one. The fusion of art and politics proved difficult to maintain beyond the first moments of this *prise de parole* ("taking the floor"). At the beginning of the 1960s there was deep uncertainty about what literature could accomplish. Writing was extolled as the very model of sovereign action, and at the same time experienced as an empty shell of impotent talk. The simultaneity of these extreme reactions reflected historical circumstances, not only the disproportion between the rates of cultural and political evolution, but also the Québécois' problematic relation to their language. Aquin's novels, the most important and self-conscious fiction of the 1960s, dramatize the writer's struggle to define his political role and the historical importance of literary form.

In *Prochain épisode* (1965; "next episode," but the English translation keeps the French title), Aquin's first published book, the narrator, a failed revolutionary languishing in a psychiatric clinic after his arrest, seeks distraction from his despair by writing a spy novel. Unable to give its characters independent life, he compensates by making himself the focus of the story, which becomes a mirror for his own earlier attempts to overcome a pervasive inability to act. Yet this retrospective meditation is driven by the prospect of an "episode" to come, destined to complete the narrator's revolutionary work. *Prochain épisode* echoes the French *nouveau roman* (new novel) in its technically sophisticated account of impossible closure, but it belongs at the same time to a more idealistic tradition emphasizing the healing of painful dualities. The tension between these two aspects is fundamental, for beyond the pathos of Aquin's political themes lies a paradox that informs the author's nationalism, always balanced by his rejection of all provincialism, but which found its most articulate expression on the literary plane: what needs to be undone or opened up—the stable and objectified constructs of a culture—has not yet been realized. A new literature emerging in postmodern culture, like a nation asserting its specificity in the midst of advanced Western society, is compelled to ask at what point its self-identification can be taken sufficiently for granted that the limitations of that image can be exposed.

The exemplary importance of Aquin's career lies in his refusal to postpone this question in the name of nation-building or blithely to assume it is easily resolved. The first temptation was present in the remarkable expansion of cultural institutions in the 1960s and 1970s, offering writers unprecedented opportunity and sometimes indiscriminate rewards for publication. The second was a factor in the extraordinarily rapid and widespread endorsement of avant-garde literary and feminist discourses, with their radical challenge to the identities of self, gender, and text. It is true that a new literature can hardly arise without some anticipatory structures, while the deep conservatism of culture and religion in traditional Quebec, once it was shaken off, had to give way to a reaction of commensurate force. (Within a generation, for example, Quebec's birthrate, long among the highest in the West, fell to below replacement level.) Yet it sometimes seemed, at the end of the 1970s, that the institutional consecration of literature as such overshadowed individual achievements, and that the avant-garde view of the text as pure process, as *écriture,* consigned the very idea of the text as work to premature obsolescence.

The problematic identity and value of the work remained a central focus of Aquin's novels, even to the point of paralysis. But in his last novels, *L'antipho-*

naire (1969; *The Antiphonary*) and *Neige noire* (1974; "black snow," translated as *Hamlet's Twin*), Aquin's writing attains a degree of intelligence and stylistic resonance such that paralysis is turned inside out and becomes an enabling energy for the new generation of readers that returned to his works after the author's suicide in 1977. Just as defeat of the independence referendum in 1980 prompted a fresh reading of the lyric poets, tempered by the insight that, as André Belleau put it, "literature is that which never happens" (*Surprendre les voix,* p. 105), Aquin's unfinished novel *Obombre* crystallized a deepened awareness of the ironies of culture: the fragmentary text is introduced by a sentence Aquin found in the German Romantic philosopher Friedrich Schelling: "The beginning is not the beginning until the end" (*Liberté,* May–June 1981, p. 16).

Aquin's appeal to Romantic philosophy is especially significant, since the birth of Quebec literature in the 1830s occurred during the flowering of French Romanticism, although it could not coincide with it. At the time, Quebec writers had neither the social nor the cultural resources to do more than adopt the externals of Romantic diction along with a simplified and cautious version of its subjectivism. Among its other legacies, Aquin's work made possible a critical reappropriation of literary history, a longer perspective on the enduring tension between the means and ends of artistic expression. In the 1980s this view allowed for a pluralistic acceptance of different language levels and of divergent literary allegiances. Michel Tremblay (1942–), for example, uses local popular speech patterns to spectacular effect in his plays while composing novels in a style more accessible to an international audience. Anne Hébert (1916–), who first made her reputation as a poet in the 1950s, offers another striking instance of artistic mobility in her late novel *Les fous de Bassan* (1982; *In the Shadow of the Wind*). Her narrative technique borrows freely from American and French sources, ranging from William Faulkner to Hélène Cixous. The story takes place in an English-speaking community in Quebec, but the style is so closely wedded to French rhythm and idiom that the book becomes a highly original pursuit of linguistic and cultural borderlines on the literary map now being redrawn in different ways by so many younger writers.

This new vitality also informs the commitment of both individual artists and public institutions to the wider community of French-speaking peoples. No longer to be considered as the legacy of France's colonialism or chauvinism, this diverse grouping of peoples in Europe, Africa, the Caribbean, and elsewhere sees in the French language a common yet pluralistic medium of communication shared by speakers of varied backgrounds, accents, and outlooks. The struggle to maintain a French entity in Quebec finds its appropriate counterpart in a determination to undo any monocultural idea of "French" itself.

See also 1968 (February).

Bibliography: Hubert Aquin, "Après le 15 novembre 1976," in *Romanciers du Québec* (Quebec: Québec Français, 1980). Aquin, *Prochain Episode,* trans. Penny Williams (Toronto: McClelland and Stewart, 1967). André Belleau, *Surprendre les voix* (Montreal:

Boréal, 1986). Patricia Merivale, "Hubert Aquin (1929–1977)," in *Dictionary of Literary Biography,* ed. W. H. New, vol. 53 (Detroit: Gale Research, 1986). André Sénécal, *A Reader's Guide to Québec Studies* (Quebec: Ministry of International Affairs, 1988). Larry Shouldice, ed. and trans., *Contemporary Québec Criticism* (Toronto: University of Toronto Press, 1979). William Toye, ed., *The Oxford Companion to Canadian Literature* (Toronto: Oxford University Press, 1983).

Patrick Coleman

✐〇 *1985, 27 September*
The 500th Program of "Apostrophes" Is Broadcast on Antenne 2

Friday Night Books

That if Bernard Pivot did not exist he would quickly have had to be reinvented was no doubt a thought that crossed more than one French publisher's mind while watching the 500th broadcast of "Apostrophes" on 27 September 1985. Luckily his existence was unquestionable, and had been ever since, ten years earlier, this most successful of literary chat shows, in every sense Pivot's invention, saw the light of television's day. Pivot invented not just a program but also literature with it in his image—the average sensual man's average sensual literature. Fan of wine and *football* (he wrote a book on the Beaujolais region, another on the Saint-Etienne soccer team), Pivot is equally an avid supporter of reading (before becoming "Bernard Pivot," he also wrote a first and only novel, *L'amour en vogue* {1959; *Love's the Thing*], a rather ordinary love story: all Pivot is in the setting, his much-loved hometown of Lyons, and the occupation of the first-person narrator, head-tickler for a fairground ghost train): just *reading,* the pleasure of that and not of the text; no theories, no academic discourse, no credentials (Pivot has no degrees)—nothing but the man in the street as reader, sharing his excitement with a few million other such men and women live every Friday night. "I'm not a critic. I'm just happy to try to give people the taste of reading" ("Pivot présente la nouvelle cuvée d'*Apostrophes*" ["Pivot Presents the Latest Vintage of *Apostrophes*"], p. 105). Exactly.

The studio set is simple, merely the space for a handful of authors to sit facing one another, Pivot in the middle, the books for the week at his side, a small audience of relatives and friends forming the barely visible background. The authors are sent each other's works to read: the point is discussion—or rather, passion, an exchange of convictions, likes, dislikes, sensations, what Pivot calls "a kind of spontaneous theatrical performance" ("Entretien avec Bernard Pivot" ["Conversation with Bernard Pivot"], p. 70). Take Marie Cardinal, Pierre Mertens, Hortense Dufour, Guy Hocquenghem, Jean-Jacques Brochier, Jacques Testart, all with recent novels; put them together under the title "La vie en noir" ("Life on the Dark Side"); and there you have a typical "Apostrophes" (this one, in fact, 4 September 1987, the 590th). The title theme is approximate: how do you link the story of a mother whose daughter is a drug addict (Cardinal's *Les grands désordres,* 1987; *Major Troubles*) with that of Adam, Eve, and AIDS (Hocquenghem's *Eve,* 1987) and then with that of the German writer Gottfried Benn (Mertens' *Les éblouissements,* 1987; *Bedazzlements*)? What is important is the spectacle of the author and the creation before our eyes of his or her book as "the book of the author," in the same way that we talk of "the book of the film": something to which we are subsequently incited and which gains its impact from its reactivation of what we first saw, the true substance. No longer dead, the author has now become the very condition of the book's reality, its television life. Cardinal's cumbersome gesturing, Brochier's lip-curling urbanity, Dufour's twitchy nervousness, Hocquenghem's diffident sincerity—this is what is to define their work, how they come over and their novels with them, *as* them.

In the midst of which Pivot stops to read this and that passage, head raised on the final words, arms waving, book in one hand, glasses off in the other: "Ça, c'est fort . . ." (that's really strong). It is an exclamation and a question, the exact reflection of Pivot's bushy-eyebrowed, self-amused, ingenuously enthusiastic, quizzical certitude. Books are an extravaganza of powerful affects, in ceaseless supply as authors come and go with them, week in, week out; Pivot in the middle receives and reflects, provokes and precipitates, jubilates (a kind of Lacanian "book phase"), brings it all to a continual head, his and ours, represents literature as today it is and to great effect. "Apostrophes," indeed, has been hugely successful, and there are articles galore, books even, about "the Pivot effect." The show attracts 2 million to 5 million viewers and in 1986 had an average audience share of 10.2 percent and a best score of 15.5 percent (equal to and better than "Dynasty" that year in France). For ninety minutes of literary talk these figures are spectacular; so much so that "Apostrophes" has now bred two further shows, two short Sunday and Monday evening late-spots called— what else?—"Apos" and "Strophes." In 1986 Pivot was the fifth highest-paid French television personality, with a salary of 80,000 francs per month; the next year it was said to be 120,000 . . . All of which is not bad for a program that costs peanuts to produce and the members of whose cast—the authors— receive nothing; most, after all, would pay to appear.

They would pay because "Apostrophes" brings their books into contemporary being. More than publicity, or rather supreme publicity, it actualizes and authenticates: a book is real, it exists, it means something precisely inasmuch as it is "apostrophizable." This reality can be measured in copies sold (bookshops throughout France stock and make a special display of the program's books of the week); but it is more, too, than that simple measure: for a moment, the book becomes part of what has been read (millions have seen it through Pivot); it is recognizable, discussable, knowable—it has *happened.* "Apostrophes" is the culmination of today's commerce—the whole circulation—of the literary, a culmination that simultaneously continues and shows up all the institutions of literature that precede and surround it, from the Académie Française to the literary prizes and so on. The Académie, which celebrated its 350th anniversary in the same year as the 500th "Apostrophes" (naturally Pivot laid on an Académie show), is an anachronism that combines innate political conservatism (one specialty is the election of notorious right-wing public figures: the likes of Michel Droit or Alain Peyrefitte) with the best-selling enterprise of individual members (novelists such as Jean d'Ormesson and Henri Troyat) and an overall commitment to ignoring the significant writing going on around it (hard to imagine, say, the election of Hélène Cixous); the prizes, the Goncourt et al., have defied anachronism by resolutely turning themselves into large promotional ventures in which publishing-trade pressures outweigh—in fact largely define—literary judgment, and mediatization is the name of the game (thus the Goncourt guarantees sales of 250,000 or more). Pivot stands over them all: bigger and more real by virtue of television and his audience; independent by virtue of the same from anachronism or lobby—what do these other institutions amount to when set against television and "Apostrophes"? Pivot is incorruptible, genuinely and totally (there is a hushed moment in every piece on him at which his imperviousness to inducements from authors, publishers, and politicians is stressed): just like you and me, he selects what he likes, invites only the people whose books we will find interesting, will want to find out about. As indeed we will: why else would he have invited them? We are as free as he is, television is our power too (Pivot talks of "the democracy of the big eye"; "Entretien," p. 71)—there is no putting one over on Bernard, on us!

With so many books pouring out (some 12,000 new titles a year in France), Pivot is of recognized public utility, picking and reading and watching for us. He pursues this task, moreover, beyond the confines of "Apostrophes." His monthly magazine, *Lire,* has close to a million readers and consists of extracts from chosen new books, interviews, games, and—the opening pages—Pivot's literary diary. Obviously, the choice excludes whole areas of writing almost completely—poetry, for instance. Which is right: what, after all, is the temporality of poetry? Its televisuality? Novels—most, anyway—can be made into stories, themes, issues, the same issues that essay and documentary works already offer, these latter thus constituting some 60 percent of the books featured on the show each year. The book-event needs a book with events (Barthes's "from work to text," the text as order of the signifier, resistant to consumption, shifts to Pivot's "from book to event," the book as signified, programmed to appear). And then there are the author-events so crucial to the former: the various ordinary performances week by week; the dramatic extremes (a wine-soaked Bukowski plunging up his neighbor's skirts before being expelled from the set); the occasional great-author nights (the presence of Solzhenitsyn, Yourcenar, Mailer . . .). And then again, supreme and unfailing, the "Apostrophes"-event itself, the weekly moment of French literature today, its *occurrence.*

Why the success? Why should the discussion of a few books make appealing television, and why should "Apostrophes" figure in the ratings along with top comedy and variety programs, "Sexy-folies," "Le grand échiquier," and "Coco-ricocoboy"? It is certain that "Literature" remains a value, an official investment of the culture in its institutions, its education, its received ideas, something like a property of France and the French language. In what other Western industrial society do presidents feel the need to be writers, to discourse on books, to keep up a literary profile? While ordering the evacuation of the Sorbonne in 1968, Charles de Gaulle is also polishing a deft sentence or two to the Princess Bibesco to thank her for having him read her books. With sales of his war memoirs in the millions, de Gaulle, of course, is a national monument, the embodiment of the culture—of France—in what is still one of its most influential versions of itself. But then we are always reminded too that Georges Pompidou edited an anthology of French poetry; and Valéry Giscard d'Estaing (who would have liked to have been Maupassant) and François Mitterrand (whose writing—*Le grain et la paille* [1975; *The Wheat and the Chaff*] and *L'abeille et l'architecte* [1978; *The Bee and the Architect*]—stakes his claim for a place in the tradition of French literary moralists) have both been more than keen to be on "Apostrophes" (needless to say, Giscard's Maupassant revelation was made to Pivot).

The value and the investment are there; the point is to make them good today, which is Pivot's success. The national property is made over to the public: literature for the small shareholder. Not that *literature* is then a term much used, although it has its reserved place on special occasions (those great authors); it is now just a matter of books—here they are, democratically, picked by Pivot, any book, provided it's *fort*. Books need no longer intimidate us; we can watch them on their authors, the authors of whom Pivot is so respectfully disrespectful, in control, getting them to do their best for us, tickling their heads a little.

The two other major cultural events of 1985 in France were the 100th anniversary of the death of Victor Hugo (Socialist Minister of Culture Jack Lang launched "Victor Hugo Year") and the marriage of top television personality Yves Mourousi (a gigantic celebration by the media of the media). Pivot and "Apostrophes" are somewhere in the middle, between Hugo and Mourousi. Their aim, what they respond to and create, is a medium literature, writers and works as bearers of effective intermediary messages, good for Friday-night circulation: literature as *porte-parole*. Which then makes it no surprise that the most appearances on "Apostrophes" have been notched up by those whose very profession is that of the *porte-parole*, the "word-carriers," consecrated media mouthpieces: Max Gallo, spokesman for the Mauroy Socialist government in 1983–84 and editor of *Le matin;* and Jean d'Ormesson, ideologue of *Le Figaro* right.

In the same year as "Apostrophes"'s 500th, the Nobel Prize for literature went to Claude Simon. The contrary of Gallo or d'Ormesson, Simon has pursued a project of writing far from the expediencies and maneuverings of the Parisian scene, across a range of more than twenty novels that represent a worked intensity of experience and language, a particular literary achievement not easily adaptable to any given tele-vision. The prize raises sales, and Simon's name becomes, momentarily, an event; but his work carries on an idea of writing, of literature, before or beyond the "Apostrophes" mean to which it is destined nevertheless also to be reduced by the power that television, that "Apostrophes," now wields. Thus Simon, like all the others, had been persuaded, even before the Nobel, to forgo his seclusion and appear on the show.

All are as one under Pivot's gaze and ours; the flow of books—those 12,000 new titles yearly—becomes the flow of the program itself—those 500-plus "Apostrophes." Literature today is a massive accelerated production, coming and going every week. In 1985, alongside Simon's Nobel, are Dominique Pierre's *La cité de la joie* (*The City of Joy*), Patrick Modiano's *Quartier perdu* (*Out-of-the-Way District*), Jean d'Ormesson's *Le vent du soir* (*The Evening Wind*), Françoise Sagan's *De guerre lasse* (*Worn Down*), Simone Signoret's *Adieu Volodia* . . . to mention just a tiny few of the titles from among that year's successes in what is called "the quality novel." And then alongside these, we must remember the teeming world of popular books, with its accredited and regularly best-selling authors (Guy des Cars, Gérard de Villiers . . .) and its sudden phenomena (singer Rika Zaraï's *Ma médecine naturelle* [*My Natural Medicine*] sells millions and turns into a cultural fact of French life in the 1980s). And so on. From within this massive production singular writers of an older experimental generation or of a different literary ambition will occasionally be taken up and accelerated into instantaneity, their moment of success. As with Simon, thanks to the Nobel and its aftermath. As with Marguerite Duras, whose *L'amant* (*The Lover*) in 1984 went through the Prix Goncourt to media glory and sales of 750,000 by the year's end, helped no doubt by its eroticism, its French colonial setting, and the public's awareness of its author from literature at school (*Moderato cantabile*, 1958, is a widely read class text).

The seriousness and quality of Duras' writing are beyond question, but her success came at a time when the avant-garde of literature as defined in the 1960s—literature conceived as a specific form of practice with radical cultural-political implications—was being recast by its central figures to accommodate a wider readership. "We must give up the dubious notion of the avant-garde and abandon such comforting certitudes as 'the less I'm read, the more genius I have'"; thus Danièle Sallenave (quoted, appropriately, in *Lire*, September 1987, p. 17), whose *La vie fantôme* (*Ghostly Life*) in 1986 put her briefly in the Pivot public eye. The extreme case, inevitably, is that of Philippe Sollers; founder and energizer of the most influential avant-garde journal of this half-century, *Tel quel*, he has gone from a series of uncompromising texts (such as *Nombres*, 1968; *Numbers*) via phases of adulation of the pope and the United States to a trilogy—a trinity—of novels that combine sex, antifeminism, and the chronicles of multinational Parisian cultural life to the taste of a greatly extended audience (*Femmes* [1983; *Women*], the novel of "an American journalist ranging across the world and multiple female partners," is an immediate best-seller). Sollers's significance is now the degree to which he spectacularizes the current reality of the writer as medium, assumes his work as simply the sum of his appearances: penning a piece on Madonna, posing for a car commercial, popping up with Pivot.

"What is literature?" asked Sartre just after the war, defining its value in terms of freedom and commitment. Some forty years later, the question is about what state it is in, "where it is at"—*où en est la littérature?* The necessary challenge to the assumptions of literature as value too readily gives way to the refusal of all idea of value; the problems of posing and creating values for the practices of writing that "literature" names, or named, and that must henceforth be grasped in full awareness of determinations such as class, race, and sex, all the intersecting particularizations that make up those practices, are collapsed into a free-floating postmodern mobility in which everything is equaled out to the benefit of Sollers and his heroes and all the others on the media scene. "Eclecticism is the degree zero of contemporary general culture: one listens to reggae, watches a western, eats McDonald's food for lunch and local cuisine for dinner, wears Paris perfume in Tokyo and 'retro' clothes in Hong-Kong: knowledge is a matter of TV games," writes "one," alias Jean-François Lyotard (*Le postmoderne*, p. 22); while Jean Baudrillard talks of "the new strategies of indifference" and hymns the end of representation—of political, social, literary value—in our world of simulation, appearances as all (*La gauche divine*, passim). No wonder Max Gallo in 1983, after two years of Socialist government (for Baudrillard a striking example of the anachronism of the political), was deploring in an article in *Le monde* the silence of left-wing intellectuals and asking where they were. He hadn't understood that, like himself, they were all *chez Pivot*, which is where what matters happens, so many microevents.

Meanwhile, out in front of the screens, is a macroreality that provides the accompaniment to "Apostrophes." In its celebration year, some 4 million French people over the age of fifteen were reckoned to be illiterate; 20 percent of localities with more than 10,000 inhabitants had no public library; of the country's 600 bookstores (there are a further 20,000 or so outlets where a few books can be bought, supermarkets and the like), half were in Paris; and half the sales of new titles of significant interest occurred in just four of the capital's districts; France's best-selling publication was the TV guide *Télé 7 jours*, and watching television was about to overtake working as the major waking activity (the lifetime estimates now are 63,000 hours of TV against 55,000 hours of work per French working person); the Socialist government departed from its long-standing assertion of the need to maintain television as a "public service" and authorized the creation of two private channels, leaving the subsequent right-wing government to sell off the first channel (TF1, previously enshrined as the voice of the nation) and carry out a reorganization destined to allow the law of the market full sway.

The appeal to "modernization" that such latter moves are taken to represent coincides with exigencies of "cultural identity" in quite traditional terms. In 1980 Parlement called for a "politics" of the French language and established a commission to look into its development, an undertaking paralleled only by the Abbé Grégoire's inquiry during the Revolution as to the necessity of achieving "uniformity" for French. The defense of the language subsequently urged ran from the enactment of legislation for its protection in the workplace (a spot-check at Air France revealed widespread linguistic promiscuity), through the drawing up of rules for secondary and higher education, to demands for increased budgets for the diffusion of French abroad. In the midst of all of which television was singled out for its part in what the Académie Française in its testimony called "the deterioration of the language," for the shoddiness of media French and the nefarious tendency to capitulate to Anglo-American. The wider, international arm of the defense is then given by *la francophonie* (francophony), which, once proposed with a conviction of the value of French as the language of revolutionary ideals and principles of liberation, has today become the term for an identity to be forged and maintained against U.S. political and cultural expansionism, for a strategic and economic post-colonial grouping in which France can hold on to a role as world power; this at the moment when the last remnants of its empire are torn by struggles for independence—two days after the 500th, for example, *indépendentistes* in New Caledonia gained the majority in three out of four electoral regions.

Pivot and his "Apostrophes" fit reassuringly in a France that is, profoundly, culturally and politically traditional while socially and economically modernizing itself according to the usual tenets of contemporary capitalism. The values of "Literature" and "French" are there intact, taken for granted and defended (Pivot is the organizer of the national spelling championships); and at the same time the values of television are preeminent (Pivot's very existence depends on them). Pivot helps writing today, gets some of it read, and holds it to a common place, drops the questions as to the possibilities of literature now, all the cultural-political questions of writing, into the foregone conclusions of media, market, and moment. Himself genuinely popular, Pivot can nevertheless neither negotiate the terms of a new popular literature nor propose critical perspectives for the understanding of current writing practices. His can be only the equalizing middle ground of the "interesting," on which terrain he welcomes books and authors, viewers and readers in a—happily—unproblematic *exchange:* just television, Pivot and us. And thus it is that every Friday night, a ritual *serment de Paris,* "Apostrophes" pledges French culture today, in his media image and at the end of one history of literature.

See also 1954, 1960, 1973.

Bibliography: John Ardagh, *France in the 1980s* (London: Secker & Warburg, 1982). Roland Barthes, "The Death of the Author," in *Image, Music, Text,* trans. Stephen Heath (New York: Hill and Wang, 1977), pp. 142–148. Barthes, "From Work to Text," in ibid., pp. 155–164. Jean Baudrillard, *La gauche divine* (Paris: Grasset, 1985). Régis Debray, *Teachers, Writers, Celebrities: The Intellectuals of Modern France,* trans. David Macey (London: NLB/Verso, 1981). Max Gallo, "Les intellectuels, la politique et la modernité," *Le monde,* 26 July 1983. Jean-François Lyotard, *The Postmodern Condition: A Report on Knowledge,* trans. Geoff Bennington and Brian Massumi (Minneapolis: University of Minnesota Press, 1984). Lyotard, *Le postmoderne expliqué aux enfants* (Paris: Galilée, 1986). Bernard Pivot, "Entretien avec Bernard Pivot," *Cahiers du cinéma,* Supplement "Télévision," Autumn 1981, pp. 68–71. Pivot, "Pivot présente la nouvelle cuvée d'*Apostrophes*," *Télé 7 jours,* 29 August–4 September 1987, pp. 104–105. Jean-Paul Sartre, *"What Is Literature?" and Other Essays,* trans. Bernard Frechtman (Cambridge, Mass.: Harvard University Press, 1988).

Stephen Heath

The Bicentennial of the French Revolution Is Celebrated

How Can One Be French?

The French avant-garde, which has been running out of steam since the 1960s, now survives only under the protection of the university: having deliberately made itself inaccessible, it has found its final consecration in the Ph.D. thesis. Everything exists, said Mallarmé, only to end up in a book. Books, in turn, exist only to end up in dissertations. By declaring itself intransitive and beyond genre (writers no longer write *something*—a novel or a poem—they simply write), literature has reduced the distance that once separated it from what was written about it. Over the years, what is said about novels has supplanted the novels themselves. From its current, dominant position, criticism can thus aspire to become the primary genre of the century—what the sonnet was to the sixteenth century, tragedy to the seventeenth, and the novel to the nineteenth. In France, the central works of our generation are those of Althusser, Barthes, Blanchot, Deleuze, Derrida, Foucault, and Lacan.

Literary discourse is breaking free of its traditional academic confines. Critics no longer simply teach French; they have become philosophers, linguists, semiologists, psychoanalysts, historians, scholars of poetics and semantics. This professional migration explains, at least in part, the militant response to Barthes's *Sur Racine* in 1963 and the ensuing debate over the new criticism. But the shift in affiliation has also been accompanied by a geographic migration. The new literary discourse is not only moving away from the classroom; it is spreading beyond the borders of France, particularly to the United States, where literature departments fight for analytical models. During the last thirty years, the Americans' markedly French point of reference has been tied less to actual literary production than to fundamental research on language, text, and meaning. The structuralists have been succeeded by the poststructuralists and the deconstructionists: Barthes, de Certeau, Derrida, Foucault, Genette, Girard, Goldmann, Kristeva, Lyotard, Marin, Riffaterre, Serres, Todorov. The fact that a critical anthology such as this one was conceived in the United States bears witness to thirty years of successful transatlantic export of French models for textual analysis.

The journal *Tel quel* provided this generation's most brilliant forum for expression. In 1968, its leader, Philippe Sollers, published a volume of essays, *Logiques,* prefaced by a "Programme" in which he declared: "Theory considers 'literature' (and the culture in which it exists as a whole) closed" (*Logiques,* p. 14). Faithful to the role of Minerva's owl, theory looks down at what it concludes: instead of playing the literary game as usual, the theoretician reveals its rules, its matrix, its overall theory.

Of all the literary genres, the novel has been the most frequent target of theory, particularly since the emergence of the *nouveau roman.* In 1965, in "Le roman et l'expérience des limites" ("The Novel or the Experience of Limits," reprinted in *Logiques*), Sollers called for a form of writing that would resist the social demand for fiction: "We do not want, like children, to be told stories, we want perhaps to fix our eyes, at the risk of being blinded, on the point from which all stories stem" (p. 249). Fifteen years later, in *Vision à New York (Vision in New York),* he continued to contrast the pathetic "demand for serious plot," "the obsessive demand for limited psychological identity, the need for character," with what he called "the envelope of all possible stories" (p. 76). It is this envelope that must be made visible: formal transgressions of the novel's rules should force the source from which it issues to appear.

Sollers's 1983 novel, *Femmes (Women)*, was therefore seen as a betrayal and a regression. In *Femmes,* Sollers told a story. Whereas he had previously denounced the demand for novels, he now denounced the demand for theory. At the same time, however, he endowed the novel with what used to be the monopoly of theory: the truth about the novel. *Femmes* declared the novel able to speak more truth than could be spoken about it. By returning to character and plot, Sollers had renounced experimenting on limits, at least as far as the boundaries between novel and theory were concerned. There was also criticism of the novel's content: a romanticized chronicle of the Parisian intelligentsia of the 1960s, it not only betrayed the avant-garde agenda of *Tel quel* on a formal level; it also buried (literally) the figures who had nourished its theoretical inspiration—Barthes's and Lacan's deaths, as well as Althusser's murdering of his wife are featured prominently under different names. Moreover, the geographical mapping of its plot provided a rather lucid analysis of the situation of French literature on the international stage.

At the beginning of Laclos's *Les liaisons dangereuses,* the Marquise de Merteuil offers to compose Valmont's memoirs. *Femmes* takes the Marquise's formula to another plane: it involves not a woman writing the memoirs of a man, but a Frenchman signing those of an American. The book is narrated by an American living in Paris. He is called Will (like Shakespeare) and he is a journalist (like Hemingway—or, why not, Saint-Simon). In French, his adopted language, Will writes a novel that his friend S., an avant-garde writer, agrees to publish under his own name. In the meantime, S. corrects Will's French. The reader cannot help wondering why Will doesn't write his novel in English. The question is never asked, but an answer is suggested at the end of the book. Will must return to the United States. He leaves his manuscript with S., asking him to bring it to Gallimard. "And for New York?" asks S. (p. 658). Things, says Will, don't look encouraging. The book is too good to have a future in New York. Thus, in order to leave the avant-garde and become a novelist, Sollers had to identify with an American writer, one, moreover, who refuses to use his own language. The team of Will and S. evokes a French literature that is defined by the improbable conjunction of two negative parameters: a Frenchman can't write it and an American can't read it.

In conjunction with *Femmes,* Sollers published a very inspired description of the island of Ré, on France's Atlantic coast. It opened with these words: "In general, I am rather unhappy in France: a feeling of confinement and of stagnation" (*Théorie des exceptions* [*A Theory of Exceptions*], p. 188). At the beginning of *Vision à New York*, Sollers had already exclaimed: "France and Paris are for me more of . . . an exile" (p. 19). In *Femmes*, Will expresses a similar feeling. During a survey on what is happening in France, someone asks, "And literature?" He answers, "At a standstill, I'd say" (p. 642). The description of Ré sustains a fantasy of escape, which ends with the transformation of the island into a "boat headed for America," "the small craft of fiction itself" (pp. 194–195). Ré is the symmetrical counterpart (departure) of Ellis Island (arrival). *Femmes*, following the island's metaphor, is the launching of a fictitious transatlantic crossing, a daring escape from French finitude. French literature—or the experience of its geographic limits.

This crossing is not always a happy one. In Sollers's next novel, *Portrait du joueur* (*Portrait of the Gambler*, 1984), the motif of French stagnation recurs insistently: "Admit at least that nothing is happening in France anymore" (p. 95). But its staging has changed. The opinion is expressed by someone who is no longer just playing American. The simple act of saying that nothing is happening in France is enough to make clear to the reader, like a Wagnerian leitmotif, the character's American accent. America remains, nevertheless, the long-term Cythera of Sollers's novelistic journey. Stendhal was willing to wait fifty years to win his case in appeal. Sollers doesn't set a date, but he knows that the trial will be set in New York—one day. The heroine of *Les folies françaises* (*French Follies*, 1988), asks her father: "Do you think people will be able to read you in New York?" "No. Not for the moment. One day."

Les folies françaises is an excellent illustration of the way Sollers's novels invent themselves. As in a daydream, the novel anticipates its American reception, which becomes, at least obliquely, its subject. The narrator is a writer—"I, Philippe Sollers, writer"—who has enough work behind him and enough fame for a thirty-year-old American student, Saul, to come to Paris to write his biography. A portrait of Saul: "Sympathetic, cultivated, ignorant, like most Americans. He believes that philosophy rules the world. He detests literature, but it is his passion . . . He knows all the theories of which I am, it seems, a fallen angel" (p. 38). Sollers (the character and the author) has no trouble turning the situation to his advantage in a kind of farce of analyst analyzed: transformed into a fictitious character, the critic loses his superiority and has to concede, overcome by novelistic truth. Still, the originality of this allegorical battle between Novel and Theory lies less in the opposition of novelist and critic than in the international dimension given it.

Saul is a minor character. But he is not the only American figure in the novel to be entrusted with the future of French literature. The narrator's daughter, named France, is central to the action. She has left New York and her American mother to pursue her "literary studies" (p. 17) in Paris. Her father, a specialist, enjoys initiating her into this new culture. "I can easily see you becoming a professor of literature. It would be one of the best jokes of my life" (p. 23). He introduces her to Villon, Versailles, Molière, La Fontaine, and other French *folies*. On the last page, France returns to her native English-speaking territories, married and with a diploma, ready to teach French literature to anglophone students. The French in Sollers's work do not speak to the French. America has become the future of French literature.

In a way that is not fundamentally opposed to his 1965 definition, Sollers's novel has taken for its subject the experience of the limits of its language. In 1965, the limits of the novel had already been conceived—following *Finnegans Wake*—as a departure from natural language, the transgression that suddenly makes the language we live in seem "a dead language" (p. 240). Sollers's essay on Joyce in *Théorie des exceptions* expands on this idea: "Joyce marks the limits of all national or maternal language" ("Joyce et Cie" [1975], *Théorie*, p. 80). Joyce was the first modernist to revive the classical notion that literature is inspired by the feeling of being cramped in a living language, by the desire to escape its restrictions: the experience of limits, rooted in the experience of language's finitude, makes all spoken language seem dead. Its password begins an exodus, a departure toward a secret, silent language, a language that, Sollers says, one knows "without knowing how to speak it" (*Vision à New York*, p. 16).

This same exodus from the Egypt of spoken language is the subject of several books by Pascal Quignard. His first novel, *Carus* (1979), which could be subtitled *De finibus linguae gallicae* ("On the Limits of French Language"), works the pathos of a language moved by its own fragility, inspired by its finitude, its own disappearance. *Carus* tells the story of a musician's depression and the ways in which his loved ones (among them the narrator) try to distract and cure him. A. suffers from a kind of linguistic anorexia: "I won't be able to speak" (p. 135). He suffers *from* his language and *in* his language. "All of this *says* nothing to me anymore" (p. 114). And further: "Words mean nothing" (p. 119). He feels his "tongue a little heavy, like a man who has drunk too much" (p. 235). When his crisis finally begins to pass, the narrator notes: "I saw that he was better. He made an effort in the use of language" (p. 137). A.'s loved ones arrange a convivial environment (almost always meeting for meals) where, day after day, around a kind of communion table set for this Good Friday of language, a random dialogue continues, full of baroquely pessimistic philosophical debates, of maniacal grammatical commentaries, of depressive childishness—all delivered with a formal freedom reminiscent of the brusqueness of the Banquets, Convivia, Symposia, and other Renaissance table talk.

Ieurre, the philologist of the circle, formulates the clearest diagnosis. "If this language had not fallen into disuse, he would not be ill" (p. 104). Nobody, however, explicitly describes the disuse. The only indication of it is found in the narrator's calendar—his journal cites exclusively American dates: Columbus Day, Veterans' Day, Thanksgiving Day, Washington's Birthday, Memorial Day, Independence Day, Labor Day. The book's events, recounted in French, occurring in France, are dated in another language, as if the French language, besieged by a foreign calendar, were about to slip into a temporality it cannot control. A language falls into disuse when it no longer has the strength to measure time, to give the hour, the day, the date, the holidays. "We are not a sufficient marker," A. remarks (p. 336). An American friend suggests that a trip to the United States could restore A.'s speech: "Heroic response from A.: 'I will not leave a sinking ship. I will keep my tongue in my mouth. I will stay calm: sword in hand'" (p. 102). The narrator, however, spends a month in America—"for the money," he says without elaborating (p. 255). But during this month, his journal lies fallow. Time spent in foreign-speaking territory does not bear fruit in one's own language.

In many ways, *Carus* is a lament. The novel is written at the bedside of a dying language, as if recording the last breath of the language in which it is written. Its characters are joined together by the disuse that has struck their native tongue. During one of the last meals, Ieurre develops a theory on this subject. People, he says, and especially philologists—those who love their language, who intone it as one intones a religious service—are prisoners of the object of their love. A language is a cruel, pitiless superego, jealous like the god of the Jansenists and, like him, immortal. Languages never die, their servants do. By some strange error, we mourn a language as dead when it has exterminated its speakers (p. 364).

This theory does not make the least reference to the American linguistic threat. It is no longer a question of a modern discord between the two languages, the confrontation of two competing vernaculars, in which English has driven French away; rather, it is the language itself that forbids speech: it does not want to be spoken. A foreign language appears here that is not the one everyone speaks, but one that no one speaks anymore: no longer the calendar's American but the language of the book's title, Latin: *Carus,* dear. Unlike the "false friends" of the world's vernacular, *caritas,* true charity, is named in a language that no mouth speaks.

During the 1930s, many French writers tried to revive literature by a "defense and illustration" of spoken language: Céline, Queneau, and others chose to write the way people speak. *Carus* takes the opposite course. Following in the footsteps of Mallarmé, who (in a speech at Oxford) defined the "lecture" (reading aloud to others) as "a genre to spread beyond borders," A. sees in "the poetry read aloud in the Bauhaus of Beaubourg or the universities of the United States" the result of a language that has been trapped by a "refusal of writing" (p. 260).

The narrative meditation "Où sont les ombres?" ("Where Did the Shadows Go?"), published by Quignard in *L'infini* (no. 30, Summer 1990), takes as its theme Grégoire de Tours's story of the death of the last Roman king, Sygarius, whom Clovis defeated at Soissons. After Sygarius's death, Clovis banned Latin altogether: "The language itself had to be annihilated" (p. 29). *De finibus litterarum latinarum.* This ban, however, is described by Quignard not as the defeat of Latin by French but as a triumph of writing over speech: Clovis is a sort of Pilate, the tool of fate that allowed Latin to join the "languages with no mouths to speak them" (p. 6). Although it is written in the language of the then conqueror, Quignard's story nevertheless requires from the reader linguistic identifications that go against his own narcissism: its plan of reference is the Latin repressed in the catacombs of writing. This meditation, ironically, could actually conclude the historic parcourse of French literature; at its close, French looks back, in an orphic circle, to its origin, to the Latin it silenced and is on the verge of rejoining.

Novels such as those of Sollers or Quignard present a French literature that is more concerned with its language than it has been at any other time. This feeling is in keeping with the objective situation of the French language in the contemporary world (what, in an early essay on Dante, Sollers called the "cartography" of languages). Without going as far as Sollers does when, in his last novel, *La fête à Venise* (1991; *A Venetian Feast*), he jokes about the French who still don't realize that "they have been wiped off the map since 1945" (p. 200), we must acknowledge the worldwide decline of Voltaire's tongue. In *Qu'est-ce que la littérature? (What Is Literature?)*, Sartre asked his famous question, "For whom do we write?" Almost half a century later, Sartre's heirs seem tormented by a much more narrow question: For whom do we write in French? For whom do we write in a language whose universality is a memory shared only with itself? But this situation also provides a good starting point.

This solicitude for Voltaire's language is recent. Many of those who now fear that they are its last heirs began by choosing as their exemplars writers who had shown neither respect nor tenderness for it. Whether they chose Artaud or Céline, Michaux, Leiris, Ponge, Bataille, or Queneau (or, outside the purely literary domain, Lacan), their models were remarkable for what Sollers himself praised as great irregularities of language. In their desire to bring down the exchange value, they cultivated the idiolect to the point of barbarism. The structure and system of the language were exposed to insult. No literature thus far had enacted such violence on its own verbal body, tried so feverishly to devalue itself, or hated itself to the point of rupture. One cannot help wondering if today's anxiety is language's revenge for the violence inflicted on it twenty years ago.

Still, when Sollers announces that the French have already been wiped off the map, he goes beyond the mere geopolitical reality—the cubbyhole to which the French language might very well be relegated in the future. His provocation is a reminder of what has always been the most eminent vocation of literature: the administration of absence. "All literature," Jean Paulhan once said to Marguerite Duras, "even the most mediocre, or the most boring, is an effort to see the world as if we weren't in it" (*Les yeux verts* [*Green Eyes*], p. 146).

In *Les lettres persanes (Persian Letters)*, Montesquieu used the fictional voices of Persians visiting Paris to describe France as though it were a world to which he did not belong. Roger Caillois called this "mental process that consists in pretending to be a foreigner to the society in which one lives" (p. xiii) a sociological revolution. One could call its generalization and radicalization a *literary* revolution: the writer today feigns not foreignness but absence. A more recent editor of Montesquieu, Paul Vernière, finds a slightly different message in his work: "Man has the right to be what he is, without shame, in a world where no one will ask the ridiculous question: 'How can one be Persian?'" (p. xxxiv). In effect, in an enlightened world what lends itself to ridicule is not difference but the idea of being surprised by it. Being Persian should not inspire laughter; and the person who laughs should inspire fear. But beyond the right of individuals to be what they are, to affirm their identity—and without calling this right into question—literature affirms something more strange: the opposite possibility—for *individuals not* to be what they are. The right to defamiliarization. After removing oneself, through sociology, from the society in which one lives, one can remove oneself, through literature, from what one is, from what one is supposed to be. Montesquieu asked: "How can one be Persian?" But the pseudo-Will manages to have his French ghostwriter, S., write: "I am not French" (*Femmes*, p. 36).

Languages distinguish between nations. In today's world, the production and consumption of literature continue to respect the geography of language. But whatever the geopolitics of language, the literary space does not compete with worldly powers. In the watermark of the world, it inscribes the anagram of the unreal. Literature cleanses everything of the sin of existence, of being in the world—everything, including language: whereas in Poe's time the death of a beautiful woman was the most poetical topic in the world, in our own the death of one's language is well on its way to becoming the most literary.

Like the little girl Sartre writes about, who returned on tiptoe to the garden she had just left, wanting to know what it was like when she wasn't there to watch it, literature is perhaps, in the end, what happens to language when, convinced of its own finitude, it tries to cash in on what Maurice Blanchot called its "right to die" and is seduced by the classical dream of joining the family of dead languages, of seeing the world as though the words it uses are no longer spoken, of acting as though a language were able to end its own story, to have the last word on itself.

See also On Writing Literary History, *p. xxi.*

Bibliography: Roger Caillois, in Montesquieu, *Oeuvres complètes,* vol. 1 (Paris: Gallimard, 1951). Marguerite Duras, *Les yeux verts* (Paris: Cahiers du cinéma, 1987). René Girard, *Deceit, Desire, and the Novel,* trans. Yvonne Freccero (Baltimore: Johns Hopkins Press, 1965). Denis Hollier, "On Literature Considered as a Dead Language," *Modern Language Quarterly,* 55, 1 (1993), 20–29. Pascal Quignard, *Carus* (Paris: Gallimard, 1979). Quignard, "Où sont les ombres?" *L'infini,* 30 (1990), 3–30. Jean-Paul Sartre, *"What Is Literature?" and Other Essays,* trans. Bernard Frechtman (Cambridge, Mass.: Harvard University Press, 1988). Philippe Sollers, *Femmes* (Paris: Gallimard, 1983). Sollers, *La fête à Venise* (Paris: Gallimard, 1991). Sollers, *Les folies françaises* (Paris: Gallimard, 1988). Sollers, *Logiques* (Paris: Seuil, 1968). Sollers, *Portrait du joueur* (Paris: Gallimard, 1984). Sollers, *Théorie des exceptions* (Paris: Gallimard, 1986). Sollers, *Vision à New York* (Paris: Denoël, 1981). Paul Vernière, in Montesquieu, *Les lettres persanes* (Paris: Bordas, 1992).

Denis Hollier

125 B.C.   The Romans begin the conquest of Gaul.

52   Vercingetorix, leader of the revolt against the Romans, capitulates at Alesia. Latin progressively becomes the spoken language throughout the land.

A.D. 360   Lutetia becomes Paris.

406   The Franks invade Gaul.

476   Fall of the Western Roman Empire.

486   End of Roman domination in Gaul.

496?   Clovis, king of the Franks (Merovingian dynasty), converts to Christianity.

507   Paris becomes the capital of France. The Salic Law excludes females from dynastic succession.

732   Charles Martel defeats the Arabs near Poitiers.

751   Pepin the Short is elected king, beginning the Carolingian dynasty (751–987).

771   Charlemagne becomes sole king of the Franks.

778   Charlemagne's offensive against the Umayyad emirate is stopped at Roncesvalles, in the Pyrenees.

800   Charlemagne is crowned emperor of the West by Pope Leo III in Rome. During his reign (800–814), minuscule writing replaces majuscule (Gothic) writing.

840   Death of Louis the Pious, son of Charlemagne.

843   Treaty of Verdun: The Frankish empire is divided among the three grandsons of Charlemagne.

845–862   The Norsemen (Northmen or Normans) pillage Paris and ravage the Ile-de-France region.

911   King Charles the Simple grants Norsemen the right to settle on the lands they occupy.

987	The election and coronation of Hugh Capet at Reims ushers in the Capetian dynasty (987–1328).
1020–21	First dated pieces of Romanesque sculpture, in the lintel of the church of Saint-Genis-des-Fontaines, in the Pyrenees.
1066	William of Normandy (the Conqueror) becomes king of England after his victory at Hastings.
1095	Pope Urban II preaches the First Crusade at the Council of Clermont.
1097–1099	Crusaders found the states of Antioch, Tripoli, Edessa, and Jerusalem.
1115	St. Bernard founds the Cistercian abbey of Clairvaux.
1120	Abbé Suger initiates the Gothic style with his renovation of Saint-Denis, necropolis of the French kings since the Merovingians.
1152	The Second Council of Beaugency annuls the marriage of Louis VII and Eleanor of Aquitaine. Eleanor marries Henry Plantagenet, who adds her dowry, the vast Aquitainian fief, to his Norman and Angevin possessions.
1154	With the extinction of the Norman line in England, Henry Plantagenet of the house of Anjou becomes Henry II of England and ruler of an Anglo-French empire. A century of conflicts ensues.
1163	Bishop Maurice de Sully starts the construction of Notre-Dame de Paris.
1180	Philip II Augustus, son of Louis VII, is crowned king of France.
1194	Royal archives are established in Paris.
1199	John Lackland succeeds his brother Richard I in England but loses his French possessions to Philip II Augustus.
1204	Crusaders take Constantinople.
1204–1206	Philip Augustus reunites Normandy, Maine, Anjou, Touraine, and Poitou to the French throne.
1210–1311	Construction of Reims cathedral, prototype of the mature Gothic style.
1214	At the Fourth Lateran Council, Pope Innocent III establishes the statutes of the University of Paris, the first in France.
1258–1274	Robert de Sorbon's school, the Sorbonne, becomes the center of theological studies and the seat of the University of Paris.
1270	Louis IX (canonized as St. Louis in 1297) dies in Tunis during the Eighth Crusade.
1305	The French Pope Clement V moves the papacy to Avignon.
1327	Petrarch meets Laura of Noves in Avignon.
1328	Philip II of Valois accedes to the throne of France, ushering in the Valois dynasty (1328–1589).

1337	Edward III of England, grandson of France's Philip IV the Fair (1285–1328) through his mother, claims the French crown, thus starting the Hundred Years' War (1337–1453).
1347–1351	French-English truce.
1348	The Black Death (bubonic plague) sweeps Europe.
1373	The flowing tracery of the late Gothic style appears for the first time in France at Amiens cathedral.
1392	As Charles VI loses his sanity, a bitter civil war breaks out between the Armagnacs (partisans of the house of Orléans) and the Burgundians (partisans of the duke of Burgundy).
1415	On 25 October Henry V of England defeats the French at Agincourt.
1429	Joan of Arc delivers Orléans from English occupation and persuades the dauphin to be crowned as Charles VII at Reims.
1430	Henry V of England is crowned king of France in Notre-Dame de Paris. Joan of Arc, captured by the Burgundians, is sold to the English.
1431	Joan of Arc is tried and burned at the stake in Rouen.
1437	Charles VII retakes Paris.
1461	Louis XI succeeds Charles VII and annexes Burgundy.
1470	Guillaume Fichet installs the first printing press in France at the Sorbonne.
1495	Charles VIII initiates the Italian Wars (1495–1559), during which there is a reverse invasion of France by Italian art.
1498	Louis XII, a Valois-Orléans, succeeds his cousin Charles VII.
1515	Francis I, a Valois-Angoulême, becomes the first modern king of France (1515–1547). Charles V Hapsburg becomes emperor of Germany and king of Spain.
1519	While a guest of the French court, Leonardo da Vinci dies at Le Clos-Lucé, near Amboise.
1521	Francis I forbids the sale of books without examination by the University of Paris.
1525	At the Battle of Pavia, Francis I is taken prisoner by Charles V.
1530	At the urging of the humanist Guillaume Budé, Francis I creates a college of twelve Royal Readers.
1534	On 17 October the Affaire des Placards terminates the king's support for Evangelism. John Calvin escapes to Switzerland.
1534–1543	Jacques Cartier reaches Newfoundland and claims Canada in the name of Francis I.
1539	The Edict of Villers-Cotterêts prescribes the use of French in all official decrees and court sentences.

1540 Ignatius Loyola founds the Society of Jesus in Montmartre.

1546 Pierre Lescot redesigns the Louvre for Francis I. Etienne Dolet, humanist and defender of religious freedom, is hanged and burned for heresy.

1547 Henri II succeeds Francis I.

1559 Henri II is mortally wounded in a tournament. Three of his sons will succeed him on the throne. The first, Francis II, Mary Stuart's husband, dies in 1560.

1562–1598 Wars of Religion.

1563 Charles IX (1560–1574) prohibits printing without permission.

1570 Under the Treaty of Saint-Germain, Catherine de Médicis, widow of Henri II, grants Protestants amnesty and freedom of worship.

1572 The Catholic party threatens to overthrow the king. On St. Bartholomew's Eve (23 August), Charles IX orders a massacre in which more than 3,000 Protestants are killed in Paris. Henri of Navarre, head of the Calvinist party, narrowly escapes.

1574 Henri III succeeds Charles IX.

1576 Henri, duc de Guise, founds the Catholic League to combat Protestantism.

1582 The Gregorian calendar replaces the Julian calendar.

1588 12 May (Journée des Barricades): Insurrection against the king in Paris. 23–24 Dec.: Assassination of the duc de Guise and his brother the cardinal of Lorraine.

1589 Henri III is stabbed to death by a member of the League. Death of Catherine de Médicis. The Bourbon dynasty (1589–1792, 1814–1830) begins as Henri of Navarre becomes Henri IV of France.

1594 Henri IV converts to Catholicism.

1598 Henri IV signs the Edict of Nantes, spelling out the status of Protestants in France.

1605–1608 French colonies are planted in North America: Acadia (1605) and New France (a Norman shipbuilder, Samuel Champlain, founds Quebec in 1608).

1610 Henri IV is assassinated. Marie de Médicis acts as regent for their nine-year-old son, Louis XIII.

1620 Creation of the Royal Printing Office.

1634 Armand du Plessis, cardinal de Richelieu, minister to Louis XIII (1610–1643), founds the Académie Française.

1635 Guadeloupe and Martinique become French colonies.

1637 Jansenists found the society of the Solitaries of Port-Royal, centered first in Paris, then at the Port-Royal-des-Champs abbey, in the Chevreuse valley.

1643	Anne of Austria acts as regent for the five-year-old Louis XIV (1643–1715) and appoints the Italian Jules Cardinal Mazarin as minister.
1648	Foundation of the Royal Academy of Painting and Sculpture in Paris.
1648–1653	During the Fronde, a revolt directed against the unpopular Mazarin, the court flees to Saint-Germain. Louis XIV returns to Paris in 1652 and Mazarin the following year.
1661	Upon Mazarin's death, Louis XIV decides to govern France himself.
1663–1671	Louis XIV's minister, Jean-Baptiste Colbert, founds the Academies of Inscriptions and Letters (1663), of Sciences (1666), of Music (1669), and of Architecture (1671), thereby replacing the authority of the guilds by that of the state.
1664	Louis XIV disperses the nuns from Port-Royal-de-Paris.
1666–1681	Pierre de Riquet builds the 148-mile Midi Canal, the first lock canal in Europe.
1667–68	Louis XIV launches a war of conquest to claim the inheritance rights of his wife (Maria Teresa of Spain) over the Spanish Lowlands. A triple alliance concluded by William of Orange with England and Sweden stops this "Devolution War."
1669–1679	Port-Royal-des-Champs, a brilliant intellectual center, becomes also a center of opposition to absolutism.
1672	Louis XIV moves his court to Versailles permanently.
1680	Foundation of the Comédie-Française.
1681–82	Robert Cavelier de La Salle sails down the Mississippi River to the Gulf of Mexico and takes possession of Louisiana.
1685	On 18 October Louis XIV revokes the Edict of Nantes. More than 200,000 Protestants emigrate.
1697	The French take the western half of Hispaniola (later Saint-Domingue, modern Haiti).
1701	French monopoly on the slave trade in the New World.
1701–1713	Louis XIV fights the War of the Spanish Succession against his grandson, Philip V of Spain.
1702–1704	Camisards (Protestants of the mountainous Cévennes region) rebel against the severe repression following the revocation of the Edict of Nantes.
1709–10	Louis XIV disbands the Jansenist convent at Port-Royal-des-Champs and orders it razed.
1715	Upon Louis XIV's death, Philip of Orléans becomes regent to Louis XV, who will reach his majority in 1723.
1724	Foundation of the Paris Bourse (stock exchange).
1733–1738	The Polish War of Succession gives Lorraine to France.

1737   Institution of yearly painting "Salons" at the Louvre.

1752   First condemnation of the *Encyclopédie* by the Roman Catholic church.

1759   Second condemnation of the *Encyclopédie*. The French lose Quebec to the British.

1762   Jacques-Ange Gabriel begins construction of the Petit Trianon at Versailles. Louisiana is ceded to Spain.

1763   Under the Treaty of Paris, ending the Seven Years' War, France cedes to England all of Canada, settlements east of the Mississippi, and trading posts in India; gains trading posts in Africa; and receives back Martinique and Guadeloupe.

1766   Louis Antoine Bougainville embarks on a scientific expedition around the world.

1767   Genoa sells Corsica to France.

1774   Louis XV (the Beloved) dies and is succeeded by his grandson, Louis XVI (1774–1792).

1777   The marquis de La Fayette joins the American troops in the War of Independence against England. A year later, France signs a treaty of friendship and trade with the United States.

1783   First hot-air balloon flights by Etienne and Joseph de Montgolfier in Annonay and by François Pilâtre de Rozier in Paris.

1787–88   Disastrous war expenditures and profligate court spending cause the nobles to revolt. The king convokes the Estates General. Civil rights are extended to non-Catholics.

1789   5 May: First meeting of the Estates General. 17 June: The middle-class Third Estate proclaims itself the National Assembly. 20 June: The Tennis Court Oath. 9 July: The National Assembly becomes the Constituent National Assembly, establishing a constitutional monarchy. The court is moved back to Paris. 14 July: The storming of the Bastille prison launches a popular rebellion that soon spreads to the provinces. 4 Aug.: The Assembly abolishes all feudal privileges. 26 Aug.: Declaration of the Rights of Man.

1790   14 July: During the commemoration of Bastille Day, Louis XVI swears to uphold the constitution. 27 Nov.: The Assembly requires all clergy to swear an oath of allegiance to the constitution.

1791   21 June: Louis XVI and his family are arrested while trying to emigrate. 1 Oct.: A Legislative Assembly succeeds the Constituent Assembly. 14 Sept.: Avignon votes to be returned to France.

1792   The guillotine is adopted. 25 April: Claude Rouget de Lisle composes the "Marseillaise." 10 Aug.: The Legislative Assembly convokes a new Constituent Assembly, the Convention. 2–5 Sept.: The Prussian invasion triggers the "September Massacres" (more than 1,200 prisoners are executed in Paris). 21 Sept.: The Convention abolishes the monarchy and proclaims the Republic. 22 Sept.:

Beginning of the Revolutionary calendar, used for thirteen years. The Louvre palace becomes a museum.

1793   21 Jan.: Execution of Louis XVI. March: An uprising of Breton royalists (the "Chouans") in Vendée unleashes the wave of summary executions known as the Terror (1,376 executions in Paris). 13 July: Charlotte Corday assassinates Jean-Paul Marat. 27 July: Maximilien Robespierre, member of the Jacobin Club, is put in power.

1794   27 Jan.: French becomes the official language in all public acts. 27 July (9 Thermidor): The Terror ends with Robespierre's arrest and execution.

1795   Installation of the Directory, an executive body of five members.

1796–97   Twenty-six-year-old General Napoleon Bonaparte captures Savoy, Milan, and Mantua. Before he reaches Vienna, the Austrians sign the Treaty of Campoformio.

1798   Bonaparte conducts a successful campaign on land in Egypt, but his fleet is destroyed by English Admiral Horatio Nelson at Aboukir Bay. Foundation of the Institut du Caire.

1799   Bonaparte seizes power on 18 Brumaire (9 November), marking the beginning of the Consulate (1799–1804).

1800   The Bank of France is created as a private institution. Spain returns Louisiana to France.

1801   Bonaparte and Pope Pius VII sign a concordat restoring and reorganizing Catholicism in France.

1802   A plebiscite elects Bonaparte consul for life.

1803   To fund his war chest, Bonaparte sells Louisiana to the United States for $15 million. A revolt of black slaves headed by François Toussaint-Louverture expels the French from Saint-Domingue (now Haiti).

1804   Promulgation of the Civil Code (later known as the Napoleonic Code). 2 Dec.: Napoleon is crowned emperor by Pope Pius VII at Notre-Dame de Paris.

1805   21 Oct.: The British fleet defeats the Franco-Spanish fleet at Cape Trafalgar. 2 Dec.: Napoleon defeats the Austro-Russian army at Austerlitz.

1806   Jean-François Chalgrin constructs the Arc de Triomphe de l'Etoile.

1812   Napoleon enters Moscow but is forced to withdraw.

1814   By the Treaty of Paris France loses nearly all its conquests made since the Revolution. Napoleon abdicates and goes into exile at Elba. Louis XVIII, brother of Louis XVI, becomes king and signs a constitutional charter.

1815   Napoleon escapes from Elba, rallies support, and marches to Paris, where he seizes power. Defeated at Waterloo on June 18, he abdicates a second time. Louis XVIII returns.

1821   Napoleon dies at Saint Helena. (His ashes, returned to France in 1840, are installed in the Invalides in 1861.)

1824   Louis XVIII's brother, Charles X, begins a reign marked by reactionary policies.

1830   5 July: The French take Algiers. 25 July: Freedom of the press is abolished. 27–29 July: Les Trois Glorieuses, or Revolution of 1830, puts an end to the reign of Charles X. Louis-Philippe d'Orléans becomes the "Citizen King," beginning the July Monarchy (1830–1848).

1836   Construction of the railroad from Paris to Saint-Germain-en-Laye.

1838   Louis Daguerre improves on Nicéphore Niepce's invention of photography.

1848   24 Feb. (Revolution of 1848): Fall of Louis-Philippe after two days of rioting in the streets of Paris. 25 Feb.: The Second Republic is proclaimed. The right to vote is given to French males over age twenty-one. 22–26 June (June Days): Parisian workers rise against the bourgeois Republic. 10 Dec.: Louis-Napoleon, nephew of Napoleon, is elected president.

1849   A reactionary Legislative Assembly suspends the right of assembly, interdicts strikes, curtails freedom of the press, and abolishes universal suffrage.

1851   Louis-Napoleon seizes power in an administrative coup on 2 December, approved by a plebiscite on 21 December.

1852   Following a plebiscite on 2 December, Louis-Napoleon proclaims himself Emperor Napoleon III (beginning of the Second Empire, 1852–1870). Aristide Boucicaut opens the first department store in Paris, Au Bon Marché. Foundation of major banking institutions, Crédit Foncier and Crédit Immobilier.

1852–1870   Georges Eugène Haussmann starts vast development projects (large avenues, sewage system, parks, gardens, train stations) in Paris. The capital is divided into twenty districts (*arrondissements*).

1854   Victor Baltard uses glass and metal for construction of the pavilions of Paris' central market, les Halles.

1854–1856   The French side with the British in the Crimean War against Russia.

1855   Paris World Exhibition.

1857   Conquest of Senegal by Louis Faidherbe. Beginning of work on the Mont-Cenis tunnel through the Alps.

1858   The French and British seize Tientsin, proclaim it an "international city," and install foreign concessions.

1859   Ferdinand de Lesseps begins construction of the Suez Canal.

1859–1863   Colonial expansion in Indochina: the French occupy Saigon (1859), take Cochinchina (1862), and impose a protectorate over Cambodia (1863).

1860 Savoy and Nice are ceded to France. A Franco-British corps occupies Tientsin and Peking.

1862 Charles Garnier begins construction of the new Paris Opéra.

1863 Foundation of Crédit Lyonnais.

1864 Foundation of the International, an international workers' association led by Karl Marx.

1868 Dissolution of the French section of the International.

1869 Opening of the Suez Canal.

1870 19 July: France declares war on Prussia. 2 Sept.: Napoleon III is defeated at Sedan. 4 Sept.: Beginning of the Third Republic (1870–1940). 18 Sept.: The Prussians take Paris.

1871 18 Jan.: The Second Reich, proclaimed at Versailles, annexes Alsace and Lorraine. 28–29 Jan.: Formation, in Paris, of the Commune, a revolutionary government hostile to capitulation. March: The Commune enacts the first socialist program in Europe. 22–28 May ("Bloody Week"): Suppression of the Commune (25,000 dead).

1874 A painting by Claude Monet, *Impression—soleil levant*, prompts the term *Impressionism*.

1875–1882 Pierre Savorgnan de Brazza sails up the Ogooué River in West Africa and places the Congo region under a French protectorate.

1879 Louis Pasteur discovers the principles of vaccines.

1881 France establishes a protectorate over Tunisia.

1882 The Jules Ferry Laws secularize elementary education and make it free and compulsory.

1883 Establishment of a French protectorate over Annam and Tonkin leads to a Franco-Chinese war. The French bomb and occupy Madagascar (which will become a French colony in 1896).

1887 An Indochinese Union comprising Annam, Cambodia, and Tonkin is created. The New Hebrides are controlled by a Franco-British commission (to become a condominium in 1906).

1889 The Second International is created at the Congress of Paris. The Eiffel Tower is inaugurated at the Paris World's Fair. The "Marseillaise" is made the national anthem.

1892 Etienne Marey invents chronophotography, first step toward cinematography.

1892–93 The Panama Canal scandal triggers a press campaign by Louis Drumont against Jewish financing.

1893 France imposes a protectorate over Dahomey. Laos is added to the Indochinese Union.

1894   Captain Alfred Dreyfus, condemned for espionage, is deported to Devil's Island, in Guyana.

1895   Auguste and Louis Lumière invent the cinematograph in Lyons and present a first public projection in Paris. (Two years later, Georges Méliès builds the first cinema studio in Montreuil.)

1898   The Dreyfus Affair's domination of French politics leads to the foundation of the right-wing Action Française. Construction of the first Métro line. 14 June: French-English convention to outline African colonial borders.

1902   Foundation of the Goncourt Academy.

1904–05   Strong secularization policy: Ecclesiastical orders are prohibited from teaching, diplomatic relations are broken with the Vatican (1904). Law of Separation of Church and State (1905).

1907   Picasso's *Les demoiselles d'Avignon* marks the birth of cubism.

1909   Louis Blériot crosses the English Channel in an airplane.

1910   Constitution of the federation known as French Equatorial Africa.

1912   The French establish a formal protectorate over Morocco.

1914   Beginning of World War I (1.3 million French soldiers dead, 1.1 million wounded). 1 Aug.: France mobilizes. 3 Aug.: Germany declares war on France. 5–12 Sept.: The Battle of the Marne stops the Germans' "race to the sea." Beginning of trench warfare.

1916   The battle of Verdun. First offensive use of tanks.

1918   Under a German-Allied armistice, signed on 11 November, Alsace-Lorraine is restored to France.

1919   The Allies sign the Treaty of Versailles (Germany is barred from negotiations). France adds arms-limitation and war-payment clauses. In Moscow, Lenin founds the Third International or Comintern.

1920   A split between the Second International and Third International at the Congress of Tours leads to creation of the Socialist and Communist parties.

1923   France occupies the Ruhr valley.

1925   Exhibition of Art Deco in Paris.

1927–28   Joseph Le Brix and Dieudonné Costes fly around the world.

1933   Adolf Hitler becomes chancellor of Germany. Germany leaves the International Conference on Disarmament and the League of Nations and begins rearmament. Irène and Frédéric Joliot-Curie artificially produce radioactive substances.

1934   6 Feb.: Fascist demonstrations in the Place de la Concorde. 9 Feb.: Left-wing counterdemonstrations.

1936   The Popular Front, a left-wing coalition, wins a majority in the national elections. Creation of the International Brigades, composed of foreign volunteers joining the Republican forces during the Spanish Civil War (1936–1940). Henri Langlois founds the French Cinémathèque.

1937 Paris World's Fair. Fall of the Popular Front.

1938 Inauguration of the Musée de l'Homme, housed in the new Palais de Chaillot. Edouard Daladier (France) and Neville Chamberlain (Great Britain) sign the Munich Agreement with Hitler and Mussolini on 30 September.

1939 1 Sept.: Germany invades Poland. England and France declare war on Germany.

1940 14 June: The Germans enter Paris. 18 June: From London, General Charles de Gaulle broadcasts a call to resistance. 22 June: Marshal Philippe Pétain signs an armistice. France is divided into an occupied (north and west) and a (southern) free zone. The Third Republic is replaced by a French State (1940–1946), with Vichy as the seat of government. Laws on the status of Jews. Britain recognizes de Gaulle as head of the Free French Forces.

1941 Creation of the most important French Resistance movement, the National Front (originally Communist).

1942 The Germans occupy the free zone on 11 November. The Vichy government becomes openly collaborationist.

1944 May: A provisional Government of the French Republic, headed by de Gaulle, takes over the Vichy administration. 6 June (D-Day): The Allies land in Normandy. 25 Aug.: Liberation of Paris. Women are given the right to vote.

1945 General surrender of the German armies on 8 May. De Gaulle is confirmed as head of the French government. Bloody uprising in Algeria.

1946 De Gaulle resigns. The Fourth Republic (1946–1958) is established. A French Union is created, making all citizens of French overseas territories French citizens. First annual film festival at Cannes.

1947 Bloody incidents in Tunisia.

1952 Violent anti-French riots in Casablanca, Morocco, and Bizerte, Tunisia.

1954 3 Feb.–7 May: The Viet Minh (Vietnam Liberation Front) routs the French army at Dien Bien Phu. The Geneva agreements conclude the Indochina war and recognize the independence of Laos and Cambodia. Nov.: In Algeria, terrorist attacks organized by the independentist FLN (National Front of Liberation) lead to a "civil" war.

1956 France recognizes the independence of Morocco (3 March) and of Tunisia (20 May).

1957   The Treaty of Rome creates the six-nation European Economic Community (Common Market).

1958   13 May: A military putsch in Algiers brings de Gaulle back to power. 21 Dec.: De Gaulle establishes the Fifth Republic.

1959   De Gaulle proclaims the "rights of Algerians to self-determination."

1960   June: France proclaims the independence of the Central African Republic, Chad, Congo, Dahomey, Gabon, the Ivory Coast, Mali, Niger, and Upper Volta. France test-fires its first atomic bombs.

1962   The Evian agreements recognize Algeria's independence. First satellite television transmission between Pleumeur-Bodou (Brittany) and the United States.

1963   Opening of France's first nuclear power station, at Avoine-Chinon.

1965   De Gaulle is reelected president.

1966   France withdraws its forces from the North Atlantic Treaty Organization, whose headquarters move from Paris to Brussels. Opening of the Rance tidal power station in Brittany.

1967   Neuwirth Law on contraception. De Gaulle's stormy visit to Quebec. First public demonstration of the Franco-British supersonic aircraft Concorde.

1968   May–June: An economic, social, political, and cultural crisis, marked by student riots in the Latin Quarter and a paralyzing general strike, shakes the Fifth Republic. Universities are granted administrative autonomy.

1969   De Gaulle resigns. President Georges Pompidou modifies Gaullist policy in a climate of social malaise.

1970   Death of de Gaulle.

1971   The first French nuclear submarine, *Le redoutable,* is launched at Cherbourg, in Normandy.

1972   Salaries for men and women are equalized.

1973   The government establishes Commissions on Terminology to coin French technological words.

1974   Valéry Giscard d'Estaing is elected president. The Veil Law legalizes abortion. Another law lowers the voting age to eighteen years.

1977   The architecturally controversial Georges Pompidou National Center of Art and Culture (Beaubourg Center) opens in Paris.

1980   Marguerite Yourcenar, resident and naturalized citizen of the United States, becomes the first woman elected to the Académie Française.

1981   Socialist François Mitterrand becomes president. Capital punishment is abolished.

1986 Inauguration of the La Villette Center for Science and Industry, and of the Orsay Museum (19th-century art).

1987 Creation of the Institute of the Arab World in Paris.

1988 François Mitterrand is reelected president.

1989 Celebration of the bicentennial of the storming of the Bastille and of the Declaration of the Rights of Man.

METROPOLITAN FRANCE TODAY

VAL-D'OISE
SEINE-ST.DENIS
SEINE-ET-MARNE
HAUTS-DE-SEINE
Paris
Seine
YVELINES
VAL-DE-MARNE
ESSONNE

English Channel

Calais
BELGIUM
GERMANY
PAS-DE-CALAIS
Lille
NORD
LUXEMBOURG
Amiens
SOMME
AISNE
ARDENNES
Guernsey
Cherbourg
CHANNEL IS.
(To Great Britain)
Sark
Jersey
Le Havre
SEINE-MARITIME
Rouen
OISE
Verdun
Metz
MOSELLE
Bayeux
Caen
CALVADOS
EURE
VAL-D'OISE
Reims
MARNE
MEUSE
Nancy
BAS-RHIN
Strasbourg
Brest
CÔTES-DU-NORD
ORNE
EURE-ET-LOIR
YVELINES
Paris
SEINE-ET-MARNE
Troyes
AUBE
HAUTE-MARNE
VOSGES
HAUT-RHIN
FINISTÈRE
ILLE-ET-VILAINE
MAYENNE
SARTHE
Le Mans
LOIRET
Orléans
YONNE
HAUTE-SAÔNE
TERRITOIRE DE BELFORT
MORBIHAN
LOIRE-ATLANTIQUE
MAINE-ET-LOIRE
Angers
Blois
LOIR-ET-CHER
CÔTE-D'OR
Dijon
DOUBS
SWITZERLAND
Belle-Île
Nantes
INDRE-ET-LOIRE
CHER
NIÈVRE
Bourges
Nevers
JURA
VENDÉE
DEUX-SÈVRES
Poitiers
VIENNE
INDRE
SAÔNE-ET-LOIRE
ATLANTIC OCEAN
Île de Ré
CHARENTE-MARITIME
ALLIER
Vichy
RHÔNE
AIN
HAUTE-SAVOIE
Île d'Oléron
CHARENTE
HAUTE-VIENNE
Limoges
CREUSE
Clermont-Ferrand
PUY-DE-DÔME
LOIRE
Lyons
SAVOIE
Bay of Biscay
CORRÈZE
CANTAL
HAUTE-LOIRE
ISÈRE
Grenoble
ITALY
Bordeaux
DORDOGNE
Bergerac
ARDÈCHE
DRÔME
HAUTES-ALPES
GIRONDE
LOT
LOZÈRE
VAUCLUSE
ALPES-DE-HAUTE-PROVENCE
ALPES-MARITIMES
MONACO
Nice
LANDES
LOT-ET-GARONNE
TARN-ET-GARONNE
AVEYRON
GARD
Avignon
Nîmes
BOUCHES-DU-RHÔNE
VAR
Toulon
GERS
TARN
Montpellier
HÉRAULT
Marseilles
PYRÉNÉES-ATLANTIQUES
HAUTE-GARONNE
Toulouse
Carcassonne
Golfe du Lion
HAUTES-PYRÉNÉES
ARIÈGE
AUDE
ANDORRA
PYRÉNÉES-ORIENTALES
Mediterranean Sea
SPAIN

N

0   50   100   150   200
miles

CORSICA
Bastia
HAUTE-CORSE
Ajaccio
CORSE-DU-SUD

✐ Acknowledgments

Both the conception and the completion of this book involved a strong sense of collective effort, and I am grateful for the generous support of all those who undertook to be a part of it. I want first to express my personal gratitude to Lindsay Waters, General Editor at Harvard University Press, whose energy triggered the project in the first place; to Ann Hawthorne, whose commitment to the project supported her conviction that clarity was not a utopian goal; and to Rosalind Krauss, who was present at every stage of the enterprise.

I want to thank the editorial board for their confidence in this project and for the collaborative spirit that promoted a collective, and therefore polyphonic, work. The table of contents for the entire volume was worked out by all of us together. Within this framework R. Howard Bloch oversaw the general organization for the Middle Ages, François Rigolot and Nancy J. Vickers for the 16th century, Joan DeJean and Philip E. Lewis for the 17th, Nancy K. Miller for the 18th, Peter Brooks for the first part of the 19th, and Barbara Johnson for its second part, while I organized the 20th century.

I want also to express my warmest gratitude to the 165 contributors for having entered into a venture that would inevitably submit their autonomous authorial status to demanding editorial trials.

Special thanks also to those who intervened as consultants at various moments of the preparation of the volume: Timothy Hampton for the 16th century; John D. Lyons for the 17th; Christie McDonald for the 18th; and Alice Yaeger Kaplan, Jeffrey Mehlman, and Ann Smock for the 20th.

Ruth Larson, my assistant at Yale, spent an entire year under the pressure of the project. She managed to keep the traffic under control even during the worst moments of the editorial rush. Renée Morel composed the chronology and completed the monumental task of mapping the index. I also received significant help from Carol Reitan and Katharine Streip in Berkeley and, for the iconography, from Juliette Hollier-Larousse in Paris.

Articles written in French were translated by Scott Durham (1401), Karen Duval (17–18 October 1534), Jane Hale (1661), Erec R. Koch (1814), Ruth

Larson (1181, November 1925, 1935, 1962), Christopher L. Miller (13 January 1791), David Pelizzari (December 1827), Katharine Streip (1152, 1677, December 1925), Allan S. Weiss (Summer 1791), Mark J. Wortman (13 September 1555, 1895).

The management of this project was immensely facilitated by research grants from the Florence J. Gould Foundation, Inc., the Georges Lurcy Charitable and Educational Trust, the University of California at Berkeley, and Yale University.

D.H.

✍ Contributors

Jean Alter (1657, 1699)
Department of Romance Languages
University of Pennsylvania

Janet Gurkin Altman (1725)
Department of French and Italian
University of Iowa, Iowa City

Wilda Anderson (1754)
Department of French
Johns Hopkins University

Dudley Andrew (1954)
Institute for Cinema and Culture
University of Iowa, Iowa City

Jean-Marie Apostolidès (1661)
Department of French and Italian
Stanford University

Alan Astro (1946)
Department of Foreign Languages
Trinity University

John Atherton (November 1933)
Institut d'Anglais Charles V
Université Paris VII

Ora Avni (1837, 1869)
Department of French
Yale University

Michel Beaujour (1550, 1924)
  Department of French
  New York University

Réda Bensmaïa (1962)
  Department of French and Italian
  University of Minnesota, Minneapolis

John Benton [*deceased*] (778)
  Department of Humanities
  California Institute of Technology

Charles Bernheimer (1880)
  Department of Romance Languages
  University of Pennsylvania

Leo Bersani (1922)
  Department of French
  University of California, Berkeley

Bernard Beugnot (1651)
  Département d'Etudes Françaises
  Université de Montréal

Robert J. Bezucha (1840)
  Department of History
  Amherst College

Thomas Bishop (28 October 1959)
  Department of French
  New York University

R. Howard Bloch (842)
  Department of French
  University of California, Berkeley

Renate Blumenfeld-Kosinski (1214)
  Department of French and Romance Philology
  Columbia University

Yve-Alain Bois (1973)
  Art History Department
  Johns Hopkins University

Norbert Bonenkamp (1873)
  Department of Romance Languages
  Harvard University

Barbara C. Bowen (1460)
  Department of French and Italian
  Vanderbilt University

Frank Paul Bowman (1799)
  Department of Romance Languages
  University of Pennsylvania

Daniel Brewer (1751)
  Department of French and Italian
  University of California, Irvine

Victor Brombert (1889)
  Department of Romance Languages and Literatures
  Princeton University

Peter Brooks (March 1782, 1800, 1830)
  Whitney Humanities Center
  Yale University

Kevin Brownlee (1225, 1342)
  Department of Romance Languages
  University of Pennsylvania

E. Jane Burns (1209)
  Department of Romance Languages
  University of North Carolina at Chapel Hill

E. S. Burt (25 July 1794)
  Department of French and Italian
  University of California, Irvine

Jay L. Caplan (23 April 1759)
  Department of Romance Languages
  Amherst College

Jean-Claude Carron (1538)
  Department of French
  University of California, Los Angeles

Terence Cave (1512)
  St. John's College
  Oxford University

Mary Ann Caws (1966)
  Ph.D. Program in French, English, and Comparative Literature
  Graduate Center, City University of New York

Brigitte Cazelles (1050)
  Department of French and Italian
  Stanford University

Jacqueline Cerquiglini (1401)
  Département de Français
  Université de Genève

Ross Chambers (1851)
  Department of Romance Languages
  University of Michigan, Ann Arbor

Roger Chartier (1677)
  Ecole des Hautes Etudes en Sciences Sociales, Paris

Paul A. Chilton (1609)
  Department of French Studies
  University of Warwick

James Clifford (February 1933)
  History of Consciousness Program
  University of California, Santa Cruz

Patrick Coleman (1762, 1976)
  Department of French
  University of California, Los Angeles

Douglas Collins (December 1933)
  Department of Romance Languages and Literatures
  University of Washington

Antoine Compagnon (13 September 1555, 1895)
  Department of French and Romance Philology
  Columbia University

Tom Conley (1913)
  Department of French and Italian
  University of Minnesota

James Creech (1721)
  Department of French and Italian
  Miami University

Thomas Crow (1707)
  Department of Art History
  University of Michigan, Ann Arbor

Michael Danahy (23 July 1859)
  Hollins College

Natalie Zemon Davis (1526)
  Department of History
  Princeton University

Carolyn J. Dean (March 1931)
  Department of History
  Northwestern University

Gérard Defaux (17–18 October 1534, 1673)
  Department of French
  Johns Hopkins University

Joan DeJean (1654, 1700)
    Department of Romance Languages
    University of Pennsylvania

Lance K. Donaldson-Evans (1573)
    Department of Romance Languages
    University of Pennsylvania

Joseph J. Duggan (1095)
    Department of Comparative Literature
    University of California, Berkeley

Edwin M. Duval (1532)
    Department of French
    Yale University

Doranne Fenoaltea (1544)
    Department of Romance Languages
    University of Florida, Gainesville

Margaret Ferguson (1549)
    Department of English and Comparative Literature
    Columbia University

Joan M. Ferrante (1180)
    Department of English and Comparative Literature
    Columbia University

Lucienne Frappier-Mazur (1843)
    Department of Romance Languages
    University of Pennsylvania

Carla Freccero (1527)
    Department of French and Italian
    Dartmouth College

Michael Fried (August–September 1759)
    Humanities Center
    Johns Hopkins University

Jane Gallop (1975)
    Department of Humanities
    Rice University

Jean Gaudon (December 1827)
    Département de Lettres Modernes
    Université Paris XII

Sima Godfrey (1874)
    Department of Romance Languages
    University of North Carolina at Chapel Hill

Lionel Gossman (1697, December 1761)
  Department of Romance Languages
  Princeton University

Jean-Joseph Goux (November 1925)
  Department of French Studies
  Brown University

Kathryn Gravdal (1175)
  Department of French and Romance Philology
  Columbia University

Mary Jean Green (1914–1918)
  Department of French and Italian
  Dartmouth College

Mitchell Greenberg (1637)
  Department of French and Italian
  Miami University

Stephen Greenblatt (1563)
  Department of English
  University of California, Berkeley

Jacques Guicharnaud (1680, 27 April 1784)
  Department of French
  Yale University

Madelyn Gutwirth (1787)
  Department of Foreign Languages
  West Chester University

Marcel Gutwirth (1660)
  French Department
  Graduate Center, City University of New York

Timothy Hampton (1517)
  Department of French
  Yale University

Stephen Heath (1985)
  Jesus College
  Cambridge University

Francis M. Higman (September 1541)
  Institut d'Histoire de la Réformation
  Université de Genève

Denis Hollier (1836, 1905, June 1931, 1934, May 1968, 1989)
  Department of French
  Yale University

Louise K. Horowitz (1619)
  Department of French
  Rutgers University–Camden

Richard Howard (1911)
  Department of English and Comparative Literature
  University of Cincinnati

Jean-Charles Huchet (1152)

Marie-Hélène Huet (8 June 1794)
  Department of Romance Languages
  Amherst College

David F. Hult (1277)
  Department of French
  Johns Hopkins University

Jefferson Humphries (1853, 1884)
  Department of French and Italian
  Louisiana State University

Michel Jeanneret (Fall 1534, 1578)
  Département de Français
  Université de Genève

Barbara Johnson (1820, 1866, June 1885)
  Department of Romance Languages
  Harvard University

Ann Rosalind Jones (July 1555)
  Comparative Literature Program
  Smith College

Herbert Josephs (19 April 1774)
  Department of Romance and Classical Languages
  Michigan State University, East Lansing

Peggy Kamuf (1754?)
  Department of French and Italian
  University of Southern California

Alice Yaeger Kaplan (6 February 1945)
  Department of Romance Studies
  Duke University

Vincent Kaufmann (December 1925)
  Département de Français
  Université de Genève

Donald R. Kelley (1566)
  Department of History
  University of Rochester

Douglas Kelly (1267)
  Department of French and Italian
  University of Wisconsin–Madison

Laura Kendrick (1123)
  English Department
  Rutgers University

Samuel Kinser (1942)
  Department of History
  Northern Illinois University

Rosalind Krauss (9 January 1959)
  Art Department
  Hunter College and the Graduate Center, City University of New York

Lawrence D. Kritzman (1542)
  Department of French and Italian
  Dartmouth College

Dominick LaCapra (1857)
  Department of History
  Cornell University

Ullrich Langer (1572)
  Department of French and Italian
  University of Wisconsin–Madison

Alexandre Leupin (1181)
  Department of French and Italian
  Louisiana State University

Philip E. Lewis (1664)
  Department of Romance Studies
  Cornell University

Patrizia Lombardo (1808)
  Department of French and Italian
  University of Pittsburgh

Sylvère Lotringer (1935)
  Department of French and Romance Philology
  Columbia University

John D. Lyons (1627, 1678, 1689)
  Department of French Language and Literature
  University of Virginia

Eric MacPhail (June 1553)
  Department of French and Italian
  Indiana University–Bloomington

Donald Maddox (1300)
  Department of Romance Languages
  University of Connecticut, Storrs

Louis Marin (1674)
  Centre de Recherches sur les Arts et le Langage
  Ecole des Hautes Etudes en Sciences Sociales, Paris

Elaine Marks (1929)
  Department of French and Italian
  University of Wisconsin–Madison

Gita May (1750)
  Department of French and Romance Philology
  Columbia University

Sarah Maza (1816)
  Department of History
  Northwestern University

Christie V. McDonald (1769)
  Département d'Etudes Françaises
  Université de Montréal

Margaret M. McGowan (1581)
  School of European Studies
  University of Sussex

Jeffrey Mehlman (1898)
  Department of Modern Foreign Languages and Literatures
  Boston University

Françoise Meltzer (1892)
  Department of Romance Languages and Literature, Department of
  Comparative Literature
  University of Chicago

Christopher L. Miller (1847, February 1968)
  Department of French and Program in African and Afro-American Studies
  Yale University

D. A. Miller (1839)
  Department of Comparative Literature
  University of California, Berkeley

Nancy K. Miller (1735)
  Department of English
  Lehman College and the Graduate Center, City University of New York

Toril Moi (1949)
  Literature Program
  Duke University

Timothy Murray (1634)
  Department of English
  Cornell University

Charles Muscatine (1210)
  Department of English
  University of California, Berkeley

Robert J. Nelson (1687)
  Department of French
  University of Illinois, Urbana

Stephen G. Nichols (1127)
  Department of Romance Languages
  University of Pennsylvania

Glyn P. Norton (July 1541)
  Department of Romance Languages
  Williams College

David O'Connell (1920)
  Department of Foreign Languages
  Georgia State University, Atlanta

Thomas G. Pavel (1647)
  Cowell College
  University of California, Santa Cruz

Sandy Petrey (1789, 1834, 1877)
  Department of Comparative Studies
  State University of New York, Stony Brook

Mark Poster (1772)
  Department of History
  University of California, Irvine

Gerald Prince (1953)
  Department of Romance Languages
  University of Pennsylvania

Esther Rashkin (1886)
  Department of Languages and Literatures
  University of Utah

Nancy Freeman Regalado (1456)
  Department of French
  New York University

Richard L. Regosin (1595)
  Department of French and Italian
  University of California, Irvine

Martine Reid (13 January 1791)
Department of French
Yale University

Timothy J. Reiss (March 1553, 1640)
Department of Comparative Literature
New York University

Walter E. Rex (1704)
Department of French
University of California, Berkeley

Alain Rey (1694)
Directeur Littéraire des Dictionnaires *Robert,* Paris

François Rigolot (1493, Summer 1536, February 1827)
Department of Romance Languages and Literatures
Princeton University

Pierre Ronzeaud (1648)
Centre des Lettres et Sciences Humaines
Université de Provence (Aix-Marseilles I)

Ronald C. Rosbottom (February 1761)
Department of Romance Languages
Ohio State University, Columbus

Kristin Ross (1871)
Board of Studies in Literature
University of California, Santa Cruz

Daniel S. Russell (1536)
Department of French and Italian
University of Pittsburgh

Ronnie Scharfman (1939)
Department of Humanities
State University of New York–Purchase

Naomi Schor (1833, 1876)
Department of Romance Studies
Duke University

English Showalter, Jr. (1734)
Department of French
Rutgers University

Richard Sieburth (February 1885)
Department of French
New York University

Ann Smock (1928, 1940–1944)
  Department of French
  University of California, Berkeley

Gabrielle M. Spiegel (1202)
  Department of History
  University of Maryland, College Park

Domna C. Stanton (1685)
  Department of Romance Languages
  University of Michigan

Joan Hinde Stewart (1787)
  Department of Foreign Languages and Literatures
  North Carolina State University, Raleigh

Philip Stewart (1770)
  Department of Romance Studies
  Duke University

Allan Stoekl (March 1937)
  Department of Comparative Literature
  Yale University

Donald Stone, Jr. (1552)
  Department of Romance Languages
  Harvard University

Susan Rubin Suleiman (12 July 1937, 1960)
  Department of Romance Languages
  Harvard University

Virginia E. Swain (May 1782)
  Department of French and Italian
  Dartmouth College

Michael Syrotinski (1941)
  Department of Foreign Languages
  Illinois State University

Richard Terdiman (1848, 1852)
  Board of Studies in Literature
  University of California, Santa Cruz

Chantal Thomas (Summer 1791)
  Centre National de la Recherche Scientifique, Lyons

Tzvetan Todorov (1814)
  Centre National de la Recherche Scientifique, Paris

Jack Undank (1727, 1771)
  Department of French
  Rutgers University

Steven Ungar (15 October 1945)
  Department of French and Italian and Department of Comparative Literature
  University of Iowa

Eugene Vance (1165)
  Department of Modern Languages
  Emory University

Georges Van Den Abbeele (1668)
  Department of French and Italian
  Miami University

Aram Vartanian (January 1759)
  Department of French Language and Literature
  University of Virginia

Nancy J. Vickers (1528)
  Department of French and Italian
  University of Southern California

Anthony Vidler (1802)
  Department of Architecture
  Princeton University

Evelyn Birge Vitz (1215)
  Department of French
  New York University

Hayden White (1823)
  History of Consciousness Program
  University of California, Santa Cruz

Dudley B. Wilson (1562)
  Department of French
  University of Durham

Nathaniel Wing (1835, 7 December 1859)
  Department of French and Italian
  Louisiana State University

Terence R. Wooldridge (1539)
  Department of French
  University of Toronto

✐ Index

Works whose authorship is known are given under the authors' names. Anonymous works and periodicals are listed by title.